# Webster's II *Pocket* Dictionary

Third Edition

Visit our website: www.houghtonmifflinbooks.com

ISBN-13: 978-0-618-40690-6
ISBN-10: 0-618-40690-5

Manufactured in the United States of America

RP 10 9 8 7 6 5 4 3

# Contents

# How to Use This Dictionary

**The Main Entry:** Entry words, divided into syllables by centered dots, appear in alphabetical order. Two or more entries that are identical in spelling but have different histories are entered separately, each bearing a superscript number:

> **game**[1]
> **game**[2]

**Variants:** When two or more different spellings of a single word are entered, they are set in boldface type. If a variant follows the main entry, separated from it by only a comma, the two forms are used with almost equal frequency:

> **ax, axe**

If one spelling is distinctly preferred, the variant is introduced by the word "Also":

> **en•cy•clo•pe•di•a** ... Also **en•cy•clo•pae•di•a.**

**Inflected Forms:** Irregular inflected forms or those offering possible spelling problems are entered in boldface type, often in shortened form:

> **base**[2] ... **baser, basest.**
> **gam•ble** ... **-bled, -bling.**
> **well**[2] ... **better, best.**

Although regular inflections are normally not entered, the regular plural of a noun is shown when there is an irregular variant plural or when the spelling of the regular plural might present difficulty:

> **cac•tus** *pl.* **-ti** or **-tuses.**
> **gal•lows** *pl.* **-lowses** or **-lows.**
> **pi•a•no** *pl.* **-os.**

The inflected forms of verbs are given in the following order:

past tense, past participle (if it differs from the past tense), and present participle:

**fly ... flew, flown, flying.**

**Labels:** The labels below are used to indicate parts of speech:

| | | | |
|---|---|---|---|
| *n.* | noun | *pron.* | pronoun |
| *adj.* | adjective | *conj.* | conjunction |
| *def. art.* | definite article | *prep.* | preposition |
| *indef. art.* | indefinite article | *v.* | verb |
| *adv.* | adverb | *interj.* | interjection |

The following additional labels are used to indicate additional forms:

| | | | |
|---|---|---|---|
| *pl.* | plural | *p.p.* | past participle |
| *sing.* | singular | *compar.* | comparative |
| *pres.p.* | present participle | *superl.* | superlative |
| *p.t.* | past tense | *pl.n.* | plural noun |

**Pronunciation:** All pronunciations, indicated in parentheses following the forms to which they apply, are acceptable in all circumstances. When more than one is given, the first is assumed to be the most common, although the difference in frequency may be insignificant.

Below is a list of the symbols used in the pronunciations in this dictionary:

| *Symbols* | *Spellings* | *Symbols* | *Spellings* |
|---|---|---|---|
| ă | pat | ē | bee |
| ā | pay | f | fife, phase |
| âr | care | g | gag |
| ä | father | h | hat |
| är | car | hw | which |
| b | bib | ĭ | pit |
| ch | church | ī | pie, by |
| d | deed, milled | îr | deer, pier |
| ĕ | pet | j | judge |

| *Symbols* | *Spellings* |
|---|---|
| k | **k**i**ck**, **c**at, pi**que** |
| KH | **ch**utzpah |
| l | **l**id, need**le** |
| m | **m**u**m** |
| n | **n**o, sudd**en** |
| N | da**n**seur |
| ng | thi**ng** |
| ŏ | p**o**t |
| ō | t**oe** |
| ô | c**au**ght, p**aw** |
| ôr | c**ore** |
| œ | mili**eu** |
| oi | n**oi**se |
| o͝o | t**oo**k |
| o͝or | l**ure** |
| o͞o | b**oo**t |
| ou | **ou**t |
| p | **p**o**p** |
| r | **r**oa**r** |
| s | **s**au**ce** |
| sh | **sh**ip, di**sh** |
| t | **t**igh**t**, stopp**ed** |
| th | **th**in |
| *th* | **th**is |
| ŭ | c**u**t |
| ûr | **ur**ge, t**er**m, f**ir**m w**or**d, h**ear**d |
| v | **v**al**ve** |
| w | **w**ith |
| y | **y**es |
| z | **z**ebra, **x**ylem |
| zh | vi**si**on, plea**s**ure, gara**ge** |
| ə | **a**bout, it**e**m, ed**i**ble, gall**o**p, circ**u**s |
| ər | butt**er** |

A *y* between slashes (/y/) indicates that the sound is present in the pronunciation of some speakers and absent from the pronunciation of others, as in the word *duty*, where two pronunciations may occur, (do͞o′tē) and (dyo͞o′tē). In this dictionary, both pronunciations are represented: (d/y/o͞o′tē).

Stress, the relative degree of emphasis with which the syllables of a word are spoken, is indicated in three different ways. An unmarked syllable has the weakest stress in the word. The strongest, or *primary*, stress is marked with a bold mark (**′**). An intermediate level of stress, called *secondary*, is marked with a similar but lighter mark (′). Words of one syllable show no stress mark, since there is no other stress level to which the syllable is compared.

Primary stress **′** **bi•ol′o•gy** (bī-ŏl′ə-jē)
Secondary stress ′ **bi′o•log′i•cal** (bī′ə-lŏj′ĭ-kəl)

# – A –

**a, A** (ā) *n.* The 1st letter of the English alphabet.

**a** (ə; *emphatic* ā) *indef. art.* One; any.

**a•back** (ə-băk′) *adv.* **—take aback.** To startle; confuse.

**ab•a•cus** (ăb′ə-kəs) *n., pl.* **-cuses** or **-ci.** A manual computing device with rows of movable beads.

**a•ban•don** (ə-băn′dən) *v.* **1.** To give up; forsake. **2.** To desert. *—n.* A complete surrender of inhibitions. **—a•ban′doned** *adj.* **—a•ban′don•ment** *n.*

**a•base** (ə-bās′) *v.* **abased, abasing.** To humble; humiliate. **—a•base′ment** *n.*

**a•bate** (ə-bāt′) *v.* **abated, abating.** To reduce; lessen. **—a•bate′ment** *n.*

**ab•bey** (ăb′ē) *n., pl.* **-beys.** A monastery or convent.

**ab•bre•vi•ate** (ə-brē′vē-āt′) *v.* **-ated, -ating.** To make shorter. **—ab•bre′vi•a′tion** *n.*

**ab•di•cate** (ăb′dĭ-kāt′) *v.* **-cated, -cating.** To relinquish (power or responsibility) formally. **—ab′di•ca′tion** *n.*

**ab•do•men** (ăb′də-mən, ăb-dō′mən) *n.* The part of the body between the thorax and the pelvis. **—ab•dom′i•nal** *adj.*

**ab•duct** (ăb-dŭkt′) *v.* To kidnap. **—ab•duc′tion** *n.* **—ab•duc′tor** *n.*

**ab•er•ra•tion** (ăb′ə-rā′shən) *n.* Deviation or departure from the normal, typical, or expected. **—ab•er′rance, ab•er′ran•cy** *n.* **—ab•er′rant** *adj.*

**a•bet** (ə-bĕt′) *v.* **abetted, abetting. 1.** To encourage; incite. **2.** To assist. **—a•bet′tor, a•bet′ter** *n.*

**a•bey•ance** (ə-bā′əns) *n.* Temporary suspension.

**ab•hor** (ăb-hôr′) *v.* **-horred, -horring.** To dislike intensely; loathe. **—ab•hor′rence** *n.* **—ab•hor′rent** *adj.*

**a•bide** (ə-bīd′) *v.* **abode** or **abided, abiding. 1.** To await. **2.** To tolerate; bear. **3.** To remain; last. **—abide by.** To conform to; comply with. **—a•bid′ing** *adj.*

**a•bil•i•ty** (ə-bĭl′ĭ-tē) *n., pl.* **-ties. 1.** The power to perform. **2.** A skill or talent.

**ab•ject** (ăb′jĕkt′, ăb-jĕkt′) *adj.* **1.** Contemptible; base. **2.** Miserable; wretched. **—ab•jec′tion** *n.* **—ab•ject′ly** *adv.*

**ab•jure** (ăb-jo͝or′) *v.* **-jured, -juring.** To renounce under oath; forswear.

**a•ble** (ā′bəl) *adj.* **abler, ablest. 1.** Having sufficient ability. **2.** Capable or talented. **—a′bly** *adv.*

**ab•ne•gate** (ăb′nĭ-gāt′) *v.* **-gated, -gating.** To deny to oneself; renounce. **—ab′ne•ga′tion** *n.*

**ab•nor•mal** (ăb-nôr′məl) *adj.* Not normal; deviant. **—ab′nor•mal′i•ty** *n.* **—ab•nor′mal•ly** *adv.*

**a•bode** (ə-bōd′) *v.* p.t. & p.p. of **abide.** *—n.* A home.

**a•bol•ish** (ə-bŏl′ĭsh) *v.* To put an end to; annul. **—ab′o•li′tion** *n.* **—ab′o•li′tion•ist** *n.*

**a•bom•i•na•ble** (ə-bŏm′ə-nə-bəl) *adj.* Detestable; loathsome. **—a•bom′i•na•bly** *adv.* **—a•bom′i•nate′** *v.* **—a•bom′i•na′tion** *n.*

**ab•o•rig•i•ne** (ăb′ə-rĭj′ə-nē) *n.* An original inhabitant of a region. **—ab′o•rig′i•nal** *adj. & n.*

**a•bort** (ə-bôrt′) *v.* To terminate pregnancy or full development prematurely. *—n.* Premature termination of a rocket launch or space mission. **—a•bor′tive** *adj.*

**a•bor•tion** (ə-bôr′shən) *n.* **1.** Induced premature termination of pregnancy or development. **2.** Something malformed. **—a•bor′tion•ist** *n.*

**a•bound** (ə-bound′) *v.* To be great in number or amount; teem.

**a•bout** (ə-bout′) *adv.* **1.** Approximately. **2.** Toward a reverse direction. **3.** In the vicinity. *—prep.* **1.** On all sides of. **2.** Near to. **3.** In or on. **4.** Concerning. **5.** Ready. *—adj.* Astir.

**a•bove** (ə-bŭv′) *adv.* **1.** Overhead. **2.** In a higher place, rank, or position. *—prep.* **1.** Over. **2.** Superior to. **3.** In preference to. *—n.* Something that is above. *—adj.* Appearing or stated earlier.

**a•bove•board** (ə-bŭv′bôrd′, -bōrd′) *adv.* Without deceit. **—a•bove′board′** *adj.*

**ab•ra•sion** (ə-brā′zhən) *n.* **1.** A wearing away by friction. **2.** A scraped or worn area. **—a•brade′** *v.* **—a•bra′sive** *adj. & n.*

**a•bridge** (ə-brĭj′) *v.* **abridged, abridging.** To condense; shorten. **—a•bridg′ment, a•bridge′ment** *n.*

**a•broad** (ə-brôd′) *adv.* **1.** Out of one's own country. **2.** Out of doors. **3.** Broadly; widely.

**a•brupt** (ə-brŭpt′) *adj.* **1.** Unexpectedly sudden. **2.** Curt; brusque. **3.** Very steep. **—a•brupt′ly** *adv.* **—a•brupt′ness** *n.*

**ab•scess** (ăb′sĕs′) *n.* A mass of pus surrounded by inflamed tissue. **—ab′scess** *v.*

**ab•scond** (ăb-skŏnd′) *v.* To leave quickly and secretly.

**ab•sent** (ăb′sənt) *adj.* **1.** Not present. **2.** Lacking. —*v.* (ăb-sĕnt′). To keep (oneself) away. **—ab′sence** *n.* **—ab′sent•ly** *adv.*

**ab•sent-mind•ed** (ăb′sənt-mīn′dĭd) *adj.* Forgetful; preoccupied. **—ab′sent-mind′ed•ly** *adv.* **—ab′sent-mind′ed•ness** *n.*

**ab•so•lute** (ăb′sə-lo͞ot′) *adj.* **1.** Perfect; complete. **2.** Pure. **3.** Unconditional; unqualified. **4.** Positive. **—ab′so•lute′ly** *adv.*

**ab•solve** (əb-zŏlv′, -sŏlv′) *v.* **-solved, -solving. 1.** To clear of blame or guilt. **2.** To grant forgiveness for sins committed. **—ab′so•lu′tion** *n.*

**ab•sorb** (əb-sôrb′, -zôrb′) *v.* **1.** To take in; soak in or up. **2.** To engross. **—ab•sorb′en•cy** *n.* **—ab•sorb′ent** *adj.* **—ab•sorp′tion** *n.*

**ab•stain** (ăb-stān′) *v.* To refrain from; forbear. **—ab•stain′er** *n.* **—ab•sten′tion** *n.*

**ab•ste•mi•ous** (ăb-stē′mē-əs) *adj.* Eating and drinking in moderation. **—ab•ste′mi•ous•ly** *adv.* **—ab•ste′mi•ous•ness** *n.*

**ab•sti•nence** (ăb′stə-nəns) *n.* A refraining from drinking alcoholic beverages, eating certain foods, etc. **—ab′sti•nent** *adj.*

**ab•stract** (ăb-străkt′, ăb′străkt′) *adj.* **1.** Considered apart from concrete existence. **2.** Theoretical. —*v.* (ăb′străkt′). **1.** To take away; remove. **2.** To steal. **3.** To summarize. —*n.* A summary. **—ab•strac′tion** *n.* **—ab•stract′ly** *adv.*

**ab•struse** (ăb-stro͞os′) *adj.* Difficult to understand.

**ab•surd** (əb-sûrd′, -zûrd′) *adj.* Ridiculous or unreasonable. **—ab•surd′i•ty** *n.* **—ab•surd′ly** *adv.*

**a•bun•dance** (ə-bŭn′dəns) *n.* Also **a•bun•dan•cy.** A great amount; plentiful supply. **—a•bun′dant** *adj.*

**a•buse** (ə-byo͞oz′) *v.* **abused, abusing. 1.** To use improperly. **2.** To maltreat. **3.** To berate; insult. —*n.* (ə-byo͞os′). **1.** Misuse. **2.** Maltreatment. **3.** Insulting language. **—a•bu′sive** *adj.*

**a•but** (ə-bŭt′) *v.* **-butted, -butting.** To touch at an end or side of. **—a•but′ment** *n.*

**a•bys•mal** (ə-bĭz′məl) *adj.* Unfathomable; deep.

**a•byss** (ə-bĭs′) *n.* A profound depth or emptiness.

**AC** *abbr.* **1.** Air conditioning. **2.** Area code.

**ac•a•dem•ic** (ăk′ə-dĕm′ĭk) *adj.* **1.** Of a school. **2.** Conventional. **3.** Theoretical.

**a•cad•e•my** (ə-kăd′ə-mē) *n., pl.* **-mies. 1.** An association of scholars. **2.** A school. **—ac′a•deme′** *n.* **—ac′a•de•mi′cian** *n.*

**ac•cede** (ăk-sēd′) *v.* **-ceded, -ceding. 1.** To give consent; agree. **2.** To come or succeed to a public office.

**ac•cel•er•ate** (ăk-sĕl′ə-rāt′) *v.* **-ated, -ating. 1.** To move or cause to move faster. **2.** To make happen sooner than expected. **—ac•cel′er•a′tion** *n.* **—ac•cel′er•a′tor** *n.*

**ac•cent** (ăk′sĕnt′) *n.* **1. a.** The stress placed on a syllable of a word. **b.** A mark used to indicate this. **2.** A characteristic pronunciation. —*v.* **1.** To stress the pronunciation of. **2.** To emphasize. **—ac•cen′tu•a′tion** *n.*

**ac•cept** (ăk-sĕpt′) *v.* **1.** To receive willingly. **2.** To admit to a group or place. **3.** To answer affirmatively. **—ac•cept′a•bil′i•ty** *n.* **—ac•cept′a•ble** *adj.* **—ac•cep′tance** *n.*

**ac•cess** (ăk′sĕs) *n.* **1.** A means of approaching. **2.** The right to enter or use. **3.** A sudden outburst. —*v.* To obtain access to. **—ac•ces′si•bil′i•ty** *n.* **—ac•ces′si•ble** *adj.*

**ac•ces•sion** (ăk-sĕsh′ən) *n.* **1.** The attainment of rank. **2.** An increase. **3.** Agreement; assent.

**ac•ces•so•ry, ac•ces•sa•ry** (ăk-sĕs′ə-rē) *n., pl.* **-ries. 1.** Something nonessential but useful. **2.** One who though absent aids in a crime. **—ac•ces′so•ry** *adj.*

**access time** *n.* The time lag between a request for information in a computer and its delivery.

**ac•ci•dent** (ăk′sĭ-dənt, -dĕnt′) *n.* **1.** An unexpected and undesirable event. **2.** A chance circumstance. **—ac′ci•den′tal** *adj.* **—ac′ci•den′tal•ly** *adv.*

**ac•claim** (ə-klām′) *v.* To applaud, salute, or hail. *—n.* Enthusiastic applause. **—ac′cla•ma′tion** *n.*

**ac•cli•mate** (ə-klī′mĭt, ăk′lə-māt′) *v.* **-mated, -mating.** Also **ac•cli•ma•tize, -tized, -tizing.** To accustom to a new environment or situation; adapt. **—ac′-cli•ma′tion, ac•cli′ma•ti•za′tion** *n.*

**ac•cliv•i•ty** (ə-klĭv′ĭtē) *n., pl.* **-ties.** An upward slope.

**ac•co•lade** (ăk′ə-lād′, -läd′) *n.* Praise; approval.

**ac•com•mo•date** (ə-kŏm′ə-dāt′) *v.* **-dated, -dating. 1.** To do a favor for. **2.** To supply with. **3.** To have space for. **4.** To adapt; adjust. **—ac•com′mo•da′-tion** *n.*

**ac•com•pa•ni•ment** (ə-kŭm′pə-nē-mənt, ə-kŭmp′nē-) *n.* **1.** Something that accompanies. **2.** A vocal or instrumental part that supports a solo part.

**ac•com•pa•ny** (ə-kŭm′pə-nē, ə-kŭmp′nē) *v.* **-nied, -nying. 1.** To go along or occur with. **2.** To perform an accompaniment to. **—ac•com′pa•nist** *n.*

**ac•com•plice** (ə-kŏm′plĭs) *n.* One who abets a lawbreaker.

**ac•com•plish** (ə-kŏm′plĭsh) *v.* To succeed in doing. **—ac•com′plished** *adj.* **—ac•com′plish•ment** *n.*

**ac•cord** (ə-kôrd′) *v.* To agree or be in agreement. *—n.* Agreement; harmony. **—ac•cor′dance** *n.* **—ac•cord′ing•ly** *adv.*

**ac•cor•di•on** (ə-kôr′dē-ən) *n.* A bellows-operated musical instrument. **—ac•cor′di•on•ist** *n.*

**ac•cost** (ə-kôst′, ə-kŏst′) *v.* To approach and speak to first.

**ac•count** (ə-kount′) *n.* **1. a.** A narrative of events. **b.** An explanation; report. **2.** A list of monetary transactions. **3.** A business relationship involving the exchange of money or credit. **4.** Importance. **—on account of.** Because of. **—take into account.** To take into consideration. *—v.* To consider or esteem. **—account for. 1.** To make a reckoning; report. **2.** To give the reason for; explain. **3.** To be answerable for. **—ac•count′a•bil′i•ty** *n.* **—ac•count′a•ble** *adj.*

**ac•count•ing** (ə-koun′tĭng) *n.* The occupation, process, or methods of keeping the financial records of a business. **—ac•count′ant** *n.*

**ac•cou•ter** (ə-ko͞o′tər) *v.* To outfit and equip. **—ac•cou′ter•ment** *n.*

**ac•cred•it** (ə-krĕd′ĭt) *v.* **1.** To attribute to. **2.** To certify as meeting a prescribed standard. **—ac•cred′i•ta′tion** *n.*

**ac•crete** (ə-krēt′) *v.* **-creted, -creting.** To grow or make grow larger or greater. **—ac•cre′tion** *n.*

**ac•crue** (ə-kro͞o′) *v.* **-crued, -cruing.** To increase by regular growth, as interest on capital. **—ac•cru′al** *n.*

**ac•cul•tur•ate** (ə-kŭl′chə-rāt′) *v.* **-ated, -ating.** To change or make change by contact with another society. **—ac•cul′tur•a′tion** *n.*

**ac•cu•mu•late** (ə-kyo͞om′yə-lāt′) *v.* **-lated, -lating.** To amass; mount up. **—ac•cu′mu•la′tion** *n.*

**ac•cu•rate** (ăk′yər-ĭt) *adj.* Having no errors; exact; correct. **—ac′cu•ra•cy** *n.* **—ac′cu•rate•ly** *adv.* **—ac′cu•rate•ness** *n.*

**ac•cuse** (ə-kyo͞oz′) *v.* **-cused, -cusing. 1.** To charge (someone) with an error; blame. **2.** In law, to bring charges against. **—ac′cu•sa′tion** *n.* **—ac•cused′** *n.*

**ac•cus•tom** (ə-kŭs′təm) *v.* To familiarize.

**ace** (ās) *n.* **1.** A playing card, domino, etc., having one spot. **2.** In tennis, a point scored for an unreturned serve. **3.** An expert in any field, esp. a fighter pilot. *—adj.* First-rate. *—v.* **aced, acing.** To receive a grade of A on.

**a•cet•a•min•o•phen** (ə-sē′tə-mĭn′ə-fən) *n.* A substance used in medicine in place of aspirin to reduce pain and fever.

**ache** (āk) *v.* **ached, aching. 1.** To suffer a dull pain. **2.** To yearn. *—n.* A dull, steady pain.

**a•chieve** (ə-chēv′) *v.* **achieved, achieving.** To accomplish successfully; attain. **—a•chiev′a•ble** *adj.* **—a•chieve′-ment** *n.* **—a•chiev′er** *n.*

**ac•id** (ăs′ĭd) *n.* **1.** A substance capable of dissolving certain metals to form salts, reacting with bases or alkalis to form salts, or having a sour taste. **2.** LSD.

—*adj.* Biting; ill-tempered. **—a•cid'ic** *adj.* **—a•cid'i•ty** *n.*

**ac•knowl•edge** (ăk-nŏl'ĭj) *v.* **-edged, -edging. 1.** To admit the existence or truth of. **2.** To report the receipt of. **3.** To express gratitude for. **—ac•knowl'edg•ment** *n.*

**ac•me** (ăk'mē) *n.* The point of utmost attainment.

**ac•ne** (ăk'nē) *n.* A skin disease characterized by pimples.

**a•corn** (ā'kôrn', ā'kərn) *n.* The nut of the oak tree.

**a•cous•tic** (ə-ko͞o'stĭk) *adj.* Also **a•cous•ti•cal.** Of sound, the sense of hearing, or the science of sound. —*n.* **acoustics. 1.** *(takes sing. v.).* The science of sound. **2.** *(takes pl. v.).* The effect of sound, esp. in an enclosed space.

**ac•quaint** (ə-kwānt') *v.* **1.** To make familiar. **2.** To inform. **—ac•quain'tance** *n.* **—ac•quaint'ed** *adj.*

**ac•qui•esce** (ăk'wē-ĕs') *v.* **-esced, -escing.** To consent passively. **—ac'qui•es'cence** *n.* **—ac'qui•es'cent** *adj.*

**ac•quire** (ə-kwīr') *v.* **-quired, -quiring.** To gain possession of. **—ac'qui•si'tion** *n.* **—ac•quis'i•tive** *adj.*

**ac•quit** (ə-kwĭt') *v.* **-quitted, -quitting.** To clear of a charge. **—ac•quit'tal** *n.*

**a•cre** (ā'kər) *n.* A unit of land area equal to 4,840 square yards. **—a'cre•age** *n.*

**ac•rid** (ăk'rĭd) *adj.* **1.** Bitter to taste or smell. **2.** Sharp in language or tone. **—a•crid'i•ty** *n.* **—ac'rid•ly** *adj.*

**ac•ri•mo•ny** (ăk'rə-mō'nē) *n.* Animosity in speech or manner. **—ac'ri•mo'ni•ous** *adj.* **—ac'ri•mo'ni•ous•ly** *adv.* **—ac'ri•mo'ni•ous•ness** *n.*

**ac•ro•bat** (ăk'rə-băt') *n.* One skilled in feats of agility and balance. **—ac'ro•bat'ic** *adj.* **—ac'ro•bat'i•cal•ly** *adv.*

**ac•ro•nym** (ăk'rə-nĭm) *n.* A word formed from the initial letters of a name, as *NATO* from *N*orth *A*tlantic *T*reaty *O*ganization. **—ac'ro•nym'ic** *adj.*

**a•cross** (ə-krôs', ə-krŏs') *prep.* **1.** On, at, or from the other side of. **2.** From one side of to the other. —*adv.* **1.** From one side to the other. **2.** On or to the opposite side.

**act** (ăkt) *n.* **1.** The process of doing something. **2.** Something that is done. **3.** A legislative enactment. **4.** A major division of a play, opera, etc. **5.** A pose. —*v.* **1.** To perform, as in a play. **2.** To behave. **3.** To do something.

**act•ing** (ăk'tĭng) *adj.* Temporarily assuming another's duties. —*n.* The occupation of an actor.

**ac•tion** (ăk'shən) *n.* **1.** The state or process of doing. **2.** An act or deed. **3. actions.** Behavior. **4.** The operating parts of a mechanism. **5.** The plot of a story or play. **6.** A lawsuit. **7.** Combat. **8.** The most profitable activity in an area or profession.

**ac•ti•vate** (ăk'tə-vāt') *v.* **-vated, -vating. 1.** To set in motion. **2.** To make active. **—ac'ti•va'tion** *n.* **—ac'ti•va'tor** *n.*

**ac•tive** (ăk'tĭv) *adj.* **1.** In action; moving. **2.** Functioning. **3.** Participating. **4.** Characterized by energetic action. **5.** Denoting that the subject of a sentence is performing the action expressed by the verb. **—ac•tiv'i•ty** *n.*

**ac•tor** (ăk'tər) *n.* A male theatrical performer.

**ac•tress** (ăk'trĭs) *n.* A female theatrical performer.

**ac•tu•al** (ăk'cho͞o-əl) *adj.* In existence; real. **—ac'tu•al'i•ty** *n.* **—ac'tu•al•ly** *adv.* **—ac'tu•ate'** *v.*

**a•cu•men** (ăk'yə-mən, ə-kyo͞o'mən) *n.* Keenness of insight.

**ac•u•pres•sure** (ăk'yo͞o-prĕsh'ər) *n.* Massage with the fingers on the parts of the body used in acupuncture.

**ac•u•punc•ture** (ăk'yo͞o-pŭngk'chər) *n.* Traditional Chinese therapy using fine needles to pierce the body. **—ac'u•punc'tur•ist** *n.*

**a•cute** (ə-kyo͞ot') *adj.* **1.** Sharp. **2.** Keenly perceptive. **3.** Sensitive; critical. **4.** Extremely severe. **5.** Designating angles less than 90°. **—a•cute'ly** *adv.*

**a•cy•clo•vir** (ā-sī'klō-vēr', -klə-) *n.* A substance used to treat genital herpes.

**ad•age** (ăd'ĭj) *n.* A short proverb.

**ad•a•mant** (ăd'ə-mənt) *adj.* Unyielding; stubborn. **—ad'a•man'tine** *adj.* **—ad'a•mant•ly** *adv.*

**a•dapt** (ə-dăpt') *v.* To adjust to new or different conditions. **—a•dapt'a•bil'i•ty** *n.* **—a•dapt'a•ble** *adj.* **—ad'ap•ta'tion, a•dap'tion** *n.* **—a•dapt'er, a•dap'tor** *n.* **—a•dap'tive** *adj.*

**add** (ăd) *v.* **1.** To join so as to increase. **2.** To combine to form a sum. **3.** To say further. —*n.* An act or instance of add-

ing. **—add'a•ble, add'i•ble** *adj.*
**ad•den•dum** (ə-dĕn'dəm) *n., pl.* **-da.** Something to be added; a supplement.
**ad•dict** (ə-dĭkt') *v.* To give (oneself) habitually to; depend on. *—n.* (ăd'ĭkt). A person who is addicted, esp. to narcotics. **—ad•dic'tion** *n.* **—ad•dic'tive** *adj.*
**ad•di•tion** (ə-dĭsh'ən) *n.* **1.** The act or process of adding. **2.** Something added; a supplement. **—ad•di'tion•al** *adj.*
**ad•dle** (ăd'l) *v.* **-dled, -dling. 1.** To make or become confused. **2.** To spoil, as an egg.
**add-on** (ăd'ŏn', -ôn') *n.* Something extra added on or to, to make more desirable. **—add-on** *adj.*
**ad•dress** (ə-drĕs') *v.* **1.** To speak to. **2.** To mark with a destination. **3.** To direct one's efforts to. *—n.* **1.** A formal speech. **2.** The indication of destination on mail. **3.** The location of an organization or person. **4.** A number used in information storage and assigned to a specific memory location. **—ad•dress'a•ble** *adj.* **—ad'dress•ee'** *n.*
**ad•e•noids** (ăd'n-oidz') *pl.n.* Tissue growths above the throat in the nose.
**ad•e•no•vi•rus** (ăd'n-ō-vī'rəs) *n.* A virus that causes respiratory disease. **—ad'e•no•vi'ral** *adj.*
**a•dept** (ə-dĕpt') *adj.* Highly skilled. **—a•dept'ly** *adv.*
**ad•e•quate** (ăd'ĭ-kwĭt) *adj.* **1.** Able to satisfy a requirement. **2.** Satisfactory or sufficient. **—ad'e•qua•cy** *n.* **—ad'e•quate•ly** *adv.*
**ad•here** (ăd-hîr') *v.* **-hered, -hering. 1.** To stick to as if glued. **2.** To maintain loyalty; follow without deviation. **—ad•her'ence** *n.* **—ad•her'ent** *adj. & n.*
**ad•he•sive** (ăd-hē'sĭv) *adj.* Tending to adhere; sticky. *—n.* An adhesive substance. **—ad•he'sion** *n.*
**ad hoc** (ăd hŏk', hōk') *adj. & adv.* For this specific purpose or case.
**ad hom•i•nem** (hŏm'ə-nĕm', -nəm) *adj. & adv.* Appealing to personal dislikes.
**a•dieu** (ə-d/y/ōō') *interj.* Good-by; farewell. *—n., pl.* **adieus, adieux.** A farewell.
**ad in•fi•ni•tum** (ĭn'fə-nī'təm) *adj. & adv.* Without end; limitless.
**ad•ja•cent** (ə-jā'sənt) *adj.* Next to; adjoining.
**ad•jec•tive** (ăj'ĭk-tĭv) *n.* A word used to modify a noun. **—ad'jec•ti'val** *adj.*
**ad•join** (ə-join') *v.* To be next to.
**ad•journ** (ə-jûrn') *v.* To suspend until a later stated time. **—ad•journ'ment** *n.*
**ad•just** (ə-jŭst') *v.* **1.** To regulate or adapt. **2.** To settle (a debt or claim). **—ad•just'a•ble** *adj.* **—ad•just'er** *n.* **—ad•just'ment** *n.*
**ad•ju•tant** (ăj'ə-tənt) *n.* A military assistant to a commander.
**ad-lib** (ăd-lĭb') *v.* **-libbed, -libbing.** To improvise. *—n.* Something ad-libbed.
**ad•min•is•ter** (ăd-mĭn'ĭ-stər) *v.* **1.** To manage. **2.** To give or dispense. **3.** To mete out. **—ad•min'is•tra'tor** *n.*
**ad•min•is•tra•tion** (ăd-mĭn'ĭ-strā'shən) *n.* **1.** The act of administering. **2.** Management. **3.** The executive body of a government. **—ad•min'is•tra'tive** *adj.*
**ad•mi•ral** (ăd'mər-əl) *n.* A naval officer of next-to-highest rank.
**ad•mire** (ăd-mīr') *v.* **-mired, -miring. 1.** To regard with wonder and approval. **2.** To esteem; respect. **—ad'mi•ra•ble** *adj.* **—ad'mi•ra'tion** *n.* **—ad•mir'er** *n.*
**ad•mis•si•ble** (ăd-mĭs'ə-bəl) *adj.* Allowable. **—ad•mis'si•bil'i•ty** *n.*
**ad•mis•sion** (ăd-mĭsh'ən) *n.* **1.** The act of admitting. **2.** An acknowledgment or confession. **3.** The right to enter. **4.** An entrance fee.
**ad•mit** (ăd-mĭt') *v.* **-mitted, -mitting. 1.** To permit to enter. **2.** To allow; permit (with *of*). **3.** To acknowledge; confess. **4.** To concede. **—ad•mit'tance** *n.*
**ad•mon•ish** (ăd-mŏn'ĭsh) *v.* **1.** To reprove. **2.** To counsel against; warn. **—ad'mo•ni'tion, ad•mon'ish•ment** *n.* **—ad•mon'i•to'ry** *adj.*
**ad nau•se•am** (ăd nô'zē-əm, -ăm') *adv.* To a disgusting degree.
**a•do** (ə-dōō') *n.* Bustle; bother.
**ad•o•les•cence** (ăd'l-ĕs'əns) *n.* The period between puberty and maturity. **—ad'o•les'cent** *adj. & n.*
**a•dopt** (ə-dŏpt') *v.* **1.** To take (a child) into one's family and raise as one's own. **2.** To take up and use or follow. **—a•dop'tion** *n.*
**a•dore** (ə-dôr', ə-dōr') *v.* **adored, adoring. 1.** To worship. **2.** To love deeply. **—a•dor'a•ble** *adj.* **—ad'o•ra'tion** *n.*

**a•dorn** (ə-dôrn′) *v.* **1.** To enhance. **2.** To decorate, as with ornaments. **—a•dorn′ment** *n.*

**ad•re•nal gland** (ə-drē′nəl) *n.* One of two endocrine glands located above the kidneys.

**a•dren•a•line** (ə-drĕn′ə-lĭn) *n.* Epinephrine.

**a•drift** (ə-drĭft′) *adv.* Floating; without direction. **—a•drift′** *adj.*

**a•droit** (ə-droit′) *adj.* Dexterous. **—a•droit′ly** *adv.*

**a•dult** (ə-dŭlt′, ăd′ŭlt′) *n.* One who is fully grown or of legal age. *—adj.* **1.** Fully developed and mature. **2.** Sexually explicit; pornographic. **—a•dult′hood′** *n.*

**a•dul•ter•ate** (ə-dŭl′tə-rāt′) *v.* **-ated, -ating.** To make impure, as by adding improper ingredients. **—a•dul′ter•a′tion** *n.*

**a•dul•ter•y** (ə-dŭl′tə-rē, -trē) *n., pl.* **-ies.** Marital infidelity. **—a•dul′ter•ous** *adj.*

**ad•vance** (ăd-văns′) *v.* **-vanced, -vancing.** **1.** To move forward. **2.** To propose. **3.** To make progress or aid the progress of. **4.** To raise or rise in rank, amount, etc. **5.** To pay (money) beforehand. *—n.* **1.** The act of moving forward. **2.** Improvement; progress. **3.** A rise in price or value. **4.** Payment of money before legally due. *—adj.* **1.** Prior. **2.** Going before. **—ad•vance′ment** *n.*

**ad•van•tage** (ăd-văn′tĭj) *n.* **1.** A favorable position or factor. **2.** Benefit; gain. **—ad′van•ta′geous** *adj.*

**ad•ven•ture** (ăd-vĕn′chər) *n.* **1.** A risky undertaking. **2.** An exciting experience. **—ad•ven′tur•ous** *adj.*

**ad•verb** (ăd′vûrb) *n.* A word used to modify a verb, an adjective, or another adverb. **—ad•ver′bi•al** *adj.*

**ad•ver•sar•y** (ăd′vər-sĕr′ē) *n., pl.* **-ies.** An opponent; enemy. **—ad′ver•sar′i•al** *adj.*

**ad•verse** (ăd-vûrs′, ăd′vûrs′) *adj.* **1.** Actively opposed; hostile. **2.** Unfavorable.

**ad•ver•si•ty** (ăd-vûr′sĭ-tē) *n., pl.* **-ties.** Hardship; misfortune.

**ad•ver•tise** (ăd′vər-tīz′) *v.* **-tised, -tising.** To call public attention to so as to promote sales. **—ad′ver•tise′ment** *n.* **—ad′ver•tis′ing** *n.*

**ad•vice** (ăd-vīs′) *n.* Opinion about a course of action; counsel.

**ad•vis•a•ble** (ăd-vī′zə-bəl) *adj.* Prudent; expedient. **—ad•vis′a•bil′i•ty** *n.*

**ad•vise** (ăd-vīz′) *v.* **-vised, -vising.** **1.** To offer advice to; recommend. **2.** To inform. **—ad•vi′sed•ly** *adv.* **—ad•vise′ment** *n.* **—ad•vi′ser, ad•vi′sor** *n.* **—ad•vi′so•ry** *adj.*

**ad•vo•cate** (ăd′və-kāt′) *v.* **-cated, -cating.** To speak in favor of; recommend. *—n.* (-kĭt, -kāt′). **1.** One who argues for a cause or person; a supporter. **2.** A lawyer. **—ad′vo•ca•cy** *n.*

**aer•ate** (âr′āt) *v.* **-ated, -ating.** To supply or charge with air or gas. **—aer•a′tion** *n.*

**aer•i•al** (âr′ē-əl) *adj.* **1.** Of, in, or caused by the air. **2.** Lofty. **3.** Airy. *—n.* An antenna.

**aer•ie** (âr′ē, îr′ē) *n.* A high nest, as of an eagle.

**aer•o•bic** (â-rō′bĭk) *adj.* **1.** Living in the presence of oxygen. **2.** Relating to exercises conditioning the cardiopulmonary system. **—aer′obe** *n.* **—aer•o′bics** *n.*

**aer•o•nau•tics** (âr′ə-nô′tĭks) *n.* **1.** The design and construction of aircraft. **2.** Aircraft navigation. **—aer′o•nau′tic, aer′o•nau′ti•cal** *adj.*

**aer•o•space** (âr′ō-spās′) *adj.* **1.** Of the earth's atmosphere and the space beyond. **2.** Of the science or technology of flight. **—aer′o•space′** *n.*

**aes•thete, es•thete** (ĕs′thēt) *n.* One who cultivates a superior appreciation of the beautiful.

**aes•thet•ic, es•thet•ic** (ĕs-thĕt′ĭk) *adj.* **1.** Of aesthetics. **2.** Of the beautiful; artistic. *—n.* **aesthetics, esthetics.** *(takes sing. v.).* The philosophical study of the beautiful and of the fine arts.

**af•fa•ble** (ăf′ə-bəl) *adj.* **1.** Amiable. **2.** Mild; gentle. **—af′fa•bil′i•ty** *n.*

**af•fair** (ə-fâr′) *n.* **1.** Anything done or to be done. **2. affairs.** Business matters. **3.** A sexual involvement.

**af•fect**[1] (ə-fĕkt′) *v.* **1.** To bring about a change in. **2.** To touch the emotions of.

**af•fect**[2] (ə-fĕkt′) *v.* **1.** To simulate so as to impress; feign. **2.** To fancy; prefer. **—af′fec•ta′tion** *n.* **—af•fect′ed** *adj.*

**af•fec•tion** (ə-fĕk′shən) *n.* A tender feeling toward another; fondness. **—af•fec′tion•ate** *adj.*

**af•fi•da•vit** (ăf′ĭ-dā′vĭt) *n.* A written statement made under oath.

**af•fil•i•ate** (ə-fĭl′ē-āt′) *v.* **-ated, -ating. 1.** To adopt as a subordinate associate. **2.** To associate (with). —*n.* (-ĭt). An associate or subordinate. **—af•fil′i•a′tion** *n.*

**af•fin•i•ty** (ə-fĭn′ĭ-tē) *n., pl.* **-ties. 1.** An attraction. **2.** Relationship; kinship.

**af•firm** (ə-fûrm′) *v.* **1.** To maintain to be true. **2.** To confirm. **—af′fir•ma′tion** *n.*

**af•fir•ma•tive** (ə-fûr′mə-tĭv) *adj.* **1.** Giving assent. **2.** Confirming. —*n.* A word signifying assent.

**af•fix** (ə-fĭks′) *v.* **1.** To attach. **2.** To append. —*n.* (ăf′ĭks′). Something attached or added, esp. a prefix or suffix.

**af•flict** (ə-flĭkt′) *v.* To inflict suffering upon; cause distress to. **—af•flic′tion** *n.*

**af•flu•ence** (ăf′lo͞o-əns) *n.* Wealth; abundance. **—af′flu•ent** *adj.*

**af•ford** (ə-fôrd′, ə-fōrd′) *v.* **1.** To have the financial means for. **2.** To be able to spare or give up. **3.** To provide. **—af•ford′a•ble** *adj.* **—af•ford′a•bly** *adv.*

**a•fraid** (ə-frād′) *adj.* **1.** Filled with fear. **2.** Reluctant; averse.

**a•fresh** (ə-frĕsh′) *adv.* Anew; again.

**Af•ri•can-A•mer•i•can** (ăf′rĭ-kən-ə-mĕr′ĭ-kən) *adj.* Black; Afro-American. —*n.* A Black American; an Afro-American.

**Af•ro-A•mer•i•can** (ăf′rō-ə-mĕr′ĭkən) *adj.* Of or relating to American Blacks of African ancestry, their history, or their culture. —*n.* An American Black of African ancestry.

**aft** (ăft, äft) *adv.* At, in, or toward the stern of a vessel. —*adj.* Situated near or at the stern.

**af•ter** (ăf′tər) *prep.* **1.** Behind in place or order. **2.** In pursuit of. **3.** At a later time than. **4.** In the style of. **5.** Past the hour of. —*adv.* **1.** Behind. **2.** Later. —*adj.* Later; following. —*conj.* Subsequent to the time that.

**af•ter-hours** (ăf′tər-ourz′) *adj.* **1.** Occurring after closing time. **2.** Open after a legal closing time.

**af•ter•mar•ket** (ăf′tər-mär′kĭt) *n.* The need for goods and services for the maintenance of a previous purchase.

**af•ter•math** (ăf′tər-măth′) *n.* A consequence or result.

**af•ter•noon** (ăf′tər-no͞on′) *n.* The day from noon until sunset.

**af•ter-tax** (ăf′tər-tăks′) *adj.* Remaining after payment of income tax.

**af•ter•ward** (ăf′tər-wərd) *adv.* Also **af•ter•wards.** In or at a later time; subsequently.

**a•gain** (ə-gĕn′) *adv.* **1.** Once more. **2.** To a previous place or position. **3.** Furthermore.

**a•gainst** (ə-gĕnst′) *prep.* **1.** In a direction or course opposite to. **2.** So as to come into contact with. **3.** In opposition to.

**age** (āj) *n.* **1.** The length of time someone or something has existed. **2.** The time in life when one officially assumes certain rights. **3.** A distinctive period or stage. **4.** The state of being old. —*v.* **aged, aging** or **ageing.** To grow or cause to grow old. **—a′ged** *adj.*

**age•ism** (ā′jĭz-əm) *n.* Discrimination against the elderly. **—age′ist** *adj. & n.*

**a•gen•cy** (ā′jən-sē) *n., pl.* **-cies. 1.** Action; operation. **2.** A means. **3.** A business or service acting for others.

**a•gen•da** (ə-jĕn′də) *pl.n. Sing.* **-dum.** A list of things to be done.

**a•gent** (ā′jənt) *n.* **1.** One that acts. **2.** One that acts as the representative of another. **3.** A means; instrument.

**ag•glom•er•ate** (ə-glŏm′ə-rāt′) *v.* **-ated, -ating.** To form into a rounded mass. **—ag•glom′er•a′tion** *n.*

**ag•gra•vate** (ăg′rə-vāt′) *v.* **-vated, -vating. 1.** To make worse. **2.** To annoy. **—ag′gra•va′tion** *n.*

**ag•gre•gate** (ăg′rĭ-gĭt) *adj.* Gathered together into a mass. —*n.* A collective mass; total. —*v.* (-gāt′) **-gated, -gating.** To gather into a mass. **—ag′gre•ga′tion** *n.*

**ag•gres•sion** (ə-grĕsh′ən) *n.* **1.** An assault. **2.** Hostile action or behavior. **—ag•gres′sive** *adj.* **—ag•gres′sor** *n.*

**a•ghast** (ə-găst′) *adj.* Horror-stricken; appalled.

**ag•ile** (ăj′əl, ăj′īl′) *adj.* Quick; nimble. **—a•gil′i•ty** *n.*

**ag•i•tate** (ăj′ĭ-tāt′) *v.* **-tated, -tating. 1.** To stir up violently. **2.** To upset; disturb. **3.** To arouse public interest. **—ag′i•ta′tion** *n.* **—ag′i•ta′tor** *n.*

**ag•nos•tic** (ăg-nŏs′tĭk) *n.* One who doubts the possibility of knowing the existence of God. **—ag•nos′tic** *adj.*

—**ag•nos'ti•cism'** *n.*
**a•go** (ə-gō') *adj. & adv.* Gone by; past.
**ag•o•nize** (ăg'ə-nīz') *v.* **-nized, -nizing.** To suffer great distress.
**ag•o•ny** (ăg'ə-nē) *n., pl.* **-nies.** Intense pain or distress.
**a•gree** (ə-grē') *v.* **agreed, agreeing. 1.** To consent. **2.** To be in accord. **3.** To have the same opinion. **4.** To be beneficial. **5.** To correspond, as in grammatical number. **—a•gree'ment** *n.*
**a•gree•a•ble** (ə-grē'ə-bəl) *adj.* **1.** Pleasing; pleasant. **2.** Willing. **—a•gree'a•bly** *adv.*
**ag•ri•busi•ness** (ăg'rə-bĭz'nĭs) *n.* Farming engaged in as a big business.
**ag•ri•cul•ture** (ăg'rĭ-kŭl'chər) *n.* Cultivation of crops and raising livestock; farming. **—ag'ri•cul'tur•al** *adj.* **—ag'ri•cul'tur•ist** *n.*
**a•head** (ə-hĕd') *adv.* **1.** At or to the front or head. **2.** Before; in advance. **3.** Onward; forward.
**aid** (ād) *v.* To help; assist. —*n.* Help; assistance.
**aide** (ād) *n.* An assistant.
**AIDS** (ādz) *n.* Acquired Immune Deficiency Syndrome; a contagious disease that is caused by HIV and attacks the body's immune system.
**aim** (ām) *v.* **1.** To direct (a weapon, blow, etc.). **2.** To direct one's efforts or purpose. —*n.* **1.** The act of aiming. **2.** The direction of something aimed. **3.** Purpose; intention. **—aim'less** *adj.*
**ain't** (ānt) *v.* Contraction of *am not, is not, has not,* and *have not.*
**air** (âr) *n.* **1.** A gaseous mixture that surrounds the earth. **2.** An impression; appearance. **3. airs.** Affectation. **4.** A melody. —*v.* **1.** To expose to air. **2.** To give public utterance to.
**air-con•di•tion** (âr'kən-dĭsh'ən) *v.* To control, esp. lower, the temperature and humidity of (an enclosure). **—air con•di'tion•er** *n.* **—air con•di'tion•ing** *n.*
**air•craft** (âr'krăft') *n., pl.* **-craft.** Any machine or device capable of flight.
**air•plane** (âr'plān') *n.* A winged, heavier-than-air flying machine propelled by jet engines or propellers.
**air•play** (âr'plā') *n.* The broadcast of a record on the air by a radio station.
**air•port** (âr'pôrt', -pōrt') *n.* A place with cargo and passenger facilities where aircraft take off and land.
**air right** *n.* A right of way to the air space above a piece of property.
**air•time** (âr'tīm') *n.* The time during which a radio station or a TV station is broadcasting.
**air•waves** (âr'wāvz') *pl.n.* The medium used for the transmission of radio or TV signals.
**air•y** (âr'ē) *adj.* **-ier, -iest. 1.** Of or like air. **2.** Breezy. **3.** Graceful or delicate. **—air'i•ly** *adv.*
**aisle** (īl) *n.* A passageway between rows of seats.
**a•jar** (ə-jär') *adv. & adj.* Partially open.
**a•kim•bo** (ə-kĭm'bō) *adj. & adv.* With the hands on the hips.
**a•kin** (ə-kĭn') *adj.* **1.** Related. **2.** Similar.
**a•lac•ri•ty** (ə-lăk'rĭ-tē) *n.* Cheerful eagerness; sprightliness.
**a•larm** (ə-lärm') *n.* **1.** A sudden feeling of fear. **2.** A warning of danger. **3.** A device sounded to warn people of danger. —*v.* **1.** To fill with alarm; frighten. **2.** To set with a warning device. **—a•larm'ing** *adj.* **—a•larm'ing•ly** *adv.* **—a•larm'ist** *adj. & n.*
**al•ba•tross** (ăl'bə-trôs', -trŏs') *n.* A large, web-footed sea bird.
**al•be•it** (ôl-bē'ĭt) *conj.* Although.
**al•bi•no** (ăl-bī'nō) *n., pl.* **-nos.** A person or animal having abnormally pale skin, very light hair, and lacking normal eye coloring.
**al•bum** (ăl'bəm) *n.* **1.** A blank book for stamps, photographs, etc. **2.** One or more phonograph records in one binding.
**al•bu•men** (ăl-byōō'mən) *n.* The white of an egg.
**al•che•my** (ăl'kə-mē) *n.* An early kind of chemistry concerned primarily with changing common metals into gold. **—al'che•mist** *n.*
**al•co•hol** (ăl'kə-hôl') *n.* **1.** Any of a series of chemically related organic compounds. **2.** An intoxicating liquor. **—al'co•hol'ic** *adj. & n.* **—al'co•hol•ism'** *n.*
**al•cove** (ăl'kōv') *n.* A recess of a room.
**al•der•man** (ôl'dər-mən) *n.* A member of a municipal legislative body.
**ale** (āl) *n.* A beverage similar to beer.

**a•lert** (ə-lûrt′) *adj.* **1.** Vigilant; watchful. **2.** Mentally responsive; quick. —*n.* **1.** A warning signal. **2.** The period during which such a warning is in effect. —*v.* To warn. **—a•lert′ness** *n.*

**al•fal•fa** (ăl-făl′fə) *n.* A cloverlike plant cultivated for forage.

**al•fres•co** (ăl-frĕs′kō) *adj. & adv.* In the fresh air; outdoors.

**al•gae** (ăl′jē) *pl.n.* Mostly aquatic plants, as the seaweeds.

**al•ge•bra** (ăl′jə-brə) *n.* A form of mathematics dealing with symbols, equations, etc. **—al′ge•bra′ic** *adj.*

**al•gi•cide** (ăl′jə-sīd′) *n.* A chemical added to water to kill algae.

**ALGOL** (ăl′gŏl′) *n.* A mathematical language for computer programming.

**a•li•as** (ā′lē-əs, āl′yəs) *n.* An assumed name. —*adv.* Otherwise named.

**al•i•bi** (ăl′ə-bī′) *n.* **1.** A legal defense in which a defendant tries to prove he was elsewhere when a crime was committed. **2.** An excuse.

**a•li•en** (ā′lē-ən, āl′yən) *adj.* **1.** Foreign; unfamiliar. **2.** Repugnant. —*n.* **1.** An unnaturalized resident of a country. **2.** A creature supposedly from outer space.

**al•ien•ate** (āl′yə-nāt′, ā′lē-ə-) *v.* **-ated, -ating.** To make unfriendly or indifferent. **—al′ien•a′tion** *n.*

**a•light**[1] (ə-līt′) *v.* **alighted** or **alit, alighting. 1.** To come down and settle. **2.** To dismount.

**a•light**[2] (ə-līt′) *adj. & adv.* Burning; lighted.

**a•lign** (ə-līn′) *v.* **1.** To arrange in a line. **2.** To ally (oneself) with; take sides. **—a•lign′ment** *n.*

**a•like** (ə-līk′) *adj.* Similar. —*adv.* In the same way.

**al•i•mo•ny** (ăl′ə-mō′nē) *n., pl.* **-nies.** An allowance for support paid to a former spouse.

**A-line** (ā′līn′) *adj.* Relating to a garment with a flared bottom and a close-fitting top. **—A′-line′** *n.*

**a•lit** (ə-lĭt′) *v.* p.t. & p.p. of **alight.**

**a•live** (ə-līv′) *adj.* **1.** Having life; living. **2.** In operation; active. **3.** Full of life; lively.

**al•ka•li** (ăl′kə-lī′) *n.* In chemistry, a base.

**all** (ôl) *adj.* **1.** The total extent, number, or quantity of. **2.** Every. **3.** Any. **4.** Nothing but. —*pron.* Each and every one. —*n.* The whole number; totality. —*adv.* Wholly; entirely.

**al•lay** (ə-lā′) *v.* **1.** To lessen; relieve. **2.** To calm; pacify.

**al•lege** (ə-lĕj′) *v.* **-leged, -leging.** To assert, esp. without proof. **—al′le•ga′tion** *n.* **—al•leg′ed•ly** *adv.*

**al•le•giance** (ə-lē′jəns) *n.* Loyalty to a nation, sovereign, or cause.

**al•le•go•ry** (ăl′ĭ-gôr′ē, -gōr′ē) *n., pl.* **-ries.** A story in which the characters represent abstract qualities. **—al′le•gor′ic, al′le•gor′ic•al** *adj.*

**al•ler•gen** (ăl′ər-jən, -jĕn′) *n.* A substance that causes an allergy. **—al′ler•gen′ic** *adj. & n.*

**al•ler•gist** (ăl′ər-jĭst) *n.* A physician specializing in treating allergies.

**al•ler•gy** (ăl′ər-jē) *n., pl.* **-gies.** Hypersensitive reaction to a substance harmless to most people. **—al•ler′gic** *adj.*

**al•le•vi•ate** (ə-lē′vē-āt′) *v.* **-ated, -ating.** To make more bearable. **—al•le′vi•a′tion** *n.*

**al•ley** (ăl′ē) *n., pl.* **-leys.** A narrow passageway between or behind buildings.

**al•li•ance** (ə-lī′əns) *n.* **1.** An agreement to join forces or work together. **2.** A connection; union.

**al•li•ga•tor** (ăl′ĭ-gā′tər) *n.* A large reptile with a shorter snout than the related crocodiles.

**al•lit•er•a•tion** (ə-lĭt′ə-rā′shən) *n.* The occurrence of two or more words having the same initial sound. **—al•lit′er•a′tive** *adj.*

**all-night•er** (ôl′nī′tər) *n.* A project, party, or study session lasting through the night.

**al•lo•cate** (ăl′ə-kāt′) *v.* **-cated, -cating.** To allot; assign. **—al′lo•ca′tion** *n.*

**al•lot** (ə-lŏt′) *v.* **-lotted, -lotting.** To distribute; give. **—al•lot′ment** *n.*

**al•low** (ə-lou′) *v.* **1.** To let happen; permit. **2.** To acknowledge or admit. **3.** To make provision. **4.** To provide. **—al•low′a•ble** *adj.*

**al•low•ance** (ə-lou′əns) *n.* A regular provision, as of money.

**al•loy** (ăl′oi′, ə-loi′) *n.* A mixture of metals. **—al•loy′** *v.*

**all right** *adv. & adj.* **1.** Satisfactory; average. **2.** Correct. **3.** Uninjured. **4.** Very well; yes.

**all-star** (ôl′stär′) *adj.* Made up wholly of star performers. —*n.* A player chosen for an all-star team.

**all-time** (ôl′tīm′) *adj.* Of all time.

**al•lude** (ə-lo͞od′) *v.* **-luded, -luding.** To refer to indirectly. —**al•lu′sion** *n.*

**al•lure** (ə-lo͝or′) *v.* **-lured, -luring.** To entice; tempt. —*n.* The power to entice. —**al•lur′ing•ly** *adv.*

**al•ly** (ə-lī′, ăl′ī) *v.* **-lied, -lying.** To unite or join for a specific purpose. —*n., pl.* **-lies.** A nation or person that is allied to another.

**al•ma•nac** (ôl′mə-năk′, ăl′-) *n.* A calendar with weather forecasts and other useful information.

**al•might•y** (ôl-mī′tē) *adj.* Omnipotent. —*n.* **the Almighty.** God.

**al•mond** (ä′mənd, ăm′ənd) *n.* **1.** An oval, edible nut with a light-brown shell. **2.** The tree bearing this nut. **3.** A pale tan.

**al•most** (ôl′mōst′, ôl-mōst′) *adv.* Nearly; not quite.

**alms** (ämz) *pl.n.* Money or goods given to the poor.

**a•lone** (ə-lōn′) *adj.* **1.** Apart from other people; single; solitary. **2.** Sole; only. —**a•lone′** *adv.*

**a•long** (ə-lông′, ə-lŏng′) *adv.* **1.** In a line with. **2.** Forward. **3.** In association; together. —*prep.* In a line with; by the length of.

**a•long•side** (ə-lông′sīd′, ə-lŏng′-) *adv.* Along, at, or to the side. —*prep.* By the side of.

**a•loof** (ə-lo͞of′) *adj.* Distant; reserved. —**a•loof′ness** *n.*

**al•pha•bet** (ăl′fə-bĕt′, -bĭt) *n.* The letters of a language, arranged in a fixed order. —**al′pha•bet′i•cal** *adj.* —**al′pha•bet′i•cal•ly** *adv.* —**al′pha•bet•ize′** *v.*

**al•pha•nu•mer•ic** (ăl′fə-no͞o-mĕr′ĭk) *adj.* Relating to the alphabetic, numeric, and other symbols used esp. in computer work. —**al′pha•nu•mer′ics** *pl.n.*

**Al•pine** (ăl′pīn′) *adj.* **1.** Relating to the Alps. **2. alpine.** Relating to high mountains. **3.** Relating to competitive downhill racing and slalom skiing.

**al•read•y** (ôl-rĕd′ē) *adv.* By this time.

**al•so** (ôl′sō) *adv.* Besides; in addition.

**al•tar** (ôl′tər) *n.* An elevated structure used in religious ceremonies.

**al•ter** (ôl′tər) *v.* To change; modify. —**al′ter•a′tion** *n.*

**al•ter•ca•tion** (ôl′tər-kā′shən) *n.* A heated, noisy quarrel. —**al′ter•cate′** *v.*

**al•ter•nate** (ôl′tər-nāt′, ăl′-) *v.* **-nated, -nating. 1.** To do, use, occur, etc., in turn. **2.** To go back and forth. —*adj.* (-nĭt). **1.** Happening or following in turns. **2.** Every other. **3.** Substitute. —*n.* (-nĭt). A substitute. —**al′ter•na′tion** *n.*

**al•ter•na•tive** (ôl-tûr′nə-tĭv, ăl-) *n.* A choice between possibilities. —*adj.* Allowing or furnishing a choice.

**al•though** (ôl-*th*ō′) *conj.* Also **al•tho.** Regardless of the fact that.

**al•ti•tude** (ăl′tĭ-t/y/o͞od′) *n.* Height, esp. above the earth's surface.

**al•to** (ăl′tō) *n., pl.* **-tos.** A low female singing voice.

**al•to•geth•er** (ôl′tə-gĕ*th*′ər) *adv.* **1.** Entirely; completely. **2.** In all; all told. **3.** On the whole; all things considered.

**al•tru•ism** (ăl′tro͞o-ĭz′əm) *n.* Selfless concern for others. —**al′tru•ist** *n.* —**al′tru•is′tic** *adj.*

**a•lu•mi•num** (ə-lo͞o′mə-nəm) *n.* A metallic element used to form many hard, light alloys.

**a•lum•na** (ə-lŭm′nə) *n., pl.* **-nae.** A female graduate of a school, college, or university.

**a•lum•nus** (ə-lŭm′nəs) *n., pl.* **-ni.** A male graduate of a school, college, or university.

**al•ways** (ôl′wāz, -wĭz) *adv.* **1.** On every occasion. **2.** Continuously. **3.** At any time; in any event.

**am** (ăm) *v.* 1st person sing. present indicative of **be.**

**a•mass** (ə-măs′) *v.* To accumulate.

**am•a•teur** (ăm′ə-tûr′, -tər, -ə-cho͝or′) *n.* **1.** One who engages in an activity for pleasure, not pay. **2.** An inept practitioner. —**am′a•teur′ish** *adj.*

**a•maze** (ə-māz′) *v.* **amazed, amazing.** To surprise; astound. —**a•maze′ment** *n.*

**am•bas•sa•dor** (ăm-băs′ə-dər, dôr′) *n.* A diplomat of the highest rank. —**am•bas′sa•do′ri•al** *adj.*

**am•bi•ance** (ăm′bē-əns) *n.* Surroundings; atmosphere.

**am•bi•dex•trous** (ăm′bĭ-dĕk′strəs) *adj.* Able to use both hands with equal facility.

**am•big•u•ous** (ăm-bĭg′yo͞o-əs) *adj.* Having more than one meaning; unclear. **—am′bi•gu′i•ty, am•big′u•ous•ness** *n.*

**am•bi•tion** (ăm-bĭsh′ən) *n.* **1.** A strong desire to achieve something; will to succeed. **2.** A goal. **—am•bi′tious** *adj.*

**am•biv•a•lence** (ăm-bĭv′ə-ləns) *n.* The existence of conflicting feelings about a person or thing. **—am•biv′a•lent** *adj.*

**am•bu•lance** (ăm′byə-ləns) *n.* A vehicle to transport the sick or wounded.

**am•bu•la•to•ry** (ăm′byə-lə-tôr′ē, -tōr′ē) *adj.* Involving or capable of walking.

**am•bush** (ăm′bo͝osh′) *n.* **1.** A surprise attack from a concealed position. **2.** The concealed position from which such an attack is made. **—am′bush′** *v.*

**a•me•lio•rate** (ə-mēl′yə-rāt′) *v.* **-rated, -rating.** To improve. **—a•me′lio•ra′tion** *n.*

**a•men** (ā-mĕn′, ä-) *interj.* So be it.

**a•me•na•ble** (ə-mē′nə-bəl, ə-mĕn′ə-) *adj.* Agreeable; responsive.

**a•mend** (ə-mĕnd′) *v.* **1.** To improve. **2.** To correct; rectify. **3.** To alter (a law) formally. **—a•mend′ment** *n.*

**a•mends** (ə-mĕndz′) *pl.n.* Compensation for insult or injury; redress.

**a•men•i•ty** (ə-mĕn′ĭ-tē, ə-mē′nĭ-) *n., pl.* **-ties. 1.** Pleasantness. **2.** A comfort or convenience. **3. amenities.** Social courtesies.

**am•e•thyst** (ăm′ə-thĭst) *n.* A purple quartz used as a gemstone.

**a•mi•a•ble** (ā′mē-ə-bəl) *adj.* **1.** Good-natured. **2.** Cordial; friendly. **—a′mi•a•bil′i•ty** *n.*

**am•i•ca•ble** (ăm′ĭ-kə-bəl) *adj.* Friendly. **—am′i•ca•bly** *adv.*

**a•mid** (ə-mĭd′) *prep.* Also **a•midst.** Among.

**a•miss** (ə-mĭs′) *adj.* Wrong. *—adv.* In an improper way.

**am•i•ty** (ăm′ĭ-tē) *n.* Friendly relations.

**am•mo•nia** (ə-mōn′yə) *n.* A colorless, pungent gas.

**am•mu•ni•tion** (ăm′yə-nĭsh′ən) *n.* Bullets, shells, etc., that can be fired from guns.

**am•ne•sia** (ăm-nē′zhə) *n.* Loss of memory.

**am•nes•ty** (ăm′nĭ-stē) *n., pl.* **-ties.** A general pardon, esp. for political offenders.

**am•ni•o•cen•te•sis** (ăm′nē-ō-sĕn-tē′sĭs) *n., pl.* **-ses.** Examination of a fetus by withdrawing and studying fluid from within the uterus.

**a•moe•ba, a•me•ba** (ə-mē′bə) *n., pl.* **-bas** or **-bae.** A one-celled organism that has a changeable form. **—a•moe′bic** *adj.*

**a•mong** (ə-mŭng′) *prep.* Also **a•mongst. 1.** In or through the midst of. **2.** In the group or company of. **3.** With portions to each of. **4.** Between one another.

**a•mor•phous** (ə-môr′fəs) *adj.* Lacking definite form or shape.

**am•or•tize** (ăm′ər-tīz′, ə-môr′-) *v.* **-tized, -tizing.** To pay off (as a debt) by installments. **—am′or•ti•za′tion** *n.*

**a•mount** (ə-mount′) *n.* **1.** A total or sum. **2.** Quantity. *—v.* **1.** To reach as a total. **2.** To be equivalent.

**am•per•sand** (ăm′pər-sănd′) *n.* A symbol (&) meaning *and.*

**am•phib•i•an** (ăm-fĭb′ē-ən) *n.* **1.** An animal, as a frog, that can live in water and on land. **2.** A vehicle that can travel in water and on land. *—adj.* Amphibious.

**am•phib•i•ous** (ăm-fĭb′ē-əs) *adj.* Able to live or operate both in water and on land.

**am•phi•the•a•ter** (ăm′fə-thē′ə-tər) *n.* An oval building with tiers of seats rising around an arena.

**am•ple** (ăm′pəl) *adj.* **-pler, -plest. 1.** Large. **2.** Sufficient; abundant. **—am′ply** *adv.*

**am•pli•fy** (ăm′plə-fī′) *v.* **-fied, -fying. 1.** To enlarge, extend, or increase. **2.** To make louder. **—am′pli•fi•ca′tion** *n.* **—am′pli•fi′er** *n.*

**am•pli•tude** (ăm′plĭ-t/y/o͞od′) *n.* **1.** Abundance; fullness. **2.** Greatness of size; extent.

**am•pu•tate** (ăm′pyo͞o-tāt′) *v.* **-tated, -tating.** To cut off, as a limb. **—am′pu•ta′tion** *n.* **—am′pu•tee′** *n.*

**a•muck, a•mok** (ə-mŭk′) *adv.* In a fit of wildness.

**am•u•let** (ăm′yə-lĭt) *n.* A charm worn against evil or injury.

**a•muse** (ə-myo͞oz′) *v.* **amused, amusing.** To entertain; divert. **—a•muse′ment** *n.*

**an** (ăn, ən) *indef. art.* A form of *a* used before words beginning with a vowel.

**a•nach•ro•nism** (ə-năk′rə-nĭz′əm) *n.* Something that is out of its proper time. —**a•nach′ro•nis′tic** *adj.*

**an•al•ge•sic** (ăn′əl-jē′zĭk) *n.* A drug that relieves pain.

**a•nal•o•gy** (ə-năl′ə-jē) *n., pl.* **-gies.** Correspondence in some respects; partial similarity. —**a•nal′o•gous** *adj.*

**a•nal•y•sis** (ə-năl′ĭ-sĭs) *n., pl.* **-ses. 1.** The separation of a whole into its parts for study and interpretation. **2.** Psychoanalysis. —**an′a•lyst** *n.* —**an′a•lyt′ic, an′a•lyt′i•cal** *adj.* —**an′a•lyze′** *v.*

**an•ar•chy** (ăn′ər-kē) *n., pl.* **-chies. 1.** Absence of political authority. **2.** Disorder and confusion. —**an•ar′chic** *adj.*

**a•nat•o•my** (ə-năt′ə-mē) *n., pl.* **-mies. 1.** The structure of an organism. **2.** The science of the structure of organisms. —**an′a•tom′ic, an′a•tom′i•cal** *adj.*

**an•ces•tor** (ăn′sĕs′tər) *n.* A person from whom another has descended. —**an′ces′try** *n.*

**an•chor** (ăng′kər) *n.* **1.** A heavy metal device cast overboard to keep a ship in place. **2.** The chief broadcaster on a news or sports program. —*v.* **1.** To hold or be held fast or secure. **2.** To act as an anchor on a broadcast. —**an′chor•man′** *n.* —**an′chor•peo′ple** *n.* —**an′chor•per′son** *n.* —**an′chor•wom′an** *n.*

**an•cient** (ān′shənt) *adj.* **1.** Very old. **2.** Belonging to times long past.

**and** (ənd, ən; *stressed* ănd) *conj.* **1.** Together with; as well as. **2.** Added to; plus. **3.** As a result.

**and•i•ron** (ănd′ī′ərn) *n.* One of a pair of metal supports for logs in a fireplace.

**an•ec•dote** (ăn′ĭk-dōt′) *n.* A short account of an interesting or humorous incident. —**an′ec•dot′al** *adj.*

**a•ne•mi•a, a•nae•mi•a** (ə-nē′mē-ə) *n.* A deficiency in the oxygen-carrying material of the blood. —**a•ne′mic** *adj.*

**a•nem•o•ne** (ə-nĕm′ə-nē) *n.* A plant having cup-shaped flowers.

**an•es•the•sia, an•aes•the•sia** (ăn′ĭs-thē′zhə) *n.* Loss of sensation.

**an•es•thet•ic, an•aes•thet•ic** (ăn′ĭs-thĕt′ĭk) *adj.* Causing anesthesia. —*n.* An anesthetic agent. —**an•es′the•tist** *n.* —**an•es′the•tize′** *v.*

**an•gel** (ān′jəl) *n.* **1.** One of the immortal beings attendant upon God. **2.** A kind and lovable person. —**an•gel′ic** *adj.*

**an•ger** (ăng′gər) *n.* Wrath; rage. —*v.* To make or become angry.

**an•gle**[1] (ăng′gəl) *v.* **-gled, -gling.** To fish with a hook and line. —**an′gler** *n.*

**an•gle**[2] (ăng′gəl) *n.* **1.** The figure formed by two lines diverging from a common point. **2.** A point of view. —*v.* **-gled, -gling.** To move or turn at an angle.

**an•gry** (ăng′grē) *adj.* **-grier, -griest. 1.** Feeling or showing anger. **2.** Having a menacing aspect. —**an′gri•ly** *adv.*

**an•guish** (ăng′gwĭsh) *n.* Great physical or mental pain; torment. —**an′guished** *adj.*

**an•gu•lar** (ăng′gyə-lər) *adj.* **1.** Having an angle or angles. **2.** Bony and lean. —**an′gu•lar′i•ty** *n.*

**an•i•mal** (ăn′ə-məl) *n.* **1.** An organism distinguished from a plant by such characteristics as the ability to move. **2.** A bestial person; brute. —*adj.* **1.** Of animals. **2.** Sensual or physical as distinguished from spiritual.

**an•i•mate** (ăn′ə-māt′) *v.* **-mated, -mating. 1.** To give life to. **2.** To enliven. **3.** To make (a cartoon) so as to convey the illusion of motion. —*adj.* (-mĭt). Living. —**an′i•ma′tion** *n.*

**an•kle** (ăng′kəl) *n.* The joint that connects the foot with the leg.

**an•nex** (ə-nĕks′, ăn′ĕks′) *v.* To add or join, esp. to a larger thing. —*n.* (ăn′ĕks′). A building added on to a larger one. —**an′nex•a′tion** *n.*

**an•ni•hi•late** (ə-nī′ə-lāt′) *v.* **-lated, -lating.** To destroy completely. —**an•ni′hi•la′tion** *n.*

**an•ni•ver•sa•ry** (ăn′ə-vûr′sə-rē) *n., pl.* **-ries.** The annual return, often celebrated, of the date of an important event.

**an•no•tate** (ăn′ō-tāt′) *v.* **-tated, -tating.** To furnish with explanatory notes. —**an′no•ta′tion** *n.*

**an•nounce** (ə-nouns′) *v.* **-nounced, -nouncing.** To bring to public notice; proclaim. —**an•nounce′ment** *n.* —**an•nounc′er** *n.*

**an•noy** (ə-noi′) *v.* To bother or irritate. —**an•noy′ance** *n.*

**an•nu•al** (ăn′yo͞o-əl) *adj.* Yearly. —*n.* **1.** A yearly periodical. **2.** A plant that lives for one year or season.

**an•nul** (ə-nŭl′) *v.* **-nulled, -nulling.** To nullify or cancel, as a marriage. —**an•nul′ment** *n.*

**a•nom•a•ly** (ə-nŏm′ə-lē) *n., pl.* **-lies.** A deviation from the normal; abnormality. —**a•nom′a•lous** *adj.*

**a•non** (ə-nŏn′) *adv.* In a short time; soon.

**a•non•y•mous** (ə-nŏn′ə-məs) *adj.* Having an unknown or withheld name. —**an′o•nym′i•ty, a•non′y•mous•ness** *n.*

**an•o•rex•i•a** (ăn′ə-rĕk′sē-ə) *n.* **1.** Loss of appetite, esp. from disease. **2.** Life-threatening loss of appetite occurring chiefly among adolescent girls and young women. —**an′o•rec′tic** *adj. & n.* —**an′o•rex′ic** *adj. & n.*

**an•oth•er** (ə-nŭ*th*′ər) *adj.* **1.** Additional; one more. **2.** Different; some other. —*pron.* **1.** An additional or different one. **2.** One of the same kind.

**an•swer** (ăn′sər) *n.* **1.** A reply, as to a question. **2.** A solution or result. —*v.* **1.** To reply to. **2.** To respond correctly to. **3.** To serve (a purpose). **4.** To be responsible. —**an′swer•a•ble** *adj.*

**ant** (ănt) *n.* An insect, usually wingless, living in colonies.

**ant•ac•id** (ănt-ăs′ĭd) *n.* A medication that reduces stomach acid. —**ant•ac′id** *adj.*

**an•tag•o•nism** (ăn-tăg′ə-nĭz′əm) *n.* Opposition; hostility. —**an•tag′o•nist** *n.* —**an•tag′o•nis′tic** *adj.*

**an•tag•o•nize** (ăn-tăg′ə-nīz′) *v.* **-nized, -nizing.** To arouse the hostility of.

**an•te•bel•lum** (ăn′tē-bĕl′əm) *adj.* Relating to the time before the American Civil War.

**an•te•ce•dent** (ăn′tĭ-sēd′nt) *adj.* Going before; preceding. —*n.* **1.** One that precedes another. **2.** A word or phrase to which a pronoun refers.

**an•te•date** (ăn′tĭ-dāt′) *v.* **-dated, -dating.** To give a date earlier than the actual date; backdate.

**an•te•lope** (ăn′tl-ōp′) *n.* A swift-running, long-horned hoofed mammal.

**an•ten•na** (ăn-tĕn′ə) *n.* **1.** *pl.* **-nae.** One of the feelers on the head of an insect, crustacean, etc. **2.** *pl.* **-nas.** A metallic apparatus for sending and receiving electromagnetic waves; aerial.

**an•te•ri•or** (ăn-tîr′ē-ər) *adj.* **1.** Located in front. **2.** Earlier.

**an•them** (ăn′thəm) *n.* A patriotic or religious song.

**an•thol•o•gy** (ăn-thŏl′ə-jē) *n., pl.* **-gies.** A collection of literary pieces.

**an•thro•pol•o•gy** (ăn′thrə-pŏl′ə-jē) *n.* The study of the origin, culture, and development of the human race. —**an′thro•po•log′ic, an′thro•po•log′i•cal** *adj.* —**an′thro•pol′o•gist** *n.*

**an•ti•bi•ot•ic** (ăn′tĭ-bī-ŏt′ĭk, ăn′tī-) *n.* A substance, often produced by fungi or bacteria, that destroys or inhibits the growth of microorganisms.

**an•ti•bod•y** (ăn′tĭ-bŏd′ē) *n. pl.* **-ies.** A protein in the blood generated to combat foreign substances.

**an•tic** (ăn′tĭk) *n.* A playful or ludicrous act; a caper.

**an•tic•i•pate** (ăn-tĭs′ə-pāt′) *v.* **-pated, -pating. 1.** To realize beforehand; foresee. **2.** To look forward to. **3.** To prevent; forestall. —**an•tic′i•pa′tion** *n.*

**an•ti•cli•max** (ăn′tē-klī′măks′) *n.* A decline in disappointing contrast to what has preceded. —**an′ti•cli•mac′tic** *adj.*

**an•ti•dote** (ăn′tĭ-dōt′) *n.* Something that counteracts a poison or injury.

**an•tip•a•thy** (ăn-tĭp′ə-thē) *n., pl.* **-thies.** An intense dislike.

**an•ti•per•spi•rant** (ăn′tĭ-pûr′spər-ənt) *n.* A preparation applied to the skin to reduce or prevent excessive sweating.

**an•tique** (ăn-tēk′) *adj.* Belonging to an earlier period. —*n.* An object having special value because of its age. —*v.* **-tiqued, -tiquing.** To give the appearance of an antique to.

**an•tiq•ui•ty** (ăn-tĭk′wĭ-tē) *n., pl.* **-ties. 1.** Ancient times. **2.** Great age. **3. antiquities.** Relics and monuments of former times.

**an•ti•sep•tic** (ăn′tĭ-sĕp′tĭk) *adj.* **1.** Capable of destroying harmful bacteria. **2.** Thoroughly clean. **3.** Austere; drab. —*n.* An antiseptic substance.

**ant•ler** (ănt′lər) *n.* One of the paired bony growths on the head of a deer.

**an•to•nym** (ăn′tə-nĭm′) *n.* A word opposite in meaning to another.

**a•nus** (ā′nəs) *n., pl.* **anuses.** The excretory opening of the digestive system.

**an•vil** (ăn′vĭl) *n.* A block on which metals are shaped by hammering.

**anx•i•e•ty** (ăng-zī′ĭ-tē) *n., pl.* **-ties.** A feeling of uneasiness; worry.
**anx•ious** (ăngk′shəs, ăng′shəs) *adj.* **1.** Worried about some uncertainty. **2.** Desirous; eager. **—anx′ious•ly** *adv.*
**an•y** (ĕn′ē) *adj.* **1.** One, no matter which, from three or more. **2.** Some. *—pron.* **1.** Any one or ones. **2.** Any quantity or part.
**an•y•bod•y** (ĕn′ē-bŏd′ē, -bŭd′ē) *pron.* Anyone.
**an•y•how** (ĕn′ē-hou′) *adv.* **1.** In any way. **2.** In any case.
**an•y•more** (ĕn′ē-môr′, -mōr′) *adv.* At the present time; from now on.
**an•y•one** (ĕn′ē-wŭn′, -wən) *pron.* Any person.
**an•y•place** (ĕn′ē-plās′) *adv.* To, in, or at any place; anywhere.
**an•y•thing** (ĕn′ē-thĭng′) *pron.* Any object or matter whatever.
**an•y•way** (ĕn′ē-wā′) *adv.* **1.** In any manner. **2.** Nevertheless.
**an•y•where** (ĕn′ē-hwâr′) *adv.* To, in, or at any place.
**a•or•ta** (ā-ôr′tə) *n., pl.* **-tas** or **-tae.** The main artery carrying blood away from the heart.
**a•part•ment** (ə-pärt′mənt) *n.* A room or suite of rooms for dwelling.
**ap•a•thy** (ăp′ə-thē) *n.* Lack of emotion or interest; indifference. **—ap′a•thet′ic** *adj.*
**ape** (āp) *n.* A large primate such as a chimpanzee. *—v.* **aped, aping.** To mimic.
**a•pex** (ā′pĕks) *n., pl.* **apexes** or **apices.** The highest point of something.
**aph•o•rism** (ăf′ə-rĭz′əm) *n.* A maxim; adage.
**a•pi•ar•y** (ā′pē-ĕr′ē) *n., pl.* **-ies.** A place where bees are raised.
**a•piece** (ə-pēs′) *adv.* To or for each one.
**APL** *n.* A computer programming language for use at remote terminals.
**a•plomb** (ə-plŏm′, ə-plŭm′) *n.* Self-confidence; poise.
**a•pol•o•gy** (ə-pŏl′ə-jē) *n., pl.* **-gies. 1.** An expression of regret. **2.** A formal justification or defense. **—a•pol′o•get′ic** *adj.* **—a•pol′o•gist** *n.* **—a•pol′o•gize′** *v.*
**a•pos•tle** (ə-pŏs′əl) *n.* **1. Apostle.** One of Christ's 12 original disciples. **2.** One who leads a new cause.
**a•pos•tro•phe** (ə-pŏs′trə-fē) *n.* The sign (') used to indicate the omission of a letter or letters from a word, the possessive case, and certain plurals.
**ap•pall** (ə-pôl) *v.* To fill with dismay. **—ap•pall′ing** *adj.*
**ap•pa•ra•tus** (ăp′ə-rā′təs, -răt′əs) *n., pl.* **-tus** or **-tuses.** The equipment needed to perform a specific function; machine or device.
**ap•par•el** (ə-păr′əl) *n.* Clothing. *—v.* To clothe; dress.
**ap•par•ent** (ə-păr′ənt, ə-pâr′-) *adj.* Readily perceived; evident; plain. **—ap•par′ent•ly** *adv.*
**ap•pa•ri•tion** (ăp′ə-rĭsh′ən) *n.* A ghost.
**ap•peal** (ə-pēl′) *n.* **1.** An earnest request. **2.** Attraction; allure. **3.** In law, a request for a new hearing by a higher court. *—v.* **1.** To make an earnest request. **2.** To be attractive. **3.** To apply to transfer (a case) to a higher court for rehearing.
**ap•pear** (ə-pîr′) *v.* **1.** To become visible. **2.** To come into existence. **3.** To seem or look. **4.** To come before the public. **—ap•pear′ance** *n.*
**ap•pease** (ə-pēz′) *v.* **-peased, -peasing. 1.** To placate, esp. by granting concessions. **2.** To satisfy. **—ap•pease′ment** *n.*
**ap•pend** (ə-pĕnd′) *v.* To attach; add.
**ap•pend•age** (ə-pĕn′dĭj) *n.* An attached organ or part.
**ap•pen•dec•to•my** (ăp′ən-dĕk′tə-mē) *n., pl.* **-mies.** Surgical removal of the appendix.
**ap•pen•di•ci•tis** (ə-pĕn′dĭ-sī′tĭs) *n.* Inflammation of the appendix.
**ap•pen•dix** (ə-pĕn′dĭks) *n., pl.* **-dixes** or **-dices. 1.** Supplementary material at the end of a book. **2.** A tubular projection attached to the large intestine.
**ap•pe•tite** (ăp′ĭ-tīt′) *n.* A desire or craving, esp. for food or drink.
**ap•pe•tiz•er** (ăp′ĭ-tī′zər) *n.* A food or drink served before a meal.
**ap•plaud** (ə-plôd′) *v.* To express approval, esp. by clapping the hands. **—ap•plause′** *n.*
**ap•ple** (ăp′əl) *n.* A rounded, often red-skinned edible fruit.
**ap•pli•ance** (ə-plī′əns) *n.* A machine or device, esp. one for household use.

**ap•pli•cant** (ăp′lĭ-kənt) *n.* One who applies, as for a job.

**ap•pli•ca•tion** (ăp′lĭ-kā′shən) *n.* **1.** The act of applying. **2.** Something that is applied, as a cosmetic. **3. a.** A request, as for a job. **b.** A form on which such a request is made.

**ap•ply** (ə-plī′) *v.* **-plied, -plying. 1.** To put on or upon. **2.** To adapt for a special use. **3.** To devote (oneself or one's efforts). **4.** To be pertinent. **5.** To make a request, as for a job. **—ap′pli•ca•ble** *adj.* **—ap′pli•ca•bil′i•ty** *n.*

**ap•point** (ə-point′) *v.* **1.** To name for a position. **2.** To fix or set, as a time. **3.** To furnish; equip. **—ap•point′ee′** *n.* **—ap•point′ive** *adj.* **—ap•point′ment** *n.*

**ap•por•tion** (ə-pôr′shən, ə-pōr′-) *v.* To divide and assign; allot. **—ap•por′tion•ment** *n.*

**ap•praise** (ə-prāz′) *v.* **-praised, -praising.** To evaluate. **—ap•prais′al** *n.* **—ap•prais′er** *n.*

**ap•pre•cia•ble** (ə-prē′shə-bəl) *adj.* Capable of being noticed or measured; noticeable.

**ap•pre•ci•ate** (ə-prē′shē-āt′) *v.* **-ated, -ating. 1.** To value highly. **2.** To realize. **3.** To be thankful for. **4.** To go up in value. **—ap•pre′ci•a′tion** *n.* **—ap•pre′cia•tive** *adj.*

**ap•pre•hend** (ăp′rĭ-hĕnd′) *v.* **1.** To arrest. **2.** To grasp mentally; understand. **3.** To anticipate with anxiety. **—ap′pre•hen′sion** *n.* **—ap′pre•hen′sive** *adj.*

**ap•pren•tice** (ə-prĕn′tĭs) *n.* **1.** One learning a trade under a skilled craftsman. **2.** Any beginner. —*v.* **-ticed, -ticing.** To place as an apprentice. **—ap•pren′tice•ship′** *n.*

**ap•prise** (ə-prīz′) *v.* **-prised, -prising.** To inform.

**ap•proach** (ə-prōch′) *v.* **1.** To come near (to). **2.** To approximate. **3.** To make a proposal to. —*n.* **1.** The act of approaching. **2.** A way of dealing or working with something. **3.** A way of reaching; access.

**ap•pro•pri•ate** (ə-prō′prē-ĭt) *adj.* Suitable; proper. —*v.* (-āt′) **-ated, -ating. 1.** To set apart for a particular use. **2.** To take; seize. **—ap•pro′pri•ate•ly** *adv.* **—ap•pro′pri•a′tion** *n.*

**ap•prove** (ə-pro͞ov′) *v.* **-proved, -proving. 1.** To regard favorably. **2.** To consent to. **—ap•prov′al** *n.*

**ap•prox•i•mate** (ə-prŏk′sə-mĭt) *adj.* Almost exact or accurate. —*v.* (-māt′) **-mated, -mating.** To come close to; be nearly the same as. **—ap•prox′i•ma′tion** *n.*

**a•pri•cot** (ăp′rĭ-kŏt′, ā′prĭ-) *n.* A yellow-orange peachlike fruit.

**A•pril** (ā′prəl) *n.* The 4th month of the year.

**a•pron** (ā′prən) *n.* A garment worn over the front to protect one's clothes.

**apt** (ăpt) *adj.* **1.** Exactly suitable; appropriate. **2.** Likely. **3.** Quick to learn.

**APT** *n.* A computer language for programming machine tools.

**ap•ti•tude** (ăp′tĭ-t/y/o͞od′) *n.* **1.** A natural talent. **2.** Quickness in learning.

**a•quar•i•um** (ə-kwâr′ē-əm) *n., pl.* **-ums** or **-ia.** A water-filled enclosure for keeping or displaying fish.

**a•quat•ic** (ə-kwăt′ĭk, ə-kwŏt′-) *adj.* Living or happening in water.

**ar•bi•ter** (är′bĭ-tər) *n.* A judge; arbitrator.

**ar•bi•trage** (är′bĭ-träzh′) *n.* The purchase of securities on one market for immediate sale for profit on another. **—ar′bi•tra•geur′** *n.*

**ar•bi•trar•y** (är′bĭ-trĕr′ē) *adj.* **1.** Determined by whim or caprice. **2.** Based on individual judgment. **—ar′bi•trar′i•ly** *adv.*

**ar•bi•trate** (är′bĭ-trāt′) *v.* **-trated, -trating.** To hear and settle a dispute; mediate. **—ar′bi•tra′tion** *n.* **—ar′bi•tra′tor** *n.*

**arc** (ärk) *n.* A portion of a curve, esp. of a circle. —*v.* **arced** or **arcked, arcing** or **arcking.** To form an arc.

**ar•cade** (är-kād′) *n.* **1.** A series of arches supported by columns. **2.** A roofed passageway, esp. one lined with shops. **3.** An amusement center with coin-operated electronic and video games.

**arch** (ärch) *n.* A curved structure forming the upper edge of an opening or a support, as in a bridge or doorway. —*v.* To form or supply with an arch.

**ar•chae•ol•o•gy, ar•che•ol•o•gy** (är′kē-ŏl′-ə-jē) *n.* The recovery and study of material evidence of human life and culture in past ages. **—ar′chae•o•log′ic, ar′chae•o•log′i•cal** *adj.* **—ar′chae•

**ol'o•gist** *n.*

**ar•cha•ic** (är-kā'ĭk) *adj.* **1.** Belonging to a much earlier time. **2.** Suggesting an earlier style or period.

**arch•bish•op** (ärch-bĭsh'əp) *n.* A bishop of the highest rank.

**arch•di•o•cese** (ärch-dī'ə-sĭs, -sēs', -sēz') *n.* A diocese under an archbishop's jurisdiction.

**arch•er•y** (är'chə-rē) *n.* The art or skill of shooting with a bow and arrows. **—arch'er** *n.*

**ar•chi•pel•a•go** (är'kə-pĕl'ə-gō') *n., pl.* **-goes** or **-gos.** A large group of islands.

**ar•chi•tec•ture** (är'kĭ-tĕk'chər) *n.* **1.** The art and science of designing and erecting buildings. **2.** The way computer components are organized and integrated. **—ar'chi•tect'** *n.* **—ar'chi•tec'tur•al** *adj.*

**ar•chives** (är'kīvz') *pl.n.* Public records or the place where they are kept.

**arcked** (ärkt) *v.* Alternate p.t. & p.p. of **arc.**

**arck•ing** (är'kĭng) *v.* Alternate pres.p. of **arc.**

**ar•dent** (är'dnt) *adj.* Passionate; fervent. **—ar'dent•ly** *adv.* **—ar'dor** *n.*

**ar•du•ous** (är'jo͞o-əs) *adj.* Strenuous; difficult.

**are** (är) *v.* 2nd person sing. and present tense indicative pl. of **be.**

**ar•e•a** (âr'ē-ə) *n.* **1.** A space; region. **2.** A range, as of study. **3.** The measure of a region, in square units.

**a•re•na** (ə-rē'nə) *n.* The area in the center of an amphitheater or stadium where contests are held.

**aren't** (ärnt, är'ənt) *v.* Contraction of *are not.*

**ar•gue** (är'gyo͞o) *v.* **-gued, -guing. 1.** To put forth reasons for or against. **2.** To dispute; quarrel. **—ar'gu•a•ble** *adj.* **—ar'gu•ment** *n.* **—ar'gu•men'ta•tive** *adj.*

**a•ri•a** (är'ē-ə) *n.* A solo vocal piece with instrumental accompaniment, as in an opera.

**ar•id** (ăr'ĭd) *adj.* **1.** Lacking moisture; dry. **2.** Dull.

**a•right** (ə-rīt') *adv.* Properly; correctly.

**a•rise** (ə-rīz') *v.* **arose, arisen, arising. 1.** To get up or move upward. **2.** To come into being. **3.** To result or proceed (with *from*).

**ar•is•toc•ra•cy** (ăr'ĭ-stŏk'rə-sē) *n., pl.* **-cies. 1.** A hereditary ruling class or nobility. **2.** Government by such a class. **—a•ris'to•crat'** *n.* **—a•ris'to•crat'ic** *adj.*

**a•rith•me•tic** (ə-rĭth'mĭ-tĭk) *n.* Computation involving the addition, subtraction, multiplication, and division of real numbers. **—ar'ith•met'ic, ar'ith•met'i•cal** *adj.*

**ark** (ärk) *n.* The boat built by Noah for the Flood.

**arm¹** (ärm) *n.* **1.** An upper limb of the human body. **2.** A part similar to an arm.

**arm²** (ärm) *n.* **1.** A weapon. **2.** A branch of a military force. *—v.* **1.** To equip with weapons. **2.** To prepare for war.

**ar•ma•ment** (är'mə-mənt) *n.* Often **armaments.** All the military weapons and equipment of a country.

**ar•mi•stice** (är'mĭ-stĭs) *n.* A truce.

**ar•mor** (är'mər) *n.* **1.** A protective covering, as for the body. **2.** The armored vehicles of an army. **—ar'mored** *adj.*

**ar•mor•y** (är'mə-rē) *n., pl.* **-ies. 1.** An arsenal. **2.** The headquarters of a military reserve force.

**ar•my** (är'mē) *n., pl.* **-mies. 1.** A large body of soldiers organized for warfare. **2.** Any large organized group.

**a•ro•ma** (ə-rō'mə) *n.* A pleasant odor. **—ar'o•mat'ic** *adj.*

**a•rose** (ə-rōz') *v.* p.t. of **arise.**

**a•round** (ə-round') *adv.* **1.** On or to all sides or in all directions. **2.** In a circle. **3.** In or toward the opposite direction. **4.** Close at hand; nearby. *—prep.* **1.** On all sides of. **2.** So as to surround. **3.** In or to various places within or near. **4.** Approximately at.

**a•rouse** (ə-rouz') *v.* **aroused, arousing. 1.** To awaken. **2.** To stir up; stimulate. **—a•rous'al** *n.*

**ar•raign** (ə-rān') *v.* **1.** To call before a court to answer a charge. **2.** To accuse.

**ar•range** (ə-rānj') *v.* **-ranged, -ranging. 1.** To put into a deliberate order. **2.** To agree about; settle. **3.** To reset (music) for other instruments or voices. **—ar•range'ment** *n.*

**ar•ray** (ə-rā') *v.* **1.** To arrange or draw up, as troops. **2.** To dress up, esp. in fine clothes. *—n.* **1.** An orderly arrangement. **2.** An impressive collection. **3.** Splendid attire.

**ar•rear** (ə-rîr′) *n.* Often **arrears.** An overdue debt. **—in arrears.** Behind in paying debts.

**ar•rest** (ə-rĕst′) *v.* **1.** To stop or check. **2.** To seize and hold by legal authority. *—n.* The act of arresting or state of being arrested.

**ar•rive** (ə-rīv′) *v.* **-rived, -riving. 1.** To reach a destination. **2.** To come at last. **3.** To achieve success. **—ar•ri′val** *n.*

**ar•ri•viste** (ä-rē-vēst′) *n.* A social climber; upstart.

**ar•ro•gant** (ăr′ə-gənt) *adj.* Overbearingly proud; haughty. **—ar′ro•gance** *n.*

**ar•row** (ăr′ō) *n.* **1.** A pointed shaft, shot from a bow at a target. **2.** A symbol used to indicate direction.

**ar•se•nal** (är′sə-nəl) *n.* A place for storing or making weapons.

**ar•son** (är′sən) *n.* The crime of burning buildings or other property. **—ar′son•ist** *n.*

**art** (ärt) *n.* **1. a.** The activity of creating beautiful things. **b.** Works, as paintings, poetry, music, etc., resulting from this. **2. arts.** The liberal arts. **3.** A craft; skill. **4.** Cunning.

**ar•ter•y** (är′tə-rē) *n., pl.* **-ies. 1.** Any of a branching system of tubes that carry blood away from the heart. **2.** A major transport route. **—ar•te′ri•al** *adj.*

**art•ful** (ärt′fəl) *adj.* **1.** Skillful; clever. **2.** Crafty; deceitful.

**ar•thri•tis** (är-thrī′tĭs) *n.* Inflammation of a joint or joints. **—ar•thrit′ic** *adj. & n.*

**ar•ti•choke** (är′tĭ-chōk′) *n.* The edible flower head of a thistlelike plant.

**ar•ti•cle** (är′tĭ-kəl) *n.* **1.** An individual thing; item. **2.** A section of a document. **3.** A piece of nonfiction writing, as in a magazine. **4.** Any of the words *a, an,* or *the.*

**ar•tic•u•late** (är-tĭk′yə-lĭt) *adj.* **1.** Able to speak clearly. **2.** Having joints. *—v.* (-lāt′) **-lated, -lating. 1.** To pronounce distinctly. **2.** To give voice to, as an emotion. **—ar•tic′u•la′tion** *n.*

**ar•ti•fice** (är′tə-fĭs) *n.* A clever device or crafty trick.

**ar•ti•fi•cial** (är′tə-fĭsh′əl) *adj.* **1.** Made by human beings rather than natural forces. **2.** Not genuine or natural. **—ar′ti•fi′ci•al′i•ty** *n.*

**ar•til•ler•y** (är-tĭl′ə-rē) *n.* **1.** Large-caliber mounted guns. **2.** The branch of an army that uses such guns.

**art•ist** (är′tĭst) *n.* One who creates works of art, esp. a painter or sculptor.

**ar•tis•tic** (är-tĭs′tĭk) *adj.* **1.** Of art or artists. **2.** Skilled. **3.** Appreciative of the fine arts.

**art•less** (ärt′lĭs) *adj.* **1.** Without guile; ingenuous. **2.** Natural; simple.

**as** (ăz, əz) *adv.* **1.** Equally. **2.** For instance. *—conj.* **1.** To the same degree that. **2.** In the same way that. **3.** While. **4.** Since; because. **5.** Though. **—as for** (or **to).** With regard to; concerning. *—pron.* That; which; who. *—prep.* In the capacity of.

**as•cend** (ə-sĕnd′) *v.* To move upward; climb. **—as•cen′sion** *n.*

**as•cen•dant** (ə-sĕn′dənt) *adj.* Also **as•cen•dent. 1.** Rising. **2.** Dominant; superior. **—as•cen′dan•cy** *n.*

**as•cent** (ə-sĕnt′) *n.* **1.** The act of ascending. **2.** An upward slope..

**as•cer•tain** (ăs′ər-tān′) *v.* To find out.

**as•cet•ic** (ə-sĕt′ĭk) *adj.* Practicing austere self-discipline. **—as•cet′ic** *n.* **—as•cet′i•cism′** *n.*

**ash**[1] (ăsh) *n.* The gray or black residue of combustion.

**ash**[2] (ăsh) *n.* A tree having strong, durable wood.

**a•side** (ə-sīd′) *adv.* **1.** On or to one side. **2.** Apart. **—aside from.** Excluding; excepting. *—n.* **1.** A piece of dialogue that other actors on stage are supposed not to hear. **2.** A digression.

**as•i•nine** (ăs′ə-nīn′) *adj.* Stupid or silly. **—as′i•nin′i•ty** *n.*

**ask** (ăsk) *v.* **1.** To put a question to. **2.** To inquire about. **3.** To request. **4.** To invite.

**a•skew** (ə-skyōō′) *adj.* Crooked. *—adv.* To one side; awry.

**a•sleep** (ə-slēp′) *adj.* **1.** Sleeping. **2.** Inactive. **3.** Numb. *—adv.* Into a sleep.

**as•par•a•gus** (ə-spăr′ə-gəs) *n.* The young, edible stalks of a cultivated plant.

**as•par•tame** (ăs′pər-tām′, ə-spär′-) *n.* An artificial, low-calorie sweetener.

**as•pect** (ăs′pĕkt) *n.* **1.** Appearance; look. **2.** A side; facet.

**as•perse** (ə-spûrs′) *v.* **-persed, -persing.** To defame; slander. **—as•per′sion** *n.*

**as•phyx•i•ate** (ăs-fĭk'sē-āt') *v.* **-ated, -ating.** To cause or undergo unconsciousness or death from lack of oxygen. —**as•phyx'i•a'tion** *n.*

**as•pi•ra•tion** (ăs'pə-rā'shən) *n.* **1.** Expulsion of breath in speech. **2.** A strong desire, as for high achievement.

**as•pire** (ə-spīr') *v.* **-pired, -piring.** To have a great ambition; strive. —**as'pi•rant** *n.* & *adj.*

**as•pi•rin** (ăs'pər-ĭn, -prĭn) *n.* **1.** A substance used in medicine to reduce fever, pain, and inflammation. **2.** A tablet of this substance.

**ass** (ăs) *n.* **1.** A donkey. **2.** A silly or stupid person.

**as•sail** (ə-sāl') *v.* **1.** To attack with blows. **2.** To attack verbally. —**as•sail'ant** *n.*

**as•sas•sin** (ə-săs'ĭn) *n.* A murderer, esp. of a prominent person.

**as•sas•si•nate** (ə-săs'ə-nāt') *v.* **-nated, -nating.** To murder (a prominent person). —**as•sas'si•na'tion** *n.*

**as•sault** (ə-sôlt') *n.* A violent physical or verbal attack. —*v.* To attack violently.

**as•say** (ăs'ā', ă-sā') *n.* A chemical analysis, esp. of an ore. —*v.* (ă-sā', ăs'ā') **1.** To analyze, esp. chemically; test. **2.** To attempt.

**as•sem•ble** (ə-sĕm'bəl) *v.* **-bled, -bling.** **1.** To bring or gather together; congregate. **2.** To fit or join together the parts of. **3.** To translate data from symbolic language into machine language. —**as•sem'blage** *n.* —**as•sem'bler** *n.*

**as•sem•bly** (ə-sĕm'blē) *n., pl.* **-blies.** **1.** A gathering. **2.** A legislative body. **3.** The putting together of parts.

**as•sent** (ə-sĕnt') *v.* To express agreement (with *to*). —*n.* Agreement; consent.

**as•sert** (ə-sûrt') *v.* **1.** To state; declare. **2.** To defend or maintain. —**as•ser'tion** *n.* —**as•ser'tive** *adj.*

**as•sess** (ə-sĕs') *v.* **1.** To estimate the value of (property) for taxation. **2.** To charge with a tax or fine. **3.** To evaluate. —**as•sess'ment** *n.* —**as•ses'sor** *n.*

**as•set** (ăs'ĕt') *n.* **1.** A valuable quality or possession. **2. assets.** All the property owned by a person, business, etc.

**as•sid•u•ous** (ə-sĭj'o͞o-əs) *adj.* Diligent; industrious.

**as•sign** (ə-sīn') *v.* **1.** To set apart for a particular purpose. **2.** To appoint. **3.** To give out as a task. **4.** To ascribe; attribute. —**as•sign'ment** *n.*

**as•sig•na•tion** (ăs'ĭg-nā'shən) *n.* **1.** An act or instance of assigning. **2.** An assignment. **3.** A tryst.

**as•sim•i•late** (ə-sĭm'ə-lāt') *v.* **-lated, -lating.** To consume and incorporate; absorb. —**as•sim'i•la'tion** *n.*

**as•sist** (ə-sĭst') *v.* To aid; help. —*n.* An act of giving aid. —**as•sis'tance** *n.* —**as•sis'tant** *n.*

**as•so•ci•ate** (ə-sō'shē-āt', -sē-) *v.* **-ated, -ating.** **1.** To connect or join in a relationship. **2.** To connect in the mind. —*n.* (-ĭt). A partner; colleague. —*adj.* (-ĭt). Joined with others and having equal or nearly equal status. —**as•so'ci•a'tion** *n.*

**as•sort•ment** (ə-sôrt'mənt) *n.* A variety.

**as•sume** (ə-so͞om') *v.* **-sumed, -suming.** **1.** To undertake. **2.** To adopt. **3.** To feign; affect. **4.** To take for granted; suppose. —**as•sump'tion** *n.*

**as•sure** (ə-sho͝or') *v.* **-sured, -suring.** **1.** To inform confidently. **2.** To make certain. **3.** To insure. —**as•sur'ance** *n.*

**as•ter•isk** (ăs'tə-rĭsk') *n.* A symbol (*) used to indicate an omission or a reference to a footnote.

**asth•ma** (ăz'mə) *n.* A chronic disease marked by coughing and labored breathing. —**asth•mat'ic** *adj.*

**a•stig•ma•tism** (ə-stĭg'mə-tĭz'əm) *n.* An eye defect that prevents focusing of sharp, distinct images. —**as'tig•mat'ic** *adj.*

**a•stir** (ə-stûr') *adj.* Moving about.

**a•ston•ish** (ə-stŏn'ĭsh) *v.* To fill with wonder; amaze. —**a•ston'ish•ment** *n.*

**a•stound** (ə-stound') *v.* To astonish.

**as•trin•gent** (ə-strĭn'jənt) *adj.* Tending to constrict living tissue. —*n.* An astringent substance. —**as•trin'gen•cy** *n.*

**as•trol•o•gy** (ə-strŏl'ə-jē) *n.* The study of stars, planets, etc., to predict their supposed influence on human affairs. —**as•trol'o•ger** *n.* —**as'tro•log'ic, as'tro•log'i•cal** *adj.*

**as•tro•naut** (ăs'trə-nôt') *n.* A person trained to participate in a spacecraft's flight.

**as•tron•o•my** (ə-strŏn'ə-mē) *n.* The scientific study of the universe beyond the earth. —**as•tron'o•mer** *n.* —**as'tro•nom'ic, as'tro•nom'i•cal** *adj.*

**as•tute** (ə-st/y/o͞ot′) *adj.* Keen in judgment.

**a•sun•der** (ə-sŭn′dər) *adv.* Apart.

**a•sy•lum** (ə-sī′ləm) *n.* **1.** An institution for the mentally ill or aged. **2.** A place offering safety.

**at** (ăt, ət) *prep.* **1.** Near to; by; in; on. **2.** In the direction of; to. **3.** Engaged in.

**ate** (āt) *v.* p.t. of **eat.**

**a•the•ism** (ā′thē-iz′əm) *n.* Denial of the existence of God. **—a′the•ist** *n.* **—a′the•is′tic** *adj.*

**ath•lete** (ăth′lēt′) *n.* One who takes part in competitive sports. **—ath•let′ic** *adj.*

**at•las** (ăt′ləs) *n.* A bound collection of maps.

**at•mos•phere** (ăt′mə-sfîr′) *n.* **1.** The air surrounding a celestial body, esp. the earth. **2.** A general feeling or mood. **—at′mos•pher′ic** *adj.*

**a•toll** (ăt′ôl′, -ŏl′, ā′tôl′) *n.* A ringlike coral island enclosing a lagoon.

**at•om** (ăt′əm) *n.* The smallest unit of a chemical element. **—a•tom′ic** *adj.*

**at•om•iz•er** (ăt′ə-mī′zər) *n.* A device that produces a fine spray for medicine or perfume.

**a•tone** (ə-tōn′) *v.* **atoned, atoning.** To make amends for. **—a•tone′ment** *n.*

**a•tro•cious** (ə-trō′shəs) *adj.* **1.** Extremely evil or cruel. **2.** Exceptionally bad. **—a•troc′i•ty** *n.*

**at•ro•phy** (ăt′rə-fē) *n., pl.* **-phies.** Shrinking or wasting away of body tissues. *—v.* **-phied, -phying.** To cause or undergo atrophy.

**at•tach** (ə-tăch′) *v.* **1.** To fasten on; connect. **2.** To adhere. **3.** To ascribe. **4.** To bind by ties of affection or loyalty. **5.** To seize by legal writ. **—at•tach′ment** *n.*

**at•tack** (ə-tăk′) *v.* **1.** To set upon with force. **2.** To denounce; criticize. **3.** To start work on. *—n.* **1.** An assault. **2.** Seizure by a disease.

**at•tain** (ə-tān′) *v.* **1.** To accomplish. **2.** To arrive at. **—at•tain′a•ble** *adj.* **—at•tain′ment** *n.*

**at•tempt** (ə-tĕmpt′) *v.* To try. *—n.* **1.** An effort. **2.** An attack.

**at•tend** (ə-tĕnd′) *v.* **1.** To be present at. **2.** To accompany. **3.** To take care of. **4.** To heed.

**at•ten•dance** (ə-tĕn′dəns) *n.* **1.** The act of attending. **2.** The number of persons present.

**at•ten•dant** (ə-tĕn′dənt) *n.* **1.** One who waits on another. **2.** One who is present. *—adj.* Accompanying or consequent.

**at•ten•tion** (ə-tĕn′shən) *n.* **1.** Concentration of one's mental powers upon an object. **2.** Consideration; notice. **—at•ten′tive** *adj.*

**at•ten•u•ate** (ə-tĕn′yo͞o-āt′) *v.* **-ated, -ating.** To thin; weaken. **—at•ten′u•a′tion** *n.*

**at•test** (ə-tĕst′) *v.* **1.** To affirm to be true, correct, etc. **2.** To provide evidence of.

**at•tic** (ăt′ĭk) *n.* A space directly below the roof.

**at•tire** (ə-tīr′) *v.* **-tired, -tiring.** To dress; clothe. *—n.* Clothing; array.

**at•ti•tude** (ăt′ĭ-t/y/o͞od′) *n.* **1.** A posture. **2.** A state of mind or feeling.

**at•tor•ney** (ə-tûr′nē) *n., pl.* **-neys.** A lawyer.

**at•tract** (ə-trăkt′) *v.* **1.** To cause to draw near. **2.** To appeal; allure. **—at•trac′tion** *n.* **—at•trac′tive** *adj.*

**at•trib•ute** (ə-trĭb′yo͞ot) *v.* **-uted, -uting.** To regard as belonging to; ascribe. *—n.* (ăt′rə-byo͞ot′). A distinctive feature; mark. **—at•trib′ut•a•ble** *adj.* **—at′tri•bu′tion** *n.*

**at•tri•tion** (ə-trĭsh′ən) *n.* **1.** A rubbing away or wearing down by friction. **2.** A gradual, natural reduction in membership or personnel, as through retirement, death, etc.

**at•tune** (ə-t/y/o͞on′) *v.* **-tuned, -tuning. 1.** To tune. **2.** To bring into harmony.

**ATV** *n., pl.* **ATVs.** A motor vehicle with treads or wheels, designed to travel over open country.

**auc•tion** (ôk′shən) *n.* A public sale in which items are sold to the highest bidder. *—v.* To sell at an auction. **—auc′tion•eer′** *n.*

**au•da•cious** (ô-dā′shəs) *adj.* **1.** Daring; reckless. **2.** Arrogant; impudent. **—au•dac′i•ty** *n.*

**au•di•ble** (ô′də-bəl) *adj.* Capable of being heard. **—au′di•bil′i•ty** *n.* **—au′di•bly** *adv.*

**au•di•ence** (ô′dē-əns) *n.* **1.** A gathering of spectators or listeners. **2.** Those reached by a book, television program, etc. **3.** A formal hearing or conference.

**au•di•o•cas•sette** (ô′dē-ō-kə-sĕt′) *n.* A cassette containing an audiotape.

**au•di•o•tape** (ô′dē-ō-tāp′) *n.* A tape recording of sound.

**au•di•o•vis•u•al** (ô′dē-ō-vĭzh′o͞o-əl) *adj.* Using both sound and sight to present information. **—au′di•o•vis′u•als** *pl.n.*

**au•dit** (ô′dĭt) *n.* An examination of records or accounts. *—v.* **1.** To examine and verify (records or accounts). **2.** To attend (a college course) without receiving academic credit. **—au′di•tor** *n.*

**au•di•tion** (ô-dĭsh′ən) *n.* A trial performance, as of an actor. *—v.* To perform in or give an audition.

**au•di•to•ri•um** (ô′dĭ-tôr′ē-əm, -tōr′-) *n., pl.* **-riums** or **-ria.** A room or building to accommodate an audience.

**aught** (ôt) *n.* **1.** Anything. **2.** Zero.

**aug•ment** (ôg-mĕnt′) *v.* To enlarge; increase. **—aug′men•ta′tion** *n.*

**au•gur** (ô′gər) *n.* A seer or prophet. *—v.* **1.** To foretell. **2.** To betoken. **—au′gu•ry** *n.*

**au•gust** (ô-gŭst′) *adj.* Majestic; venerable.

**Au•gust** (ô′gəst) *n.* The 8th month of the year.

**aunt** (ănt, änt) *n.* **1.** The sister of one's father or mother. **2.** The wife of one's uncle.

**au•ra** (ôr′ə) *n.* A distinctive air or quality.

**au•ri•cle** (ôr′ĭ-kəl) *n.* **1.** The external part of the ear. **2.** A chamber of the heart.

**aus•pi•ces** (ô′spĭ-sēz′) *pl.n.* Sponsorship; patronage.

**aus•pi•cious** (ô-spĭsh′əs) *adj.* Propitious; fortunate. **—aus•pi′cious•ly** *adv.* **—aus•pi′cious•ness** *n.*

**aus•tere** (ô-stîr′) *adj.* **1.** Severe; stern. **2.** Ascetic; frugal. **—aus•ter′i•ty** *n.*

**au•then•tic** (ô-thĕn′tĭk) *adj.* Genuine; real. **—au•then′ti•cal•ly** *adv.* **—au′then•tic′i•ty** *n.*

**au•then•ti•cate** (ô-thĕn′tĭ-kāt′) *v.* **-cated, -cating.** To confirm as authentic. **—au•then′ti•ca′tion** *n.*

**au•thor** (ô′thər) *n.* **1.** A writer. **2.** An originator or creator. **—au′thor•ship′** *n.*

**au•thor•i•tar•i•an** (ə-thôr′ĭ-târ′ē-ən, ə-thŏr′-, ô-) *adj.* Characterized by or favoring absolute obedience to authority. *—n.* One who believes in such policies.

**au•thor•i•ta•tive** (ə-thôr′ĭ-tā′tĭv, ə-thŏr′-, ô-) *adj.* Having or arising from authority.

**au•thor•i•ty** (ə-thôr′ĭ-tē, ə-thŏr′-, ô-) *n., pl.* **-ties. 1. a.** The power to command, determine, influence, or judge. **b.** A person or group with this power. **2.** An accepted source of expert information.

**au•thor•ize** (ô′thə-rīz′) *v.* **-ized, -izing. 1.** To grant authority to. **2.** To sanction. **—au′thor•i•za′tion** *n.*

**au•to** (ô′tō) *n., pl.* **-tos.** An automobile.

**au•to•bi•og•ra•phy** (ô′tō-bī-ŏg′rə-fē) *n., pl.* **-phies.** The story of one's life written by oneself. **—au′to•bi′o•graph′ic, au′to•bi′o•graph′i•cal** *adj.* **—au′to•bi′o•graph′i•cal•ly** *adv.*

**au•toc•ra•cy** (ô-tŏk′rə-sē) *n., pl.* **-cies.** Government by a person having absolute power. **—au′to•crat′** *n.* **—au′to•crat′ic** *adj.*

**au•to•fo•cus** (ô′tō-fō′kəs) *adj.* That can focus automatically. *—n.* A camera or lens that can focus automatically.

**au•to•graph** (ô′tə-grăf′) *n.* A person's own signature or handwriting. *—v.* To sign.

**au•to•im•mune** (ô′tō-ĭ-myo͞on′) *adj.* Relating to antibodies that attack the organism that produces them. **—au′to•im•mu′ni•ty** *n.* **—au′to•im•mun•i•za′tion** *n.* **—au′to•im′mu•nize** *v.*

**au•to•mate** (ô′tə-māt′) *v.* **-mated, -mating.** To convert to or operate by self-regulating machinery. **—au′to•ma′tion** *n.*

**au•to•mat•ic** (ô′tə-măt′ĭk) *adj.* **1. a.** Acting or operating by itself. **b.** Self-regulating. **2.** Involuntary; reflex. *—n.* An automatic device. **—au′to•mat′ic•al•ly** *adv.*

**au•to•mo•bile** (ô′tə-mō-bēl′, -mō′bēl′) *n.* A self-propelled land vehicle. **—au′to•mo′tive** *adj.*

**au•ton•o•mous** (ô-tŏn′ə-məs) *adj.* Independent; self-governing. **—au′to•nom′ic** *adj.* **—au•ton′o•my** *n.*

**au•top•sy** (ô′tŏp′sē, ô′təp-) *n., pl.* **-sies.** The examination of a dead body to determine the cause of death; postmortem.

**au•tumn** (ô′təm) *n.* The season of the year between summer and winter.

—**au•tum'nal** *adj.*

**aux•il•ia•ry** (ôg-zĭl'yə-rē, -zĭl'ə-rē) *adj.* **1.** Giving assistance; aiding; helping. **2.** Subsidiary; supplementary. —*n., pl.* **-ries. 1.** One that gives aid. **2.** Also **auxiliary verb.** A verb that accompanies certain verb forms to express tense, mood, voice, or aspect.

**a•vail** (ə-vāl') *v.* To be of use; assist; help. —*n.* Use; benefit.

**a•vail•a•ble** (ə-vā'lə-bəl) *adj.* Accessible for use; obtainable. —**a•vail'a•bil'i•ty** *n.*

**av•a•lanche** (ăv'ə-lănch') *n.* A fall of a large mass of snow, rock, or other material down a mountainside.

**av•a•rice** (ăv'ə-rĭs) *n.* Greed for wealth. —**av'a•ri'cious** *adj.*

**a•venge** (ə-vĕnj') *v.* **avenged, avenging.** To take revenge for. —**a•veng'er** *n.*

**av•e•nue** (ăv'ə-n/y/ōō') *n.* A wide street.

**av•er•age** (ăv'ər-ĭj, ăv'rĭj) *n.* **1.** The sum of a set of quantities divided by the number of quantities in the set; mean. **2.** The usual type, amount, or quality. —*adj.* **1.** Of or constituting the average. **2.** Typical. —*v.* **-aged, -aging. 1.** To calculate, obtain, or amount to an average of. **2.** To distribute proportionately.

**a•verse** (ə-vûrs') *adj.* Opposed; reluctant.

**a•vert** (ə-vûrt') *v.* **1.** To turn away. **2.** To ward off or prevent.

**a•vi•a•tion** (ā'vē-ā'shən, ăv'ē-) *n.* The operation of aircraft. —**a'vi•a'tor** *n.*

**av•id** (ăv'ĭd) *adj.* Eager; enthusiastic. —**a•vid'i•ty** *n.* —**av'id•ly** *adv.*

**av•o•ca•do** (ăv'ə-kä'dō) *n., pl.* **-dos.** A tropical fruit with yellow-green pulp.

**av•o•ca•tion** (ăv'ō-kā'shən) *n.* A hobby.

**a•void** (ə-void') *v.* To keep away from; shun. —**a•void'ance** *n.*

**av•oir•du•pois** (ăv'ər-də-poiz') *n.* **1.** The system of weights in which 16 ounces equal a pound. **2.** Weight; heaviness.

**a•vow** (ə-vou') *v.* To acknowledge openly; confess. —**a•vow'al** *n.*

**AWACS** (ā'wăks) *n., pl.* **AWACS.** An aircraft equipped with radar and computers and able to track many aircraft from a great distance.

**a•wait** (ə-wāt') *v.* **1.** To wait for. **2.** To be in store for.

**a•wake** (ə-wāk') *v.* **awoke, awaked, awaking.** To rouse from sleep; wake up. —*adj.* **1.** Not asleep. **2.** Alert; watchful.

**a•wak•en** (ə-wā'kən) *v.* To wake up; rouse. —**a•wak'en•ing** *adj. & n.*

**a•ward** (ə-wôrd') *v.* To grant for high performance or quality. —*n.* **1.** A decision, as by a judge. **2.** A prize.

**a•ware** (ə-wâr') *adj.* Conscious; informed. —**a•ware'ness** *n.*

**a•way** (ə-wā') *adv.* **1.** At or to a distance. **2.** To a different place. **3.** From one's possession. **4.** Continuously. —*adj.* **1.** Absent. **2.** At a distance.

**awe** (ô) *n.* Mingled reverence, dread, and wonder. —*v.* **awed, awing.** To inspire with awe. —**awe'some** *adj.*

**aw•ful** (ô'fəl) *adj.* **1.** Extremely bad or unpleasant. **2.** Dreadful; appalling. —**aw'ful•ly** *adv.*

**awk•ward** (ôk'wərd) *adj.* **1.** Lacking grace or dexterity; clumsy. **2.** Unwieldy. **3.** Uncomfortable; inconvenient. **4.** Embarrassing. —**awk'ward•ly** *adv.* —**awk'ward•ness** *n.*

**a•woke** (ə-wōk') *v.* p.t. of **awake.**

**a•wry** (ə-rī') *adv.* **1.** Askew. **2.** Amiss; wrong. —**a•wry'** *adj.*

**ax, axe** (ăks) *n., pl.* **axes.** A chopping tool with a bladed head mounted on a handle.

**ax•i•om** (ăk'sē-əm) *n.* A self-evident or accepted principle. —**ax'i•o•mat'ic** *adj.* —**ax'i•o•mat'i•cal•ly** *adv.*

**ax•is** (ăk'sĭs) *n., pl.* **axes. 1.** A straight line about which an object rotates. **2.** A center line or part.

**ax•le** (ăk'səl) *n.* A shaft on which a wheel turns.

**aye, ay** (ī) *n.* An affirmative vote. —*adv.* Yes.

**az•ure** (ăzh'ər) *n.* Sky blue. —**az'ure** *adj.*

## — B —

**b, B** (bē) *n.* The 2nd letter of the English alphabet.

**bab•ble** (băb'əl) *v.* **-bled, -bling. 1.** To utter incoherent sound. **2.** To chatter. —*n.* Babbling sound. —**bab'bler** *n.*

**ba•boon** (bă-bōōn') *n.* A large monkey with a prominent, doglike muzzle.

**ba•by** (bā'bē) *n., pl.* **-bies.** An infant. —*v.* **-bied, -bying.** To pamper; coddle.

—**ba'by•hood'** *n.* —**ba'by•ish** *adj.*

**bach•e•lor** (băch'ə-lər, băch'lər) *n.* **1.** An unmarried man. **2. a.** An undergraduate degree. **b.** A person holding such a degree. —**bach'e•lor•hood'** *n.*

**back** (băk) *n.* **1.** The part of the body nearest the spine. **2.** The rear. **3.** The reverse side. —*v.* **1.** To move backward. **2.** To support; strengthen. **3.** To bet on. **4.** To form the back of. —**back down.** To withdraw from a former stand. —*adj.* **1.** At the rear. **2.** Of a past time. **3.** Backward. —*adv.* **1.** To or toward the rear. **2.** To or toward a former place, state, or time. **3.** In reserve, concealment, or check. **4.** In return. —**back'er** *n.* —**back'ing** *n.*

**back•bone** (băk'bōn') *n.* **1.** The vertebrate spine. **2.** A main support. **3.** Strength of character.

**back•fire** (băk'fīr') *n.* An explosion of prematurely ignited fuel or of unburned exhaust. —*v.* **-fired, -firing. 1.** To have a backfire. **2.** To produce an unwanted result.

**back•ground** (băk'ground') *n.* **1.** The area, space, or surface against which objects are seen or represented. **2.** A setting. **3.** Relative obscurity. **4.** One's experience or training.

**back•hand** (băk'hănd') *n.* **1.** A stroke of a racket with the back of the hand facing out. **2.** Handwriting slanted to the left. —*v.* To perform backhand. —**back'hand'** *adv.* —**back'hand'ed** *adj.* —**back'hand'ed•ly** *adv.* —**back'hand'ed•ness** *n.*

**back•lash** (băk'lăsh') *n.* **1.** A sudden backward whipping motion. **2.** An antagonistic reaction.

**back•log** (băk'lôg', -lôg') *n.* A reserve supply or accumulation.

**back•pack** (băk'păk') *n.* A knapsack worn on the back. —*v.* To hike while wearing a backpack. —**back'pack'er** *n.* —**back'pack'ing** *n.*

**back•slide** (băk'slīd') *v.* To revert to wrongdoing. —**back'slid'er** *n.* —**back'slid'ing** *n.*

**back•track** (băk'trăk') *v.* **1.** To retrace one's route. **2.** To reverse one's stand; retreat.

**back-up** (băk'ŭp') *n.* **1.** A reserve or substitute. **2.** Support. **3.** Background accompaniment. —**back'up'** *adj.*

**back•ward** (băk'wərd) *adv.* Also **back•wards. 1.** Toward the rear. **2.** With the back leading. **3.** In reverse. **4.** Toward a former, often worse, condition. —*adj.* **1.** Reversed. **2.** Reluctant; unwilling. **3.** Retarded in development. —**back'ward•ness** *n.*

**ba•con** (bā'kən) *n.* Salted and smoked meat from a pig's back and sides.

**bac•te•ri•a** (băk-tîr'ē-ə) *pl.n. Sing.* **-rium.** Single-celled organisms often causing disease. —**bac•te'ri•al** *adj.*

**bac•te•ri•ol•o•gy** (băk-tîr'ē-ŏl'ə-jē) *n.* The study of bacteria. —**bac•te'ri•o•log'ic, bac•te'ri•o•log'i•cal** *adj.* —**bac•te'ri•ol'o•gist** *n.*

**bad** (băd) *adj.* **worse, worst. 1.** Undesirable; not good. **2.** Inferior; poor. **3.** Unfavorable. **4.** Rotten; spoiled. **5.** Severe; intense. **6.** Sorry; regretful. —**bad'ly** *adv.* —**bad'ness** *n.*

**bade** (băd) *v.* A p.t. of **bid.**

**badge** (băj) *n.* An emblem worn as a sign of rank, membership, or honor.

**badg•er** (băj'ər) *n.* A burrowing animal with a grizzled coat. —*v.* To harry; pester.

**bad-mouth** (băd'mouth', -mou*th*) *v.* To criticize unfairly; disparage.

**baf•fle** (băf'əl) *v.* **-fled, -fling. 1.** To foil; thwart. **2.** To make helplessly puzzled. —*n.* A structure that impedes or deflects. —**baf'fle•ment** *n.* —**baf'fler** *n.*

**bag** (băg) *n.* **1.** A nonrigid container, as of paper. **2.** A suitcase or purse. —*v.* **bagged, bagging. 1.** To hang or bulge loosely. **2.** To capture or kill, as game. —**bag'gy** *adj.*

**ba•gel** (bā'gəl) *n.* A heavy, glazed, doughnut-shaped roll.

**bag•gage** (băg'ĭj) *n.* Luggage.

**bag•pipe** (băg'pīp') *n.* Often **bagpipes.** A musical instrument with an inflatable bag attached to pipes.

**bail[1]** (bāl) *n.* **1.** Money supplied as a guarantee that an arrested person will appear for trial. **2.** Release obtained by such security. —*v.* To release by providing or taking bail. —**bail'er** *n.*

**bail[2]** (bāl) *v.* To empty a boat of water by scooping or dipping. —**bail out.** To parachute from an aircraft.

**bail•iff** (bā'lĭf) *n.* A courtroom attendant who guards prisoners and maintains order.

**bail•out** (bāl′out′) *n.* A rescue esp. from financial difficulties. **—bail′ out′** *v.*

**bait** (bāt) *n.* **1.** Food used to catch fish or trap animals. **2.** An enticement; lure. —*v.* **1.** To supply with bait. **2.** To lure; entice. **3.** To harass.

**bake** (bāk) *v.* **baked, baking. 1.** To cook with dry heat, esp. in an oven. **2.** To harden with heat. **—bak′er** *n.* **—bak′er•y** *n.*

**BAL** *n.* A low-level computer assembly language.

**bal•ance** (băl′əns) *n.* **1.** A weighing device having a lever with 2 pans suspended from it. **2.** Equilibrium. **3.** Equality of or difference between totals in the debit and credit sides of an account. **4.** Remainder. **5.** Harmony; symmetry. —*v.* **-anced, -ancing. 1.** To bring into or be maintained in equilibrium. **2.** To counterbalance. **3.** To compute the difference between the debits and credits of (an account).

**bal•co•ny** (băl′kə-nē) *n., pl.* **-nies. 1.** A platform projecting from an upper story of a building. **2.** A gallery projecting over the main floor in a theater.

**bald** (bôld) *adj.* **1.** Lacking hair on the top of the head. **2.** Unadorned; plain. **—bald′ing** *adj.* **—bald′ness** *n.*

**bale** (bāl) *n.* A large bound package. —*v.* **baled, baling.** To wrap in bales. **bal′er** *n.*

**bale•ful** (bāl′fəl) *adj.* **1.** Malignant. **2.** Ominous. **—bale′ful•ly** *adv.* **—bale′ful•ness** *n.*

**balk** (bôk) *v.* **1.** To stop short and refuse to go on. **2.** To thwart; check. —*n.* A hindrance. **—balk′y** *adj.*

**ball**[1] (bôl) *n.* **1.** A round object; sphere. **2. a.** A rounded object used in a game. **b.** A game played with such an object.

**ball**[2] (bôl) *n.* **1.** A formal dance. **2.** An enjoyable time.

**bal•lad** (băl′əd) *n.* **1.** A narrative poem, often of folk origin and intended to be sung. **2.** A slow, romantic popular song. **—bal′lad•eer′** *n.*

**bal•last** (băl′əst) *n.* Heavy material put aboard a ship to enhance stability. —*v.* To stabilize with ballast.

**bal•let** (bă-lā′, băl′ā′) *n.* A dance genre with a highly formalized technique. **—bal′le•ri′na** *fem. n.*

**bal•lis•tics** (bə-lĭs′tĭks) *n.* **1.** The study of the dynamics of projectiles. **2.** The study of firearms and bullets. **—bal•lis′tic** *adj.*

**bal•loon** (bə-lo͞on′) *n.* A flexible bag that expands when inflated with a gas. —*v.* To expand like a balloon.

**bal•lot** (băl′ət) *n.* **1.** A paper or ticket used to cast a vote. **2.** The act or method of voting. **3.** A list of candidates for office. —*v.* To cast a ballot.

**balm•y** (bä′mē) *adj.* **-ier, -iest. 1.** Mild and pleasant. **2.** Insane; mad; foolish.

**ba•lo•ney** (bə-lō′nē) *n., pl.* **-neys. 1.** Bologna. **2.** Nonsense.

**bal•us•ter** (băl′ə-stər) *n.* One of the upright supports of a handrail.

**bal•us•trade** (băl′ə-strād′) *n.* A rail and the row of posts that support it.

**bam•boo** (băm-bo͞o′) *n.* A tall tropical grass with hollow, woody stems.

**ban** (băn) *v.* **banned, banning.** To prohibit, esp. officially. —*n.* A prohibition.

**ba•nal** (bə-năl′, bā′nəl, bə-näl′) *adj.* Trite; ordinary. **—ba•nal′i•ty** *n.*

**ba•nan•a** (bə-năn′ə) *n.* A crescent-shaped tropical fruit having pulpy flesh and yellow skin.

**band**[1] (bănd) *n.* **1.** A thin strip of flexible material used to bind together. **2.** A range of numerical values. —*v.* To bind or identify with a band.

**band**[2] (bănd) *n.* **1.** A group of people or animals. **2.** A group of musicians. —*v.* To assemble or unite in a group.

**band•age** (băn′dĭj) *n.* A strip of material used to protect a wound or other injury. —*v.* **-aged, -aging.** To apply a bandage to.

**ban•dit** (băn′dĭt) *n.* A robber, esp. a member of a band of robbers.

**ban•dy** (băn′dē) *v.* **-died, -dying. 1.** To toss back and forth. **2.** To discuss or exchange. —*adj.* Bent in an outward curve.

**bane** (bān) *n.* A cause of distress or ruin. **—bane′ful** *adj.*

**bang** (băng) *n.* A sudden loud noise. —*v.* To hit or close noisily.

**ban•ish** (băn′ĭsh) *v.* **1.** To force to leave a country; exile. **2.** To drive away; expel. **—ban′ish•ment** *n.*

**ban•is•ter** (băn′ĭstər) *n.* **1.** A baluster. **2.** The balustrade of a staircase.

**ban•jo** (băn′jō) *n., pl.* **-jos** or **-joes.** A stringed instrument having a hollow circular body.

**bank¹** (băngk) *n.* **1.** Any piled-up mass. **2.** A natural incline. **3.** An artificial embankment. **4.** The slope of land adjoining a lake, river, or sea. **5.** Lateral tilting of an aircraft in a turn. —*v.* **1.** To border or protect with a bank. **2.** To pile up; amass. **3.** To cover (a fire) with ashes or fuel for low burning. **4.** To tilt (an aircraft) laterally in flight.

**bank²** (băngk) *n.* **1.** An establishment for safekeeping, handling, and lending money. **2.** A supply or stock. —*v.* **1.** To deposit (money) in a bank. **2.** To transact business with a bank. **3.** To operate a bank. —**bank on.** To have confidence in. —**bank′a•ble** *adj.* —**bank′-card′** *n.* —**bank′er** *n.*

**bank•roll** (băngk′rōl′) *n.* **1.** A roll of paper money. **2.** Ready cash. —*v.* To underwrite the expenses of. —**bank′rol•ler** *n.*

**bank•rupt** (băngk′rŭpt′, -rəpt) *n.* A debtor who is judged insolvent and whose remaining property is administered for his creditors. —*adj.* **1.** Legally declared a bankrupt. **2.** Financially ruined. —*v.* To cause to become bankrupt. —**bank′rupt•cy** *n.*

**ban•ner** (băn′ər) *n.* A flag; standard. —*adj.* Oustanding.

**ban•quet** (băng′kwĭt) *n.* An elaborate feast or ceremonial dinner.

**ban•ter** (băn′tər) *n.* Good-humored teasing. —*v.* To tease or mock gently.

**bap•tism** (băp′tĭz′əm) *n.* A Christian rite in which a person is cleansed of original sin by immersion in or sprinkling with water. —**bap•tis′mal** *adj.* —**bap•tize′** *v.*

**bar** (băr) *n.* **1.** A long, rigid piece of solid material. **2.** A solid oblong block of a substance, as soap. **3.** An obstacle. **4.** A band, as one formed by light. **5.** A system of law courts. **6.** The profession of law. **7.** A vertical line dividing a musical staff into measures. **8.** A counter at which drinks are served. —*v.* **barred, barring. 1.** To obstruct with or as if with bars. **2.** To exclude. —*prep.* Excluding.

**barb** (bärb) *n.* **1.** A sharp backward-pointing projection. **2.** A cutting remark. —**barbed** *adj.*

**bar•bar•i•an** (băr-bâr′ē-ən) *n.* An uncivilized or uncultured person. —**bar•bar′i•an** *adj.* —**bar•bar′ic, bar′bar•ous** *adj.* —**bar′bar•ism** *n.* —**bar•bar′i•ty** *n.*

**bar•be•cue** (băr′bĭ-kyōō′) *n.* **1.** A grill or outdoor fireplace for roasting meat. **2.** Meat roasted over an open fire. —*v.* **-cued, -cuing.** To cook (meat) over live coals or an open fire.

**bar•ber** (băr′bər) *n.* One whose business is to cut hair or beards.

**bar•bi•tu•rate** (bär-bĭch′ər-ĭt, -ə-rāt′, bär′bĭ-t/y/ŏŏr′ĭt, -āt′) *n.* A sedative drug.

**bare** (bâr) *adj.* **barer, barest. 1.** Naked. **2.** Exposed to view; undisguised. **3.** Plain; simple. **4.** Just sufficient. —*v.* **bared, baring.** To make bare. —**bare′ly** *adv.*

**bare•faced** (bâr′făst′) *adj.* Bold; brazen.

**bar•gain** (bär′gĭn) *n.* **1.** An agreement or contract. **2.** Something offered or acquired at a low price. —*v.* To negotiate the terms of an agreement; haggle. —**bar′gain•er** *n.*

**barge** (bärj) *n.* A flat-bottomed freight boat. —*v.* **barged, barging.** To intrude (with *in* or *into*).

**bar•i•tone** (băr′ĭ-tōn′) *n.* A male voice between a bass and a tenor.

**bark¹** (bärk) *n.* The short, harsh sound made by a dog. —*v.* **1.** To utter a bark. **2.** To speak sharply.

**bark²** (bärk) *n.* The outer covering of trees. —*v.* **1.** To remove bark from. **2.** To scrape skin from.

**barn** (bärn) *n.* A farm building for storing produce and sheltering livestock. —**barn′yard′** *n.*

**bar•na•cle** (bär′nə-kəl) *n.* A marine crustacean that adheres to submerged surfaces. —**bar′na•cled** *adj.*

**ba•rom•e•ter** (bə-rŏm′ĭ-tər) *n.* An instrument for measuring atmospheric pressure. —**bar′o•met′ric, bar′o•met′ri•cal** *adj.* —**ba•rom′e•try** *n.*

**ba•roque** (bə-rōk′) *adj.* Of an artistic style marked by elaborate decoration.

**bar•racks** (băr′əks) *n., pl.* **-racks.** A building used to house soldiers.

**bar•rage** (bə-räzh′) *n.* A heavy curtain of artillery fire.

**bar•rel** (băr'əl) *n.* **1.** A large cask with bulging sides and flat ends. **2.** The cylindrical part of a firearm, through which the bullet travels.

**bar•ren** (băr'ən) *adj.* **1.** Infertile; sterile. **2.** Unproductive.

**bar•ri•cade** (băr'ĭ-kād', băr'ĭ-kād') *n.* A barrier set up across a route of access. —*v.* **-caded, -cading.** To block or confine with a barricade.

**bar•ri•er** (băr'ē-ər) *n.* **1.** A structure built to bar passage. **2.** An obstruction; hindrance.

**bar•ter** (bär'tər) *v.* To exchange (goods). —*n.* The practice of bartering.

**base**[1] (bās) *n.* **1.** The lowest part; bottom. **2.** A fundamental principle; basis. **3.** In certain sports, a goal, starting point, or safety area. **4.** A center of organization, supply, or activity. —*v.* **based, basing. 1.** To form or make a base for. **2.** To find a basis for; establish.

**base**[2] (bās) *adj.* **baser, basest.** Low; inferior. **—base'ly** *adv.* **—base'ness** *n.*

**base•ball** (bās'bôl') *n.* **1.** A game played with a bat and ball. **2.** The ball used.

**base•ment** (bās'mənt) *n.* The story below the ground floor of a building.

**ba•ses** *n.* pl. of **basis.**

**bash•ful** (băsh'fəl) *adj.* Shy; retiring. **—bash'ful•ly** *adv.* **—bash'ful•ness** *n.*

**ba•sic** (bā'sĭk) *adj.* Fundamental; essential. —*n.* A basic fact or skill. **—ba'si•cal•ly** *adv.*

**BASIC** (bā'sĭk) *n.* A common, simple programming language often used with remote or time-sharing computing centers.

**ba•sis** (bā'sĭs) *n., pl.* **-ses. 1.** A foundation. **2.** The chief component.

**bask** (băsk) *v.* To warm oneself pleasantly.

**bas•ket** (băs'kĭt) *n.* A container of interwoven material.

**bas•ket•ball** (băs'kĭt-bôl') *n.* **1.** A game in which players try to throw a large ball through an elevated hoop. **2.** The ball used.

**bass** (bās) *n.* The lowest male voice. **—bass** *adj.*

**bas•soon** (bə-so͞on', bă-) *n.* A low-pitched woodwind instrument. **—bas•soon'ist** *n.*

**bas•tard** (băs'tərd) *n.* An illegitimate child. —*adj.* Illegitimate. **—bas'tard•y** *n.*

**baste** (bāst) *v.* **basted, basting. 1.** To sew loosely. **2.** To pour liquid over.

**bas•tion** (băs'chən, -tē-ən) *n.* A well-fortified position.

**bat**[1] (băt) *n.* A stout wooden stick or club. —*v.* **batted, batting.** To hit with a bat. **—bat'ter** *n.*

**bat**[2] (băt) *n.* A mouselike flying mammal.

**batch** (băch) *n.* **1.** An amount produced at 1 time. **2.** A set of data or jobs to be run on a computer at 1 time with 1 program.

**bath** (băth, bäth) *n., pl.* **baths. 1.** The act of washing the body. **2.** A tub for bathing. **3.** A room with a bath and usually a toilet.

**bathe** (bā*th*) *v.* **bathed, bathing. 1.** To take or give a bath. **2.** To go swimming. **3.** To suffuse. **—bath'er** *n.*

**ba•ton** (bə-tŏn', bă-) *n.* A stick, esp. for conducting an orchestra.

**bat•tal•ion** (bə-tăl'yən) *n.* A large military group, esp. a force of several companies.

**bat•ter**[1] (băt'ər) *v.* To pound with heavy blows.

**bat•ter**[2] (băt'ər) *n.* A mixture of flour and liquid used in cooking.

**bat•ter•y** (băt'ə-rē) *n., pl.* **-ies. 1.** An unlawful beating. **2.** An array, esp. of artillery. **3.** A device for generating an electric current.

**bat•tle** (băt'l) *n.* A combat; struggle, as between armies. —*v.* **-tled, -tling.** To engage in battle.

**bau•ble** (bô'bəl) *n.* A trinket.

**baud** (bôd) *n.* In computer science, a unit of speed in data transmission.

**bawd•y** (bô'dē) *adj.* **-ier, -iest.** Humorously coarse; lewd. **—bawd'i•ness** *n.*

**bawl** (bôl) *v.* To cry out loudly; bellow. **—bawl out.** To scold. **—bawl'er** *n.*

**bay**[1] (bā) *n.* A wide body of water partly enclosed by land.

**bay**[2] (bā) *adj.* Reddish-brown. —*n.* A reddish-brown animal, esp. a horse.

**bay**[3] (bā) *v.* To bark with long, deep cries.

**bay•o•net** (bā'ə-nĭt, -nĕt', bā'ə-nĕt') *n.* A blade affixed to a rifle. —*v.* **-neted** or **-netted, -neting** or **-netting.** To stab

with a bayonet.
**bay•ou** (bī′o͞o, bī′ō) *n., pl.* **-ous.** A marsh connected to a lake or river.
**ba•zaar** (bə-zär′) *n.* **1.** A market, esp. in the Middle East. **2.** A fair for charity.
**BCD** *n.* A code representing alphanumeric data on magnetic tape.
**be** (bē) *v.* **1.** To exist. **2.** To occupy a place. **3.** To equal. **4.** To mean; signify. **5.** To have a specified quality.
**beach** (bēch) *n.* A sandy shore.
**bea•con** (bē′kən) *n.* A guiding or signal light.
**bead** (bēd) *n.* **1. a** A small piece of material pierced for stringing. **b. beads.** A necklace of such pieces. **2.** A drop or globule.
**beak** (bēk) *n.* The horny, projecting mouth parts of a bird; bill.
**beak•er** (bē′kər) *n.* A large drinking cup or glass vessel.
**beam** (bēm) *n.* **1.** A length of timber supporting a strucure. **2.** A radio signal for navigational guidance. **3.** A ray of light or particles. **—on the beam.** On the right track. *—v.* **1.** To emit or radiate. **2.** To smile radiantly.
**bean** (bēn) *n.* The edible seed or seed pod of some plants.
**bear**[1] (bâr) *v.* **bore, borne** or **born, bearing. 1.** To carry; support. **2.** To endure. **3.** To conduct (oneself). **4.** To have; show. **5.** *p.p.* **borne.** To give birth to. **6.** To yield; produce. **7.** To exert pressure. **—bear′a•ble** *adj.* **—bear′er** *n.*
**bear**[2] (bâr) *n.* A large, burly, shaggy-coated mammal. **—bear′ish** *adj.*
**beard** (bîrd) *n.* The hair on a man's chin and cheeks.
**bear•ing** (bâr′ĭng) *n.* **1.** Deportment; posture. **2.** A device that connects and reduces friction between machine parts. **3.** Relationship or relevance. **4.** Direction.
**bear market** *n.* A stock market characterized by falling prices.
**beast** (bēst) *n.* An animal.
**beat** (bēt) *v.* **beat, beaten** (bēt′n) or **beat, beating. 1.** To strike repeatedly. **2.** To forge. **3.** To tread. **4.** To defeat. **5.** To pulsate; throb. **6.** To mix rapidly. *—n.* **1.** A stroke; blow **2.** A throb. **3.** A rhythmic stress. **4.** A regular round. **—beat′er** *n.*
**beau•ty** (byo͞o′tē) *n., pl.* **-ties. 1.** A quality that delights the senses; loveliness. **2.** One possessing this quality. **—beau′te•ous** *adj.* **—beau′ti•ful** *adj.* **—beau′ti•fy** *v.*
**bea•ver** (bē′vər) *n.* A large aquatic rodent.
**be•came** (bĭ-kām′) *v.* p.t. of **become.**
**be•cause** (bĭ-kôz′, -kŭz′) *conj.* For the reason that; since. **—because of.** On account of.
**beck•on** (bĕk′ən) *v.* To summon by gesture.
**be•come** (bĭ-kŭm′) *v.* **-came** (-kām′), **-come, -coming. 1.** To grow or come to be. **2.** To be appropriate to. **3.** To show to advantage. **—become of.** To happen to. **—be•com′ing** *adj.*
**bed** (bĕd) *n.* **1.** A piece of furniture for sleeping. **2.** A plot of ground. **3.** A layer. **4.** A foundation. *—v.* **bedded, bedding.** To put in a bed.
**bed•ding** (bĕd′ĭng) *n.* Coverings for a bed.
**bed•lam** (bĕd′ləm) *n.* Noisy confusion.
**bed•room** (bĕd′ro͞om′, -ro͝om′) *n.* A room for sleeping.
**bed•stead** (bĕd′stĕd′) *n.* The frame supporting a bed.
**bee** (bē) *n.* **1.** A social insect that lives in hives and makes honey. **2.** A gathering for work or competition.
**beef** (bēf) *n.* **1.** The meat of a full-grown steer, bull, ox, or cow. **2.** Human strength; brawn. **3.** A complaint.
**been** (bĭn) *v.* p.p. of **be.**
**beep** (bēp) *v.* To make a brief, high-pitched sound, as from an electronic device. **—beep′er** *n.*
**beer** (bîr) *n.* An alcoholic drink brewed from malt and hops.
**bee•tle** (bēt′l) *n.* An insect with horny front wings.
**be•fall** (bĭ-fôl′) *v.* **-fell, -fallen, -falling. 1.** To come to pass. **2.** To happen to.
**be•fit** (bĭ-fĭt′) *v.* **-fitted, -fitting.** To be suitable to.
**be•fore** (bĭ-fôr′, -fōr′) *adv.* Earlier; previously. *—prep.* **1.** Ahead of. **2.** Prior to. **3.** In front of. **4.** In the presence of. **5.** Under the consideration of. **6.** In preference to. *—conj.* **1.** In advance of the time when. **2.** Sooner than.
**be•friend** (bĭ-frĕnd′) *v.* To act as a friend to.

**be•fud•dle** (bĭ-fŭd′l) *v.* **-dled, -dling.** To confuse. **—be•fud′dle•ment** *n.*
**beg** (bĕg) *v.* **begged, begging. 1.** To ask for as charity. **2.** To entreat.
**be•gan** (bĭ-găn′) *v.* p.t. of **begin.**
**be•get** (bĭ-gĕt′) *v.* **-got, -gotten** or **-got, -getting.** To father; sire. **—be•get′ter** *n.*
**beg•gar** (bĕg′ər) *n.* One who begs for money. —*v.* To impoverish.
**be•gin** (bĭ-gĭn′) *v.* **-gan, -gun, -ginning.** To start. **—be•gin′ner** *n.* **—be•gin′ning** *n.*
**be•got** (bĭ-gŏt′) *v.* p.t. and alternate p.p. of **beget.**
**be•got•ten** (bĭ-gŏt′n) *v.* p.p. of **beget.**
**be•grudge** (bĭ-grŭj′) *v.* **-grudged, -grudging. 1.** To envy. **2.** To give with reluctance.
**be•guile** (bĭ-gīl′) *v.* **-guiled, -guiling. 1.** To deceive. **2.** To divert; charm. **—be•guile′ment** *n.* **—be•guil′er** *n.*
**be•gun** (bĭ-gŭn′) *v.* p.p. of **begin.**
**be•half** (bĭ-hăf′) *n.* Interest; benefit.
**be•have** (bĭ-hāv′) *v.* **-haved, -having. 1.** To act or function. **2.** To conduct oneself, esp. properly. **—be•hav′ior** *n.* **—be•hav′ior•al** *adj.*
**be•head** (bĭ-hĕd′) *v.* To kill by cutting off the head of.
**be•hind** (bĭ-hīnd′) *adv.* **1.** In or toward the rear. **2.** In arrears; late. —*prep.* **1.** To the rear of. **2.** After. **3.** In support of.
**be•hold** (bĭ-hōld′) *v.* **-held** (-hĕld′), **-holding.** To look upon; see. **—be•hold′er** *n.*
**beige** (bāzh) *n.* Light grayish brown. **—beige** *adj.*
**be•ing** (bē′ĭng) *n.* **1.** Existence. **2.** One that exists.
**be•lat•ed** (bĭ-lā′tĭd) *adj.* Tardy. **—be•lat′ed•ly** *adv.*
**belch** (bĕlch) *v.* To expel stomach gas through the mouth; burp. —*n.* A burp. **—belch′er** *n.*
**bel•fry** (bĕl′frē) *n., pl.* **-fries.** A church bell tower.
**be•lief** (bĭ-lēf′) *n.* **1.** Trust; confidence. **2.** A conviction or opinion.
**be•lieve** (bĭ-lēv′) *v.* **-lieved, -lieving. 1.** To accept as true or real. **2.** To credit; trust. **3.** To suppose; think. **—be•liev′a•ble** *adj.* **—be•liev′er** *n.*
**be•lit•tle** (bĭ-lĭt′l) *v.* **-tled, -tling.** To speak of as small or unimportant; disparage.
**bell** (bĕl) *n.* A hollow metal object that rings when struck.
**bel•lig•er•ent** (bə-lĭj′ər-ənt) *adj.* **1.** Aggressively hostile. **2.** Waging war. —*n.* A warring nation. **—bel•lig′er•ence, bel•lig′er•en•cy** *n.* **—bel•lig′er•ent•ly** *adv.*
**bel•low** (bĕl′ō) *v.* To roar like a bull. **—bel′low** *n.*
**bel•lows** (bĕl′ōz, -əz) *n.* A device for producing and directing a strong current of air.
**bel•ly** (bĕl′ē) *n., pl.* **-lies.** The abdomen or stomach.
**bel•ly-up** (bĕl′ē-ŭp′) *adj.* Out of business; bankrupt.
**be•long** (bĭ-lông′, -lŏng′) *v.* **1.** To be the property of. **2.** To be a member of. **3.** To have a proper place. **—be•long′ings** *pl.n.*
**be•low** (bĭ-lō′) *adv.* In or to a lower place. —*prep.* **1.** Lower than. **2.** Inferior to.
**belt** (bĕlt) *n.* **1.** A band around the waist. **2.** A continuous moving band in machinery or manufacturing. **3.** A geographic region. —*v.* **1.** To encircle; gird. **2.** To strike with or as if with a belt.
**bench** (bĕnch) *n.* **1.** A long seat. **2. a.** The judge's seat in court. **b.** The court or judges. **3.** A craftsman's worktable.
**bench•mark** (bĕnch′märk′) *n.* **1.** A permanent mark used as a reference point for surveying. **2.** A standard problem for comparing computer programs or systems. **3.** A critical standard. —*v.* To test computer programs or systems with a benchmark.
**bend** (bĕnd) *v.* **bent, bending. 1.** To curve. **2.** To coerce or subdue. **3.** To yield; submit. —*n.* Something bent; a curve; crook.
**be•neath** (bĭ-nēth′) *adv.* **1.** In a lower place. **2.** Underneath. —*prep.* **1.** Below. **2.** Unworthy of.
**ben•e•dic•tion** (bĕn′ĭ-dĭk′shən) *n.* A blessing.
**ben•e•fac•tor** (bĕn′ə-făk′tər) *n.* One who gives financial or other aid. **—ben′e•fac′tion** *n.*

**be•nef•i•cent** (bə-nĕf′ĭ-sənt) *adj.* Kind; charitable. **—be•nef′i•cence** *n.*

**ben•e•fi•cial** (bĕn′ə-fĭsh′əl) *adj.* Helpful; advantageous. **—ben′e•fi′cial•ly** *adv.*

**ben•e•fit** (bĕn′ə-fĭt) *n.* **1.** An advantage. **2.** An aid; help. **3.** A payment. **4.** A fundraising event. *—v.* **1.** To be helpful or advantageous to. **2.** To derive advantage.

**be•nev•o•lence** (bə-nĕv′ə-ləns) *n.* Charitable good nature. **—be•nev′o•lent** *adj.*

**be•nign** (bĭ-nīn′) *adj.* **1.** Kindly; favorable. **2.** Not malignant.

**bent** (bĕnt) *v.* p.t. & p.p. of **bend.** *—adj.* **1.** Crooked. **2.** Determined. *—n.* An inclination.

**be•queath** (bĭ-kwēth′, -kwēth′) *v.* **1.** To leave by will. **2.** To pass on or hand down.

**be•quest** (bĭ-kwĕst′) *n.* Something left by will.

**be•rate** (bĭrāt′) *v.* **-rated, -rating.** To scold harshly.

**be•reave** (bĭ-rēv′) *v.* **-reaved** or **-reft** (-rĕft′), **-reaving.** To deprive of, as by death. **—be•reave′ment** *n.*

**ber•ry** (bĕr′ē) *n., pl.* **-ries.** A small, many-seeded fruit.

**ber•serk** (bər-sûrk′, -zûrk′) *adj.* Destructively violent. **—ber•serk′** *adv.* **—ber•serk′er** *n.*

**berth** (bûrth) *n.* **1.** A built-in bed. **2.** A docking space. **3.** A job. *—v.* To dock.

**be•seech** (bĭ-sēch′) *v.* **-sought** or **-seeched, -seeching.** To request earnestly; implore. **—be•seech′er** *n.*

**be•set** (bĭ-sĕt′) *v.* **-set, -setting.** To attack from all sides; harass.

**be•side** (bĭ-sīd′) *prep.* **1.** Next to. **2.** In comparison with. **—beside oneself.** Extremely agitated. *—adv.* In addition to.

**be•sides** (bĭ-sīdz′) *adv.* **1.** In addition; also. **2.** Furthermore. **3.** Otherwise. *—prep.* **1.** In addition to. **2.** Except for.

**be•siege** (bĭ-sēj′) *v.* **-sieged, -sieging. 1.** To encircle; crowd around. **2.** To overwhelm; flood. **—be•sieg′er** *n.*

**be•smirch** (bĭ-smûrch′) *v.* To soil; dishonor.

**be•sought** (bĭ-sôt′) *v.* p.t. & p.p. of **beseech.**

**be•speak** (bĭ-spēk′) *v.* **-spoke, -spoken** or **-spoke, -speaking.** To be or give a sign of; indicate.

**best** (bĕst) *adj.* superl. of **good.** Surpassing all others; most excellent. *—adv.* superl. of **well. 1.** Most advantageously. **2.** To the greatest extent. *—n.* **1.** The one highest in quality. **2.** The most excellent condition. **3.** The utmost. *—v.* To surpass; defeat.

**bes•tial** (bĕs′chəl, bĕs′-) *adj.* Like a beast; savage. **—bes′ti•al′i•ty** *n.*

**be•stow** (bĭ-stō′) *v.* To present; confer. **—be•stow′al** *n.*

**bet** (bĕt) *n.* An agreement between 2 parties that the party proved wrong will pay the other; wager. *—v.* **bet, betting.** To make or place a bet. **—bet′tor, bet′ter** *n.*

**be•tray** (bĭ-trā′) *v.* **1.** To be disloyal or faithless to. **2.** To reveal, esp. unintentionally. **—be•tray′al** *n.* **—be•tray′er** *n.*

**be•troth** (bĭ-trōth′, -trôth′) *v.* To promise in marriage. **—be•troth′al** *n.* **—be•trothed′** *adj. & n.*

**bet•ter** (bĕt′ər) *adj.* compar. of **good. 1.** Greater in excellence or higher in quality. **2.** More useful. **3.** Healthier. *—adv.* compar. of **well. 1.** To a greater or higher extent. **2.** More. **—had better.** Ought to. **—think better of.** To change one's mind. *—n.* **1.** Something better. **2.** Often **betters.** One's superiors. *—v.* **1.** To make or become better. **2.** To surpass. **—bet′ter•ment** *n.*

**be•tween** (bĭ-twēn′) *prep.* **1.** In the space or time separating. **2.** In the combined effort or ownership of. *—adv.* In an intermediate space, position, or time.

**bev•er•age** (bĕv′ər-ĭj, bĕv′rĭj) *n.* A liquid refreshment; drink.

**be•ware** (bĭ-wâr′) *v.* **-wared, -waring.** To guard against; be cautious of.

**be•wil•der** (bĭ-wĭl′dər) *v.* To confuse or befuddle. **—be•wil′der•ment** *n.*

**be•witch** (bĭ-wĭch′) *v.* To enchant; fascinate.

**be•yond** (bē-ŏnd′) *prep.* **1.** Farther away than. **2.** After. **3.** Outside the limits of. *—adv.* Farther along.

**bi•an•nu•al** (bī-ăn′yo͞o-əl) *adj.* Twice each year. **—bi•an′nu•al•ly** *adv.*

**bi•as** (bī′əs) *n.* **1.** A line cutting diagonally across the grain of fabric. **2.** Prejudice. *—v.* **-ased** or **-assed, -asing** or **-assing.** To prejudice or influence.

**—bi'ased** *adj.*

**bi•ath•lon** (bī-ăth'lən, -lŏn') *n.* An athletic contest consisting of cross-country skiing and rifle target-shooting. **—bi•ath'lete** *n.*

**Bi•ble** (bī'bəl) *n.* **1.** The sacred book of Christianity. **2.** The Scriptures, the sacred book of Judaism. **—Bib'li•cal** *adj.*

**bib•li•og•ra•phy** (bĭb'lē-ŏg'rə-fē) *n., pl.* **-phies.** A list of works by an author or on a subject. **—bib'li•og'ra•pher** *n.* **—bib'li•o•graph'ic, bib'li•o•graph'i•cal** *adj.*

**bi•ceps** (bī'sĕps') *n., pl.* **-ceps** or **-cepses.** The large muscle at the front of the upper arm.

**bick•er** (bĭk'ər) *v.* To quarrel.

**bi•cy•cle** (bī'sĭk'əl, -sĭ-kəl) *n.* A 2-wheeled vehicle pedaled by the rider. **—bi'cy•cle** *v.* **—bi'cy•clist** *n.*

**bid** (bĭd) *v.* **1. bid** or **bade, bidden** or **bid, bidding. a.** To direct; command. **b.** To invite; summon; ask. **2. bid, bid, bidding. a.** To seek; strive. **b.** To offer as a price. *—n.* **1.** An offer of a price. **2.** An invitation. **3.** A try; attempt. **—bid'der** *n.*

**bide** (bīd) *v.* **bided** or **bode, bided, biding. 1.** To stay. **2.** To await.

**bi•en•ni•al** (bī-ĕn'ē-əl) *adj.* **1.** Lasting 2 years. **2.** Happening every 2nd year. **—bi•en'ni•al** *n.*

**bier** (bîr) *n.* A stand for a coffin.

**bi•fo•cal** (bī-fō'kəl) *adj.* Designed to correct both near and distant vision. *—n.* **bifocals.** Eyeglasses with bifocal lenses.

**big** (bĭg) *adj.* **bigger, biggest. 1.** Of great size; large. **2.** Grown-up. **3.** Important. **—big'gish** *adj.* **—big'ness** *n.*

**big•a•my** (bĭg'ə-mē) *n., pl.* **-mies.** The crime of marrying 1 person while still married to another. **—big'a•mist** *n.* **—big'a•mous** *adj.*

**big•ot** (bĭg'ət) *n.* An intolerant person. **—big'ot•ed** *adj.* **—big'ot•ry** *n.*

**bike** (bīk) *n.* **1.** A bicycle. **2.** A motorcycle. **3.** A motorbike. **—bik'er** *n.*

**bile** (bīl) *n.* **1.** A bitter liquid secreted by the liver and aiding in digestion. **2.** Ill humor. **—bil'ious** *adj.* **—bil'ious•ness** *n.*

**bilge** (bĭlj) *n.* **1.** The lowest inner part of a ship's hull. **2.** Water that collects in this part. **3.** Stupid talk; nonsense.

**bill**[1] (bĭl) *n.* **1.** A statement of charges. **2.** A list of items offered. **3.** An advertising poster. **4.** A piece of paper money. **5.** A proposed law. *—v.* To present a statement of costs to.

**bill**[2] (bĭl) *n.* The beak of a bird.

**bil•let** (bĭl'ĭt) *n.* A lodging, as for troops. *—v.* To assign quarters to.

**bill•fold** (bĭl'fōld') *n.* A wallet.

**bil•lion** (bĭl'yən) *n.* The cardinal number written 1,000,000,000. **—bil'lion** *adj.* **—bil'lionth** *n. & adj.*

**bil•low** (bĭl'ō) *n.* **1.** A large wave. **2.** A great swell or surge. *—v.* To surge, roll, or rise in billows.

**bi•month•ly** (bī-mŭnth'lē) *adj. & adv.* **1.** Occurring every 2 months. **2.** Occurring twice a month. **—bi•month'ly** *n.*

**bin** (bĭn) *n.* A storage receptacle.

**bi•na•ry** (bī'nə-rē) *adj.* Based on or having 2.

**bind** (bīnd) *v.* **bound, binding. 1.** To tie or encircle. **2.** To bandage. **3.** To hold or restrain. **4.** To compel; oblige. **5.** To enclose and fasten (a book) between covers. **—bind'er** *n.*

**bin•oc•u•lars** (bə-nŏk'yə-lərz, bī-) *pl.n.* An optical device with a lens for each eye for magnifying distant objects.

**bi•o•chem•is•try** (bī'ō-kĕm'ĭ-strē) *n.* The chemistry of biological substances and processes. **—bi'o•chem'i•cal** *adj.* **—bi'o•chem'ist** *n.*

**bi•o•de•grad•a•ble** (bī'ō-dĭ-grā'də-bəl) *adj.* That can be decomposed by natural biological processes.

**bi•o•en•gi•neer•ing** (bī'ō-ĕn'jə-nîr'ĭng) *n.* The application of engineering to biology and medicine. **—bi'o•en'gi•neer'** *n.*

**bi•o•eth•ics** (bī'ō-ĕth'ĭks) *n.* The study of the ethics of biological research as applied in medicine. **—bi'o•eth'i•cist** *n.*

**bi•o•gas** (bī'ō-găs') *n.* a mixture of methane and carbon dioxide produced by bacteria and used for fuel.

**bi•og•ra•phy** (bī-ŏg'rə-fē, bē-) *n., pl.* **-phies.** A written account of a person's life. **—bi•og'ra•pher** *n.* **—bi'o•graph'ic, bi'o•graph'i•cal** *adj.*

**bi•o•haz•ard** (bī'ō-hăz'ərd) *n.* A biological agent or condition dangerous to human life. **—bi'o•haz'ar•dous** *adj.*

**bi•ol•o•gy** (bī-ŏl′ə-jē) *n.* The science of living things. **—bi′o•log′i•cal** *adj.* **—bi•ol′o•gist** *n.*

**bi•o•mass** (bī′ō-mas′) *n.* **1.** The total mass of living matter in an environment. **2.** Plant material and animal waste as a source for fuel.

**bi•o•med•i•cine** (bī′ō-mĕd′ĭ-sĭn) *n.* **1.** Medicine dealing with human survival and performance under abnormal stress. **2.** Medicine as it relates to all biological systems. **—bi′o•med′i•cal** *adj.*

**bi•on•ics** (bī-ŏn′ĭks) *n. (takes sing. v.)* The application of biological principles to engineering. **—bi•on′ic** *adj.*

**bi•o•re•search** (bī′ō-rĭ-sûrch′, -rē′sûrch′) *n.* Research in the biological sciences.

**bi•o•sphere** (bī′ə-sfîr′) *n.* The part of the earth in which living things exist.

**bi•par•ti•san** (bī-pär′tĭ-zən) *adj.* Of 2 parties. **—bi•par′ti•san•ship**′ *n.*

**bird** (bûrd) *n.* A warm-blooded, egg-laying, feathered vertebrate with wings.

**birth** (bûrth) *n.* **1.** The act or condition of being born. **2.** Origin; beginning.

**bis•cuit** (bĭs′kĭt) *n.* **1.** A small roll of bread. **2.** A cracker or cookie.

**bi•sect** (bī′sĕkt′, bī-sĕkt′) *v.* To divide or cut into 2. **—bi•sec′tion** *n.*

**bi•sex•u•al** (bī-sĕk′shōō-əl) *adj.* **1.** Pertaining to both sexes. **2.** Having both male and female organs; hermaphroditic. **3.** Sexually attracted to individuals of either sex. **—bi•sex′u•al** *n.*

**bish•op** (bĭsh′əp) *n.* A Christian clergyman in charge of a diocese.

**bi•son** (bī′sən, -zən) *n.* A short-horned, oxlike mammal of North America.

**bit[1]** (bĭt) *n.* **1.** A small piece or amount. **2.** A moment.

**bit[2]** (bĭt) *n.* **1.** A pointed tool for drilling and boring. **2.** The metal mouthpiece of a bridle.

**bit[3]** (bĭt) *n.* **1.** One character of a computer language having just 2 characters, as 0 and 1. **2.** A unit of information storage capacity, as of a computer memory.

**bitch** (bĭch) *n.* A female dog, wolf, or fox.

**bite** (bīt) *v.* **bit** (bĭt), **bitten** (bĭt′n) or **bit, biting. 1.** To cut or tear with the teeth. **2.** To sting. **3.** To take bait. *—n.* **1.** The act of biting. **2.** An injury resulting from biting. **3. a.** A stinging or smarting sensation. **b.** An incisive, penetrating quality. **4.** A mouthful.

**bit•ter** (bĭt′ər) *adj.* **1.** Having a sharp and unpleasant taste. **2.** Painful; resentful. **—bit′ter•ly** *adv.* **—bit′ter•ness** *n.*

**biv•ou•ac** (bĭv′ōō-ăk′, bĭv′wăk′) *n.* A temporary encampment of soldiers. *—v.* **-acked, -acking.** To encamp in a bivouac.

**bi•week•ly** (bī-wēk′lē) *adj. & adv.* **1.** Occurring every 2 weeks. **2.** Occurring twice a week. **—bi•week′ly** *n.*

**bi•year•ly** (bī-yîr′lē) *adj. & adv.* **1.** Occurring every 2 years. **2.** Occurring twice a year.

**bi•zarre** (bĭ-zär′) *adj.* Strikingly unconventional; odd.

**blab** (blăb) *v.* **blabbed, blabbing.** To chatter indiscreetly. **—blab′ber** *n.* **—blab′by** *adj.*

**black** (blăk) *adj.* **1.** Of the darkest color. **2.** Having no light. **3. Black. a.** Relating to a racial group, esp. of African origin, having brown to black skin; Negro. **b.** Afro-American; African-American. **4.** Evil. **5.** Cheerless. *—n.* **1.** A black color or pigment. **2.** An African-American; a Negro. **—black′ish** *adj.*

**black•guard** (blăg′ərd, -ärd′) *n.* A scoundrel.

**black•jack** (blăk′jăk′) *n.* **1.** A small leather-covered club. **2.** A card game.

**black•mail** (blăk′māl′) *n.* Extortion by threat of exposing something disgraceful. **—black′mail′** *v.* **—black′mail′er** *n.*

**black market** *n.* **1.** Buying and selling goods illegally. **2.** The place where such transactions are carried on.

**blad•der** (blăd′ər) *n.* A sac, esp. a sac in the pelvic cavity for storing urine.

**blade** (blād) *n.* **1.** The flat-edged cutting part of a tool. **2.** A leaf of grass. **3.** A dashing young man.

**blame** (blām) *v.* **blamed, blaming. 1.** To hold responsible. **2.** To censure. *—n.* **1.** Responsibility for a fault or error. **2.** Censure.

**blanch** (blănch) *v.* To make or become pale or white.

**bland** (blănd) *adj.* **1.** Moderate; mild. **2.** Characterless; zestless. **—bland'ness** *n.*

**blan•dish** (blăn'dĭsh) *v.* To coax by flattery; cajole. **—blan'dish•ment** *n.*

**blank** (blăngk) *adj.* **1.** Bearing no writing or marking. **2.** Not filled in. **3.** Expressing nothing; vacant. *—n.* **1.** An empty space. **2.** A space or form to be filled in. **3.** A gun cartridge with no bullet. **—blank'ly** *adv.*

**blan•ket** (blăng'kĭt) *n.* **1.** A thick cloth used as a covering, esp. on a bed. **2.** A thick layer that covers. *—adj.* Covering a wide range of conditions. *—v.* To cover with or as if with a blanket.

**blare** (blâr) *v.* **blared, blaring.** To sound loudly. *—n.* A loud sound.

**blar•ney** (blär'nē) *n.* Smooth, flattering talk.

**blas•pheme** (blăs-fēm') *v.* **-phemed, -pheming.** To speak of irreverently; profane. **—blas'phe•mous** *adj.* **—blas'phe•my** *n.*

**blast** (blăst) *n.* **1.** A strong gust; rush. **2.** A loud sound, as of a whistle. **3.** An explosion. **4.** A verbal assault. **5.** An exciting, enjoyable event. **—(at) full blast.** At full capacity. *—v.* **1.** To explode. **2.** To blight; wither. **3.** To criticize vigorously.

**bla•tant** (blāt'nt) *adj.* Offensively conspicuous; obvious. **—bla'tant•ly** *adv.*

**blaze** (blāz) *n.* **1.** A fire. **2.** Any bright, hot light. **3.** A sudden outburst. *—v.* **blazed, blazing. 1.** To burn brightly. **2.** To shine brightly. **3.** To be deeply excited.

**bleach** (blēch) *v.* To make or become white or colorless. *—n.* A chemical used for bleaching.

**bleak** (blēk) *adj.* **1.** Exposed; barren. **2.** Gloomy and somber.

**blear** (blîr) *v.* To blur; dim. **—blear'i•ness** *n.* **—blear'y** *adj.*

**bleed** (blēd) *v.* **bled** (blĕd), **bleeding. 1.** To lose or extract blood. **2.** To extort money from. **3.** To become mixed or run, as dyes in wet cloth.

**bleep** (blēp) *n.* **1.** A brief high-pitched sound, as from an electronic device. *—v.* **1.** To make such a sound, esp. on recordings to delete obscenities; blip.

**blem•ish** (blĕm'ĭsh) *n.* A flaw; defect. **—blem'ished** *adj.*

**blend** (blĕnd) *v.* To combine; mix; merge. *—n.* A combination; mixture.

**bless** (blĕs) *v.* **blessed** or **blest, blessing. 1.** To make holy; sanctify. **2.** To invoke divine favor upon. **3.** To make fortunate; favor. **—bless'ed** *adj.* **—bless'ing** *n.*

**blew** (blo͞o) *v.* p.t. of **blow.**

**blight** (blīt) *n.* **1.** A destructive plant disease. **2.** An injurious influence. **—blight** *v.*

**blind** (blīnd) *adj.* **1.** Without sight. **2.** Without reason or evidence. **3.** Hidden from sight. **4.** Closed at 1 end. *—n.* **1.** Something that shuts out light. **2.** A shelter for concealing hunters. *—v.* To deprive of sight. **—blind'ly** *adv.* **—blind'ness** *n.*

**blind•fold** (blīnd'fōld') *n.* A bandage over the eyes. **—blind'fold'** *v.*

**blind•side** (blīnd'sīd') *v.* **-sided, -siding.** To hit or attack on someone's blind side.

**blink** (blĭngk) *v.* **1.** To close and open (1 or both eyes) rapidly. **2.** To flash on and off. *—n.* **1.** The act of blinking. **2.** A flash of light; a glimmer.

**blip** (blĭp) *n.* **1.** A spot of light on a radar screen. **2.** A brief interruption of the sound on a TV transmission, as by a censor. **3.** A sudden, temporary, steep move up or down on a graph. **4.** An error or mistake. *—v.* **blipped, blipping.** To interrupt recorded sounds, as on a videotape; bleep.

**bliss** (blĭs) *n.* Serene happiness. **—bliss'ful** *adj.* **—bliss'ful•ly** *adv.*

**blis•ter** (blĭs'tər) *n.* A thin, fluid-filled swelling of the skin caused by irritation. **—blis'ter** *v.*

**blister pack** *n.* A package containing a product in a clear plastic case sealed onto cardboard; a bubble pack.

**blithe** (blīth, blīth) *adj.* Cheerful; carefree. **—blithe'ly** *adv.*

**bliz•zard** (blĭz'ərd) *n.* A heavy snowstorm with high winds.

**bloat** (blōt) *v.* To make or become swollen.

**blob** (blŏb) *n.* A rounded mass or splotch.

**bloc** (blŏk) *n.* A group united for common action.

**block** (blŏk) *n.* **1.** A solid, flat-sided piece of wood or other hard substance. **2.** A stand at an auction. **3.** A pulley or a system of pulleys set in a casing. **4.** A set of like items. **5. a.** A section of a town bounded on each side by consecutive streets. **b.** A segment of a street bounded by successive cross streets. **6.** An obstacle. —*v.* **1.** To stop the passage or view of. **2.** To plan roughly; shape. —**block'age** *n.*

**block•ade** (blŏ-kād') *n.* The closing off of access to an area. —**block•ade'** *v.*

**blond** (blŏnd) *adj.* **1.** Having fair hair. **2.** Light-colored. —*n.* A blond person.

**blood** (blŭd) *n.* **1.** The red fluid that flows through the body. **2.** Kinship. **3.** Racial or national ancestry.

**blood•shed** (blŭd'shĕd') *n.* Loss of life; casualties.

**blood•thirst•y** (blŭd'thûr'stē) *adj.* Murderous; cruel.

**blood•y** (blŭd'ē) *adj.* **-ier, -iest. 1.** Of, containing, or stained with blood. **2.** Giving rise to bloodshed. **3.** Bloodthirsty; cruel. —*v.* **-ied, -ying.** To stain with blood.

**bloom** (blo͞om) *n.* **1.** The flower or blossoms of a plant. **2.** The time of flowering. **3.** A fresh, rosy complexion. —*v.* **1.** To bear flowers. **2.** To glow. **3.** To grow or flourish.

**bloom•ers** (blo͞o'mərz) *pl.n.* Women's wide, loose pants closely gathered at the ankles or knees.

**blos•som** (blŏs'əm) *n.* A flower. —*v.* **1.** To flower; bloom. **2.** To develop; flourish.

**blot** (blŏt) *n.* A spot; a stain. —*v.* **blotted, blotting. 1.** To spot or stain. **2.** To erase; cancel (with *out*). **3.** To dry with absorbent material. —**blot'ter** *n.*

**blotch** (blŏch) *n.* A spot or blot. —**blotch** *v.*

**blouse** (blous, blouz) *n.* A loosely fitting shirtlike garment. —*v.* **bloused, blousing.** To hang loosely.

**blow** (blō) *v.* **blew** (blo͞o), **blown** (blōn), **blowing. 1.** To move as the wind does. **2.** To carry or be carried by the wind. **3.** To expel a current of air. **4.** To sound or make by expelling a current of air. **5.** To explode. **6.** To melt (a fuse). —*n.* **1.** A blast of air or wind. **2.** The act of blowing. **3.** A hard stroke; impact; hit. **4.** A shock or calamity. —**blow'er** *n.*

**blow•out** (blō'out') *n.* **1.** A sudden bursting, as of an automobile tire. **2.** The burning out of a fuse.

**blow•torch** (blō'tôrch') *n.* A gas burner that produces a flame for welding metals.

**blow•up** (blō'ŭp') *n.* **1.** An explosion. **2.** A photographic enlargement. **3.** A violent outburst of temper.

**blub•ber** (blŭb'ər) *n.* Fat, esp. whale fat.

**bludg•eon** (blŭj'ən) *n.* A short club. —*v.* **-eoned, -eoning. 1.** To club. **2.** To threaten or bully.

**blue** (blo͞o) *n.* A color like that of a clear sky. —**the blues. 1.** Low spirits. **2.** A slow, sad style of jazz ballad. —*adj.* **bluer, bluest. 1.** Of the color blue. **2.** Gloomy; dreary. —**blu'ish** *adj.*

**blue chip** *n.* **1.** A stock selling at a high price because of a long record of steady earnings. **2.** A valuable asset or property. —**blue'chip'** *adj.*

**blue-col•lar** (blo͞o'kŏl'ər) *adj.* Relating to wage earners engaged esp. in manual labor.

**blue law** *n.* A law regulating Sunday activities.

**blue-pen•cil** (blo͞o'pĕn'səl) *v.* **-ciled** or **-cilled, -ciling** or **-cilling. 1.** To edit or revise with or as with a blue pencil. **2.** To correct.

**blue•print** (blo͞o'prĭnt') *n.* A detailed plan, as of an architectural design.

**blue ribbon** *n.* **1.** A 1st prize in a competition. **2.** An award for excellence. —**blue'-rib'bon** *adj.*

**bluff** (blŭf) *v.* To mislead by a display of boldness. —*n.* **1.** The act of bluffing. **2.** A steep bank; cliff. —*adj.* Blunt. —**bluff'er** *n.*

**blun•der** (blŭn'dər) *n.* A stupid mistake. —*v.* **1.** To move awkwardly or clumsily. **2.** To make a stupid mistake.

**blunt** (blŭnt) *adj.* **1.** Having a thick, dull edge or end. **2.** Outspoken; brusque. —*v.* To make or become blunt. —**blunt'ly** *adv.*

**blur** (blûr) *v.* **blurred, blurring. 1.** To make or become indistinct; obscure. **2.** To smear or stain. **3.** To dim. —*n.* Anything hazy and indistinct. —**blur'ry** *adj.*

**blurb** (blûrb) *n.* A short publicity notice, as on a book jacket.

**blurt** (blûrt) *v.* To utter impulsively.

**blush** (blŭsh) *n.* A reddening of the face, as from shame. —**blush** *v.* —**blush'er** *n.*

**blus•ter** (blŭs'tər) *v.* **1.** To blow in violent gusts, as wind in a storm. **2.** To speak boastfully. —**blus'ter** *n.*

**board** (bôrd, bōrd) *n.* **1.** A long, flat piece of wood. **2.** Regularly provided meals. **3.** A group of administrators; council. —**on board.** Aboard. —*v.* **1.** To cover or close with boards. **2.** To furnish with or receive meals. **3.** To enter or go aboard (a vehicle or ship). —**board'er** *n.*

**boast** (bōst) *v.* **1.** To talk about or speak with excessive pride. **2.** To take pride in; enjoy the possession of. —*n.* An instance of bragging. —**boast'er** *n.* —**boast'ful** *adj.*

**boat** (bōt) *n.* **1.** A small water craft. **2.** A ship.

**bob** (bŏb) *n.* **1.** A short jerking movement. **2.** A fishing float. **3.** A short haircut. —*v.* **bobbed, bobbing. 1.** To move or jerk up and down. **2.** To cut (hair) short.

**bob•bin** (bŏb'ĭn) *n.* A spool or reel for thread.

**bob•sled** (bŏb'slĕd') *n.* A racing sled. —**bob'sled'** *v.*

**bode**[1] (bōd) *v.* **boded, boding.** To be an omen of.

**bode**[2] (bōd) *v.* A p.t. of **bide.**

**bo•de•ga** (bō-dā'gə) *n.* A grocery store specializing in Hispanic products.

**bod•ice** (bŏd'ĭs) *n.* The fitted upper part of a woman's dress.

**bod•y** (bŏd'ē) *n., pl.* **-ies. 1. a.** The physical structure, esp. of a human being or animal. **b.** A corpse. **2.** A trunk or torso. **3.** A person. **4.** A number of persons or things; group. **5.** The main or central part. **6.** Any bounded mass. —**bod'i•ly** *adj. & adv.*

**bof•fo** (bŏf'ō) *adj.* Very successful.

**bog** (bôg, bŏg) *n.* Soft, water-logged ground; a marsh. —*v.* **bogged, bogging.** To hinder or be hindered; slow (with *down*).

**bo•gus** (bō'gəs) *adj.* Counterfeit; fake.

**boil**[1] (boil) *v.* **1.** To vaporize a liquid by applying heat. **2.** To cook by boiling. **3.** To be in a state of agitation. —**boil down.** To condense; summarize. —*n.* The state of boiling. —**boil'er** *n.*

**boil**[2] (boil) *n.* A pus-filled skin swelling.

**bois•ter•ous** (boi'stər-əs, -strəs) *adj.* Noisy and unrestrained; rowdy. —**bois'ter•ous•ly** *adv.* —**bois'ter•ous•ness** *n.*

**bold** (bōld) *adj.* **1.** Fearless; courageous. **2.** Unduly forward; impudent. **3.** Clear and distinct. —**bold'ly** *adv.* —**bold'ness** *n.*

**bo•lo•gna** (bə-lō'nē, -nə) *n.* A mild, smoked sausage.

**bol•ster** (bōl'stər) *n.* A long, narrow pillow. —*v.* To prop up.

**bolt** (bōlt) *n.* **1.** A sliding bar used to fasten or lock a door. **2.** A threaded metal pin used with a nut to hold parts together. **3.** A flash of lightning. **4.** A sudden movement; dash. **5.** A large roll of cloth. —*v.* **1.** To secure or lock with a bolt. **2.** To eat hurriedly; gulp. **3.** To desert; abandon. **4.** To move or spring suddenly; dash.

**bomb** (bŏm) *n.* An explosive weapon dropped on or thrown at a target. —*v.* To attack with bombs.

**bom•bard** (bŏm-bärd') *v.* To attack heavily with artillery, bombs, or missiles. —**bom'bar•dier'** *n.* —**bom•bard'ment** *n.*

**bom•bast** (bŏm'băst') *n.* Pompous speech or writing. —**bom•bas'tic** *adj.*

**bomb•er** (bŏm'ər) *n.* An aircraft designed to drop bombs.

**bo•na fide** (bō'nə fīd', fī'dē) *adj.* Done or made in good faith; sincere.

**bond** (bŏnd) *n.* **1.** Anything that binds, ties, or fastens together. **2.** A uniting force or tie; a link. **3.** A sum of money paid as bail or surety. **4.** A certificate of debt guaranteeing payment plus interest. —*v.* **1.** To furnish bond or surety for. **2.** To join securely, as with glue.

**bond•age** (bŏn'dĭj) *n.* Slavery; servitude.

**bond paper** *n.* A superior grade of white paper made from rag pulp.

**bone** (bōn) *n.* **1.** The rigid, calcified material that makes up the skeleton. **2.** One of the pieces of the skeleton. —*v.* **boned, boning.** To remove the bones from. —**bon'y** *adj.*

**bon•fire** (bŏn'fīr') *n.* A large outdoor fire.

**bon•net** (bŏn′ĭt) *n.* A hat tied under the chin.

**bo•nus** (bō′nəs) *n., pl.* **-nuses.** An extra payment or gift.

**book** (bo͝ok) *n.* **1.** Written or printed material made of fastened pages between protective covers. **2.** A literary work. **3.** A volume in which financial transactions are recorded. —*v.* To list, reserve, or schedule in a book. —**book′ish** *adj.*

**book•keep•ing** (bo͝ok′kē′pĭng) *n.* The recording of the accounts of a business. —**book′keep′er** *n.*

**book•let** (bo͝ok′lĭt) *n.* A small bound book.

**boom**[1] (bo͞om) *v.* **1.** To make a deep, resonant sound. **2.** To flourish. —*n.* **1.** A booming sound. **2.** Prosperity; success.

**boom**[2] (bo͞om) *n.* **1.** A long spar extending from a mast to hold a sail. **2.** A long pole, esp. to support or guide objects being lifted.

**boo•mer•ang** (bo͞o′mə-răng′) *n.* A flat, curved missile that can be hurled so that it returns to the thrower. —*v.* To rebound detrimentally.

**boon** (bo͞on) *n.* Something beneficial; a blessing.

**boor** (bo͝or) *n.* A rude, clumsy person. —**boor′ish** *adj.* —**boor′ish•ness** *n.*

**boost** (bo͞ost) *v.* **1.** To raise by pushing from below. **2.** To increase; raise. **3.** To promote vigorously. —*n.* **1.** A lift or help. **2.** An increase. —**boost′er** *n.*

**boot** (bo͞ot) *n.* **1.** A piece of footwear covering the foot and part or all of the leg. **2.** A kick. —*v.* **1.** To put boots on. **2.** To kick.

**booth** (bo͞oth) *n., pl.* **booths.** A small enclosed compartment, stall, or eating area.

**boot•leg** (bo͞ot′lĕg′) *v.* **-legged, -legging.** To make, sell, or transport illegally, as liquor. —*adj.* Produced or sold illegally. —**boot′leg′ger** *n.*

**boo•ty** (bo͞o′tē) *n., pl.* **-ties.** Plunder; loot.

**booze** (bo͞oz) *n.* Intoxicating liquor. —*v.* **boozed, boozing.** To drink to excess.

**bor•der** (bôr′dər) *n.* **1.** A surrounding margin; edge. **2.** A geographic or political boundary. —*v.* **1.** To provide with a border. **2.** To lie on the border of. **3.** To verge; approach.

**bore**[1] (bôr, bōr) *v.* **bored, boring.** To make a hole in or through; drill; dig. —*n.* **1.** A hole made by drilling. **2.** The interior diameter of a tube, cylinder, etc.

**bore**[2] (bôr, bōr) *v.* **bored, boring** To tire by dullness; be uninteresting to. —*n.* A dull person or thing. —**bore′dom** *n.*

**bore**[3] (bôr, bōr) *v.* p.t. of **bear**[1].

**born** (bôrn) *v.* A p.p. of **bear**[1]. —*adj.* From birth; innate.

**borne** (bôrn, bōrn) *v.* A p.p. of **bear**[1].

**bor•row** (bŏr′ō, bôr′ō) *v.* **1.** To obtain on loan with intent to return. **2.** To adopt or use as one's own. —**bor′row•er** *n.*

**bos•om** (bo͝oz′əm, bo͞o′zəm) *n.* **1.** The chest or breasts. **2.** The center or heart. —*adj.* Intimate.

**boss** (bôs, bŏs) *n.* **1.** An employer or supervisor. **2.** A powerful politician. —*v.* **1.** To supervise. **2.** To command in a domineering manner. —**boss′y** *adj.*

**bot•a•ny** (bŏt′n-ē) *n.* The science of plants. —**bo•tan′ic, bo•tan′i•cal** *adj.* —**bot′a•nist** *n.*

**botch** (bŏch) *v.* To ruin; bungle. —**botch** *n.*

**both** (bōth) *adj.* Two together. —*pron.* The one and the other. —*conj.* As well; together. Two together.

**both•er** (bŏ*th*′ər) *v.* **1.** To irritate, esp. by small annoyances; pester; harass. **2.** To trouble or concern oneself. —*n.* A cause or state of disturbance. —**both′er•some** *adj.*

**bot•tle** (bŏt′l) *n.* A container, usually of glass, having a narrow neck and a mouth that can be sealed. —*v.* **-tled, -tling.** To place in a bottle. —**bottle up.** To confine.

**bot•tom** (bŏt′əm) *n.* **1.** The lowest or deepest part. **2.** The underside. **3.** The basic quality; essence. **4.** The buttocks. —*adj.* Lowest; fundamental. —**bot′tom•less** *adj.*

**bottom line** *n.* **1.** The lowest line on a financial statement, showing net loss or gain. **2.** The final result. **3.** The main point.

**bottom out** *v.* To descend to the lowest point before rising.

**bough** (bou) *n.* A branch of a tree.

**bought** (bôt) *v.* p.t. & p.p. of **buy.**

**bouil•lon** (bo͞ol'yŏn', -yən, bo͞o'yŏn') *n.* A clear broth made from meat.
**boul•der** (bōl'dər) *n.* A large rounded rock.
**bounce** (bouns) *v.* **bounced, bouncing.** **1.** To rebound from a collision. **2.** To cause to collide and rebound. **3.** To move energetically; bound. **4.** To write (a check) on an account with insufficient funds. —*n.* **1.** A bound or rebound. **2.** A spring or leap.
**bound**[1] (bound) *v.* To leap or spring. —*n.* **1.** A leap. **2.** A bounce.
**bound**[2] (bound) *n.* Often **bounds.** A boundary. —*v.* **1.** To limit. **2.** To demarcate. **—bound'less** *adj.*
**bound**[3] (bound) *v.* p.t. & p.p. of **bind.** —*adj.* **1.** Confined by bonds; tied. **2.** Under obligation. **3.** Equipped with a cover or binding. **4.** Certain.
**bound•a•ry** (boun'də-rē, -drē) *n., pl.* **-ries.** A border or limit.
**boun•te•ous** (boun'tē-əs) *adj.* **1.** Generous. **2.** Plentiful. **—boun'te•ous•ly** *adv.*
**boun•ty** (boun'tē) *n., pl.* **-ties. 1.** Liberality in giving. **2.** A reward or inducement. **—boun'ti•ful** *adj.*
**bou•quet** (bō-kā', bo͞o-) *n.* **1.** A bunch of flowers. **2.** An aroma.
**bour•bon** (bûr'bən) *n.* A whiskey distilled from corn.
**bour•geois** (bo͝or-zhwä', bo͝or'zhwä') *n., pl.* **-geois.** One belonging to the middle class. **—bour•geois'** *adj.* **—bour'geoi•sie'** *n.*
**bout** (bout) *n.* **1.** A contest; match. **2.** A period of time; spell.
**bou•tique** (bo͞o-tēk') *n.* A small shop specializing in fashionable merchandise.
**bo•vine** (bō'vīn', -vēn') *adj.* Of or resembling a cow or cattle. **—bo'vine'** *n.*
**bow**[1] (bou) *n.* The front section of a ship.
**bow**[2] (bou) *v.* **1.** To bend (the head or body) in order to express greeting or respect. **2.** To acquiesce; submit. —*n.* An inclination of the head or body, as in greeting.
**bow**[3] (bō) *n.* **1.** Something bent, curved, or arched. **2.** A curved stick, strung taut and used to launch arrows. **3.** A rod strung with horsehair, used in playing violins, etc. **4.** A knot having loose loops. —*v.* **1.** To bend into a bow. **2.** To play a stringed instrument with a bow.
**bow•els** (bou'əlz) *pl.n.* **1.** The intestines. **2.** The interior; depths.
**bowl**[1] (bōl) *n.* **1.** A hemispheric vessel for food or fluids. **2.** A curved, hollow part. **3.** A bowl-shaped building, esp. a sports arena.
**bowl**[2] (bōl) *v.* To throw or roll a ball in bowling. **—bowl'er** *n.*
**box**[1] (bŏks) *n.* **1.** A rectangular container, often with a lid. **2.** A separate seating compartment in a theater. —*v.* To place in a box.
**box**[2] (bŏks) *n.* A blow or cuff. —*v.* To hit or fight with the fists. **—box'er** *n.* **—box'ing** *adj. & n.*
**box•car** (bŏks'kär') *n.* An enclosed railway car for freight.
**boy** (boi) *n.* A male child or youth. **—boy'hood'** *n.* **—boy'ish** *adj.*
**boy•cott** (boi'kŏt') *v.* To abstain from dealing with, as a means of protest. **—boy'cott'** *n.*
**brace** (brās) *n.* **1.** A clamp. **2.** Any support. **3.** A cranklike device for turning a bit. **4.** *pl.* **brace.** A pair of like things. —*v.* **braced, bracing. 1.** To support. **2.** To prepare for an impact or danger. **3.** To invigorate.
**brace•let** (brās'lĭt) *n.* An ornamental band for the wrist.
**brack•et** (brăk'ĭt) *n.* **1.** A structure projecting to support a shelf or other weight. **2.** Either of a pair of symbols, [ ], used to enclose written or printed material. **3.** A classification. —*v.* **1.** To support with brackets. **2.** To place within brackets. **3.** To classify together.
**brack•ish** (brăk'ĭsh) *adj.* Salty.
**brag** (brăg) *v.* **bragged, bragging.** To talk boastfully. **—brag'gart** *n.*
**braid** (brād) *v.* **1.** To interweave strands of; plait. **2.** To decorate with an ornamental trim. —*n.* **1.** A braided length. **2.** An ornamental trim.
**Braille** (brāl) *n.* Also **braille.** A system of printing for the blind, using raised dots.
**brain** (brān) *n.* **1.** The gray nerve tissue in the skull responsible for the control of bodily activities and the exercise of emotion and thought. **2.** Often **brains.**

Intelligence. —*v.* To smash on the skull of. **—brain'less** *adj.* **—brain'y** *adj.*

**brain death** *n.* Death as evidenced by absence of central-nervous-system activity. **—brain'-dead'** *adj.*

**brain drain** *n.* The emigration of professionals for better positions.

**brain scanner** *n.* A CAT scanner used to x-ray the brain. **—brain'-scan'** *v.*

**brake** (brāk) *n.* a device for slowing or stopping motion. —*v.* **braked, braking.** To slow or stop with a brake.

**brake pad** *n.* A flat block that presses against the disk of a disc brake.

**bram•ble** (brăm'bəl) *n.* A prickly plant.

**branch** (brănch) *n.* **1.** An extension dividing off from the trunk or a limb of a plant. **2.** A division, tributary, or unit. —*v.* **1.** To spread out in branches. **2.** To subdivide; diverge.

**brand** (brănd) *n.* **1.** A trademark or label. **2.** A make; kind. **3.** A mark burned on the hide of an animal. **4.** A mark of disgrace; stigma. —*v.* **1.** To mark with a brand. **2.** To stigmatize.

**bran•dish** (brăn'dĭsh) *v.* To flourish; display.

**bran•dy** (brăn'dē) *n., pl.* **-dies.** A liquor distilled from wine or fruit juice.

**brash** (brăsh) *adj.* **1.** Hasty; rash. **2.** Impudent; saucy.

**brass** (brăs) *n.* **1.** An alloy of copper and zinc. **2. brasses.** Wind instruments made of brass. **3.** Military officers. **—brass** *adj.*

**bras•siere, bras•sière** (brə-zîr') *n.* A woman's undergarment worn to support the breasts.

**brat** (brăt) *n.* A disobedient child. **—brat'ty** *adj.*

**bra•va•do** (brə-vä'dō) *n., pl.* **-does** or **-dos.** False bravery; swagger.

**brave** (brāv) *adj.* **braver, bravest.** Displaying courage. —*n.* A Native American warrior. —*v.* **braved, braving.** To face courageously. **—brave'ly** *adv.* **—brav'er•y** *n.*

**brawl** (brôl) *n.* A noisy quarrel or fight. —*v.* To quarrel noisily.

**brawn** (brôn) *n.* **1.** Well-developed muscles. **2.** Muscular power. **—brawn'y** *adj.*

**bra•zen** (brā'zən) *adj.* **1.** Made of brass. **2.** Loud; raucous. **3.** Impudent; bold. **—bra'zen•ly** *adv.* **—bra'zen•ness** *n.*

**breach** (brēch) *n.* **1.** A violation; infraction. **2.** A gap; rift; break. —*v.* To make a hole or gap in; break through.

**bread** (brĕd) *n.* **1.** A foodstuff made from baked flour dough. **2.** The necessities of life; livelihood. —*v.* To coat with bread crumbs.

**breadth** (brĕdth) *n.* **1.** The measure from side to side; width. **2.** Wide extent or scope.

**break** (brāk) *v.* **broke** (brōk), **broken** (brō'kən), **breaking. 1.** To separate into pieces by sudden force; come apart. **2.** To make or become unusable. **3.** To force or make a way into; pierce. **4.** To disrupt. **5.** To come into being or notice. **6.** To surpass. **7.** To tame; subdue. **8.** To stop. **—break in. 1.** To train. **2.** To enter forcibly. **3.** To interrupt. **—break off.** To stop suddenly. **—break out. 1.** To erupt. **2.** To escape, as from prison. —*n.* **1.** The act of breaking. **2.** A fracture or crack. **3.** A disruption. **4.** A change. **5.** A respite; rest period. **—break'age** *n.*

**break•down** (brāk'doun') *n.* **1.** Loss of function; mechanical failure. **2.** A collapse in health. **3.** An analysis.

**break•fast** (brĕk'fəst) *n.* The 1st meal of the day. **—break'fast** *v.*

**breast** (brĕst) *n.* **1.** A mammary gland. **2.** The chest.

**breath** (brĕth) *n.* **1.** The air inhaled and exhaled in respiration. **2.** Respiration. **3.** A stirring of air. **4.** A trace. **—breath'less** *adj.* **—breath'tak'ing** *adj.*

**breathe** (brē*th*) *v.* **breathed, breathing. 1.** To inhale and exhale. **2.** To live. **3.** To pause to rest. **4.** To utter. **—breath'•a•ble** *adj.*

**breath•er** (brē'*th*ər) *n.* A short rest period.

**breech•es** (brĭch'ĭz) *pl.n.* Knee-length trousers.

**breed** (brēd) *v.* **bred** (brĕd), **breeding. 1.** To produce (offspring); reproduce. **2.** To bring about. **3.** To raise (animals). **4.** To rear; bring up. —*n.* **1.** A genetic strain. **2.** A kind; sort. **—breed'ing** *n.*

**breeze** (brēz) *n.* A gentle wind. —*v.* **breezed, breezing.** To move effortlessly. **—breez'y** *adj.*

**brev•i•ty** (brĕv′ĭ-tē) *n.* Briefness; terseness.

**brew** (bro͞o) *v.* **1.** To make (ale or beer) from malt and hops. **2.** To make by boiling or steeping. **3.** To concoct; make. —*n.* A beverage made by brewing. —**brew′er** *n.* —**brew′er•y** *n.*

**bribe** (brīb) *n.* Anything offered or given to induce someone to act dishonestly. —*v.* **bribed, bribing.** To give or offer a bribe to. —**brib′er•y** *n.*

**brick** (brĭk) *n.* A block of baked clay used in construction. —*v.* To cover with brick. —**brick** *adj.* —**brick′lay′er** *n.*

**bride** (brīd) *n.* A woman recently married or about to be married. —**bri′dal** *adj.*

**bride•groom** (brīd′gro͞om, -gro͞om′) *n.* A man recently married or about to be married.

**bridge**[1] (brĭj) *n.* **1.** A structure providing passage over a waterway or other obstacle. **2.** A connection; link; liaison. **3.** The ridge of the nose. **4.** A false tooth or set of teeth anchored by natural teeth. —*v.* **bridged, bridging.** To build or be a bridge over.

**bridge**[2] (brĭj) *n.* A card game played with 1 deck of cards dealt equally among 4 persons.

**bri•dle** (brīd′l) *n.* **1.** The harness fitted about a horse's head. **2.** Any restraint. —*v.* **-dled, -dling. 1.** To put a bridle on. **2.** To control or restrain. **3.** To display resentment.

**brief** (brēf) *adj.* Short. —*n.* A summary, esp. of a legal case. —*v.* To inform or instruct. —**brief′ly** *adv.*

**brig** (brĭg) *n.* **1.** A 2-masted sailing ship. **2.** A ship's prison.

**bri•gade** (brĭ-gād′) *n.* **1.** A military unit consisting of a number of combat battalions. **2.** Any organized group.

**bright** (brīt) *adj.* **1.** Emitting or reflecting light; shining. **2.** Brilliant; vivid. **3.** Auspicious. **4.** Happy; cheerful. **5.** Intelligent. —**bright′en** *v.* —**bright′ly** *adv.* —**bright′ness** *n.*

**bril•liant** (brĭl′yənt) *adj.* **1.** Shining. **2.** Brightly vivid in color. **3.** Glorious; splendid. **4.** Marked by extraordinary intellect. —**bril′liance, bril′lian•cy** *n.* —**bril′liant•ly** *adv.*

**brim** (brĭm) *n.* **1.** The uppermost edge of a cup. **2.** A projecting edge of a hat.

**brine** (brīn) *n.* **1.** Very salty water. **2.** The ocean. —**brin′y** *adj.*

**bring** (brĭng) *v.* **brought** (brôt), **bringing. 1.** To take with oneself to a place. **2.** To lead into a specified state. **3.** To induce. **4.** To cause to occur. —**bring about.** To cause to happen. —**bring forth.** To produce. —**bring off.** To accomplish. —**bring out. 1.** To reveal. **2.** To produce. —**bring up. 1.** To rear (a child). **2.** To mention.

**brink** (brĭngk) *n.* The edge; verge.

**brisk** (brĭsk) *adj.* **1.** Moving or acting quickly. **2.** Keen or sharp. **3.** Invigorating. —**brisk′ly** *adv.*

**bris•tle** (brĭs′əl) *n.* A short, stiff hair. —*v.* **-tled, -tling. 1.** To erect the bristles. **2.** To react with anger. **3.** To be densely covered. —**bris′tly** *adj.*

**brit•tle** (brĭt′l) *adj.* Hard but breakable; fragile. —**brit′tle•ness** *n.*

**broad** (brôd) *adj.* **1.** Wide from side to side. **2.** Spacious. **3.** Widely diffused. **4.** Covering a wide scope. **5.** Liberal; tolerant. **6.** Plain; obvious. —**broad′en** *v.* —**broad′ly** *adv.*

**broad•cast** (brôd′kăst′) *v.* **-cast** or **-casted, -casting. 1.** To transmit (a program) by radio or television. **2.** To make known widely. —*n.* A radio or television program. —*adv.* Far and wide. —**broad′cast′er** *n.*

**bro•cade** (brō-kād′) *n.* A fabric with a raised interwoven design. —**bro•cad′ed** *adj.*

**broc•co•li** (brŏk′ə-lē) *n.* A plant with an edible flower head.

**bro•chure** (brō-sho͝or′) *n.* A pamphlet.

**brogue** (brōg) *n.* **1.** A strong Irish accent. **2.** A sturdy oxford shoe.

**broil** (broil) *v.* To cook by direct radiant heat. —**broil′er** *n.*

**broke** (brōk) *v.* p.t. of **break.** —*adj.* Lacking funds.

**bro•ken** (brō′kən) *v.* p.p. of **break.** —*adj.* **1.** Fractured; shattered. **2.** Violated, as promises. **3.** Discontinuous. **4.** Spoken imperfectly. **5.** Defeated; tamed.

**bro•ker** (brō′kər) *n.* One who buys or sells for another; an agent. —*v.* To act as a broker. —**bro′ker•age** *n.*

**bro•mide** (brō′mīd′) *n.* **1.** A sedative drug. **2.** A commonplace saying.
**bron•chus** (brŏng′kəs) *n., pl.* **-chi.** Either of 2 main branches of the trachea, leading directly to the lungs. —**bron′chi•al** *adj.*
**bronze** (brŏnz) *n.* **1.** An alloy of copper and tin. **2.** Reddish brown. —*v.* **bronzed, bronzing.** To give the appearance of bronze to. —**bronze** *adj.*
**brooch** (brōch, brōōch) *n.* A large decorative pin.
**brood** (brōōd) *n.* A group of young animals, esp. of birds hatched at the same time. —*v.* **1.** To sit on and hatch (eggs). **2.** To ponder moodily. —*adj.* Kept for breeding.
**brook** (brŏŏk) *n.* A small freshwater stream.
**broom** (brōōm, brŏŏm) *n.* A long-handled brushlike implement for sweeping.
**broth** (brôth, brŏth) *n.* A thin, clear soup; stock.
**broth•er** (brŭ*th*′ər) *n.* **1.** A male having the same parents as another. **2.** One who has a close bond with another. **3.** A fellow member. —**broth′er•hood′** *n.* —**broth′er•ly** *adj.*
**brought** (brôt) *v.* p.t. & p.p. of **bring.**
**brow** (brou) *n.* **1. a** The ridge over the eyes. **b.** An eyebrow. **c.** The forehead. **2.** The edge of a steep place.
**brown** (broun) *n.* A color between red and yellow. —*v.* To make or become brown. —**brown** *adj.* —**brown′ish** *adj.*
**browse** (brouz) *v.* **browsed, browsing. 1.** To look through books casually. **2.** To feed on vegetation; graze.
**bruise** (brōōz) *v.* **bruised, bruising. 1.** To injure the skin without rupture. **2.** To dent or mar. —*n.* An injury in which the skin is not broken; contusion.
**bru•net** (brōō-nĕt′) *adj.* Dark or brown in color, as hair. —*n.* A person with brown hair.
**brunt** (brŭnt) *n.* The main impact, as of a blow.
**brush** (brŭsh) *n.* **1.** A device consisting of bristles or other material fastened into a handle, for scrubbing, grooming, etc. **2.** A light touch in passing. **3.** A brief encounter. **4.** A growth of bushes; thicket. —*v.* **1.** To scrub, groom, etc., with a brush. **2.** To apply or remove with or as if with motions of a brush. **3.** To touch lightly in passing.
**brushed** (brŭsht) *adj.* Relating to fabrics that have a nap produced by brushing.
**brusque** (brŭsk) *adj.* Abrupt; discourteously blunt. —**brusque′ly** *adv.*
**bru•tal** (brōōt′l) *adj.* Cruel; harsh. —**brutal′i•ty** *n.* —**bru′tal•ize′** *v.* —**bru′tal•ly** *adv.*
**brute** (brōōt) *n.* **1.** An animal; beast. **2.** A brutal person. —*adj.* Of beasts. —**bru′tish** *adj.*
**bub•ble** (bŭb′əl) *n.* A light, hollow ball, esp. a small globule of gas trapped in a liquid. —*v.* **-bled, -bling.** To form or give off bubbles. —**bub′bly** *adj.*
**bubble pack** *n.* A blister pack.
**buc•ca•neer** (bŭk′ə-nîr′) *n.* A pirate.
**buck•et** (bŭk′ĭt) *n.* A cylindrical container for liquids; pail.
**buck•le** (bŭk′əl) *n.* A clasp for fastening 2 strap or belt ends. —*v.* **-led, -ling.** To fasten or secure with a buckle.
**bu•col•ic** (byōō-kŏl′ĭk) *adj.* Pastoral; rustic.
**bud** (bŭd) *n.* **1.** A small, protruding plant part containing undeveloped flowers, leaves, etc. **2.** An undeveloped or incipient stage. —*v.* **budded, budding. 1.** To form or produce buds. **2.** To develop as from a bud.
**Bud•dhism** (bōō′dĭz′əm, bŏŏd′ĭz′-) *n.* A religion chiefly of Asia. —**Bud′dhist** *n. & adj.*
**budge** (bŭj) *v.* **budged, budging.** To move slightly.
**budg•et** (bŭj′ĭt) *n.* **1.** A plan for meeting expenses. **2.** The total sum of money needed or available. —*v.* To make or plan for in a budget.
**buff** (bŭf) *n.* **1.** A soft, thick leather. **2.** Light yellowish brown. **3.** An enthusiast. —*v.* To polish or shine with a soft cloth. —**buff** *adj.*
**buf•fa•lo** (bŭf′ə-lō′) *n., pl.* **-loes** or **-los** or **-lo. 1.** An oxlike African or Asian mammal. **2.** The American bison. —*v.* To intimidate.
**buf•fet**[1] (bə-fā′, bōō-) *n.* **1.** A sideboard. **2.** A meal at which guests serve themselves from a table or sideboard.
**buf•fet**[2] (bŭf′ĭt) *n.* A blow or cuff. —**buf′fet** *v.*

**buf•foon** (bə-fo͞on′) *n.* A clown; jester. **—buf•foon′er•y** *n.*

**bug** (bŭg) *n.* **1.** An insect, spider, or similar creature. **2.** A germ. **3.** A defect; flaw. **4.** An enthusiast. **5.** A hidden microphone or other device. *—v.* **bugged, bugging. 1.** To annoy; pester. **2.** To eavesdrop on, esp. with electronic devices.

**bug•a•boo** (bŭg′ə-bo͞o) *n., pl.* **-boos.** A persistent annoyance.

**bu•gle** (byo͞o′gəl) *n.* A trumpetlike instrument without valves. **—bu′gle** *v.* **—bu′gler** *n.*

**build** (bĭld) *v.* **built, building. 1.** To erect; construct. **2.** To fashion; create. **3.** To add to; develop. *—n.* Physical makeup; physique. **—build′er** *n.* **—build′ing** *n.*

**bulb** (bŭlb) *n.* **1.** A rounded underground plant part from which a new plant develops. **2.** An incandescent lamp or its glass housing. **—bul′bous** *adj.*

**bulge** (bŭlj) *n.* An outward swelling. *—v.* **bulged, bulging.** To swell up.

**bu•lim•i•a** (b/y/o͞o-lĭm′ē-ə, -lē′mē-ə) *n.* A disorder characterized by episodes of binge eating, occurring among adolescent girls and young women. **—bu•lim′ic** *adj. & n.*

**bulk** (bŭlk) *n.* **1.** Great size, mass, or volume. **2.** The major portion. *—v.* To appear massive; loom. **—bulk′y** *adj.*

**bull** (bo͝ol) *n.* The adult male of cattle or certain other large animals. *—adj.* Male. **—bul′lish** *adj.*

**bul•let** (bo͝ol′ĭt) *n.* A projectile fired from a gun.

**bul•le•tin** (bo͝ol′ĭ-tn, -tĭn) *n.* **1.** A printed or broadcast news statement. **2.** A periodical.

**bul•lion** (bo͝ol′yən) *n.* Gold or silver metal.

**bull market** *n.* A stock market characterized by rising prices.

**bully** (bo͝ol′ē) *n., pl.* **-lies.** One who is cruel to weaker people. *—v.* **-lied, -lying.** To behave like a bully.

**bum** (bŭm) *n.* A tramp; hobo. *—v.* **bummed, bumming. 1.** To beg. **2.** To loaf. *—adj.* **1.** Of poor quality. **2.** Disabled.

**bum•ble•bee** (bŭm′bəl-bē′) *n.* A large bee.

**bump** (bŭmp) *v.* **1.** To strike or collide with. **2.** To knock. **3.** To displace; oust. *—n.* **1.** A light blow. **2.** A lump.

**bump•er** (bŭm′pər) *n.* An impact-absorbing device, esp. a heavy bar attached to a motor vehicle.

**bun** (bŭn) *n.* **1.** A rounded, often sweetened roll. **2.** A tight roll of hair.

**bunch** (bŭnch) *n.* A group or cluster. **—bunch** *v.* **—bunch′y** *adj.*

**bun•dle** (bŭn′dl) *n.* Anything bound together; package. *—v.* **-dled, -dling.** To tie or otherwise secure together. **—bundle up.** To dress warmly.

**bun•ga•low** (bŭng′gə-lō′) *n.* A small cottage.

**bun•gle** (bŭng′gəl) *v.* **-gled, -gling.** To perform badly; ruin. **—bun′gler** *n.*

**bunk** (bŭngk) *n.* A narrow bed built like a shelf against a wall.

**bunt•ing** (bŭn′tĭng) *n.* **1.** A light cloth used for making flags. **2.** Flags.

**buoy** (bo͞o′ē, boi) *n.* A marker moored in water. *—v.* **1.** To mark with a buoy. **2.** To keep afloat. **3.** To uplift the spirits of.

**buoy•an•cy** (boi′ən-sē, bo͞oyən-) *n.* **1.** The tendency to float. **2.** The ability to recover quickly from setbacks. **3.** Cheerfulness. **—buoy′ant** *adj.*

**bur•den** (bûr′dn) *n.* **1. a.** Something that is carried. **b.** Something that is difficult to bear. **2.** A duty. *—v.* To load or overload; weigh down; oppress. **—bur′den•some** *adj.*

**bu•reau** (byo͝or′ō) *n., pl.* **-reaus** or **bu•reaux. 1.** A chest of drawers. **2.** A government department. **3.** An office or business.

**bu•reauc•ra•cy** (byo͝o-rŏk′rə-sē) *n., pl.* **-cies.** Government marked by numerous offices and inflexible rules of operation. **—bu′reau•crat′** *n.* **—bu′reau•crat′ic** *adj.*

**bur•geon** (bûr′jən) *v.* To sprout or grow.

**bur•glar** (bûr′glər) *n.* One who breaks into a building, esp. to steal. **—bur′glar•ize′** *v.* **—bur′gla•ry** *n.*

**bur•i•al** (bĕr′ē-əl) *n.* The burying of a dead body.

**bur•lap** (bûr′lăp′) *n.* A coarsely woven cloth.

**bur•lesque** (bər-lĕsk′) *n.* **1.** Broad or crudely comic imitation. **2.** Vaudeville entertainment, often with nudity. *—v.*

**-lesqued, -lesquing.** To imitate mockingly.

**bur•ly** (bûr′lē) *adj.* **-lier, -liest.** Heavy and strong.

**burn** (bûrn) *v.* **burned** or **burnt, burning. 1.** To be or set on fire. **2. a.** To destroy or be destroyed by fire. **b.** To damage or be damaged by fire or heat. **3.** To use as a fuel. **4.** To feel or look hot. **5.** To be consumed with strong emotion. —*n.* An injury from fire or heat. —**burn′er** *n.*

**bur•nish** (bûr′nĭsh) *v.* To polish by rubbing. —**bur′nish** *n.*

**bur•ri•to** (bo͝o-rē′tō, bə-) *n., pl.* **-tos.** A flour tortilla wrapped around a filling, as beef, beans, or cheese.

**bur•row** (bûr′ō) *n.* A hole or tunnel dug by an animal. —**bur′row** *v.*

**burst** (bûrst) *v.* **burst, bursting. 1.** To force open or fly apart suddenly; explode. **2.** To be full to the breaking point. **3.** To appear or emerge suddenly. —*n.* A rupture or explosion.

**bur•y** (bĕr′ē) *v.* **-ied, -ying. 1.** To place in the ground. **2.** To place in a grave or tomb. **3.** To hide; conceal.

**bus** (bŭs) *n., pl.* **buses** or **busses.** A motor vehicle for carrying passengers. —*v.* **bused** or **bussed, busing** or **bussing.** To transport by bus. —**bus′ing, bus′sing** *n.*

**bush** (bo͝osh) *n.* **1.** A branching, woody plant; shrub. **2.** Land covered with dense shrubby growth. —**bush′y** *adj.*

**bush•el** (bo͝osh′əl) *n.* A dry measure equal to 4 pecks.

**busi•ness** (bĭz′nĭs) *n.* **1.** An occupation. **2.** Commercial, industrial, or professional dealings. **3.** Any commercial establishment. **4.** Volume of commercial trade. **5.** One's concern or interest. **6.** An affair or matter. —**busi′ness•man** *n.* —**busi′ness•wo′man** *n.*

**bust[1]** (bŭst) *n.* **1.** A woman's bosom. **2.** A sculpture of the head and shoulders.

**bust[2]** (bŭst) *v.* **1.** To burst or break. **2.** To demote. **3.** To punch. **4.** To arrest. —*n.* **1.** A failure. **2.** An arrest.

**bus•tle** (bŭs′əl) *v.* **-tled, -tling.** To move energetically. —*n.* **1.** Flurry; haste. **2.** A pad at the upper back of a woman's skirt.

**bus•y** (bĭz′ē) *adj.* **-ier, -iest. 1.** Actively engaged; at work. **2.** Crowded with activity. **3.** Temporarily in use. —*v.* **-ied, -ying.** To make busy. —**bus′i•ly** *adv.*

**bus•y•work** (bĭz′ē-wûrk′) *n.* Activity that is meant to be time-consuming and produces little result.

**but** (bŭt; *unstressed* bət) *conj.* **1.** On the contrary. **2.** However. **3.** Except. —*prep.* With the exception of. —**but for.** Were it not for. —*adv.* No more than; only; just. —**all but.** Nearly.

**butch•er** (bo͝och′ər) *n.* **1.** One who kills and cuts up animals for food. **2.** One who sells meat. **3.** A cruel killer. —*v.* **1.** To slaughter. **2.** To kill cruelly.

**butt[1]** (bŭt) *v.* To hit with the head or horns. —**butt in.** To meddle.

**butt[2]** (bŭt) *n.* An object of ridicule.

**butt[3]** (bŭt) *n.* **1.** The larger end. **2.** A remnant; remainder.

**but•ter** (bŭt′ər) *n.* A yellowish, fatty food churned from milk or cream. —*v.* **1.** To put butter on. **2.** To flatter.

**but•ter•fly** (bŭt′ər-flī′) *n., pl.* **-flies.** An insect with four broad, usually colorful wings.

**but•tocks** (bŭt′əks) *pl.n.* The two rounded parts of the lower back.

**but•ton** (bŭt′n) *n.* A small disk sewn on a garment as a fastener or trimming. —**on the button.** Exactly. —*v.* To fasten with a button or buttons.

**but•tress** (bŭt′rĭs) *n.* **1.** A structure built against a wall for support. **2.** Any support. —**but′tress** *v.*

**buy** (bī) *v.* **bought** (bôt), **buying. 1.** To acquire for money; purchase. **2.** To bribe. —*n.* Anything bought. —**buy′er** *n.*

**buy•back** (bī′băk′) *n.* The repurchase by a corporation of shares of its own common stock.

**buzz** (bŭz) *v.* To make a droning sound like that of a bee. —**buzz** *n.* —**buzz′er** *n.*

**buzz session** *n.* An informal group discussion.

**buzz•word** (bŭz′wûrd′) *n.* An important-sounding technical word used to impress laypeople.

**by** (bī) *prep.* **1.** Next to. **2.** With the use of. **3.** Up to and beyond; past. **4.** Not later than. **5.** To the extent of. **6.** According to. **7.** Through the agency or action of. —*adv.* **1.** On hand; nearby. **2.**

Aside; away. **3.** Past. **—by and large.** For the most part.
**bye-bye, by-by** (bī′bī′) *interj.* Used to express farewell.
**by•gone** (bī′gôn′, -gŏn′) *adj.* Gone by; past.
**by•law** (bī′lô′) *n.* **1.** A secondary law. **2.** A rule for the internal affairs of an organization.
**by•line** (bī′līn′) *n.* A line at the head of a news story giving the author and place of origin.
**by-play** (bī′plā′) *n.* Secondary action occurring at the same time as the main action.
**by•stand•er** (bī′stăn′dər) *n.* A person present at an event but not participating in it.
**by•street** (bī′strēt′) *n.* A side street or road.
**byte** (bīt) *n.* A sequence of adjacent binary digits operated on as a unit by a computer.
**by•word** (bī′wûrd′) *n.* **1.** A proverb. **2.** A notorious example.

## — C —

**c, C** (sē) *n.* The 3rd letter of the English alphabet.
**cab** (kăb) *n.* **1.** A taxicab. **2.** The compartment in a truck where the driver sits.
**ca•bal** (kə-băl′) *n.* **1.** A conspiratorial group of schemers. **2.** A secret plot.
**cab•a•ret** (kăb′ə-rā′) *n.* **1.** A restaurant or night club offering live entertainment. **2.** The show provided at such an establishment.
**cab•bage** (kăb′ĭj) *n.* A plant having an edible head of leaves.
**cab•in** (kăb′ĭn) *n.* **1.** A small, roughly built house. **2.** An enclosed apartment on a ship or airplane.
**cab•i•net** (kăb′ə-nĭt) *n.* **1.** A cupboardlike repository with shelves or drawers. **2.** The leading ministers in a government. **—cab′inet** *adj.*
**ca•ble** (kā′bəl) *n.* **1.** A thick steel or fiber rope. **2.** A telegram. **3.** Cable TV. *—v.* **-bled, -bling.** To send a telegram to.
**ca•ble•cast** (kā′bə-kăst′) *n.* A telecast by cable TV. **—ca′ble•cast′** *v.*
**cable TV** *n.* A TV distribution system in which signals are delivered by cable to the receivers of subscribers; cablevision.
**ca•ca•o** (kə-kā′ō) *n.* The seed of a tropical American tree, used in making chocolate and cocoa.
**cache** (kăsh) *n.* **1.** A hole for hiding food or other necessities. **2.** A place for hiding valuables. **3.** A fast storage buffer in the central processing unit of a computer. **—cache** *v.*
**ca•chet** (kă-shā′) *n.* **1.** A seal on a document. **2.** A mark of quality or distinction.
**cack•le** (kăk′əl) *v.* **-led, -ling.** To make the shrill cry of a hen. **—cack′le** *n.* **—cack′ler** *n.*
**cac•tus** (kăk′təs) *n., pl.* **-ti** or **-tuses.** A leafless, fleshy-stemmed desert plant.
**ca•dav•er** (kə-dăv′ər) *n.* A dead body. **—ca•dav′er•ous** *adj.*
**ca•dence** (kād′ns) *n.* Rhythmic flow or movement. **—ca′denced** *adj.*
**ca•det** (kə-dĕt′) *n.* A student training to be a military officer. **—ca•det′ship′** *n.*
**ca•dre** (kä′drā) *n.* **1.** A framework. **2.** A core of trained personnel around which a larger organization can be formed.
**ca•fé** (kă-fā′, kə-) *n.* A small, informal restaurant.
**ca•fé au lait** (kă-fā′ ō lā′) *n.* **1.** Coffee served with hot milk. **2.** A light coffee color.
**caf•e•te•ri•a** (kăf′ĭtîr′ē-ə) *n.* A restaurant in which customers carry their meals from a service counter to tables.
**caf•feine** (kă-fēn′) *n.* A stimulant found in coffee and tea.
**cage** (kāj) *n.* A barred or grated enclosure for confining animals. *—v.* **caged, caging.** To confine in a cage.
**ca•gey, ca•gy** (cā′jē) *adj.* **-ier, -iest. 1.** Wary; careful. **2.** Crafty; shrewd. **—cag′i•ly** *adv.* **—cag′i•ness** *n.*
**ca•hier** (kä-yā′) *n.* **1.** Pages bound together in a binder; a notebook. **2.** A report, as from a meeting.
**ca•jole** (kə-jōl′) *v.* **-joled, -joling.** To coax; wheedle. **—ca•jol′er** *n.* **—ca•jol′er•y** *n.*
**cake** (kāk) *n.* **1.** A sweet food made from baked batter or dough. **2.** A shaped mass, as of soap. *—v.* **caked, caking.** To make into a hard mass.

**ca•lam•i•ty** (kə-lăm'ĭ-tē) *n., pl.* **-ties.** A disaster. **—ca•lam'i•tous** *adj.* **—ca•lam'i•tous•ly** *adv.* **—ca•lam'i•tous•ness** *n.*

**cal•ci•um** (kăl'sē-əm) *n.* A silvery metallic element that occurs in bone, shells, etc.

**cal•cu•late** (kăl'kyə-lāt') *v.* **-lated, -lating. 1.** To compute; figure. **2.** To estimate. **3.** To use a calculator. **—cal'cu•la•ble** *adj.* **—cal'cu•la•bly** *adv.* **—cal'cu•la'tion** *n.*

**cal•cu•lat•ed** (kăl'kyə-lā'tĭd) *adj.* **1.** Undertaken after careful consideration of the risk. **2.** Likely; apt.

**cal•cu•lat•ing** (kăl'kyə-lā'tĭng) *adj.* **1.** Performing calculations. **2. a.** Shrewd; crafty. **b.** Coldly scheming.

**cal•cu•la•tor** (kăl'kyə-lā'tər) *n.* One that performs calculations, esp. a keyboard machine for the automatic performance of mathematical operations.

**cal•dron** (kôl'drən) *n.* A large kettle.

**cal•en•dar** (kăl'ən-dər) *n.* **1.** A table showing time divisions, esp. the days of a year. **2.** A schedule.

**calf**[1] (kăf) *n., pl.* **calves** (kăvz). The young of cattle or certain other large mammals, as the elephant.

**calf**[2] (kăf) *n., pl.* **calves** (kăvz). The fleshy back part of the leg.

**cal•i•ber** (kăl'ə-bər) *n.* **1.** The diameter of the bore of a gun, bullet, or shell. **2.** Quality.

**cal•i•brate** (kăl'ə-brāt') *v.* **-brated, -brating.** To check the graduations in a measuring device. **—cal'i•bra'tion** *n.*

**cal•i•co** (kăl'ĭ-kō') *n., pl.* **-coes** or **-cos.** A printed cotton cloth.

**cal•is•then•ics** (kăl'ĭs-thĕn'ĭks) *pl.n.* Simple gymnastic exercises. **—cal'is•then'ic** *adj.*

**call** (kôl) *v.* **1.** To cry or utter loudly. **2.** To summon. **3.** To telephone. **4.** To name. **5.** To pay a brief visit. **—call off.** To cancel. *—n.* **1.** A shout or loud cry. **2.** A summons. **3.** Demand; need. **4.** A short visit. **5.** A communication by telephone. **—call'er** *n.*

**call-in** (kôl'ĭn') *adj.* Inviting listeners to make broadcasted telephone calls.

**call letters** *pl.n.* The identifying code letters or numbers of a radio or TV transmitting station.

**call loan** *n.* A loan repayable on demand at any time.

**call number** *n.* A number used in a library to classify and place a book.

**cal•lous** (kăl'əs) *adj.* Hardened; unfeeling. **—cal'lous•ly** *adv.* **—cal'lous•ness** *n.*

**cal•low** (kăl'ō) *adj.* **1.** Immature; inexperienced. **2.** Lacking feathers; unfledged. **—cal'low•ness** *n.*

**call rate** *n.* The interest rate on a call loan.

**cal•lus** (kăl'əs) *n., pl.* **-luses.** An area of skin that has grown thick and tough. *—v.* To form a callus.

**calm** (käm) *adj.* Quiet; undisturbed. *—n.* Stillness; serenity. *—v.* To make or become calm. **—calm'ly** *adv.* **—calm'ness** *n.*

**cal•o•rie** (kăl'ə-rē) *n.* **1.** A unit of heat. **2.** A unit of energy that can be derived from food. **—ca•lor'ic** *adj.*

**cal•um•ny** (kăl'əm-nē) *n., pl.* **-nies.** Slander. **—ca•lum'ni•ous** *adj.*

**calves** *n.* pl. of **calf.**

**came** (kām) *v.* p.t. of **come.**

**cam•el** (kăm'əl) *n.* A humped, long-necked desert animal.

**cam•el•back** (kăm'əl-băk') *adj.* Having a shape characterized by a hump or arching curve.

**camel's hair** *n.* **1.** The soft, fine hair of a camel. **2.** The cloth, usu. light tan, made from this hair.

**cam•e•o** (kăm'ē-ō') *n., pl.* **-os.** A gem, medallion, etc., with a carved design.

**cam•er•a** (kăm'ər-ə, kăm'rə) *n.* An apparatus for taking photographs.

**cam•i•sole** (kăm'ĭ-sōl') *n.* **1.** A woman's sleeveless undergarment. **2.** A short negligee.

**cam•ou•flage** (kăm'ə-fläzh', -fläj') *n.* Concealment of something by making it look like its surroundings. *—v.* **-flaged, -flaging.** To conceal by such means. **—cam'ou•flag'er** *n.*

**camp** (kămp) *n.* **1.** A place where people are temporarily lodged in makeshift shelters. **2.** A group supporting a cause. *—v.* To shelter in a camp. **—camp'er** *n.*

**cam•paign** (kăm-pān') *n.* A series of actions taken to achieve a goal, as in warfare or politics. *—v.* To engage in a campaign. **—cam•paign'er** *n.*

**cam•pus** (kăm′pəs) *n., pl.* **-puses.** The grounds of a school or college.

**can**[1] (kăn) *v.* **could. 1.** To be able to. **2.** To have permission to.

**can**[2] (kăn) *n.* A metal container used for airtight food storage. —*v.* **canned, canning.** To preserve in cans or jars. —**can′ner** *n.* —**can′ner•y** *n.*

**ca•naille** (kə-nī′, -nāl′) *n.* The mass of common people; the rabble.

**ca•nal** (kə-năl′) *n.* **1.** An artificial channel filled with water. **2.** In anatomy, a tube or duct.

**can•a•pé** (kăn′ə-pā′, -pē) *n.* A cracker or small, thin piece of bread spread with a topping and served as an appetizer.

**ca•nard** (kə-närd′) *n.* An unfounded or misleading story.

**ca•nar•y** (kə-nâr′ē) *n., pl.* **-ies.** A yellow songbird.

**ca•nas•ta** (kə-năs′tə) *n.* A card game for 2 to 6 players, played with 2 decks of cards.

**can•cel** (kăn′səl) *v.* **1.** To cross out. **2.** To annul or invalidate. **3.** To neutralize; offset. —**can′cel•a•ble** *adj.* —**can′cel•er** *n.* —**can′cel•la′tion** *n.*

**can•cer** (kăn′sər) *n.* **1.** A malignant growth that tends to spread. **2.** A spreading evil. —**can′cer•ous** *adj.*

**can•did** (kăn′dĭd) *adj.* **1.** Straightforward; open. **2.** Not posed. —**can′did•ly** *adv.* —**can′did•ness** *n.*

**can•di•da** (kăn′dĭ-də) *n.* Any of several yeastlike fungi that cause disease.

**can•di•di•a•sis** (kăn′dĭ-dī′ə-sĭs) *n.* An infection caused by candida.

**can•di•date** (kăn′dĭ-dāt′) *n.* A person seeking an office, prize, honor, etc. —**can′di•da•cy** *n.*

**can•dle** (kăn′dl) *n.* A stick of solid wax with an embedded wick, burned for light.

**can•dor** (kăn′dər) *n.* Frankness; sincerity.

**can•dy** (kăn′dē) *n., pl.* **-dies.** A sweet confection made with sugar. —*v.* **-died, -dying.** To cook or coat with sugar or syrup.

**cane** (kān) *n.* **1.** A hollow woody stem. **2.** A walking stick. —*v.* **caned, caning.** To beat with a cane. **2.** To weave with cane.

**ca•nine** (kā′nīn) *adj.* Of dogs. —*n.* **1.** One of the conical teeth between the incisors and the bicuspids. **2.** A dog.

**can•is•ter** (kăn′ĭ-stər) *n.* A container for holding dry foods or other items.

**can•ker** (kăng′kər) *n.* An ulcerous sore of the mouth. —**can′ker•ous** *adj.*

**can•na•bis** (kăn′ə-bĭs) *n.* **1.** The plant from which marijuana is obtained. **2.** Marijuana.

**can•ni•bal** (kăn′ə-bəl) *n.* A person who eats the flesh of human beings. —**can′ni•bal•ism** *n.* —**can′ni•bal•is′tic** *adj.*

**can•ni•bal•ize** (kăn′ə-bə-līz′) *v.* **-ized, -izing. 1.** To remove serviceable parts from for other equipment. **2.** To strip an organization of personnel or equipment for use in another organization.

**can•non** (kăn′ən) *n., pl.* **-non** or **-nons.** A heavy mounted gun.

**can•not** (kăn′ŏt, kə-nŏt′) *v.* The negative form of **can.**

**can•ny** (kăn′ē) *adj.* **-nier, -niest.** Careful and shrewd, esp. about one's own interests.

**ca•noe** (kə-no͞o′) *n.* A light, slender boat, propelled by paddles. —*v.* **-noed, -noeing.** To carry or travel by canoe. —**ca•noe′ist** *n.*

**can•on** (kăn′ən) *n.* **1.** A church law or code of laws. **2.** A secular code of law. —**ca•non′i•cal** *adj.*

**can•o•py** (kăn′ə-pē) *n., pl.* **-pies. 1.** A covering fastened over a bed, chair, etc. **2.** The transparent, movable enclosure over an aircraft cockpit.

**cant** (kănt) *n.* **1.** Insincere or hypocritically pious talk. **2.** Jargon. —**cant′ing•ly** *adv.*

**can't** (kănt) *v.* Contraction of *cannot.*

**can•tan•ker•ous** (kăn-tăng′kər-əs) *adj.* Ill-tempered.

**can•teen** (kăn-tēn′) *n.* **1.** A store for military personnel. **2.** Water flask.

**can•ter** (kăn′tər) *n.* A gait of a horse slower than the gallop but faster than the trot. —**can′ter** *v.*

**can•ti•cle** (kăn′tĭ-kəl) *n.* A song or chant with words taken from the Bible.

**can•tor** (kăn′tər) *n.* The singer of the liturgy, esp. in a synagogue.

**can•vas** (kăn′vəs) *n.* A heavy, closely woven fabric used for making tents and sails.

**can•vass** (kăn′vəs) *v.* **1.** To examine thoroughly; scrutinize. **2.** To solicit votes or opinions. —**can′vass** *n.* —**can′-**

**vass•er** *n.*

**can•yon** (kăn'yən) *n.* A narrow valley with steep cliff walls.

**cap** (kăp) *n.* **1.** A close-fitting brimless hat. **2.** A tight cover; lid. —*v.* **capped, capping.** To put a cap on.

**ca•pa•ble** (kā'pə-bəl) *adj.* Able; competent. **—ca'pa•bil'i•ty** *n.* **—ca'pa•bly** *adv.*

**ca•pac•i•ty** (kə-păs'ĭ-tē) *n., pl.* **-ties. 1.** Volume. **2.** A maximum; limit. **3.** Ability. **4.** Role; position.

**cape[1]** (kāp) *n.* A sleeveless garment worn over the shoulders.

**cape[2]** (kāp) *n.* A point of land projecting into water.

**cap•il•lar•y** (kăp'ə-lĕr'ē) *n., pl.* **-ies.** A minute blood vessel. **—cap'il•lar•y** *adj.*

**cap•i•tal** (kăp'ĭ-tl) *n.* **1.** An official seat of government. **2.** Wealth, esp. invested or available funds. **3.** A large or uppercase letter. —*adj.* **1.** First; chief. **2.** First-rate; excellent. **3.** Punishable by or involving death. **4.** Large; uppercase.

**capital asset** *n.* A long-term asset, as land or a building.

**capital expenditure** *n.* Money spent for additions or improvements to plant or equipment.

**capital gain** *n.* Profit from the sale of capital assets.

**capital goods** *pl.n.* Goods used in the production of commodities.

**cap•i•tal•ism** (kăp'ĭ-tl-ĭz'əm) *n.* An economic system in which goods are produced privately and sold for profit. **—cap'i•tal•ist** *n.* **—cap'i•tal•is'tic** *adj.* **—cap'i•tal•is'ti•cal•ly** *adv.*

**cap•i•tal•ize** (kăp'ĭ-tl-īz') *v.* **-ized, -izing. 1.** To write in or begin a word with an uppercase letter. **2.** To seize an advantage. **—cap'i•tal•i•za'tion** *n.*

**cap•i•tol** (kăp'ĭ-tl) *n.* **1.** The building in which a state's legislature meets. **2. Capitol.** The building in which the U.S. Congress meets.

**ca•pri•cious** (kə-prĭsh'əs, -prē'shəs) *adj.* Unpredictable; impulsive. **—ca•price'** *n.*

**cap•size** (kăp'sīz', kăp-sīz') *v.* **-sized, -sizing.** To overturn or cause to turn over.

**cap•sule** (kăp'səl, -so͞ol) *n.* **1.** A small case, esp. one containing medicine. **2.** A pressurized compartment, as in a spacecraft. **—cap'su•lar** *adj.*

**cap•tain** (kăp'tən) *n.* **1.** One who commands; leader. **2.** The officer in command of a ship. **3.** A commissioned army or navy officer. —*v.* To command or direct. **—cap'tain•cy** *n.* **—cap'tain•ship'** *n.*

**cap•tion** (kăp'shən) *n.* A short legend or description.

**cap•ti•vate** (kăp'tə-vāt') *v.* **-vated, -vating.** To fascinate. **—cap'ti•va'tion** *n.*

**cap•tive** (kăp'tĭv) *n.* A prisoner. —*adj.* Held prisoner. **—cap•tiv'i•ty** *n.*

**cap•ture** (kăp'chər) *v.* **-tured, -turing. 1.** To take captive. **2.** To win possession of. —*n.* The act of capturing.

**car** (kär) *n.* **1.** An automobile. **2.** A wheeled vehicle.

**ca•rafe** (kə-răf') *n.* A glass bottle for serving water or wine.

**car•a•mel** (kăr'ə-məl, -mĕl', kär'məl) *n.* **1.** A chewy candy. **2.** Burnt sugar, used for coloring.

**car•at** (kăr'ət) *n.* A unit of weight for precious stones.

**car•a•van** (kăr'ə-văn') *n.* A group of travelers, esp. across a desert.

**car•bine** (kär'bēn', -bīn') *n.* A light rifle.

**car•bo•hy•drate** (kär'bō-hī'drāt') *n.* An organic compound, such as sugar or starch, important as a foodstuff.

**car•bon** (kär'bən) *n.* A naturally abundant nonmetallic element.

**car•bu•re•tor** (kär'bə-rā'tər, -byə-) *n.* A device used in gasoline engines to mix fuel and air.

**car•cass** (kär'kəs) *n.* A dead body, esp. of an animal.

**car•cin•o•gen** (kär-sĭn'ə-jən, kär'sə-nə-jĕn') *n.* A substance that causes cancer. **—car'cin•o•gen'ic** *adj.*

**car•ci•no•ma** (kär'sə-nē'mə) *n., pl.* **-mas** or **-mata.** A kind of malignant cancer.

**card** (kärd) *n.* A small, flat piece of stiff paper, esp.: **a.** One of a set of playing cards. **b.** A post card. **c.** A greeting or business card.

**card-car•ry•ing** (kärd'kăr'ē-ĭng) *adj.* **1.** Being an enrolled member of an organization, esp. the Communist Party. **2.** Strongly devoted, as to a cause.

**car•di•ac** (kär′dē-ăk′) *adj.* Of the heart.

**car•di•gan** (kär′dĭ-gən) *n.* A sweater opening down the front.

**car•di•nal** (kär′dn-əl, kärd′nəl) *adj.* **1.** Primary; foremost. **2.** Vivid red. —*n.* **1. Cardinal.** One of the highest-ranking Roman Catholic clergymen. **2.** A vivid red. **3.** A crested, bright-red bird.

**car•di•o•graph** (kär′dē-ə-grăf′) *n.* An instrument to record the motions of the heart. **—car′di•o•gram′** *n.*

**car•di•ol•o•gy** (kär′dē-ŏl′ə-jē) *n.* The medical study of the heart and its diseases. **—car′di•o•log′ic, car′di•o•log′i•cal** *adj.* **—car′di•ol′o•gist** *n.*

**car•di•tis** (kär-dī′tĭs) *n.* Inflammation of the heart.

**care** (kâr) *n.* **1.** Mental distress and grief. **2.** Caution. **3.** Supervision. **—(in) care of.** At the address of. —*v.* **cared, car•ing. 1.** To be concerned or interested. **2.** To object; mind. **—care′free** *adj.*

**ca•reer** (kə-rîr′) *n.* **1.** A chosen pursuit. **2.** One's progress in one's occupation.

**ca•reer•ism** (kə-rîr′ĭz′əm) *n.* The practice of advancing professionally by all possible means. **—ca•reer′ist** *adj. & n.*

**care•ful** (kâr′fəl) *adj.* **1.** Cautious. **2.** Thorough; painstaking. **—care′ful•ly** *adv.* **—care′ful•ness** *n.* **—care′less** *adj.* **—care′less•ly** *adv.* **—care′less•ness** *n.*

**ca•ress** (kə-rĕs′) *n.* A gentle touch or gesture of fondness. **—ca•ress′** *v.*

**car•go** (kär′gō) *n., pl.* **-goes** or **-gos.** The freight carried by a vehicle.

**car•i•ca•ture** (kăr′ĭ-kəchŏŏr′) *n.* A comically exaggerated portrait. —*v.* **-tured, -turing.** To represent in a caricature. **—car′i•ca•tur′ist** *n.*

**car•nage** (kär′nĭj) *n.* Massive slaughter; massacre.

**car•nal** (kär′nəl) *adj.* **1.** Relating to the desires of the flesh. **2.** Worldly; earthly; temporal.

**car•na•tion** (kär-nā′shən) *n.* A plant having fragrant many-petaled flowers.

**car•ni•val** (kär′nə-vəl) *n.* **1.** A celebration; festivity. **2.** A traveling amusement show.

**car•niv•o•rous** (kär-nĭv′ər-əs) *adj.* Flesh-eating. **—car′ni•vore** *n.* **—car•niv′o•rous•ly** *adv.*

**car•ol** (kăr′əl) *v.* To sing joyously. —*n.* A festive song, esp. for Christmas. **—car′ol•er** *n.*

**ca•rouse** (kə-rouz′) *n.* Boisterous, drunken merrymaking. —*v.* **-roused, -rousing.** To go on a drinking spree. **—ca•rous′al** *n.* **—ca•rous′er** *n.*

**car•pen•ter** (kär′pən-tər) *n.* A maker of wooden objects and structures. **—car′pen•ter** *v.* **—car′pen•try** *n.*

**car•pet** (kär′pĭt) *n.* A heavy fabric covering for a floor. —*v.* To cover with a carpet.

**car•port** (kär′pôrt′, -pōrt′) *n.* A roof projecting from the side of a building, used to protect a car.

**car•riage** (kăr′ĭj) *n.* **1.** A 4-wheeled, horse-drawn vehicle. **2.** A machine part for holding or shifting another part. **3.** Posture.

**car•rot** (kăr′ət) *n.* A plant with an edible, orange root.

**car•ry** (kăr′ē) *v.* **-ried, -rying. 1.** To convey; transport. **2.** To win over. **3.** To have on one's person. **4.** To involve; imply. **5.** To conduct (oneself); behave. **6.** To support. **7.** To keep in stock. **8.** To reach. **—carry on. 1.** To continue. **2.** To act wildly. **—carry out.** To put into practice. **—car′ri•a•ble, car′ry•a•ble** *adj.* **—car′ri•er** *n.*

**car•ry•on** (kăr′ē-ŏn′) *n.* An item small enough to be carried aboard an airplane by a passenger. **—car′ry•on′** *adj.*

**car•ry•out** (kăr′ē-out′) *adj.* Take-out. **—car′ry•out′** *n.*

**car•sick** (kär′sĭk′) *adj.* Nauseated by vehicular motion. **—car′sick′ness** *n.*

**cart** (kärt) *n.* **1.** A 2-wheeled vehicle. **2.** Any small vehicle. —*v.* To convey in a cart. **—cart′a•ble** *adj.* **—cart′er** *n.*

**car•tel** (kär-tĕl′) *n.* A large-scale, esp. international, monopoly.

**car•ti•lage** (kär′tl-ĭj) *n.* A tough connective tissue attached to the bone joints. **—car′ti•lag′i•nous** *adj.*

**car•tog•ra•phy** (kär-tŏg′rə-fē) *n.* The making of maps. **—car•tog′ra•pher** *n.* **—car′to•graph′ic** *adj.*

**car•ton** (kär′tn) *n.* A cardboard box.

**car•toon** (kär-to͞on′) *n.* **1.** A satirical drawing. **2.** A short animated film. **3.** A comic strip. **—car•toon′ist** *n.*

**car•tridge** (kär′trĭj) *n.* **1.** A tubular case containing the powder and projectile for a firearm. **2.** A case containing reeled magnetic tape for play in tape recorders or players. **3.** A case with photographic film that can be loaded into a camera.

**carve** (kärv) *v.* **carved, carving. 1.** To cut and serve meat. **2.** To fashion by cutting. **—carv′er** *n.*

**cas•cade** (kă-skād′) *n.* **1.** A waterfall. **2.** Profusion; shower. *—v.* **-caded, -cading.** To fall in a cascade.

**case[1]** (kās) *n.* **1.** An instance; example. **2.** A matter. **3.** A persuasive argument or justification. **4.** The form of a noun or pronoun that indicates its relation to other words. **5.** A legal action. *—v.* **cased, casing.** To inspect.

**case[2]** (kās) *n.* **1.** A container or receptacle. **2.** A covering. *—v.* **cased, casing.** To put into a case. **—cas′ing** *n.*

**cash** (kăsh) *n.* Ready money. *—v.* To exchange for money.

**cash•book** (kăsh′bo͝ok′) *n.* A book in which cash receipts and expenditures are recorded.

**cash•ew** (kăsh′o͞o, kə-sho͞o′) *n.* A tropical kidney-shaped nut.

**cash•ier** (kă-shîr′) *n.* A business employee responsible for paying or receiving money.

**cash•mere** (kăzh′mîr′, kăsh′-) *n.* Fine wool from an Asian goat.

**ca•si•no** (kə-sē′nō) *n., pl.* **-nos.** A gambling house.

**cask** (kăsk) *n.* A barrel of liquids.

**cas•ket** (kăs′kĭt) *n.* **1.** A small case for valuables. **2.** A coffin.

**cas•se•role** (kăs′ə-rōl′) *n.* A baking dish or the food cooked in it.

**cas•sette** (kə-sĕt′) *n.* A small case for film or magnetic tape.

**cast** (kăst) *v.* **cast, casting. 1.** To throw. **2.** To direct; aim. **3.** To give or deposit (a ballot). **4.** To assign, as an actor's part. **5.** To form by molding. *—n.* **1.** A throw. **2.** A mold or form. **3.** A rigid plaster dressing for a broken bone. **4.** The actors in a play.

**caste** (kăst) *n.* Any exclusive social class.

**cast•er** (kăs′tər) *n.* A small swiveled wheel on which a heavy object can be rolled.

**cas•tle** (kăs′əl) *n.* A large, fortified building.

**cas•trate** (kăs′trāt′) *v.* **-trated, -trating.** To remove the testicles of. **—cas·tra′tion** *n.*

**ca•su•al** (kăzh′o͞o-əl) *adj.* **1.** Occurring by chance. **2.** Informal. **3.** Careless; negligent. **—ca′su•al•ly** *adv.* **—ca′su•al•ness** *n.*

**ca•su•al•ty** (kăzh′o͞o-əl-tē) *n., pl.* **-ties.** One injured or killed, as in a battle.

**cat** (kăt) *n.* **1.** A small, domesticated furry mammal. **2.** A related animal, as the lion.

**CAT** (kăt) *n.* A 3-dimensional x-ray of a structure, made from a series of cross-sectional scans.

**cat•a•clysm** (kăt′ə-klĭz′əm) *n.* A violent upheaval. **—cat′a•clys′mic, cat′a•clys′mal** *adj.*

**cat•a•logue** (kăt′l-ôg′). Also **cat•a•log.** *n.* An itemized list. *—v.* **-logued, -loguing.** To list. **—cat′a•logu′er** *n.*

**cat•a•lyst** (kăt′l-ĭst) *n.* **1.** A substance that modifies a chemical reaction without being consumed. **2.** Any person, event, or factor that causes or inspires a sudden change. **—ca•tal′y•sis** *n.* **—cat′a•lyt′ic** *adj.*

**cat•a•ract** (kăt′ə-răkt′) *n.* **1.** A great waterfall. **2.** Opacity of the lens of the eye.

**ca•tas•tro•phe** (kə-tăs′trə-fē) *n.* A sudden calamity; disaster. **—cat′a•stroph′ic** *adj.* **—cat′a•stroph′i•cal•ly** *adv.*

**catch** (kăch) *v.* **caught, catching. 1.** To capture, esp. after a chase. **2.** To snare or trap. **3.** To surprise. **4.** To grasp. **5.** To contract; get. *—n.* **1.** The act of catching. **2.** A fastening device. **3.** Something caught. **4.** An unsuspected drawback.

**Catch-22** *n.* **1.** A difficult problem for which all solutions are invalid. **2.** An illogical or senseless situation.

**catch-up** (kăch′ŭp′) *adj.* Designed to catch up to a standard or a competitor. **—catch′-up′** *n.*

**cat•e•gor•i•cal** (kăt′ĭ-gôr′ĭ-kəl) *adj.* Absolute; certain. **—cat′e•gor′i•cal•ly** *adv.* **—cat′e•gor′i•cal•ness** *n.*

**cat•e•go•ry** (kăt′ĭ-gôr′ē, -gōr′ē) *n., pl.* **-ries.** A division in a system of classification; a class. **—cat′e•go•rize′** *v.*

**—cat′e•go•ri•za′tion** *n.*
**ca•ter** (kā′tər) *v.* To provide food, as for a party. **—ca′ter•er** *n.*
**cat•er•pil•lar** (kăt′ər-pĭl′ər, kăt′ə-) *n.* The wormlike larva of a butterfly or moth.
**ca•the•dral** (kə-thē′drəl) *n.* The principal church of a bishop's see.
**cath•o•lic** (kăth′ə-lĭk, kăth′lĭk) *adj.* **1.** Universal. **2. Catholic.** Of the Roman Catholic Church. *—n.* **Catholic.** A member of the Roman Catholic Church. **—Ca•thol′i•cism′** *n.*
**cat•tle** (kăt′l) *pl.n.* Horned, hoofed mammals; livestock.
**CATV** *n.* Community-antenna television; cable TV.
**Cau•ca•sian** (kô-kā′zhən) *adj.* Relating to a racial group having light to brown skin pigmentation and straight or wavy hair. **—Cau•ca′sian** *n.*
**cau•cus** (kô′kəs) *n., pl.* **-cuses.** A meeting, esp. of the members of a political party. **—cau′cus** *v.*
**caught** (kôt) *v.* p.t. & p.p. of **catch.**
**cau•li•flow•er** (kô′lĭ-flou′ər, kŏl′ĭ-) *n.* A plant with an edible, compact head.
**caulk** (kôk) *v.* Also **calk.** To make watertight by filling cracks. **—caulk′er** *n.*
**cause** (kôz) *n.* **1.** A person or thing responsible for an action or result. **2.** A reason; motive. **3.** A social or political purpose. **4.** A lawsuit. *—v.* **caused, causing.** To bring about. **—caus′al** *adj.* **—cau•sal′i•ty** *n.* **—caus′al•ly** *adv.* **—cau•sa′tion** *n.*
**caus•tic** (kô′stĭk) *adj.* Corrosive; biting.
**cau•ter•ize** (kô′tə-rīz′) *v.* **-ized, -izing.** To burn or sear (a wound). **—cau′ter•i•za′tion** *n.*
**cau•tion** (kô′shən) *n.* **1.** Forethought; prudence. **2.** A warning. *—v.* To warn against danger. **—cau′tion•ar′y** *adj.* **—cau′tious** *adj.* **—cau′tious•ly** *adv.*
**cav•a•lier** (kăv′ə-lîr′) *n.* **1.** A knight. **2.** A gallant. *—adj.* **1.** Haughty. **2.** Carefree; offhand. **—cav′a•lier′ly** *adv.*
**cav•al•ry** (kăv′əl-rē) *n., pl.* **-ries.** Mounted or motorized troops. **—cav′al•ry•man** *n.*
**cave** (kāv) *n.* A hollow beneath the earth's surface. **—cav′ern** *n.* **—cav′er•nous** *adj.*
**cav•i•ar** (kăv′ē-är′) *n.* The salted eggs of a sturgeon.
**cav•il** (kăv′əl) *v.* To quibble or carp. **—cav′il** *n.*
**cav•i•ty** (kăv′ĭ-tē) *n., pl.* **-ties.** A hollow or hole.
**ca•vort** (kə-vôrt′) *v.* To prance.
**CB** *n., pl.* **CB's. 1.** A radio-frequency band for private use. **2.** A transmitter or receiver for such a band.
**CBW** *n.* Chemical and biological warfare.
**CCTV** *n.* Closed-circuit television.
**CD** *n., pl.* **CD's. 1.** Compact disk. **2.** Certificate of deposit.
**cease** (sēs) *v.* **ceased, ceasing.** To discontinue; stop. *—n.* Cessation. **—cease′less** *adj.* **—cease′less•ly** *adv.*
**cede** (sēd) *v.* **ceded, ceding.** To relinquish; transfer.
**ceil•ing** (sē′lĭng) *n.* **1.** The interior upper surface of a room. **2.** A maximum limit.
**cel•e•brate** (sĕl′ə-brāt′) *v.* **-brated, -brating. 1.** To observe (a day or event) with festivity. **2.** To perform (a religious ceremony). **3.** To praise. **—cel′e•bra′tion** *n.* **—cel′e•bra′tor** *n.*
**ce•leb•ri•ty** (sə-lĕb′rĭ-tē) *n., pl.* **-ties. 1.** A famous person. **2.** Fame.
**cel•er•y** (sĕl′ə-rē) *n.* A plant with juicy edible stalks.
**ce•les•tial** (sə-lĕs′chəl) *adj.* **1.** Of the sky or heavens. **2.** Heavenly; divine.
**cel•i•ba•cy** (sĕl′ə-bə-sē) *n.* The condition of being unmarried. **—cel′i•bate** *adj. & n.*
**cell** (sĕl) *n.* **1.** A small, plain room. **2.** A small enclosed space. **3.** The smallest independent unit of living matter. **4.** A device for generating electricity. **5.** A computer memory subdivision holding 1 operating unit.
**cel•lar** (sĕl′ər) *n.* An underground storage room.
**cel•lo** (chĕl′ō) *n., pl.* **-los.** Also **'cel•lo.** A violinlike instrument played between the knees. **—cel′list** *n.*
**cel•lo•phane** (sĕl′ə-fān′) *n.* A transparent material used for wrapping.
**cel•lu•lar** (sĕl′yə-lər) *adj.* **1.** Relating to a cell. **2.** Made of or containing cells. **3.** Relating to a mobile radiotelephone system used esp. in automobiles.
**Cel•si•us** (sĕl′sē-əs, -shəs) *adj.* Of a temperature scale that registers the freezing point of water as 0°C and the boiling point as 100°C.

**ce•ment** (sĭ-mĕnt′) *n.* **1.** A construction material made of powdered rock, clay, and water that hardens after pouring. **2.** Any adhesive; glue. —*v.* To bind with or as if with cement.

**cem•e•ter•y** (sĕm′ĭ-tĕr′ē) *n., pl.* **-ies.** A graveyard.

**cen•sor** (sĕn′sər) *n.* An examiner of printed or other materials, who may prohibit what is considered objectionable. —*v.* To examine and expurgate. —**cen•so′ri•al** *adj.* —**cen′sor•ship′** *n.*

**cen•sure** (sĕn′shər) *n.* Disapproval. —*v.* **-sured, -suring.** To criticize severely; blame. —**cen′sur•a•ble** *adj.* —**cen′sur•er** *n.*

**cen•sus** (sĕn′səs) *n., pl.* **-suses.** An official population count.

**cen•ten•ni•al** (sĕn-tĕn′ē-əl) *adj.* Of 100 years or a 100th anniversary. —*n.* A 100th anniversary. —**cen•ten′ni•al•ly** *adv.*

**cen•ter** (sĕn′tər) *n.* **1.** A middle point. **2.** A place of concentrated activity. —*v.* **1.** To place at the center. **2.** To concentrate or cluster.

**cen•ti•grade** (sĕn′tĭ-grād′) *adj.* Celsius.

**cen•tral** (sĕn′trəl) *adj.* **1.** At, near, or being the center. **2.** Essential. —**cen′tral•ly** *adv.*

**cen•tu•ry** (sĕn′chə-rē) *n., pl.* **-ries.** A period of 100 years.

**CEO** *n., pl.* **CEO's.** The chief executive officer of a company.

**ce•ram•ics** (sə-răm′ĭks) *pl.n.* **1.** Pottery and other objects made by shaping and baking clay. **2.** *(takes sing. v.)* The art of making such objects. —**ce•ram′ic** *adj.*

**ce•re•al** (sîr′ē-əl) *n.* **1.** An edible grain. **2.** A food prepared from such grain. —**ce′re•al** *adj.*

**cer•e•bral** (sĕr′ə-brəl, sə-rē′-) *adj.* Of the brain. —**ce•re′bral•ly** *adv.*

**cer•e•mo•ny** (sĕr′ə-mō′nē) *n., pl.* **-nies.** **1.** A formal act or set of acts prescribed by ritual or custom. **2.** Formality; etiquette. —**cer′e•mo′ni•al** *adj.* —**cer′e•mo′ni•al•ly** *adv.* —**cer′e•mo′ni•ous** *adj.* —**cer′e•mo′ni•ous•ly** *adv.*

**cer•tain** (sûr′tn) *adj.* **1.** Definite; sure; indisputable. **2.** Inevitable. **3.** Not identified. —**cer′tain•ly** *adv.* —**cer′tain•ty** *n.*

**cer•tif•i•cate** (sər-tĭf′ĭ-kĭt) *n.* A document testifying to a fact or promise.

**cer•ti•fy** (sûr′tə-fī′) *v.* **-fied, -fying.** **1.** To confirm formally as true. **2.** To guarantee. —**cer′ti•fi′a•ble** *adj.* —**cer′ti•fi′a•bly** *adv.* —**cer′ti•fi•ca′tion** *n.* —**cer′ti•fied** *adj.*

**cess•pool** (sĕs′po͞ol′) *n.* A covered hole for sewage.

**chafe** (chāf) *v.* **chafed, chafing.** **1.** To make or become worn or sore from rubbing. **2.** To make or become annoyed.

**cha•grin** (shə-grĭn′) *n.* Deep disappointment; humiliation. —*v.* To humiliate.

**chain** (chān) *n.* **1.** A flexible series of connected links. **2.** Any series of related things. —*v.* **1.** To bind with a chain. **2.** To confine.

**chair** (châr) *n.* **1.** A seat with a back. **2.** An important office, as that of a judge or chairperson. **3.** A chairperson.

**chair•man** (châr′mən) *n.* A man who presides over a meeting. —**chair′man•ship′** *n.*

**chair•per•son** (châr′pûr′sən) *n.* One who presides over a meeting or an organization.

**chair•wom•an** (châr′wo͝om′ən) *n.* A woman who presides over a meeting or an organization.

**chalk** (chôk) *n.* A soft mineral used in pieces for marking on a blackboard. —*v.* To mark with chalk. —**chalk** *adj.* —**chalk′i•ness** *n.* —**chalk′y** *adj.*

**chal•lenge** (chăl′ənj) *n.* **1.** A call to engage in a contest. **2.** A demand for an explanation or identification. **3.** A test of one's abilities. **4.** A formal objection. —*v.* **-lenged, -lenging.** To put or be a challenge to. —**chal′lenge•a•ble** *adj.* —**chal′leng•er** *n.*

**cham•ber** (chām′bər) *n.* **1.** A room. **2.** A judge's office. **3.** A hall, esp. for a legislative assembly.

**cham•pagne** (shăm-pān′) *n.* A sparkling white wine.

**cham•pi•on** (chăm′pē-ən) *n.* **1.** One that holds first place. **2.** An advocate; defender. —*v.* To fight for; support. —**cham′pi•on** *adj.* —**cham′pi•on•ship′** *n.*

**chance** (chăns) *n.* **1.** Randomness; unpredictability. **2.** Luck; fate. **3.** Probability. **4.** An opportunity. **5.** A risk.

—*v.* **chanced, chancing. 1.** To happen by chance. **2.** To risk. **—chance** *adj.* **—chanc'y** *adj.*

**chan•cel•lor** (chăn'sə-lər) *n.* **1.** A state official of high rank. **2.** The head of certain universities. **—chan'cel•lor•ship'** *n.*

**chan•de•lier** (shăn'də-lîr') *n.* A branched, hanging fixture for lights.

**change** (chānj) *v.* **changed, changing. 1.** To make or become different; alter. **2.** To exchange. **3.** To put on fresh clothes. —*n.* **1.** The process or condition of changing. **2.** Money given in exchange for money of higher denomination. **3.** Any small coins. **—change'a•ble** *adj.* **—change'less** *adj.* **—chang'er** *n.*

**change•o•ver** (chānj'ō'vər) *n.* Conversion to a different purpose or from 1 system to another.

**chan•nel** (chăn'əl) *n.* **1.** The bed of a stream. **2.** The deeper part of a river or harbor. **3.** A strait. **4.** A passage or route. **5.** A specified frequency band, esp. for a TV station. **6.** An area on a magnetic disk or tape storing information. —*v.* **1.** To make or form channels in. **2.** To direct or guide.

**chant** (chănt) *n.* **1.** A melody in which a number of words are sung on each note. **2.** A monotonous voice. —*v.* To say or sing in a chant. **—chant'er** *n.*

**cha•os** (kā'ŏs') *n.* Total disorder. **—cha•ot'ic** *adj.* **—cha•ot'i•cal•ly** *adv.*

**chap**[1] (chăp) *v.* **chapped, chapping.** To roughen, esp. from cold.

**chap**[2] (chăp) *n.* A man; fellow.

**cha•peau** (shă-pō') *n., pl.* **-peaus** or **-peaux.** A hat.

**chap•el** (chăp'əl) *n.* A place of worship subordinate to a church.

**chap•er•on** (shăp'ə-rōn') *n.* An older person who for propriety accompanies young unmarried people. —*v.* To act as chaperon for.

**chap•fal•len** (chăp'fô'lən) *adj.* In low spirits; dejected.

**chap•lain** (chăp'lĭn) *n.* A cleric attached to a chapel or military unit.

**chap•ter** (chăp'tər) *n.* **1.** A main division of a book. **2.** A branch of a club, fraternity, etc.

**Chapter 11** *n.* A section in bankruptcy law allowing an insolvent company to reorganize under court supervision and pay its debts.

**char•ac•ter** (kăr'ək-tər) *n.* **1.** A distinguishing feature. **2.** The essential nature of a person or group. **3.** Integrity; fortitude. **4.** Reputation. **5.** An eccentric person. **6.** A person portrayed in a drama, novel, etc. **7.** A symbol in a writing system.

**char•ac•ter•is•tic** (kăr'ək-tə-rĭs'tĭk) *adj.* Distinctive; typical. —*n.* A distinguishing feature or attribute. **—char'ac•ter•is'ti•cal•ly** *adv.*

**char•ac•ter•ize** (kăr'ək-tə-rīz') *v.* **-ized, -izing. 1.** To describe. **2.** To be a distinguishing trait of. **—char'ac•ter•i•za'tion** *n.*

**char•coal** (chär'kōl') *n.* A black, porous material made by burning wood in an airless kiln.

**charge** (chärj) *v.* **charged, charging. 1.** To entrust. **2.** To command. **3.** To blame or accuse. **4.** To set as a price. **5.** To demand payment from. **6.** To attack violently. **7.** To load or fill. —*n.* **1.** Care; custody. **2.** A command. **3.** An accusation. **4.** Cost; price. **5.** An attack. **6.** A load; burden.

**char•gé d'af•faires** (shär-zhā' də-fâr') *n., pl.* **chargés d'affaires.** A government official temporarily substituting for an absent ambassador.

**cha•ris•ma** (kə-rĭz'mə) *n.* Power to attract followers. **—char'is•mat'ic** *adj.*

**char•i•ty** (chăr'ĭ-tē) *n., pl.* **-ties. 1.** Help given to the poor. **2.** An organization that helps the poor. **3.** A kindly act. **—char'i•ta•ble** *adj.* **—char'i•ta•bly** *adv.*

**char•la•tan** (shär'lə-tən) *n.* A pretender; impostor.

**charm** (chärm) *n.* **1.** The power of pleasing or attracting. **2.** A small ornament worn on a bracelet. **3.** A formula, object, etc., thought to have magical power. —*v.* **1.** To attract; delight. **2.** To bewitch. **—charm'er** *n.* **—charm'ing** *adj.*

**chart** (chärt) *n.* **1.** A map. **2.** A graph or table. —*v.* **1.** To make a chart of. **2.** To plan.

**char•ter** (chär'tər) *n.* **1.** A document creating a corporation, chapter, etc. **2.** The hiring of an aircraft, vessel, etc. —*v.* **1.** To grant a charter to. **2.** To hire or lease.

**char•treuse** (shär-trōōz′, -trōōs′) *n.* A strong greenish yellow.

**char•y** (châr′ē) *adj.* **-ier, -iest. 1.** Cautious; wary. **2.** Shy. **3.** Not giving freely; sparing. **—char′i•ly** *adv.* **—char′i•ness** *n.*

**chase** (chās) *v.* **chased, chasing. 1.** To pursue; follow. **2.** To hunt. **3.** To drive away. *—n.* The act of chasing. **—chas′er** *n.*

**chasm** (kăz′əm) *n.* **1.** A deep cleft in the earth. **2.** A sudden interruption in continuity. **3.** A pronounced difference of opinion.

**chas•sis** (shăs′ē) *n., pl.* **-sis. 1.** The rectangular frame of a car. **2.** The framework of a radio, television set, etc.

**chaste** (chāst) *adj.* **1.** Modest. **2.** Abstaining from illicit sexual intercourse. **—chaste′ly** *adv.* **—chaste′ness** *n.* **—chas′ti•ty** *n.*

**chas•tise** (chăs-tīz′) *v.* **-tised, -tising. 1.** To punish. **2.** To criticize severely. **—chas•tise′ment** *n.*

**chat** (chăt) *v.* **chatted, chatting.** To converse light and casually. *—n.* An informal conversation. **—chat′ty** *adj.*

**cha•teau** (shă-tō′) *n., pl.* **-teaux.** A French castle.

**chat•ter** (chăt′ər) *v.* **1.** To talk foolishly; babble. **2.** To make a chirping noise. **—chat′ter** *n.* **—chat′ter•er** *n.*

**chauf•feur** (shō′fər, shō-fûr′) *n.* One employed to drive a private automobile. **—chauf′feur** *v.*

**chau•vin•ism** (shō′və-nĭz′əm) *n.* **1.** Fanatical devotion to one's country. **2.** Prejudiced belief in the superiority of one's own group or cause. **—chau′vin•ist** *n.* **—chau′vin•is′tic** *adj.*

**cheap** (chēp) *adj.* **1.** Inexpensive. **2.** Of low quality. **3.** Stingy. *—adv.* Inexpensively. **—cheap′en** *v.* **—cheap′ly** *adv.* **—cheap′ness** *n.*

**cheat** (chēt) *v.* **1.** To swindle. **2.** To act dishonestly. *—n.* **1.** A fraud or swindle. **2.** One guilty of swindle or dishonesty. **—cheat′er** *n.*

**check** (chĕk) *n.* **1.** An abrupt stop. **2.** A restraint. **3.** A verification. **4.** A bill. **5.** A written bank draft. **6.** A pattern of small squares. *—v.* **1.** To stop; halt. **2.** To hold in restraint. **3.** To examine for accuracy. **4.** To make a check mark on. **5.** To deposit for temporary safekeeping. **—check′a•ble** *adj.*

**check•ers** (chĕk′ərz) *n.* A board game played by 2 persons. **—check′er•board′** *n.*

**check•list** (chĕk′lĭst′) *n.* A list on which items can be compared, scheduled, or verified.

**check•off** (chĕk′ôf′, -ŏf′) *n.* Collection of union dues by an authorized deduction from wages.

**check-out** (chĕk′out′) *n.* **1.** The act, time, or place of checking out, as in a library or a motel. **2.** A test, as for a machine. **3.** An inspection or investigation.

**check•point** (chĕk′point′) *n.* A place where surface traffic is stopped for inspection.

**check•room** (chĕk′rōōm′) *n.* A place where coats, hats, and other items can be stored temporarily.

**cheek** (chēk) *n.* **1.** The fleshy part of either side of the face. **2.** Impudence. **—cheek′i•ly** *adv.* **—cheek′i•ness** *n.* **—cheek′y** *adj.*

**cheer** (chîr) *n.* **1,** Gaiety; happiness. **2.** A joyful shout. *—v.* **1.** To fill with happiness. **2.** To encourage with cheers. **—cheer′ful** *adj.* **—cheer′ful•ly** *adv.* **—cheer′ful•ness** *n.* **—cheer′i•ly** *adv.* **—cheer′i•ness** *n.* **—cheer′less** *adj.* **—cheer′y** *adj.*

**cheese** (chēz) *n.* A solid food prepared from milk curd.

**chef** (shĕf) *n.* A chief cook.

**chem•i•cal** (kĕm′ĭ-kəl) *adj.* **1.** Of chemistry. **2.** Involving or produced by chemicals. *—n.* A substance produced by or used in chemistry. **—chem′i•cal•ly** *adv.*

**che•mise** (shə-mēz′) *n.* A woman's loose, shirtlike undergarment.

**chem•is•try** (kĕm′ĭ-strē) *n., pl.* **-tries.** The science of the composition and reactions of matter. **—chem′ist** *n.*

**che•mo•sur•ger•y** (kē′mō-sûr′jə-rē, kĕm′ō-) *n.* The selective destruction of tissue by chemicals.

**cher•ish** (chĕr′ĭsh) *v.* To hold dear. **—cher′ish•er** *n.*

**cher•ry** (chĕr′ē) *n., pl.* **-ries. 1.** A small, rounded fruit. **2.** Deep red. **—cher′ry** *adj.*

**chess** (chĕs) *n.* A board game for 2 players. **—chess'man'** *n.*
**chest** (chĕst) *n.* **1.** The part of the body between the neck and abdomen. **2.** A sturdy box. **3.** A bureau.
**chest•nut** (chĕs'nŭt', -nət) *n.* **1.** An edible nut. **2.** Reddish brown. **—chest'nut** *adj.*
**chew** (cho͞o) *v.* To grind with the teeth. **—chew'er** *n.*
**chic** (shēk) *adj.* **-er, -est. 1.** Sophisticated; stylish. **2.** Dressed fashionably; modish. *—n.* **1.** Sophistication; elegance. **2.** Stylishness. **—chic'ness** *n.*
**Chi•ca•na** (chĭ-kä'nə, shĭ-) *n.* A female Mexican-American.
**Chi•ca•no** (chĭ-kä'nō, shĭ-) *n., pl.* **-nos.** A male Mexican-American. **—Chi'ca•nis'mo** *n.* **—Chi•ca'no** *adj.*
**chick•en** (chĭk'ən) *n.* The common domestic fowl or its edible flesh. **—chick** *n.*
**chide** (chīd) *v.* **chided, chiding.** To scold. **—chid'er** *n.*
**chief** (chēf) *n.* A leader. *—adj.* Principal; most important. **—chief'ly** *adv.* **—chief'tain** *n.*
**child** (chīld) *n., pl.* **children. 1.** Any person between birth and puberty. **2.** A son or daughter. **—child'hood'** *n.* **—child'ish** *adj.* **—child'ish•ly** *adv.* **—child'ish•ness** *n.* **—child'less** *adj.*
**child•proof** (chīld'pro͞of') *adj.* Designed to be secure from a child's meddling.
**chill** (chĭl) *n.* **1.** A moderate coldness. **2.** A sensation of coldness; a shiver. *—adj.* Cold. *—v.* To make or become cold. **—chill'y** *adj.* **—chill'i•ness** *n.*
**chime** (chīm) *n.* Often **chimes.** A set of tuned bells or their sound. *—v.* **chimed, chiming.** To sound harmoniously. **—chim'er** *n.*
**chim•ney** (chĭm'nē) *n.* A passage through which smoke escapes from a fireplace.
**chim•pan•zee** (chĭm'păn-zē', chĭm-păn'zē) *n.* A gregarious African ape.
**chin** (chĭn) *n.* The central portion of the lower jaw. *—v.* **chinned, chinning.** To pull oneself up on an overhead bar.
**chi•na** (chī'nə) *n.* Pottery, esp. high-quality porcelain.
**chintz** (chĭnts) *n.* A printed and glazed cotton fabric, usually of bright colors. **—chintz'i•ness** *n.* **—chintz'y** *adj.*
**chip** (chĭp) *n.* **1.** A small piece broken or cut off. **2.** A mark; dent. **3.** A disk; counter. **4.** A minute piece of semiconducting material used in an electronic component or integrated circuit. *—v.* **chipped, chipping.** To break so as to form chips. **—chip in.** To contribute.
**chip•munk** (chĭp'mŭngk') *n.* A small squirrellike rodent.
**chi•ro•prac•tic** (kī'rə-prăk'tĭk) *n.* A system of therapy by manipulation of the spinal column and other bodily structures. **—chi'ro•prac'tor** *n.*
**chis•el** (chĭz'əl) *n.* A cutting and shaping tool with a sharp edge. *—v.* **1.** To shape with a chisel. **2.** To swindle. **—chis'el•er** *n.*
**chit** (chĭt) *n.* A statement of an amount owed for food and drink; a check.
**chiv•al•ry** (shĭv'əl-rē) *n., pl.* **-ries.** Bravery, courtesy, etc., as idealized by knighthood. **—chiv'al•rous** *adj.* **—chiv'al•rous•ly** *adv.*
**chive** (chīv) *n.* A grasslike plant with onion-flavored leaves.
**choc•o•late** (chô'kə-lĭt) *n.* **1.** Roasted and ground cacao seeds. **2.** A candy or beverage made from this. **—choc'o•late** *adj.*
**choice** (chois) *n.* **1.** The act or right of choosing. **2.** Something chosen. *—adj.* **choicer, choicest.** Of fine quality.
**choir** (kwīr) *n.* An organized group of singers, esp. in a church.
**choke** (chōk) *v.* **choked, choking. 1.** To interfere with the breathing of; suffocate. **2.** To repress or check. **3.** To obstruct. *—n.* The act or sound of choking.
**chol•er•a** (kŏl'ər-ə) *n.* An acute, often fatal epidemic disease.
**cho•les•ter•ol** (kə-lĕs'tə-rôl', -rōl') *n.* A soapy crystalline substance, occurring notably in animal fats.
**choose** (cho͞oz) *v.* **chose, chosen, choosing. 1.** To select. **2.** To desire. **—choos'er** *n.* **—choos'y** *adj.*
**chop** (chŏp) *v.* **chopped, chopping. 1.** To cut by striking with a sharp tool. **2.** To cut into bits. *—n.* **1.** A sharp blow. **2.** A small cut of meat from the rib, shoulder, etc. **—chop'per** *n.*
**chop•py** (chŏp'ē) *adj.* **-pier, -piest.** Shifting abruptly, as waves. **—chop'pi•ness** *n.*

**chore** (chôr, chōr) *n.* A task.

**cho•re•og•ra•phy** (kôr′ē-ŏg′rə-fē) *n.* The creation of ballets or dances. **—cho′re•o•graph′** *v.* **—cho′re•og′ra•pher** *n.* **—cho′re•o•graph′ic** *adj.*

**cho•rus** (kôr′əs, kōr′-) *n., pl.* **-ruses. 1.** A group of singers. **2.** A repeated refrain. *—v.* To sing or utter together. **—cho′ral** *adj.*

**chose** (chōz) *v.* p.t. of **choose.**

**cho•sen** (chō′zən) *v.* p.p. of **choose.** *—adj.* Preferred above others.

**chow•der** (chou′dər) *n.* A thick seafood soup.

**chris•ten** (krĭs′ən) *v.* **1.** To baptize. **2.** To name. **—chris′ten•er** *n.* **—chris′ten•ing** *n.*

**Chris•ti•an•i•ty** (krĭs′chē-ăn′ĭ-tē) *n.* The religion founded on the teachings of Jesus. **—Chris′tian** *adj. & n.*

**chron•ic** (krŏn′ĭk) *adj.* Prolonged; lingering. **—chron′i•cal•ly** *adv.*

**chron•i•cle** (krŏn′ĭ-kəl) *n.* A historical record. *—v.* **-cled, -cling.** To record. **—chron′i•cler** *n.*

**chro•nol•o•gy** (krə-nŏl′ə-jē) *n., pl.* **-gies. 1.** The determination of sequences of events. **2.** A list of successive events; order of occurrence. **—chron′o•log′i•cal** *adj.* **—chron′o•log′i•cal•ly** *adv.*

**chry•san•the•mum** (krĭ-săn′thə-məm) *n.* A plant with showy flowers.

**chub•by** (chŭb′ē) *adj.* **-bier, -biest.** Plump. **—chub′bi•ly** *adv.* **—chub′bi•ness** *n.*

**chuck•le** (chŭk′əl) *v.* **-led, -ling.** To laugh quietly. **—chuck′le** *n.* **—chuck′ler** *n.*

**chuk•ka** (chŭk′ə) *n.* A short, ankle-length boot, usually of suede, with 2 pairs of eyelets.

**chum** (chŭm) *n.* A close friend. *—v.* **chummed, chumming.** To be a close friend. **—chum′my** *adj.*

**chunk** (chŭngk) *n.* A thick piece. **—chunk′i•ness** *n.* **—chunk′y** *adj.*

**church** (chûrch) *n.* **1.** A building for public worship. **2.** A congregation. **3.** Any Christian denomination; sect.

**churn** (chûrn) *n.* A vessel in which butter is made. *—v.* **1.** To shake. **2.** To make (butter). **—churn′er** *n.*

**chutz•pah** (ᴋʜo͝ot′spə, ho͝ot′-) *n.* Brazenness; gall.

**ciao** (chou) *interj.* An Italian expression of greeting and farewell.

**ci•der** (sī′dər) *n.* Apple juice.

**ci•gar** (sĭ-gär′) *n.* Chopped tobacco leaves rolled into a cylinder for smoking.

**cig•a•rette** (sĭg′ə-rĕt′) *n.* A small roll of finely chopped tobacco enclosed in paper for smoking.

**cin•der** (sĭn′dər) *n.* **1.** A burned substance not reduced to ashes. **2. cinders.** Ashes.

**cin•e•ma** (sĭn′ə-mə) *n.* **1.** A motion picture. **2.** A motion-picture theater.

**cin•na•mon** (sĭn′ə-mən) *n.* A spice made from the bark of a tropical tree.

**ci•pher** (sī′fər) *n.* **1.** The mathematical symbol (0); zero.

**cir•cle** (sûr′kəl) *n.* **1.** A closed curve everywhere equidistant from a central point. **2.** Anything similarly shaped. **3.** A group sharing an interest, activity, etc. *—v.* **-cled, -cling.** To make a circle around. **—cir′cler** *n.*

**cir•cuit** (sûr′kĭt) *n.* **1.** A closed, usually circular, curve. **2.** A repeated route, sequence, or round. **3.** A closed path followed by an electric current.

**cir•cu•lar** (sûr′kyə-lər) *adj.* **1.** Of or shaped like a circle. **2.** Returning to a starting point. *—n.* A printed notice for mass distribution. **—cir′cu•lar′i•ty** *n.*

**cir•cu•late** (sûr′kyə-lāt′) *v.* **-lated, -lating.** To move about freely or in a circle. **—cir′cu•la′tion** *n.* **—cir′cu•la′tor** *n.* **—cir′cu•la•tor′y** *adj.* **—cir′cu•la•tive** *adj.*

**cir•cum•cise** (sûr′kəm-sīz′) *v.* **-cised, -cising.** To remove the foreskin of. **—cir′cum•ci′sion** *n.*

**cir•cum•fer•ence** (sər-kŭm′fər-əns) *n.* The distance around a circle or other figure.

**cir•cum•spect** (sûr′kəm-spĕkt′) *adj.* Prudent; cautious. **—cir′cum•spec′tion** *n.*

**cir•cum•stance** (sûr′kəm-stăns′) *n.* **1.** One of the conditions or facts attending an event. **2.** Often **circumstances.** Financial means. **3.** Details. **—cir′cum•stan′tial** *adj.*

**cir•cus** (sûr′kəs) *n.* A traveling show of acrobats, clowns, trained animals, etc.

**cite** (sīt) *v.* **cited, citing. 1.** To quote as an authority or example. **2.** To commend. **—ci•ta′tion** *n.*

**cit•i•zen** (sĭt′ĭ-zən) *n.* A person belonging by birth or naturalization to a given place or nation. **—cit′i•zen•ry** *n.* **—cit′i•zen•ship** *n.*

**cit•rus** (sĭt′rəs) *adj.* Of fruit such as the orange, lemon, etc. *—n., pl.* **-ruses.** A citrus tree.

**cit•y** (sĭt′ē) *n., pl.* **-ies.** A large town.

**civ•ic** (sĭv′ĭk) *adj.* Of a city or citizenship. *—n.* **civics** *(takes sing. v.)* The study of the rights and duties of citizenship.

**civ•il** (sĭv′əl) *adj.* **1.** Of citizens. **2.** Of ordinary community life. **3.** Polite. **—civ′il•ly** *adv.* **—civ′il•ness** *n.*

**ci•vil•ian** (sĭ-vĭl′yən) *n.* A person in civil life, not in the armed forces. **—ci•vil′-ian** *adj.*

**ci•vil•i•ty** (sĭ-vĭl′ĭ-tē) *n., pl.* **-ties. 1.** Politeness. **2.** A courteous act.

**civ•i•li•za•tion** (sĭv′ə-lĭ-zā′shən) *n.* Any human society having an advanced cultural development. **—civ′i•lize′** *v.*

**clad** (klăd) *v.* A p.t. & p.p. of **clothe.**

**claim** (klām) *v.* **1.** To demand as one's due. **2.** To state to be true. *—n.* **1.** A demand. **2.** Title or right. **3.** Something claimed.

**clair•voy•ance** (klâr-voi′əns) *n.* The power to perceive things beyond the natural range of human senses. **—clair•voy′ant** *n. & adj.*

**clam** (klăm) *n.* A mollusk. *—v.* **clammed, clamming.** To hunt for clams.

**clam•my** (klăm′ē) *adj.* **-mier, -miest.** Disagreeably chilly and moist. **—clam′mi•ly** *adv.* **—clam′mi•ness** *n.*

**clam•or** (klăm′ər) *n.* A loud outcry; hubbub. *—v.* To make a clamor. **—clam′or•ous** *adj.*

**clamp** (klămp) *n.* A device used to fasten or grip things. *—v.* To fasten with a clamp. **—clamp′er** *n.*

**clan** (klăn) *n.* A large family or group of related families. **—clan′nish** *adj.* **—clan′nish•ly** *adv.*

**clan•des•tine** (klăn-dĕs′tĭn) *adj.* Concealed; secret.

**clap** (klăp) *v.* **clapped, clapping. 1.** To strike (the hands) together, as in applauding. **2.** To come together with a sharp noise. *—n.* The act or sound of clapping.

**clap•board** (klăb′ərd, klăp′bôrd′, -bōrd′) *n.* Board placed in overlapping rows on the outside of houses.

**claque** (klăk) *n.* **1.** A group of persons hired to applaud at a performance. **2.** A group of fawning admirers.

**clar•et** (klăr′ĭt) *n.* A red table wine.

**clar•i•fy** (klăr′ə-fī′) *v.* **-fied, -fying.** To make or become clear. **—clar′i•fi•ca′tion** *n.*

**clar•i•net** (klăr′ə-nĕt′) *n.* A tube-shaped woodwind instrument. **—clar′i•net′ist** *n.*

**clar•i•ty** (klăr′ĭ-tē) *n.* Clearness.

**clash** (klăsh) *v.* **1.** To collide noisily. **2.** To conflict; disagree. *—n.* **1.** A loud metallic noise. **2.** A conflict.

**clasp** (klăsp) *n.* **1.** A fastener; clip. **2. a.** An embrace. **b.** A grip of the hand. *—v.* **1.** To fasten. **2.** To grip. **—clasp′er** *n.*

**class** (klăs) *n.* **1.** A group; kind; sort. **2.** A division by quality or grade. **3.** A social stratum. **4.** A group of students in the same year. *—v.* To classify.

**class action** *n.* A lawsuit in which the plaintiffs file for themselves and for many others with the same claims against the defendant.

**class-con•scious** (klăs′kŏn′shəs) *adj.* Aware of belonging to a particular socioeconomic class. **—class′-con′scious•ness** *n.*

**clas•sic** (klăs′ĭk) *adj.* **1.** Of ancient Greece or Rome. **2.** Traditional. **3.** Supreme; exemplary. *—n.* An artist, author, or work of the highest rank. **—clas′si•cal** *adj.* **—clas′si•cal•ly** *adv.*

**clas•si•fy** (klăs′ə-fī′) *v.* **-fied, -fying.** To put in classes or groupings. **—clas′si•fi•ca′tion** *n.* **—clas′si•fi′er** *n.*

**clat•ter** (klăt′ər) *n.* A rattling sound. **—clat′ter** *v.*

**clause** (klôz) *n.* **1.** A group of words with a subject and verb that forms part of a sentence. **2.** A provision.

**claus•tro•pho•bi•a** (klô′strə-fō′bē-ə) *n.* Fear of confined spaces. **—claus′tro•pho′bic** *adj.*

**claw** (klô) *n.* **1.** A sharp, curved nail on the toe of an animal. **2.** A pincerlike part. *—v.* To scratch with claws.

**clay** (klā) *n.* A readily molded earth used in making bricks and pottery. **—clay′ey, clay′ish** *adj.*

**clean** (klēn) *adj.* **1.** Free from impurities. **2.** Thorough; complete. *—v.* To rid of dirt or other impurities. **—clean′er** *n.* **—clean′ly** *adj.* **—clean′li•ness** *n.*

**cleanse** (klĕnz) *v.* **cleansed, cleansing.** To clean; purify. **—cleans′er** *n.*

**clear** (klîr) *adj.* **1.** Free from anything that dims or obscures. **2.** Unobstructed. **3.** Easily perceptible. **4.** Free from doubt, burden, or guilt. *—adv.* **1.** Distinctly. **2.** Entirely. *—v.* **1.** To make or become clear. **2.** To gain as net profit. **—clear′ance** *n.* **—clear′er** *n.* **—clear′ly** *adv.* **—clear′ness** *n.*

**clear•ing** (klîr′ĭng) *n.* A tract of land cleared of trees.

**cleat** (klēt) *n.* A projection used to prevent slipping.

**cleave** (klēv) *v.* **cleft** (klĕft) or **cleaved, cleaving.** To split or separate. **—cleav′age** *n.* **—cleav′er** *n.*

**clef** (klĕf) *n.* A written musical symbol indicating the pitch of the notes.

**cleft** (klĕft) *v.* A p.t. & p.p. of **cleave.** *—adj.* Split. *—n.* A crack.

**clem•ent** (klĕm′ənt) *adj.* **1.** Merciful. **2.** Mild, as the weather. **—clem′en•cy** *n.*

**clench** (klĕnch) *v.* To bring together tightly. *—n.* A tight grip or grasp.

**cler•gy** (klûr′jē) *n., pl.* **-gies.** Persons ordained for religious service.

**cler•i•cal** (klĕr′ĭ-kəl) *adj.* **1.** Of clerks or office workers. **2.** Of the clergy.

**clerk** (klûrk) *n.* **1.** A person who performs office work. **2.** A salesperson. *—v.* To work as a clerk.

**clev•er** (klĕv′ər) *adj.* **1.** Mentally quick and resourceful. **2.** Dexterous. **—clev′er•ly** *adv.* **—clev′er•ness** *n.*

**cli•ché** (klē-shā′) *n.* A trite expression.

**click** (klĭk) *n.* **1.** A short, sharp sound. **2.** An act of clicking. *—v.* **1.** To make a short, sharp sound. **2.** To succeed. **3.** To function well. **4.** To press down and release a button on a computer mouse. **—click′er** *n.*

**cli•ent** (klī′ənt) *n.* **1.** One for whom professional services are rendered. **2.** A customer.

**cli•en•tele** (klī′ən-tĕl′, klē′än-) *n.* The customers of a professional person considered as a group.

**cliff** (klĭf) *n.* A high, steep face of rock.

**cli•mate** (klī′mĭt) *n.* The prevailing weather. **—cli•mat′ic** *adj.*

**cli•max** (klī′măks′) *n.* The point of greatest intensity or excitement. *—v.* To reach a climax. **—cli•mac′tic** *adj.*

**climb** (klīm) *v.* To move up or ascend. **—climb down.** To descend. *—n.* The act of climbing. **—climb′er** *n.*

**clinch** (klĭnch) *v.* **1.** To fasten securely. **2.** To settle decisively; win. **3.** To embrace tightly. *—n.* The act of clinching. **—clinch′er** *n.*

**cling** (klĭng) *v.* **clung** (klŭng), **clinging.** To hold fast. **—cling′er** *n.*

**clin•ic** (klĭn′ĭk) *n.* **1.** A specialized hospital. **2.** An outpatient division. **3.** A center that offers counsel or instruction. **—clin′i•cal** *adj.*

**clip**[1] (klĭp) *v.* **clipped, clipping. 1.** To cut off. **2.** To cut short. *—n.* A brisk pace. **—clip′per** *n.*

**clip**[2] (klĭp) *n.* **1.** A clasp. **2.** A container for ammunition. *—v.* **clipped, clipping.** To fasten.

**clique** (klēk, klĭk) *n.* An exclusive group.

**cloak** (klōk) *n.* **1.** A loose outer garment. **2.** Anything that conceals. *—v.* To conceal.

**clock** (klŏk) *n.* An instrument for measuring time. *—v.* To record the time or speed of. **—clock′wise′** *adv. & adj.*

**clod** (klŏd) *n.* **1.** A lump of earth. **2.** A stupid person. **—clod′dish** *adj.*

**clog** (klŏg) *n.* **1.** An obstacle. **2.** A heavy, usu. wooden shoe. *—v.* **clogged, clogging. 1.** To impede. **2.** To make or become obstructed. **—clog′gy** *adj.*

**clois•ter** (kloi′stər) *n.* **1.** A covered walk. **2.** A monastery or convent. *—v.* To seclude.

**close** (klōs) *adj.* **closer, closest. 1.** Near. **2.** Compact. **3.** Nearly even. **4.** Fitting tightly. **5.** Complete; thorough. **6.** Intimate. **7.** Confined. **8.** Secretive. **9.** Miserly. **10.** Lacking fresh air. *—v.* (klōz) **closed, closing. 1.** To shut. **2.** To end; finish. **3.** To come near. **4.** To agree. *—n.* (klōz). A conclusion. *—adv.* (klōs). In a close manner. **—close′ly** *adv.* **—close′ness** *n.*

**closed-cap•tioned** (klōzd′kăp′shənd) *adj.* Relating to a TV broadcast in which captions appear only on those screens equipped with a decoder.

**closed shop** *n.* A business or factory whose employees are required to be union members; a union shop.

**clos•et** (klŏz′ĭt, klô′zĭt) *n.* A small room for storage and clothes. —*v.* To shut up in a private room.

**clos•ing** (klō′zĭng) *n.* A meeting between seller and buyer in a real-estate deal to transfer title.

**clot** (klŏt) *n.* A coagulated mass. —**clot** *v.*

**cloth** (klôth, klŏth) *n., pl.* **cloths. 1.** Fabric. **2.** A piece of fabric used for a specific purpose, as a tablecloth.

**clothe** (klō*th*) *v.* **clothed** or **clad, clothing.** To dress.

**clothes** (klōz, klō*thz*) *pl.n.* Articles of dress. —**cloth′ing** *n.*

**clothes•horse** (klōz′hôrs′) *n.* **1.** A frame on which to hang clothes. **2.** One who is excessively concerned with dress.

**clo•ture** (klō′chər) *n.* Also **clo•sure** (klō′zhər). A parliamentary procedure by which debate is ended and an immediate vote taken. —**clo′ture** *v.*

**cloud** (kloud) *n.* **1.** A visible body of fine water droplets in the sky. **2.** Any hovering mass, as of dust. —*v.* **1.** To cover with clouds. **2.** To make or become gloomy or troubled. —**cloud′i•ness** *n.* —**cloud′less** *adj.* —**cloud′y** *adj.*

**clout** (klout) *n.* **1.** A blow. **2.** Influence. —*v.* To strike heavily.

**clove**[1] (klōv) *n.* A spice from the flower of an Asian tree.

**clove**[2] (klōv) *n.* A section of a bulb, as of garlic.

**clown** (kloun) *n.* **1.** A comic entertainer. **2.** A fool. —*v.* To behave like a clown. —**clown′ish** *adj.* —**clown′ish•ly** *adv.*

**cloy** (kloi) *v.* To surfeit. —**cloy′ing** *adj.* —**cloy′ing•ly** *adv.*

**club**[1] (klŭb) *n.* **1.** A heavy stick. **2.** A playing card marked with a black cloverleaf. —*v.* **clubbed, clubbing.** To strike with a club.

**club**[2] (klŭb) *n.* A social group or hobby.

**clue** (klo͞o) *n.* Also **clew.** Anything that helps solve a problem or mystery.

**clump** (klŭmp) *n.* **1.** A clustered mass. **2.** A heavy dull sound. —*v.* To walk with a heavy dull sound.

**clum•sy** (klŭm′zē) *adj.* **-sier, -siest.** Graceless; awkward. —**clum′si•ly** *adv.* —**clum′si•ness** *n.*

**clung** (klŭng) *v.* p.t. & p.p. of **cling.**

**clus•ter** (klŭs′tər) *n.* A close group; bunch. —*v.* To gather or grow in clusters.

**cluster headache** *n.* A severe headache like a migraine, occurring several times a day for several weeks.

**clutch** (klŭch) *v.* To grasp or attempt to grasp tightly. —*n.* **1.** A tight grasp. **2. clutches.** Control. **3.** A device for engaging engine gears.

**clut•ter** (klŭt′ər) *n.* A disordered state; jumble. —*v.* To litter.

**coach** (kōch) *n.* **1.** A closed carriage, bus, train, etc. **2.** One who is a trainer, esp. in athletics. —*v.* To teach or train.

**co•ag•u•late** (kō-ăg′yə-lāt′) *v.* **-lated, -lating.** To thicken; clot. —**co•ag′u•lant** *adj. & n.* —**co•ag′u•la′tion** *n.*

**coal** (kōl) *n.* A black carbon-containing mineral burned as a fuel.

**co•a•li•tion** (kō′ə-lĭsh′ən) *n.* An alliance or union. —**co′a•li′tion•ist** *n.*

**co-an•chor** (kō-ăng′kər) *n.* A newscaster or sportscaster who shares the duties of anchor. —**co-an′chor** *v.*

**coarse** (kôrs, kōrs) *adj.* **coarser, coarsest. 1.** Crude. **2.** Rough-textured. —**coarse′ly** *adv.* —**coars′en** *v.* —**coarse′ness** *n.*

**coast** (kōst) *n.* The seashore. —*v.* **1.** To slide down a slope. **2.** To move effortlessly. —**coast′al** *adj.* —**coast′er** *n.*

**coat** (kōt) *n.* **1.** An outer garment with sleeves. **2.** A natural outer covering. **3.** A covering layer. —*v.* To cover with a coat. —**coat′ed** *adj.*

**coax** (kōks) *v.* To urge by pleading or flattery. —**coax′er** *n.*

**cob** (kŏb) *n.* The core of an ear of corn.

**cob•ble** (kŏb′əl) *v.* **-bled, -bling.** To mend (shoes). —**cob′bler** *n.*

**COBOL** (kō′bôl′) *n.* A computer language for business applications.

**co•caine** (kō-kān′) *n.* A narcotic drug from coca leaves.

**cock** (kŏk) *n.* **1.** A male bird, esp. a rooster. **2.** A faucet or valve. **3.** The hammer in a firearm. —*v.* **1.** To set the hammer of (a gun) for firing. **2.** To tilt or turn up.

**cock•a•ma•mie, cock•a•ma•my** (kŏk′ə-mā′mē) *adj.* **1.** Worthless. **2.** Ridiculous.

**cock•a•poo** (kŏk′ə-po͞o′) *n.* A dog that is a cross between a cocker spaniel and a poodle.

**cock•pit** (kŏk′pĭt′) *n.* The pilots' space in an airplane.

**cock•roach** (kŏk′rōch′) *n.* A common flat-bodied insect, usu. considered a pest.

**cock•tail** (kŏk′tāl′) *n.* **1.** A mixed alcoholic drink. **2.** An appetizer.

**co•coa** (kō′kō) *n.* Roasted powdered cacao seeds, or a drink made from this powder.

**co•co•nut** (kō′kə-nŭt′, -nət) *n.* Also **co•coa•nut.** The large, hard-shelled, edible nut of a tropical palm tree.

**co•coon** (kə-ko͞on′) *n.* The pupal case spun by the larva of a moth or other insect.

**cod** (kŏd) *n., pl.* **cod** or **cods.** Also **cod•fish.** A food fish of north Atlantic waters.

**cod•dle** (kŏd′l) *v.* **-dled, -dling.** To pamper.

**code** (kōd) *n.* **1.** A set of laws or rules. **2.** A system of signals. —*v.* **coded, coding.** To put in a code.

**co•ed•u•ca•tion** (kō-ĕj′ə-kā′shən) *n.* The education of both men and women at the same institution. **—co′ed′** *n. & adj.* **—co′-ed•u•ca′tion•al** *adj.*

**co-e•qual** (kō-ē′kwəl) *adj.* Equal. **—co-equal** *n.* **—co-e′qual•ly** *adv.*

**co•erce** (kō-ûrs′) *v.* **-erced, -ercing.** To compel; force. **—co•erc′er** *n.* **—co•er′cion** *n.* **—co•er′cive** *adj.*

**cof•fee** (kô′fē, kŏf′ē) *n.* A beverage prepared from the seeds of a tropical tree.

**cof•fin** (kô′fĭn, kŏf′ĭn) *n.* A box in which a corpse is buried.

**cog** (kŏg) *n.* **1.** A tooth on the rim of a wheel. **2.** A subordinate member of an organization.

**co•gnac** (kōn′yăk′, kŏn′-, kôn′-) *n.* A fine French brandy.

**cog•ni•zance** (kŏg′nĭ-zəns) *n.* Awareness. **—cog′ni•zant** *adj.*

**co•her•ent** (kō-hîr′ənt, -hĕr′-) *adj.* **1.** Sticking together. **2.** Orderly; intelligible. **—co•her′ence, co•her′en•cy** *n.*

**co•he•sion** (kō-hē′zhən) *n.* The condition of sticking together; union. **—co•here′** *v.* **—co•he′sive** *adj.* **—co•he′sive•ly** *adv.* **—co•he′sive•ness** *n.*

**co•hort** (kō′hôrt′) *n.* **1.** A group or band. **2.** A companion.

**coil** (koil) *n.* **1.** A series of connected spirals. **2.** A spiral or ring. —*v.* To wind in coils. **—coil′er** *n.*

**coin** (koin) *n.* A piece of metal stamped and issued as money. —*v.* **1.** To make (coins) from metal. **2.** To invent (a word or phrase). **—coin′age** *n.*

**co•in•cide** (kō′ĭn-sīd′) *v.* **-cided, -ciding.** **1.** To happen at the same time. **2.** To correspond exactly. **—co•in′ci•dence** *n.* **—co•in′ci•den′tal, co•in′ci•dent** *adj.*

**coke** (kōk) *n.* The solid residue of coal after removal of gases.

**col•an•der** (kŭl′ən-dər, kŏl′-) *n.* A perforated kitchen bowl for draining.

**cold** (kōld) *adj.* **1.** Having a low temperature. **2.** Uncomfortably chilled. **3.** Lacking warmth; reserved; unemotional. —*n.* **1.** Relative lack of warmth. **2.** A chilly sensation. **3.** A viral respiratory infection. **—cold′ly** *adv.* **—cold′ness** *n.*

**cole•slaw** (kōl′slô′) *n.* Also **cole slaw.** A salad made from shredded raw cabbage.

**col•lab•o•rate** (kə-lăb′ə-rāt′) *v.* **-rated, -rating.** **1.** To work together. **2.** To cooperate with an occupying enemy force. **—col•lab′o•ra′tion** *n.* **—col•lab′o•ra′tive** *adj.* **—col•lab′o•ra′tor** *n.*

**col•lapse** (kə-lăps′) *v.* **-lapsed, -lapsing.** **1.** To fall down; cave in. **2.** To break down. **—col•lapse′** *n.* **—col•laps′i•ble** *adj.*

**col•lar** (kŏl′ər) *n.* A band of a garment that encircles the neck. —*v.* To seize or detain.

**col•lat•er•al** (kə-lăt′ər-əl) *adj.* **1.** Side-by-side. **2.** Secondary. —*n.* Property acceptable as security for a loan.

**col•league** (kŏl′ēg′) *n.* A fellow worker or member of a profession.

**col•lect** (kə-lĕkt′) *v.* **1.** To assemble; accumulate. **2.** To obtain payment of. —*adj. & adv.* With payment to be made by the receiver. **—col•lec′tion** *n.* **—col•lec′tive** *adj. & n.* **—col•lec′tive•ly** *adv.* **—col•lec′tor** *n.*

**col•lege** (kŏl′ĭj) *n.* A school of higher learning. **—col•le′gian** *n.* **—col•le′giate** *adj.*

**col•lide** (kə-līd′) *v.* **-lided, -liding.** To come together violently. **—col•li′sion** *n.*

**col•lie** (kŏl'ē) *n.* A large, long-haired dog.

**col•lo•qui•al** (kə-lō'kwē-əl) *adj.* Used in conversation but not formal writing. **—col•lo'qui•al•ism'** *n.* **—col•lo'qui•al•ly** *adv.*

**col•lu•sion** (kə-lo͞o'zhən) *n.* A secret, deceitful agreement. **—col•lu'sive** *adj.*

**co•logne** (kə-lōn') *n.* A perfumed liquid.

**co•lon**[1] (kō'lən) *n.* A punctuation mark (:).

**co•lon**[2] (kō'lən) *n., pl.* **-lons** or **-la.** A section of the large intestine. **—co•lon'ic** *adj.*

**colo•nel** (kûr'nəl) *n.* An officer ranking above a lieutenant colonel. **—colo'nel•cy, colo'nel•ship'** *n.*

**col•on•nade** (kŏl'ə-nād') *n.* A row of columns.

**col•o•ny** (kŏl'ə-nē) *n., pl.* **-nies. 1.** A group of settlers far from but subject to a parent country. **2.** A region politically controlled by another country. **3.** A group living together. **—co•lo'ni•al** *adj.* **—co•lo'ni•al•ism** *n.* **—col'o•nist** *n.* **—col'o•ni•za'tion** *n.* **—col'o•nize** *v.* **—col'o•niz'er** *n.*

**col•or** (kŭl'ər) *n.* **1.** The perceived quality of the light reflected or emitted by an object. **2.** A dye, paint, etc. **3.** Skin tone; complexion. **4. colors.** A flag. **5.** Vividness or picturesqueness. *—v.* **1.** To impart color to. **2.** To influence. **3.** To misrepresent. **4.** To blush. **—col'or•a'tion** *n.* **—col'or•ful** *adj.* **—col'or•ful•ly** *adv.* **—col'or•less** *adj.* **—col'or•less•ly** *adv.*

**co•los•sal** (kə-lŏs'əl) *adj.* Enormous; gigantic. **—co•los'sal•ly** *adv.*

**colt** (kōlt) *n.* A young male horse.

**col•umn** (kŏl'əm) *n.* **1.** An upright rod-shaped structure; pillar. **2.** A vertical section of print on a page. **3.** A regular feature article. **4.** A long row, as of troops. **—col'um•nist** *n.*

**co•ma** (kō'mə) *n., pl.* **-mas.** A deep, prolonged unconsciousness. **—co'ma•tose** *adj.*

**comb** (kōm) *n.* **1.** A thin, toothed object for arranging the hair. **2.** A fleshy crest on a bird's head. *—v.* **1.** To arrange with a comb. **2.** To search thoroughly.

**com•bat** (kəm-băt', kŏm'băt') *v.* To fight against; contend. *—n.* Fighting, esp. armed battle. **—com•bat'ant** *adj. & n.* **—com•bat'ive** *adj.*

**com•bi•na•tion** (kŏm'bə-nā'shən) *n.* **1.** The act of combining. **2.** A group; aggregate. **3.** A sequence of numbers used to open a lock.

**com•bine** (kəm-bīn') *v.* **-bined, -bining.** To unite; merge; blend. *—n.* (kŏm'bīn') A machine that harvests and threshes grain. **—com•bin'er** *n.*

**com•bus•ti•ble** (kəm-bŭs'tə-bəl) *adj.* Capable of burning. *—n.* A combustible substance. **—com•bus'ti•bil'i•ty** *n.* **—com•bus'ti•bly** *adv.* **—com•bus'tion** *n.*

**come** (kŭm) *v.* **came** (kām), **coming. 1.** To advance; approach. **2.** To arrive. **3.** To happen. **4.** To issue; originate.

**com•e•dy** (kŏm'ĭ-dē) *n., pl.* **-dies. 1.** A humorous drama. **2.** Humor. **—co•me'dic** *adj.* **—co•me'di•an** *n.*

**come•ly** (kŭm'lē) *adj.* **-lier, -liest.** Attractive; handsome. **—come'li•ness** *n.*

**com•et** (kŏm'ĭt) *n.* A celestial body having a long, bright tail.

**com•fort** (kŭm'fərt) *v.* To soothe, console. *—n.* **1.** Ease or well-being. **2.** Consolation; solace. **3.** One that brings ease. **—com'fort•a•ble** *adj.* **—com'fort•a•bly** *adv.* **—com'fort•er** *n.*

**com•ic** (kŏm'ĭk) *adj.* Also **com•i•cal. 1.** Of comedy. **2.** Amusing; humorous. *—n.* A comedian. **—com'i•cal•ly** *adv.*

**com•ma** (kŏm'ə) *n.* A punctuation mark (,).

**com•mand** (kə-mănd') *v.* **1.** To give orders (to). **2.** To rule. *—n.* **1.** An order. **2.** The authority to command. **3.** A unit, etc., under 1 officer. **4.** An electronic signal actuating an apparatus. **—com'man•dant** *n.* **—com•mand'er** *n.* **—com•mand'ing** *adj.* **—com•mand'ing•ly** *adv.*

**com•mand•ment** (kə-mănd'mənt) *n.* A command; edict.

**com•mem•o•rate** (kə-mĕm'ə-rāt') *v.* **-rated, -rating. 1.** To honor the memory of. **2.** To serve as a memorial to. **—com•mem'o•ra'tion** *n.* **—com•mem'o•ra•tive** *adj.*

**com•mence** (kə-mĕns') *v.* **-menced, -mencing.** To begin; start.

**com•mence•ment** (kə-mĕns'mənt) *n.* **1.** A beginning. **2.** A graduation ceremony.

**com•mend** (kə-mĕnd′) *v.* **1.** To recommend. **2.** To praise. **—com•mend′a•ble** *adj.* **—com•mend′a•bly** *adv.* **—com′men•da′tion** *n.*

**com•ment** (kŏm′ĕnt) *n.* A remark; observation; note. *—v.* To make a comment (on).

**com•men•tar•y** (kŏm′ən-tĕr′ē) *n., pl.* **-ies.** A series of explanations.

**com•men•ta•tor** (kŏm′ən-tā′tər) *n.* A radio or television reporter.

**com•merce** (kŏm′ərs) *n.* The buying and selling of goods; trade.

**com•mer•cial** (kə-mûr′shəl) *adj.* **1.** Of or engaged in commerce. **2.** Having profit as a major aim. *—n.* An advertisement. **—com•mer′cial•ism** *n.* **—com•mer′cial•ize** *v.*

**com•mis•er•ate** (kə-mĭz′ə-rāt′) *v.* **-ated, -ating.** To sympathize. **—com•mis′er•a′tion** *n.*

**com•mis•sar•y** (kŏm′ĭ-sĕr′ē) *n., pl.* **-ies.** A food store on a military post.

**com•mis•sion** (kə-mĭsh′ən) *n.* **1.** Authorization to carry out a task. **2.** A group authorized to perform certain duties. **3.** A committing; perpetration. **4.** An allowance to a salesman or agent for his services. **5.** A document conferring the rank of a military officer. *—v.* **1.** To grant a commission to. **2.** To place an order for.

**com•mis•sion•er** (kə-mĭsh′ə-nər) *n.* **1.** A member of a commission. **2.** An official in charge of a public service.

**com•mit** (kə-mĭt′) *v.* **-mitted, -mitting. 1.** To do; perform. **2.** To consign; entrust. **3.** To place in confinement. **4.** To pledge; bind. **—com•mit′ment** *n.*

**com•mit•tee** (kə-mĭt′ē) *n.* A group delegated to perform a function.

**com•mode** (kə-mōd′) *n.* **1.** A low cabinet. **2.** A toilet.

**com•mod•i•ty** (kə-mŏd′ĭ-tē) *n., pl.* **-ties.** An agricultural or mining product.

**com•mo•dore** (kŏm′ə-dôr′, -dōr′) *n.* A naval officer.

**com•mon** (kŏm′ən) *adj.* **1.** Belonging to all; joint. **2.** Widespread; prevalent. **3.** Ordinary. **4.** Average. **5.** Vulgar; coarse. *—n.* A tract of public land. **—com′mon•ly** *adv.* **—com′mon•ness** *n.*

**com•mon•place** (kŏm′ən-plās′) *adj.* Ordinary; common. *—n.* Something ordinary, esp. an obvious remark.

**com•mon•weal** (kŏm′ən-wēl′) *n.* The public good.

**com•mon•wealth** (kŏm′ən-wĕlth′) *n.* **1.** The people of a nation or state. **2.** A republic. **3.** A federation.

**com•mo•tion** (kə-mō′shən) *n.* Violent motion; agitation.

**com•mu•nal** (kə-myo͞o′nəl, kŏm′yə-) *adj.* **1.** Of a commune or community. **2.** Public. **—com′mu•nal′i•ty** *n.* **—com•mu′nal•ly** *adv.*

**com•mu•ni•cate** (kə-myo͞o′nĭ-kāt′) *v.* **-cated, -cating. 1.** To make known; impart. **2.** To transmit, as a disease. **—com•mu′ni•ca•ble** *adj.*

**com•mu•ni•ca•tion** (kə-myo͞o′nĭ-kā′shən) *n.* **1.** Transmission. **2.** The exchange of thoughts, messages, etc. **3.** Something communicated. **4. communications.** A means of communicating. **—com•mu′ni•ca′tive** *adj.*

**com•mun•ion** (kə-myo͞on′yən) *n.* **1.** A sharing, as of thoughts or feelings. **2.** A religious or spiritual fellowship. **3. Communion.** The Eucharist.

**com•mu•nism** (kŏm′yə-nĭz′əm) *n.* **1.** An economic system in which factories, farms, etc., are owned in common by the workers. **2. Communism.** Revolutionary struggle toward this system. **—com′mu•nist** *n. & adj.* **—com′mu•nis′tic** *adj.*

**com•mu•ni•ty** (kə-myo͞o′nĭ-tē) *n., pl.* **-ties.** A group of people with common interests living in the same area.

**com•mute** (kə-myo͞ot′) *v.* **-muted, -muting. 1.** To change (a penalty or payment) to a less severe one. **2.** To travel to and from work. **—com′mu•ta′tion** *n.* **—com•mute′** *n.* **—com•mut′er** *n.*

**com•pact** (kəm-păkt′) *adj.* **1.** Closely packed. **2.** Expressed briefly. *—v.* To pack firmly together. *—n.* (kŏm′păkt′). **1.** A small cosmetic case. **2.** An agreement. **—com•pact′ly** *adv.* **—com•pact′ness** *n.*

**compact disk** *n.* A small, round optical plate storing digitally recorded music.

**com•pan•ion** (kəm-păn′yən) *n.* **1.** A comrade; associate. **2.** One of a pair; mate. **—com•pan′ion•ship′** *n.*

**com•pa•ny** (kŭm′pə-nē) *n., pl.* **-nies. 1.** A group of people. **2.** A guest or guests. **3.** A business enterprise. **4.** A subdivision of a regiment.

**com•par•a•tive** (kəm-păr′ə-tĭv) *adj.* **1.** Involving comparison. **2.** Compared to others; relative. **—com•par′a•tive•ly** *adv.*

**com•pare** (kəm-pâr′) *v.* **-pared, -paring. 1.** To represent as similar (with *to*). **2.** To examine the similarities or differences (with *with*). **—beyond** (or **without) compare.** Unequaled. **—com′pa•ra•ble** *adj.* **—com•par′er** *n.* **—com•par′i•son** *n.*

**com•part•ment** (kəm-pärt′mənt) *n.* A space or subdivision sectioned off.

**com•pass** (kŭm′pəs, kŏm′-) *n.* **1.** A device for finding direction. **2.** A device for drawing circles. **3.** A range or scope.

**com•pas•sion** (kəm-păsh′ən) *n.* Sympathy for the suffering; pity. **—com•pas′sion•ate** *adj.*

**com•pat•i•ble** (kəm-păt′ə-bəl) *adj.* Capable of living or performing together. **—com•pat′i•bil′i•ty, com•pat′i•ble•ness** *n.* **—com•pat′i•bly** *adv.*

**com•pa•tri•ot** (kəm-pā′trē-ət, -ŏt′) *n.* A fellow citizen.

**com•pel** (kəm-pĕl′) *v.* **-pelled, -pelling.** To force.

**com•pen•sate** (kŏm′pən-sāt′) *v.* **-sated, -sating. 1.** To make up for. **2.** To pay. **—com•pen•sa′tion** *n.* **—com•pen′sa•to•ry** *adj.*

**com•pete** (kəm-pēt′) *v.* **-peted, -peting.** To contend with another; vie.

**com•pe•tent** (kŏm′pĭ-tənt) *adj.* **1.** Properly qualified; capable. **2.** Adequate. **—com′pe•tence** *n.* **—com′pe•tent•ly** *adv.*

**com•pe•ti•tion** (kŏm′pĭ-tĭsh′ən) *n.* **1.** A vying with others; struggle. **2.** A contest of skill. **—com•pet′i•tive** *adj.* **—com•pet′i•tive•ness** *n.* **—com•pet′i•tor** *n.*

**com•pile** (kəm-pīl′) *v.* **-piled, -piling.** To compose from diverse sources. **—com′pi•la′tion** *n.* **—com•pil′er** *n.*

**com•pla•cen•cy** (kəm-plā′sən-sē) *n.* Also **com•pla•cence.** Self-satisfaction; smugness. **—com•pla′cent** *adj.* **—com•pla′cent•ly** *adv.*

**com•plain** (kəm-plān′) *v.* **1.** To express pain, dissatisfaction, or resentment. **2.** To make a formal accusation. **—com•plain′er** *n.* **—com•plaint′** *n.*

**com•ple•ment** (kŏm′plə-mənt) *n.* **1.** Something that completes or balances. **2.** Full quantity or allowance. *—v.* To complete; balance. **—com′ple•men′ta•ry** *adj.*

**com•plete** (kəm-plēt′) *adj.* **1.** Having all parts. **2.** Concluded; ended. **3.** Thorough; perfect. *—v.* **-pleted, -pleting. 1.** To make whole. **2.** To finish. **—com•plete′ly** *adv.* **—com•ple′tion** *n.*

**com•plex** (kəm-plĕks′, kŏm′plĕks′) *adj.* **1.** Consisting of connected parts. **2.** Intricate; complicated. *—n.* (kŏm′plĕks′) **1.** A whole made of connected parts. **2.** A painful or disruptive set of fixed ideas. **—com•plex′i•ty** *n.*

**com•plex•ion** (kəm-plĕk′shən) *n.* The color and texture of the skin.

**com•pli•cate** (kŏm′plĭ-kāt′) *v.* **-cated, -cating.** To make complex or difficult. **—com′pli•ca′tion** *n.*

**com•plic•i•ty** (kəm-plĭs′ĭ-tē) *n.* The state of being an accomplice, as in wrongdoing.

**com•pli•ment** (kŏm′plə-mənt) *n.* **1.** An expression of praise or admiration. **2.** A formal act of courtesy or respect. *—v.* To pay a compliment to.

**com•pli•men•ta•ry** (kŏm′plə-mĕn′tə-rē, -trē) *adj.* **1.** Expressing a compliment. **2.** Given free.

**com•ply** (kəm-plī′) *v.* **-plied, -plying.** To act in accordance; conform. **—com•pli′ance** *n.* **—com•pli′ant** *adj.*

**com•po•nent** (kəm-pō′nənt) *n.* A part; constituent.

**com•pose** (kəm-pōz′) *v.* **-posed, -posing. 1.** To make up the parts of. **2.** To make by putting parts together. **3.** To create or write, esp. music. **4.** To make calm. **—com•pos′er** *n.* **—com′po•si′tion** *n.*

**com•pos•ite** (kəm-pŏz′ĭt) *adj.* Made up of distinct parts. *—n.* A composite structure. **—com•pos′ite•ly** *adv.*

**com•po•sure** (kəm-pō′zhər) *n.* Self-possession.

**compound** (kŏm-pound′) *v.* **1.** To combine; mix. **2.** To increase. *—adj.* (kŏm′pound′). Consisting of 2 or more parts. *—n.* (kŏm′pound′). **1.** A compound entity. **2.** A combination. **3.** A pure substance consisting of atoms of different elements bound together.

**com•pre•hend** (kŏm′prĭ-hĕnd′) *v.* **1.** To understand. **2.** To include. **—com′pre•**

**hen′si•ble** *adj.* —**com′pre•hen′sion** *n.*

**com•pre•hen•sive** (kŏm′prĭ-hĕn′sĭv) *adj.* Totally inclusive. —**com′pre•hen′sive•ly** *adv.*

**com•press** (kəm-prĕs′) *v.* To press together. —*n.* (kŏm′prĕs′). A pad applied to an injury. —**com•press′i•ble** *adj.* —**com•pres′sion** *n.*

**com•prise** (kəm-prīz′) *v.* **-prised, -prising. 1.** To consist of. **2.** To include; contain.

**com•pro•mise** (kŏm′prə-mīz′) *n.* A settlement in which both sides make concessions. —*v.* **-mised, -mising. 1.** To settle by compromise. **2.** To expose to suspicion. —**com′pro•mis′er** *n.*

**comp•trol•ler** (kən-trō′lər) *n.* A controller.

**com•pul•sion** (kəm-pŭl′shən) *n.* **1.** The act of compelling or the state of being compelled. **2.** An irresistible impulse to act. —**com•pul′sive** *adj.* —**com•pul′sive•ly** *adv.*

**com•pul•so•ry** (kəm-pŭl′sə-rē) *adj.* Obligatory; required. —**com•pul′so•ri•ly** *adv.*

**com•punc•tion** (kəm-pŭngk′shən) *n.* Uneasiness caused by guilt; remorse.

**com•pute** (kəm-pyo͞ot′) *v.* **-puted, -puting. 1.** To calculate. **2.** To determine by or use a computer. —**com•put′a•ble** *adj.* —**com′pu•ta′tion** *n.*

**com•put•er** (kəm-pyo͞o′tər) *n.* One that computes, esp. an electronic machine that performs high-speed calculations and processes them according to a program. —**com•put′er•ize** *v.*

**com•rade** (kom′răd′) *n.* A friend or associate. —**com′rade•ship′** *n.*

**con** (kŏn) *adv.* Against. —**con** *n.*

**con•cave** (kŏn-kāv′) *adj.* Curved inward. —**con•cav′i•ty** *n.*

**con•ceal** (kən-sēl′) *v.* To keep secret; hide. —**con•ceal′er** *n.* —**con•ceal′ment** *n.*

**con•ceit** (kən-sēt′) *n.* **1.** Self-importance; vanity. **2.** A fanciful comparison or notion. —**con•ceit′ed** *adj.*

**con•ceive** (kən-sēv′) *v.* **-ceived, -ceiving. 1.** To become pregnant. **2.** To imagine; understand. —**con•ceiv′a•ble** *adj.* —**con•ceiv′a•bly** *adv.* —**con•ceiv′er** *n.*

**con•cen•trate** (kŏn′sən-trāt′) *v.* **-trated, -trating. 1.** To draw inward; focus. **2.** To think attentively. **3.** To make or become denser. —*n.* A concentrated substance. —**con′cen•tra′tion** *n.*

**con•cept** (kŏn′sĕpt) *n.* An idea.

**con•cep•tion** (kən-sĕp′shən) *n.* **1.** The fact of becoming pregnant. **2.** A beginning; start. **3.** A thought.

**con•cern** (kən-sûrn′) *v.* **1.** To relate to; affect. **2.** To engage the interests of. **3.** To cause uneasiness in. —*n.* **1.** Something of interest. **2.** Earnest regard. **3.** Anxiety; worry. **4.** A business. —**con•cerned′** *adj.* —**con•cern′ing** *prep.*

**con•cert** (kŏn′sûrt′) *n.* **1.** A public musical performance. **2.** Agreement. —*v.* To plan or arrange together. —**con•cert′ed** *adj.*

**con•cer•to** (kən-chĕr′tō) *n., pl.* **-ti** or **-tos.** A composition for an orchestra and 1 or more solo instruments.

**con•ces•sion** (kən-sĕsh′ən) *n.* **1.** The act of conceding. **2.** Something conceded. **3.** The privilege of maintaining a subsidiary business within certain premises.

**conch** (kŏngk, kŏnch) *n., pl.* **conchs** or **conches.** A large spiral sea shell.

**con•cil•i•ate** (kən-sĭl′ē-āt′) *v.* **-ated, -ating.** To overcome the animosity of. —**con•cil′i•a′tion** *n.* —**con•cil′i•a′tor** *n.* —**con•cil′i•a•to′ry** *adj.*

**con•cise** (kən-sīs′) *adj.* Expressing much in few words; succinct. —**con•cise′ly** *adv.* —**con•cise′ness** *n.*

**con•clave** (kŏn′klāv, kŏng′-) *n.* A secret meeting.

**con•clude** (kən-klo͞od′) *v.* **-cluded, -cluding. 1.** To bring to an end. **2.** To agree. **3.** To decide; resolve. —**con•clu′sion** *n.* —**con•clu′sive** *adj.* —**con•clu′sive•ly** *adv.*

**con•cord** (kŏn′kôrd′, kŏng′-) *n.* Harmony. —**con•cord′ant** *adj.*

**con•cor•dance** (kən-kôr′dns) *n.* **1.** Agreement. **2.** An index of all the words in a book.

**con•course** (kŏn′kôrs′, -kōrs′, kŏng′-) *n.* **1.** A crowd. **2.** A large open space for crowds.

**con•crete** (kŏn-krēt′) *adj.* **1.** Particular; specific. **2.** Real; tangible. **3.** Hard; solid. —*n.* A construction material made of gravel and mortar or cement. —**con•crete′ly** *adv.* —**con•cre′tion** *n.*

**con•cur** (kən-kûr′) *v.* **-curred, -curring. 1.** To have the same opinion. **2.** To coincide. **—con•cur′rence** *n.* **—con•cur′rent** *adj.*

**con•cus•sion** (kən-kŭsh′ən) *n.* **1.** A violent jarring; shock. **2.** A brain injury from a blow.

**con•demn** (kən-dĕm′) *v.* **1.** To express disapproval of; censure. **2.** To sentence. **3.** To mark for destruction. **—con′dem•na′tion** *n.*

**con•dense** (kən-dĕns′) *v.* **-densed, -densing. 1.** To compress. **2.** To abridge. **3.** To form a liquid from a vapor. **—con•den′sa•ble** *adj.* **—con′den•sa′tion** *n.* **—con•den′ser** *n.*

**con•de•scend** (kŏn′dĭ-sĕnd′) *v.* To be patronizing; stoop. **—con′de•scen′sion** *n.*

**con•di•tion** (kən-dĭsh′ən) *n.* **1.** A state of being. **2.** State of health. **3.** A disease. **4.** A prerequisite. **5.** A qualification. **6.** Often **conditions.** The existing circumstances. —*v.* **1.** To make conditional. **2.** To put into a proper condition. **—con•di′tion•al** *adj.*

**con•dole** (kən-dōl′) *v.* **-doled, -doling.** To express sympathy to one in grief. **—con•do′lence** *n.* **—con•dol′er** *n.*

**con•duct** (kən-dŭkt′) *v.* **1.** To direct; manage. **2.** To lead or guide. **3.** To transmit. **4.** To behave. —*n.* (kŏn′dŭkt). **1.** The way a person acts. **2.** Management. **—con•duc′tion** *n.* **—con•duc′tive** *adj.*

**con•duc•tor** (kən-dŭk′tər) *n.* **1.** The person in charge of a train, bus, etc. **2.** The director of a musical ensemble. **3.** A substance that conducts electricity, etc.

**cone** (kōn) *n.* **1.** A circular-based figure tapering evenly to a point. **2.** A rounded seed-bearing structure. **—con′ic, con′i•cal** *adj.*

**con•fec•tion** (kən-fĕk′shən) *n.* A sweet food. **—con•fec′tion•er** *n.* **—con•fec′tion•er′y** *n.*

**con•fed•er•ate** (kən-fĕd′ər-ĭt) *n.* **1.** An ally. **2.** An accomplice. —*adj.* United; allied. —*v.* (-ə-rāt′) **-ated, -ating.** To unite. **—con•fed′er•a•cy** *n.* **—con•fed′er•a′tive** *adj.*

**con•fer** (kən-fûr′) *v.* **-ferred, -ferring. 1.** To bestow. **2.** To hold a conference.

**con•fer•ence** (kŏn′fər-əns, -frəns) *n.* **1.** A meeting; consultation. **2.** A league.

**con•fess** (kən-fĕs′) *v.* **1.** To disclose a misdeed or fault. **2.** To concede the truth of. **3.** To declare openly; profess. **—con•fess′ed•ly** *adv.* **—con•fes′sion** *n.* **—con•fes′sor** *n.*

**con•fet•ti** (kən-fĕt′ē) *n.* Bits of colored paper scattered at celebrations.

**con•fi•dant** (kŏn′fĭ-dănt′, -dänt′, kŏn′fĭ-dănt′, -dänt) *n.* One to whom secrets are confided.

**con•fide** (kən-fīd′) *v.* **-fided, -fiding. 1.** To tell in confidence. **2.** To put into another's keeping. **—con•fid′er** *n.*

**con•fi•dence** (kŏn′fĭ-dəns) *n.* **1.** Trust. **2.** Secrecy; privacy. **3.** Something confided. **4.** A feeling of assurance or certainty. **—con′fi•dent** *adj.* **—con′fi•den′tial** *adj.* **—con′fi•dent•ly** *adv.*

**con•fig•u•ra•tion** (kən-fĭg′yə-rā′shən) *n.* The arrangement of the parts; form.

**con•fine** (kən-fīn′) *v.* **-fined, -fining. 1.** To restrict. **2.** To imprison. **—con•fine′ment** *n.* **—con•fin′er** *n.*

**con•firm** (kən-fûrm′) *v.* **1.** To verify. **2.** To strengthen. **3.** To ratify. **4.** To admit as a church member. **—con′fir•ma′tion** *n.*

**con•fis•cate** (kŏn′fĭ-skāt′) *v.* **-cated, -cating.** To seize by authority. **—con′fis•ca′tion** *n.* **—con′fis•ca′tor** *n.*

**con•flict** (kŏn′flĭkt′) *n.* **1.** A prolonged battle. **2.** A disagreement. —*v.* (kən-flĭkt′). To come into opposition; differ.

**con•form** (kən-fôrm′) *v.* **1.** To make or become similar. **2.** To be in agreement. **3.** To act in accordance with customs or rules. **—con•form′ist** *n.* **—con•form′i•ty** *n.*

**con•found** (kən-found′, kŏn-) *v.* To confuse. **—con•found′er** *n.*

**con•front** (kən-frŭnt′) *v.* **1.** To come face to face with. **2.** To face; oppose. **—con′fron•ta′tion** *n.*

**con•fuse** (kən-fyo͞oz′) *v.* **-fused, -fusing. 1.** To perplex. **2.** To mix up. **—con•fus′ed•ly** *adv.* **—con•fus′ing•ly** *adv.* **—con•fu′sion** *n.*

**con•gen•ial** (kən-jēn′yəl) *adj.* Sympathetic; agreeable. **—con•ge′ni•al′i•ty** *n.* **—con•gen′ial•ly** *adv.*

**con•gen•i•tal** (kən-jĕn′ĭ-tl) *adj.* Existing at birth but not hereditary. **—con•gen′i•tal•ly** *adv.*

**con•glom•er•ate** (kən-glŏm′ə-rāt′) *v.* **-ated, -ating.** To form into a dense mass. —*n.* (-ər-ĭt) **1.** A heterogeneous mass. **2.** A business corporation made up of diverse companies. —**con•glom′er•a′tion** *n.*

**con•grat•u•late** (kən-grăch′ə-lāt′) *v.* **-lated, -lating.** To express pleasure at the achievement or good fortune of. —**con•grat′u•la′tion** *n.* —**con•grat′u•la•to′ry** *adj.*

**con•gre•gate** (kŏng′grĭ-gāt′) *v.* **-gated, -gating.** To come together in a crowd. —**con′gre•ga′tion** *n.*

**con•gress** (kŏng′grĭs) *n.* **1.** A formal assembly. **2.** A national legislature. —**con•gres′sion•al** *adj.* —**con′gress•man** *n.* —**con′gress•wom′an** *n.*

**con•ju•gate** (kŏn′jə-gāt′) *v.* **-gated, -gating.** To inflect (a verb). —**con′ju•ga′tion** *n.*

**con•junc•tion** (kən-jŭngk′shən) *n.* **1.** A connection. **2.** Simultaneous occurrence. **3.** A word connecting other words or word groups. —**con•junc′tive** *adj.*

**con•jure** (kŏn′jər, kən-jŏŏr′) *v.* **-jured, -juring. 1.** To entreat. **2.** To summon or effect by or as if by magic. —**con′ju•ra′tion** *n.* —**con′jur•er** *n.*

**con•nect** (kə-nĕkt′) *v.* To join; link; unite. —**con•nect′ed•ly** *adv.* —**con•nec′tion** *n.* —**con•nec′tive** *adj.*

**con•nive** (kə-nīv′) *v.* **-nived, -niving. 1.** To feign ignorance of a wrong. **2.** To cooperate secretly. —**con•niv′ance** *n.* —**con•niv′er** *n.*

**con•nois•seur** (kŏn′ə-sûr′) *n.* An informed judge in matters of taste.

**con•note** (kə-nōt′) *v.* **-noted, -noting.** To suggest in addition to literal meaning. —**con′no•ta′tion** *n.* —**con′no•ta′tive** *adj.*

**con•quer** (kŏng′kər) *v.* **1.** To defeat or subdue. **2.** To overcome. —**con′quer•a•ble** *adj.* —**con′quer•or** *n.* —**con′quest** *n.*

**con•science** (kŏn′shəns) *n.* The faculty of recognizing right and wrong in one's own conduct.

**con•sci•en•tious** (kŏn′shē-ĕn′shəs) *adj.* **1.** Scrupulous; honest. **2.** Painstaking; careful. —**con′sci•en′tious•ly** *adv.* —**con′sci•en′tious•ness** *n.*

**con•scious** (kŏn′shəs) *adj.* **1.** Not asleep; awake. **2.** Aware; cognizant. **3.** Intentional. —**con′scious•ly** *adv.* —**con′scious•ness** *n.*

**con•script** (kŏn′skrĭpt′) *n.* One compulsorily enrolled for military service. —*v.* (kən-skrĭpt′). To draft for military service. —**con•scrip′tion** *n.*

**con•se•crate** (kŏn′sĭ-krāt′) *v.* **-crated, -crating. 1.** To make or declare sacred. **2.** To dedicate. —**con′se•cra′tion** *n.*

**con•sec•u•tive** (kən-sĕk′yə-tĭv) *adj.* Following successively without interruption. —**con•sec′u•tive•ly** *adv.*

**con•sen•sus** (kən-sĕn′səs) *n.* Collective opinion.

**con•sent** (kən-sĕnt′) *v.* To agree. —*n.* Acceptance or approval. —**con•sent′er** *n.*

**con•se•quence** (kŏn′sĭ-kwĕns′, -kwəns) *n.* **1.** An effect. **2.** Importance.

**con•se•quent** (kŏn′sĭ-kwĕnt′, -kwənt) *adj.* Following as a result. —**con′se•quent′ly** *adv.*

**con•ser•va•tive** (kən-sûr′və-tĭv) *adj.* **1.** Favoring preservation of the existing order. **2.** Moderate; cautious. **3.** Traditional. —*n.* A conservative person. —**con•ser′va•tism** *n.*

**con•ser•va•to•ry** (kən-sûr′və-tôr′ē, -tōr′ē) *n.* pl. **-ries.** A school of music or dramatic art.

**con•serve** (kən-sûrv′) *v.* **-served, -serving. 1.** To protect; preserve. **2.** To preserve (fruits). —**con•serv′a•ble** *adj.* —**con′ser•va′tion** *n.*

**con•sid•er** (kən-sĭd′ər) *v.* **1.** To deliberate upon; examine. **2.** To think or deem.

**con•sid•er•a•ble** (kən-sĭd′ər-ə-bəl) *adj.* Fairly large or significant. —**con•sid′er•a•bly** *adv.*

**con•sid•er•ate** (kən-sĭd′ər-ĭt) *adj.* Having regard for the needs or feelings of others. —**con•sid′er•ate•ness** *n.*

**con•sid•er•a•tion** (kən-sĭd′ə-rā′shən) *n.* **1.** Deliberation. **2.** A factor. **3.** Thoughtfulness. —**con•sid′er•ing** *prep. & adv.*

**con•sign** (kən-sīn′) *v.* **1.** To entrust. **2.** To deliver. **3.** To allot. —**con•sign′ment** *n.* —**con•sign′or** *n.*

**con•sist** (kən-sĭst′) *v.* **1.** To be composed (with *of*). **2.** To be inherent; lie (with *in*).

**con•sis•ten•cy** (kən-sĭs′tən-sē) *n., pl.* **-cies.** Also **con•sis•tence. 1.** Agreement or compatability. **2.** Steadiness; invariability. **3.** Thickness. **—con•sis'tent** *adj.* **—con•sis'tent•ly** *adv.*

**console** (kən-sōl') *v.* **-soled, -soling.** To comfort. **—con'so•la'tion** *n.* **—con•sol'er** *n.*

**con•sol•i•date** (kən-sŏl'ĭ-dāt') *v.* **-dated, -dating. 1.** To solidify. **2.** To unite; combine. **—con•sol'i•da'tor** *n.*

**con•som•mé** (kŏn'sə-mā') *n.* A clear soup.

**con•so•nant** (kŏn'sə-nənt) *adj.* In agreement. *—n.* A letter representing a speech sound produced by obstructing the air flow.

**con•sort** (kŏn'sôrt') *n.* A spouse, esp. of a monarch. *—v.* (kən-sôrt') To keep company; associate.

**con•sor•ti•um** (kən-sôr'tē-əm, -shē-əm) *n., pl.* **-tia. 1.** An association of businesses in a venture, esp. in international finance. **2.** The right of 1 spouse for the company and affection of the other.

**con•spic•u•ous** (kən-spĭk'yo͞o-əs) *adj.* Easily seen; obvious. **—con•spic'u•ous•ly** *adv.* **—con•spic'u•ous•ness** *n.*

**con•spire** (kən-spīr') *v.* **-spired, -spiring.** To plan secretly; plot. **—con•spir'a•cy** *n.* **—con•spir'a•tor** *n.* **—con•spir'a•to'ri•al** *adj.* **—con•spir'er** *n.*

**con•sta•ble** (kŏn'stə-bəl, kŭn'-) *n.* A police officer.

**con•stant** (kŏn'stənt) *adj.* **1.** Persistent. **2.** Unchanging. **3.** Steadfast. *—n.* A thing that is unchanging. **—con'stan•cy** *n.* **—con'stant•ly** *adv.*

**con•stel•la•tion** (kŏn'stə-lā'shən) *n.* A group of stars.

**con•ster•na•tion** (kŏn'stər-nā'shən) *n.* Alarm.

**con•sti•pa•tion** (kŏn'stə-pā'shən) *n.* Difficult evacuation of the bowels. **—con'sti•pate'** *v.*

**con•stit•u•ent** (kən-stĭch'o͞o-ənt) *adj.* Serving as part of a whole. *—n.* **1.** One represented by an elected official. **2.** A component. **—con•stit'u•en•cy** *n.*

**con•sti•tute** (kŏn'stĭ-t/y/o͞ot') *v.* **-tuted, -tuting. 1.** To make up; compose. **2.** To establish.

**con•sti•tu•tion** (kŏn'stĭ-t/y/o͞o'shən) *n.* **1.** Composition; make-up. **2.** The basic law of a politically organized body. **—con'sti•tu'tion•al** *adj.* **—con'sti•tu•tion•al'i•ty** *n.*

**con•strain** (kən-strān') *v.* **1.** To compel; oblige. **2.** To confine. **3.** To make uneasy. **—con•strain'a•ble** *adj.* **—con•strain'er** *n.* **—con•straint'** *n.*

**con•strict** (kən-strĭkt') *v.* To make narrower; squeeze. **—con•stric'tion** *n.* **—con•stric'tive** *adj.* **—con•stric'tor** *n.*

**con•struct** (kən-strŭkt') *v.* To build. **—con•struc'tion** *n.* **—con•struc'tor** *n.*

**con•struc•tive** (kən-strŭk'tĭv) *adj.* Useful; helpful. **—con•struc'tive•ly** *adv.*

**con•sul** (kŏn'səl) *n.* An official appointed by a government to reside in a foreign city and represent its citizens there. **—con'su•lar** *adj.* **—con'su•late** *n.*

**con•sult** (kən-sŭlt') *v.* **1.** To seek the advice of. **2.** To confer. **—con•sult'ant** *n.* **—con•sul•ta'tion** *n.* **—con•sult'a•tive** *adj.*

**con•sume** (kən-so͞om') *v.* **-sumed, -suming. 1.** To eat up. **2.** To expend. **3.** To destroy. **—con•sum'a•ble** *adj.* **—con•sum'er** *n.*

**con•sum•mate** (kŏn'sə-māt') *v.* **-mated, -mating.** To complete; achieve. *—adj.* (kən-sŭm'ĭt). Perfect; complete. **—con•sum'mate•ly** *adv.*

**con•sump•tion** (kən-sŭmp'shən) *n.* **1.** The act or process of consuming. **2.** The amount consumed. **3.** Tuberculosis.

**con•tact** (kŏn'tăkt') *n.* **1.** A coming together or touching. **2.** A relationship; association. **3.** Connection. *—v.* **1.** To come or put into contact. **2.** To get in touch with.

**con•ta•gion** (kən-tā'jən) *n.* Disease transmission by contact. **—con•ta'gious** *adj.*

**con•tain** (kən-tān') *v.* **1.** To enclose. **2.** To have within; include. **3.** To be able to hold. **4.** To restrict. **—con•tain'er** *n.* **—con•tain'ment** *n.*

**con•tam•i•nate** (kən-tăm'ə-nāt') *v.* **-nated, -nating.** To make impure. **—con•tam'i•na'tion** *n.*

**con•tem•plate** (kŏn'təm-plāt') *v.* **-plated, -plating. 1.** To ponder or consider. **2.** To intend; expect. **—con'tem•pla'tion** *n.* **—con•tem'pla•tive** *adj.*

**con•tem•po•rar•y** (kən-tĕm'pə-rĕr'ē) *adj.* **1.** Belonging to the same period of time. **2.** Current; modern. *—n., pl.* **-ies.**

**1.** One of the same time or age. **2.** A person of the present time. **—con•tem′po•ra′ne•ous** *adj.*

**con•tempt** (kən-tĕmpt′) *n.* **1.** Bitter scorn; disdain. **2.** Open disrespect to a court, legislature, etc. **—con•temp′tu•ous** *adj.* **—con•temp′tu•ous•ly** *adv.* **—con•temp′tu•ous•ness** *n.*

**con•tempt•i•ble** (kən-tĕmp′tə-bəl) *adj.* Deserving contempt.

**con•tend** (kən-tĕnd′) *v.* **1.** To compete; struggle. **2.** To maintain. **—con•tend′er** *n.*

**con•tent[1]** (kŏn′tĕnt′) *n.* **1.** Often **contents.** That which is contained in something. **2.** Substance; meaning.

**con•tent[2]** (kən-tĕnt′) *adj.* Satisfied. *—v.* To satisfy. *—n.* Satisfaction. **—con•tent′ed** *adj.* **—con•tent′ment** *n.*

**con•ten•tion** (kən-tĕn′shən) *n.* **1.** Competition. **2.** Dispute. **—con•ten′tious** *adj.* **—con•ten′tious•ness** *n.*

**con•test** (kŏn′tĕst′) *n.* **1.** A struggle; fight. **2.** A competition. *—v.* (kən-tĕst′) **1.** To compete for. **2.** To challenge. **—con•test′ant** *n.*

**con•text** (kŏn′tĕkst) *n.* **1.** Situation; environment. **2.** The surrounding words. **—con•tex′tu•al** *adj.*

**con•tig•u•ous** (kən-tĭg′yo͞o-əs) *adj.* **1.** Touching. **2.** Next to. **—con′ti•gu′i•ty** *n.*

**con•ti•nent** (kŏn′tə-nənt) *n.* One of the principal land masses of the earth. **—con′ti•nen′tal** *adj.*

**con•tin•gen•cy** (kən-tĭn′jən-sē) *n., pl.* **-cies.** A possible event.

**con•tin•gent** (kən-tĭn′jənt) *adj.* **1.** Possible. **2.** Conditional. *—n.* **1.** A quota, as of troops. **2.** A representative group.

**con•tin•ue** (kən-tĭn′yo͞o) *v.* **-ued, -uing. 1.** To persist. **2.** To last. **3.** To remain. **4.** To resume. **5.** To extend. **6.** To postpone or adjourn. **—con•tin′u•al** *adj.* **—con•tin′u•al•ly** *adv.* **—con•tin′u•ance** *n.* **—con•tin′u•a′tion** *n.*

**con•ti•nu•i•ty** (kŏn′tə-n/y/o͞o′ĭ-tē) *n., pl.* **-ties. 1.** Continuousness. **2.** An uninterrupted succession.

**con•tin•u•ous** (kən-tĭn′yo͞o-əs) *adj.* Extending without interruption; unbroken. **—con•tin′u•ous•ly** *adv.*

**con•tort** (kən-tôrt′) *v.* To twist out of shape. **—con•tor′tion** *n.*

**con•tour** (kŏn′to͝or′) *n.* **1.** The outline of a figure, body, or mass. **2.** A line joining points of equal elevation.

**con•tra•band** (kŏn′trə-bănd′) *n.* Smuggled goods.

**con•tra•cep•tion** (kŏn′trə-sĕp′shən) *n.* Prevention of conception. **—con′tra•cep′tive** *adj. & n.*

**con•tract** (kŏn′trăkt′) *n.* A legal agreement. *—v.* (kən-trăkt′, kŏn′trăkt′) **1.** To enter into or establish by contract. **2.** To catch (a disease). **3.** To shrink. **4.** To shorten by omitting letters. **—con•trac′tion** *n.* **—con′trac′tor** *n.*

**con•tra•dict** (kŏn′trə-dĭkt′) *v.* **1.** To assert the opposite of. **2.** To be inconsistent with. **—con′tra•dic′tion** *n.* **—con′tra•dic′to•ry** *adj.*

**con•tral•to** (kən-trăl′tō) *n., pl.* **-tos.** The lowest female voice.

**con•trap•tion** (kən-trăp′shən) *n.* An elaborate device.

**con•trar•y** (kŏn′trĕr′ē) *adj.* **1.** Opposite. **2.** Adverse. **3.** Perverse; willful. *—n., pl.* **-ries.** The opposite. *—adv.* In opposition. **—con′tra′ri•ly** *adv.* **—con′trar′i•wise′** *adv.*

**con•trast** (kən-trăst′) *v.* **1.** To set in opposition in order to show differences. **2.** To show differences when compared. *—n.* (kŏn′trăst′) Dissimilarity.

**con•trib•ute** (kən-trĭb′yo͞ot) *v.* **-uted, -uting.** To give to or participate in a common fund or effort. **—con′tri•bu′tion** *n.* **—con•trib′u•tor** *n.* **—con•trib′u•to′ry** *adj.*

**con•trite** (kən-trīt′) *adj.* Repentant. **—con•trite′ly** *adv.* **—con•tri′tion** *n.*

**con•trive** (kən-trīv′) *v.* **-trived, -triving. 1.** To devise. **2.** To make. **3.** To manage or effect. **—con•triv′ance** *n.*

**con•trol** (kən-trōl′) *v.* **-trolled, -trolling.** To regulate; direct. *—n.* **1.** Power to regulate, direct, or dominate. **2.** Restraint; reserve. **3.** An instrument for regulating a machine. **—con•trol′la•ble** *adj.*

**con•trol•ler** (kən-trō′lər) *n.* **1.** One who controls. **2.** A regulating mechanism, as on a ship. **3.** Also **comptroller.** The chief financial officer of an organization.

**con•tro•ver•sy** (kŏn′trə-vûr′sē) *n., pl.* **-sies.** A public dispute. **—con′tro•ver′sial** *adj.*

**con•va•lesce** (kŏn′və-lĕs′) *v.* **-lesced, -lescing.** To recuperate from an illness. **—con′va•les′cence** *n.* **—con′va•les′cent** *adj. & n.*

**con•vene** (kən-vēn′) *v.* **-vened, -vening.** To meet together; assemble.

**con•ven•ient** (kən-vēn′yənt) *adj.* **1.** Suited to one's comfort or needs. **2.** Easy to reach; accessible. **—con•ven′ience** *n.* **—con•ven′ient•ly** *adv.*

**con•vent** (kŏn′vənt′) *n.* A religious community, esp. of nuns.

**con•ven•tion** (kən-vĕn′shən) *n.* **1.** A formal assembly. **2.** An international agreement. **3.** An accepted or prescribed practice.

**con•ven•tion•al** (kən-vĕn′shə-nəl) *adj.* **1.** Customary. **2.** Commonplace or ordinary. **—con•ven′tion•al•ism′** *n.* **—con•ven′tion•al′i•ty** *n.* **—con•ven′tion•al•ly** *adv.*

**con•verge** (kən-vûrj′) *v.* **-verged, -verging.** To tend toward a common point. **—con•ver′gence, con•ver′gen•cy** *n.* **—con•ver′gent** *adj.*

**con•ver•sa•tion** (kŏn′vər-sā′shən) *n.* A spoken exchange; talk. **—con′ver•sa′tion•al** *adj.*

**con•verse[1]** (kən-vûrs′) *v.* **-versed, -versing.** To talk.

**con•verse[2]** (kən-vûrs′, kŏn′vûrs′) *adj.* Reversed. *—n.* The opposite. **—con•verse′ly** *adv.*

**con•vert** (kən-vûrt′) *v.* **1.** To change into another form; transform. **2.** To persuade or be persuaded to adopt a new religion. **3.** To adapt. *—n.* (kŏn′vûrt′). A converted person. **—con•ver′sion** *n.* **—con•vert′er, con•ver′tor** *n.*

**con•vert•i•ble** (kən-vûr′tə-bəl) *adj.* Capable of being converted. *—n.* An automobile with a movable top.

**con•vex** (kŏn′vĕks′, kən-vĕks′) *adj.* Curved outward. **—con•vex′i•ty** *n.*

**con•vey** (kən-vā′) *v.* **1.** To carry. **2.** To transmit. **—con•vey′er, con•vey′or** *n.*

**con•vey•ance** (kən-vā′əns) *n.* **1.** The act of transporting. **2.** A vehicle.

**con•vict** (kən-vĭkt′) *v.* To find or prove guilty. *—n.* (kŏn′vĭkt′). A person serving a prison sentence.

**con•vic•tion** (kən-vĭk′shən) *n.* **1.** The state of being convicted. **2.** A belief.

**con•vince** (kən-vĭns′) *v.* **-vinced, -vincing.** To bring to belief; persuade. **—con•vinc′er** *n.* **—con•vinc′ing** *adj.* **—con•vinc′ing•ly** *adv.*

**con•viv•i•al** (kən-vĭv′ē-əl) *adj.* Sociable; jovial. **—con•viv′i•al′i•ty** *n.*

**con•vo•lu•tion** (kŏn′və-lo͞o′shən) *n.* **1.** A coiling or twisting together. **2.** An intricacy. **—con′vo•lut′ed** *adj.*

**con•voy** (kŏn′voi′, kən-voi′) *v.* To escort for protection. *—n.* An accompanying force.

**con•vulse** (kən-vŭls′) *v.* **-vulsed, -vulsing.** **1.** To shake violently. **2.** To cause involuntary muscular contractions. **—con•vul′sion** *n.* **—con•vul′sive** *adj.*

**cook** (ko͝ok) *v.* To heat (food) for eating. *—n.* One who prepares food for eating. **—cook′er•y** *n.*

**cook•ie, cook•y** (ko͝ok′ē) *n., pl.* **-ies.** A small, sweet cake.

**cool** (ko͞ol) *adj.* **1.** Moderately cold. **2.** Calm; controlled. **3.** Indifferent. *—v.* To make or become cool. *—n.* **1.** Moderate cold. **2.** Composure. **—cool′ly** *adv.* **—cool′ness** *n.*

**coop** (ko͞op) *n.* A cage, as for poultry. *—v.* To confine.

**co•op•er•ate** (kō-ŏp′ə-rāt′) *v.* **-ated, -ating.** To work together. **—co•op′er•a′tion** *n.*

**co•op•er•a•tive** (kō-ŏp′ər-ə-tĭv, -ə-rā′tĭv, -ŏp′rə-) *adj.* **1.** Willing to cooperate. **2.** Engaged in joint economic activity. *—n.* An enterprise collectively owned and operated. **—co•op′er•a•tive•ly** *adv.*

**co-opt** (kō-ŏpt′, kō′ŏpt′) *v.* **1.** To elect as a fellow member. **2.** To appoint summarily. **3.** To appropriate. **4.** To assimilate. **—co′-op•ta′tion** *n.* **—co-op′ta•tive** *adj.*

**co•or•di•nate** (kō-ôr′dn-ĭt) *adj.* Of equal rank or order. *—v.* (-āt′) **-nated, -nating.** To harmonize in a common action. **—co•or′di•nate•ly** *adv.* **—co•or′di•na′tion** *n.* **—co•or′di•na′tor** *n.*

**cope** (kōp) *v.* **coped, coping.** To contend, esp. with success.

**co•pi•ous** (kō′pē-əs) *adj.* Abundant. **—co′pi•ous•ly** *adv.* **—co′pi•ous•ness** *n.*

**cop•per** (kŏp′ər) *n.* A reddish-brown metallic element.

**cop•y** (kŏp′ē) *n., pl.* **-ies.** **1.** A reproduction; duplicate. **2.** A manuscript to be set in type. —*v.* **-ied, -ying. 1.** To make a copy of. **2.** To imitate.

**cop•y•right** (kŏp'ē-rīt') *n.* The exclusive right to publish, sell, or distribute a literary or artistic work. **—cop'y•right'** *v.*

**cor•al** (kôr'əl, kŏr'əl) *n.* **1.** A stony substance formed from the massed skeletons of minute marine organisms. **2.** Yellowish red or pink. **—cor'al** *adj.*

**cord** (kôrd) *n.* **1.** A thick string or small rope. **2.** An insulated electric wire. **3.** Fabric with raised ribs. **4.** A unit of cut fuel wood, equal to 128 cubic feet. —*v.* To fasten with a cord.

**cor•dial** (kôr'jəl) *adj.* Hearty; warm. —*n.* **1.** A stimulant. **2.** A liqueur. **—cor'-dial'i•ty** *n.* **—cor'dial•ly** *adv.*

**cor•du•roy** (kôr'də-roi') *n.* A ribbed cotton fabric.

**core** (kôr, kōr) *n.* **1.** The central part of certain fruits. **2.** The center; essence. —*v.* **cored, coring.** To remove the core of. **—cor'er** *n.*

**cork** (kôrk) *n.* **1.** The light, porous bark of a cork oak. **2.** A bottle stopper. —*v.* To stop with a cork.

**cork•screw** (kôrk'skrōō') *n.* A spiral-shaped device for drawing corks from bottles. —*adj.* Spiral.

**corn¹** (kôrn) *n.* A cereal grass bearing seeds on large ears. —*v.* To preserve in brine. **—corn'y** *adj.*

**corn²** (kôrn) *n.* A horny thickening of the skin, usually on a toe.

**cor•ne•a** (kôr'nē-ə) *n.* A transparent, convex structure covering the lens of the eye. **—cor'ne•al** *adj.*

**cor•ner** (kôr'nər) *n.* **1.** The place where 2 streets or other lines meet. **2.** A region. **3.** Complete control of a stock or commodity. —*v.* **1.** To drive into a corner. **2.** To form a corner in (a stock or commodity).

**cor•nu•co•pi•a** (kôr'nə-kō'pē-ə) *n.* A cone-shaped horn overflowing with fruit and flowers.

**cor•ol•lar•y** (kôr'ə-lĕr-ē, kŏr'-) *n., pl.* **-ies. 1.** A proposition that follows from one already proven. **2.** A consequence; result.

**cor•o•nar•y** (kôr'ə-nĕr-ē, kŏr'-) *adj.* Of the heart or the arteries that supply it with blood.

**cor•o•na•tion** (kôr'ə-nā'shən, kŏr'-) *n.* The crowning of a sovereign.

**cor•o•ner** (kôr'ə-nər, kŏr'-) *n.* A public officer who investigates deaths.

**cor•o•net** (kôr'ə-nĕt', kŏr'-) *n.* A small crown.

**cor•po•ral¹** (kôr'pər-əl) *adj.* Of the body.

**cor•po•ral²** (kôr'pər-əl, -prəl) *n.* A noncommissioned officer of the lowest rank.

**cor•po•ra•tion** (kôr'pə-rā'shən) *n.* A body of persons legally recognized as a separate entity, usually to conduct a business enterprise. **—cor'po•rate** *adj.*

**cor•po•re•al** (kôr-pôr'ē-əl, -pōr'-) *adj.* **1.** Bodily. **2.** Material; tangible.

**corps** (kôr, kōr) *n., pl.* **corps. 1.** A branch of the armed forces. **2.** A body of persons.

**corpse** (kôrps) *n.* A dead body, esp. of a human being.

**cor•pu•lence** (kôr'pyə-ləns) *n.* Fatness; obesity. **—cor'pu•lent** *adj.*

**cor•pus•cle** (kôr'pə-səl, -pŭs'əl) *n.* A body cell capable of free movement in a fluid. **—cor•pus'cu•lar** *adj.*

**cor•ral** (kə-răl') *n.* An enclosure for livestock. —*v.* **-ralled, -ralling. 1.** To drive into and hold in a corral. **2.** *Informal.* To seize.

**cor•rect** (kə-rĕkt') *v.* **1.** To remove the mistakes from. **2.** To mark the errors in. **3.** To admonish or punish. **4.** To adjust. —*adj.* **1.** Accurate or true. **2.** Proper. **—cor•rec'tion** *n.* **—cor•rec'tive** *adj. & n.* **—cor•rect'ly** *adv.* **—cor•rect'ness** *n.*

**cor•re•la•tion** (kôr'ə-lā'shən, kŏr'-) *n.* A relationship; correspondence. **—cor're•late'** *v.*

**cor•re•spond** (kôr'ĭ-spŏnd', kŏr'-) *v.* **1.** To be similar or equal (with *to*). **2.** To communicate by letter (with *with*). **—cor're•spon'dence** *n.* **—cor're•spon'dent** *n. & adj.*

**cor•ri•dor** (kôr'ĭ-dər, -dôr', kŏr'-) *n.* A long passageway.

**cor•rob•o•rate** (kə-rŏb'ə-rāt') *v.* **-rated, -rating.** To strengthen or support (other evidence). **—cor•rob'o•ra'tion** *n.*

**cor•rode** (kə-rōd') *v.* **-roded, -roding.** To wear away gradually. **—cor•ro'sion** *n.* **—cor•ro'sive** *adj.*

**cor•ru•gate** (kôr′ə-gāt′, kŏr′-) *v.* **-gated, -gating.** To make folds or ridges in. **—cor′ru•ga′tion** *n.*

**cor•rupt** (kə-rŭpt′) *adj.* **1.** Immoral; perverted. **2.** Bribe-taking. **3.** Decaying. —*v.* To make or become corrupt. **—cor•rupt′i•ble** *adj.* **—cor•rup′tion** *n.* **—cor•rup′tive** *adj.* **—cor•rupt′ly** *adv.*

**cor•sage** (kôr-säzh′) *n.* A small bouquet worn by a woman.

**cor•set** (kôr′sĭt) *n.* A close-fitting, supportive undergarment.

**cor•tex** (kôr′tĕks′) *n.* The outer layer of an organ or part.

**cos•met•ic** (kŏz-mĕt′ĭk) *n.* A preparation designed to beautify the body. **—cos•met′ic** *adj.*

**cos•met•i•cize** (kŏz-mĕt′ĭ-sīz′) *v.* **-cized, -cizing.** To make superficially attractive or acceptable.

**cos•mo•pol•i•tan** (kŏz′mə-pŏl′ĭ-tn) *adj.* **1.** Common to the whole world. **2.** At home in all places; broadened by travel. —*n.* A cosmopolitan person.

**cos•mos** (kŏz′məs, -mōs′) *n.* The universe regarded as an orderly whole. **—cos′mic** *adj.*

**cost** (kôst) *n.* **1.** A price. **2.** A loss or penalty. —*v.* **cost, costing.** To require a specified payment. **—cost′ly** *adj.*

**cost accountant** *n.* An accountant who keeps records of the costs of production and distribution. **—cost accounting** *n.*

**cost-ef•fec•tive** (kôst′ĭ-fĕk′tĭv) *adj.* Economical in terms of the goods or services received for the money spent. **—cost′-ef•fec′tive•ness** *n.*

**cost-plus** (kôst′plŭs′) *n.* The cost of production plus a fixed rate of profit. **—cost′-plus′** *adj.*

**cos•tume** (kŏs′t/y/o͞om′) *n.* **1.** A style of dress of a particular country or period. **2.** A set of clothes.

**cot** (kŏt) *n.* A narrow bed.

**cot•tage** (kŏt′ĭj) *n.* A small country house.

**cottage cheese** *n.* A soft, white cheese made of seasoned curds of skim milk.

**cot•ton** (kŏt′n) *n.* **1.** The downy white fiber surrounding the seeds of a plant. **2.** Thread of cloth made from cotton fiber. **—cot′ton•y** *adj.*

**couch** (kouch) *n.* An article of furniture on which one can lie.

**cough** (kôf, kŏf) *v.* To expel air from the lungs violently. **—cough** *n.*

**could** (ko͝od) *v.* p.t. of **can.**

**could•n't** (ko͝od′nt) *v.* Contraction of *could not.*

**could've** (ko͝od′əv) *v.* Contraction of *could have.*

**coun•cil** (koun′səl) *n.* An administrative, legislative, or advisory body. **—coun′cil•man** *n.* **—coun′cil•or** *n.*

**coun•sel** (koun′səl) *n.* **1.** Advice or guidance. **2.** pl. **counsel.** A lawyer or group of lawyers. —*v.* **-seled** or **-selled, -seling** or **-selling.** To advise. **—coun′sel•or** *n.*

**count** (kount) *v.* **1.** To name 1 by 1 for a total. **2.** To recite numerals in order. **3.** To include. **4.** To matter. **—count on.** To rely. —*n.* **1.** The act of counting. **2.** A total. **3.** Any of the charges in an indictment. **—count′a•ble** *adj.* **—count′less** *adj.*

**count•er¹** (koun′tər) *adj.* Contrary; opposing. —*v.* To oppose. —*adv.* In a contrary manner.

**count•er²** (koun′tər) *n.* **1.** A table on which business is transacted or food served. **2.** A piece for keeping a count or a place in games.

**coun•ter•cul•ture** (koun′tər-kŭl′chər) *n.* A culture, esp. of young people, going against the general culture.

**coun•ter•feit** (koun′tər-fĭt′) *v.* **1.** To forge. **2.** To pretend. —*n.* A fraudulent imitation. **—coun′ter•feit** *adj.* **—coun′ter•feit•er** *n.*

**coun•ter•part** (koun′tər-pärt′) *n.* A matching thing; mate.

**coun•ter•pro•duc•tive** (koun′tər-prə-dŭk′tĭv) *adj.* Tending to hinder rather than help one's purpose. **—coun′ter•pro•duc′tive•ly** *adv.*

**coun•try** (kŭn′trē) *n., pl.* **-tries. 1.** A large area; region. **2.** A rural area. **3.** A nation. —*adj.* Rural.

**coun•ty** (koun′tē) *n., pl.* **-ties.** An administrative subdivision of a state.

**coup** (ko͞o) *n.* **1.** A bold, successful move. **2.** A surprise overthrow of a government.

**cou•ple** (kŭp′əl) *n.* **1.** A group of 2; pair. **2.** Two lovers or companions. **3.** A few. —*v.* **-pled, -pling.** To link together.

**cou•pon** (k/y/o͞o′pŏn′) *n.* A certificate entitling the owner to a payment, discount, or other benefit.

**cour•age** (kûr′ĭj) *n.* Resistance to fear; bravery. **—cou•ra′geous** *adj.* **—cou•ra′geous•ly** *adv.*

**cou•ri•er** (ko͝or′ē-ər, kûr′-) *n.* A messenger.

**course** (kôrs, kōrs) *n.* **1.** Onward movement in a particular direction. **2.** A route; path. **3.** Duration. **4.** A mode of action. **5.** A prescribed study or series of studies. **6.** A part of a meal served separately. **—of course.** Certainly. *—v.* **coursed, coursing.** To move swiftly; run; race.

**course•ware** (kôrs′wâr′, kōrs′-) *n.* Computer software for educational use.

**court** (kôrt, kōrt) *n.* **1.** An enclosed yard. **2.** A short street. **3.** A palace. **4.** A sovereign's attendants and advisers. **5. a.** A judge or panel of judges. **b.** A judicial session. **6.** A marked playing area, as for tennis. *—v.* To attempt to gain the love of. **—cour′ti•er** *n.* **—court′li•ness** *n.* **—court′ly** *adj.* **—court′ship** *n.* **—court′yard** *n.*

**cour•te•ous** (kûr′tē-əs) *adj.* Considerate; polite. **—cour′te•ous•ly** *adv.* **—cour′te•sy** *n.*

**court•mar•tial** (kôrt′mär′shəl) *n., pl.* **courts-martial.** A military trial or court. *—v.* **-tialed** or **-tialled, -tialing** or **-tialling.** To try by court-martial.

**cous•in** (kŭz′ĭn) *n.* A child of one's aunt or uncle.

**cove** (kōv) *n.* A small, sheltered bay.

**cov•e•nant** (kŭv′ə-nənt) *n.* A binding agreement.

**cov•er** (kŭv′ər) *v.* **1.** To place something upon, over, or in front of. **2.** To protect. **3.** To deal with; treat of. **4.** To include; encompass. *—n.* **1.** Something that covers. **2.** Shelter. **3.** Concealment. **—cov′er•age** *n.*

**cov•ert** (kŭv′ərt, kō′vərt) *adj.* Concealed; secret. **—cov′ert•ly** *adv.*

**cov•et** (kŭv′ĭt) *v.* To desire (that which is another's). **—cov′et•ous** *adj.* **—cov′et•ous•ly** *adv.*

**cow** (kou) *n.* The mature female of cattle or of other animals, as the whale or elephant. *—v.* To intimidate.

**cow•ard** (kou′ərd) *n.* One who lacks courage. **—cow′ard•ice** *n.* **—cow′ard•ly** *adj. & adv.*

**cow•er** (kou′ər) *v.* To cringe in fear.

**cowl** (koul) *n.* A monk's hood.

**coy** (koi) *adj.* Affectedly shy or devious. **—coy′ly** *adv.* **—coy′ness** *n.*

**coy•o•te** (kī-ō′tē, kī′ōt′) *n.* A small wolflike animal.

**co•zy** (kō′zē) *adj.* **-zier, -ziest.** Snug and comfortable. **—co′zi•ly** *adv.* **—co′zi•ness** *n.*

**CPR** *n.* A process to restore normal breathing after a heart attack.

**crab** (krăb) *n.* A broad-bodied crustacean with a shell-like covering.

**crack** (krăk) *v.* **1.** To break with a sharp sound; snap. **2.** To break without dividing into parts. **3.** To tell (a joke). *—n.* **1.** A sharp, snapping sound. **2.** A break; fissure. **3.** A narrow space. **4.** A chance. **5.** A sarcastic remark. **6.** A highly addictive form of cocaine. *—adj.* Superior; first-rate.

**crack•er** (krăk′ər) *n.* A thin, crisp wafer or biscuit.

**cra•dle** (krăd′l) *n.* An infant's low bed with rockers. *—v.* **-dled, -dling.** To place in a cradle.

**craft** (krăft) *n.* **1.** Skill; a trade. **2.** Guile; slyness. **3.** pl. **craft.** A boat, ship, or aircraft. **—craft′i•ness** *n.* **—crafts′man** *n.* **—crafts′man•ship′** *n.* **—crafts′wom′an** *n.* **—craft′y** *adj.*

**crag** (krăg) *n.* A steeply projecting mass of rock. **—crag′gy** *adj.*

**cram** (krăm) *v.* **crammed, cramming. 1.** To squeeze into an insufficient space; stuff. **2.** To study intensely.

**cramp** (krămp) *n.* A sudden painful muscular contraction. *—v.* To confine; hamper.

**cran•ber•ry** (krăn′bĕr′ē) *n.* A red, tart, edible berry.

**crane** (krān) *n.* **1.** A long-legged wading bird. **2.** A machine for hoisting heavy objects. *—v.* **craned, craning.** To stretch one's neck.

**cra•ni•um** (krā′nē-əm) *n., pl.* **-ums** or **nia.** The skull. **—cra′ni•al** *adj.*

**crank** (krăngk) *n.* **1.** A handle attached to a shaft, turned to start or run a machine. **2.** An eccentric person. *—v.* To operate (an engine) by a crank.

**crank•y** (krăng′kē) *adj.* **-ier, -iest. 1.** Ill-tempered; peevish. **2.** Eccentric. **—crank′i•ly** *adv.* **—crank′i•ness** *n.*

**cran•ny** (krăn′ē) *n., pl.* **-nies.** A small crevice.
**craps** (krăps) *n.* A dice game.
**crash** (krăsh) *v.* **1.** To fall, break, or collide noisily. **2.** To fail suddenly. —*n.* **1.** A sudden loud noise. **2.** A collision. **3.** A sudden business failure.
**crass** (krăs) *adj.* Grossly ignorant; coarse. —**crass′ly** *adv.* —**crass′ness** *n.*
**crate** (krāt) *n.* A slatted wooden container for storing or shipping things. —*v.* **crated, crating.** To pack into a crate.
**cra•ter** (krā′tər) *n.* A bowl-shaped depression.
**crave** (krāv) *v.* **craved, craving. 1.** To yearn for; desire intensely. **2.** To beg for. —**crav′er** *n.* —**crav′ing** *n.*
**cra•ven** (krā′vən) *adj.* Cowardly. —**cra′ven•ly** *adv.*
**crawl** (krôl) *v.* To move slowly by dragging the body along the ground; creep. —*n.* **1.** The act of crawling. **2.** A rapid swimming stroke.
**cra•zy** (krā′zē) *adj.* **-zier, -ziest. 1.** Insane. **2.** Immoderately fond. —**craze** *v. & n.* —**cra′zi•ly** *adv.* —**cra′zi•ness** *n.*
**cream** (krēm) *n.* **1.** The fatty component of milk. **2.** Yellowish white. **3.** The choicest part. —*v.* **1.** To beat till smooth. **2.** To prepare in a cream sauce. —**cream** *adj.* —**cream′er** *n.* —**cream′y** *adj.*
**crease** (krēs) *n.* A line made by pressing, folding, or wrinkling. —*v.* **creased, creasing.** To make a crease in. —**creas′er** *n.*
**cre•ate** (krē-āt′) *v.* **-ated, -ating.** To cause to exist; originate. —**cre•a′tion** *n.* —**cre•a′tive** *adj.* —**cre′a•tiv′i•ty** *n.* —**cre•a′tor** *n.*
**crea•ture** (krē′chər) *n.* A living being, esp. an animal.
**cre•dence** (krēd′ns) *n.* Belief.
**cre•den•tials** (krĭ-dĕn′shəlz) *pl.n.* Papers entitling one to credit or acceptance.
**cred•i•ble** (krĕd′ə-bəl) *adj.* Believable. —**cred′i•bil′i•ty, cred′i•ble•ness** *n.* —**cred′i•bly** *adv.*
**cred•it** (krĕd′ĭt) *n.* **1.** Belief; trust. **2.** A good reputation. **3.** A source of honor. **4.** Time allowed for payment. **5.** Entry in an account of payment received. —*v.* **1.** To believe; trust. **2.** To give credit to.
**cred•it•a•ble** (krĕd′ĭ-tə-bəl) *adj.* Deserving commendation. —**cred′it•a•bly** *adv.*
**credit card** *n.* A card authorizing the holder to buy goods or services on credit.
**cred•i•tor** (krĕd′ĭ-tər) *n.* One to whom money is owed.
**credit rating** *n.* The amount of credit that can safely be extended to a person or company.
**credit union** *n.* A cooperative organization that makes loans to its members at low interest rates.
**cred•it•wor•thy** (krĕd′ĭt-wûr′*thē*) *adj.* Having an acceptable credit rating. —**cred′it•wor′thi•ness** *n.*
**cred•u•lous** (krĕj′ə-ləs) *adj.* Disposed to believe too readily; gullible. —**cre•du′li•ty** *n.* —**cred′u•lous•ly** *adv.*
**creed** (krēd) *n.* A statement of belief.
**creek** (krēk, krĭk) *n.* A small stream.
**creep** (krēp) *v.* **crept** (krĕpt), **creeping. 1.** To move furtively or slowly. **2.** To grow along the ground. —**creep′er** *n.*
**creep•y** (krē′pē) *adj.* **-ier, -iest.** Eerie. —**creep′i•ness** *n.*
**cre•mate** (krē′māt′, krĭ-māt′) *v.* **-mated, -mating.** To incinerate (a corpse). —**cre•ma′tion** *n.* —**cre′ma′tor** *n.* —**cre′ma•to′ri•um** *n.*
**crept** (krĕpt) *v.* p.t. & p.p. of **creep.**
**cres•cen•do** (krə-shĕn′dō) *n., pl.* **-dos.** A gradual increase in volume.
**cres•cent** (krĕs′ənt) *n.* The shape of the quarter moon.
**crest** (krĕst) *n.* **1.** A tuft on the head of a bird or other animal. **2.** The highest point; summit. —*v.* To reach a crest; peak.
**crew** (kro͞o) *n.* A team of workers.
**crib** (krĭb) *n.* **1.** A child's bed with high sides. **2.** A rack or trough for fodder.
**crime** (krīm) *n.* An act in violation of the law. —**crim′i•nal** *n.* —**crim′i•nal′i•ty** *n.* —**crim′i•nal•ly** *adv.*
**crim•son** (krĭm′zən) *n.* A deep red. —*v.* To become crimson. —**crim′son** *adj.*
**cringe** (krĭnj) *v.* **cringed, cringing.** To shrink back, as with fear; cower.
**crin•kle** (krĭng′kəl) *v.* **-kled, -kling.** To wrinkle; rustle. —*n.* A rustle. —**crin′kly** *adj.*
**crip•ple** (krĭp′əl) *n.* A disabled or lame person. —*v.* **-pled, -pling.** To disable or

damage.

**cri•sis** (krī'sĭs) *n., pl.* **-ses.** A crucial situation; turning point.

**crisp** (krĭsp) *adj.* **1.** Brittle. **2.** Firm and fresh. **3.** Brisk; invigorating. **—crisp'i•ness** *n.* **—crisp'ly** *adv.* **—crisp'y** *adj.*

**cri•te•ri•on** (krī-tîr'ē-ən) *n., pl.* **-ria.** A standard of judgment.

**crit•ic** (krĭt'ĭk) *n.* **1.** A judge or reviewer of artistic works. **2.** One who finds fault.

**crit•i•cal** (krĭt'ĭ-kəl) *adj.* **1.** Tending to criticize. **2.** Characterized by careful evaluation. **3.** Of critics or criticism. **4.** Crucial. **—crit'i•cal•ly** *adv.* **—crit'i•cal•ness** *n.*

**crit•i•cize** (krĭt'ĭ-sīz') *v.* **-cized, -cizing. 1.** To judge the merits and faults of; evaluate. **2.** To find fault with. **—crit'i•cism'** *n.*

**cri•tique** (krĭ-tēk') *v.* **-tiqued, -tiquing. 1.** To comment, esp. on a literary or artistic work. **2.** To have a discussion on a specific topic. **—cri•tique'** *n.*

**cro•chet** (krō-shā') *v.* To make needlework by looping thread with a hooked needle.

**croc•o•dile** (krŏk'ə-dīl') *n.* A large tropical aquatic reptile.

**cro•ny** (krō'nē) *n., pl.* **-nies.** A close friend.

**crook** (krŏŏk) *n.* **1.** A bend or angle. **2.** A swindler; thief. *—v.* To curve; bend. **—crook'ed** *adj.* **—crook'ed•ly** *adv.*

**croon** (krōōn) *v.* To sing softly. *—n.* A crooning sound. **—croon'er** *n.*

**crop** (krŏp) *n.* **1. a.** A food grown on a farm. **b.** A harvest; yield. **2.** A short riding whip. **3.** A pouchlike enlargement of a bird's esophagus. *—v.* **cropped, cropping. 1.** To cut off the ends of. **2.** To cut short.

**cross** (krôs, krŏs) *n.* **1.** An upright post with a transverse piece near the top. **2.** A trial or affliction. **3.** A pattern formed by 2 intersecting lines. **4.** A hybrid. *—v.* **1.** To go or extend across. **2.** To intersect. **3.** To place crosswise. **4.** To obstruct. **5.** To breed. *—adj.* **1.** Lying crosswise. **2.** Contrary. **3.** Irritable. **—cross'ing** *n.*

**cross-train** (krôs'trān', krŏs'-) *v.* **1.** To train someone to do more than 1 job. **2.** To practice or exercise at more than 1 sport.

**crotch** (krŏch) *n.* The fork formed by the junction of parts. **—crotched** *adj.*

**crouch** (krouch) *v.* To stoop with the limbs close to the body. **—crouch** *n.*

**croup** (krōōp) *n.* A children's disease of the larynx, marked by a harsh cough.

**crowd** (kroud) *n.* A large number of persons or things gathered together. *—v.* **1.** To gather in numbers. **2.** To press or shove.

**crown** (kroun) *n.* **1.** A head covering worn by a monarch. **2.** A top or covering part. *—v.* **1.** To put a crown upon. **2.** To honor. **3.** To surmount; top.

**cru•cial** (krōō'shəl) *adj.* Decisive. **—cru'cial•ly** *adv.*

**cru•ci•ble** (krōō'sə-bəl) *n.* A vessel for melting materials.

**cru•ci•fix** (krōō'sə-fĭks') *n.* A cross on which is fixed an image of Christ.

**cru•ci•fy** (krōō'sə-fī') *v.* **-fied, -fying.** To put to death by nailing or binding to a cross. **—cru'ci•fix'ion** *n.*

**crude** (krōōd) *adj.* **cruder, crudest. 1.** Unrefined; raw. **2.** Lacking finish, tact, or taste. **—crude'ly** *adv.* **—cru'di•ty, crude'ness** *n.*

**cru•el** (krōō'əl) *adj.* Causing pain or suffering; merciless. **—cru'el•ly** *adv.* **—cru'el•ty** *n.*

**cruise** (krōōz) *v.* **cruised, cruising.** To sail or travel over or about. *—n.* A sea voyage for pleasure.

**cruis•er** (krōō'zər) *n.* **1.** A fast warship of medium tonnage. **2.** A police squad car.

**crum•ble** (krŭm'bəl) *v.* **-bled, -bling.** To break into small parts. **—crumb** *n.*

**crunch** (krŭnch) *v.* To chew or crush noisily. **—crunch** *n.*

**cru•sade** (krōō-sād') *n.* A zealous movement for a cause. *—v.* **-saded, -sading.** To engage in a crusade. **—cru•sad'er** *n.*

**crush** (krŭsh) *v.* **1.** To mash or squeeze so as to injure. **2.** To pound or grind. **3.** To overwhelm; subdue. *—n.* **1.** The act of crushing. **2.** A crowd. **3.** An infatuation.

**crust** (krŭst) *n.* A hard outer covering. *—v.* To cover or become covered with a crust. **—crust'y** *adj.*

**crus•ta•cean** (krŭ-stā'shən) *n.* A segmented, hard-shelled arthropod, as a lobster.

**crutch** (krŭch) *n.* A supporting stick fitted under the armpit in walking.

**crux** (krŭks, kro͝oks) *n.* A critical or crucial point.

**cry** (krī) *v.* **cried, crying. 1.** To make sobbing sounds; weep. **2.** To utter loudly. —*n., pl.* **cries. 1.** A loud utterance. **2.** A fit of weeping. **3.** An urgent appeal. —**cri•er** *n.*

**crypt** (krĭpt) *n.* An underground chamber, esp. for burial.

**cryp•tic** (krĭp'tĭk) *adj.* Veiled; mystifying. —**cryp'ti•cal•ly** *adv.*

**crys•tal** (krĭs'təl) *n.* **1.** Solid matter with a highly regular, periodically repeated structure and plane faces. **2.** Clear quartz. **3.** Fine glass. —**crys'tal•line** *adj.* —**crys'tal•li•za'tion** *n.* —**crys'tal•lize'** *v.*

**cub** (kŭb) *n.* A young bear, wolf, lion, etc.

**cube** (kyo͞ob) *n.* **1.** A solid having 6 congruent faces. **2.** The 3rd power of a number. —*v.* **cubed, cubing. 1.** To raise to the 3rd power. **2.** To cut into cubes. —**cu'bic, cu'bi•cal** *adj.*

**cu•bi•cle** (kyo͞o'bĭ-kəl) *n.* A small room.

**cu•cum•ber** (kyo͞o'kŭm'bər) *n.* A long, green-skinned vegetable.

**cud** (kŭd) *n.* Food regurgitated from the 1st stomach of a ruminant and chewed again.

**cud•dle** (kŭd'l) *v.* **-dled, -dling.** To fondle; hug.

**cudg•el** (kŭj'əl) *n.* A short, heavy club. —*v.* To beat with a cudgel.

**cue[1]** (kyo͞o) *n.* The long, tapered rod used to propel a billiard ball.

**cue[2]** (kyo͞o) *n.* A signal, esp. to begin or enter. —**cue** *v.*

**cuff** (kŭf) *n.* **1.** A fold at the bottom of a sleeve or trouser leg. **2.** A light blow; slap. —*v.* To slap.

**cu•li•nar•y** (kyo͞o'lə-nĕr'ē, kŭl'ə-) *adj.* Of kitchens or cookery.

**cull** (kŭl) *v.* To pick out; select. —**cull'er** *n.*

**cul•mi•nate** (kŭl'mə-nāt') *v.* **-nated, -nating.** To reach the highest point; climax. —**cul'mi•na'tion** *n.*

**cul•pa•ble** (kŭl'pə-bəl) *adj.* Guilty; blameworthy. —**cul'pa•bil'i•ty** *n.* —**cul'pa•bly** *adv.*

**cul•prit** (kŭl'prĭt) *n.* A person charged with or found guilty of a crime.

**cult** (kŭlt) *n.* **1.** A system or community of worship. **2.** Obsessive devotion.

**cul•ti•vate** (kŭl'tə-vāt') *v.* **-vated, -vating. 1.** To prepare (land) for raising crops. **2.** To grow or tend. **3.** To form and refine, as by education. —**cul'ti•va'tion** *n.* —**cul'ti•va'tor** *n.*

**cul•ture** (kŭl'chər) *n.* **1.** The raising of animals or growing of plants. **2.** A growth or colony of microorganisms. **3.** Socially transmitted behavior patterns. **4.** Social and artistic expression and activity. —*v.* **-tured, -turing.** To cultivate. —**cul'tur•al** *adj.* —**cul'tur•al•ly** *adv.*

**cum•ber•some** (kŭm'bər-səm) *adj.* Unwieldy. —**cum'ber•some•ness** *n.*

**cu•mu•la•tive** (kyo͞om'yə-lā'tĭv, -lə-tĭv) *adj.* Increasing by successive addition. —**cu'mu•la'tive•ly** *adv.*

**cun•ning** (kŭn'ĭng) *adj.* Shrewd; crafty. —*n.* Craftiness; skill. —**cun'ning•ly** *adv.*

**cup** (kŭp) *n.* A small, open container for drinking. —*v.* **cupped, cupping.** To shape like a cup.

**cup•board** (kŭb'ərd) *n.* A shelved cabinet for storing food or dishes.

**cu•ra•tor** (kyo͞o-rā'tər, kyo͝or'ə-tər) *n.* The director of a museum or similar institution.

**curb** (kûrb) *n.* **1.** Anything that checks or restrains. **2.** A concrete edging along a sidewalk. —*v.* To check or restrain. —**curb'er** *n.*

**curd** (kûrd) *n.* Often **curds.** The coagulated part of sour milk. —**cur'dle** *v.*

**cure** (kyo͝or) *n.* **1.** Restoration of health. **2.** A medical remedy. —*v.* **cured, curing. 1.** To restore to health. **2.** To rid of (disease). **3.** To preserve. —**cur'a•ble** *adj.* —**cur'a•tive** *adj.*

**cur•few** (kûr'fyo͞o) *n.* An order to retire from the streets at a prescribed hour.

**cu•ri•ous** (kyo͝or'ē-əs) *adj.* **1.** Eager to know. **2.** Singular; odd. —**cu'ri•os'i•ty** *n.* —**cu'ri•ous•ly** *adv.*

**curl** (kûrl) *v.* **1.** To twist into ringlets. **2.** To curve; wind. —*n.* **1.** A spiral or coil. **2.** A ringlet. —**curl'i•ness** *n.* —**curl'y** *adj.*

**cur•ren•cy** (kûr'ən-sē) *n., pl.* **-cies. 1.** Money in circulation. **2.** Common acceptance.

**cur•rent** (kûr′ənt) *adj.* **1.** Belonging to the present time. **2.** Commonly accepted; prevalent. —*n.* A steady and smooth onward movement, as of water or electricity. **—cur′rent•ly** *adv.*

**cur•ric•u•lum** (kə-rĭk′yə-ləm) *n., pl.* **-la** or **-lums.** A course of study. **—cur•ric′u•lar** *adj.*

**curse** (kûrs) *n.* **1.** A call for evil to afflict someone or something. **2.** A scourge; evil. **3.** Any profane oath. —*v.* **cursed** or **curst, cursing. 1.** To invoke evil upon; damn. **2.** To afflict. **3.** To utter curses. **—curs′ed** *adj.* **—curs′er** *n.*

**cur•sor** (kûr′sər) *n.* A movable indicator on a computer screen that marks the position where a character can be entered or deleted.

**curt** (kûrt) *adj.* Rudely brief or abrupt. **—curt′ly** *adv.* **—curt′ness** *n.*

**cur•tail** (kər-tāl′) *v.* To cut short. **—cur•tail′ment** *n.*

**cur•tain** (kûr′tn) *n.* A piece of material hanging in a window or other opening. —*v.* To provide or shut off with a curtain.

**curve** (kûrv) *n.* A line or surface that deviates from straightness in a smooth, continuous fashion. —*v.* **curved, curving.** To move in, form, or cause to form a curve. **—cur′va•ture** *n.*

**cush•ion** (ko͝osh′ən) *n.* **1.** A pad or pillow. **2.** Anything that absorbs shock. —*v.* To provide with a cushion.

**cus•to•dy** (kŭs′tə-dē) *n., pl.* **-dies. 1.** The act or right of guarding or maintaining. **2.** Detainment. **—cus•to′di•al** *adj.* **—cus•to′di•an** *n.*

**cus•tom** (kŭs′təm) *n.* **1.** A usual practice; convention. **2.** A habit. **3. customs.** A tax on imported goods. —*adj.* Made to order. **—cus′tom•ar′y** *adj.* **—cus′tom•ar′i•ly** *adv.*

**cus•tom•er** (kŭs′tə-mər) *n.* One who buys goods or services.

**cut** (kŭt) *v.* **cut, cutting. 1.** To slice with a sharp edge. **2.** To sever. **3.** To harvest. **4.** To reduce; shorten. **5.** To omit; drop. —*n.* **1.** The act or result of cutting. **2.** A dug passage. **3.** A reduction. **4.** A share. **—cut′ter** *n.*

**cute** (kyo͞ot) *adj.* **cuter, cutest.** Pretty or dainty. **—cute′ly** *adv.* **—cute′ness** *n.*

**cu•ti•cle** (kyo͞o′tĭ-kəl) *n.* The hardened skin at the base of a nail.

**cut•ler•y** (kŭt′lə-rē) *n.* **1.** Cutting instruments. **2.** Tableware.

**cy•cle** (sī′kəl) *n.* **1. a.** A regularly repeated sequence of events. **b.** The period of such a sequence. **2.** A related series of artistic works. **3.** A bicycle or motorcycle. —*v.* **-cled, -cling.** To ride a bicycle or motorcycle. **—cy′clic, cy′cli•cal** *adj.* **—cy′cli•cal•ly** *adv.* **—cy′clist** *n.*

**cy•clone** (sī′klōn′) *n.* A violent rotating windstorm. **—cy•clon′ic** *adj.*

**cyl•in•der** (sĭl′ən-dər) *n.* A figure with a rounded surface bounded by flat, parallel ends. **—cy•lin′dri•cal** *adj.*

**cym•bal** (sĭm′bəl) *n.* One of a pair of brass plates struck together as percussion instruments.

**cyn•ic** (sĭn′ĭk) *n.* One who believes all persons are motivated by selfishness. **—cyn′i•cal** *adj.* **—cyn′i•cal•ly** *adv.* **—cyn′i•cism′** *n.*

**czar** (zär) *n.* Also **tsar, tzar. 1.** A Russian emperor. **2.** A powerful ruler. **3.** An official in charge.

## — D —

**d, D** (dē) *n.* The 4th letter of the English alphabet.

**dab** (dăb) *v.* **dabbed, dabbing.** To touch or apply with short, light strokes. —*n.* **1.** A small amount. **2.** A pat.

**dab•ble** (dăb′əl) *v.* **-bled, -bling. 1.** To splash gently. **2.** To undertake something superficially. **—dab′bler** *n.*

**dag•ger** (dăg′ər) *n.* A short, pointed weapon.

**dai•ly** (dā′lē) *adj.* Occurring or published every day. —*n., pl.* **-lies.** A daily publication. **—dai′ly** *adv.*

**dain•ty** (dān′tē) *adj.* **-tier, -tiest. 1.** Delicately beautiful. **2.** Refined; fastidious. —*n., pl.* **-ties.** A delicacy. **—dain′ti•ly** *adv.*

**dair•y** (dâr′ē) *n. pl.* **-ies.** An establishment that processes or sells milk and milk products. **—dair′y** *adj.*

**da•is** (dā′ĭs, dī′-) *n., pl.* **-ises.** A raised platform.

**dam** (dăm) *n.* A barrier, esp. one across a waterway. —*v.* **dammed, damming. 1.** To construct a dam across. **2.** To obstruct.

**dam•age** (dăm'ĭj) *n.* **1.** Impairment of usefulness or value; harm. **2. damages.** Money paid for injury or loss. —*v.* **-aged, -aging.** To cause injury to.

**damn** (dăm) *v.* To condemn. **—dam'na•ble** *adj.* **—dam•na'tion** *n.* **—damned** *adj.*

**damp** (dămp) *adj.* Slightly wet. —*n.* Moisture. —*v.* **1.** To make damp. **2.** To restrain or check. **—damp'en** *v.* **—damp'er** *n.* **—damp'ness** *n.*

**dance** (dăns) *v.* **danced, dancing.** To move rhythmically to music. —*n.* **1.** A series of rhythmical motions and steps. **2.** A gathering or piece of music for dancing. **—danc'er** *n.*

**dan•der** (dăn'dər) *n.* Temper.

**dan•druff** (dăn'drəf) *n.* A scaly scurf from the scalp.

**dan•dy** (dăn'dē) *n., pl.* **-dies. 1.** A man who affects extreme elegance. **2.** Something very agreeable. —*adj.* **-dier, -diest.** Fine; good.

**dan•ger** (dān'jər) *n.* **1.** Chance of harm or evil. **2.** A source of peril. **—dan'ger•ous** *adj.* **—dan'ger•ous•ly** *adv.*

**dan•gle** (dăng'gəl) *v.* **-gled, -gling.** To hang loosely.

**dank** (dăngk) *adj.* Uncomfortably damp and chilly.

**dan•seur** (dän-sœr') *n.* A male ballet dancer.

**dan•seuse** (dän-sœz') *n., pl.* **-seuses.** A female ballet dancer.

**dap•per** (dăp'ər) *adj.* **1. a.** Neatly dressed. **b.** Stylish. **2.** Small and active.

**dare** (dâr) *v.* **dared, daring. 1.** To have the courage for. **2.** To challenge (someone) to do something bold. —*n.* A challenge. **—dar'ing** *adj.* **—dar'ing•ly** *adv.*

**dark** (därk) *adj.* **1.** Lacking light. **2.** Somber in color. **3.** Gloomy. **4.** Obscure. —*n.* Absence of light. **—dark'en** *v.* **—dark'ly** *adv.* **—dark'ness** *n.*

**darn** (därn) *v.* To mend by weaving thread across a hole. **—darn'er** *n.*

**dart** (därt) *n.* **1.** A slender, pointed missile to be thrown or shot. **2.** A sudden movement. —*v.* To move suddenly. **—dart'er** *n.*

**dash** (dăsh) *v.* **1.** To smash; destroy. **2.** To knock or thrust violently. **3.** To perform hastily (with *off*). **4.** To rush. —*n.* **1.** A small amount. **2.** A rush. **3.** A short foot race. **4.** Verve. **5.** A punctuation mark (–).

**dash•ing** (dăsh'ĭng) *adj.* **1.** Bold; gallant; spirited. **2.** Elegant; splendid.

**da•ta** (dā'tə, dăt'ə, dä'tə) *pl.n.* **1.** Information. **2.** Numerical information in a form suitable for processing by a computer.

**data bank** *n.* **1.** A database. **2.** An organization that builds, maintains, and uses a data bank.

**da•ta•base** (dā'tə-bās', dăt'ə-) *n.* A collection of data arranged for ease and speed of retrieval, as by a computer.

**data carrier** *n.* The medium, as magnetic tape, that transports data.

**data processing** *n.* Preparation of information for processing by a computer. **—data processor** *n.*

**data set** *n.* **1.** An electronic device that provides an interface in the transmission of data. **2.** A collection of related computer records. **3.** A modem.

**date** (dāt) *n.* **1.** The time at which something happens. **2.** The day of the month. **3. a.** An appointment to meet socially. **b.** A person so met. —*v.* **dated, dating. 1.** To mark with a date. **2.** To determine the date of. **3.** To originate (with *from*). **4.** To make or have social engagements with.

**date•line** (dāt'līn') *n.* A phrase at the beginning of a news article, giving the date and place of origin.

**daub** (dôb) *v.* **1.** To smear. **2.** To paint crudely. **—daub'er** *n.*

**daugh•ter** (dô'tər) *n.* One's female child. **—daugh'ter•ly** *adj.*

**daugh•ter-in-law** (dô'tər-ĭn-lô') *n., pl.* **daugh•ters-in-law.** The wife of one's son.

**daw•dle** (dôd'l) *v.* **-dled, -dling.** To waste time. **—daw'dler** *n.*

**dawn** (dôn) *n.* **1.** The first appearance of daylight. **2.** A beginning. —*v.* **1.** To begin to become light in the morning. **2.** To begin to appear or be understood. **—dawn'ing** *adj.*

**day** (dā) *n.* **1.** The period between dawn and nightfall. **2.** A 24-hour period, esp. one starting at midnight.

**day•book** (dā'bo͝ok') *n.* **1.** An account book in which daily transactions are recorded. **2.** A diary.

**day-trip•per** (dā'trĭp'ər) *n.* One who takes a trip during the day without staying overnight.

**daze** (dāz) *v.* **dazed, dazing.** To stun or dazzle. —*n.* A stunned condition.

**daz•zle** (dăz'əl) *v.* **-zled, -zling.** To overpower, as with intense light. —**daz'zle** *n.*

**dead** (dĕd) *adj.* **1.** No longer alive. **2.** No longer in existence or use. **3.** Weary and worn-out.

**dead•en** (dĕd'n) *v.* To render less intense; dull.

**dead•line** (dĕd'līn') *n.* A time limit, as for paying a debt or for completing an assignment.

**dead•ly** (dĕd'lē) *adj.* **-lier, -liest. 1.** Causing or intending to cause death. **2.** Implacable; mortal. —*adv.* To an extreme. —**dead'li•ness** *n.*

**deaf** (dĕf) *adj.* **1.** Unable to hear. **2.** Heedless. —**deaf'en** *v.* —**deaf'ness** *n.*

**deaf-mute** (dĕf'myo͞ot') *n.* Also **deaf mute.** One who can neither speak nor hear.

**deal** (dēl) *v.* **dealt** (dĕlt), **dealing. 1.** To distribute. **2.** To be concerned; treat. **3.** To do business; trade —*n.* **1.** The act of dealing. **2.** An amount. **3.** An agreement or business transaction. —**deal'er** *n.*

**deal•er•ship** (dē'lər-shĭp') *n.* A franchise to sell a particular item in a certain area.

**dean** (dēn) *n.* **1.** An administrative officer in a college or school. **2.** The senior member.

**dear** (dîr) *adj.* **1.** Beloved. **2.** High-priced. —*n.* A greatly loved person —**dear'ly** *adv.*

**dearth** (dûrth) *n.* Scarcity; lack, esp. of food.

**death** (dĕth) *n.* The act of dying or state of being dead. —**death'less** *adj.* —**death'less•ness** *n.* —**death'ly** *adj. & adv.*

**de•ba•cle** (dĭ-bä'kəl, -băk'əl) *n.* **1.** A sudden, total collapse or defeat. **2.** A complete failure.

**de•bark** (dĭ-bärk') *v.* To unload, as from a ship.

**de•bate** (dĭ-bāt') *v.* **-bated, -bating.** To discuss or argue formally. —*n.* A formal argument. —**de•bat'a•ble** *adj.* —**de•bat'er** *n.*

**de•ben•ture** (dĭ-bĕn'chər) *n.* **1.** A certificate acknowledging a debt. **2.** An unsecured bond issued by a government and backed only by the government's credit.

**de•bil•i•tate** (dĭ-bĭl'ĭ-tāt') *v.* **-tated, -tating.** To make feeble; weaken. —**de•bil'i•ta'tion** *n.*

**deb•it** (dĕb'ĭt) *n.* An item of debt. —*v.* To enter a debit in an account.

**debit card** *n.* A bankcard with which purchases are charged directly to a bank account.

**deb•o•nair** (dĕb'ə-nâr') *adj.* Suave; affable. —**deb'o•nair'ly** *adv.*

**de•bris, dé•bris** (də-brē', dā'brē') *n.* Scattered remains.

**debt** (dĕt) *n.* Something owed. —**debt'or** *n.*

**de•bug** (dē-bŭg') *v.* **-bugged, -bugging. 1.** To remove bugs from. **2.** To remove electronic eavesdropping devices from. **3.** To remove flaws in the design from.

**de•bunk** (dē-bŭngk') *v.* To expose and ridicule the falseness and stupidity of. —**de•bunk'er** *n.*

**de•but** (dā-byo͞o', dā'byo͞o') *n.* Also **dé•but.** A first public appearance.

**dec•ade** (dĕk'ād', dĕ-kād') *n.* A period of 10 years.

**dec•a•dence** (dĕk'ə-dəns, dĭ-kād'ns) *n.* A decay, esp. in morality. —**dec'a•dent** *adj.* —**dec'a•dent•ly** *adv.*

**de•cant** (dĭ-kănt') *v.* To pour liquid from 1 container into another.

**de•cant•er** (dĭ-kăn'tər) *n.* A decorative bottle used to serve wine; a carafe.

**de•cay** (dĭ-kā') *v.* **1.** To decompose; rot. **2.** To decline. —*n.* **1.** Decomposition. **2.** Deterioration.

**de•cease** (dĭ-sēs') *v.* **-ceased, -ceasing.** To die. —*n.* Death. —**de•ceased'** *adj.*

**de•ceit** (dĭ-sēt') *n.* **1.** Deception. **2.** A trick. —**de•ceit'ful** *adj.* —**de•ceit'ful•ly** *adv.*

**de•ceive** (dĭ-sēv') *v.* **-ceived, -ceiving.** To delude; mislead. —**de•ceiv'er** *n.*

**de•cel•er•ate** (dē-sĕl'ə-rāt') *v.* **-ated, -ating.** To decrease speed. —**de•cel'er•a'tion** *n.*

**De•cem•ber** (dĕ-sĕm'bər) *n.* The 12th month of the year.

**de•cent** (dē'sənt) *adj.* **1.** Proper. **2.** Modest. **3.** Adequate. **4.** Kind. —**de'cen•cy** *n.* —**de'cent•ly** *adv.*

**de•cep•tion** (dĭ-sĕp′shən) *n.* **1.** The use of deceit. **2.** The fact or state of being deceived. —**de•cep′tive** *adj.* —**de•cep′tive•ly** *adv.*

**de•cide** (dĭ-sīd′) *v.* **-cided, -ciding. 1.** To conclude, settle, or announce a verdict. **2.** To determine the outcome of. **3.** To make up one's mind. —**de•cid′er** *n.* —**de•ci′sion** *n.*

**de•cid•ed** (dĭ-sī′dĭd) *adj.* **1.** Without doubt or question; definite. **2.** Without hesitation; resolute.

**dec•i•mal** (dĕs′ə-məl) *adj.* Of or based on 10.

**de•ci•pher** (dĭ-sī′fər) *v.* To decode; interpret.

**de•ci•sive** (dĭ-sī′sĭv) *adj.* **1.** Conclusive. **2.** Resolute. **3.** Unmistakable. —**de•ci′sive•ly** *adv.* —**de•ci′sive•ness** *n.*

**deck**[1] (dĕk) *n.* **1.** An exposed floor on a ship. **2.** A pack of playing cards.

**deck**[2] (dĕk) *v.* To adorn.

**de•clare** (dĭ-klâr′) *v.* **-clared, -claring.** To state officially or formally. —**dec′la•ra′tion** *n.* —**de•clar′a•tive** *adj.* —**de•clar′er** *n.*

**dé•clas•sé** (dā′klă-sā′) *adj.* Lowered in rank or social position.

**de•cline** (dĭ-klīn′) *v.* **-clined, -clining. 1.** To refuse to do or accept (something). **2.** To slope downward. **3.** To wane. —**de•cline′** *n.*

**de•code** (dē-kōd′) *v.* **-coded, -coding.** To convert from code to plain text. —**de•cod′er** *n.*

**de•com•pose** (dē′kəm-pōz′) *v.* **-posed, -posing.** To rot. —**de•com′po•si′tion** *n.*

**de•con•ges•tant** (dē′kən-jĕs′tənt) *n.* A medication that breaks up congestion, as in the sinuses.

**dé•cor, de•cor** (dā′kôr′, dā-kôr′) *n.* **1.** The decorative style of a room or house. **2.** Stage setting; scenery.

**dec•o•rate** (dĕk′ə-rāt′) *v.* **-rated, -rating. 1.** To furnish or adorn. **2.** To confer a medal upon. —**dec′o•ra′tion** *n.* —**dec′o•ra•tive** *adj.* —**dec′o•ra′tor** *n.*

**de•coy** (dē′koi′, dĭ-koi′) *n.* **1.** A living or artificial animal used to entice game. **2.** A lure.

**de•crease** (dĭ-krēs′) *v.* **-creased, -creasing.** To diminish gradually; reduce. —*n.* (dē′krēs′). Reduction; decline.

**de•cree** (dĭ-krē′) *n.* An authoritative order; edict. —**de•cree′** *v.*

**de•crep•it** (dĭ-krĕp′ĭt) *adj.* Worn-out; broken down. —**de•crep′i•tude′** *n.*

**ded•i•cate** (dĕd′ĭ-kāt′) *v.* **-cated, -cating. 1.** To set apart for special purposes. **2.** To inscribe. **3.** To devote. —**ded′i•ca′tion** *n.*

**de•duce** (dĭ-d/y/o͞os) *v.* **-duced, -ducing.** To reach (a conclusion) by reasoning. —**de•duc′i•ble** *adj.*

**de•duct** (dĭ-dŭkt′) *v.* To subtract. —**de•duct′i•ble** *adj.* —**de•duc′tion** *n.*

**deed** (dēd) *n.* **1.** An act. **2.** A legal document, esp. one certifying ownership. —*v.* To transfer by deed.

**deem** (dēm) *v.* To judge; consider.

**deep** (dēp) *adj.* **1.** Extending far down, back, or inward. **2.** Learned; profound. **3.** Intense; extreme. **4.** Dark. **5.** Absorbed. **6.** Low. —*n.* Any deep place. —*adv.* **1.** Profoundly. **2.** Late. —**deep′en** *v.* —**deep′ly** *adv.* —**deep′ness** *n.*

**deet** (dēt) *n.* An oily, colorless liquid insect repellent.

**de•face** (dĭ-fās′) *v.* **-faced, -facing. 1.** To disfigure. **2.** To impair. **3.** To obliterate.

**de fac•to** (dĭ făk′tō, dā) *adv. & adj.* In fact; in reality.

**de•fame** (dĭ-fām′) *v.* **-famed, -faming.** To slander or libel. —**def′a•ma′tion** *n.* —**de•fam′er** *n.*

**de•fault** (dĭ-fôlt′) *n.* A failure to fulfill an obligation. —**de•fault′** *v.* —**de•fault′er** *n.*

**de•feat** (dĭ-fēt′) *v.* **1.** To win victory over. **2.** To thwart. —*n.* The act of defeating or the state of being defeated. —**de•feat′er** *n.* —**de•feat′ism** *n.*

**de•fect** (dē′fĕkt′, dĭ-fĕkt′) *n.* An imperfection; fault. —*v.* (dĭ-fĕkt′). To abandon an allegiance. —**de•fec′tion** *n.* —**de•fec′tive** *adj.* —**de•fec′tive•ly** *adv.* —**de•fec′tive•ness** *n.* —**de•fec′tor** *n.*

**de•fend** (dĭ-fĕnd′) *v.* **1.** To protect from danger. **2.** To represent (a legal defendant). —**de•fend′er** *n.*

**de•fen•dant** (dĭ-fĕn′dənt) *n.* A person accused or sued.

**de•fense** (dĭ-fĕns′) *n.* **1.** The act of defending. **2.** One that defends or protects. —**de•fense′less** *adj.* —**de•fense′less•ly** *adv.* —**de•fen′si•ble** *adj.*

—**de•fen′sive** *adj.*

**de•fer**[1] (dĭ-fûr′) *v.* **-ferred, -ferring.** To postpone. —**de•fer′ment, de•fer′ral** *n.*

**de•fer**[2] (dĭ-fûr′) *v.* **-ferred, -ferring.** To yield or submit respectfully. —**def′er•ence** *n.* —**def′er•en′tial** *adj.* —**def′-er•en′tial•ly** *adv.*

**de•fi•ant** (dĭ-fī′ənt) *adj.* Marked by resistance to authority. —**de•fi′ance** *n.* —**de•fi′ant•ly** *adv.*

**de•fi•cient** (dĭ-fĭsh′ənt) *adj.* **1.** Lacking; incomplete. **2.** Inadequate. —**de•fi′-cien•cy** *n.* —**de•fi′cient•ly** *adv.*

**def•i•cit** (dĕf′ĭ-sĭt) *n.* The amount by which a sum falls short.

**de•file** (dĭ-fīl′) *v.* **-filed, -filing. 1.** To make filthy or dirty. **2.** To corrupt. —**de•file′ment** *n.* —**de•fil′er** *n.*

**de•fine** (dĭ-fīn′) *v.* **-fined, -fining. 1.** To state the meaning of. **2.** To delineate. **3.** To specify distinctly. —**de•fin′a•ble** *adj.* —**de•fin′a•bly** *adv.* —**de•fin′er** *n.* —**def′i•ni′tion** *n.*

**def•i•nite** (dĕf′ə-nĭt) *adj.* **1.** Having distinct limits. **2.** Known positively. **3.** Clearly defined. —**def′i•nite•ly** *adv.*

**de•fin•i•tive** (dĭ-fĭn′ĭ-tĭv) *adj.* Determining finally; decisive. —**de•fin′i•tive•ly** *adv.* —**de•fin′i•tive•ness** *n.*

**de•flate** (dĭ-flāt′) *v.* **-flated, -flating. 1.** To release contained air or gas from. **2.** To lessen the confidence, pride, or certainty of. —**de•fla′tion** *n.* —**de•fla′tor** *n.*

**de•flect** (dĭ-flĕkt′) *v.* To turn aside. —**de•flec′tion** *n.*

**de•form** (dĭ-fôrm′) *v.* To misshape; disfigure. —**de′for•ma′tion** *n.* —**de•formed′** *adj.* —**de•form′i•ty** *n.*

**de•fray** (dĭ-frā′) *v.* To pay. —**de•fray′a•ble** *adj.* —**de•fray′al** *n.*

**deft** (dĕft) *adj.* Skillful; adroit. —**deft′ly** *adv.*

**de•funct** (dĭ-fŭngkt′) *adj.* Having ceased to exist.

**de•fy** (dĭ-fī′) *v.* **-fied, -fying. 1.** To oppose boldly. **2.** To resist successfully; withstand. **3.** To dare; challenge.

**de•gen•er•ate** (dĭ-jĕn′ə-rāt′) *v.* **-ated, -ating.** To deteriorate or decay. —*adj.* (-ər-ĭt). Morally degraded. —*n.* (-ər-ĭt). A degenerate person. —**de•gen′er•a•cy** *n.* —**de•gen′er•a′tion** *n.* —**de•gen′er•a•tive** *adj.*

**de•grade** (dĭ-grād′) *v.* **-graded, -grading.** To debase; corrupt. —**deg′ra•da′tion** *n.* —**de•grad′ed•ly** *adv.* —**de•grad′er** *n.*

**de•gree** (dĭ-grē′) *n.* **1.** A step or stage in a series. **2.** Extent; intensity. **3.** A unit on a subdivided scale or range, as of temperature. **4.** An academic title or rank.

**de•hy•drate** (dē-hī′drāt′) *v.* **-drated, -drating.** To remove water from. —**de′hy•dra′tion** *n.*

**de•ice** (dē-īs′) *v.* **-iced, -icing. 1.** To keep free of ice. **2.** To remove ice from.

**de•ic•er** (dē-ī′sər) *n.* A compound to prevent formation of ice.

**deign** (dān) *v.* To condescend.

**de•in•sti•tu•tion•al•i•za•tion** (dē-ĭn′stĭ-to͞o′shə-nə-lĭ-zā′shən) *n.* The release of a person from an institution to the general community for care. —**de•in′-sti•tu′tion•al•ize′** *v.*

**de•i•ty** (dē′ĭ-tē) *n., pl.* **-ties. 1.** A god. **2.** Divinity.

**de•ject•ed** (dĭ-jĕk′tĭd) *adj.* Depressed; disheartened. —**de•ject′ed•ly** *adv.* —**de•jec′tion** *n.*

**de ju•re** (dē jo͝or′ē, dā jo͝or′ā) *adv.* & *adj.* According to law; by right.

**de•lay** (dĭ-lā′) *v.* **1.** To cause to be late. **2.** To postpone. —*v.* The act of delaying or condition of being delayed. —**de•lay′er** *n.*

**de•lec•ta•ble** (dĭ-lĕk′tə-bəl) *adj.* **1.** Delightful. **2.** Delicious. —**de•lec′ta•bly** *adv.*

**del•e•gate** (dĕl′ĭ-gāt′, -gĭt) *n.* One authorized to act for another. —*v.* (-gāt′) **-gated, -gating. 1.** To send (a person) as one's representative. **2.** To commit to a subordinate. —**del′e•ga′tion** *n.*

**de•lete** (dĭ-lēt′) *v.* **-leted, -leting.** To strike out; omit. —**de•le′tion** *n.*

**del•i** (dĕl′ē) *n., pl.* **-is.** A delicatessen.

**de•lib•er•ate** (dĭ-lĭb′ə-rāt′) *v.* **-ated, -ating.** To consider carefully. —*adj.* (-ər-ĭt). **1.** Intentional. **2.** Careful in deciding. **3.** Unhurried. —**de•lib′er•ate•ly** *adv.* —**de•lib′er•ate•ness** *n.* —**de•lib′er•a′tion** *n.* —**de•lib′er•a′-tive** *adj.*

**del•i•cate** (dĕl′ĭ-kĭt) *adj.* **1.** Pleasingly small. **2.** Frail and fine. **3.** Easily damaged. **4.** Requiring or marked by careful skill. —**del′i•ca•cy** *n.* —**del′i•**

**cate•ly** *adv.*

**del•i•ca•tes•sen** (dĕl′ĭ-kə-tĕs′ən) *n.* A shop that sells cooked or prepared foods.

**de•li•cious** (dĭ-lĭsh′əs) *adj.* Highly pleasing to the taste. **—de•li′cious•ly** *adv.*

**de•light** (dĭ-līt′) *n.* Great pleasure; joy. *—v.* To give or take great pleasure or joy. **—de•light′ful** *adj.* **—de•light′ful•ly** *adv.*

**de•lin•quent** (dĭ-lĭng′kwənt) *adj.* Failing to do what is required. *—n.* A delinquent person. **—de•lin′quen•cy** *n.*

**de•lir•i•um** (dĭ-lîr′ē-əm) *n., pl.* **-ums** or **-ia. 1.** Temporary mental confusion and clouded consciousness. **2.** Ecstasy; rapture. **—de•lir′i•ous** *adj.* **—de•lir′i•ous•ly** *adv.*

**de•liv•er** (dĭ-lĭv′ər) *v.* **1.** To set free. **2.** To assist in birth. **3.** To take to an intended recipient. **4.** To utter. **—de•liv′er•ance** *n.* **—de•liv′er•er** *n.* **—de•liv′er•y** *n.*

**de•lude** (dĭ-lo͞od′) *v.* **-luded, -luding.** To mislead into error. **—de•lu′sion** *n.* **—de•lu′sive** *adj.*

**del•uge** (dĕl′yo͞oj) *v.* **-uged, -uging.** To flood. *—n.* A flood.

**de luxe, de•luxe** (dĭ-lŭks′, -lo͝oks′) *adv. & adj.* Especially elegant.

**delve** (dĕlv) *v.* **delved, delving.** To search deeply. **—delv′er** *n.*

**dem•a•gogue** (dĕm′ə-gôg′, -gŏg′) *n.* A leader who appeals to popular emotions and prejudices. **—dem′a•gog′ic** *adj.* **—dem′a•gogu′er•y** *n.*

**de•mand** (dĭ-mănd′) *v.* **1.** To ask for insistently. **2.** To claim as just or due. *—n.* **1.** The act of demanding. **2.** Something demanded. **3.** The state of being sought after. **—de•mand′er** *n.* **—de•mand′ing** *adj.*

**de•mean•or** (dĭ-mē′nər) *n.* Behavior.

**de•ment•ed** (dĭ-mĕn′tĭd) *adj.* Insane.

**de•mise** (dĭ-mīz′) *n.* Death.

**dem•o** (dĕm′ō) *n.* **1.** A demonstration. **2.** A product used in a demonstration and therefore sold at a discount.

**de•moc•ra•cy** (dĭ-mŏk′rə-sē) *n., pl.* **-cies. 1.** Government by the people. **2.** Social equality. **—dem′o•crat′** *n.* **—dem′o•crat′ic** *adj.* **—dem′o•crat′i•cal•ly** *adv.*

**de•mog•ra•phy** (dĭ-mŏg′rə-fē) *n.* The study of human populations, esp. of their size, growth, and statistics. **—de•mog′ra•pher** *n.* **—dem′o•graph′ic, dem′o•graph′i•cal** *adj.* **—dem′o•graph′i•cal•ly** *adv.* **—dem′o•graph′ics** *pl.n.*

**de•mol•ish** (dĭ-mŏl′ĭsh) *v.* To destroy. **—dem′o•li′tion** *n.*

**de•mon** (dē′mən) *n.* A devil or evil spirit. **—de′mo•ni′a•cal, de•mon′ic** *adj.*

**dem•on•strate** (dĕm′ən-strāt′) *v.* **-strated, -strating. 1.** To prove. **2.** To show. **—de•mon′stra•ble** *adj.* **—dem′on•stra′tion** *n.* **—de•mon′stra•tive** *adj.* **—dem′on•stra′tor** *n.*

**de•mor•al•ize** (dĭ-môr′ə-līz′, -mŏr′-) *v.* **-ized, -izing. 1.** To corrupt the morals of. **2.** To dishearten. **—de•mor′al•i•za′tion** *n.* **—de•mor′al•iz′er** *n.*

**de•mote** (dĭ-mōt′) *v.* **-moted, -moting.** To lower in rank. **—de•mo′tion** *n.*

**de•mur** (dĭ-mûr′) *v.* **-murred, -murring. 1.** To object. **2.** To delay.

**de•mure** (dĭ-myo͝or′) *adj.* **-murer, -murest. 1.** Modest and reserved. **2.** Feigning modesty; coy.

**den** (dĕn) *n.* **1.** The shelter of a wild animal; lair. **2.** A refuge, esp. if hidden. **3.** A small room for study or relaxation.

**den•i•grate** (dĕn′ĭ-grāt′) *v.* **-grated, -grating. 1.** To belittle. **2.** To defame. **—den′i•gra′tion** *n.*

**den•im** (dĕn′ĭm) *n.* A coarse twilled cloth.

**de•nom•i•na•tion** (dĭ-nŏm′ə-nā′shən) *n.* **1.** A name. **2.** A unit in a system of currency or weights. **3.** A religious group or sect. **—de•nom′i•na′tion•al** *adj.*

**de•nom•i•na•tor** (dĭ-nŏm′ə-nā′tər) *n.* The quantity below the line in a fraction.

**de•note** (dĭ-nōt′) *v.* **-noted, -noting. 1.** To indicate plainly. **2.** To mean. **—de′no•ta′tion** *n.*

**dé•noue•ment** (dā′no͞o-mäɴ′) *n.* **1.** The solution of a plot of a play or novel. **2.** The outcome of a series of events.

**de•nounce** (dĭ-nouns′) *v.* **-nounced, -nouncing. 1.** To speak out against; condemn. **2.** To accuse formally. **—de•nounce′ment** *n.* **—de•nounc′er** *n.* **—de•nun′ci•a′tion** *n.*

**dense** (dĕns) *adj.* **denser, densest. 1.** Compact. **2.** Thick. **3.** Stupid. **—dense′ly** *adv.* **—den′si•ty** *n.*

**dent** (dĕnt) *n.* A depression or hollow. **—dent** *v.*

**den•tal** (dĕn′tl) *adj.* Of the teeth.

**den•tist•ry** (dĕn′tĭstrē) *n.* The diagnosis and treatment of diseases of the teeth. **—den′tist** *n.*

**de•ny** (dĭ-nī′) *v.* **-nied, -nying. 1.** To declare untrue. **2.** To refuse to recognize or acknowledge. **3.** To refuse to grant. **—de•ni′al** *n.* **—de•ni′er** *n.*

**de•part** (dĭ-pärt′) *v.* **1.** To leave. **2.** To deviate. **—de•par′ture** *n.*

**de•part•ment** (dĕ-pärt′mənt) *n.* A division, as of a government, having a specialized function. **—de′part•men′tal** *adj.*

**de•pend** (dĭ-pĕnd′) *v.* **1.** To rely, as for support. **2.** To place trust. **3.** To be determined. **—de•pend′a•bil′i•ty** *n.* **—de•pend′a•ble** *adj.* **—de•pend′a•bly** *adv.* **—de•pend′ence** *n.* **—de•pend′ent** *adj.* & *n.*

**de•pict** (dĭ-pĭkt′) *v.* **1.** To represent in a picture. **2.** To describe. **—de•pic′tion** *n.*

**de•plane** (dē-plān′) *v.* **-planed, -planing.** To disembark from an airplane.

**de•plete** (dĭ-plēt′) *v.* **-pleted, -pleting.** To use up or exhaust. **—de•ple′tion** *n.*

**de•plore** (dĭ-plôr′, -plōr′) *v.* **-plored, -ploring.** To regard as unfortunate or wrong. **—de•plor′a•ble** *adj.* **—de•plor′a•bly** *adv.*

**de•port** (dĭ-pôrt′, -pōrt′) *v.* **1.** To expel from a country. **2.** To conduct (oneself). **—de′por•ta′tion** *n.* **—de•port′ment** *n.*

**de•pose** (dĭ-pōz′) *v.* **-posed, -posing. 1.** To remove from office. **2.** To testify under oath. **—dep′o•si′tion** *n.*

**de•pos•it** (dĭ-pŏz′ĭt) *v.* **1.** To place for safekeeping. **2.** To put down in layers. **3.** To give as partial payment. —*n.* Something deposited. **—de•pos′i•tor** *n.* **—de•pos′i•to′ry** *n.*

**de•pot** (dē′pō) *n.* **1.** A railroad or bus station. **2.** A warehouse.

**de•prave** (dĭ-prāv′) *v.* **-praved, -praving.** To corrupt. **—de•praved′** *adj.* **—de•prav′i•ty** *n.*

**de•pre•ci•ate** (dĭ-prē′shē-āt′) *v.* **-ated, -ating. 1.** To make or become less in value. **2.** To belittle. **—de•pre′ci•a′tion** *n.* **—de•pre′ci•a′tor** *n.*

**de•press** (dĭ-prĕs′) *v.* **1.** To sadden. **2.** To press down. **3.** To lower in value, price etc. **—de•pres′sion** *n.* **—de•pres′sive** *adj.* **—de•pres′sor** *n.*

**de•prive** (dĭ-prīv′) *v.* **-prived, -priving. 1.** To take something away from; divest. **2.** To keep something from. **—dep′ri•va′tion** *n.*

**depth** (dĕpth) *n.* **1.** The condition of being deep. **2.** The distance downward.

**dep•u•ty** (dĕp′yə-tē) *n., pl.* **-ties.** A person empowered to act for another. **—dep′u•ta′tion** *n.* **—dep′u•tize′** *v.* **—dep′u•ty** *adj.*

**de•range** (dĭ-rānj′) *v.* **-ranged, -ranging. 1.** To disturb. **2.** To make insane. **—de•range′ment** *n.*

**der•e•lict** (dĕr′ə-lĭkt′) *adj.* **1.** Neglectful. **2.** Abandoned. —*n.* A vagrant. **—der′e•lic′tion** *n.*

**de•ride** (dĭ-rīd′) *v.* **-rided, -riding.** To scoff at. **—de•ri′sion** *n.* **—de•ri′sive** *adj.* **—de•ri′sive•ly** *adv.*

**de•rive** (dĭ-rīv′) *v.* **-rived, -riving. 1.** To obtain or issue from a source. **2.** To deduce. **—der′i•va′tion** *n.* **—de•riv′a•tive** *adj.* & *n.*

**de•rog•a•to•ry** (dĭ-rŏg′ə-tôr′ē, -tōr′ē) *adj.* Detracting; disparaging. **—der′o•ga′tion** *n.*

**der•rick** (dĕr′ĭk) *n.* A large hoisting crane.

**de•scend** (dĭ-sĕnd′) *v.* **1.** To move or go down. **2.** To slope downward. **—de•scen′dent** *adj.* **—de•scent′** *n.*

**de•scen•dant** (dĭ-sĕn′dənt) *n.* An immediate or remote offspring.

**de•scribe** (dĭ-skrīb′) *v.* **-scribed, -scribing. 1.** To tell about. **2.** To trace the figure of. **—de•scrib′er** *n.* **—de•scrip′tion** *n.* **—de•scrip′tive** *adj.*

**des•ert**[1] (dĕz′ərt) *n.* A dry and barren region.

**de•sert**[2] (dĭ-zûrt′) *v.* To abandon. **—de•sert′er** *n.* **—de•ser′tion** *n.*

**de•serve** (dĭ-zûrv′) *v.* **-served, -serving.** To be worthy of; merit. **—de•serv′ing** *adj.*

**de•sign** (dĭ-zīn′) *v.* **1.** To conceive; invent. **2.** To form a plan for. **3.** To intend; scheme. —*n.* **1.** A plan. **2.** A pattern. **3.** An intention. **—de•sign′er** *n.* **—de•sign′ing** *adj.*

**des•ig•nate** (dĕz′ĭg-nāt′) *v.* **-nated, -nating. 1.** To indicate or specify. **2.** To give a name to. **3.** To appoint. *—adj.* (-nĭt). Appointed. **—des′ig•na′tion** *n.*

**de•sire** (dĭ-zīr′) *v.* **-sired, -siring.** To wish or long for; crave. *—n.* **1.** A wish. **2.** A request. **3.** Something longed for. **4.** Sexual appetite. **—de•sir′a•bil′i•ty** *n.* **—de•sir′a•ble** *adj.* **—de•sir′ous** *adj.*

**de•sist** (dĭ-sĭst′) *v.* To cease; stop.

**desk** (dĕsk) *n.* A writing table.

**desk•top** (dĕsk′tŏp′) *adj.* That can easily fit atop a desk, esp. a computer.

**des•o•late** (dĕs′ə-lĭt) *adj.* **1.** Deserted. **2.** Dismal. **3.** Forlorn. *—v.* (-lāt′) **-lated, -lating.** To make desolate. **—des′o•la′tion** *n.*

**de•spair** (dĭ-spâr′) *v.* To lose all hope. *—n.* Utter lack of hope. **—de•spair′ing•ly** *adv.*

**des•per•ate** (dĕs′pər-ĭt) *adj.* **1.** Reckless because of despair. **2.** Nearly hopeless. **3.** Extreme. **—des′per•ate•ly** *adv.* **—des′per•ate•ness, des′per•a′tion** *n.*

**des•pi•ca•ble** (dĕs′pĭ-kə-bəl, dĭ-spĭk′ə-) *adj.* Contemptible. **—des′pi•ca•bly** *adv.*

**de•spise** (dĭ-spīz′) *v.* **-spised, -spising.** To regard with contempt. **—de•spis′er** *n.*

**de•spite** (dĭ-spīt′) *prep.* In spite of.

**de•spon•den•cy** (dĭ-spŏn′dən-sē) *n., pl.* **-cies.** Also **de•spon•dence.** Depression; dejection. **—de•spon′dent** *adj.*

**des•pot** (dĕs′pət) *n.* An autocratic ruler. **—des•pot′ic** *adj.* **—des′pot•ism′** *n.*

**des•sert** (dĭ-zûrt′) *n.* A usually sweet food served at the end of a meal.

**des•ti•na•tion** (dĕs′tə-nā′shən) *n.* The place to which one is going; goal.

**des•tine** (dĕs′tĭn) *v.* **-tined, -tining. 1.** To preordain. **2.** To intend or direct.

**des•ti•ny** (dĕs′tə-nē) *n., pl.* **-nies.** Fate.

**des•ti•tute** (dĕs′tĭ-t/y/o͞ot′) *adj.* **1.** Altogether lacking; devoid. **2.** Very poor; penniless. **—des′ti•tu′tion** *n.*

**de•stroy** (dĭ-stroi′) *v.* **1.** To ruin. **2.** To demolish. **3.** To kill. **—de•stroy′er** *n.*

**de•struc•tion** (dĭ-strŭk′shən) *n.* The act of destroying or state of being destroyed. **—de•struc′tive** *adj.* **—de•struc′tive•ly** *adv.* **—de•struc′tive•ness** *n.*

**de•tach** (dĭ-tăch′) *v.* To separate; remove. **—de•tach′a•ble** *adj.*

**de•tail** (dĭ-tāl′, dē′tāl′) *n.* **1.** An individual part or item. **2.** Itemized treatment of particulars. *—v.* To relate item by item.

**de•tain** (dĭ-tān′) *v.* **1.** To keep from proceeding; delay. **2.** To confine. **—de•tain′ment, de•ten′tion** *n.*

**de•tect** (dĭ-tĕkt′) *v.* To discover the existence, presence, or fact of. **—de•tect′a•ble** *adj.* **—de•tec′tion** *n.* **—de•tec′tive** *n.* **—de•tec′tor** *n.*

**de•ter** (dĭ-tûr′) *v.* **-terred, -terring.** To prevent or discourage from acting. **—de•ter′rent** *adj. & n.*

**de•ter•gent** (dĭ-tûr′jənt) *n.* A cleansing substance.

**de•te•ri•o•rate** (dĭ-tîr′ē-ə-rāt′) *v.* **-rated, -rating.** To become or make worse. **—de•te′ri•o•ra′tion** *n.*

**de•ter•mine** (dĭ-tûr′mĭn) *v.* **-mined, -mining. 1.** To decide or establish conclusively. **2.** To limit or regulate. **3.** To be the cause of. **—deter′mi•na•ble** *adj.* **—de•ter′mi•na•bly** *adv.* **—de•ter′mi•na′tion** *n.*

**de•test** (dĭ-tĕst′) *v.* To dislike intensely; loathe. **—de•test′a•ble** *adj.* **—de′tes•ta′tion** *n.*

**de•tour** (dē′to͝or′, dĭ-to͝or′) *n.* A roundabout way. *—v.* To go by a detour.

**de•tox** (dē′tŏks) *adj.* Relating to detoxification. *—n.* A section of a hospital for patients undergoing detoxification. *—v.* To detoxify.

**de•tox•i•fy** (dē-tŏk′sə-fī′) *v.* **-fied, -fying. 1.** To counteract the poisons of. **2.** To free a person from alcohol or drug addiction. **—de•tox′i•fi•ca′tion** *n.*

**de•tract** (dĭ-trăkt′) *v.* To be a drawback; diminish. **—de•trac′tion** *n.* **—de•trac′tive** *adj.* **—de•trac′tor** *n.*

**det•ri•ment** (dĕt′rə-mənt) *n.* Harm; disadvantage. **—det′ri•men′tal** *adj.*

**de•val•u•ate** (dēvăl′yo͞o-āt′) *v.* **-ated, -ating.** Also **de•val•ue, -ued, -uing.** To lower the value of. **—de•val′u•a′tion** *n.*

**dev•as•tate** (dĕv′ə-stāt′) *v.* **-tated, -tating. 1.** To lay waste. **2.** To overwhelm. **—dev′as•ta′tion** *n.*

**de•vel•op** (dĭ-vĕl′əp) *v.* **1.** To bring, grow, or evolve to a more complete state. **2.** To appear or disclose gradually. **3.** To elaborate; expand. **—de•vel′op•er** *n.* **—de•vel′op•ment** *n.*

**de•vi•ate** (dē′vē-āt′) *v.* **-ated, -ating.** To turn away from an accepted course or standard. *—n.* (-ĭt). A sexual pervert.

—**de′vi•ance** *n.* —**de′vi•ant** *adj. & n.* —**de′vi•a′tion** *n.*

**de•vice** (dĭ-vīs′) *n.* **1.** Something, as a mechanical contrivance, made for a particular purpose. **2.** A scheme; trick.

**dev•il** (dĕv′əl) *n.* **1.** The major spirit of evil. **2.** A wicked or mischievous person. —**dev′il•ish** *adj.*

**de•vi•ous** (dē′vē-əs) *adj.* **1.** Roundabout. **2.** Deceitful. —**de′vi•ous•ly** *adv.* —**de′vi•ous•ness** *n.*

**de•vise** (dĭ-vīz′) *v.* **-vised, -vising.** To plan; invent. —**de•vis′er** *n.*

**de•void** (dĭ-void′) *adj.* Completely lacking.

**de•vote** (dĭ-vōt′) *v.* **-voted, -voting. 1.** To give or apply entirely. **2.** To dedicate.

**de•vo•tion** (dĭ-vō′shən) *n.* **1.** Ardent attachment or affection. **2.** Religious zeal. **3. devotions.** Prayers. —**de•vo′tion•al** *adj.*

**de•vour** (dĭ-vour′) *v.* To eat up or consume greedily. —**de•vour′er** *n.*

**de•vout** (dĭ-vout′) *adj.* **1.** Deeply religious; pious. **2.** Earnest. —**de•vout′ly** *adv.* —**de•vout′ness** *n.*

**dew** (d/y/ōō) *n.* Water droplets condensed onto cool surfaces. —**dew′i•ness** *n.* —**dew′y** *adj.*

**dex•ter•ous** (dĕk′stər-əs) *adj.* Also **dex•trous** (-strəs). Skillful; adroit. —**dex•ter′i•ty** *n.* —**dex′ter•ous•ly** *adv.*

**di•a•bol•ic** (dī′ə-bŏl′ĭk) *adj.* Also **di•a•bol•i•cal.** Devilish; wicked. —**di′a•bol′i•cal•ly** *adv.*

**di•ag•no•sis** (dī′əg-nō′sĭs) *n., pl.* **-ses** (-sēz). Identification, esp. of a disease. —**di′ag•nose′** *v.* —**di′ag•nos′tic** *adj.* —**di′ag•nos′ti•cal•ly** *adv.* —**di′ag•nos•ti′cian** *n.*

**di•ag•o•nal** (dī-ăg′ə-nəl) *adj.* Slanted or oblique in direction. —*n.* A diagonal line. —**di•ag′o•nal•ly** *adv.*

**di•a•gram** (dī′ə-grăm′) *n.* A simplified explanatory drawing or plan. —*v.* To represent by a diagram. —**di′a•gram•mat′ic, di′a•gram•mat′i•cal** *adj.*

**di•al** (dī′əl) *n.* **1.** A marked disk or plate on which a measurement is indicated. **2.** A rotatable disk, as of a telephone. —*v.* **1.** To indicate or select by means of a dial. **2.** To call on a telephone with a dial.

**di•a•lect** (dī′ə-lĕkt′) *n.* **1.** A regional variety of a spoken language. **2.** A jargon. —**di′a•lec′tal** *adj.*

**di•a•logue** (dī′ə-lôg′, -lŏg′) *n.* Also **di•a•log.** A conversation, esp. in a play or narrative.

**di•am•e•ter** (dī-ăm′ĭ-tər) *n.* **1.** A straight line through the center of a circle or other figure. **2.** Its length. —**di′a•met′ric, di′a•met′ri•cal** *adj.* —**di′a•met′ri•cal•ly** *adv.*

**di•a•mond** (dī′ə-mənd, dī′mənd) *n.* **1.** An extremely hard brilliant gemstone. **2.** A rhombus or lozenge. **3.** A baseball field.

**di•a•per** (dī′ə-pər, dī′pər) *n.* A folded cloth used to cover a baby's genital and anal areas. —*v.* To put a diaper on.

**di•a•phragm** (dī′ə-frăm′) *n.* **1.** A muscular membrane separating the abdomen and chest. **2.** Any similar membranous partition.

**di•ar•rhe•a, di•ar•rhoe•a** (dī′ə-rē′ə) *n.* Frequent and watery bowel movements.

**di•a•ry** (dī′ə-rē) *n., pl.* **-ries.** A daily record, esp. of personal experiences. —**di′a•rist** *n.*

**dice** (dīs) *pl.n. Sing.* **die.** Small cubes used in gambling games. —*v.* **diced, dicing.** To cut into small cubes. —**dic′er** *n.*

**di•cey** (dī′sē) *adj.* **-ier, -iest.** Risky; chancy; hazardous.

**di•chot•o•my** (dī-kŏt′ə-mē) *n., pl.* **-mies.** Division into 2 usu. contradictory parts or opinions.

**dic•tate** (dĭk′tāt′, dĭk-tāt′) *v.* **-tated, -tating. 1.** To speak for recording or transcription. **2.** To issue (a command, order, etc.) authoritatively. —**dic•ta′tion** *n.*

**dic•ta•tor** (dĭk′tā′tər) *n.* An absolute or tyrannical ruler. —**dic′ta•to′ri•al** *adj.* —**dic•ta′tor•ship′** *n.*

**dic•tion•ar•y** (dĭk′shə-nĕr′ē) *n., pl.* **-ies. 1.** A book containing an alphabetical list of words with definitions or translations. **2.** A list in machine-readable form for use by a computer.

**did** (dĭd) *v.* p.t. of **do.**

**did•dle** (dĭd′l) *v.* **-dled, -dling. 1.** To waste time. **2.** To cheat.

**did•n't** (dĭd′nt) *v.* Contraction of *did not.*

**die**[1] (dī) *v.* **died, dying. 1.** To cease living. **2.** To pass out of existence.

**die**[2] (dī) *n.* **1.** A device used for cutting out, forming, or stamping material. **2.** *Sing.* of **dice.**

**die•sel•ing** (dē′zə-lĭng, -sə-) *n.* The continued running of a motor after the ignition is turned off.

**di•et** (dī′ĭt) *n.* **1.** One's usual food and drink. **2.** A restricted selection of food. —*v.* To eat according to a diet. **—di′e•tar′y** *adj.* **—di′et•er** *n.* **—di′e•tet′ic** *adj.* **—di′e•ti′tian** *n.*

**dif•fer** (dĭf′ər) *v.* **1.** To be unlike. **2.** To disagree; dissent. **—dif′fer•ence** *n.* **—dif′fer•ent** *adj.*

**dif•fi•cult** (dĭf′ĭ-kŭlt′, -kəlt) *adj.* Hard; not easy. **—dif′fi•cul′ty** *n.*

**dig** (dĭg) *v.* **dug** (dŭg), **digging. 1.** To turn over or remove (soil) with a tool. **2.** To make or extract by removing soil. **3.** To search; probe.

**di•gest** (dī-jĕst′, dĭ-) *v.* **1.** To transform food into an assimilable condition. **2.** To absorb mentally. —*n.* (dī′jĕst′). A summary; condensation. **—di•gest′i•ble** *adj.* **—di•ges′tion** *n.* **—di•ges′tive** *adj.*

**dig•it** (dĭj′ĭt) *n.* **1.** A finger or toe. **2.** Any of the Arabic number symbols, 0 through 9.

**dig•i•tal** (dĭj′ĭ-tl) *adj.* **1.** Relating to digits, esp. fingers. **2.** Expressed in digits, esp. for use by a computer. **3.** Using or giving a reading in digits. **4.** Relating to a compact disk made from a digital master.

**dig•ni•ty** (dĭg′nĭ-tē) *n., pl.* **-ties. 1.** Nobility; honor; worth. **2.** A high rank. **3.** Calm assurance; composure.

**dike, dyke** (dīk) *n.* An embankment to contain a body of water.

**di•late** (dī-lāt′, dī′lāt′) *v.* **-lated, -lating.** To expand. **—di•la′tion, dil′a•ta′tion** *n.*

**di•lem•ma** (dĭ-lĕm′ə) *n.* A perplexing choice or predicament.

**dil•i•gence** (dĭl′ə-jəns) *n.* Persistent and energetic application to a task. **—dil′i•gent** *adj.* **—dil′i•gent•ly** *adv.*

**di•lute** (dī-lo͞ot′, dĭ-) *v.* **-luted, -luting.** To reduce the concentration of. **—di•lut′er** *n.* **—di•lu′tion** *n.*

**dim** (dĭm) *adj.* **dimmer, dimmest. 1.** Not bright; faint. **2.** Indistinct; obscure. —*v.* **dimmed, dimming.** To make or become dim. **—dim′ly** *adv.* **—dim′ness** *n.*

**dime** (dīm) *n.* A coin worth 10 cents.

**di•men•sion** (dĭmĕn′shən) *n.* **1.** A measure of spatial extent. **2.** Often **dimensions.** Extent; size; scope. **—di•men′sion•al** *adj.*

**di•min•ish** (dĭ-mĭn′ĭsh) *v.* To make or become smaller. **—di•min′ish•ment, dim′i•nu′tion** *n.*

**di•min•u•tive** (dĭ-mĭn′yə-tĭv) *adj.* Small.

**din** (dĭn) *n.* Discordant noise. —*v.* **dinned, dinning.** To impress by wearying repetition.

**dine** (dīn) *v.* **dined, dining.** To eat dinner. **—din′er** *n.*

**din•gy** (dĭn′jē) *adj.* **-gier, -giest.** Drab; shabby. **—din′gi•ness** *n.*

**din•ner** (dĭn′ər) *n.* The chief meal of the day.

**di•o•cese** (dī′ə-sĭs, -sēs′, -sēz′) *n.* The district of churches under a bishop. **—di•oc′e•san** *adj.*

**dip** (dĭp) *v.* **dipped, dipping. 1.** To plunge briefly into a liquid. **2.** To scoop up (liquid). **3.** To drop or sink. **—dip′per** *n.*

**di•plo•ma** (dĭ-plō′mə) *n.* A document certifying completion of a course of study.

**di•plo•ma•cy** (dĭ-plō′mə-sē) *n., pl.* **-cies. 1.** The art or profession of conducting international relations. **2.** Tact. **—dip′lo•mat′** *n.* **—dip′lo•mat′ic** *adj.* **—dip′lo•mat′i•cal•ly** *adv.*

**dire** (dīr) *adj.* **direr, direst.** Dreadful. **—dire′ly** *adv.*

**di•rect** (dĭ-rĕkt′, dī-) *v.* **1.** To conduct; manage. **2.** To instruct; order. **3.** To aim. —*adj.* **1.** Straight. **2.** Straightforward. **—di•rect′ly** *adv.* **—di•rec′tor** *n.*

**di•rec•tion** (dĭ-rĕk′shən, dī-) *n.* **1.** The act or function of directing. **2.** Often **directions.** Instructions. **3.** A command. **4.** The line or course along which a person or thing moves. **—di•rec′tion•al** *adj.*

**dirge** (dûrj) *n.* A funeral hymn.

**dirt** (dûrt) *n.* **1.** Earth or soil. **2.** A soiling substance. **—dirt′y** *adj.*

**dis•a•ble** (dĭs-ā′bəl) *v.* **-bled, -bling.** To weaken or cripple. **—dis′a•bil′i•ty** *n.*

**dis•ad•van•tage** (dĭs′əd-văn′tĭj) *n.* A handicap; detriment. **—dis′ad•van′taged** *adj.* **—dis•ad′van•ta′geous** *adj.*

**dis•a•gree** (dĭs′ə-grē′) *v.* **-greed, -greeing. 1.** To be different. **2.** To have a different opinion. **—dis′a•gree′ment** *n.*

**dis•a•gree•a•ble** (dĭs′ə-grē′ə-bəl) *adj.* Unpleasant; offensive. **—dis′a•gree′a•bly** *adv.*

**dis•ap•pear** (dĭs′ə-pîr′) *v.* To pass out of sight; vanish. **—dis′ap•pear′ance** *n.*

**dis•ap•point** (dĭs′ə-point′) *v.* To fail to satisfy the hopes of. **—dis′ap•point′ing•ly** *adv.* **—dis′ap•point′ment** *n.*

**dis•ap•prove** (dĭs′ə-pro͞ov′) *v.* **-proved, -proving.** To have an unfavorable opinion. **—dis′ap•prov′al** *n.*

**dis•arm** (dĭs-ärm′) *v.* **1.** To deprive of weapons. **2.** To overcome the hostility of. **—dis•ar′ma•ment** *n.* **—dis•arm′ing** *adj.* **—dis•arm′ing•ly** *adv.*

**dis•ar•ray** (dĭs′ə-rā′) *n.* Disorder.

**dis•as•ter** (dĭ-zăs′tər) *n.* **1.** An occurrence inflicting widespread destruction and distress. **2.** A total failure. **—dis•as′trous** *adj.* **—dis•as′trous•ly** *adv.*

**dis•bar** (dĭs-bär′) *v.* **-barred, -barring.** To expel from the legal profession. **—dis•bar′ment** *n.*

**dis•burse** (dĭs-bûrs′) *v.* **-bursed, -bursing.** To pay out. **—dis•burse′ment** *n.*

**disc** (dĭsk) *n.* A disk.

**dis•card** (dĭ-skärd′) *v.* To throw away; reject.

**dis•charge** (dĭs-chärj′) *v.* **-charged, -charging. 1.** To unload. **2.** To release or dismiss. **3.** To emit. **4.** To shoot. **5.** To perform (a duty). —*n.* (dĭs′chärj′). **1.** The act of discharging. **2.** Something discharged.

**dis•ci•ple** (dĭ-sī′pəl) *n.* A follower; adherent.

**dis•ci•pline** (dĭs′ə-plĭn) *n.* **1.** Training, esp. to instill good behavior. **2.** Controlled behavior. **3.** Corrective punishment. —*v.* **-plined, -plining. 1.** To train. **2.** To punish. **—dis′ci•pli•nar′i•an** *n.* **—dis′ci•pli•nar′y** *adj.*

**dis•claim** (dĭs-klām′) *v.* To deny; disown. **—dis•claim′er** *n.*

**dis•close** (dĭ-sklōz′) *v.* **-closed, -closing.** To expose to view; reveal. **—dis•clo′sure** *n.*

**dis•com•fort** (dĭs-kŭm′fərt) *n.* **1.** The condition of being uncomfortable. **2.** Something that disturbs one's comfort.

**dis•con•nect** (dĭs′kə-nĕkt′) *v.* To sever the connection of. **—dis′con•nect′ed** *adj.* **—dis′con•nec′tion** *n.*

**dis•con•so•late** (dĭs-kŏn′sə-lĭt) *adj.* Hopelessly sad. **—dis•con′so•late•ly** *adv.* **—dis•con′so•late•ness** *n.*

**dis•con•tent** (dĭs′kən-tĕnt′) *n.* Dissatisfaction. **—dis′con•tent′ed** *adj.*

**dis•con•tin•ue** (dĭs′kən-tĭn′yo͞o) *v.* **-ued, -uing.** To cease; stop. **—dis′con•tin′u•ance, dis′con•tin′u•a′tion** *n.*

**dis•cord** (dĭs′kôrd′) *n.* **1.** Dissension. **2.** Dissonance. **—dis•cor′dant** *adj.* **—dis•cor′dant•ly** *adv.*

**dis•count** (dĭs′kount′, dĭs-kount′) *v.* **1.** To deduct, as from a cost. **2.** To disregard. —*n.* (dĭs′kount′). A reduction from the full amount.

**dis•cour•age** (dĭ-skûr′ĭj) *v.* **-aged, -aging. 1.** To deprive of confidence, hope, or spirit. **2.** To dissuade. **—dis•cour′age•ment** *n.*

**dis•cour•te•ous** (dĭs-kûr′tē-əs) *adj.* Impolite. **—dis•cour′te•sy** *n.*

**dis•cov•er** (dĭ-skŭv′ər) *v.* **1.** To arrive at through search or study. **2.** To be the first to find, learn of, or observe. **—dis•cov′er•a•ble** *adj.* **—dis•cov′er•er** *n.* **—dis•cov′er•y** *n.*

**dis•cred•it** (dĭs-krĕd′ĭt) *v.* **1.** To disgrace; dishonor. **2.** To cast doubt on. —*n.* **1.** Damage to one's reputation. **2.** Loss of trust or belief. **—dis•cred′it•a•ble** *adj.*

**dis•creet** (dĭ-skrēt′) *adj.* Tactful; prudent. **—dis•creet′ly** *adv.* **—dis•cre′tion** *n.*

**dis•crep•an•cy** (dĭ-skrĕp′ən-sē) *n., pl.* **-cies.** Disagreement, as between facts. **—dis•crep′ant** *adj.*

**dis•crim•i•nate** (dĭ-skrĭm′ə-nāt′) *v.* **-nated, -nating. 1.** To distinguish. **2.** To act on the basis of prejudice. **—dis•crim′i•na′tion** *n.* **—dis•crim′i•na′tive, dis•crim′i•na•to′ry** *adj.*

**dis•cuss** (dĭ-skŭs′) *v.* **1.** To speak or write about. **2.** To talk over. **—dis•cus′sion** *n.*

**dis•dain** (dĭs-dān′) *v.* To regard with contempt. —*n.* Scornful superiority. **—dis•dain′ful** *adj.*

**dis•ease** (dĭ-zēz′) *n.* An abnormal condition that impairs normal functioning; illness. **—dis•eased′** *adj.*

**dis•em•bark** (dĭs′ĕm-bärk′) *v.* To go ashore from a ship.

**dis•fa•vor** (dĭs-fā′vər) *n.* Disapproval.

**dis•fig•ure** (dĭs-fĭg′yər) *v.* **-ured, -uring.** To deform. **—dis•fig′ure•ment** *n.*
**dis•grace** (dĭs-grās′) *n.* Loss of honor; shame. *—v.* **-graced, -gracing.** To bring shame or dishonor upon. **—dis•grace′-ful** *adj.* **—dis•grace′ful•ly** *adv.*
**dis•guise** (dĭs-gīz′) *v.* **-guised, -guising.** To modify the appearance of to prevent recognition. *—n.* **1.** The condition of being disguised. **2.** Something that serves to disguise.
**dis•gust** (dĭs-gŭst′) *v.* To excite nausea or loathing in; sicken. *—n.* Profound repugnance. **—dis•gust′ed** *adj.* **—dis•gust′ing** *adj.*
**dish** (dĭsh) *n.* **1.** An open, shallow container for food. **2.** A particular preparation of food.
**dis•heart•en** (dĭs-här′tn) *v.* To discourage. **—dis•heart′en•ing•ly** *adv.*
**dis•hon•est** (dĭs-ŏn′ĭst) *adj.* Not honest. **—dis•hon′est•ly** *adv.* **—dis•hon′es•ty** *n.*
**dis•hon•or** (dĭs-ŏn′ər) *n.* Loss of honor; disgrace. *—v.* To deprive of honor; disgrace. **—dis•hon′or•a•ble** *adj.* **—dis•hon′or•a•bly** *adv.*
**dis•il•lu•sion** (dĭs′ĭ-lo͞o′zhən) *v.* To free of illusion. **—dis′il•lu′sion•ment** *n.*
**dis•in•fect** (dĭs′ĭn-fĕkt′) *v.* To cleanse of germs. **—dis′in•fec′tant** *n.*
**dis•in•for•ma•tion** (dĭs-ĭn′fər-mā′shən) *n.* Lies deliberately spread to obscure embarrassing facts or discredit opponents. **—dis′in•form′** *v.*
**dis•in•her•it** (dĭs′ĭn-hĕr′ĭt) *v.* To prevent from inheriting.
**dis•in•te•grate** (dĭs-ĭn′tĭ-grāt′) *v.* **-grated, -grating.** To separate into fragments. **—dis•in′te•gra′tion** *n.*
**dis•in•ter•est•ed** (dĭs-ĭn′trĭ-stĭd, -ĭn′tə-rĕs′-tĭd) *adj.* Impartial. **—dis•in′ter•est•ed•ly** *adv.*
**disk** (dĭsk) *n.* **1.** Any thin, flat, circular plate. **2.** A compact disk. **3.** A floppy disk; diskette. **4.** A magnetic disk.
**disk•ette** (dĭ-skĕt′) *n.* A small, flexible, plastic magnetic plate storing computer data; a floppy disk.
**dis•like** (dĭs-līk′) *n.* Distaste or aversion. **—dis•like′** *v.*
**dis•lo•cate** (dĭs′lō-kāt′, dĭs-lō′kāt) *v.* **-cated, -cating.** **1.** To displace from the normal position. **2.** To upset; disturb. **—dis′lo•ca′tion** *n.*
**dis•mal** (dĭz′məl) *adj.* Causing gloom. **—dis′mal•ly** *adv.*
**dis•man•tle** (dĭs-măn′tl) *v.* **-tled, -tling.** To take apart. **—dis•man′tle•ment** *n.*
**dis•may** (dĭs-mā′) *v.* **1.** To make anxious or afraid. **2.** To discourage. *—n.* Consternation.
**dis•miss** (dĭs-mĭs′) *v.* **1.** To discharge, as from employment. **2.** To direct to leave. **3.** To reject. **—dis•miss′al** *n.*
**dis•o•bey** (dĭs′ə-bā′) *v.* To fail or refuse to obey. **—dis′o•be′di•ence** *n.* **—dis′-o•be′di•ent** *adj.*
**dis•or•der** (dĭs-ôr′dər) *n.* **1.** Lack of order. **2.** A public disturbance. **3.** An illness. **—dis•or′der•ly** *adj.*
**dis•own** (dĭs-ōn′) *v.* To repudiate.
**dis•par•age** (dĭ-spăr′ĭj) *v.* **-aged, -aging.** To belittle. **—dis•par′age•ment** *n.* **—dis•par′ag•ing•ly** *adv.*
**dis•pa•rate** (dĭs′pər-ĭt, dĭ-spăr′ĭt) *adj.* Distinct; dissimilar. **—dis′pa•rate•ly** *adv.* **—dis•par′i•ty** *n.*
**dis•patch** (dĭ-spăch′) *v.* **1.** To send. **2.** To perform promptly. *—n.* **1.** The act of dispatching. **2.** Efficient performance. **3.** A message. **4.** A shipment. **—dis•patch′er** *n.*
**dis•pel** (dĭ-spĕl′) *v.* **-pelled, -pelling.** To drive away.
**dis•pense** (di-spĕns′) *v.* **-pensed, -pensing.** **1.** To distribute; give out. **2.** To exempt. **—dis′pen•sa′tion** *n.* **—dis•pens′er** *n.*
**dis•perse** (dĭ-spûrs′) *v.* **-persed, -persing.** **1.** To scatter. **2.** To distribute. **—dis•per′sal, dis•per′sion** *n.*
**dis•place** (dĭs-plās′) *v.* **-placed, -placing.** **1.** To remove from a place or position. **2.** To take the place of. **—dis•place′-ment** *n.*
**dis•play** (dĭ-splā′) *v.* To place in view; show. *—n.* **1.** An act of displaying. **2.** Something displayed. **3.** An electronic device giving information in a visual form.
**dis•please** (dĭs-plēz′) *v.* **-pleased, -pleasing.** To annoy or irritate. **—dis•pleas′ure** *n.*
**dis•pose** (dĭ-spōz′) *v.* **-posed, -posing.** **1.** To arrange. **2.** To settle; conclude. **3.** To incline. **—dis•pos′a•ble** *adj.* **—dis•pos′al** *n.* **—dis′po•si′tion** *n.*
**dis•prove** (dĭs-pro͞ov′) *v.* **-proved, -proving.** To prove false; refute. **—dis•**

**proof′** *n.*

**dis•pute** (dĭ-spyo͞ot′) *v.* **-puted, -puting. 1.** To argue; debate. **2.** To question. —*n.* **1.** An argument; debate. **2.** A quarrel. —**dis•put′a•ble** *adj.* —**dis•pu′tant** *adj. & n.* —**dis′pu•ta′tion** *n.*

**dis•qual•i•fy** (dĭs-kwŏl′ə-fī′) *v.* **-fied, -fying.** To declare or render unqualified. —**dis•qual′i•fi•ca′tion** *n.*

**dis•re•gard** (dĭs′rĭ-gärd′) *v.* To ignore. —*n.* Willful lack of regard.

**dis•re•spect** (dĭs′rĭ-spĕkt′) *n.* Lack of respect; rudeness. —**dis′re•spect′ful** *adj.*

**dis•rupt** (dĭs-rŭpt′) *v.* To throw into confusion. —**dis•rup′tion** *n.* —**dis•rup′tive** *adj.*

**dis•sat•is•fy** (dĭs-săt′ĭs-fī′) *v.* **-fied, -fying.** To make discontented. —**dis•sat′is•fac′tion** *n.*

**dis•sect** (dĭ-sĕkt′, dī-, dī′sĕkt′) *v.* **1.** To cut apart for study. **2.** To analyze. —**dis•sec′tion** *n.*

**dis•sent** (dĭ-sĕnt′) *v.* To disagree. —*n.* **1.** Disagreement. **2.** Political or religious nonconformity. —**dis•sen′sion** *n.* —**dis•sent′er** *n.*

**dis•sim•i•lar** (dĭ-sĭm′ə-lər) *adj.* Unlike. —**dis•sim′i•lar′i•ty** *n.*

**dis•si•pate** (dĭs′ə-pāt′) *v.* **-pated, -pating. 1.** To dispel or scatter. **2.** To waste. **3.** To indulge oneself intemperately. —**dis′si•pa′tion** *n.*

**dis•so•ci•ate** (dĭ-sō′shē-āt′, -sē-) *v.* **-ated, -ating.** To remove from association; separate. —**dis•so′ci•a′tion** *n.* —**dis•so′ci•a′tive** *adj.*

**dis•solve** (dĭ-zŏlv′) *v.* **-solved, -solving. 1.** To enter or cause to enter into solution. **2.** To melt. **3.** To dispel. **4.** To terminate or dismiss.

**dis•so•nance** (dĭs′ə-nəns) *n.* Discord. —**dis′so•nant** *adj.* —**dis′so•nant•ly** *adv.*

**dis•suade** (dĭ-swād′) *v.* **-suaded, -suading.** To discourage by persuasion. —**dis•sua′sion** *n.* —**dis•sua′sive** *adj.*

**dis•tance** (dĭs′təns) *n.* **1.** Separation in space or time. **2.** The length of a line joining two points. **3.** Coldness; aloofness. —**dis′tant** *adj.* —**dis′tant•ly** *adv.*

**dis•taste** (dĭs-tāst′) *n.* Dislike. —**dis•taste′ful** *adj.* —**dis•taste′ful•ly** *adv.*

**dis•till** (dĭs-tĭl′) *v.* To extract, purify, or produce by vaporizing and condensing. —**dis′til•la′tion** *n.* —**dis•till′er** *n.* —**dis•till′er•y** *n.*

**dis•tinct** (dĭ-stĭngkt′) *adj.* **1.** Individual. **2.** Different; unlike. —**dis•tinct′ly** *adv.*

**dis•tinc•tion** (dĭ-stĭngk′shən) *n.* **1.** A difference. **2.** A distinguishing factor or characteristic. **3.** Personal excellence. **4.** Honor.

**dis•tinc•tive** (dĭ-stĭngk′tĭv) *adj.* **1.** Serving to identify. **2.** Characteristic. —**dis•tinc′tive•ly** *adv.*

**dis•tin•guish** (dĭ-stĭng′gwĭsh) *v.* **1.** To recognize as distinct. **2.** To perceive distinctly; discern. **3.** To set apart. —**dis•tin′guish•a•ble** *adj.* —**dis•tin′guished** *adj.*

**dis•tort** (dĭ-stôrt′) *v.* **1.** To twist out of proper shape. **2.** To misrepresent. —**dis•tor′tion** *n.*

**dis•tract** (dĭ-străkt′) *v.* **1.** To divert. **2.** To unsettle emotionally. —**dis•trac′tion** *n.* —**dis•trac′tive** *adj.*

**dis•tress** (dĭ-strĕs′) *v.* To cause anxiety or suffering to. —*n.* **1.** Anxiety or suffering. **2.** Misfortune.

**dis•trib•ute** (dĭ-strĭb′yo͞ot) *v.* **-uted, -uting. 1.** To divide and dispense in portions. **2.** To pass or send out. **3.** To spread through an area. —**dis′tri•bu′tion** *n.* —**dis•trib′u•tive** *adj.* —**dis•trib′u•tor, dis•trib′ut•er** *n.*

**dis•trict** (dĭs′trĭkt) *n.* **1.** A territorial division, esp. for administrative purposes. **2.** An area; region.

**dis•trust** (dĭs-trŭst′) *n.* Lack of trust; suspicion. —*v.* To lack confidence in. —**dis•trust′ful** *adj.*

**dis•turb** (dĭ-stûrb′) *v.* **1.** To upset or disarrange. **2.** To intrude upon. —**dis•tur′bance** *n.* —**dis•turb′ing•ly** *adv.*

**ditch** (dĭch) *n.* A trench dug in the ground. —*v.* To discard.

**dive** (dīv) *v.* **dived** or **dove** (dōv), **dived, diving. 1.** To plunge headfirst into water. **2.** To submerge. **3.** To drop sharply. —*n.* An act or instance of diving. —**div′er** *n.*

**di•verge** (dĭ-vûrj′, dī-) *v.* **-verged, -verging. 1.** To tend in different directions from a common point. **2.** To differ; deviate. —**di•ver′gence** *n.* —**di•ver′gent** *adj.*

**di•verse** (dī-vûrs′, dĭ-, dī′vûrs′) *adj.* **1.** Unlike. **2.** Varied. **—di•verse′ly** *adv.* **—di•ver′si•fi•ca′tion** *n.* **—di•ver′si•fy′** *v.* **—di•ver′si•ty** *n.*

**di•vert** (dĭ-vûrt′, dī-) *v.* **1.** To turn aside; deflect. **2.** To distract. **3.** To entertain. **—di•ver′sion** *n.* **—di•vert′er** *n.*

**di•vide** (dĭ-vīd′) *v.* **-vided, -viding. 1.** To separate or become separated into parts. **2.** To disunite. **3.** To apportion or share. **4.** To determine how many times one quantity is contained in another. **—di•vid′a•ble** *adj.* **—di•vid′er** *n.* **—di•vis′i•ble** *adj.* **—di•vi′sion** *n.* **—di•vi′sive** *adj.* **—di•vi′sor** *n.*

**div•i•dend** (dĭv′ĭ-dĕnd′) *n.* **1.** A quantity to be divided. **2.** A share of profits received by a stockholder.

**di•vine**[1] (dĭ-vīn′) *adj.* **-viner, -vinest. 1.** Of God or a god. **2.** Supremely good. **—di•vine′ly** *adv.* **—di•vin′i•ty** *n.*

**di•vine**[2] (dĭ-vīn′) *v.* **-vined, -vining. 1.** To foretell or prophesy. **2.** To guess. **—div′i•na′tion** *n.* **—di•vin′er** *n.*

**di•vorce** (dĭ-vôrs′, -vōrs′) *n.* The dissolution of a marriage by law. **—di•vorce′** *v.*

**di•vulge** (dĭ-vŭlj′) *v.* **-vulged, -vulging.** To reveal. **—di•vulg′er** *n.*

**diz•zy** (dĭz′ē) *adj.* **-zier, -ziest.** Giddy. **—diz′zi•ly** *adv.* **—diz′zi•ness** *n.* **—diz′zy** *v.*

**do** (do͞o) *v.* **did, done, doing, does. 1.** To perform. **2.** To fulfill; complete. **3.** To create, compose, or make. **4.** To effect. **5.** To exert. **6.** To deal with. **7.** To work at. **8.** To be adequate. **9.** To get along; fare. **—do′er** *n.*

**doc•ile** (dŏs′əl) *adj.* Tractable; submissive. **—do•cil′i•ty** *n.*

**dock**[1] (dŏk) *n.* **1.** A pier or wharf. **2.** The place for the defendant in a courtroom. *—v.* To maneuver into a dock.

**dock**[2] (dŏk) *v.* **1.** To clip or cut off. **2.** To withhold a part of (salary).

**doc•tor** (dŏk′tər) *n.* **1.** One who holds the highest academic degree of a university. **2.** A physician, chiropractor, osteopath, optometrist, podiatrist, dentist, or veterinarian. **—doc′tor•al** *adj.* **—doc′tor•ate** *n.*

**doc•trine** (dŏk′trĭn) *n.* A tenet; teaching. **—doc′tri•nal** *adj.*

**doc•u•ment** (dŏk′yə-mənt) *n.* **1.** A paper bearing evidence, proof, or information. **2.** Something, such as a computer file, that contains information. **—doc′u•men′ta•ry** *adj. & n.* **—doc′u•men•ta′tion** *n.*

**dodge** (dŏj) *v.* **dodged, dodging. 1.** To avoid by moving aside. **2.** To evade. *—n.* **1.** A quick move or shift. **2.** A trick; stratagem. **—dodg′er** *n.*

**does** (dŭz) *v.* 3rd person sing. present tense of **do.**

**does•n't** (dŭz′ənt) *v.* Contraction of *does not.*

**dog** (dôg, dŏg) *n.* A domesticated mammal related to wolves and foxes. *—v.* **dogged, dogging.** To track or trail persistently.

**dog•ged** (dô′gĭd, dŏg′ĭd) *adj.* Stubborn. **—dog′ged•ly** *adv.* **—dog′ged•ness** *n.*

**dog•ma** (dŏg′mə, dŏg′-) *n.* A strict doctrine or system of beliefs. **—dog•mat′ic** *adj.* **—dog•mat′i•cal•ly** *adv.* **—dog′ma•tism′** *n.*

**dole** (dōl) *n.* Relief payments to the needy or unemployed. *—v.* **doled, doling.** To distribute in small portions.

**doll** (dŏll) *n.* A child's toy shaped like a person.

**dol•lar** (dŏl′ər) *n.* The basic U.S. monetary unit.

**do•main** (dō-mān′) *n.* A sphere; field.

**dome** (dōm) *n.* A hemispheric roof.

**do•mes•tic** (də-mĕs′tĭk) *adj.* **1.** Of the family or household. **2.** Tame. **3.** Of a country's internal affairs. **4.** Indigenous. *—n.* A household servant. **—do•mes′ti•cal•ly** *adv.* **—do•mes′ti•cate** *v.* **—do′mes•tic′i•ty** *n.*

**dom•i•nate** (dŏm′ə-nāt′) *v.* **-nated, -nating. 1.** To control or rule. **2.** To be most prominent among. **3.** To overlook from a height. **—dom′i•nance** *n.* **—dom′i•nant** *adj.* **—dom′i•na′tion** *n.* **—dom′i•na′tor** *n.*

**dom•i•neer** (dŏm′ə-nîr′) *v.* To tyrannize.

**do•min•ion** (də-mĭn′yən) *n.* **1.** Control; sovereignty. **2.** A realm; domain.

**do•nate** (dō′nāt′, dō-nāt′) *v.* **-nated, -nating.** To contribute. **—do•na′tion** *n.* **—do′nor** *n.*

**done** (dŭn) *v.* p.p. of **do.**

**don't** (dōnt) *v.* Contraction of *do not.*

**doom** (do͞om) *n.* **1.** Condemnation to a severe penalty. **2.** A terrible fate. *—v.* To condemn.

**door** (dôr, dōr) *n.* **1.** A movable panel used to close an entranceway. **2.** An entranceway.
**dope** (dōp) *n.* **1.** A narcotic. **2.** A stupid person. **3.** Factual information. —*v.* **doped, doping.** To drug. **—dop'er** *n.*
**dor•mant** (dôr'mənt) *adj.* **1.** Sleeping. **2.** Inactive. **—dor'man•cy** *n.*
**dor•mi•to•ry** (dôr'mĭ-tôr'ē, -tōr'ē) *n., pl.* **-ries.** A large bedroom or building for a number of people.
**dose** (dōs) *n.* An amount of medicine to be taken at one time. **—dos'age** *n.* **—dose** *v.* **—dos'er** *n.*
**dot** (dŏt) *n.* A spot; point. —*v.* **dotted, dotting.** To mark with a dot or dots.
**dou•ble** (dŭb'əl) *adj.* **1.** Twice as much. **2.** Of or for two. —*n.* **1.** Something increased twofold. **2.** A duplicate. —*v.* **-bled, -bling. 1.** To make twice as great. **2.** To be twice as much as. **3.** To duplicate or fold in two. **4.** To serve in an additional capacity. —*adv.* **1.** Twice. **2.** In two. **—doub'ly** *adv.*
**doubt** (dout) *v.* **1.** To be uncertain about. **2.** To consider unlikely. —*n.* **1.** Uncertainty. **2. doubts.** Suspicion. **—doubt'er** *n.* **—doubt'ful** *adj.* **—doubt'ful•ly** *adv.* **—doubt'less** *adj.*
**dough** (dō) *n.* **1.** A mixture of flour and other ingredients baked as bread, pastry, etc. **2.** Money. **—dough'y** *adj.*
**douse** (dous) *v.* **doused, dousing. 1.** To plunge into liquid. **2.** To drench; soak. **3.** To extinguish.
**dove[1]** (dŭv) *n.* **1.** A bird resembling a pigeon. **2.** An innocent child. **3.** A messenger of peace and comfort. **4.** One who advocates peace and negotiation instead of war. **—dov'ish** *adj.* **—dov'ish•ness** *n.*
**dove[2]** (dōv) *v.* A p.t. of **dive.**
**dow•a•ger** (dou'ə-jər) *n.* A titled or rich widow.
**down[1]** (doun) *adv.* From a higher to a lower place, position, condition, etc. —*adj.* **1.** Moving or directed downward. **2.** In a low position. —*prep.* In a descending direction along, upon, or through. —*v.* To put, strike, or throw down. **—down'ward** *adv. & adj.*
**down[2]** (doun) *n.* Fine, soft feathers. **—down'y** *adj.*
**down•fall** (doun'fôl') *n.* A sudden loss of wealth, reputation, etc.; ruin.
**down•grade** (doun'grād') *n.* A descending slope. —*v.* To lower the importance of.
**down•load** (doun'lōd') *v.* To transfer data from a large computer to a small one.
**down•size** (doun'sīz') *v.* **-sized, -sizing.** To make smaller.
**down•stream** (doun'strēm') *adj.* In the direction of a stream's current. —*adv.* **1.** Down a stream. **2.** In the future; at a distance from realization.
**down•time** (doun'tīm') *n.* The period when a factory or computer is inactive, esp. for repairs or adjustment.
**doze** (dōz) *v.* **dozed, dozing.** To sleep lightly. **—doze** *n.* **—doz'er** *n.*
**doz•en** (dŭz'ən) *n.* **1.** *pl.* **dozen.** A set of 12. **2.** *pl.* **dozens.** A great many. **—doz'enth** *adj.*
**drab** (drăb) *adj.* **drabber, drabbest.** Dull; dreary. **—drab'ly** *adv.* **—drab'ness** *n.*
**draft** (drăft) *n.* **1.** A current of air. **2.** The depth of a vessel's keel below the water line. **3.** A document for transferring money. **4.** A gulp, swallow, or drink. **5.** Conscription for military service. **6.** A preliminary outline, version, or design. —*v.* **1.** To select for an assignment, as military service. **2.** To draw up a plan or rough outline for. **—draft'y** *adj.*
**drag** (drăg) *v.* **dragged, dragging. 1.** To pull or draw along the ground. **2.** To search the bottom of (a body of water), as with a hook. **3.** To prolong tediously (with *out*). —*n.* **1.** The act of dragging. **2.** Something that retards motion or progress.
**drag•net** (drăg'nĕt') *n.* **1.** A net, esp. one for trawling. **2.** A large-scale search for a criminal.
**drain** (drān) *v.* **1.** To draw or flow off gradually. **2.** To empty. **3.** To exhaust. —*n.* A pipe or channel. **—drain'age** *n.*
**dra•ma** (drä'mə, drăm'ə) *n.* **1. a.** A play. **b.** Works for the theater. **2.** A situation of interesting conflict or emotion. **—dra•mat'ic** *adj.* **—dram'a•tist** *n.* **—dram'a•ti•za'tion** *n.* **—dram'a•tize'** *v.*
**drank** (drăngk) *v.* p.t. of **drink.**
**drape** (drāp) *v.* **draped, draping. 1.** To dress or hang with cloth in loose folds. **2.** To arrange in loose folds. —*n.*

Often **drapes.** A long curtain. **—drap'er•y** *n.*

**dras•tic** (drăs'tĭk) *adj.* Severe; extreme. **—dras'ti•cal•ly** *adv.*

**draw** (drô) *v.* **drew** (dro͞o), **drawn, drawing. 1.** To pull. **2.** To take or pull out. **3.** To suck or take in (air). **4.** To attract. **5.** To formulate. **6.** To withdraw (money). **7.** To evoke; elicit. **8.** To make (pictures or lines), as with a pencil; sketch. *—n.* A contest ending in a tie. **—draw'ing** *n.*

**draw•back** (drô'băk') *n.* A disadvantage.

**draw•er** (drôr) *n.* A boxlike compartment in furniture.

**drawl** (drôl) *v.* To speak with lengthened or drawn-out vowels. **—drawl** *n.*

**drawn** (drôn) *v.* p.p. of **draw.** *—adj.* Haggard.

**dread** (drĕd) *v.* **1.** To fear greatly. **2.** To anticipate with anxiety. *—n.* **1.** Profound fear. **2.** Anxious or fearful anticipation. **—dread'ful** *adj.* **—dread'ful•ly** *adv.*

**dream** (drēm) *n.* **1.** A series of images, ideas, etc., occurring in sleep. **2.** A reverie. **3.** A wild fancy or hope. *—v.* **dreamed** or **dreamt** (drĕmt), **dreaming. 1.** To experience a dream. **2.** To aspire or hope (with *of*). **3.** To imagine. **—dream'er** *n.* **—dream'y** *adj.*

**drea•ry** (drîr'ē) *adj.* **-rier, -riest.** Also *poetic* **drear.** Gloomy; dismal. **—drea'ri•ly** *adv.*

**dredge** (drĕj) *n.* A machine used to scoop or remove dirt, sand, etc., from under water. *—v.* **dredged, dredging.** To deepen or scoop with a dredge.

**dregs** (drĕgz) *pl.n.* The sediment of a liquid.

**drench** (drĕnch) *v.* To wet thoroughly. **—drench'er** *n.*

**dress** (drĕs) *v.* **1.** To put on clothing. **2.** To adorn or arrange. **3.** To treat (a wound). *—n.* **1.** Clothing. **2.** A one-piece skirted outer garment for women.

**dress•er** (drĕs'ər) *n.* A chest of drawers.

**drew** (dro͞o) *v.* p.t. of **draw.**

**drib•ble** (drĭb'əl) *v.* **-bled, -bling. 1.** To flow unsteadily; trickle. **2.** To drool. *—n.* A trickle.

**dri•er** (drī'ər) *adj.* Alternate comparative of **dry.**

**drift** (drĭft) *v.* **1.** To carry or be carried along by a current. **2.** To wander aimlessly. **3.** To pile up. *—n.* **1.** Drifting material. **2.** A bank or pile, as of snow. **3.** A trend or general meaning. **—drift'er** *n.* **—drift'y** *adj.*

**drill** (drĭl) *n.* **1.** An implement with a pointed end for boring holes. **2.** Disciplined, repetitious training. **3.** A training exercise. *—v.* **1.** To make a hole in with a drill. **2.** To train by repetition. **—drill'er** *n.*

**drink** (drĭngk) *v.* **drank** (drăngk), **drunk** (drŭngk), **drinking. 1.** To swallow (a liquid). **2.** To absorb. **3.** To imbibe alcoholic liquors, esp. to excess. *—n.* **1.** A beverage. **2.** Alcoholic liquor. **—drink'a•ble** *adj.* **—drink'er** *n.*

**drip** (drĭp) *v.* **dripped, dripping.** To fall or allow to fall in drops. *—n.* The process or sound of dripping.

**drive** (drīv) *v.* **drove** (drōv), **driven** (drĭv'ən), **driving. 1.** To push, propel, or press forcibly. **2.** To force to act or work. **3.** To operate (a vehicle). *—n.* **1.** A trip in a vehicle. **2.** A campaign. **3.** A strong tendency or instinct. **—driv'er** *n.*

**driv•el** (drĭv'əl) *v.* **-eled** or **-elled, -eling** or **-elling.** To slobber; drool. *—n.* **1.** Saliva flowing from the mouth. **2.** Senseless talk. **—driv'el•er** *n.*

**driz•zle** (drĭz'əl) *v.* **-zled, -zling.** To rain gently in fine drops. **—driz'zle** *n.* **—driz'zly** *adj.*

**drone** (drōn) *n.* **1.** A male bee. **2.** A loafer. **3.** A humming sound. *—v.* **droned, droning. 1.** To hum. **2.** To speak monotonously.

**drool** (dro͞ol) *v.* To let saliva run from the mouth. *—n.* Saliva; drivel.

**droop** (dro͞op) *v.* To hang downward. **—droop** *n.* **—droop'y** *adj.*

**drop** (drŏp) *n.* **1.** A small, rounded mass of liquid. **2.** A minute quantity. **3.** A sudden fall or decline. **4.** Vertical distance downward. *—v.* **dropped, dropping. 1.** To descend, fall, or let fall. **2.** To decrease. **—drop'per** *n.*

**drought** (drout) *n.* A long period with no rain.

**drove** (drōv) *v.* p.t. of **drive.** *—n.* A flock or herd.

**drown** (droun) *v.* **1.** To kill or die by suffocation in water. **2.** To overwhelm or muffle.

**drowse** (drouz) *v.* **drowsed, drowsing.** To be half asleep; doze. **—drow'si•ly** *adv.* **—drow'si•ness** *n.* **—drow'sy** *adj.*

**drug** (drŭg) *n.* **1.** A medicine. **2.** A narcotic, esp. one that is addictive. *—v.* **drugged, drugging.** To administer or add a drug to. **—drug'gist** *n.*

**drum** (drŭm) *n.* **1.** A percussion instrument consisting of a hollow cylinder with a membrane stretched tightly over it. **2.** A cylindrical metal container. *—v.* **drummed, drumming.** To beat or thump rhythmically. **—drum'mer** *n.*

**drunk** (drŭngk) *v.* p.p. of **drink.** *—adj.* Intoxicated with alcoholic liquor. *—n.* An intoxicated person. **—drunk'ard** *n.* **—drunk'en** *adj.* **—drunk'en•ly** *adv.* **—drunk'en•ness** *n.*

**dry** (drī) *adj.* **drier** or **dryer, driest** or **dryest. 1.** Free from liquid or moisture. **2.** Having little or no rain. **3.** Needing drink. **4.** Not sweet. **5.** Dull; boring. *—v.* **dried, drying.** To make or become dry. **—dry'ly** *adv.* **—dry'ness** *n.*

**dry•er** (drī'ər) *n.* An appliance for removing moisture, esp. by heating.

**dub** (dŭb) *v.* **dubbed, dubbing. 1.** To name or rename. **2.** To provide (a film) with a new sound track.

**du•bi•ous** (d/y/o͞o'bē-əs) *adj.* **1.** Undecided. **2.** Doubtful. **—du'bi•ous•ly** *adv.* **—du'bi•ous•ness** *n.*

**duch•ess** (dŭch'ĭs) *n.* **1.** A duke's wife. **2.** A noblewoman with the highest rank.

**duck** (dŭk) *n.* A web-footed water bird. *—v.* **1.** To lower quickly, esp. so as to avoid something. **2.** To evade; dodge. **3.** To submerge briefly.

**duct** (dŭkt) *n.* A tubular passage for a liquid or gas.

**dude** (d/y/o͞od) *n.* A dandy.

**due** (d/y/o͞o) *adj.* **1.** Payable immediately or on demand. **2.** Owed. **3.** Fitting or appropriate. *—n.* **1.** Something owed or deserved. **2. dues.** A charge or fee for membership. *—adv.* Straight.

**du•el** (d/y/o͞o'əl) *n.* A prearranged combat between two persons. *—v.* To fight in a duel. **—du'el•er, du'el•ist** *n.*

**du•et** (d/y/o͞o-ĕt') *n.* A musical composition for two performers.

**dug** (dŭg) *v.* p.t. & p.p. of **dig.**

**duke** (d/y/o͞ok) *n.* A nobleman with the highest rank. **—duke'dom** *n.*

**dull** (dŭl) *adj.* **1.** Lacking mental agility. **2.** Sluggish. **3.** Blunt. **4.** Not keenly felt. **5.** Boring. **6.** Not bright. **7.** Muffled. *—v.* To make or become dull. **—dull'ness** *n.* **—dul'ly** *adv.*

**du•ly** (do͞o'lē) *adv.* **1.** In a proper manner. **2.** At the expected time.

**dumb** (dŭm) *adj.* **1.** Unable to speak; mute. **2.** Speechless. **3.** Stupid. **—dumb'ly** *adv.* **—dumb'ness** *n.*

**dum•my** (dŭm'ē) *n., pl.* **-mies. 1.** An imitation of a real object, used as a substitute. **2.** A figure imitating the human form.

**dump** (dŭmp) *v.* **1.** To drop in a large mass. **2.** To discard. **3.** To reproduce internally stored computer data onto external storage, as a printout. *—n.* **1.** A place where refuse is dumped. **2.** A storage place. **3.** An instance or result of dumping computer data.

**dunce** (dŭns) *n.* A stupid person.

**dun**[1] (dŭn) *v.* **dunned, dunning.** To ask persistently for payment. **—dun** *n.*

**dun**[2] (dŭn) *n.* **1.** A neutral or dull brownish gray. **2.** A horse of this color.

**dune** (d/y/o͞on) *n.* A ridge of wind-blown sand.

**dun•ga•ree** (dŭng'gə-rē') *n.* **1.** A sturdy denim fabric. **2. dungarees.** Trousers of this fabric.

**dun•geon** (dŭn'jən) *n.* A dark cell for prisoners.

**du•pli•cate** (d/y/o͞o'plĭ-kĭt) *n.* An identical copy; facsimile. *—v.* (-kāt') **-cated, -cating. 1.** To make a duplicate of. **2.** To make or perform again. **—du'pli•ca'tion** *n.*

**du•plic•i•ty** (d/y/o͞o-plĭs'ĭ-tē) *n., pl.* **-ties.** Deliberate deceptiveness.

**du•ra•ble** (d/y/o͝or'ə-bəl) *adj.* Able to withstand wear and tear; lasting. **—du'ra•bil'i•ty** *n.*

**du•ra•tion** (d/y/o͞o-rā'shən) *n.* **1.** Continuance in time. **2.** The time during which something exists.

**du•ress** (d/y/o͞o-rĕs') *n.* Compulsion by threat; coercion.

**dur•ing** (d/y/o͝or'ĭng) *prep.* **1.** Throughout the course or duration of. **2.** Within the time of.

**dusk** (dŭsk) *n.* The darker stage of twilight. **—dusk'y** *adj.*

**dust** (dŭst) *n.* **1.** Fine particulate matter. **2.** A cloud of such matter. *—v.* **1.** To remove dust. **2.** To sprinkle with a powdery substance. **—dust'er** *n.* **—dust'y** *adj.*

**du•ty** (d/y/ōō'tē) *n., pl.* **-ties. 1.** Moral obligation. **2.** A task or assignment. **3.** A tax charged by a government, esp. on imports. **—du'te•ous** *adj.* **—du'ti•ful** *adj.*

**dwarf** (dwôrf) *n., pl.* **dwarfs** or **dwarves.** An abnormally small person, animal, or plant. *—v.* To cause to appear small by comparison.

**dwell** (dwĕl) *v.* **dwelt** or **dwelled, dwelling. 1.** To live; reside. **2.** To linger over; emphasize (with *on* or *upon*). **—dwell'ing** *n.*

**dwin•dle** (dwĭn'dl) *v.* **-dled, -dling.** To waste away; diminish.

**dye** (dī) *n.* **1.** A substance used to color materials, hair, etc. **2.** A color imparted by dyeing. *—v.* **dyed, dyeing.** To color with or become colored by a dye.

**dy•nam•ic** (dī-năm'ĭk) *adj.* Also **dy•nam•i•cal. 1.** Energetic; vigorous. **2.** Of energy, force, or motion in relation to force. **—dy•nam'i•cal•ly** *adv.*

**dy•na•mite** (dī'nə-mīt') *n.* A powerful explosive.

**dy•na•mo** (dī'nə-mō') *n., pl.* **-mos. 1.** A generator, esp. one for producing direct current. **2.** An energetic person.

**dy•nas•ty** (dī'nə-stē) *n., pl.* **-ties.** A succession of rulers from the same family or line. **—dy•nas'tic** *adj.*

## – E –

**e, E** (ē) *n.* The 5th letter of the English alphabet.

**each** (ēch) *adj.* One of 2 or more considered individually; every. *—pron.* Every individual one of a group; each one. *—adv.* Apiece.

**ea•ger** (ē'gər) *adj.* Impatiently desirous. **—ea'ger•ly** *adv.* **—ea'ger•ness** *n.*

**ea•gle** (ē'gəl) *n.* A large bird of prey.

**ear**[1] (îr) *n.* **1.** The organ of hearing in vertebrates. **2.** Attention; heed. **—ear'ache'** *n.*

**ear**[2] (îr) *n.* The seed-bearing spike of a cereal plant.

**ear•drum** (îr'drŭm') *n.* The tympanic membrane.

**earl** (ûrl) *n.* A British peer ranking below a marquis. **—earl'dom** *n.*

**ear•ly** (ûr'lē) *adj.* **-lier, -liest. 1.** Near the beginning of a given period of time. **2.** Occurring before the usual time. **—ear'ly** *adv.*

**earn** (ûrn) *v.* To gain or deserve for one's labor or as a result of one's behavior. **—earn'er** *n.* **—earn'ings** *pl.n.*

**ear•nest**[1] (ûr'nĭst) *adj.* **1.** Serious. **2.** Sincere. **—in earnest.** With serious intent. **—ear'nest•ly** *adv.* **—ear'nest•ness** *n.*

**ear•nest**[2] (ûr'nĭst) *n.* A token or assurance of something to come.

**ear•ring** (îr'rĭng, -ĭng) *n.* An ear ornament.

**earth** (ûrth) *n.* **1.** The land surface of the world. **2.** Soil; dirt. **3. Earth.** The 3rd planet from the sun. **—earth'en** *adj.* **—earth'ly** *adj.*

**earth•quake** (ûrth'kwāk') *n.* A trembling movement of the earth's surface.

**ease** (ēz) *n.* **1.** Freedom from pain, worry, or agitation. **2.** Freedom from awkwardness; naturalness. **3.** Freedom from difficulty; facility. *—v.* **eased, easing. 1.** To comfort; relieve. **2.** To alleviate or lighten (discomfort); mitigate; lessen. **3.** To slacken; loosen.

**ea•sel** (ē'zəl) *n.* An upright frame used to support an artist's canvas.

**ease•ment** (ēz'mənt) *n.* In law, a right, such as a right of way, through another's property.

**east** (ēst) *n.* **1.** The direction of the earth's rotation. **2.** Often **East.** The eastern part of any country or region. **3. East.** Asia; the Orient. *—adj. & adv.* To, from, or in the east. **—east'er•ly** *adj. & adv.* **—east'ern, East'ern** *adj.* **—east'ern•er, East'ern•er** *n.* **—east'ward** *adj. & adv.*

**eas•y** (ē'zē) *adj.* **-ier, -iest. 1.** Capable of being accomplished without difficulty. **2.** Free from worry, anxiety, or pain. **—take it easy. 1.** To relax. **2.** To remain calm. **—eas'i•ly** *adv.*

**eat** (ēt) *v.* **ate** (āt), **eaten** (ēt'n), **eating. 1.** To consume (food). **2.** To erode or corrode. **—eat'er** *n.*

**eaves** (ēvz) *pl.n.* The overhang at the edge of a roof.
**ebb** (ĕb) *n.* A period of declining or diminishing. —*v.* To fall back or recede.
**eb•on•y** (ĕb'ə-nē) *n.* A hard, dark wood of a tropical Asian tree. —*adj.* **1.** Made of ebony. **2.** Black.
**e•bul•lience** (ĭ-bo͝ol'yəns, ĭ-bŭl'-) *n.* Enthusiastic liveliness. —**e•bul'lient** *adj.*
**ec•cen•tric** (ĭk-sĕn'trĭk, ĕk-) *adj.* **1.** Deviating from a conventional pattern. **2.** Not having the same center as a circle or sphere. —*n.* An odd person. —**ec'cen•tric'i•ty** *n.*
**ec•cle•si•as•ti•cal** (ĭ-klē'zē-ăs'tĭ-kəl) *adj.* Of a church. —**ec•cle'si•as'tic** *adj.* & *n.*
**ech•e•lon** (ĕsh'ə-lŏn') *n.* A level of authority in a hierarchy.
**ech•o** (ĕk'ō) *n., pl.* **-oes. 1.** Repetition of a sound by reflection of sound waves. **2.** A sound so produced. **3.** Any repetition or imitation. —*v.* **1.** To resound with an echo; reverberate. **2.** To imitate.
**ech•o•car•di•og•ra•phy** (ĕk'ō-kär'dē-ŏg'rə-fē) *n.* The use of ultrasound to form a visible image of the internal structure of the heart. —**ech'o•card'i•o•graph'** *n.*
**e•clec•tic** (ĭ-klĕk'tĭk) *adj.* Choosing or consisting of the best from diverse sources. —**e•clec'ti•cal•ly** *adv.*
**e•clipse** (ĭ-klĭps') *n.* **1.** The obscuring of one celestial body by another. **2.** A falling into obscurity; decline. —*v.* **eclipsed, eclipsing.** To obscure.
**e•clip•tic** (ĭ-klĭp'tĭk) *n.* The apparent path of the sun among the stars.
**e•col•o•gy** (ĭ-kŏl'ə-jē) *n.* The science of the relationships between organisms and their environments. —**ec'o•log'i•cal** *adj.* —**ec'o•log'i•cal•ly** *adv.* —**e•col'o•gist** *n.*
**e•con•o•met•rics** (ĭ-kŏn'ə-mĕt'rĭks) *n.* The use of statistics in economic problems. —**e•con'o•met'ric** *adj.*
**ec•o•nom•ic** (ĕk'ə-nŏm'ĭk, ē'kə-) *adj.* **1.** Of the production, development, and management of material wealth. **2.** Of the necessities of life. —*n.* **economics.** The science of the production, distribution, and consumption of commodities. —**ec'o•nom'i•cal** *adj.* —**ec'o•nom'i•cal•ly** *adv.* —**e•con'o•mist** *n.*
**e•con•o•my** (ĭ-kŏn'ə-mē) *n., pl.* **-mies. 1.** The careful or thrifty management of resources. **2.** A system for the management of resources. —**e•con'o•mize'** *v.*
**ec•o•sys•tem** (ĕk'ō-sĭs'təm, ē'kō-) *n.* An ecological community and its physical environment considered as a unit.
**ec•ru** (ĕk'ro͞o, ā'kro͞o) *n.* A grayish to pale yellow; beige.
**ec•sta•sy** (ĕk'stə-sē) *n., pl.* **-sies.** Overwhelming delight; rapture. —**ec•stat'ic** *adj.*
**ec•u•men•i•cal** (ĕk'yə-mĕn'ĭ-kəl) *adj.* Of the general unity of all Christian sects. —**ec'u'me•nism** *n.*
**ec•ze•ma** (ĕk'sə-mə, ĕg'zə-) *n.* A red, itching, oozing, noncontagious inflammation of the skin. —**ec•zem'a•tous** *adj.*
**e•de•ma** (ĭ-dē'mə) *n.* Excessive accumulation of liquid in tissue. —**e•dem'a•tous** *adj.*
**edge** (ĕj) *n.* **1.** The sharp side of a cutting blade. **2.** A rim or brink. **3.** A margin; border. **4.** An advantage. —**on edge.** Highly tense; irritable; impatient. —*v.* **edged, edging. 1.** To give an edge to. **2.** To move gradually. —**edg'i•ness** *n.* —**edg'ing** *n.* —**edg'y** *adj.*
**ed•i•ble** (ĕd'ə-bəl) *adj.* Fit to be eaten.
**ed•it** (ĕd'ĭt) *v.* To prepare something for publication. —**ed'i•tor** *n.*
**e•di•tion** (ĭ-dĭsh'ən) *n.* **1.** The form in which a book is published. **2.** The entire number of copies of a publication printed at one time.
**ed•i•to•ri•al** (ĕd'ĭ-tôr'ē-əl, -tōr'-) *n.* An article in a publication expressing the opinion of its editors or publishers. —*adj.* Of an editor. —**ed'i•to'ri•al•ize'** *v.* —**ed'i•to'ri•al•ly** *adv.*
**ed•u•cate** (ĕj'ə-kāt') *v.* **-cated, -cating.** To provide with knowledge, esp. through formal schooling; teach. —**ed'u•ca•ble** *adj.* —**ed'u•ca'tion** *n.* —**ed'u•ca'tion•al** *adj.* —**ed'u•ca'tion•al•ly** *adv.* —**ed'u•ca'tor** *n.*
**eel** (ēl) *n.* A long, snakelike fish.
**ee•rie, ee•ry** (îr'ē) *adj.* **-rier, -riest. 1.** Causing fear or dread. **2.** Supernatural. —**ee'ri•ly** *adv.* —**ee'ri•ness** *n.*
**ef•fect** (ĭ-fĕkt') *n.* **1.** A result. **2.** Influence. **3.** Basic meaning; purport. **4. effects.** Possessions; belongings. —**in effect.** Actually; virtually. —*v.* To

bring about. —**ef•fec'tive** *adj.* —**ef•fec'tive•ly** *adv.* —**ef•fec'tive•ness** *n.*

**ef•fem•i•nate** (ĭ-fĕm'ə-nĭt) *adj.* Being overly soft or excessively delicate; unmanly.

**ef•fi•cient** (ĭ-fĭsh'ənt) *adj.* **1.** Acting effectively with little waste or effort. **2.** Exhibiting a high ratio of output to input. —**ef•fi'cien•cy** *n.* —**ef•fi'cient•ly** *adv.*

**ef•fi•gy** (ĕf'ə-jē) *n., pl.* **-gies.** A crude image or figure of a hated person or thing, esp. for hanging or burning.

**ef•flu•ent** (ĕf'lo͞o-ənt) *n.* A stream flowing out from a body of water, esp. of waste from a sewer. —**ef'flu•ence** *n.*

**ef•fort** (ĕf'ərt) *n.* **1.** The use of physical or mental energy; exertion. **2.** An attempt. **3.** An achievement.

**ef•front•er•y** (ĭ-frŭn'tə-rē) *n., pl.* **-ies.** Shameless boldness.

**ef•fu•sive** (ĭ-fyo͞o'sĭv) *adj.* Showing unrestrained or excessive emotion. —**ef•fu'sive•ness** *n.*

**e•gal•i•tar•i•an** (ĭ-găl'ĭ-târ'ē-ən) *n.* One maintaining equal political, economic, and legal rights for all. —**e•gal'i•tar'i•an** *adj.* —**e•gal'i•tar'i•an•ism** *n.*

**egg**[1] (ĕg) *n.* **1.** A female reproductive cell; ovum. **2.** The thin-shelled ovum of a bird, used as food.

**egg**[2] (ĕg) *v.* —**egg on.** To urge or incite.

**egg•plant** (ĕg'plănt') *n.* A plant with large, purple-skinned fruit.

**e•go** (ē'gō, ĕg'ō) *n.* **1.** The self. **2.** Conceit; egotism. —**e'go•cen'tric** *adj.*

**e•go•ism** (ē'gō-ĭz'əm, ĕg'ō-) *n.* **1.** The belief that self-interest is the most important motive force. **2.** Egotism. —**e'go•ist** *n.* —**e'go•is'tic, e'go•is'ti•cal** *adj.*

**e•go•tism** (ē'gə-tĭz'əm, ĕg'ə-) *n.* **1.** The tendency to speak excessively about oneself. **2.** An exaggerated sense of self-importance; conceit. —**e'go•tist** *n.* —**e'go•tis'tic, e'go•tis'ti•cal** *adj.* —**e'go•tis'ti•cal•ly** *adv.*

**e•gress** (ē'grĕs') *n.* An exit.

**eight** (āt) *n.* The cardinal number written 8. —**eight** *adj. & pron.* —**eighth** *n. & adj.*

**eight•een** (ā-tēn') *n.* The cardinal number written 18. —**eight•een'** *adj. & pron.* —**eight•eenth'** *n. & adj.*

**eight•y** (ā'tē) *n.* The cardinal number written 80. —**eight'i•eth** *n. & adj.* —**eight'y** *adj. & pron.*

**ei•ther** (ē'*th*ər, ī'*th*ər) *pron.* One or the other. —*conj.* Used before the 1st of 2 or more stated alternatives, the following 1 signaled by *or.* —*adj.* Any 1 (of 2). —*adv.* Likewise; also.

**eke** (ēk) *v.* **eked, eking.** To supplement; add to (with *out*).

**e•lab•o•rate** (ĭ-lăb'ər-ĭt) *adj.* Planned with attention to detail; complicated. —*v.* (-ə-rāt') **-rated, -rating.** To work out in detail; develop thoroughly.

**e•lapse** (ĭ-lăps) *v.* **elapsed, elapsing.** To pass; slip by, as time.

**e•las•tic** (ĭ-lăs'tĭk) *adj.* **1.** Capable of returning to an initial shape after deformation; springy. **2.** Adaptable to change; flexible. —*n.* **1.** An elastic fabric. **2.** A rubber band. —**e'las•tic'i•ty** *n.*

**e•late** (ĭ-lāt') *v.* **elated, elating.** To raise the spirits of; make happy. —**e•la'tion** *n.*

**el•bow** (ĕl'bō') *n.* **1.** The joint of the arm between the forearm and upper arm. **2.** Something having a bend similar to an elbow. —*v.* To push or shove.

**eld•er** (ĕl'dər) *adj.* A compar. of **old.** —*n.* **1.** An older person. **2.** An older, influential person of a family, tribe, etc. —**eld'er•ly** *adj.*

**e•lect** (ĭ-lĕkt') *v.* To select, esp. by vote. —*adj.* Chosen. —**e•lec'tion** *n.* —**e•lec'tion•eer'** *v.* —**e•lec'tor** *n.* —**e•lec'tor•al** *adj.*

**e•lec•tive** (ĭ-lĕk'tĭv) *adj.* **1.** Filled or obtained by voting. **2.** Permitting a choice; optional. —*n.* A school course or subject that is optional, not required.

**e•lec•tor•ate** (ĭ-lĕk'tər-ĭt) *n.* The body of qualified voters.

**e•lec•tric** (ĭ-lĕk'trĭk) *adj.* Also **e•lec•tri•cal.** Of, producing, derived from, or powered by electricity. —**e•lec'tri•cal•ly** *adv.*

**e•lec•tric•i•ty** (ĭ-lĕk-trĭs'ĭ-tē, ē'lĕk-) *n.* **1.** The class of physical phenomena arising from the existence and interactions of electric charge. **2.** Electric current. —**e•lec'tri'cian** *n.* —**e•lec'tri•fy'** *v.*

**e•lec•tro•cute** (ĭ-lĕk'trə-kyo͞ot') *v.* **-cuted, -cuting.** To kill cr execute with electricity. **—e•lec'tro•cu'tion** *n.*

**e•lec•tron** (ĭ-lĕk'trŏn') *n.* A subatomic particle having a negative electric charge.

**e•lec•tron•ic** (ĭ-lĕk-trŏn'ĭk, ē'lĕk-) *adj.* **1.** Of electrons or electronics. **2.** Implemented on or controlled by a computer. —*n.* **electronics.** The commercial industry of electronic devices and systems.

**el•e•gance** (ĕl'ĭ-gəns) *n.* **1.** Refinement and grace. **2.** Tasteful opulence. **—el'e•gant** *adj.*

**el•e•ment** (ĕl'ə-mənt) *n.* **1.** A fundamental consituent or principle of something. **2.** In chemistry and physics, a substance composed of atoms having an identical number of protons in each nucleus. **3. elements.** The forces that collectively constitute the weather. **—el'e•men'tal** *adj.*

**el•e•men•ta•ry** (ĕl'ə-mĕn'tə-rē, -trē) *adj.* **1.** Fundamental, essential, or irreducible. **2.** Of the basic aspects of a subject.

**el•e•phant** (ĕl'ə-fənt) *n.* A large mammal with tusks and a long, flexible trunk.

**el•e•vate** (ĕl'ə-vāt') *v.* **-vated, -vating. 1.** To raise to a higher place; lift up. **2.** To raise to a higher moral level. **—el'e•va'tion** *n.*

**el•e•va•tor** (ĕl'ə-vā'tər) *n.* **1.** An enclosure raised and lowered to transport freight or people. **2.** A granary with devices for hoisting and discharging grain.

**e•lev•en** (ĭ-lĕv'ən) *n.* The cardinal number written 11. **—e•lev'en** *adj. & pron.* **—e•lev'enth** *n. & adj.*

**el•i•gi•ble** (ĕl'ĭ-jə-bəl) *adj.* Qualified; worthy of choice. **—el'i•gi•bil'i•ty** *n.*

**e•lim•i•nate** (ĭ-lĭm'ə-nāt') *v.* **-nated, -nating. 1.** To get rid of; remove. **2.** To omit from consideration. **—e•lim'i•na'tion** *n.*

**el•lipse** (ĭ-lĭps') *n.* An oval figure formed around 2 foci, the sum of the distances from the foci to any point on the perimeter being a constant. **—el•lip'tic** *adj.*

**e•lite, é•lite** (ĭ-lēt') *n.* **1.** The best members of a group. **2.** A small, privileged group. **—e•lit'ism** *n.* **—e•lit'ist** *adj. & n.*

**elk** (ĕlk) *n., pl.* **elks** or **elk.** A large deer of northern regions.

**elm** (ĕlm) *n.* A shade tree with arching branches.

**el•o•cu•tion** (ĕl'ə-kyōō'shən) *n.* **1.** The art of formal public speaking. **2.** A style or manner of speaking.

**e•lon•gate** (ĭ-lông'gāt', ĭ-lŏng'-) *v.* **-gated, -gating.** To lengthen; grow in length. **—e'lon•ga'tion** *n.*

**e•lope** (ĭ-lōp') *v.* **eloped, eloping.** To run away with a lover, esp. to get married. **—e•lope'ment** *n.*

**el•o•quent** (ĕl'ə-kwənt) *adj.* Persuasive and fluent in speech. **—el'o•quence** *n.*

**else** (ĕls) *adj.* **1.** Other; different. **2.** In addition; more. —*adv.* **1.** In a different time, place, or manner. **2.** If not; otherwise.

**else•where** (ĕls'hwâr') *adv.* In or to another place.

**e•lu•ci•date** (ĭ-lōō'sĭ-dāt') *v.* **-dated, -dating.** To make plain; clarify. **—e•lu'ci•da'tion** *n.*

**e•lude** (ĭ-lōōd') *v.* **eluded, eluding. 1.** To escape from or avoid. **2.** To escape the understanding or memory of. **—e•lu'sive** *adj.* **—e•lu'sive•ness** *n.*

**e-mail, e•mail** (ē'māl') *n.* A message or messages sent electronically over a computer network. **—e-mail** *v.*

**e•man•ci•pate** (ĭ-măn'sə-pāt') *v.* **-pated, -pating.** To free from oppression or bondage. **—e•man'ci•pa'tion** *n.* **—e•man'ci•pa'tor** *n.*

**em•balm** (ĕm-bäm') *v.* To prevent the decay of (a corpse) by treatment with preservatives. **—em•balm'er** *n.*

**em•bark** (ĕm-bärk') *v.* **1.** To board or cause to board a vessel. **2.** To set out on a venture; commence. **—em'bar•ka'tion** *n.*

**em•bar•rass** (ĕm-băr'əs) *v.* **1.** To make feel ill at ease. **2.** To impede. **—em•bar'rass•ing** *adj.* **—em•bar'rass•ment** *n.*

**em•bas•sy** (ĕm'bə-sē) *n., pl.* **-sies. 1.** A mission to a foreign government. **2.** An ambassador and his staff. **3.** The headquarters of an ambassador.

**em•bel•lish** (ĕm-bĕl'ĭsh) *v.* To make more beautiful; adorn; add details to. **—em•bel'lish•ment** *n.*

**em•ber** (ĕm'bər) *n.* A piece of live coal or wood.

**em•bez•zle** (ĕm-bĕz′əl) *v.* **-zled, -zling.** To take (money or property) by fraud. **—em•bez′zle•ment** *n.* **—em•bez′zler** *n.*

**em•blem** (ĕm′bləm) *n.* **1.** A symbol. **2.** A distinctive badge, design, etc.

**em•bod•y** (ĕm-bŏd′ē) *v.* **-ied, -ying. 1.** To invest with bodily form; make corporeal. **2.** To personify. **—em•bod′i•ment** *n.*

**em•bo•lism** (ĕm′bə-lĭz′əm) *n.* Blockage of a blood vessel by a bubble, clot, or foreign body.

**em•boss** (ĕm-bôs′, -bŏs′) *v.* To cover with a raised design.

**em•brace** (ĕm-brās′) *v.* **-braced, -bracing. 1.** To hug. **2.** To include. **3.** To adopt, as a cause. **4.** To accept eagerly. *—n.* An affectionate hug.

**em•broi•der** (ĕm-broi′dər) *v.* **1.** To ornament (fabric) with needlework. **2.** To embellish (a story). **—em•broi′der•y** *n.*

**em•broil** (ĕm-broil′) *v.* **1.** To involve in an argument. **2.** To throw into confusion. **—em•broil′ment** *n.*

**em•bry•o** (ĕm′brē-ō′) *n., pl.* **-os.** An organism in its earliest stages of development. **—em′bry•on′ic** *adj.*

**em•cee** (ĕm′sē′) *n.* A master of ceremonies. **—em′cee′** *v.*

**em•er•ald** (ĕm′ər-əld, ĕm′rəld) *n.* **1.** A brilliant, transparent green gemstone. **2.** Strong yellowish green. **—em′er•ald** *adj.*

**e•merge** (ĭ-mûrj′) *v.* **emerged, emerging. 1.** To rise up or come into sight. **2.** To come into existence. **—e•mer′gence** *n.* **—e•mer′gent** *adj.*

**e•mer•gen•cy** (ĭ-mûr′jən-sē) *n., pl.* **-cies.** A sudden, unexpected occurrence demanding immediate action.

**e•met•ic** (ĭ-mĕt′ĭk) *n.* An agent that causes vomiting. **—e•met′ic** *adj.*

**em•i•grate** (ĕm′ĭ-grāt′) *v.* **-grated, -grating.** To leave 1 country to settle in another. **—em′i•grant** *n.* **—em′i•gra′tion** *n.*

**ém•i•gré** (ĕm′ĭ-grā′) *n.* One who has emigrated for political reasons. **—ém•i•gré** *adj.*

**em•i•nence** (ĕm′ə-nəns) *n.* A position of superiority or distinction. **—em′i•nent** *adj.*

**e•mit** (ĭ-mĭt′) *v.* **emitted, emitting. 1.** To release or send forth. **2.** To utter.

**e•mol•lient** (ĭ-mŏl′yənt) *n.* An agent that softens or smoothes, esp. a skin softener. **—e•mol′lient** *adj.*

**e•mol•u•ment** (ĭ-mŏl′yə-mənt) *n.* Payment for work.

**e•mote** (ĭ-mōt′) *v.* **emoted, emoting.** To be excessively emotional and theatrical.

**e•mo•tion** (ĭ-mō′shən) *n.* **1.** A feeling, passion, or sensibility. **2.** Any strong subjective feeling. **—e•mo′tion•al** *adj.*

**em•pa•thy** (ĕm′pə-thē) *n.* Identification with another's feelings. **—em′pa•thet′ic, em•path′ic** *adj.* **—em′pa•thize′** *v.*

**em•pha•sis** (ĕm′fə-sĭs) *n., pl.* **-ses.** Special importance placed upon something; stress. **—em′pha•size′** *v.* **—em•phat′ic** *adj.*

**em•phy•se•ma** (ĕm′fĭ-sē′mə, -zē′-) *n.* A disease of the lungs. **—em′phy•sem′a•tous** *adj.*

**em•pire** (ĕm′pīr′) *n.* A political unit of territories or nations ruled by a single authority. **—em′per•or** *n.* **—em′press** *n.*

**em•pir•i•cal** (ĕm-pîr′ĭ-kəl) *adj.* **1.** Relying on observation or experiment. **2.** Guided by experience rather than theory.

**em•ploy** (ĕm-ploi′) *v.* **1.** To use. **2.** To apply (one's time or energies) to some activity. **3.** To provide with a job. **—em•ploy′ee** *n.* **—em•ploy′er** *n.* **—em•ploy′ment** *n.*

**emp•ty** (ĕmp′tē) *adj.* **1.** Containing nothing. **2.** Having no occupants; vacant. **3.** Lacking purpose or substance; meaningless. *—v.* **-tied, -tying.** To remove the contents of. **—emp′ti•ness** *n.*

**EMT** *n., pl.* **EMTs** A person certified to give emergency first aid.

**en•a•ble** (ĕ-nā′bəl) *v.* **-bled, -bling.** To supply with the means to do something.

**e•nam•el** (ĭ-năm′əl) *n.* **1.** A glassy, opaque coating baked on metal, ceramic ware, etc. **2.** A paint that dries to a hard, glossy surface. *—v.* To coat with enamel.

**en•chant** (ĕn-chănt′) *v.* **1.** To bewitch. **2.** To delight completely; charm. **—en•chant′er** *n.* **—en•chant′ment** *n.*

**en•cir•cle** (ĕn-sûr′kəl) *v.* **-cled, -cling.** To surround. **—en•cir′cle•ment** *n.*

**en•close** (ĕn-klōz′, ĭn-) *v.* **-closed, -closing.** Also **in•close. 1.** To surround; fence in. **2.** To insert in the same container with a letter or package. **—en•clo′sure** *n.*

**en•com•pass** (ĕn-kŭm′pəs) *v.* **1.** To surround. **2.** To include; contain.

**en•coun•ter** (ĕn-koun′tər) *n.* **1.** A meeting, esp. when unplanned. **2.** A hostile confrontation. —*v.* **1.** To meet esp. unexpectedly. **2.** To confront in battle.

**en•cour•age** (ĕn-kûr′ĭj) *v.* **-aged, -aging. 1.** To impart bravery or confidence to. **2.** To give support to; foster. **—en•cour′age•ment** *n.*

**en•croach** (ĕn-krōch′) *v.* To intrude on the possessions or rights of another; trespass. **—en•croach′ment** *n.*

**en•cy•clo•pe•di•a** (ĕn-sī′klə-pē′dē-ə) *n.* Also **en•cy•clo•pae•di•a.** A reference work with articles on many subjects. **—en•cy′clo•pe′dic, en•cy′clo•pae′dic** *adj.*

**end** (ĕnd) *n.* **1.** An extremity; tip. **2.** A boundary; limit. **3.** The point at which something is completed; conclusion. **4.** A result; outcome. **5.** A purpose; goal. —*v.* To bring or come to an end. **—end′less** *adj.* **—end′less•ly** *adv.*

**en•dan•gered** (ĕn-dān′jərd) *adj.* Threatened with extinction.

**en•deav•or** (ĕn-dĕv′ər) *v.* To make an attempt; strive. **—en•deav′or** *n.*

**en•dorse** (ĕn-dôrs′) *v.* **-dorsed, -dorsing.** Also **in•dorse. 1.** To write one's signature on the back of (a check, stock certificate, etc.). **2.** To approve; sanction. **—en•dorse′ment** *n.*

**en•dow** (ĕn-dou′) *v.* **1.** To provide with property or income. **2.** To equip with a talent or quality. **—en•dow′ment** *n.*

**en•dure** (ĕn-d/y/ŏŏr′) *v.* **-dured, -during. 1.** To put up with; withstand. **2.** To continue in existence; last. **—en•dur′a•ble** *adj.* **—en•dur′ance** *n.* **—en•dur′ing** *adj.*

**en•e•my** (ĕn′ə-mē) *n., pl.* **-mies.** A foe.

**en•er•gy** (ĕn′ər-jē) *n., pl.* **-gies. 1.** Vigor or power. **2.** Capacity for action or accomplishment. **—en′er•get′ic** *adj.*

**en•force** (ĕn-fôrs′, -fōrs′) *v.* **-forced, -forcing.** To compel obedience to. **—en•force′a•ble** *adj.* **—en•force′ment** *n.*

**en•gage** (ĕn-gāj′) *v.* **-gaged, -gaging. 1.** To employ; hire. **2.** To attract and hold the attention of. **3.** To pledge, esp. by a promise to marry. **4.** To enter into conflict with. **5.** To interlock or cause to interlock. **6.** To become occupied. **—en•gage′ment** *n.*

**en•gine** (ĕn′jən) *n.* **1.** A machine that converts energy into mechanical motion. **2.** A locomotive.

**en•gi•neer** (ĕn′jə-nîr′) *n.* **1.** One skilled at engineering. **2.** One who operates an engine. —*v.* **1.** To act as engineer. **2.** To plan or accomplish by skillful acts or contrivance.

**en•gi•neer•ing** (ĕn′jə-nîr′ĭng) *n.* The application of scientific principles to practical ends.

**en•grave** (ĕn-grāv′) *v.* **-graved, -graving.** To carve, cut, or etch into a material. **—en•grav′er** *n.* **—en•grav′ing** *n.*

**en•gross** (ĕn-grōs′) *v.* To occupy the complete attention of. **—en•gross′ing** *adj.*

**en•hance** (ĕn-hăns′) *v.* **-hanced, -hancing.** To increase, as in value or beauty.

**e•nig•ma** (ĭ-nĭg′mə) *n.* **1.** An obscure riddle. **2.** A person or thing that is puzzling. **—en′ig•mat′ic** *adj.* **—en′ig•mat′i•cal•ly** *adv.*

**en•joy** (ĕn-joi′) *v.* **1.** To experience joy in. **2.** To have as one's lot. **—en•joy′a•ble** *adj.* **—en•joy′ment** *n.*

**en•large** (ĕn-lärj′) *v.* **-larged, -larging.** To make or become larger. **—en•large′ment** *n.*

**en•list** (ĕn-lĭst′) *v.* **1.** To engage the assistance of. **2.** To enter the armed forces voluntarily. **—en•list′ment** *n.*

**e•nor•mous** (ĭ-nôr′məs) *adj.* Huge; immense. **—e•nor′mous•ly** *adv.*

**e•nough** (ĭ-nŭf′) *adj.* Sufficient to meet a need. —*n.* An adequate quantity. —*adv.* **1.** To a satisfactory degree. **2.** Very; quite.

**en•rich** (ĕn-rĭch′) *v.* To make rich or richer; add to the quality or enjoyment of. **—en•rich′ment** *n.*

**en•roll, en•rol** (ĕn-rōl′) *v.* **-rolled, -rolling.** To enter one's name or the name of another in a register, record, or roll. **—en•roll′ment** *n.*

**en•sem•ble** (ŏn-sŏm′bəl) *n.* A group of parts that contribute to a single effect, as a coordinated costume or a group of musicians.

**en•tan•gle** (ĕn-tăng′gəl) *v.* **-gled, -gling. 1.** To twist together; snarl. **2.** To complicate; confuse. **3.** To involve inextricably. **—en•tan′gle•ment** *n.*

**en•ter** (ĕn′tər) *v.* **1.** To come or go into. **2.** To penetrate; pierce. **3.** To enroll. **4.** To become a participant in; join. **5.** To place on record.

**en•ter•prise** (ĕn′tər-prīz′) *n.* **1.** An undertaking; project. **2.** Readiness to venture; initiative. **—en′ter•pris′ing** *adj.*

**en•ter•tain** (ĕn′tər-tān′) *v.* **1.** To hold the attention of; amuse. **2.** To extend hospitality toward. **3.** To hold in mind. **—en′ter•tain′er** *n.* **—en′ter•tain′ing** *adj.* **—en′ter•tain′ment** *n.*

**en•thu•si•asm** (ĕn-thōō′zē-ăz′əm) *n.* **1.** Great interest or excitement. **2.** Something that inspires a lively interest. **—en•thu′si•ast′** *n.* **—en•thu′si•as′tic** *adj.*

**en•tire** (ĕn-tīr′) *adj.* Whole; complete. **—en•tire′ly** *adv.* **—en•tire′ty** *n.*

**en•ti•tle** (ĕn-tīt′l) *v.* **-tled, -tling. 1.** To give a name to. **2.** To give (one) a right.

**en•ti•tle•ment** (ĕn-tī′tl-mənt) *n.* A government program benefiting a specific group.

**en•ti•ty** (ĕn′tĭ-tē) *n., pl.* **-ties. 1.** The fact of existence. **2.** Something that exists independently.

**en•trance** (ĕn′trəns) *n.* **1.** The act of entering. **2.** A passage or opening. **3.** Admission.

**en•trée, en•tree** (ŏn′trā) *n.* The main course of a meal.

**en•tre•pre•neur** (ŏn′trə-prə-nûr′) *n.* A person who organizes, operates, and assumes the risk for business ventures. **—en′tre•pre•neur′i•al** *adj.* **—en′tre•pre•neur′ship** *n.*

**en•try** (ĕn′trē) *n., pl.* **-tries. 1.** An entrance. **2.** An item included in a list. **3.** A participant in a competition.

**en•try-lev•el** (ĕn′trē-lĕv′əl) *adj.* Relating to the lowest level of a corporate hierarchy.

**en•vel•op** (ĕn-vĕl′əp) *v.* **-oped, -oping. 1.** To enclose. **2.** To surround.

**en•ve•lope** (ĕn′və-lōp′, ŏn-) *n.* **1.** Something that envelops; cover. **2.** A paper container for a letter.

**en•vi•a•ble** (ĕn′vē-ə-bəl) *adj.* Highly desirable. **—en′vi•a•ble•ness** *n.* **—en′vi•a•bly** *adv.*

**en•vi•ron•ment** (ĕn-vī′rən-mənt) *n.* **1.** Surroundings. **2.** The external conditions that affect the growth and development of organisms. **—en•vi′ron•men′tal** *adj.*

**en•vi•ron•men•tal•ist** (ĕn-vī′rən-mĕn′tl-ĭst) *n.* One that advocates protection of the natural environment. **—en•vi′ron•men′tal•ism** *n.*

**en•voy** (ĕn′voi′, ŏn′-) *n.* **1.** A messenger. **2.** A diplomatic representative.

**en•vy** (ĕn′vē) *n.* Discontent aroused by another's possessions or qualities, with a strong desire to have them for oneself. **—en′vi•ous** *adj.* **—en′vi•ous•ly** *adv.*

**ep•ic** (ĕp′ĭk) *n.* A long narrative poem about heroic characters and deeds. *—adj.* Grand; heroic.

**ep•i•dem•ic** (ĕp′ĭ-dĕm′ĭk) *adj.* Spreading rapidly among many in an area. *—n.* A contagious disease that spreads rapidly.

**ep•i•lep•sy** (ĕp′ə-lĕp′sē) *n.* A neurological disorder characterized by convulsions. **—ep′i•lep′tic** *adj. & n.*

**ep•i•logue** (ĕp′ə-lôg′, -lŏg′) *n.* Also **ep•i•log.** A short concluding section at the end of a literary work.

**ep•i•neph•rine** (ĕp′ə-nĕf′rĭn) *n.* **1.** A hormone that stimulates involuntary nerve action. **2.** A compound used as a heart stimulant and asthma medication.

**e•pis•co•pal** (ĭ-pĭs′kə-pəl) *adj.* Of a bishop.

**ep•i•sode** (ĕp′ĭ-sōd′) *n.* **1.** An incident in a continuous experience. **2.** A portion of a narrative that relates an event.

**ep•och** (ĕp′ək) *n.* A particular period of history, esp. one that is memorable.

**e•pox•y** (ĭ-pŏks′ē) *n., pl.* **-ies.** A kind of tough, strongly adhesive glue. *—v.* **-ied, -ying.** To glue with epoxy.

**e•qual** (ē′kwəl) *adj.* **1.** Having the same capability. **2.** Alike; identical. **3.** Having the same status, rights, etc. **4.** Qualified; fit. *—n.* One that is equal to another. *—v.* **1.** To be equal to, esp. in value. **2.** To do or produce something equal to. **—e•qual'i•ty** *n.* **—e'qual•ly** *adv.*

**e•qua•tion** (ĭ-kwā'zhən, -shən) *n.* A mathematical statement that 2 quantities are equal.

**e•qua•tor** (ĭ-kwā'tər) *n.* The imaginary circle dividing the earth's surface between the N and S hemispheres. **—e'qua•to'ri•al** *adj.*

**e•qui•lib•ri•um** (ē-kwə-lĭb'rē-əm) *n.* Any condition in which all acting influences are stable; balance.

**e•qui•nox** (ē'kwə-nŏks', ĕk'wə-) *n.* Either of the 2 times during a year when the lengths of day and night are approximately equal. **—eq•ui•noc'tial** *adj. & n.*

**e•quip** (ĭ-kwĭp') *v.* **equipped, equipping.** To supply with what is needed or wanted. **—e•quip'ment** *n.*

**e•quiv•a•lent** (ĭ-kwĭv'ə-lənt) *adj.* Equal; similar in effect. **—e•quiv'a•lence** *n.*

**e•ra** (îr'ə, ĕr'ə) *n.* A period of time.

**e•rase** (ĭ-rās') *v.* **erased, erasing. 1.** To rub, scrape, or blot out. **2.** To remove all traces of. **—e•ras'er** *n.* **—e•ra'sure** *n.*

**e•rect** (ĭ-rĕkt') *adj.* Standing upright; vertical. *—v.* **1.** To construct; build. **2.** To raise upright; set on end. **—e•rec'tion** *n.*

**e•ro•sion** (ĭ-rō'zhən) *n.* A natural process by which earth or rock is gradually worn away and removed by wind, water, etc. **—e•rode'** *v.*

**e•rot•ic** (ĭ-rŏt'ĭk) *adj.* Of sexual love. **—e•rot'i•ca** *pl.n.*

**er•rand** (ĕr'ənd) *n.* A short trip taken for a specific purpose.

**er•rat•ic** (ĭ-răt'ĭk) *adj.* Irregular; inconsistent. **—er•rat'i•cal•ly** *adv.*

**er•ror** (ĕr'ər) *n.* **1.** A mistake. **2.** A transgression; wrongdoing.

**er•u•dite** (ĕr'/y/ə-dīt') *adj.* Deeply learned. **—er'u•di'tion** *n.*

**e•rupt** (ĭ-rŭpt') *v.* To emerge or eject violently. **—e•rup'tion** *n.*

**es•ca•late** (ĕs'kə-lāt') *v.* **-lated, -lating.** To increase or intensify. **—es'ca•la'tion** *n.*

**es•cape** (ĭ-skāp') *v.* **-caped, -caping. 1.** To break from confinement; get free. **2.** To avoid; elude. *—n.* **1.** The act of escaping. **2.** Temporary freedom from trouble. **—es'cap•ee'** *n.*

**es•cort** (ĕs'kôrt') *n.* **1.** A person or vehicle accompanying another to give guidance or protection or to pay honor. **2.** A male companion of a woman at a social function. *—v.* (ĭ-skôrt'). To accompany as an escort.

**e•soph•a•gus** (ĭ-sŏf'ə-gəs) *n.* A tube for the passage of food from the pharynx to the stomach.

**es•pe•cial** (ĭ-spĕsh'əl) *adj.* Special; exceptional. **—es•pe'cial•ly** *adv.*

**es•say** (ĕs'ā, ĕ-sā') *v.* To try. *—n.* **1.** An attempt. **2.** (ĕs'ā') A short literary composition on a single subject. **—es'say'ist** *n.*

**es•sence** (ĕs'əns) *n.* **1.** The intrinsic properties of a thing. **2.** A concentrated extract of a substance.

**es•sen•tial** (ĭ-sĕn'shəl) *adj.* **1.** Constituting the essence of something; basic. **2.** Indispensable; necessary. *—n.* An essential thing.

**es•tab•lish** (ĭ-stăb'lĭsh) *v.* **1.** To settle securely in a position. **2.** To found or create. **3.** To prove. **—es•tab'lish•ment** *n.*

**es•tate** (ĭ-stāt') *n.* **1.** A sizable piece of land with a large house. **2.** All of one's possessions.

**es•teem** (ĭ-stēm') *v.* To regard favorably; respect. *—n.* Favorable regard; respect.

**es•ti•mate** (ĕs'tə-māt') *v.* **-mated, -mating. 1.** To calculate approximately the cost, quantity, or extent of. **2.** To evaluate. *—n.* (-mĭt). **1.** A rough or preliminary calculation, as the cost of work to be undertaken. **2.** An opinion. **—es'ti•ma'tion** *n.*

**es•trange** (ĭ-strānj') *v.* **-tranged, -tranging.** To alienate the affections of. **—es•trange'ment** *n.*

**etch** (ĕch) *v.* To make (a pattern) on a surface with acid. **—etch'er** *n.* **—etch'ing** *n.*

**e•ter•nal** (ĭ-tûr'nəl) *adj.* **1.** Without beginning or end. **2.** Lasting; timeless. **—e•ter'nal•ly** *adv.* **—e•ter'ni•ty** *n.*

**e•ther** (ē'thər) *n.* Also **ae•ther. 1.** A liquid used as an anesthetic. **2.** The heavens.

**e•the•re•al** (ĭ-thîr'ē-əl) *adj.* **1.** Highly refined; delicate. **2.** Heavenly; spiritual.

**eth•ic** (ĕth'ĭk) *n.* A principle of right or good conduct or a body of such principles. —*n.* **ethics. 1.** *(takes sing. v.)* The study of the nature of morals and moral choices. **2.** Any set of moral principles or values. **—eth′i•cal** *adj.* **—eth′i•cal•ly** *adv.*

**eth•nic** (ĕth′nĭk) *adj.* Of a specific race or national group. —*n.* A member of an ethnic group. **—eth•nic′i•ty** *n.*

**et•i•quette** (ĕt′ĭ-kĕt′, -kĭt) *n.* Prescribed social behavior and manners.

**et•y•mol•o•gy** (ĕt′ə-mŏl′ə-jē) *n., pl.* **-gies.** The origin and historical development of a word. **—et′y•mo•log′i•cal** *adj.* **—et′y•mol′o•gist** *n.*

**Eu•ro•cur•ren•cy** (yo͝or′ō-kûr′ən-sē) *n., pl.* **-cies.** Non-European currency used in European money markets.

**Eu•ro•dol•lar** (yo͝or′ō-dŏl′ər) *n.* A U.S. dollar on deposit in a foreign, esp. European, bank.

**eu•tha•na•sia** (yo͞o′thə-nā′zhə, -zhē-ə) *n.* Mercy killing. **—eu•than′a•tize′, eu′tha•nize′** *v.*

**e•vac•u•ate** (ĭ-văk′yo͞o-āt′) *v.* **-ated, -ating. 1.** To remove the contents of. **2.** To withdraw. **—e•vac′u•a′tion** *n.* **—e•vac′u•ee′** *n.*

**e•vade** (ĭ-vād′) *v.* **evaded, evading.** To escape or avoid by cleverness. **—e•va′sion** *n.* **—e•va′sive** *adj.* **—e•va′sive•ness** *n.*

**e•val•uate** (ĭ-văl′yo͞o-āt′) *v.* **-ated, -ating.** To ascertain or judge. **—e•val′u•a′tion** *n.*

**e•van•gel•i•cal** (ē′văn-jĕl′ĭ-kəl) *adj.* Also **e•van•gel•ic.** Of the Christian Gospel.

**e•van•gel•ism** (ĭ-văn′jə-lĭz′əm) *n.* The preaching of the Gospel. **—e•van′gel•ist** *n.*

**e•vap•o•rate** (ĭ-văp′ə-rāt′) *v.* **-rated, -rating. 1.** To change into a vapor. **2.** To vanish. **—e•vap′o•ra′tion** *n.*

**eve** (ēv) *n.* The evening or day preceding a holiday or a certain event.

**e•ven** (ē′vən) *adj.* **1.** Flat; smooth; level. **2.** Uniform; steady; regular. **3.** Tranquil; calm. **4.** Equal; balanced. **5.** Exactly divisible by 2. —*v.* To make or become even. **—e′ven•ly** *adv.* **—e′ven•ness** *n.*

**eve•ning** (ēv′nĭng) *n.* Late afternoon and early night.

**e•vent** (ĭ-vĕnt′) *n.* **1.** An occurrence, esp. a significant one. **2.** One of the items in a sports program. **—e•vent′ful** *adj.*

**ev•er** (ĕv′ər) *adv.* **1.** At any time. **2.** In any way.

**ev•er•green** (ĕv′ər-grēn′) *adj.* Having foliage that remains green all year. —*n.* An evergreen tree or plant.

**eve•ry** (ĕv′rē) *adj.* **1.** Each without exception. **2.** Not lacking anything necessary; complete. **—eve′ry•bod′y, eve′ry•one′** *pron.* **—eve′ry•place′, eve′ry•where′** *adv.*

**e•vict** (ĭ-vĭkt′) *v.* To expel (a tenant) by legal process; force out. **—e•vic′tion** *n.*

**ev•i•dence** (ĕv′ĭ-dəns) *n.* The data on which a judgment or proof can be based. —*v.* **-denced, -dencing.** To indicate clearly.

**ev•i•dent** (ĕv′ĭ-dənt) *adj.* Easily recognized; obvious. **—ev′i•dent•ly** *adv.*

**e•vil** (ē′vəl) *adj.* **1.** Wicked. **2.** Injurious; harmful. —*n.* Wickedness.

**ev•o•lu•tion** (ĕvə-lo͞o′shən) *n.* A gradual process in which something changes, esp. into a more complex form.

**ewe** (yo͞o) *n.* A female sheep.

**ex•act** (ĭg-zăkt′) *adj.* Strictly accurate.

**ex•ac•ta** (ĭg-zăk′tə) *n.* A type of wager in which the bettor must pick the 1st and 2nd finishers of a race.

**ex•ag•ger•ate** (ĭg-zăj′ə-rāt′) *v.* **-ated, -ating.** To enlarge (something) disproportionately; overstate. **—ex•ag′ger•a′tion** *n.*

**ex•am•ine** (ĭg-zăm′ĭn) *v.* **-ined, -ining. 1.** To inspect or analyze in detail. **2.** To test knowledge or skills. **3.** To interrogate formally. **—ex•am′i•na′tion** *n.* **—ex•am′in•er** *n.*

**ex•am•ple** (ĭg-zăm′pəl) *n.* **1.** One that is representative of a group; a sample. **2.** A model. **3.** One that serves as a warning. **—ex•em′pla•ry** *adj.*

**ex•ceed** (ĭk-sēd′) *v.* **1.** To be greater than; surpass. **2.** To go or be beyond the limits of. **—ex•ceed′ing** *adj.*

**ex•cel•lent** (ĕk′sə-lənt) *adj.* Exceptionally good; superb. **—ex′cel•lence** *n.* **—ex′cel•lent•ly** *adv.*

**ex•cept** (ĭk-sĕpt′) *prep.* With the exclusion of; but. —*conj.* Were it not for the fact that; only. —*v.* To leave out; exclude.

**ex•cep•tion** (ĭk-sĕp′shən) *n.* **1.** An exclusion or omission. **2.** A case that does not conform to normal rules.

**ex•cep•tion•al** (ĭk-sĕp′shə-nəl) *adj.* Uncommon; extraordinary.
**ex•cerpt** (ĕk′sûrpt′) *n.* A passage selected from a speech, book, etc.
**ex•cess** (ĭk-sĕs′, ĕk′sĕs′) *n.* **1.** An amount beyond what is required; superfluity. **2.** Overindulgence. —*adj.* Being more than is required. **—ex•ces′sive** *adj.*
**ex•change** (ĭks-chānj′) *v.* **-changed, -changing. 1.** To give and receive reciprocally; trade. **2.** To replace (1 thing by another). —*n.* **1.** An act of exchanging. **2.** A place where things are exchanged.
**ex•cise** (ĕk′sīz′) *n.* A tax on certain commodities within a country.
**ex•cite** (ĭk-sīt′) *v.* **-cited, -citing. 1.** To stimulate; stir to activity. **2.** To arouse strong feeling in (a person); provoke. **—ex•cit′ed•ly** *adv.* **—ex•cite′ment** *n.*
**ex•claim** (ĭk-sklām′) *v.* To cry out or speak suddenly. **—ex′cla•ma′tion** *n.*
**ex•clude** (ĭk-sklo͞od′) *v.* **-cluded, -cluding. 1.** To prevent from entering a place, group, etc.; bar. **2.** To force out; expel. **—ex•clu′sion** *n.*
**ex•clu•sive** (ĭk-sklo͞o′sĭv) *adj.* **1.** Not divided or shared with others. **2.** Admitting only certain people; select. **—ex•clu′sive•ly** *adv.* **—ex′clu•siv′i•ty** *n.*
**ex•crete** (ĭk-skrēt′) *v.* **-creted, -creting.** To eliminate (waste matter) from the body. **—ex•cre′tion** *n.* **—ex′cre•to′ry** *adj.*
**ex•cru•ci•at•ing** (ĭk-skro͞o′shē-ā′tĭng) *adj.* Intensely painful.
**ex•cur•sion** (ĭk-skûr′zhən) *n.* A short journey or pleasure trip; outing.
**ex•cuse** (ĭk-skyo͞oz′) *v.* **-cused, -cusing. 1.** To forgive. **2.** To overlook; condone. **3.** To free, as from an obligation. —*n.* (-skyo͞os′). An explanation.
**ex•e•cute** (ĕk′sĭ-kyo͞ot′) *v.* **-cuted, -cuting. 1.** To carry out; perform. **2.** To subject to capital punishment. **—ex′e•cu′tion** *n.* **—ex′e•cu′tion•er** *n.*
**ex•ec•u•tive** (ĭg-zĕk′yə-tĭv) *n.* One having administrative authority in an organization.
**ex•empt** (ĭg-zĕmpt′) *v.* To free from an obligation or duty. **—ex•empt′** *adj.* **—ex•emp′tion** *n.*
**ex•er•cise** (ĕk′sər-sīz′) *n.* **1.** An act of employing. **2.** Physical activity to develop fitness. **3.** A lesson, problem, etc., designed to increase some skill. **4.** Often **exercises.** A public ceremony. —*v.* **-cised, -cising. 1.** To put into operation; employ. **2.** To subject to or engage in exercises for physical fitness.
**ex•ert** (ĭg-zûrt′) *v.* To put into vigorous action. **—ex•er′tion** *n.*
**ex•hale** (ĕks-hāl′, ĕk-sāl′) *v.* **-haled, -haling. 1.** To breathe out. **2.** To emit (vapor, smoke, etc.). **—ex′ha•la′tion** *n.*
**ex•haust** (ĭg-zôst′) *v.* **1.** To let out (air or fumes). **2.** To use up; expend. **3.** To wear out completely; tire. —*n.* Vapor or fumes exhausted. **—ex•haus′tion** *n.*
**ex•haus•tive** (ĭg-zô′stĭv) *adj.* Comprehensive; thorough.
**ex•hib•it** (ĕg-zĭb′ĭt, ĭg-) *v.* To show; display. —*n.* That which is exhibited. **—ex′hi•bi′tion** *n.*
**ex•hort** (ĭg-zôrt′) *v.* To urge by strong appeal. **—ex′hor•ta′tion** *n.*
**ex•ile** (ĕg′zīl′, ĕk′sīl′) *n.* **1.** Banishment. **2.** One who has been banished from his country. —*v.* **-iled, -iling.** To send (someone) into exile.
**ex•ist** (ĭg-zĭst′) *v.* **1.** To be or live. **2.** To occur. **—ex•is′tence** *n.* **—ex•is′tent** *adj.*
**ex•it** (ĕg′zĭt, ĕk′sĭt) *n.* **1.** The act of going out; departure. **2.** A way out. **—ex′it** *v.*
**ex•o•dus** (ĕk′sə-dəs) *n.* A departure, usually of a large number of people.
**ex•or•bi•tant** (ĭg-zôr′bĭ-tənt) *adj.* Excessive; immoderate. **—ex•or′bi•tance** *n.*
**ex•or•cise** (ĕk′sôr-sīz′, -sər-) *v.* **-cised, -cising.** To expel (an evil spirit) by prayer. **—ex′or•cism** *n.* **—ex′or•cist** *n.*
**ex•ot•ic** (ĭg-zŏt′ĭk) *adj.* **1.** Not indigenous; foreign. **2.** Having the charm of the unfamiliar; unusual.
**ex•pand** (ĭk-spănd′) *v.* **1.** To unfold; spread out. **2.** To increase in size, extent, etc. **—ex•pan′sion** *n.*
**ex•panse** (ĭk-spăns′) *n.* A wide and open extent, as of land.
**ex•pect** (ĭk-spĕkt′) *v.* **1.** To look forward to; anticipate. **2.** To consider reasonable or due. **—ex•pec′tan•cy** *n.* **—ex•pec′tant•ly** *adv.* **—ex′pec•ta′tion** *n.*
**ex•pe•di•ent** (ĭk-spē′dē-ənt) *adj.* **1.** Appropriate; suitable. **2.** Serving to promote one's interest without regard for principle. —*n.* Something expedient.

—**ex•pe′di•en•cy, ex•pe′di•ence** *n.* —**ex•pe′di•ent•ly** *adv.*

**ex•pe•dite** (ĕk′spĭ-dīt′) *v.* **-dited, -diting.** To speed the progress of; facilitate. —**ex′pe•dit′er** *n.* —**ex′pe•di′tious** *adj.*

**ex•pe•di•tion** (ĕk′spĭ-dĭsh′ən) *n.* A trip or march made by a group, as for military action. —**ex′pe•di′tion•ar′y** *adj.*

**ex•pel** (ĭk-spĕl′) *v.* **-pelled, -pelling. 1.** To drive out; eject forcefully. **2.** To dismiss by official decision.

**ex•pend** (ĭk-spĕnd′) *v.* To pay out; use up; consume. —**ex•pend′a•ble** *adj.* —**ex•pen′di•ture** *n.*

**ex•pense** (ĭk-spĕns′) *n.* **1.** Often **ex•penses.** Money needed for a purpose. **2.** Cost; sacrifice. —**ex•pen′sive** *adj.* —**ex•pen′sive•ly** *adv.*

**ex•pe•ri•ence** (ĭk-spîr′ē-əns) *n.* **1.** An event or series of events participated in or lived through. **2. a.** Activity through which knowledge or skill is gained. **b.** Knowledge or skill gained through an activity. —*v.* **-enced, -encing.** To have as an experience; undergo. —**ex•pe′ri•enced** *adj.*

**ex•per•i•ment** (ĭk-spĕr′ə-mənt) *n.* A test made to demonstrate a known truth, examine a hypothesis, etc. —*v.* To conduct an experiment; try or test. —**ex•per′i•men′tal** *adj.* —**ex•per′i•men•ta′tion** *n.*

**ex•pert** (ĕk′spûrt′) *n.* A person with skill or specialized knowledge. —*adj.* Highly skilled or knowledgeable. —**ex′per•tise′** *n.* —**ex•pert′ly** *adv.* —**ex•pert′ness** *n.*

**ex•pire** (ĭk-spīr′) *v.* **-pired, -piring. 1.** To die. **2.** To come to an end. **3.** To exhale. —**ex′pi•ra′tion** *n.*

**ex•plain** (ĭk-splān′) *v.* **1.** To make plain or comprehensible. **2.** To offer reasons for; account for. —**ex′pla•na′tion** *n.*

**ex•plic•it** (ĭk-splĭs′ĭt) *adj.* Precisely expressed; clear and specific. —**ex•plic′it•ly** *adv.* —**ex•plic′it•ness** *n.*

**ex•plode** (ĭk-splōd′) *v.* **-ploded, -ploding.** To burst or make burst suddenly and violently. —**ex•plo′sion** *n.*

**ex•ploit** (ĕk′-sploit′) *n.* A noteworthy act or deed; feat. —*v.* (ĕk-sploit′). **1.** To use fully or advantageously. **2.** To make selfish or unethical use of. —**ex•ploit′a•tive** *adj.* —**ex′ploi•ta′tion** *n.*

**ex•plore** (ĭk-splôr′, -splōr′) *v.* **-plored, -ploring. 1.** To investigate systematically. **2.** To travel into (an area) for the purpose of discovery. —**ex′plo•ra′tion** *n.* —**ex•plor′a•to′ry** *adj.* —**ex•plor′er** *n.*

**ex•plo•sive** (ĭk-splō′sĭv) *adj.* **1.** Of an explosion. **2.** Tending to explode. —*n.* A substance that explodes or causes explosion. —**ex•plo′sive•ly** *adv.*

**ex•port** (ĭk-spôrt′, -spōrt′, ĕk′spôrt′, -spōrt′) *v.* To send abroad, esp. for sale. —*n.* (ĕk′spôrt′, -spōrt′). Something exported. —**ex•port′er** *n.*

**ex•pres•sion** (ĭk-sprĕsh′ən) *n.* **1.** Communication of an idea, emotion, etc. **2.** a facial aspect or tone of voice conveying feeling. **3.** A word or phrase. —**ex•pres′sive** *adj.* —**ex•pres′sive•ly** *adv.*

**ex•pul•sion** (ĭk-spŭl′shən) *n.* The act of expelling or state of being expelled.

**ex•qui•site** (ĕk′skwĭ-zĭt, ĭk-skwĭz′ĭt) *adj.* **1.** Delicately beautiful. **2.** Sensitive; discriminating. **3.** Keen; intense. —**ex′qui•site•ly** *adv.*

**ex•tant** (ĕk′stənt, ĕk-stănt′) *adj.* Still in existence.

**ex•tend** (ĭk-stĕnd′) *v.* **1.** To spread, stretch, or enlarge. **2.** To exert to full capacity. **3.** To offer; tender. —**ex•tend′i•ble, ex•ten′si•ble** *adj.*

**ex•ten•sion** (ĭk-stĕn′shən) *n.* **1.** The act of extending or condition of being extended. **2.** An extended or added part.

**ex•ten•sive** (ĭk-stĕn′sĭv) *adj.* Great in extent, range, etc. —**ex•ten′sive•ly** *adv.*

**ex•tent** (ĭk-stĕnt′) *n.* **1.** The distance over which something stretches or spreads; size. **2.** Degree to which something stretches or spreads; scope.

**ex•te•ri•or** (ĭk-stîr′ē-ər) *adj.* Outer; external. —*n.* An outer part or surface.

**ex•ter•mi•nate** (ĭk-stûr′mə-nāt′) *v.* **-nated, -nating.** To destroy completely; wipe out. —**ex•ter′mi•na′tion** *n.* —**ex•ter′mi•na′tor** *n.*

**ex•ter•nal** (ĭk-stûr′nəl) *adj.* Of the outside or an outer part.

**ex•tinct** (ĭk-stĭngkt′) *adj.* No longer existing; having died out. —**ex•tinc′tion** *n.*

**ex•tin•guish** (ĭk-stĭng′gwĭsh) *v.* To put out (a fire, light, etc.).
**ex•tol** (ĭk-stōl′) *v.* **-tolled, -tolling.** To praise highly.
**ex•tort** (ĭk-stôrt′) *v.* To obtain (money, information, etc.) by coercion or intimidation. **—ex•tor′tion** *n.* **—ex•tor′tion•ist** *n.*
**ex•tra** (ĕk′strə) *adj.* Additional. *—n.* **1.** Something additional. **2.** A special edition of a newspaper. *—adv.* Very; unusually.
**ex•tract** (ĭk-străkt′) *v.* **1.** To draw forth or pull out by force. **2.** To pick out for separate mention; excerpt. *—n.* (ĕk′străkt′). An extracted substance or concentrated preparation. **—ex•trac′tion** *n.*
**ex•traor•di•nar•y** (ĭk-strôr′dn-ĕr′ē, ĕk′strə-ôr′-) *adj.* Unusual; exceptional.
**ex•trav•a•gant** (ĭk-străv′ə-gənt) *adj.* **1.** Spending too much; wasteful. **2.** Immoderate; excessive. **—ex•trav′a•gance** *n.* **—ex•trav′a•gant•ly** *adv.*
**ex•treme** (ĭk-strēm) *adj.* **1.** Farthest; most remote. **2.** Final; last. **3.** Very great; intense. **4.** To the utmost degree; radical. **5.** Drastic; severe. *—n.* **1.** The greatest or utmost degree. **2.** Either of the 2 ends of a scale, series, etc. **—ex•treme′ly** *adv.*
**ex•trem•i•ty** (ĭk-strĕm′ĭ-tē) *n., pl.* **-ties. 1.** The outermost point or part. **2.** A bodily limb or appendage.
**ex•tro•vert** (ĕk′strə-vûrt′) *n.* One interested in others or in outside activities as opposed to self. **—ex′tro•vert′ed** *adj.*
**ex•u•ber•ant** (ĭg-zo͞o′bər-ənt) *adj.* Full of high spirits. **—ex•u′ber•ance** *n.*
**eye** (ī) *n.* **1.** An organ of vision. **2.** Ability to perceive or discern. *—v.* **eyed, eyeing** or **eying.** To look at; regard.
**eye•ball** (ī′bôl′) *n.* The ball-shaped portion of the eye.
**eye•brow** (ī′brou′) *n.* The hairs covering the ridge over the eye.
**eye•glass** (ī′glăs′) *n.* **1.** A lens used to aid vision. **2. eyeglasses.** A pair of mounted lenses worn to correct faulty vision.
**eye•lash** (ī′lăsh′) *n.* A hair fringing the edge of an eyelid.
**eye•let** (ī′lĭt) *n.* A small, often rimmed hole used for fastening with a cord or for decoration.
**eye•lid** (ī′lĭd′) *n.* A fold of skin that closes over an eye.
**eye•sight** (ī′sīt′) *n.* The ability to see; vision.

## — F —

**f, F** (ĕf) *n.* The 6th letter of the English alphabet.
**fa•ble** (fā′bəl) *n.* A brief moral story.
**fab•ric** (făb′rĭk) *n.* Cloth.
**fab•ri•cate** (făb′rĭ-kāt′) *v.* **-cated, -cating. 1.** To make or fashion. **2.** To make up (a deception). **—fab′ri•ca′tion** *n.*
**fab•u•lous** (făb′yə-ləs) *adj.* **1.** Legendary. **2.** Excellent or wonderful.
**fa•çade, fa•cade** (fə-säd′) *n.* The front of a building.
**face** (fās) *n.* **1.** The front of the head. **2.** A facial expression. **3.** Dignity; prestige. *—v.* **faced, facing. 1.** To turn or be turned in the direction of. **2.** To meet; encounter. **3.** To meet boldly; confront. **—fa′cial** *adj.*
**fac•et** (făs′ĭt) *n.* **1.** One of the flat surfaces cut on a gemstone. **2.** An aspect; phase.
**fa•ce•tious** (fə-sē′shəs) *adj.* Joking; humorous. **—fa•ce′tious•ly** *adv.* **—fa•ce′tious•ness** *n.*
**fac•ile** (făs′əl) *adj.* **1.** Superficial. **2.** Easy.
**fa•cil•i•tate** (fə-sĭl′ĭ-tāt′) *v.* **-tated, -tating.** To make easier. **—fa•cil′i•ta′tion** *n.* **—fa•cil′i•ta′tor** *n.*
**fa•cil•i•ty** (fə-sĭl′ĭ-tē) *n., pl.* **-ties. 1.** An aptitude or skill. **2.** Something that provides a service or assistance.
**fac•sim•i•le** (făk-sĭm′ə-lē) *n.* An exact copy or reproduction.
**fact** (făkt) *n.* **1.** Something actually happening; a certainty. **2.** Truth; reality. **—fac′tu•al** *adj.* **—fac′tu•al•ly** *adv.*
**fac•tion** (făk′shən) *n.* A group forming a usually contentious minority. **—fac′tion•al** *adj.* **—fac′tion•al•ism′** *n.*
**fac•tor** (făk′tər) *n.* One that actively contributes to a result or process.
**fac•to•ry** (făk′tə-rē) *n., pl.* **-ries.** A building in which goods are manufactured.
**fact sheet** *n.* A summary of background information.
**fac•ul•ty** (făk′əl-tē) *n., pl.* **-ties. 1.** An inherent power or ability. **2.** The teach-

ers in a school.

**fade** (fād) *v.* **faded, fading. 1.** To lose color or brightness; dim. **2.** To wither.

**Fahr•en•heit** (făr'ən-hīt') *adj.* Of a temperature scale that registers the freezing point of water as 32°F and the boiling point as 212°F.

**fail** (fāl) *v.* **1.** To be deficient or unsuccessful. **2.** To decline, weaken, or cease. **3.** To disappoint. **4.** To omit or neglect. **—fail'ure** *n.*

**faint** (fānt) *adj.* **1.** Lacking strength. **2.** Indistinct; dim. **3.** Suddenly dizzy. *—n.* A brief loss of consciousness. **—faint** *v.* **—faint'ly** *adv.* **—faint'ness** *n.*

**fair[1]** (fâr) *adj.* **1.** Beautiful; lovely. **2.** Sunny. **3.** Light in color, as hair. **4.** Just; equitable. **5.** Moderately good. **—fair'ly** *adv.* **—fair'ness** *n.*

**fair[2]** (fâr) *n.* A gathering for buying and selling goods.

**fair•y** (fâr'ē) *n., pl.* **-ies.** A supernatural being of folklore.

**faith** (fāth) *n.* **1. a.** Confident belief; trust. **b.** Religious conviction. **2.** Loyalty; allegiance. **—faith'ful** *adj.* **—faith'ful•ly** *adv.* **—faith'ful•ness** *n.* **—faith'less** *adj.*

**fake** (fāk) *adj.* False; fraudulent. *—n.* **1.** A counterfeit. **2.** An impostor. **—fake** *v.* **—fak'er** *n.* **—fak'er•y** *n.*

**fall** (fôl) *v.* **fell** (fĕl), **fallen** (fô'lən), **fall•ing. 1.** To drop without restraint. **2.** To come down from an erect position; collapse. **3.** To be killed or wounded. **4.** To be conquered. **5.** To diminish. **6.** To occur at a specified time or place. *—n.* **1.** The act of falling. **2.** That which has fallen. **3.** Often **Fall.** Autumn. **4.** An overthrow, as of a government.

**fal•la•cy** (făl'ə-sē) *n., pl.* **-cies.** An erroneous idea or opinion. **—fal•la'cious** *adj.* **—fal•la'cious•ly** *adv.*

**fal•li•ble** (făl'ə-bəl) *adj.* Capable of erring. **—fal'li•bil'i•ty** *n.* **—fal'li•bly** *adv.*

**fall•out** (fôl'out') *n.* **1. a.** The slow descent of minute radioactive particles through the air. **b.** The particles themselves. **2.** An incidental, esp. undesirable, result or side effect.

**false** (fôls) *adj.* **falser, falsest. 1.** Contrary to fact or truth. **2.** Insincere. **3.** Artificial. **—false'hood'** *n.* **—false'ly** *adv.* **—false'ness** *n.* **—fal'si•fi•ca'tion** *n.* **—fal'si•ty'** *v.*

**fal•ter** (fôl'tər) *v.* **1.** To waver or weaken. **2.** To stammer. **3.** To stumble. **—fal'ter•ing•ly** *adv.*

**fame** (fām) *n.* Public esteem; renown. **—famed** *adj.*

**fa•mil•iar** (fə-mĭl'yər) *adj.* **1.** Well-known; often encountered; common. **2.** Having knowledge of. **3.** Friendly; intimate. **—fa•mil'iar'i•ty** *n.* **—fa•mil'iar•ize'** *v.* **—fa•mil'iar•ly** *adv.*

**fam•i•ly** (făm'ə-lē, făm'lē) *n., pl.* **-lies. 1.** Parents and their children. **2.** Relatives. **3.** A group or category of like things. **—fa•mil'ial** *adj.*

**fam•ine** (făm'ĭn) *n.* A drastic shortage of food.

**fa•mous** (fā'məs) *adj.* Widely known. **—fa'mous•ly** *adv.*

**fan[1]** (făn) *n.* An implement for creating a cooling breeze. *—v.* **fanned, fanning. 1.** To direct a current of air upon. **2.** To stir up. **3.** To spread out.

**fan[2]** (făn) *n.* An ardent admirer.

**fa•nat•ic** (fə-năt'ĭk) *n.* A person possessed by an excessive or irrational zeal. **—fa•nat'ic, fa•nat'i•cal** *adj.* **—fa•nat'i•cal•ly** *adv.* **—fa•nat'i•cism'** *n.*

**fan•cy** (făn'sē) *n., pl.* **-cies. 1.** Imagination. **2.** An unfounded opinion; notion. **3.** A capricious idea; whim. **4.** Taste or preference. *—adj.* **-cier, -ciest. 1.** Elegant. **2.** Illusory. **3.** Executed with skill. *—v.* **-cied, -cying. 1.** To imagine. **2.** To like. **3.** To suppose; guess. **—fan'ci•ful** *adj.* **—fan'ci•ful•ly** *adv.* **—fan'ci•ly** *adv.* **—fan'ci•ness** *n.*

**fang** (făng) *n.* A long, pointed tooth. **—fanged** *adj.*

**fan•light** (făn'līt') *n.* A half-circle window, with sash bars set like the ribs of a fan.

**fan•tas•tic** (făn-tăs'tĭk) *adj.* **1.** Grotesque. **2.** Unreal; imaginary. **3.** Wonderful; superb. **—fan•tas'ti•cal•ly** *adv.*

**fan•ta•sy** (făn'tə-sē, -zē) *n., pl.* **-sies. 1.** Imagination. **2.** An illusion or delusion. **3.** A story based on fantastic elements.

**far** (fär) *adv.* **farther, farthest. 1.** To, from, or at a considerable distance. **2.** To a considerable degree; much. **3.** Not at all. *—adj.* **farther, farthest. 1.** Distant. **2.** More distant; opposite.

**fare** (fâr) *v.* **fared, faring.** To get along. —*n.* **1.** A transportation charge. **2.** A passenger transported. **3.** Food and drink.

**farm** (färm) *n.* A tract of land for producing crops or raising livestock. —*v.* To cultivate land or raise livestock. —**farm'er** *n.* —**farm'house'** *n.* —**farm'ing** *n.* —**farm'yard'** *n.*

**fas•ci•nate** (făs'ə-nāt') *v.* **-nated, -nating.** To attract irresistibly. —**fas'ci•nat'ing•ly** *adv.* —**fas'ci•na'tion** *n.*

**fas•cism** (făsh'ĭz'əm) *n.* A dictatorship of the extreme right. —**fas'cist** *n. & adj.*

**fash•ion** (făsh'ən) *n.* **1.** Kind; sort. **2.** Manner. **3.** The current style. —*v.* To make. —**fash'ion•a•ble** *adj.* —**fash'ion•a•bly** *adv.* —**fash'ion•er** *n.*

**fast**[1] (făst) *adj.* **1.** Rapid. **2.** Firmly attached or fastened. **3.** Loyal. **4.** Proof against fading. —*adv.* **1.** Firmly. **2.** Deeply. **3.** Quickly. —**fast'ness** *n.*

**fast**[2] (făst) *v.* To abstain from food. —**fast** *n.*

**fast•back** (făst'băk') *n.* A car with a curving downward slope from roof to rear.

**fas•ten** (făs'ən) *v.* **1.** To attach. **2.** To make secure. —**fas'ten•er** *n.*

**fast food** *n.* Restaurant food prepared and served quickly. —**fast'-food'** *adj.*

**fas•tid•i•ous** (fă-stĭd'ē-əs, fə-) *adj.* **1.** Exacting; meticulous. **2.** Difficult to please. —**fas•tid'i•ous•ness** *n.*

**fast lane** *n.* Fast track.

**fast track** *n.* A rapid, arduous course in career advancement. —**fast'-track'** *v.*

**fat** (făt) *n.* **1.** A compound in animal and plant tissue. **2.** Solidified animal or vegetable oil. **3.** Plumpness. —*adj.* **1.** Plump. **2.** Oily; greasy. —**fat'ness** *n.* —**fat'ten** *v.* —**fat'ty** *adj.*

**fa•tal** (fāt'l) *adj.* **1.** Deadly. **2.** Ruinous; disastrous. —**fa•tal'i•ty** *n.* —**fa'tal•ly** *adv.*

**fate** (fāt) *n.* **1.** The supposed force that predetermines events. **2.** Fortune. **3.** Outcome. **4.** Doom or ruin. —**fat'ed** *adj.* —**fate'ful** *adj.* —**fate'ful•ly** *adv.*

**fa•ther** (fä'*th*ər) *n.* **1.** A male parent. **2.** A male ancestor. **3.** An originator. —*v.* To beget. —**fa'ther•hood'** *n.* —**fa'ther•less** *adj.* —**fa'ther•ly** *adj. & adv.*

**fa•tigue** (fə-tēg') *n.* **1.** Weakness or weariness. **2. fatigues.** Military work dress. —*v.* **-tigued, -tiguing.** To tire out; weary.

**fat•u•ous** (făch'o͞o-əs) *adj.* Stupid; foolish; inane. —**fa•tu'i•ty** *n.* —**fat'u•ous•ly** *adv.*

**fau•cet** (fô'sĭt) *n.* A device for regulating the flow of a liquid, as from a pipe.

**fault** (fôlt) *n.* **1.** A defect. **2.** A mistake. **3.** Responsibility for something wrong. **4.** A break in the continuity of a rock formation. —**to a fault.** Excessively. —*v.* To find a fault in. —**fault'less** *adj.* —**fault'less•ly** *adv.* —**fault'y** *adj.*

**faux** (fō) *adj.* False.

**faux pas** (fō pä') *n., pl.* **faux pas.** A social blunder.

**fa•vor** (fā'vər) *n.* **1.** High esteem. **2.** An act of kindness. **3.** Approval or support. —*v.* **1.** To show favor toward. **2.** To resemble. —**fa'vor•a•ble** *adj.* —**fa'vor•a•ble•ness** *n.* —**fa'vor•a•bly** *adv.* —**fa'vor•ite** *n. & adj.* —**fa'vor•it•ism'** *n.*

**fawn**[1] (fôn) *n.* A young deer.

**fawn**[2] (fôn) *v.* **1.** To show affection, as a dog wagging its tail. **2.** To seek favor by flattery. —**fawn'er** *n.* —**fawn'ing•ly** *adv.*

**fax** (făks) *n., pl.* **faxes. 1.** The electronic transmission of images or printed matter. **2.** The material thus transmitted. —**fax** *v.*

**faze** (fāz) *v.* **fazed, fazing.** To upset the composure of; disconcert.

**fear** (fîr) *n.* **1.** A feeling of alarm caused by expectation of danger. **2.** A state of dread or awe. —*v.* To be afraid of. —**fear'ful** *adj.* —**fear'ful•ly** *adv.* —**fear'ful•ness** *n.* —**fear'less** *adj.* —**fear'less•ly** *adv.* —**fear'less•ness** *n.* —**fear'some** *adj.*

**fea•si•ble** (fē'zə-bəl) *adj.* Capable of being accomplished; practicable. —**fea'si•bil'i•ty, fea'si•ble•ness** *n.* —**fea'si•bly** *adv.*

**feast** (fēst) *n.* **1.** A large meal; banquet. **2.** A religious festival. —*v.* To have a feast. —**feast'er** *n.*

**feat** (fēt) *n.* A remarkable achievement.

**feath•er** (fĕ*th*'ər) *n.* One of the structures forming the covering of birds. —**feath'er** *v.* —**feath'er•i•ness** *n.* —**feath'er•y** *adj.*

**fea•ture** (fē'chər) *n.* **1.** The shape or aspect of the face. **2.** Any distinctive characteristic. **3.** The main presentation at a motion-picture theater. **4.** An article in a newspaper or periodical. —*v.* **-tured, -turing.** To make prominent.

**Feb•ru•ar•y** (fĕb'ro͞o-ĕr'ē, fĕb'yo͞o-) *n., pl.* **-ies** or **-ys.** The 2nd month of the year.

**fe•ces** (fē'sēz) *pl.n.* Excrement. **—fe'cal** *adj.*

**fed** (fĕd) *v.* p.t. & p.p. of **feed.**

**fed•er•al** (fĕd'ər-əl) *adj.* **1.** Of a league or a union of states recognizing a central government. **2. Federal.** Of the central government of the U.S. **—fed'er•al•ism'** *n.* **—fed'er•al•ist** *n.* **—fed'er•ate'** *v.* **—fed'er•a'tion** *n.*

**fe•do•ra** (fĭ-dôr'ə, -dōr'ə) *n.* A soft felt hat.

**fee** (fē) *n.* **1.** A fixed charge. **2.** A payment for professional services.

**fee•ble** (fē'bəl) *adj.* **-bler, -blest.** Frail; weak. **—fee'ble•ness** *n.* **—fee'bly** *adv.*

**feed** (fēd) *v.* **fed** (fĕd), **feeding. 1.** To give food to. **2.** To eat. —*n.* Food for animals.

**feed•back** (fēd'băk') *n.* **1.** The return of a portion of the output to the input for quality control. **2.** The return of information about the result of a process.

**feel** (fēl) *v.* **felt** (fĕlt), **feeling. 1.** To perceive by touch. **2.** To touch. **3.** To experience (an emotion). **4.** To believe in. —*n.* **1.** The sense of touch. **2.** The way something feels. **—feel'ing** *n. & adj.* **—feel'ing•ly** *adv.*

**feet** (fēt) *n.* pl. of **foot.**

**feign** (fān) *v.* To pretend. **—feign'er** *n.*

**fe•lic•i•ty** (fĭ-lĭs'ĭ-tē) *n., pl.* **-ties.** Great happiness. **—fe•lic'i•tous** *adj.*

**fe•line** (fē'līn') *adj.* **1.** Of cats or related animals. **2.** Catlike. —*n.* A feline animal.

**fell** (fĕl) *v.* p.t. of **fall.**

**fel•low** (fĕl'ō) *n.* **1.** A man or boy. **2.** A comrade; associate. **3.** An equal; peer. **4.** A member of a learned society. **—fel'low•ship'** *n.*

**fel•on** (fĕl'ən) *n.* A criminal.

**fel•o•ny** (fĕl'ə-nē) *n., pl.* **-nies.** A serious crime, such as murder or rape. **—fe•lo'ni•ous** *adj.* **—fe•lo'ni•ous•ly** *adv.*

**felt¹** (fĕlt) *n.* A fabric of matted, compressed fibers of wool, fur, etc.

**felt²** (fĕlt) *v.* p.t. & p.p. of **feel.**

**fe•male** (fē'māl') *adj.* **1.** Of the sex that produces ova or bears young. **2.** Feminine. —*n.* A female person, plant, or animal. **—fe'male'ness** *n.*

**fem•i•nine** (fĕm'ə-nĭn) *adj.* **1.** Of the female sex. **2.** Characterized by qualities attributed to women. **—fem'i•nin'i•ty** *n.*

**fem•i•nism** (fĕm'ə-nĭz'əm) *n.* Advocacy for women of the same rights granted to men. **—fem'i•nist** *adj. & n.*

**fen** (fĕn) *n.* Swampy land; marsh.

**fence** (fĕns) *n.* **1.** An enclosure made of posts, boards, wire, etc. **2.** A receiver of stolen goods. —*v.* **fenced, fencing. 1.** To close in or off by a fence. **2.** To act as a fence for stolen goods. **—fenc'er** *n.* **—fenc'ing** *n.*

**fend•er** (fĕn'dər) *n.* **1.** A metal guard over the wheel of an automobile. **2.** A fireplace screen.

**fer•ment** (fûr'mĕnt') *n.* **1.** Something that causes fermentation, as a yeast or enzyme. **2.** Unrest. —*v.* (fər-mĕnt'). **1.** To produce by fermentation. **2.** To undergo or cause to undergo fermentation. **—fer•ment'a•ble** *adj.*

**fer•men•ta•tion** (fûr'mĕn-tā'shən) *n.* Chemical conversion of compounds, esp. the conversion of sugar to carbon dioxide and alcohol by yeast.

**fern** (fûrn) *n.* A flowerless plant having divided leaves.

**fe•ro•cious** (fə-rō'shəs) *adj.* Extremely savage; fierce. **—fe•ro'cious•ly** *adv.* **—fe•roc'i•ty** *n.*

**fer•ry•boat** (fĕr'ē-bōt') *n.* A boat used to transport passengers or goods. **—fer'ry** *v. & n.*

**fer•tile** (fûr'tl) *adj.* **1.** Capable of reproduction. **2.** Rich in material for plant growth. **3.** Highly productive; inventive. **—fer'tile•ly** *adv.* **—fer•til'i•ty** *n.* **—fer'til•i•za'tion** *n.* **—fer'til•ize'** *v.* **—fer'til•iz'er** *n.*

**fer•vent** (fûr'vənt) *adj.* Showing deep feeling; earnest. **—fer'ven•cy, fer'vor** *n.* **—fer'vent•ly** *adv.*

**fes•ter** (fĕs'tər) *v.* **1.** To generate pus. **2.** To rankle.

**fes•ti•val** (fĕs'tə-vəl) *n.* **1.** A day of feasting or special observances. **2.** A program of cultural events. **—fes'tive** *adj.* **—fes'tive•ly** *adv.* **—fes•tiv'i•ty** *n.*

**fetch** (fĕch) *v.* To go after and return with. **—fetch'er** *n.*

**fetch•ing** (fĕch'ĭng) *adj.* Very attractive.

**fete, fête** (fāt, fĕt) *n.* **1.** A festival. **2.** An elaborate party. —*v.* **feted, feting.** To honor with a fete.

**fet•id** (fĕt'ĭd, fē'tĭd) *adj.* Foul-smelling.

**fet•ish** (fĕt'ĭsh) *n.* **1.** An object believed to have magical power. **2.** An object of obsessive attention. **—fet'ish•ism'** *n.* **—fet'ish•ist** *n.*

**fet•ter** (fĕt'ər) *n.* **1.** A chain attached to the ankles. **2. fetters.** A restraint. **—fet'ter** *v.*

**fe•tus** (fē'təs) *n., pl.* **-tuses.** The unborn young of a mammal. **—fe'tal** *adj.*

**feud** (fyo͞od) *n.* A protracted quarrel. **—feud** *v.*

**fe•ver** (fē'vər) *n.* **1.** A sickness characterized by high body temperature. **2.** Heightened activity or excitement. **—fe'ver•ish** *adj.* **—fe'ver•ish•ly** *adv.* **—fe'ver•ish•ness** *n.*

**few** (fyo͞o) *adj.* **fewer, fewest.** Consisting of or amounting to a small number. —*n. & pron. (takes pl. v.).* A small number. **—few'ness** *n.*

**fi•an•cé** (fē'än-sā', fē-än'sā') *n.* A man engaged to be married.

**fi•an•cée** (fē'än-sā', fē-än'sā') *n.* A woman engaged to be married.

**fi•as•co** (fē-ăs'kō) *n., pl.* **-coes** or **-cos.** A complete failure.

**fi•ber** (fī'bər) *n.* A slender, elongated structure; a filament or strand. **—fi'brous** *adj.*

**fi•ber•fill** (fī'bər-fĭl') *n.* Manufactured fibers used as filling.

**fiche** (fēsh) *n.* A microfiche.

**fick•le** (fĭk'əl) *adj.* Changeable; capricious. **—fick'le•ness** *n.*

**fic•tion** (fĭk'shən) *n.* **1.** Something invented or imagined. **2.** Literature that includes novels, short stories, etc. **—fic'tion•al** *adj.* **—fic'tion•al•ly** *adv.* **—fic•ti'tious** *adj.*

**fid•dle** (fĭd'l) *n.* A violin. —*v.* **-dled, -dling. 1.** To play a violin. **2.** To fidget. **—fid'dler** *n.*

**fi•del•i•ty** (fĭ-dĕl'ĭ-tē, fī-) *n., pl.* **-ties. 1.** Faithfulness; loyalty. **2.** Accuracy.

**fidg•et** (fĭj'ĭt) *v.* To move nervously or restlessly. —*n.* Often **fidgets.** Restlessness. **—fidg'et•y** *adj.*

**fi•du•ci•ar•y** (fĭ-d/y/o͞o'shē-ĕr'ē, -shə-rē, fī-) *n., pl.* **-ies.** One having a special trust from or obligation to others, as a company director. —*adj.* **1.** Relating to one who holds something in trust for another. **2.** Relating to a trustee or trusteeship.

**field** (fēld) *n.* **1.** A broad, level expanse of open land, esp. one devoted to a particular crop. **2.** An area of activity or knowledge. **—field'er** *adj.*

**fiend** (fēnd) *n.* **1.** A demon. **2.** A wicked person. **—fiend'ish** *adj.* **—fiend'ish•ly** *adv.* **—fiend'ish•ness** *n.*

**fierce** (fîrs) *adj.* **fiercer, fiercest.** Violent; ferocious. **—fierce'ly** *adv.* **—fierce'ness** *n.*

**fif•teen** (fĭf-tēn') *n.* The cardinal number written 15. **—fif•teen'** *adj. & pron.* **—fif•teenth'** *n. & adj.*

**fif•ty** (fĭf'tē) *n.* The cardinal number written 50. **—fif'ty** *adj. & pron.* **—fif'ti•eth** *n. & adj.*

**fight** (fīt) *v.* **fought** (fôt), **fighting. 1.** To participate in combat. **2.** To quarrel; argue. **3.** To oppose. —*n.* **1.** A battle; combat. **2.** A quarrel. **—fight'er** *n.*

**fig•ure** (fĭg'yər) *n.* **1.** A written symbol other than a letter, esp. a number. **2.** An amount. **3.** An outline or shape. **4.** A well-known person. **5.** An expression, as a simile. —*v.* **-ured, -uring. 1.** To compute. **2.** To make a likeness of.

**fig•u•ra•tive** (fĭg'yər-ə-tĭv) *adj.* Relating to figures of speech; not to be taken literally; metaphorical. **—fig'u•ra•tive•ly** *adv.*

**fig•ure•head** (fĭg'yər-hĕd') *n.* **1.** One holding a title of leadership but having no authority. **2.** A carved figure on the prow of a ship.

**fil•a•ment** (fĭl'ə-mənt) *n.* A thin threadlike structure.

**file[1]** (fīl) *n.* **1.** A receptacle for keeping papers, cards, etc. **2.** A line of persons, animals, or things. **3.** A collection of related computer data stored as a unit. **—file** *v.* **—fil'er** *n.*

**file[2]** (fīl) *n.* A tool with ridged surfaces, used in smoothing. —*v.* **filed, filing.** To work with a file. **—fil'er** *n.* **—fil'ing** *n.*

**fil•i•bus•ter** (fĭl'ə-bŭs'tər) *n.* A prolonged speech made to obstruct legislative action. **—fil'i•bus'ter** *v.*

**fill** (fĭl) *v.* **1.** To make or become full. **2.** To supply the materials for. **3.** To pervade. —*n.* **1.** A full supply. **2.** A built-up piece of land. —**fill'ing** *n.*

**fil•ly** (fĭl'ē) *n., pl.* **-lies.** A young female horse.

**film** (fĭlm) *n.* **1.** Any thin layer, covering, or coating. **2.** A thin sheet with a photosensitive coating used to make photographic negatives or transparencies. **3.** A motion picture. —**film** *v.* —**film'i•ly** *adv.* —**film'i•ness** *n.* —**film'y** *adj.*

**film•card** (fĭlm'kärd') *n.* A microfiche.

**fil•ter** (fĭl'tər) *n.* A porous substance or device through which a liquid is strained. —*v.* **1.** To pass through a filter. **2.** To remove by filtering. —**fil'ter•a•ble** *adj.* —**fil•tra'tion** *n.*

**filth** (fĭlth) *n.* **1.** Dirty matter. **2.** A dirty condition. —**filth'i•ness** *n.* —**filth'y** *adj.*

**fin** (fĭn) *n.* One of the swimming and balancing appendages of a fish, whale, etc.

**fi•nal** (fī'nəl) *adj.* Concluding; last. —*n.* The last of a series of athletic contests, school examinations, etc. —**fi'nal•ist** *n.* —**fi•nal'i•ty** *n.* —**fi'nal•ize'** *v.* —**fi'nal•ly** *adv.*

**fi•nance** (fə-năns', fī-, fī'năns') *n.* **1.** The management of money. **2. finances.** Monetary resources. —*v.* **-nanced, -nancing.** To supply the capital for. —**fi•nan'cial** *adj.* —**fi•nan'cial•ly** *adv.* —**fin'an•cier'** *n.*

**find** (fīnd) *v.* **found** (found), **finding. 1.** To come upon. **2.** To determine. **3.** To consider; regard. —*n.* What is found, esp. a rare discovery. —**find'er** *n.* —**find'ing** *n.*

**fine**[1] (fīn) *adj.* **finer, finest. 1.** Of superior quality; excellent. **2.** Enjoyable; pleasant. **3.** Sharp. **4.** Consisting of extremely small particles. **5.** Subtle or precise. —*adv.* Very well. —**fine'ly** *adv.* —**fine'ness** *n.*

**fine**[2] (fīn) *n.* A sum of money imposed as a penalty. —*v.* **fined, fining.** To impose a fine on.

**fi•nesse** (fə-nĕs') *n.* Artful performance or behavior.

**fine-tune** (fīn't/y/o͞on') *v.* **-tuned, -tuning.** To adjust to the highest level of efficiency.

**fin•ger** (fĭng'gər) *n.* One of the five digits of the hand. —*v.* To touch with the fingers; handle. —**fin'ger•print'** *n.* & *v.*

**fin•ick•y** (fĭn'ĭ-kē) *adj.* Very fussy.

**fin•ish** (fĭn'ĭsh) *v.* **1.** To terminate. **2.** To complete a task. **3.** To use up. —*n.* The conclusion of something; end. —**fin'ish•er** *n.*

**fi•nite** (fī'nīt') *adj.* Having boundaries; limited. —**fi'nite'ly** *adv.* —**fi'nite'ness** *n.*

**fir** (fûr) *n.* An evergreen tree or its wood.

**fire** (fīr) *n.* **1.** A burning. **2.** Enthusiasm. —*v.* **fired, firing. 1.** To ignite. **2.** To stimulate. **3.** To shoot (a weapon). **4.** To discharge from a position. —**fier'y** *adj.*

**fire•arm** (fīr'ärm') *n.* A pistol, rifle, etc.

**fire•place** (fīr'plās') *n.* An open recess for a fire; hearth.

**firm**[1] (fûrm) *adj.* **1.** Unyielding to pressure; solid. **2.** Fixed in place. **3.** Indicating resolution. —*v.* To make or become firm. —*adv.* Resolutely; unwaveringly. —**firm'ly** *adv.* —**firm'ness** *n.*

**firm**[2] (fûrm) *n.* A commercial partnership.

**fir•ma•ment** (fûr'mə-mənt) *n.* The sky.

**first** (fûrst) *adj.* **1.** Located before all others. **2.** Earliest. **3.** Foremost in importance or quality. —*adv.* **1.** Before or above all others in time or rank. **2.** For the 1st time. —*n.* **1.** The ordinal number 1 in a series. **2.** The one occurring or ranking 1st. **3.** The beginning. **4.** The lowest forward gear in a vehicle. —**first'ly** *adv.*

**fis•cal** (fĭs'kəl) *adj.* Of finances. —**fis'cal•ly** *adv.*

**fish** (fĭsh) *n., pl.* **fish** or **fishes. 1.** An aquatic vertebrate having fins and gills. **2.** Its edible flesh. —*v.* To catch or try to catch fish. —**fish'er•man** *n.* —**fish'er•y** *n.* —**fish'i•ness** *n.* —**fish'ing** *n.* —**fish'y** *adj.*

**fis•sion** (fĭsh'ən) *n.* The act or process of splitting into parts. —**fis'sion•a•ble** *adj.*

**fis•sure** (fĭsh'ər) *n.* A narrow groove, crack, or cleft.

**fist** (fĭst) *n.* The hand closed tightly.

**fit** (fĭt) *v.* **fitted** or **fit, fitted, fitting. 1.** To be or make the proper size and shape (for). **2.** To be suitable. **3.** To equip. —*adj.* **fitter, fittest. 1.** Appropriate; proper. **2.** Healthy. —*n.* The manner in which clothing fits. —**fit'ly** *adv.* —**fit'ness** *n.* —**fit'ting** *adj. & n.* —**fit'ting•ly** *adv.* —**fit'ting•ness** *n.*

**fit•ful** (fĭt'fəl) *adj.* Intermittent; irregular. —**fit'ful•ly** *adv.* —**fit'ful•ness** *n.*

**five** (fīv) *n.* The cardinal number written 5. —**fifth** *n. & adj.* —**five** *adj. & pron.*

**fix** (fĭks) *v.* **1.** To place or fasten securely. **2.** To repair. **3.** To direct steadily, as a stare. **4.** To put together; prepare. —*n.* **1.** A predicament; dilemma. **2.** A position, as of a ship or aircraft, as determined by observations or radio. —**fix'a•tive** *n.* —**fixed** *adj.* —**fix'ed•ly** *adv.* —**fix'er** *n.*

**fix•a•tion** (fĭk-sā'shən) *n.* A strong attachment to a person or thing.

**fix•ture** (fĭks'chər) *n.* Something attached as a permanent appendage, apparatus, or appliance.

**flab•by** (flăb'ē) *adj.* **-bier, -biest.** Lacking firmness. —**flab'bi•ly** *adv.* —**flab'bi•ness** *n.*

**flack** (flăk) *n.* A press agent. —**flack** *v.* —**flack'er•y** *n.*

**flag[1]** (flăg) *n.* A piece of fabric used as a symbol, signal, etc. —*v.* **flagged, flagging. 1.** To mark with a flag. **2.** To signal with or as with a flag.

**flag[2]** (flăg) *v.* **flagged, flagging. 1.** To hang limply; droop. **2.** To become languid; tire. **3.** To grow dull.

**fla•grant** (flā'grənt) *adj.* Extremely conspicuous; shocking. —**fla'grance, fla'gran•cy** *n.* —**fla'grant•ly** *adv.*

**flair** (flâr) *n.* A natural aptitude.

**flak** (flăk) *n.* **1. a.** Antiaircraft artillery. **b.** The shellburst from such artillery. **2. a.** Excessive or abusive criticism. **b.** Dissension; opposition.

**flake** (flāk) *n.* A thin piece or fragment. —*v.* **flaked, flaking.** To come off in flakes. —**flak'y** *adj.*

**flam•boy•ant** (flăm-boi'ənt) *adj.* Highly elaborate; showy. —**flam•boy'ance** *n.* —**flam•boy'ant•ly** *adv.*

**flame** (flām) *n.* **1.** Active, blazing combustion. **2.** A violent or intense passion. —*v.* **flamed, flaming. 1.** To burn brightly. **2.** To burst into or as into flame.

**flame-re•tard•ant** (flām'rĭ-tär'dnt) *adj.* Resistant to catching fire.

**flam•ma•ble** (flăm'ə-bəl) *adj.* Easily ignitable.

**flank** (flăngk) *n.* A side or lateral part. —*v.* **1.** To be at the side of. **2.** To go around the flank of.

**flan•nel** (flăn'əl) *n.* A soft woven cloth of wool or a wool blend.

**flap** (flăp) *v.* **flapped, flapping. 1.** To wave up and down, as wings; beat. **2.** To swing loosely. —*n.* **1.** An appendage attached on one side, as of an envelope. **2.** The action or sound of flapping. **3.** A control on an aircraft wing.

**flare** (flâr) *v.* **flared, flaring. 1.** To flame up with a bright, wavering light. **2.** To expand outward, as a bell. —*n.* **1.** A brief blaze. **2.** A device that produces a bright light, as for signaling. **3.** An expanding contour.

**flash** (flăsh) *v.* **1.** To occur suddenly in or as in flame. **2.** To be or cause to be lighted intermittently. **3.** To move rapidly. **4.** To signal with light. —*n.* **1.** A brief, intense light. **2.** An instant. **3.** A brief news dispatch.

**flash•y** (flăsh'ē) *adj.* **-ier, -iest.** Showy; gaudy.

**flask** (flăsk) *n.* A small, bottle-shaped container.

**flat[1]** (flăt) *adj.* **flatter, flattest. 1.** Having a smooth, even, level surface. **2.** Lying prone; prostrate. **3.** Unequivocal. **4.** Fixed, as a rate. **5.** Flavorless. **6.** Deflated, as a tire. **7.** In music, being below the intended pitch. —*adv.* **1.** Horizontally. **2.** Prostrate. **3.** In music, below the intended pitch. —*n.* **1.** A flat object, surface, or part. **2.** A deflated tire. —**flat'ly** *adv.* —**flat'ness** *n.* —**flat'ten** *v.*

**flat[2]** (flăt) *n.* An apartment.

**flat•ter** (flăt'ər) *v.* To compliment, often insincerely. —**flat'ter•er** *n.* —**flat'ter•ing** *adj.* —**flat'ter•y** *n.*

**flat•ware** (flăt'wâr') *n.* **1.** Tableware that is fairly flat and formed in 1 piece, such as a plate. **2.** Table utensils, such as knives and forks.

**flaunt** (flônt) *v.* To exhibit ostentatiously; show off. —**flaunt'er** *n.*

**fla•vor** (flā'vər) *n.* A distinctive taste. —*v.* To give flavor to. —**fla'vor•ing** *n.*

**flaw** (flô) *n.* An imperfection; defect. **—flaw′less** *adj.*

**flax** (flăks) *n.* **1.** A plant yielding linseed oil and fiber. **2.** The textile fiber from this plant, made into linen. **3.** A grayish yellow. **—flax′en** *adj.* **—flax′en•haired′** *adj.*

**flay** (flā) *v.* To strip off the skin of. **—flay′er** *n.*

**flea** (flē) *n.* A bloodsucking, parasitic insect.

**fleck** (flĕk) *n.* A tiny mark or spot. *—v.* To spot or streak.

**flee** (flē) *v.* **fled** (flĕd), **fleeing.** To run away, as from danger. **—fle′er** *n.*

**fleece** (flēs) *n.* The coat of wool of a sheep. *—v.* **fleeced, fleecing. 1.** To shear the fleece from. **2.** To swindle. **—fleec′i•ness** *n.* **—fleec′y** *adj.*

**fleet**[1] (flēt) *n.* A number of ships, esp. warships.

**fleet**[2] (flēt) *adj.* Moving swiftly; rapid. **—fleet′ing** *adj.* **—fleet′ing•ly** *adv.* **—fleet′ly** *adv.* **—fleet′ness** *n.*

**flesh** (flĕsh) *n.* **1.** The soft tissue of the body. **2.** Meat. **3.** The pulpy part of a fruit or vegetable. **—flesh′i•ness** *n.* **—flesh′y** *adj.*

**flew** (flo͞o) *v.* p.t. of **fly**[1].

**flex** (flĕks) *v.* **1.** To bend. **2.** To contract (a muscle). **—flex′i•bil′i•ty** *n.* **—flex′i•ble** *adj.* **—flex′i•bly** *adv.*

**flex•time** (flĕks′tīm′) *n.* A system in which employees may set their own times of work.

**flick** (flĭk) *n.* A light, quick motion or touch. **—flick** *v.*

**flick•er** (flĭk′ər) *v.* To yield irregular light. *—n.* **1.** A brief or wavering light. **2.** A brief sensation.

**flight**[1] (flīt) *n.* **1.** Motion through the earth's atmosphere. **2.** A group flying together, as of birds or aircraft. **3.** A scheduled airline run. **4.** A soaring, as of the imagination. **5.** A series of stairs.

**flight**[2] (flīt) *n.* A running away.

**flight•y** (flī′tē) *adj.* **-ier, -iest.** Capricious. **—flight′i•ness** *n.*

**flim•sy** (flĭm′zē) *adj.* **-sier, -siest.** Not strong or substantial. **—flim′si•ly** *adv.* **—flim′si•ness** *n.*

**flinch** (flĭnch) *v.* To shrink or wince, as from pain or fear.

**fling** (flĭng) *v.* **flung** (flŭng), **flinging.** To throw or move forcefully. *—n.* A toss; a throw.

**flint** (flĭnt) *n.* Quartz that sparks when struck with steel.

**flip** (flĭp) *v.* **flipped, flipping.** To toss or turn with a light quick motion. *—n.* A nimble turn or motion. *—adj.* Pert.

**flip•pant** (flĭp′ənt) *adj.* Showing disrespectful levity or indifference. **—flip′pan•cy** *n.*

**flirt** (flûrt) *v.* **1.** To amuse oneself in playful courtship. **2.** To move jerkily; dart. *—n.* A person who flirts. **—flir•ta′tion** *n.* **—flir•ta′tious** *adj.* **—flir•ta′tious•ly** *adv.*

**float** (flōt) *v.* **1.** To drift or be suspended on water, in space, etc. **2.** To move easily and lightly. *—n.* **1.** Something that floats. **2.** A vehicle bearing an exhibit in a parade. **—float′er** *n.*

**flock** (flŏk) *n.* A group of animals. *—v.* To congregate or travel in a flock.

**floe** (flō) *n.* A large, flat mass of ice on the surface of a body of water.

**flog** (flŏg, flôg) *v.* **flogged, flogging.** To beat, esp. with a whip. **—flog′ger** *n.*

**flood** (flŭd) *n.* **1.** An overflowing of water onto land. **2.** Any abundant flow. *—v.* **1.** To cover with a flood; inundate. **2.** To fill abundantly.

**floor** (flôr, flōr) *n.* **1.** The surface of a room on which one stands. **2.** The lowermost surface, as of a forest or ocean. **3.** The right to address an assembly. **4.** A story of a building. *—v.* **1.** To provide with a floor. **2.** To knock down.

**flop** (flŏp) *v.* **flopped, flopping. 1.** To fall down heavily. **2.** To move about clumsily. **3.** To fail. *—n.* **1.** The action of flopping. **2.** A failure.

**flop•py** (flŏp′ē) *adj.* **-pier, -piest.** Tending to flop; loose and flexible. *—n., pl.* **-pies.** A floppy disk. **—flop′pi•ly** *adv.* **—flop′pi•ness** *n.*

**floppy disk** *n.* A flexible plastic disk coated with magnetic material used to store computer data.

**flo•ral** (flôr′əl, flōr′-) *adj.* Of flowers.

**flor•id** (flôr′ĭd, flōr′-) *adj.* **1.** Ruddy. **2.** Heavily embellished.

**flo•rist** (flôr′ĭst, flōr′-, flŏr′-) *n.* One who sells flowers.

**floss** (flôs, flŏs) *n.* **1.** Silk from the cocoon of a silkworm. **2.** Any soft, fibrous substance. —**floss'y** *adj.*

**flounce**[1] (flouns) *n.* Gathered or pleated material used for trimming, as on a garment.

**flounce**[2] (flouns) *v.* **flounced, flouncing. 1.** To move with exaggerated motions. **2.** To struggle or flounder.

**floun•der** (floun'dər) *v.* To move clumsily or in confusion. —**floun'der** *n.*

**flour** (flour) *n.* A powdery substance obtained by grinding grain. —*v.* To coat with flour. —**flour'y** *adj.*

**flour•ish** (flûr'ĭsh) *v.* **1.** To grow well; thrive. **2.** To make bold, sweeping movements. —*n.* A dramatic action or gesture.

**flout** (flout) *v.* To show contempt for.

**flow** (flō) *v.* **1.** To move in or as in a stream. **2.** To be plentiful. **3.** To hang gracefully. —*n.* **1.** The act of flowing. **2.** A continuous movement or circulation.

**flow•er** (flou'ər) *n.* **1.** A plant blossom. **2.** Highest development; peak. —*v.* **1.** To bloom. **2.** To develop fully. —**flow'er•y** *adj.*

**flown** (flōn) *v.* p.p. of **fly.**

**flub** (flŭb) *v.* **flubbed, flubbing.** To ruin; botch.

**fluc•tu•ate** (flŭk'cho͞o-āt') *v.* **-ated, -ating.** To vary irregularly. —**fluc'tu•a'tion** *n.*

**flue** (flo͞o) *n.* A pipe or tube through which hot gas or steam may pass.

**flu•ent** (flo͞o'ənt) *adj.* Having facility in the use of a language. —**flu'en•cy** *n.* —**flu'ent•ly** *adv.*

**fluff** (flŭf) *n.* **1.** Something having a soft or frothy consistency, as down or nap. **2.** Something inconsequential. **3.** An error. —*v.* **1.** To make light and puffy by shaking or patting. **2.** To make a mistake. —**fluff'y** *adj.*

**flu•id** (flo͞o'ĭd) *n.* A substance that flows readily; liquid. —**flu•id'i•ty** *n.* —**flu'id•ly** *adv.*

**flume** (flo͞om) *n.* **1.** A narrow gorge with a stream. **2.** An artificial channel or chute for water.

**flung** (flŭng) *v.* p.t. & p.p. of **fling.**

**fluo•res•cence** (flo͞o-rĕs'əns, flô-, flō-) *n.* The emission of electromagnetic radiation, esp. of visible light. —**fluo•res'cent** *adj.*

**fluor•i•date** (flo͝or'ĭ-dāt', flôr'-) *v.* **-dated, -dating.** To add a fluorine compound to drinking water to prevent tooth decay. —**fluor'i•da'tion** *n.*

**fluor•ide** (flo͝or'īd', flôr'-) *n.* A compound containing fluorine.

**fluor•ine** (flo͝or'ēn', -ĭn) *n.* A pale-yellow chemical element.

**flur•ry** (flûr'ē) *n., pl.* **-ries. 1.** A gust of wind. **2.** A light snowfall. **3.** A burst of activity.

**flush** (flŭsh) *v.* **1.** To redden; blush. **2.** To wash out by a gush of water. —*n.* **1.** A brief flow or gushing. **2.** A reddish tinge; a blush. —*adj.* **1.** Blushing. **2.** Prosperous. **3.** Having surfaces in the same plane; even. —*adv.* **1.** So as to be even. **2.** Squarely; solidly.

**flus•ter** (flŭs'tər) *v.* To upset. —*n.* A state of agitation.

**flute** (flo͞ot) *n.* **1.** A musical woodwind instrument. **2.** A groove. —*v.* **fluted, fluting.** To make a groove in.

**flut•ter** (flŭt'ər) *v.* **1.** To wave or flap rapidly, esp. in the air. **2.** To behave in a restless manner. —*n.* **1.** An act of fluttering. **2.** A condition of excitement or agitation. —**flut'ter•er** *n.* —**flut'ter•y** *adj.*

**flux** (flŭks) *n.* **1.** Continual change or flow. **2.** A substance used, as in soldering, to facilitate melting and fusing.

**fly**[1] (flī) *v.* **flew** (flo͞o), **flown** (flōn), **flying. 1.** To move or cause to move through the air wth the aid of wings or winglike parts. **2.** To hasten; rush. —**fli'er** *n.*

**fly**[2] (flī) *n., pl.* **flies.** A winged insect.

**foal** (fōl) *n.* The young offspring of a horse. —*v.* To give birth to (a foal).

**foam** (fōm) *n.* A mass of gas bubbles trapped in a film of liquid. —*v.* To form foam; froth. —**foam'i•ness** *n.* —**foam'y** *adj.*

**fo•cus** (fō'kəs) *n.* **1.** A point in an optical system at which rays of light come together or from which they appear to spread. **2.** The condition or adjustment in which an eye or optical instrument gives its best image. **3.** A center of interest or activity. —**fo'cus** *v.*

**fod•der** (fŏd'ər) *n.* Feed for livestock.

**foe** (fō) *n.* An enemy; adversary; opponent.

**fog** (fôg, fŏg) *n.* Cloudlike masses of condensed water vapor limiting visibility. —*v.* **fogged, fogging.** To cover or be obscured by or as by fog. **—fog'gi•ly** *adv.* **—fog'gi•ness** *n.* **—fog'gy** *adj.*

**foi•ble** (foi'bəl) *n.* A minor personal peculiarity.

**foil**[1] (foil) *v.* To thwart.

**foil**[2] (foil) *n.* A fencing sword with a blunt point.

**foist** (foist) *v.* **1.** To pass off (something inferior) as genuine, etc. **2.** To impose, as by coercion.

**fold** (fōld) *v.* **1.** To bend over so that one part lies on another. **2.** To bring to a closed position. **3.** To wrap; envelop. —*n.* **1.** The act of folding. **2.** The junction of two folded parts.

**fo•li•age** (fō'lē-ĭj) *n.* Plant leaves.

**folk** (fōk) *n.* People.

**folk•lore** (fōk'lôr', -lōr') *n.* Traditions, tales, etc., of a people. **—folk'lor'ist** *n.*

**fol•low** (fŏl'ō) *v.* **1.** To come or go after. **2.** To pursue. **3.** To move along the course of. **4.** To engage in. **5.** To result. **6.** To be attentive to. **7.** To understand. **—fol'low•er** *n.* **—fol'low•ing** *n.*

**fol•ly** (fŏl'ē) *n., pl.* **-lies.** An act of foolishness.

**fond** (fŏnd) *adj.* **1.** Affectionate. **2.** Cherished. **—fond'ly** *adv.* **—fond'ness** *n.*

**fon•dle** (fŏn'dl) *v.* **-dled, -dling.** To caress.

**font**[1] (fŏnt) *n.* **1.** A basin for holy water. **2.** A source of abundance.

**font**[2] (fŏnt) *n.* A complete set of printing type in 1 size and face.

**food** (fo͞od) *n.* Any material that is taken in to maintain life and growth.

**fool** (fo͞ol) *n.* One lacking judgment, sense, etc. —*v.* **1.** To trick. **2.** To play; joke. **—fool'ish** *adj.* **—fool'ish•ly** *adv.* **—fool'ish•ness** *n.*

**foot** (fo͝ot) *n., pl.* **feet. 1.** The part of the leg that rests on or touches the ground. **2.** Something resembling a foot in position or function. **3.** A unit of length equal to 12 inches. —*v.* To walk. **—foot'less** *adj.* **—foot'print'** *n.*

**foot•ball** (fo͝ot'bôl') *n.* A game played with an inflated oblong ball on a rectangular field.

**foot•ing** (fo͝ot'ĭng) *n.* **1.** A secure place. **2.** A basis; foundation.

**for** (fôr, *unstressed* fər) *prep.* **1.** Directed to. **2.** As a result of. **3.** Through the duration of. **4.** On behalf of. **5.** In place of. **6.** In favor or support of. —*conj.* Because; since.

**for•age** (fôr'ĭj) *n.* Food for animals. —*v.* **-aged, -aging.** To search for food or supplies.

**for•ay** (fôr'ā') *n.* A raid. **—for'ay'** *v.*

**for•bear** (fôr-bâr') *v.* **-bore** (-bôr', -bōr'), **-borne** (-bôrn', -bōrn'), **-bearing. 1.** To refrain from. **2.** To be tolerant or patient. **—for•bear'ance** *n.*

**for•bid** (fər-bĭd') *v.* **-bade** (-băd', -bād') or **-bad** (-băd'), **-bidden** (-bĭd'n) or **-bid, -bidding.** To prohibit.

**force** (fôrs, fōrs) *n.* **1.** Strength; power. **2.** Coercion. —*v.* **forced, forcing. 1.** To compel to perform an action. **2.** To extort. **—force'ful** *adj.* **—force'ful•ly** *adv.* **—for'ci•ble** *adj.* **—for'ci•ble•ness** *n.* **—for'ci•bly** *adv.*

**ford** (fôrd, fōrd) *n.* A shallow place in a body of water where a crossing can be made on foot. —*v.* To cross at such a place.

**fore•bear** (fôr'bâr', fōr-) *n.* An ancestor; forefather.

**fore•bode** (fôr-bōd', fōr-) *v.* **-boded, -boding.** To portend. **—fore•bod'ing** *n. & adj.*

**fore•cast** (fôr'kăst', fōr'-) *v.* **-cast** or **-casted, -casting.** To predict; foreshadow. —*n.* A prediction. **—fore'cast'er** *n.*

**fore•close** (fôr-klōz', fōr-) *v.* **-closed, -closing.** To reclaim mortgaged property, esp. for nonpayment. **—fore•clo'sure** *n.*

**fore•fa•ther** (fôr'fä'*th*ər, fōr'-) *n.* An ancestor.

**fore•front** (fôr'frŭnt', fōr'-) *n.* The foremost part of something.

**fore•go** (fôr-gō', fōr-) *v.* To precede. **—fore•go'ing** *adj. & n.*

**fore•head** (fôr'ĭd, -hĕd', fōr'-) *n.* The part of the face between eyebrows and hairline.

**for•eign** (fôr'ĭn, fōr'-) *adj.* **1.** Of or from a country other than one's own. **2.** Situated in an abnormal place. **—for'eign•er** *n.* **—for'eign•ness** *n.*

**fore•man** (fôr′mən, fōr′-) *n.* One in charge of a group of workers.
**fore•most** (fôr′mōst′, fōr′-) *adj.* Ahead of all others; first. **—fore′most′** *adv.*
**fo•ren•sic** (fə-rĕn′sĭk) *adj.* **1.** Of legal proceedings. **2.** Of debate or argument.
**fore•see** (fôr-sē′, fōr-) *v.* To know beforehand. **—fore•see′a•ble** *adj.* **—fore′sight′** *n.* **—fore′sight′ed** *adj.*
**for•est** (fôr′ĭst, fōr′-) *n.* A growth of trees covering a large area. **—for′est•er** *n.* **—for′est•ry** *n.*
**fore•tell** (fôr-tĕl′, fōr-) *v.* To predict.
**fore•thought** (fôr′thôt′, fōr′-) *n.* Planning beforehand.
**for•ev•er** (fôr-ĕv′ər, fər-) *adv.* **1.** Eternally. **2.** Incessantly.
**fore•word** (fôr′wərd, fōr′-) *n.* An introductory note; preface.
**for•feit** (fôr′fĭt) *n.* A penalty or fine. *—v.* To surrender as a forfeit. **—for′fei•ture** *n.*
**for•gave** (fər-gāv′, fôr-) *v.* p.t. of **forgive.**
**forge**[1] (fôrj, fōrj) *n.* A place where metals are heated and hammered. *—v.* **forged, forging. 1.** To form (metal) in a forge. **2.** To reproduce for fraudulent purposes. **—forge′a•ble** *adj.* **—forg′er** *n.* **—for′ger•y** *n.*
**forge**[2] (fôrj, fōrj) *v.* **forged, forging.** To advance gradually but firmly.
**for•get** (fər-gĕt′, fôr-) *v.* **-got** (-gŏt′), **-gotten** (gŏt′n) or **-got, -getting. 1.** To be unable to remember. **2.** To neglect. **—for•get′ful** *adj.* **—for•get′ful•ness** *n.*
**for•give** (fər-gĭv′, fôr-) *v.* **-gave** (gāv′), **-given** (gĭv′ən), **-giving.** To excuse for a fault or offense. **—for•giv′a•ble** *adj.* **—for•give′ness** *n.*
**for•go, fore•go** (fôr-gō′, fōr-) *v.* **-went** (-wĕnt′), **-gone** (-gôn′, -gŏn′), **-going.** To abstain from.
**fork** (fôrk) *n.* **1.** A pronged implement used for raising, eating, etc. **2.** A separation into branches. **—fork** *v.* **—forked** *adj.*
**for•lorn** (fər-lôrn′, fôr-) *adj.* **1.** Deserted. **2.** Pitiful. **—for•lorn′ly** *adv.*
**form** (fôrm) *n.* **1.** The contour of something. **2.** A mold. **3.** Kind; variety. **4.** A document for the collection of informaton. **—form** *v.* **—for•ma′tion** *n.* **—for′ma•tive** *adj.*
**for•mal** (fôr′məl) *adj.* **1.** Following accepted conventions or rules. **2.** Calling for elegant clothes. **3.** Ceremonious. *—n.* An occasion requiring formal attire. **—for•mal′i•ty** *n.* **—for′mal•ly** *adv.*
**for•mat** (fôr′măt′) *n.* The organization and arrangement of something.
**for•mer** (fôr′mər) *adj.* Earlier. **—for′mer•ly** *adv.*
**for•mi•da•ble** (fôr′mĭ-də-bəl) *adj.* Arousing dread or awe. **—for′mi•da•bly** *adv.*
**for•mu•la** (fôr′myə-lə) *n., pl.* **-las** or **-lae** (-lē′). A set form of words or symbols.
**for•mu•late** (fôr′myə-lāt′) *v.* **-lated, -lating.** To state in systematic terms. **—for′mu•la′tion** *n.*
**for•ni•cate** (fôr′nĭ-kāt′) *v.* **-cated, -cating.** To have illicit sexual intercourse. **—for′ni•ca′tion** *n.*
**for•sake** (fôr-sāk′, fər-) *v.* **-sook** (-so͝ok′), **-saken** (-sā′kən), **-saking. 1.** To give up. **2.** To abandon. **—for•sak′er** *n.*
**for•swear** (fôr-swâr′, fōr-) *v.* **forswore** (fôr-swôr′, fōr-swōr′), **forsworn** (fôr-swôrn′, fōr-swōrn′), **forswearing. 1.** To renounce. **2.** To commit perjury.
**fort** (fôrt, fōrt) *n.* A fortified place, esp. a permanent post. **—for′tress** *n.*
**forte**[1] (fôrt, fōrt, fôr′tā′) *n.* Something in which one excels.
**for•te**[2] (fôr′tā′) *adv.* To be played loudly and forcefully. *—n.* Such a musical note.
**forth** (fôrth, fōrth) *adv.* **1.** Forward; onward. **2.** Out into view.
**forth•com•ing** (fôrth-kŭm′ĭng, fōrth-) *adj.* **1.** About to happen. **2.** Available when needed. **3.** Friendly; considerate.
**forth•right** (fôrth′rīt′, fōrth′-) *adj.* Straightforward; frank.
**forth•with** (fôrth-wĭ*th*′, -wĭth′, fōrth-) *adv.* Immediately.
**for•ti•fy** (fôr′tə-fī′) *v.* **-fied, -fying.** To strengthen. **—for′ti•fi•ca′tion** *n.* **—for′ti•fi′er** *n.*
**for•ti•tude** (fôr′tĭ-t/y/o͞od′) *n.* Strength of mind; courage.
**fort•night** (fôrt′nīt′) *n.* Two weeks. **—fort′night′ly** *adj. & adv.*
**FOR•TRAN** (fôr′trăn′) *n.* A computer language for problems expressed in algebraic terms.

**for•tu•i•tous** (fôr-t/y/o͞o′ĭ-təs) *adj.* **1.** Accidental. **2.** Fortunate. **—for•tu′i•tous•ly** *adv.* **—for•tu′i•ty** *n.*

**for•tune** (fôr′chən) *n.* **1.** Good or bad luck. **2.** Wealth or riches. **—for′tu•nate** *adj.* **—for′tu•nate•ly** *adv.*

**for•ty** (fôr′tē) *n.* The cardinal number written 40. **—for′ti•eth** *n. & adj.* **—for′ty** *adj. & pron.*

**fo•rum** (fôr′əm, fōr′-) *n.* Any public place or medium used for discussion.

**for•ward** (fôr′wərd) *adj.* **1.** At or toward the front. **2.** Bold. **3.** Progressive; advanced. *—adv.* **1.** Toward the front. **2.** In the future. *—v.* To send on.

**fos•sil** (fŏs′əl) *n.* A remnant of an organism of a past age embedded in the earth's crust. *—adj.* Of fossils.

**fos•ter** (fô′stər, fŏs′tər) *v.* **1.** To bring up; rear. **2.** To cultivate. *—adj.* Receiving parental care although not related.

**fought** (fôt) *v.* p.t. & p.p. of **fight.**

**foul** (foul) *adj.* **1.** Offensive. **2.** Dirty; filthy. **3.** Immoral; wicked. **4.** Unfair. *—n.* An infraction of the rules in sports. *—adv.* In a foul manner. *—v.* **1.** To make or become foul. **2.** To entangle or become entangled, as a rope. **3.** To commit a foul in sports. **—foul′ly** *adv.* **—foul′ness** *n.*

**found[1]** (found) *v.* To originate or establish. **—foun•da′tion** *n.* **—foun•da′tion•al** *adj.* **—found′er** *n.*

**found[2]** (found) *v.* p.t. & p.p. of **find.**

**foun•der** (foun′dər) *v.* **1.** To become disabled or lame. **2.** To collapse or break down. **3.** To sink below water. **4.** To cave in; sink.

**found•ling** (found′lĭng) *n.* A child abandoned by unknown parents.

**foun•tain** (foun′tən) *n.* **1.** A spring, esp. the source of a stream. **2.** An artificial jet of water. **—fount** *n.*

**four** (fôr, fōr) *n.* The cardinal number written 4. **—four** *adj. & pron.* **—fourth** *n. & adj.*

**four•teen** (fôr-tēn′, fōr-) *n.* The cardinal number written 14. **—four•teen′** *adj. & pron.* **—four•teenth′** *n. & adj.*

**fowl** (foul) *n.* **1.** Any bird used as food or hunted as game. **2.** The common domesticated chicken.

**fox** (fŏks) *n.* An animal related to the dogs and wolves.

**fox•hole** (fŏks′hōl′) *n.* A pit dug for refuge against enemy fire.

**fox•y** (fŏk′sē) *adj.* **-ier, -iest.** Sly; clever. **—fox′i•ness** *n.*

**foy•er** (foi′ər, foi′ā′) *n.* A lobby or entrance hall.

**fra•cas** (frā′kəs) *n.* A brawl.

**frac•tion** (frăk′shən) *n.* A part of something. **—frac′tion•al** *adj.*

**frac•ture** (frăk′chər) *n.* A break or crack. *—v.* **-tured, -turing.** To break; crack.

**frag•ile** (frăj′əl, -īl′) *adj.* **1.** Easily broken. **2.** Physically weak; frail. **3.** Tenuous; flimsy. **—fra•gil′i•ty, frag′ile•ness** *n.*

**frag•ment** (frăg′mənt) *n.* **1.** A part broken off. **2.** Something incomplete. **—frag•ment′** *v.* **—frag′men•tar′y** *adj.* **—frag′men•ta′tion** *n.*

**fra•grance** (frā′grəns) *n.* A pleasing odor. **—fra′grant** *adj.* **—fra′grant•ly** *adv.*

**frail** (frāl) *adj.* Weak. **—frail′ty** *n.*

**frame** (frām) *v.* **framed, framing. 1.** To construct; build. **2.** To design. **3.** To enclose. *—n.* Something composed of parts fitted and joined together; a structure. **—fram′er** *n.* **—frame′work′** *n.*

**fran•chise** (frăn′chīz′) *n.* **1.** A privilege or authorization. **2.** A constitutional or statutory right.

**frank** (frăngk) *adj.* Straightforward; direct. *—v.* To send (mail) free of charge. **—frank′ly** *adv.* **—frank′ness** *n.*

**fran•tic** (frăn′tĭk) *adj.* Emotionally distraught; frenzied. **—fran′ti•cal•ly** *adv.*

**fra•ter•ni•ty** (frə-tûr′nĭ-tē) *n., pl.* **-ties. 1.** Brotherhood; brotherliness. **2.** A social club of male college students. **—fra•ter′nal** *adj.* **—frat′er•nize′** *v.*

**fraud** (frôd) *n.* **1.** Deception for unlawful gain. **2.** A swindle; trick. **—fraud′u•lence** *n.* **—fraud′u•lent** *adj.* **—fraud′u•lent•ly** *adv.*

**fraught** (frôt) *adj.* Attended; full of.

**fray[1]** (frā) *n.* A brawl.

**fray[2]** (frā) *v.* To unravel or tatter.

**freak** (frēk) *n.* An abnormal person or thing. **—freak′ish** *adj.*

**freck•le** (frĕk′əl) *n.* A small spot of dark pigment on the skin. *—v.* **-led, -ling.** To mark or become marked with freckles. **—freck′ly** *adj.*

**free** (frē) *adj.* **freer, freest. 1.** At liberty; not imprisoned or enslaved. **2.** Not under obligation. **3.** Costing nothing. **4.** Unoccupied. —*adv.* **1.** In a free manner. **2.** Without charge. —*v.* **freed, freeing. 1.** To set free. **2.** To disengage; untangle. —**free'dom** *n.* —**free'ly** *adv.*

**free agent** *n.* A professional sports player free to sign a contract with any team.

**free lance** *n.* A person, esp. a writer or artist, working without a long-term commitment. —**free'-lance'** *v.* —**free'-lanc'er** *n.*

**freeze** (frēz) *v.* **froze** (frōz), **frozen** (frō'zən), **freezing. 1.** To form ice. **2.** To preserve (food) by cooling. **3.** To fix (prices or wages) at a current level. —*n.* An act of freezing. —**freez'er** *n.*

**freight** (frāt) *n.* **1.** Goods carried by a vehicle; cargo. **2.** The transportation of goods. **3.** The charge for transporting such goods. —**freight'er** *n.*

**fre•net•ic** (frə-nĕt'ĭk) *adj.* Frantic; frenzied. —**fre•net'i•cal•ly** *adv.*

**fren•zy** (frĕn'zē) *n., pl.* **-zies.** Violent agitation. —**fren'zied** *adj.*

**fre•quent** (frē'kwənt) *adj.* Occurring often or at close intervals. —*v.* (frē-kwĕnt'). To pay frequent visits to. —**fre'quen•cy** *n.* —**fre•quent'er** *n.* —**fre'quent•ly** *adv.* —**fre'quent•ness** *n.*

**fres•co** (frĕs'kō) *n., pl.* **-coes** or **-cos.** The art of painting on wet plaster.

**fresh** (frĕsh) *adj.* **1.** New; original. **2.** Recently made or harvested. **3.** Not saline. **4.** Impudent. —*adv.* Recently; newly. —**fresh'en** *v.* —**fresh'en•er** *n.* —**fresh'ly** *adv.* —**fresh'ness** *n.*

**fresh•man** (frĕsh'mən) *n.* A 1st-year student.

**fret**[1] (frĕt) *v.* **fretted, fretting.** To worry. —*n.* Irritation; annoyance. —**fret'ful** *adj.* —**fret'ful•ly** *adv.* —**fret'ful•ness** *n.*

**fret**[2] (frĕt) *n.* A design within a band or border. —**fret** *v.* —**fret'work'** *n.*

**fri•ar** (frī'ər) *n.* A member of a Roman Catholic mendicant order.

**fric•tion** (frĭk'shən) *n.* **1.** The rubbing of one object against another. **2.** A conflict. —**fric'tion•al** *adj.*

**Fri•day** (frī'dē, -dā') *n.* The 6th day of the week.

**fried** (frīd) *v.* p.t. & p.p. of **fry.**

**friend** (frĕnd) *n.* **1.** A person one knows, likes, and trusts. **2. Friend.** A member of the Society of Friends; Quaker. —**friend'less** *adj.* —**friend'li•ness** *n.* —**friend'ly** *adj.* —**friend'ship'** *n.*

**frieze** (frēz) *n.* A decorative band, as along a wall.

**frig•ate** (frĭg'ĭt) *n.* A fast-sailing warship.

**fright** (frīt) *n.* **1.** Sudden fear. **2.** Something very ugly or alarming. —**fright'en** *v.* —**fright'ful** *adj.* —**fright'ful•ly** *adv.*

**frig•id** (frĭj'ĭd) *adj.* Extremely cold. —**frig'id•ness, fri•gid'i•ty** *n.*

**frill** (frĭl) *n.* A ruffle. —**frill'y** *adj.*

**fringe** (frĭnj) *n.* A decorative border of hanging threads, etc. —*v.* **fringed, fringing.** To decorate with a fringe. —**fringe'less** *adj.*

**frisk** (frĭsk) *v.* To move about briskly and playfully. —**frisk'er** *n.* —**frisk'i•ly** *adv.* —**frisk'i•ness** *n.* —**frisk'y** *adj.*

**friv•o•lous** (frĭv'ə-ləs) *adj.* Unworthy of serious attention. —**fri•vol'i•ty** *n.*

**frizz** (frĭz) *v.* To form or be formed into tight curls. —**frizz** *n.* —**friz'zi•ly** *adv.* —**friz'zi•ness** *n.* —**friz'zy** *adj.*

**fro** (frō) *adv.* Away; back.

**frock** (frŏk) *n.* A dress.

**frog** (frôg, frŏg) *n.* **1.** A tailless amphibian with hind legs adapted for leaping. **2.** Hoarseness.

**frol•ic** (frŏl'ĭk) *n.* Gaiety; merriment. —*v.* **-icked, -icking.** To engage in merrymaking. —**frol'ick•er** *n.* —**frol'ic•some** *adj.*

**from** (frŭm, frŏm) *prep.* **1.** Beginning at. **2.** With a specified point as the first of two limits. **3.** Because of. **4.** Out of.

**front** (frŭnt) *n.* **1.** The forward part or surface. **2.** Demeanor or bearing. **3.** A false appearance or manner. **4.** The most forward line of combat force. —*adj.* Of or in the front. —*v.* **1.** To face. **2.** To serve as a front for. —**front'age** *n.* —**fron'tal** *adj.*

**fron•tier** (frŭn-tîr') *n.* **1.** A boundary between countries. **2.** A region beyond a settled area. —**fron•tiers'man** *n.*

**frost** (frôst, frŏst) *n.* **1.** A covering of ice crystals. **2.** Weather conditions when this covering forms. —*v.* **1.** To cover or become covered with frost. **2.** To decorate with icing. —**frost'i•ness** *n.* —**frost'y** *adj.*

**frost•ing** (frô'stĭng, frŏs'tĭng) *n.* **1.** Icing. **2.** A speckled surface on glass or metal.

**froth** (frôth, frŏth) *n.* Foam. —*v.* To foam. —**froth'i•ly** *adv.* —**froth'i•ness** *n.* —**froth'y** *adj.*

**frown** (froun) *v.* To wrinkle the brow, as in displeasure. —**frown** *n.* —**frown'er** *n.*

**froze** (frōz) *v.* p.t. of **freeze.**

**fro•zen** (frō'zən) *v.* p.p. of **freeze.**

**fru•gal** (fro͞o'gəl) *adj.* Thrifty. —**fru•gal'i•ty** *n.* —**fru'gal•ly** *adv.*

**fruit** (fro͞ot) *n.* **1.** An edible plant crop or product. **2.** Result; outcome. —*v.* To produce fruit. —**fruit'ful** *adj.* —**fruit'i•ness** *n.* —**fruit'less** *adj.* —**fruit'y** *adj.*

**fru•i•tion** (fro͞o-ĭsh'ən) *n.* **1.** The bearing of fruit. **2.** Achievement.

**frus•trate** (frŭs'trāt') *v.* **-trated, -trating.** To prevent from accomplishing something. —**frus•tra'tion** *n.*

**fry** (frī) *v.* **fried, frying.** To cook over direct heat in oil or fat. —**fry'er** *n.*

**fu•el** (fyo͞o'əl) *n.* Anything burned to produce energy or heat. —*v.* To provide with or take in fuel.

**fu•gi•tive** (fyo͞o'jĭ-tĭv) *adj.* **1.** Running or having run away. **2.** Passing quickly; fleeting. —*n.* One who flees. —**fu'gi•tive•ly** *adv.*

**ful•crum** (fo͝ol'krəm) *n.* The point or support on which a lever turns.

**ful•fill** (fo͝ol-fĭl') *v.* **-filled, -filling. 1.** To effect. **2.** To satisfy. **3.** To complete. —**ful•fill'er** *n.* —**ful•fill'ment** *n.*

**full** (fo͝ol) *adj.* **1.** Containing all that is possible; filled. **2.** Having a great deal or many. —*adv.* **1.** To a complete extent; entirely. **2.** Very. —**full'y** *adv.* —**full'ness** *n.*

**ful•mi•nate** (fŭl'mə-nāt', fo͝ol'-) *v.* **-nated, -nating. 1.** To denounce severely. **2.** To explode. —**ful'mi•na'tion** *n.*

**ful•some** (fo͝ol'səm) *adj.* Excessive or insincere. —**ful'some•ly** *adv.* —**ful'some•ness** *n.*

**fum•ble** (fŭm'bəl) *v.* **-bled, -bling. 1.** To grope awkwardly and uncertainly; blunder. **2.** To drop. —**fum'ble** *n.* —**fum'bler** *n.*

**fume** (fyo͞om) *n.* **1.** An exhalation of smoke, gas, etc. **2.** A strong or acrid odor. —*v.* **fumed, fuming. 1.** To give off or treat with fumes. **2.** To show anger.

**fu•mi•gate** (fyo͞o'mĭ-gāt') *v.* **-gated, -gating.** To subject to fumes, esp. to exterminate vermin or insects. —**fu'mi•ga'tion** *n.* —**fu'mi•ga'tor** *n.*

**fun** (fŭn) *n.* Enjoyment; amusement.

**func•tion** (fŭngk'shən) *n.* **1.** The proper action for which a person or thing is fitted. **2.** An official ceremony or elaborate social occasion. —*v.* To have or perform a function; serve. —**func'tion•al** *adj.*

**fund** (fŭnd) *n.* A source of supply, esp. of money.

**fun•da•men•tal** (fŭn'də-mĕn'tl) *adj.* Elemental; basic. —**fun'da•men'tal** *n.* —**fun'da•men'tal•ly** *adv.*

**fu•ner•al** (fyo͞o'nər-əl) *n.* Burial ceremonies. —**fu•ne're•al** *adj.*

**fun•gus** (fŭng'gəs) *n., pl.* **-gi** or **-guses.** A group of plants that includes the yeasts, molds, and mushrooms. —**fun'gal, fun'gous** *adj.*

**fun•nel** (fŭn'əl) *n.* **1.** A conical utensil used to channel a substance into a small-mouthed container. **2.** A smokestack. —**fun'nel** *v.*

**fun•ny** (fŭn'ē) *adj.* **-nier, -niest. 1.** Causing laughter or amusement. **2.** Strange; odd.

**fur** (fûr) *n.* **1.** The thick hair covering the body of various animals. **2.** The pelt of an animal, used for garments. —**furred** *adj.* —**fur'ry** *adj.*

**fu•ri•ous** (fyo͝or'ē-əs) *adj.* **1.** Extremely angry. **2.** Fierce; violent. —**fu'ri•ous•ly** *adv.*

**fur•long** (fûr'lông', -lŏng') *n.* A unit of length, equal to ⅛ mile.

**fur•lough** (fûr'lō) *n.* A leave of absence. —**fur'lough** *v.*

**fur•nace** (fûr'nĭs) *n.* An enclosed chamber in which heating fuel is burned.

**fur•nish** (fûr'nĭsh) *v.* **1.** To provide furniture for. **2.** To supply; give.

**fur•ni•ture** (fûr'nĭ-chər) *n.* Movable articles in a room or establishment.

**fu•ror** (fyo͝or'ôr', -ər) *n.* A state of intense excitement.

**fur•row** (fûr'ō) *n.* **1.** A trench made by a plow. **2.** A deep wrinkle, as on the forehead. —**fur'row** *v.* —**fur'row•y** *adj.*

**fur•ther** (fûr'*th*ər) *adj.* **1.** More distant in time or degree. **2.** Additional. —*adv.* **1.** To a greater extent; more. **2.** In addition; also. —*v.* To help the progress of; advance. —**fur'ther•ance** *n.*

**fur•ther•more** (fûr'*th*ər-môr', -mōr') *adv.* Moreover; in addition.

**fur•tive** (fûr'tĭv) *adj.* Stealthy; sly. —**fur'tive•ly** *adv.* —**fur'tive•ness** *n.*

**fu•ry** (fyo͝or'ē) *n., pl.* **-ries. 1.** Violent, intense anger. **2. Furies.** The 3 winged goddesses who pursue and punish wrongdoers.

**fuse[1]** (fyo͞oz) *n.* A length of combustible material that is lighted at one end to detonate an explosive at the other.

**fuse[2]** (fyo͞oz) *v.* **fused, fusing.** To mix together by melting; blend. —*n.* A device containing an element that protects an electric circuit by melting when overloaded. —**fu'si•ble** *adj.* —**fu'sion** *n.*

**fu•se•lage** (fyo͞o'sə-läzh', fyo͞o'zə-) *n.* The central body of an airplane.

**fuss** (fŭs) *n.* Needlessly nervous or useless activity. —*v.* To trouble or worry over trifles. —**fus'sy** *adj.*

**fu•tile** (fyo͞ot'l, fyo͞o'tīl') *adj.* Having no useful result; ineffectual. —**fu'tile•ly** *adv.* —**fu•til'i•ty** *n.*

**fu•ton** (fo͞o'tŏn) *n., pl.* **futons** or **futon.** A foldable, cotton-filled mattress laid on the floor for a bed.

**fu•ture** (fyo͞o'chər) *n.* **1.** The period of time yet to be. **2.** That which will happen in time to come. —**fu'ture** *adj.* —**fu•tu'ri•ty** *n.*

**fuzz** (fŭz) *n.* A mass of fine particles, hairs, etc.

## — G —

**g, G** (jē) *n.* The 7th letter of the English alphabet.

**gab** (găb) *v.* **gabbed, gabbing.** To chatter. —*n.* Chatter; prattle. —**gab'by** *adj.*

**gab•ar•dine** (găb'ər-dēn', găb'ər-dēn') *n.* A worsted fabric.

**ga•ble** (gā'bəl) *n.* A triangular wall section at the ends of a pitched roof. —**ga'bled** *adj.*

**gad** (găd) *v.* **gadded, gadding.** To roam about restlessly; rove. —**gad'a•bout'** *n.*

**gad•fly** (găd'flī') *n.* **1.** A large, stinging fly. **2.** An annoying person.

**gadg•et** (găj'ĭt) *n.* A small mechanical device. —**gadg'et•ry** *n.*

**gaff** (găf) *n.* An iron hook used to land large fish.

**gaffe** (găf) *n.* A social error.

**gag** (găg) *n.* **1.** Something forced into the mouth to prevent speech. **2.** A joke. —*v.* **gagged, gagging. 1.** To prevent from uttering sounds by using a gag. **2.** To choke or retch.

**gage** (gāj) *n.* **1.** A pledge. **2.** Something thrown down as a challenge to fight.

**gag•gle** (găg'əl) *n.* **1.** A flock of geese. **2.** A group.

**gai•e•ty** (gā'ĭ-tē) *n.* Merriment.

**gai•ly** (gā'lē) *adv.* **1.** Cheerfully. **2.** Colorfully.

**gain** (gān) *v.* **1.** To acquire. **2.** To win. **3.** To earn **4.** To increase. **5.** To progress. —*n.* A profit; advantage; increase.

**gain•ful** (gān'fəl) *adj.* Profitable; lucrative. —**gain'ful•ly** *adv.*

**gain•say** (gān-sā') *v.* **-said** (-sĕd'), **-saying.** To deny or contradict.

**gait** (gāt) *n.* A manner of walking or running.

**gai•ter** (gā'tər) *n.* **1.** A leather or cloth covering for the legs. **2.** An ankle-high shoe.

**ga•la** (gā'lə, găl'ə, gä'lə) *n.* A festive occasion. —*adj.* Festive.

**gal•ax•y** (găl'ək-sē) *n., pl.* **-ies. 1.** A large cluster of stars. **2. the Galaxy.** The galaxy of which the earth's sun is a part. **3.** An assembly of distinguished persons. —**ga•lac'tic** *adj.*

**gale** (gāl) *n.* **1.** A very strong wind. **2.** An outburst, as of laughter.

**gall[1]** (gôl) *n.* **1.** Bile. **2.** Bitterness. **3.** Impudence; effrontery.

**gall[2]** (gôl) *n.* **1.** A skin sore. **2.** Exasperation; irritation. —*v.* **1.** To chafe. **2.** To irritate.

**gal•lant** (găl'ənt) *adj.* **1.** Dashing. **2.** Courageous; daring. **3.** Chivalrous; courteous. —**gal'lant•ly** *adv.* —**gal'lant•ry** *n.*

**gall•blad•der** (gôl'blăd'ər) *n.* Also **gall bladder.** A small, pear-shaped muscular sac located under the liver.

**gal•le•on** (găl'ē-ən) *n.* A large, three-masted old Spanish ship.
**gal•ler•y** (găl'ə-rē) *n., pl.* **-ies. 1.** A long balcony. **2.** Any enclosed narrow passageway. **3.** The balcony of a theater. **4.** A place in which artwork is displayed or sold.
**gal•ley** (găl'ē) *n.* **1.** An ancient ship propelled by sails and oars. **2.** The kitchen of a ship or airliner.
**gal•li•vant** (găl'ə-vănt') *v.* To roam about frivolously.
**gal•lon** (găl'ən) *n.* A unit of measure equal to 4 quarts.
**gal•lop** (găl'əp') *n.* A fast gait of a horse. —*v.* To move or ride at a gallop.
**gal•lows** (găl'ōz) *n., pl.* **-lowses** or **-lows.** A frame from which condemned prisoners are hanged.
**gall•stone** (gôl'stōn') *n.* A small, hard mass formed in the gallbladder.
**ga•lore** (gə-lôr', -lōr') *adj.* In abundance.
**ga•losh•es** (gə-lŏsh'ĭz) *pl.n.* Waterproof overshoes.
**gal•va•nize** (găl'və-nīz') *v.* **-nized, -nizing. 1.** To stimulate with an electric current. **2.** To spur; startle. **3.** To coat (metal) with zinc. **—gal•van'ic** *adj.* **—gal'va•ni•za'tion** *n.*
**gam•bit** (găm'bĭt) *n.* **1.** An opening move in chess in which one or more pieces are sacrificed. **2.** A strategem.
**gam•ble** (găm'bəl) *v.* **-bled, -bling. 1.** To bet money on a game of chance. **2.** To play a game of chance. **3.** To risk. —*n.* **1.** A bet. **2.** A risk. **—gam'bler** *n.*
**gam•bol** (găm'bəl) *v.* To frolic.
**game[1]** (gām) *n.* **1.** A pastime; diversion. **2.** A sport or contest. **3.** Wildlife hunted for food or sport. —*adj.* **gamer, gamest. 1.** Plucky; resolute. **2.** Ready and willing.
**game[2]** (gām) *adj.* Lame.
**games•man•ship** (gāmz'mən-shĭp') *n.* The practice of winning at something by using unethical but not illegal means.
**gam•ete** (găm'ēt', gə-mēt') *n.* A reproductive cell, as a mature sperm or egg.
**gam•in** (găm'ĭn) *n.* A street urchin.
**gam•ut** (găm'ət) *n.* The complete range of anything.
**gam•y** (gā'mē) *adj.* **-ier, -iest. 1.** Having the flavor or odor of game. **2.** Plucky; hardy.
**gan•der** (găn'dər) *n.* **1.** A male goose. **2.** A simpleton. **3.** A quick look; glance.
**gang** (găng) *n.* A group of people. **—gang up (on).** To harass or attack as a group.
**gan•gling** (găng'glĭng) *adj.* Also **gan•gly, -glier, -gliest.** Tall, thin, and ungraceful.
**gan•gli•on** (găng'glē-ən–) *n., pl.* **-glia** or **-glons.** A bundle of nerve cells.
**gang•plank** (găng'plăngk') *n.* A removable bridge between a ship and a pier.
**gan•grene** (găng'grēn', găng-grēn') *n.* Death and decay of bodily tissue. **—gan'gre•nous** *adj.*
**gang•ster** (găng'stər) *n.* A member of a criminal group.
**gang•way** (găng'wā') *n.* **1.** A passageway. **2.** A gangplank.
**gap** (găp) *n.* **1.** An opening; fissure; cleft. **2.** A blank space; an interval.
**gape** (gāp, găp) *v.* **gaped, gaping. 1.** To open the mouth wide; yawn. **2.** To stare, as with the mouth open. **—gap'ing** *adj.*
**ga•rage** (gə-räzh', -räj') *n.* **1.** A structure for housing cars. **2.** A commercial establishment where cars are repaired. **—ga•rage'** *v.*
**garb** (gärb) *n.* Clothing. —*v.* To clothe; array.
**gar•bage** (gär'bĭj) *n.* **1.** Food wastes. **2.** Refuse; rubbish.
**gar•ble** (gär'bəl) *v.* **-bled, -bling.** To distort (an account or message) so as to be unintelligible; jumble.
**gar•ban•zo** (gär-bän'zō) *n., pl.* **-zos.** The seed of the chickpea.
**gar•den** (gär'dn) *n.* **1.** A plot of land used for growing flowers, vegetables, or fruit. **2.** A public park. —*adj.* Of a garden. —*v.* To work in a garden. **—gar'den•er** *n.*
**gar•de•ni•a** (gär-dēn'yə) *n.* **1.** A shrub with glossy leaves and fragrant white flowers. **2.** Its flower.
**gar•gan•tu•an** (gär-găn'cho͞o-ən) *adj.* Of immense size.
**gar•gle** (gär'gəl) *v.* **-gled, -gling.** To rinse the throat, as with a medicated liquid. —*n.* A medicated solution for gargling.
**gar•goyle** (gär'goil') *n.* A roof spout carved to represent a grotesque creature.

**gar•ish** (gâr′ĭsh) *adj.* Gaudy. —**gar′-ish•ly** *adv.*
**gar•land** (gär′lənd) *n.* A wreath of flowers, leaves, etc. —*v.* To adorn with a garland.
**gar•lic** (gär′lĭk) *n.* A plant bulb with a strong, distinctive odor and flavor, used as a seasoning.
**gar•ment** (gär′mənt) *n.* An article of clothing.
**gar•ner** (gär′nər) *v.* To amass; acquire.
**gar•net** (gär′nĭt) *n.* A deep-red gem.
**gar•nish** (gär′nĭsh) *v.* To decorate or adorn. —*n.* A decoration for food.
**gar•nish•ment** (gär′nĭsh-mənt) *n.* A proceeding whereby money or property of a debtor is attached and applied to the payment of the debt. —**gar′nish•ee′** *n.*
**gar•ret** (găr′ĭt) *n.* An attic.
**gar•ri•son** (găr′ĭ-sən) *n.* **1.** A military post. **2.** The troops stationed at such a post.
**gar•ru•lous** (găr′/y/ə-ləs) *adj.* Talking much. —**gar•ru′li•ty, gar′ru•lous•ness** *n.*
**gar•ter** (gär′tər) *n.* An elastic band to hold up hose.
**gas** (găs) *n., pl.* **gases** or **gasses. 1.** The state of matter distinguished from the solid and liquid states by low density, the ability to diffuse readily, and the tendency to expand. **2.** A substance in this state. **3.** Gasoline. —*v.* **gassed, gassing. 1.** To supply with gas. **2.** To poison with gas. —**gas′e•ous** *adj.*
**gash** (găsh) *n.* A long, deep cut. —**gash** *v.*
**gas•ket** (găs′kĭt) *n.* A seal used between machine parts or joints to prevent the escape of a gas or fluid.
**gas•o•hol** (găs′ə-hôl′) *n.* A fuel consisting of a blend of ethanol and unleaded gasoline.
**gas•o•line** (găs′ə-lēn′, găs′ə-lēn′) *n.* A flammable liquid derived from petroleum and used as a motor fuel.
**gasp** (găsp) *v.* **1.** To draw in the breath sharply. **2.** To breathe with difficulty. —**gasp** *n.*
**gas•tric** (găs′trĭk) *adj.* Of the stomach.
**gas•tron•o•my** (gă-strŏn′ə-mē) *n.* The art of good eating. —**gas′tro•nom′ic** *adj.*
**gate** (gāt) *n.* **1.** A hinged door in a wall or fence. **2.** The total admission at a public spectacle. —**gate′way′** *n.*
**gath•er** (găth′ər) *v.* **1.** To bring or come together. **2.** To accumulate; collect. **3.** To harvest. **4.** To infer. —**gath′er•ing** *n.*
**gauche** (gōsh) *adj.* Lacking social grace; tactless. —**gauche′ly** *adv.* —**gauche′-ness** *n.* —**gau′che•rie′** *n.*
**gaud•y** (gô′dē) *adj.* **-ier, -iest.** Tasteless and showy. —**gaud′i•ly** *adv.*
**gauge** (gāj) *n.* **1.** A standard of measurement. **2.** A standard dimension, quantity, or capacity. —*v.* **gauged, gauging. 1.** To measure. **2.** To estimate. —**gaug′er** *n.*
**gaunt** (gônt) *adj.* Very thin and bony; emaciated. —**gaunt′ly** *adv.*
**gaunt•let**[1] (gônt′lĭt, gänt′-) *n.* A protective glove.
**gaunt•let**[2] (gônt′lĭt, gänt′-) *n.* A double line of men armed with clubs with which to beat a person forced to run between them.
**gauze** (gôz) *n.* A thin, transparent fabric. —**gauz′y** *adj.*
**gave** (gāv) *v.* p.t. of **give.**
**gav•el** (găv′əl) *n.* A mallet used by a presiding officer or auctioneer.
**gawk** (gôk) *n.* An awkward, stupid person. —*v.* To stare stupidly. —**gawk′y** *adj.*
**gay** (gā) *adj.* **1.** Merry; lively. **2.** Given to social pleasures. **3.** Homosexual, esp. male homosexual.
**gaze** (gāz) *v.* **gazed, gazing.** To stare. —**gaze** *n.*
**ga•ze•bo** (gə-zē′bō, -zā′-) *n.* A small, roofed, open-sided structure offering shade.
**ga•zelle** (gə-zĕl′) *n.* A slender, swift-running antelope.
**gaz•et•teer** (găz′ĭ-tîr′) *n.* A geographic dictionary.
**gaz•pa•cho** (gə-spä′chō, gəz-pä′-) *n.* A chilled soup made with tomatoes and herbs.
**gear** (gîr) *n.* **1.** A toothed wheel that meshes with another in machinery. **2.** Equipment. —*v.* **1.** To connect by gears. **2.** To adjust.
**Gei•ger counter** (gī′gər) *n.* An electronic instrument used to measure radioactivity.
**gei•sha** (gā′shə, gē′-) *n., pl.* **-sha** or **-shas.** A Japanese female entertainer.

**gel•a•tin** (jĕl'ə-tn) *n.* Also **gel•a•tine.** A transparent, sticky protein formed from animal tissue, used in foods, drugs, and photographic film. —**ge•lat'i•nous** *adj.*

**geld•ing** (gĕl'dĭng) *n.* A castrated animal, esp. a horse. —**geld** *v.*

**gel•id** (jĕl'ĭd) *adj.* Very cold; icy.

**gem** (jĕm) *n.* A precious stone.

**gen•der** (jĕn'dər) *n.* A grammatical category, as masculine, feminine, and neuter, into which words are divided.

**gene** (jēn) *n.* A functional hereditary unit on a chromosome.

**ge•ne•al•o•gy** (jē'nē-ŏl'ə-jē) *n., pl.* **-gies. 1.** A record of ancestry. **2.** The study of ancestry. —**ge'ne•a•log'i•cal** *adj.* —**ge'ne•al'o•gist** *n.*

**gen•er•a** (jĕn'ər-ə) *n.* pl. of **genus.**

**gen•er•al** (jĕn'ər-əl) *adj.* **1.** Of the whole or every member of a group. **2.** Widespread. **3.** Being usually the case. **4.** Diversified. **5.** Lacking detail. —*n.* A high-ranking military officer. —**in general.** For the most part. —**gen'er•al•ly** *adv.*

**gen•er•al•i•ty** (jĕn'ə-răl'ĭ-tē) *n., pl.* **-ties. 1.** A general principle. **2.** A vague statement.

**gen•er•al•ize** (jĕn'ər-ə-līz') *v.* **-ized, -izing. 1.** To render general. **2.** To infer. **3.** To speak or think in generalities. —**gen'er•al•i•za'tion** *n.*

**gen•er•ate** (jĕn'ə-rāt') *v.* **-ated, -ating.** To produce. —**gen'er•a'tive** *adj.*

**gen•er•a•tion** (jĕn'ə-rā'shən) *n.* **1.** A group of contemporaneous individuals. **2.** The average time interval between the birth of parents and the birth of their offspring.

**gen•er•a•tor** (jĕn'ə-rā'tər) *n.* A machine that converts mechanical energy into electrical energy.

**ge•ner•ic** (jĭ-nĕr'ĭk) *adj.* **1.** Of an entire group or class. **2.** Of a genus. —**ge•ner'i•cal•ly** *adv.*

**gen•er•ous** (jĕn'ər-əs) *adj.* **1.** Liberal in giving; unselfish. **2.** Abundant. —**gen'er•os'i•ty** *n.* —**gen'er•ous•ly** *adv.*

**gen•e•sis** (jĕn'ĭ-sĭs) *n., pl.* **-ses.** An origin.

**ge•net•ics** (jə-nĕt'ĭks) *n.* The biology of heredity. —**ge•net'ic** *adj.* —**ge•net'i•cist** *n.*

**gen•ial** (jēn'yəl) *adj.* Cheerful and friendly; kindly. —**ge'ni•al'i•ty** *n.* —**gen'ial•ly** *adv.*

**gen•i•ta•li•a** (jĕn'ĭ-tā'lē-ə, -tāl'yə) *pl.n.* The genitals. —**gen'i•tal** *adj.*

**gen•i•tals** (jĕn'ĭ-tlz) *pl.n.* The external sex organs.

**gen•ius** (jēn'yəs) *n., pl.* **-iuses. 1.** Great intellectual and creative power. **2.** A person having this power.

**gen•o•cide** (jĕn'ə-sīd') *n.* The systematic killing of a racial, political, or cultural group.

**gen•re** (zhän'rə) *n.* **1.** Type; class. **2.** A kind of artistic or literary work of a particular style.

**gen•teel** (jĕn-tēl') *adj.* **1.** Refined in manner; polite. **2.** Fashionable. —**gen•til'i•ty** *n.*

**gen•tian** (gĕn'shən) *n.* A plant with showy blue flowers.

**gen•tle** (jĕn'tl) *adj.* **-tler, -tlest. 1.** Considerate or kindly. **2.** Not harsh; moderate; mild. **3.** Easily managed. —**gen'tle•ness** *n.* —**gen'tly** *adv.*

**gen•tle•man** (jĕn'tl-mən) *n.* **1.** A polite or considerate man. **2.** A polite term for any man.

**gen•try** (jĕn'trē) *n.* People of good birth and social position.

**gen•u•flect** (jĕn'yə-flĕkt') *v.* To bend the knee, as in worship. —**gen'u•flec'tion** *n.*

**gen•u•ine** (jĕn'yo͞o-ĭn) *adj.* **1.** Not artificial; real. **2.** Sincere; frank.

**ge•nus** (jē'nəs) *n., pl.* **genera.** A category of related organisms usually including several species.

**ge•og•ra•phy** (jē-ŏg'rə-fē) *n., pl.* **-phies.** The study of the earth and its features, including human life. —**ge•og'ra•pher** *n.* —**ge'o•graph'ic, ge'o•graph'i•cal** *adj.*

**ge•ol•o•gy** (jē-ŏl'ə-jē) *n., pl.* **-gies.** The scientific study of the origin, history, and structure of the earth. —**ge'o•log'ic, ge'o•log'i•cal** *adj.* —**ge•ol'o•gist** *n.*

**ge•om•e•try** (jē-ŏm'ĭ-trē) *n., pl.* **-tries.** The branch of mathematics dealing with points, lines, angles, surfaces, and solids. —**ge'o•met'ric** *adj.*

**ge•ra•ni•um** (jə-rā'nē-əm) *n.* A plant with showy clusters of flowers.

**ger•bil** (jûr′bəl) *n.* A small, mouselike rodent often kept as a pet.

**ger•i•at•rics** (jĕr′ē-ăt′rĭks) *n.* The medical study of old age. **—ger′i•at′ric** *adj. & n.*

**germ** (jûrm) *n.* **1.** A microscopic organism that causes disease. **2.** Something that may serve as the basis of further development. **—ger′mi•nal** *adj.*

**ger•mane** (jər-mān′) *adj.* To the point; pertinent. **—ger•mane′ness** *n.*

**ger•mi•cide** (jûr′mĭ-sīd′) *n.* Anything that kills germs.

**ger•mi•nate** (jûr′mə-nāt′) *v.* **-nated, -nating.** To begin to grow; sprout. **—ger′mi•na′tion** *n.*

**ger•und** (jĕr′ənd) *n.* A verbal form that can be used as a noun, in English ending in *-ing.*

**ges•ta•tion** (jĕ-stā′shən) *n.* The carrying of offspring in the uterus.

**ges•tic•u•late** (jĕ-stĭk′yə-lāt′) *v.* **-lated, -lating.** To make gestures. **—ges•tic′u•la′tion** *n.*

**ges•ture** (jĕs′chər) *n.* A movement of the limbs or body, to express feelings, ideas, etc. *—v.* **-tured, -turing.** To make or signal by gestures.

**get** (gĕt) *v.* **got** (gŏt), **got** or **gotten** (gŏt′n), **getting. 1.** To obtain or acquire. **2.** To cause to move, come, or go. **3.** To arrive. **4.** To go after; fetch. **5.** To bring or take. **6.** To cause to become or to be in a specific condition. **7.** To become or grow. **8.** To understand. **9.** To have the obligation. **—get along.** To manage. **—get around.** To avoid doing; circumvent. **—get away.** To escape. **—get by.** To manage. **—get over.** To recover from.

**gew•gaw** (gyo͞o′gô′) *n.* A trinket; bauble.

**gey•ser** (gī′zər) *n.* A hot spring that ejects a column of water.

**ghast•ly** (găst′lē) *adj.* **-lier, -liest. 1.** Dreadful; horrible. **2.** Deathly pale.

**ghet•to** (gĕt′ō) *n., pl.* **-tos** or **-toes.** A usually poor section of a city inhabited by people of the same race, religion, or social background, often because of discrimination.

**ghost** (gōst) *n.* **1.** The disembodied spirit of a dead person. **2.** A slight trace. **—ghost′ly** *adj.*

**ghost•writ•er** (gōst′rī′tər) *n.* One who writes for and gives credit of authorship to another. **—ghost′write′** *v.*

**GI** (jē′ī′) *n., pl.* **GIs** or **GI's.** An enlisted person in the U.S. Army.

**gi•ant** (jī′ənt) *n.* A being of enormous size and strength. *—adj.* Huge.

**gib•ber•ish** (jĭb′ər-ĭsh) *n.* Rapid, meaningless talk.

**gib•bet** (jĭb′ĭt) *n.* A gallows.

**gib•bon** (gĭb′ən) *n.* An ape with a slender body and long arms.

**gib•bous** (gĭb′əs) *adj.* Humped; protuberant. **—gib′bous•ly** *adv.*

**gibe** (jīb) *v.* **gibed, gibing.** Also **jibe.** To mock; taunt.

**gib•let** (jĭb′lĭt) *n.* The edible heart, liver, or gizzard of a fowl.

**gid•dy** (gĭd′ē) *adj.* **-dier, -diest. 1.** Lightheaded; dizzy. **2.** Frivolous; flighty. **—gid′di•ness** *n.*

**gift** (gĭft) *n.* **1.** A present. **2.** The act of giving. **3.** A natural ability; talent.

**gift•ed** (gĭf′tĭd) *adj.* Talented.

**gi•gan•tic** (jī-găn′tĭk) *adj.* Enormous; huge.

**gig•gle** (gĭg′əl) *v.* **-gled, -gling.** To laugh in a nervous, high-pitched manner. *—n.* A nervous, high-pitched laugh. **—gig′gly** *adj.*

**gild** (gĭld) *v.* **gilded** or **gilt, gilding.** To cover with a thin layer of gold.

**gill** (gĭl) *n.* The respiratory organ of fishes.

**gilt** (gĭlt) *v.* Alternate p.t. & p.p. of **gild.** *—n.* A thin layer of gold.

**gilt-edged** (gĭlt′ĕjd′) *adj.* Also **gilt-edge. 1.** Having gilded edges. **2.** Of the highest quality.

**gim•let** (gĭm′lĭt) *n.* A small tool for boring holes.

**gim•mick** (gĭm′ĭk) *n.* A deceptive, often dishonest, device.

**gimp** (gĭmp) *n.* **1.** A limp. **2.** One that limps. **—gimp** *v.* **—gimp′y** *adj.*

**gin**[1] (jĭn) *n.* An alcoholic liquor flavored with juniper berries.

**gin**[2] (jĭn) *n.* A mechanical device used to remove seeds from cotton fibers. *—v.* **ginned, ginning.** To remove seeds from (cotton) with such a gin.

**gin•ger** (jĭn′jər) *n.* The root of a tropical plant, used as flavoring.

**gin•ger•ly** (jĭn′jər-lē) *adj.* Cautiously careful; timid. *—adv.* Carefully; timidly.

**ging•ham** (gĭng′əm) *n.* A cotton fabric with a checked pattern.

**gin•gi•vi•tis** (jĭn′jə-vī′tĭs) *n.* Inflammation of the gums.

**gi•raffe** (jə-răf′) *n.* An African mammal with a long neck.

**gird** (gûrd) *v.* **girded** or **girt, girding. 1.** To encircle. **2.** To prepare for action.

**gird•er** (gûr′dər) *n.* A beam used as a main support in a building.

**gir•dle** (gûr′dl) *n.* **1.** An encircling band, as a belt. **2.** A light corset.

**girl** (gûrl) *n.* A female child or young woman. **—girl′hood′** *n.* **—girl′ish** *adj.*

**girth** (gûrth) *n.* **1.** Circumference. **2.** A strap encircling an animal's body.

**gist** (jĭst) *n.* The central idea.

**give** (gĭv) *v.* **gave** (gāv), **given** (gĭv′ən), **giving. 1.** To make a present of. **2.** To hand over; deliver. **3.** To place in the hands of. **4.** To produce. **5.** To provide (something required or expected). **6.** To relinquish. **7.** To emit or issue. **8.** To allot; assign. **9.** To bend or yield. **—give back.** To return. **—give in.** To concede. **—give out.** To break down; fail. **—give up. 1.** To surrender. **2.** To stop. **—give way. 1.** To make room for. **2.** To collapse. **3.** To relinquish. *—n.* Resilient springiness.

**give•back** (gĭv′băk′) *n.* A return to the employer of a benefit won by a union in previous contracts.

**giv•en** (gĭv′ən) *adj.* **1.** Specified. **2.** Bestowed. **3.** Acknowledged. **4.** Habitually inclined.

**giz•zard** (gĭz′ərd) *n.* A part of the digestive tract in birds.

**gla•cier** (glā′shər) *n.* A huge mass of moving ice originating from compacted snow. **—gla′cial** *adj.*

**glad** (glăd) *adj.* **gladder, gladdest. 1.** Feeling, showing, or giving joy; happy. **2.** Pleased. **—glad′den** *v.* **—glad′ly** *adv.* **—glad′ness** *n.*

**glade** (glād) *n.* An open space in a forest.

**glad•i•a•tor** (glăd′ē-ā′tər) *n.* A professional combatant fighting for public entertainment in ancient Rome.

**glad•i•o•lus** (glăd′ē-ō′ləs) *n., pl.* **-li** or **-luses.** A plant with a spike of showy, variously colored flowers.

**glam•our, glam•or** (glăm′ər) *n.* Alluring charm and excitement. **—glam′or•ize′** *v.* **—glam′or•ous** *adj.*

**glance** (glăns) *v.* **glanced, glancing. 1.** To strike and be deflected. **2.** To look briefly. *—n.* A quick look.

**gland** (glănd) *n.* A body organ or structure that secretes a substance. **—glan′du•lar** *adj.*

**glare** (glâr ) *v.* **glared, glaring. 1.** To stare fixedly. **2.** To shine blindingly. *—n.* **1.** An angry stare. **2.** A blinding light.

**glass** (glăs) *n.* **1.** Transparent or translucent materials that solidify from the molten state without crystallization. **2.** Something made of glass. **3.** Often **glasses.** A device containing lenses and used as an aid to vision. **—glass′y** *adj.*

**glau•co•ma** (glou-kō′mə, glô-) *n.* A disease of the eye. **—glau•co′ma•tous** *adj.*

**glaze** (glāz) *n.* A thin, smooth, glassy coating. *—v.* **glazed, glazing. 1.** To furnish with glass. **2.** To apply a glaze to.

**gla•zier** (glā′zhər) *n.* One who cuts and fits window glass.

**gleam** (glēm) *n.* **1.** A brief flash or glow of light. **2.** A brief indication. *—v.* To send out a gleam.

**glean** (glēn) *v.* To collect bit by bit, as grain left behind by reapers.

**glee** (glē) *n.* Joy. **—glee′ful** *adj.*

**glee club** *n.* A group of singers performing short pieces of choral music.

**glen** (glĕn) *n.* A narrow valley.

**glib** (glĭb) *adj.* **glibber, glibbest.** Fluent and often superficial. **—glib′ly** *adv.* **—glib′ness** *n.*

**glide** (glīd) *v.* **glided, gliding. 1.** To move smoothly and easily. **2.** To fly without propulsion. *—n.* A smooth, effortless movement or descent.

**glid•er** (glī′dər) *n.* A light, engineless aircraft.

**glim•mer** (glĭm′ər) *v.* To emit a dim, flickering light. *—n.* **1.** A dim, flickering light. **2.** A brief indication.

**glimpse** (glĭmps) *n.* A brief look. *—v.* **glimpsed, glimpsing.** To catch a brief view of.

**glint** (glĭnt) *n.* A gleam. *—v.* To gleam.

**glis•sade** (glĭ-säd′, -sād′) *n.* **1.** A gliding ballet step. **2.** A controlled glide, as down a steep icy slope. **—glis•sade′** *v.*

**glis•ten** (glĭs′ən) *v.* To shine; gleam.

**glitch** (glĭch) *n.* A minor malfunction.
**glit•ter** (glĭt′ər) *v.* To sparkle. —*n.* **1.** Brightness. **2.** Showy splendor.
**glitz** (glĭts) *n.* Vulgar showiness. **—glitz′i•ness** *n.* **—glitz′y** *adj.*
**gloam•ing** (glō′mĭng) *n.* Twilight.
**gloat** (glōt) *v.* To show malicious pleasure or satisfaction.
**glob** (glŏb) *n.* **1.** A small drop; globule. **2.** A rounded mass.
**globe** (glōb) *n.* **1.** A spherical object. **2.** The earth. **—glob′al** *adj.* **—glob′al•ly** *adv.*
**glob•ule** (glŏb′yo͞ol) *n.* A small spherical mass. **—glob′u•lar** *adj.*
**gloom** (glo͞om) *n.* **1.** Darkness. **2.** Melancholy; depression. **—gloom′i•ly** *adv.* **—gloom′y** *adj.*
**glo•ry** (glôr′ē, glōr′ē) *n., pl.* **-ries. 1.** Great honor; renown. **2.** Adoration; praise. **3.** Magnificent splendor. **—glo′ri•fy′** *v.* **—glo′ri•ous** *adj.*
**gloss[1]** (glôs, glŏs) *n.* Surface shine; luster. **—gloss′y** *adj.*
**gloss[2]** (glôs, glŏs) *n.* A commentary or footnote.
**glos•sa•ry** (glô′sə-rē, glŏs′-) *n., pl.* **-ries.** A list of specialized terms with definitions.
**glot•tis** (glŏt′ĭs) *n., pl.* **-tises.** The space between the vocal cords. **—glot′tal** *adj.*
**glove** (glŭv) *n.* **1.** A covering for the hand with separate sheaths for the fingers. **2.** A padded mitt, as for boxing, baseball, etc.
**glow** (glō) *v.* **1.** To shine brightly. **2.** To have a bright or ruddy color. **3.** To be elated. —*n.* **1.** A bright, steady light. **2.** Brightness. **3.** A warm feeling. **—glow′ing** *adj.*
**glow•er** (glou′ər) *v.* To stare angrily or sullenly. —*n.* An angry or sullen stare.
**glox•in•i•a** (glŏk-sĭn′ē-ə) *n.* A South American plant having showy flowers.
**gloze** (glōz) *v.* **glozed, glozing.** To minimize; downplay.
**glu•cose** (glo͞o′kōs′) *n.* A sugar, dextrose.
**glue** (glo͞o) *n.* An adhesive substance or solution. —*v.* **glued, gluing.** To fasten with glue.
**glum** (glŭm) *adj.* **glummer, glummest.** Dejected; gloomy. **—glum′ly** *adv.*
**glut** (glŭt) *v.* **glutted, glutting.** To eat or fill to excess. —*n.* An oversupply.
**glu•ti•nous** (glo͞ot′n-əs) *adj.* Resembling glue or paste; sticky.
**glut•ton** (glŭt′n) *n.* One that eats to excess. **—glut′ton•ous** *adj.* **—glut′ton•y** *n.*
**gnarl** (närl) *n.* A knot on a tree.
**gnash** (năsh) *v.* To grind (the teeth) together.
**gnat** (năt) *n.* A small, winged, biting insect.
**gnaw** (nô) *v.* **gnawed, gnawed** or **gnawn, gnawing.** To wear away by nibbling.
**gnome** (nōm) *n.* A fabled dwarflike creature that lives underground and guards treasures. **—gnom′ish** *adj.*
**gnu** (n/y/o͞o) *n.* A large, bearded antelope.
**go** (gō) *v.* **went** (wĕnt), **gone** (gôn, gŏn), **going. 1.** To move or start to move. **2.** To move to or from a given place. **3.** To function. **4.** To belong (somewhere). **5.** To fail. **6.** To be used up. **7.** To become. **8.** To fit; harmonize.
**goad** (gōd) *n.* **1.** A stick used for prodding animals. **2.** A stimulus; spur. **—goad** *v.*
**goal** (gōl) *n.* **1.** An objective. **2.** The finish line of a race. **3.** The place where a ball or puck scores.
**goat** (gōt) *n.* A horned, bearded mammal.
**goat•ee** (gō-tē′) *n.* A small pointed beard.
**gob** (gŏb) *n.* A lump or mass.
**gob•ble[1]** (gŏb′əl) *v.* **-bled, -bling.** To devour greedily.
**gob•ble[2]** (gŏb′əl) *v.* **-bled, -bling.** To make the guttural sound of a male turkey. **—gob′bler** *n.*
**gob•ble•dy•gook** (gŏb′əl-dē-go͝ok′) *n.* Also **gob•ble•de•gook.** Unintelligible jargon.
**go-be•tween** (gō′bĭ-twēn′) *n.* An intermediary.
**gob•let** (gŏb′lĭt) *n.* A drinking glass with a stem.
**gob•lin** (gŏb′lĭn) *n.* A grotesque, mischievous elf or sprite.
**god** (gŏd) *n.* **1.** A supernatural being worshiped by a people. **2. God.** The creator and ruler of the universe in monotheistic religions.

**god•child** (gŏd′chīld′) *n.* One for whom another serves as sponsor at baptism. **—god′daugh′ter** *n.* **—god′son′** *n.*

**god•head** (gŏd′hĕd′) *n.* **1.** Divinity. **2. Godhead.** The essential nature of God.

**god•ly** (gŏd′lē) *adj.* **-lier, -liest. 1.** Pious; devout. **2.** Divine. **—god′less** *adj.* **—god′li•ness** *n.*

**god•par•ent** (gŏd′pâr′ənt) *n.* A person who sponsors a child at its baptism. **—god′fa′ther** *n.* **—god′moth′er** *n.*

**god•send** (gŏd′sĕnd′) *n.* A stroke of luck.

**gog•gle** (gŏg′əl) *v.* **-gled, -gling.** To stare. *—n.* **goggles.** Large, protective eyeglasses.

**go-go, go•go** (gō′gō′) *adj.* **1.** Relating to a discotheque or the music played there. **2.** Energetic; lively. **3.** Relating to risky stock market speculation.

**goi•ter** (goi′tər) *n.* Also **goi•tre.** An enlargement of the thyroid gland. **—goi′trous** *adj.*

**gold** (gōld) *n.* **1.** A soft, yellow metallic element that is used as an international monetary standard. **2.** Money; riches. **3.** Yellow color. **—gold′en** *adj.*

**gold•brick** (gōld′brĭk′) *n.* A person, esp. a soldier, who avoids assigned work. **—gold′brick′** *v.* **—gold′brick′er** *n.*

**gold•en•rod** (gōl′dən-rŏd′) *n.* A plant with small yellow flowers.

**gold•finch** (gōld′fĭnch′) *n.* A small bird with yellow and black plumage.

**gold•fish** (gōld′fĭsh′) *n.* A small freshwater fish.

**golf** (gŏlf, gôlf) *n.* A game played on an outdoor course, the object being to propel a small ball with the use of a club into various holes. **—golf** *v.* **—golf′er** *n.*

**go•nad** (gō′năd′) *n.* An organ that produces sex cells.

**gon•do•la** (gŏn′dl-ə, gŏn-dō′lə) *n.* A narrow barge used on the canals of Venice. **—gon′do•lier′** *n.*

**gone** (gôn, gŏn) *v.* p.p. of **go.**

**gong** (gông, gŏng) *n.* A metal disk that produces a sonorous tone when struck.

**gon•o•coc•cus** (gŏn′ə-kŏk′əs) *n., pl.* **-cocci.** A bacterium that causes gonorrhea.

**gon•or•rhe•a** (gŏn′ə-rē′ə) *n.* An infectious venereal disease.

**good** (go͝od) *adj.* **better** (bĕt′ər), **best** (bĕst). **1.** Having positive or desirable qualities. **2.** Suitable; serviceable. **3.** Not spoiled; whole or sound. **4.** Of high quality. **5.** Beneficial. **6.** Competent; skilled. **7.** Pleasant; enjoyable. **8.** Virtuous; upright. **9.** Well-behaved; obedient. *—n.* **1.** That which is good. **2.** Welfare; benefit. **3.** Virtue; merit. **—good′ness** *n.*

**good-by, good-bye** (go͝od-bī′) *interj.* Farewell. **—good-by′, good-bye′** *n.*

**good•ly** (go͝od′lē) *adj.* **-lier, -liest. 1.** Handsome; comely. **2.** Rather large; considerable.

**goods** (go͝odz) *pl.n.* Merchandise.

**goose** (go͞os) *n., pl.* **geese. 1.** A large water bird related to the duck. **2.** A silly person.

**go•pher** (gō′fər) *n.* Any of various burrowing rodents.

**gore¹** (gôr) *v.* **gored, goring.** To stab with a horn or tusk.

**gore²** (gôr) *n.* Blood, esp. from a wound. **—gor′y** *adj.*

**gore³** (gôr) *n.* A triangular piece of cloth, esp. in a skirt or sail.

**gorge** (gôrj) *n.* A deep, narrow ravine. *—v.* **gorged, gorging. 1.** To stuff; glut. **2.** To eat greedily.

**gor•geous** (gôr′jəs) *adj.* **1.** Resplendent; magnificent. **2.** Strikingly beautiful. **—gor′geous•ly** *adv.*

**go•ril•la** (gə-rĭl′ə) *n.* A large African ape.

**gos•ling** (gŏz′lĭng) *n.* A young goose.

**gos•pel** (gŏs′pəl) *n.* **1.** Often **Gospel.** The teachings of Christ and the Apostles. **2. Gospel.** Any of the first four books of the New Testament. **3.** Something accepted as unquestionably true.

**gos•sa•mer** (gŏs′ə-mər) *n.* **1.** A fine film of floating cobwebs. **2.** A sheer gauzy fabric. **—gos′sa•mer** *adj.*

**gos•sip** (gŏs′əp) *n.* **1.** Rumor of a personal nature. **2.** One who engages in such talk. *—v.* To engage in gossip.

**gos•sip•mon•ger** (gŏs′əp-mŭng′gər, -mŏng′-) *n.* A person who passes on gossip.

**got** (gŏt) *v.* p.t. & p.p. of **get.**

**got•ten** (gŏt′n) *v.* A p.p. of **get.**

**gouge** (gouj) *n.* **1.** A chisel with a troughlike blade. **2.** A groove or hole. *—v.* **gouged, gouging.** To cut or scoop out with a gouge.

**gou•lash** (gōō'läsh', -läsh') *n.* A hearty stew of Hungarian origin, seasoned with paprika.

**gourd** (gôrd, gōrd, gōōrd) *n.* **1.** A vine related to the pumpkin. **2.** The dried shell of a fruit from this vine.

**gour•mand** (gōōr'mənd) *n.* A person who likes to eat well and to excess.

**gour•man•dise** (gōōr'mən-dēz') *n.* An enthusiasm for good food.

**gour•met** (gōōr-mā') *n.* A person who likes fine food.

**gout** (gout) *n.* A disease marked by painful swelling of the joints. **—gout'y** *adj.*

**gov•ern** (gŭv'ərn) *v.* **1.** To control; guide. **2.** To rule by exercise of sovereign authority. **3.** To regulate or determine. **—gov'ern•a•bil'i•ty** *n.* **—gov'ern•a•ble** *adj.* **—gov'er•nance** *n.*

**gov•er•ness** (gŭv'ər-nĭs) *n.* A woman who supervises the children of a private household.

**gov•ern•ment** (gŭv'ərn-mənt) *n.* **1.** The administration of policy by a ruling body. **2.** The office or authority whereby political power is exercised. **3.** A prevailing political system or policy. **4.** A governing body. **—gov'ern•ment'al** *adj.*

**gov•er•nor** (gŭv'ər-nər) *n.* The chief executive of a state. **—gov'er•nor•ship'** *n.*

**gown** (goun) *n.* **1.** A loose, flowing garment, esp. a nightgown. **2.** A woman's formal dress.

**grab** (grăb) *v.* **grabbed, grabbing.** To grasp suddenly; snatch; seize. **—grab** *n.* **—grab'ber** *n.*

**grace** (grās) *n.* **1.** Beauty of movement or form. **2.** Mercy; clemency. **3.** Temporary immunity. **4.** Divine love and protection. —*v.* **graced, gracing.** To honor or favor. **—grace'ful** *adj.* **—grace'ful•ly** *adv.* **—grace'less** *adj.*

**gra•cious** (grā'shəs) *adj.* **1.** Tactful and courteous. **2.** Merciful; compassionate. **3.** Tasteful. **—gra'cious•ly** *adv.* **—gra'cious•ness** *n.*

**grack•le** (grăk'əl) *n.* **1.** A kind of blackbird with iridescent plumage. **2.** An Asian mynah bird.

**gra•da•tion** (grā-dā'shən) *n.* A progression of successive stages.

**grade** (grād) *n.* **1.** A stage in a process; position in a scale. **2.** A school class. **3.** A mark indicating a student's level of achievement. **4.** A military rank. —*v.* **graded, grading.** **1.** To arrange in degrees; rank. **2.** To asisgn an academic grade to. **3.** To level or smooth.

**grad•u•al** (grăj'ōō-əl) *adj.* Occurring by stages or degrees. **—grad'u•al•ly** *adv.*

**grad•u•ate** (grăj'ōō-āt') *v.* **-ated, -ating.** **1.** To grant or be granted an academic degree. **2.** To divide into intervals. —*n.* (-ĭt). A recipient of an academic degree. **—grad'u•a'tion** *n.*

**graf•fi•ti** (grə-fē'tē) *pl.n. Sing.* **-fito.** A crude drawing or inscription written or carved on a wall.

**graft**[1] (grăft) *v.* **1.** To unite (a shoot, bud, or plant) with a growing plant. **2.** To transplant (tissue) into a bodily part. —*n.* A detached shoot grafted onto a growing plant.

**graft**[2] (grăft) *n.* **1.** The unscrupulous use of one's position or knowledge to derive profit or advantages. **2.** Money thus obtained.

**grail** (grāl) *n.* **1. Grail.** The chalice used by Jesus at the Last Supper. **2.** The object of prolonged, arduous effort.

**grain** (grān) *n.* **1.** A small, hard seed. **2.** A mass of particles. **3.** Cereal grasses collectively. **4.** A tiny quantity. **5.** Texture, esp. of wood. **—grain'i•ness** *n.* **—grain'y** *adj.*

**gram** (grăm) *n.* A metric unit of mass and weight.

**gram•mar** (grăm'ər) *n.* **1.** The study of syntax and word inflection. **2.** A system of usage rules for language. **—gram•mar'i•an** *n.* **—gram•mat'i•cal** *adj.* **—gram•mat'i•cal•ly** *adv.*

**gran•a•ry** (grăn'ə-rē, grā'nə-) *n., pl.* **-ries.** A building for storing grain.

**grand** (grănd) *adj.* **1.** Large and impressive. **2.** Magnificent; sumptuous. **3.** Illustrious. **4.** Dignified; stately. **5.** Inclusive; complete. **—grand'ly** *adv.*

**grand•child** (grănd'chīld, grăn'-) *n.* A child of one's son or daughter. **—grand'daugh'ter** *n.* **—grand'son'** *n.*

**gran•dee** (grăn-dē') *n.* **1.** A Spanish or Portuguese nobleman of the highest rank. **2.** A high-ranking person.

**gran•deur** (grăn′jər, -jo͝or′) *n.* Greatness; splendor.

**grand•par•ent** (grănd′pâr′ənt, grăn′-) *n.* A parent of one's mother or father. **—grand′fa′ther** *n.* **—grand′moth′er** *n.*

**grand•stand** (grănd′stănd′, grăn′-) *n.* A stand for spectators at a stadium.

**gran•ite** (grăn′ĭt) *n.* A common, hard rock, used for building.

**gran•o•la** (grə-nō′lə) *n.* Rolled oats mixed with various ingredients for a snack or breakfast cereal.

**grant** (grănt) *v.* **1.** To allow; consent to. **2.** To accord, as a favor. **3.** To bestow; confer. **4.** To acknowledge. —*n.* Something granted.

**grants•man•ship** (grănts′mən-shĭp′) *n.* Skill at winning grants, esp. for research projects.

**gran•u•late** (grăn′yə-lāt′) *v.* **-lated, -lating.** To form into granules.

**gran•ule** (grăn′yo͞ol) *n.* A small grain.

**grape** (grāp) *n.* A juicy, smooth-skinned, edible fruit.

**grape•fruit** (grāp′fro͞ot) *n.* A large, yellow-skinned citrus fruit.

**grape•vine** (grāp′vīn′) *n.* A vine on which grapes grow.

**graph** (grăf) *n.* A drawing that exhibits a relationship between two sets of numbers. —*v.* To represent by or plot on a graph.

**graph•ic** (grăf′ĭk) *adj.* Also **graphical. 1.** Written, printed, drawn, or engraved. **2.** Vividly outlined; lifelike. **—graph′i•cal•ly** *adv.*

**graph•ite** (grăf′īt′) *n.* The soft, crystallized form of carbon, used in lead pencils.

**grap•nel** (grăp′nəl) *n.* A small anchor.

**grap•ple** (grăp′əl) *n.* A clawed implement, formerly used to secure enemy ships while boarding. —*v.* **-pled, -pling. 1.** To seize firmly. **2.** To attempt to cope.

**grasp** (grăsp) *v.* **1.** To take hold of; seize. **2.** To comprehend. —*n.* **1.** Hold; grip. **2.** Comprehension.

**grass** (grăs) *n.* **1.** Any of numerous plants with narrow leaves. **2.** Ground, as a lawn, covered with such plants. **—grass′y** *adj.*

**grass•hop•per** (grăs′hŏp′ər) *n.* An insect with long legs for jumping.

**grate**[1] (grāt) *v.* **grated, grating. 1.** To shred by rubbing. **2.** To make a rasping sound. **3.** To irritate. **—grat′er** *n.* **—grat′ing** *adj.*

**grate**[2] (grāt) *n.* A framework of parallel bars over an opening.

**grate•ful** (grāt′fəl) *adj.* Appreciative; thankful. **—grate′ful•ly** *adv.* **—grate′ful•ness** *n.*

**grat•i•fy** (grăt′ə-fī′) *v.* **-fied, -fying.** To please, favor, or indulge. **—grat′i•fi•ca′tion** *n.*

**grat•is** (grăt′ĭs, grä′tĭs, grā′-) *adv.* Without charge; free. **—gra′tis** *adj.*

**grat•i•tude** (grăt′ĭ-t/y/o͞od′) *n.* Thankfulness.

**gra•tu•i•tous** (grə-t/y/o͞o′ĭ-təs) *adj.* **1.** Free; gratis. **2.** Unnecessary or unwarranted. **—gra•tu′i•tous•ly** *adv.*

**gra•tu•i•ty** (grə-t/y/o͞o′ĭ-tē) *n., pl.* **-ties.** A tip for service.

**grave**[1] (grāv) *n.* A burial excavation. **—grave′stone′** *n.* **—grave′yard′** *n.*

**grave**[2] (grāv) *adj.* **graver, gravest. 1.** Extremely serious; important; weighty. **2.** Fraught with danger. **—grave′ly** *adv.*

**grav•el** (grăv′əl) *n.* A mixture of rock fragments.

**grav•i•ta•tion** (grăv′ĭ-tā′shən) *n.* **1.** The natural attraction between massive bodies. **2.** A movement toward a source of attraction. **—grav′i•tate′** *v.* **—grav′i•ta′tion•al** *adj.*

**grav•i•ty** (grăv′ĭ-tē) *n.* **1.** The force of gravitation, esp. the attractive central force exerted by a celestial body such as the earth. **2.** Seriousness; importance.

**gra•vy** (grā′vē) *n., pl.* **-vies.** The juices that drip from cooking meat.

**gray, grey** (grā) *adj.* **1.** Of a color between black and white. **2.** Dull or dark; gloomy. —*n.* A neutral color. **—gray′ish** *adj.*

**gray matter.** *n.* The nerve tissue of the brain and spinal cord.

**graze**[1] (grāz) *v.* **grazed, grazing.** To feed on growing grass.

**graze**[2] (grāz) *v.* **grazed, grazing.** To touch lightly in passing.

**grease** (grēs) *n.* **1.** Melted animal fat. **2.** Any thick oil or viscous lubricant. —*v.* **greased, greasing.** To coat, lubricate, or soil with grease. **—greas′y** *adj.*

**great** (grāt) *adj.* **1.** Extremely large; bulky; big. **2.** Remarkable; outstanding. **3.** Eminent; distinguished. **—great'ly** *adv.* **—great'ness** *n.*

**greed** (grēd) *n.* Rapacious desire; avarice. **—greed'i•ly** *adv.* **—greed'y** *adj.*

**green** (grēn) *n.* **1.** A color whose hue is that of the emerald or grass. **2.** Leafy plants. **3.** A grassy lawn. *—adj.* **1.** Of the color green. **2.** Not ripe; immature. **3.** Lacking experience. **—green'er•y** *n.* **—green'ish** *adj.*

**green-eyed** (grēn'īd') *adj.* Jealous.

**green•house** (grēn'hous') *n.* A structure in which plants are grown.

**greet** (grēt) *v.* To address in a friendly way; welcome. **—greet'ing** *n.*

**gre•gar•i•ous** (grĭ-gâr'ē-əs) *adj.* **1.** Tending to live or move in herds. **2.** Enjoying the company of others; sociable.

**gre•nade** (grə-nād') *n.* An explosive missile thrown by hand.

**grew** (gro͞o) *v.* p.t. of **grow.**

**grey•hound** (grā'hound') *n.* A large, slender, swift-running dog.

**grid** (grĭd) *n.* **1.** A grating. **2.** A pattern of lines forming squares on a map.

**grid•dle** (grĭd'l) *n.* A flat pan used for cooking.

**grid•i•ron** (grĭd'ī'ərn) *n.* **1.** A grill framework for broiling. **2.** A football field.

**grid•lock** (grĭd'lŏk') *n.* **1.** A traffic jam so severe that no movement is possible. **2.** A deadlock or impasse. **—grid'locked'** *adj.*

**grief** (grēf) *n.* Acute sorrow or anguish.

**griev•ance** (grē'vəns) *n.* A complaint or protest.

**grieve** (grēv) *v.* **grieved, grieving. 1.** To cause grief to; distress. **2.** To lament; mourn. **—griev'ous** *adj.* **—griev'ous•ly** *adv.*

**grill** (grĭl) *n.* A cooking utensil composed of thin metal bars. *—v.* To broil on a grill.

**grille** (grĭl) *n.* Also **grill.** A metal grate used as a screen.

**grim** (grĭm) *adj.* **grimmer, grimmest. 1.** Stern; forbidding. **2.** Ghastly; sinister. **—grim'ly** *adv.*

**grim•ace** (grĭm'ĭs, grĭ-mās') *n.* A facial contortion expressing pain, contempt, or disgust. **—grim'ace** *v.*

**grime** (grīm) *n.* Black dirt or soot. **—grim'y** *adj.*

**grin** (grĭn) *v.* **grinned, grinning.** To smile broadly. *—n.* The expression produced by grinning.

**grind** (grīnd) *v.* **ground** (ground), **grinding. 1.** To crush into fine particles. **2.** To shape, sharpen, or refine with friction. **3.** To rub together; gnash. **4.** To turn a crank. **—grind'er** *n.* **—grind'stone'** *n.*

**grip** (grĭp) *n.* **1.** A tight hold. **2.** A handle. **—come to grips.** To confront and resolve a problem. *—v.* **gripped, gripping.** To grasp and keep a tight hold on.

**gripe** (grīp) *v.* **griped, griping. 1.** To cause or suffer sharp pain in the bowels. **2.** To complain; grumble.

**grippe, grip** (grĭp) *n.* Influenza. **—grip'py** *adj.*

**gris•ly** (grĭz'lē) *adj.* **-lier, -liest.** Horrifying; gruesome.

**grist** (grĭst) *n.* Grain to be or already ground.

**gris•tle** (grĭs'əl) *n.* Cartilage, esp. in meat.

**grit** (grĭt) *n.* **1.** Minute rough granules. **2.** Spirit; pluck. *—v.* **gritted, gritting.** To clamp (the teeth) together. **—grit'ty** *adj.*

**grits** (grĭts) *pl.n.* Coarsely ground grain.

**griz•zly** (grĭz'lē) *adj.* **-zlier, -zliest.** Grayish. *—n., pl.* **-zlies.** Also **grizzly bear.** A large brown bear.

**groan** (grōn) *v.* To moan in pain, annoyance, or disapproval. *—n.* Such a moan.

**gro•cer** (grō'sər) *n.* A storekeeper who sells foodstuffs and household supplies. **—gro'cer•y** *n.*

**grog•gy** (grŏg'ē) *adj.* **-gier, -giest.** Unsteady and dazed; shaky.

**groin** (groin) *n.* The crease at the juncture of the thigh and abdomen.

**grom•met** (grŏm'ĭt) *n.* A reinforced eyelet in cloth, leather, etc.

**groom** (gro͞om, gro͝om) *n.* **1.** A man employed to take care of horses. **2.** A bridegroom. *—v.* **1.** To make neat and trim; brush. **2.** To train.

**groove** (gro͞ov) *n.* **1.** A long, narrow channel. **2.** A settled routine. *—v.* **grooved, grooving.** To cut a groove in.

**grope** (grōp) *v.* **groped, groping. 1.** To feel one's way uncertainly. **2.** To search blindly. **—grop'ing•ly** *adv.*

**gross** (grōs) *adj.* **1.** Exclusive of deductions. **2.** Glaringly obvious; flagrant. **3.** Coarse; vulgar. —*n., pl.* **gross.** Twelve dozen. —*v.* To earn a total before deductions. —**gross'ly** *adv.* —**gross'ness** *n.*

**gro•tesque** (grō-tĕsk') *adj.* **1.** Extravagant; outlandish. **2.** Bizarre; distorted. —**gro•tesque'ly** *adv.* —**gro•tesque'ness** *n.*

**grot•to** (grŏt'ō) *n., pl.* **-toes** or **-tos.** A small cave.

**grouch** (grouch) *v.* To sulk. —*n.* **1.** A grumbling or sulky mood. **2.** An irritable person. —**grouch'y** *adj.*

**ground**[1] (ground) *n.* **1.** The solid surface of the earth. **2.** Often **grounds.** An area of land designated for a particular purpose. **3.** Often **grounds.** The basis for an argument, belief, or action. **4.** **grounds.** The sediment at the bottom of a liquid. —*v.* **1.** To prevent from flying. **2.** To instruct in fundamentals. —**ground'less** *adj.*

**ground**[2] (ground) *v.* p.t. & p.p. of **grind.**

**ground•work** (ground'wûrk') *n.* Basis; preliminary work.

**group** (gro͞op) *n.* A number of individuals or things with certain similarities. —*v.* To place in or form a group.

**group•think** (gro͞op'thĭngk') *n.* Conformity to group ethics and behavior.

**grouse** (grous) *n., pl.* **grouse.** A chickenlike bird.

**grove** (grōv) *n.* A small group of trees.

**grov•el** (grŭv'əl, grŏv'-) *v.* To humble oneself; cringe. —**grov'el•er** *n.*

**grow** (grō) *v.* **grew** (gro͞o), **grown** (grōn), **growing.** **1.** To increase in size. **2.** To develop and reach maturity. **3.** To become. —**grown** *adj.* —**grown'-up'** *n. & adj.*

**growl** (groul) *n.* A low, menacing sound. —*v.* To utter such a sound.

**growth** (grōth) *n.* **1.** The process of growing. **2.** Something that has grown. **3.** An abnormal tissue formation.

**grub** (grŭb) *v.* **grubbed, grubbing.** **1.** To dig up by the roots. **2.** To toil arduously; drudge. —*n.* The larva of certain insects.

**grub•by** (grŭb'ē) *adj.* **-bier, -biest.** Dirty; unkempt. —**grub'bi•ness** *n.*

**grudge** (grŭj) *v.* **grudged, grudging.** To be reluctant to give. —*n.* Resentment or rancor. —**grudg'ing•ly** *adv.*

**gru•el** (gro͞o'əl) *n.* A watery porridge. —*v.* To exhaust. —**gru'el•ing** *adj.*

**grue•some** (gro͞o'səm) *adj.* Causing horror and repugnance; frightful. —**grue'some•ly** *adv.* —**grue'some•ness** *n.*

**gruff** (grŭf) *adj.* **1.** Brusque and stern. **2.** Hoarse. —**gruff'ly** *adv.* —**gruff'ness** *n.*

**grum•ble** (grŭm'bəl) *v.* **-bled, -bling.** To mumble in discontent. —*n.* A grumbling utterance.

**grump•y** (grŭm'pē) *adj.* **-ier, -iest.** Irritable; cranky. —**grump'i•ness** *n.*

**grunt** (grŭnt) *v.* To utter (with) a low, guttural sound. —*n.* A low, guttural sound.

**guar•an•tee** (găr'ən-tē') *n.* A formal assurance that something is as represented or that a specified act will be performed. —*v.* **-teed, -teeing.** **1.** To assume responsibility for the debt of. **2.** To furnish security for. —**guar'an•tor'** *n.*

**guard** (gärd) *v.* **1.** To protect from harm. **2.** To watch over to prevent escape. **3.** To take precautions. —*n.* One that guards.

**guard•ed** (gär'dĭd) *adj.* **1.** Protected. **2.** Cautious; restrained. —**guard'ed•ly** *adv.*

**guard•i•an** (gär'dē-ən) *n.* **1.** A custodian. **2.** A person legally responsible for the care of the affairs of an incompetent person. —**guard'i•an•ship'** *n.*

**gu•ber•na•to•ri•al** (g/y/o͞o'bər-nə-tôr'ē-əl, -tōr'-) *adj.* Of a governor.

**guer•ril•la, gue•ril•la** (gə-rĭl'ə) *n.* A member of an irregular military force. —*adj.* Of or by guerrillas.

**guess** (gĕs) *v.* **1.** To predict (a result or event) or assume (a fact) without sufficient information. **2.** To estimate correctly. —*n.* **1.** An instance of guessing. **2.** A conjecture arrived at by guessing. —**guess'work'** *n.*

**guest** (gĕst) *n.* **1.** A visitor. **2.** A patron; customer.

**guf•faw** (gə-fô') *n.* A hearty laugh. —**guf•faw'** *v.*

**guide** (gīd) *n.* **1.** One who shows the way. **2.** An example or model. **3.** A sign or indicator. —*v.* **guided, guiding.** **1.** To show the way to; conduct. **2.** To manage the affairs of others; govern. **3.** To counsel. **—gui'dance** *n.*

**guide•line** (gīd'līn') *n.* A statement of policy or procedure.

**guided missile.** *n.* Any missile capable of being guided while in flight.

**guild** (gĭld) *n.* An association of persons of the same trade.

**guile** (gīl) *n.* Insidious cunning; craftiness. **—guile'ful** *adj.*

**guil•lo•tine** (gĭl'ə-tēn', gē'ə-) *n.* A machine to behead a condemned prisoner. *—v.* **-tined, -tining.** To behead with a guillotine.

**guilt** (gĭlt) *n.* **1.** The fact of being responsible for a wrongdoing. **2.** Remorseful awareness of having done something wrong. **—guilt'i•ly** *adv.* **—guilt'less** *adj.* **—guilt'y** *adj.*

**guin•ea pig** (gĭn'ē). **1.** A variously colored rodent. **2.** A subject for experimentation.

**guise** (gīz) *n.* **1.** Outward appearance. **2.** False appearance; pretense.

**gui•tar** (gĭ-tär') *n.* A stringed musical instrument. **—gui•tar'ist** *n.*

**gulch** (gŭlch) *n.* A shallow canyon or ravine.

**gulf** (gŭlf) *n.* **1.** A large area of a sea partially enclosed by land. **2.** A deep, wide chasm; abyss.

**gull**[1] (gŭl) *n.* **1.** A coastal water bird.

**gull**[2] (gŭl) *n.* An easily deceived person; dupe. *—v.* To deceive; dupe. **—gul'li•ble** *adj.*

**gul•let** (gŭl'ĭt) *n.* The esophagus.

**gul•ly** (gŭl'ē) *n., pl.* **-lies.** A channel cut in the earth by water.

**gulp** (gŭlp) *v.* **1.** To gasp, as in nervousness. **2.** To swallow in large amounts. *—n.* **1.** The act of gulping. **2.** A large mouthful.

**gum**[1] (gŭm) *n.* A viscous plant substance. *—v.* **gummed, gumming.** To seal or fill with gum. **—gum'my** *adj.*

**gum**[2] (gŭm) *n.* The firm connective tissue at the base of the teeth.

**gum•bo** (gŭm'bō) *n., pl.* **-bos.** Soup or stew made with okra.

**gun** (gŭn) *n.* A weapon consisting of a metal tube from which a projectile is fired. *—v.* **gunned, gunning.** To shoot (with *down*). **—gun'ner** *n.*

**gun•ny** (gŭn'ē) *n.* A coarse fabric; burlap.

**gun•pow•der** (gŭn'pou'dər) *n.* An explosive powder used in firearms.

**gun•ship** (gŭn'shĭp') *n.* A helicopter or cargo plane equipped with machine guns and rockets.

**gup•py** (gŭp'ē) *n., pl.* **-pies.** A small tropical freshwater fish.

**gur•gle** (gûr'gəl) *v.* **-gled, -gling. 1.** To flow making intermittent, bubbling sounds. **2.** To make such sounds. **—gur'gle** *n.*

**gur•ney** (gûr'nē) *n., pl.* **-neys.** A wheeled stretcher used in hospitals.

**gu•ru** (gŏŏr'ōō, gŏŏ-rōō') *n., pl.* **-rus.** A spiritual, esp. Hindu, leader or guide.

**gush** (gŭsh) *v.* **1.** To flow forth suddenly. **2.** To display sentiment effusively. *—n.* A sudden, copious outflow. **—gush'er** *n.*

**gus•set** (gŭs'ĭt) *n.* A triangular insert, esp. in a garment.

**gust** (gŭst) *n.* An abrupt rush of wind. **—gust'y** *adj.*

**gus•ta•to•ry** (gŭs'tə-tôr'ē, -tōr'ē) *adj.* Of the sense of taste.

**gus•to** (gŭs'tō) *n.* Vigorous enjoyment; relish.

**gut** (gŭt) *n.* **1.** The intestine or stomach. **2. guts.** Courage; fortitude. *—v.* **gutted, gutting.** To destroy the interior of.

**gut•ter** (gŭt'ər) *n.* A channel for draining off water.

**gut•tur•al** (gŭt'ər-əl) *adj.* **1.** Of the throat. **2.** Produced in the throat. **—gut'tur•al•ly** *adv.*

**guy**[1] (gī) *n.* A rope or cable used to steady or guide something.

**guy**[2] (gī) *n.* A man.

**guz•zle** (gŭz'əl) *v.* **-zled, -zling.** To drink greedily.

**gym•na•si•um** (jĭm-nā'zē-əm) *n.* A building equipped for gymnastics and sports.

**gym•nas•tics** (jĭm-năs'tĭks) *pl.n.* Body-building exercises. **—gym'nast'** *n.* **—gym•nas'tic** *adj.*

**gy•ne•col•o•gy** (gī'nĭ-kŏl'ə-jē, jĭn'ĭ-, jī'nĭ-) *n.* The medical science of the diseases and functions of women. **—gy'ne•co•log'i•cal** *adj.* **—gy'ne•col'o•gist** *n.*

**gyp•sum** (jĭp'səm) *n.* A white mineral used to make plaster.

**gy•rate** (jī'rāt') *v.* **-rated, -rating.** To revolve; circle; spiral. **—gy•ra'tion** *n.*

**gy•ro**[1] (jī′rō) *n., pl.* **-ros.** A gyroscope.

**gy•ro**[2] (jī′rō, jē′-) *n., pl.* **-ros.** A sandwich made with pita bread and roasted meat.

**gy•ro•scope** (jī′rə-skōp′) *n.* A spinning disk, suspended to rotate freely around an axis, used to maintain equilibrium.

# — H —

**h, H** (āch) *n.* The 8th letter of the English alphabet.

**hab•er•dash•er** (hăb′ər-dăsh′ər) *n.* A dealer in men's furnishings. **—hab′er•dash′er•y** *n.*

**hab•it** (hăb′ĭt) *n.* **1.** An activity repeated so frequently it is done without thinking. **2.** A customary manner or practice. **3.** An addiction. **4.** A distinctive dress or costume. **—ha•bit′u•al** *adj.* **—ha•bit′u•ate′** *v.*

**hab•i•tat** (hăb′ĭ-tăt′) *n.* The area or environment in which a plant or animal normally lives or occurs.

**hack**[1] (hăk) *v.* **1.** To cut or chop roughly; mangle. **2.** To cough in short spasms.

**hack**[2] (hăk) *n.* **1.** A worn-out horse. **2.** A vehicle for hire; taxicab. **3.** One hired to do routine writing. *—adj.* Banal; trite.

**hack•er** (hăk′ər) *n.* **1.** One that hacks. **2.** One who is inexperienced or inept at something. **3.** A computer enthusiast.

**hack•ney** (hăk′nē) *n., pl.* **-neys. 1.** A horse for riding. **2.** A carriage for hire.

**hack•neyed** (hăk′nēd) *adj.* Overused; trite.

**hack•saw** (hăk′sô′) *n.* A saw for cutting metal.

**had** (hăd) *v.* p.t. & p.p. of **have.**

**had•n't** (hăd′nt) *v.* Contraction of *had not.*

**hag** (hăg) *n.* An ugly old woman.

**hag•gard** (hăg′ərd) *adj.* Appearing worn and exhausted; gaunt.

**hag•gle** (hăg′əl) *v.* **-gled, -gling.** To urge or dispute in an attempt to bargain. **—hag′gler** *n.*

**hail**[1] (hāl) *n.* Pellets of ice and hard snow. *—v.* To precipitate hail. **—hail′stone′** *n.*

**hail**[2] (hāl) *v.* **1.** To salute or greet. **2.** To call out to. *—n.* A greeting or expression of acclaim.

**hair** (hâr) *n.* **1.** A fine, threadlike outgrowth, esp. from the skin of a mammal. **2.** A minute distance or narrow margin. **—hair′i•ness** *n.* **—hair′y** *adj.*

**hale**[1] (hāl) *adj.* **haler, halest.** Healthy; robust.

**hale**[2] (hāl) *v.* **haled, haling.** To compel to go; force.

**half** (hăf) *n., pl.* **halves.** One of 2 equal parts. *—adj.* **1.** Being a half. **2.** Partial; incomplete. *—adv.* **1.** To the extent of 50%. **2.** Not completely; partly. **—half′way′** *adj.*

**half•heart•ed** (hăf′här′tĭd) *adj.* Lacking interest or enthusiasm; uninspired. **—half′heart′ed•ly** *adv.*

**half•way house** (hăf′wā′) *n.* A rehabilitation center to help deinstitutionalized persons readjust to the outside world.

**hal•ite** (hăl′īt′, hā′līt′) *n.* Common salt, usually in chunks, used esp. to melt ice on sidewalks; rock salt.

**hall** (hôl) *n.* **1.** A corridor; lobby. **2.** A large public building. **3.** A large room. **—hall′way′** *n.*

**hal•le•lu•jah** (hăl′ə-lo͞o′yə) *interj.* Expressive of praise or joy.

**hall•mark** (hôl′märk′) *n.* **1.** A stamp of quality on gold or silver articles. **2.** A mark of excellence. **3.** A distinguishing characteristic.

**hal•low** (hăl′ō) *v.* To consecrate. **—hal′lowed** *adj.*

**hal•lu•ci•na•tion** (hə-lo͞o′sə-nā′shən) *n.* False perception; delusion. **—hal•lu′ci•nate′** *v.* **—hal•lu′ci•na•to′ry** *adj.*

**ha•lo** (hā′lō) *n., pl.* **-los** or **-loes. 1.** A ring of light around the head, as in a picture of a saint. **2.** A circular band of light around a light source, as the sun or moon.

**halt**[1] (hôlt) *n.* A suspension of movement; a stop.

**halt**[2] (hôlt) *v.* To limp or hobble. *—adj.* Lame.

**hal•ter** (hôl′tər) *n.* **1.** A strap that fits around the head of an animal. **2.** A noose used for execution by hanging. **3.** A backless bodice for women. *—v.* To put a halter on; control with a halter.

**halve** (hăv) *v.* **halved, halving. 1.** To divide into 2 equal parts. **2.** To reduce by half.

**halves** (hăvz) *n.* pl. of **half.**
**hal•yard** (hăl′yərd) *n.* A rope used to raise a sail, flag, etc.
**ham** (hăm) *n.* **1.** The thigh of the hind leg of a hog. **2.** An actor who exaggerates excessively. **3.** A licensed amateur radio operator.
**ham•burg•er** (hăm′bûr′gər) *n.* **1.** Ground beef. **2.** A cooked patty of such meat.
**ham•let** (hăm′lĭt) *n.* A small village.
**ham•mer** (hăm′ər) *n.* A hand tool with an iron head, used for pounding, driving nails, etc. —*v.* To strike, pound, or drive with or as with a hammer.
**ham•mock** (hăm′ək) *n.* A hanging bed suspended by cords.
**ham•per[1]** (hăm′pər) *v.* To restrain movement, action, etc.; impede.
**ham•per[2]** (hăm′pər) *n.* A large basket.
**ham•ster** (hăm′stər) *n.* A rodent often used in laboratory research.
**hand** (hănd) *n.* **1.** The terminal part of the arm below the wrist. **2.** A lateral direction; side. **3.** Handwriting. **4.** A round of applause. **5.** Help. **6.** The cards held by or dealt to a player. **7.** A laborer. —*v.* To pass with the hands. **—hand′ful′** *n.*
**hand•book** (hănd′bo͝ok′) *n.* A manual or small reference book.
**hand•cuff** (hănd′kŭf′) *n.* Often **handcuffs.** A restraining device that can be locked about the wrist. —*v.* To restrain with handcuffs.
**hand•gun** (hănd′gŭn′) *n.* A firearm, esp. a pistol, that can be used with 1 hand.
**hand•i•cap** (hăn′dē-kăp′) *n.* **1.** An advantage or penalty given different contestants in a race to equalize their chances of winning. **2.** A deficiency that prevents or restricts normal achievement. —*v.* **-capped, -capping. 1.** To assign a handicap or handicaps to (a contestant). **2.** To hinder.
**hand•i•work** (hăn′dē-wûrk′) *n.* **1.** Work performed by hand. **2.** The results of one's efforts.
**hand•ker•chief** (hăng′kər-chĭf) *n.* A small cloth used in wiping the nose, mouth, etc.
**han•dle** (hăn′dl) *v.* **-dled, -dling. 1.** To touch, lift, or turn with the hands. **2.** To manipulate. **3.** To manage; deal with or in. —*n.* A part that is held with the hand.
**hand•out** (hănd′out′) *n.* **1.** Something given to a beggar. **2.** A leaflet distributed gratis. **3.** A prepared news or publicity release.
**hand•some** (hăn′səm) *adj.* **1.** Pleasing and dignified in appearance. **2.** Generous; liberal. **—hand′some•ly** *adv.*
**hands-on** (hăndz′ŏn′, -ôn′) *adj.* **1.** Allowing manual examination or use. **2.** Practical; down-to-earth.
**hand•y** (hăn′dē) *adj.* **-ier, -iest. 1.** Manually adroit. **2.** Readily accessible. **3.** Easy to use. **—hand′i•ly** *adv.*
**hang** (hăng) *v.* **hung** (hŭng) or **hanged, hanging. 1.** To fasten or be fastened from above. **2.** To suspend or be suspended so as to allow free movement. **3.** To execute or be executed by suspending by the neck.
**han•gar** (hăng′ər) *n.* A shed, esp. for aircraft.
**hang•man** (hăng′mən) *n.* One employed to execute prisoners by hanging.
**hank** (hăngk) *n.* A coil or loop.
**han•ker** (hăng′kər) *v.* To crave.
**hap•haz•ard** (hăp-hăz′ərd) *adj.* Dependent on or characterized by mere chance. **—hap•haz′ard•ly** *adv.*
**hap•less** (hăp′lĭs) *adj.* Luckless; unfortunate.
**hap•pen** (hăp′ən) *v.* **1.** To take place. **2.** To come upon or appear by chance; turn up.
**hap•pen•ing** (hăp′ə-nĭng) *n.* An event.
**hap•py** (hăp′ē) *adj.* **-pier, -piest. 1.** Characterized by good fortune; prosperous. **2.** Having pleasure; gratified. **—hap′pi•ly** *adv.* **—hap′pi•ness** *n.*
**ha•rangue** (hə-răng′) *n.* A speech characterized by vehement expression. **—ha•rangue′** *v.*
**har•ass** (hăr′əs, hə-răs′) *v.* To disturb or irritate persistently. **—har′ass•ment** *n.*
**har•bin•ger** (här′bĭn-jər) *n.* A forerunner.
**har•bor** (här′bər) *n.* **1.** A shelter for ships; port. **2.** A refuge. —*v.* **1.** To give shelter to; protect. **2.** To hold a thought or feeling about.
**hard** (härd) *adj.* **1.** Not easily penetrated; rigid. **2.** Difficult. **3.** Severe; harsh. **4.** Callous; unfeeling. **5.** Real.
**hard•back** (härd′băk′) *adj.* Relating to a book bound in cloth or cardboard;

hardbound; hardcover. **—hard'back'** *n.*

**hard•ball** (härd'bôl') *n.* **1.** Baseball. **2.** The use of any means, however ruthless, to obtain an objective.

**hard-bit•ten** (härd'bĭt'n) *adj.* Toughened by experience.

**hard•board** (härd'bôrd', -bōrd') *n.* Construction board made of compressed wood chip fibers.

**hard-boiled** (härd'boild') *adj.* **1.** Cooked by boiling in a shell to solidity. **2.** Unfeeling; callous. **3.** Unsentimental; tough.

**hard copy** *n.* Readable printed copy of the output of a computer.

**hard-core** (härd'kôr', -kōr') *adj.* **1.** Stubbornly resistant. **2.** Intractable; insoluble. **3.** Extremely graphic and explicit.

**hard•hat** (härd'hăt') *n.* **1.** A lightweight helmet worn by construction workers. **2.** A construction worker. **3.** A very patriotic person with a conventional morality. **4.** An ultraconservative. **—hard'hat'** *adj.*

**hard line** *n.* A firm, uncompromising policy or stance. **—hard'-line'** *adj.* **—hard'-lin'er** *n.*

**hard•ly** (härd'lē) *adv.* **1.** Barely; just. **2.** Probably or almost surely not.

**hard news** *n.* News of important events delivered by the media.

**hard•ship** (härd'shĭp) *n.* Extreme privation; suffering.

**hard•ware** (härd'wâr') *n.* Metal goods and utensils.

**har•dy** (här'dē) *adj.* **-dier, -diest. 1.** Rugged; strong. **2.** Capable of surviving severe cold, drought, etc., as a plant. **3.** Courageous. **—har'di•ness** *n.*

**hare** (hâr) *n.* A mammal related to and resembling the rabbits.

**hare•lip** (hâr'lĭp') *n.* A congenital fissure in the upper lip. **—hare'lipped'** *adj.*

**har•em** (hâr'əm, hăr'-) *n.* **1.** A section of a house reserved for women in a Muslim household. **2.** The women occupying a harem.

**hark** (härk) *v.* To listen attentively.

**har•lot** (här'lət) *n.* A prostitute.

**harm** (härm) *n.* **1.** Injury or damage. **2.** Wrong; evil. —*v.* To damage; injure; impair. **—harm'ful** *adj.* **—harm'less** *adj.*

**har•mon•i•ca** (här-mŏn'ĭ-kə) *n.* A small wind instrument.

**har•mon•y** (här'mə-nē) *n., pl.* **-nies. 1.** Agreement or accord, as of feeling. **2.** A pleasing combination of parts or elements. **3.** Combination and progression of chords in musical structure. **—har•mon'ic** *adj.* **—har•mo'ni•ous** *adj.* **—har'mo•nize'** *v.*

**har•ness** (här'nĭs) *n.* Gear by which a draft animal pulls a vehicle or implement. —*v.* **1.** To put a harness on. **2.** To control and direct the force of.

**harp** (härp) *n.* A musical instrument with strings played by plucking. **—harp'ist** *n.*

**har•poon** (här-po͞on') *n.* A spearlike weapon used esp. in whaling. —*v.* To strike with a harpoon.

**harp•si•chord** (härp'sĭ-kôrd', -kōrd') *n.* A keyboard instrument, resembling a piano, whose strings are plucked. **—harp'si•chord'ist** *n.*

**har•ri•dan** (hăr'ĭ-dn) *n.* A disagreeable old woman.

**har•ri•er**[1] (hăr'ē-ər) *n.* **1.** One that harries. **2.** A kind of narrow-winged hawk.

**har•ri•er**[2] (hăr'ē-ər) *n.* **1.** A small hound used to hunt hares. **2.** A cross-country runner.

**har•row** (hăr'ō) *n.* An implement used to break up plowed ground. —*v.* **1.** To break up (soil) with a harrow. **2.** To distress greatly; torment.

**har•ry** (hăr'ē) *v.* **-ried, -rying.** To distress by constant attacks; harass.

**harsh** (härsh) *adj.* **1.** Severe; stern. **2.** Unpleasant; irritating. **—harsh'ly** *adv.* **—harsh'ness** *n.*

**hart** (härt) *n.* An adult male deer.

**har•vest** (här'vĭst) *n.* **1.** The gathering in of a crop. **2.** A gathered crop. —*v.* **1.** To gather (a crop). **2.** To gain, win, or acquire; reap.

**has** (hăz) *v.* 3rd person sing. present indicative of **have.**

**hash** (hăsh) *n.* **1.** Chopped meat and potatoes. **2.** A jumble; hodgepodge. —*v.* **1.** To chop up; mince. **2.** To discuss.

**has•n't** (hăz'ənt) *v.* Contraction of *has not.*

**hasp** (hăsp) *n.* A hinged metal fastener that fits over a staple.

**has•sle** (hăs′əl) *n.* **1.** An argument or fight. **2.** Trouble; bother.

**has•sock** (hăs′ək) *n.* A cushion used as a footstool.

**haste** (hāst) *n.* **1.** Swiftness. **2.** Eagerness; urgency. **3.** Careless or headlong hurrying. —**hast′i•ly** *adv.* —**hast′i•ness** *n.* —**hast′y** *adj.*

**has•ten** (hā′sən) *v.* To move or cause to move swiftly; hurry.

**hat** (hăt) *n.* A covering for the head, esp. one with a brim.

**hatch**[1] (hăch) *n.* A small door or trap door, esp. one on board a ship. —**hatch′way′** *n.*

**hatch**[2] (hăch) *v.* **1.** To emerge or cause to emerge from an egg. **2.** To cause (an egg or eggs) to produce young. —**hatch′er•y** *n.*

**hatch•back** (hăch′băk′) *n.* An automobile with a hatch in a sloping back that opens upward.

**hatch•et** (hăch′ĭt) *n.* A short-handled ax.

**hate** (hāt) *v.* **hated, hating. 1.** To loathe; detest. **2.** To dislike. —*n.* Strong dislike; animosity. —**hate′ful** *adj.* —**ha′tred** *n.*

**haugh•ty** (hô′tē) *adj.* **-tier, -tiest.** Proud and vain to the point of arrogance. —**haugh′ti•ly** *adv.* —**haugh′ti•ness** *n.*

**haul** (hôl) *v.* To pull or drag. —*n.* **1.** The act of hauling. **2.** The distance over which a load is carted or the load carted. **3.** An amount collected; a take.

**haunch** (hônch, hŏnch) *n.* The hip, buttock, and upper thigh.

**haunt** (hônt, hŏnt) *v.* **1.** To visit or appear to in the form of a ghost. **2.** To frequent. —*n.* A place much frequented.

**hau•teur** (hō-tûr′) *n.* Haughtiness; arrogance.

**have** (hăv) *v.* **had** (hăd), **having. 1.** Used as an auxiliary before a past participle to form the past, present, and future perfect tenses. **2.** To possess; own. **3.** To be obliged to. **4.** To keep. **5.** To accept or take. **6.** To be made of or contain. **7.** To experience. **8.** To give birth to. **9.** To hold in one's mind.

**ha•ven** (hā′vən) *n.* **1.** A harbor. **2.** A place of sanctuary.

**have•n't** (hăv′ənt) *v.* Contraction of *have not.*

**hav•er•sack** (hăv′ər-săk′) *n.* A canvas bag to transport supplies on a hike.

**hav•oc** (hăv′ək) *n.* Widespread destruction or confusion.

**hawk**[1] (hôk) *n.* A bird of prey.

**hawk**[2] (hôk) *v.* To peddle (wares).

**haw•ser** (hô′zər) *n.* A cable used in mooring or towing a ship.

**hay** (hā) *n.* Grass and other plants cut and dried for fodder. —*v.* To cut and process grass and other plants to make hay. —**hay′stack′** *n.*

**haz•ard** (hăz′ərd) *n.* **1.** A chance or accident. **2.** A danger; risk. —*v.* To run the risk of; venture. —**haz′ard•ous** *adj.* —**haz′ard•ous•ly** *adv.*

**haze**[1] (hāz) *n.* **1.** A foglike mixture of dust, smoke, and vapor suspended in the air. **2.** A vague state of mind. —**haz′i•ness** *n.* —**haz′y** *adj.*

**haze**[2] (hāz) *v.* **hazed, hazing.** To harass with humiliating tasks or practical jokes.

**ha•zel** (hā′zəl) *n.* **1.** A small tree bearing edible nuts. **2.** Light yellowish brown. —**ha′zel** *adj.*

**he** (hē) *pron.* **1.** The 3rd person sing. pronoun in the subjective case, masculine gender. **2.** The male person last mentioned. **3.** One whose gender is not known or not specified. —*n.* A male.

**head** (hĕd) *n.* **1.** The upper or anterior bodily extremity. **2.** Intellect; mind. **3.** A leader. **4.** The foremost position. **5.** The upper or higher end of something. —*adj.* Foremost in importance. —*v.* **1.** To be chief of. **2.** To proceed or set out.

**head•ache** (hĕd′āk′) *n.* A pain in the head. —**head′ach′y** *adj.*

**head•ing** (hĕd′ĭng) *n.* A word or words at the beginning of a chapter, paragraph, etc.

**head•light** (hĕd′līt′) *n.* A lamp on the front of a vehicle.

**head•line** (hĕd′līn′) *n.* The title of a newspaper article.

**head•long** (hĕd′lông′, -lŏng′) *adv.* **1.** With the head leading. **2.** Impetuously. **3.** At breakneck speed.

**head•quar•ters** (hĕd′kwôr′tərz) *pl.n.* A command center or center of operations.

**head•rest** (hĕd′rĕst′) *n.* A cushion or support for the head, for comfort or to prevent injury.

**head•strong** (hĕd′strông′, -strŏng′) *adj.* Willful; obstinate.

**head•way** (hĕd′wā′) *n.* Progress.

**head•y** (hĕd′ē) *adj.* **-ier, -iest. 1.** Intoxicating. **2.** Headstrong; obstinate.

**heal** (hēl) *v.* To restore or return to health.

**health** (hĕlth) *n.* **1.** The condition or functioning of an organism at any given time. **2.** Freedom from disease and abnormality. **—health′ful** *adj.* **—health′y** *adj.*

**heap** (hēp) *n.* A pile. *—v.* **1.** To put in a heap. **2.** To fill to overflowing.

**hear** (hîr) *v.* **heard** (hûrd), **hearing. 1.** To perceive by the ear. **2.** To listen attentively. **3.** To learn.

**hear•ing** (hîr′ĭng) *n.* **1.** The capacity to hear. **2.** An opportunity to be heard.

**hear•say** (hîr′sā′) *n.* Information or a rumor heard from another.

**hearse** (hûrs) *n.* A vehicle for conveying a dead body to a cemetery.

**heart** (härt) *n.* **1.** The organ that pumps blood into the arteries. **2.** The seat of emotions, as affection, compassion, courage, etc. **3.** The innermost area; essence.

**heart•ache** (härt′āk′) *n.* Emotional anguish; deep sorrow. **—heart′break′** *n.* **—heart′break′ing** *adj.*

**heart•en** (här′tn) *v.* To encourage.

**heart•felt** (härt′fĕlt′) *adj.* Deeply or sincerely felt.

**hearth** (härth) *n.* **1.** The floor of a fireplace. **2.** Family life; the home.

**heart•less** (härt′lĭs) *adj.* Pitiless; cruel.

**heart•y** (här′tē) *adj.* **-ier, -iest. 1.** Exuberant. **2.** Complete or thorough. **3.** Vigorous. **4.** Nourishing. **—heart′i•ly** *adv.*

**heat** (hēt) *n.* **1.** Hotness. **2.** The sensation of being hot. **3.** A height of feeling or energy. **4.** A time in which a female animal is ready to mate. **5.** A single course in a race or competition. *—v.* To make or become warm or hot. **—heat′er** *n.*

**heath** (hēth) *n.* An uncultivated tract of land covered with low-growing shrubs.

**hea•then** (hē′*th*ən) *n., pl.* **-thens** or **-then.** A disparaging term for a person whose religion does not acknowledge the God of Judaism, Christianity, or Islam. **—hea′then** *adj.*

**heave** (hēv) *v.* **heaved** or **hove** (hōv), **heaving. 1.** To raise or lift. **2.** To throw, esp. with great effort. **3.** To rise and fall. **4.** To utter with effort. **5.** To vomit. *—n.* The act or effort of heaving.

**heav•en** (hĕv′ən) *n.* **1.** Often **heavens.** The sky or universe as seen from the earth. **2.** The abode of God. **3.** A place or thing that affords supreme happiness. **—heav′en•ly** *adj.* **—heav′en•ward** *adv. & adj.*

**heav•y** (hĕv′ē) *adj.* **-ier, -iest. 1.** Having relatively great weight. **2.** Large in number, amount, etc.; substantial. **3.** Dense or thick. **4.** Rough; violent. **5.** Difficult or oppressive. **6.** Deeply concerned or sad. **—heav′i•ly** *adv.* **—heav′i•ness** *n.*

**heck•le** (hĕk′əl) *v.* **-led, -ling.** To harass, as with questions or objections. **—heck′ler** *n.*

**hec•tic** (hĕk′tĭk) *adj.* Marked by feverish activity, confusion, or haste.

**he'd** (hēd) *v.* **1.** Contraction of *he had.* **2.** Contraction of *he would.*

**hedge** (hĕj) *n.* A row of closely planted shrubs forming a boundary. *—v.* **hedged, hedging. 1.** To enclose with hedges. **2.** To avoid committing oneself.

**hedge•hog** (hĕj′hôg′, -hŏg′) *n.* A small mammal covered with dense spines.

**heed** (hēd) *v.* To pay attention (to). *—n.* Close attention or consideration. **—heed′ful** *adj.* **—heed′ful•ly** *adv.* **—heed′less** *adj.* **—heed′less•ly** *adv.*

**heel**[1] (hēl) *n.* **1.** The rounded rear portion of the human foot. **2.** The part of footwear that covers the heel. *—v.* To furnish with a heel.

**heel**[2] (hēl) *v.* To tip or cause to tip to one side.

**heft•y** (hĕf′tē) *adj.* **-ier, -iest. 1.** Heavy. **2.** Large and powerful. **—heft** *n.*

**heif•er** (hĕf′ər) *n.* A young cow.

**height** (hīt) *n.* **1.** The highest or uppermost point; summit. **2.** The highest or most advanced degree; zenith; climax. **3.** The distance from the base to the top; altitude. **4.** Measurement from head to foot; stature. **5.** Often **heights.** A high place.

**height•en** (hīt′n) *v.* **1.** To intensify. **2.** To make or become higher.

**hei•nous** (hā′nəs) *adj.* Reprehensible.

**heir** (âr) *n.* A male who inherits the property of another.
**heir•ess** (âr'ĭs) *n.* A female who inherits the property of another.
**heir•loom** (âr'lo͞om) *n.* A possession passed down in a family.
**held** (hĕld) *v.* p.t. & p.p. of **hold.**
**hel•i•cop•ter** (hĕl'ĭ-kŏp'tər) *n.* An aircraft with blades that rotate horizontally about a vertical central axis.
**hel•i•pad** (hĕl'ə-păd') *n.* A heliport.
**hel•i•port** (hĕl'ə-pôrt, -pōrt') *n.* A place for helicopters to land and take off.
**he•li•um** (hē'lē-əm) *n.* A colorless, odorless gaseous element used to provide lift for balloons.
**hell** (hĕl) *n.* **1.** The place of punishment for the wicked after death. **2.** Torment; anguish. **—hell'ish** *adj.*
**he'll** (hēl) *v.* **1.** Contraction of *he will.* **2.** Contraction of *he shall.*
**hel•lo** (hĕ-lō', hə-) *interj.* Expressive of greeting.
**helm** (hĕlm) *n.* The steering gear of a ship. **—helms'man** *n.*
**hel•met** (hĕl'mĭt) *n.* A protective head covering.
**help** (hĕlp) *v.* **1.** To aid. **2.** To contribute to; further. **3.** To give relief to. **4.** To avoid. *—n.* **1.** Aid; assistance. **2.** Relief; remedy. **3.** A person employed to assist. **—help'er** *n.* **—help'ful** *adj.* **—help'ful•ly** *adv.* **—help'ful•ness** *n.*
**help•ing** (hĕl'pĭng) *n.* A portion of food for one person.
**help•less** (hĕlp'lĭs) *adj.* **1.** Defenseless; dependent. **2.** Powerless. **—help'less•ly** *adv.* **—help'less•ness** *n.*
**hem** (hĕm) *n.* An edge or border of a piece of cloth. *—v.* **hemmed, hemming. 1.** To fold back and stitch down the edge of. **2.** To encircle; enclose.
**he•ma•tol•o•gy** (hē'mə-tŏl'ə-jē) *n.* The science dealing with the blood and its diseases. **—he'ma•to•log'ic, he'ma•to•log'i•cal** *adj.* **—he'ma•to•log'i•cal•ly** *adv.* **—he'ma•tol'o•gist** *n.*
**hem•i•sphere** (hĕm'ĭ-sfîr') *n.* **1.** A half of a sphere. **2.** Either the N or S half of the earth or the E or W half. **—hem'i•spher'ic, hem'i•spher'i•cal** *adj.*
**he•mo•phil•i•a** (hē'mə-fĭl'ē-ə, -fēl'yə) *n.* A hereditary disorder affecting males, characterized by excessive bleeding. **—he'mo•phil'i•ac** *n.* **—he'mo•phil'ic** *adj.*
**hem•or•rhage** (hĕm'ər-ĭj) *n.* Bleeding, esp. heavy bleeding. *—v.* **-rhaged, -rhaging.** To bleed heavily.
**hem•or•rhoid** (hĕm'ə-roid') *n.* An itching or painful mass of dilated veins in swollen anal tissue. **—hem'or•rhoid'al** *adj.*
**hemp** (hĕmp) *n.* A plant with a coarse fiber used to make rope, cord, etc.
**hen** (hĕn) *n.* A female bird, esp. of the domestic fowl.
**hence** (hĕns) *adv.* **1.** Therefore. **2.** From now. **3.** Forth from this place.
**hence•forth** (hĕns'fôrth') *adv.* Also **hence•for•ward.** From now on.
**hench•man** (hĕnch'mən) *n.* A trusted follower.
**hen•na** (hĕn'ə) *n.* A reddish-brown dye obtained from a shrub.
**hep•a•ti•tis** (hĕp'ə-tī'tĭs) *n.* Inflammation of the liver.
**her** (hûr) *pron.* The objective case of *she.* *—adj.* The possessive case of *she,* used as a modifier before a noun.
**her•ald** (hĕr'əld) *n.* One who proclaims important news or gives indication of something to come. *—v.* To proclaim; foretell. **—he•ral'dic** *adj.*
**herb** (ûrb, hûrb) *n.* **1.** A plant with a fleshy rather than woody stem. **2.** A plant used in medicine or as seasoning. **—her•ba'ceous** *adj.* **—herb'age** *n.* **—herb'al** *adj.*
**her•bi•cide** (hûr'bĭ-sīd', ûr'-) *n.* A substance used to destroy plants, esp. weeds. **—her'bi•cid'al** *adj.*
**herd** (hûrd) *n.* A group of animals that remain or are kept together. *—v.* To congregate, gather, or drive in a herd. **—herd'er** *n.* **—herds'man** *n.*
**here** (hîr) *adv.* **1.** At, in, or to this place. **2.** At this time.
**here•af•ter** (hîr-ăf'tər) *adv.* After this. *—n.* Life after death.
**here•by** (hîr-bī') *adv.* By this means.
**he•red•i•tar•y** (hə-rĕd'ĭ-tĕr'ē) *adj.* **1.** Passing down by inheritance. **2.** Genetically transmitted.
**he•red•i•ty** (hə-rĕd'ĭ-tē) *n., pl.* **-ties.** The genetic transmission of characteristics from parents to offspring.
**here•in** (hîr-ĭn') *adv.* In this.
**here's** (hîrz) *v.* Contraction of *here is.*

**her•e•sy** (hĕr'ĭ-sē) *n., pl.* **-sies.** An opinion or doctrine at variance with established beliefs, esp. religious beliefs. **—her'e•tic** *n.* **—he•ret'i•cal** *adj.*

**here•to•fore** (hîr'tə-fôr', -fōr') *adv.* Up to the present time.

**her•i•tage** (hĕr'ĭ-tĭj) *n.* **1.** Property inherited. **2.** Tradition passed down from preceding generations.

**her•maph•ro•dite** (hər-măf'rə-dīt') *n.* **1.** One having as a defect the organs and characteristics of both sexes. **2.** An organism, such as an earthworm, ordinarily possessing both male and female organs. **3.** Something composed of disparate parts. **—her•maph'ro•dit'ic** *adj.* **—her•maph'ro•dit'i•cal•ly** *adv.*

**her•met•ic** (hər-mĕt'ĭk) *adj.* Also **her•met•i•cal.** Completely sealed; airtight. **—her•met'i•cal•ly** *adv.*

**her•mit** (hûr'mĭt) *n.* One who lives in solitude and seclusion.

**he•ro** (hîr'ō) *n., pl.* **-roes.** **1.** A man noted for his courage. **2.** The principal male character in a novel, poem, or dramatic work. **—he•ro'ic** *adj.* **—her'o•ism'** *n.*

**her•o•in** (hĕr'ō-ĭn) *n.* A narcotic derived from morphine.

**her•o•ine** (hĕr'ō-ĭn) *n.* **1.** A woman noted for her courage. **2.** The principal female character in a novel, poem, or dramatic work.

**her•pes** (hûr'pēz) *n.* Any of several viral diseases affecting the skin or mucous membranes. **—her•pet'ic** *adj.*

**herpes la•bi•a•lis** (lā'bē-ā'lĭs) *n.* A cold sore.

**herpes sim•plex** (sĭm'plĕks') *n.* A viral infection affecting the lips or external genitalia.

**her•pes•vi•rus** (hûr'pēz-vī'rəs) *n.* Any of several viruses causing herpes.

**her•ring** (hĕr'ĭng) *n., pl.* **-ring** or **-rings.** A food fish of Atlantic waters.

**hers** (hûrz) *pron.* The possessive case of *she,* used by itself or as a predicate adjective.

**her•self** (hûr-sĕlf') *pron.* **1.** The reflexive form of *she.* **2.** The emphatic form of *she* or *her.*

**he's** (hēz) *v.* **1.** Contraction of *he is.* **2.** Contraction of *he has.*

**hes•i•tate** (hĕz'ĭ-tāt') *v.* **1.** To be slow to act or decide; waver. **2.** To pause briefly, as in uncertainty. **—hes'i•tan•cy** *n.* **—hes'i•tant** *adj.* **—hes'i•ta'tion** *n.*

**het•er•o•dox** (hĕt'ər-ə-dŏks') *adj.* Holding unorthodox opinions. **—het'er•o•dox'y** *n.*

**het•er•o•ge•ne•ous** (hĕt'ər-ə-jē'nē-əs, -jēn'-yəs) *adj.* Also **het•er•og•e•nous.** Having dissimilar elements; not homogeneous. **—het'er•o•ge•ne'ity** *n.*

**het•er•o•sex•u•al** (hĕt'ə-rō-sĕk'shōō-əl) *adj.* **1.** Relating to different sexes. **2.** Attracted to the opposite sex. **—het'er•o•sex'u•al** *n.* **—het'er•o•sex'u•al'i•ty, het'er•o•sex'** *n.*

**hew** (hyōō) *v.* **hewed, hewn** (hyōōn) or **hewed, hewing.** To shape or cut down with an ax.

**hex** (hĕks) *n.* An evil spell; curse. *—v.* To bring bad luck to.

**hex•a•gon** (hĕk'sə-gŏn') *n.* A polygon having six sides. **—hex•ag'o•nal** *adj.*

**hey** (hā) *interj.* **1.** Expressive of surprise. **2.** Used to attract attention.

**hey•day** (hā'dā') *n.* The period of greatest popularity, success, etc.

**hi** (hī) *interj.* Expressive of greeting.

**hi•a•tus** (hī-ā'təs) *n., pl.* **-tuses** or **-tus.** **1.** A gap. **2.** An interruption in time.

**hi•ber•nate** (hī'bər-nāt') *v.* **-nated, -nating.** To pass the winter in a dormant or torpid state. **—hi'ber•na'tion** *n.*

**hic•cup** (hĭk'ŭp, -əp) *n.* A spasm of the diaphragm resulting in a sudden inhalation quickly cut off by a spasm in the glottis. *—v.* **-cupped, -cupping.** To have such a spasm or spasms.

**hide¹** (hīd) *v.* **hid** (hĭd), **hidden** (hĭd'n) or **hid, hiding.** **1.** To put or keep out of sight; conceal. **2.** To seek refuge.

**hide²** (hīd) *n.* The skin of an animal.

**hide•bound** (hīd'bound') *adj.* **1.** Having dry, stiff, tough skin adhering closely to the flesh. **2.** Stubbornly narrow-minded and inflexible.

**hid•e•ous** (hĭd'ē-əs) *adj.* **1.** Physically repulsive; ugly. **2.** Despicable.

**hi•er•ar•chy** (hī'ə-rär'kē, hī'rär'-) *n., pl.* **-chies.** A body of persons, esp. clergy, classified according to rank or authority. **—hi'er•ar'chi•cal, hi'er•ar'chic** *adj.*

**hier•o•glyph•ic** (hī′ər-ə-glĭf′ĭk, hī′rə-) *n.* A picture or symbol used in writing, esp. in the writing system of ancient Egypt.

**high** (hī) *adj.* **1.** Tall; elevated. **2.** Above average, as in degree, amount, etc. **3.** Piercing in tone or sound. **4.** Costly; expensive. **5.** Excited; elated. **6.** Being at or near its peak. **7.** Of great importance. *—adj.* At, in, or to a high position, price, or level. *—n.* **1.** A high degree, level, point, etc. **2.** The transmission gear giving the greatest output speed. **—high′ly** *adv.*

**high•flown** (hī′flōn′) *adj.* **1.** Lofty; exalted. **2.** Pretentious.

**high•hand•ed** (hī′hăn′dĭd) *adj.* In an arrogant or arbitrary manner.

**high•light** (hī′līt′) *n.* An outstanding event or prominent detail. *—v.* **1.** To give prominence to. **2.** To be the highlight of.

**high-rise** (hī′rīz′) *adj.* **1.** Relating to a multistoried building with elevators. **2.** Relating to a bicycle with long handlebars. **—high′-rise′** *n.*

**high-strung** (hī′strŭng′) *adj.* Acutely nervous.

**high-tech** (hī′tĕk′) *adj.* Relating to highly advanced, specialized technology. **—high tech** *n.*

**high•way** (hī′wā′) *n.* A main public road.

**hi•jack** (hī′jăk′) *v.* **1.** To rob (a vehicle) by stopping it in transit. **2.** To seize or commandeer (a moving vehicle). **—hi′jack′er** *n.*

**hike** (hīk) *v.* **hiked, hiking. 1.** To go on an extended walk. **2.** To raise or go up. *—n.* **1.** A walk. **2.** A rise, as in prices. **—hik′er** *n.*

**hi•lar•i•ous** (hĭ-lâr′ē-əs, hī-) *adj.* Boisterously funny. **—hi•lar′i•ty** *n.*

**hill** (hĭl) *n.* A naturally elevated area of land smaller than a mountain. **—hill′side′** *n.* **—hill′top′** *n.* **—hill′y** *adj.*

**hilt** (hĭlt) *n.* The handle of a weapon or tool.

**him** (hĭm) *pron.* The objective case of *he.*

**him•self** (hĭm-sĕlf′) *pron.* **1.** The reflexive form of *he.* **2.** The emphatic form of *he* or *him.*

**hind**[1] (hīnd) *adj.* Located at the rear; posterior.

**hind**[2] (hīnd) *n.* A female deer.

**hin•der** (hĭn′dər) *v.* **1.** To hamper. **2.** To prevent. **—hin′drance** *n.*

**hind•most** (hīnd′mōst′) *adj.* Farthest to the rear.

**Hin•du•ism** (hĭn′do͞o-ĭz′əm) *n.* The major religion of India. **—Hin′du** *n. & adj.*

**hinge** (hĭnj) *n.* A jointed device on which a door, gate, etc., turns or swings. *—v.* **hinged, hinging. 1.** To attach by a hinge. **2.** To depend.

**hint** (hĭnt) *n.* A subtle suggestion; clue. *—v.* To give a hint.

**hip** (hĭp) *n.* The laterally projecting prominence of the pelvis from the waist to the thigh.

**hip•po•drome** (hĭp′ə-drōm′) *n.* An arena.

**hip•po•pot•a•mus** (hĭp′ə-pŏt′ə-məs) *n., pl.* **-muses** or **-mi.** A large African river mammal.

**hire** (hīr) *v.* **hired, hiring. 1.** To engage the services of (a person) for a fee; employ. **2.** To rent or rent out. *—n.* The payment for services or use of something.

**hir•sute** (hûr′so͞ot′, hîr′-, hər-so͞ot′) *adj.* Hairy.

**his** (hĭz) *adj.* The possessive case of *he,* used as a modifier before a noun.

**His•pan•ic** (hĭ-spăn′ĭk) *adj.* **1.** Relating to Spain or Spanish-speaking America. **2.** Relating to a Spanish-speaking people or culture. *—n.* **1.** A Spanish-speaking person. **2.** A U.S. citizen or resident of Hispanic descent.

**hiss** (hĭs) *n.* A sharp, sibilant sound similar to a sustained *s.* *—v.* **1.** To make a hiss. **2.** To direct hisses at in disapproval.

**his•to•ry** (hĭs′tə-rē) *n., pl.* **-ries. 1.** A chronological record of events. **2.** The branch of knowledge that analyzes past events. **—his•to′ri•an** *n.* **—his•tor′ic, his•tor′i•cal** *adj.* **—his•tor′i•cal•ly** *adv.*

**his•tri•on•ic** (hĭs′trē-ŏn′ĭk) *adj.* Theatrical; affected. *—n.* **histrionics.** Showy, exaggerated emotional behavior.

**hit** (hĭt) *v.* **hit, hitting. 1.** To come or cause to come in contact with; strike. **2.** To affect adversely. **3.** To propel with a blow. **4.** To get to; reach. *—n.* **1.** A collision or impact. **2.** A shot, blow, or throw. **3.** A successful or popular venture. **—hit′ter** *n.*

**hitch** (hĭch) *v.* **1.** To fasten with a loop, hook, or noose. **2.** To connect or attach. **3.** To raise with a tug or jerk. *—n.* **1.** A short jerking motion. **2.** An impediment or delay. **3.** A term of military service.

**hith•er** (hĭ*th*′ər) *adv.* To or toward this place.

**hith•er•to** (hĭ*th*′ər-to͞o′) *adv.* Until this time.

**HIV** *n.* A retrovirus that causes AIDS.

**hive** (hīv) *n.* **1.** A structure for housing bees, esp. honeybees. **2.** A colony of bees.

**HMO** *n., pl.* **HMOs.** A medical insurance plan for enrolled members and their families.

**hoard** (hôrd, hōrd) *n.* A supply for future use; cache. *—v.* To save, keep, or store away. **—hoard′er** *n.*

**hoarse** (hôrs, hōrs) *adj.* **hoarser, hoarsest.** Grating in sound; husky; croaking.

**hoar•y** (hôr′ē, hōr′ē) *adj.* **-ier, -iest. 1.** White or grayish. **2.** Very old; aged.

**hoax** (hōks) *n.* A trick or action intended to deceive. *—v.* To deceive or cheat by a hoax.

**hob•ble** (hŏb′əl) *v.* **-bled, -bling. 1.** To limp. **2.** To fetter; restrain.

**hob•by** (hŏb′ē) *n., pl.* **-bies.** A pastime.

**hob•nob** (hŏb′nŏb′) *v.* **-nobbed, -nobbing.** To associate familiarly (with *with*).

**ho•bo** (hō′bō) *n., pl.* **-boes** or **-bos.** A tramp; vagrant.

**hock**[1] (hŏk) *n.* The joint of the hind leg of a horse or other four-footed animal.

**hock**[2] (hŏk) *v.* To pawn.

**hock•ey** (hŏk′ē) *n.* A game played on ice with curved sticks and a puck.

**hod** (hŏd) *n.* **1.** A trough for transporting loads, as of bricks. **2.** A coal scuttle.

**hoe** (hō) *n.* A tool used for weeding, cultivating, and gardening. **—hoe** *v.*

**hog** (hôg, hŏg) *n.* **1.** A pig. **2.** A greedy or selfish person. *—v.* **hogged, hogging.** To take more than one's share of.

**hogs•head** (hôgz′hĕd′, hŏgz′-) *n.* A large barrel or cask.

**hoist** (hoist) *v.* To raise or haul up. *—n.* **1.** A device for hoisting. **2.** A pull; lift.

**hold**[1] (hōld) *v.* **held** (hĕld), **holding. 1.** To have and keep in possession; grasp; clasp. **2.** To bear; support. **3.** To contain. **4.** To restrain. **5.** To believe; assert; affirm. **6.** To stand up under stress; last. *—n.* **1.** A grip; clasp. **2.** A strong influence. **—hold′er** *n.*

**hold**[2] (hōld) *n.* The interior of a ship where cargo is stored.

**hold•ing** (hōl′dĭng) *n.* **1.** Land rented or leased. **2.** Often **holdings.** Legally possessed property.

**hole** (hōl) *n.* **1.** A cavity. **2.** An opening; gap. **3.** An animal's burrow.

**hol•i•day** (hŏl′ĭ-dā′) *n.* A day on which a particular event is celebrated. **—hol′i•day** *adj.*

**hol•ler** (hŏl′ər) *v.* To yell or shout.

**hol•low** (hŏl′ō) *adj.* **1.** Having a cavity within. **2.** Concave; sunken. **3.** Without substance or validity. *—n.* **1.** A cavity. **2.** A valley. *—v.* To make or become hollow.

**hol•ly** (hŏl′ē) *n., pl.* **-lies.** A shrub bearing bright-red berries.

**hol•o•caust** (hŏl′ə-kôst′, hō′lə-) *n.* Great or total destruction, esp. by fire.

**hol•o•gram** (hŏl′ə-grăm′, hō′lə-) *n.* The visible 3-dimensional image produced by holography.

**hol•o•graph** (hŏl′ə-grăf′, hō′lə-) *n.* **1.** A manuscript written wholly and signed by the author. **2.** A hologram.

**ho•log•raph•y** (hō-lŏg′rə-fē) *n.* The technique of using lasers to record an image on a plate from which a 3-dimensional image can be projected.

**hol•ster** (hōl′stər) *n.* A leather case for a pistol.

**ho•ly** (hō′lē) *adj.* **-lier, -liest. 1.** Associated with a divine power; sacred. **2.** Blessed. **3.** Saintly. **4.** Regarded with special respect. **—ho′li•ness** *n.*

**hom•age** (hŏm′ĭj, ŏm′-) *n.* Honor or respect publicly expressed.

**home** (hōm) *n.* **1.** The place where one resides. **2.** A family living in a dwelling; household. **3.** A customary environment; habitat. **4.** A place of origin. *—adj.* Of a household or house. *—adv.* **1.** At or to one's home. **2.** To the center or heart of something. **—home′ward** *adv. & adj.* **—home′y** *adj.*

**home•ly** (hōm′lē) *adj.* **-lier, -liest. 1.** Familiar. **2.** Not pretty; plain.

**home•spun** (hōm′spŭn′) *adj.* **1.** Spun or woven at home. **2.** Simple; unpretentious. —*n.* A coarse woolen cloth.

**hom•i•cide** (hŏm′ĭ-sīd′, hō′mĭ-) *n.* **1.** The killing of one person by another. **2.** A person who kills another. —**hom′i•ci′dal** *adj.*

**hom•i•ly** (hŏm′ə-lē) *n., pl.* **-lies.** A sermon.

**ho•mo•ge•ne•ous** (hō′mə-jē′nē-əs, -jēn′yəs) *adj.* Uniform in composition throughout. —**ho′mo•ge•ne′i•ty** *n.* —**ho′mo•ge′ne•ous•ly** *ad.* —**ho•mog′e•nize′** *v.*

**ho•mo•sex•u•al** (hō′mə-sĕk′sho͞o-əl, -mō-) *adj.* Relating to or having sexual attraction for members of one's own sex; gay; lesbian. —**ho′mo•sex′u•al** *n.* —**ho′mo•sex′u•al′i•ty** *n.*

**hone** (hōn) *n.* A fine-grained whetstone. —*v.* **honed, honing.** To sharpen on a hone.

**hon•est** (ŏn′ĭst) *adj.* **1.** Truthful and trustworthy. **2.** Not deceptive; genuine. **3.** Frank; sincere. —**hon′est•ly** *adv.* —**hon′es•ty** *n.*

**hon•ey** (hŭn′ē) *n., pl.* **-eys.** A sweet fluid produced by bees.

**hon•ey•comb** (hŭn′ē-kōm′) *n.* A wax structure made by honeybees to hold honey. —*v.* To fill with holes; riddle.

**hon•ey•moon** (hŭn′ē-mo͞on′) *n.* A trip taken by a newly married couple. —*v.* To spend a honeymoon.

**hon•or** (ŏn′ər) *n.* **1.** Esteem; respect. **2.** Glory; distinction. **3.** Great privilege. **4.** Personal integrity. —*v.* **1.** To esteem; show respect for. **2.** To confer distinction upon. **3.** To accept or pay as valid, as a check. —**hon′or•a•ble** *adj.* —**hon′or•a•bly** *adv.*

**hon•o•rar•i•um** (ŏn′ə-râr′ē-əm) *n., pl.* **-iums** or **-ia.** Payment to a professional person for services for which fees are not legally required.

**hon•or•ar•y** (ŏn′ə-rĕr′ē) *adj.* Conferred as an honor without the usual duties, privileges, etc.

**hood** (ho͝od) *n.* **1.** A loose covering for the head. **2.** The metal lid over an automobile engine. —**hood′ed** *adj.*

**hood•lum** (ho͞od′ləm, ho͝od′-) *n.* A thug.

**hood•wink** (ho͝od′wĭngk′) *v.* To deceive; trick.

**hoof** (ho͝of, ho͞of) *n., pl.* **hoofs** or **hooves** (ho͝ovz, ho͞ovz). The horny covering of the feet of horses, cattle, etc.

**hook** (ho͝ok) *n.* A curved device, usually of metal, used to catch, drag, or fasten something. —*v.* To get hold of with a hook.

**hoop** (ho͞op, ho͝op) *n.* A circular band.

**hoot** (ho͞ot) *v.* **1.** To utter the cry of an owl. **2.** To make a derisive cry. —*n.* **1.** The cry of an owl. **2.** A cry of derision.

**hooves** (ho͝ovz, ho͞ovz) *n.* A pl. of **hoof.**

**hop** (hŏp) *v.* **hopped, hopping.** To jump, esp. on one foot. —*n.* A light, springy jump, esp. on one foot.

**hope** (hōp) *v.* **hoped, hoping.** To desire (something) with confidence of fulfillment. —*n.* **1.** A desire supported by confidence of its fulfillment. **2.** That which is desired. **3.** Expectation; confidence. —**hope′ful** *adj.* —**hope′ful•ly** *adv.* —**hope′less** *adj.* —**hope′less•ly** *adv.* —**hope′less•ness** *n.*

**hop•per** (hŏp′ər) *n.* A receptacle in which materials are stored.

**horde** (hôrd, hōrd) *n.* A throng or swarm.

**ho•ri•zon** (hə-rī′zən) *n.* The apparent intersection of the earth and sky.

**hor•i•zon•tal** (hôr′ĭ-zŏn′tl, hŏr′-) *adj.* **1.** Parallel to the plane of the horizon. **2.** Flat.

**hor•mone** (hôr′mōn′) *n.* A substance formed by one organ that stimulates another to function. —**hor•mo′nal** *adj.*

**horn** (hôrn) *n.* **1.** One of the hard structures projecting from the head of cattle, sheep, etc. **2.** A wind instrument made of brass. —**horned** *adj.* —**horn′y** *adj.*

**hor•net** (hôr′nĭt) *n.* A large wasp.

**hor•o•scope** (hôr′ə-skōp′, hŏr′-) *n.* An astrological forecast of a person's future.

**hor•ren•dous** (hô-rĕn′dəs, hə-) *adj.* Hideous; dreadful.

**hor•ri•ble** (hôr′ə-bəl, hŏr′-) *adj.* **1.** Causing horror. **2.** Unpleasant. —**hor′ri•bly** *adv.*

**hor•rid** (hôr′ĭd, hŏr′-) *adj.* **1.** Causing horror. **2.** Unpleasant, disagreeable, etc. —**hor′rid•ly** *adv.*

**hor•ror** (hôr′ər, hŏr′-) *n.* **1.** An intense feeling of repugnance and fear; terror.

**2.** Intense dislike; abhorrence. **—hor′ri•fy′** *v.*

**hors de combat** (ôr də kôN-bä′) *adj. & adv.* Out of action; disabled.

**hors d'oeuvre** (ôr dûrv′) *n., pl.* **hors d'oeuvres** or **hors d'oeuvre.** An appetizer served before a meal.

**horse** (hôrs) *n.* **1.** A large hoofed mammal used for riding, carrying loads, etc. **2.** A supportive device.

**horse•back** (hôrs′băk′) *adv.* On the back of a horse.

**horse•pow•er** (hôrs′pou′ər) *n.* A unit of power equal to 745.7 watts.

**horse•shoe** (hôrs′sho͞o′, hôrsh′-) *n.* A U-shaped iron plate nailed to a horse's hoof.

**hor•ti•cul•ture** (hôr′tĭ-kŭl′chər) *n.* The science of cultivating plants. **—hor′ti•cul′tur•al** *adj.* **—hor′ti•cul′tur•ist** *n.*

**hose** (hōz) *n.* **1.** *pl.* **hose.** Stockings or socks. **2.** *pl.* **hoses.** A flexible tube for spraying water. *—v.* **hosed, hosing.** To water with a hose.

**ho•sier•y** (hō′zhə-rē) *n.* Hose.

**hos•pice** (hŏs′pĭs) *n.* **1.** A shelter for travelers, children, etc., maintained by monks. **2.** A shelter or program for terminally ill patients.

**hos•pi•ta•ble** (hŏs′pĭ-tə-bəl, hŏ-spĭt′ə-bəl) *adj.* Cordial and generous to guests. **—hos′pi•tal′i•ty** *n.*

**hos•pi•tal** (hŏs′pĭ-tl, -pĭt′l) *n.* An institution providing treatment for the sick and injured. **—hos′pi•tal•i•za′tion** *n.* **—hos′pi•tal•ize′** *v.*

**host**[1] (hōst) *n.* One who entertains guests.

**host**[2] (hōst) *n.* A great number.

**host**[3] (hōst) *n.* Also **Host.** The consecrated bread of the Eucharist.

**hos•tage** (hŏs′tĭj) *n.* A person held as a security.

**hos•tel** (hŏs′təl) *n.* **1.** Inexpensive, supervised lodging, esp. for young people. **2.** An inn.

**host•ess** (hō′stĭs) *n.* A female who entertains guests.

**hos•tile** (hŏs′təl, -tīl′) *adj.* **1.** Of an enemy. **2.** Feeling or showing enmity.

**hos•til•i•ty** (hŏ-stĭl′ĭ-tē) *n., pl.* **-ties. 1.** Antagonism; enmity. **2. hostilities.** Open warfare.

**hot** (hŏt) *adj.* **hotter, hottest. 1.** Being at a high temperature. **2.** Warmer than is normal or desirable. **3.** Spicy. **4.** Angry. **5.** Currently popular. **—hot′ly** *adv.*

**ho•tel** (hō-tĕl′) *n.* A public house that provides lodging and board.

**hot•head•ed** (hŏt′hĕd′ĭd) *adj.* **1.** Having a fiery temper. **2.** Impetuous; rash. **—hot′head′** *n.*

**hot•house** (hŏt′hous′) *n.* A greenhouse.

**hot line** *n.* **1.** A direct communications link, esp. between government heads, to use in a crisis. **2.** A telephone line enabling a caller to talk confidentially about a personal problem.

**hound** (hound) *n.* A dog originally bred and used for hunting. *—v.* To pursue relentlessly.

**hour** (our) *n.* **1.** The 24th part of a day. **2.** The time of day. **3.** A customary or specified time. **—hour′ly** *adj. & adv.*

**house** (hous) *n., pl.* **houses. 1.** A building used as a dwelling. **2.** A household. **3.** A commercial firm. **4.** A legislative assembly. *—v.* **housed, housing. 1.** To provide living quarters for. **2.** To contain.

**house•hold** (hous′hōld′) *n.* The members of a family and others living under the same roof. **—house′hold′** *adj.*

**house•keep•er** (hous′kē′pər) *n.* One who has charge of domestic tasks in a house. **—house′keep′ing** *n.*

**house•wife** (hous′wīf′) *n.* A woman who manages her own house.

**hous•ing** (hou′zĭng) *n.* **1.** A dwelling or dwellings collectively. **2.** A protective covering, as for a mechanical part.

**hov•el** (hŭv′əl, hŏv′-) *n.* A small, miserable dwelling.

**hov•er** (hŭv′ər, hŏv′-) *v.* **1.** To fly or float as if suspended. **2.** To linger close to a place.

**how** (hou) *adv.* **1.** In what manner or way. **2.** In what state or condition. **3.** To what extent, amount, or degree. **4.** For what purpose.

**how•ev•er** (hou-ev′ər) *adv.* **1.** By whatever manner or means. **2.** To whatever degree or extent. *—conj.* Nevertheless; yet.

**howl** (houl) *v.* **1.** To utter a long, wailing cry. **2.** To laugh heartily. *—n.* A long, wailing cry.

**hub** (hŭb) *n.* **1.** The center portion of a wheel. **2.** A center of activity.

**hub•bub** (hŭb′ŭb′) *n.* A confused din.

**hu•bris** (hyōō′brĭs) *n.* Overbearing pride.

**huck•le•ber•ry** (hŭk′əl-bĕr′ē) *n.* A blackish, edible berry resembling a blueberry.

**huck•ster** (hŭk′stər) *n.* A peddler.

**hud•dle** (hŭd′l) *v.* **-dled, -dling. 1.** To crowd in a close group. **2.** To hunch up; crouch.

**hue** (hyōō) *n.* Color; tint; shade.

**huff** (hŭf) *n.* A fit of anger. —*v.* To blow; breathe heavily. —**huff′y** *adj.*

**hug** (hŭg) *v.* **hugged, hugging. 1.** To clasp; embrace. **2.** To keep close to. —*n.* A close embrace.

**huge** (hyōōj) *adj.* **huger, hugest.** Very large; enormous. —**huge′ness** *n.*

**hulk** (hŭlk) *n.* **1.** The hull of a ship, esp. an old or wrecked ship. **2.** A large, clumsy person or object. —**hulk′ing** *adj.*

**hull** (hŭl) *n.* **1.** The outer covering of a fruit, seed, or nut. **2.** The main body of a ship. —*v.* To remove the hulls of (fruit or seeds).

**hum** (hŭm) *v.* **hummed, humming. 1.** To produce a continuous droning sound. **2.** To sing with closed lips. —*n.* A continuous droning sound.

**hu•man** (hyōō′mən) *adj.* Relating to people. —*n.* Also **human being.** A person. —**hu′man•ly** *adv.*

**hu•mane** (hyōō-mān′) *adj.* Compassionate; kind. —**hu•mane′ly** *adv.*

**hu•man•i•tar•i•an** (hyōō-măn′ĭ-târ′ē-ən) *n.* One devoted to the promotion of human welfare. —*adj.* Concerned with human welfare.

**hu•man•i•ty** (hyōō-măn′ĭ-tē) *n.* **1.** The human race. **2.** The condition of being human. **3.** Kindness; mercy.

**hum•ble** (hŭm′bəl) *adj.* **-bler, -blest. 1.** Modest; meek. **2.** Deeply respectful. **3.** Lowly. —*v.* **-bled, -bling.** To abase. —**hum′bly** *adv.*

**hum•bug** (hŭm′bŭg′) *n.* **1.** A hoax. **2.** Nonsense.

**hum•drum** (hŭm′drŭm′) *adj.* Monotonous; uneventful.

**hu•mid** (hyōō′mĭd) *adj.* Having a high concentration of moisture. —**hu•mid′i•fy** *v.* —**hu•mid′i•ty** *n.*

**hu•mil•i•ate** (hyōō-mĭl′ē-āt′) *v.* **-ated, -ating.** To destroy the dignity or pride of; shame; disgrace. —**hu•mil′i•a′tion** *n.*

**hu•mil•i•ty** (hyōō-mĭl′ĭ-tē) *n.* The quality of being humble.

**hu•mor** (hyōō′mər) *n.* **1.** The quality of being comical. **2.** The ability to perceive, enjoy, etc., what is comical. **3.** State of mind; mood. —*v.* To indulge. —**hu′mor•ist** *n.* —**hu′mor•ous** *adj.*

**hump** (hŭmp) *n.* A rounded protuberance. —*v.* To make into a hump; round.

**hunch** (hŭnch) *v.* To arch into a hump. —*n.* A strong feeling or guess; premonition.

**hunch•back** (hŭnch′băk′) *n.* One having an abnormally humped back.

**hun•dred** (hŭn′drĭd) *n., pl.* **-dreds** or **-dred.** The cardinal number written 100. —**hun′dred** *adj. & pron.* —**hun′dredth** *n. & adj.*

**hung** (hŭng) *v.* Alternate p.t. & p.p. of **hang.**

**hun•ger** (hŭng′gər) *n.* **1.** A strong desire or need for food. **2.** A strong desire; craving. —*v.* **1.** To be hungry. **2.** To desire; yearn. —**hun′gri•ly** *adv.* —**hun′gry** *adj.*

**hunk** (hŭngk) *n.* A large piece; chunk.

**hunt** (hŭnt) *v.* **1.** To pursue (animals) for food, sport, etc. **2.** To search for; seek. —*n.* **1.** The act or sport of hunting. **2.** A search or pursuit. —**hunt′er** *n.* —**hunt′ress** *n.*

**hur•dle** (hûr′dl) *n.* **1.** A barrier in obstacle races. **2.** Any obstacle or problem that must be overcome. —*v.* **-dled, -dling.** To jump over (a barrier). —**hur′dler** *n.*

**hurl** (hûrl) *v.* To throw forcefully; fling.

**hur•rah** (hōō-rä′, -rô′) *interj.* Also **hoo•ray, hur•ray.** Expressive of elation, approval, etc. —**hur•rah′** *n.*

**hur•ri•cane** (hûr′ĭ-kān′) *n.* A severe tropical cyclone.

**hur•ry** (hûr′ē) *v.* **-ried, -rying.** To move or cause to move with speed or haste; rush. —*n., pl.* **-ries.** Haste; a rush. —**hur′ried•ly** *adv.*

**hurt** (hûrt) *v.* **hurt, hurting. 1.** To feel or cause to feel physical pain. **2.** To offend or distress. **3.** To damage; harm. —*n.* Something that hurts; a pain, injury, or wound. —**hurt′ful** *adj.*

**hur•tle** (hûr′tl) *v.* **-tled, -tling. 1.** To move with forceful speed. **2.** To collide violently; crash.

**hus•band** (hŭz′bənd) *n.* A male spouse. —*v.* To spend or use wisely.

**hus•band•ry** (hŭz′bən-drē) *n.* **1.** Farming; agriculture. **2.** Careful management.

**hush** (hŭsh) *v.* To make or become silent. —*n.* A silence; stillness.

**husk** (hŭsk) *n.* A dry or leaflike outer covering, as of an ear of corn. —*v.* To remove the husk from.

**husk•y**[1] (hŭs′kē) *adj.* **-ier, -iest.** Hoarse.

**husk•y**[2] (hŭs′kē) *adj.* **-ier, -iest.** Large and strong.

**hus•tle** (hŭs′əl) *v.* **-tled, -tling. 1.** To jostle; shove. **2.** To hurry along. **3.** To work busily and quickly. —*n.* Energetic activity.

**hut** (hŭt) *n.* A makeshift or crude dwelling; shack.

**hutch** (hŭch) *n.* **1.** A coop for small animals. **2.** A cupboard with open shelves above it.

**hy•a•cinth** (hī′ə-sĭnth) *n.* A plant with fragrant flowers.

**hy•brid** (hī′brĭd) *n.* The offspring of genetically dissimilar parents or stock. —**hy′brid** *adj.*

**hy•drant** (hī′drənt) *n.* An upright pipe serving as an outlet from a water main.

**hy•drau•lic** (hī-drô′lĭk) *adj.* **1.** Of or operated by a fluid, esp. water, under pressure. **2.** Of hydraulics. —*n.* **hydraulics** *(takes sing. v.).* The physical science and technology of the behavior of fluids.

**hy•dro•car•bon** (hī′drə-kär′bən) *n.* Any organic compound containing only carbon and hydrogen.

**hy•dro•e•lec•tric** (hī′drō-ĭ-lĕk′trĭk) *adj.* Generating electricity from the energy of running or falling water.

**hy•dro•gen** (hī′drə-jən) *n.* A colorless, highly flammable gaseous element used in rocket fuels.

**hy•dro•pho•bi•a** (hī′drə-fō′bē-ə) *n.* Rabies.

**hy•dro•plane** (hī′drə-plān′) *n.* **1.** A seaplane. **2.** A high-speed motorboat that skims the water.

**hy•e•na** (hī-ē′nə) *n.* A carnivorous African or Asian mammal.

**hy•giene** (hī′jēn′) *n.* The science of health and the prevention of disease. —**hy′gi•en′ic** *adj.*

**hymn** (hĭm) *n.* A song of praise, esp. to a deity.

**hym•nal** (hĭm′nəl) *n.* A book of hymns.

**hy•per•bo•le** (hī-pûr′bə-lē) *n.* Exaggeration used as a figure of speech.

**hy•per•link** (hī′pər-lĭngk) *n.* A text segment or image that serves as a cross-reference, as between hypertext documents.

**hy•per•text** (hī′pər-tĕkst) *n.* A text retrieval system that provides access to locations in webpages by clicking on embedded hyperlinks.

**hy•per•ten•sion** (hī′pər-tĕn′shən) *n.* Abnormally high blood pressure.

**hy•per•ven•ti•late** (hī′pər-vĕn′tl-āt′) *v.* **-lated, -lating.** To breathe abnormally fast and deeply, esp. to the fainting point. —**hy′per•ven′ti•la′tion** *n.*

**hy•phen** (hī′fən) *n.* A punctuation mark (-) used between parts of a compound word or between syllables of a divided word.

**hyp•no•sis** (hĭp-nō′sĭs) *n.* An artificially induced sleeplike condition. —**hyp•not′ic** *adj.* —**hyp′no•tism′** *n.* —**hyp′no•tize′** *v.*

**hy•po•al•ler•gen•ic** (hī′pō-ăl′ər-jĕn′ĭk) *adj.* Designed to provoke little or no allergic reaction.

**hy•po•chon•dri•a** (hī′pə-kŏn′drē-ə) *n.* The persistent conviction that one is or is likely to become ill. —**hy′po•chon′dri•ac′** *n. & adj.*

**hy•poc•risy** (hĭ-pŏk′rĭ-sē) *n.* The feigning of beliefs, feelings, or virtues one does not hold. —**hyp′o•crite′** *n.* —**hyp′o•crit′i•cal** *adj.*

**hy•po•der•mic** (hī′pə-dûr′mĭk) *adj.* Injected beneath the skin. —*n.* A hypodermic injection.

**hy•pot•e•nuse** (hī-pŏt′n/y/o͞os′) *n.* The side of a right triangle opposite the right angle.

**hy•poth•e•sis** (hī-pŏth′ĭ-sĭs) *n., pl.* **-ses.** An assumption subject to verification or proof. —**hy•poth′e•size′** *v.* —**hy′po•thet′i•cal** *adj.*

**hys•ter•i•a** (hĭ-stĕr′ē-ə) *n.* Uncontrollable fear or other strong emotion. —**hys•ter′i•cal** *adj.* —**hys•ter′i•cal•ly** *adv.*

**hys•ter•ics** (hĭ-stĕr′ĭks) *n.* A fit of uncontrollable laughing and crying.

# — I —

**i, I** (ī) *n.* The 9th letter of the English alphabet.

**I** (ī) *pron.* The 1st person sing. pronoun in the subjective case.

**i•bi•dem** (ĭb′ĭ-dĕm′, ĭ-bī′dəm) Also **ibid.** *adv.* In the same place.

**i•bu•pro•fen** (ī′byo͞o-prō′fən) *n.* **1.** A substance used in medicine to relieve fever, pain, and inflammation. **2.** A tablet of this substance.

**ice** (īs) *n.* **1.** Frozen water. **2.** A dessert of flavored crushed ice. —*v.* **iced, icing. 1.** To chill. **2.** To cover with ice or icing. —**i′ci•ly** *adv.* —**i′cy** *adj.*

**ich•thy•ol•o•gy** (ĭk′thē-ŏl′ə-jē) *n.* The study of fishes. —**ich′thy•o•log′gic, ich′thy•o•log′i•cal** *adj.* —**ich′thy•ol′-o•gist** *n.*

**i•ci•cle** (īsĭ-kəl) *n.* A tapering spike of ice.

**i•con•o•clast** (ī-kŏn′ə-klăst′) *n.* **1.** One who destroys sacred images. **2.** One who destroys popular or traditional ideas. —**i•con′o•clasm** *n.* —**i•con′o•clas′tic** *adj.*

**ICU** *abbr.* Intensive care unit.

**I'd** (īd) *v.* **1.** Contraction of *I had.* **2.** Contraction of *I would.*

**i•de•a** (ī-dē′ə) *n.* **1.** A mental conception; thought. **2.** An opinion. **3.** A plan or method. —**i′de•a′tion•al** *adj.*

**i•de•al** (ī-dē′əl, ī-dēl′) *n.* **1.** A standard or model of absolute perfection. **2.** An honorable principle. —*adj.* **1.** Perfect or nearly perfect. **2.** Existing only in the mind. —**i•de′al•ly** *adv.*

**i•de•al•ism** (ī-dē′ə-lĭz′əm) *n.* Seeing things in ideal forms rather than as they actually are. —**i•de′al•list** *n.* —**i•de′al•is′tic** *adj.* —**i•de′al•ize′** *v.*

**i•den•ti•cal** (ī-dĕn′tĭ-kəl) *adj.* The same; equal. —**i•den′ti•cal•ly** *adv.*

**i•den•ti•fy** (ī-dĕn′tə-fī′) *v.* **-fied, -fying. 1.** To establish the identify of. **2.** To consider as identical; equate. **3.** To associate (oneself) with. —**i•den′ti•fi′•a•ble** *adj.* —**i•den′ti•fi•ca′tion** *n.*

**i•den•ti•ty** (ī-dĕn′tĭ-tē) *n., pl.* **-ties. 1.** The set of characteristics by which a person or thing is known. **2.** Individuality.

**i•de•ol•o•gy** (ī′dē-ŏl′ə-jē, ĭd′ē-) *n., pl.* **-gies.** The body of ideas forming the basis of an individual, group, or culture. —**i′de•o•log′i•cal** *adj.*

**id est** (ĭd ĕst′) Also **i.e.** That is.

**id•i•ot** (ĭd′ē-ət) *n.* **1.** A mentally deficient person. **2.** An imbecile; blockhead. —**id′i•o•cy** *n.* —**id′i•ot′ic** *adj.*

**i•dle** (īd′l) *adj.* **idler, idlest. 1.** Inactive. **2.** Lazy. **3.** Useless or groundless. —*v.* **idled, idling.** To pass time without working. —**i•dly** *adv.*

**i•dol** (īd′l) *n.* **1.** An image of a deity; false god. **2.** One that is adored. —**i•dol′a•try** *n.* —**i′dol•ize′** *v.*

**i•dyll, i•dyl** (īd′l) *n.* **1.** A literary work praising rustic life. **2. a.** A carefree experience. **b.** A romantic interlude. —**i•dyl′lic** *adj.* —**i•dyl′li•cal•ly** *adv.* —**i•dyl′list** *n.*

**i.e.** *abbr.* Id est: that is.

**if** (ĭf) *conj.* **1.** In the event that. **2.** Even though. **3.** Whether.

**ig•nite** (ĭg-nīt′) *v.* **-nited, -niting.** To cause or begin to burn. —**ig•ni′tion** *n.*

**ig•no•min•i•ous** (ĭg′nə-mĭn′ē-əs) *adj.* **1.** Dishonorable; despicable. **2.** Humiliating; degrading. —**ig′no•min′i•ous•ly** *adv.* —**ig′no•min′y** *n.*

**ig•no•rant** (ĭg′nər-ənt) *adj.* **1.** Without education or knowledge. **2.** Unaware or uninformed. —**ig′no•rance** *n.* —**ig′-no•rant•ly** *adv.*

**ig•nore** (ĭg-nôr′, -nōr′) *v.* **-nored, -noring.** To disregard.

**ill** (ĭl) *adj.* **worse** (wûrs), **worst** (wûrst). **1.** Not healthy; sick. **2.** Unfavorable. **3.** Hostile. **4.** Cruel. —*adv.* **worse, worst. 1.** Not well. **2.** With difficulty. —*n.* **1.** Evil. **2.** Disaster or harm.

**I'll** (īl) *v.* Contraction of *I will.*

**il•le•gal** (ĭ-lē′gəl) *adj.* Prohibited by law. —**il′le•gal′i•ty** *n.* —**il•le′gal•ly** *adv.*

**il•le•git•i•mate** (ĭl′ĭ-jĭt′ə-mĭt) *adj.* **1.** Illegal. **2.** Born out of wedlock. —**il′le•git′i•ma•cy** *n.* —**il′le•git′i•mate•ly** *adv.*

**il•lic•it** (ĭ-lĭs′ĭt) *adj.* Unlawful. —**il•lic′-it•ly** *adv.*

**il•lit•er•ate** (ĭ-lĭt′ər-ĭt) *adj.* Unable to read and write. —**il•lit′er•a•cy** *n.* —**il•lit′er•ate** *n.*

**ill•ness** (ĭl′nĭs) *n.* Sickness.

**il•log•i•cal** (ĭ-lŏj′ĭ-kəl) *adj.* Contradicting logic; irrational. **—il•log′i•cal•ly** *adv.*

**il•lu•mi•nate** (ĭ-lo͞o′mə-nāt′) *v.* **-nated, -nating. 1.** To provide with light. **2.** To clarify. **—il•lu′mi•na′tion** *n.* **—il•lu′mi•na′tor** *n.*

**il•lu•sion** (ĭ-lo͞o′zhən) *n.* **1.** A false appearance or perception. **2.** Delusion; misconception. **—il•lu′sive, il•lu′so•ry** *adj.*

**il•lus•trate** (ĭl′ə-strāt′, ĭ-lŭs′trāt′) *v.* **-trated, -trating. 1.** To explain by example. **2.** To provide (a text) with pictures, photographs, etc. **—il′lus•tra′tion** *n.* **—il•lus′tra•tive** *adj.* **—il′lus•tra′tor** *n.*

**il•lus•tri•ous** (ĭ-lŭs′trē-əs) *adj.* Eminent; famous. **—il•lus′tri•ous•ly** *adv.* **—il•lus′tri•ous•ness** *n.*

**I'm** (īm) *v.* Contraction of *I am.*

**im•age** (ĭm′ĭj) *n.* **1.** A likeness; resemblance. **2.** A figure of speech. **3.** A mental picture. *—v.* **-aged, -aging.** To mirror; reflect. **—im′age•ry** *n.*

**i•mag•i•na•tion** (ĭ-măj′ə-nā′shən) *n.* **1.** The power of forming a mental image of something that is not present, has not been experienced, or is not real. **2.** Creativity; inventiveness; resourcefulness. **—i•mag′i•na•ble** *adj.* **—i•mag′i•nar′y** *adj.* **—i•mag′i•na•tive** *adj.* **—i•mag′i•na•tive•ly** *adv.* **—i•mag′ine** *v.*

**im•bro•glio** (ĭm-brōl′yō) *n., pl.* **-glios. 1.** A difficult or intricate situation. **2.** A confused or complicated quarrel.

**im•bue** (ĭm-byo͞o′) *v.* **-bued, -buing. 1.** To saturate or stain. **2.** To inspire.

**im•i•tate** (ĭm′ĭ-tā′) *v.* **-tated, -tating. 1.** To copy or emulate. **2.** To mimic or counterfeit. **—im′i•ta′tion** *n.* **—im′i•ta′tive** *adj.* **—im′i•ta′tor** *n.*

**im•mac•u•late** (ĭ-măk′yə-lĭt) *adj.* **1.** Pure. **2.** Impeccably clean. **—im•mac′u•late•ly** *adv.* **—im•mac′u•late•ness** *n.*

**im•ma•ture** (ĭm′ə-tyo͞o′, -cho͝or′) *adj.* **1.** Not fully developed; unripe. **2.** Exhibiting less than normal maturity. **—im′ma•tur′i•ty** *n.*

**im•me•di•ate** (ĭ-mē′dē-ĭt) *adj.* **1.** Next in line or sequence. **2.** Without delay. **3.** Near to the present. **—im•me′di•a•cy** *n.* **—im•me′di•ate•ly** *adv. & conj.* **—im•me′di•ate•ness** *n.*

**im•mense** (ĭ-mĕns′) *adj.* Vast; huge. **—im•mense′ly** *adv.* **—im•men′si•ty** *n.*

**im•merse** (ĭ-mûrs′) *v.* **-mersed, -mersing. 1.** To plunge into liquid. **2.** To absorb; engross. **—im•mer′sion** *n.*

**im•mi•grate** (ĭm′ĭ-grāt′) *v.* **-grated, -grating.** To settle in a foreign country. **—im′mi•grant** *n.* **—im′mi•gra′tion** *n.*

**im•mi•nent** (ĭm′ə-nənt) *adj.* About to occur; impending. **—im′mi•nence** *n.* **—im′mi•nent•ly** *adv.*

**im•mor•tal** (ĭ-môr′tl) *adj.* **1.** Not subject to death. **2.** Having eternal fame; everlasting. **3.** Of eternal life. *—n.* **1.** One exempt from death. **2.** One whose fame is enduring. **—im′mor•tal′i•ty** *n.* **—im•mor′tal•ize′** *v.* **—im•mor′tal•ly** *adv.*

**im•mune** (ĭ-myo͞on′) *adj.* **1.** Exempt **2.** Resistant to a disease. **—im•mu′ni•ty** *n.* **—im′mu•ni•za•tion** *n.* **—im′mu•nize′** *v.*

**im•pact** (ĭm′păkt′) *n.* **1.** A collision. **2.** A strong impression; effect. *—v.* To affect.

**impact statement** *n.* A statement, often required by law, listing the effects of a building project upon the environment and on cultural, historical, or archaeological sites.

**im•pair** (ĭm-pâr′) *v.* To diminish in strength, value, etc.; weaken. **—im•pair′ment** *n.*

**im•pal•pa•ble** (ĭm-păl′pə-bəl) *adj.* **1.** Intangible **2.** Imperceptible. **—im•pal′pa•bly** *adv.*

**im•part** (ĭm-pärt′) *v.* **1.** To transmit or give. **2.** To disclose.

**im•par•tial** (ĭm-pär′shəl) *adj.* Unbiased; unprejudiced. **—im′par•ti•al′i•ty** *n.* **—im•par′tial•ly** *adv.*

**im•passe** (ĭm′păs′) *n.* **1.** A way or passage with no exit. **2. a.** A difficult situation with no relief. **b.** A deadlock; stalemate.

**im•pas•sive** (ĭm-păs′ĭv) *adj.* Revealing no emotion; calm. **—im•pas′sive•ly** *adv.* **—im′pas•siv′i•ty** *n.*

**im•pa•tience** (ĭm-pā′shəns) *n.* **1.** Lack of patience. **2.** Eagerness, desire, or anticipation. **—im•pa′tient** *adj.* **—im•pa′tient•ly** *adv.*

**im•peach** (ĭm-pēch′) *v.* **1.** To charge with misconduct in office before a proper tribunal. **2.** To discredit. **—im•peach′a•ble** *adj.* **—im•peach′ment** *n.*

**im•pec•ca•ble** (ĭm-pĕk′ə-bəl) *adj.* Faultness; flawless. **—im•pec′ca•bly** *adv.* **—im•pec′ca•bil′i•ty** *n.*

**im•pe•cu•ni•ous** (ĭm′pĭ-kyōō′nē-əs) *adj.* Having no money. **—im•pe•cu′ni•ous•ly** *adv.* **—im′pe•cu′ni•ous•ness** *n.*

**im•pede** (ĭm-pēd′) *v.* **-peded, -peding.** To obstruct; block. **—im•ped′i•ment** *n.*

**im•pel** (ĭm-pĕl′) *v.* **-pelled, -pelling.** To urge; compel.

**im•pen•e•tra•ble** (ĭm-pĕn′ĭ-trə-bəl) *adj.* **1.** Not capable of being entered. **2.** Incomprehensible. **—im•pen′e•tra•bil′i•ty** *n.* **—im•pen′e•tra•bly** *adv.*

**im•per•a•tive** (ĭm-pĕr′ə-tĭv) *adj.* **1.** Expressing a command. **2.** Urgent or obligatory. **—im•per′a•tive** *n.* **—im•per′a•tive•ly** *adv.*

**im•per•fect** (ĭm-pûr′fĭkt) *adj.* **1.** Defective; flawed. **2.** Of a verb tense expressing continuous or incomplete action —*n.* The imperfect tense of a verb. **—im′per•fec′tion** *n.* **—im•per′fect•ly** *adv.*

**im•pe•ri•al•ism** (ĭm-pîr′ē-ə-lĭz′əm) *n.* The policy of extending rule over other nations. **—im•pe′ri•al•ist** *n.* & *adj.* **—im•pe′ri•al•is′tic** *adj.*

**im•per•il** (ĭm-pĕr′əl) *v.* **-iled** or **-illed, -iling** or **-illing.** To put in peril; endanger.

**im•per•son•al** (ĭm-pûr′sə-nəl) *adj.* **1.** Not referring to a particular person. **2.** Emotionless; aloof; heartless. **—im•per′son•al′i•ty** *n.* **—im•per′son•al•ly** *adv.*

**im•per•son•ate** (ĭm-pûr′sə-nāt′) *v.* **-ated, -ating.** To act the part of. **—im•per′son•a′tion** *n.* **—im•per′son•a•′tor** *n.*

**im•per•ti•nent** (ĭm-pûr′tn-ənt) *adj.* **1.** Impudent; insolent. **2.** Not pertinent. **—im•per′ti•nence** *n.* **—im•per′ti•nent•ly** *adv.*

**im•per•turb•a•ble** (ĭm′pər-tûr′bə-bəl) *adj.* Calm and collected. **—im′per•turb′a•bil′i•ty** *n.* **—im′per•turb′a•bly** *adv.*

**im•per•vi•ous** (ĭm-pûr′vē-əs) *adj.* **1.** Not allowing penetration. **2.** Unfeeling. **—im•per′vi•ous•ly** *adv.*

**im•pet•u•ous** (ĭm-pĕch′ōō-əs) *adj.* **1.** Impulsive; hasty. **2.** Rushing with violence. **—im•pet′u•os′i•ty, im•pet′u•ous•ness** *n.* **—im•pet′u•ous•ly** *adv.*

**im•pe•tus** (ĭm′pĭ-təs) *n., pl.* **-tuses. 1.** An impelling force; stimulus. **2.** Force associated with a moving body.

**im•pinge** (ĭm-pĭnj′) *v.* **-pinged, -pinging.** To encroach; infringe.

**im•plac•a•ble** (ĭm-plăk′ə-bəl, -plā′kə-) *adj.* Inexorable; relentless. **—im•plac′a•bly** *adv.*

**im•plant** (ĭm-plănt′) *v.* **1.** To fix firmly. **2.** To instill.

**im•ple•ment** (ĭm′plə-mənt) *n.* A tool or utensil. —*v.* To carry into effect. **—im′ple•men•ta′tion** *n.*

**im•pli•cate** (ĭm′plĭ-kāt′) *v.* **-cated, -cating. 1.** To involve; entangle. **2.** To imply. **—im′pli•ca′tion** *n.*

**im•plic•it** (ĭm-plĭs′ĭt) *adj.* **1.** Implied or understood. **2.** Inherent in the nature of something. **3.** Unquestioning. **—im•plic′it•ly** *adv.*

**im•plore** (ĭm-plôr′, -plō′) *v.* **-plored, -ploring.** To beseech.

**im•ply** (ĭm-plī′) *v.* **-plied, -plying. 1.** To entail. **2.** To express indirectly; suggest.

**im•po•lite** (ĭm′pə-līt′) *adj.* Not polite; rude; discourteous. **—im′po•lite′ly** *adv.* **—im′po•lite′ness** *n.*

**im•pol•i•tic** (ĭm-pŏl′ĭ-tĭk) *adj.* Not wise or expedient **—im•pol′i•tic•ly** *adv.*

**im•port** (ĭm-pôrt′, -pōrt′, -ĭm′pôrt′, -pōrt′) *v.* **1.** To bring in from a foreign country. **2.** To signify. —*n.* (ĭm′pôrt′). **1.** Something imported. **2.** Significance. **—im•port′a•ble** *adj.* **—im′por•ta′tion** *n.*

**im•por•tant** (ĭm-pôr′tnt) *adj.* **1.** Significant; essential; weighty. **2.** Prominent; noteworthy. **—im•por′tance** *n.* **—im•por′tant•ly** *adv.*

**im•por•tune** (ĭm′pôr-t/y/ōōn′) *v.* **-tuned, -tuning.** To bother with repeated requests. **—im•por′tu•nate** *adj.* **—im•por′tu•nate•ly** *adv.* **—im′por•tune′** *adj.* **—im′por•tune′ly** *adv.*

**im•pose** (ĭm-pōz′) *v.* **-posed, -posing. 1.** To set or establish (a tax, etc.). **2.** To apply or force upon by authority. **3.** To take unfair advantage of. **—im•pos′er** *n.* **—im′po•si′tion** *n.*

**im•pos•ing** (ĭm-pō′zĭng) *adj.* Impressive; awesome.

**im•pos•si•ble** (ĭm-pŏs′ə-bəl) *adj.* **1.** Not capable of existing or happening. **2.** Intolerable. **—im•pos′si•bil′i•ty** *n.* **—im•pos′si•bly** *adv.*

**im•pos•tor** (ĭm-pŏs′tər) *n.* A person who deceives under an assumed identity.

**im•po•tent** (ĭm′pə-tənt) *adj.* **1.** Lacking physical strength. **2.** Ineffectual. **3.** Incapable of sexual intercourse. **—im′po•tence** *n.* **—im′po•tent•ly** *adv.*

**im•pound** (ĭm-pound′) *v.* To seize, esp. legally.

**im•preg•nate** (ĭm-prĕg′nāt) *v.* **-nated, -nating. 1.** To make pregnant. **2.** To fill throughout. **—im′preg•na′tion** *n.*

**im•pre•sa•ri•o** (ĭm′prĭ-sär′ē-ō′, -sâr′-) *n., pl.* **-os.** A producer or director, esp. of an opera company.

**im•press** (ĭm-prĕs) *v.* **1.** To stamp. **2.** To fix in the mind. **3.** To affect deeply. **—im•pres′sion** *n.* **—im•pres′sion•a•ble** *adj.* **—im•pres′sive** *adj.* **—im•pres′sive•ly** *adv.*

**im•promp•tu** (ĭm-prŏmp′t/y/o͞o) *adj.* Performed or conceived without rehearsal. **—im•promp′tu** *adv. & n.*

**im•prop•er** (ĭm-prŏp′ər) *adj.* **1.** Not suitable; unseemly. **2.** Incorrect; wrong. **—im•prop′er•ly** *adv.* **—im′pro•pri′e•ty** *n.*

**im•prove** (ĭm-pro͞ov′) *v.* **-proved, -proving.** To make or become better. **—im•prove′ment** *n.*

**im•pu•dent** (ĭm′pyə-dənt) *adj.* Impertinent; rude. **—im′pu•dence** *n.* **—im′pu•dent•ly** *adv.*

**im•pulse** (ĭm′pŭls′) *n.* **1.** An impelling force or the motion it produces. **2.** A sudden urge. **3.** A stimulus. **—im•pul′sive** *adj.* **—im•pul′sive•ly** *adv.* **—im•pul′sive•ness** *n.*

**in** (ĭn) *prep.* **1.** Within; inside. **2.** During. **3.** Into. **4.** Among; out of. *—adv.* **1.** To or toward the inside. **2.** Into a given place, state, etc. **3.** Indoors. **4.** Inward.

**in•ad•ver•tent** (ĭn′əd-vûr′tnt) *adj.* **1.** Not duly attentive. **2.** Accidental; unintentional. **—in′ad•ver′tence, in′ad•ver′ten•cy** *n.* **—in′ad•ver′tent•ly** *adv.*

**in•ane** (ĭn-ān′) *adj.* Lacking substance; silly. **—in•ane′ly** *adv.* **—in•an′i•ty** *n.*

**in•as•much as** (ĭn′əz-mŭch′) *conj.* Because of the fact that; since.

**in•au•gu•rate** (ĭn-ô′gyə-rāt′) *v.* **-rated, -rating. 1.** To induct into office. **2.** To begin officially. **—in•au′gu•ral** *adj. & n.* **—in•au′gu•ra′tion** *n.*

**in•can•des•cent** (ĭn′kən-dĕ′sənt) *adj.* **1.** Emitting visible light from being heated. **2.** Shining brilliantly. **—in′can•des′cence** *n.* **—in′can•des′cent•ly** *adv.*

**in•ca•pac•i•tate** (ĭn′kə-păs′ĭ-tāt) *v.* **-tated, -tating. 1.** To deprive of strength; disable. **2.** To disqualify. **—in′ca•pac′i•ta′tion** *n.*

**in•car•nate** (ĭn-kär′nĭt) *adj.* **1.** Embodied in a mortal form. **2.** Personified. *—v.* (-nāt′) **-nated, -nating. 1.** To give bodily form to. **2.** To personify. **—in′car•na′tion** *n.*

**in•cen•tive** (ĭn-sĕn′tĭv) *n.* Something motivating action; stimulus.

**in•cep•tion** (ĭn-sĕp′shən) *n.* The beginning of something.

**in•ces•sant** (ĭn-sĕs′ənt) *adj.* Constant; unceasing. **—in•ces′sant•ly** *adv.*

**in•cest** (ĭn′sĕst′) *n.* Sexual union between close relatives. **—in•ces′tu•ous** *adj.*

**inch** (ĭnch) *n.* A unit of length equal to 1/12 of a foot. *—v.* To move by small degrees.

**in•ci•dence** (ĭn′sĭ-dəns) n. The extent or frequency of occurrence.

**in•ci•dent** (ĭn′sĭ-dənt) *n.* An occurrence. *—adj.* Tending to arise in connection with. **—in′ci•den′tal** *adj.*

**in•cin•er•ate** (ĭn-sĭn′ə-rāt′) *v.* **-ated, -ating.** To consume by burning. **—in•cin′er•a′tor** *n.*

**in•ci•sion** (ĭn-sĭzh′ən) *n.* **1.** A surgical cut into tissue. **2.** The scar from such a cut.

**in•ci•sive** (ĭn-sī′sĭv) *adj.* **1.** Cutting; penetrating. **2.** Trenchant. **—in•ci′sive•ly** *adv.*

**in•cite** (ĭn-sīt′) *v.* **-cited, -citing.** To provoke to action; stir up.

**in•cle•ment** (ĭn-klĕm′ənt) *adj.* **1.** Stormy. **2.** Severe.

**in•cline** (ĭn-klīn′) *v.* **-clined, -clining. 1.** To lean; slant. **2.** To influence. **3.** To tend. *—n.* (ĭn′klīn′) An inclined surface; a slope. **—in′cli•na′tion** *n.*

**in•clude** (ĭn-klo͞od′) *v.* **-cluded, -cluding. 1.** To contain. **2.** To regard as part of a general category. **—in•clu′sion** *n.* **—in•clu′sive** *adj.* **—in•clu′sive•ly** *adv.* **—in•clu′sive•ness** *n.*

**in•come** (ĭn'kŭm') *n.* Money received from investments, salary, etc.

**in•com•mu•ni•ca•do** (ĭn'kə-myōō'nĭ-kä'dō) *adv. & adj.* Without being able to communicate with others.

**in•cor•po•rate** (ĭn-kôr'pə-rāt') *v.* **-rated, -rating. 1.** To form a legal corporation. **2.** To combine together into a whole. **—in•cor'po•ra'tion** *n.*

**in•cor•ri•gi•ble** (ĭn-kôr'ĭ-jə-bəl, ĭn-kŏr'-) *adj.* Incapable of being corrected or reformed. **—in•cor'ri•gi•bly** *adv.*

**in•crease** (ĭn-krēs') *v.* **-creased, -creasing.** To make or become greater. *—n.* (ĭn'krēs') **1.** Addition; enlargement. **2.** The amount of such increase. **—in•creas'ing•ly** *adv.*

**in•cred•i•ble** (ĭn-krĕd'ə-bəl) *adj.* Unbelievable; remarkable. **—in•cred'i•bil'i•ty** *n.* **—in•cred'i•ble•ness** *n.* **—in•cred'i•bly** *adv.*

**in•cred•u•lous** (ĭn-krĕj'ə-ləs) *adj.* Disbelieving; expressing disbelief. **—in'cre•du'li•ty** *n.* **—in•cred'u•lous•ly** *adv.* **—in•cred'u•lous•ness** *n.*

**in•cre•ment** (ĭn'krə-mənt, ĭng-') *n.* An increase in number or size. **—in'cre•men'tal** *adj.* **—in'cre•men'tal•ly** *adv.*

**in•cum•bent** (ĭn-kŭm'bənt) *adj.* Required; obligatory. *—n.* A person who holds an office. **—in•cum'ben•cy** *n.*

**in•cur** (ĭn-kûr') *v.* **-curred, -curring.** To bring upon oneself.

**in•de•cent** (ĭn-dē'sənt) *adj.* **1.** Offensive to good taste; unseemly. **2.** Offensive to good morals; immodest. **—in•de'cen•cy** *n.* **—in•de'cent•ly** *adv.*

**in•de•ci•sive** (ĭn'dĭ-sī'sĭv) *adj.* **1.** Not decisive; inconclusive. **2.** Unable or unwilling to make up one's mind. **3.** Not clearly defined; indefinite. **—in'de•ci'sion** *n.* **—in'de•ci'sive•ly** *adv.* **—in'de•ci'sive•ness** *n.*

**in•deed** (ĭn-dēd') *adv.* **1.** Certainly. **2.** In fact. **3.** Admittedly.

**in•dem•ni•ty** (ĭn-dĕm'nĭ-tē) *n., pl.* **-ties. 1.** Insurance against loss. **2.** Compensation for loss incurred. **—in•dem'ni•fy'** *v.* **—in•dem'ni•fi•ca'tion** *n.*

**in•dent** (ĭn-dĕnt') *v.* **1.** To notch; make jagged. **2.** To set in from the margin. **—in'den•ta'tion** *n.*

**in•de•pen•dent** (ĭn'dĭ-pĕn'dənt) *adj.* **1.** Politically autonomous. **2.** Free from control by others. **3.** Not affiliated with. *—n.* A voter not committed to any political party. **—in•de•pen'dence** *n.* **—in'de•pen'dent•ly** *adv.*

**in•dex** (ĭn'dĕks') *n., pl.* **-dexes** or **-dices. 1.** An alphabetized list of the names and subjects in a printed work, with page references. **2.** An indicator; a sign. *—v.* **1.** To furnish with an index. **2.** To enter in an index.

**in•di•cate** (ĭn'dĭ-kāt') *v.* **-cated, -cating. 1.** To point out. **2.** To serve as a sign of. **3.** To state. **—in'di•ca'tion** *n.* **—in•dic'a•tive** *adj.* **—in'di•ca'tor** *n.*

**in•dict** (ĭn-dīt) *v.* To accuse formally of a crime. **—in•dict'ment** *n.*

**in•dif•fer•ent** (ĭn-dĭf'ər-ənt, -dĭf'rənt) *adj.* **1.** Impartial. **2.** Callous; unfeeling. **3.** Having no interest in; apathetic. **4.** Mediocre. **—in•dif'fer•ence** *n.* **—in•dif'fer•ent•ly** *adv.*

**in•dig•e•nous** (ĭn-dĭj'ə-nəs) *adj.* Natural to; native.

**in•di•gent** (ĭn'dĭ-jənt) *adj.* Impoverished, needy. *—n.* A destitute person. **—in'di•gence** *n.* **—in'di•gent•ly** *adv.*

**in•dig•na•tion** (ĭn'dĭg-nā'shən) *n.* Anger aroused by something unjust. **—in•dig'nant** *adj.* **—in•dig'nant•ly** *adv.*

**in•di•vid•u•al** (ĭn'də-vĭj'ōō-əl) *adj.* **1.** Of, by, or for 1 person. **2.** Single; separate. **3.** Distinctive. *—n.* **1.** A single person, organism, or thing. **2.** A particular person. **—in'di•vid'u•al'i•ty** *n.* **—in'di•vid'u•al•ly** *adv.*

**in•di•vid•u•al•ist** (ĭn'də-vĭj'ōō-ə-lĭst) *n.* A person of independent thought and action. **—in'di•vid'u•al•ism'** *n.* **—in'di•vid'u•al•is'tic** *adj.*

**in•dom•i•ta•ble** (ĭn-dŏm'ĭ-tə-bəl) *adj.* Unyielding; unconquerable.

**in•duce** (ĭn-d/y/ōōs') *v.* **-duced, -ducing. 1.** To persuade. **2.** To cause. **3.** To infer by logic. **—in•duce'ment** *n.*

**in•duct** (ĭn-dŭkt') *v.* To install formally, esp. in office or into military service. **—in'duc•tee'** *n.* **—in•duc'tion** *n.*

**in•dulge** (ĭn-dŭlj') *v.* **-dulged, -dulging. 1.** To yield to desires of. **2.** To gratify. **—in•dul'gence** *n.* **—in•dul'gent** *adj.*

**in•dus•tri•ous** (ĭn-dŭs'trē-əs) *adj.* Diligent; hardworking. **—in•dus'tri•ous•ly** *adv.* **—in•dus'tri•ous•ness** *n.*

**in•dus•try** (ĭn'də-strē) *n., pl.* **-tries. 1.** The production of goods. **2.** A specific branch of manufacture and trade. **3.**

Diligence. **—in•dus'tri•al** *adj.* **—in•dus'tri•al•ist** *n.* **—in•dus'tri•al•ize'** *v.*

**in•ept** (ĭn-ĕpt') *adj.* **1.** Clumsy. **2.** Incompetent. **—in•ep'ti•tude'** *n.*

**in•ert** (ĭn-ûrt') *adj.* **1.** Not able to move or act. **2.** Sluggish or inactive. **—in•er'tia** *n.*

**in•ev•i•ta•ble** (ĭn-ĕv'ĭ-tə-bəl) *adj.* Not able to be avoided or prevented. **—in•ev'i•ta•bil'i•ty** *n.* **—in•ev'i•ta•bly** *adv.*

**in•ex•o•ra•ble** (ĭn-ĕk'sər-ə-bəl) *adj.* Relentless. **—in•ex'o•ra•bly** *adv.*

**in•fa•mous** (ĭn'fə-məs) *adj.* **1.** Having a bad reputation. **2.** Loathsome; disgraceful. **—in'fa•my** *n.*

**in•fant** (ĭn'fənt) *n.* A baby. **—in'fan•cy** *n.* **—in'fan•tile'** *adj.*

**in•fan•try** (ĭn'fən-trē) *n., pl.* **-tries.** Army units trained to fight on foot. **—in'fan•try•man** *n.*

**in•fat•u•ate** (ĭn-făch'o͞o-āt') *v.* **-ated, -ating.** To inspire with foolish passion. **—in•fat'u•a'tion** *n.*

**in•fect** (ĭn-fĕkt') *v.* **1.** To contaminate with germs; pollute. **2.** To communicate a disease to. **3.** To affect as if by contagion; catch on. **—in•fec'tion** *n.* **—in•fec'tious** *adj.*

**in•fer** (ĭn-fûr') *v.* **-ferred, -ferring.** To conclude from evidence; deduce. **—in'fer•ence** *n.* **—in'fer•en'tial** *adj.* **—in'fer•en'tial•ly** *adv.*

**in•fe•ri•or** (ĭn-fîr'ē-ər) *adj.* **1.** Lower. **2.** Lower in degree or rank. **3.** Lower in quality. **—in•fe'ri•or'i•ty** *n.*

**in•fin•i•tive** (ĭn-fĭn'ĭ-tĭv) *n.* An uninflected verb form, esp. when preceded by *to.*

**in•fin•i•ty** (ĭn-fĭn'ĭ-tē) *n., pl.* **-ties.** That which is unbounded by space, time, or quantity. **—in'fi•nite** *adj.*

**in•flam•ma•ble** (ĭn-flăm'ə-bəl) *adj.* Flammable. **—in•flam'ma•bil'i•ty** *n.* **—in•flam'ma•bly** *adv.*

**in•flam•ma•tion** (ĭn'flə-mā'shən) *n.* Localized redness, swelling, and pain. **—in•flame'** *v.* **—in•flam'ma•to'ry** *adj.*

**in•flate** (ĭn-flāt) *v.* **-flated, -flating. 1.** To fill and swell with a gas. **2.** To raise abnormally, as prices. **—in•fla'tion** *n.* **—in•fla'tion•ar'y** *adj.*

**in•flict** (ĭn-flĭkt') *v.* To impose.

**in•flu•ence** (ĭn'flo͞o-əns) *n.* **1.** A power affecting a person or events. **2.** A person or thing exercising such power. *—v.* **-enced, -encing.** To have power over; affect. **—in'flu•en'tial** *adj.*

**in•form** (ĭn-fôrm') *v.* To impart information to. **—in•form'ant, in•form'er** *n.*

**in•for•mal** (ĭn-fôr'məl) *adj.* **1.** Performed without ceremony. **2.** Of or for ordinary use; casual. **—in'for•mal'i•ty** *n.* **—in•for'mal•ly** *adv.*

**in•for•ma•tion** (ĭn'fər-mā'shən) *n.* **1.** Knowledge. **2.** News. **—in'for•ma'tion•al** *adj.* **—in•form'a•tive** *adj.*

**in•fra•struc•ture** (ĭn'frə-strŭk'chər) *n.* **1.** A base or foundation for an organization. **2.** The equipment needed for a system to function.

**in•gen•ious** (ĭn-jēn'yəs) *adj.* **1.** Inventive. **2.** Resourceful; clever. **—in'ge•nu'i•ty** *n.*

**in•gra•ti•ate** (ĭn-grā'shē-āt') *v.* **-ated, -ating.** To work (oneself) into another's good graces.

**in•gre•di•ent** (ĭn-grē'dē-ənt) *n.* A component; a part of a mixture.

**in•hab•it** (ĭn-hăb'ĭt) *v.* To reside in. **—in•hab'i•ta•ble** *adj.* **—in•hab'i•tant** *n.*

**in•hale** (ĭn-hāl') *v.* **-haled, -haling.** To breathe in. **—in'ha•la'tion** *n.*

**in•her•ent** (ĭn-hîr'ənt, -hĕr'-) *adj.* Existing as an essential part. **—in•her'ent•ly** *adv.*

**in•her•it** (ĭn-hĕr'ĭt) *v.* **1.** To receive, esp. as an heir. **2.** To receive genetically from an ancestor. **—in•her'i•tance** *n.*

**in•hib•it** (ĭn-hĭb'ĭt) *v.* To restrain; repress. **—in'hi•bi'tion** *n.*

**in-house** (ĭn'hous') *adj.* Coming from within an organization.

**in•i•tial** (ĭ-nĭsh'əl) *adj.* Occurring 1st. *—n.* **1.** Often **initials.** The 1st letters of a person's name. **2.** The 1st letter of a word. *—v.* **-tialed, -tialing.** To sign with one's initials. **—in•i'tial•ly** *adv.*

**in•i•ti•ate** (ĭ-nĭsh'ē-āt') *v.* **-ated, -ating. 1.** To begin. **2.** To admit into membership, as with ceremonies. *—n.* (-ĭt). One who has been initiated. **—in•i'ti•a'tion** *n.*

**in•i•tia•tive** (ĭ-nĭsh'ə-tĭv) *n.* **1.** The ability to follow through with a plan; enterprise. **2.** The 1st step.

**in•ject** (ĭn-jĕkt') *v.* To force something into. **—in•jec'tion** *n.*

**in•junc•tion** (ĭn-jŭngk'shən) *n.* **1.** A directive or order. **2.** A court order prohibiting a specific course of action.

**in•jure** (ĭn′jər) *v.* **-jured, -juring. 1.** To harm; hurt. **2.** To commit an offense against. **—in•ju′ri•ous** *adj.* **—in′ju•ry** *n.*

**in•jus•tice** (ĭn-jŭs′tĭs) *n.* **1.** Lack of justice. **2.** An unjust act.

**ink** (ĭngk) *n.* A pigmented liquid for writing. **—ink′y** *adj.*

**in•lay** (ĭn-lā′) *v.* To set into a surface to form a design. *—n.* (ĭn′lā′). **1.** An inlaid object or design. **2.** A solid filling fitted to a cavity in a tooth. **—in′laid′** *adj.*

**inn** (ĭn) *n.* **1.** A hotel. **2.** A tavern.

**in•nate** (ĭ-nāt′, ĭn′āt′) *adj.* **1.** Inborn. **2.** Inherent. **—in•nate′ly** *adv.*

**in•ner** (ĭn′ər) *adj.* **1.** Located farther inside. **2.** Of the soul, emotions, or mind. **—in′ner•most′** *adj.*

**in•no•cent** (ĭn′ə-sənt) *adj.* **1.** Without guile. **2.** Not guilty of a crime. **3.** Not experienced; naive. **—in′no•cence** *n.* **—in′no•cent** *n.* **—in′no•cent•ly** *adv.*

**in•noc•u•ous** (ĭ-nŏk′yo͞o-əs) *adj.* **1.** Harmless. **2.** Insignificant.

**in•no•vate** (ĭn′ə-vāt′) *v.* **-vated, -vating.** To begin or introduce (something new). **—in′no•va′tion** *n.* **—in′no•va′tive** *adj.* **—in′no•va′tor** *n.*

**in•nu•en•do** (ĭn′yo͞o-ĕn′dō) *n., pl.* **-does.** An indirect, often derogatory implication.

**in•oc•u•late** (ĭ-nŏk′yə-lāt′) *v.* **-lated, -lating.** To introduce the virus of a disease into (the body) in order to immunize. **—in•oc′u•la′tion** *n.*

**in•quest** (ĭn′kwĕst′) *n.* A legal or judicial inquiry.

**in•quire** (ĭn-kwīr′) *v.* **-quired, -quiring. 1.** To ask. **2.** To investigate. **—in•quir′er** *n.* **—in•quir′ing•ly** *adv.* **—in•quir′y** *n.*

**in•quis•i•tive** (ĭn-kwĭz′ĭ-tĭv) *adj.* **1.** Unduly curious. **2.** Eager to learn.

**in re** (ĭn rā′) *prep.* In the matter of; concerning.

**in•sane** (ĭn-sān′) *adj.* **1.** Of or afflicted with mental disorder. **2.** Mad. **—in•san′i•ty** *n.*

**in•scribe** (ĭn-skrīb′) *v.* **-scribed, -scribing. 1.** To write or engrave. **2.** To dedicate to another. **—in•scrip′tion** *n.*

**in•sect** (ĭn′sĕkt′) *n.* A small animal with a 3-segmented body and 6 legs.

**in•se•cure** (ĭn′sĭ-kyo͝or′) *adj.* **1.** Not safe. **2.** Unstable; shaky. **3.** Lacking self-confidence. **—in′se•cure′ly** *adv.* **—in′se•cu′ri•ty** *n.*

**in•sert** (ĭn-sûrt′) *v.* **1.** To put or thrust into. **2.** To put in between other parts. *—n.* (ĭn′sûrt′). Something inserted. **—in•ser′tion** *n.*

**in•side** (ĭn-sīd′, ĭn′sīd′) *n.* **1.** The inner part. **2.** An inner surface. *—adj.* Inner. *—adv.* (ĭn-sīd′). Within. *—prep.* (ĭn-sīd′). **1.** Within. **2.** Into.

**in•sid•i•ous** (ĭn-sĭd′ē-əs) *adj.* **1.** Cunning. **2.** Treacherous. **3.** Sly; beguiling.

**in•sight** (ĭn′sīt′) *n.* **1.** Discernment. **2.** An elucidating glimpse.

**in•sig•ni•a** (ĭn-sĭg′nē-ə) *n., pl.* **-nia** or **-nias.** A badge of office, rank, etc.

**in•sin•u•ate** (ĭn-sĭn′yo͞o-āt′) *v.* **-ated, -ating. 1.** To introduce insidiously. **2.** To worm (oneself) by subtle means. **3.** To hint covertly. **—in•sin′u•a′tion** *n.*

**in•sip•id** (ĭn-sĭp′ĭd) *adj.* Dull; vapid. **—in•sip′id•ly** *adv.*

**in•sist** (ĭn-sĭst′) *v.* **1.** To emphasize an assertion, demand, or course. **2.** To assert or demand persistently. **—in•sis′tence** *n.* **—in•sis′tent** *adj.*

**in•so•lent** (ĭn′sə-lənt) *adj.* **1.** Insulting in manner; arrogant. **2.** Impudent. **—in′so•lence** *n.* **—in′so•lent•ly** *adv.*

**in•som•ni•a** (ĭn-sŏm′nē-ə) *n.* Chronic inability to sleep. **—in•som′ni•ac′** *n.*

**in•spect** (ĭn-spĕkt′) *v.* To examine carefully and critically. **—in•spec′tion** *n.* **—in•spec′tor** *n.*

**in•spire** (ĭn-spīr′) *v.* **-spired, -spiring. 1.** To arouse the mind or emotions of. **2.** To stimulate; impel. **3.** To inhale. **—in′spi•ra′tion** *n.* **—in′spi•ra′tion•al** *adj.*

**in•stall** (ĭn-stôl′) *v.* Also **in•stal. -stalled, -stalling. 1.** To set in position for use. **2.** To put in an office. **3.** To establish. **—in′stal•la′tion** *n.*

**in•stall•ment** (ĭn-stôl′mənt) *n.* Also **in•stal•ment. 1.** One of several payments of a debt. **2.** A portion of anything issued at intervals.

**in•stance** (ĭn′stəns) *n.* **1.** A case or example. **2.** A prompting; request.

**in•stant** (ĭn′stənt) *n.* **1.** A very brief time. **2.** A particular point in time. *—adj.* **1.** Immediate. **2.** Urgent. **3.** Prepared for rapid completion with minimal effort.

—**in′stan•ta′ne•ous** *adj.* —**in′stan•ta′ne•ous•ly** *adv.* —**in′stant•ly** *adv.*

**in•sti•gate** (ĭn′stĭ-gāt′) *v.* **-gated, -gating.** To incite. —**in′sti•ga′tion** *n.* —**in′sti•ga′tor** *n.*

**in•stinct** (ĭn′stĭngkt′) *n.* **1.** A powerful and natural impulse. **2.** An innate aptitude. —**in•stinc′tive** *adj.* —**in•stinc′tive•ly** *adv.* —**in•stinc′tu•al** *adj.*

**in•sti•tute** (ĭn′stĭ-t/y/o͞ot′) *v.* **-tuted, -tuting. 1.** To establish. **2.** To initiate. —*n.* **1.** An organization founded to promote some cause. **2.** An educational institution.

**in•sti•tu•tion** (ĭn′stĭ-t/y/o͞o′shən) *n.* **1.** An established custom or practice. **2.** An organization, esp. one dedicated to public service. **3.** A place of confinement. —**in′sti•tu′tion•al** *adj.*

**in•struct** (ĭn-strŭkt′) *v.* **1.** To teach. **2.** To direct. —**in•struc′tion** *n.* —**in•struc′tion•al** *adj.* —**in•struc′tive** *adj.* —**in•struc′tor** *n.*

**in•stru•ment** (ĭn′strə-mənt) *n.* **1.** A means. **2.** A tool. **3.** A device for producing music. —**in′stru•men′tal** *adj.* —**in′stru•men′tal•ly** *adv.*

**in•su•late** (ĭn′sə-lāt′, ĭns′yə-) *v.* **-lated, -lating. 1.** To detach; isolate. **2.** To prevent the passage of heat, electricity, or sound into or out of by interposition of a nonconducting material. —**in′su•la′tion** *n.* —**in′su•la′tor** *n.*

**in•sult** (ĭn-sŭlt′) *v.* To treat in a contemptuous way. —*n.* (ĭn′sult′). An offensive remark or act.

**in•sure** (ĭn-sho͝or′) *v.* **-sured, -suring. 1.** To protect against loss, damage, etc. **2.** To guarantee. —**in•sur′ance** *n.* —**in•sur′er** *n.*

**in•tact** (ĭn-tăkt′) *adj.* **1.** Not impaired. **2.** Whole.

**in•te•ger** (ĭn′tĭ-jər) *n.* **1.** A whole number. **2.** An intact unit.

**in•te•gral** (ĭn′tĭ-grəl) *adj.* **1.** Essential for completion. **2.** Whole; entire. —**in′te•gral•ly** *adv.*

**in•te•grate** (ĭn′tĭ-grāt′) *v.* **-grated, -grating. 1.** To make into a whole. **2.** To unite. **3.** To open to all groups. —**in′te•gra′tion** *n.* —**in′te•gra′tive** *adj.*

**in•te•grat•ed circuit** (ĭn′tĭ-grā′tĭd) *n.* A tiny wafer etched or imprinted with electronic components.

**in•teg•ri•ty** (ĭn-tĕg′rĭ-tē) *n.* **1.** Adherence to a code of values. **2.** Soundness; completeness.

**in•tel•lect** (ĭn′tl-ĕkt′) *n.* **1.** The ability to learn, reason, and understand. **2.** A person of great intellectual ability. —**in′tel•lec′tu•al** *adj. & n.*

**in•tel•li•gence** (ĭn-tĕl′ə-jəns) *n.* **1.** The capacity to acquire and apply knowledge; intellect. **2.** News, esp. secret information. —**in•tel′li•gent** *adj.* —**in•tel′li•gent•ly** *adv.*

**in•tend** (ĭn-tĕnd′) *v.* **1.** To have in mind; plan. **2.** To mean.

**in•tense** (ĭn-tĕns′) *adj.* **1.** Of great concentration or force. **2.** Extreme in degree, strength, or size. **3.** Deeply felt; emotional. —**in•tense′ly** *adv.* —**in•tense′ness** *n.* —**in•ten′si•fy′** *v.* —**in•ten′si•ty** *n.* —**in•ten′sive** *adj.*

**in•tent** (ĭn-tĕnt′) *n.* **1.** Aim; purpose. **2.** Volition. **3.** Meaning. —*adj.* **1.** Firmly fixed; determined. **2.** Engrossed. —**in•ten′tion** *n.* —**in•ten′tion•al** *adj.* —**in•ten′tion•al•ly** *adv.*

**in•ter•cede** (ĭn′tər-sēd′) *v.* **-ceded, -ceding. 1.** To plead on another's behalf. **2.** To mediate.

**in•ter•cept** (ĭn′tər-sĕpt′) *v.* To stop or interrupt the progress of. —**in′ter•cep′tion** *n.*

**in•ter•course** (ĭn′tər-kôrs, -kōrs′) *n.* **1.** Social communication. **2.** Sexual relations.

**in•ter•est** (ĭn′trĭst, -tər-ĭst) *n.* **1.** A feeling of curiosity, fascination, etc. **2.** Advantage; benefit. **3.** A right or legal share in something. **4.** A charge for a financial loan. —*v.* To arouse or hold the attention of.

**in•ter•face** (ĭn′tər-fās′) *n.* **1.** A surface forming a boundary. **2.** The point at which or the device by which different systems interact. —**in′ter•face′** *v.*

**in•ter•fere** (ĭn′tər-fîr′) *v.* **-fered, -fering. 1.** To hinder; impede. **2.** To intrude; meddle. —**in′ter•fer′ence** *n.*

**in•ter•im** (ĭn′tər-ĭm) *n.* An intervening period of time. —*adj.* Temporary.

**in•te•ri•or** (ĭn-tîr′ē-ər) *adj.* **1.** Situated inside; inner. **2.** Inland. —*n.* **1.** The inner area of something. **2.** The inland part.

**in•ter•jec•tion** (ĭn′tər-jĕk′shən) *n.* **1.** An exclamation. **2.** A part of speech consisting of exclamatory words. **3.** An interruption. **—in′ter•ject′** *v.*

**in•ter•me•di•ar•y** (ĭn′tər-me′dē-ĕr′ē) *n., pl.* **-ies.** A mediator or agent. *—adj.* **1.** Acting as a mediator. **2.** In between.

**in•ter•me•di•ate** (ĭn′tər-me′dē-ĭt) *adj.* In between; in the middle.

**in•ter•mis•sion** (ĭn′tər-mĭsh′ən) *n.* An interval, as the period between the acts of a drama, etc.

**in•ter•mit•tent** (ĭn′tər-mĭt′nt) *adj.* Stopping and starting at intervals. **—in′ter•mit′tent•ly** *adv.*

**in•ter•nal** (ĭn-tûr′nəl) *adj.* **1.** Inner; interior. **2.** Intrinsic; inherent. **3.** Of the domestic affairs of a country. **—in•ter′nal•ly** *adv.*

**in•ter•na•tion•al** (ĭn′tər-năsh′ə-nəl) *adj.* Of, or involving 2 or more nations or nationalities. **—in′ter•na′tion•al•ly** *adv.*

**In•ter•net** (ĭn′tər-nĕt′) *n.* A system connecting computers around the world using a common software program for transmitting data.

**in•ter•pret** (ĭn-tûr′prĭt) *v.* **1.** To clarify. **2.** To explain the significance of. **3.** To translate. **—in•ter′pret•a•ble** *adj.* **—in•ter′pre•ta′tion** *n.* **—in•ter′pret•er** *n.*

**in•ter•ro•gate** (ĭn-tər′ə-gāt′) *v.* **-gated, -gating.** To question, esp. formally. **—in•ter′ro•ga′tion** *n.* **—in′ter•rog′a•tive** *adj. & n.* **—in•ter′ro•ga′tor** *n.*

**in•ter•rupt** (ĭn′tə-rŭpt′) *v.* **1.** To break the continuity of. **2.** To hinder by breaking in upon. **—in′ter•rup′tion** *n.*

**in•ter•sect** (ĭn′tər-sĕkt′) *v.* To cut through. **—in′ter•sec′tion** *n.*

**in•ter•val** (ĭn′tər-vəl) *n.* **1.** An intervening space or time period. **2.** A difference in pitch.

**in•ter•vene** (ĭn′tər-vēn′) *v.* **-vened, -vening.** **1.** To occur between 2 things or periods of time. **2.** To mediate. **3.** To interfere in the affairs of another. **—in′ter•ven′tion** *n.*

**in•ter•view** (ĭn′tər-vyōō′) *n.* **1.** A formal discussion. **2.** A conversation between a reporter and one from whom information is sought. **—in′ter•view′** *v.* **—in′ter•view′er** *n.*

**in•tes•tine** (ĭn-tĕs′tĭn) *n.* The lower portion of the digestive tract. **—in•tes′ti•nal** *adj.* **—in•tes′ti•nal•ly** *adv.*

**in•ti•mate** (ĭ′tə-mĭt) *adj.* **1.** Close or familiar. **2.** Of love or sexual relations. **3.** Very personal; private. **—in′ti•ma•cy** *n.* **—in′ti•mate•ly** *adv.*

**in•tim•i•date** (ĭn-tĭm′ĭ-dāt′) *v.* **-dated, -dating.** **1.** To make timid; frighten. **2.** To discourage as by threats. **—in•tim′i•da′tion** *n.*

**in•to** (ĭn′tōō) *prep.* **1.** To the inside of. **2.** To the condition or form of. **3.** To a time or place. **4.** Against.

**in•tox•i•cate** (ĭn-tŏk′sĭ-kāt′) *v.* **-cated, -cating.** **1.** To induce drunkenness. **2.** To stimulate or excite. **—in•tox′i•cant** *n.* **—in•tox′i•ca′tion** *n.*

**in•tran•si•tive** (ĭn-trăn′sĭ-tĭv, -zĭ-) *adj.* Designating a verb that does not take a direct object.

**in•trep•id** (ĭn-trĕp′ĭd) *adj.* Resolutely courageous; fearless. **—in•trep′id•ly** *adv.*

**in•tri•cate** (ĭn′trĭ-kĭt) *adj.* **1.** Having many complex elements. **2.** Puzzling; confusing. **—in′tri•ca•cy** *n.* **—in′tri•cate•ly** *adv.*

**in•trigue** (ĭn′trēg′, ĭn-trēg′) *n.* **1.** A secret scheme. **2.** A clandestine love affair. **3.** Mystery; suspense. *—v.* (ĭn-trēg′) **-trigued, -triguing.** **1.** To engage in covert schemes. **2.** To arouse the curiosity of.

**in•trin•sic** (ĭn-trĭn′zĭk, -sĭk) *adj.* Of the essential nature of a thing. **—in•trin′si•cal•ly** *adv.*

**in•tro•duce** (ĭn′trə-d/y/ōōs′) *v.* **-duced, -ducing.** **1.** To make acquainted. **2.** To bring into use, notice, etc. **3.** To insert. **4.** To preface. **—in′tro•duc′tion** *n.* **—in′tro•duc′to•ry** *adj.*

**in•tro•spec•tion** (ĭn′trə-spĕk′shən) *n.* Contemplation of one's own thoughts and sensations. **—in′tro•spec′tive** *adj.*

**in•tro•vert** (ĭn′trə-vûrt′) *n.* One whose thoughts and interests are directed inward. **—in′tro•ver′sion** *n.*

**in•trude** (ĭn-trōōd′) *v.* **-truded, -truding.** To come in rudely or inappropriately. **—in•trud′er** *n.* **—in•tru′sion** *n.* **—in•tru′sive** *adj.* **—in•tru′sive•ly** *adv.*

**in•tui•tion** (ĭn′t/y/ōō-ĭsh′ən) *n.* Knowledge of something without reasoning; instinctive understanding. **—in•tu′it** *v.* **—in•tu′i•tive** *adj.*

**in•un•date** (ĭn′ŭn-dāt′) *v.* **-dated, -dating.** To flood; overwhelm. **—in′-**

**un•da'tion** *n.*

**in u•ter•o** (ĭn yo͞o'tə-rō) *adv. & adj.* In the womb.

**in•vade** (ĭn-vād') *v.* **-vaded, vading. 1.** To enter by force in order to conquer. **2.** To encroach. **—in•va'sion** *n.*

**in•va•lid** (ĭn'və-lĭd) *n.* A chronically ill or disabled person. *—adj.* Physically disabled.

**in•vent** (ĭn-vĕnt') *v.* **1.** To devise first; originate. **2.** To fabricate. **—in•ven'tion** *n.* **—in•ven'tive** *adv.* **—in•ven'tor** *n.*

**in•ven•to•ry** (ĭn'vən-tôr'ē, -tōr'ē) *n., pl.* **-ries.** A detailed list of things, esp. goods in stock. **—in'ven•to'ry** *v.*

**in•vert** (ĭn-vûrt') *v.* **1.** To turn inside out or upside down. **2.** To reverse. **—in•ver'sion** *n.*

**in•ver•te•brate** (ĭn-vûr'tə-brĭt, -brāt') *adj.* Having no backbone. **—in•ver'te•brate** *n.*

**in•vest** (ĭn-vĕst') *v.* **1.** To commit (money) in order to gain profit. **2.** To endow with authority or power. **—in•vest'ment** *n.* **—in•ves'tor** *n.*

**in•ves•ti•gate** (ĭn-vĕs'tĭ-gāt') *v.* **-gated, -gating.** To examine systematically. **—in•ves'ti•ga'tion** *n.* **—in•ves'ti•ga'tive** *adj.* **—in•ves'ti•ga'tor** *n.*

**in•vin•ci•ble** (ĭn-vĭn'sə-bəl) *adj.* Unconquerable. **—in•vin'ci•bil'i•ty** *n.* **—in•vin'ci•bly** *adv.*

**in•vi•o•la•ble** (ĭn-vī'ə-lə-bəl) *adj.* **1.** That cannot or must not be violated. **2.** Impregnable. **—in•vi'o•la•bil'i•ty** *n.* **—in•vi'o•la•bly** *adv.* **—in•vi'o•late** *adj.*

**in•vite** (ĭn-vīt') *v.* **-vited, -viting. 1.** To request the presence of. **2.** To request formally. **3.** To provoke. **4.** To attract. **—in'vi•ta'tion** *n.*

**in•voice** (ĭn'vois') *n.* A list of goods shipped; a bill.

**in•voke** (ĭn-vōk') *v.* **-voked, -voking. 1.** To call upon (a higher power) for assistance. **2.** To appeal to.

**in•volve** (ĭn-vŏlv') *v.* **-volved, -volving. 1.** To include. **2.** To have as a necessary feature. **3.** To engross. **—in•volve'ment** *n.*

**in•ward** (ĭn-wərd) *adj.* **1.** Inner. **2.** Toward the interior. *—adv.* Also **in•wards. 1.** Toward the inside or center. **2.** Toward the self. **—in'ward•ly** *adv.*

**i•o•dine** (ī'ə-dīn', -dĭn, -dēn') *n.* A nonmetallic element used in medicine.

**i•on** (ī'ən, -ī'ŏn') *n.* An electrically charged atom. **—i'on•i•za•tion** *n.* **—i'on•ize** *v.*

**i•rate** (ī-rāt', ī'rāt') *adj.* Angry; enraged. **—i'rate•ly** *adv.*

**ire** (īr) *n.* Wrath; anger. **—ire'ful** *adj.*

**i•ris** (ī'rĭs) *n.* **1.** The colored part of the eye. **2.** A plant with variously colored flowers.

**irk** (ûrk) *v.* To vex; irritate. **—irk'some** *adj.*

**i•ron** (ī'ərn) *n.* **1.** A silvery-white metallic element. **2.** An appliance used to press fabric. *—adj.* Of or like iron. *—v.* To press (fabric) with a heated iron.

**i•ro•ny** (ī'rə-nē) *n., pl.* **-nies.** The use of words to convey the opposite of their literal meaning. **—i•ron'ic, i•ron'i•cal** *adj.* **—i•ron'i•cal•ly** *adv.*

**ir•ref•u•ta•ble** (ĭ-rĕf'yə-tə-bəl, ĭr'ĭ-fyo͞o'-) *adj.* That cannot be refuted or disproved. **—ir•ref'u•ta•bil'i•ty** *n.* **—ir•ref'u•tab•ly** *adv.*

**ir•rel•e•vant** (ĭ-rĕl'ə-vənt) *adj.* Having no relevance or effect. **—ir•rel'e•vance, ir•rel'e•van•cy** *n.* **—ir•rel'e•vant•ly** *adv.*

**ir•rep•a•ra•ble** (ĭ-rĕp'ər-ə-bəl) *adj.* That cannot be repaired. **—ir•rep'a•ra•bil'i•ty** *n.* **—ir•rep'a•ra•bly** *adv.*

**ir•rev•o•ca•ble** (ĭ-rĕv'ə-kə-bəl) *adj.* That cannot be revoked or retracted. **—ir•rev'o•ca•bil'i•ty, ir•rev'o•ca•ble•ness** *n.* **—ir•rev'o•ca•bly** *adv.*

**ir•ri•gate** (ĭr'ĭ-gāt') *v.* **-gated, -gating.** To supply with water. **—ir'ri•ga'tion** *n.*

**ir•ri•ta•ble** (ĭr'ĭ-tə-bəl) *adj.* Easily annoyed. **—ir'ri•ta•bil'i•ty** *n.* **—ir'ri•ta•bly** *adv.*

**ir•ri•tate** (ĭr'ĭ-tāt') *v.* **-tated, -tating. 1.** To exasperate. **2.** To chafe. **—ir'ri•tant** *adj. & n.* **—ir'ri•tat'ing•ly** *adv.* **—ir'ri•ta'tion** *n.*

**is** (ĭz) *v.* 3rd person sing. present indicative of **be.**

**Is•lam** (ĭs-läm', ĭz-, ĭs'läm, ĭz'-) *n.* A monotheistic religion based upon the teachings of Muhammad; the Muslim religion. **—Is•lam'ic** *adj.*

**is•land** (ī'lənd) *n.* A land mass surrounded by water. **—is'land•er** *n.*

**is•n't** (ĭz'ənt) *v.* Contraction of *is not.*

**i•so•late** (ī'sə-lāt) *v.* **-lated, -lating.** To separate and set apart. **—i'so•la'tion** *n.*

**i•sos•ce•les** (ī-sŏs'ə-lēz') *adj.* Having 2 equal sides.

**is•sue** (ĭsh'o͞o) *n.* **1.** An act of flowing. **2.** Something produced or published. **3.** The result of an action. **4.** Offspring. **5.** A point of discussion. *—v.* **-sued, -suing. 1.** To go or come out. **2.** To distribute, as supplies. **3.** To be descended. **4.** To result from. **5.** To publish or be published. **—is'su•er** *n.*

**isth•mus** (ĭs'mə-s) *n., pl.* **-muses** or **-mi.** A strip of land connecting 2 larger masses of land.

**it** (ĭt) *pron.* The 3rd person sing. pronoun in the subjective or objective case, neuter gender.

**i•tal•ic** (ĭ-tăl'ĭk, ī-tăl'-) *adj.* Being a type with the letters slanting to the right. **—i•tal'ic** *n.* **—i•tal'i•cize'** *v.*

**itch** (ĭch) *n.* **1.** An irritating sensation of the skin. **2.** A restless craving. **—itch** *v.* **—itch'i•ness** *n.* **—itch'y** *adj.*

**i•tem** (ī'təm) *n.* **1.** A single unit. **2.** A bit of information. **—i'tem•ize'** *v.*

**i•tin•er•ar•y** (ī-tĭn'ə-rĕr'ē, ĭtĭn'-) *n., pl.* **-ies. 1.** A route. **2.** A record of a journey. **3.** A traveler's guidebook.

**its** (ĭts) *adj.* The possessive case of *it,* used as a modifier before a noun.

**it's** (ĭts) *v.* **1.** Contraction of *it is.* **2.** Contraction of *it has.*

**it•self** (ĭt-sĕlf') *pron.* The reflexive and emphatic form of *it.*

**I've** (īv) *v.* Contraction of *I have.*

**i•vo•ry** (ī'vərē, īv'rē) *n., pl.* **-ries. 1.** The hard, white substance forming the tusks of certain animals. **2.** Creamy white. **—i'vo•ry** *adj.*

## — J —

**j, J** (jā) *n.* The 10th letter of the English alphabet.

**jab** (jăb) *v.* **jabbed, jabbing. 1.** To poke abruptly. **2.** To punch with short, quick blows. **—jab** *n.*

**jab•ber** (jăb'ər) *v.* To talk quickly, stupidly, or idly. **—jab'ber** *n.* **—jab'ber•er** *n.*

**jab•ber•wock•y** (jăb'ər-wŏk'ē) *n.* Nonsense speech or writing having the appearance of making sense.

**jack** (jăk) *n.* **1.** A device for raising heavy objects. **2.** A kind of socket that accepts a plug at one end to make an electrical connection. **3.** A playing card showing a knave.

**jack•al** (jăk'əl, -ôl') *n.* A doglike mammal of Africa and Asia.

**jack•ass** (jăk'ăs') *n.* **1.** A male donkey. **2.** A foolish person.

**jack•daw** (jăk'dô') *n.* A bird resembling a crow.

**jack•et** (jăk'ĭt) *n.* **1.** A short coat. **2.** An outer covering.

**jack•ham•mer** (jăk'hăm'ər) *n.* A hand-held pneumatic machine for drilling rock.

**jack•pot** (jăk'pŏt') *n.* A top prize or reward.

**jade** (jād) *n.* A hard gemstone that is usually pale green or white.

**jag•uar** (jăg'wär', -yo͞o-är') *n.* A large tropical American wildcat.

**jail** (jāl) *n.* A prison. *—v.* To detain in custody; imprison. **—jail'er** *n.*

**jam** (jăm) *v.* **jammed, jamming. 1.** To squeeze; cram. **2.** To become or cause to become locked, stuck, or unworkable. *—n.* A predicament.

**jamb** (jăm) *n.* The side posts of a door or window frame.

**jan•i•tor** (jăn'ĭ-tər) *n.* A caretaker of a building.

**Jan•u•ar•y** (jăn'yo͞o-ĕr'ē) *n., pl.* **-ies.** The 1st month of the year.

**jar¹** (jär) *n.* A wide-mouthed bottle.

**jar²** (jär) *v.* **jarred, jarring. 1.** To make a harsh sound. **2.** To shake from impact. **3.** To clash. *—n.* **1.** A jolt. **2.** A harsh, grating sound.

**jar•gon** (jär'gən) *n.* The specialized language of a group, profession, etc.

**jas•mine** (jăz'mĭn) *n.* A fragrant flowering shrub.

**jaun•dice** (jôn'dĭs, jän'-) *n.* Yellowish discoloration of tissues and bodily fluids caused by a malfunction of the liver.

**jaun•diced** (jôn'dĭst, jän'-) *adj.* Affected by envy, jealousy, etc.

**jaun•ty** (jôn'tē, jän'-) *adj.* **-tier, -tiest. 1.** Dapper. **2.** Carefree; self-confident. **—jaun'ti•ly** *adv.*

**jave•lin** (jăv'lĭn, jăv'ə-) *n.* A light spear for throwing.

**jaw** (jô) *n.* **1.** Either of two bony structures holding the teeth. **2. jaws.** Anything resembling a pair of jaws.
**jay** (jā) *n.* A noisy, crowlike bird.
**jay•walk** (jā′wôk′) *v.* To cross a street carelessly. **—jay′walk′er** *n.*
**jazz** (jăz) *n.* A kind of American music, of African origin, featuring solo and ensemble improvisations.
**jeal•ous** (jĕl′əs) *adj.* **1.** Fearful of losing another's affection. **2.** Envious. **—jeal′ous•ly** *adv.* **—jeal′ous•y** *n.*
**jeans** (jēnz) *pl.n.* Pants made of heavy, usually blue cotton cloth.
**jeep** (jēp) *n.* A small, rugged motor vehicle.
**jeer** (jîr) *v.* To shout derisively; taunt. **—jeer** *n.*
**je•june** (jəjōōn′) *adj.* **1.** Lacking in nutrition. **2.** Uninteresting. **3.** Immature. **—je•june′ly** *—adv.*
**jell** (jĕl) *v.* To pass from a liquid to a semisolid state; congeal.
**jel•ly** (jĕl′ē) *n., pl.* **-lies.** A soft food made by using gelatin to cause a liquid to set. *—v.* **-lied, -lying.** To make into jelly.
**jel•ly•fish** (jĕl′ē-fĭsh′) *n.* A gelatinous, umbrella-shaped sea animal.
**jeop•ard•ize** (jĕp′ər-dīz′) *v.* **-ized, -izing.** To endanger; risk. **—jeop′ard•y** *n.*
**jerk** (jûrk) *v.* To move with a sharp, abrupt motion. *—n.* **1.** A sudden, abrupt motion. **2.** A stupid person. **—jerk′i•ly** *adv.* **—jerk′i•ness** *n.* **—jerk′y** *adj.*
**jer•ry•build** (jĕr′ē-bĭld′) *v.* **-built, -building.** To build shoddily and cheaply. **—jer′ry•build•er** *n.*
**jer•sey** (jûr′zē) *n., pl.* **-seys. 1.** A plain-knitted fabric. **2.** A knitted pullover shirt, jacket, or sweater.
**jest** (jĕst) *n.* A joke. *—v.* To joke. **—jest′er** *n.*
**jet**[1] (jĕt) *n.* **1.** A dense black coal used for jewelry. **2.** A deep black.
**jet**[2] (jĕt) *n.* **1.** A stream forced from a small-diameter opening. **2.** A jet-propelled aircraft. *—v.* **jetted, jetting. 1.** To gush out; squirt. **2.** To travel by jet aircraft.
**jet•sam** (jĕt′səm) *n.* Cargo thrown overboard to lighten a ship in distress.
**jet•ti•son** (jĕt′ĭ-sən, -zən) *v.* To cast overboard; discard.
**jet•ty** (jĕt′ē) *n., pl.* **-ties.** A wharf; pier.
**Jew** (jōō) *n.* **1.** An adherent of Judaism. **2.** A descendant of the Hebrew people. **—Jew′ish** *adj.* **—Jew′ry** *n.*
**jew•el** (jōōəl) *n.* **1.** An ornament of gems. **2.** A precious stone; a gem. **3.** A treasured person or thing. **—jew′el•er** *n.* **—jew′el•ry** *n.*
**jibe** (jīb) *v.* **jibed, jibing.** To be in accord; agree.
**jig** (jĭg) *n.* A lively dance. *—v.* **jigged, jigging.** To dance a jig.
**jig•ger** (jĭg′ər) *n.* **1.** One that jigs. **2.** A small measure for liquor, usually 1.5 ounces.
**jig•saw** (jĭg′sô′) *n.* A saw used to cut sharp curves.
**jilt** (jĭlt) *v.* To discard (a lover) unexpectedly.
**jin•gle** (jĭng′gəl) *v.* **-gled, -gling.** To make a tinkling sound. *—n.* **1.** A tinkling sound. **2.** A simple, catchy rhyme.
**jinx** (jĭngks) *n.* A cause of bad luck. *—v.* To bring bad luck to.
**jit•ney** (jĭt′nē) *n., pl.* **-neys.** A small bus transporting passengers for a small fare.
**jit•ter** (jĭt′ər) *v.* To be nervous; fidget. **—jit′ter•y** *adj.*
**job** (jŏb) *n.* **1.** An activity performed for payment. **2. a.** A piece of work. **b.** The object to be worked on. *—v.* **jobbed, jobbing. 1.** To work by the piece. **2.** To sell wholesale.
**jock•ey** (jŏk′ē) *n., pl.* **-eys.** One who rides racehorses. *—v.* To maneuver for position.
**jo•cose** (jō-kōs′) *adj.* Merry; humorous. **—jo•cose′ly** *adv.* **—jo•cos′i•ty** *n.*
**joc•u•lar** (jŏk′yə-lər) *adj.* Humorous; facetious. **—joc′u•lar′i•ty** *n.* **—joc′u•lar•ly** *adv.*
**jog** (jŏg) *v.* **1.** To jolt or nudge. **2.** To run at a steady slow trot. *—n.* **1.** A jolt or nudge. **2.** A trot. **—jog′ger** *n.* **—jog′ging** *n.*
**join** (join) *v.* **1.** To put together or into close association. **2.** To connect. **3.** To take part; participate.
**joint** (joint) *n.* **1.** A point or position at which 2 or more things are joined. **2.** A connection between movable bodily parts. **3.** A marijuana cigarette. *—adj.* Shared by or common to 2 or more.

**joke** (jōk) *n.* **1.** An amusing remark or story. **2.** A mischievous trick. —*v.* **joked, joking. 1.** To tell or play jokes. **2.** To be facetious.

**jok•er** (jō'kər) *n.* **1.** One who tells or plays jokes. **2.** A playing card typically used as a wild card.

**jol•ly** (jŏl'ē) *adj.* **-lier, -liest.** Merry; festive. —**jol'li•ty** *n.*

**jolt** (jōlt) *v.* **1.** To shake. **2.** To jar with a sudden blow. —*n.* A sudden jerking.

**josh** (jŏsh) *v.* To tease; joke.

**jos•tle** (jŏs'əl) *v.* **-tled, -tling. 1.** To collide. **2.** To push or elbow. —*n.* A shove.

**jot** (jŏt) *n.* The smallest bit. —*v.* **jotted, jotting.** To write down briefly.

**jour•nal** (jûr'nəl) *n.* **1.** A daily record. **2.** A newspaper or periodical.

**jour•nal•ism** (jûr'nə-lĭz'əm) *n.* The collecting, writing, editing, and publishing of news in periodicals. —**jour'nal•ist** *n.* —**jour'nal•is'tic** *adj.*

**jour•ney** (jûr'nē) *n., pl.* **-neys.** Travel; a trip. —*v.* To travel.

**joust** (joust) *n.* **1.** Combat between mounted knights with lances. **2.** A tournament —**joust** *v.*

**jo•vi•al** (jō'vē-əl) *adj.* Cheery; convivial; festive. —**jo'vi•al'i•ty** *n.*

**jowl**[1] (joul) *n.* **1.** The jaw. **2.** The cheek.

**jowl**[2] (joul) *n.* The flesh under the lower jaw.

**joy** (joi) *n.* **1.** Delight; happiness; gladness. **2.** A source of pleasure. —**joy'ful** *adj.* —**joy'•ful•ly** *adv.* —**joy'ous** *adj.* —**joy'ous•ly** *adv.*

**ju•bi•la•tion** (jo͞o'bə-lā'shən) *n.* Rejoicing; joy; exultation. —**ju'bi•lant** *adj.*

**ju•bi•lee** (jo͞o'bə-lē') *n.* A 50th anniversary.

**Ju•da•ism** (jo͞o'dē-ĭz'əm) *n.* The monotheistic religion of the Hebrew people. —**Ju•da'ic** *adj.*

**judge** (jŭj) *v.* **judged, judging. 1.** To pass judgment upon in a court of law. **2.** To determine after deliberation; decide. **3.** To form an opinion about. **4.** To criticize; censure. —*n.* **1.** A public official who decides cases in a court of law; justice. **2.** A connoisseur.

**judg•ment** (jŭj'mənt) *n.* Also **judge•ment. 1.** The capacity to make reasonable decisions; discernment. **2.** An idea; opinion; estimation. **3.** Criticism. **4.** A judicial decision. —**judg•men'tal** *adj.*

**ju•di•cial** (jo͞o-dish'əl) *adj.* Of courts of law or the administration of justice.

**ju•di•ci•ar•y** (jo͞o-dish'ē-ĕr'ē) *adj.* Of courts, judges, or their decisions. —*n., pl.* **-ies.** The judicial branch of government.

**ju•di•cious** (jo͞o-dĭsh'əs) *adj.* Exhibiting sound judgment; wise. —**ju•di'cious•ly** *adv.* —**ju•di'cious•ness** *n.*

**ju•do** (jo͞o'dō) *n.* A modern form of jujitsu.

**jug** (jŭg) *n.* A pitcher or rounded vessel for holding liquids.

**jug•gle** (jŭg'əl) *v.* **-gled, -gling. 1.** To keep (2 or more objects) in the air at 1 time by alternately tossing and catching them. **2.** To manipulate in order to deceive. —**jug'gler** *n.*

**jug•u•lar** (jŭg'yə-lər) *adj.* Of the neck or throat.

**juice** (jo͞os) *n.* **1.** Fluid contained in plant or animal tissue. **2.** Electric current. —*v.* **juiced, juicing.** To extract the juice from. —**juice'less** *adj.* —**juic'y** *adj.*

**ju•jit•su** (jo͞o-jit'so͞o) *n.* A Japanese art of hand-to-hand combat.

**ju•lep** (jo͞o'lĭp) *n.* **1.** A mint julep. **2.** A sweet, syrupy drink.

**Ju•ly** (jo͞o-lī') *n., pl.* **-lys.** The 7th month of the year.

**jum•ble** (jŭm'bəl) *v.* **-bled, -bling. 1.** To move or mix in a confused manner. **2.** To confuse. —**jum'ble** *n.*

**jump** (jŭmp) *v.* **1.** To spring up; leap; bound. **2.** To throw oneself down, off, out, etc. **3.** To spring at in attack. **4.** To start; jerk. **5.** To skip over; omit. —*n.* **1.** A leap. **2.** A sudden rise. **3.** A level or stage. —**jump'er** *n.*

**junc•tion** (jŭngk'shən) *n.* **1.** The act or process of joining. **2.** A place where 2 things join.

**junc•ture** (jŭngk'chər) *n.* **1.** Junction. **2.** A point in time.

**June** (jo͞on) *n.* The 6th month of the year.

**jun•gle** (jŭng'gəl) *n.* Densely overgrown land.

**jun•ior** (jo͞on'yər) *adj.* **1.** Younger. **2.** Designed for youthful persons. **3.** Of lower standing. **4.** Designating the 3rd year of a high school or college. —*n.* **1.** A younger person. **2.** A subordinate.

**3.** A 3rd-year student.

**ju•ni•per** (jo͞o′nə-pər) *n.* An evergreen tree or shrub with berrylike fruit.

**junk[1]** (jŭngk) *n.* Scrapped materials; rubbish. —*v.* To throw away.

**junk[2]** (jŭngk) *n.* A Chinese flat-bottomed ship.

**junk bond** *n.* A high-risk, high-yield debt security with no rating.

**jun•ket** (jŭng′kĭt) *n.* **1.** A sweet, custardlike food. **2.** An outing. **3.** A trip taken by an official.

**Ju•pi•ter** (jo͞o′pĭ-tər) *n.* The 5th planet from the sun.

**ju•ris•dic•tion** (jo͝or′ĭs-dĭk′shən) *n.* **1.** The authority to apply the law. **2.** The extent of such authority. —**ju′ris•dic′tion•al** *adj.*

**ju•ris•pru•dence** (jo͝or′ĭs-pro͞od′ns) *n.* The science of law.

**ju•rist** (jo͝or′ĭst) *n.* One skilled in law.

**ju•ror** (jo͝or′ər′, -ôr′) *n.* One who serves on a jury.

**ju•ry** (jo͝or′ē) *n., pl.* **-ries.** A group of persons chosen to judge and give a decision, esp. in a court of law.

**just** (jŭst) *adj.* **1.** Honorable and fair; equitable. **2.** Merited. **3.** Legitimate. **4.** Suitable; fitting. **5.** Sound; accurate. —*adv.* **1.** Exactly. **2.** Only a moment ago. **3.** Barely; merely. —**just′ly** *adv.* —**just′ness** *n.*

**jus•tice** (jŭs′tĭs) *n.* **1.** Moral rightness; equity. **2.** Fairness. **3.** The administration and procedure of law. **4.** A judge.

**jus•ti•fy** (jŭs′tə-fī′) *v.* **-fied, -fying. 1.** To demonstrate to be just, right, or valid. **2.** To warrant or defend. —**jus′ti•fi′a•ble** *adj.* —**jus′ti•fi′a•bly** *adv.* —**jus′ti•fi•ca′tion** *n.*

**jut** (jŭt) *v.* **jutted, jutting.** To project; protrude.

**ju•ve•nile** (jo͞o′və-nəl, -nīl′) *adj.* **1.** Young. **2.** Immature. —*n.* A young person.

**jux•ta•pose** (jŭk′stə-pōz′) *v.* **-posed, -posing.** To put side by side. —**jux′ta•po•si′tion** *n.*

## — K —

**k, K** (kā) *n.* The 11th letter of the English alphabet.

**ka•bu•ki** (kə-bo͞o′kē) *n.* Popular Japanese drama with song and dance.

**ka•chi•na** (kə-chē′nə) *n.* A doll representing an ancestral spirit of the Hopi.

**Kad•dish** (kä′dĭsh) *n.* A Jewish prayer recited daily in the synagogue and by mourners.

**kale** (kāl) *n.* A type of cabbage.

**ka•lei•do•scope** (kə-lī′də-skōp′) *n.* **1.** A small tube in which light shines through loose bits of colored glass that form designs when the tube is rotated. **2.** A series of changing events. —**ka•lei′do•scop′ic** *adj.*

**kan•ga•roo** (kăng′gə-ro͞o′) *n.* An Australian marsupial with large hind limbs adapted for leaping.

**ka•pok** (kā′pŏk′) *n.* A silky fiber from the fruit of a tropical tree, used in pillows, etc.

**kar•at** (kăr′ət) *n.* Also **car•at.** A measure comprising 24 units used to specify the proportion of pure gold in an alloy.

**ka•ra•te** (kə-rä′tē) *n.* A Japanese system of unarmed self-defense.

**kar•ma** (kär′mə) *n.* **1.** In Hinduism and Buddhism, the sum and consequences of one's actions during the successive phases of one's existence. **2.** Fate; destiny. —**kar′mic** *adj.*

**ka•ty•did** (kā′tē-dĭd′) *n.* A green insect related to the grasshoppers.

**kay•ak** (kī′ăk′) *n.* An Eskimo canoe with a covering that closes around the paddler's waist.

**keel** (kēl) *n.* The principal structural member of a ship, extending from bow to stern and forming the backbone of the vessel. —**keel over. 1.** To capsize. **2.** To faint.

**keen** (kēn) *adj.* **1.** Having a sharp cutting edge. **2.** Intellectually acute. **3.** Acutely sensitive. **4.** Eager; enthusiastic. —**keen′ly** *adv.* —**keen′ness** *n.*

**keep** (kēp) *v.* **kept** (kĕpt), **keeping. 1.** To retain possession of. **2.** To support. **3.** To manage; maintain. **4.** To remain or cause to continue in some condition. **5.** To preserve and protect. **6.** To detain. **7.** To refrain from divulging. **8.** To celebrate; observe. **9.** To remain fresh or unspoiled. —*n.* **1.** Care; charge. **2.** Means of support. —**keep′er** *n.*

**keep•sake** (kēp′sāk′) *n.* A memento.

**keg** (kĕg) *n.* A small cask.

**kelp** (kĕlp) *n.* Brown, often very large seaweed.

**ken•nel** (kĕn′əl) *n.* **1.** A dog shelter. **2.** An establishment where dogs are bred or boarded.

**Ke•ogh plan** (kē′ō) *n.* A retirement plan for the self-employed.

**ke•pi** (kā′pē, kĕp′ē) *n.* A French military cap with a flat, circular top and a visor.

**kept** (kĕpt) *v.* p.t. & p.p. of **keep.**

**ker•chief** (kûr′chĭf, -chēf′) *n., pl.* **-chiefs** or **-chieves. 1.** A scarf, worn as a head covering. **2.** A handkerchief.

**ker•nel** (kûr′nəl) *n.* **1.** A grain or seed. **2.** The inner, often edible part of a nut. **3.** The core; essence.

**ker•o•sene** (kĕr′ə-sēn′, kăr′-, kĕr′ə-sēn′, kăr′-) *n.* A thin oil used as a fuel.

**ketch** (kĕch) *n.* A two-masted sailing vessel.

**ketch•up** (kĕch′əp, kăch′-) *n.* A thick, spicy tomato sauce.

**ket•tle** (kĕt′l) *n.* A metal pot for boiling.

**ket•tle•drum** (kĕt′l-drŭm′) *n.* A large drum with a parchment head.

**key**[1] (kē) *n.* **1.** A metal implement to open or close a lock. **2.** A crucial fact; clue; explanation. **3.** A button or lever depressed with the finger to operate a machine or to produce or change the sound of a musical instrument. **4.** In music, a tonal system of 7 tones in fixed relationship to a tonic. **5.** A general tone or level of intensity. *—v.* To tune up; adjust. *—adj.* Crucial; essential.

**key**[2] (kē) *n.* A small offshore island or reef.

**key•board** (kē′bôrd′, -bōrd′) *n.* A set of keys, as on a piano, computer terminal, etc.

**key money** *n.* Payment made surreptitiously to assure an apartment rental.

**key•note** (kē′nōt′) *n.* A central element.

**key•punch** (kē′pŭnch′) *n.* A keyboard machine for punching holes in cards or tapes in data-processing systems. **—key′punch′er** *n.*

**key•stone** (kē′stōn′) *n.* The central wedge-shaped stone of an arch.

**key•stroke** (kē′strōk′) *n.* The stroke of a key, as of a typewriter or computer keyboard.

**khak•i** (kăk′ē, kä′kē) *n., pl.* **-is. 1.** Light olive or yellowish brown. **2.** A cloth of this color. **—khak′i** *adj.*

**kib•butz** (kĭ-bo͝ots′) *n., pl.* **kibbutzim** (kĭb′o͝ot-sēm′). A collective farm in Israel.

**kick** (kĭk) *v.* **1.** To strike with the foot. **2.** To recoil, as a gun. *—n.* **1.** The act of kicking. **2.** A temporary interest.

**kick•back** (kik′băk′) *n.* A payment to a person able to influence or control a source of income.

**kid** (kĭd) *n.* **1.** A young goat. **2.** Leather from the skin of a young goat. **3.** A child. *—v.* **kidded, kidding.** To tease or deceive playfully. **—kid′der** *n.*

**kid•nap** (kĭd′năp′) *v.* **-naped** or **-napped, -naping** or **-napping.** To abduct and detain (a person), often for ransom. **—kid′nap′er, kid′nap′per** *n.*

**kid•ney** (kĭd′nē) *n., pl.* **-neys.** Either of a pair of organs that maintain proper water balance and excrete urine.

**kill** (kĭl) *v.* **1.** To put to death; slay. **2.** To thwart; veto. *—n.* That which is killed or destroyed, as an animal in hunting. **—kill′er** *n.*

**kill•ing** (kĭl′ĭng) *n.* **1.** A murder. **2.** A sudden large profit.

**kiln** (kĭl, kĭln) *n.* An oven for hardening or drying, esp. ceramics.

**ki•lo•cy•cle** (kĭl′ə-sī′kəl) *n.* One thousand cycles per second.

**kil•o•gram** (kĭl′ə-grăm′) *n.* The fundamental unit of mass in the metric system, about 2.20 pounds.

**kil•o•me•ter** (kĭl′ə-mē′tər, kĭ-lŏm′ə-tər) *n.* One thousand meters.

**kil•o•watt** (kĭl′ə-wŏt′) *n.* One thousand watts.

**kilt** (kĭlt) *n.* A man's skirt worn in the Scottish Highlands.

**ki•mo•no** (kə-mō′nə, -nō) *n., pl.* **-nos. 1.** A wide-sleeved Japanese robe. **2.** A type of dressing gown.

**kin** (kĭn) *n.* One's relatives collectively. **—kin′folk′** *n.*

**kind**[1] (kīnd) *adj.* Showing sympathy or understanding; helpful or giving. **—kind′ness** *n.*

**kind**[2] (kīnd) *n.* A class or category; sort; type.

**kin•der•gar•ten** (kĭn′dər-gär′tn, -dn) *n.* A program or class for 4- to 6-year-old children as preparation for school.

**kin•dle** (kĭn′dl) *v.* **-dled, -dling. 1.** To start (a fire). **2.** To arouse; inspire.

**kin•dling** (kĭnd′lĭng) *n.* Material used to start a fire.

**kind•ly** (kīnd′lē) *adj.* **-lier, -liest.** Sympathetic; considerate; helpful. *—adv.* **1.** In a kind manner. **2.** Pleasantly; accommodatingly. **—kind′li•ness** *n.*

**kin•dred** (kĭn′drĭd) *n.* A person's relatives. *—adj.* Similar or related.

**kin•e•scope** (kĭn′ĭ-skōp′) *n.* A cathode-ray tube that translates received TV signals into a visible picture.

**king** (kĭng) *n.* **1.** A male monarch. **2.** A playing card bearing a picture of a king. **—king′li•ness** *n.* **—king′ly** *adj.*

**king•dom** (kĭng′dəm) *n.* **1.** A country ruled by a king or queen. **2.** A broad category of living or natural forms.

**king•fish•er** (kĭng′fĭsh′ər) *n.* A large-billed bird that feeds on fish.

**kink** (kĭngk) *n.* **1.** A curl or twist. **2.** A painful muscle spasm. *—v.* To form kinks (in). **—kink′y** *adj.*

**kin•ship** (kĭn′shĭp′) *n.* **1.** Relationship by blood. **2.** A close connection.

**ki•osk** (kē-ŏsk′, kē′ŏsk′) *n.* A small structure used as a newsstand, etc.

**kip•per** (kĭp′ər) *n.* A salted, smoked herring.

**kis•met** (kĭz′mĕt′, -mĭt) *n.* Fate; fortune.

**kiss** (kĭs) *v.* To touch with the lips in affection, greeting, etc. *—n.* **1.** A touching with the lips. **2.** A small piece of candy.

**kit** (kĭt) *n.* **1.** A set of instruments or equipment. **2.** A set of parts to be assembled.

**kitch•en** (kĭch′ən) *n.* A room in which food is cooked. **—kitch′en•ette′** *n.*

**kite** (kīt) *n.* **1.** A light framework covered with paper and designed to hover in the wind. **2.** A predatory bird with a long tail.

**kitsch** (kĭch) *n.* Pretentious bad taste.

**kit•ten** (kĭt′n) *n.* A young cat.

**kit•ty** (kĭt′ē) *n., pl.* **-ties.** A pool or fund of money.

**klep•to•ma•ni•a** (klĕp′tə-mā′nē-ə) *n.* An obsessive impulse to steal. **—klep′to•ma′ni•ac′** *n.*

**knack** (năk) *n.* A specific ability.

**knap•sack** (năp′săk′) *n.* A supply bag worn on the back.

**knave** (nāv) *n.* An unprincipled, crafty person. **—knav′ish** *adj.*

**knead** (nēd) *v.* **1.** To mix and work (a substance). **2.** To massage.

**knee** (nē) *n.* The joint between the upper and lower parts of the leg.

**knee•cap** (nē′kăp′) *n.* The patella.

**kneel** (nēl) *v.* **knelt** (nĕlt) or **kneeled, kneeling.** To rest on bent knees.

**knell** (nĕl) *v.* **1.** To ring a bell; toll. **2.** To signal by tolling. *—n.* **1.** The slow sounding of a bell. **2.** An omen of sorrow.

**knew** (n/y/o͞o) *v.* p.t. of **know.**

**knick•ers** (nĭk′ərz) *pl.n.* Full breeches gathered below the knee.

**knick•knack** (nĭk′năk′) *n.* A decorative trinket.

**knife** (nīf) *n., pl.* **knives** (nīvz). A cutting blade with a handle. *—v.* **knifed, knifing.** To cut, stab, or wound.

**knight** (nīt) *n.* **1.** A medieval gentleman-soldier. **2.** The holder of a nonhereditary title conferred by a sovereign. *—v.* To raise (a person) to knighthood. **—knight′hood′** *n.* **—knight′ly** *adj.*

**knish** (kə-nĭsh′) *n.* A piece of dough stuffed with cheese, meat, or vegetables and baked or fried.

**knit** (nĭt) *v.* **knit** or **knitted, knitting. 1.** To make by intertwining yarn in a series of loops. **2.** To join closely. *—n.* A knitted fabric or garment.

**knob** (nŏb) *n.* A rounded protuberance or a rounded handle. **—knob′by** *adj.*

**knock** (nŏk) *v.* **1.** To strike hard. **2.** To criticize adversely. **3.** To collide; bump. **—knock** *n.*

**knoll** (nōl) *n.* A small hill.

**knot** (nŏt) *n.* **1.** A tightly tied intersection, as of string. **2.** Any bond. **3.** A cluster of persons or things. **4.** A hard lump from which a tree branch grows. **5.** A unit of speed, 1 nautical mile per hour. *—v.* **knotted, knotting. 1.** To snarl or tangle. **2.** To form a knot (in).

**knot•ty** (nŏt′ē) *adj.* **-tier, -tiest. 1.** Covered with or having knots; gnarled. **2.** Difficult; intricate.

**know** (nō) *v.* **knew** (no͞o), **known** (nōn), **knowing. 1.** To perceive directly; be aware of. **2.** To be capable of. **3** To understand. **4.** To be acquainted with.

**know•ing** (nō′ĭng) *adj.* **1.** Possessing knowledge or understanding. **2.** Clever;

shrewd. **—know'ing•ly** *adv.*

**knowl•edge** (nŏl'ĭj) *n.* **1.** Familiarity, awareness, or understanding. **2.** That which is known. **3.** Learning. **—knowl'edge•a•ble** *adj.*

**knuck•le** (nŭk'əl) *n.* Any joint of a finger. —*v.* **-led, -ling. —knuckle down.** To apply oneself. **—knuckle under.** To yield to pressure.

**ko•a•la** (kō-ä'lə) *n.* A furry, tree-dwelling Australian marsupial.

**Ko•ran** (kə-răn', -rän', kô-, kō-) *n.* The holy book of Islam, containing the revelation of Allah to Muhammad.

**ko•sher** (kō'shər) *adj.* **1.** Conforming to Jewish dietary laws. **2.** Proper; legitimate.

**ku•dos** (k/y/ōō'dōz', -dōs') *n.* Acclaim or prestige.

**kum•quat** (kŭm'kwŏt') *n.* A small, edible orangelike fruit.

# – L –

**l, L** (ĕl) *n.* The 12th letter of the English alphabet.

**la•bel** (lā'bəl) *n.* A tag attached to an article to designate its owner, contents, etc. —*v.* **1.** To attach a label to. **2.** To classify.

**la•bor** (lā'bər) *n.* **1.** Physical or mental work. **2.** Work for wages. **3.** Workers collectively. —*v.* **1.** To work. **2.** To proceed slowly; plod. **—la'bor•er** *n.* **—la•bo'ri•ous** *adj.*

**lab•o•ra•to•ry** (lăb'rə-tôr'ē, -tōr'ē) *n., pl.* **-ries.** A place for scientific research or experiment.

**la•bor-in•ten•sive** (lā'bər-ĭn-tĕn'sĭv) *adj.* Requiring a large expenditure of labor in comparison to capital.

**lab•y•rinth** (lăb'ə-rĭnth') *n.* A network of interconnecting passages. **—lab'y•rin'thine'** *adj.*

**lace** (lās) *n.* **1.** A cord. **2.** A delicate fabric in a weblike pattern. —*v.* **laced, lacing.** To fasten with a lace.

**lac•er•ate** (lăs'ə-rāt') *v.* **-ated, -ating.** To tear; mangle. **—lac'er•a'tion** *n.*

**lack** (lăk) *n.* A deficiency or absence. —*v.* To be without or be wanting.

**lack•ey** (lăk'ē) *n., pl.* **-eys. 1.** A footman. **2.** A servile follower.

**lack•lus•ter** (lăk'lŭs'tər) *adj.* Lacking brightness and vitality; dull.

**la•con•ic** (lə-kŏn'ĭk) *adj.* Terse; concise.

**lac•quer** (lăk'ər) *n.* A coating used to give surfaces a high gloss. **—lac'quer** *v.*

**lac•tic** (lăk'tĭk) *adj.* Of or derived from milk.

**la•cu•na** (lə-kyōō'nə) *n., pl.* **-nae** or **-nas.** An empty space or missing part; gap.

**lad** (lăd) *n.* A young man.

**lad•der** (lăd'ər) *n.* A device consisting of 2 long poles crossed by parallel rungs, used to climb.

**la•dle** (lād'l) *n.* A long-handled spoon with a deep bowl. —*v.* **-dled, -dling.** To lift out with a ladle.

**la•dy** (lā'dē) *n., pl.* **-dies. 1.** A woman of refinement. **2.** The female head of a household. **3.** A feminine title of rank.

**la•dy•bug** (lā'dē-bŭg') *n.* A small beetle, reddish with black spots.

**lag** (lăg) *v.* **lagged, lagging. 1.** To fail to keep up a pace. **2.** To slacken. —*n.* **1.** A falling behind. **2.** A gap. **—lag'gard** *n.*

**la•ger** (lä'gər) *n.* A kind of beer, aged 6 weeks to 6 months.

**la•goon** (lə-gōōn') *n.* A body of brackish water, esp. one separated from the sea by sandbars or reefs.

**laid** (lād) *v.* p.t. & p.p. of **lay[1]**.

**lain** (lān) *v.* p.p. of **lie[1]**.

**lair** (lâr) *n.* The den of a wild animal.

**lais•sez faire** (lĕs'ā fâr') *n.* An economic theory opposing government interference in commerce. **—lais'sez-faire'** *adj.*

**lake** (lāk) *n.* A large inland body of water.

**lamb** (lăm) *n.* A young sheep.

**lam•baste** (lăm-bāst') *v.* **-basted, -basting. 1.** To thrash. **2.** To scold.

**lam•bent** (lăm'bənt) *adj.* **1.** Flickering lightly over a surface. **2.** Effortlessly brilliant. **3.** Gently glowing; luminous. **—lam'ben•cy** *n.* **—lam'bent•ly** *adv.*

**lame** (lām) *adj.* **lamer, lamest. 1.** Crippled, esp. in a leg or foot. **2.** Ineffectual. —*v.* **lamed, laming.** To make lame. **—lame'ness** *n.*

**la•mé** (lă-mā') *n.* A brocaded fabric having metallic threads.

**la•ment** (lə-mĕnt') *v.* **1.** To mourn. **2.** To wail; complain. —*n.* **1.** An expression of mourning. **2.** A dirge. **—la•men'ta•ble** *adj.* **—lam'en•ta'tion** *n.*

**lam•i•nate** (lăm'ə-nāt') *v.* **-nated, -nating. 1.** To bond together in thin layers. **2.** To divide into thin layers. **—lam'i•na'tion** *n.*

**lamp** (lămp) *n.* A device for providing light.

**lam•poon** (lăm-po͞on') *n.* Satire, esp. that intended to ridicule. —*v.* To ridicule in a lampoon.

**lance** (lăns) *n.* A spear with a long shaft. —*v.* **lanced, lancing.** To cut into with a surgical knife.

**land** (lănd) *n.* **1.** The solid part of the earth's surface. **2.** A portion or region of this. —*v.* To arrive or cause to arrive on land or at a certain place.

**land•la•dy** (lănd'lā'dē) *n., pl.* **-ladies.** A woman who owns and leases property.

**land•lord** (lănd'lôrd') *n.* A man who owns and leases property.

**land•scape** (lănd'skāp') *n.* **1.** A view of rural scenery. **2.** A pictorial representation of this.

**land•slide** (lănd'slīd') *n.* **1.** The slip and fall of a mass of earth and rock. **2.** An election or a majority of votes sweeping a candidate or party into office. **3.** A great victory.

**lane** (lān) *n.* A narrow way or road.

**lan•guage** (lăng'gwĭj) *n.* **1.** Speech. **2.** Any system of signs, symbols, etc., used for communication.

**lan•guish** (lăng'gwĭsh) *v.* **1.** To lose strength or vigor. **2.** To become listless or disconsolate. **—lan'guid** *adj.* **—lan'guor** *n.* **—lan'•guor•ous** *adj.*

**lank** (lăngk) *adj.* Long and lean; gaunt. **—lank'y** *adj.*

**lan•o•lin** (lăn'ə-lĭn) *n.* A yellowish fat obtained from sheep's wool and used in ointments and soaps.

**lan•tern** (lăn'tərn) *n.* A case for holding and protecting a light.

**lap¹** (lăp) *n.* The front part of a seated person from the lower trunk to the knees.

**lap²** (lăp) *v.* **lapped, lapping.** To fold or wrap over or around. —*n.* **1.** An overlapping part. **2.** A complete circuit of a racecourse.

**lap³** (lăp) *v.* To lift and take in (a liquid or food) with the tongue. **—lap** *n.*

**la•pel** (lə-pĕl) *n.* A front of a coat, jacket, etc., folded back against the chest.

**lap•is laz•u•li** (lăp'ĭs lăz'ə-lē) *n.* An opaque, deep-blue gemstone.

**lapse** (lăps) *v.* **lapsed, lapsing. 1.** To fall away gradually. **2.** To become invalid. —*n.* **1.** A slipping into a lower state. **2.** A minor slip or failure. **3.** A passing or interval of time.

**lar•ce•ny** (lär'sə-nē) *n. pl.* **-nies.** Theft. **—lar'ce•nous** *adj.*

**lard** (lärd) *n.* The white solid rendered fat of a hog. —*v.* **1.** To cover with lard. **2.** To make rich with fat. **3.** To embellish. **—lard'y** *adj.*

**large** (lärj) *adj.* **larger, largest.** Of considerable size, capacity, etc.; big. **—at large. 1.** At liberty. **2.** Not representing or assigned to a specific country, district, etc. **—large'ly** *adv.*

**lar•i•at** (lăr'ē-ət) *n.* A lasso.

**lark** (lärk) *n.* A carefree romp or prank.

**lar•yn•gi•tis** (lăr'ən-jī'tĭs) *n.* Inflammation of the larynx.

**lar•ynx** (lăr'ĭngks) *n.* The upper part of the respiratory tract, containing the vocal cords. **—la•ryn'ge•al** *adj.*

**las•civ•i•ous** (lə-siv'ē-əs) *adj.* Lewd; lecherous.

**la•ser** (lāzər) *n.* A device that produces highly amplified coherent light.

**lash¹** (lăsh) *n.* **1.** A whip or thong of a whip. **2.** A blow with a whip. **3.** An eyelash. —*v.* To strike with or as with a whip.

**lash²** (lăsh) *v.* To secure, as with a rope.

**lass** (lăs) *n.* A girl or young woman.

**las•si•tude** (lăs'ĭ-t/y/o͞od') *n.* Listless weakness or exhaustion.

**las•so** (lăs'o͞o) *n., pl.* **-sos -soes.** A long rope with a running noose, used esp. to catch horses. **—las'so** *v.*

**last¹** (lăst) *adj.* **1.** Being, coming, or remaining after all others. **2.** Most recent; latest. **3.** Conclusive and authoritative. —*adv.* **1.** Most recently. **2.** In conclusion. —*n.* One that is last. **—last'ly** *adv.*

**last²** (lăst) *v.* To endure.

**latch** (lăch) *n.* A fastening or lock, as for a gate.

**late** (lāt) *adj.* **later, latest. 1.** Coming or occurring after the expected time. **2.** Recent. **3.** Recently deceased. —*adv.* **1.**

After the expected time. **2.** Recently. **—late'ly** *adv.*

**la•tent** (lāt'nt) *adj.* Present or potential but not manifest. **—la'ten•cy** *n.*

**lat•er•al** (lăt'ər-əl) *adj.* Of, at, on, or toward the side.

**la•tex** (lā'tĕks') *n.* The viscous sap of certain plants and trees. **—la'tex'** *adj.*

**lathe** (lāth) *n.* A machine on which a piece is spun and shaped by a cutting tool.

**lath•er** (lăth'ər) *n.* **1.** Foam, esp. that formed by soap and water. **2.** Frothy sweat. *—v.* **1.** To produce lather. **2.** To apply lather to.

**lat•i•tude** (lăt'ĭ-t/y/o͞od') *n.* **1.** Extent; range. **2.** Freedom from limitations. **3.** The angular distance N or S of the equator.

**lat•ter** (lăt'ər) *adj.* **1.** Second of 2. **2.** Further advanced; later.

**lat•tice** (lăt'ĭs) *n.* An open framework made of interwoven strips. **—lat'tice•work'** *n.*

**laud** (lôd) *v.* To praise; commend. **—laud'a•ble** *adj.*

**laugh** (lăf) *v.* To produce sounds expressive of mirth or derision. *—n.* The sound or act of laughing. **—laugh'a•ble** *adj.* **—laugh'ter** *n.*

**launch¹** (lônch) *v.* **1.** To set in motion. **2.** To move (a boat) into the water. *—n.* An act of launching.

**launch²** (lônch) *n.* An open motorboat.

**laun•der** (lôn'dər, län'-) *v.* To wash and iron (clothes or linens). **—laun'dry** *n.*

**lau•re•ate** (lôr'ē-ĭt, lŏr'-) *adj.* **1.** Crowned with laurel as an honor. **2.** Worthy of honor. *—n.* **1.** One honored for accomplishments, esp. in the arts or sciences. **2.** A poet laureate. **—lau're•ate•ship'** *n.*

**la•va** (lä'və, lăv'ə) *n.* Molten rock from a volcano.

**lav•a•to•ry** (lăv'ə-tôr'ē, -tōr'ē) *n., pl.* **-ries.** A room with a toilet and sink.

**lav•en•der** (lăv'ən-dər) *n.* **1.** An aromatic plant having fragrant purplish flowers. **2.** Pale to light purple. **—lav'en•der** *adj.*

**lav•ish** (lăv'ĭsh) *adj.* Extravagant. *—v.* To give, spend, etc., unstintingly.

**law** (lô) *n.* **1.** A rule established by authority, society, or custom. **2.** A body of such rules. **3.** The profession relating to such rules. **4.** A generalization based on observed phenomena. **—law'ful** *adj.* **—law'less** *adj.* **—law'mak'er** *n.*

**lawn** (lôn) *n.* A closely mown area planted with grass.

**law•suit** (lô's/y/o͞ot') *n.* A case brought before a law court.

**law•yer** (lô'yər) *n.* A professional who practices law.

**lax** (lăks) *adj.* **1.** Negligent; remiss. **2.** Not strict. **—lax'i•ty, lax'ness** *n.*

**lax•a•tive** (lăk'sə-tĭv) *n.* A substance stimulating the evacuation of the bowels. **—lax'a•tive** *adj.*

**lay¹** (lā) *v.* **laid** (lād), **laying. 1.** To place on a surface. **2.** To produce and deposit (eggs). **3.** To set or place in a desired position. **4.** To prepare; contrive. *—n.* The relative position of something.

**lay²** (lā) *v.* p.t. of **lie¹.**

**lay³** (lā) *adj.* Relating to the laity; not clerical. **2.** Not of a particular trade or profession. **—lay'-peo'ple** *pl.n.*

**lay•er** (lā'ər) *n.* A single thickness.

**lay•ette** (lā-ĕt') *n.* Clothing and other equipment for a newborn baby.

**lay•man** (lā'mən) *n., pl.* **-men. 1.** A man who is not a member of the clergy. **2.** A man who is not a member of a skilled or learned profession.

**lay•off** (lā'ôf', -ŏf') *n.* **1.** A suspension or dismissal of employees. **2.** A period of temporary inactivity.

**lay•out** (lā'out') *n.* An arrangement or plan.

**lay•o•ver** (lā'ō'vər) *n.* A usu. short stop or break in a journey.

**lay•wom•an** (lā'wo͝om'ən) *n., pl.* **-women.** A woman who is not a member of the clergy.

**la•zy** (lā'zē) *adj.* **-zier, -ziest. 1.** Indolent; slothful. **2.** Slow-moving; sluggish. **—la'zi•ness** *n.*

**LCD** *n.* A digital display consisting of liquid crystal material between sheets of glass.

**lea** (lē, lā) *n.* A meadow.

**lead¹** (lēd) *v.* **led** (lĕd), **leading. 1.** To guide, conduct, escort, or direct. **2.** To influence. **3.** To be ahead or at the head of. **4.** To pursue; live. *—n.* **1.** The 1st place. **2.** A clue. **3.** The amount by which one is ahead. **4.** The main part in a play, movie, etc. **—lead'er** *n.*

**—lead'er•ship'** *n.*

**lead²** (lĕd) *n.* **1.** A soft, dense, dull-gray metallic element. **2.** Graphite used as a marking substance in a pencil. **—lead'en** *adj.*

**leaf** (lēf) *n., pl.* **leaves. 1.** A usually green, flattened plant structure attached to a stem. **2.** A thin sheet of paper, as a page of a book. **3.** A thin sheet of gold. *—v.* To turn or glance at pages rapidly. **—leaf'y** *adj.*

**league** (lēg) *n.* An association or alliance.

**leak** (lēk) *n.* **1. a.** A flaw, crack, or hole permitting escape of fluid or light. **b.** Such escape. **2.** A disclosure of confidential information. *—v.* **1.** To escape through a leak. **2.** To disclose or become known through a breach of secrecy. **—leak'age** *n.* **—leak'y** *adj.*

**lean¹** (lēn) *v.* **leaned, leaning. 1.** To bend; incline. **2.** To rely on for assistance.

**lean²** (lēn) *adj.* **1.** Thin. **2.** Containing little or no fat. **—lean'ness** *n.*

**lean-to** (lēn'to͞o') *n., pl.* **-tos.** A shed or shelter having a roof with only 1 slope.

**leap** (lēp) *v.* **leaped** or **leapt** (lĕpt, lēpt), **leaping. 1.** To jump off the ground. **2.** To jump forward; bound. *—n.* A jump.

**learn** (lûrn) *v.* **learned** or **learnt, learning. 1.** To gain knowledge or mastery. **2.** To become informed. **—learn'ed** *adj.* **—learn'er** *n.* **—learn'ing** *n.*

**lease** (lēs) *n.* A contract granting use of land or holdings in exchange for rent. *—v.* **leased, leasing.** To grant by or hold under lease.

**leash** (lēsh) *n.* A restraining chain, strap, etc., for an animal. **—leash** *v.*

**least** (lēst) *adv. & adj.* superl. of **little. 1.** Lowest in importance or rank. **2.** Smallest in magnitude. *—n.* The one that is smallest or slightest.

**leath•er** (lĕ*th*'ər) *n.* The tanned hide of an animal. **—leath'er** *adj.* **—leath'er•y** *adj.*

**leave¹** (lēv) *v.* **left** (lĕft), **leaving. 1.** To go away from; depart. **2.** To let or cause to remain. **3.** To bequeath.

**leave²** (lēv) *n.* **1.** Permission, esp. to be absent from duty. **2.** Farewell.

**leaves** (lēvz) *n.* pl. of **leaf.**

**lech•er** (lĕch'ər) *n.* A person given to excessive sexual indulgence. **—lech'er•ous** *adj.* **—lech'er•y** *n.*

**lec•tern** (lĕk'tərn) *n.* A stand with a slanted top serving as a support for a speaker's notes or books.

**lec•ture** (lĕk'chər) *n.* **1.** An instructional speech. **2.** A solemn scolding. **—lec'ture** *v.* **—lec'tur•er** *n.*

**led** (lĕd) *v.* p.t. & p.p. of **lead¹.**

**LED** *n.* A diode converting electricity into light used in digital displays.

**ledge** (lĕj) *n.* A shelflike projection.

**ledg•er** (lĕj'ər) *n.* A book in which monetary transactions are posted.

**lee** (lē) *n.* **1.** The side away from the wind. **2.** Cover; shelter. **—lee** *adj.*

**leer** (lîr) *n.* A suggestive or cunning look. **—leer** *v.*

**lee•way** (lē'wā') *n.* A margin of freedom; latitude.

**left¹** (lĕft) *adj.* Of, at, or on the side of the body that faces north when the subject is facing east. *—n.* **1.** The left side or hand. **2.** Often **the Left.** The persons and groups pursuing egalitarian political goals by reform or revolution. *—adv.* Toward or on the left.

**left²** (lĕft) *v.* p.t. & p.p. of **leave¹.**

**leg** (lĕg) *n.* **1.** A limb of an animal, used for locomotion or support. **2.** Something resembling a leg.

**leg•a•cy** (lĕg'ə-sē) *n., pl.* **-cies. 1.** A bequest. **2.** Something handed down; heritage. **—leg'a•tee'** *n.*

**le•gal** (lē'gəl) *adj.* **1.** Of law or lawyers. **2.** Authorized by law. **—le•gal'i•ty** *n.* **—le'gal•i•za'tion** *n.* **—le'gal•ize'** *v.* **—le'gal•ly** *adv.*

**le•ga•tion** (lĭ-gā'shən) *n.* **1.** A diplomatic mission headed by a minister. **2.** The premises occupied by the mission.

**leg•end** (lĕj'ənd) *n.* **1.** A story handed down from the past. **2.** An inscription. **—leg'en•dar•y** *adj.*

**leg•er•de•main** (lĕj'ər-də-mān') *n.* Sleight of hand; trickery.

**leg•i•ble** (lĕj'ə-bəl) *adj.* Capable of being read. **—leg'i•bil'i•ty** *n.* **—leg'i•bly** *adv.*

**le•gion** (lē'jən) *n.* **1.** A large military division. **2.** A multitude.

**leg•is•late** (lĕj'ĭ-slāt') *v.* **-lated, -lating.** To pass a law. **—leg'is•la'tion** *n.* **—leg'is•la'tive** *adj.* **—leg'is•la'tor** *n.*

**leg•is•la•ture** (lĕj'ĭ-slā'chər) *n.* A body of persons vested with the power to legislate.

**le•git•i•mate** (lə-jĭt'ə-mĭt) *adj.* **1.** Lawful. **2.** Reasonable. **3.** Authentic; genuine. **4.** Born in wedlock. **—le•git'i•ma•cy** *n.*

**lei•sure** (lē'zhər, lĕzh'ər) *n.* Freedom from work; time not spent in compulsory activity. **—lei'sure•ly** *adj. & adv.*

**leit•mo•tif, leit•mo•tiv** (līt'mō-tēf') *n.* **1.** A melodic passage or phrase associated with a particular character. **2.** A dominant and recurring theme.

**lem•ming** (lĕm'ĭng) *n.* A species of European rodent notorious for its mass migrations into the sea.

**lem•on** (lĕm'ən) *n.* A yellow citrus fruit with sour, juicy pulp. **—lem'on•y** *adj.*

**lend** (lĕnd) *v.* **lent** (lĕnt), **lending. 1.** To give out or allow for temporary use. **2.** To impart. **—lend'er** *n.*

**length** (lĕngkth, lĕngth) *n.* **1.** The measure of something along its greatest dimension. **2.** Duration or extent. **—length'en** *v.* **—length'wise'** *adv. & adj.* **—length'y** *adj.*

**le•ni•ent** (lē'nē-ənt, lēn'yənt) *adj.* Merciful; generous. **—le'ni•en•cy, le'ni•ence** *n.*

**lens** (lĕnz) *n.* **1.** A piece of glass or other transparent material used to make light rays converge or diverge to form an image. **2.** A transparent part of the eye that focuses light entering the eye on the retina.

**lent** (lĕnt) *v.* p.t. & p.p. of **lend.**

**leop•ard** (lĕp'ərd) *n.* A large wild cat, usually having a spotted coat.

**lep•ro•sy** (lĕp'rə-sē) *n.* A chronic disease causing ulcers and sores on the body. **—lep'er** *n.* **—lep'rous** *adj.*

**Les•bi•an** (lĕz'bē-ən) *adj.* **1.** Relating to the isle of Lesbos or its people or culture. **2. lesbian.** Relating to female homosexuality. *—n.* **1.** An inhabitant of Lesbos. **2. lesbian.** A female homosexual. **—les'bi•an•ism'** *n.*

**le•sion** (lē'zhən) *n.* A wound, injury, or mass of diseased tissue.

**less** (lĕs) *adv. & adj.* A compar. of **little. 1.** Smaller. **2.** Lower in importance. *—n.* A smaller amount. *—prep.* Minus. **—less'en** *v.*

**les•see** (lĕ-sē') *n.* One that holds a lease from a lessor.

**les•son** (lĕs'ən) *n.* **1.** Something learned or to be learned. **2.** A period of instruction. **3.** An instructive example or experience.

**les•sor** (lĕs'ôr', lĕ-sôr') *n.* One that lets a property under a lease to a lessee.

**let** (lĕt) *v.* **let, letting. 1.** To allow. **2.** To rent or lease.

**le•thal** (lē'thəl) *adj.* Deadly.

**leth•ar•gy** (lĕth'ər-jē) *n. pl.* **-gies.** Sluggishness and indifference; drowsiness. **—le•thar'gic** *adj.*

**let•ter** (lĕt'ər) *n.* **1.** A written symbol representing a speech sound. **2.** A written communication. **3. letters.** Literature or learning. *—v.* To mark or write with letters.

**lev•ee** (lĕv'ē) *n.* **1.** An embankment to prevent a river from flooding. **2.** A landing place on a river.

**lev•el** (lĕv'əl) *n.* **1.** Relative position or rank. **2.** A flat, horizontal surface. **3.** Elevation; height. **4.** An instrument for ascertaining whether a surface is horizontal. *—adj.* **1.** Having a flat, smooth surface. **2.** Horizontal. **3.** Even. **4.** Uniform; consistent. *—v.* **1.** To make or become horizontal, flat, or even. **2.** To raze. **3.** To aim. **—lev'el•er** *n.*

**le•ver** (lĕv'ər, lē'vər) *n.* A simple machine consisting of a rigid bar that turns on a fixed fulcrum.

**lev•er•age** (lĕv'ər-ĭj, lē'vər-) *n.* **1.** The mechanical advantage of a lever. **2.** Positional advantage.

**le•vi•a•than** (lə-vī'ə-thən) *n.* **1.** A sea monster. **2.** A whale. **3.** Something unusually large of its kind.

**lev•i•tate** (lĕv'ĭ-tāt') *v.* **-tated, -tating.** To rise or raise into the air and float. **—lev'i•ta'tion** *n.*

**lev•i•ty** (lĕv'ĭ-tē) *n., pl.* **-ties.** Frivolity.

**lev•y** (lĕv'ē) *v.* **-ied, -ying. 1.** To impose or collect (a tax). **2.** To wage (a war). *—n.* **1.** The act or process of levying. **2.** Money or property levied.

**lewd** (lo͞od) *adj.* **1.** Licentious; lustful. **2.** Obscene.

**lex•i•con** (lĕk'sĭ-kŏn') *n.* **1.** A dictionary. **2.** A vocabulary used in a particular subject.

**li•a•bil•i•ty** (lī'ə-bĭl'ĭ-tē) *n., pl.* **-ties. 1.** The state of being liable. **2. liabilities.** Debts. **3.** A drawback.

**li•a•ble** (lī'ə-bəl) *adj.* **1.** Legally obligated; responsible. **2.** Likely; apt.

**li•ai•son** (lē'ā-zŏn', lē-ā'-) *n.* **1.** Communication between groups or units. **2.** An illicit relationship.

**li•ba•tion** (lī-bā'shən) *n.* **1.** The pouring of a liquid offering, esp. wine, in a religious ritual. **2.** An alcoholic beverage.

**li•bel** (lī'bəl) *n.* A written, printed, or pictorial statement that unjustly damages a person's reputation. —*v.* To defame or malign. **—li'bel•ous** *adj.*

**lib•er•al** (lĭb'ər-əl, lĭb'rəl) *adj.* **1.** Favoring individual freedom and nonrevolutionary reform. **2.** Broad-minded or tolerant. **3.** Generous; bountiful. —*n.* One holding liberal political views. **—lib'er•al•ism'** *n.* **—lib'er•al'i•ty** *n.* **—lib'er•al•ize'** *v.*

**lib•er•ate** (lĭb'ə-rāt) *v.* **-ated, -ating.** To set free. **—lib'er•a'tion** *n.* **—lib'er•a'tor** *n.*

**lib•er•ty** (lĭb'ər-tē) *n., pl.* **-ties. 1.** Freedom from restriction or control; independence. **2.** Freedom from confinement. **3.** Often **liberties.** Unwarranted familiarity.

**li•brar•y** (lī'brĕr'ē) *n., pl.* **-ies. 1.** A repository for books, records, prints, etc. **2.** A permanent collection of such materials. **—li•brar'i•an** *n.*

**li•bret•to** (lĭ-brĕt'ō) *n., pl.* **-tos** or **-ti.** The dialogue of an opera or other dramatic musical work. **—li•bret'tist** *n.*

**lice** (līs) *n.* pl. of **louse.**

**li•cense** (lī'səns) *n.* **1.** Legal permission to do or own something. **2.** Excessive or undisciplined freedom. —*v.* **licensed, licensing.** To grant a license to or for.

**li•cen•tious** (lī-sĕn'shəs) *adj.* Unrestrained; immoral.

**lick** (lĭk) *v.* **1.** To pass the tongue over. **2.** To defeat. **—lick** *n.*

**lid** (lĭd) *n.* **1.** A cover for any hollow receptacle. **2.** An eyelid.

**lie[1]** (lī) *v.* **lay** (lā), **lain** (lān), **lying. 1.** To assume a recumbent position; recline. **2.** To be or remain in a specific condition.

**lie[2]** (lī) *n.* A deliberate falsehood. —*v.* **lied, lying.** To tell a lie. **—li'ar** *n.*

**lien** (lēn, lē'ən) *n.* The right to take a debtor's property as security or payment for a debt.

**lieu** (lo͞o) *n.* Place; stead. **—in lieu of.** In place of.

**lieu•ten•ant** (lo͞o-tĕn'ənt) *n.* **1.** A commissioned officer in the armed forces. **2.** A chief assistant; deputy.

**life** (līf) *n., pl.* **lives. 1.** The quality by which living organisms are distinguished from dead organisms or inanimate matter. **2.** Living organisms collectively. **3.** The interval between birth and death **4.** A manner of living. **5.** Liveliness. **—life'less** *adj.* **—life'time'** *n.*

**lift** (lĭft) *v.* **1.** To raise; elevate. **2.** To ascend; rise. —*n.* **1.** The act of raising or rising. **2.** A rising of spirits. **3.** A short ride in a vehicle.

**lig•a•ment** (lĭg'ə-mənt) *n.* A band of tough, fibrous tissue that connects bones or supports an organ.

**light[1]** (līt) *n.* **1.** Electromagnetic radiation. **2.** Illumination or a source of illumination. **3.** Daylight or visible light. **4.** A means for igniting a fire. **5.** An aspect or point of view. —*v.* **lighted** or **lit** (lĭt), **lighting. 1.** To ignite. **2.** To illuminate. —*adj.* **1.** Radiant; bright. **2.** Not dark; pale.

**light[2]** (līt) *adj.* **1.** Not heavy. **2.** Not serious. **3.** Frivolous; silly. **4.** Small in intensity or amount. —*adv.* With little baggage. —*v.* **lighted** or **lit** (lĭt), **lighting. 1.** To dismount. **2.** To land. **—light'ly** *adv.*

**light•en[1]** (līt'n) *v.* To make or become light or lighter; brighten.

**light•en[2]** (līt'n) *v.* **1.** To make or become less heavy. **2.** To make or become less oppressive.

**light•house** (līt'hous') *n.* A tower topped by a powerful light for guiding ships.

**light•ning** (līt'nĭng) *n.* A large natural electric discharge in the atmosphere. —*adj.* Very fast or sudden.

**light•year** (līt'yîr') *n.* Also **light year.** The distance that light travels in 1 year, approx. 6 trillion miles.

**like[1]** (līk) *v.* **liked, liking. 1.** To enjoy. **2.** To want or wish. **3.** To be fond of. **—lik'a•ble, like'a•ble** *adj.* **—lik'ing** *n.*

**like[2]** (līk) *prep.* **1.** Similar to. **2.** Typical of. **3.** Disposed to. **4.** Indicative of. —*adj.* **1.** Similar. **2.** Equivalent. —*n.* Similar or related persons or things.

**like•ly** (lĭk′lē) *adj.* **-lier, -liest. 1.** Probable; apt. **2.** Suitable. **3.** Seemingly true; credible. —*adv.* Probably. —**like′li•hood′** *n.*

**like•ness** (lĭk′nĭs) *n.* **1.** A resemblance. **2.** An image.

**like•wise** (lĭk′wĭz′) *adv.* **1.** In the same way; similarly. **2.** Also; too.

**li•lac** (lī′lək, -lŏk, -lăk) *n.* **1.** A shrub bearing fragrant purplish or white flowers. **2.** Pale purple. —**li′lac** *adj.*

**lilt** (lĭlt) *n.* A cheerful, rhythmic manner of speaking.

**limb** (lĭm) *n.* **1.** One of the jointed appendages of an animal, as an arm, leg, or wing. **2.** A tree branch.

**lim•ber** (lĭm′bər) *adj.* **1.** Bending easily; pliable. **2.** Agile.

**lime** (līm) *n.* A tart, green citrus fruit.

**lim•er•ick** (lĭm′ər-ĭk) *n.* A humorous 5-line poem.

**lim•it** (lĭm′ĭt) *n.* **1.** The point, edge, or line where something ends. **2.** The greatest amount or number allowed. —*v.* To place a limit on. —**lim′i•ta′tion** *n.* —**lim′it•less** —*adj.*

**lim•o** (lĭm′ō) *n., pl.* **-os.** A limousine.

**lim•ou•sine** (lĭm′ə-zēn′, lĭm′ə-zēn′) *n.* A large passenger vehicle, esp. a luxurious car driven by a chauffeur.

**limp** (lĭmp) *v.* To walk lamely. —*adj.* Lacking rigidity; flabby. —**limp** *n.*

**lim•pid** (lĭm′pĭd) *adj.* Crystal clear; transparent.

**line**[1] (līn) *n.* **1.** A thin, continuous mark. **2.** A border or boundary. **3.** A cable, rope, wire, etc. **4.** A course of progress or movement. **5.** Often **lines.** Outline or styling. **6.** One's occupation. **7.** A group of persons or things arranged in a row. **8.** A system of transportation. **9.** Merchandise of a similar nature. —*v.* **lined, lining. 1.** To mark with lines. **2.** To place in a series or row. **3.** To form a bordering line along.

**line**[2] (līn) *v.* **lined, lining.** To sew or fit a covering to the inside surface of. —**lin′ing** *n.*

**lin•e•age** (lĭn′ē-ĭj) *n.* Ancestry.

**lin•en** (lĭn′ən) *n.* **1.** Cloth made of flax. **2.** Articles made from this cloth. —**lin′en** *adj.*

**lin•ger** (lĭng′gər) *v.* **1.** To remain; tarry. **2.** To persist. **3.** To procrastinate.

**lin•ge•rie** (län′zhə-rā′, län′zhə-rē) *n.* Women's underwear.

**lin•guis•tics** (lĭng-gwĭs′tĭks) *n.* The science of language. —**lin′guist** *n.* —**lin•guis′tic** *adj.*

**lin•i•ment** (lĭn′ə-mənt) *n.* A soothing medicinal fluid applied to the skin.

**link** (lĭngk) *n.* **1.** One of the rings forming a chain. **2.** A bond or tie. **3.** A hyperlink. —*v.* To connect or become connected with or as if with a link. —**link′age** *n.*

**li•no•le•um** (lĭ-nō′lē-əm) *n.* A durable, washable material used as a floor covering.

**lint** (lĭnt) *n.* Bits of fiber and fluff; fuzz.

**li•on** (lī′ən) *n.* A very large, wild cat.

**lip** (lĭp) *n.* **1.** Either of 2 fleshy, muscular folds that surround the opening of the mouth. **2.** The rim of a container, wound, etc.

**liq•uid** (lĭk′wĭd) *n.* A substance capable of flowing. —*adj.* **1.** Of a liquid. **2.** Readily converted into cash. —**liq′ue•fy′, liq′ui•fy′** *v.*

**liq•ui•date** (lĭk′wĭ-dāt′) *v.* **-dated, -dating. 1.** To pay off or settle. **2.** To wind up the affairs of (a business firm). **3.** To convert (assets) into cash. **4.** To kill; execute. —**liq′ui•da′tion** *n.*

**liq•uor** (lĭk′ər) *n.* A strong, distilled, alcoholic beverage.

**lisp** (lĭsp) *n.* A speech defect in which *s* and *z* are pronounced *th.* —**lisp** *v.*

**list**[1] (lĭst) *n.* A printed or written series of persons or things. —*v.* To make a list of or enter in a list. —**list′ing** *n.*

**list**[2] (lĭst) *n.* A tilt. —*v.* To lean or tilt.

**lis•ten** (lĭs′ən) *v.* **1.** To make an effort to hear something. **2.** To pay attention. —**lis′ten•er** *n.*

**list•less** (lĭst′lĭs) *adj.* Indifferent; languid. —**list′less•ly** *adv.* —**list′less•ness** *n.*

**lit** (lĭt) *v.* **1.** A p.t. & p.p. of **light**[1]. **2.** A p.t. & p.p. of **light**[2].

**li•ter** (lē′tər) *n.* A metric unit of volume.

**lit•er•a•cy** (lĭt′ər-ə-sē) *n.* The ability to read and write. —**lit′er•ate** *adj.*

**lit•er•al** (lĭt′ər-əl) *adj.* Exact; word for word. —**lit′er•al•ly** *adv.*

**lit•er•a•ture** (lĭt′ər-ə-chər) *n.* **1.** Imaginative or creative writing. **2.** A body of writing on a given subject. —**lit′er•ar′y** *adj.*

**lit•i•gate** (lĭt′ĭ-gāt′) *v.* **-gated, -gating.** To engage in or subject to legal proceedings. **—lit′i•gant** *n.* **—lit′i•ga′tion** *n.* **—lit′i•ga′tor** *n.*

**li•ti•gious** (lĭ-tĭj′əs) *adj.* Relating or inclined to litigation.

**lit•ter** (lĭt′ər) *n.* **1.** A stretcher. **2.** The young produced at 1 birth by certain mammals. **3.** Discarded waste. *—v.* To discard rubbish carelessly.

**lit•tle** (lĭt′l) *adj.* **-tler, -tlest. 1.** Small in size, quantity, or degree. **2.** Also compar. of **less,** superl. of **least. a.** Brief; short. **b.** Insignificant; not important. *—adv.* **less, least.** Not much. *—n.* A small quantity.

**live¹** (lĭv) *v.* **lived, living. 1.** To have life. **2.** To reside. **3.** To pass; spend.

**live²** (līv) *adj.* **1.** Alive. **2.** Glowing. **3.** Carrying electric current. **4.** Not exploded. **5.** Of current interest.

**live•li•hood** (līv′lē-hŏŏd′) *n.* Means of support.

**live•ly** (līv′lē) *adj.* **-lier, -liest. 1.** Full of energy; vigorous. **2.** Intense; keen. **3.** Cheerful. **—live′li•ness** *n.*

**li•ven** (lī′vən) *v.* To make or become lively.

**liv•er** (lĭv′ər) *n.* A glandular organ that secretes bile.

**lives** (līvz) *n.* pl. of **life.**

**live•stock** (līv′stŏk′) *n.* Domestic animals, as cattle, horses, or sheep.

**liv•id** (lĭv′ĭd) *adj.* **1.** Discolored, as from a bruise. **2.** Ashen, as with anger.

**liv•ing** (lĭv′ĭng) *adj.* **1.** Alive. **2.** Of persons who are alive. **3.** Of or characteristic of daily life. **4.** Currently in use. *—n.* **1.** The state of being alive. **2.** Livelihood.

**liz•ard** (lĭz′ərd) *n.* A reptile having a long, scaly body and usu. 4 well-distinguished limbs.

**load** (lōd) *n.* **1.** A supported weight or mass. **2.** Material or an amount of material transported by a vehicle or animal. *—v.* **1.** To place (a load) in or on a structure, device, or conveyance. **2.** To charge (a firearm) with ammunition.

**loaf¹** (lōf) *n., pl.* **loaves.** A shaped mass of bread or other baked food.

**loaf²** (lōf) *v.* To spend time lazily or aimlessly. **—loaf′er** *n.*

**loan** (lōn) *n.* **1.** A sum of money lent at interest. **2.** Anything lent for temporary use. *—v.* To lend.

**loathe** (lō*th*) *v.* **loathed, loathing.** To detest; abhor. **—loath′some** *adj.*

**loaves** (lōvz) *n.* pl. of **loaf¹.**

**lob•by** (lŏb′ē) *n., pl.* **-bies. 1.** A hall or waiting room. **2.** Persons engaged in influencing legislation. *—v.* **-bied, -bying.** To seek to influence legislators. **—lob′by•ist** *n.*

**lobe** (lōb) *n.* A rounded projection. **—lo′bar** *adj.*

**lob•ster** (lŏb′stər) *n.* A large, edible marine crustacean.

**lo•cal** (lō′kəl) *adj.* **1.** Of a limited place. **2.** Affecting a limited part of the body. **3.** Making many stops. *—n.* **1.** A local branch of an organization. **2.** A train, bus, etc., making frequent stops. **—lo′cal•ize′** *v.*

**lo•cal•i•ty** (lō-kăl′ĭ-tē) *n., pl.* **-ties.** A neighborhood, place, or region.

**lo•cate** (lō′kāt′, lō-kāt′) *v.* **-cated, -cating. 1.** To find or determine the position of. **2.** To situate or place. **—lo•ca′tion** *n.*

**lock¹** (lŏk) *n.* **1.** A mechanism used to secure a door, lid, etc. **2.** A section of a canal closed off with gates. **3.** A mechanism in a firearm. *—v.* **1.** To fasten or become fastened with a lock. **2.** To become entangled; interlock. **3.** To jam or force together so as to make unmovable. **—lock′er** *n.*

**lock²** (lŏk) *n.* A curl of hair.

**lo•co•mo•tion** (lō′kə-mō′shən) *n.* The act of moving or ability to move from place to place.

**lo•co•mo•tive** (lō′kə-mō′tĭv) *n.* An engine that moves railroad cars. *—adj.* Of locomotion.

**lode** (lōd) *n.* A vein of mineral ore.

**lodge** (lŏj) *n.* **1.** A cottage, cabin, or inn. **2.** A local chapter of a fraternal society. *—v.* **lodged, lodging. 1.** To rent quarters temporarily. **2.** to live in a rented room. **3.** To be or become embedded. **—lodg′er** *n.* **—lodg′ing** *n.*

**loft** (lôft, lŏft) *n.* **1.** An attic. **2.** A gallery or balcony.

**loft•y** (lôf′tē, lŏf′-) *adj.* **-ier, -iest. 1.** Towering. **2.** Noble.

**log** (lôg, lŏg) *n.* **1.** A section of a felled tree. **2.** Any record of performance, as of a ship's progress. *—v.* **logged, logging. 1.** To cut (trees) into logs. **2.** To enter (something) in a ship's or aircraft's log. **—log'ger** *n.*

**log•ic** (lŏj'ĭk) *n.* **1.** The study of reasoning. **2.** Valid reasoning. **—log'i•cal** *adj.* **—lo•gi'cian** *n.*

**lo•go** (lō'gō') *n.* A logotype.

**lo•go•type** (lô'gə-tīp', lŏg'ə-) *n.* The name, symbol, or trademark of a company borne on a single piece of type.

**loin** (loin) *n.* The part of the sides and back of the body between the ribs and hipbones.

**loi•ter** (loi'tər) *v.* **1.** To stand idly about; loaf. **2.** To proceed slowly.

**loll** (lŏl) *v.* **1.** To recline indolently. **2.** to hang laxly.

**lone** (lōn) *adj.* Solitary; isolated.

**lone•ly** (lōn'lē) *adj.* **-lier, -liest. 1.** Solitary. **2.** Desolate. **3.** Dejected by the awareness of being alone. **—lone'li•ness** *n.*

**lone•some** (lōn'səm) *adj.* Feeling or producing a feeling of loneliness.

**long[1]** (lông, lŏng) *adj.* **1.** Having great length. **2.** Of great duration. **3.** Far-reaching. **4.** Having an abundance of. —*adv.* For an extended period of time.

**long[2]** (lông, lŏng) *v.* To yearn. **—long'ing** *n.*

**lon•gev•i•ty** (lŏn-jĕv'ĭ-tē) *n.* Long duration of life.

**lon•gi•tude** (lŏn'jĭ-t/y/o͞od') *n.* Angular distance east or west. **—lon'gi•tu'di•nal** *adj.*

**look** (lo͝ok) *v.* **1.** To use one's eyes to see. **2.** To turn one's eyes upon. **3.** To seem or seem to be. **4.** To face in a specified direction. **—look for. 1.** To search for. **2.** To expect. —*n.* **1.** The action of looking; a gaze or glance. **2.** Appearance. **3. looks.** Personal appearance.

**loom[1]** (lo͞om) *v.* **1.** To come into view as a massive, distorted, or indistinct image. **2.** To seem imminent.

**loom[2]** (lo͞om) *n.* A weaving machine on which cloth is produced.

**loop** (lo͞op) *n.* **1.** A length of line, thread, etc., that is folded over and joined at the ends. **2.** Any roughly oval turn or figure. —*v.* To form or form into a loop.

**loop•hole** (lo͞op'hōl') *n.* **1.** A small hole in a wall. **2.** A means of evasion.

**loose** (lo͞os) *adj.* **looser, loosest. 1.** Slack. **2.** Not tightly fitted. **3.** Immoral. **4.** Not literal or exact. —*v.* **loosed, loosing. 1.** To set free. **2.** To make less tight or firm. **3.** To let fly (a missile). **—loose'ly** *adv.*

**loos•en** (lo͞o'sən) *v.* **1.** To make or become loose. **2.** To free from restraint, strictness, etc.

**loot** (lo͞ot) *n.* Spoils. —*v.* To pillage. **—loot'er** *n.*

**lop** (lŏp) *v.* **lopped, lopping.** To cut off from; trim.

**lope** (lōp) *v.* **loped, loping.** To run or ride with a steady, easy gait. **—lope** *n.*

**lop•sid•ed** (lŏp'sī'dĭd) *adj.* Not symmetrical.

**lo•qua•cious** (lō-kwā'shəs) *adj.* Very talkative. **—lo•qua'cious•ness, lo•quac'i•ty** *n.*

**lord** (lôrd) *n.* **1.** A ruler or master. **2. Lord.** The general masculine title of nobility and other rank in Britain. **3. Lord.** God. —*v.* To domineer. **—lord'ly** *adj.*

**lore** (lôr, lōr) *n.* Tradition or belief.

**lose** (lo͞oz) *v.* **lost** (lôst, lŏst), **losing. 1.** To mislay. **2.** To be unable to maintain or keep. **3.** To be deprived of. **4.** To fail to win.

**loss** (lôs, lŏs) *n.* **1.** The act or fact of losing. **2.** Someone or something lost.

**lost** (lôst, lŏst) *adj.* **1.** Strayed or missing. **2.** Ruined, **3.** No longer possessed. **4.** Uncertain; bewildered. **5.** Not used; wasted.

**lot** (lŏt) *n.* **1.** An object used in making a determination by chance. **2.** Fate. **3.** Often **lots.** A large amount or number. **4.** A piece of land. —*adv.* Very much.

**lo•tion** (lō'shən) *n.* A liquid for external application.

**lot•ter•y** (lŏt'ə-rē) *n., pl.* **-ies.** A contest in which the winner is chosen in a drawing of lots.

**loud** (loud) *adj.* **1.** Characterized by high volume and intensity of sound. **2.** Having offensively bright colors. **—loud, loud'ly** *adv.* **—loud'ness** *n.*

**lounge** (lounj) *v.* **lounged, lounging.** To pass time in a relaxed way. —*n.* A waiting room.

**louse** (lous) *n., pl.* **lice.** A small insect that lives as a parasite on various animals.

**lou•ver** (lo͞o'vər) *n.* **1.** An opening fitted with slanted slats. **2.** A slat in such an opening. **—lou'vered** *adj.*

**love** (lŭv) *n.* **1.** An intense affectionate concern for or passionate attraction to another person. **2.** A beloved person. **3.** A strong liking for something. *—v.* **loved, loving.** To feel love for. **—lov'a•ble, love'a•ble** *adj.* **—lov'er** *n.*

**love•ly** (lŭv'lē) *adj.* **-lier, -liest. 1.** Beautiful. **2.** Enjoyable; delightful. **—love'li•ness** *n.*

**low**[1] (lō) *adj.* **1.** Having little height. **2.** Of less than usual depth; shallow. **3.** Of inferior quality or character. **4.** Dejected. **5.** Below average, as in degree, intensity, etc. **6.** Not loud. *—adv.* **1.** In a low position, level, etc. **2.** At or to a low volume, intensity, etc. *—n.* **1.** At low level, position, etc. **2.** The transmission gear giving the smallest output speed.

**low**[2] (lō) *v.* To moo. **—low** *n.*

**low•er**[1] (lou'ər) *v.* **1.** To scowl. **2.** To appear dark and threatening.

**low•er**[2] (lō'ər) *adj.* Below someone or something. *—v.* **1.** To move down to a less high level. **2.** To reduce.

**low•ly** (lō'lē) *adj.* **-lier, -liest.** Low in rank, position, etc.

**loy•al** (loi'əl) *adj.* Faithful to a person, ideal, etc. **—loy'al•ty** *n.*

**lu•bri•cate** (lo͞o'brĭ-kāt') *v.* **-cated, -cating.** To apply oil or grease to. **—lu'bri•cant** *n.* **—lu'bri•ca'tion** *n.*

**lu•cid** (lo͞o'sĭd) *adj.* **1.** Easily understood. **2.** Rational. **—lu•cid'i•ty, lu'cid•ness** *n.*

**luck** (lŭk) *n.* **1.** Chance; fortune. **2.** Good fortune. **—luck'y** *adj.*

**lu•cra•tive** (lo͞o'krə-tĭv) *adj.* Profitable.

**lu•di•crous** (lo͞o'dĭ-krəs) *adj.* Laughable; ridiculous.

**lug** (lŭg) *v.* **lugged, lugging.** To drag or carry (something) laboriously.

**lug•gage** (lŭg'ĭj) *n.* Baggage.

**luke•warm** (lo͝ok'wôrm') *adj.* **1.** Mildly warm. **2.** Halfhearted.

**lull** (lŭl) *v.* **1.** To cause to sleep; soothe. **2.** To deceive into trustfulness. *—n.* A calm or inactive period.

**lull•a•by** (lŭl'ə-bī') *n., pl.* **-bies.** A song with which to lull a child to sleep.

**lum•ber**[1] (lŭm'bər) *n.* Timber sawed into boards.

**lum•ber**[2] (lŭm'bər) *v.* To move heavily.

**lu•mi•nous** (lo͞o'mə-nəs) *adj.* **1.** Emitting light, esp. self-generated light. **2.** Full of light. **—lu'mi•nos'i•ty** *n.*

**lump** (lŭmp) *n.* **1.** An irregularly shaped mass. **2.** An abnormal swelling in the body. **3.** An aggregate; collection. *—v.* To put together in a single group or pile. **—lump'y** *adj.*

**lu•nar** (lo͞o'nər) *adj.* Of the moon.

**lu•na•tic** (lo͞o'nə-tĭk) *adj.* **1.** Of or for the insane. **2.** Wildly foolish. **—lu'na•tic** *n.*

**lunch** (lŭnch) *n.* A meal eaten at midday. **—lunch** *v.* **—lunch'eon** *n.*

**lung** (lŭng) *n.* A spongy, saclike organ in most vertebrates that functions in respiration.

**lunge** (lŭnj) *n.* Any sudden forward movement. *—v.* **lunged, lunging.** To move with a lunge.

**lurch** (lûrch) *v.* **1.** To stagger. **2.** To roll or tip abruptly. *—n.* **1.** A staggering movement. **2.** An abrupt rolling or tipping.

**lure** (lo͝or) *n.* **1.** Anything that attracts. **2.** An artificial bait for fish. *—v.* **lured, luring.** To entice.

**lu•rid** (lo͝or'ĭd) *adj.* Shocking; sensational.

**lurk** (lûrk) *v.* **1.** To lie in wait. **2.** To move furtively.

**lus•cious** (lŭsh'əs) *adj.* **1.** Delicious **2.** Sensually appealing.

**lush** (lŭsh) *adj.* Luxurious; opulent.

**lust** (lŭst) *n.* **1.** Sexual craving. **2.** Any overwhelming craving. *—v.* To have an inordinate desire. **—lust'ful** *adj.*

**lus•ter** (lŭs'tər) *n.* **1.** Sheen; gloss. **2.** Brilliance or radiance. **—lus'trous** *adj.*

**lux•u•ri•ant** (lŭg-zho͝or'ē-ənt, lŭk-sho͝or'-) *adj.* **1.** Growing abundantly. **2.** Elaborate; ornate. **—lux•u'ri•ance** *n.*

**lux•u•ry** (lŭg'zhə-rē, lŭk'shə-) *n., pl.* **-ries. 1.** Something not necessary that provides comfort or enjoyment. **2.** A sumptuous environment or lifestyle. **—lux•u'ri•ous** *adj.*

**ly•ing** (lī'ĭng) *v.* **1.** pres.p. of **lie**[1]. **2.** pres.p. of **lie**[2].

**lymph** (lĭmf) *n.* A clear bodily liquid. **—lym•phat'ic** *adj.*

**lynch** (lĭnch) *v.* To execute without due process of law.

**lyr•ic** (lĭr'ĭk) *adj.* **1.** Of poetry that is a direct, often songlike expression of feelings. **2.** Exuberant; unrestrained.

—*n.* **1.** A lyric poem. **2. lyrics.** The words of a song. **—lyr'i•cal** *adj.* **—lyr'i•cist** *n.*

# — M —

**m, M** (ĕm) *n.* The 13th letter of the English alphabet.

**ma•ca•bre** (mə-kä'brə, -bər) *adj.* Gruesome; ghastly.

**mac•a•ro•ni** (măk'ə-rō'nē) *pl.n.* Also **mac•ca•ro•ni.** Dried pasta, usually tube-shaped.

**mac•a•roon** (măk'ə-ro͞on') *n.* A cookie made with almond paste or coconut.

**mace** (mās) *n.* **1.** A medieval spiked war club. **2.** A ceremonial staff of authority.

**ma•chet•e** (mə-shĕt'ē, -chĕt'ē) *n.* A large knife used esp. for chopping.

**mach•i•na•tion** (măk'ə-nā'shən) *n.* A hostile or evil scheme or plot.

**ma•chine** (mə-shēn') *n.* **1.** A mechanical system or device that assists in the performance of work. **2.** A powerful political group under the control of 1 or more leaders. —*v.* **-chined, -chining.** To cut, shape, or finish by machine. **—ma•chin'er•y** *n.* **—ma•chin'ist** *n.*

**ma•chis•mo** (mä-chēz'mō) *n.* An exaggerated sense of masculinity.

**ma•cho** (mä'chō) *adj.* Characterized by machismo.

**mac•ro** (măk'rō') *n.* An instruction in computer language that represents a longer sequence of instructions.

**mad** (măd) *adj.* **madder, maddest. 1.** Insane. **2.** Frantic. **3.** Angry; resentful. **4.** Affected by rabies. **—mad'den** *v.* **—mad'ly** *adv.* **—mad'man'** *n.* **—mad'ness** *n.*

**Mad•am** (măd'əm) *n.* A courteous form of address to a woman.

**made** (mād) *v.* p.t. & p.p. of **make.**

**Ma•don•na** (mə-dŏn'ə) *n.* **1.** The Virgin Mary. **2.** An artistic representation of the Virgin Mary.

**mael•strom** (māl'strəm) *n.* **1.** A large whirlpool. **2.** Turmoil; confusion.

**mag•a•zine** (măg'ə-zēn', măg'ə-zēn') *n.* **1.** A storehouse for ammunition. **2.** A periodical containing articles, stories, etc. **3.** A compartment in some types of firearms for holding cartridges.

**mag•got** (măg'ət) *n.* The larva of an insect, esp. of a fly, found in decaying matter or as a parasite.

**mag•ic** (măj'ĭk) *n.* **1.** The production of seemingly supernatural effects. **2.** Any mysterious quality that lends enchantment. **3.** Sleight of hand, as for entertainment. **—mag'ic, mag'i•cal** *adj.* **—ma•gi'cian** *n.*

**mag•is•trate** (măj'ĭ-strāt', -strĭt) *n.* A civil officer who administers the law.

**mag•nan•i•mous** (măg-năn'ə-məs) *adj.* Generous and noble; above revenge or resentment. **—mag'na•nim'i•ty** *n.*

**mag•nate** (măg'nāt') *n.* A powerful or influential person.

**mag•ne•si•um** (măg-nē'zē-əm) *n.* A light, silvery metallic element.

**mag•net** (măg'nĭt) *n.* **1.** A metal body that attracts iron. **2.** Anything that attracts. **—mag•net'ic** *adj.* **—mag'net•ism** *n.* **—mag'net•ize'** *v.*

**mag•nif•i•cent** (măg-nĭf'ĭ-sənt) *adj.* **1.** Splendid; lavish; sumptuous. **2.** Outstanding; impressive. **—mag•nif'i•cence** *n.*

**mag•ni•fy** (măg'nə-fī') *v.* **-fied, fying. 1.** To make greater in size; enlarge. **2.** To exaggerate. **3.** To increase the apparent size of, esp. by means of a lens. **—mag'ni•fi•ca'tion** *n.* **—mag'ni•fi'er** *n.*

**mag•ni•tude** (măg'nĭ-t/y/o͞od') *n.* **1.** Greatness in size, extent, or significance. **2.** The relative brightness of a celestial body.

**ma•hog•a•ny** (mə-hŏg'ə-nē) *n., pl.* **-nies.** A tropical American tree with hard, reddish-brown wood.

**maid** (mād) *n.* **1.** A young girl. **2.** A female servant.

**maid•en** (mād'n) *n.* An unmarried girl. —*adj.* First or earliest. **—maid'en•ly** *adj.*

**mail[1]** (māl) *n.* **1.** Letters, packages, etc., handled by a postal system. **2.** A postal system. —*v.* To send by mail. **—mail'box'** *n.* **—mail'man'** *n.*

**mail[2]** (māl) *n.* Armor made of small overlapping metal rings.

**maim** (mām) *v.* **1.** To mutilate; disable; cripple. **2.** To impair.

**main** (mān) *adj.* Most important; principal; major. —*n.* **1.** The principal pipe or conduit in a utility system. **2.** Physical strength. **—main'ly** *adv.*

**main•frame** (mān'frām') *n.* A large, powerful computer, often serving several connected terminals.

**main•stay** (mān'stā') *n.* A principal support.

**main•stream** (mān'strēm') *adj.* Relating to the prevalent attitudes and values of a society. **—main'stream'** *n.*

**main•tain** (mān-tān') *v.* **1.** To continue; carry on. **2.** To preserve. **3.** To keep in repair. **4.** To support. **5.** To assert or declare. **—main'te•nance** *n.*

**mai•tre d'** (mā'trə dē', mā'tər) *n.* The headwaiter of a restaurant.

**maj•es•ty** (măj'ĭ-stē) *n., pl.* **-ties. 1. Majesty.** A title used in speaking of or to a monarch. **2.** Dignity, splendor, and grandeur. **—ma•jes'tic** *adj.*

**ma•jor** (mā'jər) *adj.* Greater in importance or extent. *—n.* **1.** A military officer ranking next above a captain. **2.** The principal field of specialization of a college student. *—v.* To pursue academic studies in a major field.

**ma•jor•i•ty** (mə-jôr'ĭ-tē, -jŏr-) *n., pl.* **-ties. 1.** The greater number or part of something. **2.** The excess of a greater number over a smaller. **3.** The status of legal age.

**make** (māk) *v.* **made** (mād), **making. 1.** To create; construct. **2.** To compel. **3.** To appoint. **4.** To do; execute. **5.** To achieve; attain. **6.** To prepare. **7.** To constitute. *—n.* **1.** The style in which a thing is made. **2.** A specific line of manufactured goods. **—mak'er** *n.*

**make•shift** (māk'shĭft') *n.* A temporary substitute. **—make'shift'** *adj.*

**make•up** (māk'ŭp') *n.* Also **make-up. 1.** The way in which something is arranged or constructed. **2.** Cosmetics.

**mal•ad•just•ment** (măl'ə-jŭst'mənt) *n.* **1.** Faulty adjustment, as in a machine. **2.** Inability to adjust to one's environment or circumstances. **—mal'ad•just'ed** *adj.*

**mal•a•droit** (măl'ə-droit') *adj.* **1.** Lacking dexterity; clumsy. **2.** Lacking good judgment; tactless.

**mal•a•dy** (măl'ə-dē) *n., pl.* **-dies.** A disease, disorder, or ailment.

**mal•aise** (mă-lāz', -lĕz') *n.* A vague feeling of illness or depression.

**ma•lar•i•a** (mə-lâr'ē-ə) *n.* An infectious disease transmitted by the anopheles mosquito. **—ma•lar'i•al** *adj.*

**ma•lar•key** (mə-lär'kē) *n.* Exaggerated or foolish talk.

**mal•con•tent** (măl'kən-tĕnt') *adj.* Discontented. *—n.* A discontented person.

**male** (māl) *adj.* **1.** Of the sex capable of fertilizing ova. **2.** Masculine. *—n.* One that is male.

**ma•lev•o•lent** (mə-lĕv'ə-lənt) *adj.* Exhibiting ill will or malice. **—ma•lev'o•lence** *n.*

**mal•fea•sance** (măl-fē'zəns) *n.* Wrongdoing, esp. by a public official.

**mal•func•tion** (măl-fŭngk'shən) *v.* To fail to function normally. **—mal•func'tion** *n.*

**mal•ice** (măl'ĭs) *n.* Ill will; spite. **—ma•li'cious** *adj.*

**ma•lign** (mə-līn') *v.* To speak evil of; defame. *—adj.* Evil.

**ma•lig•nant** (mə-lĭg'nənt) *adj.* **1.** Malevolent. **2.** Relating to a pathological growth that tends to spread; cancerous. **—ma•lig'nan•cy** *n.*

**ma•lin•ger** (mə-lĭng'gər) *v.* To feign illness to avoid duty or work. **—ma•lin'ger•er** *n.*

**mall** (môl, măl) *n.* **1.** A shady public walk. **2.** A shop-lined street closed to vehicles. **3. a.** A shopping center. **b.** A large building complex containing shops and restaurants.

**mal•le•a•ble** (măl'ē-ə-bəl) *adj.* **1.** Capable of being shaped, as by hammering. **2.** Amenable; pliable. **—mal'le•a•bil'i•ty** *n.*

**mal•let** (măl'ĭt) *n.* **1.** A hammer used for striking a chisel or wedge. **2.** A large-headed tool used to strike a surface without damage.

**mal•nu•tri•tion** (măl'n/y/o͞o-trĭsh'ən) *n.* Poor nutrition, esp. because of a poorly balanced diet.

**mal•o•dor•ous** (măl-ō'dər-əs) *adj.* Ill-smelling.

**mal•prac•tice** (măl-prăk'tĭs) *n.* Improper conduct or treatment, esp. by a physician.

**malt** (môlt) *n.* Sprouted and dried grain, usually barley, used in brewing.

**mal•treat** (măl-trēt') *v.* To treat cruelly; abuse. **—mal•treat'ment** *n.*

**mam•mal** (măm′əl) *n.* A vertebrate animal the female of which suckles her young. **—mam•ma′li•an** *adj. & n.*
**mam•ma•ry** (măm′ə-rē) *adj.* Relating to a milk-producing gland.
**mam•moth** (măm′əth) *n.* An extinct animal resembling an elephant. *—adj.* Huge; gigantic.
**man** (măn) *n., pl.* **men. 1.** An adult male human being. **2.** A human being; a person. **3.** The human race. **4.** A piece used in board games. *—v.* **manned, manning. 1.** To supply with men. **2.** To take one's place for work at. **—man′hood′** *n.* **—man′li•ness** *n.* **—man′ly** *adj.*
**man•a•cle** (măn′ə-kəl) *n.* Often **manacles.** Handcuffs. *—v.* **-cled, -cling.** To restrain with manacles.
**man•age** (măn′ĭj) *v.* **-aged, -aging. 1.** To direct; control. **2.** To administer or regulate. **3.** To contrive or arrange. **4.** To get along. **—man′age•a•ble** *adj.* **—man′age•ment** *n.* **—man′ag•er** *n.* **—man′a•ge′ri•al** *adj.*
**ma•ña•na** (mä-nyä′nə) *adv.* **1.** Tomorrow. **2.** At an unspecified future date.
**man•date** (măn′dāt′) *n.* **1.** The wishes of a political electorate, expressed to its representatives. **2. a.** A commission authorizing a nation to administer a territory. **b.** A territory under such administration.
**man•da•to•ry** (măn′də-tôr′ē, -tōr′ē) *adj.* Required; obligatory.
**man•do•lin** (măn′də-lĭn′, măn′dl-ĭn) *n.* A stringed instrument with a pear-shaped body.
**mane** (mān) *n.* The long hair on the neck of a horse, male lion, etc.
**ma•neu•ver** (mə-n/y/o͞o′vər) *n.* **1. a.** A strategic military movement. **b.** Often **maneuvers.** A large-scale military training exercise. **2.** A stratagem. *—v.* **1.** To perform a military maneuver. **2.** To scheme; manipulate.
**man•ger** (mān′jər) *n.* A feeding trough for horses or cattle.
**man•gle** (măng′gəl) *v.* **-gled, -gling. 1.** To mutilate by battering, hacking, etc. **2.** To ruin through ineptitude.
**man•han•dle** (măn′hăn′dəl) *v.* To handle roughly. **—man′han′dler** *n.*
**man•hole** (măn′hōl′) *n.* An entrance hole to a sewer, boiler, etc.
**ma•ni•a** (mā′nē-ə) *n.* An intense enthusiasm; craze; obsession. **—man′ic** *adj.*
**ma•ni•ac** (mā′nē-ăk′) *n.* An insane person; lunatic. **—ma′ni•ac′, ma•ni′a•cal** *adj.*
**man•i•cure** (măn′ĭ-kyo͝or′) *n.* Treatment of the hands and fingernails. *—v.* **-cured, -curing.** To care for (the fingernails). **—man′i•cur′ist** *n.*
**man•i•fest** (măn′ə-fĕst′) *adj.* Clearly apparent; obvious. *—v.* To show plainly; reveal. *—n.* A list of cargo or passengers. **—man′i•fes•ta′tion** *n.*
**man•i•fes•to** (măn′ə-fĕs′tō) *n., pl.* **-toes** or **-tos.** A public declaration of principles or intentions.
**man•i•fold** (măn′ə-fōld′) *adj.* Of many kinds; varied; numerous. *—n.* A pipe having apertures for multiple connections.
**man•i•kin, man•ni•kin** (măn′ĭ-kĭn) *n.* **1.** A model of the human body. **2.** A mannequin.
**ma•nip•u•late** (mə-nĭp′yə-lāt′) *v.* **-lated, -lating. 1.** To control skillfully. **2.** To manage shrewdly or deviously. **—ma•nip′u•la′tion** *n.* **—ma•nip′u•la′tor** *n.*
**man•kind** (măn′kīnd′) *n.* The human race.
**man•ne•quin** (măn′ĭ-kĭn) *n.* **1.** A model used for displaying clothes. **2.** A woman who models clothes.
**man•ner** (măn′ər) *n.* **1.** A way of doing something; custom. **2.** One's natural bearing. **3. manners.** Polite social behavior. **4.** Kind or sort.
**man•ner•ism** (măn′ə-rĭz′əm) *n.* **1.** A distinctive trait; idiosyncrasy. **2.** An exaggerated or affected habit.
**man•ner•ly** (măn′ər-lē) *adj.* Polite.
**man•or** (măn′ər) *n.* A landed estate. **—ma•no′ri•al** *adj.*
**man•sion** (măn′shən) *n.* A large, stately house.
**man•slaugh•ter** (măn′slô′tər) *n.* An unintentional homicide.
**man•tel** (măn′tl) *n.* **1.** A facing around a fireplace. **2.** A mantelpiece.
**man•tel•piece** (măn′tl-pēs′) *n.* The shelf over a fireplace.
**man•til•la** (măn-tē′yə, -tĭl′ə) *n.* A shawl worn by women in Spain and Latin America.
**man•tle** (măn′tl) *n.* **1.** A loose, sleeveless cloak. **2.** Anything that covers or con-

ceals. —*v.* **-tled, -tling.** To cover with or as with a mantle; cloak.

**man•u•al** (măn′yo͞o-əl) *adj.* **1.** Of or operated by the hands. **2.** Employing human rather than mechanical energy. —*n.* **1.** A handbook. **2.** An organ keyboard. **—man′u•al•ly** *adv.*

**man•u•fac•ture** (măn′yə-făk′chər) *v.* **-tured, -turing. 1.** To make into a finished product, esp. through a large-scale industrial operation. **2.** To concoct or fabricate. —*n.* The process of manufacturing. **—man′u•fac′tur•er** *n.*

**ma•nure** (mə-n/y/o͝or′) *n.* Animal dung used to fertilize soil. —*v.* **-nured, -nuring.** To apply manure to.

**man•u•script** (măn′yə-skrĭpt′) *n.* **1.** A document written by hand. **2.** A typewritten or handwritten version of a book, article, etc., submitted for publication.

**man•y** (mĕn′ē) *adj.* **more** (môr, mōr), **most** (mōst). Consisting of a large number; numerous. —*n. (takes pl. v.).* A large number. —*pron. (takes pl. v.).* A large number of persons or things.

**map** (măp) *n.* A representation of a region of the earth. —*v.* **mapped, mapping. 1.** To make a map of. **2.** To plan, esp. in detail.

**ma•ple** (mā′pəl) *n.* **1.** A North American tree with sap that is boiled to produce a sweet syrup or sugar. **2.** The hard wood of such a tree.

**mar** (mär) *v.* **marred, marring.** To damage, deface, or spoil.

**mar•a•thon** (măr′ə-thŏn′) *n.* **1.** A long-distance race. **2.** A contest of endurance. **—mar′a•thon′** *adj.*

**ma•raud** (mə-rôd′) *v.* To raid for plunder. **—ma•raud′er** *n.*

**mar•ble** (mär′bəl) *n.* **1.** A metamorphic rock often irregularly colored by impurities. **2.** A small ball used in children's games.

**march** (märch ) *v.* To walk or make walk in a military manner with measured steps in cadence. —*n.* **1.** The act of marching. **2.** The distance covered. **3.** A musical composition to accompany marching.

**March** (märch) *n.* The 3rd month of the year.

**mare** (mâr) *n.* A female horse.

**mar•ga•rine** (mär′jə-rĭn) *n.* A butter substitute made with vegetable oils.

**mar•gin** (mär′jən) *n.* **1.** An edge; border. **2.** The blank border on a printed page. **3.** A surplus measure or amount. **4.** A measure or degree of difference. **—mar′gin•al** *adj.*

**mar•i•jua•na, mar•i•hua•na** (măr′ə-wä′nə) *n.* The dried flowers and leaves of the hemp plant, smoked to induce euphoria.

**ma•rine** (mə-rēn′) *adj.* Of the sea, sea life, or maritime activities. —*n.* **Marine.** A member of the U.S. Marine Corps.

**Marine Corps.** A branch of the U.S. Armed Forces.

**mar•i•o•nette** (măr′ē-ə-nĕt′) *n.* A puppet manipulated by strings.

**mar•i•tal** (măr′ĭ-tl) *adj.* Of marriage.

**mar•i•time** (măr′ĭ-tīm′) *adj.* **1.** Located by or near the sea. **2.** Of shipping or navigation.

**mark** (märk) *n.* **1.** A visible impression on something, as a spot, dent, or line. **2.** A written or printed symbol. **3.** A grade, as in school. **4.** A target; goal. **5.** An indication of some quality. **6.** A label, seal, etc., placed on an article. —*v.* **1.** To make a mark on. **2.** To pay attention to. **3.** To characterize; set off. **4.** To grade (school papers). **—marked** *adj.* **—mark′ed•ly** *adv.* **—mark′er** *n.*

**mark•down** (märk′doun′) *n.* A reduction in the selling price.

**mar•ket** (mär′kĭt) *n.* **1.** A place where merchandise is offered for sale. **2.** A store selling a particular type of merchandise. **3.** The process of buying and selling. **4.** Demand for goods. —*v.* **1.** To offer for sale; sell. **2.** To buy household supplies. **—mar′ket•a•ble** *adj.*

**marks•man** (märks′mən) *n.* One who practices shooting at a target. **—marks′man•ship′** *n.*

**mark•up** (märk′ŭp′) *n.* The amount added to the cost price in calculating the selling price.

**mar•ma•lade** (mär′mə-lād′) *n.* A jelly-like preserve made of fruits.

**ma•roon**[1] (mə-ro͞on′) *v.* To abandon (a person), as on a deserted island, with little hope of rescue or escape.

**ma•roon**[2] (mə-ro͞on′) *n.* Dark red.

**mar•quee** (mär-kē′) *n.* A rooflike structure projecting over an entrance.
**mar•row** (măr′ō) *n.* The soft material that fills bone cavities.
**mar•ry** (măr′ē) *v.* **-ried, -rying. 1.** To take as a husband or wife. **2.** To unite as husband and wife. **—mar′riage** *n.* **—mar′riage•a•ble** *adj.*
**Mars** (märz) *n.* The 4th planet from the sun. **—Mar′tian** *adj. & n.*
**marsh** (märsh) *n.* Low-lying, wet land; a swamp. **—marsh′y** *adj.*
**mar•shal** (mär′shəl) *n.* A federal or city officer who carries out court orders. —*v.* To arrange or place in order.
**marsh•mal•low** (märsh′mĕl′ō, -măl′ō) *n.* A confection made with corn syrup, gelatin, and starch.
**mar•su•pi•al** (mär-sōō′pē-əl) *n.* A mammal of which the female carries her young in an external pouch. **—mar•su′pi•al** *adj.*
**mar•tial** (mär′shəl) *adj.* Of war or warriors; warlike; military.
**mar•ti•net** (mär′tn-ĕt′) *n.* A rigid disciplinarian.
**mar•tyr** (mär′tər) *n.* One who chooses to suffer or die rather than renounce religious principles. **—mar′tyr** *v.* **—mar′tyr•dom** *n.*
**mar•vel** (mär′vəl) *n.* Something that evokes surprise, admiration, or wonder. —*v.* To feel wonder or astonishment. **—mar′vel•ous** *adj.*
**mas•car•a** (mă-skăr′ə) *n.* A cosmetic used to darken the eyelashes.
**mas•cot** (măs′kŏt′, -kət) *n.* A person, animal, or object believed to bring good luck.
**mas•cu•line** (măs′kyə-lĭn) *adj.* **1.** Of men or boys; male. **2.** Mannish. **3.** Of the gender of words referring normally to males. **—mas′cu•lin′i•ty** *n.*
**mash** (măsh) *n.* **1.** A fermentable starchy mixture from which alcohol can be distilled. **2.** A soft, pulpy mixture, esp. one fed to livestock. —*v.* To convert (something) into a soft, pulpy mixture.
**mask** (măsk) *n.* **1.** A cover worn on the face. **2.** Anything that disguises or conceals. —*v.* To cover, disguise, or protect with a mask.
**mas•och•ism** (măs′ə-kĭz′əm) *n.* The deriving of sexual pleasure from being subjected to pain or humiliation. **—mas′o•chist** *n.* **—mas′och•is′tic** *adj.*
**ma•son** (mā′sən) *n.* **1.** One who builds with stone or brick. **2. Mason.** A Freemason. **—ma′son•ry** *n.*
**mas•quer•ade** (măs′kə-rād′) *n.* **1.** A costume ball at which masks are worn. **2.** A disguise. —*v.* **-aded, -ading.** To wear a disguise; pretend. **—mas′quer•ad′er** *n.*
**mass** (măs) *n.* **1.** A unified body of matter with no specific shape. **2.** A large amount or number. **3.** The major part of something. **4.** The physical bulk of a solid body. —*v.* To gather, form, or assemble into a mass.
**Mass** (măs) *n.* In Roman Catholic and some Protestant churches, the celebration of the Eucharist.
**mas•sa•cre** (măs′ə-kər) *n.* Savage and indiscriminate killing; slaughter. **—mas′sa•cre** *v.*
**mas•sage** (mə-säzh′) *n.* The rubbing or kneading of the body to aid circulation or relax the muscles. **—mas•sage′** *v.*
**mas•sive** (măs′ĭv) *adj.* Large; bulky.
**mast** (măst) *n.* **1.** A tall vertical pole to support a ship's sails and rigging. **2.** Any vertical pole.
**mas•ter** (măs′tər) *n.* **1.** A person having control over others; an employer or owner. **2.** The captain of a merchant ship. **3.** One highly skilled, as in a trade. —*v.* **1.** To make oneself a master of (an art, craft, or science). **2.** To overcome or subdue. **—mas′ter•ful** *adj.* **—mas′ter•ly** *adj.* **—mas′ter•y** *n.*
**mas•ter•piece** (măs′tər-pēs′) *n.* **1.** An outstanding work of art. **2.** Anything superlative.
**mas•ti•cate** (măs′tə-kāt′) *v.* **-cated, -cating.** To chew. **—mas′ti•ca′tion** *n.*
**mas•tur•ba•tion** (măs′tər-bā′shən) *n.* Excitation of the genitals by means other than sexual intercourse. **—mas′tur•bate′** *v.*
**mat¹** (măt) *n.* **1.** A flat piece of material used as a floor covering, table pad, etc. **2.** A dense or tangled mass. —*v.* **matted, matting. 1.** To cover, protect, or decorate with a mat. **2.** To form into a mat.
**mat²** (măt) *n.* A border placed around a picture.

**mat•a•dor** (măt′ə-dôr′) *n.* A bullfighter that kills the bull.
**match¹** (măch) *n.* **1.** One equal or similar to another. **2.** A game or contest. **3.** A marriage. —*v.* **1.** To be or make similar or equal to. **2.** To harmonize with; fit together. **3.** To place in competition with. —**match′less** *adj.*
**match²** (măch) *n.* A narrow strip of wood or cardboard coated on one end with a compound that ignites easily by friction. —**match′book′** *n.*
**mate** (māt) *n.* **1.** One of a matched pair. **2.** A spouse. **3.** A deck officer on a merchant ship. —*v.* **mated, mating. 1.** To join closely; couple. **2.** To unite in marriage or for breeding.
**ma•te•ri•al** (mə-tîr′ē-əl) *n.* **1.** The substance out of which a thing is constructed. **2. materials.** Tools or apparatus for a certain task. —*adj.* **1.** Of the physical as distinct from the spiritual. **2.** Of importance to an argument; relevant.
**ma•te•ri•al•ism** (mə-tîr′ē-əl-ĭzm) *n.* Preoccupation with money and possessions. —**ma•te′ri•al•ist** *adj. & n.* —**ma•te′ri•al•is′tic** *adj.*
**ma•te•ri•al•ize** (mə-tîr′ē-əl-īz′) *v.* **-ized, -izing.** To assume or cause to assume material or effective form.
**ma•te•ri•el, ma•té•ri•el** (mə-tîr′ē-ĕl′) *n.* The equipment and apparatus of an organization, esp. of an army.
**ma•ter•ni•ty** (mə-tûr′nə-tē) *n.* Motherhood. —**ma•ter′nal** *adj.*
**math•e•mat•ics** (măth′ə-măt′ĭks) *n.* The study of numbers, forms, sets, etc., and their associated relationships. —**math′e•mat′i•cal** *adj.* —**math′e•ma•ti′cian** *n.*
**mat•i•nee, mat•i•née** (măt′n-ā′) *n.* An afternoon dramatic or musical performance.
**ma•tri•arch** (mā′trē-ärk′) *n.* A woman who rules a family, clan, or tribe. —**ma′tri•ar′chal** *adj.* —**ma′tri•ar′chy** *n.*
**ma•tric•u•late** (mə-trĭk′yə-lāt′) *v.* **-lated, -lating.** To enroll in a college or university. —**ma•tric′u•la′tion** *n.*
**mat•ri•mo•ny** (măt′rə-mō′nē) *n.* Marriage. —**mat′ri•mo′ni•al** *adj.*
**ma•trix** (mā′trĭks) *n., pl.* **-trices** or **-trixes.** A situation or substance within which something forms or is contained.
**ma•tron** (mā′trən) *n.* **1.** A married woman. **2.** A woman who supervises a public institution. —**ma′tron•ly** *adj. & adv.*
**mat•ter** (măt′ər) *n.* **1.** That which constitutes any physical body or the universe as a whole; substance. **2.** The substance of thought or expression. **3.** Any subject of concern or action. —*v.* To be of importance.
**mat•tress** (măt′rĭs) *n.* A pad filled with soft material, used as or on a bed.
**ma•ture** (mə-t/y/o͝or′, -cho͝or′) *adj.* **-turer, -turest. 1.** Fully grown or developed. **2.** Fully aged or ripened. **3.** Payable; due. —*v.* **-tured, -turing.** To bring or come to full development. —**ma•tur′i•ty** *n.*
**mat•zo** (mät′sə, -sô) *n., pl.* **-zos.** A brittle, flat piece of unleavened bread.
**maud•lin** (môd′lĭn) *adj.* Effusively sentimental.
**maul** (môl) *v.* To handle roughly; bruise or tear. —**maul′er** *n.*
**mau•so•le•um** (mô′sə-lē′əm, mô′zə-) *n., pl.* **-leums** or **-lea.** A large, stately tomb.
**mav•en** (mā′vən) *n.* An expert.
**mav•er•ick** (măv′ər-ĭk, măv′rĭk) *n.* **1.** An unbranded calf. **2.** An independent, as in politics.
**maw** (mô) *n.* The stomach, mouth, or gullet of a voracious animal.
**mawk•ish** (mô′kĭsh) *adj.* Excessively and objectionably sentimental.
**max•im** (măk′sĭm) *n.* A principle or rule of conduct; a saying.
**max•i•mize** (măk′sə-mīz′) *v.* To make as great as possible. —**max′i•mi•za′tion** *n.* —**max′i•miz′er** *n.*
**max•i•mum** (măk′sə-məm) *n., pl.* **-mums** or **-ma.** The greatest or greatest possible quantity, degree, or number. —*adj.* Of or having the greatest quantity or highest degree that can be attained.
**may** (mā) *v.* Used as an auxiliary to indicate: **1.** A requesting or granting of permission. **2.** Possibility. **3.** Ability or capacity. **4.** Desire or fervent wish.
**May** (mā) *n.* The 5th month of the year.
**may•be** (mā′bē) *adv.* Perhaps; possibly.

**may•hem** (mā'hĕm', mā'əm) *n.* The offense of willfully maiming a person.
**may•or** (mā'ər, mâr) *n.* The chief magistrate of a city. **—may'or•al** *adj.* **—may'or•al•ty** *n.*
**maze** (māz) *n.* An intricate network of pathways; a labyrinth.
**me** (mē) *pron.* The objective case of *I.*
**mead** (mēd) *n.* An alcoholic drink made from fermented honey.
**mead•ow** (mĕd'ō) *n.* A tract of grassland.
**mea•ger** (mē'gər) *adj.* **1.** Thin; lean. **2.** Lacking in quantity; scant.
**meal**[1] (mēl) *n.* Coarsely ground grain. **—meal'y** *adj.*
**meal**[2] (mēl) *n.* The food served in 1 sitting.
**mean**[1] (mēn) *v.* **meant** (mĕnt), **meaning. 1.** To be defined as; denote; represent. **2.** To intend. **3.** To have as a purpose. **4.** To be of a specific importance; matter.
**mean**[2] (mēn) *adj.* **1.** Low in quality; inferior. **2.** Ignoble; base. **3.** Miserly. **4.** Lacking in kindness and good will; cruel. **—mean'ness** *n.*
**mean**[3] (mēn) *n.* **1.** The middle point between 2 extremes. **2.** An average. **3. means.** A course of action or instrument by which some act can be accomplished. **4. means.** Money, property, or other wealth. *—adj.* Occupying a middle or intermediate position.
**me•an•der** (mē-ăn'dər) *v.* **1.** To follow a winding course. **2.** To wander aimlessly.
**mean•ing** (mē'nĭng) *n.* That which is signified by something; sense. **—mean'ing•ful** *adj.* **—mean'ing•less** *adj.*
**meant** (mĕnt) *v.* p.t. & p.p. of **mean.**
**mean•time** (mēn'tīm') *n.* The time between 1 occurrence and another. *—adv.* In the intervening time. **—mean'while'** *n. & adv.*
**meas•ure** (mĕzh'ər) *n.* **1.** The dimensions, quantity, or capacity of anything. **2.** A unit specified by a scale, as an inch, or by variable conditions, as a day's march. **3.** A device used for measuring. **4.** The extent, amount, or degree of something. **5.** Limit; bounds. **6.** An action taken for a specified purpose. *—v.* **-ured, -uring. 1.** To ascertain or mark off the dimensions, quantity, or capacity of. **2.** To have a specified measure. **—meas'ur•a•ble** *adj.* **—meas'ure•ment** *n.*
**meat** (mēt) *n.* **1.** The edible flesh of animals. **2.** The essence or principal part of something. **—meat'y** *adj.*
**Mec•ca** (mĕk'ə) *n.* **1.** The holy city of Islam. **2. mecca.** A center of interest.
**me•chan•ic** (mĭ-kăn'ĭk) *n.* One who works with machines and tools.
**me•chan•i•cal** (mĭ-kăn'ĭ-kəl) *adj.* **1.** Of, operated by, or produced by a machine or machines. **2.** Like a machine.
**me•chan•ics** (mĭ-kăn'ĭks) *n.* **1.** The analysis of the action of forces on matter or material systems. **2.** The technical aspect of an activity.
**mech•a•nism** (mĕk'ə-nĭz'əm) *n.* **1.** A machine or the arrangement of its parts. **2.** Any system of interacting parts. **3.** An instrument or process by which something is done.
**med•al** (mĕd'l) *n.* A flat piece of metal having a special shape and design, often given as an award.
**me•dal•lion** (mĭ-dăl'yən) *n.* A large medal.
**med•dle** (mĕd'l) *v.* **-dled, -dling.** To interfere in other people's business. **—med'dler** *n.*
**me•di•a** (mē'dē-ə) *n.* A pl. of **medium.**
**me•di•an** (mē'dē-ən) *adj.* Of the middle. *—n.* A median point, plane, line, or part. **—me'di•al** *adj.*
**me•di•ate** (mē'dē-āt') *v.* **-ated, -ating.** To act as an intermediary, esp. to seek to resolve (differences). **—me'di•a'tion** *n.* **—me'di•a'tor** *n.*
**med•i•cate** (mĕd'ĭ-kāt') *v.* **-cated, -cating.** To treat with medicine. **—med'i•ca'tion** *n.*
**med•i•cine** (mĕd'ĭ-sĭn) *n.* **1.** The science of diagnosing, treating, or preventing disease. **2.** A drug or other agent used to treat disease. **—me•dic'i•nal** *adj.*
**me•di•e•val** (mē'dē-ē'vəl, mĕd'ē'vəl) *adj.* Also **me•di•ae•val.** Of the Middle Ages.
**me•di•o•cre** (mē'dē-ō'kər) *adj.* Of medium and unimpressive quality. **—me'di•oc'ri•ty** *n.*
**me•di•um** (mē'dē-əm) *n., pl.* **-dia** or **-ums. 1.** Something midway between extremes. **2.** An intervening substance.

3. A means; agency. 4. A means of mass communication. 5. *pl.* **-ums** *only.* One thought to have powers of communicating with the dead. 6. An environment. —*adj.* Intermediate in degree, amount, quantity, or quality.

**med•ley** (mĕd′lē) *n., pl.* **-leys. 1.** A jumbled assortment; mixture. **2.** A musical arrangement of various melodies.

**meek** (mēk) *adj.* **1.** Humble and patient. **2.** Submissive. **—meek′ly** *adv.* **—meek′ness** *n.*

**meet**[1] (mēt) *v.* **met** (mĕt), **meeting. 1.** To come upon; encounter. **2.** To connect with; join. **3.** To assemble; get together. **4.** To satisfy (a demand, need, etc.) **5.** To be introduced to. —*n.* A meeting or contest.

**meet**[2] (mēt) *adj.* Fitting; proper.

**meet•ing** (mē′tĭng) *n.* A coming together; assembly.

**meg•a•phone** (mĕg′ə-fōn′) *n.* A horn-shaped device used to project the voice.

**mel•an•chol•y** (mĕl′ən-kŏl′ē) *n.* Sadness; gloom. —*adj.* Sad; gloomy. **—mel′an•chol′ic** *adj.*

**me•lee, mê•lée** (mā′lā′, mā-lā′) *n.* A confused fight or brawl.

**mel•low** (mĕl′ō) *adj.* **1.** Sweet, juicy, and full-flavored because of ripeness. **2.** Rich and soft in quality. **3.** Relaxed and at ease. —*v.* To make or become mellow.

**mel•o•dra•ma** (mĕl′ə-drä′mə, -drăma′ə) *n.* **1.** A sentimental and sensational drama. **2.** Exaggeratedly emotional or sentimental behavior. **—mel′o•dra•mat′ic** *adj.*

**mel•o•dy** (mĕl′ə-dē) *n., pl.* **-dies.** A pleasing arrangement of musical sounds; tune. **—me•lod′ic** *adj.* **—me•lo′di•ous** *adj.*

**mel•on** (mĕl′ən) *n.* Any of several edible fruits.

**melt** (mĕlt) *v.* **1.** To change or be changed from a solid to a liquid by heat. **2.** To dissolve. **3.** To blend gradually. **4.** To soften. **5.** To disappear.

**melt•down** (mĕlt′doun′) *n.* The melting of the core of a nuclear reactor.

**mem•ber** (mĕm′bər) *n.* **1.** A distinct part of a whole. **2.** One who belongs to a group. **—mem′ber•ship′** *n.*

**mem•brane** (mĕm′brān′) *n.* A thin, pliable layer of animal or plant tissue. **—mem′bra•nous** *adj.*

**me•men•to** (mə-mĕn′tō) *n., pl.* **-tos** or **-toes.** A reminder; souvenir.

**mem•o** (mĕm′ō) *n., pl.* **-os.** A memorandum.

**mem•oir** (mĕm′wär′, -wôr′) *n.* **1. memoirs.** An autobiography; biography. **2.** A written reminder; memorandum.

**mem•o•ra•ble** (mĕm′ər-ə-bəl) *adj.* Worth being remembered; remarkable.

**mem•o•ran•dum** (mĕm′ə-răn′dəm) *n., pl.* **-dums** or **-da. 1.** A written reminder. **2.** A written record or communication.

**me•mo•ri•al** (mə-môr′ē-əl, -mōr′-) *n.* An established remembrance of a person or event; monument. —*adj.* Commemorative. **—me•mo′ri•al•ize′** *v.*

**mem•o•rize** (mĕm′ə-rīz′) *v.* **-rized, -rizing.** To commit to memory; learn by heart. **—mem′o•ri•za′tion** *n.*

**mem•o•ry** (mĕm′ə-rē) *n., pl.* **-ries. 1.** The ability to remember. **2.** A remembrance; recollection. **3.** All that a person can remember. **4.** The period of time covered by recollection.

**men** (mĕn) *n.* pl. of **man.**

**men•ace** (mĕn′ĭs) *n.* A threat. —*v.* **-aced, -acing.** To threaten.

**me•nag•er•ie** (mə-năj′ə-rē, -năzh′-) *n.* A collection of live wild animals.

**mend** (mĕnd) *v.* **1.** To correct; repair. **2.** To heal. **3.** To correct errors. —*n.* A mended place.

**men•da•cious** (mĕn-dā′shəs) *adj.* Lying; untruthful. **—men•dac′i•ty** *n.*

**men•di•cant** (mĕn′dĭ-kənt) *adj.* Begging. —*n.* A beggar.

**me•ni•al** (mē′nē-əl, mēn′yəl) *adj.* Of or appropriate to a servant. —*n.* A servant.

**men•o•pause** (mĕnə-pôz′) *n.* The cessation of menstruation.

**mensch** (mĕnsh) *n.* An admirable person.

**men•stru•ate** (mĕn′stro͞o-āt′) *v.* **-ated, -ating.** To discharge blood from the uterus monthly. **—men′stru•al** *adj.* **—men′stru•a′tion** *n.*

**men•tal** (mĕn′tl) *adj.* Of the mind; intellectual. **—men′tal•ly** *adv.*

**men•tal•i•ty** (mĕn-tăl′ĭ-tē) *n., pl.* **-ties. 1.** Intellectual capability; intelligence. **2.**

A habitual frame of mind.

**men•thol** (mĕn′thôl′) *n.* An organic compound obtained from peppermint oil. **—men′tho•lat′ed** *adj.*

**men•tion** (mĕn′shən) *v.* To cite or refer to; speak of. *—n.* An act of mentioning.

**men•u** (mĕn′yo͞o) *n.* **1.** A list of dishes available for a meal. **2.** A list on a computer monitor allowing the user to choose an operation in a program.

**me•ow** (mē-ou′) *n.* The cry of a cat. **—me•ow′** *v.*

**mer•ce•nar•y** (mûr′sə-nĕr′ē) *adj.* **1.** Motivated solely by a desire for money. **2.** Hired for service in a foreign army. **—mer′ce•nar′y** *n.*

**mer•chan•dise** (mûr′chən-dīz′, -dīs′) Also **mer•chan•dize.** *n.* Goods that can be bought or sold. *—v.* **-dised, -dising.** To buy and sell.

**mer•chant** (mûr′chənt) *n.* **1.** One whose occupation is the retail sale of goods for profit. **2.** A shopkeeper.

**merchant marine.** A nation's ships that are engaged in commerce.

**mer•cu•ry** (mûr′kyə-rē) *n.* **1.** A silvery-white, poisonous metallic element, liquid at room temperature, used in thermometers, barometers, vapor lamps, and batteries. **2. Mercury.** The planet nearest the sun. **—mer•cu′ri•al** *adj.*

**mer•cy** (mûr′sē) *n., pl.* **-cies. 1.** Kindness; clemency. **2.** A fortunate act or occurrence. **—mer′ci•ful** *adj.* **—mer′ci•less** *adj.*

**mere** (mîr) *adj.* Being nothing more than; only. **—mere′ly** *adv.*

**mer•e•tri•cious** (mĕr′ĭ-trĭsh′əs) *adj.* **1.** Relating to a prostitute. **2.** Attractive in a vulgar manner; showy; gaudy.

**merge** (mûrj) *v.* **merged, merging.** To blend together so as to lose identity; unite. **—merg′er** *n.*

**me•rid•i•an** (mə-rĭd′ē-ən) *n.* **1.** An imaginary great circle on the earth's surface passing through both geophysical poles. **2.** The highest stage of development; zenith. **—me•rid′i•an** *adj.*

**me•ringue** (mə-răng′) *n.* A dessert topping made of beaten egg whites and sugar.

**mer•it** (mĕr′ĭt) *n.* **1.** Superior value; excellence. **2. merits.** The actual facts of a legal case or other issue. **3.** A praiseworthy feature or quality. *—v.* To earn; deserve; warrant. **—mer′i•to′ri•ous** *adj.*

**mer•maid** (mûr′mād′) *n.* A fabled sea creature with the head and torso of a woman and the tail of a fish.

**mer•ry** (mĕr′ē) *adj.* **-rier, -riest. 1.** Gay; jolly. **2.** Festive; lively. **—mer′ri•ly** *adv.* **—mer′ri•ment** *n.* **—mer′ry•mak′ing** *n.*

**me•sa** (mā′sə) *n.* A flat-topped elevation with clifflike sides.

**mesh** (mĕsh) *n.* **1.** Any of the open spaces in a net, sieve, etc. **2.** A net or network. **3.** The engagement of gear teeth. *—v.* **1.** To entangle or ensnare. **2.** To engage or become engaged, as gear teeth. **3.** To coordinate; harmonize.

**mes•mer•ize** (mĕz′mə-rīz′) *v.* **-ized, -izing.** To enthrall.

**mess** (mĕs) *n.* **1.** A disorderly accumulation; jumble. **2.** A muddle; chaos. **3.** A group who regularly eat meals together. *—v.* **1.** To make disorderly; clutter. **2.** To bungle or mismanage. **—mess′i•ness** *n.* **—mess′y** *adj.*

**mes•sage** (mĕs′ĭj) *n.* A communication transmitted from 1 person or place to another.

**mes•sen•ger** (mĕs′ən-jər) *n.* One who transmits messages or performs errands.

**mes•si•ah** (mĭ-sī′ə) *n.* **1.** A deliverer or liberator. **2. Messiah.** Jesus Christ.

**met** (mĕt) *v.* p.t. & p.p. of **meet.**

**me•tab•o•lism** (mə-tăb′ə-lĭz′əm) *n.* The physical and chemical process involved in the maintenance of life. **—met′a•bol′ic** *adj.* **—me•tab′o•lize′** *v.*

**met•al** (mĕt′l) *n.* Any of the usually lustrous elements that are often ductile and malleable, with high tensile strength. **—me•tal′lic** *adj.*

**met•al•lur•gy** (mĕt′l-ûr′jē) *n.* The study and technology of metals. **—met′al•lur′gic, met′al•lur′gi•cal** *adj.* **—met′al•lur′gist** *n.*

**met•a•mor•pho•sis** (mĕt′ə-môr′fə-sĭs) *n., pl.* **-ses. 1.** A complete, often sudden change in appearance, character, etc. **2.** Changes in form and life function during natural development. **—met′a•mor′phose′** *v.*

**met•a•phor** (mĕtə-fôr′, -fər) *n.* A figure of speech in which a term is used to describe an object by implicit comparison or analogy, as in the phrase *evening of life.* **—met′a•phor′ic, met′a•phor′i•cal** *adj.*

**met•a•phys•ics** (mĕt′ə-fĭz′ĭks) *n.* The philosophical investigation of the ultimate nature or 1st causes of things. **—met′a•phys′i•cal** *adj.*

**mete** (mēt) *v.* **meted, meting.** To deal out; allot.

**me•te•or** (mē′tē-ər, -ôr′) *n.* **1.** The bright trail or streak seen in the sky when a meteoroid falls into the earth's atmosphere and burns. **2.** A meteoroid. **—me′te•or′ic** *adj.*

**me•te•or•ite** (mē′tē-ə-rīt′) *n.* The stony or metallic material of a meteoroid that passes through the atmosphere and reaches the earth.

**me•te•or•oid** (mē′tē-ə-roid′) *n.* A celestial body that appears as a meteor when entering the earth's atmosphere.

**me•te•or•ol•o•gy** (mē′tē-ə-rŏl′ə-jē) *n.* The science of the earth's atmosphere, esp. weather conditions. **—me′te•or′o•log′i•cal** *adj.* **—me′te•or•ol′o•gist** *n.*

**me•ter**[1] (mē′tər) *n.* The measured rhythm of verse. **—met′ri•cal** *adj.*

**me•ter**[2] (mē′tər) *n.* The fundamental metric unit of length, approx. 39.37 inches.

**me•ter**[3] (mē′tər) *n.* A device designed to measure and indicate, record, or control. *—v.* To measure or control with a meter.

**meth•od** (mĕth′əd) *n.* A systematic means or manner or procedure. **—me•thod′i•cal** *adj.*

**me•tic•u•lous** (mĭ-tĭk′yə-ləs) *adj.* Extremely careful and precise; scrupulous.

**met•ric** (mĕt′rĭk) *adj.* Related to or using the metric system of measurement.

**met•ro•nome** (mĕt′rə-nōm′) *n.* An adjustable device that marks time at a steady beat. **—met′ro•nom′ic** *adj.*

**me•trop•o•lis** (mĭ-trŏp′ə-lĭs) *n., pl.* **-lises.** A major city or a large urban center. **—met′ro•pol′i•tan** *adj.*

**met•tle** (mĕt′l) *n.* **1.** Character and temperament. **2.** Courage and fortitude; spirit.

**mewl** (myo͞ol) *v.* To cry weakly.

**mez•za•nine** (mĕz′ə-nēn′, mĕz′ə-nēn′) *n.* **1.** A partial story between 2 main stories of a building. **2.** The lowest balcony in a theater.

**mi•as•ma** (mī-ăz′mə, mē-) *n.* **1.** A thick, vaporous atmosphere. **2.** A noxious atmosphere or influence. **—mi•as′mic** *adj.*

**mice** (mīs) *n.* pl. of **mouse.**

**mi•crobe** (mī′krōb′) *n.* A minute life form; a microorganism, esp. one that causes disease. **—mi•cro′bi•al, mi•cro′bic** *adj.*

**mi•cro•chip** (mī′krə-chĭp′) *n.* An integrated circuit on a minute slice of semiconducting material.

**mi•cro•com•put•er** (mī′krō-kəm-pyo͞o′tər) *n.* A very small computer built around a microprocessor.

**mi•cro•cosm** (mī′krə-kŏz′əm) *n.* A small, representative system analogous to a larger system. **—mi′cro•cos′mic** *adj.*

**mi•cro•fiche** (mī′krō-fēsh′) *n.* A sheet of microfilm.

**mi•cro•film** (mī′krə-fĭlm′) *n.* A film upon which printed materials are photographed greatly reduced in size.

**mi•cro•or•gan•ism** (mī′krō-ôr′gə-nĭz′əm) *n.* An organism that can be seen only with a microscope.

**mi•cro•phone** (mī′krə-fōn′) *n.* An instrument that converts sound waves into electric signals, as in broadcasting.

**mi•cro•proc•es•sor** (mī′krō-prŏs′ĕs-ər) *n.* A central processing unit of a computer contained on a single microchip.

**mi•cro•scope** (mīkrə-skōp′) *n.* An instrument that uses lenses to produce magnified images of small objects. **—mi′cro•scop′ic** *adj.*

**mi•cro•wave** (mī′krə-wāv′) *n.* **1.** An electromagnetic wave between infrared and shortwave radio lengths. **2.** An oven in which microwaves cook the food. **—mi′cro•wave′** *v.*

**mid** (mĭd) *adj.* Middle; central.

**mid•day** (mĭd′dā′) *n.* Noon. **—mid′day′** *adj.*

**mid•dle** (mĭd′l) *adj.* **1.** Equally distant from extremes; central. **2.** Medium; moderate. *—n.* A middle area or point.

**middle class** *n.* The members of society occupying an intermediate social and economic position. **—mid'dle-class'** *adj.*

**mid•dle•man** (mĭd'l-măn') *n.* An intermediary, esp. one who buys from producers and sells to retailers or consumers.

**mid•land** (mĭd'lənd) *n.* The middle part of a country or region.

**mid•night** (mĭd'nīt') *n.* Twelve o'clock at night.

**mid•riff** (mĭd'rĭf) *n.* **1.** The diaphragm. **2.** The part of the body extending from the chest to the waistline. **—mid'riff'** *adj.*

**mid•ship•man** (mĭd'shĭp'mən, mĭd-shĭp'mən) *n.* A student training to be an officer in the U.S. Navy or Coast Guard.

**midst** (mĭdst, mĭtst) *n.* The middle part; center. *—prep.* Among.

**mid•way** (mĭd'wā') *n.* The area of a fair, carnival, etc., where side shows are located. *—adv. & adj.* In the middle; halfway.

**mid•wife** (mĭd'wīf') *n.* A woman who assists women in childbirth. **—mid'-wife'ry** *n.*

**mien** (mēn) *n.* Manner; appearance; aspect.

**miff** (mĭf) *v.* To offend; upset.

**might[1]** (mīt) *n.* **1.** Great or supreme power. **2.** Great physical strength. **—might'y** *adj.*

**might[2]** (mīt) *v.* p.t. of **may.**

**mi•graine** (mī'grān') *n.* Severe, recurrent headache, often on only 1 side of the head.

**mi•grant** (mī'grənt) *n.* **1.** One that migrates. **2.** One who travels from place to place in search of work. **—mi'grant** *adj.*

**mi•grate** (mī'grāt') *v.* **-grated, -grating.** To move from one country or region and settle in another, esp. seasonally. **—mi•gra'tion** *n.* **—mi'gra•to'ry** *adj.*

**mild** (mīld) *adj.* **1.** Gentle or meek; kind. **2.** Not extreme; moderate; temperate. **3.** Not sharp or strong in taste. **—mild'ly** *adv.* **—mild'ness** *n.*

**mil•dew** (mĭl'd/y/ōō') *n.* A white or grayish coating formed by fungi. **—mil'dew'** *v.*

**mile** (mīl) *n.* A unit of length equal to 5,280 feet.

**mile•age, mil•age** (mī'lĭj) *n.* **1.** Distance measured or expressed in miles. **2.** An allowance by the mile for travel expenses.

**mile•stone** (mīl'stōn') *n.* An important event or turning point.

**mi•lieu** (mĭl-yōō', mē-lyœ') *n.* Environment or surroundings.

**mil•i•tant** (mĭl'ĭ-tənt) *adj.* Warlike; combative; aggressive. *—n.* One who is militant. **—mil'i•tan•cy** *n.*

**mil•i•ta•rism** (mĭl'ĭ-tə-rĭz'əm) *n.* The glorification of the military or its predominance in state affairs. **—mil'i•ta•rist** *n.* **—mil'i•ta•ris'tic** *adj.*

**mil•i•tar•y** (mĭl'ĭ-tĕr'ē) *adj.* Of soldiers, the armed forces, or warfare. *—n.* **the military.** The armed forces; soldiers collectively.

**mil•i•tate** (mĭl'ĭ-tāt') *v.* **-tated, -tating.** To operate or work.

**mi•li•tia** (mə-lĭsh'ə) *n.* Those who are called to military service in an emergency.

**milk** (mĭlk) *n.* **1.** A whitish liquid produced by the mammary glands of female mammals for feeding their young. **2.** A milklike fluid. *—v.* To draw milk from (a female mammal). **—milk'y** *adj.*

**mill** (mĭl) *n.* **1.** A building with machinery for grinding grain. **2.** A machine for grinding, crushing, etc. **3.** A factory. *—v.* **1.** To grind or crush in a mill. **2.** To move around in a confused or disorderly manner. **—mill'er** *n.*

**mil•len•ni•um** (mə-lĕn'ē-əm) *n., pl.* **-niums** or **-nia. 1.** A span of 1000 years. **2.** A 1000-year reign of Christ on earth, expected by early Christians. **3.** A hoped-for period of prosperity and justice. **—mil•len'ni•al** *adj.*

**mil•li•ner** (mĭl'ə-nər) *n.* One who makes or sells women's hats. **—mil'li•ner'y** *n.*

**mil•lion** (mĭl'yən) *n., pl.* **-lion** or **-lions. 1.** The cardinal number written 1,000,000. **2.** Often **millions.** An indefinitely large number. **—mil'lion** *adj. & pron.* **—mil'lionth** *n. & adj.*

**mil•lion•aire** (mĭl'yə-nâr') *n.* One whose wealth amounts to 1,000,000 or more dollars, pounds, etc.

**mill•stone** (mĭl′stōn′) *n.* **1.** A cylindrical stone for grinding grain. **2.** A heavy burden.

**mime** (mīm) *n.* **1.** The art of pantomime. **2.** A performer in pantomime. **3.** A mimic. —*v.* **mimed, miming. 1.** To mimic. **2.** To portray in pantomime.

**mim•ic** (mĭm′ĭk) *v.* **-icked, -icking.** To imitate another's speech, gestures, etc., as in mockery; ape. —*n.* One who mimics others. **—mim′ick•er** *n.* **—mim′ic•ry** *n.*

**min•a•ret** (mĭn′ə-rĕt′) *n.* A tall, slender tower on a mosque.

**mince** (mĭns) *v.* **minced, mincing. 1.** To cut into very small pieces. **2.** To moderate or restrain (words). **3.** To walk in a prim way.

**mind** (mīnd) *n.* **1.** The consciousness that directs mental and physical behavior. **2.** Memory. **3.** Conscious thoughts; attention. **4.** Opinion or intentions. **5.** Intellect; intelligence. —*v.* **1.** To pay attention to; obey. **2.** To take care of; tend. **—mind′ful** *adj.* **—mind′less** *adj.*

**mine**[1] (mīn) *n.* **1.** An excavation in the earth to extract metals or other minerals. **2.** An abundant supply. **3.** An explosive device detonated by contact or a time fuse. —*v.* **mined, mining. 1.** To dig from a mine. **2.** To lay explosive mines in or under. **—min′er** *n.*

**mine**[2] (mīn) *pron.* The possessive case of *I,* used by itself or as a predicate adjective.

**min•er•al** (mĭn′ər-əl) *n.* **1.** A natural, inorganic, crystalline substance such as stone, coal, salt, etc. **2.** Any substance that is neither animal nor vegetable; inorganic matter. **3.** An ore. —*adj.* Of minerals.

**min•er•al•o•gy** (mĭn′ə-rŏl′ə-jē, -răl′-) *n.* The scientific study of minerals. **—min′er•al′o•gist** *n.*

**min•e•stro•ne** (mĭn′ĭ-strō′nē) *n.* An Italian soup with vegetables, pasta, and herbs.

**min•gle** (mĭng′gəl) *v.* **-gled, -gling.** To mix together; associate.

**min•i•a•ture** (mĭn′ē-ə-cho͝or′, -chər, mĭn′ə-) *n.* **1.** A greatly reduced copy or model. **2.** A small painting. —*adj.* On a small or greatly reduced scale.

**min•i•mum** (mĭn′ə-məm) *n., pl.* **-mums** or **-ma. 1.** The smallest possible or allowable quantity or degree. **2.** The lowest amount or degree reached or recorded. **—min′i•mal** *adj.* **—min′i•mize′** *v.* **—min′i•mum** *adj.*

**min•ion** (mĭn′yən) *n.* An obsequious follower or dependent.

**min•is•ter** (mĭn′ĭ-stər) *n.* **1.** A member of the clergy; pastor. **2.** A head of a governmental department. **3.** A diplomat ranking next below an ambassador. —*v.* To attend to the needs of others. **—min′is•te′ri•al** *adj.* **—min′is•tra′tion** *n.*

**min•is•try** (mĭn′ĭ-strē) *n., pl.* **-tries. 1.** The act of ministering or serving. **2. a.** The profession of a minister of religion. **b.** The clergy. **3.** A governmental department presided over by a minister.

**mi•nor** (mī′nər) *adj.* **1.** Lesser in amount, size, or importance. **2.** Not yet of full legal age. —*n.* One under full legal age.

**mi•nor•i•ty** (mə-nôr′ĭ-tē, -nŏr′-, mī-) *n., pl.* **-ties. 1.** A group numbering less than half of a total. **2.** A racial, religious, or other group regarded as being different from the larger group of which it is a part. **3.** The state or period of being under legal age.

**min•strel** (mĭn′strəl) *n.* A musician.

**mint**[1] (mĭnt) *n.* A place where coins are manufactured. —*v.* **1.** To produce (money) by stamping metal. **2.** To invent; fabricate. —*adj.* In original condition; unused.

**mint**[2] (mĭnt) *n.* **1.** A plant having an aromatic oil used for flavoring. **2.** A candy made with mint flavoring.

**mint ju•lep** *n.* A julep made with bourbon and mint.

**min•u•end** (mĭn′yo͞o-ĕnd′) *n.* The quantity from which another is to be subtracted.

**mi•nus** (mī′nəs) *prep.* **1.** Less. **2.** Lacking; without. —*adj.* **1.** Less than 0; negative. **2.** Slightly lower or less than. —*n.* A loss, deficiency, or disadvantage.

**min•us•cule** (mĭn′ə-skyo͞ol′, mĭ-nŭs′-kyo͞ol′) *adj.* Very small; tiny; minute.

**min•ute**[1] (mĭn′ĭt) *n.* **1.** A unit of time equal to 60 seconds. **2.** A moment. **3.**

**minutes.** An official record of proceedings at a meeting.
**min•ute²** (mī-n/y/o͞ot′, mĭ-) *adj.* **1.** Exceptionally small; tiny. **2.** Characterized by close examination.
**mi•nu•ti•a** (mĭ-n/y/o͞o′shē-ə, -shə) *n., pl.* **-tiae.** A small or trivial detail.
**mir•a•cle** (mĭr′ə-kəl) *n.* **1.** An event that is held to be supernatural because it appears inexplicable. **2.** Something that causes great admiration, wonder, etc. **—mi•rac′u•lous** *adj.*
**mi•rage** (mĭ-räzh′) *n.* An optical illusion of water, often with inverted reflections of distant objects.
**mire** (mīr) *n.* **1.** A bog. **2.** Swampy, slimy soil or mud. *—v.* **mired, miring.** To sink or become stuck in mire.
**mir•ror** (mĭr′ər) *n.* **1.** A polished surface that reflects a virtual image. **2.** Anything that gives a true picture of something else. *—v.* To reflect in or as in a mirror.
**mirth** (mûrth) *n.* Gaiety or merriment. **—mirth′ful** *adj.*
**mis•ad•ven•ture** (mĭs′əd-vĕn′chər) *n.* A mishap; misfortune.
**mis•an•thrope** (mĭs′ən-thrōp′, mĭz′-) *n.* A hater of the human race. **—mis′an•throp′ic** *adj.* **—mis•an′thro•py** *n.*
**mis•ap•pre•hend** (mĭs-ăp′rĭ-hĕnd′) *v.* To interpret incorrectly; misunderstand. **—mis′ap•pre•hen′sion** *n.*
**mis•ap•pro•pri•ate** (mĭs′ə-prō′prē-āt′) *v.* To take dishonestly for one's own use. **—mis′ap•pro′pri•a′tion** *n.*
**mis•be•have** (mĭs′bĭ-hāv′) *v.* To behave badly. **—mis′be•hav′ior** *n.*
**mis•cal•cu•late** (mĭs-kăl′kyə-lāt′) *v.* To calculate incorrectly. **—mis•cal′cu•la′tion** *n.*
**mis•car•ry** (mĭs′kăr′ē, mĭs-kăr′ē) *v.* **1.** To fail; go wrong. **2.** To give birth too early; abort. **—mis•car′riage** *n.*
**mis•ceg•e•na•tion** (mĭ-sĕj′ə-nā′shən, mĭs′ĭ-jə-) *n.* The interbreeding of different human races.
**mis•cel•la•ne•ous** (mĭs′ə-lā′nē-əs) *adj.* Made up of a variety of different elements; mixed. **—mis′cel•la′ny** *n.*
**mis•chance** (mĭs-chăns′) *n.* A mishap; bad luck.
**mis•chief** (mĭs′chĭf) *n.* **1.** An inclination to misbehave or cause trouble. **2.** Harm or damage. **—mis′chie•vous** *adj.*
**mis•con•ceive** (mĭs′kən-sēv′) *v.* To interpret incorrectly; misunderstand. **—mis′con•cep′tion** *n.*
**mis•con•duct** (mĭs-kŏn′dŭkt) *n.* **1.** Improper behavior; impropriety. **2.** Malfeasance.
**mis•con•strue** (mĭs′kən-stro͞o′) *v.* To misinterpret.
**mis•count** (mĭs-kount′) *v.* To count incorrectly; miscalculate.
**mis•cre•ant** (mĭs′krē-ənt) *n.* An evil person; villain. **—mis′cre•ant** *adj.*
**mis•de•mean•or** (mĭs′dĭ-mē′nər) *n.* An offense less serious than a felony.
**mi•ser** (mī′zər) *n.* A stingy person, esp. one who hoards money. **—mi′ser•ly** *adj.*
**mis•er•a•ble** (mĭz′ər-ə-bəl, mĭz′rə-) *adj.* **1.** Very unhappy; wretched. **2.** Wretchedly inadequate or inferior; deplorable.
**mis•er•y** (mĭz′ə-rē) *n., pl.* **-ies.** Extreme suffering; wretchedness.
**mis•fire** (mĭs-fīr′) *v.* **1.** To fail to explode. **2.** To fail to achieve an anticipated result. **—mis′fire′** *n.*
**mis•fit** (mĭs′fĭt′, mĭs-fĭt′) *n.* **1.** A poor fit. **2.** A maladjusted person.
**mis•for•tune** (mĭs-fôr′chən) *n.* **1.** Bad fortune. **2.** An unfortunate occurrence.
**mis•giv•ing** (mĭs-gĭv′ĭng) *n.* Often **misgivings.** A feeling of uncertainty or doubt; fear.
**mis•guide** (mĭs-gīd′) *v.* To give misleading direction to; lead astray.
**mis•hap** (mĭs′hăp′, mĭs-hăp′) *n.* An unfortunate accident.
**mis•in•form** (mĭs′ĭn-fôrm′) *v.* To give false or inaccurate information to. **—mis•in′for•ma′tion** *n.*
**mis•in•ter•pret** (mĭs′ĭn-tûr′prĭt) *v.* **1.** To explain inaccurately. **2.** To err in understanding. **—mis′in•ter′pre•ta′tion** *n.*
**mis•judge** (mĭs-jŭj′) *v.* To judge or estimate wrongly. **—mis•judg′ment** *n.*
**mis•lay** (mĭs-lā′) *v.* **1.** To lose. **2.** To put away something that is afterward forgotten.
**mis•lead** (mĭs-lēd′) *v.* **1.** To deceive. **2.** To lead into error of action or belief. **—mis•lead′ing** *adj.*
**mis•man•age** (mĭs-măn′ĭj) *v.* To manage badly or carelessly. **—mis•man′age•ment** *n.*

**mis•no•mer** (mĭs-nō′mər) *n.* A name that is wrongly applied.
**mi•sog•y•ny** (mĭ-sŏj′ə-nē) *n.* Hatred of women. **—mi•sog′y•nist** *n.*
**mis•place** (mĭs-plās′) *v.* **1.** To put in a wrong place. **2.** To mislay. **3.** To place unwisely.
**mis•print** (mĭs′prĭnt′) *n.* An error in printing.
**mis•pro•nounce** (mĭs′prə-nouns′) *v.* To pronounce incorrectly.
**mis•quote** (mĭs-kwōt′) *v.* To quote incorrectly.
**mis•read** (mĭs-rēd′) *v.* **1.** To read incorrectly. **2.** To misinterpret.
**mis•rep•re•sent** (mĭs-rĕp′rĭ-zĕnt′) *v.* To give a false or misleading representation of. **—mis•rep′re•sen•ta′tion** *n.*
**miss**[1] (mĭs) *v.* **1.** To fail to hit, reach, etc. **2.** To fail to attend. **3.** To omit. **4.** To avoid. **5.** To discover or feel the absence of. *—n.* A failure to hit, reach, etc.
**miss**[2] (mĭs) *n., pl.* **misses. 1. Miss.** A title preceding the name of an unmarried woman or girl. **2.** An unmarried woman or girl.
**mis•sile** (mĭs′əl) *n.* Any object or weapon fired, thrown, or dropped.
**miss•ing** (mĭs′ĭng) *adj.* Absent; lost; lacking.
**mis•sion** (mĭsh′ən) *n.* **1.** A body of envoys to a foreign country, esp. a permanent diplomatic staff and office. **2.** A body of missionaries, their ministry, or the place of its exercise. **3.** A combat assignment. **4.** A function or task.
**mis•sion•ar•y** (mĭsh′ə-nĕr′ē) *n., pl.* **-ies.** One sent to do religious work in a territory or foreign country. *—adj.* Of church missions or missionaries.
**mis•sive** (mĭs′ĭv) *n.* A letter or message.
**mis•spell** (mĭs-spĕl′) *v.* To spell incorrectly. **—mis•spell′ing** *n.*
**mis•state** (mĭs-stāt′) *v.* To state wrongly or falsely. **—mis•state′ment** *n.*
**mis•step** (mĭs-stĕp′) *n.* **1.** A wrong step. **2.** A mistake in conduct.
**mist** (mĭst) *n.* **1.** A mass of fine droplets of water in the atmosphere. **2.** Fine drops of any liquid sprayed into the air. **—mist′y** *adj.*
**mis•take** (mĭ-stāk′) *n.* **1.** An error or blunder. **2.** A misconception or misunderstanding. **—mis•take′** *v.* **—mis•tak′en** *adj.*
**Mis•ter** (mĭs′tər) *n.* A title preceding a man's surname.
**mis•treat** (mĭs-trēt′) *v.* To treat roughly or wrongly; abuse. **—mis•treat′ment** *n.*
**mis•tress** (mĭs′trĭs) *n.* **1.** A woman in a position of authority, control, or ownership. **2.** A man's female lover.
**mis•tri•al** (mĭs-trī′əl, -trīl′) *n.* A trial that becomes invalid because of basic error in procedure.
**mis•trust** (mĭs-trŭst′) *n.* Lack of trust; suspicion. *—v.* To regard without confidence. **—mis•trust′ful** *adj.*
**mis•un•der•stand** (mĭs′ŭn-dər-stănd′) *v.* To fail to understand or understand incorrectly. **—mis•un′der•stand′ing** *n.*
**mis•use** (mĭs-yo͞os′) *n.* Improper use; misapplication. *—v.* (-yo͞oz′). **1.** To misapply. **2.** To abuse.
**mit•i•gate** (mĭt′ĭ-gāt′) *v.* **-gated, -gating.** To make or become less severe; alleviate. **—mit′i•ga′tion** *n.*
**mitt** (mĭt) *n.* A large baseball glove.
**mit•ten** (mĭt′n) *n.* A hand covering that encases the thumb separately and the four fingers together.
**mix** (mĭks) *v.* **1.** To blend into a single mass. **2.** To combine or join. **3.** To associate socially; mingle. **—mix′ture** *n.*
**mne•mon•ic** (nĭ-mŏn′ĭk) *adj.* Assisting the memory.
**moan** (mōn) *n.* A low, sustained, mournful sound. **—moan** *v.*
**moat** (mōt) *n.* A protective ditch, usually filled with water, esp. around a medieval town or castle.
**mob** (mŏb) *n.* **1.** A large, disorderly crowd. **2.** An organized gang of criminals. *—v.* **mobbed, mobbing. 1.** To crowd around and jostle or attack. **2.** To crowd into (a place).
**mo•bile** (mō′bəl, -bēl′, bīl′) *adj.* **1.** Movable. **2.** Moving quickly from one condition to another. **—mo•bil′i•ty** *n.*
**mo•bi•lize** (mō′bə-līz′) *v.* **-lized, -lizing.** To assemble or prepare for war or a similar emergency. **—mo′bi•li•za′tion** *n.*
**mob•ster** (mŏb′stər) *n.* A member of a criminal gang.
**moc•ca•sin** (mŏk′ə-sĭn) *n.* A soft leather slipper or shoe.

**mo•cha** (mō′kə) *n.* **1.** A rich Arabian coffee. **2.** A coffee flavoring, often mixed with chocolate.

**mock** (mŏk) *v.* **1.** To treat with scorn or contempt; deride. **2.** To mimic in derision. —*adj.* Simulated; sham. **—mock′er•y** *n.*

**mode** (mōd) *n.* **1.** A way, manner, or style of doing or acting. **2.** The current fashion or style.

**mod•el** (mŏd′l) *n.* **1.** A miniature reproduction of something. **2.** A type or design. **3.** A preliminary pattern. **4.** An example to be emulated. **5.** One who poses for an artist, photographer, etc. —*v.* **1.** To plan or construct. **2.** To display (clothes) by wearing. **3.** To work as a model. **—mod′el** *adj.*

**mo•dem** (mō′dĕm′) *n.* A device that converts data from one form to another, as when transmitted from a computer to a telephone.

**mod•er•ate** (mŏd′ər-ĭt) *adj.* **1.** Not excessive or extreme. **2.** Temperate. **3.** Average; mediocre. **4.** Avoiding political extremes. —*n.* One who holds moderate political views. —*v.* (-ə-rāt′) **-ated, -ating. 1.** To make or become less severe or extreme. **2.** To preside over (a meeting, discussion, etc.). **—mod′er•a′tion** *n.* **—mod′er•a′tor** *n.*

**mod•ern** (mŏd′ərn) *adj.* Of or characteristic of recent times or the present. **—mod′ern•is′tic** *adj.* **—mo•der′ni•ty** *n.* **—mod′ern•i•za′tion** *n.* **—mod′ern•ize′** *v.*

**mod•est** (mŏd′ĭst) *adj.* **1.** Having a moderate estimation of oneself. **2.** Shy; reserved. **3.** Unpretentious. **4.** Moderate in size or amount. **—mod′es•ty** *n.*

**mod•i•cum** (mŏd′ĭ-kəm) *n.* A small amount.

**mod•i•fy** (mŏd′ə-fī′) *v.* **-fied, -fying. 1.** To change; alter. **2.** To make or become less extreme or severe. **—mod′i•fi•ca′tion** *n.* **—mod′i•fi′er** *n.*

**mod•u•late** (mŏj′ə-lāt′) *v.* **-lated, -lating. 1.** To regulate; temper. **2.** To change or vary the pitch, intensity, or tone of. **—mod′u•la′tion** *n.*

**mod•ule** (mŏj′o͞ol) *n.* **1.** A standardized unit used with others of its kind. **2.** A self-contained unit designed for a specific task.

**mo•gul** (mō′gəl) *n.* A small mound on a ski slope.

**moist** (moist) *adj.* Slightly wet or damp; humid. **—mois′ten** *v.* **—mois′ture** *n.*

**mo•las•ses** (mə-lăs′ĭz) *n.* A thick syrup produced in refining sugar.

**mold**[1] (mōld) *n.* **1.** A form for shaping a fluid or plastic substance. **2.** Something made or shaped from a mold. **3.** General shape or form. —*v.* To shape in a mold.

**mold**[2] (mōld) *n.* A fungous growth formed on organic matter. —*v.* To become covered with mold. **—mold′y** *adj.*

**mold•ing** (mōl′dĭng) *n.* A decorative strip, esp. on a wall.

**mole** (mōl) *n.* A small growth on the human skin.

**mol•e•cule** (mŏl′ĭ-kyo͞ol′) *n.* The simplest structural unit that displays the characteristic physical and chemical properties of a compound. **—mo•lec′u•lar** *adj.*

**mo•lest** (mə-lĕst′) *v.* **1.** To interfere with or annoy. **2.** To accost sexually. **—mo′les•ta′tion** *n.* **—mo•lest′er** *n.*

**mol•li•fy** (mŏl′ə-fī′) *v.* **-fied, -fying. 1.** To placate; calm. **2.** To soften or ease. **—mol′li•fi•ca′tion** *n.*

**mol•lusk** (mŏl′əsk) *n.* Also **mol•lusc.** A soft-bodied, usually shell-bearing invertebrate.

**molt** (mōlt) *v.* To shed an outer covering, as feathers, for replacement by a new growth.

**mol•ten** (mōl′tən) *adj.* Melted.

**mo•ment** (mō′mənt) *n.* **1.** A brief interval of time. **2.** A specific point in time. **3.** Importance.

**mo•men•tar•y** (mō′mən-tĕr′ē) *adj.* Brief; short-lived. **—mo′men•tar′i•ly** *adv.*

**mo•men•tous** (mō-mĕn′təs) *adj.* Of utmost importance or significance.

**mo•men•tum** (mōmĕn′təm) *n.* Force or speed of motion; impetus.

**mon•arch** (mŏn′ərk) *n.* **1.** A sovereign, as a king. **2.** A large orange and black butterfly. **—mon•ar′chic, mon•ar′chi•cal** *adj.*

**mon•ar•chy** (mŏn′ər-kē) *n., pl.* **-chies. 1.** Government by a monarch. **2.** A state ruled by a monarch. **—mon′ar•chism′** *n.* **—mon′ar•chist** *n. & adj.*

**mon•as•ter•y** (mŏn'ə-stĕr'ē) *n., pl.* **-ies.** The dwelling place of a community of monks. **—mo•nas'tic** *adj.*

**Mon•day** (mŭn'dē, -dā') *n.* The 2nd day of the week.

**mon•e•tar•y** (mŏn'ĭ-tĕr'ē, mŭn'-) *adj.* **1.** Of money. **2.** Of a nation's currency or coinage.

**mon•ey** (mŭn'ē) *n., pl.* **-eys** or **-ies. 1.** Something, as gold, that is legally established as an exchangeable equivalent of all other commodities. **2.** Currency. **3.** Wealth.

**mon•ger** (mŭng'gər, mŏng'-) *n.* **1.** One who deals in a commodity. **2.** One who promotes something undesirable.

**Mon•gol•oid** (mŏng'gə-loid', mŏn'-) *adj.* Of a major ethnic division of the human species having yellowish-brown to white skin color. **—Mon'gol•oid'** *n.*

**mon•grel** (mŭng'grəl, mŏng'-) *n.* A plant or animal of mixed breed.

**mon•i•tor** (mŏn'ĭ-tər) *n.* **1.** A student who assists a teacher. **2.** Any device used to record or control a process. *—v.* To check, watch, or keep track of, often by means of an electronic device.

**monk** (mŭngk) *n.* A member of a religious brotherhood living in a monastery.

**mon•key** (mŭng'kē) *n., pl.* **-keys.** Any member of the primates except man, esp. one of the long-tailed small- to medium-sized species. *—v.* To play or tamper with something.

**mon•o•chrome** (mŏn'ə-krōm') *n.* The state of being in a single color. **—mon'o•chrome'** *adj.*

**mon•o•cle** (mŏn'ə-kəl) *n.* An eyeglass for 1 eye.

**mo•nog•a•my** (mə-nŏg'ə-mē) *n.* The custom of being married to only 1 person at a time. **—mo•nog'a•mist** *n.* **—mo•nog'a•mous** *adj.*

**mon•o•gram** (mŏn'ə-grăm') *n.* A design composed of 2 or more initials of a name. **—mon'o•gram'** *v.*

**mon•o•lith** (mŏn'ə-lĭth') *n.* A large, single block of stone. **—mon'o•lith'ic** *adj.*

**mon•o•logue** (mŏn'ə-lôg', -lŏg') *n.* A long speech by a single actor, character in a story, or person in a group.

**mo•nop•o•ly** (mə-nŏp'ə-lē) *n., pl.* **-lies. 1.** Exclusive ownership or control. **2.** A company or group having such control. **3.** A commodity or service thus controlled. **—mo•nop'o•lis'tic** *adj.* **—mo•nop'o•lize'** *v.*

**mon•o•syl•la•ble** (mŏn'ə-sĭl'ə-bəl) *n.* A word of 1 syllable. **—mon'o•syl•lab'ic** *adj.*

**mon•o•the•ism** (mŏn'ə-thē-ĭz'əm) *n.* The belief that there is only 1 God. **—mon'o•the•is'tic** *adj.*

**mo•not•o•nous** (mə-nŏt'n-əs) *adj.* **1.** Unvarying in pitch. **2.** Repetitiously dull. **—mo•not'o•ny** *n.*

**mon•soon** (mŏn-sōōn') *n.* A seasonal wind system, esp. the system that produces dry and wet seasons in south Asia.

**mon•ster** (mŏn'stər) *n.* **1.** An animal or plant of abnormal or grotesque form. **2.** Any very large animal, plant, or object. **3.** One who inspires horror or disgust. *—adj.* Gigantic; huge. **—mon•stros'i•ty** *n.* **—mon'strous** *adj.*

**mon•tage** (mŏn-täzh') *n.* **1.** A picture made by arranging several pictures together. **2.** A rapid sequence of images. **3.** A jumble.

**month** (mŭnth) *n.* One of the 12 divisions of the year.

**month•ly** (mŭnth'lē) *adj.* **1.** Of, occurring, coming due, or published every month. **2.** Lasting for a month. *—n., pl.* **-lies.** A monthly publication. **—month'ly** *adv.*

**mon•u•ment** (mŏn'yə-mənt) *n.* **1.** A structure erected as a memorial. **2.** A tombstone. **3.** An exceptional example of something. **—mon'u•men'tal** *adj.*

**moo** (mōō) *v.* To emit the deep, bellowing sound made by a cow. **—moo** *n.*

**mood** (mōōd) *n.* A state of mind or feeling.

**mood•y** (mōō'dē) *adj.* **-ier, -iest. 1.** Given to changeable emotional states. **2.** Gloomy; uneasy.

**moon** (mōōn) *n.* **1.** The natural satellite of the earth. **2.** Any natural satellite of a planet. **3.** A month. *—v.* **1.** To dream aimlessly. **2.** To exhibit infatuation. **—moon'light'** *n.*

**moon•shine** (mōōn'shīn') *n.* **1.** The light of the moon. **2.** Illegally distilled whiskey.

**moor**[1] (mo͝or) *v.* To secure or make fast, as with cables or anchors.

**moor**[2] (mo͝or) *n.* A broad tract of open, often boggy land.

**moose** (mo͞os) *n., pl.* **moose.** A very large deer of North America.

**moot** (mo͞ot) *adj.* Subject to debate; arguable.

**mop** (mŏp) *n.* A device made of absorbent material attached to a handle, used for cleaning floors. **—mop** *v.*

**mope** (mōp) *v.* **moped, moping.** To be gloomy or dejected.

**mo•ped** (mō′pĕd′) *n.* A light motorbike that can be pedaled.

**mor•al** (môr′əl, mŏr′-) *adj.* **1.** Of or concerned with the discernment of what is right and wrong. **2.** Virtuous; upright. **3.** Arising from conscience. *—n.* **1.** The principle taught by a story. **2. morals.** Rules or habits of conduct. **—mor′al•ist** *n.* **—mor′a•lis′tic** *adj.* **—mo•ral′i•ty** *n.* **—mor′al•ize′** *v.*

**mo•rale** (mə-răl′) *n.* The attidue of a person or group with respect to confidence, cheerfulness, discipline, etc.

**mo•rass** (mə-răs′, mô-) *n.* **1.** A bog or marsh. **2.** Any perplexing situation.

**mor•a•to•ri•um** (môr′ə-tôr′ē-əm, -tōr′-, mŏr′-) *n., pl.* **-riums** or **-ria. 1.** An authorization to a debtor permitting temporary suspension of payments. **2.** A delay of any action.

**mor•bid** (môr′bĭd) *adj.* **1.** Of or caused by disease. **2.** Characterized by preoccupation with unwholesome matters. **—mor•bid′i•ty** *n.*

**mor•dant** (môr′dnt) *adj.* **1.** Bitingly sarcastic. **2.** Incisive and trenchant.

**more** (môr, mōr) *adj.* **1. a.** compar. of **many.** Greater in number. **b.** compar. of **much.** Greater in size, amount, extent, or degree. **2.** Additional; extra. *—n.* A greater or additional degree or amount. *—adv.* **1.** To a greater degree. **2.** In addition; further; again; longer.

**more•o•ver** (môr-ō′vər, mōr-, môr′ō′vər, mōr′-) *adv.* Further; besides.

**mo•res** (môr′āz′, -ēz, mōr′-) *pl.n.* The traditional customs of a social group, often having the force of law.

**morgue** (môrg) *n.* A place in which dead bodies are temporarily kept.

**mor•i•bund** (môr′ə-bŭnd′, mŏr′-) *adj.* At the point of death; dying.

**Mor•mon** (môr′mən) *n.* A member of the Church of Jesus Christ of Latter-day Saints.

**morn** (môrn) *n.* The morning.

**morn•ing** (môr′nĭng) *n.* The first or early part of the day, esp. from sunrise to noon.

**mo•ron** (môr′ŏn′, mōr′-) *n.* A stupid person; a dolt.

**mo•rose** (mə-rōs′, mô-) *adj.* Sullenly melancholy; gloomy.

**mor•phine** (môr′fēn′) *n.* A drug extracted from opium, used as an anesthetic and sedative.

**mor•sel** (môr′səl) *n.* A small piece, esp. of food.

**mor•tal** (môr′tl) *adj.* **1.** Subject to death. **2.** Causing death; fatal. **3.** Unrelenting; implacable. **4.** Extreme; dire. *—n.* A human being. **—mor′tal•ly** *adv.*

**mor•tal•i•ty** (môr-tăl′ĭ-tē) *n., pl.* **-ties. 1.** The condition of being subject to death. **2.** Death rate.

**mor•tar** (môr′tər) *n.* **1.** A receptacle in which substances are crushed or ground. **2.** A muzzle-loading cannon. **3.** A mixture of cement of lime with sand and water, used in building.

**mort•gage** (môr′gĭj) *n.* A pledge of property to a creditor as security against a debt. *—v.* **-gaged, -gaging.** To pledge (property) by mortgage. **—mort′ga•gee′** *n.* **—mort′ga•gor** *n.*

**mor•ti•cian** (môr-tĭsh′ən) *n.* A funeral director.

**mor•ti•fy** (môr′tə-fī′) *v.* **-fied, -fying. 1.** To shame; humiliate. **2.** To discipline (one's body and appetite) by self-denial. **3.** To become gangrenous. **—mor′ti•fi•ca′tion** *n.*

**mor•tu•ar•y** (môr′cho͞o-ĕr′ē) *n., pl.* **-ies.** A place where dead bodies are prepared for burial.

**mo•sa•ic** (mō-zā′ĭk) *n.* **1.** A picture composed of small colored pieces set in mortar. **2.** Something that resembles or suggests a mosaic.

**Mos•lem** (mŏz′ləm, mŏs′-) *n.* See **Muslim. —Mos′lem** *adj.*

**mosque** (mŏsk) *n.* A Muslim house of worship.

**mos•qui•to** (mə-skē′tō) *n., pl.* **-toes** or **-tos.** A winged insect of which the females bite and suck blood.

**moss** (môs, mŏs) *n.* A small, green plant often forming a matlike growth. **—moss'y** *adj.*

**most** (mōst) *adj.* **1. a.** superl. of **many.** Greatest in number. **b.** superl. of **much.** Greatest in amount, size, or degree. **2.** In the greatest number of instances. *—n.* **1.** The greatest amount, quantity, or degree. **2.** *(takes pl. v.).* The majority. *—adv.* **1.** In the highest degree, quantity, or extent. **2.** Very. **—most'ly** *adv.*

**mote** (mōt) *n.* A speck, esp. of dust.

**mo•tel** (mō-tĕl') *n.* A hotel for motorists.

**moth** (môth, mŏth) *n.* An insect related to the butterfly but generally night-flying.

**moth•er** (mŭ*th*'ər) *n.* A female parent. *—adj.* **1.** Being or characteristic of a mother. **2.** Native. *—v.* To care for; nourish and protect. **—moth'er•hood'** *n.* **—moth'er•ly** *adj.*

**moth•er-in-law** (mŭ*th*'ər-ĭn-lô') *n., pl.* **mothers-in-law.** The mother of one's spouse.

**mo•tif** (mō-tēf') *n.* A recurrent thematic element in art or literature.

**mo•tile** (mōt'l, mō'tīl') *adj.* Moving or able to move. **—mo•til'i•ty** *n.*

**mo•tion** (mō'shən) *n.* **1.** The action or process of change of position. **2.** A gesture. **3.** A formal proposal put to vote under parliamentary procedures. *—v.* To direct or signal by making a gesture. **—mo'tion•less** *adj.*

**motion picture** *n.* A series of filmed images projected so rapidly as to create the illusion of motion. **—mo'tion-pic'ture** *adj.*

**mo•ti•vate** (mō'tə-vāt') *v.* **-vated, -vating.** To provide with an incentive; impel. **—mo'ti•va'tion** *n.*

**mo•tive** (mō'tĭv) *n.* An impulse acting as an incitement to action; incentive; cause. *—adj.* Producing motion.

**mot•ley** (mŏt'lē) *adj.* **1.** Having components of great variety; heterogeneous; varied. **2.** Multicolored.

**mo•to•cross** (mō'tō-krôs', -krŏs') *n.* A motorcycle race over rough terrain.

**mo•tor** (mō'tər) *n.* **1.** Anything that imparts or produces motion. **2.** A device that converts any form of energy into mechanical energy; engine. *—adj.* **1.** Causing or producing motion. **2.** Relating to movements of the muscles. *—v.* To drive a motor vehicle. **—mo'tor•ist** *n.*

**mo•tor•cade** (mō'tər-kād') *n.* A procession of motor vehicles.

**mo•tor•cy•cle** (mō'tər-sī'kəl) *n.* A 2-wheeled vehicle propelled by an engine. **—mo'tor•cy'clist** *n.*

**mot•tle** (mŏt'l) *v.* **-tled, -tling.** To cover (a surface) with colored spots or streaks.

**mot•to** (mŏt'ō) *n., pl.* **-toes** or **-tos.** A brief phrase used to express a principle, goal, or ideal.

**mound** (mound) *n.* **1.** A pile or bank of earth. **2.** A natural elevation, as a small hill.

**mount** (mount) *v.* **1.** To climb or ascend. **2.** To get up on. **3.** To place in an appropriate setting. **4. a.** To set (guns) in position. **b.** To launch and carry out. *—n.* **1.** A horse on which to ride. **2.** An object to which another is affixed for accessibility, display, or use.

**moun•tain** (moun'tən) *n.* A large natural elevation of the earth's surface. **—moun'tain•ous** *adj.*

**mourn** (môrn, mōrn) *v.* To feel or express sorrow for; grieve. **—mourn'er** *n.* **—mourn'ful** *adj.* **—mourn'ing** *n.*

**mouse** (mous) *n., pl.* **mice** (mīs). **1.** A small, usually long-tailed rodent. **2.** A movable hand-held device that is connected to a computer and is moved about on a flat surface to direct the cursor on the screen.

**mouth** (mouth) *n., pl.* **mouths** (mou*th*z). **1.** The body opening with which food is taken in. **2.** A natural opening, as a harbor entrance. *—v.* (mou*th*). To utter mechanically, without conviction.

**mouth•piece** (mouth'pēs') *n.* **1.** A part of an instrument that functions in the mouth. **2.** A spokesman.

**move** (mo͞ov) *v.* **moved, moving. 1.** To change position. **2.** To settle in a new place. **3.** To affect deeply. **4.** To take some action. **5.** To make a formal motion in parliamentary procedure. *—n.* **1.** An act of moving. **2.** A change of residence. **3.** A player's turn to move a piece in a board game. **4.** One of a series of actions undertaken to achieve some end. **—mov'a•ble** *adj.* **—mov'er** *n.*

**move•ment** (mo͞ov′mənt) *n.* **1.** An act of moving. **2.** The activities of a group toward a specific goal. **3.** Activity, esp. in business or commerce. **4.** A primary section of a musical composition. **5.** A mechanism that produces or transmits motion.

**mov•ie** (mo͞o′vē) *n.* **1.** A motion picture. **2. the movies.** A showing of a motion picture.

**mow**[1] (mō) *v.* **mowed, mowed** or **mown** (mōn), **mowing.** To cut down (grain, grass, etc.). **—mow down.** To fell in great numbers, as in battle. **—mow′er** *n.*

**mow**[2] (mou) *n.* A place for storing hay or grain.

**mox•ie** (mŏk′sē) *n.* **1.** Spirit in the face of difficulty. **2.** Energy or pep.

**moz•za•rel•la** (mŏt′sə-rĕl′ə) *n.* A soft, white Italian curd cheese.

**much** (mŭch) *adj.* **more** (môr, mōr), **most** (mōst). Great in quantity, degree, or extent. *—n.* **1.** A large quantity or amount. **2.** Anything impressive or important. *—adv.* **more, most. 1.** To a great degree. **2.** Just about; almost.

**muck** (mŭk) *n.* **1.** A moist mixture of mud and filth. **2.** Moist animal dung.

**muck•rake** (mŭk′rāk′) *v.* **-raked, -raking.** To expose political or commercial corruption. **—muck′rak′er** *n.*

**mu•cous** (myo͞o′kəs) *adj.* Also **mu•cose.** Producing or secreting mucus.

**mu•cus** (myo͞o′kəs) *n.* A viscous bodily secretion.

**mud** (mŭd) *n.* Wet, sticky, soft earth. **—mud′dy** *adj.*

**mud•dle** (mŭd′l) *v.* **-dled, -dling. 1.** To mix up; confuse. **2.** To mismanage or bungle. *—n.* A confusion, jumble, or mess.

**muff**[1] (mŭf) *v.* To perform (an act) clumsily; bungle.

**muff**[2] (mŭf) *n.* A small, tubelike cover for keeping the hands warm.

**muf•fin** (mŭf′ĭn) *n.* A small, cup-shaped bread.

**muf•fle** (mŭf′əl) *v.* **-fled, -fling. 1.** To wrap up snugly. **2.** To deaden (a sound). **—muf′fler** *n.*

**mug**[1] (mŭg) *n.* A drinking vessel.

**mug**[2] (mŭg) *v.* **mugged, mugging.** To waylay and beat severely. **—mug′ger** *n.*

**mug•gy** (mŭg′ē) *adj.* **-gier, -giest.** Warm and humid.

**mulch** (mŭlch) *n.* Organic material spread around plants for protection.

**mule**[1] (myo͞ol) *n.* The sterile offspring of a male donkey and a mare.

**mule**[2] (myo͞ol) *n.* A slipper with no heel strap.

**mul•ish** (myo͞o′lĭsh) *adj.* Stubborn.

**mull** (mŭl) *v.* To ponder or ruminate on (with *over*).

**mul•ti•far•i•ous** (mŭl′tə-fâr′ē-əs) *adj.* Having great variety; of many kinds.

**mul•ti•me•di•a** (mŭl′tē-mē′dē-ə) *adj.* Involving several media.

**mul•ti•ple** (mŭl′tə-pəl) *adj.* Of or having more than 1 element, component, etc. *—n.* A quantity into which another can be divided with 0 remainder.

**mul•ti•pli•cand** (mŭl′tə-plĭ-kănd′) *n.* A number to be multiplied by another.

**mul•ti•plic•i•ty** (mŭl′tə-plĭs′ĭ-tē) *n.* A large number or variety.

**mul•ti•ply** (mŭl′tə-plī′) *v.* **-plied, -plying. 1.** To increase in number, amount, or degree. **2.** To add (a pair of numbers) a given number of times to find their product. **—mul′ti•pli•ca′tion** *n.* **—mul′ti•pli′er** *n.*

**mul•ti•tude** (mŭl′tĭ-t/y/o͞od′) *n.* A great, indefinite number. **—mul′ti•tu′di•nous** *adj.*

**mum•ble** (mŭm′bəl) *v.* **-bled, -bling.** To speak or utter indistinctly. **—mum′ble** *n.*

**mum•my** (mŭm′ē) *n., pl.* **-mies.** A body embalmed after death, as by the ancient Egyptians.

**munch** (mŭnch) *v.* To chew steadily and noisily.

**munch•ies** (mŭn′chēz) *pl.n.* **1.** Snack food. **2.** A craving for snacks.

**mun•dane** (mŭn-dān′, mŭn′dān′) *adj.* **1.** Not spiritual, worldly. **2.** Typical of the ordinary.

**mu•nic•i•pal** (myo͞o-nĭs′ə-pəl) *adj.* **1.** Of a city or its government. **2.** Having local self-government. **—mu•nic′i•pal′i•ty** *n.*

**mu•nif•i•cent** (myo͞o-nĭf′ĭ-sənt) *adj.* Extremely generous. **—mu•nif′i•cence** *n.*

**mu•ni•tions** (myo͞o-nĭsh′ənz) *pl.n.* War materiel.

**mu•ral** (myo͝or′əl) *n.* A large picture or

decoration that is applied directly to a wall.

**mur•der** (mûr′dər) *n.* The deliberate killing of 1 human being by another. —*v.* **1.** To kill (a human being). **2.** To ruin. **—mur′der•er** *n.* **—mur′der•ess** *n.* **—mur′der•ous** *adj.*

**murk•y** (mûr′kē) *adj.* **-ier, -iest. 1.** Dark; gloomy. **2.** Cloudy and dark with smoke, mist, etc.

**mur•mur** (mûr′mər) *n.* **1.** A low, indistinct, and continuous sound. **2.** An indistinct complaint. —*v.* To make or utter in a murmur.

**mus•cle** (mŭs′əl) *n.* **1. a.** A tissue composed of fibers capable of contracting and relaxing to effect bodily movement. **b.** A part made of such tissue. **2.** Strength. —*v.* **-cled, -cling.** To force one's way. **—mus′cu•lar** *adj.*

**muse** (myo͞oz) *v.* **mused, musing.** To ponder; consider reflectively or at length.

**mu•se•um** (myo͞o-zē′əm) *n.* A building in which works of artistic, historical, and scientific interest are exhibited.

**mush** (mŭsh) *n.* **1.** Boiled cornmeal. **2.** Anything thick, soft, and pulpy. **3.** Maudlin sentimentality. **—mush′y** *adj.*

**mush•room** (mŭsh′ro͞om′, -ro͝om′) *n.* A fleshy fungus having an umbrella-shaped cap, esp. one that is edible. —*v.* To multiply or grow rapidly.

**mu•sic** (myo͞o′zĭk) *n.* The art of organizing sounds so as to create an aesthetic combination of rhythm, melody, and harmony. **—mu′si•cal** *adj.* **—mu•si′-cian** *n.*

**musk** (mŭsk) *n.* An odorous animal secretion used in perfume. **—musk′y** *adj.*

**mus•ket** (mŭs′kĭt) *n.* A 17th- and 18th-century firearm. **—mus′ket•eer′** *n.*

**Mus•lim** (mŭz′ləm, mo͝oz′-) *n.* A believer in Islam. **—Mus′lim** *adj.*

**mus•lin** (mŭz′lĭn) *n.* A sturdy cotton fabric.

**muss** (mŭs) *v.* To make untidy; rumple. —*n.* Disorder; mess. **—muss′y** *adj.*

**mus•sel** (mŭs′əl) *n.* A bivalve mollusk, often edible.

**must** (mŭst) *v.* An auxiliary to indicate: **1.** Necessity or obligation. **2.** Probability. **3.** Inevitability or certainty. —*n.* An absolute requirement.

**mus•tache, mous•tache** (mŭs′tăsh′, mə-stăsh′) *n.* The hair growing on the upper lip.

**mus•tard** (mŭs′tərd) *n.* **1.** A plant with yellow flowers and often pungent seeds. **2.** A condiment made from mustard seeds.

**mus•ter** (mŭs′tər) *v.* **1.** To summon (troops). **2.** To gather up. —*n.* A gathering, esp. of troops, for inspection.

**must•y** (mŭs′tē) *adj.* **-ier, -iest.** Having a stale odor.

**mu•ta•gen** (myo͞o′tə-jən) *n.* An agent that causes biological mutation. **—mu′ta•gen′ic** *adj.*

**mu•ta•tion** (myo͞o-tā′shən) *n.* **1.** An alteration or change, as in nature or form. **2.** In biology, any heritable alteration of an organism. **—mu′tant** *n. & adj.*

**mute** (myo͞ot) *adj.* **1.** Incapable of producing speech. **2.** Not speaking or spoken; silent. —*n.* **1.** A person incapable of speech. **2.** A device used to muffle the tone of a musical instrument. —*v.* **muted, muting.** To soften the sound, color, or shade of.

**mu•ti•late** (myo͞ot′l-āt′) *v.* **-lated, -lating.** To injure or disfigure by seriously damaging a limb, part, etc. **—mu′ti•la′tion** *n.*

**mu•ti•ny** (myo͞ot′n-ē) *n., pl.* **-nies.** Open rebellion against constituted authority, esp. by sailors or soldiers. **—mu′ti•neer′** *n.* **—mu′ti•nous** *adj.*

**mutt** (mŭt) *n.* A mongrel dog.

**mut•ter** (mŭt′ər) *v.* **1.** To speak in low, indistinct tones. **2.** To complain or grumble. —*n.* A muttering utterance.

**mut•ton** (mŭt′n) *n.* The flesh of a grown sheep.

**mu•tu•al** (myo͞o′cho͞o-əl) *adj.* **1.** Having the same feelings each for the other. **2.** Given and received in equal amounts. **3.** Possessed in common. **—mu′tu•al′i•ty** *n.*

**muz•zle** (mŭz′əl) *n.* **1.** The projecting jaws and nose of certain animals. **2.** A protective device fitted over an animal's snout. **3.** The front end of the barrel of a firearm. —*v.* **-zled, -zling. 1.** To put a muzzle on (an animal). **2.** To prevent (someone) from expressing opinions.

**my** (mī) *adj.* The possessive case of *I,* used before a noun as an attributive adjective.

**my•col•o•gy** (mī-kŏl′ə-jē) *n.* The scientific study of fungi. **—my•col′o•gist** *n.*

**my•na, my•nah** (mī′nə) *n.* Any of several birds resembling starlings and capable of mimicking human speech.

**my•o•pi•a** (mī-ō′pē-ə) *n.* **1.** Shortsightedness. **2.** Lack of foresight in thinking or planning. **—my•op′ic** *adj.* **—my•op′i•cal•ly** *adv.*

**myr•i•ad** (mĭr′ē-əd) *adj.* Amounting to a very large, indefinite number. —*n.* A vast number.

**myrrh** (mûr) *n.* An aromatic gum resin used in perfume and incense.

**myr•tle** (mûr′tl) *n.* Any of several evergreen shrubs or trees.

**my•self** (mī-sĕlf′) *pron.* **1.** The reflexive form of *I.* **2.** The emphatic form of *I* or *me.*

**mys•ter•y** (mĭs′tə-rē) *n., pl.* **-ies. 1.** Anything that arouses curiosity because it is unexplained, inexplicable, or secret. **2.** The quality of being inexplicable or secret. **—mys•te′ri•ous** *adj.*

**mystery play** A medieval drama based on a biblical event.

**mys•tic** (mis′tĭk) *adj.* **1.** Of mystics or mysticism. **2.** Inspiring a quality of mystery. —*n.* One who believes in mysticism. **—mys′ti•cal** *adj.*

**mys•ti•cism** (mĭs′tĭ-sĭz′əm) *n.* A spiritual discipline aiming at union with the divine through deep meditation or contemplation.

**mys•ti•fy** (mĭs′tə-fī′) *v.* **-fied, -fying.** To perplex; bewilder. **—mys′ti•fi•ca′tion** *n.*

**mys•tique** (mĭ-stēk′) *n.* Mystical attitudes or beliefs associated with a particular person, thing, or idea.

**myth** (mĭth) *n.* **1.** A traditional story about ancestors, heroic figures, or supernatural beings. **2.** A fictitious or imaginary story, person, thing, explanation, etc. **—myth′i•cal** *adj.*

**my•thol•o•gy** (mĭ-thŏl′ə-jē) *n., pl.* **-gies. 1.** A body of myths about the origin and history of a people. **2.** The study of myths. **—myth′o•log′i•cal** *adj.*

# — N —

**n, N** (ĕn) *n.* The 14th letter of the English alphabet.

**nab** (năb) *v.* **nabbed, nabbing. 1.** To arrest. **2.** To grab or snatch.

**na•cho** (nä′chō′) *n., pl.* **-os.** A piece of tortilla topped with cheese or chili-pepper sauce and broiled.

**na•dir** (nā′dər, -dîr′) *n.* **1.** A celestial point opposite the zenith. **2.** The lowest point.

**nag**[1] (năg) *v.* **nagged, nagging. 1.** To annoy by constant complaining. **2.** To complain or find fault constantly. —*n.* One who nags. **—nag′ging•ly** *adv.*

**nag**[2] (năg) *n.* A horse.

**nail** (nāl) *n.* **1.** A thin, pointed piece of metal used as a fastener. **2.** A fingernail or toenail. —*v.* To fasten with nails.

**na•ive, na•ïve** (nä-ēv′) *adj.* Lacking sophistication; ingenuous. **—na′ive•té′, na′ïve•té′** *n.*

**na•ked** (nā′kĭd) *adj.* Without clothing on the body; nude. **—na′ked•ness** *n.*

**name** (nām) *n.* **1.** A word or words by which any entity is designated. **2.** Reputation; renown. —*v.* **named, naming. 1.** To give a name to. **2.** To call by the name of. **3.** To appoint. **—name′less** *adj.* **—name′ly** *adv.*

**name•sake** (nām′sāk′) *n.* One named after another.

**nap**[1] (năp) *n.* A brief sleep. —*v.* **napped, napping.** To sleep for a brief period.

**nap**[2] (năp) *n.* A fuzzy surface on certain textiles.

**nape** (nāp) *n.* The back of the neck.

**nap•kin** (năp′kĭn) *n.* A piece of fabric or paper used at table to protect the clothes or wipe the lips.

**nar•cot•ic** (när-kŏt′ĭk) *n.* An often addictive drug that dulls the senses and induces sleep. **—nar•cot′ic** *adj.*

**nar•rate** (năr′āt′, nă-rāt′) *v.* **-rated, -rating. 1.** To tell (a story). **2.** To give an account or commentary. **—nar•ra′tion** *n.* **—nar′ra•tive** *n.* **—nar′ra′tor** *n.*

**nar•row** (năr′ō) *adj.* **1.** Of small or limited width. **2.** Limited in area or scope. **3.** Rigid in views or ideas; limited in outlook. —*v.* To make or become nar-

row or narrower. —*n.* **narrows.** A narrow body of water connecting two larger ones. —**nar'row•ly** *adv.*
**na•sal** (nā'zəl) *adj.* Of the nose.
**nas•cence** (nā'səns) *n.* A coming into existence; birth. —**nas'cent** *adj.*
**nas•ty** (năs'tē) *adj.* **-tier, -tiest. 1.** Disgusting to see, smell, or touch; filthy. **2.** Malicious; spiteful. **3.** Unpleasant; disagreeable. —**nas'ti•ly** *adv.* —**nas'ti•ness** *n.*
**na•tal** (nāt'l) *adj.* Of birth.
**na•tion** (nā'shən) *n.* **1.** A group of people under a single government. **2.** A people having common origins or traditions; federation or tribe. —**na'tion•al** *adj. & n.* —**na'tion•al•ism'** *n.* —**na'tion•al•ist** *n.* —**na'tion•al•is'tic** *adj.* —**na'tion•al'i•ty** *n.* —**na'tion•al•ly** *adv.*
**na•tive** (nā'tĭv) *adj.* **1.** Inborn; innate. **2.** Originating in a certain place; indigenous. —*n.* **1.** One born in a place. **2.** An original inhabitant of a place.
**na•tiv•i•ty** (nə-tĭv'ĭ-tē, nā-) *n., pl.* **-ties.** Birth.
**nat•u•ral** (năch'ər-əl, năch'rəl) *adj.* **1.** Present in or produced by nature; not artificial. **2.** Of nature. **3.** Free from affectation. **4.** Consonant with particular circumstances; expected and accepted. —*n.* One with talent for a particular endeavor. —**nat'u•ral•ly** *adv.* —**nat'u•ral•ness** *n.*
**nat•u•ral•ist** (năch'ər-ə-lĭst, năch'rə-) *n.* One who studies plants and animals.
**nat•u•ral•ize** (năch'ər-ə-līz', năch'rə-) *v.* **-ized, -izing.** To grant full citizenship to. —**nat'u•ral•i•za'tion** *n.*
**na•ture** (nā'chər) *n.* **1.** The fundamental character of a person or thing. **2.** The order, disposition, and behavior of all entities composing the physical universe. **3.** The physical world, including living things, natural phenomena, etc.
**naught** (nôt) *n.* Nothing; zero.
**naugh•ty** (nô'tē) *adj.* **-tier, -tiest.** Disobedient; mischievous. —**naugh'ti•ly** *adv.* —**naugh'ti•ness** *n.*
**nau•se•a** (nô'zē-ə, -zhə, -sē-ə, -shə) *n.* **1.** A stomach disturbance. **2.** Strong disgust. —**nau'se•ate'** *v.* —**nau'seous** *adj.*
**nau•ti•cal** (nô'tĭ-kəl) *adj.* Of ships, sailors, or navigation.
**na•vel** (nā'vəl) *n.* The mark on the abdomen of mammals where the umbilical cord was attached before birth.
**nav•i•gate** (năv'ĭ-gāt') *v.* **-gated, -gating. 1.** To control the course of a ship or aircraft. **2.** To voyage over water; sail. —**nav'i•ga•ble** *adj.* —**nav'i•ga'tion** *n.* —**nav'i•ga'tor** *n.*
**na•vy** (nā'vē) *n., pl.* **-vies.** All of a nation's warships. —**na'val** *adj.*
**nay** (nā) *adv.* No. —*n.* A negative vote.
**near** (nîr) *adv.* To, at, or within a short distance or interval in space or time. —*adj.* **1.** Close. **2.** Closely related; intimate. —*prep.* Close to. —*v.* To come close or closer to; draw near. —**near'by'** *adj. & adv.* —**near'ly** *adv.* —**near'ness** *n.*
**near•sight•ed** (nîr'sī'tĭd) *adj.* Unable to see distant objects clearly. —**near'sight'ed•ness** *n.*
**neat** (nēt) *adj.* **1.** Tidy. **2.** Orderly in appearance or procedure. —**neat'ly** *adv.* —**neat'ness** *n.*
**neb•u•la** (nĕb'yə-lə) *n.* A diffuse mass of interstellar dust or gas.
**neb•u•lous** (nĕb'yə-ləs) *adj.* Lacking definite form; vague; unclear. —**neb'u•lous•ly** *adv.*
**nec•es•sar•y** (nĕs'ĭ-sĕr'ē) *adj.* **1.** Needed for the continuing existence or functioning of something; essential; requisite. **2.** Inevitable. —*n., pl.* **-ies.** Often **necessaries.** Something that is essential. —**nec'es•sar'i•ly** *adv.*
**ne•ces•si•ty** (nə-sĕs'ĭ-tē) *n., pl.* **-ties. 1.** Something necessary. **2.** Pressing or urgent need. —**ne•ces'si•tate'** *v.*
**neck** (nĕk) *n.* **1.** The part of the body joining the head to the trunk. **2.** A narrow projecting or connecting part of anything, as of a bottle.
**neck•lace** (nĕk'lĭs) *n.* An ornament worn around the neck.
**neck•tie** (nĕk'tī') *n.* A narrow band of fabric knotted or tied and worn around the neck of a shirt.
**nec•tar** (nĕk'tər) *n.* **1.** The drink of the gods. **2.** A sweet liquid secreted by flowers.
**nec•tar•ine** (nĕk'tə-rēn') *n.* A smooth-skinned variety of peach.
**need** (nēd) *n.* **1.** A state in which something necessary is required. **2.** Something required or wanted. **3.** Poverty. **4.**

Necessity; obligation. —*v.* To require or want. **—need'ful** *adj.* **—need'i•ness** *n.* **—need'less** *adj.* **—need'less•ly** *adv.* **—need'y** *adj.*

**nee•dle** (nēd'l) *n.* **1.** A slender implement for knitting, sewing, etc. **2.** A pointer or indicator, as on a magnet. **3.** A stiff, narrow leaf, as of a pine. —*v.* **-dled, -dling.** To goad, provoke, or tease.

**need•n't** (nēd'nt) *v.* Contraction of *need not.*

**ne•far•i•ous** (nə-fâr'ē-əs) *adj.* Evil; wicked. **—ne•far'i•ous•ness** *n.*

**ne•gate** (nĭ-gāt') *v.* **-gated, -gating. 1.** To render ineffective; nullify. **2.** To rule out; deny. **—ne•ga'tion** *n.*

**neg•a•tive** (nĕg'ə-tĭv) *adj.* **1.** Expressing negation, refusal, or denial. **2.** Lacking the quality of being positive or affirmative. **3.** Of an electric charge that tends to repel electrons. —*n.* **1.** A negative word or statement. **2.** An image in which the light areas appear dark and the dark areas appear light. **—neg'a•tive•ly** *adv.*

**ne•glect** (nĭ-glĕkt') *v.* **1.** To disregard; ignore. **2.** To fail to give proper attention to. —*n.* **1.** The act of neglecting something. **2.** The state of being neglected. **—ne•glect'ful** *adj.*

**neg•li•gee** (nĕg'lĭ-zhā') *n.* A woman's dressing gown.

**neg•li•gent** (nĕg'lĭ-jənt) *adj.* Habitually guilty of neglect. **—neg'li•gence** *n.*

**neg•li•gi•ble** (nĕg'lĭ-jə-bəl) *adj.* Not worth considering; trifling.

**ne•go•ti•ate** (nĭ-gō'shē-āt') *v.* **-ated, -ating. 1.** To confer with another or others in order to come to terms; bargain. **2.** To transfer ownership of (financial documents) in return for value received. **—ne•go'tia•ble** *adj.* **—ne•go'ti•a'tion** *n.* **—ne•go'ti•a'tor** *n.*

**Ne•gro** (nē'grō) *n., pl.* **-groes.** A member of a racial group having brown to black skin color; a black. —*adj.* Of a Negro.

**neigh** (nā) *v.* To utter the cry of a horse. **—neigh** *n.*

**neigh•bor** (nā'bər) *n.* One living near another. —*v.* To live or be situated nearby. **—neigh'bor•hood'** *n.* **—neigh'bor•ing** *adj.* **—neigh'bor•ly** *adj.*

**nei•ther** (nē'*th*ər, nī'-) *adj.* Not one or the other. —*pron.* Not the one nor the other. —*conj.* Not either.

**nem•e•sis** (nĕm'ĭ-sĭs) *n., pl.* **-ses 1.** An inflicter of retribution; avenger. **2.** An unbeatable rival, as in sports.

**ne•on** (nē'ŏn') *n.* A gaseous chemical element, used in display and television tubes.

**ne•o•nate** (nē'ə-nāt') *n.* A newborn child.

**ne•o•phyte** (nē'ə-fīt') *n.* A beginner.

**neph•ew** (nĕf'yo͞o) *n.* The son of one's brother or sister.

**nep•o•tism** (nĕp'ə-tĭz'əm) *n.* Favoritism shown to relatives, esp. in politics.

**Nep•tune** (nĕp't/y/o͞on') *n.* The 8th planet from the sun.

**nerd** (nûrd) *n.* A socially inept person. **—nerd'y** *adj.*

**nerve** (nûrv) *n.* **1.** A bundle of fibers capable of transmitting sensory stimuli and motor impulses through the body. **2.** Courage. **3.** Impudence.

**nerv•ous** (nûr'vəs) *adj.* **1.** High-strung; excitable. **2.** Of the nerves. **3.** Uneasy; anxious. **—ner'vous•ly** *adv.* **—ner'vous•ness** *n.*

**nest** (nĕst) *n.* **1.** The structure made by a bird or other creature for holding its eggs and young. **2.** A snug place. **3.** A set of objects that can be stacked together. —*v.* **1.** To build or occupy a nest. **2.** To fit or place snugly together.

**nes•tle** (nĕs'əl) *v.* **-tled, -tling.** To settle snugly and comfortably.

**net**[1] (nĕt) *n.* **1.** An openwork meshed fabric. **2.** Something made of net. —*v.* **netted, netting.** To catch in a net. **—net'ting** *n.*

**net**[2] (nĕt) *adj.* Remaining after all costs have been deducted. —*n.* Total gain, as of profit. —*v.* **netted, netting.** To bring in as profit.

**net•tle** (nĕt'l) *n.* A plant with stinging hairs. —*v.* **-tled, -tling.** To irritate; vex.

**net•work** (nĕt'wûrk') *n.* **1.** Something resembling a net in having a number of parts, passages, or lines that branch out or interconnect. **2.** A system of computers that are connected together to share information.

**neu•ral** (n/y/o͝or'əl) *adj.* Of the nerves.

**neu•rol•o•gy** (n/y/o͞o-rŏl'ə-jē) *n.* The medical science of the nervous system and its disorders. **—neu'ro•log'i•cal** *adj.* **—neu•rol'o•gist** *n.*

**neu•ro•sis** (n/y/o͞o-rō'sĭs) *n., pl.* **-ses.** A disorder of the mind or emotions, involving anxiety, phobia, etc. **—neu•rot'ic** *adj. & n.*

**neu•ter** (n/y/o͞o'tər) *adj.* Neither masculine nor feminine.

**neu•tral** (n/y/o͞o'trəl) *adj.* **1.** Not favoring or belonging to either side in a dispute. **2.** Indifferent. **3.** Designating a color with no hue. *—n.* One that is neutral. **—neu•tral'i•ty** *n.* **—neu'tral•ize'** *v.* **—neu'tral•ly** *adv.*

**neu•tron** (n/y/o͞o'trŏn') *n.* An electrically neutral particle found in the nuclei of all atoms except hydrogen.

**nev•er** (nĕv'ər) *adv.* Not ever. **—nev'er•more'** *adv.*

**nev•er•the•less** (nĕv'ər-*thə*-lĕs') *adv.* Nonetheless; however.

**new** (n/y/o͞o) *adj.* **1.** Not old; recent. **2.** Unfamiliar. **3.** Different and distinct from what was before. **4.** Modern; current. *—adv.* Freshly; recently. **—new'ly** *adv.* **—new'ness** *n.*

**new•born** (n/y/o͞o'bôrn') *adj.* **1.** Very recently born. **2.** Born anew.

**new•ly•wed** (n/y/o͞o'lē-wĕd') *n.* A person recently married.

**news** (n/y/o͞oz) *n. (takes sing. v.)* A report about recent events.

**news•cast** (n/y/o͞oz'kăst') *n.* A broadcast of news events. **—news'cast'er** *n.*

**news•let•ter** (n/y/o͞oz'lĕt'ər) *n.* A printed report giving news or information to a special group.

**news•pa•per** (n/y/o͞oz'pā'pər) *n.* A daily or weekly publication containing news, advertising, etc.

**news•reel** (n/y/o͞oz'rēl') *n.* A short film of current events.

**news•stand** (n/y/o͞oz'stănd') *n.* A shop or booth at which newspapers or periodicals are sold.

**new wave** *n.* A new movement in a particular area, as popular music.

**next** (nĕkst) *adj.* **1.** Nearest; adjacent. **2.** Immediately succeeding. *—adv.* **1.** In the time, order, or place immediately following. **2.** On the first subsequent occasion. *—prep.* Close to; nearest.

**nex•us** (nĕk'səs) *n., pl.* **-us** or **-uses.** A means of connection; link.

**nib•ble** (nĭb'əl) *v.* **-bled, -bling.** To eat with small, quick bites. *—n.* A small bite.

**nice** (nīs) *adj.* **nicer, nicest. 1.** Pleasing; appealing. **2.** Considerate; well-mannered. **3.** Respectable; virtuous. **4.** Fastidious; exacting. **—nice'ly** *adv.* **—nice'ness** *n.* **—ni'ce•ty** *n.*

**niche** (nĭch) *n.* A recess in a wall, as for a statue.

**nick** (nĭk) *n.* A notch or indentation on a surface. *—v.* To cut a nick in.

**nick•el** (nĭk'əl) *n.* **1.** A silvery, metallic chemical element. **2.** A U.S. coin worth 5 cents.

**nick•name** (nĭk'nām') *n.* A descriptive, informal, or affectionate name used instead of a real name. *—v.* **-named, -naming.** To call by a nickname.

**nic•o•tine** (nĭk'ə-tēn') *n.* A poisonous substance derived from tobacco.

**niece** (nēs) *n.* A daughter of one's brother or sister.

**nig•gard•ly** (nĭg'ərd-lē) *adj.* **-lier, -liest. 1.** Stingy. **2.** Meager. **—nig'gard•ly** *adv.*

**nig•gle** (nĭg'əl) *v.* **-gled, -gling.** To be preoccupied with trifles or petty details.

**nigh** (nī) *adj.* **nigher, nighest.** Close; near. *—adv.* **1.** Near. **2.** Nearly; almost. *—prep.* Not far from; near to.

**night** (nīt) *n.* The period of darkness between sunset and sunrise. **—night'fall'** *n.* **—night'ly** *adj. & adv.* **—night'time'** *n.*

**night•gown** (nīt'goun') *n.* A loose gown worn in bed.

**night•life** (nīt'līf') *n.* Entertainment available or pursued in the evening.

**night•mare** (nīt'mâr') *n.* A frightening dream or event.

**night•shirt** (nīt'shûrt') *n.* A long shirt worn in bed.

**night•stick** (nīt'stĭk') *n.* A club carried by a policeman.

**ni•hil•ism** (nī'ə-lĭz'əm) *n.* A doctrine that holds that all values are baseless and that nothing is knowable or can be communicated. **—ni'hil•ist** *n.* **—ni'hil•is'tic** *adj.*

**nil** (nĭl) *n.* Nothing; naught.

**nim•ble** (nĭm'bəl) *adj.* **-bler, -blest. 1.** Quick and agile; deft. **2.** Clever in thinking, responding, etc. **—nim'bly** *adv.*

**nin•com•poop** (nĭn'kəm-po͞op', nĭng'-) *n.* A silly or stupid person; fool.

**nine** (nīn) *n.* The cardinal number written 9. **—nine** *adj. & pron.* **—ninth** *n. & adj.*

**nine•teen** (nīn-tēn') *n.* The cardinal number written 19. **—nine'teen'** *adj. & pron.* **—nine'teenth'** *n. & adj.*

**nine•ty** (nīn'tē) *n.* The cardinal number written 90. **—nine'ty** *adj. & pron.* **—nine'ti•eth** *n. & adj.*

**nin•ja** (nĭn'jə) *n.* A member of a class of 14th-century Japanese mercenaries trained in the martial arts.

**nip**[1] (nĭp) *v.* **nipped, nipping. 1.** To squeeze, pinch, or bite. **2.** To sting, as cold. **3.** To check growth or development. *—n.* **1.** A bite or pinch. **2.** A stinging quality, as of frosty air. **—nip'py** *adj.*

**nip**[2] (nĭp) *n.* A small drink or sip of liquor. *—v.* **nipped, nipping.** To drink (liquor) in small portions.

**nip•ple** (nĭp'əl) *n.* **1.** A small projection near the center of the mammary gland. **2.** The rubber cap on a nursing bottle. **3.** Anything resembling a nipple.

**nir•va•na** (nîr-vä'nə, nər-) *n.* **1. Nirvana.** The Buddhist state of perfect bliss. **2.** An ideal condition of rest, joy, etc.

**nit** (nĭt) *n.* The egg of a parasitic insect, as a louse.

**nit•pick** (nĭt'pĭk') *v.* To be concerned with or find fault with insignificant details. **—nit'pick'er** *n.*

**ni•tro•gen** (nī'trə-jən) *n.* One of the elements, a colorless, odorless gas.

**ni•tro•glyc•er•in** (nī'trō-glĭs'ər-ĭn) *n.* Also **ni•tro•glyc•er•ine.** A dangerously explosive pale-yellow liquid.

**nit•wit** (nĭt'wĭt') *n.* A stupid or silly person.

**nix** (nĭks) *n.* Nothing. *—v.* To forbid; veto.

**no** (nō) *adv.* **1.** Not so. Used to express refusal. **2.** Not at all. Used with the comparative. *—adj.* **1.** Not any. **2.** Not at all. *—n., pl.* **noes. 1.** A negative response; denial; refusal. **2.** A negative vote.

**no•ble** (nō'bəl) *adj.* **-bler, -blest. 1.** Of high hereditary rank. **2.** Showing greatness of character; illustrious. **3.** Grand; stately; magnificent. *—n.* A person of noble rank. **—no•bil'i•ty** *n.* **—no'ble•man** *n.* **—no'ble•ness** *n.* **—no'ble•wom'an** *n.* **—no'bly** *adv.*

**no•bod•y** (nō'bŏd'ē, -bə-dē) *pron.* No person; no one. *—n., pl.* **-bodies.** One without fame or influence.

**noc•tur•nal** (nŏk-tûr'nəl) *adj.* **1.** Of the night. **2.** Active or functioning at night.

**nod** (nŏd) *v.* **nodded, nodding. 1.** To bow the head briefly. **2.** To express (greeting, approval, etc.) by bowing the head. **3.** To let the head fall forward as if sleepy. *—n.* A nodding motion.

**node** (nōd) *n.* **1.** A knob, knot, protuberance, or swelling. **2.** The point on a plant stem where a leaf is attached. **—nod'al** *adj.*

**nod•ule** (nŏj'o͞ol) *n.* A small node. **—nod'u•lar** *adj.*

**noise** (noiz) *n.* A sound or sounds, esp. when loud or disagreeable. **—nois'y** *adj.*

**noi•some** (noi'səm) *adj.* **1.** Offensive, disgusting, or foul. **2.** Harmful or injurious.

**no•mad** (nō'măd') *n.* **1.** One of a people having no permanent home and moving from place to place. **2.** A wanderer. **—no•mad'ic** *adj.*

**no•men•cla•ture** (nō'mən-klā'chər, nō-mĕn'klə-chər) *n.* A system of names, esp. in an art or science.

**nom•i•nal** (nŏm'ə-nəl) *adj.* **1.** In name only. **2.** Insignificant. **—nom'i•nal•ly** *adv.*

**nom•i•nate** (nŏm'ə-nāt') *v.* **-nated, -nating. 1.** To propose as a candidate. **2.** To appoint to an office, honor, etc. **—nom'i•na'tion** *n.* **—nom'i•nee'** *n.*

**nom•i•na•tive** (nŏm'ə-nə-tĭv) *adj.* Of the grammatical case that indicates the subject of a verb; subjective. *—n.* The nominative or subjective case.

**non•cha•lant** (nŏn'shə-länt') *adj.* Appearing casually unconcerned. **—non'cha•lance'** *n.* **—non'cha•lant'ly** *adv.*

**non•com•mit•tal** (nŏn'kə-mĭt'l) *adj.* Revealing no preference or purpose.

**non•de•script** (nŏn'dĭ-skrĭpt') *adj.* Lacking in distinctive qualities; hard to describe.

**none** (nŭn) *pron.* **1.** No one; nobody. **2.** No part; not any. *—adj.* Not one; no. *—adv.* In no way; not at all.

**non•en•ti•ty** (nŏn-ĕn′tĭ-tē) *n., pl.* **-ties.** An insignificant person or thing.

**none•the•less** (nŭn′*thə*-lĕs′) *adv.* Nevertheless.

**non•pa•reil** (nŏn′pə-rĕl′) *adj.* Without rival; matchless. **—non′pa•reil′** *n.*

**non•plus** (nŏn-plŭs′) *v.* **-plused** or **-plussed, -plusing** or **-plussing.** To perplex; baffle.

**non•sense** (nŏn′sĕns′, -səns) *n.* Foolish or absurd behavior or language. **—non•sen′si•cal** *adj.*

**non se•qui•tur** (nŏn sĕk′wĭ-tər, -to͝or′) *n.* A statement that does not follow logically from what preceded it.

**noo•dle** (no͞od′l) *n.* A thin strip of dried dough.

**nook** (no͝ok) *n.* **1.** A corner, esp. in a room. **2.** A quiet or secluded spot.

**noon** (no͞on) *n.* Twelve o'clock in the daytime; midday. **—noon′day′** *n.* **—noon′tide′** *n.* **—noon′time′** *n.*

**noose** (no͞os) *n.* A loop in a rope formed by a knot that tightens when pulled.

**nor** (nôr; *unstressed* nər) *conj.* And not; or not; not either.

**norm** (nôrm) *n.* A standard regarded as typical.

**nor•mal** (nôr′məl) *adj.* Conforming to a usual or typical pattern. *—n.* Anything normal; the standard. **—nor•mal′i•ty, nor′mal•cy** *n.* **—nor′mal•ly** *adv.*

**north** (nôrth) *n.* **1.** The direction along a meridian 90° counterclockwise from east. **2.** Often **North.** The N part of any country or region. *—adj. & adv.* To or from the north. **—north′er•ly** *adj. & adv.* **—north′ern, North′ern** *adj.* **—north′ern•er, North′ern•er** *n.* **—north′ward** *adj. & adv.*

**north•east** (nôrth-ēst′) *n.* The direction or area halfway between north and east. *—adj. & adv.* To, from, or in the northeast. **—north•east′ern** *adj.* **—north•east′er•ly** *adj. & adv.*

**north•west** (nôrth-wĕst′) *n.* The direction or area halfway between north and west. *—adj. & adv.* To, from, or in the northwest. **—north•west′ern** *adj.* **—north•west′er•ly** *adj. & adv.*

**nose** (nōz) *n.* **1.** The facial structure containing the nostrils and organs of smell. **2.** The sense of smell. **3.** Anything like a nose in shape or position. *—v.* **nosed, nosing. 1.** To find out by or as by smell. **2.** To pry curiously. **—nos′i•ness** *n.* **—nos′y, nos′ey** *adj.*

**nose•gay** (nōz′gā′) *n.* A small bunch of flowers.

**nos•tal•gi•a** (nŏ-stăl′jə, nə-) *n.* **1.** A longing for things of the past. **2.** Homesickness. **—nos•tal′gic** *adj.*

**nos•tril** (nŏs′trəl) *n.* Either of the external openings of the nose.

**nos•trum** (nŏs′trəm) *n.* A favorite but untested remedy.

**not** (nŏt) *adv.* In no way; to no degree.

**no•ta•ble** (nō′tə-bəl) *adj.* Worthy of notice; remarkable. *—n.* A person of note or distinction. **—no′ta•bil′i•ty** *n.* **—no′ta•bly** *adv.*

**no•ta•rize** (nō′tə-rīz′) *v.* **-rized, -rizing.** To witness and authenticate (a document).

**no•ta•ry** (nō′tə-rē) *n.* A person legally empowered to witness and certify documents.

**no•ta•tion** (nō-tā′shən) *n.* **1.** A system of symbols used to represent numbers, quantities, etc. **2.** The use of such a system.

**notch** (nŏch) *n.* A V-shaped cut. *—v.* To cut notches in.

**note** (nōt) *n.* **1.** A brief written record or communication. **2.** A commentary to a passage in a text. **3.** A promissory note. **4.** A tone of definite pitch or the symbol of such a tone in musical notation. **5.** Importance; consequence. **6.** Notice; observation. *—v.* **noted, noting. 1.** To observe carefully; notice. **2.** To write down; make a note of. **3.** To make mention of; remark. **—note′wor′thy** *adj.*

**note•book** (nōt′bo͝ok′) *n.* A book of blank pages for notes.

**not•ed** (nō′tĭd) *adj.* Distinguished by reputation; eminent.

**noth•ing** (nŭth′ĭng) *n.* **1.** No thing; not anything. **2.** A person or thing of no consequence. **3.** Zero; naught. *—adv.* Not at all. **—noth′ing•ness** *n.*

**no•tice** (nō′tĭs) *n.* **1.** The act of observing; attention. **2.** An announcement or indication of some event. **3.** A critical review, as of a play. *—v.* **-ticed, -ticing. 1.** To observe; be aware of. **2.** To take note of; remark on. **—no′tice•a•ble** *adj.* **—no′tice•a•bly** *adv.*

**no•ti•fy** (nō′tə-fī′) *v.* **-fied, -fying. 1.** To let (someone) know; inform. **2.** To tell by a notice; proclaim. **—no′ti•fi•ca′tion** *n.*

**no•tion** (nō′shən) *n.* **1.** A general impression or feeling. **2.** A view or theory. **3.** Intention or inclination. **4. notions.** Small items for household and clothing use.

**no•to•ri•ous** (nō-tôr′ē-əs, -tōr′-) *adj.* Known widely and regarded unfavorably; infamous. **—no′to•ri′e•ty** *n.* **—no•to′ri•ous•ly** *adv.*

**not•with•stand•ing** (nŏt′wĭth-stăn′dĭng, -wĭth-) *prep.* In spite of. *—adv.* All the same; nevertheless.

**noun** (noun) *n.* A word used to name a person, place, thing, quality, or act.

**nour•ish** (nûr′ĭsh) *v.* To provide (a living thing) with food that it needs to grow and live. **—nour′ish•ment** *n.*

**nov•el**[1] (nŏv′əl) *n.* A long fictional prose narrative. **—nov′el•ist** *n.*

**nov•el**[2] (nŏv′əl) *adj.* Strikingly new, unusual, or different. **—nov′el•ty** *n.*

**No•vem•ber** (nō-vĕm′bər) *n.* The 11th month of the year.

**nov•ice** (nŏv′ĭs) *n.* **1.** A beginner. **2.** One who has entered a religious order but has not yet taken final vows.

**now** (nou) *adv.* **1.** At the present time. **2.** At once; immediately. *—conj.* Since; seeing that. *—n.* The present time.

**now•a•days** (nou′ə-dāz′) *adv.* In or during the present time.

**no•where** (nō′hwâr′) *adv.* Not anywhere.

**nox•ious** (nŏk′shəs) *adj.* Injurious to health.

**noz•zle** (nŏz′əl) *n.* A projecting spout.

**nu•ance** (n/y/ōō-äns′, n/y/ōō′äns′) *n.* A slight variation, as in meaning, color, or tone.

**nub** (nŭb) *n.* **1.** A lump or knob. **2.** The gist or point. **—nub′by** *adj.*

**nu•bile** (n/y/ōō′bĭl, -bīl′) *adj.* Relating to marriage, esp. of a young woman.

**nu•cle•us** (n/y/ōō′klē-əs) *n., pl.* **-clei. 1.** A central part around which other parts are grouped; core. **2.** A complex structure within a living cell, controlling its metabolism, reproduction, etc. **3.** The positively charged central region of an atom. **—nu′cle•ar** *adj.*

**nude** (n/y/ōōd) *adj.* Without clothing; naked. *—n.* The nude human figure or a representation of it. **—nud′ism′** *n.* **—nud′ist** *n. & adj.* **—nu′di•ty** *n.*

**nudge** (nŭj) *v.* **nudged, nudging.** To push gently. **—nudge** *n.*

**nug•get** (nŭg′ĭt) *n.* A small lump, esp. of natural gold.

**nui•sance** (n/y/ōō′səns) *n.* A source of inconvenience or annoyance; a bother.

**null** (nŭl) *adj.* Having no legal force; invalid. **—nul′li•fi•ca′tion** *n.* **—nul′li•fy′** *v.* **—nul′li•ty** *n.*

**numb** (nŭm) *adj.* **1.** Insensible, as from excessive chill. **2.** Stunned, as from shock. **—numb** *v.* **—numb′ly** *adv.* **—numb′ness** *n.*

**num•ber** (nŭm′bər) *n.* **1.** A member of the set of integers. **2.** A sum or quantity of units. **3.** One item in a sequence or series. *—v.* **1.** To add up to. **2.** To count. **3.** To include in. **4.** To assign a number to. **—num′ber•less** *adj.*

**nu•mer•al** (n/y/ōō′mər-əl) *n.* A symbol used to represent a number. **—nu′mer•al** *adj.* **—nu•mer′i•cal** *adj.* **—nu•mer′i•cal•ly** *adv.*

**nu•mer•a•tor** (n/y/ōō′mə-rā′tər) *n.* The number written above the line in a fraction.

**nu•mer•ous** (n/y/ōō′mər-əs) *adj.* Many. **—nu•′mer•ous•ly** *adv.*

**nun** (nŭn) *n.* A woman who belongs to a religious community. **—nun′ner•y** *n.*

**nup•tial** (nŭp′shəl, -chəl) *adj.* Of marriage or the wedding ceremony. *—n.* Often **nuptials.** A wedding ceremony.

**nurse** (nûrs) *n.* **1.** A person trained to care for the sick. **2.** A woman employed to take care of children. *—v.* **nursed, nursing. 1.** To suckle. **2.** To care for or tend (a child or invalid).

**nurs•er•y** (nûr′sə-rē, nûrs′rē) *n., pl.* **-ies. 1.** A room for children. **2.** A place where plants are grown.

**nur•ture** (nûr′chər) *n.* **1.** Anything that nourishes; food. **2.** Upbringing; rearing. *—v.* **-tured, -turing.** To nourish.

**nut** (nŭt) *n.* **1.** A fruit or seed with a hard shell. **2.** An eccentric person. **3.** A small metal block that holds a bolt or screw. **—nut′crack′er** *n.* **—nut′shell′** *n.* **—nut′ty** *adj.*

**nu•tri•ent** (n/y/ōō′trē-ənt) *n.* A nourishing substance. **—nu′tri•ent** *adj.*

**nu•tri•ment** (n/y/ōō′trə-mənt) *n.* Food.

**nu•tri•tion** (n/y/o͞o-trĭsh′ən) *n.* The process of nourishing or being nourished. —**nu•tri′tion•al** *adj.* —**nu•tri′tion•al•ly** *adv.* —**nu•tri′tious** *adj.* —**nu′tri•tive** *adj.*

**nuz•zle** (nŭz′əl) *v.* **-zled, -zling. 1.** To rub or push against gently with the nose or snout. **2.** To nestle or cuddle together.

**ny•lon** (nī′lŏn′) *n.* **1.** A high-strength, resilient synthetic material. **2. nylons.** Stockings made of nylon.

**nymph** (nĭmf) *n.* **1.** A female spirit representing a feature of nature. **2.** A young stage of an insect.

# — O —

**o, O** (ō) *n.* The 15th letter of the English alphabet.

**oaf** (ōf) *n.* A big, clumsy, thickheaded person. —**oaf′ish** *adj.*

**oak** (ōk) *n.* An acorn-bearing tree with hard, durable wood. —**oak′en** *adj.*

**oar** (ôr, ōr) *n.* A long pole with a blade at one end, used to row a boat. —**oar′-lock′** *n.*

**o•a•sis** (ō-ā′sĭs) *n., pl.* **-ses.** A fertile spot in a desert.

**oat** (ōt) *n.* A cereal grass having edible seeds. —**oat′meal′** *n.*

**oath** (ōth) *n., pl.* **oaths. 1.** A formal promise to do something. **2.** A curse; profanity.

**ob•du•rate** (ŏb′d/y/o͝o-rĭt) *adj.* Stubborn; unyielding. —**ob′du•ra•cy** *n.*

**ob•e•lisk** (ŏb′ə-lĭsk) *n.* A four-sided column tapering and ending in a pyramid.

**o•bese** (ō-bēs′) *adj.* Extremely fat. —**o•be′si•ty** *n.*

**o•bey** (ō-bā′) *v.* To do what one is ordered to do. —**o•be′di•ence** *n.* —**o•be′di•ent** *adj.* —**o•be′di•ent•ly** *adv.*

**ob•fus•cate** (ŏb′fə-skāt′, ŏb-fŭs′kāt′) *v.* **-cated, -cating.** To confuse; obscure. —**ob′fus•ca′tion** *n.*

**o•bit•u•ar•y** (ō-bĭch′o͞o-ĕr′ē) *n., pl.* **-ies.** A notice of death.

**ob•ject**[1] (əb-jĕkt′) *v.* **1.** To present a dissenting or opposing argument. **2.** To disapprove of something. —**ob•jec′tion** *n.* —**ob•jec′tion•a•ble** *adj.*

**ob•ject**[2] (ŏb′jĭkt, -jĕkt′) *n.* **1.** A material thing. **2.** An aim or purpose. **3.** A noun that receives or is affected by the action of a verb or that follows and is governed by a preposition.

**ob•jec•tive** (əb-jĕk′tĭv) *adj.* **1.** Of a material object as distinguished from a mental concept, idea, or belief. **2.** Uninfluenced by emotion or personal prejudice. **3.** Denoting the grammatical case of a noun or pronoun serving as the object of a verb or preposition. **4.** Serving as the goal of a course of action. —*n.* **1.** An aim or purpose; a goal. **2.** In grammar, the objective case. —**ob•jec′tive•ly** *adv.* —**ob′jec•tiv′i•ty** *n.*

**ob•li•ga•tion** (ŏb′lĭ-gā′shən) *n.* **1.** The act of binding oneself by a social, legal, or moral tie. **2.** A binding contract, promise, etc. —**ob′li•gate′** *v.* —**o•blig′a•to′ry** *adj.*

**o•blige** (ə-blīj′) *v.* **obliged, obliging. 1.** To constrain by physical, legal, or moral means. **2.** To make grateful or thankful. **3.** To do a favor for.

**o•blique** (ō-blēk′, ə-) *adj.* **1.** Slanting or sloping. **2.** Indirect or evasive. —**o•blique′ly** *adv.* —**o•bliq′ui•ty** *n.*

**o•blit•er•ate** (ə-blĭt′ə-rāt′) *v.* **-ated, -ating.** To destroy completely; wipe out; erase. —**o•blit′er•a′tion** *n.*

**o•bliv•i•on** (ə-blĭv′ē-ən) *n.* The state of being completely forgotten. —**o•bliv′i•ous** *adj.*

**ob•long** (ŏb′lông′, -lŏng′) *adj.* Shaped like or resembling a rectangle or ellipse. —**ob′long′** *n.*

**ob•lo•quy** (ŏb′lə-kwē) *n., pl.* **-quies. 1.** Abusively detractive language; calumny. **2.** Discredit; disgrace.

**ob•nox•ious** (ŏb-nŏk′shəs, əb-) *adj.* Offensive; odious. —**ob•nox′ious•ly** *adv.* —**ob•nox′ious•ness** *n.*

**o•boe** (ō′bō) *n.* A woodwind instrument with a double-reed mouthpiece. —**o′bo•ist** *n.*

**ob•scene** (ŏb-sēn′, əb-) *adj.* **1.** Offensive to decency. **2.** Inciting lustful feelings; lewd. **3.** Disgusting. —**ob•scene′ly** *adv.* —**ob•scen′i•ty** *n.*

**ob•scure** (ŏb-skyo͝or′, əb-) *adj.* **-scurer, -scurest. 1.** Dark; gloomy. **2.** Indistinctly heard or perceived. **3.** Out of sight; hidden. **4.** Difficult to understand. —*v.* **-scured, -scuring. 1.** To make indistinct or unclear. **2.** To conceal; hide. **—ob•scure'ly** *adv.* **—ob•scu'ri•ty** *n.*

**ob•se•qui•ous** (ŏb-sē'kwē-əs, əb-) *adj.* Servile and fawning. **—ob•se'qui•ous•ly** *adv.* **—ob•se'qui•ous•ness** *n.*

**ob•ser•vance** (əb-zûr'vəns) *n.* **1.** Compliance with a law, custom, etc. **2.** The celebration of a holiday or religious festival.

**ob•ser•va•to•ry** (əb-zûr'və-tôr'ē, -tōr'ē) *n., pl.* **-ries.** A building equipped for making observations, as in astronomy or meteorology.

**ob•serve** (əb-zûrv') *v.* **-served, -serving. 1.** To perceive, notice, or watch attentively. **2.** To make a comment. **3.** To abide by. **4.** To celebrate (a holiday, rite, etc.). **—ob•serv'a•ble** *adj.* **—ob•ser'vant** *adj.* **—ob'ser•va'tion** *n.* **—ob•serv'er** *n.*

**ob•ses•sion** (əb-sĕsh'ən, ŏb-) *n.* Compulsive preoccupation with a fixed idea or unwanted feeling. **—ob•sess'** *v.* **—ob•ses'sive** *adj.*

**ob•so•lete** (ŏb'sə-lēt', ŏb'sə-lēt') *adj.* No longer in use. **—ob'so•les'cence** *n.* **—ob'so•les'cent** *adj.*

**ob•sta•cle** (ŏb'stə-kəl) *n.* One that opposes or stands in the way of progress toward some goal.

**ob•stet•rics** (ŏb-stĕt'rĭks, əb-) *n.* The branch of medicine concerned with pregnancy and childbirth. **—ob•stet'ric** *adj.* **—ob'ste•tri'cian** *n.*

**ob•sti•nate** (ŏb'stə-nĭt) *adj.* Stubborn; inflexible. **—ob'sti•na•cy** *n.* **—ob'sti•nate•ly** *adv.*

**ob•strep•er•ous** (ŏb-strĕp'ər-əs, əb-) *adj.* Unruly.

**ob•struct** (əb-strŭkt', ŏb-) *v.* **1.** To block (a passage) with obstacles. **2.** To impede or retard. **3.** To get in the way of so as to hide. **—ob•struc'tion** *n.* **—ob•struc'tive** *adj.*

**ob•tain** (əb-tān', ŏb-) *v.* To get or acquire. **—ob•tain'a•ble** *adj.*

**ob•trude** (ŏb-trōōd', əb-) *v.* **-truded, -truding.** To force (oneself or one's ideas) upon others; intrude. **—ob•tru'sion** *n.* **—ob•tru'sive** *adj.*

**ob•tuse** (ŏb-t/y/ōōs', əb-) *adj.* **1.** Not sharp or pointed; blunt. **2.** Slow to understand. **—ob•tuse'ness** *n.*

**obtuse angle** *n.* An angle greater than 90° and less than 180°.

**ob•verse** (ŏb-vûrs', ŏb'vûrs') *adj.* Facing the observer. *—n.* The side of a coin that bears the principal design.

**ob•vi•ate** (ŏb'vē-āt') *v.* **-ated, -ating.** To prevent by making unnecessary.

**ob•vi•ous** (ŏb'vē-əs) *adj.* Easily perceived or understood. **—ob'vi•ous•ly** *adv.* **—ob'vi•ous•ness** *n.*

**oc•ca•sion** (ə-kā'zhən) *n.* **1.** A significant event. **2.** The time of an occurrence. **3.** A favorable time; opportunity. **4.** Ground; reason. *—v.* To provide occasion for. **—oc•ca'sion•al** *adj.* **—oc•ca'sion•al•ly** *adv.*

**Oc•ci•dent** (ŏk'sĭ-dənt, -dĕnt') *n.* Europe and the W Hemisphere. **—Oc'ci•den'tal** *adj. & n.*

**oc•clude** (ə-klōōd') *v.* **-cluded, -cluding.** To close off; obstruct. **—oc•clu'sion** *n.*

**oc•cult** (ə-kŭlt', ŏk'ŭlt') *adj.* **1.** Of or dealing with magic, astrology, supernatural powers, etc. **2.** Not readily explained; mysterious.

**oc•cu•pa•tion** (ŏk'yə-pā'shən) *n.* **1.** A means of making a living; a profession or job. **2.** The act of occupying or state of being occupied. **3.** The invasion and seizure of a nation by a foreign military force. **—oc'cu•pa'tion•al** *adj.*

**oc•cu•py** (ŏk'yə-pī') *v.* **-pied, -pying. 1.** To seize possession of (a place or region). **2.** To reside in. **3.** To engage or busy (oneself). **—oc'cu•pan•cy** *n.* **—oc'cu•pant** *n.*

**oc•cur** (ə-kûr') *v.* **-curred, -curring. 1.** To take place. **2.** To exist or appear. **3.** To come to mind. **—oc•cur'rence** *n.*

**o•cean** (ō'shən) *n.* **1.** The entire body of salt water that covers about 72% of the earth's surface. **2.** Often **Ocean.** Any of the principal divisions of this body of water. **—o'ce•an'ic** *adj.* **—o'cean•og'ra•phy** *n.*

**oc•e•lot** (ŏs'ə-lŏt', ō'sə-) *n.* A spotted American wildcat.

**o'clock** (ə-klŏk') *adv.* According to the clock.

**oc•ta•gon** (ŏk'tə-gŏn') *n.* A polygon with eight sides. **—oc•tag'o•nal** *adj.*

**oc•tane** (ŏk'tān') *n.* A hydrocarbon occurring in petroleum and used in gasoline to prevent knocking.

**oc•tave** (ŏk'tĭv, -tāv') *n.* The interval of eight degrees between two musical tones.

**oc•tet** (ŏk-tĕt′) *n.* Also **octette. 1.** A musical composition written for eight voices or instruments. **2.** Any group of eight.

**Oc•to•ber** (ŏk-tō′bər) *n.* The 10th month of the year.

**oc•to•ge•nar•i•an** (ŏk′tə-jə-nâr′ē-ən) *n.* Someone between eighty and ninety years of age.

**oc•to•pus** (ŏk′tə-pəs) *n., pl.* **-puses** or **-pi.** A sea animal with eight sucker-bearing tentacles.

**oc•u•lar** (ŏk′yə-lər) *adj.* Of the eye.

**oc•u•list** (ŏk′yə-lĭst) *n.* A physician who treats diseases of the eyes; ophthalmologist.

**O.D.** (ō′dē′) *v.* **O.D.'d, O.D.'ing.** To overdose. **—O.D.** *n.*

**odd** (ŏd) *adj.* **1. a.** Strange; unusual. **b.** Eccentric in conduct. **2.** In addition to what is usual or approximated. **3.** Being one of an incomplete pair or set; extra. **4.** Not divisible by two. **—odd′i•ty** *n.* **—odd′ly** *adv.*

**odds** (ŏdz) *pl.n.* **1.** An advantage given to a weaker side. **2.** A ratio expressing the probability of an outcome.

**ode** (ōd) *n.* A lyric poem characterized by noble style.

**o•di•ous** (ō′dē-əs) *adj.* Hateful; repugnant. **—o′di•um** *n.*

**o•dom•e•ter** (ō-dŏm′ĭ-tər) *n.* An instrument that records how far a vehicle goes.

**o•dor** (ō′dər) *n.* Scent; smell. **—o′dor•if′er•ous** *adj.* **—o′dor•less** *adj.* **—o′dor•ous** *adj.*

**od•ys•sey** (ŏd′ĭ-sē) *n.* An extended adventurous journey.

**of** (ŭv; *unstressed* əv) *prep.* **1.** From. **2.** Owing to. **3.** Away fom. **4.** From the total or group comprising. **5.** Composed or made from. **6.** Belonging or connected to. **7.** Possessing; having. **8.** Specified as; named or called. **9.** Before; until.

**off** (ôf, ŏf) *adv.* **1.** At a distance from. **2.** Distant in time. **3.** So as to be unattached, disconnected, or removed. **4.** So as to be away from work. *—adj.* **1.** More distant or removed. **2.** Not on, attached, or connected. **3.** Away from work. *—prep.* **1.** Away from. **2.** Extending or branching out from. **3.** Below the usual level of.

**of•fal** (ô′fəl, ŏf′əl) *n.* **1.** Waste parts, esp. of a butchered animal. **2.** Refuse; rubbish.

**of•fend** (ə-fĕnd′) *v.* To anger or annoy; affront; displease. **—of•fend′er** *n.*

**of•fense** (ə-fĕns′) *n.* **1. a.** A violation of a moral or social code. **b.** A crime. **2.** The act of attacking. **—of•fen′sive** *adj. & n.* **—of•fen′sive•ly** *adv.*

**of•fer** (ô′fər, ŏf′ər) *v.* **1.** To present for acceptance or rejection; suggest. **2.** To present for sale. **3.** To propose as payment; bid. **4.** To volunteer. **—of′fer** *n.* **—of′fer•ing** *n.*

**of•fice** (ô′fĭs, ŏf′ĭs) *n.* **1.** A place of business. **2.** A duty or function. **3.** A position of authority. **4.** A public position, esp. an elective one.

**of•fi•cer** (ô′fĭ-sər, ŏf′ĭ-) *n.* **1.** One who holds an office of authority or trust. **2.** One holding a commission in the armed forces.

**of•fi•cial** (ə-fĭsh′əl) *adj.* **1.** Of or authorized by a proper authority; authoritative. **2.** Formal or ceremonious. *—n.* One who holds an office. **—of•fi′cial•dom** *n.* **—of•fi′cial•ly** *adv.*

**of•fi•ci•ate** (ə-fĭsh′ē-āt′) *v.* **-ated, -ating.** To perform official duties and functions, esp. as a priest or minister.

**of•fi•cious** (ə-fĭsh′əs) *adj.* Excessively forward in offering one's services or advice to others. **—of•fi′cious•ly** *adv.* **—of•fi′cious•ness** *n.*

**off•set** (ôf′sĕt′, ŏf′-) *n.* **1.** Something that balances, counteracts, or compensates. **2.** Printing by indirect image transfer. *—v.* **-set, -setting. 1.** To counterbalance, counteract, or compensate for. **2.** To print by offset. **—off′set′** *adj.*

**off•shoot** (ôf′sho͞ot′, ŏf′-) *n.* Something that branches out or originates from a source.

**off•spring** (ôf′sprĭng′, ŏf′-) *n., pl.* **-spring.** Progeny; young.

**of•ten** (ô′fən, ŏf′ən) *adv.* Frequently; repeatedly.

**o•gle** (ō′gəl, ô′-) *v.* **ogled, ogling.** To stare in an impertinent or amorous manner. **—o′gle** *n.*

**o•gre** (ō′gər) *n.* **1.** A fabled giant that eats human flesh. **2.** A cruel person.

**oh** (ō) *interj.* Expressive of surprise, fear, etc.

**oil** (oil) *n.* A natural or synthetic combustible liquid or liquefiable substance, used in a great variety of products, esp. lubricants and fuels. —*v.* **1.** To lubricate with oil. **2.** To take on fuel oil. **—oil'y** *adj.*

**oint•ment** (oint'mənt) *n.* A viscous salve used for cosmetic or medical purposes.

**OK** (ō-kā') *n., pl.* **OK's.** Approval; agreement. —*v.* **OK'ed** *or* **OK'd, OK'ing.** To approve; agree to. —*interj.* Expressive of approval or agreement. **—OK** *adj. & adv.*

**o•kay** (ō-kā') *interj.* OK. —*v.* **okayed, okaying.** To approve.

**old** (ōld) *adj.* **1.** Far advanced in years or life. **2.** Ancient; antique. **3.** Of age. **4.** Mature; experienced. **5.** Of an earlier time. **6.** Worn-out. —*n.* Former times; yore. **—old'en** *adj.*

**old-fash•ioned** (ōld'făsh'ənd) *adj.* Having the beliefs, style, etc., of an earlier era.

**Old World** The E Hemisphere, esp. Europe. **—old'-world', Old'-World'** *adj.*

**o•le•o** (ō'lē-ō) *n.* Margarine.

**ol•fac•to•ry** (ŏl-făk'tə-rē, -trē, ōl-) *adj.* Of the sense of smell.

**ol•i•gar•chy** (ŏl'ĭ-gär'kē) *n., pl.* **-chies.** Government by the few, esp. by a small faction. **—ol'i•garch'** *n.* **—ol'i•gar'chic** *adj.*

**ol•ive** (ŏl'ĭv) *n.* **1.** The edible fruit of an Old World tree, pressed to extract a yellowish oil. **2.** Dull yellowish green. **—ol'ive** *adj.*

**om•buds•man** (ŏm'bŭdz'mən, -bədz-, -bo͝odz'-) *n.* One who investigates complaints and works toward fair settlement.

**om•e•let, om•e•lette** (ŏm'lĭt, ŏm'ə-lĭt) *n.* A dish consisting of beaten eggs cooked and often folded around a filling.

**o•men** (ō'mən) *n.* A prophetic sign.

**om•i•nous** (ŏm'ə-nəs) *adj.* Of an evil omen; foreboding; threatening. **—om'i•nous•ly** *adv.*

**o•mit** (ō-mĭt') *v.* **omitted, omitting. 1.** To leave out. **2.** To neglect; fail (to do). **—o•mis'sion** *n.*

**om•nip•o•tent** (ŏm-nĭp'ə-tənt) *adj.* All-powerful. **—om•nip'o•tence** *n.*

**om•niv•o•rous** (ŏm-nĭv'ər-əs) *adj.* Eating all kinds of food. **—om'ni•vore'** *n.* **—om•niv'o•rous•ly** *adv.* **—om•niv'o•rous•ness** *n.*

**on** (ŏn, ôn) *prep.* **1.** Atop; in contact with. **2.** Toward or against. **3.** During. **4.** In the state, condition, or process of. **5.** Concerning; about. —*adv.* **1. a.** In the direction of. **b.** Forward. **2.** In or into operation. **3.** In or into a position of being attached to or covering.

**once** (wŭns) *adv.* **1.** One time only. **2.** Formerly. **3.** At any time; ever. **—at once. 1.** Simultaneously. **2.** Immediately. —*conj.* As soon as; when.

**one** (wŭn) *adj.* **1.** Being a single thing. **2.** Of a single kind; undivided. **3.** Designating an unspecified person or thing; a certain. **4.** Single in kind; alike or the same. —*n.* **1.** The cardinal number written 1. **2.** A single person or thing; unit. —*pron.* A person or thing. **—one'ness** *n.*

**on•er•ous** (ŏn'ər-əs, ō'nər-) *adj.* Troublesome; burdensome.

**on-line** (ŏn'līn', ôn'-) *adj.* **1.** Under the control of a central computer. **2.** In progress; going on. **—on'-line'** *adv.*

**one•self** (wŭn-sĕlf') *pron.* The reflexive form of the pronoun *one.*

**on•ion** (ŭn'yən) *n.* A plant with an edible bulb of pungent flavor.

**on•ly** (ōn'lē) *adj.* Alone in kind; sole. —*adv.* **1.** Alone. **2. a.** No more than; at least. **b.** Merely. **3.** Exclusively; solely. —*conj.* But.

**on•set** (ŏn'sĕt', ôn'-) *n.* **1.** An attack. **2.** A beginning.

**on•slaught** (ŏn'slôt', ôn'-) *n.* A violent attack.

**on•to** (ŏn'to͞o', -tə, ôn'-) *prep.* On top of; upon.

**o•nus** (ō'nəs) *n.* A burden, esp. a disagreeable responsibility.

**on•ward** (ŏn'wərd, ôn'-) *adv.* Also **on•wards.** Forward; in advance; ahead. —*adj.* Moving forward.

**on•yx** (ŏn'ĭks) *n.* A kind of quartz that occurs in bands of different colors.

**oo•dles** (o͞od'lz) pl.n. A great amount; lots.

**ooze**[1] (o͞oz) *v.* **oozed, oozing.** To leak out slowly; exude. **—ooze** *n.*

**ooze**[2] (o͞oz) *n.* Soft, thin mud. **—ooz'y** *adj.*

**o•pal** (ō′pəl) *n.* A translucent mineral having iridescent colors and often used as a gem.

**o•paque** (ō-pāk′) *adj.* **1. a.** Impenetrable by light. **b.** Not reflecting light. **2.** Obtuse; dense. **—o•pac′i•ty, o•paque′ness** *n.*

**o•pen** (ō′pən) *adj.* **1.** Affording unobstructed passage; not shut or closed. **2.** Having no cover; exposed. **3.** Not sealed. **4.** Accessible to all; unrestricted. **5.** Candid; receptive. *—v.* **1.** To become or cause to become open. **2.** To spread out or apart. **3.** To remove wrapping from. **4.** To begin. **5.** To become more responsive or understanding. *—n.* The outdoors. **—o′pen•er** *n.* **—o′pen•ing** *n.* **—o′pen•ly** *adv.* **—o′pen•ness** *n.*

**op•er•a** (ŏp′rə, ŏp′ər-ə) *n.* A dramatic presentation set to music. **—op′er•at′ic** *adj.*

**op•er•ate** (ŏp′ə-rāt′) *v.* **-ated, -ating. 1.** To function effectively; work. **2.** To perform surgery. **3.** To manage; run. **—op′er•a•ble** *adj.* **—op′er•a′tion** *n.* **—op′er•a′tion•al** *adj.* **—op′er•a′tor** *n.*

**op•er•a•tive** (ŏp′ər-ə-tĭv, -ə-rā′tĭv, ŏp′rə-) *adj.* **1.** Exerting influence or force. **2.** Functioning; working. *—n.* **1.** A skilled worker. **2.** A secret agent.

**oph•thal•mol•o•gy** (ŏf′thəl-mŏl′ə-jē, -thăl-, ŏp′-) *n.* The medical specialty encompassing the eye. **—oph•thal′mic** *adj.* **—oph′thal•mol′o•gist** *n.*

**o•pi•ate** (ō′pē-ĭt, -āt′) *n.* **1.** A narcotic containing opium. **2.** Any sedative or narcotic drug.

**o•pin•ion** (ə-pĭn′yən) *n.* **1.** A belief, conclusion, or judgment not substantiated by proof. **2.** An evaluation based on special knowledge.

**o•pin•ion•at•ed** (ə-pĭn′yə-nā′tĭd) *adj.* Holding stubbornly to one's own opinions.

**o•pi•um** (ō′pē-əm) *n.* A narcotic drug made from the dried juice of a certain poppy.

**o•pos•sum** (ə-pŏs′əm, pŏs′əm) *n.* Also **pos•sum.** A furry, tree-dwelling marsupial.

**op•po•nent** (ə-pō′nənt) *n.* One that opposes, as in a fight; adversary.

**op•por•tune** (ŏp′ər-t/y/o͞on′) *adj.* **1.** Suitable; appropriate. **2.** Timely.

**op•por•tun•ist** (ŏp′ər-t/y/o͞o′nĭst) *n.* One who takes advantage of any opportunity, usually unethically. **—op′por•tun′ism′** *n.* **—op′por•tun•is′tic** *adj.*

**op•por•tu•ni•ty** (ŏp′ər-t/y/o͞o′nĭ-tē) *n., pl.* **-ties.** A favorable combination of circumstances.

**op•pose** (ə-pōz′) *v.* **-posed, -posing. 1.** To resist; fight. **2.** To contrast. **—op′po•si′tion** *n.*

**op•po•site** (ŏp′ə-zĭt) *adj.* **1.** Located directly across from. **2.** Facing the other way. **3.** Diametrically opposed; altogether different. *—n.* One that is contrary to another. **—op′po•site** *adv.*

**op•press** (ə-prĕs′) *v.* **1.** To govern in a cruel or arbitrary way. **2.** To weigh heavily upon. **—op•pres′sion** *n.* **—op•pres′sive** *adj.* **—op•pres′sor** *n.*

**op•pro•bri•um** (ə-prō′brē-əm) *n.* **1.** Disgrace; ignominy. **2.** Reproach or contempt. **—op•pro′bri•ous** *adj.*

**op•ti•cian** (ŏp-tĭsh′ən) *n.* One who makes or sells lenses and eyeglasses.

**op•tics** (ŏp′tĭks) *n.* The scientific study of light and vision. **—op′tic, op′ti•cal** *adj.*

**op•ti•mism** (ŏp′tə-mĭz′əm) *n.* A tendency to expect the best possible outcome. **—op′ti•mist** *n.* **—op′ti•mis′tic** *adj.*

**op•ti•mum** (ŏp′tə-məm) *n., pl.* **-ma** or **-mums.** The best or most favorable condition. **—op′ti•mal** *adj.* **—op′ti•mal•ly** *adv.*

**op•tion** (ŏp′shən) *n.* **1.** The act of choosing; choice. **2.** The freedom to choose. **3.** The right to buy or sell within a specified time and at a specified price. **—op′tion•al** *adj.* **—op′tion•al•ly** *adv.*

**op•tom•e•try** (ŏp-tŏm′ĭ-trē) *n.* The profession of treating visual defects esp. with corrective lenses. **—op•tom′e•trist** *n.*

**op•u•lent** (ŏp′yə-lənt) *adj.* **1.** Wealthy; rich. **2.** Abundant; copious. **—op′u•lence** *n.*

**or** (ôr; *unstressed* ər) *conj.* Used to indicate: **1.** An alternative. **2.** An equivalent expression. **3.** Uncertainty or indefiniteness.

**or•a•cle** (ôr′ə-kəl, ŏr′-) *n.* **1. a.** A shrine consecrated to a prophetic god. **b.** A priest or priestess at such a shrine. **2.** A wise adviser. **—o•rac′u•lar** *n.*

**o•ral** (ôr′əl, ōr′-) *adj.* **1.** Spoken. **2.** Of the mouth. **—o′ral•ly** *adv.*

**or•ange** (ôr′ĭnj, ŏr′-) *n.* **1.** A round, reddish-yellow citrus fruit. **2.** Reddish yellow. **—or•ange** *adj.*

**o•rang•u•tan** (ō-răng′ə-tăn′, ə-răng′-) *n.* A shaggy-haired, long-armed ape.

**o•ra•tion** (ô-rā′shən, ō-rā′-) *n.* A formal speech. **—o•rate′** *v.* **—or′a•tor** *n.*

**or•a•to•ry** (ôr′ə-tôr′ē, -tōr′ē, ŏr′-) *n.* Eloquent public speaking; rhetoric.

**orb** (ôrb) *n.* A sphere; globe.

**or•bit** (ôr′bĭt) *n.* **1.** The path of a celestial body, artificial satellite, etc., as it revolves around another body. **2.** A cavity in the skull for the eye. *—v.* To put into an orbit or move in orbit. **—or′bit•al** *adj.*

**or•chard** (ôr′chərd) *n.* A tract of land where fruit trees are cultivated.

**or•ches•tra** (ôr′kĭ-strə, -kĕs′trə) *n.* **1.** A large ensemble of musicians. **2.** The main floor of a theater. **—or•ches′tral** *adj.*

**or•chid** (ôr′kĭd) *n.* **1.** A tropical plant with irregularly shaped flowers. **2.** The flower of such a plant.

**or•dain** (ôr-dān′) *v.* **1.** To invest as a minister, priest, etc. **2.** To decree; order. **—or•dain′ment** *n.* **—or′di•na′tion** *n.*

**or•deal** (ôr-dēl′) *n.* A severely difficult experience.

**or•der** (ôr′dər) *n.* **1.** A logical arrangement among the separate elements of a group. **2.** A sequence of things. **3.** Customary procedure. **4.** A command or direction. **5.** A portion of food in a restaurant. **6.** A monastic institution. **7.** A group of people bound by some common bond or social aim. *—v.* **1.** To issue a command or instruction to. **2.** To request to be supplied with (something). **3.** To put in a systematic arrangement.

**or•der•ly** (ôr′dər-lē) *adj.* **1.** Tidy; neat. **2.** Peaceful; well-behaved. *—n., pl.* **-lies. 1.** A hospital attendant. **2.** A soldier who attends an officer.

**or•di•nal** (ôr′dn-əl) *adj.* Of a specified position in a series.

**or•di•nance** (ôr′dn-əns) *n.* A statute or regulation.

**or•di•nar•y** (ôr′dn-ĕr′ē) *adj.* **1.** Usual; normal. **2.** Average; commonplace. **—or′di•nar′i•ness** *n.* **—or′di•nar′i•ly** *adv.*

**ord•nance** (ôrd′nəns) *n.* Military supplies, esp. weapons and ammunition.

**ore** (ôr, ōr) *n.* A metal-yielding mineral.

**or•gan** (ôr′gən) *n.* **1.** A musical keyboard instrument played by forcing air through pipes. **2.** A part of an organism, adapted for a specific function. **3.** An instrument of communication, esp. a periodical publication. **—or′gan•ist** *n.*

**or•gan•ic** (ôr-găn′ĭk) *adj.* **1.** Of a bodily organ. **2.** Of a living organism. **3.** In chemistry, of carbon compounds. **—or•gan′i•cal•ly** *adv.*

**or•gan•ism** (ôr′gə-nĭz′əm) *n.* Any living being; a plant or animal.

**or•gan•ize** (ôr′gə-nīz′) *v.* **-ized, -izing. 1.** To form a functional, structured whole. **2.** To arrange; systematize. **3.** To induce employees to form or join a union. **—or′gan•i•za′tion** *n.* **—or′gan•i•za′tion•al** *adj.* **—or′gan•iz′er** *n.*

**or•gasm** (ôr′găz′əm) *n.* A sexual climax. **—or•gas′mic** *adj.*

**or•gy** (ôr′jē) *n., pl.* **-gies. 1.** Unrestrained drinking or sexual activity. **2.** Excessive indulgence in any activity. **—or′gi•as′tic** *adj.*

**o•ri•ent** (ôr′ē-ənt, -ĕnt′, ōr′-) *n.* **Orient.** The countries of Asia, esp. of E Asia. *—v.* **1.** To align or position. **2.** To adjust to a situation. **—O′ri•en′tal** *adj. & n.* **—o′ri•en•ta′tion** *n.*

**or•i•fice** (ôr′ə-fĭs, ŏr′-) *n.* An opening; mouth.

**o•ri•ga•mi** (ôr′ĭ-gä′mē) *n.* **1.** The Japanese art of folding paper into shapes. **2.** A shape, such as a bird or flower, so made.

**or•i•gin** (ôr′ə-jĭn, ŏr′-) *n.* **1.** A source. **2.** Ancestry. **3.** A coming into being.

**o•rig•i•nal** (ə-rĭj′ə-nəl) *adj.* **1.** First in order or existence. **2.** Fresh and novel. **3.** Creative; inventive. *—n.* **1.** The 1st form of anything. **2.** An authentic work of art. **—o•rig′i•nal′i•ty** *n.* **—o•rig′i•nal•ly** *adv.*

**o•rig•i•nate** (ə-rĭj′ə-nāt′) *v.* **-nated, -nating.** To come or bring into being; begin. **—o•rig′i•na′tion** *n.*

**o•ri•ole** (ôr′ē-ōl′, ōr′-) *n.* An orange and black songbird.

**or•na•ment** (ôr′nə-mənt) *n.* A decoration or adornment. —*v.* (-mĕnt′). To decorate; adorn. **—or′na•men′tal** *adj.* **—or′na•men•ta′tion** *n.*

**or•nate** (ôr-nāt′) *adj.* **1.** Elaborately ornamented. **2.** Showy in style; florid. **—or•nate′ly** *adv.*

**or•ner•y** (ôr′nə-rē) *adj.* Stubborn and mean-spirited. **—or′ner•i•ness′** *n.*

**or•ni•thol•o•gy** (ôr′nə-thŏl′ə-jē) *n.* The study of birds. **—or′ni•tho•log′i•cal** *adj.* **—or′ni•thol′o•gist** *n.*

**or•phan** (ôr′fən) *n.* A child whose parents are dead. **—or′phan•age** *n.*

**or•tho•dox** (ôr′thə-dŏks′) *adj.* Adhering to traditional and established beliefs. **—or′tho•dox′y** *n.*

**or•tho•pe•dics** (ôr′thə-pē′dĭks) *n.* The medical treatment of skeletal-system disorders. **—or′tho•pe′dic** *adj.* **—or′-tho•pe′dist** *n.*

**os•cil•late** (ŏs′ə-lāt′) *v.* **-lated, -lating.** To swing back and forth. **—os′cil•la′tion** *n.* **—os′cil•la•to′ry** *adj.*

**os•cu•late** (ŏs′kyə-lāt′) *v.* **-lated, -lating.** To kiss. **—os′cu•la′tion** *n.*

**os•mo•sis** (ŏz-mō′sĭs, ŏs-) *n.* The diffusion of fluid through a porous membrane. **—os•mot′ic** *adj.*

**os•prey** (ŏs′prē, -prā) *n., pl.* **-preys.** A large fish-eating hawk.

**os•si•fy** (ŏs′ə-fī′) *v.* **-fied, -fying.** To change into bone. **—os′si•fi•ca′tion** *n.*

**os•ten•si•ble** (ŏ-stĕn′sə-bəl) *adj.* Apparent; pretended. **—os•ten′si•bly** *adv.*

**os•ten•ta•tion** (ŏs′tĕn-tā′shən, -tən-) *n.* Pretentious showiness. **—os′ten•ta′-tious** *adj.* **—os′ten•ta′tious•ly** *adv.*

**os•te•op•a•thy** (ŏs′tē-ŏp′ə-thē) *n.* A medical therapy that treats disease through manipulative techniques. **—os′te•o•path′** *n.* **—os′te•o•path′ic** *adj.*

**os•tra•cize** (ŏs′trə-sīz′) *v.* **-cized, -cizing.** To banish or exclude from a group. **—os′tra•cism′** *n.*

**os•trich** (ŏs′trĭch, ôs′-) *n.* A large, long-legged, flightless African bird.

**oth•er** (ŭ*th*′ər) *adj.* **1.** Being or designating the remaining one. **2.** Different. **3.** Additional; extra. —*pron.* **1.** The remaining one. **2.** A different or additional person or thing. —*adv.* Differently.

**oth•er•wise** (ŭ*th*′ər-wīz′) *adv.* **1.** In another way; differently. **2.** Under other circumstances. —*adj.* Other than supposed.

**ot•ter** (ŏt′ər) *n.* A weasel-like aquatic mammal with dark-brown fur.

**ouch** (ouch) *interj.* Used to express sudden pain.

**ought** (ôt) *v.* An auxiliary verb to indicate: **1.** Obligation. **2.** Expediency. **3.** Desirability. **4.** Probability.

**ounce** (ouns) *n.* **1.** A unit of weight equal to 16 drams. **2.** A unit of liquid measure equal to 8 fluid drams or 1.804 cubic inches. **3.** A tiny bit.

**our** (our) *adj.* The possessive case of *we,* used before a noun as an attributive adjective.

**ours** (ourz) *pron.* The possessive case of *we,* used by itself or as a predicate adjective.

**our•selves** (our-sĕlvz′, är-) *pron.* **1.** The reflexive form of *we.* **2.** The emphatic form of *we* or *us.*

**oust** (oust) *v.* To eject; force out. **—oust′er** *n.*

**out** (out) *adv.* **1.** Away from inside. **2.** Away from the center. **3.** Away from a usual place. **4.** To depletion or extinction. —*adj.* **1.** Exterior; external. **2.** Unable to be used. —*prep.* **1.** Through; forth from. **2.** Beyond or outside of. —*n.* A means of escape.

**out•age** (ou′tĭj) *n.* A temporary suspension of operation, as of electric power.

**out•burst** (out′bûrst′) *n.* A sudden, violent show of emotion or activity.

**out•cast** (out′kăst′) *n.* One that has been excluded. **—out′cast′** *adj.*

**out•class** (out-klăs′) *v.* To surpass decisively.

**out•come** (out′kŭm′) *n.* A result; consequence.

**out•do** (out-do͞o′) *v.* **-did** (-dĭd′), **-done** (-dŭn′), **-doing.** To exceed in performance.

**out•door** (out′dôr′, -dōr′) *adj.* Located or done in the open air. **—out•doors′** *adv. & n.*

**out•field** (out′fēld′) *n.* The grassy playing area beyond the infield of a baseball diamond.

**out•fit** (out′fĭt′) *n.* A set of equipment or clothing, esp. for a special purpose.

—*v.* To provide with an outfit.
**out•go•ing** (out′gō′ĭng) *adj.* **1.** Departing. **2.** Friendly; sociable.
**out•ing** (ou′tĭng) *n.* A pleasure trip.
**out•land•ish** (out-lăn′dĭsh) *adj.* Conspicuously odd; bizarre. **—out•land′ish•ly** *adv.* **—out•land′ish•ness** *n.*
**out•law** (out′lô′) *n.* **1.** A person excluded from normal legal protection. **2.** One who lives lawlessly. —*v.* **1.** To ban. **2.** To deprive of the protection of the law.
**out•lay** (out′lā′) *n.* An expenditure.
**out•let** (out′lĕt′, -lĭt) *n.* **1.** A passage for escape or exit. **2.** A means of releasing emotions, energies, etc. **3.** A market for commercial goods. **4.** An electric receptacle with a socket for a plug.
**out•line** (out′līn′) *n.* **1.** A line forming the boundary of an object. **2.** A drawing in which objects are depicted only in lines. **3.** A general description or summary. —*v.* **-lined, -lining. 1.** To draw the outline of. **2.** To give the main points of.
**out•look** (out′lo͝ok′) *n.* **1.** The view seen from a place. **2.** A point of view; attitude. **3.** An expectation.
**out•ly•ing** (out′lī′ĭng) *adj.* Distant or remote.
**out•pa•tient** (out′pā′shənt) *n.* One who receives medical treatment at a facility but is not hospitalized. **—out′pa′tient** *adj.*
**out•put** (out′po͝ot′) *n.* An amount of something produced, esp. during a given period of time.
**out•rage** (out′rāj′) *n.* **1.** An extremely vicious or wicked act. **2.** Great anger aroused by such an act. —*v.* **-raged, -raging. 1.** To give offense to. **2.** To make extremely angry. **—out•ra′geous** *adj.*
**out•right** (out′rīt′, -rīt′) *adv.* **1.** Wholly; openly. **2.** Without delay. —*adj.* **1.** Unqualified. **2.** Complete.
**out•side** (out-sīd′, out′sīd′) *n.* **1.** The outer surface; exterior. **2.** The external aspect. **3.** The space beyond a boundary or limit. —*adj.* **1.** Coming from without. **2.** External. **3.** Slight; remote. —*adv.* On or to the outside. —*prep.* **1.** On or to the outer side of. **2.** Except. **—out•sid′er** *n.*
**out•skirts** (out′skûrts′) *pl.n.* The surrounding areas.
**out•spo•ken** (out-spō′kən) *adj.* Frank and direct. **—out•spo′ken•ly** *adv.* **—out•spo′ken•ness** *n.*
**out•stand•ing** (out′stăn′dĭng, out-stăn′dĭng) *adj.* **1.** Prominent; distinguished. **2.** Not paid or settled.
**out•ward** (out′wərd) *adj.* **1.** Toward the outside. **2.** Outer. —*adv.* Also **out•wards.** Toward the outside. **—out′ward•ly** *adv.*
**o•va** (ō′və) *n.* pl. of **ovum.**
**o•val** (ō′vəl) *adj.* Egg-shaped; elliptical. **—o′val** *n.*
**o•va•ry** (ō′və-rē) *n., pl.* **-ries.** A female reproductive gland. **—o•var′i•an, o•var′i•al** *adj.*
**o•va•tion** (ō-vā′shən) *n.* Enthusiastic applause.
**ov•en** (ŭv′ən) *n.* A compartment for baking, heating, or drying.
**o•ver** (ō′vər) *prep.* **1.** Above. **2.** Above and across. **3.** On the other side of. **4.** Upon. **5.** Throughout or during. **6.** Concerning. —*adv.* **1.** Above. **2.** Across an intervening distance. **3.** So as to be completely covered. **4.** From an upward to an inverted or reversed position. **5.** Again. **6.** In addition or excess. —*adj.* **1.** Finished. **2. a.** Upper; higher. **b.** Outer. **3.** In excess. **—o′ver•ly** *adv.*
**o•ver•alls** (ō′vər-ôlz′) *pl.n.* Loose-fitting trousers with shoulder straps.
**o•ver•bear•ing** (ō′vər-bâr′ĭng) *adj.* Domineering; arrogant. **—o′ver•bear′ing•ly** *adv.*
**o•ver•blown** (ō′vər-blōn′) *adj.* **1.** Blown up with conceit; inflated. **2.** Very fat.
**o•ver•book** (ō′vər-bo͝ok′) *v.* To book passengers, esp. for an airplane, beyond seating capacity.
**o•ver•cast** (ō′vər-kăst′, ō′vər-kăst′) *adj.* Clouded; gloomy.
**o•ver•coat** (ō′vər-kōt′) *n.* A heavy outdoor coat.
**o•ver•come** (ō′vər-kŭm′) *v.* **1.** To defeat. **2.** To surmount. **3.** To overpower or exhaust.
**o•ver•do** (ō′vər-do͞o′) *v.* **1.** To exaggerate. **2.** To do too much.
**o•ver•dose** (ō′vər-dōs′) *v.* **-dosed, -dosing. 1.** To take an excessive, esp. a lethal, dose of a drug. **2.** To indulge excessively in an activity. **—o′ver•dose′** *n.*

**o•ver•draw** (ō′vər-drô′) *v.* **-drew** (-dro͞o′), **-drawn** (-drôn′), **-drawing.** To draw against an account in excess of credit. **—o′ver•draft′** *n.*

**o•ver•drive** (ō′vər-drīv′) *n.* An automobile gearing system that reduces the power needed to maintain driving speed.

**o•ver•flow** (ō′vər-flō′) *v.* **1.** To flow over the top or banks (of). **2.** To flood. *—n.* (ō′vər-flō′). **1.** A flood. **2.** An excess.

**o•ver•hang** (ō′vər-hăng′) *v.* To project over, out, or beyond. **—o′ver•hang′** *n.*

**o•ver•haul** (ō′vər-hôl′, ō′vər-hôl′) *v.* To dismantle for needed repairs. **—o′ver•haul′** *n.*

**o•ver•head** (ō′vər-hĕd′) *adj.* Above the level of the head. *—n.* The operating expenses of a business. *—adv.* Over or above the level of the head.

**o•ver•kill** (ō′vər-kĭl′) *n.* A greatly excessive action or response.

**o•ver•lap** (ō′vər-lăp′) *v.* **-lapped, -lapping. 1.** To extend over. **2.** To coincide partly. **—o′ver•lap′** *n.*

**o•ver•look** (ō′vər-lo͝ok′) *v.* **1.** To afford a view over. **2.** To miss or disregard. **3.** To supervise.

**o•ver•night** (ō′vər-nīt′) *adj.* Lasting for a night. *—adv.* (ō′vər-nīt′). **1.** During the night. **2.** Suddenly.

**o•ver•qual•i•fied** (ō′vər-kwŏl′ə-fīd′) *adj.* Having qualifications beyond what is necessary or desirable. **—o′ver•qual′i•fy′** *v.*

**o•ver•re•act** (ō′vər-rē-ăkt′) *v.* **-acted, -acting.** To react unduly strongly. **—o′ver•re•ac′tion** *n.*

**o•ver•ride** (ō′vər-rīd′) *v.* **-rode** (-rōd′), **-ridden** (-rĭd′n), **-riding. 1.** To prevail over. **2.** To declare null and void. **—o′ver•ride′** *n.*

**o•ver•rule** (ō′vər-ro͞ol′) *v.* **-ruled, -ruling.** To disallow; invalidate.

**o•ver•seas** (ō′vər-sēz′, ō′vər-sēz′) *adv.* Beyond the sea; abroad. **—o′ver•seas′** *adj.*

**o•ver•see** (ō′vər-sē′) *v.* **-saw** (-sô′), **-seen** (-sēn′), **-seeing.** To supervise. **—o′ver•se′er** *n.*

**o•ver•sight** (ō′vər-sīt′) *n.* An unintentional mistake.

**o•vert** (ō-vûrt′, ō′vûrt′) *adj.* Not concealed; open. **—o•vert′ly** *adv.*

**o•ver•take** (ō′vər-tāk′) *v.* **-took** (-to͝ok′), **-taken, -taking.** To catch up with.

**o•ver•throw** (ō′vər-thrō′) *v.* **-threw** (-thro͞o′), **-thrown** (-thrōn), **-throwing. 1.** To bring about the downfall of. **2.** To throw something over and beyond. **—o′ver•throw′** *n.*

**o•ver•time** (ō′vər-tīm′) *n.* Time, esp. working hours, beyond an established limit. **—o′ver•time′** *adv. & adj.*

**o•ver•ture** (ō′vər-cho͝or′) *n.* **1.** An instrumental introduction to an extended musical work. **2.** An offer or proposal.

**o•ver•turn** (ō′vər-tûrn′) *v.* **-turned, -turning. 1.** To turn over or cause to turn over. **2.** To overthrow; defeat.

**o•ver•view** (ō′vər-vyo͞o′) *n.* **1.** A broad, comprehensive view. **2.** A summary.

**o•ver•ween•ing** (ō′vər-wē′nĭng) *adj.* Arrogant.

**o•ver•weight** (ō′vər-wāt′) *adj.* Weighing more than is normal or acceptable.

**o•ver•whelm** (ō′vər-hwĕlm′) *v.* **1.** To engulf. **2.** To overpower. **—o′ver•whelm′ing** *adj.*

**o•ver•work** (ō′vər-wûrk′) *v.* **-worked, -working. 1.** To force to work too much. **2.** To use or rework to excess.

**o•void** (ō′void′) *adj.* Egg-shaped.

**o•vu•late** (ō′vyə-lāt′, ŏv′yə-) *v.* **-lated, -lating.** To produce ova. **—o′vu•la′tion** *n.*

**o•vum** (ō′vəm) *n., pl.* **ova.** A female reproductive cell; an egg.

**owe** (ō) *v.* **owed, owing. 1.** To be in debt to. **2.** To be obliged for. **—owing to.** Because of.

**owl** (oul) *n.* A night-flying bird of prey. **—owl′et** *n.* **—owl′ish** *adj.*

**own** (ōn) *adj.* Of or belonging to. *—v.* **1.** To possess. **2.** To acknowledge or confess. **—own′er** *n.* **—own′er•ship′** *n.*

**ox** (ŏks) *n., pl.* **oxen.** An adult castrated bull.

**ox•ide** (ŏk′sīd′) *n.* A compound of an element or radical with oxygen.

**ox•i•dize** (ŏk′sĭ-dīz′) *v.* **-dized, -dizing. 1.** To combine with oxygen. **2.** To rust. **—ox′i•di•za′tion** *n.* **—ox′i•diz′er** *n.*

**ox•y•gen** (ŏk′sĭ-jən) *n.* A colorless, tasteless, odorless gaseous element, constituting 21% of the atmosphere by volume, required for nearly all combustion and combustive processes.

**ox•y•mo•ron** (ŏk′sē-môr′ŏn′, -mōr′-) *n., pl.* **-mora** or **-morons.** The juxtaposition of incongruous or contradictory words.

**oys•ter** (oi′stər) *n.* An edible bivalve mollusk.

**o•zone** (ō′zōn′) *n.* A blue, gaseous form of oxygen found in the atmosphere.

## — P —

**p, P** (pē) *n.* The 16th letter of the English alphabet.

**pace** (pās) *n.* **1.** A step made in walking. **2.** Rate of progress. **3.** A horse's gait. —*v.* **paced, pacing. 1.** To go at a pace. **2.** To measure by paces. **3.** To set the speed for. —**pac′er** *n.*

**pace•mak•er** (pās′mā′kər) *n.* **1.** One that sets the pace. **2.** An electronic, surgically implanted device that regulates the heartbeat.

**pach•y•derm** (păk′ĭ-dûrm′) *n.* A large, thick-skinned animal, as the elephant or rhinoceros.

**pac•i•fism** (păs′ə-fĭz′əm) *n.* Opposition to war or violence as a means of resolving disputes. —**pac′i•fist** *n. & adj.*

**pac•i•fy** (păs′ə-fī′) *v.* **-fied, -fying. 1.** To calm; appease. **2.** To establish peace in; subdue. —**pac′i•fi•ca′tion** *n.* —**pac′i•fi′er** *n.*

**pack** (păk) *n.* **1.** A bundle. **2.** A package containing a standard number of similar items. —*v.* **1.** To combine into a bundle. **2.** To cover. **3.** To fill up tight; cram. **4.** To compact firmly. —**pack′age** *n. & v.* —**pack′er** *n.* —**pack′et** *n.*

**pact** (păkt) *n.* **1.** A treaty. **2.** A compact; bargain.

**pad** (păd) *n.* **1.** A cushion or something functioning as a cushion. **2.** Sheets of paper, stacked and glued together at one end. —*v.* **padded, padding.** To line or fill with padding.

**pad•dle** (păd′l) *n.* An oar for a canoe. —*v.* **-dled, -dling. 1.** To row with a paddle. **2.** To play in shallow water. —**pad′dler** *n.*

**pad•dock** (păd′ək) *n.* **1.** An enclosure for grazing horses. **2.** An area at a racetrack where horses or cars receive preparation.

**pad•lock** (păd′lŏk′) *n.* A detachable lock. —**pad′lock′** *v.*

**pae•an** (pē′ən) *n.* A fervent expression, esp. a song, of joy or praise.

**pa•gan** (pā′gən) *n.* **1.** One who is not a Christian, Muslim, or Jew, especially one who belongs to a religion that worships more than one god. **2.** A disparaging term for one who has no religion. —**pa′gan** *adj.* —**pa′gan•ism′** *n.*

**page** (pāj) *n.* A leaf of a book. —*v.* **paged, paging.** To number the pages of.

**pag•eant** (păj′ənt) *n.* An elaborate public spectacle. —**pag′eant•ry** *n.*

**pa•go•da** (pə-gō′də) *n.* A many-storied Buddhist building erected as a memorial or shrine.

**paid** (pād) *v.* p.t. & p.p. of **pay.**

**pail** (pāl) *n.* A bucket.

**pain** (pān) *n.* **1.** An unpleasant feeling or hurting arising from injury, disease, etc. **2.** Suffering or distress. **3. pains.** Trouble; effort. —*v.* To cause or suffer pain. —**pain′ful** *adj.* —**pain′ful•ly** *adv.* —**pain′less** *adj.* —**pain′less•ly** *adv.* —**pain′less•ness** *n.*

**pain•kill•er** (pān′kĭl′ər) *n.* A drug that relieves pain.

**paint** (pānt) *n.* A mixture of a pigment in a liquid. —*v.* **1.** To coat with paint. **2.** To paint pictures. —**paint′er** *n.* —**paint′ing** *n.*

**pair** (pâr) *n., pl.* **pairs** or **pair. 1.** Two persons or items, similar in form or function. **2.** Something composed of two corresponding parts. —*v.* To arrange in or form a pair or pairs.

**pais•ley** (pāz′lē) *n.* A colorful, swirled pattern of abstract curved shapes. —**pais′ley** *adj.*

**pa•ja•mas** (pə-jä′məz, -jăm′əz) *pl.n.* An outfit of jacket and trousers, for sleeping or lounging.

**pal•ace** (păl′ĭs) *n.* The official residence of a royal person. —**pa•la′tial** *adj.*

**pal•ate** (păl′ĭt) *n.* **1.** The roof of the mouth. **2.** The sense of taste. —**pal′at•a•ble** *adj.* —**pal′a•tal** *adj.*

**pale¹** (pāl) *n.* **1.** A stake or picket. **2.** The area enclosed by a fence or boundary.

**pale²** (pāl) *adj.* **paler, palest. 1.** Pallid. **2.** Of a low intensity of color; light. **3.** Dim. —*v.* **paled, paling.** To make or become pale. —**pale′ness** *n.*

**pal•ette** (păl′ĭt) *n.* **1.** A board upon which an artist mixes colors. **2.** The range of qualities inherent in a work of art or music.

**pal•in•drome** (păl′ĭn-drōm′) *n.* A word or writing that reads the same backward as forward. **—pal′in•dro′mic** *adj.*

**pall** (pôl) *v.* **1.** To make or become boring or wearisome. **2.** To cloy.

**pal•li•ate** (păl′ē-āt′) *v.* **-ated, -ating. 1.** To excuse. **2.** To alleviate. **—pal′li•a′tion** *n.* **—pal′li•a′tive** *adj. & n.*

**pal•lid** (păl′ĭd) *adj.* Pale; wan.

**pal•lor** (păl′ər) *n.* Extreme or unnatural paleness.

**palm**[1] (päm) *n.* The inner surface of the hand. —*v.* To conceal in the palm.

**palm**[2] (päm) *n.* A tropical tree usually having an unbranched trunk with fanlike leaves.

**pal•pa•ble** (pă′pə-bəl) *adj.* **1.** Capable of being felt; tangible. **2.** Easily perceived; obvious **—pal′pa•bil′i•ty** *n.* **—pal′pa•bly** *adv.*

**pal•pi•tate** (păl′pĭ-tāt′) *v.* **-tated, -tating. 1.** To shake. **2.** To beat rapidly; throb. **—pal′pi•ta′tion** *n.*

**pal•sy** (pô′zē) *n., pl.* **-sies. 1.** Paralysis. **2.** An enfeebled or debilitated condition. **3.** An emotional fit marked by the inability to act. **—pal′sy** *v.*

**pal•try** (pôl′trē) *adj.* **-trier, -triest.** Petty; trifling.

**pam•per** (păm′pər) *v.* To coddle; cater to. **—pam′per•er** *n.*

**pam•phlet** (păm′flĭt) *n.* A booklet with a paper cover and no binding. **—pam′phle•teer′** *n.*

**pan** (păn) *n.* A shallow, wide, open container used for holding liquids, for cooking, etc. —*v.* **panned, panning.** To wash (gravel, sand, etc.) in a pan to separate precious metal.

**pan•a•ce•a** (păn′ə-sē′ə) *n.* A cure-all.

**pa•nache** (pə-năsh′, -näsh′) *n.* **1.** A bunch of feathers. **2.** Dash; swagger; verve.

**pan•cake** (păn′kāk′) *n.* A batter cake cooked on a skillet.

**pan•cre•as** (păng′krē-əs, păn′-) *n.* A gland that secretes juice that aids digestion. **—pan′cre•at′ic** *adj.*

**pan•da** (păn′də) *n.* A bearlike mammal of the mountains of China and Tibet.

**pan•de•mo•ni•um** (păn′də-mō′nē-əm) *n.* Wild uproar.

**pan•der** (păn′dər) *v.* **-dered, -dering. 1.** To act as a liaison in sexual intrigues. **2.** To exploit or cater to the base desires of others. **—pan′der** *n.*

**pane** (pān) *n.* A sheet of glass in a window or door.

**pan•el** (păn′əl) *n.* **1.** A flat piece, as a board, forming part of a surface or overlaying it. **2.** A group of people selected to make a judgment, etc. —*v.* To cover with panels. **—pan′el•ing** *n.* **—pan′el•ist** *n.*

**pang** (păng) *n.* A sudden feeling of pain or distress.

**pan•han•dle** (păn′hăn′dl) *v.* **-dled, -dling.** To beg. **—pan′han′dler** *n.*

**pan•ic** (păn′ĭk) *n.* An overpowering terror. —*v.* **-icked, -icking.** To affect or be affected with panic. **—pan′ick•y** *adj.*

**pan•o•ram•a** (păn′ə-răm′ə, -rä′mə) *n.* **1.** A view over a wide area. **2.** A view or picture of a long series of events. **—pan′o•ram′ic** *adj.* **—pan′o•ram′i•cal•ly** *adv.*

**pant** (pănt) *v.* **1.** To breathe in short gasps. **2.** To yearn demonstratively. —*n.* A short, quick gasp.

**pan•to•mime** (păn′tə-mīm′) *n.* A theatrical performance in which the actors use motions and gestures rather than speech. —*v.* **-mimed, -miming.** To act in pantomime.

**pan•try** (păn′trē) *n., pl.* **-tries.** A small room off a kitchen for storage.

**pants** (pănts) *pl.n.* A pair of trousers.

**pap** (păp) *n.* Soft or semiliquid food.

**pa•pal** (pā′pəl) *adj.* Of the pope. **—pa′pal•ly** *adv.* **—pa′pa•cy** *n.*

**pa•per** (pā′pər) *n.* **1.** A thin material derived mainly from wood and rags. **2.** An official document. **3.** An essay, report, etc. **4.** A newspaper. —*v.* To cover with wallpaper. —*adj.* Made of paper. **—pa′per•y** *adj.*

**pa•per•weight** (pā′pər-wāt′) *n.* An object used to hold down loose papers.

**pa•pier-mâ•ché** (pā′pər-mə-shā′) *n.* Paper pulp mixed with glue or paste, that can be molded when wet.

**pa•poose** (pă-po͞os′) *n.* A Native American infant or very young child.

**pa•py•rus** (pə-pī′rəs) *n., pl.* **-ruses** or **-ri. 1.** A grasslike plant. **2.** Paper made from the pith of this plant.

**par** (pär) *n.* **1.** An accepted average. **2.** An equal status. **3.** The face value of a stock, bond, etc.

**par•a•ble** (păr'ə-bəl) *n.* A simple story illustrating a moral.

**par•a•chute** (păr'ə-sho͞ot') *n.* An umbrella-shaped apparatus used to slow the fall of persons or things from great heights. —*v.* **-chuted, -chuting.** To drop or descend by parachute. **—par'a•chut'ist** *n.*

**pa•rade** (pə-rād') *n.* A public procession held on a ceremonial occasion. —*v.* **-raded, -rading. 1.** To march in or as in a parade. **2.** To flaunt. **—pa•rad'er** *n.*

**par•a•digm** (păr'ə-dīm') *n.* An example or model. **—par'a•dig•mat'ic** *adj.*

**par•a•dise** (păr'ə-dīs', -dīz') *n.* **1.** Heaven. **2.** A place of perfect happiness or beauty.

**par•a•dox** (păr'ə-dŏks') *n.* A seemingly contradictory statement that may nonetheless be true. **—par'a•dox'i•cal** *adj.* **—par'a•dox'i•cal•ly** *adv.*

**par•af•fin** (păr'ə-fĭn) *n.* A waxy mixture used to make candles, sealing materials, etc.

**par•a•gon** (păr'ə-gŏn', -gən) *n.* A model of excellence.

**par•a•graph** (păr'ə-grăf') *n.* A distinct division of a written work or composition, begun on a new line. —*v.* To arrange in paragraphs.

**par•a•keet** (păr'ə-kēt') *n.* A small parrot.

**par•al•lel** (păr'ə-lĕl') *adj.* **1.** Being an equal distance at every point so as never to intersect. **2.** Corresponding. —*n.* **1.** A surface or line that is parallel. **2.** A set of parallel lines. **3.** Anything that closely resembles something else. —*v.* **1.** To extend parallel to. **2.** To correspond to.

**par•al•lel•o•gram** (păr'ə-lĕl'ə-grăm') *n.* A four-sided plane figure with opposite sides parallel.

**pa•ral•y•sis** (pə-răl'ĭ-sĭs) *n., pl.* **-ses.** Loss of movement or sensation in a bodily part. **—par'a•lyt'ic** *adj.* & *n.* **—par'a•lyze'** *v.*

**par•a•mount** (păr'ə-mount') *adj.* Primary; foremost.

**par•a•noi•a** (păr'ə-noi'ə) *n.* A mental disorder characterized by delusions of persecution or grandeur. **—par'a•noi'ac** *n.* **—par'a•noid'** *adj.*

**par•a•pher•na•lia** (păr'ə-fər-nāl'yə, -fə-) *n.* **1.** Personal belongings. **2.** Equipment; gear.

**par•a•phrase** (păr'ə-frāz') *n.* A restatement in other words. **—par'a•phrase'** *v.*

**par•a•ple•gi•a** (păr'ə-plē'jē-ə, -jə) *n.* Paralysis of the lower half of the body. **—par'a•ple'gic** *adj.* & *n.*

**par•a•site** (păr'ə-sīt') *n.* An often harmful organism that lives on or in a different organism. **—par'a•sit'ic, par'a•sit'i•cal** *adj.*

**par•a•sol** (păr'ə-sôl', -sŏl') *n.* A light umbrella.

**par•a•troops** (păr'ə-tro͞ops') *pl.n.* Infantry trained and equipped to parachute. **—par'a•troop'er** *n.*

**par•boil** (pär'boil') *v.* To cook partially.

**par•cel** (pä'səl) *n.* **1.** A bundle; package. **2.** A portion or plot of land. —*v.* To divide into portions.

**parch** (pärch) *v.* **1.** To make or become very dry, esp. by heat. **2.** To make thirsty.

**par•don** (pär'dn) *v.* **1.** To forgive. **2.** To excuse —*n.* The act of pardoning. **—par'don•a•ble** *adj.* **—par'don•a•bly** *adv.*

**pare** (pâr) *v.* **pared, paring.** To peel.

**par•ent** (pâr'ənt) *n.* A father or mother. **—par'ent•age** *n.* **—pa•ren'tal** *adj.* **—par'ent•hood'** *n.*

**pa•ren•the•sis** (pə-rĕn'thĭ-sĭs) *n., pl.* **-ses.** One of a pair of upright curved lines, (), used to mark off additional remarks in printing and writing. **—par'en•thet'ic, par'en•thet'i•cal** *adj.* **—par'en•thet'i•cal•ly** *adv.*

**par•fait** (pär-fā') *n.* A frozen dessert.

**pa•ri•ah** (pə-rī'ə) *n.* A social outcast.

**par•ish** (păr'ĭsh) *n.* An administrative part of a diocese. **—pa•rish'ion•er** *n.*

**par•i•ty** (păr'ĭ-tē) *n., pl.* **-ties. 1.** Equality. **2.** Similarity. **3.** A level for farm-product prices, maintained by governmental support.

**park** (pärk) *n.* Enclosed grounds for recreational use. —*v.* To leave (a vehicle) for a time in a certain location.

**par•ka** (pä'kə) *n.* A hooded jacket.

**par•lance** (pär'ləns) *n.* A manner of speaking; idiom.

**par•ley** (pär′lē) *n., pl.* **-leys.** A conference, esp. between opponents. **—par′ley** *v.*

**par•lia•ment** (pär′lə-mənt) *n.* A legislative body. **—par′lia•men′ta•ry** *adj.*

**par•lor** (pär′lər) *n.* **1.** A room for the entertainment of visitors. **2.** A room designed for some special function or business.

**pa•ro•chi•al** (pə-rō′kē-əl) *adj.* Of a parish. **—pa•ro′chi•al•ly** *adv.*

**par•o•dy** (păr′ə-dē) *n., pl.* **-dies.** A comic imitation of a work of literature or music. **—par′o•dy** *v.*

**pa•role** (pə-rōl′) *n.* The early release of a prisoner on condition of good behavior. **—pa•role′** *v.* **—pa•rol′ee′** *n.*

**par•ox•ysm** (păr′ək-sĭz′əm) *n.* A sudden outburst. **—par′ox•ys′mal** *adj.*

**par•quet** (pär-kā′) *n.* A floor made of inlaid pieces of wood in a design.

**par•rot** (păr′ət) *n.* A bird having a hooked bill, brightly colored plumage, and sometimes the ability to mimic speech. *—v.* To repeat without understanding.

**par•ry** (păr′ē) *v.* **-ried, -rying. 1.** To ward off an attack, as in fencing. **2.** To evade or turn aside. **—par′ry** *n.*

**par•si•mo•ny** (pär′sə-mō′nē) *n.* Unusual frugality. **—par′si•mo′ni•ous** *adj.*

**pars•ley** (pär′slē) *n.* A cultivated herb used as a garnish and seasoning.

**par•son** (pä′sən) *n.* A member of the clergy. **—par′son•age** *n.*

**part** (pärt) *n.* **1.** A portion or division of a whole. **2.** Duty. *—v.* To divide. *—adv.* Partially. *—adj.* Not full or complete. **—part′ly** *adv.*

**par•take** (pär-tāk′) *v.* **-took** (-to͝ok′), **-taken** (-tā′kən), **-taking.** To take or be given a portion. **—par•tak′er** *n.*

**par•tial** (pär′shəl) *adj.* **1.** Incomplete. **2.** Prejudiced. **3.** Especially fond. **—par′ti•al′i•ty** *n.* **—par′tial•ly** *adv.*

**par•tic•i•pate** (pär-tĭs′ə-pāt) *v.* **-pated, -pating.** To join or share with others. **—par•tic′i•pant** *n.* **—par•tic′i•pa′tion** *n.*

**par•ti•ci•ple** (pär′tĭ-sĭp′əl) *n.* A form of a verb that can function as an adjective or noun. **—par′ti•cip′i•al** *adj.*

**par•ti•cle** (pär′tĭ-kəl) *n.* A very small piece; speck.

**par•tic•u•lar** (pər-tĭk′yə-lər) *adj.* **1.** Of a single person, group, or thing. **2.** Worthy of note. **3.** Concerned with details; fussy. *—n.* An individual item, fact, or detail. **—par•tic′u•lar′i•ty** *n.* **—par•tic′u•lar•ly** *adv.*

**par•ti•san** (pär′tĭ-zən) *n.* **1.** A supporter of a cause, etc. **2.** A guerrilla. **—par′ti•san** *adj.* **—par′ti•san•ship′** *n.*

**par•ti•tion** (pär-tĭsh′ən) *n.* **1.** The act or process of dividing something into parts. **2.** A partial wall dividing a room or larger area. **—par•ti′tion** *v.*

**part•ner** (pärt′nər) *n.* A person associated with another in some common activity, esp. in a business. **—part′ner•ship′** *n.*

**par•took** (pär-to͝ok′) *v.* p.t. of **partake.**

**par•tridge** (pär′trĭj) *n.* A game bird.

**par•ty** (pär′tē) *n., pl.* **-ties. 1.** A social gathering. **2.** A group of persons participating in some common activity. **—par′ty** *adj. & v.*

**pass** (păs) *v.* **1.** To go by or ahead; proceed. **2.** To run; extend. **3.** To hand over to someone else. **4.** To move past in time; elapse. **5.** To be communicated, exchanged, transferred, or conveyed. **6.** To come to an end; be terminated. **7.** To undergo (an examination, etc.) with favorable results. **8.** To approve; adopt. *—n.* **1.** The act of passing. **2.** A narrow passage between mountains. **3.** An authorization to be admitted without charge. **4.** Written leave of absence, esp. from military duty. **5.** A predicament. **—pass′a•ble** *adj.* **—pass′a•bly** *adv.*

**pas•sage** (păs′ĭj) *n.* **1.** The act of passing. **2.** Movement; transit. **3.** The process of elapsing. **4.** A journey. **5.** The right to travel. **6.** A segment of a literary work or musical composition. **—pas′sage•way′** *n.*

**pas•sen•ger** (păs′ən-jər) *n.* A person traveling in a train, aircraft, ship, etc.

**pas•sion** (păsh′ən) *n.* **1.** A powerful emotion or appetite. **2.** Sexual desire. **—pas′sion•ate** *adj.* **—pas′sion•ate•ly** *adv.*

**pas•sive** (păs′ĭv) *adj.* **1.** Not active but acted upon. **2.** Accepting without resistance. **—pas′sive•ly** *adv.* **—pas•siv′i•ty, pas′sive•ness** *n.*

**pass•port** (păs′pôrt′, -pōrt′) *n.* An official document for traveling abroad.

**pass•word** (păs′wûrd′) *n.* **1.** A secret word allowing the speaker access. **2.** A sequence of characters for accessing a computer.

**past** (păst) *adj.* **1.** Gone by; over. **2.** Having occurred in an earlier time. **3.** Denoting a verb form used to express action before the time it is expressed. —*n.* **1.** The time before the present. **2.** A person's background, career, etc. **3.** A verb form in the past tense. —*adv.* So as to pass by. —*prep.* **1.** By and beyond. **2.** Beyond in position, time, extent, or amount.

**pas•ta** (päs′tə) *n.* **1.** Dried dough of flour and water, as macaroni. **2.** A dish made with this dough.

**paste** (pāst) *n.* **1.** A smooth, sticky substance used to fasten things together. **2.** A hard, brilliant glass used for artificial gems. —*v.* **pasted, pasting.** To fasten with paste.

**pas•tel** (pă-stĕl′) *n.* A delicate hue. **—pas•tel′** *adj.*

**pas•teur•i•za•tion** (păs′chər-ĭ-zā′shən) *n.* The destruction of most disease-producing bacteria in milk, beer, and other liquids by sterilization. **—pas′teur•ize′** *v.*

**pas•tiche** (pă-stēsh′, pä-) *n.* **1.** An artistic work satirically imitating that of another artist. **2.** A hodgepodge.

**pas•time** (păs′tīm′) *n.* An activity pleasantly occupying one's free time.

**pas•tor** (păs′tər) *n.* A minister or priest in charge of a parish or congregation.

**pas•tor•al** (păs′tər-əl) *adj.* **1.** Of shepherds. **2.** Of the country; rural. **3.** Of a pastor.

**pas•tra•mi** (pə-strä′mē) *n.* A highly seasoned smoked cut of beef.

**pas•try** (pā′strē) *n., pl.* **-tries.** Baked foods, such as pies or tarts, made with a rich dough.

**pas•ture** (păs′chər) *n.* Land used for grazing. —*v.* **-tured, -turing. 1.** To put in a pasture. **2.** To graze.

**pat** (păt) *v.* **patted, patting.** To tap gently. —*n.* **1.** A light stroke or tap. **2.** A small mass. —*adj.* Of a set form.

**patch** (păch) *n.* **1.** A piece of material used to cover a hole or worn place. **2.** A small piece or part of anything. —*v.* To put a patch or patches on. **—patch′work** *n.*

**pâté** (pä-tā) *n.* **1.** A meat paste. **2.** A small pastry filled with meat.

**pat•ent** (păt′nt) *n.* A grant assuring an inventor the sole right to make, use, and sell an invention. —*adj.* (pāt′nt) **1.** Obvious; plain. **2.** Protected by a patent. —*v.* To obtain a patent on.

**pa•ter•nal** (pə-tûr′nəl) *adj.* **1.** Of a father. **2.** On the father's side of a family. **—pa•ter′ni•ty** *n.*

**path** (păth, päth) *n.* **1.** A track or way made by footsteps. **2.** A course of action or conduct.

**path•o•gen** (păth′ə-jən) *n.* An agent causing disease, esp. a bacterium, fungus, or virus. **—path′o•gen′ic, path′o•ge•net′ic** *adj.* **—path′o•gen′e•sis, —pa•thog′e•ny** *n.*

**pa•thol•o•gy** (pă-thŏl′ə-jē) *n., pl.* **-gies.** The study of disease. **—path′o•log′i•cal** *adj.* **—path′o•log′i•cal•ly** *adv.* **—pa•thol′o•gist** *n.*

**pa•thos** (pā′thŏs′, -thôs′) *n.* A quality in something or someone that arouses pity. **—pa•thet′ic** *adj.* **—pa•thet′i•cal•ly** *adv.*

**pa•tient** (pā′shənt) *adj.* Capable of bearing affliction, delay, etc., with calmness. —*n.* One under medical treatment. **—pa′tience** *n.* **—pa′tient•ly** *adv.*

**pat•i•na** (păt′n-ə, pə-tē′nə) *n.* A thin layer of corrosion on copper or bronze.

**pat•i•o** (păt′ē-ō′, pä′tē-ō′) *n., pl.* **-os.** An inner, roofless courtyard.

**pa•tri•arch** (pā′trē-ärk′) *n.* **1.** The paternal leader of a family or tribe. **2.** A venerable old man. **—pa′tri•ar•′chal** *adj.*

**pat•ri•mo•ny** (păt′rə-mō′nē) *n., pl.* **-nies.** An inheritance. **—pat′ri•mo′ni•al** *adj.*

**pa•tri•ot** (pā′trē-ət, -ŏt′) *n.* One who loves and defends his or her country. **—pa′tri•ot′ic** *adj.* **—pa′tri•ot′i•cal•ly** *adv.* **—pa′tri•ot•ism** *n.*

**pa•trol** (pə-trōl′) *n.* **1.** Moving about an area, esp. for security. **2.** A person or group performing such an action. —*v.* **-trolled, -trolling.** To engage in a patrol.

**pa•tron** (pā′trən) *n.* **1.** A benefactor. **2.** A regular customer. **—pa′tron•age** *n.*

**pa•tron•ize** (pā′trə-nīz′, păt′rə-) *v.* **-ized, -izing. 1.** To go to regularly as a customer. **2.** To treat condescendingly. **—pa′tron•iz′er** *n.*

**pa•troon** (pə-tro͞on′) *n.* A landholder in the Dutch colony of what is now New York and New Jersey.

**pat•ter** (păt′ər) *v.* To make a quick, light, tapping sound. **—pat′ter** *n.*

**pat•tern** (păt′ərn) *n.* **1.** A model to be followed in making things. **2.** An artistic or decorative design. *—v.* To make by following a pattern.

**pau•ci•ty** (pô′sĭ-tē) *n.* Short supply.

**paunch** (pônch, pänch) *n.* The belly, esp. a protruding one. **—paunch′y** *adv.*

**pau•per** (pô′pər) *n.* A very poor person.

**pause** (pôz) *v.* **paused, pausing.** To stop action briefly. *—n.* A temporary stop.

**pave** (pāv) *v.* **paved, paving.** To cover (a road, etc.) with a hard, smooth surface that will bear travel. **—pav′er** *n.*

**pa•vil•ion** (pə-vĭl′yən) *n.* **1.** An ornate tent. **2.** An open structure with a roof, used for amusement or shelter.

**paw** (pô) *n.* The clawed foot of an animal, as a dog or cat. *—v.* To strike, touch, or scrape with a paw.

**pawn** (pôn) *n.* Something given as security for a loan. **—pawn** *v.* **—pawn′-shop′** *n.*

**pay** (pā) *v.* **paid** (pād), **paying 1.** To give (money) in exchange for goods or services. **2.** To discharge (a debt). **3.** To yield as return. **4.** To let out (a rope or cable) bit by bit. *—n.* **1.** Salary; wages. **2.** Paid employment. **—pay′a•ble** *adj.* **—pay•ee′** *n.* **—pay′ment** *n.*

**pay•load** (pā′lōd′) *n.* **1.** The explosive charge in the head of a missile. **2.** The passengers, crew, and instruments carried in a plane or rocket.

**pay•off** (pā′ôf′, -ŏf′) *n.* **1.** Full payment of salary or wages. **2.** The climax of a narrative. **3.** Final revenge. **4.** A bribe.

**pay•o•la** (pā-ō′lə) *n.* Bribery, esp. of a disk jockey to play certain records.

**pea** (pē) *n.* A vine with round, edible green seeds.

**peace** (pēs) *n.* **1.** The absence of war or other hostilities. **2.** Calm; tranquillity. **—peace′a•ble** *adj.* **—peace′ful** *adj.* **—peace′ful•ly** *adv.*

**peach** (pēch) *n.* A sweet, juicy fruit with yellowish-pink skin.

**pea•cock** (pē′kŏk′) *n.* A large bird having brilliant blue or green plumage and long tail feathers.

**peak** (pēk) *n.* **1.** A point that projects upward. **2.** The pointed summit of a mountain. **3.** The point of greatest development, value, etc. **—peak** *v.* **—peaked** *adj.*

**peal** (pēl) *n.* A loud sound or series of sounds, as a ringing of bells. *—v.* To resound.

**pea•nut** (pē′nŭt′) *n.* A vine bearing edible nutlike seeds in pods that ripen underground.

**pear** (pâr) *n.* An edible fruit with a rounded base and a tapering stem end.

**pearl** (pûrl) *n.* A smooth, often rounded, lustrous gem formed in the shells of oysters. **—pearl′y** *adj.*

**peas•ant** (pĕz′ənt) *n.* A member of the class of small farmers and farm laborers. **—peas′ant•ry** *n.*

**peat** (pēt) *n.* Partially carbonized moss or other matter, found in bogs and used as fuel. **—peat•y** *adj.*

**peb•ble** (pĕb′əl) *n.* A small stone worn smooth by erosion. **—peb′bly** *adj.*

**pe•can** (pĭ-kän′, -kăn′, pē′kăn) *n.* The smooth, oval, edible nut of a tree native to the southern U.S.

**peck¹** (pĕk) *v.* To strike with or as with the beak. *—n.* A stroke or mark made with or as with the beak.

**peck²** (pĕk) *n.* A dry measure, equal to 8 quarts.

**pec•tin** (pĕk′tĭn) *n.* A substance in ripe fruits, such as apples, used to jell foods, drugs, and cosmetics.

**pec•to•ral** (pĕk′tər-əl) *adj.* Of the breast or chest.

**pe•cu•liar** (pĭ-kyo͞ol′yər) *adj.* **1.** Unusual; odd. **2.** Distinct and particular. **3.** Exclusive. **—pe•cu′li•ar′i•ty** *n.* **—pe•cu′-liar•ly** *adv.*

**ped•a•gog•ic** (pĕd′ə-gŏj′ĭk, -gō′jĭk) *adj.* **1.** Relating to teaching. **2.** Pedantic. **—ped′a•gog′i•cal•ly** *adv.* **—ped′a•gog′ics** *n.* **—ped′a•gogue′** *n.*

**ped•al** (pĕd′l) *n.* A lever worked by the foot. *—adj.* Of a foot or footlike part. *—v.* To operate the pedal or pedals of.

**ped•ant** (pĕd′nt) *n.* **1.** One who pays too much attention to book learning. **2.** One who makes an ostentatious display of learning. **—pe•dan′tic** *adj.*

—**pe•dan'ti•cal•ly** *adv.* —**ped'ant•ry** *n.*

**ped•dle** (pĕd'l) *v.* **-dled, -dling.** To travel about selling (wares). —**ped'dler** *n.*

**ped•es•tal** (pĕd'ĭ-stəl) *n.* A support or base, as for a column or statue.

**pe•des•tri•an** (pə-dĕs'trē-ən) *n.* One traveling on foot. —*adj.* **1.** Of pedestrians. **2.** Commonplace; ordinary.

**pe•di•at•rics** (pē'dē-ăt'rĭks) *n.* The branch of medicine that deals with the care and treatment of children. —**pe'di•at'ric** *adj.* —**pe'di•a•tri'cian** *n.*

**ped•i•gree** (pĕd'ĭ-grē') *n.* A line of ancestors; lineage. —**ped'i•greed'** *adj.*

**peek** (pēk) *v.* To look, peer, glance, or show briefly. —*n.* A brief or furtive look.

**peel** (pēl) *n.* The skin or rind, esp. of a fruit. —*v.* **1.** To remove the skin, rind, or bark from. **2.** To come off in thin layers. —**peel'er** *n.*

**peep[1]** (pēp) *v.* **1.** To utter soft, high-pitched sounds, like those of a baby bird. **2.** To speak in a thin, hesitant voice. —**peep** *n.* —**peep'er** *n.*

**peep[2]** (pēp) *v.* **1.** To steal a quick glance. **2.** To look through a small opening. **3.** To become gradually visible. —**peep'er** *n.*

**peer[1]** (pîr) *v.* To look intently.

**peer[2]** (pîr) *n.* **1.** An equal. **2.** A member of the nobility. —**peer'age** *n.* —**peer'less** *adj.*

**peeve** (pēv) *v.* **peeved, peeving.** To annoy or make irritable. —**peeve** *n.* —**pee'vish** *adj.* —**pee'vish•ly** *adv.* —**pee'vish•ness** *n.*

**peg** (pĕg) *n.* A small cylindrical pin, as of wood, used to fasten things. —*v.* **pegged, pegging.** To put or insert a peg into.

**pel•let** (pĕl'ĭt) *n.* A small ball or mass, as of medicine.

**pel•lu•cid** (pə-lo͞o'sĭd) *adj.* **1.** Transparent. **2.** Clear. —**pel•lu'cid•ly** *adv.*

**pelt[1]** (pĕlt) *n.* An animal skin.

**pelt[2]** (pĕlt) *v.* To strike repeatedly with or as with blows or missiles.

**pel•vis** (pĕl'vĭs) *n.* A basin-shaped, bony structure in the abdomen that supports the backbone. —**pel'vic** *adj.*

**pen[1]** (pĕn) *n.* An instrument for writing or drawing with ink. —*v.* **penned, penning.** To write.

**pen[2]** (pĕn) *n.* A small fenced enclosure. —*v.* **penned** or **pent** (pĕnt), **penning.** To confine in a pen.

**pen•al•ty** (pĕn'əl-tē) *n., pl.* **-ties. 1.** A punishment for a crime. **2.** A handicap or disadvantage. —**pe'nal** *adj.* —**pe'nal•ize'** *v.*

**pen•ance** (pĕn'əns) *n.* An act of repentance.

**pen•chant** (pĕn'chənt) *n.* A strong liking or inclination.

**pen•cil** (pĕn'səl) *n.* A writing implement of graphite encased in wood, etc. —*v.* To write or mark with a pencil.

**pen•dant** (pĕn'dənt) *n.* A hanging ornament.

**pend•ing** (pĕn'dĭng) *adj.* Not yet decided. —*prep.* Until.

**pen•du•lum** (pĕn'jə-ləm, pĕn'dyə-, pĕn'də-) *n.* A suspended mass that swings under the influence of gravity. —**pen'du•lar, pen'du•lous** *adj.*

**pen•e•trate** (pĕn'ĭ-trāt') *v.* **-trated, -trating. 1.** To go or enter into; pierce. **2.** To permeate. —**pen'e•tra•ble** *adj.* —**pen'e•trat'ing** *adj.* —**pen'e•trat'ing•ly** *adv.* —**pen'e•tra'tion** *n.*

**pen•guin** (pĕng'gwĭn, pen'-) *n.* A flightless sea bird having flipperlike wings.

**pen•i•cil•lin** (pĕn'ĭ-sĭl'ĭn) *n.* An antibiotic compound used to treat many diseases and infections.

**pen•in•su•la** (pə-nĭn's/y/ə-lə) *n.* A long projection of land into water. —**pen•in'su•lar** *adj.*

**pe•nis** (pē'nĭs) *n.* The male sexual organ.

**pen•i•tent** (pĕn'ĭ-tənt) *adj.* Repentant of misdeeds. —**pen'i•tence** *n.* —**pen'i•tent•ly** *adv.*

**pen•i•ten•tia•ry** (pĕn'ĭ-tĕn'shə-rē) *n., pl.* **-ries.** A prison for those convicted of major crimes.

**pen•nant** (pĕn'ənt) *n.* A long narrow flag.

**pen•ny** (pĕn'ē) *n., pl.* **-nies.** A coin; the cent. —**pen'ni•less** *adj.*

**pen•sion** (pĕn'shən) *n.* A sum of money paid regularly, esp. to a retired person. —*v.* To give a pension to. —**pen'sion•er** *n.*

**pen•sive** (pĕn'sĭv) *adj.* Deeply thoughtful. —**pen'sive•ly** *adv.* —**pen'sive•ness** *n.*

**pent** (pĕnt) *v.* Alternate p.t. & p.p. of **pen[2].**

**pen•ta•gon** (pĕn′tə-gŏn′) *n.* A plane figure having five sides and five angles. **—pen•tag′o•nal** *adj.*

**pen•tam•e•ter** (pĕn-tăm′ĭ-tər) *n.* A line of verse composed of five metrical feet.

**pen•tath•lon** (pĕn-tăth′lən, -lŏn′) *n.* An athletic contest of 5 events: running, horseback riding, swimming, fencing, and pistol shooting. **—pen•tath′lete** *n.*

**pe•nult** (pē′nŭlt′, pĭ-nŭlt′) *n.* **1.** The next to the last syllable of a word. **2.** The next to the last item in a series. **—pe•nul′ti•mate** *adj. & n.*

**pe•nu•ri•ous** (pə-n/y/ŏŏr′ē-əs) *adj.* Miserly. **—pe•nu′ri•ous•ness** *n.*

**pen•u•ry** (pĕn′yə-rē) *n.* Extreme poverty.

**pe•on** (pē′ŏn′, pē′ən) *n.* **1.** An unskilled Latin American worker. **2.** A menial worker; drudge.

**peo•ple** (pē′pəl) *n.* **1.** A body of persons of the same country, culture, etc. **2.** The mass of ordinary persons. **3.** Relatives; family. *—v.* **-pled, -pling.** To populate.

**pep** (pĕp) *n.* Energy; high spirits. **—pep** *v.*

**pep•per** (pĕp′ər) *n.* **1.** The berry of a vine, used as a condiment. **2.** The bell-shaped edible fruit of several plants. *—v.* **1.** To season with pepper. **2.** To sprinkle or spray with many small objects.

**pep•per•o•ni** (pĕp′ə-rō′nē) *n.* A highly spiced Italian sausage.

**pep•tic** (pĕp′tĭk) *adj.* Of digestion.

**per** (pûr) *prep.* **1.** Through; by means of. **2.** To, for, or by each. **3.** According to; by.

**per•ceive** (pər-sēv′) *v.* **-ceived, -ceiving.** **1.** To become aware of through the senses. **2.** To understand. **—per•cep′ti•ble** *adj.* **—per•cep′ti•bly** *adv.* **—per•cep′tion** *n.* **—per•cep′tive** *adj.* **—per•cep′tu•al** *adj.* **—per•cep′tu•al•ly** *adv.*

**percent, per cent** (pər-sĕnt′) For or out of each hundred. **—per•cent′age** *n.*

**perch** (pûrch) *n.* A rod, branch, etc., serving as a roost for a bird. **—perch** *v.*

**per•co•late** (pûr′kə-lāt′) *v.* **-lated, -lating.** To filter. **—per′co•late** *n.* **—per′co•la′tion** *n.* **—per′co•la′tor** *n.*

**per•cus•sion** (pər-kŭsh′ən) *n.* The striking together of 2 objects, esp. when noise is produced.

**per di•em** (pər dē′əm, dī′əm) *adv.* By the day; per day. *—n., pl.* **per diems.** An allowance for daily expenses. *—adj.* Reckoned or paid by the day.

**per•emp•to•ry** (pə-rĕmp′tə-rē) *adj.* Not admitting denial; imperative. **—per•emp′to•ri•ly** *adv.* **—per•emp′to•ri•ness** *n.*

**per•en•ni•al** (pə-rĕn′ē-əl) *adj.* **1.** Everlasting; perpetual. **2.** In botany, having a life span of more than two years. *—n.* A perennial plant. **—per•en′ni•al•ly** *adv.*

**per•fect** (pûr′fĭkt) *adj.* **1.** Without defect. **2.** Complete. *—v.* (pər-fĕkt′) To make perfect. **—per•fect′i•ble** *adj.* **—per•fect′i•bil′i•ty** *n.* **—per•fec′tion** *n.* **—per′fect•ly** *adv.*

**per•fi•dy** (pûr′fĭ-dē) *n.* Treachery; faithlessness. **—per•fid′i•ous** *adj.* **—per•fid′i•ous•ly** *adv.*

**per•fo•rate** (pûr′fə-rāt′) *v.* **-rated, -rating.** To pierce, punch, etc., a hole or holes in. **—per′fo•ra′tion** *n.* **—per′fo•ra′tor** *n.*

**per•form** (pər-fôrm′) *v.* **1.** To carry out (an action). **2.** To present or enact (a musical work, dramatic role, etc.) publicly. **—per•for′mance** *n.* **—per•form′er** *n.*

**per•fume** (pûr′fyōōm′, pər-fyōōm′) *n.* **1.** A fragrant liquid. **2.** A pleasing odor. *—v.* (pər-fyōōm′) **-fumed, -fuming.** To apply or fill with a fragrance.

**per•func•to•ry** (pər-fŭngk′tə-rē) *adj.* Done with little interest or care. **—per•func′to•ri•ly** *adv.* **—per•func′to•ri•ness** *n.*

**per•haps** (pər-hăps′) *adv.* Maybe; possibly.

**per•il** (pĕr′əl) *n.* **1.** Danger. **2.** Something dangerous. **—per′il•ous** *adj.* **—per′il•ous•ly** *adv.*

**pe•rim•e•ter** (pə-rĭm′ĭ-tər) *n.* **1.** A closed curve bounding a plane area. **2.** The length of such a boundary.

**pe•ri•od** (pîr′ē-əd) *n.* **1.** An interval of time. **2.** A punctuation mark (.) indicating a full stop, placed esp. at the end of sentences. *—adj.* Of a certain historical age or time.

**pe•ri•od•ic** (pîr′ē-ŏd′ĭk) *adj.* **1.** Having periods or repeated cycles. **2.** Intermittent. **—pe′ri•od′i•cal•ly** *adv.*

**pe•ri•od•i•cal** (pîr′ē-ŏd′ĭ-kəl) *adj.* Periodic. *—n.* A publication that appears at regular intervals.

**pe•riph•er•y** (pə-rĭf′ə-rē) *n., pl.* **-ies. 1.** The outermost part within a boundary. **2.** A region immediately beyond a boundary. **3.** A zone constituting an imprecise boundary. **4.** Perimeter. **—pe•riph′er•al** *adj.* **—pe•riph′er•al•ly** *adv.*

**per•i•scope** (pĕr′ĭ-skōp′) *n.* An optical instrument that allows observation of objects that are not in a direct line of sight.

**per•ish** (pĕr′ĭsh) *v.* To die, esp. in a violent manner.

**per•jure** (pûr′jər) *v.* **-jured, -juring.** To testify falsely under oath. **—per′jur•er** *n.* **—per′ju•ry** *n.*

**perk** (pûrk) *n.* A perquisite.

**per•ma•nent** (pûr′mə-nənt) *adj.* Fixed and lasting. **—per′ma•nence, per′ma•nen•cy** *n.* **—per′ma•nent•ly** *adv.*

**per•me•ate** (pûr′mē-āt′) *v.* **-ated, -ating.** To spread or flow throughout; pervade. **—per′me•a•ble** *adj.* **—per′me•a•bly** *adv.* **—per′me•a′tion** *n.*

**per•mis•sion** (pər-mĭsh′ə-n) *n.* Consent; authorization. **—per•mis′si•ble** *adj.* **—per•mis′si•bly** *adv.*

**per•mis•sive** (pər-mĭs′ĭv) *adj.* **1.** Granting permission. **2.** Allowing freedom; lenient.

**per•mit** (pər-mĭt′) *v.* **-mitted, -mitting. 1.** To allow. **2.** To afford opportunity to. *—n.* (pûr′mĭt, pər-mĭt′). A document granting permission.

**per•ni•cious** (pər-nĭsh′əs) *adj.* **1.** Destructive; evil. **2.** Deadly.

**per•pen•dic•u•lar** (pûr′pən-dĭk′yə-lər) *adj.* **1.** Intersecting at or forming right angles. **2.** Vertical. **—per′pen•dic′u•lar** *n.* **—per′pen•dic′u•lar•ly** *adv.*

**per•pe•trate** (pûr′pĭ-trāt′) *v.* **-trated, -trating.** To be guilty of; commit. **—per′pe•tra′tion** *n.* **—per′pe•tra′tor** *n.*

**per•pet•u•al** (pər-pĕch′o͞o-əl) *adj.* **1.** Lasting forever or for an indefinitely long time. **2.** Ceaselessly repeated. **—per•pet′u•al•ly** *adv.* **—per•pet′u•ate′** *v.* **—per•pet′u•a′tion** *n.* **—per′pe•tu′i•ty** *n.*

**per•plex** (pər-plĕks′) *v.* To puzzle; bewilder. **—per•plex′i•ty** *n.*

**per•qui•site** (pûr′kwĭ-zĭt) *n.* **1.** A bonus or benefit in addition to a regular wage. **2.** Something claimed as a privilege.

**per se** (pər sā′, sē′) *adv.* In or of itself; intrinsically.

**per•se•cute** (pûr′sĭ-kyo͞ot′) *v.* **-cuted, -cuting.** To oppress or harass with ill-treatment. **—per′se•cu′tion** *n.* **—per′se•cu′tor** *n.*

**per•se•vere** (pûr′sə-vîr′) *v.* **-vered, -vering.** To persist in or hold to a course, belief, etc., in spite of obstacles. **—per′se•ver′ance** *n.*

**per•sist** (pər-sĭst′, -zĭst′) *v.* **1.** To hold firmly to some purpose or undertaking, despite obstacles. **2.** To last. **—per•sis′tence** *n.* **—per•sis′tent** *adj.* **—per•sis′tent•ly** *adv.*

**per•son** (pûr′sən) *n.* **1.** A human being. **2.** The living body of a human being. **3.** The personality of a human being.

**per•son•a•ble** (pûr′sə-nə-bəl) *adj.* Pleasing in appearance or personality.

**per•son•al** (pûr′sə-nəl) *adj.* **1.** Of a particular person; private. **2.** Done in person. **3.** Of a person's movable property. **—per′son•al•ize′** *v.* **—per′son•al•ly** *adv.*

**per•son•al•i•ty** (pûr′sə-năl′ĭ-tē) *n., pl.* **-ties.** The totality of distinctive traits of an individual.

**per•son•i•fy** (pər-sŏn′ə-fī′) *v.* **-fied, -fying. 1.** To think of or represent (an idea or inanimate object) as a person. **2.** To be the embodiment or example of. **—per•son′i•fi•ca′tion** *n.*

**per•son•nel** (pûr′sə-nĕl′) *n.* The body of persons employed in an organization.

**per•spec•tive** (pər-spĕk′tĭv) *n.* **1.** The technique of representing objects on a flat surface so that they have the 3-dimensional quality as when seen with the eye. **2.** A point of view.

**per•spi•cac•i•ty** (pûr′spĭ-kăs′ĭ-tē) *n.* The ability to perceive or understand clearly. **—per′spi•ca′cious** *adj.* **—per′spi•ca′cious•ly** *adv.*

**per•spire** (pər-spīr′) *v.* **-spired, -spiring.** To excrete saline moisture through the pores of the skin; sweat. **—per′spi•ra′tion** *n.*

**per•suade** (pər-swād′) *v.* **-suaded, -suading.** To cause (someone) to do or believe something by reasoning, arguing, etc. **—per•suad′a•ble** *adj.* **—per•suad′er** *n.* **—per•sua′sion** *n.* **—per•sua′sive** *adj.*

**pert** (pûrt) *adj.* **1.** Bold and saucy. **2.** High-spirited; vivacious.

**per•tain** (pər-tān′) *v.* To have reference; relate; belong.

**per•ti•na•cious** (pûr′tn-ā′shəs) *adj.* Stubbornly persistent. **—per′ti•nac′i•ty** *n.*

**per•ti•nent** (pûr′tn-ənt) *adj.* Relevant. **—per′ti•nence, per′ti•nen•cy** *n.* **—per′ti•nent•ly** *adv.*

**per•turb** (pər-tûrb′) *v.* To make uneasy or anxious. **—per′tur•ba′tion** *n.*

**pe•ruse** (pə-ro͞oz′) *v.* **-rused, -rusing.** To read or examine, esp. with care. **—pe•rus′al** *n.* **—pe•rus′er** *n.*

**per•vade** (pər-vād′) *v.* **-vaded, -vading.** To spread throughout; permeate. **—per•va′sive** *adj.*

**per•verse** (pər-vûrs′) *adj.* **1.** Contrary to what is considered right or good. **2.** Willful; obstinate. **—per•verse′ly** *adv.* **—per•ver′si•ty** *n.*

**per•vert** (pər-vûrt′) *v.* To cause to turn from the right course of action; corrupt or debase. *—n.* (pûr′vûrt′) Someone who is perverted. **—per•ver′sion** *n.* **—per•vert′ed** *adj.*

**pes•si•mism** (pĕs′ə-mĭz′əm) *n.* A tendency to take a gloomy view of a situation. **—pes′si•mist** *n.* **—pes′si•mis′tic** *adj.*

**pest** (pĕst) *n.* An annoying person or harmful thing; nuisance. **—pes′ter** *v.*

**pes•ti•cide** (pĕs′tĭ-sīd′) *n.* A chemical used to kill pests, esp. insects and rodents.

**pes•ti•lence** (pĕs′tə-ləns) *n.* A fatal epidemic disease. **—pes′ti•lent, pes′ti•len′tial** *adj.*

**pes•tle** (pĕs′əl, pĕs′təl) *n.* A hand tool for crushing substances in a mortar.

**pet** (pĕt) *n.* **1.** An animal kept for companionship. **2.** A favorite. *—adj.* **1.** Kept as a pet. **2.** Especially cherished. *—v.* **petted, petting.** To stroke or pat gently; caress.

**pe•tal** (pĕt′l) *n.* A usually colored leaflike part of a flower. **—pet′aled** *adj.*

**pe•tard** (pĭ-tärd′) *n.* **1.** A small bomb used to make a hole in a wall. **2.** A firecracker.

**pe•tite** (pə-tēt′) *adj.* Small, slender, and trim. Used of a girl or woman. *—n.* A clothing size for such a person.

**pe•ti•tion** (pə-tĭsh′ən) *n.* A request, esp. to a person or group in authority, often in a formal document. **—pe•ti′tion** *v.* **—pe•ti′tion•er** *n.*

**pet•ri•fy** (pĕt′rə-fī′) *v.* **-fied, -fying.** To convert (wood or other organic matter) into a stony mass. **—pet′ri•fac′tion** *n.*

**pe•tro•le•um** (pə-trō′lē-əm) *n.* A yellow-to-black, thick, flammable liquid mixture found principally below the earth's surface, processed for use as natural gas, gasoline, fuel oil, etc.

**pet•ty** (pĕt′ē) *adj.* **-tier, -tiest. 1.** Trivial or insignificant. **2.** Narrow-minded; selfish. **—pet′ti•ly** *adv.* **—pet′ti•ness** *n.*

**pet•u•lant** (pĕch′ə-lənt) *adj.* Irritable; peevish. **—pet′u•lance** *n.* **—pet′u•lant•ly** *adv.*

**pew** (pyo͞o) *n.* A bench in a church.

**pew•ter** (pyo͞o′tər) *n.* An alloy of tin used for tableware, etc. **—pew′ter** *adj.*

**pha•lanx** (fā′lăngks′, făl′ăngks′) *n., pl.* **-lanxes** or **-langes. 1.** A formation of concentrated heavy infantry used esp. by Alexander the Great. **2.** A close-knit, compact body of people. **3.** *pl.* **-langes.** A bone of a finger or toe.

**phal•lus** (făl′ə-s) *n., pl.* **-li** or **-luses.** A penis. **—phal′lic** *adj.*

**phan•tom** (făn′təm) *n.* **1.** A ghost; specter. **2.** An unreal mental image.

**phar•ma•col•o•gy** (fär′mə-kŏl′ə-jē) *n.* The science of drugs.

**phar•ma•cy** (fär′mə-sē) *n., pl.* **-cies. 1.** The preparation and dispensing of drugs. **2.** A drugstore. **—phar′ma•ceu′ti•cal** *adj.* **—phar′ma•cist** *n.*

**phar•ynx** (făr′ingks) *n.* The section of the digestive tract from the nasal cavities to the larynx, there joining the esophagus.

**phase** (fāz) *n.* **1.** A distinct stage of development. **2.** An aspect; part. *—v.* **phased, phasing.** To carry out by one stage at a time.

**pheas•ant** (fĕz′ənt) *n.* A long-tailed, often brightly colored bird.

**phe•nom•e•non** (fĭ-nŏm′ə-nŏn′) *n., pl.* **-na** or **-nons. 1.** Any occurrence or fact that is directly perceptible. **2.** An unusual or outstanding person or thing. **—phe•nom'e•nal** *adj.*

**pher•o•mone** (fĕr'ə-mōn') *n.* A chemical secreted by an animal that affects the behavior of other members of the species.

**phi•lan•der** (fĭ-lăn'dər) *v.* To engage in casual or frivolous love affairs. **—phi•lan'der•er** *n.*

**phi•lan•thro•py** (fĭ-lăn'thrə-pē) *n., pl.* **-pies. 1.** Love of the human race in general. **2.** A charitable action or institution. **—phil'an•throp'ic** *adj.* **—phi•lan'thro•pist** *n.*

**phi•los•o•phy** (fĭ-lŏs'ə-fē) *n., pl.* **-phies. 1.** Speculative inquiry concerning the source and nature of human knowledge. **2.** Any system of ideas based on such thinking. **3.** The set of values of an individual, culture, etc. **—phi•los'o•pher** *n.* **—phil'o•soph'i•cal** *adj.* **—phil'o•soph'i•cal•ly** *adv.* **—phi•los'o•phize'** *v.*

**phlegm** (flĕm) *n.* Mucus from the respiratory tract.

**pho•bi•a** (fō'bē-ə) *n.* An illogical fear of a specific thing or situation. **—pho'bic** *adj.*

**phoe•nix, phe•nix** (fē'nĭks) *n.* **1.** A fabulous bird that consumes itself by fire after 500 years and rises anew from the ashes. **2.** A paragon.

**phone** (fōn) *n.* A telephone. —*v.* **phoned, phoning.** To telephone.

**pho•net•ics** (fə-nĕt'ĭks) *n.* The study of the sounds of speech and their representation by symbols. **—pho•net'ic** *adj.*

**pho•no•graph** (fō'nə-grăf') *n.* A machine that reproduces sound from a record. **—pho'no•graph'ic** *adj.*

**pho•ny** (fō'nē) *adj.* **-nier, -niest.** Not genuine; fake. **—pho'ni•ness** *n.* **—pho'ny** *n.*

**phos•pho•res•cence** (fŏs'fə-rĕs'əns) *n.* The generation and emission of light by a living thing. **—phos'pho•resce'** *v.* **—phos'pho•res'cent** *adj.*

**phos•pho•rus** (fŏs'fər-əs) *n.* A nonmetallic element used in safety matches, fertilizers, glass, and steel. **—phos•phor'ic** *adj.*

**pho•to•cop•i•er** (fō'tə-kŏp'ē-ər) *n.* A machine that photographically reproduces written material. **—pho'to•cop'y** *n. & v.*

**pho•to•graph** (fō'tə-grăf') *n.* An image recorded by a camera and reproduced on a photosensitive surface. —*v.* To take a photograph of. **—pho•tog'ra•pher** *n.* **—pho'to•graph'ic** *adj.* **—pho'to•graph'i•cal•ly** *adv.* **—pho•tog'ra•phy** *n.*

**pho•ton** (fō'tŏn') *n.* The quantum of electromagnetic energy.

**pho•to•syn•the•sis** (fō'tō-sĭn'thĭ-sĭs) *n.* The chemical process by which plants that contain chlorophyll use light to convert carbon dioxide and water to carbohydrates.

**phrase** (frāz) *n.* A sequence of words intended to have meaning. **—phrase** *v.* **—phras'al** *adj.*

**phra•se•ol•o•gy** (frā'zē-ŏl'ə-jē) *n., pl.* **-gies.** The way in which words are used; style.

**phre•net•ic** (frə-nĕt'ĭk) *adj.* Frenetic.

**phy•lum** (fī'ləm) *n., pl.* **-la.** One of the broad categories used in the classification of animals and plants.

**phys•i•cal** (fĭz'ĭ-kəl) *adj.* **1.** Of the body. **2.** Of material things. **3.** Of physics. **—phys'i•cal•ly** *adv.*

**phy•si•cian** (fĭ-zĭsh'ən) *n.* A medical doctor.

**phys•ics** (fĭz'ĭks) *n.* The science of matter and energy and the relations between them. **—phys'i•cist** *n.*

**phys•i•og•no•my** (fĭz'ē-ŏg'nə-mē, -ŏn'ə-mē) *n., pl.* **-mies.** Facial features.

**phys•i•ol•o•gy** (fĭz'ē-ŏl'ə-jē) *n.* The science of life processes, activities, and functions. **—phys'i•o•log'i•cal** *adj.* **—phys'i•ol'o•gist** *n.*

**phy•sique** (fĭ-zēk') *n.* The body, considered in terms of its structure and development.

**pi** (pī) *n.; pl.* **pis.** The number 3.1416, representing the ratio of the circumference to the diameter of a circle.

**pi•an•o** (pē-ăn'ō) *n., pl.* **-os.** A musical keyboard instrument with hammers that strike wire strings. **—pi•an'ist** *n.*

**pi•ca¹** (pī'kə) *n.* A type size for typewriters, 10 characters per inch.

**pi•ca²** (pī'kə) *n.* A craving for unnatural food.

**pic•a•resque** (pĭk'ə-rĕsk', pē'kə-) *adj.* **1.** Relating to clever rogues. **2.** Relating to a realistic, satiric literary genre describing such people. **—pic'a•resque'** *n.*

**pic•a•yune** (pĭk'ē-yo͞on') *adj.* Of little value or importance. **—pic'a•yune'** *n.*

**pic•co•lo** (pĭk'ə-lō') *n., pl.* **-los.** A small flute.

**pick**[1] (pĭk) *v.* **1.** To select from a group. **2.** To harvest. **3.** To remove the covering of; pluck. **4.** To break up or pierce with a pointed instrument. *—n.* **1.** A choice or selection. **2.** The best part. **—pick'er** *n.*

**pick**[2] (pĭk) *n.* A long-handled tool for breaking hard surfaces.

**pick•et** (pĭk'ĭt) *n.* **1.** A pointed stake or spike driven into the ground to secure a tent, tether an animal, etc. **2.** A soldier on guard against enemy approach. **3.** A worker on strike, stationed outside a place of employment. **—pick'et** *v.* **—pick'et•er** *n.*

**pick•le** (pĭk'əl) *n.* **1.** A food, esp. a cucumber, preserved in brine or vinegar. **2.** A difficulty. *—v.* **-led, -ling.** To preserve in brine or vinegar.

**pic•nic** (pĭk'nĭk) *n.* A meal eaten outdoors on an excursion. *—v.* **-nicked, -nicking.** To go on a picnic. **—pic'nick•er** *n.*

**pic•to•ri•al** (pĭk-tôr'ē-əl, -tōr'-) *adj.* Relating to, composed of, or illustrated by pictures. *—n.* An illustrated periodical.

**pic•ture** (pĭk'chər) *n.* **1.** A painting, drawing, photograph, etc., on a flat surface. **2.** A television or motion picture. *—v.* **-tured, -turing. 1.** To make a picture of. **2.** To form a mental picture of; visualize. **—pic•to'ri•al** *adj.*

**pic•tur•esque** (pĭk'chə-rĕsk') *adj.* Striking or interesting; attractive.

**pie** (pī) *n.* A baked pastry shell filled with fruit, meat, etc.

**piece** (pēs) *n.* **1.** A unit of a larger quantity; portion. **2.** An artistic work. *—v.* **pieced, piecing. 1.** To mend by adding a piece to. **2.** To join the pieces of.

**piece•meal** (pēs'mēl') *adv.* Gradually. *—adj.* Made or done piece by piece.

**pied** (pīd) *adj.* Patchy in color; splotched.

**pied-à-terre** (pyā-dä-târ') *n., pl.* **pieds-à-terre.** A secondary or temporary lodging.

**pier** (pîr) *n.* **1.** A platform extending over water, used to moor ships or boats. **2.** A supporting structure.

**pierce** (pîrs) *v.* **pierced, piercing. 1.** To cut with or as with a sharp instrument; stab. **2.** To penetrate through. **—pierc'ing•ly** *adv.*

**pi•e•ty** (pī'ĭ-tē) *n., pl.* **-ties.** Devotion and reverence.

**pig** (pĭg) *n.* **1.** A hoofed mammal with short legs and a blunt snout, esp. one raised for meat. **2.** An oblong block of metal.

**pi•geon** (pĭj'ən) *n.* A bird with a deep-chested body and short legs.

**pig iron** *n.* Crude iron cast in blocks or pigs.

**pig•ment** (pĭg'mənt) *n.* **1.** A coloring substance or matter. **2.** A substance that produces color in plant or animal tissue.

**pig•men•ta•tion** (pĭg'mən-tā'shən) *n.* Coloration of tissues by pigment.

**pike**[1] (pīk) *n.* A long, heavy, thrusting spear formerly used by the infantry.

**pike**[2] (pīk) *n.* A freshwater game and food fish.

**pike**[3] (pīk) *n.* A turnpike; toll road.

**pile**[1] (pīl) *n.* **1.** A quantity of objects in a heap. **2.** A large accumulation or quantity. **3.** A nuclear reactor. *—v.* **piled, piling.** To stack in or form a pile.

**pile**[2] (pīl) *n.* A heavy beam driven into the earth as a support.

**pile**[3] (pīl) *n.* The nap of certain fabrics, as velvet, etc.

**pil•fer** (pĭl'fər) *v.* To steal; filch. **—pil'fer•age** *n.* **—pil'fer•er** *n.*

**pil•grim** (pĭl'grəm) *n.* A traveler, esp. one who goes to a holy place. **—pil'grim•age** *n.*

**pill** (pĭl) *n.* **1.** A medicine tablet to be take by mouth. **2.** A dull, tedious person.

**pil•lage** (pĭl'ĭj) *v.* **-laged, -laging.** To plunder. *—n.* Spoils. **—pil'lag•er** *n.*

**pil•lar** (pĭl'ər) *n.* A vertical support; a column.

**pil•low** (pĭl'ō) *n.* A cloth case stuffed with feathers, foam, etc., used to cushion the head or as a decoration. *—v.* **1.** To rest (one's head) on or as on a pillow. **2.** To act as a pillow for.

**pi•lot** (pī'lət) *n.* **1.** One who operates or is licensed to operate an aircraft or a ship. **2.** One who guides or directs. —*v.* To serve as the pilot of. —*adj.* Serving as a model for future development.

**pimp** (pĭmp) *n.* A procurer for prostitutes. —*v.* To procure.

**pim•ple** (pĭm′pəl) *n.* A small swelling of the skin. —**pim′pled, pim′ply** *adj.*

**pin** (pĭn) *n.* **1.** A short, straight, stiff piece of wire with a sharp point, used for fastening. **2.** Anything like a pin in shape or use. **3.** An ornament fastened to the clothing with a pin or clasp. —*v.* **pinned, pinning. 1.** To fasten with or as with a pin or pins. **2.** To hold fast; immobilize.

**pin•cers** (pĭn′sərz) *n.* A grasping tool having a pair of jaws and pivoted handles.

**pinch** (pĭnch) *v.* **1.** To squeeze between the thumb and a finger, the jaws of a tool, etc. **2.** To bind (a part of the body) painfully. **3.** To be miserly. —*n.* **1.** The act of pinching. **2.** An amount that can be held between thumb and forefinger. **3.** A difficult circumstance.

**pine[1]** (pīn) *n.* A cone-bearing evergreen tree.

**pine[2]** (pīn) *v.* **pined, pining.** To suffer intense longing.

**pine•ap•ple** (pīn′ăp′əl) *n.* A tropical plant with swordlike leaves and a large edible fruit.

**pink** (pĭngk) *n.* **1.** A plant with fragrant flowers, related to the carnation. **2.** Light red. **3.** The highest degree. —**pink, pink′ish** *adj.*

**pin•na•cle** (pĭn′ə-kəl) *n.* **1.** A tall, pointed formation. **2.** The highest point; summit.

**pint** (pīnt) *n.* **1.** A unit of liquid measure equal to 16 fluid ounces. **2.** A unit of dry measure equal to ½ quart.

**pi•o•neer** (pī′ə-nîr′) *n.* **1.** One who first enters or settles a region. **2.** An innovator in any field. **3.** An engineer in an army. —**pi′o•neer′** *v.*

**pi•ous** (pī′əs) *adj.* Reverently and earnestly religious; devout. —**pi′ous•ly** *adv.* —**pi′ous•ness** *n.*

**pipe** (pīp) *n.* **1.** A tubular conveyance for a fluid or gas. **2.** A tube of wood or clay with a small bowl at one end, used for smoking. **3. a.** A wind instrument, such as a flute. **b.** A tube in an organ. —*v.* **piped, piping. 1.** To convey (liquid or gas) by pipes. **2.** To play (a tune) on pipes. —**pip′er** *n.*

**pi•quant** (pē′kənt, -känt′, pē-känt′) *adj.* Pleasantly pungent. —**pi′quan•cy** *n.*

**pique** (pēk) *n.* Resentment caused by wounded feelings. —*v.* **piqued, piquing. 1.** To cause resentment. **2.** To provoke; arouse.

**pi•ra•nha** (pĭ-rän′yə, -răn′-, -rä′nə) *n.* A voracious, carnivorous tropical American freshwater fish.

**pi•rate** (pī′rĭt) *n.* A person who robs ships at sea or plunders the land from the sea. —**pi′ra•cy** *n.* —**pi′rate** *v.*

**pir•ou•ette** (pĭr′o͞o-ĕt′) *n.* A full turn of the body on the toes. —**pir′ou•ette′** *v.*

**pis al•ler** (pē ză-lā′) *n.* The last recourse; the final expedient.

**pis•til** (pĭs′təl) *n.* The seed-bearing reproductive organ of a flower.

**pis•tol** (pĭs′təl) *n.* A small gun held and fired with one hand.

**pis•ton** (pĭs′tən) *n.* A cylinder that fits into a larger cylinder and moves back and forth under fluid pressure.

**pit[1]** (pĭt) *n.* **1.** A hole in the ground. **2.** An indentation in the skin, esp. one left by disease. **3.** The musicians' section in front of a stage. —*v.* **pitted, pitting. 1.** To make holes or scars in. **2.** To set in competition; match.

**pit[2]** (pĭt) *n.* The seed of certain fruits, as a peach or cherry; stone. —*v.* **pitted, pitting.** To remove the pits from.

**pi•ta** (pē′tə) *n.* Round, flat bread with a pocket inside.

**pitch[1]** (pĭch) *n.* A dark, sticky substance obtained from coal tar, etc., used for waterproofing, roofing, etc.

**pitch[2]** (pĭch) *v.* **1.** To throw; hurl. **2.** To put up, as a tent. **3.** To fix the level of. **4.** To plunge; fall, esp. forward. **5.** To dip bow and stern alternately, as a ship in rough seas. —*n.* **1.** An act or instance of pitching. **2. a.** Any downward slant. **b.** The degree of such a slant. **3.** The quality of a musical tone by which someone can judge it to be high or low. **4.** A set talk designed to persuade.

**pitch•er** (pĭch′ər) *n.* A container for liquids, with a handle and a spout for pouring.

**pitch•fork** (pĭch′fôrk′) *n.* A large fork with prongs, used to pitch hay and break ground.

**pit•e•ous** (pĭt'e-əs) *adj.* Exciting pity; pathetic.

**pit•fall** (pĭt'fôl') *n.* **1.** A trap that is a lightly covered hole in the ground. **2.** A danger or difficulty not easily avoided.

**pith** (pĭth) *n.* **1.** The spongelike substance in plant stems. **2.** An essential part. **3.** Force; strength. **—pith'y** *adj.*

**pit•i•a•ble** (pĭt'ē-ə-bəl) *adj.* Arousing pity. **—pit'i•a•bly** *adv.*

**pit•y** (pĭt'ē) *n., pl.* **-ies. 1.** Sorrow or grief for another's suffering. **2.** A cause for regret. *—v.* **-ied, -ying.** To feel sorry (for). **—pit'i•ful** *adj.* **—pit'i•ful•ly** *adv.* **—pit'i•less** *adj.* **—pit'i•less•ness** *n.* **—pit'y•ing•ly** *adv.*

**piv•ot** (pĭv'ət) *n.* A short shaft about which another part turns or swings. *—v.* To turn on or as if on a pivot. **—piv'ot•al** *adj.*

**pix•el** (pĭk'səl, -sĕl') *n.* Any of the discrete elements forming an image on a video display screen.

**piz•za** (pēt'sə) *n.* A shallow, baked pie crust covered with tomato sauce, cheese, and spices.

**plac•ard** (plăk'ärd', -ərd) *n.* A poster for public display.

**pla•cate** (plā'kāt', plăk'āt') *v.* **-cated, -cating.** To allay the anger of; appease. **—pla•ca'tion** *n.*

**place** (plās) *n.* **1.** A portion of space. **2.** A dwelling; residence. **3.** A position of a person or thing as occupied by a substitute. **4.** A position in a series; standing. *—v.* **placed, placing. 1.** To put in place; position; set. **2.** To rank (someone or something) in order.

**pla•ce•bo** (plə-sē'bō) *n., pl.* **-bos** or **-boes. 1.** A substance of no medicinal value given to humor a patient. **2.** An inactive substance used as a control in an experiment.

**place•ment** (plās'mənt) *n.* The act or business of finding jobs for applicants.

**pla•cen•ta** (plə-sĕn'tə) *n., pl.* **-tas** or **-tae.** The organ connected to the fetus by the umbilical cord. **—pla•cen'tal** *adj.*

**plac•id** (plăs'ĭd) *adj.* Calm or composed. **—plac'id•ly** *adv.*

**pla•gia•rize** (plā'jə-rīz') *v.* **-rized, -rizing.** To use (the ideas or writings of another) as one's own. **—pla'gia•rism'** *n.* **—pla'gia•riz'er** *n.*

**plague** (plāg) *n.* **1.** An infectious, usually fatal, epidemic disease. **2.** A cause for annoyance. *—v.* **plagued, plaguing.** To harass or annoy.

**plaid** (plăd) *n.* Cloth with a checked pattern.

**plain** (plān) *adj.* **1.** Open to view; clear. **2.** Easily understood. **3.** Straightforward. **4.** Not mixed with other substances; pure. **5.** Unsophisticated; simple. *—n.* A level, treeless area of land. *—adv.* In a clear or intelligible manner. **—plain'ly** *adv.* **—plain'ness** *n.*

**plain•tiff** (plān'tĭf) *n.* The party that institutes a suit in a court of law.

**plain•tive** (plān'tĭv) *adv.* Mournful. **—plain'tive•ly** *adv.* **—plaint** *n.*

**plait** (plāt, plăt) *n.* A braid. *—v.* To braid.

**plan** (plăn) *n.* **1.** A detailed method for the accomplishment of an object. **2.** A drawing made to scale. *—v.* **planned, planning.** To make a plan or plans. **—plan'ner** *n.*

**plane¹** (plān) *n.* **1.** A flat or level surface. **2.** A level of development. **3.** An airplane.

**plane²** (plān) *n.* A tool for smoothing wood. *—v.* **planed, planing.** To smooth or finish with a plane.

**plan•et** (plăn'ĭt) *n.* A celestial body illuminated by a star around which it revolves, esp. 1 of the 9 that orbit the sun. **—plan'e•tar'y** *adj.*

**plan•e•tar•i•um** (plăn'ĭ-târ'ē-əm) *n.* A device for projecting images of celestial bodies onto the ceiling of a dome.

**plank** (plăngk) *n.* **1.** A thick piece of lumber. **2.** One of the principles of a political party. *—v.* To cover with planks.

**plank•ton** (plăngk'tən) *n.* Organisms, usu. microscopic, that drift in water.

**plant** (plănt) *n.* **1.** A living thing that differs from an animal by its ability to make its own food and its inability to move from place to place. **2.** A factory. *—v.* **1.** To place in the ground to grow. **2.** To sow or supply with or as if with seeds or plants. **—plant'er** *n.*

**plan•ta•tion** (plăn-tā'shən) *n.* A large estate or farm.

**plaque** (plăk) *n.* **1.** A flat slab or plate ornamented for mounting. **2.** A small pin worn as a decoration or badge. **3.** A thin film of mucus and microorganisms on the teeth.

**plas•ma** (plăz'mə) *n.* The clear, yellowish fluid portion of blood or lymph. **—plas•mat'ic, plas'mic** *adj.*

**plas•ter** (plăs'tər) *n.* A paste that hardens to a smooth solid used for coating walls, etc. *—v.* **1.** To cover with plaster. **2.** To cover conspicuously. **—plas'ter•er** *n.*

**plas•tic** (plăs'tĭk) *adj.* **1.** Capable of being shaped or formed; pliable. **2.** Produced by shaping or modeling. *—n.* A material that can be molded, cast, etc., into shapes and films or drawn into filaments. **—plas•tic'i•ty** *n.*

**plas•tique** (plă-stēk') *n.* A puttylike explosive that can be detonated by remote control.

**plate** (plāt) *n.* **1.** A shallow dish from which food is eaten. **2.** Dishes and other articles covered with gold or silver. **3.** A thin, flat sheet of metal. **4.** A support fitted to the gums to anchor artificial teeth. *—v.* **plated, plating. 1.** To cover with a thin layer of metal. **2.** To armor. **—plat'ed** *adj.*

**pla•teau** (plă-tō') *n.* An elevated, level expanse of land.

**plat•form** (plăt'fôrm') *n.* **1.** A floor or horizontal surface higher than an adjoining area. **2.** A declaration of principles, as by a political party.

**plat•i•num** (plăt'n-əm) *n.* A silver-white metallic chemical element.

**plat•i•tude** (plăt'ĭ-t/y/o͞od') *n.* A trite, banal statement. **—plat'i•tu'di•nar'i•an** *n.* **—plat'i•tu'di•nize'** *v.* **—plat'i•tu'di•nous** *adj.*

**pla•toon** (plə-to͞on') *n.* A subdivision of a military company.

**plat•ter** (plăt'ər) *n.* A large, shallow dish or plate for serving food.

**plau•dit** (plô'dĭt) *n.* An expression of praise.

**plau•si•ble** (plô'zə-bəl) *adj.* Appearing true or reasonable. **—plau'si•bil'i•ty, plau'si•ble•ness** *n.* **—plau'si•bly** *adv.*

**play** (plā) *v.* **1.** To have fun; amuse oneself. **2.** To take part in (a game or sport). **3.** To act in a drama. **4.** To perform on (a musical instrument). **5.** To move lightly or irregularly. *—n.* **1.** A dramatic work or its performance. **2.** Activity for enjoyment or recreation. **3.** A manner of playing a game or sport. **4.** Free movement, as of mechanical parts. **—play'er** *n.* **—play'ful** *adj.* **—play'ful•ly** *adv.*

**play•wright** (plā'rīt') *n.* One who writes plays.

**pla•za** (plä'zə, plăz'ə) *n.* A public square in a town or city.

**plea** (plē) *n.* **1.** An appeal or urgent request. **2.** An excuse.

**plead** (plēd) *v.* **pleaded** or **pled** (plĕd), **pleading. 1.** To appeal earnestly; implore. **2.** To give as an excuse or defense. **3.** To put forward a plea in a court of law. **4.** To argue (a case) in a law court. **—plead'er** *n.*

**pleas•ant** (plĕz'ənt) *adj.* Pleasing; agreeable. **—pleas'ant•ly** *adv.* **—pleas'ant•ness** *n.*

**please** (plēz) *v.* **pleased, pleasing. 1.** To give enjoyment or satisfaction to. **2.** To be willing to. **—pleas'er** *n.* **—pleas'ing•ly** *adv.*

**pleas•ure** (plĕzh'ər) *n.* **1.** Enjoyment; satisfaction. **2.** Preference or wish. **—pleas'ur•a•ble** *adj.* **—pleas'ur•a•bly** *adv.*

**pleat** (plēt) *n.* A fold in cloth made by doubling the material upon itself.

**pleb•i•scite** (plĕb'ĭ-sīt', -sĭt) *n.* A direct vote by an entire people on a public issue.

**pled** (plĕd). *v.* Alternate p.t. & p.p. of **plead.**

**pledge** (plĕj) *n.* **1.** A solemn promise. **2.** Something given or held as security in a loan, contract, etc. *—v.* **pledged, pledging. 1.** To promise solemnly. **2.** To bind by a pledge. **3.** To deposit as security.

**plen•ty** (plĕn'tē) *n.* A large amount; abundance. **—plen'ti•ful** *adj.* **—plen'ti•ful•ly** *adv.*

**pleth•o•ra** (plĕth'ər-ə) *n.* Excess.

**pli•a•ble** (plī'ə-bəl) *adj.* **1.** Easily bent. **2.** Easily influenced. **—pli'a•bil'i•ty** *n.*

**pli•ant** (plī'ənt) *adj.* Pliable. **—pli'an•cy** *n.*

**pli•ers** (plī'ərz) *pl.n.* A tool with a pair of pivoted jaws, used for holding, bending, cutting, etc.

**plight** (plīt) *n.* A condition of difficulty or danger.

**plod** (plŏd) *v.* **plodded, plodding. 1.** To walk heavily or with great effort. **2.** To work monotonously. **—plod'der** *n.* **—plod'ding•ly** *adv.*

**plot** (plŏt) *n.* **1.** A small piece of ground. **2.** The series of actions or events in a novel, play, etc. **3.** A secret plan. *—v.* **plotted, plotting. 1.** To represent graphically, as on a chart. **2.** To plan secretly. **—plot'ter** *n.*

**plow** (plou) *n.* **1.** A farm implement used for breaking up soil and cutting furrows. **2.** An implement of similar function, as a snowplow. **—plow** *v.*

**ploy** (ploi) *n.* A stratagem to gain advantage over an opponent.

**pluck** (plŭk) *v.* **1.** To pull off or out; pick. **2.** To sound (the strings of an instrument) by pulling them. *—n.* **1.** The act of plucking. **3.** Resourceful courage; spirit. **—pluck'y** *adj.*

**plug** (plŭg) *n.* **1.** An object used to stop a hole. **2.** A fitting, commonly with metal socket prongs, used to make electric connections. **—plug** *v.*

**plum** (plŭm) *n.* **1.** A smooth-skinned, fleshy fruit. **2.** Something desirable.

**plum•age** (plo͞o'mĭj) *n.* **1.** A bird's feathers. **2.** Feathers as an ornament. **3.** Elaborate dress; finery.

**plumb** (plŭm) *n.* A weight hanging from the end of a line to find depth or true vertical. *—adj.* **1.** Exactly vertical. **2.** Also **plum.** Utter; absolute. *—v.* **1.** To test alignment or straighten. **2.** To determine depth. **3.** To examine closely. **4.** To seal with lead. **5.** To work as a plumber. **—plumb, plum** *adv.* **—plumb'er** *n.*

**plumb•ing** (plŭm'ĭng) *n.* The pipes and fixtures of a water or sewage system. **—plumb'er** *n.*

**plume** (plo͞om) *n.* **1.** A feather, esp. a showy one. **2.** Something resembling a feather. *—v.* **plumed, pluming.** To decorate with or as with plumes. **—plum'age** *n.*

**plum•met** (plŭm'ĭt) *v.* To drop straight down; plunge.

**plump** (plŭmp) *adj.* Rounded and full in form; chubby. *—v.* To make or become rounded. **—plump'ly** *adv.* **—plump'ness** *n.*

**plun•der** (plŭn'dər) *v.* To rob, esp. by force; pillage. *—n.* Stolen property; booty. **—plun'der•er** *n.*

**plunge** (plŭnj) *v.* **plunged, plunging. 1.** To throw forcefully into a substance or place. **2.** To enter suddenly into a given state or activity. **3.** To descend steeply. **—plung'er** *n.*

**plu•ral** (plo͝or'əl) *adj.* Of or composed of more than 1. *—n.* **1.** The plural number or form of a word. **2.** A word in this form. **—plu•ral'i•ty** *n.* **—plu'ral•ly** *adv.*

**plus** (plŭs) *prep.* **1.** Added to. **2.** Increased by. *—adj.* **1.** Of addition. **2.** Positive. *—n.* An addition or a positive quantity.

**plush** (plŭsh) *n.* A fabric with a thick pile. *—adj.* Luxurious.

**Plu•to** (plo͞o'tō) *n.* The 9th planet from the sun.

**ply[1]** (plī) *n., pl.* **plies.** A layer or strand of which rope, yarn, etc., is composed.

**ply[2]** (plī) *v.* **plied, plying. 1.** To engage in (a trade or task). **2.** To traverse (a route) regularly. **3.** To keep supplying. **4.** To use or handle (a tool, etc.).

**pneu•mat•ic** (n/y/o͞o-măt'ĭk) *adj.* Of air or another gas.

**pneu•mon•ia** (n/y/o͞o-mōn'yə) *n.* A disease marked by inflammation of the lungs.

**poach[1]** (pōch) *v.* To cook in simmering liquid.

**poach[2]** (pōch) *v.* To trespass on another's property in order to hunt or fish. **—poach'er** *n.*

**pock•et** (pŏk'ĭt) *n.* **1.** A pouch sewn onto a garment with 1 edge open. **2.** A receptacle or cavity. *—adj.* **1.** Suitable for being carried in a pocket. **2.** Small. *—v.* To place in a pocket.

**pock•et•book** (pŏk'ĭt-bo͝ok') *n.* **1.** A purse. **2.** A paperback.

**pod** (pŏd) *n.* A seed case, as of a pea, that splits open.

**po•di•a•try** (pə-dī'ə-trē) *n.* The treatment of foot ailments. **—po•di'a•trist** *n.*

**po•di•um** (pō'dē-əm) *n., pl.* **-dia** (-dē-ə) or **-diums.** A platform for a lecturer; lectern.

**po•em** (pō'əm) *n.* A work of poetry. **—po'et** *n.*

**po•et•ry** (pō'ĭ-trē) *n.* **1.** Verse as distinguished from prose. **2.** The art or work of a poet. **—po•et'ic, po•et'i•cal** *adj.*

—**po•et'i•cal•ly** *adv.*

**po•grom** (pə-grŏm', pō'grəm) *n.* An official persecution of a minority group, esp. of Jews.

**poign•ant** (poin'yənt) *adj.* **1.** Keenly distressing. **2.** Affecting; touching. —**poign'ant•ly** *adv.*

**point** (point) *n.* **1.** The sharp end of something. **2.** An extension of land projecting into water. **3.** A dot or period. **4.** A position or place. **5.** A specific moment in time. **6.** An essential or primary factor. **7.** A purpose; reason. —*v.* **1.** To aim. **2.** To indicate with or as with the finger. —**point'ed** *adj.* —**point'ed•ly** *adv.* —**point'ed•ness** *n.* —**point'er** *n.* —**point'less** *adj.* —**point'less•ly** *adv.*

**poise** (poiz) *v.* **poised, poising.** To balance or be balanced. —*n.* **1.** Balance. **2.** Composure.

**poi•son** (poi'zən) *n.* A substance that causes injury or death. —*v.* To give poison to. —**poi'son•ous** *adj.*

**poke** (pōk) *v.* **poked, poking.** To push, thrust, or jab. —**poke** *n.*

**pok•er**[1] (pō'kər) *n.* One that pokes, esp. a metal rod to stir a fire.

**pok•er**[2] (pō'kər) *n.* Any of several card games for 2 or more players who bet on the values of their hands.

**pole**[1] (pōl) *n.* **1.** Either extremity of an axis that intersects a sphere. **2.** Either point at the ends of a magnet where the force is strongest. —**po'lar** *adj.* —**po•lar'i•ty** *n.*

**pole**[2] (pōl) *n.* A long piece of wood or other material.

**po•lice** (pə-lēs') *n., pl.* **police.** A governmental department that maintains order and enforces the law. —*v.* **-liced, -licing.** To guard or patrol to maintain order. —**po•lice'man** *n.* —**po•lice'-wom'an** *n.*

**pol•i•cy**[1] (pŏl'ĭ-sē) *n., pl.* **-cies.** A method or course of action followed by a government, an individual, etc.

**pol•i•cy**[2] (pŏl'ĭ-sē) *n., pl.* **-cies.** A written contract of insurance.

**pol•ish** (pŏl'ĭsh) *v.* To make or become smooth or shiny, as by rubbing. —*n.* **1.** Shininess of surface. **2.** A substance used to polish a surface. —**pol'ish•er** *n.*

**po•lite** (pə-līt') *adj.* **-liter, -litest.** Having or showing good manners; courteous. —**po•lite'ly** *adv.* —**po•lite'ness** *n.*

**pol•i•tics** (pŏl'ĭ-tĭks) *n.* **1.** The art or science of government. **2.** The policies or affairs of a government. **3. a.** The conducting of political affairs. **b.** The profession of a person so involved. —**po•lit'i•cal** *adj.* —**po•lit'i•cal•ly** *adv.* —**pol'i•ti'cian** *n.*

**poll** (pōl) *n.* **1.** The casting and registering of votes in an election. **2.** Often **polls.** The place where votes are cast and counted. **3.** A survey made to determine public opinion. —**poll** *v.* —**poll'er** *n.*

**pol•len** (pŏl'ən) *n.* The powderlike material produced by flowering plants, the male element in fertilization. —**pol'li•nate'** *v.* —**pol'li•na'tion** *n.*

**pol•lute** (pə-lo͞ot') *v.* **-luted, -luting.** To make harmful to living things, esp. by means of waste that contaminates air, soil, or water. —**pol•lut'ant** *n.* —**pol•lu'tion** *n.*

**po•lyg•a•my** (pə-lĭg'ə-mē) *n.* The practice of having more than one spouse at one time. —**po•lyg'a•mist** *n.* —**po•lyg'a•mous** *adj.*

**po•lyph•o•ny** (pə-lĭf'ə-nē) *n.* The combination of 2 or more independent melodic parts. —**pol'y•phon'ic** *adj.*

**pomp** (pŏmp) *n.* Magnificent or stately display.

**pom•pous** (pŏm'pəs) *adj.* Self-important; pretentious. —**pom•pos'i•ty, pom'pous•ness** *n.* —**pom'pous•ly** *adv.*

**pond** (pŏnd) *n.* A small body of water.

**pon•der** (pŏn'dər) *v.* To think or consider carefully.

**pon•der•ous** (pŏn'dər-əs) *adj.* Having great weight; unwieldy.

**pon•tiff** (pŏn'tĭf) *n.* **1.** The pope. **2.** A bishop. —**pon•tif'i•cal** *adj.*

**po•ny** (pō'nē) *n., pl.* **-nies.** A small horse.

**poo•dle** (po͞od'l) *n.* A hunting dog having thick, tightly curled hair.

**pool**[1] (po͞ol) *n.* **1.** A small pond. **2.** A puddle of any liquid.

**pool**[2] (po͞ol) *n.* **1.** A grouping of resources for mutual benefit. **2.** A game played on a billiard table. —*v.* To combine (money, etc.) for mutual benefit.

**poor** (po͝or) *adj.* **1.** Having little money. **2.** Inferior. **3.** Pitiable. **—poor'ly** *adv.*

**pop** (pŏp) *v.* **popped, popping.** To make or cause to make a sudden sharp, explosive sound. *—n.* **1.** A sudden sharp, explosive sound. **2.** A carbonated beverage.

**pope** (pōp) *n.* Often **Pope.** The head of the Roman Catholic Church.

**pop•u•lace** (pŏp'yə-lĭs) *n.* The common people.

**pop•u•lar** (pŏp'yə-lər) *adj.* **1.** Widely liked or appreciated. **2.** Of the people at large. **3.** Widespread. **—pop'u•lar'i•ty** *n.* **—pop'u•lar•ize'** *v.* **—pop'u•lar•ly** *adv.*

**pop•u•late** (pŏp'yə-lāt') *v.* **-lated, -lating.** To live in; inhabit. **—pop'u•la'tion** *n.*

**por•ce•lain** (pôrs'lĭn, pōrs'-, pôr'sə-lĭn, pōr'-) *n.* A hard, translucent ceramic; china.

**porch** (pôrch, pōrch) *n.* A roofed platform at an entrance to a building.

**pore** (pôr, pōr) *n.* A tiny opening, esp. in skin or a leaf.

**pork** (pôrk, pōrk) *n.* The meat of a pig, used as food.

**por•nog•ra•phy** (pôr-nŏg'rə-fē) *n.* Indecent literature or art. **—por'no•graph'ic** *adj.*

**po•rous** (pôr'əs, pōr'-) *adj.* Having pores into or through which a gas or liquid can pass. **—po•ros'i•ty, po'rous•ness** *n.*

**por•poise** (pôr'pəs) *n., pl.* **-poises** or **-poise. 1.** A gregarious oceanic mammal resembling a small whale. **2.** A dolphin.

**port¹** (pôrt, pōrt) *n.* A town having a harbor where ships may dock.

**port²** (pôrt, pōrt) *n.* The left side of a ship or aircraft. *—adj.* On the port.

**por•ta•ble** (pôr'tə-bəl, pōr'-) *adj.* Easily carried or moved. **—por'ta•bil'i•ty** *n.*

**por•tal** (pôr'tl, pōr'-) *n.* A doorway or entrance.

**por•tend** (pôr-tĕnd', pōr-) *v.* To serve as an advance indication of.

**por•tent** (pôr'tĕnt', pōr'-) *n.* **1.** An indication of something about to occur. **2.** Great or ominous significance. **—por•ten'tous** *adj.*

**por•ter** (pôr'tər, pōr'-) *n.* **1.** A railroad attendant. **2.** A doorman.

**port•fo•li•o** (pôrt-fō'lē-ō', pōrt-) *n., pl.* **-os. 1.** A portable case for holding papers, etc. **2.** The office or post of a minister of state.

**por•tion** (pôr'shən, pōr'-) *n.* **1.** A part of a whole. **2.** A share. *—v.* To divide into parts or shares.

**por•trait** (pôr'trĭt, -trāt', pōr'-) *n.* A painting, photograph, etc., of a person. **—por'trai•ture** *n.*

**por•tray** (pôr-trā', pōr-) *v.* To show by a picture, words, or a dramatic role. **—por•tray'al** *n.*

**pose** (pōz) *v.* **posed, posing. 1.** To hold a position, as in modeling. **2.** To affect a particular attitude. **3.** To propound. **—pose** *n.*

**po•si•tion** (pə-zĭsh'ən) *n.* **1.** A place or location. **2.** A point of view. **3.** Status; rank. **4.** A job. *—v.* To place.

**pos•i•tive** (pŏz'ĭ-tĭv) *adj.* **1.** Expressing affirmation; favorable. **2.** Absolutely certain. **3.** Confident. **4.** Of a quantity greater than 0. **5.** Of the opposite of something negative. **6.** Tending to attract electrons. **7.** Indicating the presence of a disease or microorganism. *—n.* **1.** A positive answer. **2.** A photographic image in which the lights and darks appear as they do in nature. **3.** The uncompared degree of an adjective or adverb. **4.** A positive number. **—pos'i•tive•ly** *adv.* **—pos'i•tive•ness** *n.*

**pos•sess** (pə-zĕs') *v.* **1.** To have or own. **2.** To have as an attribute. **3.** To have knowledge of. **4.** To exert control over; dominate. **—pos•ses'sion** *n.*

**pos•ses•sive** (pə-zĕs'ĭv) *adj.* **1.** Relating to ownership or possession. **2.** Desiring to control. **3.** Relating to the grammatical case of a noun or pronoun indicating possession. *—n.* In grammar, the possessive case. **—pos•ses'sive•ly** *adv.* **—pos•ses'sive•ness** *n.*

**pos•si•ble** (pŏs'ə-bəl) *adj.* Capable of happening, existing, or being accomplished. **—pos'si•bil'i•ty** *n.* **—pos'si•bly** *adv.*

**post¹** (pōst) *n.* A stake set upright in the ground to serve as a marker or support. *—v.* To put up (an announcement) in a place of public view.

**post²** (pōst) *n.* **1.** A military base where troops are stationed. **2.** A position or station. —*v.* **1.** To assign to a position or station. **2.** To put forward; present.

**post**[3] (pōst) *v.* **1.** To mail (a letter). **2.** To inform of the latest news.

**post•age** (pō′stĭj) *n.* The charge for mailing something.

**post•al** (pō′stəl) *adj.* Of the post office or mail service.

**post•er** (pō′stər) *n.* A large placard.

**pos•te•ri•or** (pŏ-stîr′ē-ər, pō-) *adj.* **1.** Located behind. **2.** Following in time.

**pos•ter•i•ty** (pŏ-stĕr′ĭ-tē) *n.* Descendants.

**post•hu•mous** (pŏs′chə-məs) *adj.* **1.** Occurring after one's death. **2.** Born after the death of the father. **—post′hu•mous•ly** *adv.*

**post office** A governmental office where mail is sorted, stamps are sold, etc.

**post•pone** (pōst-pōn′, pōs-pōn′) *v.* **-poned, -poning.** To delay until a future time. **—post•pone′ment** *n.*

**post•script** (pōst′skrĭpt′, pōs′skrĭpt′) *n.* A message added at the end of a letter after the writer's signature.

**pos•tu•late** (pŏs′chə-lāt′) *v.* **-lated, -lating.** To assume with no proof. **—pos′tu•late** *n.* **—pos′tu•la′tion** *n.*

**pos•ture** (pŏs′chər) *n.* A characteristic way of bearing one's body; carriage. —*v.* **-tured, -turing.** To assume an exaggerated pose.

**pot** (pŏt) *n.* **1.** A round, deep container, as for cooking. **2.** A container in which plants are grown. **3.** The total amount staked by all the players in 1 hand of a card game. **—pot** *v.*

**po•tas•si•um** (pə-tăs′ē-əm) *n.* A soft, silver-white, light metallic element.

**po•ta•to** (pə-tā′tō) *n., pl.* **-toes.** The starchy, edible tuber of a cultivated plant.

**po•tent** (pōt′nt) *adj.* **1.** Powerful. **2.** Able to perform sexually. **—po′ten•cy** *n.* **—po′tent•ly** *adv.*

**po•ten•tial** (pə-tĕn′shəl) *adj.* Possible but not yet realized; latent. —*n.* Capacity for further growth. **—po•ten′ti•al′i•ty** *n.* **—po•ten′tial•ly** *adv.*

**po•tion** (pō′shən) *n.* A drink or dose of liquid.

**pot•ter•y** (pŏt′ə-rē) *n., pl.* **-ies.** Ware, such as vases, pots, etc., shaped from clay and hardened by heat. **—pot′ter** *n.*

**pouch** (pouch) *n.* **1.** A flexible receptacle used for carrying various things. **2.** A saclike structure.

**poul•try** (pōl′trē) *n.* Domestic fowl.

**pound**[1] (pound) *n., pl.* **pound** or **pounds.** A unit of weight equal to 16 ounces.

**pound**[2] (pound) *v.* **1.** To strike heavily; hammer. **2.** To pulverize or crush.

**pound**[3] (pound) *n.* An enclosure for stray animals.

**pour** (pôr, pōr) *v.* To flow or cause to flow.

**pov•er•ty** (pŏv′ər-tē) *n.* **1.** The condition of being poor. **2.** A lack or deficiency.

**pow•der** (pou′dər) *n.* **1.** A substance consisting of pulverized particles. **2.** A preparation in this form, as a cosmetic, medicine, etc. —*v.* **1.** To pulverize. **2.** To apply powder to. **—pow′der•y** *adj.*

**pow•er** (pou′ər) *n.* **1.** The ability to act effectively. **2.** Strength; might. **3.** The ability to exercise control; authority. **4.** Mechanical energy derived from water, fuel, wind, etc. —*v.* To supply with power, esp. mechanical power. **—pow′er•ful** *adj.* **—pow′er•ful•ly** *adv.* **—pow′er•less** *adj.* **—pow′er•less•ly** *adv.* **—pow′er•less•ness** *n.*

**prac•ti•ca•ble** (prăk′tĭ-kə-bəl) *adj.* Feasible. **—prac′ti•ca•bil′i•ty** *n.*

**prac•ti•cal** (prăk′tĭ-kəl) *adj.* **1.** Acquired through practice or action. **2.** Capable of being used. **3.** Designed to serve a purpose; useful. **4.** Level-headed. **—prac′ti•cal′i•ty** *n.* **—prac′ti•cal•ly** *adv.*

**prac•tice** (prăk′tĭs) *v.* **-ticed, -ticing. 1.** To do or perform (something) habitually. **2.** To work on over and over in order to learn or acquire a skill. **3.** To work at (a profession). **—prac′tice** *n.* **—prac•ti′tion•er** *n.*

**prag•mat•ic** (prăg-măt′ĭk) *adj.* Dealing with facts or actual occurrences; practical. **—prag•mat′i•cal•ly** *adv.* **—prag′ma•tism** *n.*

**prai•rie** (prâr′ē) *n.* An extensive area of flat grassland.

**praise** (prāz) *n.* **1.** An expression of approval or admiration. **2.** The act of acclaiming, honoring, or exalting. **—praise** *v.*

**prance** (prăns) *v.* **pranced, prancing.** To move about in a lively manner; strut. **—prance** *n.* **—pranc′er** *n.*

**prank** (prăngk) *n.* A mischievous trick. **—prank′ster** *n.*

**prat•tle** (prăt′l) *v.* **-tled, -tling.** To talk meaninglessly; babble. **—prat′tle** *n.*

**pray** (prā) *v.* **1.** To address a prayer to a deity. **2.** To beg earnestly.

**prayer** (prâr) *n.* **1.** A reverent petition made to God. **2.** The act of praying. **—prayer′ful** *adj.* **—prayer′ful•ly** *adv.*

**preach** (prēch) *v.* **1.** To deliver (a sermon). **2.** To advocate. **—preach′er** *n.*

**pre•car•i•ous** (prĭ-kâr′ē-əs) *adj.* Dangerously insecure, unsafe, or uncertain. **—pre•car′i•ous•ly** *adv.* **—pre•car′i•ous•ness** *n.*

**pre•cau•tion** (prĭ-kô′shən) *n.* An action taken in advance to protect against possible failure or danger. **—pre•cau′tion•ar′y** *adj.*

**pre•cede** (prĭ-sēd′) *v.* **-ceded, -ceding.** To come before in time, place, or rank. **—prec′e•dence** *n.*

**prec•e•dent** (prĕs′ĭ-dənt) *n.* An act or instance that can be used as an example in dealing later with similar cases.

**pre•cept** (prē′sĕpt′) *n.* A rule or principle of action or conduct.

**pre•cinct** (prē′sĭngkt′) *n.* **1.** A part of a city patrolled by a police unit. **2.** An election district. **3.** Often **precincts.** A place marked off by definite boundaries.

**pre•cious** (prĕsh′əs) *adj.* **1.** Valuable. **2.** Beloved. **3.** Affectedly dainty. **—pre′cious•ly** *adv.*

**prec•i•pice** (prĕs′ə-pĭs) *n.* A very steep or overhanging cliff.

**pre•cip•i•tate** (prĭ-sĭp′ĭ-tāt′) *v.* **-tated, -tating. 1.** To hurl downward. **2.** To cause to happen before anticipated. **3.** To condense, as vapor into rain or snow, and drop. *—adj.* (-tĭt, -tāt′). Moving or acting rapidly and heedlessly. *—n.* (-tāt′, -tĭt). A solid separated from a solution. **—pre•cip′i•tate•ly** *adv.* **—pre•cip′i•ta′tion** *n.*

**pre•cip•i•tous** (prĭ-sĭp′ĭ-təs) *adj.* **1.** Like a precipice; very steep. **2.** Precipitate. **—pre•cip′i•tous•ly** *adv.* **—pre•cip′i•tous•ness** *n.*

**pre•cise** (prĭ-sīs′) *adj.* **1.** Clearly expressed. **2.** Correct. **3.** Distinct; very. **—pre•cise′ly** *adv.* **—pre•cise′ness, pre•ci′sion** *n.*

**pre•clude** (prĭ-klo͞od′) *v.* **-cluded, -cluding.** To prevent.

**pre•co•cious** (prĭ-kō′shəs) *adj.* Showing skills at an earlier age than is usual. **—pre•co′cious•ness, pre•coc′i•ty** *n.*

**pre•cur•sor** (prĭ-kûr′sər, prē′kûr′sər) *n.* **1.** A forerunner. **2.** A predecessor.

**pred•a•tor** (prĕd′ə-tər, -tôr′) *n.* An animal that preys upon others. **—pred′a•to′ry** *adj.*

**pred•e•ces•sor** (prĕd′ĭ-sĕs′ər, prē′dĭ-) *n.* One who precedes another.

**pre•dic•a•ment** (prĭ-dĭk′ə-mənt) *n.* A troublesome, embarrassing, or dangerous situation.

**pred•i•cate** (prĕd′ĭ-kāt′) *v.* **-cated, -cating. 1.** To base or establish (a concept or action). **2.** To declare; assert. *—n.* (-kĭt). The part of a sentence or clause that tells something about the subject. **—pred′i•ca′tion** *n.* **—pred′i•ca′tive** *adj.*

**pre•dict** (prĭ-dĭkt′) *v.* To foretell; prophesy. **—pre•dict′a•ble** *adj.* **—pre•dic′tion** *n.* **—pre•dic′tor** *n.*

**pred•i•lec•tion** (prĕd′l-ĕk′shən, prēd′-) *n.* A preference.

**pre•dom•i•nate** (prĭ-dŏm′ə-nāt′) *v.* **-nated, -nating. 1.** To be most numerous, important, or outstanding. **2.** To have authority or power; prevail. **—pre•dom′i•nance** *n.* **—pre•dom′i•nant** *adj.* **—pre•dom′i•nant•ly** *adv.* **—pre•dom′i•nate** *adj.* **—pre•dom′i•nate•ly** *adv.*

**pre-em•i•nent** (prē-ĕm′ə-nənt) *adj.* Superior to all others; outstanding. **—pre-em′i•nence** *n.* **—pre-em′i•nent•ly** *adv.*

**pre-empt** (prē-ĕmpt′) *v.* To take possession of before another. **—pre-emp′tion** *n.* **—pre-emp′tive** *adj.*

**pref•ace** (prĕf′ĭs) *n.* An introduction to a book, speech, etc. **—pref′ace** *v.* **—pref′a•to′ry** *adj.*

**pre•fect** (prē′fĕkt′) *n.* A high administrative official. **—pre′fec′ture** *n.*

**pre•fer** (prĭ-fûr′) *v.* **-ferred, -ferring.** To like better. **—pref′er•a•ble** *adj.* **—pref′er•a•bly** *adv.* **—pref′er•ence** *n.* **—pref′er•en′tial** *adj.*

**pre•fix** (prē′fĭks′) *n.* A form put before a word, changing the meaning. —*v.* To add at the beginning or front.

**preg•nant** (prĕg′nənt) *adj.* **1.** Carrying a developing fetus within the uterus. **2.** Full of meaning or significance. **—preg′nan•cy** *n.*

**prej•u•dice** (prĕj′ə-dĭs) *n.* **1.** A preconceived opinion; bias. **2.** Detriment or injury. **—prej′u•dice** *v.* **—prej′u•di′cial** *adj.*

**pre•lim•i•nar•y** (prĭ-lĭm′ə-nĕr′ē) *adj.* Introductory; prefatory. —*n., pl.* **-ies.** Something antecedent or preparatory.

**pre•lude** (prĕl′yo͞od′, prā′lo͞od′) *n.* A preliminary part; preface.

**pre•ma•ture** (prē′mə-cho͝or′, -t/y/o͝or′) *adj.* Occurring before the usual time. **—pre′ma•ture′ly** *adv.* **—pre′ma•ture′ness, pre′ma•tu′ri•ty** *n.*

**pre•med•i•tate** (prē-mĕd′ĭ-tāt′) *v.* **-tated, -tating.** To arrange or plot in advance. **—pre•med′i•ta′tion** *n.* **—pre•med′i•ta′tor** *n.*

**pre•mier** (prĭ-mîr′, -myîr′, prē′mîr) *n.* A prime minister.

**pre•mière** (prĭ-mîr′, -myâr′) *n.* The first public presentation of a movie, etc.

**prem•ise** (prĕm′ĭs) *n.* **1.** A proposition upon which an argument is based. **2. premises.** Land and the buildings on it.

**pre•mi•um** (prē′mē-əm) *n.* **1.** A prize. **2.** A bonus. **3.** The amount paid for an insurance policy.

**pre•mo•ni•tion** (prē′mə-nĭsh′ən, prĕm′ə-) *n.* **1.** An advance warning. **2.** A foreboding. **—pre•mon′i•to′ry** *adj.*

**pre•oc•cu•py** (prē-ŏk′yə-pī′) *v.* **-pied, -pying.** To engross. **—pre•oc′cu•pa′tion** *n.*

**pre•pare** (prĭ-pâr′) *v.* **-pared, -paring. 1.** To make or get ready. **2.** To put together. **—prep′a•ra′tion** *n.* **—pre•par′a•to′ry** *adj.* **—pre•par′ed•ness** *n.*

**prep•o•si•tion** (prĕp′ə-zĭsh′ən) *n.* A word that indicates the relation of a noun to a verb, an adjective, or another noun. **—prep′o•si′tion•al** *adj.*

**pre•pos•ter•ous** (prĭ-pŏs′tər-əs) *adj.* Absurd; ridiculous.

**pre•req•ui•site** (prē-rĕk′wĭ-zĭt) *adj.* Required as a prior condition to something. **—pre•req′ui•site** *n.*

**pre•rog•a•tive** (prĭ-rŏg′ə-tĭv) *n.* An exclusive right or privilege.

**pre•scribe** (prĭ-skrīb′) *v.* **-scribed, -scribing. 1.** To impose or direct. **2.** To order the use of (a drug, remedy, etc.). **—pre•scrip′tion** *n.* **—pre•scrip′tive** *adj.*

**pres•ence** (prĕz′əns) *n.* **1.** The condition of being present. **2.** Immediate nearness. **3.** Personal appearance; bearing.

**pres•ent**[1] (prĕz′ənt) *n.* A period of time between past and future; now. —*adj.* **1.** Occurring now. **2.** Being at hand. **3.** Of a verb form expressing current time.

**pre•sent**[2] (prĭ-zĕnt′) *v.* **1.** To introduce. **2.** To exhibit or display. **3.** To give or offer. —*n.* **pres•ent** (prĕz′ənt). A gift. **—pre•sent′a•ble** *adj.* **—pre•sent′a•bly** *adv.* **—pres′en•ta′tion** *n.*

**pre•sen•ti•ment** (prĭ-zĕn′tə-mənt) *n.* A premonition.

**pre•serve** (prĭ-zûrv′) *v.* **-served, -serving. 1.** To protect. **2.** To keep in unchanged condition. **3.** To treat or prepare so as to prevent decay. —*n.* **1.** Often **preserves.** Fruit cooked with sugar. **2.** An area for the protection of wildlife or natural resources. **—pres′er•va′tion** *n.* **—pre•ser′va•tive** *adj. & n.* **—pre•serv′er** *n.*

**pre•side** (prĭ-zīd′) *v.* **-sided, -siding.** To act as chairman or chairwoman.

**pres•i•dent** (prĕz′ĭ-dənt, -dĕnt′) *n.* **1.** Often **President.** The chief executive of a republic. **2.** The chief officer of a corporation, etc. **—pres′i•den•cy** *n.* **—pres′i•den′tial** *adj.*

**press** (prĕs) *v.* **1.** To exert weight or force (against). **2.** To iron (clothing). **3.** To embrace. **4.** To urge on. **5.** To require haste. **6.** To put forward insistently. **7.** To push forward. —*n.* **1.** A machine or device that applies pressure. **2.** A printing press. **3.** A printing or publishing establishment. **4.** Printed matter, esp. newspapers and periodicals. **5.** A crowding forward. **6.** The urgency of business, etc. **—press′ing** *adj.*

**pres•sure** (prĕsh′ər) *n.* **1.** The application of continuous force on 1 body by another. **2.** A compelling influence. **3.** Urgent claim or demand. —*v.* **-sured, -suring.** To force.

**pres•sur•ize** (prĕsh′ə-rīz′) *v.* **-ized, -izing.** To maintain normal air pressure in (an aircraft, etc.). —**pres′sur•i•za′tion** *n.*

**pres•tige** (prĕ-stēzh′, -stēj′) *n.* Prominence or influential status. —**pres•tig′-ious** *adj.*

**pre•sume** (prĭ-zōōm′) *v.* **-sumed, -suming. 1.** To take for granted. **2.** To venture; dare. —**pre•sum′a•ble** *adj.* —**pre•sum′a•bly** *adv.*

**pre•sump•tion** (prĭ-zŭmp′shən) *n.* **1.** Arrogant or offensive behavior. **2.** An assumption or supposition. —**pre•sump′tive** *adj.* —**pre•sump′tu•ous** *adj.* —**pre•sump′tu•ous•ly** *adv.* —**pre•sump′tu•ous•ness** *n.*

**pre•sup•pose** (prē′sə-pōz′) *v.* To assume. —**pre′sup•po•si′tion** *n.*

**pre•tend** (prĭ-tĕnd′) *v.* **1.** To make believe. **2.** To claim falsely; profess. **3.** To put forward a claim. —**pre•tend′er** *n.* —**pre′tense′** *n.*

**pre•ten•sion** (prĭ-tĕn′shən) *n.* **1.** A doubtful claim. **2.** Showy behavior. —**pre•ten′tious** *adj.* —**pre•ten′-tious•ly** *adv.* —**pre•ten′tious•ness** *n.*

**pre•text** (prē′tĕkst′) *n.* An excuse.

**pret•ty** (prĭt′ē) *adj.* **-tier, -tiest. 1.** Pleasing or attractive. **2.** Excellent; fine; good. —*adv.* To a fair degree; somewhat. —*v.* **-tied, -tying.** To make pretty. —**pret′ti•fy′** *v.* —**pret′ti•ly** *adv.* —**pret′ti•ness** *n.*

**pre•vail** (prĭ-vāl′) *v.* **1.** To be victorious. **2.** To be most common or frequent. **3.** To persuade.

**prev•a•lent** (prĕv′ə-lənt) *adj.* Widely existing or commonly occurring. —**prev′a•lence** *n.* —**prev′a•lent•ly** *adv.*

**pre•var•i•cate** (prĭ-văr′ĭ-kāt′) *v.* **-cated, -cating.** To speak evasively or lie. —**pre•var′i•ca′tion** *n.* —**pre•var′i•ca′-tor** *n.*

**pre•vent** (prĭ-vĕnt′) *v.* **1.** To keep from happening; avert. **2.** To hinder; impede. —**pre•vent′a•ble, pre•vent′i•ble** *adj.* —**pre•ven′tion** *n.* —**pre•ven′tive, pre•ven′ta•tive** *adj. & n.*

**pre•view** (prē′vyōō′) *n.* Also **pre•vue.** An advance showing of a motion picture, etc.

**pre•vi•ous** (prē′vē-əs) *adj.* Existing or occurring earlier. —**pre′vi•ous•ly** *adv.*

**prey** (prā) *n.* **1.** An animal hunted or caught for food. **2.** A victim. —*v.* **1.** To seize as prey. **2.** To victimize. **3.** To plunder.

**price** (prīs) *n.* **1.** The sum of money asked or given for something. **2.** Value or worth. —*v.* **priced, pricing. 1.** To fix a price for. **2.** To find out the price of. —**price′less** *adj.* —**price′less•ly** *adv.* —**price′less•ness** *n.*

**prick** (prĭk) *n.* **1.** A small mark or puncture. **2.** Something that punctures, as a thorn, pin, etc. —**prick** *v.*

**prick•le** (prĭk′əl) *n.* **1.** A small spine or thorn. **2.** A stinging sensation. —**prick′le** *v.* —**prick′ly** *adj.*

**pride** (prīd) *n.* **1.** Self-respect. **2.** Satisfaction over one's accomplishments or possessions. **3.** A cause or source of this. **4.** Conceit; arrogance. **5.** A group of lions. —*v.* **prided, priding.** To esteem (oneself) for. —**pride′ful** *adj.*

**priest** (prēst) *n.* A member of the clergy. —**priest′hood′** *n.* —**priest′ly** *adj.*

**prim** (prĭm) *adj.* **primmer, primmest.** Precise, neat, or proper to the point of affectation. —**prim′ly** *adv.* —**prim′-ness** *n.*

**pri•ma•ry** (prī′mĕr′ē, -mə-rē) *adj.* **1.** First in time, order, or importance. **2.** Fundamental. —*n., pl.* **-ries.** A preliminary election for nominating political-party candidates. —**pri•mar′i•ly** *adv.*

**pri•mate** (prī′māt) *n.* **1.** A mammal of the group that includes the monkeys, apes, and man. **2.** A bishop of high rank.

**prime** (prīm) *adj.* First in quality, degree, or sequence. —*n.* **1.** The earliest stage of something. **2.** The period of ideal or peak condition. —*v.* **primed, priming.** To make ready; prepare for operation. —**prim′al** *adj.*

**prim•er**[1] (prĭm′ər) *n.* **1.** An elementary reading textbook. **2.** A basic handbook.

**prim•er**[2] (prī′mər) *n.* **1.** A device for setting off an explosive. **2.** An undercoat of paint, etc., used to prime a surface.

**prim•i•tive** (prĭm′ĭ-tĭv) *adj.* **1.** Of an early stage of development, evolution, etc. **2.** Of an early stage in the evolution of human culture. —**prim′i•tive** *n.* —**prim′i•tive•ly** *adv.*

**prin•ci•pal** (prĭn′sə-pəl) *adj.* First in importance; chief. —*n.* **1.** The head of a school. **2.** A main participant, as in a play, business deal, etc. **3.** Capital as distinguished from revenue or interest.

**4.** One who empowers another to act for him. **—prin′ci•pal•ly** *adv.*

**prin•ci•pal•i•ty** (prĭn′sə-păl′ĭ-tē) *n., pl.* **-ties.** A territory ruled by a prince or princess.

**prin•ci•ple** (prĭn′sə-pəl) *n.* **1.** A basic truth or law. **2.** An ethical standard. **—prin′ci•pled** *adj.*

**print** (prĭnt) *n.* **1.** A mark made by pressure. **2.** Something marked with an impression. **3. a.** Lettering or other impressions produced in ink. **b.** The state or form of matter so produced. **4.** A design or picture reproduced by printing. **5.** A photographic copy. *—v.* **1.** To reproduce by means of inked type, plates, etc., on a paper surface. **2.** To publish. **3.** To write in characters similar to those used in print. **4.** To produce (a photograph) from a negative. **—print′a•ble** *adj.* **—print′er** *n.*

**pri•or** (prī′ər) *adj.* **1.** Preceding in time or order. **2.** Preceding in importance. **—pri•or′i•ty** *n.*

**prism** (prĭz′əm) *n.* A transparent solid used to refract light or break it up into a spectrum. **—pris•mat′ic** *adj.*

**pris•on** (prĭz′ən) *n.* A place of confinement for criminals. **—pris′on•er** *n.*

**pris•tine** (prĭs′tēn′, prĭ-stēn′) *adj.* **1.** Primitive or original. **2.** Pure.

**pri•vate** (prī′vĭt) *adj.* **1.** Belonging to a particular person or persons. **2.** Secret; confidential. *—n.* A soldier of the lowest rank. **—pri′va•cy** *n.* **—pri′vate•ly** *adv.*

**pri•va•tion** (prī-vā′shən) *n.* Lack of the basic necessities of life.

**priv•i•lege** (prĭv′ə-lĭj) *n.* A special immunity or benefit. **—priv′i•leged** *adj.*

**prize** (prīz) *n.* **1.** Something won in a competition, etc. **2.** Anything worth striving for. *—v.* **prized, prizing.** To value highly.

**prob•a•ble** (prŏb′ə-bəl) *adj.* **1.** Likely to happen. **2.** Apparently true; plausible. **—prob′a•bil′i•ty** *n.* **—prob′a•bly** *adv.*

**pro•ba•tion** (prō-bā′shən) *n.* A trial period for testing a person's behavior, etc. **—pro•ba′tion•al, pro•ba′tion•ar′y** *adj.*

**probe** (prōb) *n.* **1.** An instrument used to explore a wound or body cavity. **2.** An investigation. **—probe** *v.*

**prob•lem** (prŏb′ləm) *n.* A question or situation that presents uncertainty or difficulty. **—prob′lem•at′i•cal** *adj.*

**pro bo•no, pro-bo•no** (prō bō′nō) *adj.* Done without fee; gratis.

**pro•ceed** (prō-sēd′, prə-) *v.* **1.** To advance or continue. **2.** To undertake and carry on some action. **3.** To issue forth. **4.** To take legal action. **—pro•ce′dure** *n.* **—pro•ce′dur•al** *adj.*

**pro•ceeds** (prō′sēdz′) *pl.n.* Profits.

**proc•ess** (prŏs′ĕs, prō′sĕs′) *n.* **1.** A system of operations in the production of something. **2.** A series of actions that bring about a particular result. **3.** Ongoing movement; progression. **4. a.** A court summons or writ. **b.** The entire course of a judicial proceeding. *—v.* **1.** To put through the steps of a prescribed procedure. **2.** To prepare or convert by subjecting to some special process. **—proc′es′sor, proc′es′ser** *n.*

**pro•ces•sion** (prə-sĕsh′ən) *n.* A group of persons, vehicles, etc., moving along in an orderly manner.

**pro•claim** (prō-klām′, prə-) *v.* To announce officially and publicly. **—pro•claim′er** *n.* **—proc′la•ma′tion** *n.*

**pro•cliv•i•ty** (prō-klĭv′ĭ-tē) *n., pl.* **-ties.** A natural inclination.

**pro•cras•ti•nate** (prō-krăs′tə-nāt′, prə-) *v.* **-nated, -nating.** To put off doing something. **—pro•cras′ti•na′tion** *n.* **—pro•cras′ti•na′tor** *n.*

**pro•cre•ate** (prō′krē-āt′) *v.* **-ated, -ating.** To beget or reproduce. **—pro′cre•a′tion** *n.* **—pro′cre•a′tive** *adj.* **—pro′cre•a′tor** *n.*

**pro•cure** (prō-kyŏŏr′, prə-) *v.* **-cured, -curing. 1.** To obtain; acquire. **2.** To bring about. **3.** To act as go-between in sexual intrigues. **—pro•cur′er** *n.* **—pro•cure′ment** *n.*

**prod** (prŏd) *v.* **prodded, prodding. 1.** To jab or poke. **2.** To urge or goad. **—prod** *n.*

**prod•i•gal** (prŏd′ĭ-gəl) *adj.* **1.** Wasteful; extravagant. **2.** Profuse; lavish. **—prod′i•gal** *n.* **—prod′i•gal′i•ty** *n.*

**pro•di•gious** (prə-dĭj′əs) *adj.* **1.** Enormous. **2.** Extraordinary. **—pro•di′gious•ly** *adv.* **—pro•di′gious•ness** *n.* **—prod′i•gy** *n.*

**pro•duce** (prə-d/y/ōōs′, prō-) *v.* **-duced, -ducing. 1.** To bring forth; yield. **2.** To manufacture. **3.** To cause or give rise to. **4.** To bring forward; exhibit. —*n.* (prŏd′-yo͞os, prō′dyo͞os) Something produced; a product, esp. fruits and vegetables. **—pro•duc′er** *n.* **—pro•duc′tion** *n.* **—pro•duc′tive** *adj.* **—pro•duc′tive•ly** *adv.* **—pro′duc•tiv′i•ty** *n.*

**prod•uct** (prŏd′əkt) *n.* **1.** Anything produced by labor. **2.** The result obtained by performing multiplication.

**pro•fane** (prō-fān′, prə-) *adj.* **1.** Blasphemous. **2.** Secular. **—pro•fane′** *v.* **—pro•fan′i•ty** *n.*

**pro•fess** (prə-fĕs′, prō-) *v.* **1.** To declare openly. **2.** To claim knowledge of. **3.** To make a show of; pretend. **—pro•fessed′** *adj.* **—pro•fess′ed•ly** *adv.*

**pro•fes•sion** (prə-fĕsh′ən) *n.* **1.** An occupation that requires training and specialized study. **2.** A declaration.

**pro•fes•sion•al** (prə-fĕsh′ə-nəl) *adj.* **1.** Of a profession. **2.** Engaged in 1 of the learned professions, as law. **3.** Participating for pay in a sport. **—pro•fes′sion•al** *n.* **—pro•fes′sion•al•ly** *adv.*

**pro•fes•sor** (prə-fĕs′ər) *n.* A college teacher of the highest rank. **—pro′fes•so′ri•al** *adj.* **—pro•fes′sor•ship′** *n.*

**pro•fi•cient** (prə-fĭsh′ənt) *adj.* Skillful; expert. **—pro•fi′cien•cy** *n.* **—pro•fi′cient•ly** *adv.*

**pro•file** (prō′fīl′) *n.* **1.** A side view, esp. of the human head. **2.** Data, esp. graphs, presenting important features of something, as of a corporation. **3.** A short biographical outline.

**prof•it** (prŏf′ĭt) *n.* **1.** A benefit. **2.** The net return received on a business undertaking. —*v.* **1.** To make a profit. **2.** To benefit. **—prof′it•a•bil′i•ty** *n.* **—prof′it•a•ble** *adj.* **—prof′it•a•bly** *adv.* **—prof′it•less** *adj.*

**prof•li•gate** (prŏf′lĭ-gĭt, -gāt′) *adj.* **1.** Dissolute. **2.** Recklessly extravagant. **—prof′li•ga•cy** *n.* **—prof′li•gate** *n.*

**pro for•ma** (prō fôr′mə) *adj.* **1.** Done perfunctorily. **2.** Provided in advance, as according to schedule.

**pro•found** (prə-found′, prō-) *adj.* **1.** Of a great depth; deep. **2.** Wise and full of insight. **3.** Deeply felt or held. **4.** Total; absolute. **—pro•found′ly** *adv.* **—pro•fun′di•ty** *n.*

**pro•fuse** (prə-fyo͞os′, prō-) *adj.* Copious or abundant. **—pro•fuse′ly** *adv.* **—pro•fu′sion, pro•fuse′ness** *n.*

**prog•e•ny** (prŏj′ə-nē) *n.* Offspring.

**prog•no•sis** (prŏg-nō′sĭs) *n., pl.* **-ses.** A medical prediction of the course of a disease.

**pro•gram** (prō′grăm′, grəm) *n.* **1.** A listing of events for a public presentation. **2.** A schedule. **3.** Instructions coded for a computer. —*v.* **-grammed** or **-gramed, -gramming** or **-graming. 1.** To include in a program. **2.** To provide (a computer) with instructions. **—pro′gram•mat′ic** *adj.* **—pro′gram′mer** *n.*

**prog•ress** (prŏg′rĕs′, -rəs) *n.* **1.** Movement toward a goal. **2.** Development. **3.** Steady improvement. —*v.* **pro•gress** (prə-grĕs′) **1.** To advance; proceed. **2.** To improve. **—pro•gres′sion** *n.* **—pro•gres′sive** *adj.*

**pro•hib•it** (prō-hĭb′ĭt) *v.* **1.** To forbid by authority. **2.** To prevent. **—pro•hib′i•tive** *adj.* **—pro′hi•bi′tion** *n.*

**proj•ect** (prŏj′ĕkt′, -ĭkt) *n.* An undertaking requiring concerted effort. —*v.* **pro•ject** (prə-jĕkt′) **1.** To protrude. **2.** To throw forward. **3.** To plan. **—pro•jec′tion** *n.* **—pro•jec′tor** *n.*

**pro•jec•tile** (prə-jĕk′təl, -tīl′) *n.* An object, as a bullet, projected with force.

**pro•le•tar•i•at** (prō′lĭ-târ′ē-ĭt) *n.* The class of industrial wage earners. **—pro′le•tar′i•an** *n.*

**pro•lif•ic** (prə-lĭf′ĭk) *adj.* Producing in abundance.

**prom•e•nade** (prŏm′ə-nād′, -näd′) *n.* **1.** A leisurely walk; stroll. **2.** A public place for such walking. **—prom′e•nade′** *v.*

**prom•i•nent** (prŏm′ə-nənt) *adj.* **1.** Projecting outward. **2.** Conspicuous. **3.** Widely known; eminent. **—prom′i•nence** *n.* **—prom′i•nent•ly** *adv.*

**pro•mis•cu•ous** (prə-mĭs′kyo͞o-əs) *adj.* Indiscriminate, esp. in sexual relations. **—prom′is•cu′i•ty, pro•mis′cu•ous•ness** *n.* **—pro•mis′cu•ous•ly** *adv.*

**prom•ise** (prŏm′ĭs) *n.* **1.** A declaration assuring that one will or will not do something. **2.** Indication of future excellence or success. —*v.* **-ised, -ising. 1.** To pledge assurance. **2.** To afford a basis for expecting.

**prom•on•to•ry** (prŏm′ən-tôr′ē, -tōr′ē) *n., pl.* **-ries.** A high ridge jutting out into water.

**pro•mote** (prə-mōt′) *v.* **-moted, -moting. 1.** To raise in position or rank. **2.** To contribute to the progress or growth of; further. **3.** To urge the adoption of; advocate. **4.** To attempt to sell or popularize. **—pro•mot′er** *n.* **—pro•mo′tion** *n.* **—pro•mo′tion•al** *adj.*

**prompt** (prŏmpt) *adj.* **1.** On time. **2.** Done without delay. *—v.* **1.** To press into action; incite. **2.** To give rise to; inspire. **3.** To assist with a reminder; remind. **—prompt′er** *n.* **—promp′ti•tude′, prompt′ness** *n.* **—prompt′ly** *adv.*

**prone** (prōn) *adj.* **1.** Lying flat, esp. with the front downward. **2.** Tending; inclined. **—prone′ness** *n.*

**prong** (prông, prŏng) *n.* A pointed part, as a tine of a fork.

**pro•noun** (prō′noun′) *n.* A word that functions as a substitute for a noun.

**pro•nounce** (prə-nouns′) *v.* **-nounced, -nouncing. 1.** To utter (a word or speech sound). **2.** To state officially; declare. **—pro•nounce′ment** *n.* **—pro•nun′ci•a′tion** *n.*

**pro•nounced** (prə-nounst′) *adj.* Strongly marked; distinct.

**proof** (pro͞of) *n.* **1.** The evidence establishing the validity of an assertion. **2.** The alcoholic strength of a liquor. *—adj.* Fully resistant.

**prop** (prŏp) *n.* A support or stay. **—prop** *v.*

**prop•a•gan•da** (prŏp′ə-găn′də) *n.* Material disseminated by the supporters of a doctrine, cause, faction, or side.

**prop•a•gate** (prŏp′ə-gāt′) *v.* **-gated, -gating. 1.** To reproduce or cause to reproduce. **2.** To spread information about. **—prop′a•ga′tion** *n.* **—prop′a•ga′tor** *n.*

**pro•pel** (prə-pĕl′) *v.* **-pelled, -pelling.** To cause to move or continue in motion. **—pro•pel′lant** *n.* **—pro•pel′ler** *n.*

**pro•pen•si•ty** (prə-pĕn′sĭ-tē) *n., pl.* **-ties.** An inclination; tendency.

**prop•er** (prŏp′ər) *adj.* **1.** Suitable; fitting. **2.** Correct; exact. **3.** Designating a noun that is the name of a particular person, place, or thing. **—prop′er•ly** *adv.* **—prop′er•ness** *n.*

**prop•er•ty** (prŏp′ər-tē) *n., pl.* **-ties. 1.** A possession or possessions. **2.** A characteristic trait or quality. **—prop′er•tied** *adj.*

**proph•e•cy** (prŏf′ĭ-sē) *n., pl.* **-cies. 1.** A prediction. **2.** The utterance of a prophet. **—proph′e•sy′** *v.*

**proph•et** (prŏf′ĭt) *n.* **1.** One who speaks by divine inspiration. **2.** A predictor. **—pro•phet′ic** *adj.*

**pro•pi•tious** (prə-pĭsh′əs) *adj.* Favorable; suitable. **—pro•pi′tious•ly** *adv.*

**pro•po•nent** (prə-pō′nənt) *n.* An advocate.

**pro•por•tion** (prə-pôr′shən, -pōr′-) *n.* **1.** A part considered in relation to the whole. **2.** Harmonious relation. **3.** Often **proportions.** Dimensions; size. *—v.* **1.** To adjust so that proper relations are attained. **2.** To form with symmetry. **—pro•por′tion•al** *adj.*. **—pro•por′tion•al•ly** *adv.* **—pro•por′tion•ate** *adj.*

**pro•pose** (prə-pōz′) *v.* **-posed, -posing. 1.** To suggest. **2.** To intend. **3.** To make an offer, esp. of marriage. **—pro•pos′al** *n.* **—pro•pos′er** *n.* **—prop′o•si′tion** *n.*

**pro•pound** (prə-pound′) *v.* To put forward for consideration. **—pro•pound′er** *n.*

**pro•pri•e•tor** (prə-prī′ĭ-tər) *n.* An owner. **—pro•pri′e•tar′y** *adj.* **—pro•pri′e•tor•ship′** *n.*

**pro•pri•e•ty** (prə-prī′ĭ-tē) *n., pl.* **-ties.** Appropriateness.

**pro•pul•sion** (prə-pŭl′shən) *n.* A driving force. **—pro•pul′sive** *adj.*

**pro•sa•ic** (prō-zā′ĭk) *adj.* **1.** Relating to prose. **2.** Straightforward; matter-of-fact. **3.** Unimaginative.

**prose** (prōz) *n.* Ordinary writing as distinguished from poetry.

**pros•e•cute** (prŏs′ĭ-kyo͞ot′) *v.* **-cuted, -cuting. 1.** To initiate and conduct court action against. **2.** To persist in so as to complete. **—pros′e•cu′tion** *n.* **—pros′e•cu′tor** *n.*

**pros•pect** (prŏs′pĕkt′) *n.* **1.** A chance for success. **2.** A potential customer or candidate. **3.** An outlook. *—v.* To explore, esp. for mineral deposits. **—pro•spec′tive** *adj.* **—pros′pec′tor** *n.*

**pros•per** (prŏs′pər) *v.* To be successful. **—pros•per′i•ty** *n.* **—pros′per•ous** *adj.*

**pros•ti•tute** (prŏs′tĭ-t/y/o͞ot′) *n.* A whore. —*v.* **-tuted, -tuting.** To offer (oneself or another) for sexual hire. **—pros′ti•tu′tion** *n.*

**pros•trate** (prŏs′trāt′) *v.* **-trated, -trating. 1.** To kneel or lie face down, as in adoration or submission. **2.** To exhaust. —*adj.* **1.** Lying flat. **2.** Exhausted. **—pros•tra′tion** *n.*

**pro•tect** (prə-tĕkt′) *v.* To keep from harm or injury; guard. **—pro•tec′tion** *n.* **—pro•tec′tive** *adj.* **—pro•tec′tor** *n.*

**pro•té•gé** (prō′tə-zhā′, prō′tə-zhā′) *n.* A man or boy supported and advanced by an influential person.

**pro•té•gée** (prō′tə-zhā′, prō′tə-zhā′) *n.* A woman or girl supported and advanced by an influential person.

**pro•tein** (prō′tēn′) *n.* Any of a group of compounds that occur in all living matter and are essential for the growth and repair of animal tissue.

**pro tem•po•re** (prō tĕm′pə-rē) *adv.* Also **pro tem.** For the time being.

**pro•test** (prə-tĕst′, prō-tĕst′, prō′tĕst′) *v.* **1.** To object to (something). **2.** To affirm solemnly. —*n.* (prō′tĕst′) **1.** The act of protesting. **2.** A solemn objection. **—prot′es•ta′tion** *n.* **—pro•test′er** *n.*

**Prot•es•tant** (prŏt′ĭ-stənt) *n.* A Christian belonging to a Western church descending from those that seceded from the Church of Rome. **—Prot′es•tant•ism′** *n.*

**pro•to•col** (prō′tə-kôl′) *n.* **1.** The forms of ceremony and etiquette used by diplomats and heads of state. **2.** A standard procedure for regulating data transmission between computers.

**pro•to•plasm** (prō′tə-plăz′əm) *n.* A substance constituting the living matter of plant and animal cells.

**pro•trude** (prō-tro͞od′) *v.* **-truded, -truding.** To push outward; project. **—pro•tru′sion** *n.*

**proud** (proud) *adj.* **1.** Feeling satisfaction. **2.** Haughty; arrogant. **3.** Majestic; magnificent. **—proud′ly** *adv.*

**prove** (pro͞ov) *v.* **proved, proved** or **proven** (pro͞o′vən), **proving. 1.** To establish the truth of by argument or evidence. **2.** To try out; test. **3.** To turn out. **—prov′a•ble** *adj.* **—prov′er** *n.*

**prov•erb** (prŏv′ûrb′) *n.* A short, common saying that illustrates a truth. **—pro•ver′bi•al** *adj.*

**pro•vide** (prə-vīd′) *v.* **-vided, -viding. 1.** To furnish; supply. **2.** To make ready; prepare. **3.** To serve as. **—pro•vid′er** *n.*

**prov•i•dent** (prŏv′ĭ-dənt, -dĕnt′) *adj.* Providing for future needs. **—prov′i•den′tial** *adj.* **—prov′i•den′tial•ly** *adv.* **—prov′i•dent•ly** *adv.*

**prov•ince** (prŏv′ĭns) *n.* **1.** An administrative or political unit of a country. **2.** An area of interest. **—pro•vin′cial** *adj.*

**pro•vi•sion** (prə-vĭzh′ən) *n.* **1.** The act of supplying or fitting out. **2.** That which is supplied. **3.** A preparatory measure. **4. provisions.** A stock of necessary supplies, esp. food. **5.** A stipulation. —*v.* To supply with provisions.

**pro•vi•sion•al** (prə-vĭzh′ə-nəl) *adj.* Provided for the time being. **—pro•vi′sion•al•ly** *adv.*

**pro•voke** (prə-vōk′) *v.* **-voked, -voking. 1.** To incite to anger. **2.** To incite to action. **—prov′o•ca′tion** *n.* **—pro•voc′a•tive** *adj.* **—pro•voc′a•tive•ly** *adv.*

**prow•ess** (prou′ĭs) *n.* Bravery and resourcefulness.

**prowl** (proul) *v.* To roam stealthily, as in search of prey. **—prowl** *n.* **—prowl′er** *n.*

**prox•im•i•ty** (prŏk-sĭm′ĭ-tē) *n.* Nearness; closeness.

**prox•y** (prŏk′sē) *n., pl.* **-ies.** An agent.

**prude** (pro͞od) *n.* One who is excessively modest or proper. **—prud′er•y** *n.* **—prud′ish** *adj.* **—prud′ish•ly** *adv.*

**pru•dence** (pro͞od′ns) *n.* Wisdom in handling practical matters. **—pru′dent, pru•den′tial** *adj.* **—pru′dent•ly, pru•den′tial•ly** *adv.*

**prune** (pro͞on) *v.* **pruned, pruning.** To cut branches, etc., from (a tree or plant).

**pru•ri•ent** (pro͝or′ē-ənt) *adj.* Excessively interested in sexual matters. **—pru′ri•ence** *n.*

**pry[1]** (prī) *v.* **pried, prying.** To look curiously or inquisitively; snoop.

**pry[2]** (prī) *v.* **pried, prying.** To move with a lever. —*n., pl.* **pries.** A lever.

**psalm** (säm) *n.* A sacred song, esp. a short poem from the Bible. **—psalm′-**

ist *n.*

**pseu•do•nym** (sōōd'n-ĭm') *n.* A fictitious name.

**psy•che** (sī'kē) *n.* The human mind or soul. —**psy'chic** *adj.*

**psy•chi•a•try** (sĭ-kī'ə-trē, sī-) *n.* The medical treatment of mental illness. —**psy'chi•at'ric** *adj.* —**psy•chi'a•trist** *n.*

**psy•cho•a•nal•y•sis** (sī'kō-ə-năl'ĭ-sĭs) *n.* **1.** A system of psychotherapy. **2.** A theory of human psychology. —**psy'cho•an'a•lyst** *n.* —**psy'cho•an'a•lyt'ic** *adj.* —**psy'cho•an'a•lyze'** *v.*

**psy•chol•o•gy** (sī-kŏl'ə-jē) *n., pl.* **-gies. 1.** The science of mental processes and behavior. **2.** The behavioral characteristics of an individual or a group. —**psy'cho•log'i•cal** *adj.* —**psy•chol'o•gist** *n.*

**psy•cho•sis** (sī-kō'sĭs) *n., pl.* **-ses.** A severe mental disorder. —**psy•chot'ic** *n. & adj.*

**psy•cho•ther•a•py** (sī'kō-thĕr'ə-pē) *n.* The psychological treatment of mental, emotional, and nervous disorders. —**psy'cho•ther'a•pist** *n.*

**pu•ber•ty** (pyōō'bər-tē) *n.* The stage of development when an individual becomes physiologically capable of reproduction.

**pub•lic** (pŭb'lĭk) *adj.* **1.** Of the community or the people. **2.** Widely known. —*n.* The people. —**pub'lic•ly** *adv.*

**pub•li•ca•tion** (pŭb'lĭ-kā'shən) *n.* **1.** The process of publishing. **2.** Published material.

**pub•lic•i•ty** (pŭ-blĭs'ĭ-tē) *n.* Public interest or notice. —**pub'li•cist** *n.* —**pub'li•cize'** *v.*

**pub•lish** (pŭb'lĭsh) *v.* **1.** To prepare and issue (printed material) for public distribution or sale. **2.** To announce to the public. —**pub'lish•er** *n.*

**pud•dle** (pŭd'l) *n.* A small pool of liquid.

**pu•er•ile** (pyōō'ər-əl, pyŏŏr'əl, -īl') *adj.* Immature; childish.

**puff** (pŭf) *n.* **1.** A short, forceful discharge, as of smoke or air. **2.** A swelling. **3.** Something that is light or inflated, as pastry. —**puff** *v.* —**puff'i•ness** *n.* —**puff'y** *adj.*

**pug•na•cious** (pŭg-nā'shəs) *adj.* Eager to fight; aggressive. —**pug•nac'i•ty** *n.*

**puis•sance** (pwĭs'əns, pyōō'ĭ-səns, pyōō-ĭs'əns) *n.* Power; might. —**puis'sant** *adj.*

**pul•chri•tude** (pŭl'krĭ-t/y/ōōd') *n.* Physical beauty and appeal. —**pul'chri•tu'di•nous** *adj.*

**pull** (pŏŏl) *v.* **1.** To apply force so as to draw something toward the force. **2.** To move with force. **3.** To tug; jerk. —*n.* **1.** The action or process of pulling. **2.** Force exerted in pulling. **3.** Something used for pulling, as a handle. **4.** Special influence.

**pul•ley** (pŏŏl'ē) *n., pl.* **-leys.** A wheel with a grooved rim in which a pulled rope or chain is run, used esp. for lifting weight.

**pul•mo•nar•y** (pŏŏl'mə-nĕr'ē, pŭl'-) *adj.* Of the lungs.

**pulp** (pŭlp) *n.* **1.** A soft, moist mass. **2.** The soft, moist part of fruit, a tooth, etc. —**pulp'y** *adj.*

**pul•pit** (pŏŏl'pĭt, pŭl'-) *n.* An elevated platform used by a preacher.

**pulse** (pŭls) *n.* The throbbing of arteries produced by the regular contractions of the heart. —*v.* **pulsed, pulsing.** To throb. —**pul'sate'** *v.* —**pul•sa'tion** *n.*

**pul•ver•ize** (pŭl'və-rīz') *v.* **-ized, -izing.** To crush or grind to a powder.

**pump** (pŭmp) *n.* A device used to move something, as a liquid or gas, from 1 place or container to another. —*v.* To move with or as with a pump.

**pun** (pŭn) *n.* A play on words. —*v.* **punned, punning.** To make a pun.

**punch**[1] (pŭnch) *n.* A tool for piercing or stamping. —*v.* To perforate with a punch.

**punch**[2] (pŭnch) *v.* **1.** To hit, as with the fist. **2.** To herd (cattle). —*n.* A blow with the fist. —**punch'er** *n.*

**punc•til•i•ous** (pŭngk-tĭl'ē-əs) *adj.* Attentive to details of formal conduct. —**punc•til'i•ous•ly** *adv.*

**punc•tu•al** (pŭngk'chōō-əl) *adj.* Prompt. —**punc'tu•al'i•ty** *n.* —**punc'tu•al•ly** *adv.*

**punc•tu•ate** (pŭngk'chōō-āt') *v.* **-ated, -ating. 1.** To provide (a text) with periods, commas, etc., to clarify meaning. **2.** To interrupt periodically. —**punc'tu•a'tion** *n.*

**punc•ture** (pŭngk'chər) *v.* **-tured, -turing. 1.** To pierce. **2.** To deflate by or as by piercing. —*n.* **1.** An act of puncturing. **2.** A hole made by puncturing.

**pun•gent** (pŭn′jənt) *adj.* **1.** Sharp and acrid to taste or smell. **2.** Biting; caustic. —**pun′gen•cy** *n.* —**pun′gent•ly** *adv.*

**pun•ish** (pŭn′ĭsh) *v.* **1.** To subject to a penalty for an offense. **2.** To inflict a penalty for (an offense). **3.** To injure; hurt. —**pun′ish•a•ble** *adj.* —**pun′ish•ment** *n.* —**pu′ni•tive** *adj.*

**punt¹** (pŭnt) *n.* An open, flat-bottomed boat propelled by a long pole in shallow, slow waters. —**punt** *v.*

**punt²** (pŭnt) *n.* A kick in which a football is dropped from the hands and kicked before it hits the ground. —**punt** *v.*

**pu•ny** (pyo͞o′nē) *adj.* **-nier, -niest.** Weak. —**pu′ni•ly** *adv.* —**pu′ni•ness** *n.*

**pu•pil¹** (pyo͞o′pəl) *n.* A student.

**pu•pil²** (pyo͞o′pəl) *n.* The opening in the iris of the eye.

**pup•pet** (pŭp′ĭt) *n.* A small figure moved by strings or by hand.

**pur•chase** (pûr′chĭs) *v.* **-chased, -chasing.** To buy. —*n.* **1.** That which is bought. **2.** The act of buying. —**pur′chas•er** *n.*

**pure** (pyo͝or) *adj.* **purer, purest. 1.** Free from foreign elements, impurities, etc.; not mixed. **2.** Chaste. —**pure′ly** *adv.* —**pure′ness, pu′ri•ty** *n.* —**pu′ri•fi•ca′tion** *n.* —**pu′ri•fy′** *v.*

**purge** (pûrj) *v.* **purged, purging. 1.** To purify. **2.** To rid of sin. **3.** To rid (a nation, etc.) of persons considered undesirable. **4.** To cause evacuation of the bowels. —**pur•ga′tion** *n.* —**pur′ga•tive** *adj. & n.* —**purge** *n.*

**pu•ri•tan** (pyo͝or′ĭ-tn) *n.* One who advocates strict religious and moral discipline. —**pu′ri•tan′i•cal** *adj.* —**pu′ri•tan′i•cal•ly** *adv.*

**pur•ple** (pûr′pəl) *n.* A bluish-red color. —**pur′ple** *adj.* —**pur′plish** *adj.*

**pur•port** (pər-pôrt′, -pōrt′) *v.* **1.** To claim. **2.** To give the impression of being. —*n.* (pûr′pôrt′, -pōrt′). Meaning or significance. —**pur•port′ed•ly** *adv.*

**pur•pose** (pûr′pəs) *n.* **1.** The intended result; goal; aim. **2.** Determination; resolution. —*v.* **-posed, -posing.** To resolve or intend. —**pur′pose•ful** *adj.* —**pur′pose•ly** *adv.*

**purse** (pûrs) *n.* **1.** A small pouch for carrying money. **2.** A sum of money offered as a present or prize.

**pur•sue** (pər-so͞o′) *v.* **-sued, -suing. 1.** To follow in an effort to overtake. **2.** To engage in (a vocation, hobby, etc.). —**pur•su′ance** *n.* —**pur•su′er** *n.* —**pur•suit′** *n.*

**pur•vey** (pər-vā′, pûr′vā′) *v.* To supply or furnish. —**pur•vey′ance** *n.* —**pur•vey′or** *n.*

**pus** (pŭs) *n.* A yellowish-white fluid formed in infected tissue.

**push** (po͝osh) *v.* **1.** To exert force against (an object) to move it. **2.** To shove. —*n.* **1.** The act of pushing; a thrust. **2.** A vigorous effort. —**push′er** *n.*

**put** (po͝ot) *v.* **put, putting. 1.** To place; set. **2.** To assign; attribute. **3.** To impose or levy. **4.** To express or state. **5.** To apply.

**pu•ta•tive** (pyo͞o′tə-tĭv) *adj.* Generally regarded as such; supposed. —**pu′ta•tive•ly** *adv.*

**pu•tre•fy** (pyo͞o′trə-fī′) *v.* **-fied, -fying.** To decompose; decay. —**pu′tre•fac′tion** *n.* —**pu′trid** *adj.*

**put•ty** (pŭt′ē) *n.* **1.** A doughlike cement. **2.** A yellowish or light brownish gray. —**put′ty** *v.*

**puz•zle** (pŭz′əl) *v.* **-zled, -zling. 1.** To bewilder; perplex. **2.** To ponder over a problem. —*n.* **1.** A device that tests ingenuity. **2.** Perplexity; bewilderment. —**puz′zle•ment** *n.* —**puz′zler** *n.*

**pyg•my** (pĭg′mē) *n., pl.* **-mies.** Also **pig•my.** One of unusually small size. —*adj.* Unusually small.

**pyr•a•mid** (pîr′ə-mĭd) *n.* A solid figure with a polygonal base and triangular faces meeting in a common vertex. —*v.* To increase rapidly. —**py•ram′i•dal** *adj.*

**pyre** (pīr) *n.* A pile of wood, esp. for burning a corpse.

**py•ro•ma•ni•a** (pī′rō-mā′nē-ə, -mān′yə) *n.* The uncontrollable impulse to start fires. —**py′ro•ma′ni•ac′** *adj. & n.*

# — Q —

**q, Q** (kyo͞o) *n.* The 17th letter of the English alphabet.

**quack**[1] (kwăk) *n.* The sound of a duck. **—quack** *v.*

**quack**[2] (kwăk) *n.* One who pretends to have knowledge, esp. in medicine; charlatan. **—quack** *adj.* **—quack'er•y** *n.*

**quad•ran•gle** (kwŏd'răng'gəl) *n.* **1.** A plane figure with 4 sides and 4 angles. **2.** A courtyard bordered by buildings.

**quad•rant** (kwŏd'rənt) *n.* **1.** A quarter of a circle, an arc of 90°. **2.** An early instrument for measuring altitudes.

**quad•ri•lat•er•al** (kwŏd'rə-lăt'ər-əl) *n.* A 4-sided plane figure. *—adj.* Four-sided.

**qua•drille** (kwŏ-drĭl', kwə-, kə-) *n.* A square dance for 4 couples.

**quad•ru•ped** (kwŏd'rə-pĕd') *n.* A 4-footed animal.

**quad•ru•ple** (kwŏ-dro͞o'pəl, -drŭp'əl, kwŏd'-ro͞o-pəl) *adj.* **1.** Having 4 parts. **2.** Multiplied by 4. *—n.* A number 4 times as much as another. *—v.* **-pled, -pling.** To increase by 4 times.

**quaff** (kwŏf, kwăf, kwôf) *v.* To drink heartily. **—quaff** *n.* **—quaff'er** *n.*

**quag•mire** (kwăg'mīr', kwŏg'-) *n.* A bog with a soft, muddy surface.

**quail**[1] (kwāl) *n., pl.* **quail** or **quails.** A small, short-tailed chickenlike bird.

**quail**[2] (kwāl) *v.* To lose courage.

**quaint** (kwānt) *adj.* Agreeably odd. **—quaint'ly** *adv.* **—quaint'ness** *n.*

**quake** (kwāk) *v.* **quaked, quaking. 1.** To tremble. **2.** To shiver, as with emotion. *—n.* An earthquake.

**qual•i•fy** (kwŏl'ə-fī') *v.* **-fied, -fying. 1.** To describe. **2.** To be or make competent for a position, office, etc. **3.** To limit. **4.** To modify. **—qual'i•fi•ca'tion** *n.*

**qual•i•ty** (kwŏl'ĭ-tē) *n., pl.* **-ties. 1.** A characteristic; a property. **2.** The essential nature. **3.** Degree of excellence. **—qual'i•ta'tive** *adj.* **—qual'i•ta'tive•ly** *adv.*

**qualm** (kwäm, kwôm) *n.* **1.** A feeling of sickness. **2.** Doubt or misgiving.

**quan•da•ry** (kwŏn'də-rē, -drē) *n., pl.* **-ries.** A state of uncertainty or perplexity.

**quan•ti•fy** (kwŏn'tə-fī') *v.* **-fied, -fying.** To determine or express the quantity of. **—quan'ti•fi'a•ble** *adj.* **—quan'ti•fi•ca'tion** *n.*

**quan•ti•ty** (kwŏn'tĭ-tē) *n., pl.* **-ties. 1.** A number or amount. **2.** A considerable amount. **—quan'ti•ta'tive** *adj.* **—quan'ti•ta'tive•ly** *adv.*

**quan•tum** (kwŏn'təm) *n.* **1.** A quantity of something. **2.** A specified portion of something.

**quar•an•tine** (kwôr'ən-tēn', kwŏr'-) *n.* Isolation to prevent the spread of a disease. *—v.* **-tined, -tining.** To place in quarantine.

**quark** (kwôrk, kwärk) *n.* A subatomic particle.

**quar•rel** (kwôr'əl, kwŏr'-) *n.* An angry dispute. *—v.* To argue or disagree. **—quar'rel•some** *adj.*

**quar•ry** [1] (kwôr'ē, kwŏr'ē) *n., pl.* **-ries.** An object of pursuit.

**quar•ry** [2] (kwôr'ē, kwŏr'ē) *n., pl.* **-ries.** An open pit from which stone is obtained. *—v.* **-ried, -rying.** To dig from a quarry.

**quart** (kwôrt) *n.* A unit of liquid and dry measure equal to 2 pints.

**quar•ter** (kwôr'tər) *n.* **1.** One of 4 equal parts. **2.** A coin equal to ¼ of the dollar. **3.** Mercy. **4. quarters.** A place of residence. *—v.* To divide into 4 equal parts. *—adj.* Being 1 of 4 equal parts.

**quar•ter•ly** (kwôr'tər-lē) *adj.* **1.** Made up of 4 parts. **2.** Occurring at 3-month intervals. *—n., pl.* **-lies.** A quarterly publication. *—adv.* In or by quarters.

**quar•ter•mas•ter** (kwôr'tər-măs'tər) *n.* **1.** A military officer responsible for supplies. **2.** A naval officer responsible for navigation.

**quar•tet** (kwôr-tĕt') *n.* **1.** A group or set of 4, esp. of musicians. **2.** A musical composition for 4 instruments.

**quartz** (kwôrts) *n.* A hard, crystalline mineral found in granite or as pure crystals.

**qua•sar** (kwā'zär', -sär', -zər, -sər) *n.* A starlike celestial object that emits radio waves.

**quash**[1] (kwŏsh) *v.* To set aside or annul.

**quash**[2] (kwŏsh) *v.* To suppress completely.

**qua•si** (kwā'zī', -sī', kwä'zē, -sē) *adv.* To some degree; almost. *—adj.* Resembling.

**qua•ver** (kwā′vər) *v.* **1.** To tremble. **2.** To speak in a quivering voice. **—qua′ver** *n.*

**quea•sy** (kwē′zē) *adj.* **-sier, -siest. 1.** Nauseated. **2.** Uneasy. **—quea′si•ness** *n.*

**queen** (kwēn) *n.* **1.** A female monarch. **2.** The wife or widow of a king. **3.** A playing card bearing the figure of a queen. **4.** The fertile female of bees, ants, etc. **—queen′li•ness** *n.* **—queen′ly** *adj.*

**queer** (kwîr) *adj.* **1.** Strange; peculiar. **2.** Eccentric. **—queer′ly** *adv.*

**quell** (kwĕl) *v.* **1.** To put down forcibly. **2.** To pacify.

**quench** (kwĕnch) *v.* **1.** To put out; extinguish. **2.** To slake; satisfy.

**que•ry** (kwîr′ē) *n., pl.* **-ries.** A question. **—que′ry** *v.*

**quest** (kwĕst) *n.* A search.

**ques•tion** (kwĕs′chən) *n.* **1.** An expression of inquiry that invites a reply. **2.** A controversial subject. **3.** A difficult matter; problem. **4.** A proposal under discussion. **5.** Uncertainty; doubt. —*v.* **1.** To ask a question. **2.** To interrogate. **3.** To express doubt about.

**ques•tion•a•ble** (kwĕs′chə-nə-bəl) *adj.* **1.** Uncertain. **2.** Of dubious morality.

**ques•tion•naire** (kwĕs′chə-nâr′) *n.* A printed set of questions.

**queue** (kyōō) *n.* A line of people awaiting a turn. **—queue** *v.*

**quib•ble** (kwĭb′əl) *v.* **-bled, -bling.** To make petty distinctions or objections. **—quib′ble** *n.* **—quib′bler** *n.*

**quiche** (kēsh) *n.* A rich unsweetened custard, esp. one containing cheese, baked in a pastry shell.

**quick** (kwĭk) *adj.* **1.** Speedy. **2.** Prompt. **3.** Alert; keen. **4.** Hasty. **—quick** *adv.* **—quick′ly** *adv.* **—quick′ness** *n.*

**quick•en** (kwĭk′ən) *v.* **1.** To make or become more rapid; accelerate. **2.** To come to life. **3.** To excite and stimulate.

**quick•sand** (kwĭk′sănd′) *n.* A shifting mass of loose sand and water that yields easily to weight.

**quick•sil•ver** (kwĭk′sĭl′vər) *n.* The element mercury.

**quid•di•ty** (kwĭd′ĭ-tē) *n., pl.* **-ties. 1.** The real nature of a thing. **2.** A hairsplitting distinction.

**quid•nunc** (kwĭd′nŭngk′) *n.* A nosy person.

**quid pro quo** (kwĭd′ prō kwō′) *n.* An equal or fair exchange.

**qui•es•cent** (kwī-ĕs′ənt, kwē-) *adj.* Calm or still; inactive. **—qui•es′cence** *n.* **—qui•es′cent•ly** *adv.*

**qui•et** (kwī′ĭt) *adj.* **1.** Silent. **2.** Still. **3.** Untroubled; peaceful. **4.** Restrained. —*n.* Tranquillity; repose. —*v.* To become or cause to become quiet. **—qui′et•ly** *adv.* **—qui′et•ness** *n.* **—qui′e•tude′** *n.*

**quill** (kwĭl) *n.* **1.** A large, stiff feather. **2.** A sharp spine as of a porcupine.

**quilt** (kwĭlt) *n.* A padded bed covering.

**qui•nine** (kwī′nīn′) *n.* A bitter alkaloid used to treat malaria.

**quin•tes•sence** (kwĭn-tĕs′əns) *n.* The purest form or the essence of something.

**quin•tet** (kwĭn-tĕt′) *n.* **1.** A group or set of 5, esp. of musicians. **2.** A musical composition for 5 instruments.

**quin•tu•ple** (kwĭn-t/y/ōō′pəl, -tŭp′əl, kwĭn′tə-pəl) *adj.* **1.** Having 5 parts. **2.** Multiplied by 5. —*n.* A number 5 times as much as another. —*v.* **-pled, -pling.** To increase by 5 times.

**quip** (kwĭp) *n.* A witty or sarcastic remark. **—quip** *v.*

**quirk** (kwûrk) *n.* **1.** A sudden turn or twist. **2.** A peculiarity or eccentricity. **—quirk′i•ness** *n.*

**quis•ling** (kwĭz′lĭng) *n.* A traitor who serves as the puppet of the enemy occupying his or her country.

**quit** (kwĭt) *v.* **quit, quitting. 1.** To leave abruptly. **2.** To relinquish. **3.** To stop. **—quit•ter** *n.*

**quite** (kwīt) *adv.* **1.** Completely. **2.** Actually; really. **3.** Somewhat.

**quiv•er** (kwĭv′ər) *v.* To shake; tremble; vibrate. **—quiv′er** *n.*

**quiz** (kwĭz) *v.* **quizzed, quizzing. 1.** To question closely. **2.** To test by posing questions. —*n., pl.* **quizzes. 1.** A questioning. **2.** A short test. **—quiz′zer** *n.*

**quiz•zi•cal** (kwĭz′ĭ-kəl) *adj.* **1.** Puzzled. **2.** Comical; odd.

**quorum** (kwôr′əm, kwōr′-) *n.* The minimum number of members who must be present for the valid transaction of business.

**quota** (kwō′tə) *n.* **1. a.** An allotment. **b.** A production assignment. **2.** The maximum number of persons who may be admitted.

**quote** (kwōt) *v.* **quoted, quoting. 1.** To repeat the words of (another). **2.** To cite. **3.** To state (a price). **—quo•ta′tion** *n.* **—quote** *n.*

**quo•tient** (kwō′shənt) *n.* The quantity resulting from division of one quantity by another.

## — R —

**r, R** (är) *n.* The 18th letter of the English alphabet.

**rab•bi** (răb′ī) *n.* A Jewish spiritual leader. **—rab•bin′i•cal** *adj.* **—rab′bin•ate′** *n.*

**rab•ble** (răb′əl) *n.* A mob.

**rab•id** (răb′ĭd) *adj.* Fanatical. **—rab′id•ly** *adv.*

**race**[1] (rās) *n.* **1.** A distinct human population with a common origin. **2.** A distinct variety, esp. of plants or animals.

**race**[2] (rās) *n.* **1.** A contest of speed. **2.** A contest for supremacy. **3.** Steady onward movement. *—v.* **raced, racing. 1.** To compete in a race. **2.** To rush. **3.** To run an engine too swiftly. **—rac′er** *n.*

**ra•cial** (rā′shəl) *adj.* **1.** Relating to race. **2.** Arising from differences between races. **—ra′cial•ly** *adv.*

**rac•ism** (rā′sĭz′əm) *n.* **1.** Belief in the superiority of one's own race. **2.** Discrimination based on this belief. **—rac′ist** *n. & adj.*

**rack** (răk) *n.* **1.** A stand to hold various articles. **2.** A toothed bar that meshes with another toothed structure, such as a pinion or gearwheel. **3.** An instrument of torture. *—v.* **1.** To torture. **2.** To torment. **3.** To strain with great effort.

**rack•et**[1] (răk′ĭt) *n.* Also **rac•quet.** A light bat with a netted hoop, used in games.

**rack•et**[2] (răk′ĭt) *n.* **1.** An uproar; noise. **2.** An illegal or dishonest business. **—rack′et•eer′** *n.*

**ra•dar** (rā′där) *n.* A method of detecting distant objects by reflecting radio waves off their surfaces.

**ra•di•ate** (rā′dē-āt′) *v.* **-ated, -ating. 1.** To emit (heat, light, atomic particles, etc.), esp. in the form of rays. **2.** To glow or beam. **3.** To spread out from a center. **—ra′di•ance** *n.* **—ra′di•ant** *adj.* **—ra′di•a′tion** *n.* **—ra′di•a′tor** *n.*

**rad•i•cal** (răd′ĭ-kəl) *adj.* **1.** Going to the root or source; fundamental; drastic. **2.** Favoring revolutionary changes. *—n.* **1.** One who advocates political or social revolution. **2.** A group of atoms that is only stable as part of a compound. **—rad′i•cal•ism′** *n.* **—rad′i•cal•ly** *adv.*

**ra•di•i** (rā′dē-ī′) *n.* pl. of **radius.**

**ra•di•o** (rā′dē-ō) *n., pl.* **-os. 1.** The use of electromagnetic waves to transmit electric signals without wires. **2.** The equipment used for transmitting or receiving radio signals. **—ra′di•o** *v.*

**ra•di•o•ac•tiv•i•ty** (rā′dē-ō-ăk-tĭv′ĭ-tē) *n.* **1.** The process or property by which atomic nuclei emit radiation. **2.** The radiation released. **—ra′di•o•ac′tive** *adj.*

**ra•di•ol•o•gy** (rā′dē-ŏl′ə-jē) *n.* The medical use of radiation, esp. of x-rays. **—ra′di•ol′o•gist** *n.*

**ra•di•um** (rā′dē-əm) *n.* A rare, highly radioactive metallic element.

**ra•di•us** (rā′dē-əs) *n., pl.* **-dii** or **-diuses.** A straight line from the center of a circle to the circumference. **—ra′di•al** *adj.*

**raf•fle** (răf′əl) *n.* A lottery in which people buy chances on a prize. **—raf′fle** *v.*

**raft** (răft) *n.* A flat, floating structure of planks, logs, etc.

**raft•er** (răf′tər) *n.* A sloping beam that supports a roof.

**rag** (răg) *n.* A scrap of cloth. **—rag′ged** *adj.* **—rag′ged•ness** *n.*

**rage** (rāj) *n.* **1.** Violent anger. **2.** A fad. *—v.* **raged, raging. 1.** To show violent anger. **2.** To continue with great violence. **3.** To spread unchecked.

**raid** (rād) *n.* A surprise attack. **—raid** *v.* **—raid′er** *n.*

**rail** (rāl) *n.* **1.** A horizontal bar supported by vertical posts. **2.** A banister, fence, etc., made of rails. **3.** A bar used as a track for railroad cars. **4.** The railroad.

**rail•road** (rāl′rōd′) *n.* **1.** A road made of parallel steel rails, providing a track for trains. **2.** A system of transportation using tracks, stations, trains, etc.

**rain** (rān) *n.* **1.** Condensed atmospheric vapor falling to earth in drops. **2.** Rainy weather. —*v.* To fall or release as rain. —**rain′fall′** *n.* —**rain′y** *adj.*

**rain•bow** (rān′bō′) *n.* An arc-shaped spectrum of colors seen in the sky, caused by sunlight refracted by rain drops.

**raise** (rāz) *v.* **raised, raising. 1.** To elevate; lift. **2.** To make erect. **3.** To build. **4.** To cause to appear. **5.** To increase in amount, worth, degree, etc. **6.** To breed or rear. **7.** To collect. **8.** To cause (dough) to puff up. —*n.* **1.** An act of raising or increasing. **2.** An increase in salary.

**rai•sin** (rā′zĭn) *n.* A sweet, sun-dried grape.

**rake** (rāk) *n.* A long-handled implement with teeth, used to gather leaves and grass. —**rake** *v.*

**ral•ly** (răl′ē) *v.* **-lied, -lying. 1.** To call or join together. **2.** To reassemble. **3.** To recover (one's strength). —*n., pl.* **-lies. 1.** A mass assembly. **2.** A renewal of strength.

**ram** (răm) *n.* **1.** A male sheep. **2.** A device used to batter or crush. —*v.* **rammed, ramming. 1.** To crash or smash into. **2.** To cram; stuff.

**ram•ble** (răm′bəl) *v.* **-bled, -bling. 1.** To wander aimlessly; stroll or roam. **2.** To follow a winding course. **3.** To speak or write with many digressions. —*n.* A leisurely stroll. —**ram′bler** *n.*

**ram•i•fi•ca•tion** (răm′ə-fĭ-kā′shən) *n.* **1.** A branching out or dividing into branches. **2.** A complicating outcome of a problem, plan, or statement. —**ram′i•fy** *v.*

**ramp** (rămp) *n.* A sloping passage connecting different levels.

**ram•page** (răm′pāj′) *n.* Violent, frenzied behavior. —*v.* (răm-pāj′) **-paged, -paging.** To move about ferociously.

**ran** (răn) *v.* p.t. of **run.**

**ranch** (rănch) *n.* A large farm for raising cattle, etc. —*v.* To work on a ranch. —**ranch′er** *n.*

**ran•cid** (răn′sĭd) *adj.* Having the disagreeable odor or taste of spoiled fats and oils.

**ran•cor** (răng′kər) *n.* Bitter resentment. —**ran′cor•ous** *adj.*

**ran•dom** (răn′dəm) *adj.* Having no pattern or objective; haphazard. —**ran′dom•ly** *adv.* —**ran′dom•ness** *n.*

**rang** (răng) *v.* p.t. of **ring.**

**range** (rānj) *n.* **1.** The extent of perception, knowledge, experience, or ability. **2.** The extent of variation. **3.** Open grazing land. **4.** A series of mountains. **5.** A stove. —*v.* **ranged, ranging. 1.** To arrange in order, esp. in rows. **2.** To classify. **3.** To roam freely. **4.** To vary. —**rang′er** *n.*

**rank** (răngk) *n.* **1.** Relative standing in a group. **2.** Official or eminent position. **3.** A row, line, or series. —*v.* **1.** To place in or form a row. **2.** To hold a particular rank.

**ran•kle** (răng′kəl) *v.* **-kled, -kling.** To irritate or cause resentment; embitter.

**ran•sack** (răn′săk′) *v.* **1.** To search thoroughly. **2.** To pillage.

**ran•som** (răn′səm) *n.* **1.** The release of a person in return for payment. **2.** The price demanded or paid. —**ran′som** *v.*

**rant** (rănt) *v.* **ranted, ranting.** To speak or exclaim violently or extravagantly. —**rant** *n.*

**rap** (răp) *v.* **rapped, rapping. 1.** To strike quickly and lightly. **2.** To talk. —*n.* **1.** A knock. **2.** A criticism. **3.** A talk.

**rape** (rāp) *n.* The crime of forcing a person to submit to sexual intercourse. —**rape** *v.* —**rap′ist** *n.*

**rap•id** (răp′ĭd) *adj.* Very fast; swift. —*n.* Often **rapids.** A fast-moving part of a river. —**ra•pid′i•ty** *n.* —**rap′id•ly** *adv.*

**rap•port** (ră-pôr′, -pōr′, rə-) *n.* A relationship of mutual trust or emotional affinity.

**rapt** (răpt) *adj.* Absorbed; engrossed.

**rap•ture** (răp′chər) *n.* Ecstasy. —**rap′tur•ous** *adj.*

**rare** (râr) *adj.* **rarer, rarest. 1.** Unusual. **2.** Special. **3.** Cooked a short time. —**rare′ly** *adv.* —**rare′ness, rar′i•ty** *n.*

**ras•cal** (răs′kəl) *n.* **1.** A dishonest person. **2.** A mischievous person. —**ras′cal•ly** *adj.*

**rash**[1] (răsh) *adj.* Too bold or hasty; reckless. —**rash′ly** *adv.* —**rash′ness** *n.*

**rash**[2] (răsh) *n.* A skin eruption.

**rasp** (răsp) *v.* **1.** To file or scrape with a coarse file. **2.** To speak in a grating voice. **3.** To grate upon; irritate. —**rasp** *n.* —**rasp′ing•ly** *adv.* —**rasp′y** *adj.*

**rat** (răt) *n.* A long-tailed rodent larger than a mouse.

**ratch•et** (răch'ĭt) *n.* A mechanism having a hinged catch that engages a wheel with sloping teeth, permitting motion in 1 direction only.

**rate** (rāt) *n.* **1.** A measure of a part to a whole; proportion. **2. a.** A payment. **b.** A cost per unit. **3.** Level of quality. —*v.* **rated, rating. 1.** To calculate the value of. **2.** To classify or be classified.

**rath•er** (răth'ər, rä'thər) *adv.* **1.** Preferably. **2.** Somewhat. **3.** On the contrary.

**rat•i•fy** (răt'ə-fī') *v.* **-fied, -fying.** To give formal sanction to. **—rat'i•fi•ca'tion** *n.*

**ra•tio** (rā'shō, rā'shē-ō') *n., pl.* **-tios.** Proportion; rate.

**ra•tion** (răsh'ən, rā'shən) *n.* A fixed portion or allowance. —*v.* **1.** To supply with. **2.** To restrict or limit.

**ra•tion•al** (răsh'ə-nəl) *adj.* **1.** Having or using the ability to reason. **2.** Based upon reason; logical. **—ra'tion•al'i•ty** *n.* **—ra'tion•al•ly** *adv.*

**rat•tle** (răt'l) *v.* **-tled, -tling. 1.** To make a succession of short, sharp sounds. **2.** To fluster. —*n.* **1.** Short, rapid sounds. **2.** A baby's toy.

**rau•cous** (rô'kəs) *adj.* Rough-sounding; harsh. **—rau'cous•ly** *adv.* **—rau'cous•ness** *n.*

**rav•age** (răv'ĭj) *v.* **-aged, -aging.** To destroy or devastate. —*n.* Heavy destruction. **—rav'ag•er** *n.*

**rave** (rāv) *v.* **raved, raving. 1.** To speak wildly or incoherently. **2.** To speak about enthusiastically. —*n.* An enthusiastic review; praise.

**rav•el** (răv'əl) *v.* To separate the threads of (cloth); fray.

**ra•ven** (rā'vən) *n.* A large crowlike bird. —*adj.* Black and shiny.

**rav•en•ous** (răv'ə-nəs) *adj.* Extremely hungry. **—rav'en•ous•ly** *adv.*

**ra•vine** (rə-vēn') *n.* A deep, narrow gorge.

**rav•ish** (răv'ĭsh) *v.* **1.** To rape. **2.** To enrapture or entrance. **—rav'ish•ing** *adj.*

**raw** (rô) *adj.* **1.** Uncooked. **2.** In a natural condition. **3.** Untrained. **4.** Cold and damp. **5.** Sore; inflamed. **—raw'ness** *n.*

**ray** (rā) *n.* **1.** A narrow beam of light. **2.** A trace; hint. **3.** A line or part extending from a point.

**raze** (rāz) *v.* **razed, razing.** To tear down or demolish.

**ra•zor** (rā'zər) *n.* A sharp-edged instrument for shaving.

**reach** (rēch) *v.* **1.** To extend. **2.** To touch or take hold of, esp. with the hand. **3.** To arrive at. **4.** To amount to; achieve. —*n.* **1.** The act of stretching out a bodily part. **2.** The extent something can reach.

**re•act** (rē-ăkt') *v.* **1.** To act in response to. **2.** To be affected by circumstances. **—re•ac'tion** *n.*

**read** (rēd) *v.* **read** (rĕd), **reading. 1.** To comprehend the meaning of (something written). **2.** To utter aloud (something written). **3.** To learn by reading. **4.** To indicate or register. **—read'a•bil'i•ty** *n.* **—read'a•ble** *adj.* **—read'er** *n.*

**read•y** (rĕd'ē) *adj.* **-ier, -iest. 1.** Prepared or available. **2.** Willing. **—read'i•ly** *adv.* **—read'i•ness** *n.*

**re•al** (rē'əl, rēl) *adj.* **1.** Existing in fact or actuality. **2.** Genuine; authentic. —*adv.* Very. **—real'ly** *adv.*

**real estate.** Land and anything on it, as natural resources, buildings, etc.

**re•al•i•ty** (rē-ăl'ĭ-tē) *n., pl.* **-ties. 1.** The quality or state of being real; actual existence. **2.** The totality of things that actually exist. **—re'al•ism'** *n.* **—re'al•ist** *n.* **—re'al•is'tic** *adj.* **—re'al•is'ti•cal•ly** *adv.*

**re•al•ize** (rē'ə-līz') *v.* **-ized, -izing. 1.** To comprehend completely; grasp. **2.** To make real; achieve. **3.** To obtain as profit. **—re'al•iz'a•ble** *adj.* **—re'al•i•za'tion** *n.*

**re•al•ty** (rē'əl-tē) *n.* Real estate.

**realm** (rĕlm) *n.* **1.** A kingdom. **2.** A field of interest or expertise.

**ream** (rēm) *n.* **1.** A quantity of paper. **2.** Often **reams.** Very much.

**ream•er** (rē'mər) *n.* **1.** A tool used to shape or enlarge a hole. **2.** A conically shaped utensil for extracting juice from citrus fruit. **—ream** *v.*

**reap** (rēp) *v.* To harvest by cutting. **—reap'er** *n.*

**rear**[1] (rîr) *n.* The back part. —*adj.* Of or at the rear.

**rear**[2] (rîr) *v.* **1.** To care for during youth; bring up. **2.** To build. **3.** To rise on the hind legs, as a horse.

**rea•son** (rē'zən) *n.* **1.** The cause or motive for an action, decision, or conviction. **2.** The capacity for rational thinking. —*v.* **1.** To think or argue logically. **2.** To reach a conclusion by logical thinking. **—rea'son•a•ble** *adj.* **—rea'son•a•bly** *adv.*

**re•bate** (rē'bāt') *n.* A return of part of an amount paid. **—re'bate'** *v.*

**re•bel** (rĭ-bĕl') *v.* **-belled, -belling. 1.** To engage in armed revolt against a government. **2.** To defy any authority. —*n.* **reb•el** (rĕb'əl). One who rebels. —*adj.* Of rebels. **—re•bel'lion** *n.* **—re•bel'lious** *adj.*

**re•buff** (rĭ-bŭf') *n.* A blunt repulse or refusal. —*v.* **1.** To refuse bluntly. **2.** To drive back; repel.

**re•buke** (rĭ-byo͞ok') *v.* **-buked, -buking.** To criticize sharply; scold. **—re•buke'** *n.*

**re•but** (rĭ-bŭt') *v.* **-butted, -butting.** To present an opposing argument; refute. **—re•but'tal** *n.*

**re•call** (rĭ-kôl') *v.* **1.** To call back. **2.** To remember or recollect. **3.** To cancel; take back. **—re•call'** *n.*

**re•ca•pit•u•late** (rē'kə-pĭch'ə-lāt') *v.* **-lated, -lating.** To review; summarize. **—re'ca•pit'u•la'tion** *n.*

**re•cede** (rĭ-sēd') *v.* **-ceded, -ceding. 1.** To move back; ebb. **2.** To slope backward.

**re•ceipt** (rĭ-sēt') *n.* **1.** Often **receipts.** The amount of something received. **2.** A written acknowledgment that something has been received.

**re•ceive** (rĭ-sēv') *v.* **-ceived, -ceiving. 1.** To take or acquire. **2.** To experience. **3.** To admit or welcome. **4.** To accept electromagnetic signals, as in radio, telegraphy, etc. **—re•ceiv'er** *n.* **—re•cep'tion** *n.* **—re•cep'tive** *adj.* **—re•cip'i•ent** *n.*

**re•cent** (rē'sənt) *adj.* Of a time immediately prior to the present. **—re'cent•ly** *adv.*

**re•cep•ta•cle** (rĭ-sĕp'tə-kəl) *n.* A container.

**re•cess** (rē'sĕs', rĭ-sĕs') *n.* **1.** A temporary halt of activities. **2.** A small hollow. —*v.* **1.** To make a recess in. **2.** To suspend for recess.

**re•ces•sion** (rĭ-sĕsh'ən) *n.* A temporary economic decline.

**re•cid•i•vism** (rĭ-sĭd'ə-vĭz'əm) *n.* The return to a former pattern of behavior, esp. criminal behavior. **—re•cid'i•vist** *n.* **—re•cid'i•vis'tic** *adj.*

**rec•i•pe** (rĕs'ə-pē') *n.* A set of directions for making something, esp. food.

**re•cip•ro•cate** (rĭ-sĭp'rə-kāt') *v.* **-cated, -cating. 1.** To give or take mutually or in response. **2.** To show or feel in response. **—re•cip'ro•cal** *adj.* **—re•cip'ro•ca'tion** *n.* **—rec'i•proc'i•ty** *n.*

**re•cite** (rĭ-sīt') *v.* **-cited, -citing. 1.** To repeat aloud something memorized. **2.** To enumerate. **—rec'i•ta'tion** *n.*

**reck•less** (rĕk'lĭs) *adj.* Without care or caution; rash. **—reck'less•ly** *adv.* **—reck'less•ness** *n.*

**reck•on** (rĕk'ən) *v.* **1.** To count or compute. **2.** To consider. **—reck'on•ing** *n.*

**re•cline** (rĭ-klīn') *v.* **-clined, -clining.** To sit or lean back; lie down. **—re•clin'er** *n.*

**re•cluse** (rĕk'lo͞os', rĭ-klo͞os') *n.* One who withdraws from the world to live in solitude. **—re•clu'sive** *adj.*

**rec•og•nize** (rĕk'əg-nīz') *v.* **-nized, -nizing. 1.** To identify or perceive from past experience. **2.** To admit the acquaintance of; greet. **3.** To acknowledge. **—rec'og•ni'tion** *n.* **—rec'og•niz'a•ble** *adj.* **—rec'og•niz'a•bly** *adv.*

**re•coil** (rĭ-koil') *v.* **1.** To spring back. **2.** To shrink back in fear or disgust. **—re'coil'** *n.*

**rec•ol•lect** (rĕk'ə-lĕkt') *v.* To remember. **—rec'ol•lec'tion** *n.*

**rec•om•mend** (rĕk'ə-mĕnd') *v.* **1.** To commend as worthy or desirable. **2.** To advise. **—rec'om•men•da'tion** *n.*

**rec•om•pense** (rĕk'əm-pĕns') *n.* **1.** Amends made for damage or loss. **2.** Compensation for something given or done. **—rec'om•pense'** *v.*

**rec•on•cile** (rĕk'ən-sīl') *v.* **-ciled, -ciling. 1.** To reestablish friendship between. **2.** To settle, as a dispute. **3.** To be or make resigned to. **4.** To make compatible. **—rec'on•cil'a•ble** *adj.* **—rec'on•cil'i•a'tion** *n.*

**rec•on•dite** (rĕk'ən-dīt', rĭ-kŏn'dīt') *adj.* **1.** Not easily understood; abstruse. **2.** Concealed; hidden.

**re•con•nais•sance** (rĭ-kŏn'ə-səns, -zəns) *n.* An information-gathering exploration of an area, esp. for military purposes.

**rec•ord** (rĕk′ərd) *n.* **1.** A written account; document. **2.** The best performance known. **3.** A disk coded to reproduce sound. —*v.* **re•cord** (rĭ-kôrd′). **1.** To write down for preservation. **2.** To register (sound) in permanent form on a record or a tape. **—re•cord′er** *n.*

**re•count** (rĭ-kount′) *v.* To narrate; relate.

**re•coup** (rĭ-ko͞op′) *v.* **-couped, -couping. 1.** To make up for; reimburse. **2.** To regain a former favorable position.

**re•course** (rē′kôrs′, -kōrs′, rĭ-kôrs′, -kōrs′) *n.* A turning to or request for aid.

**re•cov•er** (rĭ-kŭv′ər) *v.* **1.** To get back. **2.** To regain health. **—re•cov′er•a•ble** *adj.* **—re•cov′er•y** *n.*

**rec•re•a•tion** (rĕk′rē-ā′shən) *n.* Refreshment through diverting activity; play. **—rec′re•a′tion•al** *adj.*

**re•crim•i•nate** (rĭ-krĭm′ə-nāt′) *v.* **-nated, -nating.** To counter one accusation with another. **—re•crim′i•na′tion** *n.* **—re•crim′i•na•to′ry** *adj.*

**re•cruit** (rĭ-kro͞ot′) *v.* To engage or enlist as a soldier or supporter. —*n.* A new member of a military force or an organization. **—re•cruit′er** *n.* **—re•cruit′ment** *n.*

**rec•tan•gle** (rĕk′tăng′gəl) *n.* A parallelogram with a right angle. **—rec•tan′gu•lar** *adj.*

**rec•ti•fy** (rĕk′tə-fī′) *v.* **-fied, -fying.** To set right; correct. **—rec′ti•fi•ca′tion** *n.*

**rec•tor** (rĕk′tər) *n.* **1.** A cleric in charge of a parish. **2.** The principal of certain schools, esp. religious institutions. **—rec′to•ry** *n.*

**rec•tum** (rĕk′təm) *n.* The lower end of the large intestine. **—rec′tal** *adj.*

**re•cum•bent** (rĭ-kŭm′bənt) *adj.* **1.** Lying down; reclining. **2.** Resting; idle. **—re•cum′ben•cy** *n.*

**re•cu•per•ate** (rĭ-k/y/o͞o′pə-rāt′) *v.* **-ated, -ating.** To regain health; recover. **—re•cu′per•a′tion** *n.*

**re•cur** (rĭ-kûr′) *v.* **-curred, -curring.** To happen again. **—re•cur′rent** *adj.* **—re•cur′rent•ly** *adv.*

**re•cy•cle** (rē-sī′kəl) *v.* **-cycled, -cycling. 1.** To put or pass through a cycle again. **2.** To reprocess for use again.

**red** (rĕd) *n.* A color like blood. —*adj.* **redder, reddest. 1.** Having such a color. **2.** Ruddy; flushed. **—red′den** *v.* **—red′dish** *adj.* **—red′ness** *n.*

**re•deem** (rĭ-dēm′) *v.* **1.** To recover ownership of by paying a sum. **2.** To pay off. **3.** To fulfill. **4.** To make amends for. **5.** To save from sin. **—re•deem′a•ble** *adj.* **—re•deem′er** *n.* **—re•demp′tion** *n.*

**red•o•lent** (rĕd′l-ənt) *adj.* **1.** Emitting fragrance; aromatic. **2.** Suggestive; reminiscent.

**re•doubt•a•ble** (rĭ-dou′tə-bəl) *adj.* **1.** Arousing fear or awe. **2.** Worthy of respect or honor. **—re•doubt′a•bly** *adv.*

**re•duce** (rĭ-d/y/o͞os′) *v.* **-duced, -ducing. 1.** To lessen in extent, amount, etc.; diminish. **2.** To break down into basic components. **3.** To bring into a given condition or state. **4.** To lose weight. **—re•duc′i•ble** *adj.* **—re•duc′tion** *n.*

**re•dun•dant** (rĭ-dŭn′dənt) *adj.* **1.** Superfluous. **2.** Repetitive. **—re•dun′dan•cy** *n.*

**reed** (rēd) *n.* **1.** A tall, hollow-stemmed marsh grass. **2.** A vibrating strip in certain musical instruments.

**reef** (rēf) *n.* A ridge of rock, sand, or coral near the surface of water.

**reek** (rēk) *v.* To give off a strong or unpleasant odor.

**reel**[1] (rēl) *n.* A spool or frame that turns on an axis, used for winding rope, fishing line, etc. **—reel** *v.*

**reel**[2] (rēl) *v.* To stagger, lurch, or sway.

**re•fer** (rĭ-fûr′) *v.* **-ferred, -ferring. 1.** To direct to a source for help or information. **2.** To attribute to. **3.** To submit to an authority for decision. **4.** To direct the attention of. **5.** To allude. **—ref′er•ence** *n.* **—re•fer′ral** *n.*

**ref•e•ree** (rĕf′ə-rē′) *n.* **1.** One to whom something is referred; an arbitrator. **2.** An umpire. **—ref′e•ree′** *v.*

**re•fine** (rĭ-fīn′) *v.* **-fined, -fining. 1.** To purify, as sugar, petroleum, ore, etc. **2.** To make or become polished, cultured, etc. **3.** To improve. **—re•fine′ment** *n.* **—re•fin′er•y** *n.*

**re•flect** (rĭ-flĕkt′) *v.* **1.** To throw back (heat, light, or sound). **2.** To mirror. **3.** To think seriously. **4.** To bring blame or reproach, esp. as a result of one's actions. **—re•flec′tion** *n.* **—re•flec′tive** *adj.*

**re•flex** (rē′flĕks′) *adj.* Designating an involuntary action or response. —*n.* An involuntary response to a stimulus.

**re•flex•ive** (rĭ-flĕk′sĭv) *adj.* Designating a verb having an identical subject and direct object. **—re•flex′ive** *n.*

**re•form** (rĭ-fôrm′) *v.* **1.** To improve. **2.** To abolish abuses in. —*n.* A change for the better. **—ref′or•ma′tion** *n.* **—re•form′er** *n.*

**re•fract** (rĭ-frăkt′) *v.* To deflect heat, light, or sound waves at the boundary between two mediums. **—re•frac′tion** *n.* **—re•frac′tive** *adj.*

**re•frain**[1] (rĭ-frān′) *v.* To hold oneself back.

**re•frain**[2] (rĭ-frān′) *n.* A recurrent verse in a song or poem.

**re•fresh** (rĭ-frĕsh′) *v.* **1.** To revive, as with food, drink, etc. **2.** To renew by stimulation. **—re•fresh′er** *n.* **—re•fresh′ing** *adj.* **—re•fresh′ment** *n.*

**re•frig•er•ate** (rĭ-frĭj′ə-rāt′) *v.* **-ated, -ating.** To cool or freeze. **—re•frig′er•a′tion** *n.* **—re•frig′er•a′tor** *n.*

**ref•uge** (rĕf′yo͞oj) *n.* **1.** Protection or shelter; sanctuary. **2.** Anything to which one may turn for help. **—ref′u•gee′** *n.*

**re•fund** (rĭ-fŭnd′, rē′fŭnd′) *v.* To return or repay. —*n.* (rē′fŭnd′). A repayment of funds.

**re•fur•bish** (rē-fûr′bĭsh) *v.* To make clean, bright, or fresh again. **—re•fur′bish•ment** *n.*

**re•fuse**[1] (rĭ-fyo͞oz′) *v.* **-fused, -fusing.** To decline to do, accept, give, or allow. **—re•fus′al** *n.*

**re•fuse**[2] (rĕf′yo͞os) *n.* Trash; rubbish.

**re•fute** (rĭ-fyo͞ot′) *v.* **-futed, -futing.** To prove false; disprove. **—ref′u•ta′tion** *n.*

**re•gain** (rē-gān′) *v.* **1.** To recover possession of. **2.** To reach again.

**re•gal** (rē′gəl) *adj.* Royal. **—re′gal•ly** *adv.*

**re•gale** (rĭ-gāl′) *v.* **-galed, -galing. 1.** To delight. **2.** To entertain sumptuously.

**re•gard** (rĭ-gärd′) *v.* **1.** To observe closely. **2.** To consider in a particular way. **3.** To love or admire. **4.** To concern or refer to. **5.** To take into account. —*n.* **1.** Attention; concern. **2.** Respect or affection. **3. regards.** Good wishes. **4.** Reference.

**re•gard•less** (rĭ-gärd′lĭs) *adv.* In spite of everything; anyway.

**re•gime** (rā-zhēm′, rĭ-) *n.* A system of management of government.

**reg•i•men** (rĕj′ə-mən, -mĕn′) *n.* **1.** The systematic course of a natural process. **2.** A system, as of therapy or diet.

**reg•i•ment** (rĕj′ə-mənt) *n.* An infantry unit. —*v.* (rĕj′ə-mĕnt′). **1.** To systematize. **2.** To force uniformity and discipline upon. **—reg′i•men′tal** *adj.* **—reg′i•men•ta′tion** *n.*

**re•gion** (rē′jən) *n.* An area; district. **—re′gion•al** *adj.* **—re′gion•al•ly** *adv.*

**reg•is•ter** (rĕj′ĭ-stər) *n.* **1.** A formal record or list. **2.** A device to regulate the flow of heated or cooled air into a room. **3.** The range of a voice or instrument. —*v.* **1.** To enter in a register. **2.** To indicate. **3.** To have one's name placed on a voting list. **—reg′is•trar′** *n.* **—reg′is•tra′tion** *n.* **—reg′is•try** *n.*

**re•gress** (rĭ-grĕs′) *v.* To go backward to a previous condition. **—re•gres′sive** *adj.* **—re•gres′sion** *n.*

**re•gret** (rĭ-grĕt′) *v.* **-gretted, -gretting. 1.** To feel sorry or disappointed about. **2.** To mourn. —*n.* **1.** An expression of grief or disappointment. **2. regrets.** A courteous declining to accept an invitation. **—re•gret′ful** *adj.* **—re•gret′ful•ly** *adv.* **—re•gret′ta•ble** *adj.* **—re•gret′ta•bly** *adv.*

**reg•u•lar** (rĕg′yə-lər) *adj.* **1.** Customary or normal. **2.** Symmetrical. **3.** Conforming to set procedure or principle. **4.** Orderly. **5.** Occurring at fixed intervals; periodic. **6.** Of the permanent army of a nation. —*n.* A soldier in the permanent army. **—reg′u•lar′i•ty** *n.* **—reg′u•lar•ly** *adv.*

**reg•u•late** (rĕg′yə-lāt′) *v.* **-lated, -lating. 1.** To control according to a rule. **2.** To adjust. **—reg′u•la′tion** *n.* **—reg′u•la•to′ry** *adj.* **—reg′u•la′tor** *n.*

**re•ha•bil•i•tate** (rē′hə-bĭl′ĭ-tāt′) *v.* **-tated, -tating. 1.** To restore to good condition. **2.** To reinstate. **—re′ha•bil′i•ta′tion** *n.* **—re′ha•bil′i•ta′tive** *adj.*

**re•hash** (rē-hăsh′) *v.* To go over a subject again; repeat old material.

**re•hearse** (rĭ-hûrs′) *v.* **-hearsed, -hearsing.** To practice in preparation for a performance. **—re•hears′al** *n.*

**reign** (rān) *n.* **1.** The exercise of sovereign power. **2.** The term of a sovereign's rule. —*v.* To rule with sovereign power.

**re•im•burse** (rē'ĭm-bûrs') *v.* **-bursed, -bursing. 1.** To repay. **2.** To compensate, as for money spent. **—re'im•burse'ment** *n.*

**rein** (rān) *n.* **1.** Often **reins.** Two narrow straps attached to a bridle and used to control a horse. **2.** Any means of restraint. —*v.* To check or hold back.

**re•in•force** (rē'ĭn-fôrs', -fōrs') *v.* **-forced, -forcing.** To strengthen; support. **—re'in•force'ment** *n.*

**re•in•state** (rē'ĭn-stāt') *v.* **-stated, -stating.** To restore to a previous position. **—re'in•state'ment** *n.*

**re•it•er•ate** (rē-ĭt'ə-rāt') *v.* **-ated, -ating.** To say over again. **—re•it'er•a'tion** *n.*

**re•ject** (rĭ-jĕkt') *v.* **1.** To refuse; repudiate. **2.** To refuse to grant; deny. **3.** To discard; throw away. —*n.* (rē'jĕkt). Something rejected. **—re•jec'tion** *n.*

**re•joice** (rĭ-jois') *v.* **-joiced, -joicing.** To feel or fill with joy.

**re•join** (rĭ-join') *v.* To say as a reply; respond. **—re•join'der** *n.*

**re•lapse** (rĭ-lăps') *v.* **-lapsed, -lapsing.** To return to a former state, esp. illness. —*n.* (rē'lăps, rĭ-lăps'). The act of relapsing.

**re•late** (rĭ-lāt') *v.* **-lated, -lating. 1.** To tell. **2.** To have reference to. **3.** To be connected by kinship. **—re•la'tion** *n.* **—re•la'tion•al** *adj.* **—re•la'tion•ship'** *n.*

**rel•a•tive** (rĕl'ə-tĭv) *adj.* **1.** Considered in comparison to something else. **2.** Dependent upon something else for significance. —*n.* One related by kinship. **—rel'a•tive•ly** *adv.* **—rel'a•tiv'i•ty** *n.*

**re•lax** (rĭ-lăks') *v.* **1.** To make or become loose. **2.** To relieve from strain. **3.** To rest. **—re'lax•a'tion** *n.*

**re•lay** (rē'lā) *n.* A fresh group, as of workers, to relieve others. —*v.* (rē'lā, rĭ-lā'). To pass or send along from one group to another.

**re•lease** (rĭ-lēs') *v.* **-leased, -leasing. 1.** To set free; liberate. **2.** To unfasten. —*n.* **1.** The act of releasing or state of being released. **2.** A device releasing a mechanism.

**rel•e•gate** (rĕl'ĭ-gāt') *v.* **-gated, -gating. 1.** To consign to a lower position, etc. **2.** To assign to a particular category. **—rel'e•ga'tion** *n.*

**re•lent** (rĭ-lĕnt') *v.* To become gentler in attitude; abate. **—re•lent'less** *adj.* **—re•lent'less•ly** *adv.* **—re•lent'less•ness** *n.*

**rel•e•vant** (rĕl'ə-vənt) *adj.* Pertinent. **—rel'e•vance, rel'e•van•cy** *n.*

**rel•ic** (rĕl'ĭk) *n.* **1.** Something that has survived deterioration. **2.** A remnant belief or custom from an earlier culture. **3.** A keepsake. **4.** An object of religious veneration.

**re•lieve** (rĭ-lēv') *v.* **-lieved, -lieving. 1.** To alleviate; ease. **2.** To free from pain, anxiety, etc. **3.** To aid. **4.** To free from duty by providing a substitute. **5.** To make less monotonous. **—re•lief'** *n.*

**re•lig•ion** (rĭ-lĭj'ən) *n.* An organized system of beliefs and rituals centering on a supernatural being or beings. **—re•lig'ious** *adj.*

**re•lin•quish** (rĭ-lĭng'kwĭsh) *v.* **1.** To let go. **2.** To surrender; renounce.

**rel•ish** (rĕl'ĭsh) *n.* **1.** An appetite for something. **2.** A spicy condiment. —*v.* To take pleasure in.

**re•luc•tant** (rĭ-lŭk'tənt) *adj.* Unwilling. **—re•luc'tance** *n.* **—re•luc'tant•ly** *adv.*

**re•ly** (rĭ-lī') *v.* **-lied, -lying. —rely on** (or **upon). 1.** To depend. **2.** To trust confidently. **—re•li'a•bil'i•ty** *n.* **—re•li'a•ble** *adj.* **—re•li'ance** *n.* **—re•li'ant** *adj.*

**re•main** (rĭ-mān') *v.* **1.** To continue without change. **2.** To stay or be left over. **3.** To endure or persist. **—re•main'der** *n.*

**re•mark** (rĭ-märk') *v.* **1.** To say casually; comment. **2.** To take notice of. —*n.* **1.** Notice; mention. **2.** A comment. **—re•mark'a•ble** *adj.* **—re•mark'a•bly** *adv.*

**rem•e•dy** (rĕm'ĭ-dē) *n., pl.* **-dies.** Something that relieves, cures, or corrects. —*v.* **-died, -dying. 1.** To relieve or cure. **2.** To rectify. **—re•me'di•al** *adj.*

**re•mem•ber** (rĭ-mĕm'bər) *v.* **1.** To recall to or retain in the mind. **2.** To give (someone) a gift, tip, etc. **—re•mem'brance** *n.*

**re•mind** (rĭ-mīnd') *v.* To cause to remember. **—re•mind'er** *n.*

**rem•i•nisce** (rĕm′ə-nĭs′) *v.* **-nisced, -niscing.** To recollect and tell of past experiences. **—rem′i•nis′cence** *n.* **—rem′i•nis′cent** *adj.*

**re•miss** (rĭ-mĭs′) *adj.* Negligent.

**re•mit** (rĭ-mĭt′) *v.* **-mitted, -mitting. 1.** To send (money). **2.** To pardon; forgive. **3.** To diminish; abate. **—re•mis′sion** *n.* **—re•mit′tance** *n.*

**rem•nant** (rĕm′nənt) *n.* **1.** Something left over. **2.** A surviving trace.

**re•morse** (rĭ-môrs′) *n.* Anguish for past misdeeds; bitter regret. **—re•morse′ful** *adj.* **—re•morse′less** *adj.*

**re•mon•strate** (rĭ-mŏn′strāt′) *v.* **-strated, -strating.** To make objections; argue against.

**re•mote** (rĭ-mōt′) *adj.* **-moter, -motest. 1.** Far away. **2.** Slight. **3.** Aloof. **—re•mote′ly** *adv.* **—re•mote′ness** *n.*

**re•move** (rĭ-mo͞ov′) *v.* **-moved, -moving. 1.** To move from one place to another. **2.** To take away. **3.** To dismiss from office. —*n.* Distance apart. **—re•mov′a•ble** *adj.* **—re•mov′al** *n.*

**re•mu•ner•ate** (rĭ-myo͞o′nə-rāt′) *v.* **-ated, -ating.** To pay for goods, work, etc. **—re•mu′ner•a′tion** *n.* **—re•mu′ner•a′tive** *adj.*

**ren•ais•sance** (rĕn′ĭ-säns′, -zäns′) *n.* A rebirth; revival.

**rend** (rĕnd) *v.* **rent** or **rended, rending. 1.** To tear apart violently. **2.** To remove forcibly. **3.** To disturb or distress.

**ren•der** (rĕn′dər) *v.* **1.** To submit. **2.** To give or make available. **3.** To represent in art. **4.** To liquefy (fat) by heating. **—ren•di′tion** *n.*

**ren•e•gade** (rĕn′ĭ-gād′) *n.* **1.** An apostate. **2.** An outlaw.

**re•nege** (rĭ-nĭg′, -nĕg′, -nēg′) *v.* **-neged, -neging.** To break a promise or commitment.

**re•new** (rĭ-n/y/o͞o′) *v.* **1.** To make as if new again; restore. **2.** To resume. **3.** To replenish. **—re•new′a•ble** *adj.* **—re•new′al** *n.*

**re•nounce** (rĭ-nouns′) *v.* **-nounced, -nouncing. 1.** To give up (a title or activity), esp. formally. **2.** To reject; disown. **—re•nounce′ment** *n.* **—re•nun′ci•a′tion** *n.*

**ren•o•vate** (rĕn′ə-vāt′) *v.* **-vated, -vating.** To renew; repair. **—ren′o•va′tion** *n.*

**re•nown** (rĭ-noun′) *n.* Fame. **—re•nowned′** *adj.*

**rent** (rĕnt) *n.* Periodic payment for the use of another's property. —*v.* To pay for and use (another's property). **—rent′al** *n. & adj.*

**re•pair** (rĭ-pâr′) *v.* To restore to sound condition. —*n.* **1.** The work of repairing. **2.** General condition.

**rep•a•ra•tion** (rĕp′ə-rā′shən) *n.* **1.** The act of making amends. **2.** Something done or paid to make amends. **3. reparations.** War payments required from a defeated nation.

**re•past** (rĭ-păst′) *n.* A meal or the food at a meal. **—re•past′** *v.*

**re•peal** (rĭ-pēl′) *v.* To revoke or annul officially. **—re•peal′** *n.*

**re•peat** (rĭ-pēt′) *v.* To say or do again. —*n.* **1.** The act of repeating. **2.** Something repeated. **—re•peat′ed** *adj.* **—re•peat′ed•ly** *adv.*

**re•pel** (rĭ-pĕl′) *v.* **-pelled, -pelling. 1.** To drive back; ward off. **2.** To cause aversion in. **—re•pel′lent** *adj. & n.*

**re•pent** (rĭ-pĕnt′) *v.* To feel regret or penitence for (what one has done or failed to do). **—re•pen′tance** *n.* **—re•pen′tant** *adj.*

**re•per•cus•sion** (rē′pər-kŭsh′ən) *n.* **1.** An indirect effect or result. **2.** A reciprocal action; rebound.

**rep•er•toire** (rĕp′ər-twär′) *n.* **1.** The stock of works an entertainer or group can perform. **2.** One's collection of talents and skills.

**rep•e•ti•tion** (rĕp′ĭ-tĭsh′ən) *n.* **1.** The act of repeating. **2.** Something repeated. **—rep′e•ti′tious** *adj.* **—rep′e•ti′tious•ly** *adv.* **—re•pet′i•tive** *adj.* **—re•pet′i•tive•ly** *adv.*

**re•place** (rĭ-plās′) *v.* **1.** To put back in place. **2.** To take the place of. **—re•place′ment** *n.*

**rep•li•ca** (rĕp′lĭ-kə) *n.* A copy; duplicate.

**re•ply** (rĭ-plī′) *v.* **-plied, -plying.** To answer. —*n., pl.* **-plies.** An answer; response.

**re•port** (rĭ-pôrt′, -pōrt′) *n.* **1.** An account, usually prepared in organized form. **2.** Rumor. **3.** An explosive noise. —*v.* **1.** To present an account of. **2.** To tell about; relate. **3.** To complain about to the proper authorities. **4.** To gather information for news stories. **5.** To present oneself. **—re•port'er** *n.*

**rep•re•hen•si•ble** (rĕp'rĭ-hĕn'sə-bəl) *adj.* Deserving censure; blameworthy. **—rep're•hen'si•bly** *adv.*

**rep•re•sent** (rĕp'rĭ-zĕnt') *v.* **1.** To stand for; symbolize. **2.** To depict; portray. **3.** To serve as the agent for. **4.** To act as a spokesman for, esp. in a legislative body. **—rep're•sen•ta'tion** *n.* **—rep're•sen'ta•tive** *n. & adj.*

**re•press** (rĭ-prĕs') *v.* **1.** To restrain. **2.** To suppress. **3.** To force (memories, ideas, or fears) into the subconscious mind. **—re•pres'sion** *n.* **—re•pres'sive** *adj.*

**re•prieve** (rĭ-prēv') *v.* **-prieved, -prieving.** To postpone or cancel punishment. *—n.* A postponement; respite.

**rep•ri•mand** (rĕp'rə-mănd') *v.* To rebuke or censure severely or formally. **—rep'ri•mand'** *n.*

**re•pri•sal** (rĭ-prī'zəl) *n.* **1.** Retaliatory seizure of enemy property. **2.** Retaliatory injury equal to injury received.

**re•proach** (rĭ-prōch') *v.* To blame. *—n.* **1.** Blame. **2.** Disgrace; shame. **—re•proach'ful** *adj.*

**re•pro•duce** (rē'prə-d/y/o͞os') *v.* **-duced, -ducing. 1.** To produce a copy of. **2.** To produce offspring. **—re'pro•duc'tion** *n.* **—re'pro•duc'tive** *adj.*

**re•proof** (rĭ-pro͞of') *n.* A rebuke.

**re•prove** (rĭ-pro͞ov') *v.* **-proved, -proving.** To rebuke; chide. **—re•prov'ing•ly** *adv.*

**rep•tile** (rĕp'tĭl, -tīl') *n.* A cold-blooded vertebrate, such as a snake, turtle, or lizard. **—rep•til'i•an** *adj. & n.*

**re•pub•lic** (rĭ-pŭb'lĭk) *n.* A political order that has no monarch and is based on a constitutional form of government, esp. a representative one. **—re•pub'li•can** *adj. & n.*

**re•pu•di•ate** (rĭ-pyo͞o'dē-āt') *v.* **-ated, -ating. 1.** To reject the validity of. **2.** To disown. **—re•pu'di•a'tion** *n.*

**re•pug•nant** (rĭ-pŭg'nənt) *adj.* Distasteful; repulsive. **—re•pug'nance** *n.*

**re•pulse** (rĭ-pŭls') *v.* **-pulsed, -pulsing.** To repel; reject. *—n.* **1.** The act of repulsing. **2.** Rejection; refusal. **—re•pul'sion** *n.*

**re•pul•sive** (rĭ-pŭl'sĭv) *adj.* Causing extreme dislike; disgusting. **—re•pul'sive•ly** *adv.* **—re•pul'sive•ness** *n.*

**rep•u•ta•tion** (rĕp'yə-tā'shən) *n.* **1.** The estimation in which one is held by the public. **2.** A specific character or trait.

**re•pute** (rĭ-pyo͞ot') *v.* **-puted, -puting.** To assign a reputation to; consider. *—n.* **1.** Reputation. **2.** A good reputation. **—rep'u•ta•ble** *adj.* **—rep'u•ta•bly** *adv.* **—re•put'ed** *adj.* **—re•put'ed•ly** *adv.*

**re•quest** (rĭ-kwĕst') *v.* To ask for. *—n.* **1.** An expressed desire. **2.** Something asked for.

**re•quire** (rĭ-kwīr') *v.* **-quired, -quiring. 1.** To need. **2.** To demand. **—re•quire'ment** *n.*

**req•ui•site** (rĕk'wĭ-zĭt) *adj.* Required. *—n.* A necessity; something essential. **—req'ui•si'tion** *n. & v.*

**re•quite** (rĭ-kwīt') *v.* **-quited, -quiting. 1.** To make repayment or return for. **—re•quit'al** *n.* **—re•quit'a•ble** *adj.*

**re•scind** (rĭ-sĭnd') *v.* To make void; repeal; annul.

**res•cue** (rĕs'kyo͞o) *v.* **-cued, -cuing.** To save, as from danger. *—n.* An act of saving. **—res'cu•er** *n.*

**re•search** (rĭ-sûrch', rē'sûrch') *n.* Diligent investigation or inquiry. **—re•search'** *v.* **—re•search'er** *n.*

**re•sem•ble** (rĭ-zĕm'bəl) *v.* **-bled, -bling.** To have a similarity to. **—re•sem'blance** *n.*

**re•sent** (rĭ-zĕnt') *v.* To feel indignant at. **—re•sent'ful** *adj.* **—re•sent'ful•ly** *adv.* **—re•sent'ment** *n.*

**re•serve** (rĭ-zûrv') *v.* **-served, -serving. 1.** To save; hold back. **2.** To set apart for a particular person or use, as land or accommodations. *—n.* **1.** Something saved for future use. **2.** Reticence; discretion. **3.** Often **reserves.** The part of an army subject to call in an emergency. **—res'er•va'tion** *n.* **—re•served'** *adj.*

**res•er•voir** (rĕz'ər-vwär', -vwôr', -vôr') *n.* **1.** A body of water stored for use. **2.** A lake or chamber for storing a fluid. **3.** A large supply of something built up over a period of time.

**re•side** (rĭ-zīd') *v.* **-sided, -siding.** To live or dwell. **—re•sid'er** *n.*

**res•i•dence** (rĕz'ĭ-dəns, -dĕns') *n.* **1.** A dwelling. **2.** The act or duration of residing somewhere. **—res'i•dent** *n.* **—res'i•den'tial** *adj.*

**res•i•due** (rĕz'ĭ-d/y/o͞o') *n.* That which remains after removal of a part.

**re•sign** (rĭ-zīn') *v.* **1.** To submit (oneself); acquiesce. **2.** To give up (a position). **—res'ig•na'tion** *n.* **—re•signed'** *adj.*

**re•sil•ience** (rĭ-zĭl'yəns) *n.* Also **re•sil•ien•cy. 1.** The ability to recover quickly, as from illness. **2.** Elasticity. **—re•sil'ient** *adj.*

**re•sist** (rĭ-zĭst') *v.* **1.** To work against; oppose. **2.** To withstand. **—re•sis'tance** *n.* **—re•sist'er** *n.*

**res•o•lu•tion** (rĕz'ə-lo͞o'shən) *n.* **1.** Determination. **2.** A course of action decided upon. **3.** A formal decision put before an assembly. **4.** Outcome or solution. **—res'o•lute'** *adj.* **—res'o•lute'ly** *adv.*

**re•solve** (rĭ-zŏlv') *v.* **-solved, -solving. 1.** To decide firmly; intend. **2.** To decide by formal vote. **3.** To solve. *—n.* **1.** Firmness of purpose; resolution. **2.** A determination or decision. **—re•solv'a•ble** *adj.* **—re•solved'** *adj.*

**res•o•nance** (rĕz'ə-nəns) *n.* The intensification and prolongation of a tone by vibration; echoing. **—res'o•nant** *adj.*

**re•sort** (rĭ-zôrt') *v.* To seek assistance; have recourse. *—n.* **1.** A place frequented for recreation. **2.** A recourse.

**re•sound** (rĭ-zound') *v.* **1.** To reverberate. **2.** To sound loudly; ring. **—re•sound'ing** *adj.* **—re•sound'ing•ly** *adv.*

**re•source** (rē'sôrs', rĭ-sôrs') *n.* **1.** A supply that can be drawn upon. **2.** An ability to deal with or adapt to a situation. **3.** Often **resources.** Available capital; assets. **—re•source'ful** *adj.* **—re•source'ful•ness** *n.*

**re•spect** (rĭ-spĕkt') *v.* **1.** To hold in esteem. **2.** To relate or refer to. *—n.* **1.** Esteem. **2.** A particular feature or detail. **3.** Reference. **—re•spect'a•bil'i•ty** *n.* **—re•spect'a•ble** *adj.* **—re•spect'a•bly** *adv.* **—re•spect'ful** *adj.* **—re•spect'ful•ly** *adv.* **—re•spect'ful•ness** *n.*

**re•spire** (rĭ-spīr') *v.* **-spired, -spiring.** To inhale and exhale; breathe. **—res'pi•ra'tion** *n.* **—res'pi•ra'tor** *n.*

**res•pite** (rĕs'pĭt) *n.* A short interval of rest or relief. *—v.* **-spited, -spiting. 1.** To delay; postpone. **2.** To grant a reprieve.

**re•splen•dent** (rĭ-splĕn'dənt) *adj.* Filled with splendor; brilliant. **—re•splen'dence** *n.*

**re•spond** (rĭ-spŏnd') *v.* **1.** To answer. **2.** To act in return. **3.** To react positively. **—re•sponse'** *n.* **—re•spon'sive** *adj.* **—re•spon'sive•ly** *adv.* **—re•spon'sive•ness** *n.*

**re•spon•si•ble** (rĭ-spŏn'sə-bəl) *adj.* **1.** Involving the ability or authority to act on one's own. **2.** Reliable. **3.** Accountable; answerable. **—re•spon'si•bil'i•ty** *n.* **—re•spon'si•bly** *adv.*

**rest**[1] (rĕst) *n.* **1.** Cessation from work, activity, or motion. **2.** Ease or refreshment resulting from sleep or relaxation. *—v.* **1.** To refresh (oneself). **2.** To be still, quiet, or inactive. **3. a.** To be supported. **b.** To place or lay. **4.** To depend. **—rest'ful** *adj.* **—rest'less** *adj.* **—rest'less•ly** *adv.* **—rest'less•ness** *n.*

**rest**[2] (rĕst) *n.* Remainder. *—v.* To be or continue to be.

**res•tau•rant** (rĕs'tər-ənt, -tə-ränt') *n.* A place where meals are served to the public.

**res•ti•tu•tion** (rĕs'tĭ-t/y/o͞o'shən) *n.* **1.** Compensation for loss, damage, or injury. **2.** The return of something to its rightful owner.

**res•tive** (rĕs'tĭv) *adj.* **1.** Impatient or nervous under restriction, delay, or pressure. **2.** Difficult to control.

**re•store** (rĭ-stôr', -stōr') *v.* **-stored, -storing. 1.** To bring back into existence or use. **2.** To bring back to a previous condition; renovate. **3.** To reinstate. **4.** To give back. **—res'to•ra'tion** *n.* **—re•stor'er** *n.*

**re•strain** (rĭ-strān') *v.* **1.** To control; check. **2.** To limit; confine. **—re•straint'** *n.*

**re•strict** (rĭ-strĭkt') *v.* To keep within limits. **—re•stric'tion** *n.* **—re•stric'tive** *adj.*

**re•sult** (rĭ-zŭlt') *v.* **1.** To occur or exist as a consequence. **2.** To end in a particular way. *—n.* The consequence; outcome. **—re•sul'tant** *adj.*

**re•sume** (rĭ-zo͞om') *v.* **-sumed, -suming. 1.** To continue after interruption. **2.** To take again. **—re•sump'tion** *n.*

**re•su•mé** (rĕz'o͞o-mā', rĕz'o͞o-mā') *n.* A brief accounting of one's personal history and experience.

**re•surge** (rĭ-sûrj′) *v.* **-surged, -surging. 1.** To rise again. **2.** To surge or sweep back again. **—re•sur′gence** *n.* **—re•sur′gent** *adj.*

**res•ur•rect** (rĕz′ə-rĕkt′) *v.* **1.** To raise or rise from the dead. **2.** To bring back into practice or notice; revive. **—res′-ur•rec′tion** *n.*

**re•sus•ci•tate** (rĭ-sŭs′ĭ-tāt′) *v.* **-tated, -tating.** To revive. **—re•sus′ci•ta′tion** *n.*

**re•tail** (rē′tāl′) *n.* The sale of goods to the consumer. **—re′tail′** *v. & adj.* **—re′tail′er** *n.*

**re•tain** (rĭ-tān′) *v.* **1.** To keep. **2.** To continue to practice, employ, etc. **3.** To hire by paying a fee. **4.** To remember. **—re•tain′er** *n.* **—re•ten′tion** *n.* **—re•ten′tive** *adj.*

**re•tal•i•ate** (rĭ-tăl′ē-āt′) *v.* **-ated, -ating.** To return like for like, esp. evil. **—re•tal′i•a′tion** *n.* **—re•tal′i•a•to′ry** *adj.*

**re•tard** (rĭ-tärd′) *v.* **-tarded, -tarding.** To slow the progress of; impede.

**retch** (rĕch) *v.* To vomit; heave.

**ret•i•cent** (rĕt′ĭ-sənt) *adj.* Not inclined to speak out; reserved. **—ret′i•cence** *n.*

**ret•i•na** (rĕt′n-ə) *n., pl.* **-nas** or **-nae.** A light-sensitive membrane lining the inner eyeball.

**re•tire** (rĭ-tīr′) *v.* **-tired, -tiring. 1.** To go to bed. **2.** To withdraw from business or public life. **—re•tired′** *adj.* **—re•tire′ment** *n.*

**re•tort** (rĭ-tôrt′) *v.* **1.** To reply. **2.** To present a counterargument. —*n.* A quick, incisive reply.

**re•tract** (rĭ-trăkt′) *v.* **1.** To disavow. **2.** To draw back. **—re•tract′a•ble** *adj.* **—re•trac′tion** *n.*

**re•treat** (rĭ-trēt′) *n.* **1.** A withdrawal, esp. of a military force. **2.** A quiet, private place; refuge. —*v.* To withdraw.

**re•trieve** (rĭ-trēv′) *v.* **-trieved, -trieving. 1.** To regain. **2.** To fetch. **3.** To bring back game, as a dog does. **—re•triev′-a•ble** *adj.* **—re•triev′al** *n.* **—re•triev′er** *n.*

**ret•ro•ac•tive** (rĕt′rō-ăk′tĭv) *adj.* Applying to a period prior to enactment.

**ret•ro•spect** (rĕt′rə-spĕkt′) *n.* A review of the past. **—ret′ro•spec′tive** *adj.* **—ret′ro•spec′tive•ly** *adv.*

**re•turn** (rĭ-tûrn′) *v.* **1.** To go or come back. **2.** To respond. **3.** To send or put back. **4.** To yield (profit or interest). —*n.* **1.** The act of returning. **2.** Something brought or sent back. **3.** Often **returns.** A profit or yield. **4.** Often **returns.** The vote in an election. **—re•turn′a•ble** *adj.*

**re•un•ion** (rē-yo͞on′yən) *n.* A gathering of a group whose members have been separated.

**re•vamp** (rē-vămp′) *v.* To patch up or restore.

**re•veal** (rĭ-vēl′) *v.* **1.** To disclose. **2.** To bring to view; expose. **—rev′e•la′tion** *n.*

**rev•eil•le** (rĕv′ə-lē) *n.* The morning bugle call to awaken soldiers.

**rev•el** (rĕv′əl) *v.* **1.** To enjoy greatly. **2.** To party riotously; carouse. —*n.* A noisy festivity. **—rev′el•er** *n.* **—rev′el•ry** *n.*

**re•venge** (rĭ-vĕnj′) *v.* **-venged, -venging.** To retaliate; avenge. —*n.* Vengeance; retaliation. **—re•venge′ful** *adj.*

**rev•e•nue** (rĕv′ə-n/y/o͞o) *n.* Income, esp. of a government.

**re•ver•ber•ate** (rĭ-vûr′bə-rāt′) *v.* **-ated, -ating.** To reecho. **—re•ver′ber•a′-tion** *n.*

**re•vere** (rĭ-vîr′) *v.* **-vered, -vering.** To regard with awe or great respect. **—rev′er•ence** *n.* **—rev′er•end** *adj.* **—rev′er•ent** *adj.* **—rev′er•en′tial** *adj.*

**rev•er•ie** (rĕv′ə-rē) *n.* Abstracted musing; daydreaming.

**re•verse** (rĭ-vûrs′) *adj.* **1.** Turned backward. **2.** Causing backward movement. —*n.* **1.** The opposite of something. **2.** The back or rear of something. **3.** A defeat; misfortune. —*v.* **-versed, -versing. 1.** To turn to or in the opposite direction. **2.** To revoke or annul (a decision or decree). **—re•ver′sal** *n.* **—re•vers′i•ble** *adj.*

**re•vert** (rĭ-vûrt′) *v.* To return to a former condition, practice, or belief.

**re•view** (rĭ-vyo͞o′) *v.* **1.** To look over again. **2.** To look back on. **3.** To examine critically. **4.** To write a critical evaluation on (a new work or performance). —*n.* **1.** A reexamination. **2.** A retrospective survey. **3.** A restudying of subject matter. **4.** An inspection or examination for evaluation. **5.** A report estimating the quality of a work or performance. **—re•view′er** *n.*

**re•vile** (rĭ-vīl′) *v.* **-viled, -viling.** To denounce with abusive language. **—re•vile′ment** *n.*

**re•vise** (rĭ-vīz′) *v.* **-vised, -vising.** To change or modify; update. **—re•vi′sion** *n.*

**re•vive** (rĭ-vīv′) *v.* **-vived, -viving. 1.** To bring back to consciousness. **2.** To regain vigor or spirit. **3.** To restore to use. **—re•viv′al** *n.*

**re•voke** (rĭ-vōk′) *v.* **-voked, -voking.** To annul by withdrawing.

**re•volt** (rĭ-vōlt′) *v.* **1.** To rebel against authority. **2.** To fill or be filled with disgust. *—n.* An uprising; rebellion.

**rev•o•lu•tion** (rĕv′ə-lo͞o′shən) *n.* **1. a.** Orbital motion about a point or an axis. **b.** A single complete cycle of such motion. **2.** A momentous or complete change. **3.** A political overthrow brought about from within. **—rev′o•lu′tion•ar′y** *adj. & n.* **—rev′o•lu′tion•ize′** *v.*

**re•volve** (rĭ-vŏlv′) *v.* **-volved, -volving. 1.** To turn or go round; rotate. **2.** To recur in cycles.

**re•volv•er** (rĭ-vŏl′vər) *n.* A pistol having a revolving cylinder with several cartridge chambers.

**re•vue** (rĭ-vyo͞o′) *n.* A musical show of satirical skits and songs.

**re•vul•sion** (rĭ-vŭl′shən) *n.* A change in feeling, esp. to disgust.

**re•ward** (rĭ-wôrd′) *n.* **1.** Recompense for service, conduct, etc. **2.** Money offered for some special service. *—v.* To give a reward to, esp. in return for.

**rhap•so•dy** (răp′sə-dē) *n., pl.* **-dies. 1.** Excessively enthusiastic expression of feeling in speech or writing. **2.** A musical composition of irregular form. **—rhap•sod′ic** *adj.* **—rhap′so•dize** *v.*

**rhet•o•ric** (rĕt′ər-ĭk) *n.* The art of effective use of language. **—rhe•tor′i•cal** *adj.*

**rhi•noc•er•os** (rī-nŏs′ər-əs) *n.* A large, thick-skinned mammal with a horned snout.

**rhyme** (rīm) Also **rime.** *n.* **1.** Correspondence of end sounds of words or lines of verse. **2.** A poem with this correspondence. *—v.* **rhymed, rhyming.** To form a rhyme.

**rhythm** (rĭ*th*′əm) *n.* Any kind of movement with a regular recurrence of strong and weak elements, esp. in music or verse. **—rhyth′mic, rhyth′mi•cal** *adj.* **—rhyth′mi•cal•ly** *adv.*

**rib** (rĭb) *n.* **1.** One of the long, curved bones extending from the spine to the breastbone. **2.** A riblike part used for support.

**rib•bon** (rĭb′ən) *n.* A strip of fine fabric.

**rice** (rīs) *n.* A cereal grass having a starchy edible seed.

**rich** (rĭch) *adj.* **1.** Possessing great wealth. **2.** Valuable. **3.** Elaborate. **4.** Plentiful; abundant. **—rich′ly** *adv.* **—rich′ness** *n.*

**rich•es** (rĭch′ĭz) *pl.n.* Wealth.

**rid** (rĭd) *v.* **rid** or **ridded, ridding.** To free from something; clear away. **—rid′dance** *n.*

**rid•den** (rĭd′n) *v.* p.p. of **ride.**

**rid•dle**[1] (rĭd′l) *v.* **-dled, -dling.** To pierce with numerous holes.

**rid•dle**[2] (rĭd′l) *n.* A puzzling question or problem.

**ride** (rīd) *v.* **rode** (rōd), **ridden** (rĭd′n), **riding. 1.** To be conveyed by an animal or vehicle. **2.** To sit on or in and drive. **3.** To be supported upon. *—n.* A journey by any means of conveyance. **—rid′er** *n.*

**ridge** (rĭj) *n.* **1.** A long, narrow land elevation. **2.** Any narrow raised strip. *—v.* **ridged, ridging.** To mark with or form into ridges.

**rid•i•cule** (rĭd′ĭ-kyo͞ol′) *n.* Derision; mockery. *—v.* **-culed, -culing.** To make fun of; deride.

**ri•dic•u•lous** (rĭ-dĭk′yə-ləs) *adj.* Absurd or preposterous. **—ri•dic′u•lous•ly** *adv.* **—ri•dic′u•lous•ness** *n.*

**rife** (rīf) *adj.* **1.** Common or frequent in occurrence. **2.** Abounding.

**ri•fle**[1] (rī′fəl) *n.* A shoulder firearm with a bore that has spiral grooves. *—v.* **-fled, -fling.** To cut spiral grooves within (a gun barrel).

**ri•fle**[2] (rī′fəl) *v.* **-fled, -fling. 1.** To search with intent to steal. **2.** To rob.

**rift** (rĭft) *n.* **1.** A narrow fissure in rock. **2.** A break in friendly relations.

**rig** (rĭg) *v.* **rigged, rigging. 1.** To fit out; equip. **2.** To equip (a ship) with ropes, chains, and tackle. **3.** To make in an expedient manner. **4.** To manipulate dishonestly. *—n.* **1.** The arrangement of masts, spars, and sails on a sailing vessel. **2.** A vehicle with one or more horses harnessed to it. **3.** The special apparatus used for drilling oil wells.

**right** (rīt) *adj.* **1.** In accordance with justice or law; proper. **2.** Factual; correct. **3.** Sound or normal. **4.** Of the side that faces east when a person or thing faces north. —*n.* **1.** That which is just, legal, proper, or fitting. **2.** The right-hand side. **3. the Right.** Political conservatives. **4.** That which is due to anyone by law or nature. —*adv.* **1.** Directly. **2.** Properly; correctly. **3.** Exactly. **4.** Immediately. **5.** Completely. —*v.* **1.** To stand or set upright. **2.** To redress. **—right'ful** *adj.* **—right'ful•ly** *adv.* **—right'ful•ness** *n.* **—right'ly** *adv.* **—right'ness** *n.*

**right•eous** (rī'chəs) *adj.* Virtuous; upright. **—right'eous•ly** *adv.* **—right'eous•ness** *n.*

**rig•id** (rĭj'ĭd) *adj.* **1.** Stiff; inflexible. **2.** Not moving; fixed. **3.** Severe; harsh. **—ri•gid'i•ty** *n.*

**rig•or** (rĭg'ər) *n.* **1.** Strictness or severity, as judgment. **2.** A hardship. **—rig'or•ous** *adj.* **—rig'or•ous•ly** *adv.*

**rile** (rīl) *v.* **riled, riling.** To vex; irritate.

**rim** (rĭm) *n.* **1.** A border or edge. **2.** The outer part of a wheel around which a tire is fitted. —*v.* **rimmed, rimming.** To furnish with a rim.

**rind** (rīnd) *n.* A tough covering, as the skin of some fruits.

**ring[1]** (rĭng) *n.* **1.** A circular object with a vacant circular center. **2.** A small circular band worn on a finger. **3.** Any circular band. **4.** An area in which prize fights, exhibitions, etc., are held. **5.** A group of persons acting privately. —*v.* To encircle.

**ring[2]** (rĭng) *v.* **rang** (răng), **rung** (rŭng), **ringing. 1.** To give forth a clear, resonant sound. **2.** To cause (a bill, chimes, etc.) to sound. **3.** To call (someone) on the telephone. —*n.* **1.** The sound created by a bell, etc. **2.** A telephone call.

**rinse** (rĭns) *v.* **rinsed, rinsing. 1.** To wash lightly. **2.** To remove (soap, dirt, etc.) with water. —*n.* **1.** The act of washing lightly. **2.** A solution used in conditioning or tinting the hair.

**ri•ot** (rī'ət) *n.* A disturbance created by a mob. —*v.* To take part in a riot. **—ri'ot•er** *n.* **—ri'ot•ous** *adj.* **—ri'ot•ous•ly** *adv.*

**rip** (rĭp) *v.* **ripped, ripping. 1.** To tear. **2.** To remove by pulling. —*n.* A torn or split place.

**ripe** (rīp) *adj.* Fully developed; mature. **—rip'en** *v.* **—ripe'ness** *n.*

**rip•ple** (rĭp'əl) *v.* **-pled, -pling. 1.** To form small waves. **2.** To rise and fall gently in tone or volume. —*n.* **1.** A small wave. **2.** An indistinct vibrating sound.

**rise** (rīz) *v.* **rose** (rōz), **risen** (rĭz'ən), **rising. 1.** To stand up. **2.** To get out of bed. **3.** To ascend. **4.** To increase in amount, value, etc. **5.** To appear above the horizon. **—rise** *n.*

**risk** (rĭsk) *n.* The possibility of loss or danger. —*v.* To expose to loss or damage. **—risk'y** *adj.*

**rit•u•al** (rĭch'o͞o-əl) *n.* **1.** The prescribed form for a solemn ceremony. **2.** A body of ceremonies, esp. religious. **—rit'u•al** *adj.* **—rit'u•al•ly** *adv.*

**ri•val** (rī'vəl) *n.* One who competes against another for the same object. —*adj.* Competing. —*v.* **1.** To attempt to equal or surpass. **2.** To equal; be a match for. **—ri'val•ry** *n.*

**riv•er** (rĭv'ər) *n.* A large natural stream of water.

**riv•et** (rĭv'ĭt) *n.* A bolt or pin used to fasten metal plates together. —*v.* **1.** To fasten with a rivet. **2.** To engross (the attention).

**road** (rōd) *n.* **1.** An open way for the passage of vehicles. **2.** A course toward the achievement of something.

**roam** (rōm) *v.* To travel aimlessly; wander.

**roar** (rôr, rōr) *v.* **1.** To utter a loud, deep sound. **2.** To express with a roar. **3.** To laugh loudly. —*n.* **1.** A loud, deep sound. **2.** Loud laughter.

**roast** (rōst) *v.* **1.** To cook with dry heat. **2.** To expose to great heat. —*n.* A cut of meat for roasting. —*adj.* Roasted. **—roast'er** *n.*

**rob** (rŏb) *v.* **robbed, robbing. 1.** To steal (from). **2.** To deprive of unlawfully. **—rob'ber** *n.* **—rob'ber•y** *n.*

**robe** (rōb) *n.* **1.** A long, loose, flowing garment. **2.** A blanket or covering. —*v.* **robed, robing.** To dress in a robe.

**rob•in** (rŏb'ĭn) *n.* A red-breasted songbird.

**ro•bot** (rō'bət, -bŏt') *n.* An automaton or programmed machine that performs

work.
**ro•bust** (rō-bŭst′, rō′bŭst′) *adj.* Healthy and strong; vigorous. **—ro•bust′ly** *adv.* **—ro•bust′ness** *n.*
**rock**[1] (rŏk) *n.* A hard natural mass of mineral matter; stone. **—rock′y** *adj.*
**rock**[2] (rŏk) *v.* **1.** To move or sway from side to side. **2.** To shake violently.
**rock•et** (rŏk′ĭt) *n.* **1.** A device propelled by ejection of matter, esp. matter produced by internal gaseous combustion. **2.** A rocket-propelled explosive weapon. —*v.* To move swiftly.
**rod** (rŏd) *n.* **1.** A thin piece or pole of metal, wood, etc. **2.** A metal bar in a machine. **3.** A linear measure equal to 5.5 yards or 5.03 meters.
**rode** (rōd) *v.* p.t. of **ride.**
**ro•dent** (rōd′nt) *n.* A gnawing mammal, as a mouse, squirrel, or beaver.
**role, rôle** (rōl) *n.* **1.** A character played by an actor. **2.** A function.
**roll** (rōl) *v.* **1.** To move by turning over and over. **2.** To move on wheels. **3.** To gain momentum. **4.** To wrap round upon itself. **5.** To enfold in a covering. **6.** To spread or flatten with a roller. **7.** To form in a ball. —*n.* **1.** Something rolled up in the form of a cylinder. **2.** A list of names. **3.** A small rounded bread or cake. **4.** A swaying or rocking motion.
**rol•lick•ing** (rŏl′ĭ-kĭng) *adj.* High-spirited; boisterous.
**ro•mance** (rō-măns′, rō′măns′) *n.* **1.** A fictitious tale of heroes and adventure. **2.** A sentimental novel dealing with love. **3.** A love affair.
**ro•man•tic** (rō-măn′tĭk) *adj.* **1.** Expressive of personal feelings and sentiment. **2.** Given to feelings of love. **3.** Conducive to romance. **4.** Imaginative but impractical. **5.** Imaginary. —*n.* A romantic person. **—ro•man′ti•cal•ly** *adv.* **—ro•man′ti•cize′** *v.*
**roof** (ro͞of, ro͝of) *n.* **1.** The top covering of a building. **2.** The upper part of the mouth. —*v.* To cover with a roof.
**room** (ro͞om, ro͝om) *n.* **1.** Space. **2.** An area of a building set off by walls. —*v.* To occupy a room; lodge. **—room′er** *n.* **—room′mate′** *n.*
**roost** (ro͞ost) *n.* A perch on which birds rest at night. —*v.* To rest or sleep on a perch.
**roost•er** (ro͞o′stər) *n.* The adult male domestic fowl.
**root**[1] (ro͞ot, ro͝ot) *n.* **1.** The underground portion of a plant. **2.** The embedded part of an organ, as a tooth, hair, etc. **3.** An essential element; core. **4.** Origin. **5.** A number that when multiplied by itself an indicated number of times equals a specified number. —*v.* **1.** To put forth roots. **2.** To implant by or as by roots.
**root**[2] (ro͞ot, ro͝ot) *v.* To dig with or as with the snout.
**rope** (rōp) *n.* A flexible, heavy cord. —*v.* **roped, roping. 1.** To fasten with rope. **2.** To enclose with a rope. **3.** To lasso.
**rose**[1] (rōz) *n.* **1.** A prickly plant with showy, fragrant flowers. **2.** Dark pink.
**rose**[2] (rōz) *v.* p.t. of **rise.**
**ros•y** (rō′zē) *adj.* **-ier, -iest. 1.** Having the pink or red color of a rose. **2.** Cheery; optimistic. **3.** Flushed; bright. **—ros′i•ly** *adv.*
**rot** (rŏt) *v.* **rotted, rotting.** To decompose; decay. —*n.* **1.** The process of rotting. **2.** Decay. **—rot′ten** *adj.* **—rot′ten•ly** *adv.* **—rot′ten•ness** *n.*
**ro•tate** (rō′tāt′) *v.* **-tated, -tating. 1.** To turn on an axis. **2.** To alternate in sequence. **—ro′ta•ry** *adj.* **—ro•ta′tion** *n.* **—ro•ta′tion•al** *adj.* **—ro′ta′tor** *n.*
**rouge** (ro͞ozh) *n.* **1.** A red cosmetic for the cheeks or lips. **2.** A reddish polishing powder for metal. —*v.* **rouged, rouging.** To color with rouge.
**rough** (rŭf) *adj.* **1.** Not smooth. **2.** Turbulent. **3.** Not gentle. **4.** In a crude or unfinished state. —*v.* **1.** To make rough. **2.** To treat roughly. **—rough′en** *v.* **—rough′ly** *adv.* **—rough′ness** *n.*
**rough•age** (rŭf′ĭj) *n.* The coarse parts of certain foods.
**round** (round) *adj.* **1.** Spherical; circular; curved. **2.** Complete. **3.** Expressed as a whole number. **4.** Approximate; not exact. —*n.* **1.** Something round. **2.** A cut of beef. **3.** A complete course, succession, or series. **4.** Often **rounds.** A course of customary actions, duties, etc. **5.** A single outburst of applause. **6.** A single shot. **7.** A period of play in various sports. —*v.* **1.** To make or become round. **2.** To complete. **3.** To go around. —*adv.* **1.** Around. **2.** Throughout. —*prep.* Around. **—round′ness** *n.*

**round•a•bout** (round'ə-bout') *adj.* Indirect; circuitous.

**round•ly** (round'lē) *adv.* **1.** Vigorously; bluntly. **2.** Thoroughly.

**rouse** (rouz) *v.* **roused, rousing. 1.** To wake up. **2.** To excite; spur.

**rout** (rout) *n.* **1.** A disorderly flight following defeat. **2.** An overwhelming defeat. —*v.* **1.** To put to flight. **2.** To defeat overwhelmingly.

**route** (ro͞ot, rout) *n.* A road or course for travel. —*v.* **1.** To send along. **2.** To schedule on a certain route.

**rou•tine** (ro͞o-tēn') *n.* **1.** A prescribed procedure. **2.** Customary activities. —*adj.* **1.** Habitual; regular. **2.** Uninteresting or unoriginal. **—rou•tine'ly** *adv.*

**rove** (rōv) *v.* **roved, roving.** To wander; roam. **—rov'er** *n.*

**row¹** (rō) *n.* A linear arrangement.

**row²** (rō) *v.* **rowed, rowing.** To propel with oars. —*n.* A trip in a rowboat. **—row'er** *n.*

**row³** (rou) *n.* A noisy quarrel.

**row•boat** (rō'bōt') *n.* A small boat propelled by oars.

**row•dy** (rou'dē) *n., pl.* **-dies.** A rough, disorderly person. —*adj.* **-dier, -diest.** Disorderly; rough.

**roy•al** (roi'əl) *adj.* Of a monarch. **—roy'al•ly** *adv.*

**roy•al•ty** (roi'əl-tē) *n., pl.* **-ties. 1.** Monarchs and their families collectively. **2.** The power of monarchs. **3.** A share paid to an author, etc., out of the proceeds from the sale of his work.

**rub** (rŭb) *v.* **rubbed, rubbing. 1.** To apply pressure and friction to (a surface). **2.** To contact repeatedly and with friction; scrape. **3.** To become or cause to become irritated. —*n.* **1.** The act of rubbing. **2.** An obstacle.

**rub•ber** (rŭb'ər) *n.* **1.** An elastic material, either natural or synthetic. **2.** Often **rubbers.** A low overshoe. **—rub'ber•y** *adj.*

**rub•bish** (rŭb'ĭsh) *n.* **1.** Garbage; litter. **2.** Nonsense.

**rub•ble** (rŭb'əl) *n.* **1.** Fragments of stone. **2.** Debris.

**ru•by** (ro͞o'bē) *n., pl.* **-bies. 1.** A deep-red gemstone. **2.** A dark red.

**rud•der** (rŭd'ər) *n.* A hinged plate at the rear of a vessel or aircraft, used for steering.

**rude** (ro͞od) *adj.* **ruder, rudest. 1.** Impolite; discourteous. **2.** Makeshift; crude. **—rude'ly** *adv.* **—rude'ness** *n.*

**ru•di•ment** (ro͞o'də-mənt) *n.* Often **rudiments.** A fundamental element, principle, or skill. **—ru'di•men'ta•ry** *adj.*

**rue** (ro͞o) *v.* **rued, ruing.** To regret; repent. **—rue'ful** *adj.* **—rue'ful•ly** *adv.*

**ruf•fle** (rŭf'əl) *n.* **1.** A strip of frilled or pleated fabric. **2.** A slight disturbance. —*v.* **-fled, -fling. 1.** To disturb the smoothness of; ripple. **2.** To gather into a ruffle. **3.** To fluster.

**rug** (rŭg) *n.* A heavy floor covering of fabric, animal skin, etc.

**rug•ged** (rŭg'ĭd) *adj.* **1.** Rough; irregular. **2.** Hard; severe. **3.** Vigorously healthy. **—rug'ged•ness** *n.*

**ru•in** (ro͞o'ĭn) *n.* **1.** Total destruction. **2.** Often **ruins.** The remains of something destroyed. —*v.* **1.** To reduce to ruin. **2.** To harm irreparably. **—ru'in•a'tion** *n.* **—ru'in•ous** *adj.* **—ru'in•ous•ly** *adv.*

**rule** (ro͞ol) *n.* **1.** Governing power. **2.** A principle that governs conduct or procedure; a regulation. **3.** A standard method. —*v.* **ruled, ruling. 1.** To control; govern. **2.** To decide judicially; decree. **3.** To mark with straight parallel lines. **—rul'ing** *n.*

**rul•er** (ro͞o'lər) *n.* **1.** One who rules. **2.** A straight-edged strip for drawing straight lines and measuring lengths.

**rum** (rŭm) *n.* An alcoholic liquor distilled from molasses.

**ru•mi•nate** (ro͞o'mə-nāt') *v.* **-nated, -nating. 1.** To chew cud, as cattle, sheep, and deer do. **2.** To meditate; muse. **—ru'mi•na'tion** *n.* **—ru'mi•nant** *n. & adj.*

**ru•mor** (ro͞o'mər) *n.* Unverified information; gossip. —*v.* To spread rumor.

**rump** (rŭmp) *n.* **1.** The fleshy hind part of an animal. **2.** The buttocks.

**rum•ple** (rŭm'pəl) *v.* **-pled, -pling.** To wrinkle or crease. **—rum'ply** *adj.*

**run** (rŭn) *v.* **ran** (răn), **run, running. 1.** To move on foot at a pace faster than walking. **2.** To retreat rapidly. **3.** To hurry. **4.** To take part in a race. **5.** To compete for elected office. **6.** To be in operation. **7.** To manage. **8.** To flow. **9.** To melt. **10.** To extend, stretch, or reach. **11.** To extend in time. **12.** To vary or range in quality, price, size, etc. —*n.* **1.** An act of running. **2.** A point scored in baseball. **3.** Unrestricted freedom or use of a place. **4.** A trip between points on a route. **5.** A movement or flow. **6.** A tear or unraveled length in a fabric. **7.** An unbroken series or sequence.

**rung**[1] (rŭng) *n.* **1.** A step of a ladder. **2.** A crosspiece supporting the legs or back of a chair. **3.** A spoke in a wheel.

**rung**[2] (rŭng) *v.* p.p. of **ring.**

**run•ner** (rŭn′ər) *n.* **1.** One who runs, as a messenger. **2.** A device in or on which something slides, as the blade of a skate. **3.** A long narrow carpet.

**runt** (rŭnt) *n.* An undersized animal or person.

**rup•ture** (rŭp′chər) *n.* **1.** A breaking open or bursting. **2.** A tear in bodily tissue. —**rup′ture** *v.*

**ru•ral** (ro͝or′əl) *adj.* Of the country. —**ru′ral•ly** *adv.*

**ruse** (ro͞oz) *n.* A trick.

**rush** (rŭsh) *v.* **1.** To move or act swiftly. **2.** To attack; charge. —*n.* **1.** A sudden forward motion. **2.** General haste. **3.** A sudden onslaught.

**rust** (rŭst) *n.* **1.** A reddish oxide formed on iron by exposure to air and water. **2.** A plant disease caused by parasitic fungi. **3.** Reddish brown. —*v.* **1.** To corrode. **2.** To deteriorate through inactivity. —**rust′i•ness** *n.* —**rust′y** *adj.*

**rus•tic** (rŭs′tĭk) *adj.* **1.** Rural. **2.** Unsophisticated; simple. —*n.* A country person. —**rus•tic′i•ty** *n.*

**rus•tle**[1] (rŭs′əl) *v.* **-tled, -tling.** To make or cause to make soft whispering sounds. —**rus′tle** *n.* —**rus′tling•ly** *adv.*

**rus•tle**[2] (rŭs′əl) *v.* **-tled, -tling.** To steal cattle. —**rus′tler** *n.*

**rut** (rŭt) *n.* **1.** A sunken groove made by the passage of wheels. **2.** A fixed routine.

**ruth•less** (ro͞oth′lĭs) *adj.* Having no compassion; merciless. —**ruth′less•ly** *adv.* —**ruth′less•ness** *n.*

**rye** (rī) *n.* **1.** A cereal grass, used in making flour and whiskey. **2.** Whiskey made from rye.

# — S —

**s, S** (ĕs) *n.* The 19th letter of the English alphabet.

**Sab•bath** (săb′əth) *n.* The weekly day of rest, Sunday for most Christians and Saturday for Jews.

**sa•ber** (sā′bər) *n.* A heavy cavalry sword.

**sab•o•tage** (săb′ə-täzh′) *n.* Deliberate subversion. —**sab′o•tage′** *v.* —**sab′o•teur′** *n.*

**sac** (săk) *n.* A pouchlike structure.

**sac•cha•rin** (săk′ər-ĭn) *n.* A sweet powder used as a calorie-free sweetener.

**sac•cha•rine** (săk′ər-ĭn, -ə-rēn′) *adj.* **1.** Sweet. **2.** Cloying in attitude or character.

**sack**[1] (săk) *n.* A large bag.

**sack**[2] (săk) *v.* To loot. —**sack** *n.*

**sac•ra•ment** (săk′rə-mənt) *n.* A ceremonial act prescribed by a religion; rite. —**sac′ra•men′tal** *adj.* & *n.* —**sac′ra•men′tal•ly** *adv.*

**sa•cred** (sā′krĭd) *adj.* **1.** Holy; religious. **2.** Worthy of respect; venerable. —**sa′cred•ly** *adv.* —**sa′cred•ness** *n.*

**sac•ri•fice** (săk′rə-fīs′) *n.* **1.** The offering of something valued, as to a god. **2.** The willing acceptance of a loss. —*v.* **-ficed, -ficing. 1.** To offer as a sacrifice. **2.** To forfeit; give up. —**sac′ri•fic′er** *n.* —**sac′ri•fi′cial** *adj.*

**sac•ro•sanct** (săk′rō-săngkt′) *adj.* Sacred and inviolable.

**sad** (săd) *adj.* **sadder, saddest. 1.** Unhappy. **2.** Deplorable. —**sad•den** *v.* —**sad′ly** *adv.* —**sad′ness** *n.*

**sad•dle** (săd′l) *n.* A leather seat for a rider, as on a horse. —*v.* **-dled, -dling. 1.** To put a saddle on. **2.** To encumber.

**sa•dism** (sā′dĭz′əm, săd′ĭz′-) *n.* Sexual pleasure derived from inflicting pain. —**sa′dist** *n.* —**sa•dis′tic** *adj.*

**sa•fa•ri** (sə-fär′ē) *n.* A trip or expedition, esp. for hunting or exploring.

**safe** (sāf) *adj.* **safer, safest. 1.** Not dangerous. **2.** Unhurt. —*n.* A strongbox. —**safe′ly** *adv.* —**safe′ty** *n.*

**sag** (săg) *v.* **sagged, sagging.** To sink or bend downward; droop. —**sag** *n.*

**sa•ga•cious** (sə-gā′shəs) *n.* Perceptive; wise. —**sa•ga′cious•ly** *adv.* —**sa•gac′i•ty** *n.*

**sage** (sāj) *n.* A wise and venerable person. —*adj.* **sager, sagest.** Wise. —**sage'ly** *adv.*

**said** (sĕd) *v.* p.t. & p.p. of **say.** —*adj.* Aforementioned.

**sail** (sāl) *n.* **1.** A length of fabric that catches the wind and so propels a vessel. **2.** A trip in a sailing craft. —*v.* **1.** To move or travel by means of a sail. **2.** To navigate. **3.** To glide; soar. —**sail'boat'** *n.*

**sail•or** (sā'lər) *n.* One who works on a ship.

**saint** (sānt) *n.* A very holy or unselfish person. —**saint'hood'** *n.* —**saint'li•ness** *n.* —**saint'ly** *adj.*

**sake** (sāk) *n.* **1.** Purpose. **2.** Benefit.

**sal•ad** (săl'əd) *n.* A dish consisting of a mixture of usu. raw vegetables.

**sal•a•ry** (săl'ə-rē, săl'rē) *n., pl.* **-ries.** A fixed payment for services. —**sal'a•ried** *adj.*

**sale** (sāl) *n.* **1.** The exchange of property for money. **2.** Availability for purchase. **3.** An offering of goods, esp. at lowered prices. —**sal'a•ble** *adj.* —**sales'man** *n.* —**sales'man•ship'** *n.* —**sales'per'son** *n.* —**sales'wom'an** *n.*

**sa•li•ent** (sā'lē-ənt, sāl'yənt) *adj.* **1.** Projecting or protruding. **2.** Conspicuous; prominent. —*n.* A section of a battle line bulging out toward the enemy. —**sa'li•ence** *n.* —**sa'li•ent•ly** *adv.*

**sa•li•va** (sə-lī'və) *n.* The thick, secreted liquid that keeps the mouth and throat moist. —**sal'i•var'y** *adj.* —**sal'i•vate** *v.*

**sal•low** (săl'ō) *adj.* **-er, -est.** Of a sickly yellow color or complexion. —**sal'low•ly** *adv.* —**sal'low•ness** *n.*

**sa•lon** (sə-lŏn', săl'ŏn', să-lôN') *n.* **1.** A large room for receiving guests. **2.** A gallery for exhibiting art. **3.** A shop offering a fashion-related service.

**sa•loon** (sə-lo͞on') *n.* **1.** A bar or tavern. **2.** A hall for receptions or exhibitions. **3.** An officers' dining room on a ship. **4.** A lounge for passengers on a cruise ship.

**sal•sa** (säl'sə) *n.* Popular Latin American dance music.

**salt** (sôlt) *n.* **1.** Sodium chloride, used as a food seasoning and preservative. **2.** Flavor or zest. —*v.* To season or cure with salt. —**salt** *adj.* —**salt'i•ness** *n.* —**salt'y** *adj.*

**sa•lu•bri•ous** (sə-lo͞o'brē-əs) *adj.* Healthful. —**sa•lu'bri•ous•ly** *adv.* —**sa•lu'bri•ous•ness, sa•lu'bri•ty** *n.*

**sal•u•tar•y** (săl'yə-tĕr'ē) *adj.* Beneficial; wholesome.

**sal•u•ta•tion** (săl'yə-tā'shən) *n.* An expression of greeting.

**sa•lute** (sə-lo͞ot') *v.* **-luted, -luting. 1.** To greet, esp. with a gesture of respect. **2.** To honor. —*n.* A formal or respectful greeting.

**sal•vage** (săl'vĭj) *n.* **1.** The rescue of a ship. **2. a.** The saving of imperiled property. **b.** The property saved. —*v.* **-vaged, -vaging.** To save from loss or destruction. —**sal'vage•a•ble** *adj.*

**sal•va•tion** (săl-vā'shən) *n.* **1.** Deliverance from evil or difficulty. **2.** A means of such deliverance. **3.** Deliverance from sin; redemption.

**salve** (săv, säv) *n.* A medicinal ointment. —*v.* **salved, salving.** To soothe.

**sal•vo** (săl'vō) *n., pl.* **-vos** or **-voes. 1.** A simultaneous discharge of firearms. **2.** A sudden outburst. **3.** A salute; tribute.

**same** (sām) *adj.* **1.** Being the very one. **2.** Similar or corresponding. —*pron.* The same person, thing, or event. —*adv.* In like manner. —**same'ness** *n.*

**sam•ple** (săm'pəl) *n.* A part representative of a whole. —*v.* **-pled, -pling.** To test or examine by a sample. —**sam'pler** *n.*

**sanc•ti•fy** (săngk'tə-fī') *v.* **-fied, -fying.** To make holy; purify. —**sanc'ti•fi•ca'tion** *n.* —**sanc'ti•fi'er** *n.*

**sanc•ti•mo•ni•ous** (săngk'tə-mō'nē-əs) *adj.* Making a pretense of piety. —**sanc'ti•mo'ni•ous•ly** *adv.* —**sanc'ti•mo'ni•ous•ness, sanc'ti•mo'ny** *n.*

**sanc•tion** (săngk'shən) *n.* **1.** Authoritative approval. **2.** A penalty intended to enforce compliance. —*v.* To authorize.

**sanc•ti•ty** (săngk'tĭ-tē) *n., pl.* **-ties. 1.** Saintliness. **2.** Sacredness.

**sanc•tu•ar•y** (săngk'cho͞o-ĕr'ē) *n., pl.* **-ies. 1.** A holy place, as in a church. **2.** A refuge or asylum.

**sand** (sănd) *n.* Loose particles of disintegrated rock. —*v.* To sandpaper. —**sand'er** *n.* —**sand'y** *adj.*

**san•dal** (săn'dl) *n.* A shoe consisting of a sole fastened to the foot by straps.

**sand•pa•per** (sănd'pā'pər) *n.* Paper coated with sand, used for smoothing.

**sand•wich** (sănd′wĭch, săn′-) *n.* Slices of bread with a filling between them. —*v.* To squeeze.
**sane** (sān) *adj.* **saner, sanest. 1.** Of sound mind. **2.** Reasonable. —**sane′ly** *adv.* —**sane′ness** *n.* —**san′i•ty** *n.*
**sang** (săng) *v.* p.t. of **sing.**
**san•guine** (săng′gwĭn) *adj.* Optimistic. —**san′guine•ly** *adv.*
**san•i•tar•y** (săn′ĭ-tĕr′ē) *adj.* **1.** Of or used to preserve health. **2.** Hygienic. —**san′i•tize′** *v.* —**san′i•tar•i•ly** *adv.*
**san•i•ta•tion** (săn′ĭ-tā′shən) *n.* **1.** Hygiene; cleanliness. **2.** Sewage disposal.
**sank** (săngk) *v.* p.t. of **sink.**
**sap[1]** (săp) *n.* **1.** The watery fluid in a plant. **2.** A fool. —**sap′py** *adj.*
**sap[2]** (săp) *v.* **sapped, sapping. 1.** To undermine. **2.** To weaken gradually.
**sap•id** (săp′ĭd) *n.* **1.** Having a pleasant flavor. **2.** Engaging the mind. —**sa•pid′i•ty** *n.*
**sa•pi•ent** (sā′pē-ənt) *adj.* Intelligent and wise. —**sa′pi•ence** *n.*
**sap•phire** (săf′īr′) *n.* A blue gemstone.
**sar•casm** (săr′kăz′əm) *n.* **1.** A mocking remark. **2.** Scornful irony. —**sar•cas′tic** *adj.*
**sar•don•ic** (săr-dŏn′ĭk) *adj.* Scornfully mocking. —**sar•don′i•cal•ly** *adv.* —**sar•don′i•cism** *n.*
**sash** (săsh) *n.* **1.** A band worn about the waist or over the shoulder. **2.** A frame in which the panes of a window or door are set.
**sat** (săt) *v.* p.t. & p.p. of **sit.**
**sa•tan•ic** (sə-tăn′ĭk, sā-) *adj.* **1.** Of or suggestive of the Devil. **2.** Profoundly cruel or evil. —**Sa′tan** *n.* —**sa•tan′i•cal** *adj.*
**satch•el** (săch′əl) *n.* A small valise or bag.
**sate** (sāt) *v.* **sated, sating.** To indulge fully; satisfy.
**sat•el•lite** (săt′l-īt′) *n.* **1.** A small body, natural or artificial, orbiting a planet. **2.** A nation dominated by another.
**sa•ti•ate** (sā′shē-āt′) *v.* **-ated, -ating.** To satisfy (an appetite or desire) fully. —**sa′ti•a′tion** *n.*
**sat•is•fy** (săt′ĭs-fī′) *v.* **-fied, -fying. 1.** To fulfill the needs or desires of. **2.** To relieve of doubt. **3.** To comply with. **4.** To pay or compensate. —**sat′is•fac′tion** *n.* —**sat′is•fac′to•ri•ly** *adv.* —**sat′is•fac′to•ry** *adj.*
**sat•u•rate** (săch′ə-rāt′) *v.* **-rated, -rating.** To soak or fill to capacity. —**sat′u•ra′tion** *n.*
**Sat•ur•day** (săt′ər-dē, -dā′) *n.* The 7th day of the week.
**sauce** (sôs) *n.* **1.** A liquid dressing for food. **2.** Stewed fruit.
**sau•cer** (sô′sər) *n.* A shallow dish for holding a cup.
**sau•cy** (sô′sē) *adj.* **-cier, -ciest.** Impudent. —**sau′ci•ly** *adv.* —**sau′ci•ness** *n.*
**sau•na** (sô′nə, sou′-) *n.* **1.** A kind of steambath. **2.** The room for such a bath.
**saun•ter** (sôn′tər) *v.* To stroll. —**saun′ter** *n.*
**sau•sage** (sô′sĭj) *n.* Chopped and seasoned meat stuffed into a casing.
**sav•age** (săv′ĭj) *adj.* **1.** Not civilized. **2.** Ferocious; brutal. —*n.* **1.** An uncivilized person. **2.** A brutal person. —**sav′age•ly** *adv.* —**sav′age•ry** *n.*
**sa•van•na, sa•van•nah** (sə-văn′ə) *n.* A flat, treeless tropical or subtropical grassland.
**save** (sāv) *v.* **saved, saving. 1.** To rescue from danger. **2.** To preserve or safeguard. **3.** To store. **4.** To spare. —*prep. & conj.* Except. —**sav′er** *n.* —**sav′ing** *adj. & n.*
**sav•ior** (sāv′yər) *n.* One who saves; rescuer.
**sa•vor** (sā′vər) *n.* A taste or aroma. —*v.* **1.** To have a particular savor. **2.** To relish. —**sa′vor•i•ness** *n.* —**sa′vor•y** *adj.*
**sav•vy** (săv′ē) *v.* **-vied, -vying.** To understand. —*adj.* **-vier, -viest.** Practical and perceptive. —**sav′vy** *n.*
**saw[1]** (sô) *n.* A cutting tool having a metal blade with a sharp-toothed edge. —*v.* **sawed, sawed** or **sawn** (sôn), **sawing.** To cut with a saw. —**saw′yer** *n.*
**saw[2]** (sô) *v.* p.t. of **see.**
**sawn** (sôn) *v.* A p.p. of **saw.**
**sax•o•phone** (săk′sə-fōn′) *n.* A single-reed wind instrument with a usu. curved conical metal tube.
**say** (sā) *v.* **said** (sĕd), **saying. 1.** To utter aloud; speak. **2.** To state or declare. —*n.* **1.** One's chance to speak. **2.** Authority.
**say•ing** (sā′ĭng) *n.* A proverb.

**scab** (skăb) *n.* **1.** A crust over a healing wound. **2.** A strikebreaker. **—scab'by** *adj.*

**scaf•fold** (skăf'əld, -ōld') *n.* **1.** A mobile platform for supporting workers. **2.** A platform for executions. **—scaf'fold•ing** *n.*

**scald** (skôld) *v.* **1.** To burn with hot liquid or steam. **2.** To heat almost to the boiling point. *—n.* An injury caused by scalding.

**scale**[1] (skāl) *n.* **1.** One of the small, thin plates covering fishes, reptiles, etc. **2.** A flake. *—v.* **scaled, scaling. 1.** To clear of scales. **2.** To remove or come off in scales. **—scal'y** *adj.*

**scale**[2] (skāl) *n.* **1.** A series of regularly spaced marks, steps, or levels, used in measurement. **2.** A progressive classification. **3.** A series of consecutive musical tones. *—v.* **scaled, scaling. 1.** To climb. **2.** To reproduce or adjust in accordance with a scale.

**scale**[3] (skāl) *n.* Often **scales.** A weighing machine.

**scal•lop** (skŏl'əp, skăl'-) *n.* **1.** An edible marine mollusk. **2.** One of a series of ornamental curves. *—v.* **1.** To border with scallops. **2.** To bake in a casserole with milk or a sauce. **—scal'lop•er** *n.*

**scalp** (skălp) *n.* The skin covering the top of the head. *—v.* **1.** To cut the scalp from. **2.** To sell at an excessive price. **—scalp'er** *n.*

**scal•pel** (skăl'pəl) *n.* A surgical knife.

**scam** (skăm) *n.* A fraudulent business deal; swindle.

**scan** (skăn) *v.* **scanned, scanning. 1.** To examine closely. **2.** To look over quickly. **3.** To analyze (verse) into metrical patterns. *—n.* An act of scanning. **—scan'ner** *n.*

**scan•dal** (skăn'dl) *n.* **1.** Public disgrace. **2.** Outrage; shame. **3.** Gossip. **—scan'dal•ize'** *v.* **—scan'dal•ous** *adj.* **—scan'dal•ous•ly** *adv.*

**scant** (skănt) *adj.* **1.** Barely enough; meager. **2.** Being just short of a specific measure. **—scant'i•ly** *adv.* **—scant'y** *adj.*

**scar** (skăr) *n.* A mark left by a healed wound. *—v.* **scarred, scarring.** To mark or become marked with a scar.

**scarce** (skârs) *adj.* **scarcer, scarcest. 1.** Infrequently seen or found. **2.** Not abundant. **—scarce'ness** *n.* **—scar'ci•ty** *n.*

**scarce•ly** (skârs'lē) *adv.* **1.** Barely. **2.** Hardly.

**scare** (skâr) *v.* **scared, scaring.** To frighten. *—n.* **1.** A fright. **2.** Panic. **—scar'y** *adj.*

**scarf** (skärf) *n., pl.* **scarfs** or **scarves.** A piece of cloth worn about the neck or head.

**scar•let** (skär'lĭt) *n.* Vivid red. **—scar'let** *adj.*

**scath•ing** (skā'*th*ĭng) *adj.* Harshly critical. **—scath'ing•ly** *adv.*

**scat•ter** (skăt'ər) *v.* **1.** To disperse. **2.** To distribute loosely.

**scav•enge** (skăv'ənj) *v.* **-enged, -enging. 1.** To feed on decaying matter. **2.** To collect or search through (refuse). **—scav'en•ger** *n.*

**sce•nar•i•o** (sĭ-nâr'ē-ō', -när'-, -năr'-) *n., pl.* **-os. 1.** The outline of a plot. **2.** A screenplay. **3.** An outline of a projected scheme. **—sce•nar'ist** *n.*

**scene** (sēn) *n.* **1.** A view. **2.** A setting. **3.** A subdivision of a film or play showing 1 continuous action. **4.** A display of temper.

**scen•er•y** (sē'nə-rē) *n.* **1.** Landscape. **2.** The painted backdrops on a stage. **—sce'nic** *adj.*

**scent** (sĕnt) *n.* **1.** A distinctive odor. **2.** A perfume. *—v.* **1.** To smell. **2.** To perfume.

**scep•ter** (sĕp'tər) *n.* A staff held by a sovereign.

**sched•ule** (skĕj'o͞ol, -o͞o-əl, skĕj'əl) *n.* **1.** A list of items, events, or appointments. **2.** A timetable. *—v.* **-uled, -uling. 1.** To enter on a schedule. **2.** To plan for a certain time.

**scheme** (skēm) *n.* **1.** A plan or design. **2.** A plot. *—v.* **schemed, scheming.** To plot. **—sche•mat'ic** *adj.* **—schem'er** *n.*

**schism** (sĭz'əm) *n.* **1.** A separation into factions, esp. within a church. **2.** A group participating in such a faction. **—schis•mat'ic** *adj. & n.*

**schiz•oid** (skĭt'soid') *adj.* Relating to or resembling schizophrenia. *—n.* A schizophrenic person.

**schmaltz, schmalz** (shmälts) *n.* **1.** Chicken fat. **2.** Maudlin sentimentality, esp. in art or music.

**schol•ar** (skŏl′ər) *n.* **1.** A learned person. **2.** A student. **—schol′ar•ly** *adj.* **—scho•las′tic** *adj.*

**schol•ar•ship** (skŏl′ər-shĭp′) *n.* **1.** Knowledge from study. **2.** Financial assistance to a student.

**school**[1] (sko͞ol) *n.* **1.** An institution for instruction and learning. **2.** A student body. **3.** A group sharing a unifying belief. *—v.* **1.** To instruct. **2.** To train or discipline.

**school**[2] (sko͞ol) *n.* A group of fish.

**schoo•ner** (sko͞o′nər) *n.* **1.** A sailing ship with fore-and-aft rigging. **2.** A beer glass that holds at least 1 pint.

**sci•ence** (sī′əns) *n.* **1.** The study of natural phenomena or the knowledge so acquired. **2.** Any branch of knowledge. **3.** An activity requiring study and method. **—sci′en•tif′ic** *adj.* **—sci′en•tif′i•cal•ly** *adv.* **—sci′en•tist** *n.*

**sci•on** (sī′ən) *n.* A descendant.

**scis•sors** (sĭz′ərz) *n.* A cutting implement of 2 blades joined by a swivel pin.

**scoff** (skŏf, skôf) *v.* To mock at or scorn. *—n.* An expression of scorn. **—scoff′er** *n.*

**scold** (skōld) *v.* To reprimand harshly. *—n.* One who scolds.

**scoop** (sko͞op) *n.* **1.** A small, shovellike utensil. **2.** The bucket of a steam shovel or dredge. **3.** An exclusive news story. *—v.* **1.** To take up with a scoop. **2.** To hollow out.

**scope** (skōp) *n.* **1.** A range, as of one's mind. **2.** Opportunity to function.

**scorch** (skôrch) *v.* To burn the surface of. *—n.* A slight or surface burn. **—scorch′ing•ly** *adv.*

**score** (skôr, skōr) *n.* **1.** A notch or incision. **2.** A record of points made. **3.** A result of a test. **4.** A debt. **5.** A group of 20. **6.** The written form of a musical composition. *—v.* **scored, scoring. 1.** To mark with lines. **2.** To gain (a point). **3.** To record a score. **4.** To achieve; win. **5.** To assign a grade to. **6.** In music, to arrange. **—scor′er** *n.*

**scorn** (skôrn) *n.* **1.** Contempt. **2.** Derision. *—v.* To treat as contemptible. **—scorn′ful** *adj.* **—scorn′ful•ly** *adv.*

**scoun•drel** (skoun′drəl) *n.* A villain.

**scour** (skour) *v.* **1.** To clean by scrubbing. **2.** To search thoroughly.

**scourge** (skûrj) *n.* **1.** A whip. **2.** A cause of affliction. *—v.* **scourged, scourging. 1.** To flog. **2.** To ravage. **—scourg′er** *n.*

**scout** (skout) *n.* One sent in advance to gather information. *—v.* **1.** To reconnoiter. **2.** To observe and evaluate.

**scowl** (skoul) *v.* To wrinkle the brow in anger or disapproval. **—scowl** *n.*

**scram•ble** (skrăm′bəl) *v.* **-bled, -bling. 1.** To move hurriedly. **2.** To compete frantically. **3.** To mix confusedly. **4.** To stir-fry (eggs) with the yolks and whites mixed. **—scram′ble** *n.* **—scram′bler** *n.*

**scrap** (skrăp) *n.* A fragment or shred. *—v.* **scrapped, scrapping.** To discard.

**scrape** (skrāp) *v.* **scraped, scraping. 1.** To rub forcefully. **2.** To smooth, injure, or remove by rubbing hard. **3.** To amass. *—n.* **1.** The act or result of scraping. **2.** A predicament. *n.*

**scratch** (skrăch) *v.* **1.** To make a shallow cut or mark on. **2.** To dig or wound with nails or claws. **3.** To rub (the skin) to relieve itching. **4.** To strike out. *—n.* A mark or wound produced by scratching. **—scratch′y** *adj.*

**scrawl** (skrôl) *v.* To write hastily or illegibly. **—scrawl** *n.*

**scraw•ny** (skrô′nē) *adj.* **-nier, -niest.** Skinny. **—scraw′ni•ness** *n.*

**scream** (skrēm) *v.* To cry out loudly and shrilly. *—n.* A loud piercing sound.

**screech** (skrēch) *v.* To make a high-pitched, strident scream. **—screech** *n.* **—screech′er** *n.* **—screech′y** *adj.*

**screen** (skrēn) *n.* **1.** Something that serves to divide, conceal, or protect. **2.** A window insertion of framed mesh. **3.** A surface upon which a picture is projected for viewing. *—v.* **1.** To conceal or protect. **2.** To sift out. **3.** To show on a screen.

**screw** (skro͞o) *n.* **1.** A naillike metal fastener with incised grooves. **2.** A propeller. *—v.* **1.** To fasten with a screw. **2.** To turn or twist.

**screw•driv•er** (skro͞o′drī′vər) *n.* A tool for turning screws.

**scrib•ble** (skrĭb′əl) *v.* **-bled, -bling.** To write hurriedly and carelessly. **—scrib′ble** *n.* **—scrib′bler** *n.*

**scribe** (skrīb) *n.* A writer.

**scrim•mage** (skrĭm′ĭj) *n.* **1.** A rough-and-tumble struggle. **2.** The contest be-

tween 2 football teams while the ball is in play. **3.** A practice session, as between 2 units of the same team.
**script** (skrĭpt) *n.* **1.** Handwriting. **2.** The text of a play, film, etc.
**Scrip•ture** (skrĭp′chər) *n.* Often **Scriptures.** Sacred writings, esp. the Bible. **—Scrip′tur•al** *adj.*
**scroll** (skrōl) *n.* A rolled document.
**scrounge** (skrounj) *v.* **scrounged, scrounging.** To forage for. **—scroung′er** *n.*
**scrub¹** (skrŭb) *v.* **scrubbed, scrubbing.** To clean by rubbing hard, as with a brush. **—scrub** *n.* **—scrub′ber** *n.*
**scrub²** (skrŭb) *n.* Stunted trees or shrubs. **—scrub** *adj.* **—scrub′by** *adj.*
**scruff** (skrŭf) *n.* The back of the neck.
**scru•ple** (skrōō′pəl) *n.* An ethical objection. **—scru′pu•lous** *adj.*
**scru•ti•ny** (skrōōt′n-ē) *n.* Close examination; careful surveillance. **—scru′ti•nize′** *v.* **—scru′ti•niz′er** *n.*
**scu•ba** (skōō′bə) *n.* An apparatus containing compressed air for breathing underwater while swimming.
**scuff** (skŭf) *v.* To scrape with the feet while walking. *—n.* A worn spot.
**scuf•fle** (skŭf′əl) *v.* **-fled, -fling. 1.** To fight in confusion at close quarters. **2.** To shuffle. **—scuf′fle** *n.* **—scuf′fler** *n.*
**sculp•ture** (skŭlp′chər) *n.* **1.** The art of making statues or other shaped figures. **2.** A statue or other artistically shaped figure. *—v.* **-tured, -turing.** To create (sculpture) by molding, carving, etc. **—sculpt** *v.* **—sculp′tor** *n.* **—sculp′tress** *n.*
**scum** (skŭm) *n.* Impure matter, esp. on a liquid surface. **—scum′my** *adj.*
**scur•ry** (skûr′ē) *v.* **-ried, -rying.** To scamper.
**scut•tle** (skŭt′l) *v.* **-tled, -tling. 1.** To sink (a ship) deliberately. **2.** To run hastily.
**scythe** (sī*th*) *n.* A long, curved blade for mowing or reaping. **—scythe** *v.*
**sea** (sē) *n.* **1.** The waters covering most of the earth. **2.** A relatively large body of water completely or partly landlocked. **3.** A vast amount or extent.
**seal¹** (sēl) *n.* **1.** A stamped emblem or design that indicates approval or authentication. **2.** A device, as a gummed paper, for closing envelopes or packages. *—v.* **1.** To affix a seal to. **2.** To close; make fast. **3.** To settle; conclude.
**seal²** (sēl) *n.* An aquatic, carnivorous, fur-bearing mammal with flippers.
**seam** (sēm) *n.* **1.** A line formed by sewing together 2 pieces of cloth. **2.** A fissure or wrinkle. **3.** A thin layer, as of coal. *—v.* **1.** To join with a seam. **2.** To mark with lines. **—seam′er** *n.* **—seam′less** *adj.*
**sear** (sîr) *v.* **1.** To wither; dry up. **2.** To burn the surface of.
**search** (sûrch) *v.* To look through, investigate, or check in hopes of finding something lost or sought. **—search** *n.* **—search′er** *n.*
**sea•son** (sē′zən) *n.* **1.** One of the 4 equal divisions of the year, spring, summer, fall, and winter. **2.** A special time of year. *—v.* **1.** To improve or enhance the flavor of. **2.** To accustom. **3.** To make usable, as by aging. **—sea′son•al** *adj.*
**seat** (sēt) *n.* **1.** A surface or place for sitting, as a chair. **2.** The part on which one rests in sitting. **3.** The buttocks. **4.** A location. **5.** Center; capital. *—v.* **1.** To place in a seat. **2.** To have seats for.
**se•clude** (sĭ-klōōd′) *v.* **-cluded, -cluding.** To set apart; isolate. **—se•clu′sion** *n.*
**sec•ond¹** (sĕk′ənd) *n.* **1.** A unit of time equal to 1/60 of a minute. **2.** A moment.
**sec•ond²** (sĕk′ənd) *adj.* **1.** Next after the 1st. **2.** Subordinate. *—n.* **1.** One that is next after the 1st. **2.** An assistant or attendant. *—v.* **1.** To attend; assist. **2.** To endorse (a motion or nomination). **—sec′ond, sec′ond•ly** *adv.* **—sec′ond•ar′y** *adj.*
**se•cret** (sē′krĭt) *adj.* **1.** Kept from being generally known. **2.** Operating covertly. *—n.* Something kept hidden from others. **—se′cre•cy** *n.* **—se′cre•tive** *adj.* **—se′cre•tive•ness** *n.* **—se′cret•ly** *adv.*
**sec•re•tar•y** (sĕk′rĭ-tĕr′ē) *n., pl.* **-ies. 1.** One employed to handle correspondence and do clerical work. **2.** An officer in charge of a governmental department. **3.** A writing desk. **—sec′re•tar′i•al** *adj.*
**se•crete¹** (sĭ-krēt′) *v.* **-creted, -creting.** To generate and release (a bodily substance). **—se•cre′tion** *n.* **—se•cre′to•ry** *adj.*
**se•crete²** (sĭ-krēt′) *v.* **-creted, -creting.** To conceal.

**sect** (sĕkt) *n.* **1.** A distinct, more strictly defined group within a larger group. **2.** A religious denomination. **—sec•tar′i•an** *adj. & n.*

**sec•tion** (sĕk′shən) *n.* A part; portion. —*v.* To divide into parts. **—sec′tion•al** *adj.*

**sec•tor** (sĕk′tər, -tôr′) *n.* A part; section.

**sec•u•lar** (sĕk′yə-lər) *adj.* Not pertaining to religion; worldly. **—sec′u•lar•ly** *adv.*

**se•cure** (sĭ-kyŏŏr′) *adj.* **-curer, -curest. 1.** Free from danger; safe. **2.** Free from doubt. **3.** Stable. **4.** Certain. —*v.* **-cured, -curing. 1.** To guard. **2.** To fasten. **3.** To acquire. **—se•cure′ly** *adv.*

**se•cu•ri•ty** (sĭ-kyŏŏr′ĭ-tē) *n., pl.* **-ties. 1.** Safety. **2.** Confidence. **3.** Something deposited as assurance of the fulfillment of an obligation. **4. securities.** Stocks, bonds, notes, etc.

**se•dan** (sĭ-dăn′) *n.* **1.** A closed automobile with 2 or 4 doors and front and rear seats. **2.** An enclosed chair carried on poles by 2 people.

**se•date** (sĭ-dāt′) *adj.* Serenely deliberate; composed. **—se•date′ly** *adv.*

**sed•a•tive** (sĕd′ə-tĭv) *adj.* Having a calming effect. —*n.* A sedative drug. **—se•da′tion** *n.*

**sed•en•tar•y** (sĕd′n-tĕr′ē) *adj.* Characterized by much sitting.

**sed•i•ment** (sĕd′ə-mənt) *n.* Material that settles to the bottom of a liquid. **—sed′i•men′ta•ry** *adj.* **—sed′i•men•ta′tion** *n.*

**se•di•tion** (sĭ-dĭsh′ən) *n.* **1.** Conduct or language arousing rebellion against the state. **2.** Rebellion against the state. **—se•di′tion•ist** *n.* **—se•di′tious** *adj.* **—se•di′tious•ness** *n.*

**se•duce** (sĭ-d/y/ŏŏs′) *v.* **-duced, -ducing. 1.** To entice into wrongful behavior. **2.** To induce to have sexual intercourse. **—se•duc′er** *n.* **—se•duc′tion** *n.* **—se•duc′tive** *adj.*

**see**[1] (sē) *v.* **saw** (sô), **seen, seeing. 1.** To perceive with the eye. **2.** To understand. **3.** To regard. **4.** To undergo. **5.** To find out. **6.** To visit. **7.** To escort. **8.** To make sure.

**see**[2] (sē) *n.* The jurisdiction or office of a bishop.

**seed** (sēd) *n., pl.* **seeds** or **seed. 1.** A fertilized plant ovule capable of developing into a new plant. **2.** A source or beginning. **3.** Offspring. —*v.* **1.** To plant seeds in. **2.** To remove seeds from.

**seed•y** (sē′dē) *adj.* **-ier, -iest. 1.** Having many seeds. **2.** Worn and shabby. **—seed′i•ness** *n.*

**seek** (sēk) *v.* **sought** (sôt), **seeking. 1.** To search for. **2.** To try to obtain. **3.** To attempt. **—seek′er** *n.*

**seem** (sēm) *v.* To give the impression of being; appear. **—seem′ing** *adj.* **—seem′ing•ly** *adv.*

**seen** (sēn) *v.* p.p. of **see**[1].

**seep** (sēp) *v.* To pass slowly through small openings. **—seep′age** *n.*

**see•saw** (sē′sô′) *n.* A long, balanced plank that goes up and down when ridden at the ends. **—see′saw′** *v.*

**seethe** (sē*th*) *v.* **seethed, seething.** To churn and foam as if boiling.

**seg•ment** (sĕg′mənt) *n.* A division or section. —*v.* (sĕg-mĕnt′). To divide into segments. **—seg′men′tal** *adj.* **—seg′men•ta′tion** *n.*

**seg•re•gate** (sĕg′rĭ-gāt′) *v.* **-gated, -gating.** To isolate from others; keep separate. **—seg′re•ga′tion** *n.*

**seis•mic** (sīz′mĭk) *adj.* Relating to, subject to, or caused by an earthquake.

**seize** (sēz) *v.* **seized, seizing. 1.** To take suddenly and forcibly. **2.** To overwhelm. **3.** To confiscate. **—sei′zure** *n.*

**sel•dom** (sĕl′dəm) *adv.* Infrequently. **—sel′dom•ness** *n.*

**se•lect** (sĭ-lĕkt′) v. To choose. —*adj.* **1.** Chosen. **2.** Of special quality. **—se•lec′tion** *n.* **—se•lec′tive** *adj.* **—se•lec′tiv′i•ty** *n.*

**self** (sĕlf) *n., pl.* **selves. 1.** One's own being. **2.** One's own welfare or advantage.

**self-con•scious** (sĕlf′kŏn′shəs) *adj.* **1.** Excessively conscious of one's appearance or manner. **2.** Not natural; stilted. **—self′-con′scious•ly** *adv.* **—self′-con′scious•ness** *n.*

**self•ish** (sĕl′fĭsh) *adj.* Concerned only with oneself; egotistic. **—self′ish•ly** *adv.* **—self′ish•ness** *n.*

**self•less** (sĕlf′lĭs) *adj.* Unselfish. **—self′less•ly** *adv.* **—self′less•ness** *n.*

**sell** (sĕl) *v.* **sold** (sōld), **selling. 1.** To exchange for money. **2.** To offer for sale. **3.** To be sold or be on sale. **—sell′er** *n.*

**selves** (sĕlvz) *n.* pl. of **self.**

**se•man•tics** (sĭ-măn'tĭks) *n.* The study of the meanings of words. **—se•man'tic** *adj.*

**sem•blance** (sĕm'bləns) *n.* An outward appearance.

**se•men** (sē'mən) *n.* The male reproductive fluid; sperm. **—sem'i•nal** *adj.*

**se•mes•ter** (sə-mĕs'tər) *n.* One of 2 divisions of an academic year.

**sem•i•co•lon** (sĕm'ĭ-kō'lən) *n.* A mark of punctuation (;).

**sem•i•nar** (sĕm'ə-när') *n.* **1.** A class of advanced students doing original research under a professor's guidance. **2.** A conference.

**sem•i•nar•y** (sĕm'ə-nĕr'ē) *n., pl.* **-ies. 1.** A school, esp. of theology, for training clerics. **2.** A school of higher education, esp. a private school for young women. **—sem•i•nar'i•an** *n.*

**sen•ate** (sĕn'ĭt) *n.* A legislative and deliberative assembly. **—sen'a•tor** *n.* **—sen'a•to'ri•al** *adj.*

**send** (sĕnd) *v.* **sent, sending. 1.** To cause to be conveyed. **2.** To direct to go. **3.** To emit. **4.** To propel. **—send'er** *n.*

**se•nes•cence** (sĭ-nĕs'əns) *n.* Old age. **—se•nes'cent** *adj.*

**se•nile** (sē'nīl', sĕn'īl') *adj.* **1.** Of old age. **2.** Weakened, esp. mentally, by old age. **—se•nil'i•ty** *n.*

**sen•ior** (sēn'yər) *adj.* **1.** Designating the older of 2. **2.** Above others in rank or length of service. *—n.* A student in the 4th year of high school or college. **—sen•ior'i•ty** *n.*

**sen•sa•tion** (sĕn-sā'shən) *n.* **1.** An impression from a sense organ or a bodily part. **2.** Feeling. **3.** Heightened public interest and excitement, or an event causing this. **—sen•sa'tion•al** *adj.* **—sen•sa'tion•al•ism'** *n.*

**sense** (sĕns) *n.* **1.** Any of the functions of hearing, sight, smell, touch, and taste. **2.** Sensation; feeling. **3.** Perception. **4.** Good judgment. **5.** Meaning. *—v.* **sensed, sensing.** To perceive. **—sense'less** *adj.* **—sense'less•ly** *adv.* **—sense'less•ness** *n.* **—sen'so•ry** *adj.*

**sen•si•bil•i•ty** (sĕn'sə-bĭl'ĭ-tē) *n., pl.* **-ties. 1.** The ability to feel. **2.** Delicate sensitivity.

**sen•si•ble** (sĕn'sə-bəl) *adj.* **1.** Perceptible. **2.** Aware. **3.** Showing good sense. **—sen'si•bly** *adv.*

**sen•si•tive** (sĕn'sĭ-tĭv) *adj.* **1.** Responsive to stimulation. **2.** Keen; perceptive. **3.** Quick to take offense; touchy. **4.** Easily irritated. **—sen'si•tive•ly** *adv.* **—sen'si•tiv'i•ty, sen'si•tive•ness** *n.*

**sen•sor** (sĕn'sər, -sôr') *n.* A device, such as a photoelectric cell, that receives and responds to a signal.

**sen•su•al** (sĕn'shōō-əl) *adj.* Of or indulging in the appetites of the senses. **—sen'su•al'i•ty, sen'su•al•ness** *n.* **—sen'su•al•ly** *adv.*

**sen•su•ous** (sĕn'shōō-əs) *adj.* Of or appealing to the senses. **—sen'su•ous•ly** *adv.* **—sen'su•ous•ness** *n.*

**sent** (sĕnt) *v.* p.t. & p.p. of **send.**

**sen•tence** (sĕn'təns) *n.* **1.** A grammatical group of words containing a subject and a verb. **2.** A legal judgment or punishment. *—v.* **-tenced, -tencing.** To pass sentence upon. **—sen•ten'tial** *adj.*

**sen•tient** (sĕn'shənt, -shē-ənt) *adj.* Having sense perception; conscious. *—n.* **1.** A sentient person or thing. **2.** The mind. **—sen'tient•ly** *adv.*

**sen•ti•ment** (sĕn'tə-mənt) *n.* **1.** An opinion or attitude. **2.** A feeling. **3.** Affection; tenderness. **4.** False or conventional emotion. **—sen'ti•men'tal** *adv.* **—sen'ti•men'tal•ism', sen'ti•men•tal'i•ty** *n.* **—sen'ti•men'tal•ly** *adv.*

**sen•try** (sĕn'trē) *n., pl.* **-tries.** A guard posted to prevent the passage of unauthorized persons.

**sep•a•rate** (sĕp'ə-rāt') *v.* **-rated, -rating. 1.** To set, keep, or come apart. **2.** To differentiate between. *—adj.* (sĕp'ər-ĭt). **1.** Set apart; not connected. **2.** Dissimilar; distinct. **—sep'a•ra•ble** *adj.* **—sep'a•rate•ly** *adv.* **—sep'a•rate•ness** *n.* **—sep'a•ra'tion** *n.*

**Sep•tem•ber** (sĕp-tĕm'bər) *n.* The 9th month of the year.

**sep•ul•cher** (sĕp'əl-kər) *n.* A burial vault. **—se•pul'chral** *adj.*

**se•quel** (sē'kwəl) *n.* **1.** A work continuing the narrative of an earlier work. **2.** A consequence.

**se•quence** (sē'kwəns) *n.* **1.** Succession. **2.** An order of occurrence. **3.** A related or continuous series. **—se•quen'tial** *adj.* **—se•quen'tial•ly** *adv.*

**se•ques•ter** (sĭ-kwĕs′tər) *v.* To remove; set apart. —**se′ques•tra′tion** *n.*
**ser•e•nade** (sĕr′ə-nād′, sĕr′ə-nād′) *n.* Music meant to please or charm a sweetheart or other listener. —*v.* **-naded, -nading.** To perform a serenade (for). —**ser′e•nad′er** *n.*
**ser•en•dip•i•ty** (sĕr′ən-dĭp′ĭ-tē) *n.* The making of fortunate, accidental discoveries. —**ser′en•dip′i•tous** *adj.*
**se•rene** (sə-rēn′) *adj.* Tranquil; dignified. —**se•rene′ly** *adv.* —**se•ren′i•ty** *n.*
**serf** (sûrf) *n.* A feudal farm laborer, owned by a lord. —**serf′dom** *n.*
**ser•geant** (sär′jənt) *n.* A low-ranking noncommissioned officer.
**se•ri•al** (sîr′ē-əl) *adj.* Of, forming, or published in a series. —*n.* A work published or produced in installments. —**se′ri•al•ize′** *v.* —**se′ri•al•ly** *adv.*
**se•ries** (sîr′ēz) *n., pl.* **-ries.** A group of related things coming one after another; succession.
**se•ri•ous** (sêr′ē-əs) *adj.* **1.** Grave; sober. **2.** Sincere. **3.** Causing anxiety; critical. —**se′ri•ous•ly** *adv.* —**se′ri•ous•ness** *n.*
**ser•mon** (sûr′mən) *n.* **1.** A homily during a religious service. **2.** A long moral lecture.
**ser•pent** (sûr′pənt) *n.* A snake. —**ser′pen•tine′** *adj.*
**se•rum** (sîr′əm) *n., pl.* **-rums** or **-ra. 1.** A clear fluid derived from blood. **2.** Such fluid from an immunized animal, used as an antitioxin. —**se′rous** *adj.*
**ser•vant** (sûr′vənt) *n.* One employed to perform domestic services.
**serve** (sûrv) *v.* **served, serving. 1.** To work for; be a servant to. **2.** To act; function. **3.** To wait on. **4.** To be of assistance to. **5.** To undergo military service. **6.** To meet a need. **7.** To present or deliver. **8.** To put (a ball) in play. —*n.* The right or act of serving in a court game. —**serv′er** *n.*
**ser•vice** (sûr′vĭs) *n.* **1.** The occupation of a servant. **2.** The act of serving. **3.** A government department. **4.** The armed forces. **5.** Maintenance and repairs. **6.** A set of dishes or utensils. —*v.* **-viced, -vicing. 1.** To repair; maintain. **2.** To provide services to. —**ser′vice•a•ble** *adj.*
**ser•vile** (sûr′vəl, -vīl′) *adj.* Slavish; submissive. —**ser•vil′i•ty** *n.*
**ser•vi•tude** (sûr′vĭ-t/y/o͞od′) *n.* **1.** Slavery; bondage. **2.** Forced labor as a punishment for crime.
**ses•sile** (sĕs′īl) *adj.* Permanently attached or fixed; unmoving.
**ses•sion** (sĕsh′ən) *n.* A meeting, as of a class or legislature.
**set¹** (sĕt) *v.* **set, setting. 1.** To put. **2.** To fix, esp. a broken bone. **3.** To arrange tableware upon (a table). **4.** To compose (type). **5.** To prescribe, establish, or assign. **6.** To sit on eggs, as a hen. **7.** To disappear below the horizon. **8.** To harden. —*adj.* **1.** Fixed. **2.** Unyielding. **3.** Ready. —*n.* The act of setting.
**set²** (sĕt) *n.* **1.** A group; collection. **2.** The scenery for a play or motion-picture scene. **3.** An apparatus, esp. a radio or television.
**set•tle** (sĕt′l) *v.* **-tled, -tling. 1.** To arrange or fix definitely. **2.** To establish residence in. **3.** To calm. **4.** To sink or come to rest. **5.** To pay (a debt). **6.** To decide. —**set′tler** *n.*
**set•tle•ment** (sĕt′l-mənt) *n.* **1.** The act of settling. **2.** A colony. **3.** A small community. **4.** An agreement.
**sev•en** (sĕv′ən) *n.* The cardinal number written 7. —**sev′en** *adj. & pron.* —**sev′enth** *n. & adj.*
**sev•en•teen** (sĕv′ən-tēn′) *n.* The cardinal number written 17. —**sev′en•teen′** *adj. & pron.* —**sev′en•teenth′** *n. & adj.*
**sev•en•ty** (sĕv′ən-tē) *n.* The cardinal number written 70. —**sev′en•ti•eth** *n. & adj.* —**sev′en•ty** *adj. & pron.*
**sev•er** (sĕv′ər) *v.* To separate; cut. —**sev′er•ance** *n.*
**sev•er•al** (sĕv′ər-əl) *adj.* **1.** More than 2, but not many. **2.** Single; distinct. —*n.* Several ones; a few. —**sev′er•al•ly** *adv.*
**se•vere** (sə-vîr′) *adj.* **-verer, -verest. 1.** Harsh; stern; strict. **2.** Grave; forbidding. **3.** Plain; unadorned. **4.** Intense; sharp. **5.** Rigorous. —**se•vere′ly** *adv.* —**se•ver′i•ty, se•vere′ness** *n.*
**sew** (sō) *v.* **sewed, sewn** or **sewed, sewing.** To make, repair, or fasten with a needle and thread. —**sew′er** *n.* —**sew′ing** *n.*
**sew•age** (so͞o′ĭj) *n.* Waste carried off in sewers.

**sew•er** (sōō′ər) *n.* A pipe or other passageway for carrying off sewage or rainwater.

**sewn** (sōn) *v.* A p.p. of **sew.**

**sex** (sĕks) *n.* **1.** Either of 2 divisions of organisms according to reproductive function, male and female. **2.** The urge or instinct to copulate. **3.** Sexual intercourse. **—sex′less** *adj.* **—sex′u•al** *adj.* **—sex′u•al′i•ty** *n.* **—sex′u•al•ly** *adv.* **—sex′y** *adj.*

**sex•ism** (sĕk′sĭz′əm) *n.* Discrimination based on sex. **—sex′ist** *adj. & n.*

**shab•by** (shăb′ē) *adj.* **-bier, -biest. 1.** Threadbare; worn-out. **2.** Wearing worn garments. **3.** Despicable. **—shab′bi•ly** *adv.* **—shab′bi•ness** *n.*

**shack** (shăk) *n.* A small, crudely built cabin.

**shack•le** (shăk′əl) *n.* A metal fastening for restraining a prisoner's ankle or wrist. *—v.* **-led, -ling.** To put shackles on. **—shack′ler** *n.*

**shade** (shād) *n.* **1.** Diminished or partial light, esp. when caused by blocking the sun's rays. **2.** A device to block the sun's rays. **3.** The degree to which a color is darkened. **4.** A slight variation or amount. *—v.* **shaded, shading. 1.** To screen from light. **2.** To change by slight degrees. **—shad′y** *adj.*

**shad•ow** (shăd′ō) *n.* **1.** A darkened area caused by an object blocking rays of light. **2.** Gloom. **3.** A faint indication. *—v.* **1.** To shade. **2.** To follow, esp. in secret. **—shad′ow•er** *n.* **—shad′ow•i•ness** *n.* **—shad′ow•y** *adj.*

**shaft** (shăft) *n.* **1.** The body of a spear or arrow. **2.** A long, narrow object or machine part; bar. **3.** A long, narrow passage.

**shag•gy** (shăg′ē) *adj.* **-gier, -giest.** Bushy and matted. **—shag′gi•ness** *n.*

**shake** (shāk) *v.* **shook** (shŏŏk), **shaken, shaking. 1.** To move or cause to move to and fro jerkily. **2.** To tremble. **3.** To weaken or discourage. **4.** To clasp (hands or another's hand), as in greeting. *—n.* An act of shaking. **—shak′a•ble, shake′a•ble** *adj.* **—shak′er** *n.* **—shak′i•ly** *adv.* **—shak′i•ness** *n.* **—shak′y** *adj.*

**shall** (shăl) *v.* **should** (shŏŏd). An auxiliary to indicate the future tense and obligation.

**shal•low** (shăl′ō) *adj.* Not deep. *—n.* A shallow part of a body of water. **—shal′low•ness** *n.*

**sham** (shăm) *n.* One that is false or counterfeit. *—adj.* Not genuine; counterfeit. *—v.* **shammed, shamming.** To feign.

**sham•bles** (shăm′bəlz) *n.* A scene of complete disorder.

**shame** (shām) *n.* **1.** A painful emotion caused by a sense of guilt, unworthiness, or disgrace. **2.** A dishonor or disgrace. **3.** A great disappointment. *—v.* **shamed, shaming. 1.** To cause to feel shame. **2.** To bring dishonor upon. **3.** To force by making ashamed. **—shame′ful** *adj.* **—shame′ful•ly** *adv.* **—shame′ful•ness** *n.* **—shame′less** *adj.* **—shame′less•ly** *adv.* **—shame′less•ness** *n.*

**sham•poo** (shăm-pōō′) *n.* A sudsy soap, esp. one for the hair. **—sham•poo′** *v.*

**shank** (shăngk) *n.* The lower leg or a similar part.

**shan't, sha'nt** (shănt, shänt) *v.* Contractions of *shall not.*

**shape** (shāp) *n.* **1.** The outline of a thing; form. **2.** Developed or definite form. **3.** Condition. *—v.* **shaped, shaping. 1.** To give a form to. **2.** To develop. **—shape′less** *adj.* **—shape′less•ness** *n.* **—shape′ly** *adj.* **—shape′li•ness** *n.*

**shard** (shärd) *n.* Also **sherd** (shûrd). A piece of broken pottery; potsherd.

**share** (shâr) *n.* A part given or due to each participant, member, owner, etc. *—v.* **shared, sharing. 1.** To give out in shares. **2.** To have, use, or experience in common. **3.** To participate. **—shar′er** *n.*

**shark** (shärk) *n.* **1.** A large, voracious fish. **2.** A swindler or cheat.

**sharp** (shärp) *adj.* **1.** Having a thin, keen edge or a fine point. **2.** Abrupt. **3.** Astute. **4.** Alert. **5.** In music, raised a half tone in pitch. *—adv.* **1.** In a sharp manner. **2.** Punctually. *—n.* A musical note raised by a half tone. **—sharp′en** *v.* **—sharp′en•er** *n.* **—sharp′ly** *adv.* **—sharp′ness** *n.*

**shat•ter** (shăt′ər) *v.* To break or burst suddenly into pieces.

**shave** (shāv) *v.* **shaved, shaved** or **shaven, shaving. 1.** To remove body hair from with a razor. **2.** To cut thin

slices from. —*n.* The act or result of shaving. —**shav'er** *n.* —**shav'ing** *n.*
**shawl** (shôl) *n.* A cloth for covering the head and shoulders.
**she** (shē) *pron.* The 3rd person sing. pronoun in the subjective case, feminine gender.
**sheaf** (shēf) *n., pl.* **sheaves.** A bundle, esp. of cut grain.
**shear** (shîr) *v.* **sheared, sheared** or **shorn** (shôrn, shōrn), **shearing.** To clip off (fleece, hair, etc.).
**shears** (shîrz) *pl.n.* Large-sized scissors.
**sheath** (shēth) *n., pl.* **sheaths.** A long, tight-fitting case, as for the blade of a knife.
**sheathe** (shē*th*) *v.* **sheathed, sheathing.** To put into a sheath.
**sheaves** (shēvz) *n.* pl. of **sheaf.**
**shed**[1] (shĕd) *v.* **shed, shedding. 1.** To pour forth. **2.** To diffuse or radiate. **3.** To cast off.
**shed**[2] (shĕd) *n.* A small structure for storage or shelter.
**she'd** (shēd) *v.* Contraction of *she had* or *she would.*
**sheen** (shēn) *n.* Shininess.
**sheep•ish** (shē'pĭsh) *adj.* Embarrassed. —**sheep'ish•ly** *adv.* —**sheep'ish•ness** *n.*
**sheer**[1] (shîr) *v.* To swerve.
**sheer**[2] (shîr) *adj.* **1.** Thin and transparent. **2.** Pure. **3.** Very steep. —**sheer'ly** *adv.* —**sheer'ness** *n.*
**sheet** (shēt) *n.* **1.** A large piece of cloth for covering a bed. **2.** A broad, thin piece, as of paper or glass.
**sheik, sheikh** (shēk, shāk) *n.* **1.** A Muslim religious official. **2.** The leader of an Arab family, village, or tribe.
**shelf** (shĕlf) *n., pl.* **shelves. 1.** A board fixed at right angles to a wall for holding objects. **2.** A ledge.
**shell** (shĕl) *n.* **1.** A hard outer covering, as of a mollusk, egg, or nut. **2.** A framework. **3.** A narrow racing boat. **4.** A projectile or piece of ammunition. —*v.* **1.** To remove from a shell, pod, etc. **2.** To bombard.
**shel•lac** (shə-lăk') *n.* A thin varnish. —*v.* **-lacked, -lacking.** To apply shellac.
**shel•ter** (shĕl'tər) *n.* Something that provides cover or protection. —*v.* To provide cover or protection for.
**shelves** (shĕlvz) *n.* pl. of **shelf.**
**shep•herd** (shĕp'ərd) *n.* One that tends sheep. —*v.* To herd, guard, or care for.
**sher•bet** (shûr'bĭt) *n.* A sweet-flavored water ice.
**sher•iff** (shĕr'ĭf) *n.* The chief law-enforcement officer in a county.
**sher•ry** (shĕr'ē) *n., pl.* **-ries.** A fortified Spanish wine.
**shield** (shēld) *n.* **1.** Protective armor carried on the forearm. **2.** Any protective covering. —*v.* To protect or defend.
**shift** (shĭft) *v.* **1.** To move or transfer. **2.** To provide for one's needs. —*n.* **1.** A change, transference, or displacement. **2.** A working period.
**shift•y** (shĭf'tē) *adj.* **-ier, -iest.** Tricky. —**shift'i•ness** *n.*
**shim•mer** (shĭm'ər) *v.* To shine with a tremulous light. —*n.* A glimmering. —**shim'mer•y** *adj.*
**shin** (shĭn) *n.* The front part of the leg between knee and ankle. —*v.* **shinned, shinning.** To climb by gripping and pulling with the hands and legs.
**shine** (shīn) *v.* **shone** (shōn) or **shined, shining. 1.** To emit or reflect light. **2.** To excel. **3.** To aim the beam or glow of. **4.** To make bright by polishing. —*n.* **1.** Brightness. **2.** A polishing. —**shin'i•ness** *n.* —**shin'y** *adj.*
**shin•gle** (shĭng'gəl) *n.* **1.** A piece of wood, asbestos, etc., for roofing or siding. **2.** A small board bearing a sign. —*v.* **-gled, -gling.** To cover with shingles. —**shin'gler** *n.*
**ship** (shĭp) *n.* **1.** A large vessel for deepwater navigation. **2.** An airplane. —*v.* **shipped, shipping. 1.** To place on a ship. **2.** To transport. —**ship'ment** *n.* —**ship'per** *n.* —**ship'ping** *adj. & n.*
**shirk** (shûrk) *v.* To put off or avoid (work or duty). —**shirk'er** *n.*
**shirt** (shûrt) *n.* A garment for the upper body.
**shiv•er** (shĭv'ər) *v.* **1.** To tremble, as from cold. **2.** To shatter. —**shiv'er** *n.*
**shoal** (shōl) *n.* **1.** A shallow. **2.** A school of fish.
**shock** (shŏk) *n.* **1.** A violent collision or impact. **2.** A violent surprise or emotional upset. **3.** An offense to one's sense of propriety. **4.** The sensation of an electric current on the body. —*v.* **1.** To disturb deeply; astonish. **2.** To outrage. **3.** To subject to an electric shock.

—**shock'ing** *adj.* —**shock'ing•ly** *adv.*

**shod•dy** (shŏd'ē) *adj.* **-dier, -diest.** Inferior; cheap. —**shod'di•ly** *adv.* —**shod'di•ness** *n.*

**shoe** (sho͞o) *n.* **1.** A durable covering for the human foot. **2.** A horseshoe. —*v.* **shod,** (shŏd), **shod** or **shodden** (shŏd'n), **shoeing.** To furnish with shoes.

**shone** (shōn) *v.* A p.t. & p.p. of **shine.**

**shook** (sho͝ok) *v.* p.t. of **shake.**

**shoot** (sho͞ot) *v.* **shot** (shŏt), **shooting. 1.** To hit, wound, or kill with a missile. **2.** To fire. **3.** To move or send forth swiftly. **4.** To project. **5.** To sprout. —*n.* A sprout. —**shoot'er** *n.*

**shop** (shŏp) *n.* **1.** A small retail store. **2.** A business or industrial establishment. —*v.* **shopped, shopping.** To inspect and buy goods, as in a store. —**shop'per** *n.*

**shore[1]** (shôr, shōr) *n.* Land along the water's edge.

**shore[2]** (shôr, shōr) *v.* **shored, shoring.** To prop up.

**shorn** (shôrn, shōrn) *v.* A p.p. of **shear.**

**short** (shôrt) *adj.* **1.** Having little length or height. **2.** Brief. **3.** Lacking; insufficient. **4.** Curt. —*n.* **1.** A short film. **2. shorts.** Short drawers or trousers. **3.** A short circuit. —*v.* To cause a short circuit in. —**short'age** *n.* —**short'en** *v.* —**short'ly** *adv.* —**short'ness** *n.*

**shot[1]** (shŏt) *n.* **1.** The firing of a weapon. **2.** pl. **shots** or **shot.** A pellet, bullet, etc. **3.** A marksman. **4.** Range. **5.** An attempt. **6.** A photograph or single cinematic view. **7.** A hypodermic injection. **8.** A drink of liquor.

**shot[2]** (shŏt) *v.* p.t. & p.p. of **shoot.**

**should** (sho͝od) *v.* p.t. of **shall,** an auxiliary expressing obligation, necessity, anticipation, contingency, or uncertainty.

**shoul•der** (shōl'dər) *n.* **1.** The part of the body between the neck and the upper arm or forelimb. **2.** The edge of a roadway. —*v.* **1.** To carry on the shoulders. **2.** To push with the shoulder.

**should•n't** (sho͝od'nt) *v.* Contraction of *should not.*

**shout** (shout) *n.* A loud cry. —**shout** *v.* —**shout'er** *n.*

**shove** (shŭv) *v.* **shoved, shoving.** To push roughly or rudely. —*n.* A push. —**shov'er** *n.*

**shov•el** (shŭv'əl) *n.* A digging tool with a handle and a scoop. —*v.* To dig or move with a shovel.

**show** (shō) *v.* **showed, shown** (shōn) or **showed, showing. 1.** To cause to be seen. **2.** To conduct. **3.** To point out. **4.** To reveal. **5.** To grant. **6.** To instruct. **7.** To be evident. —*n.* **1.** A display. **2.** An appearance. **3.** A public exhibition or entertainment.

**show•er** (shou'ər) *n.* **1.** A brief fall of rain. **2.** An outpouring. **3.** A party held to present gifts. **4.** A bath in which water is sprayed. —*v.* **1.** To spray. **2.** To bestow abundantly. **3.** To pour down. **4.** To bathe in sprayed water.

**shown** (shōn) *v.* A p.p. of **show.**

**show•y** (shō'ē) *adj.* **-ier, -iest.** Conspicuous; gaudy. —**show'i•ly** *adv.* —**show'i•ness** *n.*

**shrank** (shrăngk) *v.* A p.t. of **shrink.**

**shred** (shrĕd) *n.* **1.** A long strip torn off. **2.** A small amount. —*v.* **shredded** or **shred, shredding.** To cut into shreds. —**shred'der** *n.*

**shrewd** (shro͞od) *adj.* **1.** Discerning; astute. **2.** Cunning. —**shrewd'ly** *adv.* —**shrewd'ness** *n.*

**shriek** (shrēk) *n.* A shrill cry. —*v.* To utter such a cry.

**shrill** (shrĭl) *adj.* High-pitched and piercing.

**shrine** (shrīn) *n.* A saint's tomb or other hallowed place.

**shrink** (shrĭngk) *v.* **shrank** (shrăngk) or **shrunk** (shrŭngk), **shrunk** or **shrunken** (shrŭng'kən), **shrinking. 1.** To contract; dwindle. **2.** To draw back. —**shrink'age** *n.*

**shriv•el** (shrĭv'əl) *v.* To shrink and wrinkle.

**shroud** (shroud) *n.* **1.** A cloth used to wrap a body for burial. **2.** Something that conceals.

**shrub** (shrŭb) *n.* A low, many-stemmed woody plant. —**shrub'ber•y** *n.* —**shrub'by** *adj.*

**shrug** (shrŭg) *v.* **shrugged, shrugging.** To raise (the shoulders) as a gesture of doubt, bewilderment, or indifference. —*n.* Such a gesture.

**shrunk** (shrŭngk) *v.* A p.t. & p.p. of **shrink.**

**shrunken** (shrŭng'kən) *v.* A p.p. of **shrink.**

**shud•der** (shŭd'ər) *v.* To tremble, as from disgust. —**shud'der** *n.*

**shuf•fle** (shŭf'əl) *v.* **-fled, -fling. 1.** To move with a slow, foot-dragging gait. **2.** To mix together. —*n.* A shuffling gait. —**shuf'fler** *n.*

**shun** (shŭn) *v.* **shunned, shunning.** To avoid deliberately and consistently. —**shun'ner** *n.*

**shut** (shŭt) *v.* **shut, shutting. 1.** To close. **2.** To block passage.

**shut•ter** (shŭt'ər) *n.* A hinged cover or screen for a window. —*v.* To furnish or close with a shutter.

**shut•tle** (shŭt'l) *n.* **1.** A device used in weaving to carry the thread back and forth. **2.** A train, bus, or plane making frequent trips between 2 points. —*v.* **-tled, -tling.** To move back and forth.

**shy** (shī) *adj.* **shier, shiest. 1.** Timid. **2.** Bashful; reserved. **3.** Wary. **4.** Short; lacking. —*v.* **shied, shying.** To draw back, as from fear or caution. —**shy'ly** *adv.* —**shy'ness** *n.*

**sib•ling** (sĭb'lĭng) *n.* A brother or sister.

**sick** (sĭk) *adj.* **1.** Ill; not well. **2.** Nauseated. **3.** Of or for sick persons. **4.** Morbid. **5.** Disgusted. **6.** Weary. —**sick'en** *v.* —**sick'en•ing** *adj.* —**sick'ness** *n.*

**sick•le** (sĭk'əl) *n.* A tool with a semicircular blade on a short handle, used to cut grass.

**side** (sīd) *n.* **1.** A surface, esp. one joining a top and a bottom. **2.** The left or right half. **3.** The adjacent space. **4.** An edge or boundary. **5.** An area separated from another by some feature. **6.** A contending group, team, or opinion. **7.** An aspect. —*v.* **sided, siding.** To align oneself on or with a side. —**side'ways** *adj. & adv.*

**siege** (sēj) *n.* **1.** The surrounding of a place by an army bent on capturing it. **2.** A prolonged period.

**si•er•ra** (sē-ĕr'ə) *n.* A range of mountains having a rugged, serrated outline.

**si•es•ta** (sē-ĕs'tə) *n.* A rest or nap taken esp. after the midday meal.

**sieve** (sĭv) *n.* A strainer or sifter.

**sift** (sĭft) *v.* **1.** To separate fine particles from coarse ones; strain. **2.** To examine closely. —**sift'er** *n.*

**sigh** (sī) *v.* To exhale in a long, deep breath, as in expressing sorrow. —*n.* The act or sound of sighing.

**sight** (sīt) *n.* **1.** The ability to see. **2.** The act of seeing. **3.** The field of one's vision. **4.** Something seen. **5.** A device to assist in aiming, as on a gun. —*v.* **1.** To see. **2.** To aim. —**sight'ed** *adj.* —**sight'less** *adj.*

**sign** (sīn) *n.* **1.** An indication. **2.** A meaningful action or gesture. **3.** A message-bearing board, poster, or placard. **4.** A symbol. —*v.* **1.** To write (one's name) on. **2.** To hire, transfer, etc., by written contract. —**sign'er** *n.*

**sig•nal** (sĭg'nəl) *n.* **1.** A sign or other indicator used to convey a message. **2.** A radio wave. —*adj.* Remarkable. —*v.* To make a signal (to).

**sig•na•ture** (sĭg'nə-chər) *n.* A person's autograph.

**sig•nif•i•cant** (sĭg-nĭf'ĭ-kənt) *adj.* **1.** Having a meaning. **2.** Full of meaning. **3.** Important. —**sig•nif'i•cance** *n.* —**sig•nif'i•cant•ly** *adv.*

**sig•ni•fy** (sĭg'nə-fī') *v.* **-fied, -fying. 1.** To denote. **2.** To make known. —**sig'ni•fi•ca'tion** *n.*

**si•lence** (sī'ləns) *n.* The absence of sound; stillness. —*v.* **-lenced, -lencing. 1.** To make silent. **2.** To suppress. —**si'lent** *adj.* —**si'lent•ly** *adv.*

**sil•hou•ette** (sĭl'o͞o-ĕt') *n.* A drawing consisting of an outline filled in with a solid color. —**sil'hou•ette'** *v.*

**silk** (sĭlk) *n.* Thread or fabric of lustrous fiber produced by an Asian caterpillar, the silkworm. —**silk'en** *adj.* —**silk'y** *adj.*

**sill** (sĭl) *n.* The horizontal bottom of a window frame.

**sil•ly** (sĭl'ē) *adj.* **-lier, -liest.** Senseless; scatter-brained. —**sil'li•ness** *n.*

**silt** (sĭlt) *n.* A sediment consisting of fine particles. —**silt** *v.*

**sil•ver** (sĭl'vər) *n.* **1.** A white metallic element valued for jewelry, tableware, and coinage. **2.** Coins of this metal. **3.** Tableware of this metal. **4.** A lustrous gray color. —*adj.* Of silver. —*v.* To cover with silver. —**sil'ver•y** *adj.*

**sim•i•lar** (sĭm'ə-lər) *adj.* Alike though not identical. —**sim'i•lar'i•ty** *n.* —**sim'i•lar•ly** *adv.*

**sim•i•le** (sĭm′ə-lē) *n.* A figure of speech comparing 2 dissimilar things.
**sim•mer** (sĭm′ər) *v.* **1.** To cook below or at the boiling point. **2.** To seethe.
**sim•ple** (sĭm′pəl) *adj.* **-pler, -plest. 1.** Consisting of 1 thing or part only. **2.** Easy. **3.** Bare; mere. **4.** Plain. **5.** Unaffected. **6.** Straightforward. **7.** Humble or lowly. **8.** Stupid. **—sim•plic′i•ty** *n.* **—sim′ply** *adv.*
**sim•pli•fy** (sĭm′plə-fī′) *v.* **-fied, -fying.** To make simpler. **—sim′pli•fi•ca′tion** *n.*
**sim•u•late** (sĭm′yə-lāt′) *v.* **-lated, -lating.** To pretend; feign. **—sim′u•la′tion** *n.* **—sim′u•la′tive** *adj.* **—sim′u•la′tor** *n.*
**si•mul•ta•ne•ous** (sī′məl-tā′nē-əs, sĭm′-əl-) *adj.* Happening or done at the same time. **—si′mul•ta′ne•ous•ly** *adv.*
**sin** (sĭn) *n.* A breaking of a law enforced by religion. *—v.* **sinned, sinning.** To commit a sin. **—sin′ful** *adj.* **—sin′ful•ness** *n.* **—sin′ner** *n.*
**since** (sĭns) *adv.* **1.** From then until now. **2.** Between then and now. *—prep.* During the time after. *—conj.* **1.** From the time when. **2.** Because; inasmuch as.
**sin•cere** (sĭn-sîr′) *adj.* **-cerer, -cerest. 1.** True. **2.** Not hypocritical; honest. **—sin•cere′ly** *adv.* **—sin•cer′i•ty** *n.*
**si•ne•cure** (sī′nĭ-kyo͝or′, sĭn′ĭ-) *n.* A position requiring little or no work but providing a comfortable salary.
**sin•ew** (sĭn′yo͞o) *n.* **1.** A tendon. **2.** Muscular power. **—sin′ew•y** *adj.*
**sing** (sĭng) *v.* **sang** (săng), **sung** (sŭng), **singing. 1.** To utter words or sounds in musical tones. **2.** To perform (vocal music). **3.** To proclaim or tell in song. **—sing′er** *n.*
**singe** (sĭnj) *v.* **singed, singeing.** To burn superficially.
**sin•gle** (sĭng′gəl) *adj.* **1.** One only; sole. **2.** Individual. **3.** Designed for 1 person. **4.** Unmarried. *—n.* **1.** A separate unit; individual. **2.** A 1-dollar bill. *—v.* **-gled, -gling.** To separate (with *out*). **—sin′gly** *adv.*
**sin•gu•lar** (sĭng′gyə-lər) *adj.* **1.** Being or denoting only 1. **2.** Extraordinary. **3.** Curious; peculiar. *—n.* The grammatical form indicating only 1. **—sin′gu•lar′i•ty** *n.* **—sing′gu•lar•ly** *adv.*
**sin•is•ter** (sĭn′ĭ-stər) *adj.* Suggesting veiled evil or menace. **—sin′is•ter•ly** *adv.*
**sink** (sĭngk) *v.* **sank** (săngk) or **sunk** (sŭngk), **sunk** or **sunken** (sŭng′kən), **sinking. 1.** To submerge beneath the surface of a liquid. **2.** To descend or decline slowly. **3.** To dig or drill. **4.** To worsen or weaken. *—n.* A water basin with a drainpipe. **—sink′a•ble** *adj.* **—sink′er** *n.*
**sip** (sĭp) *v.* **sipped, sipping.** To drink in small quantities. *—n.* A small quantity of liquid sipped.
**si•phon** (sī′fən) *n.* A tube for drawing liquid from 1 container to a lower one. *—v.* To draw off with a siphon.
**sir** (sûr) *n.* **1.** Often **Sir.** A respectful form of address for a man. **2. Sir.** A title used before the name of baronets and knights.
**sire** (sīr) *n.* A father or forefather. *—v.* **sired, siring.** To beget.
**si•ren** (sī′rən) *n.* A warning device producing a loud wailing noise.
**sis•ter** (sĭs′tər) *n.* **1.** A female having the same mother and father as another. **2.** A female comrade or fellow member. **3.** A nun. **—sis′ter•hood′** *n.* **—sis′ter•ly** *adj.*
**sis•ter-in-law** (sĭs′tər-ĭn-lô′) *n., pl.* **sisters-in-law. 1.** The sister of one's spouse. **2.** The wife of one's brother.
**sit** (sĭt) *v.* **sat** (săt), **sitting. 1.** To rest on the buttocks or hindquarters. **2.** To perch. **3.** To be situated; lie. **4.** To pose. **5.** To be in session. **—sit′ter** *n.*
**site** (sīt) *n.* Location.
**sit•u•a•tion** (sĭch′o͞o-ā′shən) *n.* **1.** A location. **2.** A state of affairs. **3.** A job. **—sit′u•ate′** *v.* **—sit′u•a′tion•al** *adj.*
**six** (sĭks) *n.* The cardinal number written 6. **—six** *adj. & pron.* **—sixth** *n. & adj.*
**six•teen** (sĭk-stēn′) *n.* The cardinal number written 16. **—six•teen′** *adj. & pron.* **—six•teenth′** *n. & adj.*
**six•ty** (sĭks′tē) *n.* The cardinal number written 60. **—six′ti•eth** *n. & adj.* **—six′ty** *adj. & pron.*
**size** (sīz) *n.* **1.** Physical dimensions; magnitude. **2.** Any of a series of graduated categories of dimension, as for garments. *—v.* **sized, sizing.** To arrange according to size. **—siz′a•ble** *adj.*
**siz•zle** (sĭz′əl) *v.* **-zled, -zling. 1.** To make the hissing sound characteristic of frying fat. **2.** To seethe with anger. **3.** To be very hot. **—siz′zler** *n.*

**skate** (skāt) *n.* **1.** A bladelike metal runner fixed to a shoe for gliding over ice. **2.** A roller skate. **—skate** *v.* **—skat'er** *n.*

**skein** (skān) *n.* **1.** A length of yarn or rope wound into a loose coil. **2.** A flock of geese in flight.

**skel•e•ton** (skĕl'ĭ-tn) *n.* **1.** The structure of bones that supports the body. **2.** Any structure or framework. **—skel'e•tal** *adj.*

**skep•tic** (skĕp'tĭk) *n.* One who questions or doubts accepted conclusions. **—skep'ti•cal** *adj.* **—skep'ti•cism** *n.*

**sketch** (skĕch) *n.* **1.** A rough drawing or design. **2.** An outline. *—v.* To make a sketch (of). **—sketch'er** *n.* **—sketch'y** *adj.*

**ski** (skē) *n., pl.* **skis.** One of a pair of long, flat runners attached to a boot for gliding over snow. *—v.* To travel on skis. **—ski'er** *n.*

**skid** (skĭd) *n.* **1.** The act of sliding or slipping over a surface. **2.** A plank or log used for sliding or rolling heavy objects. *—v.* **skidded, skidding.** To slip or slide sideways because of loss of traction.

**skill** (skĭl) *n.* **1.** Proficiency; expertness. **2.** An ability or technique. **—skilled** *adj.* **—skill'ful** *adj.* **—skill'ful•ly** *adv.* **—skill'ful•ness** *n.*

**skil•let** (skĭl'ĭt) *n.* A frying pan.

**skim** (skĭm) *v.* **skimmed, skimming. 1.** To remove (floating matter) from (a liquid). **2.** To glide lightly over. **3.** To glance through quickly.

**skimp•y** (skĭm'pē) *adj.* **-ier, -iest. 1.** Inadequate in size, amount, or quality. **2.** Unduly thrifty. **—skimp** *v.* **—skimp'i•ly** *adv.* **—skimp'i•ness** *n.*

**skin** (skĭn) *n.* **1.** The external covering of the body. **2.** An animal pelt. **3.** An outer layer, as the rind of fruit. *—v.* **skinned, skinning. 1.** To remove skin from. **2.** To bruise.

**skin•ny** (skĭn'ē) *adj.* **-nier, -niest.** Very thin. **—skin'ni•ness** *n.*

**skip** (skĭp) *v.* **skipped, skipping. 1.** To leap or spring lightly (over). **2.** To hop on alternating feet. **3.** To pass from point to point omitting what intervenes. **4.** To omit. *—n.* An act of skipping. **—skip'per** *n.*

**skir•mish** (skûr'mĭsh) *n.* A minor battle. **—skir'mish** *v.*

**skirt** (skûrt) *n.* A garment, or part of a garment, that hangs from the waist down. *—v.* **1.** To pass along the edge of. **2.** To avoid.

**skit** (skĭt) *n.* A short, humorous theatrical or literary piece.

**skulk** (skŭlk) *v.* **1.** To lie in hiding. **2.** To move stealthily. **3.** To malinger. **—skulk'er** *n.*

**skull** (skŭl) *n.* The bony framework of the head.

**sky** (skī) *n., pl.* **skies.** The upper atmosphere.

**slab** (slăb) *n.* A flat, thick piece.

**slack** (slăk) *adj.* **1.** Sluggish. **2.** Not busy. **3.** Loose. **4.** Negligent. *—v.* To slacken. *—n.* **1.** A lull. **2. slacks.** Trousers for casual wear. **—slack'ness** *n.*

**slack•en** (slăk'ən) *v.* **1.** To slow down. **2.** To loosen.

**slain** (slān) *v.* p.p. of **slay.**

**slake** (slāk) *v.* **1.** To quench; satisfy. **2.** To moderate; lessen.

**slam** (slăm) *v.* **slammed, slamming.** To strike, hurl, or shut with force and loud noise. *—n.* A heavy blow or impact.

**slan•der** (slăn'dər) *n.* The utterance of lies harmful to a person. *—v.* To utter damaging lies about. **—slan'der•er** *n.* **—slan'der•ous** *adj.* **—slan'der•ous•ly** *adv.*

**slang** (slăng) *n.* Colorful, often humorous language used in place of standard terms. **—slang'i•ness** *n.* **—slang'y** *adj.*

**slant** (slănt) *v.* **1.** To incline; slope. **2.** To alter so as to fit a bias. *—n.* **1.** An incline. **2.** A bias. **—slant'ing•ly** *adv.*

**slap** (slăp) *n.* A smacking blow made with the open hand. *—v.* **slapped, slapping.** To strike with a slap.

**slash** (slăsh) *v.* **1.** To cut or lash with sweeping strokes. **2.** To reduce drastically. *—n.* A sweeping stroke or gash. **—slash'er** *n.*

**slat** (slăt) *n.* A narrow strip.

**slate** (slāt) *n.* **1.** A fine-grained, layered rock used for tiles and writing surfaces. **2.** A list of candidates. *—v.* **slated, slating.** To schedule.

**slather** (slă*th*'ər) *v.* **1.** To use great amounts of. **2.** To spread thickly on.

**slaugh•ter** (slô'tər) *v.* **1.** To kill (animals) for food. **2.** To kill (persons) cruelly. —*n.* An act of slaughtering.

**slave** (slāv) *n.* A person, usually a laborer, owned by another. —*v.* **slaved, slaving.** To work hard. **—slav'er•y** *n.* **—slav'ish** *adj.* **—slav'ish•ly** *adv.* **—slav'ish•ness** *n.*

**slay** (slā) *v.* **slew** (slo͞o), **slain** (slān), **slaying.** To kill violently. **—slay'er** *n.*

**slea•zy** (slē'zē) *adj.* **-zier, -ziest.** Cheap; shoddy. **—slea'zi•ly** *adv.* **—slea'zi•ness** *n.*

**sled** (slĕd) *n.* A vehicle on runners for moving over ice and snow. —*v.* **sledded, sledding.** To ride a sled.

**sledge** (slĕj) *n.* A large sleigh drawn by animals, used for work. **—sledge** *v.*

**sledge•ham•mer** (slĕj'hăm'ər) *n.* A long, heavy hammer used to drive wedges and posts. **—sledge'ham'mer** *v.*

**sleek** (slēk) *adj.* **1.** Glossy. **2.** Neat. —*v.* To polish. **—sleek'ness** *n.*

**sleep** (slēp) *n.* A natural, recurring state of restful unconsciousness. —*v.* **slept** (slĕpt), **sleeping.** To be in the state of sleep. **—sleep'er** *n.* **—sleep'i•ly** *adv.* **—sleep'i•ness** *n.* **—sleep'less** *adj.*

**sleet** (slēt) *n.* Partially frozen rain. —*v.* To shower sleet. **—sleet'y** *adj.*

**sleeve** (slēv) *n.* The arm of a garment. **—sleeve'less** *adj.*

**sleigh** (slā) *n.* A light, horse-drawn sled for passengers.

**sleight** (slīt) *n.* **1.** Deftness; dexterity. **2.** A clever trick or deception.

**slen•der** (slĕn'dər) *adj.* **1.** Gracefully slim. **2.** Meager. **—slen'der•ly** *adv.*

**slept** (slĕpt) *v.* p.t. & p.p. of **sleep.**

**slew¹** (slo͞o) *n.* A large amount.

**slew²** (slo͞o) *v.* p.t. of **slay.**

**slice** (slīs) *n.* **1.** A thin, broad piece. **2.** A share. —*v.* **sliced, slicing. 1.** To cut into slices. **2.** To cut from a larger piece. **—slic'er** *n.*

**slick** (slĭk) *adj.* **1.** Smooth, glossy, and slippery. **2.** Shrewd; wily. **3.** Superficially attractive but without substance.

**slide** (slīd) *v.* **slid** (slĭd), **slid** or **slidden** (slĭd'n), **sliding.** To move in smooth, continuous contact with a surface. —*n.* **1.** A sliding movement. **2.** A playground apparatus for children to slide upon. **3.** An image for projection on a screen. **4.** An avalanche. **—slid'er** *n.*

**slight** (slīt) *adj.* **1.** Small; meager. **2.** Insignificant. **3.** Slender. —*v.* **1.** To treat with disrespect. **2.** To neglect. —*n.* A snub. **—slight'ly** *adv.* **—slight'ness** *n.*

**slim** (slĭm) *adj.* **slimmer, slimmest. 1.** Slender. **2.** Scant; meager. —*v.* **slimmed, slimming.** To make or become slim. **—slim'ly** *adv.* **—slim'ness** *n.*

**slime** (slīm) *n.* A moist, sticky substance. **—slim'y** *adj.*

**sling** (slĭng) *n.* **1.** A looped strap in which a stone is whirled and then let fly. **2.** A looped rope, band, etc., for supporting, cradling, or hoisting. —*v.* **slung** (slŭng), **slinging.** To hurl from a sling; fling. **—sling'er** *n.*

**slink** (slĭngk) *v.* **slunk, slinking.** To move furtively.

**slip¹** (slĭp) *v.* **slipped, slipping. 1.** To move quietly. **2.** To slide accidentally. **3.** To escape. **4.** To decline. **5.** To place smoothly and quietly. **6.** To err. —*n.* **1.** The act of slipping. **2.** A slight error. **3.** A docking place for a ship. **4.** A woman's undergarment. **—slip'page** *n.* **—slip'per•y** *adj.*

**slip²** (slĭp) *n.* **1.** A plant cutting. **2.** A small piece of paper.

**slip•per** (slĭp'ər) *n.* A light, low shoe.

**slit** (slĭt) *n.* A long, narrow cut or opening. —*v.* **slit, slitting.** To make a slit in.

**slith•er** (slĭ*th*'ər) *v.* **1.** To slip and slide. **2.** To glide along. **—slith'er** *n.*

**sliv•er** (slĭv'ər) *n.* A slender piece.

**slob•ber** (slŏb'ər) *v.* To drool. —*n.* Saliva running from the mouth.

**slo•gan** (slō'gən) *n.* **1.** A motto. **2.** An often repeated phrase used in advertising.

**slope** (slōp) *v.* **sloped, sloping.** To incline upward or downward. —*n.* An inclined line or surface.

**slop•py** (slŏp'ē) *adj.* **-pier, -piest. 1.** Muddy. **2.** Untidy; messy. **—slop'pi•ly** *adv.* **—slop'pi•ness** *n.*

**slot** (slŏt) *n.* A long narrow opening.

**sloth** (slōth, slôth, slŏth) *n.* Laziness. **—sloth'ful** *adj.*

**slouch** (slouch) *n.* **1.** A drooping posture or gait. **2.** A lazy or inept person. **—slouch** *v.*

**slov•en•ly** (slŭv'ən-lē) *adj.* **-lier, -liest.** Untidy; messy. **—slov'en•li•ness** *n.*

**slow** (slō) *adj.* **1.** Moving at a low speed. **2.** Taking a long time. **3.** Registering behind the correct time. **4.** Sluggish. **5.** Stupid. —*v.* To make or become slower. —**slow, slow'ly** *adv.* —**slow'ness** *n.*

**sludge** (slŭj) *n.* **1.** Mire or ooze. **2.** Treated sewage. —**sludg'y** *adj.*

**slug**[1] (slŭg) *n.* **1.** A bullet. **2.** A shot of liquor. **3.** A false coin.

**slug**[2] (slŭg) *v.* **slugged, slugging.** To strike heavily. —**slug'ger** *n.*

**slug•gish** (slŭg'ĭsh) *adj.* Slow; inactive. —**slug'gard** *n.* —**slug'gish•ly** *adv.* —**slug'gish•ness** *n.*

**sluice** (slo͞os) *n.* An artificial water channel, or 1 of the gates regulating the flow through it.

**slum** (slŭm) *n.* A poor, overcrowded residential district.

**slum•ber** (slŭm'bər) *v.* To sleep. —*n.* Sleep. —**slum'ber•er** *n.*

**slump** (slŭmp) *v.* **1.** To decline suddenly; collapse. **2.** To droop or slouch. —**slump** *n.*

**slung** (slŭng) *v.* p.t. & p.p. of **sling.**

**slunk** (slŭngk) *v.* p.t. & p.p. of **slink.**

**slur** (slûr) *v.* **slurred, slurring. 1.** To pass over lightly. **2.** To pronounce indistinctly. **3.** To disparage. —*n.* A disparaging remark.

**slush** (slŭsh) *n.* Partially melted snow or ice. —**slush'i•ness** *n.* —**slush'y** *adj.*

**sly** (slī) *adj.* **slier** or **slyer, sliest** or **slyest. 1.** Cunning. **2.** Secretive or underhand. **3.** Roguish. —**sly'ly** *adv.* —**sly'ness** *n.*

**smack**[1] (smăk) *v.* **1.** To open (the lips) with a sharp sound. **2.** To kiss or slap noisily. —*n.* **1.** The sound produced by smacking the lips. **2.** A noisy kiss. **3.** A loud slap. —*adv.* Squarely; solidly.

**small** (smôl) *adj.* **1.** Little. **2.** Insignificant. **3.** Limited in scope. **4.** Petty. —**small'ness** *n.*

**smart** (smärt) *v.* To cause or feel a stinging pain. —*n.* A stinging pain. —*adj.* **1.** Mentally alert; bright. **2.** Impertinent. **3.** Fashionable. —**smart'ly** *adv.* —**smart'ness** *n.*

**smash** (smăsh) *v.* **1.** To break into pieces. **2.** To throw violently so as to shatter. **3.** To destroy; wreck. —*n.* **1.** The act or sound of smashing. **2.** A collision or crash. —**smash'er** *n.*

**smear** (smîr) *v.* **1.** To daub with a sticky or greasy substance. **2.** To soil. **3.** To vilify. —*n.* **1.** A smudge or blot. **2.** Slander.

**smell** (smĕl) *v.* **1.** To perceive by odor. **2.** To have an odor. **3.** To stink. —*n.* **1.** The olfactory sense. **2.** Odor. —**smell'y** *adj.*

**smelt** (smĕlt) *v.* To melt (ores), separating the metallic constituents. —**smelt'er** *n.*

**smile** (smīl) *n.* A happy or amused facial expression formed by an upward curving of the mouth. —*v.* **smiled, smiling. 1.** To form a smile. **2.** To express favor or approval.

**smirk** (smûrk) *v.* To smile archly or complacently. —**smirk** *n.*

**smite** (smīt) *v.* **smote** (smōt), **smitten** (smĭt'n), **smiting. 1.** To strike. **2.** To afflict. —**smit'er** *n.*

**smock** (smŏk) *n.* A loose, coatlike outer garment, often worn to protect clothing while one works.

**smog** (smŏg, smôg) *n.* Fog mixed with smoke. —**smog'gy** *adj.*

**smoke** (smōk) *n.* The vapor rising from burning material. —*v.* **smoked, smoking. 1.** To emit smoke. **2.** To draw in and exhale the smoke of tobacco or the like. **3.** To preserve by exposure to smoke. —**smok'er** *n.* —**smok'i•ness** *n.* —**smok'y** *adj.*

**smol•der** (smōl'dər) *v.* **1.** To burn with no flame. **2.** To burn or exist inwardly.

**smooch** (smo͞och) *v.* To kiss. —**smooch** *n.* —**smooch'er** *n.*

**smooth** (smo͞o*th*) *adj.* **1.** Not irregular or rough. **2.** Agreeable; mild. **3.** Easy. —*v.* To make or become smooth. —**smooth'er** *n.* —**smooth'ly** *adv.* —**smooth'ness** *n.*

**smote** (smōt) *v.* p.t. of **smite.**

**smoth•er** (smŭ*th*'ər) *v.* **1.** To suffocate. **2.** To suppress. **3.** To cover heavily.

**smudge** (smŭj) *v.* **smudged, smudging.** To smear or blur. —*n.* A smear. —**smudg'y** *adj.*

**smug** (smŭg) *adj.* **smugger, smuggest.** Complacent or self-satisfied. —**smug'ly** *adv.* —**smug'ness** *n.*

**smug•gle** (smŭg'əl) *v.* **-gled, -gling. 1.** To import or export illegally. **2.** To convey secretly. —**smug'gler** *n.*

**snack** (snăk) *n.* A light meal.

**snag** (snăg) *n.* **1.** A sharp projection. **2.** An unforeseen obstacle. —*v.* **snagged, snagging.** To get caught by a snag. —**snag'gy** *adj.*
**snail** (snāl) *n.* A mollusk with a spirally coiled shell.
**snake** (snāk) *n.* A legless, long-bodied reptile. —*v.* **snaked, snaking.** To move or twist like a snake.
**snap** (snăp) *v.* **snapped, snapping. 1.** To make or cause to make a sharp cracking sound. **2.** To break suddenly. **3.** To bite or seize suddenly. **4.** To speak sharply. —*n.* **1.** A sharp cracking sound. **2.** A sudden break. **3.** A clasp or other fastening device. **4.** Briskness. **5.** A simple task. —*adj.* Abrupt. —**snap'per** *n.* —**snap'pish** *adj.* —**snap'py** *adj.*
**snare** (snâr) *n.* **1.** A small noose for trapping birds, etc. **2.** A trap; pitfall. —**snare** *v.*
**snarl**[1] (snärl) *v.* **1.** To growl with bared teeth. **2.** To speak angrily. —**snarl** *n.* —**snarl'y** *adj.*
**snarl**[2] *n.* A tangle. —**snarl** *v.* —**snarl'y** *adj.*
**snatch** (snăch) *v.* To seize or grab. —*n.* **1.** The act of snatching. **2.** A brief period. **3.** A fragment. —**snatch'er** *n.*
**sneak** (snēk) *v.* To move, give, or take in a stealthy way. —*n.* **1.** A cowardly or underhand person. **2.** A stealthy move. —**sneak'i•ness** *n.* —**sneak'y** *adj.*
**sneer** (snîr) *n.* A contemptuous raising of the upper lip. —**sneer** *v.* —**sneer'er** *n.*
**sneeze** (snēz) *v.* **sneezed, sneezing.** To expel breath in an explosive, involuntary action. —**sneeze** *n.*
**snick•er** (snĭk'ər) *n.* A snide, partly stifled laugh. —**snick'er** *v.*
**snide** (snīd) *adj.* **1.** Slyly derogatory. **2.** Mean.
**sniff** (snĭf) *v.* To inhale a short, audible breath through the nose. —**sniff** *n.* —**sniff'er** *n.*
**snipe** (snīp) *v.* **sniped, sniping.** To shoot at an enemy from a concealed place. —**sni'per** *n.*
**snip•pet** (snĭp'ĭt) *n.* A tidbit; morsel.
**sniv•el** (snĭv'əl) *v.* **-eled** or **-elled, -eling** or **-elling. 1.** To cry and sniffle. **2.** To whine tearfully. **3.** To run at the nose. **4.** To sniffle.
**snob** (snŏb) *n.* One who is convinced of one's social superiority. —**snob'ber•y** *n.*
**snoop** (sno͞op) *v.* To pry. —*n.* One who pries. —**snoop'er** *n.* —**snoop'y** *adj.*
**snore** (snôr, snōr) *v.* **snored, snoring.** To breathe noisily while sleeping. —**snore** *n.* —**snor'er** *n.*
**snort** (snôrt) *v.* To force air noisily through the nostrils. —**snort** *n.* —**snort'er** *n.*
**snout** (snout) *n.* An animal's projecting nose or facial part.
**snow** (snō) *n.* White ice crystals falling from the sky. —*v.* To fall as snow. —**snow'y** *adj.*
**snub** (snŭb) *v.* **snubbed, snubbing.** To slight, as by ignoring. —**snub** *n.* —**snub'ber** *n.*
**snuff**[1] (snŭf) *n.* Finely pulverized tobacco for snorting up the nostrils.
**snuff**[2] (snŭf) *v.* To extinguish (a candle).
**snug** (snŭg) *adj.* **snugger, snuggest. 1.** Cozy. **2.** Close-fitting or compact. —**snug, snug'ly** *adv.* —**snug'ness** *n.*
**so** (sō) *adv.* **1.** In the manner indicated. **2.** To the degree expressed. **3.** Therefore. **4.** Thereabouts. **5.** Also. **6.** Then. **7.** Indeed. —*adj.* True; factual. —*conj.* For that reason.
**soak** (sōk) *v.* **1.** To wet, as by immersing. **2.** To absorb. **3.** To be immersed. **4.** To permeate. —**soak'er** *n.*
**soap** (sōp) *n.* A cleansing agent. —*v.* To cover with soap. —**soap'i•ly** *adv.* —**soap'i•ness** *n.* —**soap'y** *adj.*
**soar** (sôr, sōr) *v.* To rise or fly upward.
**sob** (sŏb) *v.* **sobbed, sobbing.** To weep convulsively. —**sob** *n.* —**sob'bing•ly** *adv.*
**so•ber** (sō'bər) *adj.* **1.** Not drunk. **2.** Serious or grave. **3.** Plain. —*v.* To make or become sober. —**so'ber•ly** *adv.* —**so'ber•ness, so•bri'e•ty** *n.*
**so•bri•quet** (sō'brĭ-kā', -kĕt', sō'brĭ-kā', -kĕt') *n.* Also **soubriquet** (so͞o'-). **1.** A nickname. **2.** An assumed name.
**soc•cer** (sŏk'ər) *n.* A field game played by 2 teams with 11 players each and a spherical ball.
**so•cia•ble** (sō'shə-bəl) *adj.* Friendly; companionable. —**so'cia•bil'i•ty** *n.* —**so'cia•ble•ness** *n.* —**so'cia•bly** *adv.*
**so•cial** (sō'shəl) *adj.* **1.** Living in groups. **2.** Of human society. **3.** Sociable. —*n.*

A social gathering. **—so'cial•ly** *adv.*

**so•cial•ism** (sō'shə-lĭz'əm) *n.* Public ownership of factories, farms, etc. **—so'cial•ist** *n.* & *adj.* **—so'cial•is'tic** *adj.*

**so•cial•ize** (sō'shə-līz') *v.* **-ized, -izing. 1.** To place under public ownership. **2.** To take part in social activities. **—so'cial•i•za'tion** *n.*

**so•ci•e•ty** (sə-sī'ĭ-tē) *n., pl.* **-ties. 1. a.** The totality of human relationships. **b.** A human community sharing a culture. **2.** The fashionable social class. **3.** Companionship. **4.** A cultural or charitable organization.

**so•ci•ol•o•gy** (sō'sē-ŏl'ə-jē, -shē-) *n.* The study of human societies. **—so'ci•o•log'i•cal** *adj.* **—so'ci•ol'o•gist** *n.*

**sock**[1] (sŏk) *n.* A short stocking.

**sock**[2] (sŏk) *v.* To punch. **—sock** *n.*

**sock•et** (sŏk'ĭt) *n.* A cavity that receives an inserted part.

**sod** (sŏd) *n.* Grass-covered surface soil. *—v.* **sodded, sodding.** To cover with sod.

**so•da** (sō'də) *n.* Carbonated water or a soft drink containing it.

**so•di•um** (sō'dē-əm) *n.* A light, metallic element abundant in combined forms.

**so•fa** (sō'fə) *n.* A long couch with a back and arms.

**soft** (sôft, sŏft) *adj.* **1.** Not hard or firm; yielding. **2.** Not loud. **3.** Gentle; mild. **4.** Tender. **5.** Easy. **6.** Not alcoholic. *—adv.* Gently. **—soft'en** *v.* **—soft'en•er** *n.* **—soft'ly** *adv.* **—soft'ness** *n.*

**soft•ware** (sôft'wâr', sŏft'-) *n.* **1.** Written or printed data, as programs or routines, for operating computers. **2.** Documents containing instructions for operating and maintaining computers.

**sog•gy** (sŏg'ē) *adj.* **-gier, -giest. 1.** Soaked. **2.** Humid; sultry. **—sog'gi•ly** *adv.* **—sog'gi•ness** *n.*

**soil** (soil) *n.* Earth; ground. *—v.* **1.** To make or become dirty. **2.** To tarnish.

**sol•ace** (sŏl'ĭs) *n.* Comfort in sorrow and distress. **—sol'ace** *v.*

**so•lar** (sō'lər) *adj.* Of the sun.

**sold** (sōld) *v.* p.t. & p.p. of **sell.**

**sol•der** (sŏd'ər) *n.* A fusible alloy used to join metallic parts. *—v.* To join or repair with solder.

**sol•dier** (sōl'jər) *n.* One serving in an army as an enlisted person or a noncommissioned officer.

**sole**[1] (sōl) *n.* **1.** The undersurface of the foot. **2.** The undersurface of a shoe. *—v.* **soled, soling.** To furnish with a sole.

**sole**[2] (sōl) *adj.* Single; only. **—sole'ly** *adv.*

**sol•emn** (sŏl'əm) *adj.* **1.** Earnest; grave. **2.** Formal. **3.** Gloomy. **—so•lem'ni•ty, sol'emn•ness** *n.* **—sol'emn•ly** *adv.*

**so•lic•it** (sə-lĭs'ĭt) *v.* **1.** To seek to obtain. **2.** To entreat. **—so•lic'i•tous•ly** *adv.* **—so•lic'i•tude, so•lic'i•tous•ness** *n.*

**sol•id** (sŏl'ĭd) *adj.* **1.** Not liquid or gaseous. **2.** Not hollow. **3.** Of a single substance. **4.** Three-dimensional. **5.** Continuous. **6.** Strongly constructed. **7.** Firm; substantial. *—n.* **1.** A solid substance. **2.** A 3-dimensional figure. **—so•lid'i•fy'** *v.* **—so•lid'i•ty** *n.* **—sol'id•ly** *adv.*

**sol•i•dar•i•ty** (sŏl'ĭ-dăr'ĭ-tē) *n.* Unity.

**sol•i•tar•y** (sŏl'ĭ-tĕr'ē) *adj.* **1.** Existing or done alone. **2.** Single; sole. **—sol'i•tar'i•ness** *n.* **—sol'i•tude'** *n.*

**so•lo** (sō'lō) *n., pl.* **-los.** A musical composition for 1 performer. *—v.* To perform alone. **—so'lo** *adj.* & *adv.* **—so'lo•ist** *n.*

**sol•stice** (sŏl'stĭs, sōl'-) *n.* Either of 2 times of the year when the sun takes the most northerly or most southerly path across the sky.

**sol•u•ble** (sŏl'yə-bəl) *adj.* **1.** Capable of being dissolved. **2.** Capable of being solved. **—sol'u•bil'i•ty** *n.* **—sol'u•bly** *adv.*

**so•lu•tion** (sə-lōō'shən) *n.* **1.** A liquid with a substance mixed evenly and stably in it. **2.** The solving of a problem. **3.** An answer.

**solve** (sŏlv) *v.* **solved, solving.** To find an answer. **—solv'a•ble** *adj.*

**sol•vent** (sŏl'vənt) *adj.* **1.** Able to pay debts. **2.** Capable of dissolving another substance. *—n.* A liquid capable of dissolving another substance. **—sol'ven•cy** *n.*

**som•ber** (sŏm'bər) *adj.* **1.** Dark; gloomy. **2.** Melancholy. **—som'ber•ly** *adv.*

**some** (sŭm) *adj.* **1.** Certain. **2.** Being unknown or unnamed. *—pron.* An unspecified number or portion. *—adv.* Approximately.

**some•bod•y** (sŭm′bŏd′ē, -bŭd′ē, -bə-dē) *pron.* An unspecified person. —*n.* A person of importance.
**some•one** (sŭm′wŭn′, -wən) *pron.* Some person.
**som•er•sault, sum•mer•sault** (sŭm′ər-sôlt′) *n.* **1.** A stunt in which the body rolls heels over head in a complete circle. **2.** A complete reversal, as of thought or feeling. **—som′er•sault′, sum′mer•sault′** *v.*
**some•thing** (sŭm′thĭng) *pron.* An unspecified thing.
**some•times** (sŭm′tīmz′) *adv.* Now and then.
**son** (sŭn) *n.* A male offspring.
**song** (sông, sŏng) *n.* **1.** Sound produced by singing. **2.** A brief musical composition for singing. **—song′ful** *adj.*
**son•ic** (sŏn′ĭk) *adj.* Of sound or its propagation.
**son-in-law** (sŭn′ĭn-lô′) *n., pl.* **sons-in-law.** The husband of one's daughter.
**son•net** (sŏn′ĭt) *n.* A 14-line poem divided into an octet and a sestet.
**son•o•rous** (sə-nôr′əs, -nōr′-, sŏn′ər-) *adj.* Having or producing a full, deep, rich sound. **—son′o•rous•ly** *adv.* **—son′o•rous•ness** *n.*
**soon** (so͞on) *adv.* **1.** In the near future. **2.** Promptly. **3.** Early.
**soot** (so͝ot, so͞ot) *n.* Fine, black particles of carbon, produced by incomplete combustion. **—soot′y** *adj.*
**soothe** (so͞o*th*) *v.* **soothed, soothing. 1.** To calm. **2.** To ease or relieve. **—sooth′er** *n.*
**so•phis•ti•cat•ed** (sə-fĭs′tĭ-kā′tĭd) *adj.* **1.** Experienced, esp. in matters of taste; worldly. **2.** Complicated or refined. **—so•phis′ti•cate** *n.* **—so•phis′ti•ca′tion** *n.*
**soph•o•more** (sŏf′ə-môr′, -mōr′) *n.* A 2nd-year student, esp. at a 4-year institution.
**sop•o•rif•ic** (sŏp′ə-rĭf′ĭk, sō′pə-) *adj.* **1.** Inducing sleep. **2.** Drowsy. **—sop′o•rif′ic** *n.*
**so•pran•o** (sə-prăn′ō, -prä′nō) *n., pl.* **-os.** The highest natural human voice. **—so•pran′o** *adj.*
**sor•cer•y** (sôr′sə-rē) *n.* Witchcraft. **—sor′cer•er** *n.* **—sor′cer•ess** *n.*
**sor•did** (sôr′dĭd) *adj.* **1.** Filthy; squalid. **2.** Vile; selfish. **—sor′did•ly** *adv.* **—sor′did•ness** *n.*
**sore** (sôr, sōr) *adj.* **sorer, sorest. 1.** Painful; tender. **2.** Grievous. —*n.* An open skin lesion. **—sore′ly** *adv.* **—sore′ness** *n.*
**sor•row** (sŏr′ō, sôr′ō) *n.* **1.** Mental suffering because of injury or loss. **2.** A misfortune. —*v.* To feel sorrow; grieve. **—sor′row•ful** *adj.* **—sor′row•ful•ly** *adv.*
**sor•ry** (sŏr′ē, sôr′ē) *adj.* **-rier, -riest. 1.** Feeling sympathy or regret. **2.** Poor; paltry.
**sort** (sôrt) *n.* A class; kind. —*v.* To arrange according to class, kind, or size.
**sor•tie** (sôr′tē, sôr-tē′) *n.* **1.** An armed attack made against a surrounding enemy. **2.** A flight of a warplane on a combat mission. **—sor′tie** *v.*
**sought** (sôt) *v.* p.t. & p.p. of **seek.**
**soul** (sōl) *n.* **1.** The essential, spiritual, or immortal part of a person. **2.** A person. **3.** Essence; core. **4.** Deep feeling. **—soul′ful** *adj.* **—soul′ful•ness** *n.* **—soul′less** *adj.* **—soul′less•ness** *n.*
**sound[1]** (sound) *n.* A vibratory disturbance capable of being heard. —*v.* **1.** To make or cause to make a sound. **2.** To seem to be.
**sound[2]** (sound) *adj.* **1.** In good condition. **2.** Reliable. **3.** Sensible. **4.** Thorough; complete. **—sound′ly** *adv.* **—sound′ness** *n.*
**sound[3]** (sound) *n.* A wide strait or inlet of the ocean. —*v.* **1.** To measure the depth of (water). **2.** To ascertain or test the opinions of. **—sound′er** *n.* **—sound′ing** *n.*
**soup** (so͞op) *n.* A liquid food prepared from meat, fish, or vegetable stock.
**sour** (sour) *adj.* **1.** Having a sharp or acid taste. **2.** Spoiled. **3.** Bad-tempered. —*v.* To make or become sour. **—sour′ly** *adv.* **—sour′ness** *n.*
**source** (sôrs, sōrs) *n.* **1.** A point of origin. **2.** One that supplies information.
**south** (south) *n.* **1.** The direction to the left of an observer facing the sunset. **2.** The S part of any country or region. —*adj. & adv.* In, to, or from the south. **—south′er•ly** *adj. & adv.* **—south′ern** *adj.* **—south′ern•er** *n.* **—south′ward, south′wards** *adv. & adj.*
**south•east** (south-ēst′) *n.* The direction or region halfway between south and

east. *—adj. & adv.* To, from, or in the southeast. **—south′east′er•ly** *adj. & adv.* **—south•east′ern** *adj.*

**south•west** (south-wĕst′) *n.* The direction or region halfway between south and west. *—adj. & adv.* To, from, or in the southwest. **—south′west′er•ly** *adj. & adv.* **—south•west′ern** *adj.*

**sou•ve•nir** (so͞o′və-nîr′) *n.* Something kept as a remembrance.

**sov•er•eign** (sŏv′ər-ĭn) *n.* The chief of state in a monarchy. *—adj.* **1.** Supreme. **2.** Independent. **—sov′er•eign•ty** *n.*

**sow**[1] (sō) *v.* **sowed, sown** (sōn) or **sowed, sowing. 1.** To plant (seed). **2.** To strew with seed. **—sow′er** *n.*

**sow**[2] (sou) *n.* An adult female pig.

**space** (spās) *n.* **1.** The expanse in which all things exist. **2.** A distance or area; extent. **3.** A gap. **4.** A period of time. *—v.* **spaced, spacing.** To arrange with spaces between.

**spa•cious** (spā′shəs) *adj.* Having much space. **—spa′cious•ly** *adv.* **—spa′cious•ness** *n.*

**spade**[1] (spād) *n.* A digging tool having a flat blade, esp. with a tapered point. *—v.* **spaded, spading.** To dig with a spade.

**spade**[2] (spād) *n.* A playing card marked with a black, inverted heart.

**span** (spăn) *n.* **1.** The extent between 2 points. **2.** A bridge. **3.** A period of time. *—v.* **spanned, spanning.** To reach or extend over.

**spank** (spăngk) *v.* To slap on the buttocks. **—spank** *n.*

**spar**[1] (spär) *n.* A wooden or metal pole or strut to support rigging or a structural member.

**spar**[2] (spär) *v.* **sparred, sparring. 1.** To box, esp. for practice. **2.** To dispute verbally. **3.** To fight with feet and spurs. *—n.* **1.** An act of sparring. **2.** A boxing match.

**spare** (spâr) *v.* **spared, sparing. 1.** To save or relieve from pain, trouble, etc. **2.** To use frugally. **3.** To do without. *—adj.* **sparer, sparest. 1.** Extra. **2.** Meager; lean. *—n.* A replacement reserved for future use. **—spare′ness** *n.*

**spark** (spärk) *n.* **1.** A glowing particle, as one thrown off from a fire. **2.** A flash of light. **3.** A seed; germ. *—v.* **1.** To give off sparks. **2.** To set in motion.

**spar•kle** (spär′kəl) *v.* **-kled, -kling. 1.** To give off flashes of light; glitter. **2.** To give off gas bubbles. *—n.* **1.** A small spark. **2.** Vivacity. **3.** A giving off of gas bubbles. **—spar′kler** *n.*

**sparse** (spärs) *adj.* **sparser, sparsest.** Not dense; widely spaced. **—spar′si•ty** *n.*

**spasm** (spăz′əm) *n.* **1.** A sudden, involuntary muscular contraction. **2.** A sudden burst. **—spas•mod′ic** *adj.*

**spas•tic** (spăs′tĭk) *adj.* Continuously contracting. *—n.* A person suffering from chronic spasms. **—spas′ti•cal•ly** *adv.*

**spat**[1] (spăt) *v.* p.t. & p.p. of **spit.**

**spat**[2] (spăt) *n.* A brief, petty quarrel. **—spat** *v.*

**spate** (spāt) *n.* A sudden flow or rush, esp. of water.

**spa•tial** (spā′shəl) *adj.* Also **spa•cial.** Of or involving space.

**spat•u•la** (spăch′ə-lə) *n.* A small kitchen tool with a broad, flat, flexible blade for mixing, spreading, or lifting.

**spawn** (spôn) *n.* **1.** The eggs of fish, frogs, etc. **2.** Offspring. *—v.* **1.** To produce spawn. **2.** To bring forth.

**speak** (spēk) *v.* **spoke** (spōk), **spoken** (spō′kən), **speaking. 1.** To utter words; talk. **2.** To express. **3.** To make a speech. **4.** To converse in (a language). **—speak′er** *n.*

**spear** (spîr) *n.* A sharply pointed weapon with a long shaft. *—v.* To pierce with a spear.

**spe•cial** (spĕsh′əl) *adj.* **1.** Exceptional. **2.** Peculiar. **3.** Having a specific function, application, etc. **4.** Additional. *—n.* Something special. **—spe′cial•ly** *adv.*

**spe•cial•ize** (spĕsh′ə-līz′) *v.* **-ized, -izing. 1.** To employ oneself in a special study or activity. **2.** To adapt to a specific environment or function. **—spe′cial•ist** *n.* **—spe′cial•i•za′tion** *n.* **—spe′cial•ty** *n.*

**spe•cies** (spē′shēz, -sēz) *n., pl.* **species.** Kind; type, esp. of organisms.

**spe•cif•ic** (spĭ-sĭf′ĭk) *adj.* Explicit; definite; detailed. *—n.* A distinct thing; item. **—spe•cif′i•cal•ly** *adv.*

**spec•i•fy** (spĕs′ə-fī′) *v.* **-fied, -fying. 1.** To state explicitly. **2.** To describe or design in full detail. **—spec′i•fi•ca′tion** *n.*

**spec•i•men** (spĕs′ə-mən) *n.* A representative part or thing for study; example.

**spe•cious** (spē′shəs) *adj.* **1.** Deceptively attractive. **2.** Plausible but false. **—spe′cious•ly** *adv.* **—spe′cious•ness** *n.*

**speck** (spĕk) *n.* A small spot or bit. *—v.* To mark with specks.

**spec•ta•cle** (spĕk′tə-kəl) *n.* **1.** A public display. **2.** A marvel or curiosity. **3. spectacles.** Eyeglasses.

**spec•tac•u•lar** (spĕk-tăk′yə-lər) *adj.* Visually striking; showy.

**spec•ta•tor** (spĕk′tā′tər) *n.* An observer or onlooker.

**spec•ter** (spĕk′tər) *n.* A ghost. **—spec′tral** *adj.*

**spec•trum** (spĕk′trəm) *n., pl.* **-tra** or **-trums.** A broad sequence or range, esp. of light separated into its constituent colors.

**spec•u•late** (spĕk′yə-lāt′) *v.* **-lated, -lating. 1.** To reflect. **2.** To conjecture; guess. **3.** To take risks for financial profits. **—spec′u•la•tive** *adj.*

**speech** (spēch) *n.* **1.** The faculty or manner of speaking. **2.** Vocal communication. **3.** A public address. **—speech′less** *adj.*

**speed** (spēd) *n.* **1.** Rate of motion. **2.** Swiftness. **3.** Rapid movement. **4.** Methamphetamine or a related drug. *—v.* **sped** or **speeded, speeding. 1.** To move rapidly. **2.** To accelerate. **3.** To drive at an illegal rate of speed. **—speed′ing** *adj. & n.* **—speed′y** *adj.*

**spell**[1] (spĕl) *v.* **1.** To name in order the letters of (a word). **2.** To mean. **—spell′er** *n.*

**spell**[2] (spĕl) *n.* **1.** A magic formula. **2.** Fascination. **3.** A bewitched state.

**spell**[3] (spĕl) *n.* **1.** A short period of time. **2.** A short turn of work. *—v.* To relieve (someone) from work.

**spend** (spĕnd) *v.* **spent, spending. 1.** To pay out (money). **2.** To wear out. **3.** To pass (time). **—spend′er** *n.*

**sperm** (spûrm) *n.* **1.** A male reproductive cell. **2.** Semen.

**spew** (spyo͞o) *v.* **1.** To vomit. **2.** To cast out in a stream. **—spew** *n.*

**sphere** (sfîr) *n.* **1.** A ball; globe. **2.** An environment; range. **—spher′i•cal** *adj.* **—spher′i•cal•ly** *adv.*

**sphinx** (sfĭngks) *n., pl.* **sphinxes** or **sphinges. 1.** A figure with a lion's body and a human, ram's, or hawk's head. **2.** A winged monster with a lion's body and a woman's head that killed whoever could not answer its riddle. **3.** An enigmatic person.

**spice** (spīs) *n.* **1.** An aromatic substance, as cinnamon or pepper, used as flavoring. **2.** Zest. **—spice** *v.* **—spic′i•ly** *adv.* **—spic′i•ness** *n.* **—spic′y** *adj.*

**spi•der** (spī′dər) *n.* A small animal having 8 legs, a 2-segmented body, and spinnerets to make silk for webs.

**spig•ot** (spĭg′ət) *n.* A faucet.

**spike** (spīk) *n.* **1.** A heavy nail. **2.** A sharp-pointed projection. *—v.* **spiked, spiking. 1.** To secure or pierce with a spike. **2.** To thwart.

**spill** (spĭl) *v.* **spilled** or **spilt, spilling. 1.** To cause to run or fall out of a container. **2.** To shed (blood). **3.** To cause to fall. *—n.* **1.** An act of spilling. **2.** A fall.

**spin** (spĭn) *v.* **spun** (spŭn), **spinning. 1.** To draw out and twist fibers into thread. **2.** To form (a thread, web, etc.) by forcing out a substance. **3.** To rotate rapidly; whirl. *—n.* **1.** A swift whirling motion. **2.** A short ride. **—spin′ner** *n.* **—spin′ning** *adj. & n.*

**spin•dle** (spĭn′dl) *n.* **1.** A notched stick for spinning fibers into thread. **2.** A pin holding a bobbin or spool.

**spine** (spīn) *n.* **1.** The long row of bones along the back. **2.** A thorn, prickle, or quill.

**spin•ster** (spĭn′stər) *n.* A woman who has remained single.

**spi•ral** (spī′rəl) *n.* The path of a point moving around a center at an increasing or decreasing distance. *—adj.* **1.** Moving in a spiral. **2.** Coiling. *—v.* To move in a spiral. **—spi′ral•ly** *adv.*

**spire** (spīr) *n.* The top part of a steeple or other tapering structure.

**spir•it** (spĭr′ĭt) *n.* **1.** The soul. **2.** A supernatural being. **3.** An individual. **4.** Mood; feelings. **5.** Vivacity and courage. **6.** The essential meaning or feeling. **7. spirits.** Alcoholic liquor. *—v.* To carry off secretly. **—spir′it•ed** *adj.* **—spir′it•less** *adj.*

**spir•i•tu•al** (spĭr′ĭ-cho͞o-əl) *adj.* **1.** Of the spirit. **2.** Sacred. *—n.* A religious folk song. **—spir′i•tu•al′i•ty** *n.* **—spir′i•tu•al•ly** *adv.*

**spit**[1] (spĭt) *n.* Saliva. —*v.* **spat** (spăt) or **spit, spitting.** To eject from the mouth.
**spit**[2] (spĭt) *n.* **1.** A pointed rod on which meat is impaled for broiling. **2.** A narrow point of land. —*v.* **spitted, spitting.** To fix on a spit.
**spite** (spīt) *n.* Malicious ill will. **—in spite of.** Regardless of. —*v.* **spited, spiting.** To hurt maliciously. **—spite'ful** *adj.* **—spite'ful•ly** *adv.*
**splash** (splăsh) *v.* **1.** To dash or scatter (a liquid). **2.** To dash liquid upon. —*n.* **1.** A flying mass of liquid. **2.** A mark produced by scattered liquid. **—splash'er** *n.*
**splay** (splā) *adj.* **1.** Spread or turned out. **2.** Clumsily formed; awkward.
**splen•did** (splĕn'dĭd) *adj.* **1.** Brilliant. **2.** Magnificent. **—splen'did•ly'** *adv.* **—splen'dor** *n.*
**splice** (splīs) *v.* **spliced, splicing.** To join at the ends. —*n.* A joint. **—splic'er** *n.*
**splint** (splĭnt) *n.* **1.** A thin piece from a larger piece; splinter. **2.** A rigid device to prevent movement of a broken bone. **3.** A thin wooden strip used to make baskets and chair bottoms. **—splint** *v.*
**splin•ter** (splĭn'tər) *n.* A sharp, slender piece. —*v.* To break into splinters.
**split** (splĭt) *v.* **split, splitting. 1.** To break, burst, or rip apart. **2.** To disunite. **3.** To divide and share. —*n.* **1.** The act or result of splitting. **2.** A breach or rupture. —*adj.* Divided.
**splurge** (splûrj) *n.* An extravagant expense. **—splurge** *v.*
**spoil** (spoil) *v.* **spoiled, spoiling. 1.** To damage. **2.** To overindulge so as to harm the character. **3.** To decay. —*n.* **spoils.** Plunder. **—spoil'age** *n.* **—spoil'er** *n.*
**spoke**[1] (spōk) *n.* One of the rods that connect the hub and rim of a wheel.
**spoke**[2] (spōk) *v.* p.t. of **speak.**
**spo•ken** (spō'kən) *v.* p.p. of **speak.**
**sponge** (spŭnj) *n.* **1.** A primitive marine animal. **2.** This animal's porous absorbent skeleton or a substitute, used in bathing, cleaning, etc. —*v.* **sponged, sponging. 1.** To wipe or clean with a sponge. **2.** To live off others. **—spong'er** *n.* **—spon'gy** *adj.*
**spon•sor** (spŏn'sər) *n.* **1.** One who vouches or assumes responsibility for another. **2.** A television or radio advertiser. **—spon'sor** *v.* **—spon'sor•ship'** *n.*
**spon•ta•ne•ous** (spŏn-tā'nē-əs) *adj.* **1.** Happening without external cause. **2.** Voluntary. **3.** Natural and unstudied. **—spon'ta•ne'i•ty, spon•ta'ne•ous•ness** *n.* **—spon•ta'ne•ous•ly** *adv.*
**spoof** (spo͞of) *n.* **1.** A light parody. **2.** A hoax. **—spoof** *v.*
**spook** (spo͝ok) *n.* **1.** A ghost. **2.** A spy. —*v.* **1.** To haunt. **2.** To frighten and cause nervous agitation.
**spool** (spo͞ol) *n.* A cylinder upon which thread is wound.
**spoon** (spo͞on) *n.* A small, shallow bowl on a handle, used in eating food. —*v.* To lift or scoop with a spoon.
**spore** (spôr, spōr) *n.* A reproductive cell of a fern, fungus, or bacterium.
**sport** (spôrt, spōrt) *n.* **1.** An active pastime or diversion, esp. a game. **2.** Light mockery. **3.** A fun-loving person. —*v.* **1.** To play; frolic. **2.** To display. —*adj.* For sports. **—sport'y** *adj.*
**sports•man** (spôrts'mən, spōrts'-) *n.* A participant in sports. **—sports'man•like'** *adj.* **—sports'man•ship'** *n.*
**spot** (spŏt) *n.* **1.** A particular place. **2.** A mark or stain. —*v.* **spotted, spotting. 1.** To mark with spots. **2.** To detect; locate. **—spot'less** *adj.* **—spot'ter** *n.* **—spot'ty** *adj.*
**spouse** (spous, spouz) *n.* One's husband or wife.
**spout** (spout) *v.* **1.** To gush forth. **2.** To speak volubly. —*n.* **1.** A pipe through which liquid is released. **2.** A continuous stream.
**sprain** (sprān) *n.* A painful wrenching of the ligaments of a joint. **—sprain** *v.*
**sprang** (sprăng) *v.* p.t. of **spring.**
**sprawl** (sprôl) *v.* To lie or spread out awkwardly. **—sprawl** *n.* **—sprawl'er** *n.*
**spray**[1] (sprā) *n.* **1.** A mass of dispersed droplets. **2. a.** A fine jet of liquid that releases such droplets. **b.** A pressurized container. —*v.* **1.** To disperse (a liquid) in a spray. **2.** To apply a spray to. **—spray'er** *n.*
**spray**[2] (sprā) *n.* A leafy or flowery branch.
**spread** (sprĕd) *v.* **spread, spreading. 1.** To open; stretch. **2.** To move farther

apart. **3.** To distribute over a surface. **4.** To extend. **5.** To disseminate. —*n.* **1.** The act of spreading. **2.** An expanse. **3.** A range. **4.** A cloth covering. **5.** A food to be spread. —**spread'er** *n.*

**spree** (sprē) *n.* **1.** A lively outing. **2.** A bout of drinking.

**sprig** (sprĭg) *n.* A twig or shoot.

**spring** (sprĭng) *v.* **sprang** (sprăng) or **sprung** (sprŭng), **sprung, springing. 1.** To leap. **2.** To emerge suddenly. **3.** To arise; develop. **4.** To set in motion. **5.** To disclose suddenly. —*n.* **1.** An elastic device, as a coil of wire. **2.** Elasticity; resilience. **3.** The act of springing. **4.** A natural fountain or flow of water. **5.** A source. **6.** The season between winter and summer. —**spring'y** *adj.*

**sprin•kle** (sprĭng'kəl) *v.* **-kled, -kling. 1.** To scatter in drops. **2.** To rain lightly. —*n.* A light rainfall. —**sprin'kler** *n.*

**sprint** (sprĭnt) *n.* A short dash at top speed. —*v.* To run at top speed. —**sprint'er** *n.*

**sprock•et** (sprŏk'ĭt) *n.* A toothlike projection on a wheel rim to engage the links of a chain.

**sprout** (sprout) *v.* To begin to grow. —*n.* A bud or shoot.

**spruce** (spro͞os) *adj.* **sprucer, sprucest.** Neat or dapper. —*v.* **spruced, sprucing.** To make or become spruce.

**sprung** (sprŭng) *v.* p.p. & a p.t. of **spring.**

**spry** (sprī) *adj.* **sprier** or **spryer, spriest** or **spryest.** Briskly active and alert. —**spry'ly** *adv.* —**spry'ness** *n.*

**spun** (spŭn) *v.* p.t. & p.p. of **spin.**

**spunk** (spŭngk) *n.* **1.** Punk or tinder. **2.** Spirit; pluck. —**spunk'y** *adj.*

**spur** (spûr) *n.* **1.** A spiked device on a rider's heel to urge the horse forward. **2.** An incentive or goad. **3.** A pointed projection. **4.** A lateral extension. —*v.* **spurred, spurring.** To urge on.

**spu•ri•ous** (spyo͝or'ē-əs) *adj.* **1.** Not authentic; false. **2.** Forged or interpolated. **3.** Illegitimate; bastard. —**spu'ri•ous•ly** *adv.* —**spu'ri•ous•ness** *n.*

**spurn** (spûrn) *v.* To reject disdainfully. —**spurn'er** *n.*

**spurt** (spûrt) *n.* A sudden gush. —*v.* **1.** To burst forth. **2.** To squirt.

**sput•ter** (spŭt'ər) *v.* **1.** To spit out small particles. **2.** To make a sporadic coughing noise. —**sput'ter** *n.*

**spy** (spī) *n., pl.* **spies.** One who secretly watches, esp. to obtain intelligence. —*v.* **spied, spying. 1.** To act as a spy. **2.** To see.

**squab•ble** (skwŏb'əl) *n.* A trivial quarrel. —**squab'ble** *v.*

**squad** (skwŏd) *n.* A small group or team.

**squal•id** (skwŏl'ĭd) *adj.* Filthy and cluttered. —**squal'id•ly** *adv.* —**squal'id•ness, squal'or** *n.*

**squall**[1] (skwôl) *n.* A loud, harsh outcry. —**squall** *v.*

**squall**[2] (skwôl) *n.* A brief, sudden, violent windstorm. —**squall** *v.* —**squall'y** *adj.*

**squan•der** (skwŏn'dər) *v.* To spend wastefully.

**square** (skwâr) *n.* **1.** A rectangle having 4 equal sides. **2.** An instrument for drawing right angles. **3.** The product of a number multiplied by itself. **4. a.** An open area at a street intersection. **b.** A block. —*adj.* **squarer, squarest. 1.** Having 4 equal sides and 4 right angles. **2.** Forming a right angle. **3.** Honest. **4.** Settled. —*v.* **squared, squaring. 1.** To cut to a square shape. **2.** To settle. **3.** To raise (a number) to the second power. **4.** To conform. —**square'ly** *adv.* —**square'ness** *n.*

**squash** (skwŏsh, skwôsh) *v.* **1.** To flatten; crush. **2.** To suppress. —*n.* **1.** The act of squashing. **2.** A game played in a walled court with a racket and a small dead ball.

**squat** (skwŏt) *v.* **squatted** or **squat, squatting. 1.** To sit on one's heels. **2.** To settle on unoccupied land without legal claim. —*adj.* **squatter, squattest.** Short and thick. —*n.* The posture of squatting. —**squat'ter** *n.*

**squawk** (skwôk) *v.* **1.** To utter a harsh screech. **2.** To make a loud complaint. —**squawk'er** *n.*

**squeak** (skwēk) *v.* To make a loud, shrill cry or sound. **2.** To turn informer. —**squeak** *n.* —**squeak'y** *adj.*

**squeal** (skwēl) *v.* **1.** To make a loud, shrill cry or sound. **2.** To turn informer. —**squeal** *n.* —**squeal'er** *n.*

**squea•mish** (skwē'mĭsh) *adj.* Easily nauseated or disgusted. —**squeam'ish•ly** *adv.* —**squeam'ish•ness** *n.*

**squeeze** (skwēz) *v.* **squeezed, squeezing.** **1.** To press hard. **2.** To extract by applying pressure. **3.** To cram. —*n.* An act of squeezing. —**squeez'er** *n.*

**squelch** (skwĕlch) *v.* To suppress or silence. —*n.* A crushing reply.

**squint** (skwĭnt) *v.* To look with the eyes partly closed. —**squint** *n.* —**squint'er** *n.*

**squirm** (skwûrm) *v.* To twist about; writhe. —**squirm'er** *n.* —**squirm'y** *adj.*

**squirt** (skwûrt) *v.* To eject liquid in a thin swift stream. —**squirt** *n.*

**stab** (stăb) *v.* **stabbed, stabbing.** To pierce or wound with a pointed weapon. —*n.* **1.** A thrust with a pointed weapon. **2.** An attempt.

**sta•ble**[1] (stā'bəl) *adj.* **-bler, -blest. 1.** Resistant to sudden change. **2.** Maintaining equilibrium. —**sta•bil'i•ty** *n.* —**sta'bi•li•za'tion** *n.* —**sta'bi•lize'** *v.* —**sta'bi•liz'er** *n.*

**sta•ble**[2] (stā'bəl) *n.* A building for domestic animals, esp. horses. —*v.* **-bled, -bling.** To keep in a stable.

**stack** (stăk) *n.* **1.** A pile arranged in layers. **2.** A chimney. —*v.* To arrange in a stack.

**sta•di•um** (stā'dē-əm) *n., pl.* **-dia** or **-diums.** A large, often unroofed structure for athletic events.

**staff** (stăf) *n.* **1.** pl. **staffs** or **staves.** A rod or stick. **2.** pl. **staffs.** A group of assistants or employees. **3.** pl. **staves.** The set of lines on which music is written. —*v.* To provide with employees.

**stage** (stāj) *n.* **1.** A raised platform, esp. one for theatrical performances. **2.** The theater. **3.** A leg of a journey. **4.** A step in development. —*v.* **staged, staging. 1.** To present on a stage. **2.** To carry out.

**stag•ger** (stăg'ər) *v.* **1.** To move or cause to move unsteadily; totter. **2.** To overwhelm. **3.** To arrange in alternating time periods. —*n.* A tottering or reeling motion. —**stag'ger•er** *n.*

**stag•nant** (stăg'nənt) *adj.* **1.** Foul from standing still. **2.** Inactive; sluggish.

**stag•nate** (stăg'nāt') *v.* **-nated, -nating.** To lie inactive. —**stag•na'tion** *n.*

**staid** (stād) *adj.* Grave; sober.

**stain** (stān) *v.* **1.** To discolor or spot. **2.** To disgrace. **3.** To color with a penetrating dye. —*n.* **1.** A spot or smudge. **2.** A disgrace. **3.** A dye. —**stain'er** *n.* —**stain'less** *adj.*

**stair** (stâr) *n.* **1.** Often **stairs.** A staircase. **2.** One of a flight of steps.

**stair•case** (stâr'kās') *n.* A flight of steps.

**stake** (stāk) *n.* **1.** A pointed stick for driving into the ground. **2.** Often **stakes.** Money risked in a bet. **3.** A share or interest. —*v.* **staked, staking. 1.** To mark the limits of. **2.** To gamble or risk. **3.** To finance.

**stale** (stāl) *adj.* **staler, stalest. 1.** Having lost freshness. **2.** Unoriginal.

**stalk**[1] (stôk) *n.* A plant stem.

**stalk**[2] (stôk) *v.* **1.** To walk with a stiff, haughty, or menacing gait. **2.** To track (game). —**stalk'er** *n.*

**stall** (stôl) *n.* A small compartment or booth. —*v.* To stop or delay.

**stal•lion** (stăl'yən) *n.* An uncastrated adult male horse.

**stal•wart** (stôl'wərt) *adj.* Sturdy and brave.

**stam•i•na** (stăm'ə-nə) *n.* Physical or moral strength or endurance.

**stam•mer** (stăm'ər) *v.* To speak with involuntary pauses and repetitions; stutter. —**stam'mer** *n.* —**stam'mer•er** *n.*

**stamp** (stămp) *v.* **1.** To bring the foot down upon forcibly. **2.** To imprint or impress with a mark. **3.** To affix a stamp to. **4.** To cut out with a die. —*n.* **1.** The act of stamping. **2.** A mark or seal. **3.** A piece of gummed paper, as for postage. **4. a.** An implement used to impress or cut out. **b.** The impression thus formed.

**stam•pede** (stăm-pēd) *n.* A sudden headlong rush, as of startled animals. —*v.* **-peded, -peding.** To rush in a stampede.

**stance** (stăns) *n.* **1.** Manner of standing. **2.** Attitude.

**stanch** (stônch, stänch, stănch) *v.* To check the flow of.

**stand** (stănd) *v.* **stood** (sto͝od), **standing. 1.** To take or maintain an upright position on the feet. **2.** To place or be placed upright. **3.** To remain stable or unchanged. **4.** To tolerate; endure. **5.** To rank. **6.** To hold an opinion. —*n.* **1.** A fixed position. **2.** A halt or stop. **3.** A platform or other place for standing. **4.** A counter, rack, or pedestal. **5.** A growth of trees.

**stan•dard** (stăn′dərd) *n.* **1.** A flag or banner. **2.** A measure of value; criterion. **3.** A degree or level. **—stan′dard** *adj.*

**stan•dard•ize** (stăn′dər-dīz′) *v.* **-ized, -izing.** To cause or adapt to fit a standard. **—stan′dard•i•za′tion** *n.*

**stand•ing** (stăn′dĭng) *n.* **1.** Status. **2.** Length of time. *—adj.* **1.** Upright. **2.** Permanent. **3.** Stagnant.

**stank** (stăngk) *v.* p.t. of **stink.**

**sta•ple**[1] (stā′pəl) *n.* **1.** A major commodity or product. **2.** A major part. **3.** Fiber. **—sta′ple** *adj.*

**sta•ple**[2] (stā′pəl) *n.* A U-shaped metal loop with pointed ends, used esp. as a paper fastener. **—sta′ple** *v.* **—sta′pler** *n.*

**star** (stär) *n.* **1.** A relatively stationary celestial object visible at night as a point of light. **2.** A graphic design with radiating points. **3.** A superior performer. **4.** A leading actor. **5.** An asterisk. *—v.* **starred, starring. 1.** To mark with a star. **2.** To play the leading role. **—star′ry** *adj.*

**star•board** (stär′bərd) *n.* The right-hand side of a ship or aircraft as one faces forward. **—star′board** *adj. & adv.*

**starch** (stärch) *n.* A food substance found in corn, potatoes, and wheat, and used in powdered form as a fabric stiffener. *—v.* To stiffen with starch. **—starch′y** *adj.*

**stare** (stâr) *v.* **stared, staring.** To look with a steady gaze. **—stare** *n.*

**stark** (stärk) *adj.* **1.** Utter; extreme. **2.** Bare; bleak. *—adv.* Utterly. **—stark′ly** *adv.* **—stark′ness** *n.*

**start** (stärt) *v.* **1.** To begin. **2.** To set in motion. **3.** To move suddenly. *—n.* **1. a.** A beginning. **b.** A place or time of beginning. **2.** A position of advantage. **3.** A sudden movement. **—start′er** *n.*

**star•tle** (stär′tl) *v.* **-tled, -tling.** To cause to jump, as in fright.

**starve** (stärv) *v.* **starved, starving. 1.** To die or cause to die from hunger. **2.** To suffer or cause to suffer from hunger. **—star•va′tion** *n.*

**stash** (stăsh) *v.* To hide or store away in a secret place. **—stash** *n.*

**state** (stāt) *n.* **1.** Condition. **2.** Stage; phase. **3.** A nation. **4.** National policy or power; government. **5.** A political unit of a federation. **6.** Ceremony. *—v.* **stated, stating.** To declare. **—state′hood′** *n.*

**state•ly** (stāt′lē) *adj.* **-lier, -liest.** Dignified; formal. **—state′li•ness** *n.*

**state•ment** (stāt′mənt) *n.* **1.** The act of stating. **2.** An account.

**states•man** (stāts′mən) *n.* A political leader. **—states′man•like′** *adj.* **—states′man•ship′** *n.*

**stat•ic** (stăt′ĭk) *adj.* **1.** Having no motion. **2.** Caused by accumulation of electric charge. *—n.* Random noise produced in a radio or television receiver. **—stat′i•cal•ly** *adv.*

**sta•tion** (stā′shən) *n.* **1.** A position. **2.** A center of operations. **3.** A transportation depot. **4.** Social status. **5.** A place for radio or television transmission. *—v.* To post.

**sta•tion•ar•y** (stā′shə-nĕr′ē) *adj.* Fixed; not moving.

**sta•tion•er•y** (stā′shə-nĕr′ē) *n.* **1.** Writing materials such as pens, ink, paper, and envelopes. **2.** Writing paper. **—sta′tion•er** *n.*

**sta•tis•tic** (stə-tĭs′tĭk) *n.* **1.** Any numerical datum. **2. statistics** (*takes sing. v.*). The interpretation of numerical data. **—sta•tis′ti•cal** *adj.* **—stat′is•ti′cian** *n.*

**stat•ue** (stăch′o͞o) *n.* A sculpted form or likeness.

**stat•ure** (stăch′ər) *n.* **1.** A person's height. **2.** Status; reputation.

**sta•tus** (stā′təs, stăt′əs) *n.* **1.** Legal condition. **2.** A relative position; rank. **3.** A state of affairs.

**stat•ute** (stăch′o͞ot) *n.* A law.

**stat•u•to•ry** (stăch′ə-tôr′ē, -tōr′ē) *adj.* Enacted, regulated, or defined by statute.

**staunch** (stônch, stänch) *adj.* Firm and steadfast. **—staunch′ly** *adv.* **—staunch′ness** *n.*

**stave** (stāv) *n.* **1.** One of the wooden strips that form the sides of a barrel. **2.** A staff. *—v.* **staved** or **stove** (stōv), **staving. 1.** To break a hole in. **2.** To ward off.

**staves** (stāvz) *n.* A pl. of **staff.**

**stay**[1] (stā) *v.* **1.** To remain. **2.** To stop. **3.** To wait. **4.** To endure. **5.** To postpone.

—*n.* **1.** A stop or visit. **2.** A postponement.
**stay²** (stā) *v.* To prop up. —*n.* A support or brace.
**stead•fast** (stĕd′făst′, -fəst) *adj.* **1.** Fixed; steady. **2.** Loyal; constant. **—stead′fast′ly** *adv.* **—stead′fast′ness** *n.*
**stead•y** (stĕd′ē) *adj.* **-ier, -iest. 1.** Firm. **2.** Unfaltering. **3.** Calm. —*v.* **-ied, -ying.** To make or become steady. **—stead′i•ly** *adv.* **—stead′i•ness** *n.*
**steak** (stāk) *n.* A slice of meat, usually beef.
**steal** (stēl) *v.* **stole** (stōl), **stolen** (stō′lən), **stealing. 1.** To take without right or permission. **2.** To get or effect secretly. **3.** To move stealthily.
**stealth** (stĕlth) *n.* Covert action; furtiveness. **—stealth′i•ly** *adv.* **—stealth′i•ness** *n.* **—stealth′y** *adj.*
**steam** (stēm) *n.* **1.** Water vapor. **2.** Energy. —*v.* **1.** To emit steam. **2.** To expose to steam, as in cooking. **—steam′y** *adj.*
**steed** (stēd) *n.* A horse.
**steel** (stēl) *n.* A hard, malleable alloy of iron and carbon. —*v.* To make hard or strong. **—steel** *adj.* **—steel′y** *adj.*
**steep¹** (stēp) *adj.* **1.** Sharply sloping. **2.** Excessive. **—steep′en** *v.* **—steep′ly** *adv.* **—steep′ness** *n.*
**steep²** (stēp) *v.* **1.** To soak in liquid. **2.** To saturate. **—steep′er** *n.*
**stee•ple** (stē′pəl) *n.* A tall tower.
**steer¹** (stîr) *v.* **1.** To guide; direct. **2.** To drive; move.
**steer²** (stîr) *n.* A young ox.
**stel•lar** (stĕl′ər) *adj.* **1.** Relating to the stars. **2. a.** Relating to a star performer. **b.** Outstanding.
**stem¹** (stĕm) *n.* **1.** A supporting or connecting plant part; stalk. **2.** A stemlike part, as of a pipe. **3.** The prow of a vessel. —*v.* **stemmed, stemming. 1.** To derive or develop (from). **2.** To make headway against. **—stem′less** *adj.*
**stem²** (stĕm) *v.* **stemmed, stemming.** To stop or hold back.
**stench** (stĕnch) *n.* A foul odor.
**ste•nog•ra•phy** (stə-nŏg′rə-fē) *n.* Writing in shorthand. **—ste•nog′ra•pher** *n.* **—sten′o•graph′ic** *adj.*
**step** (stĕp) *n.* **1.** A single movement of the foot in walking. **2.** A manner or rhythm of walking. **3.** A short distance. **4.** One of the horizontal surfaces in a stairway. **5.** One of a series of actions. **6.** A stage. **7.** A level; rank; degree. —*v.* **stepped, stepping. 1.** To put the foot down (on). **2.** To walk.
**steppe** (stĕp) *n.* A vast, semiarid, grass-covered plain.
**ster•e•o•type** (stĕr′ē-ə-tīp′, stîr′-) *n.* **1.** A typical example or pattern. **2.** A conventional, oversimplified conception.
**ster•ile** (stĕr′əl) *adj.* **1.** Incapable of reproducing. **2.** Unproductive. **3.** Free from germs. **—ste•ril′i•ty** *n.* **—ster′il•i•za′tion** *n.* **—ster′il•ize** *v.* **—ster′il•iz′er** *n.*
**ster•ling** (stûr′lĭng) *n.* **1.** British money. **2.** An alloy of 92.5% silver. *adj.* **1.** Of sterling. **2.** Of the highest quality.
**stern¹** (stûrn) *adj.* **1.** Unyielding. **2.** Grave or severe. **—stern′ly** *adv.*
**stern²** (stûrn) *n.* The rear part of a ship.
**ster•oid** (stĕr′oid′, stîr′-) *n.* An organic compound forming the basis of many hormones and drugs.
**stew** (st/y/o͞o) *v.* To cook (food) by boiling slowly. —*n.* A dish cooked by stewing, esp. a mixture of meat and vegetables.
**stew•ard** (st/y/o͞o′ərd) *n.* **1.** One who manages another's property or affairs. **2.** One in charge of provisions and dining arrangements. **3.** A servant or attendant on a ship or airplane.
**stick** (stĭk) *n.* **1.** A long, slender piece of wood, esp. a tree branch. **2.** A cane or baton. —*v.* **stuck** (stŭk), **sticking. 1.** To pierce. **2.** To fasten or attach. **3.** To adhere; cling. **4.** To become fixed or obstructed. **5.** To put or thrust. **6.** To burden. **7.** To persist.
**stick•y** (stĭk′ē) *adj.* **-ier, -iest. 1.** Adhesive. **2.** Muggy. **—stick′i•ly** *adv.* **—stick′i•ness** *n.*
**stiff** (stĭf) *adj.* **1.** Not flexible. **2.** Excessively formal. **3.** Not fluid. **4.** Strong or steady. **5.** Difficult. **6.** Severe. **—stiff′en** *v.* **—stiff′en•er** *n.* **—stiff′ly** *adv.* **—stiff′ness** *n.*
**sti•fle** (stī′fəl) *v.* **-fled, -fling. 1.** To smother or suffocate. **2.** To suppress. **—sti′fler** *n.*
**stig•ma** (stĭg′mə) *n., pl.* **-mata** or **-mas. 1.** A mark or token of infamy. **2.** A scar or birthmark. **3. stigmata.** Marks or sores corresponding to Jesus' wounds.

**—stig•mat'ic** *adj. & n.*

**stile¹** (stīl) *n.* A set of steps for climbing over a fence.

**stile²** (stīl) *n.* A vertical part in a frame, as in a door frame.

**still¹** (stĭl) *adj.* **1.** Silent; quiet. **2.** Without movement. *—n.* A single photograph. *—adv.* **1.** Now as before. **2.** Even. **3.** Nevertheless. *—conj.* Nevertheless. *—v.* **1.** To make or become still. **2.** To allay; calm. **—still'ness** *n.*

**still²** (stĭl) *n.* An apparatus for distilling liquids, particularly alcohols.

**stilt•ed** (stĭl'tĭd) *adj.* Pompous. **—stilt'ed•ly** *adv.*

**stim•u•late** (stĭm'yə-lāt') *v.* **-lated, -lating.** To excite. **—stim'u•lant** *adj. & n.* **—stim'u•la'tion** *n.*

**stim•u•lus** (stĭm'yə-ləs) *n., pl.* **-li. 1.** Anything causing a response. **2.** A spur; goad. **—stim'u•la'tive** *adj. & n.*

**sting** (stĭng) *v.* **stung** (stŭng), **stinging. 1.** To pierce with a sharp-pointed structure or organ. **2.** To cause or feel sharp pain. *—n.* A wound or pain caused by stinging. **—sting'er** *n.*

**stin•gy** (stĭn'jē) *adj.* **-gier, -giest.** Giving or spending reluctantly. **—stin'gi•ly** *adv.* **—stin'gi•ness** *n.*

**stink** (stĭngk) *v.* **stank** (stăngk) or **stunk** (stŭngk), **stunk, stinking.** To give off a strong foul odor. *—n.* A strong offensive odor. **—stink'er** *n.*

**stint** (stĭnt) *v.* **1.** To be sparing with. **2.** To be frugal. *—n.* A period of duty. **—stint'er** *n.*

**sti•pend** (stī'pĕnd', -pənd) *n.* A fixed, regular payment, as a salary or an allowance.

**stip•u•late** (stĭp'yə-lāt') *v.* **-lated, -lating.** To specify as a condition. **—stip'u•la'tion** *n.* **—stip'u•la'tor** *n.*

**stir** (stûr) *v.* **stirred, stirring. 1.** To mix with an implement in a circular motion. **2.** To change or move slightly. **3.** To rouse; excite. **4.** To affect strongly. *—n.* **1.** An act of stirring. **2.** A commotion. **—stir'rer** *n.* **—stir'ring** *adj.* **—stir'ring•ly** *adv.*

**stir•rup** (stûr'əp, stĭr'-) *n.* A flat-based loop to support a rider's foot.

**stitch** (stĭch) *n.* **1.** A single complete movement in sewing, knitting, etc. **2.** A sudden sharp pain. *—v.* To sew. **—stitch'er** *n.*

**stock** (stŏk) *n.* **1.** A supply, esp. of goods kept on hand. **2.** Domestic animals. **3.** The capital of a business, or shares of ownership in a business. **4.** Ancestry. **5.** A related group; family. **6. stocks.** A pillory. **7.** A supporting structure or frame. **8.** Broth. **9.** A regional theater. *—v.* To supply. *—adj.* **1.** Kept regularly available. **2.** Commonplace.

**stock•ing** (stŏk'ĭng) *n.* A close-fitting covering for the foot and leg.

**stock•y** (stŏk'ē) *adj.* **-ier, -iest.** Short and solidly built. **—stock'i•ness** *n.*

**stodg•y** (stŏj'ē) *adj.* **-ier, -iest.** Pompous; stuffy. **—stodg'i•ly** *adv.* **—stodg'i•ness** *n.*

**sto•ic** (stō'ĭk) *adj.* Indifferent to passion or pain; impassive. *—n.* A stoic person. **—sto'i•cal** *adj.* **—sto'i•cal•ly** *adv.* **—sto'i•cism'** *n.*

**stoke** (stōk) *v.* **stoked, stoking.** To stir up or tend (a fire). **—stok'er** *n.*

**stole¹** (stōl) *n.* A long scarf worn about the shoulders.

**stole²** (stōl) *v.* p.t. of **steal.**

**sto•len** (stō'lən) *v.* p.p. of **steal.**

**stol•id** (stŏl'ĭd) *adj.* Impassive. **—sto•lid'i•ty** *n.* **—stol'id•ly** *adv.*

**stom•ach** (stŭm'ək) *n.* **1.** A saclike digestive organ below the esophagus. **2.** The abdomen or belly. **3.** An appetite. *—v.* To tolerate; endure.

**stomp** (stômp, stŏmp) *v.* To tread heavily (on).

**stone** (stōn) *n.* **1.** Solid mineral matter; rock. **2.** A piece of rock. **3.** A seed with a hard covering. **4.** A mineral concretion as in the kidney. *—v.* **stoned, stoning.** To pelt or kill with stones. **—stone** *adj.* **—ston'y** *adj.*

**stood** (stŏŏd) *v.* p.t. & p.p. of **stand.**

**stool** (stōōl) *n.* **1.** A backless and armless single seat. **2.** A bowel movement.

**stoop** (stōōp) *v.* **1.** To bend from the waist. **2.** To debase oneself. *—n.* The act of stooping.

**stop** (stŏp) *v.* **stopped, stopping. 1.** To close (an opening). **2.** To obstruct. **3.** To halt or cease. **4.** To visit briefly. *—n.* **1.** An end or pause. **2.** A stay. **3.** A place stopped at. **4.** An obstruction. **—stop'page** *n.* **—stop'per** *n.*

**store** (stôr, stōr) *n.* **1.** A place where goods are offered for sale; a shop. **2.** A reserve supply. *—v.* **stored, storing. 1.**

To put away for future use. **2.** To deposit for safekeeping. **—stor'age** *n.*

**storm** (stôrm) *n.* **1.** Strong winds accompanied by rain or snow. **2.** A violent, sudden attack. *—v.* **1.** To rain or snow violently. **2.** To rage. **3.** To attack suddenly. **—storm'y** *adj.*

**sto•ry¹** (stôr'e, stōr'ē) *n., pl.* **-ries. 1.** The narration of an event or series of events. **2.** A short fictional narrative; tale. **3.** A plot. **4.** An explanation, esp. a false one.

**sto•ry²** (stôr'ē, stōr'ē) *n., pl.* **-ries.** A horizontal division of a building, from floor to ceiling.

**stout** (stout) *adj.* **1.** Bold or brave. **2.** Strong; sturdy. **3.** Corpulent. **—stout'ly** *adv.* **—stout'ness** *n.*

**stove¹** (stōv) *n.* An apparatus for cooking or heating.

**stove²** (stōv) *v.* A p.t. & p.p. of **stave.**

**stow** (stō) *v.* To store away. **—stow'a•way'** *n.*

**strad•dle** (străd'l) *v.* **-dled, -dling. 1.** To sit astride (of). **2.** To appear to favor both sides of (an issue). **—strad'dle** *n.*

**strag•gle** (străg'əl) *v.* **-gled, -gling. 1.** To stray behind. **2.** To spread out irregularly. **—strag'gler** *n.* **—strag'gly** *adj.*

**straight** (strāt) *adj.* **1.** Extending continuously without curving. **2.** Erect. **3.** Direct and candid. **4.** Unbroken. **5.** Accurate. **6.** Unmodified or undiluted. **7.** Heterosexual. *—adv.* In a straight line or manner. **—straight'en** *v.* **—straight'ness** *n.*

**straight•for•ward** (strāt-fôr'wərd) *adj.* Honest; candid. **—straight•for'ward•ness** *n.*

**strain¹** (strān) *v.* **1.** To pull or stretch to the breaking point. **2.** To exert or strive to the utmost. **3.** To injure by overexertion. **4.** To filter. *—n.* **1.** The act of straining. **2.** A great effort, exertion, or tension. **—strain'er** *n.*

**strain²** (strān) *n.* **1.** A group of the same ancestry. **2.** A kind; sort. **3.** A streak; trace. **4.** A melody.

**strait** (strāt) *n.* **1.** A narrow passage of water. **2.** Often **straits.** A position of difficulty or need. *—adj.* **1.** Narrow. **2.** Strict.

**strand¹** (strănd) *n.* A beach. *—v.* **1.** To drive aground, as a ship. **2.** To leave in a helpless position.

**strand²** (strănd) *n.* **1.** A fiber or filament in a rope, cable, etc. **2.** A string.

**strange** (strānj) *adj.* **stranger, strangest. 1.** Unfamiliar. **2.** Extraordinary. **3.** Peculiar. **4.** Exotic. **—strange'ly** *adv.* **—strange'ness** *n.*

**strang•er** (strān'jər) *n.* **1.** A person one does not know. **2.** A newcomer.

**stran•gle** (străng'gəl) *v.* **-gled, -gling.** To kill by choking or suffocating. **—stran'gler** *n.* **—stran'gu•late'** *v.* **—stran'gu•la'tion** *n.*

**strap** (străp) *n.* A long, narrow strip for binding or securing objects. *—v.* **strapped, strapping.** To fasten with a strap. **—strap'less** *adj.*

**stra•ta** (strā'tə, străt'ə) *n.* pl. of **stratum.**

**strat•a•gem** (străt'ə-jəm) *n.* A trick or artifice.

**strat•e•gy** (străt'ə-jē) *n., pl.* **-gies. 1.** The planning of military operations. **2.** A plan of action; scheme. **—stra•te'gic** *adj.* **—strat'e•gist** *n.*

**stra•tum** (strā'təm, străt'əm) *n., pl.* **-ta.** One of several parallel layers. **—stra'tal** *adj.*

**straw** (strô) *n.* **1.** Stalks of threshed grain. **2.** A slender tube for sucking up a liquid. **—straw** *adj.*

**stray** (strā) *v.* **1.** To wander. **2.** To go astray. **3.** To digress. *—n.* One that has strayed, esp. a lost domestic animal. *—adj.* **1.** Straying. **2.** Lost. **3.** Scattered.

**streak** (strēk) *n.* **1.** A long, bold line or mark. **2.** A trait. **3.** An unbroken series or period. *—v.* **1.** To mark with a streak. **2.** To rush. **—streak'i•ness** *n.* **—streak'y** *adj.*

**stream** (strēm) *n.* **1.** A body of rushing water. **2.** A current or flow. *—v.* **1.** To flow in a stream. **2.** To pour forth. **—stream'y** *adj.*

**stream•er** (strē'mər) *n.* A long, narrow banner or strip.

**stream•lined** (strēm'līnd') *adj.* **1.** Designed to offer the least resistance to fluid flow. **2.** Improved in efficiency. **—stream'line'** *v.*

**street** (strēt) *n.* A public road in a city or town.

**strength** (strĕngkth, strĕngth) *n.* **1.** Physical or moral power. **2.** Durability. **3.** Capability. **4.** Effective or binding force. **5.** Degree of concentration; intensity. **6.** An asset. **—strength'en** *v.*

—**strength'en•er** *n.*

**stren•u•ous** (strĕn'yo͞o-əs) *adj.* **1.** Requiring great effort. **2.** Energetic. —**stren'u•ous•ly** *adv.* —**stren'u•ous•ness** *n.*

**stress** (strĕs) *n.* **1.** Emphasis. **2.** Special force and loudness with which a syllable is spoken. **3.** Physical pressure. **4.** Mental or emotional strain. —*v.* **1.** To place emphasis on; accent. **2.** To strain.

**stretch** (strĕch) *v.* **1.** To lengthen by pulling. **2.** To extend. **3.** To make taut. **4.** To strain. **5.** To prolong. —*n.* **1.** The act of stretching. **2.** Elasticity. **3.** An expanse. **4.** A continuous period of time. —*adj.* Elastic. —**stretch'a•ble** *adj.*

**strew** (stro͞o) *v.* **strewed, strewn** or **strewed, strewing.** To scatter; sprinkle.

**strick•en** (strĭk'ən) *v.* A p.p. of **strike.** —*adj.* Struck or affected.

**strict** (strĭkt) *adj.* **1.** Exact. **2.** Complete; absolute. **3.** Exacting. **4.** Devout. —**strict'ly** *adv.* —**strict'ness** *n.*

**stride** (strīd) *v.* **strode** (strōd), **stridden** (strĭd'n), **striding.** To walk vigorously with long steps. —*n.* **1.** The act of striding. **2.** A long step. —**strid'er** *n.*

**strife** (strīf) *n.* Violent or bitter dissension.

**strike** (strīk) *v.* **struck** (strŭk), **struck** or **stricken** (strĭk'ən), **striking. 1.** To hit sharply. **2.** To collide with. **3.** To launch an attack. **4.** To afflict. **5.** To impress or stamp. **6.** To sound. **7.** To produce by friction. **8.** To eliminate. **9.** To find; reach. **10.** To assume (a pose). **11.** To quit working in support of labor demands. —*n.* **1.** An act of striking. **2.** An attack. **3.** A cessation of work by employees. —**strik'er** *n.*

**string** (strĭng) *n.* **1.** A cord thicker than thread. **2.** A long, thin line. **3.** A set of objects threaded together. **4. strings.** The instruments of the violin family. —*v.* **strung** (strŭng), **stringing. 1.** To furnish with a string. **2.** To thread on a string. **3.** To arrange in a series. **4.** To stretch out. —**string'i•ness** *n.* —**string'y** *adj.*

**strin•gent** (strĭn'jənt) *adj.* **1.** Rigorous; strict. **2.** Constricted; tight. **3.** Scarce in money or resources. —**strin'gen•cy** *n.* —**strin'gent•ly** *adv.*

**strip**[1] (strĭp) *v.* **stripped, stripping. 1.** To undress. **2.** To remove covering, etc., from. **3.** To deprive.

**strip**[2] (strĭp) *n.* A long, narrow piece.

**stripe** (strīp) *n.* **1.** A long, narrow band of a distinctive color. **2.** Sort; kind. —*v.* **striped, striping.** To mark with stripes. —**striped** *adj.*

**strive** (strīv) *v.* **strove** (strōv), **striven** (strĭv'ən) or **strived, striving. 1.** To exert much effort. **2.** To contend. —**striv'er** *n.*

**strode** (strōd) *v.* p.t. of **stride.**

**stroke** (strōk) *n.* **1.** An impact; blow; strike. **2.** An act of striking. **3.** Apoplexy. **4.** An inspired idea or act. **5.** A single completed movement, as in swimming or rowing. **6.** A single mark made by a pen or other marking implement. **7.** A light caressing movement. —*v.* **stroked, stroking.** To rub lightly, as with the hand; caress.

**stroll** (strōl) *v.* To walk leisurely. —**stroll** *n.* —**stroll'er** *n.*

**strong** (strông) *adj.* **1.** Powerful; forceful. **2.** In sound health. **3.** Solid. **4.** Intense. —**strong'ly** *adv.*

**strove** (strōv) *v.* p.t. of **strive.**

**struck** (strŭk) *v.* p.t. & p.p. of **strike.**

**struc•ture** (strŭk'chər) *n.* **1.** Organization; design. **2.** Something constructed, esp. a building or part. —*v.* **-tured, -turing.** To give structure to. —**struc'tur•al** *adj.* —**struc'tur•al•ly** *adv.*

**strug•gle** (strŭg'əl) *v.* **-gled, -gling. 1.** To exert energy; strive. **2.** To fight; wrestle. **3.** To contend. —*n.* Strenuous effort. **2.** A fight. **3.** Contention. —**strug'gler** *n.*

**strung** (strŭng) *v.* p.t. & p.p. of **string.**

**strut** (strŭt) *v.* **strutted, strutting.** To walk conceitedly. —*n.* **1.** A stiff, self-important gait. **2.** A bar or rod used to strengthen a framework. —**strut'ter** *n.* —**strut'ting•ly** *adv.*

**stub** (stŭb) *n.* A short blunt end remaining after something has been removed. —*v.* **stubbed, stubbing.** To strike (one's toe or foot).

**stub•ble** (stŭb'əl) *n.* **1.** Short, stiff stalks of grain remaining in a field after harvest. **2.** Something resembling this, esp. a growth of beard.

**stub•born** (stŭb'ərn) *adj.* **1.** Obstinate. **2.** Persistent. —**stub'born•ly** *adv.* —**stub'born•ness** *n.*

**stuck** (stŭk) *v.* p.t. & p.p. of **stick.**

**stud**[1] (stŭd) *n.* **1.** An upright post in the framework of a wall. **2.** A small projecting knob. **3.** A small ornamental button. —*v.* **studded, studding.** To provide with studs.

**stud**[2] (stŭd) *n.* A male animal kept for breeding.

**stu•dent** (st/y/o͞od′nt) *n.* One who studies.

**stu•di•o** (st/y/o͞o′dē-ō) *n., pl.* **-os. 1.** An artist's workroom. **2.** A single-room apartment. **3.** A room or building for motion-picture, television, or radio productions.

**stu•di•ous** (st/y/o͞o′dē-əs) *adj.* **1.** Devoted to study. **2.** Diligent. **—stu′di•ous•ly** *adv.*

**stud•y** (stŭd′ē) *v.* **-ied, -ying. 1.** To seek knowledge of. **2.** To inquire into. **3.** To examine closely. —*n., pl.* **-ies. 1.** The process of studying. **2.** A branch of knowledge. **3.** A treatise. **4.** A room for studying. **—stud′i•er** *n.*

**stuff** (stŭf) *n.* **1.** Substance; material. **2.** Unspecified objects; things. —*v.* **1.** To pack tightly; fill up. **2.** To cram. **—stuff′ing** *n.*

**stuff•y** (stŭf′ē) *adj.* **-ier, -iest. 1.** Lacking sufficient ventilation. **2.** Stodgy. **—stuff′i•ness** *n.*

**stul•ti•fy** (stŭl′tĭ-fī′) *v.* **-fied, -fying. 1.** To make useless; cripple. **2.** To make appear stupid. **—stul′ti•fi•ca′tion** *n.*

**stum•ble** (stŭm′bəl) *v.* **-bled, -bling. 1. a.** To trip and almost fall. **b.** To proceed unsteadily. **2.** To come upon accidentally. **—stum′ble** *n.* **—stum′bler** *n.* **—stum′bling•ly** *adv.*

**stump** (stŭmp) *n.* A part left after the rest has been cut off. —*v.* To perplex. **—stump′er** *n.* **—stump′y** *adj.*

**stun** (stŭn) *v.* **stunned, stunning. 1.** To daze or render senseless. **2.** To shock. **3.** To impress vividly. **—stun′ning** *adj.*

**stung** (stŭng) *v.* p.t. & p.p. of **sting.**

**stunk** (stŭngk) *v.* p.p. & a p.t. of **stink.**

**stunt**[1] (stŭnt) *v.* To check the growth of. **—stunt′ed** *adj.*

**stunt**[2] (stŭnt) *n.* A feat or spectacle.

**stu•pe•fy** (st/y/o͞o′pə-fī′) *v.* **-fied, -fying. 1.** To dull the senses of. **2.** To amaze; astonish. **—stu′pe•fa′cient** *adj. & n.* **—stu′pe•fac′tion** *n.*

**stu•pen•dous** (st/y/o͞o-pĕn′dəs) *adj.* Tremendous; overwhelming. **—stu•pen′dous•ly** *adv.*

**stu•pid** (st/y/o͞o′pĭd) *adj.* **1.** Lacking intelligence; dull. **2.** Senseless; pointless. **—stu•pid′i•ty** *n.* **—stu′pid•ly** *adv.*

**stu•por** (st/y/o͞o′pər) *n.* Mental confusion; daze. **—stu′por•ous** *adj.*

**stur•dy** (stûr′dē) *adj.* **-dier, -diest.** Durable; strong. **—stur′di•ly** *adv.* **—stur′di•ness** *n.*

**stut•ter** (stŭt′ər) *v.* To speak with a spasmodic hesitation or repetition of sounds. **—stut′ter** *n.* **—stut′ter•er** *n.*

**sty**[1] (stī) *n., pl.* **sties.** An enclosure for pigs.

**sty**[2] (stī) *n., pl.* **sties** or **styes.** An inflammation on the rim of an eyelid.

**style** (stīl) *n.* **1.** The way in which something is said or done. **2.** A kind; sort. **3.** A distinctive quality; individuality. **4.** Elegance. **5.** A fashion. —*v.* **styled, styling. 1.** To name. **2.** To design. **—styl′ish** *adj.* **—sty•lis′tic** *adj.*

**sty•mie** (stī′mē) *v.* **-mied, -mieing.** To block; thwart. **—sty′mie** *n.*

**suave** (swäv) *adj.* Smoothly gracious; urbane. **—suave′ly** *adv.* **—suav′i•ty, suave′ness** *n.*

**sub•due** (səb-d/y/o͞o′) *v.* **-dued, -duing. 1.** To conquer. **2.** To bring under control. **3.** To make less intense.

**sub•ject** (sŭb′jĭkt) *adj.* **1.** Under the power of another. **2.** Inclined; liable. **3.** Dependent; contingent. —*n.* **1.** One under the power of another. **2.** Citizen. **3.** A person or thing being spoken of or studied; topic. **4.** The part of a sentence that denotes the doer of the action. —*v.* (səb-jĕkt′). **-jected, -jecting.** To submit to something. **—sub•jec′tion** *n.*

**sub•jec•tive** (səb-jĕk′tĭv) *adj.* **1.** Mental. **2.** Particular to a given individual. **3.** Serving as the subject of a verb: nominative. **—sub•jec′tive•ly** *adv.*

**sub•let** (sŭb-lĕt′) *v.* **-let, -letting. 1.** To rent to another a property one holds by lease. **2.** To subcontract. **—sub′let′** *n.*

**sub•li•mate** (sŭb′lə-māt′) *v.* **-mated, -mating. 1.** To go from a solid to a gas without becoming liquid. **2.** To modify one's instincts in a socially acceptable manner. **—sub′li•ma′tion** *n.*

**sub•lime** (sə-blīm′) *adj.* Exalted; lofty. **—sub•lime′ly** *adv.*

**sub•ma•rine** (sŭb′mə-rēn′, sŭb′mə-rēn′) *adj.* Beneath the water surface. —*n.* A ship capable of operating submerged.

**sub•merge** (səb-mûrj′) *v.* **-merged, -merging.** To place or go under water. **—sub•mer′gence, sub•mer′sion** *n.* **—sub•mer′gi•ble** *adj.* **—sub•mer′gi•bil′i•ty** *n.*

**sub•mit** (səb-mĭt′) *v.* **-mitted, -mitting. 1.** To yield (oneself) to the authority of another; give in. **2.** To offer as a proposition. **—sub•mis′sion** *n.* **—sub•mis′sive** *adj.*

**sub•or•di•nate** (sə-bôr′dn-ĭt) *adj.* **1.** Lower in rank. **2.** Subject to another's authority. —*n.* One that is subordinate. —*v.* (-nāt′) **-nated, -nating.** To make subordinate. **—sub•or′di•na′tion** *n.*

**sub•orn** (sə-bôrn′) *v.* To induce someone to commit an unlawful act, esp. perjury. **—sub′or•na′tion** *n.* **—sub•orn′er** *n.*

**sub ro•sa** (sŭb rō′zə) *adv.* In secret; privately.

**sub•rou•tine** (sŭb′ro͞o-tēn′) *n.* A set of computer instructions performing a specific task for a main routine.

**sub•scribe** (səb-scrīb′) *v.* **-scribed, -scribing. 1.** To pledge or contribute (a sum of money). **2.** To express approval (with *to*). **3.** To receive or attend by advance purchase (with *to*). **—sub•scrib′er** *n.* **—sub•scrip′tion** *n.*

**sub•se•quent** (sŭb′sĭ-kwĕnt′, -kwənt) *adj.* Following; next. **—sub′se•quent′ly** *adv.*

**sub•serve** (səb-sûrv′) *v.* **-served, -serving.** To serve to promote an end; be useful for.

**sub•ser•vi•ent** (səb-sûr′vē-ənt) *adj.* **1.** Serving an end. **2.** Subordinate. **3.** Servile. **—sub•ser′vi•ence** *n.* **—sub•ser′vi•ent•ly** *adv.*

**sub•side** (səb-sīd′) *v.* **-sided, -siding.** To sink down; settle. **—sub•si′dence** *n.*

**sub•sid•i•ar•y** (səb-sĭd′ē-ĕr′ē) *adj.* **1.** Assisting. **2.** Secondary. —*n., pl.* **-ies.** A company contained within another company.

**sub•si•dy** (sŭb′sĭ-dē) *n., pl.* **-dies.** Monetary assistance. **—sub′si•dize′** *v.*

**sub•sist** (səb-sĭst′) *v.* To exist. **—sub•sis′tence** *n.*

**sub•stance** (sŭb′stəns) *n.* **1.** Matter or a single kind of matter. **2.** The essence; gist. **3.** Density; body.

**sub•stan•tial** (səb-stăn′shəl) *adj.* **1.** Having substance; material. **2.** Real. **3.** Solidly built. **4.** Ample; considerable. **—sub•stan′tial•ly** *adv.*

**sub•sti•tute** (sŭb′stĭ-t/y/o͞ot′) *n.* A replacement. —*v.* **-tuted, -tuting. 1.** To put or use in place of another. **2.** To take the place of another. **—sub′sti•tu′tion** *n.*

**sub•sume** (səb-so͞om′) *v.* **-sumed, -suming.** To include or classify under a more comprehensive category.

**sub•ter•ra•ne•an** (sŭb′tə-rā′nē-ən) *adj.* Underground.

**sub•tle** (sŭt′l) *adj.* **-tler, tlest. 1.** Slight; elusive. **2.** Keen. **3.** Skillfully muted or restrained. **4.** Crafty. **—sub′tle•ness, sub′tle•ty** *n.* **—sub′tly** *adv.*

**sub•tract** (səb-trăkt′) *v.* To take away; deduct. **—sub•trac′tion** *n.*

**sub•urb** (sŭb′ûrb′) *n.* A town or district outlying a city. **—sub•ur′ban** *adj.* **—sub•ur′ban•ite′** *n.*

**sub•vert** (səb-vûrt′) *v.* **1.** To undermine and overthrow. **2.** To corrupt. **—sub•ver′sion** *n.* **—sub•ver′sive** *adj. & n.* **—sub•vert′er** *n.*

**sub•way** (sŭb′wā′) *n.* An underground urban railroad.

**suc•ceed** (sək-sēd′) *v.* **1.** To follow or come after. **2.** To be successful. **—suc•ces′sor** *n.*

**suc•cess** (sək-sĕs′) *n.* **1.** The achievement of something desired or attempted. **2.** Fame or prosperity. **3.** One that succeeds. **—suc•cess′ful** *adj.* **—suc•cess′ful•ly** *adv.*

**suc•ces•sion** (sək-sĕsh′ən) *n.* **1.** The process of following in order. **2.** A series; sequence. **—suc•ces′sion•al** *adj.* **—suc•ces′sive** *adj.* **—suc•ces′sive•ly** *adv.*

**suc•cinct** (sək-sĭngkt′) *adj.* Brief and clear. **—suc•cinct′ly** *adv.* **—suc•cinct′ness** *n.*

**suc•cu•lent** (sŭk′yə-lənt) *adj.* Juicy. **—suc′cu•lence, suc′cu•len•cy** *n.* **—suc′cu•lent•ly** *adv.*

**suc•cumb** (sə-kŭm′) *v.* **1.** To yield. **2.** To die.

**such** (sŭch) *adj.* **1.** Of this or that kind. **2.** Of so great a degree or quality. —*pron.* Such a one or ones.

**suck** (sŭk) *v.* **1.** To draw (liquid) into the mouth. **2.** To draw in, as by suction. **3.** To draw nourishment from with the mouth. —*n.* The act of sucking. —**suck'er** *n.*

**suck•le** (sŭk'əl) *v.* **-led, -ling.** To feed at the breast or udder.

**suc•tion** (sŭk'shən) *n.* The pulling force of a partial vacuum. —**suc'tion** *adj.*

**sud•den** (sŭd'n) *adj.* **1.** Without warning; abrupt. **2.** Rash. **3.** Quick. —**sud'den•ly** *adv.* —**sud'den•ness** *n.*

**suds** (sŭdz) *pl.n.* Foam; lather. —**suds'y** *adj.*

**sue** (so͞o) *v.* **sued, suing. 1.** To bring suit against. **2.** To appeal.

**suede** (swād) *n.* Leather or fabric with a soft, napped surface.

**suf•fer** (sŭf'ər) *v.* **1.** To feel pain or distress. **2.** To experience. **3.** To endure. **4.** To allow. —**suf'fer•a•ble** *adj.* —**suf'fer•ance** *n.* —**suf'fer•er** *n.* —**suf'fer•ing** *adj.* & *n.* —**suf'fer•ing•ly** *adv.*

**suf•fice** (sə-fīs') *v.* **-ficed, -ficing.** To be adequate.

**suf•fi•cient** (sə-fĭsh'ənt) *adj.* Enough. —**suf•fi'cien•cy** *n.* —**suf•fi'cient•ly** *adv.*

**suf•fix** (sŭf'ĭks) *n.* An affix added to the end of a word to form a new word.

**suf•fo•cate** (sŭf'ə-kāt') *v.* **-cated, -cating. 1.** To kill by cutting off oxygen. **2.** To die from lack of air. **3.** To deprive of fresh air. —**suf'fo•ca'tion** *n.*

**suf•frage** (sŭf'rĭj) *n.* The right of voting.

**sug•ar** (sho͝og'ər) *n.* A sweet, crystalline carbohydrate. —*v.* To coat or sweeten with sugar. —**sug'ar•y** *adj.*

**sug•gest** (səg-jĕst', sə-jĕst') *v.* **1.** To offer for consideration; propose. **2.** To evoke. **3.** To imply. —**sug•ges'tion** *n.* —**sug•ges'tive** *adj.*

**su•i•cide** (so͞o'ĭ-sīd') *n.* **1.** The act of intentionally killing oneself. **2.** One who commits suicide. —**su'i•cid'al** *adj.*

**suit** (so͞ot) *n.* **1.** A coat and matching trousers or skirt. **2.** Any of the 4 sets of playing cards. **3.** Any proceeding in a court of law to recover a right or claim. —*v.* **1.** To be or make appropriate; fit or adapt. **2.** To satisfy.

**suit•a•ble** (so͞o'tə-bəl) *adj.* Appropriate. —**suit'a•bil'i•ty** *n.* —**suit'a•bly** *adv.*

**suit•case** (so͞ot'kās') *n.* A rectangular, flat piece of luggage.

**suite** (swēt) *n.* **1.** A series of connected rooms. **2.** A matched set, as of furniture.

**sulk** (sŭlk) *v.* To be sullenly aloof or withdrawn. —*n.* A mood of sulking. —**sulk'i•ly** *adv.* —**sulk'i•ness** *n.* —**sulk'y** *adj.*

**sul•len** (sŭl'ən) *adj.* Broodingly ill-humored; morose. —**sul'len•ly** *adv.* —**sul'len•ness** *n.*

**sul•try** (sŭl'trē) *adj.* **-trier, -triest. 1.** Hot and humid. **2.** Heated, as with passion. —**sul'tri•ness** *n.*

**sum** (sŭm) *n.* **1.** The amount obtained from adding. **2.** The aggregate. **3.** An amount of money. **4.** A summary. —*v.* **summed, summing.** To summarize.

**sum•ma•ry** (sŭm'ə-rē) *adj.* **1.** Condensed; concise. **2.** Hasty. —*n., pl.* **-ries.** A condensation; outline. —**sum•mar'i•ly** *adv.* —**sum'ma•rize'** *v.* —**sum•ma'tion** *n.*

**sum•mer** (sŭm'ər) *n.* The warmest season, between spring and autumn. —**sum'mer, sum'mer•y** *adj.*

**sum•mit** (sŭm'ĭt) *n.* The highest point.

**sum•mon** (sŭm'ən) *v.* **1.** To call together. **2.** To send for. **3.** To call forth; muster.

**sum•mons** (sŭm'ənz) *n., pl.* **-monses.** A call or order to come, esp. to a court.

**sump•tu•ous** (sŭmp'cho͞o-əs) *adj.* Lavish. —**sump'tu•ous•ly** *adv.* —**sump'tu•ous•ness** *n.*

**sun** (sŭn) *n.* **1.** The central star of the solar system. **2.** The heat and light emitted by the sun. —*v.* **sunned, sunning.** To expose to or bask in the sun's rays. —**sun'ny** *adj.*

**Sun•day** (sŭn'dē, -dā') *n.* The 1st day of the week.

**sun•dry** (sŭn'drē) *adj.* Various.

**sung** (sŭng) *v.* p.p. of **sing.**

**sunk** (sŭngk) *v.* A p.t. & a p.p. of **sink.**

**sunk•en** (sŭng'kən) *v.* A p.p. of **sink.** —*adj.* **1.** Depressed or hollowed. **2.** Submerged.

**sun•rise** (sŭn'rīz') *n.* The rising of the sun.

**sup** (sŭp) *v.* **supped, supping.** To dine.

**su•per** (so͞o'pər) *n.* A superintendent. —*adj.* Excellent.

**su•perb** (so͞o-pûrb') *adj.* Of unusually high quality.

**su•per•cil•i•ous** (so͞o'pər-sĭl'ē-əs) *adj.* Disdainful; arrogant. —**su'per•cil'i•**

**ous•ly** *adv.* **—su′per•cil′i•ous•ness** *n.*

**su•per•fi•cial** (so͞o′pər-fĭsh′əl) *adj.* **1.** On or near the surface. **2.** Seeing only the obvious; shallow. **3.** Trivial. **—su′per•fi′ci•al′i•ty, su′per•fi′cial•ness** *n.* **—su′per•fi′cial•ly** *adv.*

**su•per•flu•ous** (so͞o-pûr′flo͞o-əs) *adj.* Beyond what is required; unnecessary. **—su•per′flu•ous•ly** *adv.* **—su′per•flu′i•ty, su•per′flu•ous•ness** *n.*

**su•per•in•tend** (so͞o′pər-ĭn-tĕnd′) *v.* To supervise; manage. **—su′per•in•ten′dence** *n.*

**su•per•in•ten•dent** (so͞o′pər-ĭn-tĕn′dənt) *n.* **1.** A supervisor. **2.** A janitor.

**su•pe•ri•or** (so͞o-pîr′ē-ər) *adj.* **1.** Higher in rank, nature, or authority. **2.** Of great value or excellence. **3.** Haughty. —*n.* One who surpasses another, as in rank. **—su•pe′ri•or′i•ty** *n.*

**su•per•la•tive** (so͞o-pûr′lə-tĭv) *adj.* Of the highest order or degree. —*n.* The highest degree. **—su•per′la•tive•ly** *adv.* **—su•per′la•tive•ness** *n.*

**su•per•nat•u•ral** (so͞o′pər-năch′ər-əl) *adj.* Not attributable to natural or preternatural forces. **—su′per•nat′u•ral•ly** *adj.*

**su•per•son•ic** (so͞o′pər-sŏn′ĭk) *adj.* Of or at a speed greater than the speed of sound.

**su•per•sti•tion** (so͞o′pər-stĭsh′ən) *n.* Any belief, practice, or rite unreasoningly upheld by faith in magic, chance, or dogma. **—su′per•sti′tious** *adj.*

**su•per•vise** (so͞o′pər-vīz′) *v.* **-vised, -vising.** To direct the performance of (workers or work). **—su′per•vi′sion** *n.* **—su′per•vi′sor** *n.* **—su′per•vi′so•ry** *adj.*

**sup•per** (sŭp′ər) *n.* An evening meal.

**sup•ple** (sŭp′əl) *adj.* **-pler, -plest. 1.** Readily bent. **2.** Limber. **—sup′ple•ness** *n.*

**sup•ple•ment** (sŭp′lə-mənt) *n.* Something added. —*v.* To provide a supplement to. **—sup′ple•men′tal, sup′ple•men′ta•ry** *adj.*

**sup•pli•cate** (sŭp′lĭ-kāt′) *v.* **-cated, -cating. 1.** To ask for humbly. **2.** To beseech. **—sup′pli•ant** *adj. & n.* **—sup′pli•cant** *adj. & n.* **—sup′pli•ca′tion** *n.*

**sup•ply** (sə-plī′) *v.* **-plied, -plying. 1.** To provide; furnish. **2.** To fill. —*n., pl.* **-plies. 1.** An amount available; stock. **2.** Often **supplies.** Stored materials. **—sup•pli′er** *n.*

**sup•port** (sə-pôrt′, -pōrt′) *v.* **1.** To hold up or in position. **2.** To provide with necessities; maintain. **3.** To help prove. **4.** To defend; advocate. —*n.* **1.** The act of supporting. **2.** A prop. **3.** Maintenance or subsistence. **—sup•port′er** *n.* **—sup•por′tive** *adj.*

**sup•pose** (sə-pōz′) *v.* **-posed, -posing. 1.** To assume to be true. **2.** To believe probable. **3.** To expect or require. **—sup′po•si′tion** *n.*

**sup•press** (sə-prĕs′) *v.* **1.** To subdue; crush. **2.** To curtail or prohibit the activities of. **3.** To hold back; check. **—sup•pres′sion** *n.* **—sup•pres′sive** *adj.*

**su•preme** (so͞o-prēm′) *adj.* Greatest in authority, rank, or importance. **—su•prem′a•cy** *n.* **—su•preme′ly** *adv.*

**sure** (sho͝or) *adj.* **surer, surest. 1.** Certain. **2.** Having no doubt; confident. **3.** Dependable. **4.** Bound; destined. —*adv.* Undoubtedly. **—sure′ly** *adv.*

**surf** (sûrf) *n.* Foamy water caused by the breaking of waves against the shore.

**sur•face** (sûr′fəs) *n.* **1.** The outer or topmost boundary or layer. **2.** Outward appearance. —*v.* **-faced, -facing. 1.** To give a surface to. **2.** To rise to the surface. **—sur′face** *adj.*

**sur•feit** (sûr′fĭt) *v.* To feed or supply to fullness or excess. —*n.* **1.** Overindulgence. **2.** An excessive amount.

**surge** (sûrj) *v.* **surged, surging. 1.** To move in a great wave. **2.** To increase suddenly. —*n.* A sudden increase or onrush.

**sur•geon** (sûr′jən) *n.* A physician specializing in surgery.

**sur•ger•y** (sûr′jə-rē) *n., pl.* **-ies. 1.** Medical operations. **2.** An operating room or laboratory. **—sur′gi•cal** *adj.*

**sur•ly** (sûr′lē) *adj.* **-lier, -liest.** Sullenly rude. **—sur′li•ness** *n.*

**sur•mise** (sər-mīz′) *v.* **-mised, -mising.** To guess. —*n.* A guess.

**sur•name** (sûr′nām′) *n.* A family name.

**sur•pass** (sər-păs′) *v.* **1.** To go beyond; transcend. **2.** To exceed. **—sur•pass′ing** *adj.*

**sur•plus** (sûr′pləs) *adj.* Being in excess. —*n.* A quantity in excess.

**sur•prise** (sər-prīz′) *v.* **-prised, -prising. 1.** To encounter. **2.** To astonish; amaze. —*n.* **1.** Amazement or wonder. **2.** An unexpected thing. **—sur•pris′er** *n.*

**sur•ren•der** (sə-rĕn′dər) *v.* **1.** To yield possession of. **2.** To give oneself up. **—sur•ren′der** *n.*

**sur•rep•ti•tious** (sûr′əp-tĭsh′əs) *adj.* Stealthy; secret. **—sur′rep•ti′tious•ly** *adv.*

**sur•round** (sə-round′) *v.* **1.** To encircle; ring. **2.** To confine on all sides.

**sur•round•ings** (sə-roun′dĭngz) *pl.n.* The things or the area around one.

**sur•vey** (sər-vā′, sûr′vā′) *v.* **1.** To examine broadly or systematically. **2.** To determine the boundaries, area, or elevation of land. —*n.* (sûr′vā′). **1.** A detailed inspection. **2.** A general view. **3.** The process of surveying. **—sur•vey′al** *n.* **—sur•vey′or** *n.*

**sur•vive** (sər-vīv′) *v.* **-vived, -viving. 1.** To remain alive or in existence. **2.** To outlive. **—sur•viv′al** *n.* **—sur•vi′vor** *n.*

**sus•cep•ti•ble** (sə-sĕp′tə-bəl) *adj.* **1.** Readily affected. **2.** Liable; prone. **3.** Impressionable. **—sus•cep′ti•bil′i•ty** *n.* **—sus•cep′ti•bly** *adv.*

**sus•pect** (sə-spĕkt′) *v.* **1.** To mistrust. **2.** To surmise. **3.** To think guilty without proof. —*n.* (sŭs′pĕkt′). One who is suspected. —*adj.* Doubtful.

**sus•pend** (sə-spĕnd′) *v.* **1.** To bar or exclude for a period. **2.** To interrupt temporarily. **3.** To defer; put off. **4.** To hang loosely. **—sus•pen′sion** *n.*

**sus•pense** (sə-spĕns′) *n.* Anxious uncertainty. **—sus•pense′ful** *adj.*

**sus•pi•cion** (sə-spĭsh′ən) *n.* **1.** The act of suspecting. **2.** Distrust; doubt. **3.** A trace. **—sus•pi′cious** *adj.* **—sus•pi′cious•ly** *adv.*

**sus•tain** (sə-stān′) *v.* **1.** To prolong. **2.** To supply with necessities. **3.** To keep up; support. **4.** To suffer. **5.** To affirm the validity of. **—sus•tain′a•ble** *adj.*

**sus•te•nance** (sŭs′tə-nəns) *n.* **1.** Maintenance. **2.** Nourishment.

**su•ture** (so͞o′chər) *n.* A surgical stitch or stitching, as of a wound. —*v.* **-tured, -turing.** To join surgically.

**swab** (swŏb) Also **swob.** *n.* **1.** A piece of absorbent material for cleansing or applying medicine. **2.** A mop. —*v.* **swabbed, swabbing.** To clean or treat with a swab.

**swad•dle** (swŏd′l) *v.* **-dled, -dling.** To wrap (a baby) tightly in strips of cloth.

**swag•ger** (swăg′ər) *v.* **1.** To walk insolently; strut. **2.** To brag. **—swag′ger** *n.* **—swag′ger•er** *n.*

**swal•low** (swŏl′ō) *v.* **1.** To pass (food) from the mouth into the stomach. **2.** To consume. **3.** To suppress. —*n.* **1.** The act of swallowing. **2.** The amount swallowed.

**swam** (swăm) *v.* p.t. of **swim.**

**swamp** (swŏmp, swômp) *n.* Land saturated with water; marsh. —*v.* **1.** To drench or sink in water. **2.** To overwhelm. **—swamp′i•ness** *n.* **—swamp′y** *adj.*

**swap** (swŏp) *v.* **swapped, swapping.** To trade; exchange. **—swap** *n.* **—swap′per** *n.*

**swarm** (swôrm) *n.* **1.** A large mass of insects or other small organisms. **2.** A throng. —*v.* **1.** To move in a swarm. **2.** To teem.

**swarth•y** (swôr′*th*ē) *adj.* **-ier, -iest.** Dark-skinned. **—swarth′i•ness** *n.*

**swat** (swŏt) *v.* **swatted, swatting.** To slap. **—swat** *n.* **—swat′ter** *n.*

**sway** (swā) *v.* **1.** To swing from side to side. **2.** To vacillate. **3.** To influence. —*n.* **1.** A gentle swinging. **2.** Power; influence.

**swear** (swâr) *v.* **swore** (swŏr, swōr), **sworn** (swôrn, swōrn), **swearing. 1.** To make a solemn declaration or promise. **2.** To curse. **3.** To assert under oath. **4.** To administer a legal oath to. **—swear′er** *n.*

**sweat** (swĕt) *v.* **sweated** or **sweat, sweating. 1.** To perspire. **2.** To work long and hard. —*n.* **1.** Perspiration. **2.** Condensed moisture on a surface. **3.** Strenuous labor. **—sweat′y** *adj.*

**sweat•er** (swĕt′ər) *n.* A knitted garment worn on the upper body.

**sweep** (swēp) *v.* **swept** (swĕpt), **sweeping. 1.** To clean or clear with a broom. **2.** To brush. **3.** To carry or blow away. **4.** To move or traverse powerfully. **5.** To move emotionally. **6.** To extend; reach. —*n.* **1.** An act or motion of sweeping. **2.** A range or extent. **—sweep′er** *n.* **—sweep′ing** *adj.*

**sweet** (swēt) *adj.* **1.** Having a sugary taste. **2.** Pleasing or charming. **3.** Fresh.

—*n.* A candy or other sweet food. **—sweet'en** *v.* **—sweet'en•er** *n.* **—sweet'ly** *adv.* **—sweet'ness** *n.*

**swell** (swĕl) *v.* **swelled, swelled** or **swol•len** (swō'lən), **swelling. 1.** To expand; bulge. **2.** To increase. **3.** To fill with an emotion, as pride. —*n.* **1.** A bulge. **2.** A long wave. —*adj.* Fine; excellent.

**swell•ing** (swĕl'ĭng) *n.* **1.** An enlargement or increase. **2.** A swollen area on the body.

**swel•ter•ing** (swĕl'tər-ĭng) *adj.* Oppressively hot.

**swept** (swĕpt) *v.* p.t. & p.p. of **sweep.**

**swerve** (swûrv) *v.* **swerved, swerving.** To turn abruptly aside. **—swerve** *n.*

**swift** (swĭft) *adj.* **1.** Fast; fleet. **2.** Quick; prompt. **—swift'ly** *adv.* **—swift'ness** *n.*

**swill** (swĭl) *v.* To drink greedily. —*n.* Liquid animal feed. **—swill'er** *n.*

**swim** (swĭm) *v.* **swam** (swăm), **swum** (swŭm), **swimming. 1.** To propel oneself through water by bodily movements. **2.** To be flooded. **3.** To feel giddy. —*n.* A period or instance of swimming.

**swin•dle** (swĭn'dl) *v.* **-dled, -dling.** to cheat or defraud. —*n.* A fraud. **—swin'dler** *n.*

**swine** (swīn) *n., pl.* **swine. 1.** A pig. **2.** A contemptible person. **—swin'ish** *adj.*

**swing** (swĭng) *v.* **swung** (swŭng), **swing•ing. 1.** To move back and forth. **2.** To turn in place, as on a hinge. **3.** To aim a blow. **4.** To manage successfully. —*n.* **1.** A rhythmic back-and-forth movement. **2.** A sweeping blow or stroke. **3.** A seat suspended from above for playful swinging. **—swing'er** *n.*

**switch** (swĭch) *n.* **1.** A slender stick for whipping. **2.** A device used to break or open an electrical circuit. **3.** A change; shift. —*v.* **1.** To shift, transfer, or change. **2.** To turn (an electric appliance) on or off. **—switch'er** *n.*

**switch•board** (swĭch'bôrd', -bōrd') *n.* A panel containing electrical switches.

**swiv•el** (swĭv'əl) *n.* A pivot or other fastening that permits free turning. —*v.* To turn on or as on a swivel.

**swol•len** (swō'lən) *v.* A p.p. of **swell.**

**swoon** (swo͞on) *v.* To faint. —*n.* A fainting spell.

**sword** (sôrd) *n.* A weapon having a long blade.

**swore** (swôr, swōr) *v.* p.t. of **swear.**

**sworn** (swôrn, swōrn) *v.* p.p. of **swear.**

**swum** (swŭm) *v.* p.p. of **swim.**

**swung** (swŭng) *v.* p.t. & p.p. of **swing.**

**syc•o•phant** (sĭk'ə-fənt) *n.* A flatterer. **—syc'o•phan•cy** *n.*

**syl•lab•i•cate** (sĭ-lăb'ĭ-kāt') *v.* **-cated, -cating.** To divide into syllables. **—syl•lab'i•ca'tion** *n.* **—syl•lab'i•fy'** *v.*

**syl•la•ble** (sĭl'ə-bəl) *n.* A single uninterrupted sound forming part of a word or an entire word. **—syl•lab'ic** *adj.*

**sym•bol** (sĭm'bəl) *n.* Something that represents something else. **—sym•bol'ic** *adj.* **—sym•bol'i•cal•ly** *adv.* **—sym'•bol•ism'** *n.* **—sym'bol•ize'** *v.*

**sym•me•try** (sĭm'ĭ-trē) *n., pl.* **-tries.** Correspondence between parts on opposite sides of a dividing line; balance. **—sym•met'ri•cal** *adj.*

**sym•pa•thize** (sĭm'pə-thīz') *v.* **-thized, -thizing.** To feel or express sympathy. **—sym'pa•thiz'er** *n.*

**sym•pa•thy** (sĭm'pə-thē) *n., pl.* **-thies. 1.** Sameness of feeling; mutual understanding. **2.** Pity; compassion. **3.** Agreement; approval. **—sym'pa•thet'ic** *adj.*

**sym•pho•ny** (sĭm'fə-nē) *n., pl.* **-nies. 1.** A long orchestral composition. **2.** A full orchestra. **—sym•phon'ic** *adj.*

**syn•a•gogue** (sĭn'ə-gŏg') *n.* A building for Jewish worship.

**syn•chro•nize** (sĭn'krə-nīz', sĭng'-) *v.* **-nized, -nizing. 1.** To make or be simultaneous. **2.** To set at the same time or rate. **—syn'chro•ni•za'tion** *n.* **—syn'chro•niz'er** *n.*

**syn•di•cate** (sĭn'dĭ-kĭt) *n.* An association of related businesses.

**syn•o•nym** (sĭn'ə-nĭm') *n.* A word having a meaning similar to that of another.

**syn•tax** (sĭn'tăks') *n.* The way words are put together to form phrases, clauses, and sentences. **—syn•tac'tic, syn•tac'•ti•cal** *adj.*

**syn•the•sis** (sĭn'thĭ-sĭs) *n.,pl.* **-theses.** The combining of separate elements to form a whole. **—syn'the•size'** *v.*

**syn•thet•ic** (sĭn-thĕt'ĭk) *adj.* Artificial. **—syn•thet'i•cal•ly** *adv.*

**sy•ringe** (sə-rĭnj′, sîr′ĭnj) *n.* A medical instrument used to inject fluids.
**syr•up** (sûr′əp, sĭr′-) *n.* Also **sir•up.** A thick, sweet liquid. **—syr′up•y** *adj.*
**sys•tem** (sĭs′təm) *n.* **1.** A group of interrelated elements forming a whole. **2.** The human body. **3.** A set of interrelated ideas, rules, laws, etc. **4.** A deliberate procedure; method. **5.** Orderliness. **—sys′tem•at′ic** *adj.* **—sys′tem•at′i•cal•ly** *adv.* **—sys′tem•a•tize′** *v.*

## — T —

**t, T** (tē) *n.* The 20th letter of the English alphabet.
**tab** (tăb) *n.* **1.** A flap or short strip. **2.** A bill or check.
**ta•ble** (tā′bəl) *n.* **1.** An article of furniture having a flat surface set on legs. **2.** An orderly display of data. —*v.* **-bled, -bling. 1.** To place on a table. **2.** To postpone.
**ta•ble•spoon** (tā′bəl-spo͞on′) *n.* **1.** A large spoon for serving food. **2.** A household cooking measure.
**tab•let** (tăb′lĭt) *n.* **1.** A flat pellet of oral medicine. **2.** A small cake of a substance, such as soap. **3.** A pad of writing paper.
**tab•loid** (tăb′loid′) *n.* A small-format newspaper with a condensed, sensational style.
**ta•boo** (tə-bo͞o′, tă-) *n., pl.* **-boos.** A societal inhibition that arises from custom or deep-seated aversion. **—ta•boo′** *adj.*
**tab•u•late** (tăb′yə-lāt′) *v.* **-lated, -lating.** To arrange in a table or list. **—tab′u•lar** *adj.* **—tab′u•la′tion** *n.*
**tac•it** (tăs′ĭt) *adj.* **1.** Unspoken. **2.** Implied by actions or statements.
**tac•i•turn** (tăs′ĭ-tûrn′) *adj.* Habitually untalkative; uncommunicative.
**tack** (tăk) *n.* **1.** A short, flat-headed nail. **2.** The course of a ship in relation to the position of its sails. **3.** A course of action. —*v.* **1.** To fasten with a tack. **2.** To change the course of a vessel.
**tack•le** (tăk′əl) *n.* **1.** Fishing equipment. **2.** An apparatus for raising weights. —*v.* **-led, -ling. 1.** To take on; deal with. **2.** To seize and throw to the ground.
**tact** (tăkt) *n.* The ability to handle a delicate situation. **—tact′ful** *adj.* **—tact′less** *adj.*
**tac•tics** (tăk′tĭks) *n. (takes sing. v.).* The technique of securing strategic objectives, esp. in the deployment of military forces. **—tac′ti•cal** *adj.* **—tac•ti′cian** *n.*
**tag** (tăg) *n.* A strip of paper, etc., attached as identification or a label. —*v.* **tagged, tagging.** To label or identify with a tag.
**tail** (tāl) *n.* **1.** An elongated appendage at the hind part of an animal. **2.** Anything resembling an animal's tail. **3.** The bottom, rear, or hindmost part of anything. —*v.* To keep under surveillance. —*adj.* At or from the rear.
**tai•lor** (tā′lər) *n.* One who makes or repairs garments. —*v.* To make or adapt for a particular purpose.
**taint** (tānt) *v.* **1.** To stain or dishonor. **2.** To infect or spoil. —*n.* **1.** A moral defect. **2.** An infecting touch, influence, or tinge.
**take** (tāk) *v.* **took** (to͝ok), **taken** (tā′kən), **taking. 1.** To get possession of; seize. **2.** To grasp. **3.** To lead or convey to another place. **4.** To remove. **5.** To assume upon oneself. **6.** To select; choose. **7.** To travel by. **8.** To occupy. **9.** To require. **10.** To accept. **11.** To endure. **12.** To interpret or react to. **13.** To subtract. **14.** To have the intended effect. —*n.* The amount taken. **—tak′er** *n.*
**take•off** (tāk′ôf′, -ŏf′) *n.* **1.** The act of leaving the ground. **2.** An imitative caricature.
**tale** (tāl) *n.* **1.** A story. **2.** A lie.
**tal•ent** (tăl′ənt) *n.* A natural ability; aptitude.
**talk** (tôk) *v.* **1.** To articulate words. **2.** To converse; discuss. **3.** To speak. **4.** To gossip. **5.** To confer or negotiate. —*n.* **1.** Speech; conversation. **2.** An informal speech. **3.** Hearsay, rumor, or speculation. **4.** A conference or parley; negotiation. **—talk′a•tive** *adj.* **—talk′er** *n.*
**tall** (tôl) *adj.* Having greater than ordinary height; high.
**tal•ly** (tăl′ē) *n., pl.* **-lies. 1.** A notched stick used to keep a count. **2.** A reckoning or score. —*v.* **-lied, -lying. 1.** To reckon or count. **2.** To correspond; agree.

**tal•on** (tăl′ən) *n.* The claw of a bird of prey.

**tame** (tām) *adj.* **tamer, tamest. 1.** Not wild; domesticated. **2.** Insipid; flat. —*v.* **tamed, taming. 1.** To domesticate. **2.** To subdue.

**tam•per** (tăm′pər) *v.* **1.** To interfere in a harmful manner. **2.** To engage in underhand or illegal dealings. **—tam′per•er** *n.*

**tan** (tăn) *v.* **tanned, tanning. 1.** To convert (hide) into leather. **2.** To make or become brown by exposure to the sun. —*n.* A light brown. —*adj.* **tanner, tannest. 1.** Of the color tan. **2.** Having a suntan. **—tan′ner** *n.* **—tan′ner•y** *n.*

**tan•dem** (tăn′dəm) *n.* **1.** A bicycle for 2 riders. **2.** A front-to-back arrangement of 2 or more things.

**tan•gent** (tăn′jənt) *adj.* Touching but not intersecting. —*n.* **1.** A line, curve, or surface touching but not intersecting another. **2.** A sudden digression or change of course.

**tan•ger•ine** (tăn′jə-rēn′) *n.* An orangelike fruit with easily peeled skin.

**tan•gi•ble** (tăn′jə-bəl) *adj.* **1.** Discernible by touch. **2.** Real; concrete. **—tan′gi•bil′i•ty** *n.* **—tan′gi•bly** *adv.*

**tan•gle** (tăng′gəl) *v.* **-gled, -gling. 1.** To intertwine in a confused mass. **2.** To be or become entangled. —*n.* **1.** A confused, intertwined mass. **2.** A confused state or condition.

**tank** (tăngk) *n.* **1.** A large container for fluids. **2.** An enclosed, heavily armored combat vehicle.

**tank•er** (tăng′kər) *n.* A ship, plane, or truck constructed to transport oil or other liquids.

**tan•ta•lize** (tăn′tə-līz′) *v.* **-lized, -lizing.** To tease or torment by repeatedly showing something unobtainable.

**tan•ta•mount** (tăn′tə-mount′) *adj.* Equivalent in effect or value.

**tan•trum** (tăn′trəm) *n.* A fit of bad temper.

**tap[1]** (tăp) *v.* **tapped, tapping.** To strike gently. **—tap** *n.*

**tap[2]** (tăp) *n.* A faucet. —*v.* **tapped, tapping. 1.** To pierce in order to draw off liquid. **2.** To draw (liquid) from.

**tape** (tāp) *n.* A narrow strip of fabric, paper, plastic, etc. —*v.* **taped, taping. 1.** To bind or wrap with tape. **2.** To record (sound) on magnetic tape.

**ta•per** (tā′pər) *n.* **1.** A slender candle. **2.** A gradual decrease or lessening in thickness, loudness, etc. —*v.* To decrease or lessen in thickness, loudness, etc.

**tape recorder.** *n.* A device for recording and playing back sound on magnetic tape. **—tape′re•cord′** *v.*

**tap•es•try** (tăp′ĭ-strē) *n., pl.* **-tries.** A heavy textile with a woven design, used as a wall hanging.

**tar** (tär) *n.* A black, oily liquid distilled from wood, coal, or peat. —*v.* **tarred, tarring.** To coat with tar.

**tar•dy** (tär′dē) *adj.* **-dier, -diest.** Late. **—tar′di•ly** *adv.* **—tar′di•ness** *n.*

**tar•get** (tär′gĭt) *n.* **1.** A marked object that is shot at to test accuracy. **2.** Anything aimed at. **3.** A desired goal.

**tar•iff** (tăr′ĭf) *n.* **1.** A list of duties on imported or exported goods. **2.** A duty of this kind.

**tar•pau•lin** (tär-pô′lĭn, tär′pə-) *n.* A cover of material, such as canvas, that protects against moisture.

**tar•nish** (tär′nĭsh) *v.* **1.** To make or become discolored. **2.** To taint. **—tar′nish** *n.*

**tar•ry** (tăr′ē) *v.* **-ried, -rying.** To delay; linger.

**tart[1]** (tärt) *adj.* **1.** Agreeably sour. **2.** Caustic; cutting. **—tart′ly** *adv.* **—tart′ness** *n.*

**tart[2]** (tärt) *n.* **1.** A small pie with a sweet filling. **2.** A prostitute.

**task** (tăsk) *n.* **1.** A piece of assigned work. **2.** A difficult undertaking. **—task′mas′ter** *n.*

**tas•sel** (tăs′əl) *n.* An ornament consisting of a bunch of loose threads knotted at one end.

**taste** (tāst) *v.* **tasted, tasting. 1.** To distinguish the flavor of by taking into the mouth. **2.** To eat or drink a small quantity of. **3.** To have a distinct flavor. —*n.* **1.** The sense that distinguishes different flavors with the tongue. **2.** The act of tasting. **3.** A small quantity eaten or tasted. **4.** A personal preference. **5.** Discernment of what is excellent or appropriate. **—taste′ful** *adj.* **—taste′ful•ly** *adv.* **—taste′less** *adj.* **—tast′er** *n.* **—tast′y** *adj.*

**tat•tle** (tăt′l) *v.* **-tled, -tling. 1.** To reveal another's secrets. **2.** To gossip. **—tat′tler** *n.*

**tat•too** (tă-to͞o′) *n.* A permanent mark made on the skin by pricking and dyeing. **—tat•too′** *v.*

**taught** (tôt) *v.* p.t. & p.p. of **teach.**

**taunt** (tônt) *v.* To jeer mockingly. **—taunt** *n.* **—taunt′er** *n.*

**taut** (tôt) *adj.* Stretched tight; tense. **—taut′ly** *adv.* **—taut′ness** *n.*

**tav•ern** (tăv′ərn) *n.* A saloon or inn.

**taw•dry** (tô′drē) *adj.* **-drier, -driest.** Gaudy and cheap. **—taw′dri•ness** *n.*

**tax** (tăks) *n.* **1.** Compulsory payment by persons and businesses for the support of a government. **2.** An excessive demand; a strain. —*v.* **1.** To place a tax on. **2.** To make excessive demands. **—tax′a•ble** *adj.* **—tax•a′tion** *n.* **—tax′ing** *adj.*

**tax•i** (tăk′sē) *n., pl.* **-is** or **-ies.** An automobile that carries passengers for a fare. —*v.* **-ied, -iing** or **-ying. 1.** To be transported by taxi. **2.** To move slowly on the ground before takeoff or after landing. Used of an aircraft.

**tea** (tē) *n.* **1.** The dried leaves of an Asian shrub, steeped in boiling water to make a beverage. **2.** The beverage thus prepared. **3.** An afternoon social gathering.

**teach** (tēch) *v.* **taught** (tôt), **teaching. 1.** To impart knowledge to. **2.** To instruct in. **—teach′er** *n.*

**team** (tēm) *n.* **1.** Two or more harnessed draft animals. **2.** A group of players in a game. **3.** A group organized to work together. —*v.* To join in a team.

**tear[1]** (târ) *v.* **tore** (tôr, tōr), **torn** (tôrn, tōrn), **tearing. 1.** To pull apart. **2.** To make (an opening) by ripping. **3.** To lacerate. **4.** To extract forcefully; wrench. **5.** To divide; disunite. **6.** To move fast; rush. —*n.* A rip or rent.

**tear[2]** (tîr) *n.* **1.** A drop of the clear saline liquid that lubricates the eyeball. **2. tears.** The act of weeping. **—tear′ful** *adj.*

**tease** (tēz) *v.* **teased, teasing. 1.** To annoy; vex. **2.** To make fun of; bait. **3.** To fluff up, as hair. —*n.* One given to playful mocking. **—teas′er** *n.*

**tea•spoon** (tē′spo͞on′) *n.* **1.** A small spoon. **2.** A household cooking measure.

**teat** (tēt) *n.* A mammary gland or nipple.

**tech•ni•cal** (tĕk′nĭ-kəl) *adj.* **1.** Of the mechanical or industrial arts. **2.** Specialized. **3. a.** Theoretical. **b.** Scientific. **—tech′ni•cal•ly** *adv.*

**tech•nique** (tĕk-nēk′) *n.* **1.** The systematic procedure by which a task is accomplished. **2.** The degree of skill in performance. **—tech•ni′cian** *n.*

**tech•nol•o•gy** (tĕk-nŏl′ə-jē) *n., pl.* **-gies. 1.** The application of science in industry or commerce. **2.** The methods and materials thus used. **—tech′no•log′i•cal** *adj.* **—tech′no•log′i•cal•ly** *adv.* **—tech•nol′o•gist** *n.*

**te•di•ous** (tē′dē-əs) *adj.* Tiresome and long; boring. **—te′di•ous•ly** *adv.* **—te′di•um** *n.*

**tee** (tē) *n.* A small peg used in golf.

**teem** (tēm) *v.* To be full of; abound.

**teeth** (tēth) *n.* pl. of **tooth.**

**teethe** (tē*th*) *v.* **teethed, teething.** To grow teeth.

**tel•e•cast** (tĕl′ĭ-kăst′) *n.* A television broadcast. **—tel′e•cast′** *v.*

**tel•e•gram** (tĕl′ĭ-grăm′) *n.* A message sent by telegraph.

**tel•e•graph** (tĕl′ĭ-grăf′) *n.* A communications system that sends or receives messages by means of electric impulses carried through a wire. —*v.* To transmit (a message) by telegraph. **—tel′e•graph′ic** *adj.* **—te•leg′ra•phy** *n.*

**te•lep•a•thy** (tə-lĕp′ə-thē) *n.* Communication by scientifically unknown means. **—tel′e•path′ic** *adj.*

**tel•e•phone** (tĕl′ə-fōn′) *n.* An electrical device that transmits voice or acoustic signals to remote locations. —*v.* **-phoned, -phoning.** To communicate by telephone. **—tel′e•phon′ic** *adj.*

**tel•e•scope** (tĕl′ĭ-skōp′) *n.* An arrangement of lenses that permits observation of distant objects. —*v.* **-scoped, -scoping. 1.** To slide together in overlapping sections. **2.** To compress inward. **—tel′e•scop′ic** *adj.*

**tel•e•thon** (tĕl′ə-thŏn′) *n.* A long fundraising program on TV.

**tel•e•vi•sion** (tĕl′ə-vĭzh′ən) *n.* **1.** The transmission of moving images with accompanying sounds by electronic means. **2.** The receiving apparatus used in this process. —**tel′e•vise′** *v.*

**tell** (tĕl) *v.* **told** (tōld), **telling. 1.** To narrate. **2.** To express with words; communicate. **3.** To notify. **4.** To command. **5.** To identify.

**te•mer•i•ty** (tə-mĕr′ĭ-tē) *n.* Rashness; foolish boldness.

**tem•per** (tĕm′pər) *v.* **1.** A state of mind or emotions; disposition. **2.** Composure. **3.** Irascibility; rage. —**tem′pered** *adj.*

**tem•per•a•ment** (tĕm′prə-mənt, -pər-ə-) *n.* **1.** An individual's manner of thinking, behaving, and reacting; disposition. **2.** Excessive irritability. —**tem′per•a•men′tal** *adj.*

**tem•per•ance** (tĕm′pər-əns, -prəns) *n.* **1.** Moderation or self-restraint. **2.** Abstinence from alcoholic liquors.

**tem•per•ate** (tĕm′pər-ĭt, -prĭt) *adj.* **1.** Moderate; restrained. **2.** Not extreme in climate.

**tem•per•a•ture** (tĕm′pər-ə-cho͝or′, -chər, -prə-) *n.* **1.** The degree of hotness or coldness of a body or environment. **2.** Fever.

**tem•pest** (tĕm′pĭst) *n.* A violent storm. —**tem•pes′tu•ous** *adj.*

**tem•plate** (tĕm′plĭt) *n.* A pattern used as a guide in making something.

**tem•ple¹** (tĕm′pəl) *n.* A place of worship.

**tem•ple²** (tĕm′pəl) *n.* The flat region on either side of the forehead.

**tem•po** (tĕm′pō) *n., pl.* **-pos. 1.** The speed at which music is to be played. **2.** A rate of activity; pace.

**tem•po•rar•y** (tĕm′pə-rĕr′ē) *adj.* Lasting for a limited time. —**tem′po•rar′i•ly** *adv.*

**tempt** (tĕmpt) *v.* **1.** To entice. **2.** To be attractive to; provoke. **3.** To incline or dispose strongly. —**temp•ta′tion** *n.* —**tempt′er** *n.* —**tempt′ress** *n.*

**ten** (tĕn) *n.* The cardinal number written 10. —**ten** *adj. & pron.* —**tenth** *n. & adj.*

**ten•a•ble** (tĕn′ə-bəl) *adj.* Defendable or sustainable.

**te•na•cious** (tə-nā′shəs) *adj.* **1.** Persistent; stubborn. **2.** Cohesive or adhesive. **3.** Retentive. —**te•nac′i•ty** *n.*

**ten•an•cy** (tĕn′ən-sē) *n., pl.* **-cies. 1.** Possession or occupancy by rent. **2.** The period of such occupancy. —**ten′ant** *n.*

**tend¹** (tĕnd) *v.* **1.** To be disposed or inclined. **2.** To be likely.

**tend²** (tĕnd) *v.* **1.** To look after. **2.** To serve at.

**ten•den•cy** (tĕn′dən-sē) *n., pl.* **-cies.** An inclination to think or act in a certain way; bent.

**ten•der¹** (tĕn′dər) *adj.* **1.** Delicate; fragile. **2.** Young and vulnerable. **3.** Frail; weak. **4.** Sensitive or sore. **5.** Gentle and loving. —**ten′der•ly** *adv.* —**ten′der•ness** *n.*

**ten•der²** (tĕn′dər) *n.* **1.** A formal offer. **2.** Money. —*v.* To offer formally.

**ten•don** (tĕn′dən) *n.* A band of tough, fibrous tissue that connects a muscle with its bony attachment.

**ten•et** (tĕn′ĭt) *n.* A fundamental principle or dogma.

**ten•nis** (tĕn′ĭs) *n.* A game played with racket and a light ball on a court divided by a net.

**ten•or** (tĕn′ər) *n.* **1.** Flow of meaning; gist. **2.** The singing voice between baritone and alto.

**tense¹** (tĕns) *adj.* **tenser, tensest. 1.** Taut; strained. **2.** Nerve-racking. —*v.* **tensed, tensing.** To make or become tense. —**tense′ness** *n.*

**tense²** (tĕns) *n.* Any inflected form of a verb that indicates the time of the action.

**ten•sion** (tĕn′shən) *n.* **1.** A stretching or being stretched. **2.** Mental strain. **3.** A strained relation. **4.** Suspense.

**tent** (tĕnt) *n.* A portable shelter, as of canvas.

**ten•ta•tive** (tĕn′tə-tĭv) *adj.* **1.** Of an experimental nature. **2.** Uncertain. —**ten′ta•tive•ly** *adv.*

**ten•u•ous** (tĕn′yo͞o-əs) *adj.* **1.** Slender or thin; rarefied. **2.** Not substantial; flimsy. —**ten′u•ous•ly** *adv.* —**ten′u•ous•ness** *n.*

**ten•ure** (tĕn′yər, -yo͝or′) *n.* **1.** The holding of something, as an office; occupation. **2.** The period of holding.

**tep•id** (tĕp′ĭd) *adj.* Lukewarm.

**term** (tûrm) *n.* **1.** A limited or fixed period of time. **2.** A word having a precise meaning. **3. terms.** Conditions or stipulations. —*v.* To designate; name.

**ter•mi•nal** (tûr′mə-nəl) *adj.* **1.** Of or at the end. **2.** Concluding; final. —*n.* **1.** A terminating point, limit, or part. **2.** A point at which a connection to an electrical component is made. **3.** A railroad or bus station. **4.** An instrument through which data can enter or leave a computer. —**ter′mi•nal•ly** *adv.*

**ter•mi•nate** (tûr′mə-nāt′) *v.* **-nated, -nating.** To end or conclude. —**ter′mi•na′tion** *n.*

**ter•race** (tĕr′ĭs) *n.* **1.** A porch or balcony. **2.** A patio. **3.** A raised level of earth with sloping sides.

**ter•rain** (tə-rān′) *n.* **1.** A tract of land. **2.** The physical character of land.

**ter•res•tri•al** (tə-rĕs′trē-əl) *adj.* **1.** Of the earth or its inhabitants. **2.** Living or growing on land.

**ter•ri•ble** (tĕr′ə-bəl) *adj.* **1.** Causing fear; dreadful. **2.** Intense; severe. **3.** Very bad. —**ter′ri•bly** *adv.*

**ter•ri•fic** (tə-rĭf′ĭk) *adj.* **1.** Terrifying. **2.** Splendid. **3.** Very great. —**ter•rif′i•cal•ly** *adv.*

**ter•ri•fy** (tĕr′ə-fī′) *v.* **-fied, -fying.** To fill with terror. —**ter′ri•fy′ing•ly** *adv.*

**ter•ri•to•ry** (tĕr′ĭ-tôr′ē, -tōr′ē) *n., pl.* **-ries. 1.** A region. **2.** The land and waters of a state. **3.** A part of the U.S. not yet accorded statehood. —**ter′ri•to′ri•al** *adj.*

**ter•ror** (tĕr′ər) *n.* Intense fear. —**ter′ror•ize′** *v.*

**ter•ror•ism** (tĕr′ə-rĭz′əm) *n.* The political use of terror and intimidation. —**ter′ror•ist** *n. & adj.*

**terse** (tûrs) *adj.* **terser, tersest.** Concise. —**terse′ly** *adv.* —**terse′ness** *n.*

**test** (tĕst) *n.* **1.** A means of examination or proof. **2.** A series of questions designed to determine knowledge. —**test** *v.*

**tes•ti•cle** (tĕs′tĭ-kəl) *n.* The male reproductive gland.

**tes•ti•fy** (tĕs′tə-fī′) *v.* **-fied, -fying.** To give evidence under oath.

**tes•ti•mo•ni•al** (tĕs′tə-mō′nē-əl) *n.* **1.** A written affirmation of another's character. **2.** A tribute for a person's achievement.

**tes•ti•mo•ny** (tĕs′tə-mō′nē) *n., pl.* **-nies. 1.** A declaration or affirmation of fact or truth. **2.** Supporting evidence; proof.

**tes•tis** (tĕs′tĭs) *n., pl.* **-tes.** A testicle.

**teth•er** (tĕ*th*′ər) *n.* A staked rope or chain attached to an animal. —**teth′er** *v.*

**text** (tĕkst) *n.* **1.** The main body of a printed work. **2.** A textbook. —**tex′tu•al** *adj.*

**text•book** (tĕkst′bo͝ok′) *n.* A book used in teaching a particular subject.

**tex•tile** (tĕks′tīl′, -təl) *n.* Cloth; fabric, esp. woven. —*adj.* Of textiles or their manufacture.

**tex•ture** (tĕks′chər) *n.* **1.** The appearance and feel of a fabric. **2.** The structure of a substance; grain. —**tex′tur•al** *adj.*

**than** (*th*ăn) *conj.* **1.** Used to introduce the second element of a comparison or inequality. **2.** Used with the sense of 'beyond' with adverbs of degree or quantity.

**thank** (thăngk) *v.* To express gratitude to. —**thank′ful** *adj.* —**thank′less** *adj.*

**that** (*th*ăt) *adj., pl.* **those** (*th*ōz). **1.** Being the one singled out. **2.** Being the one further removed. —*pron., pl.* **those. 1. a.** The one designated. **b.** The less immediate one. **2.** Used as a relative pronoun to introduce a clause. **3.** Something. —*adv.* To such an extent. —*conj.* Used to introduce a subordinate clause stating a fact, wish, consequence, or reason.

**thaw** (thô) *v.* **1.** To melt. **2.** To become more friendly. —*n.* **1.** The process of thawing. **2.** A period during which ice and snow melt.

**the**[1] (*th*ē *before a vowel; th*ə *before a consonant*) *def. art.* Used before nouns that denote particular specified persons or things.

**the**[2] (*th*ē *before a vowel; th*ə *before a consonant*) *adv.* To that extent.

**the•a•ter** (thē′ə-tər) *n.* Also **the•a•tre. 1.** A building for the presentation of dramas, motion pictures, etc. **2.** Dramatic literature or performance. —**the•at′ri•cal** *adj.*

**theft** (thĕft) *n.* The act or an instance of stealing.

**their** (*th*âr) *adj.* The possessive case of *they*, used before a noun as an attributive adjective.

**theirs** (*th*ârz) *pron.* The possessive case of *they*, used by itself or as a predicate adjective.

**them** (*thĕm*) *pron.* The objective case of *they.*

**theme** (thēm) *n.* **1.** A topic of discourse. **2.** The subject of an artistic work. **3.** A short essay. **4.** The main melody. **—the•mat'ic** *adj.*

**them•selves** (*thĕm*-sĕlvz', *thə*m-) *pron.* **1.** The reflexive form of *they.* **2.** The emphatic form of *they* or *them.*

**then** (*thĕn*) *adv.* **1.** At that time in the past. **2.** Next in time, space, or order. **3.** At another time. **4.** In that case; accordingly. **5.** Besides. **6.** Yet. *—adj.* Being so at that time.

**the•ol•o•gy** (thē-ŏl'ə-jē) *n., pl.* **-gies.** The study of the nature of God and religious truth. **—the'o•lo'gi•an** *n.* **—the'o•log'i•cal** *adj.*

**the•o•ry** (thē'ə-rē, thîr'ē) *n., pl.* **-ries. 1.** A system of assumptions, accepted principles, and rules of procedure devised to analyze, predict, or explain a set of phenomena. **2.** Speculation. **3.** Hypothesis or supposition. **—the'o•ret'i•cal** *adj.* **—the'o•ret'i•cal•ly** *adv.*

**ther•a•py** (thĕr'ə-pē) *n., pl.* **-pies.** The treatment of illness or disability. **—ther'a•peu'tic** *adj.* **—ther'a•pist** *n.*

**there** (*thâr*) *adv.* **1.** At or in that place. **2.** To that place; thither.

**there•fore** (*thâr*'fôr', -fōr') *adv. & conj.* Consequently; hence.

**ther•mal** (thûr'məl) *adj.* Of or by heat.

**ther•mom•e•ter** (thər-mŏm'ĭ-tər) *n.* An instrument for measuring temperature.

**ther•mo•stat** (thûr'mə-stăt') *n.* A device that automatically regulates temperature.

**the•sau•rus** (thĭ-sôr'əs) *n., pl.* **-sauri** or **-sauruses.** A book of synonyms.

**these** (*thēz*) *pron. & adj.* pl. of **this.**

**the•sis** (thē'sĭs) *n., pl.* **-ses. 1.** A proposition maintained by argument. **2.** An essay written to obtain an academic degree.

**they** (*thā*) *pron.* The 3rd person pl. pronoun in the subjective case.

**they'd** (*thā*d) *v.* Contraction of *they had* or *they would.*

**they'll** (*thā*l) *v.* Contraction of *they will.*

**they're** (*thâr*) *v.* Contraction of *they are.*

**they've** (*thā*v) *v.* Contraction of *they have.*

**thick** (thĭk) *adj.* **1.** Relatively great in depth or in extent from side to side. **2.** Dense; concentrated. **3.** Having a viscous consistency. **4.** Abounding. **5.** Pronounced; heavy. **6.** Stupid. **—thick'en** *v.* **—thick'ly** *adv.* **—thick'ness** *n.*

**thief** (thēf) *n., pl.* **thieves.** One who steals. **—thiev'er•y** *n.*

**thigh** (thī) *n.* The portion of the leg between the hip and the knee.

**thim•ble** (thĭm'bəl) *n.* A small cuplike guard to protect the finger while sewing.

**thin** (thĭn) *adj.* **thinner, thinnest. 1.** Having a small distance between opposite sides. **2.** Lean or slender. **3.** Sparse. **4.** Not heavy in consistency. **5.** Lacking substance; flimsy. *—v.* **thinned, thinning.** To make or become thin or thinner. **—thin'ly** *adv.* **—thin'ness** *n.*

**thing** (thĭng) *n.* **1.** Something that exists; an entity. **2.** A real object. **3.** A creature. **4. things.** Possessions. **5.** A thought or notion.

**think** (thĭngk) *v.* **thought** (thôt), **thinking. 1.** To formulate in the mind. **2.** To ponder. **3.** To reason. **4.** To believe. **5.** To remember. **6.** To imagine. **7.** To devise or invent. **8.** To consider. **—think'er** *n.*

**third** (thûrd) *n.* **1.** The ordinal number 3 in a series. **2.** One of 3 equal parts. *—adj.* **1.** Next after second. **2.** Being 1 of 3 equal parts. *—adv.* In the 3rd place, rank, or order. **—third'ly** *adv.*

**thirst** (thûrst) *n.* **1.** A need or desire to drink. **2.** A craving. *—v.* **1.** To feel a need to drink. **2.** To have a strong craving. **—thirst'y** *adj.*

**thir•teen** (thûr-tēn') *n.* The cardinal number written 13. **—thir•teen'** *adj. & pron.* **—thir•teenth'** *n. & adj.*

**thir•ty** (thûr'tē) *n.* The cardinal number written 30. **—thir'ty** *adj. & pron.* **—thir'ti•eth** *n. & adj.*

**this** (*thĭs*) *pron., pl.* **these** (*thēz*). **1.** The person or thing present, nearby, or just mentioned. **2.** What is about to be said. **3.** The one nearer than another or compared with the other. *—adj., pl.* **these. 1.** Being just mentioned or present. **2.** Being nearer than or compared with another. **3.** Being about to be stated or described. *—adv.* To this extent.

**tho•rax** (thôr'ăks', thōr'-) *n.* The part of the body between the neck and the diaphragm. **—tho•rac'ic** *adj.*

**thorn** (thôrn) *n.* A sharp spine protruding from a plant stem. **—thorn'y** *adj.*

**thor•ough** (thûr'ō) *adj.* **1.** Fully done; finished. **2.** Complete; absolute. **3.** Careful. **—thor'ough•ly** *adv.* **—thor'ough•ness** *n.*

**thor•ough•bred** (thûr'ō-brĕd', thûr'ə-) *adj.* Bred of pure stock. **—thor'ough•bred'** *n.*

**thor•ough•fare** (thûr'ō-fâr', thûr'ə-) *n.* A main road or public highway.

**those** (*th*ōz) *pron. & adj.* pl. of **that.**

**though** (*th*ō) *conj.* **1.** Despite the fact that. **2.** However. *—adv.* However; nevertheless.

**thought** (thôt). *v.* p.t. & p.p. of **think.** *—n.* **1.** The act of thinking. **2.** An idea. **3.** Consideration; concern. **4.** A trifle. **—thought'ful** *adj.* **—thought'less** *adj.*

**thou•sand** (thou'zənd) *n.* The cardinal number written 1,000. **—thou'sand** *adj. & pron.* **—thou'sandth** *n. & adj.*

**thrash** (thrăsh) *v.* **1.** To beat or flog. **2.** To defeat utterly. **3.** To move wildly. **—thrash'ing** *n.*

**thread** (thrĕd) *n.* **1.** A fine cord of a fibrous material. **2.** A spiral ridge on a screw, nut, or bolt. *—v.* **1.** To pass 1 end of a thread through the eye of (a needle). **2.** To pass cautiously through. **3.** To machine a thread on (a screw, nut, or bolt).

**threat** (thrĕt) *n.* **1.** An expression of an intention to inflict pain, injury, etc. **2.** One regarded as a possible danger. **—threat'en** *v.*

**three** (thrē) *n.* The cardinal number written 3. **—three** *adj. & pron.*

**thresh** (thrĕsh) *v.* To remove the grain or seeds. **—thresh'er** *n.*

**thresh•old** (thrĕsh'ōld', thrĕsh'hōld') *n.* **1.** The piece of wood or stone beneath a door. **2.** An entrance or starting point.

**threw** (thro͞o) *v.* p.t. of **throw.**

**thrice** (thrīs) *adv.* Three times.

**thrift** (thrĭft) *n.* Economy; frugality. **—thrift'y** *adj.*

**thrill** (thrĭl) *v.* To feel or cause to feel a sudden intense sensation. *—n.* That which produces great excitement. **—thrill'er** *n.*

**thrive** (thrīv) *v.* **thrived, thriving. 1.** To prosper. **2.** To grow vigorously; flourish.

**throat** (thrōt) *n.* The front portion of the neck.

**throb** (thrŏb) *v.* **throbbed, throbbing.** To beat or vibrate strongly. **—throb** *n.*

**throne** (thrōn) *n.* The chair occupied by a sovereign, bishop, etc.

**throng** (thrŏng) *n.* A crowd; a multitude. *—v.* To crowd into.

**throt•tle** (thrŏt'l) *n.* **1. a.** A valve in an internal-combustion engine that regulates the amount of fuel entering the cylinders. **b.** A similar valve in a steam engine regulating the amount of steam. **2.** A lever or pedal controlling this valve. *—v.* **-tled, -tling. 1.** To regulate the speed of (an engine) with a throttle. **2.** To strangle; choke. **—throt'tler** *n.*

**through** (thro͞o) *prep.* **1.** In 1 side and out another side of. **2.** In the midst of. **3.** By way of. **4.** By means of. **5.** From the beginning to the end of. **6.** Finished with. *—adv.* **1.** From 1 end to another. **2.** From beginning to end. **3.** To a conclusion. *—adj.* **1.** Passing from 1 end to another. **2.** Unobstructed. **3.** Finished; done.

**through•out** (thro͞o-out') *prep.* In or during every part of. *—adv.* **1.** Everywhere. **2.** During the entire time.

**throw** (thrō) *v.* **threw** (thro͞o), **thrown, throwing. 1.** To propel; fling. **2.** To perplex. **3.** To move (a controlling lever). **—throw** *n.*

**thrust** (thrŭst) *v.* **1.** To push forcibly. **2.** To stab. *—n.* **1.** A forceful shove. **2.** A driving force or pressure, esp. in a jet engine. **3.** A stab.

**thud** (thŭd) *n.* A dull sound. *—v.* **thudded, thudding.** To make such a sound.

**thug** (thŭg) *n.* A ruffian; hoodlum.

**thumb** (thŭm) *n.* The short 1st digit of the hand.

**thun•der** (thŭn'dər) *n.* The explosive sound resulting from the electrical discharge of lightning. *—v.* **1.** To produce thunder. **2.** To utter loudly. **—thun'der•bolt'** *n.* **—thun'der•cloud'** *n.* **—thun'der•ous** *adj.*

**thun•der•struck** (thŭn'dər-strŭk') *adj.* Struck by sudden amazement.

**Thurs•day** (thûrz′dē, -dā′) *n.* The 5th day of the week.

**thus** (*th*ŭs) *adv.* **1.** In this way. **2.** To this extent; so. **3.** Therefore; consequently.

**thwart** (thwôrt) *v.* To prevent; frustrate.

**tic** (tĭk) *n.* A facial twitch.

**tick** (tĭk) *n.* A recurring clicking sound, esp. that made by a clock. **—tick** *v.*

**tick•et** (tĭk′ĭt) *n.* **1.** A paper slip indicating right of admission. **2.** An identifying tag. **3.** A list of candidates endorsed by a political party. **4.** A summons. *—v.* To attach a tag to.

**tick•le** (tĭk′əl) *v.* **-led, -ling. 1.** To tingle. **2.** To touch (the body) lightly, causing laughter or twitching movements. **3.** To tease or amuse. *—n.* The act or sensation of tickling. **—tick′lish** *adj.*

**tide** (tīd) *n.* **1.** The periodic rise and fall of the surface of oceans. **2.** A tendency or trend. **—tid′al** *adj.*

**tid•ings** (tī′dĭngz) *pl.n.* Information; news.

**ti•dy** (tī′dē) *adj.* **-dier, diest.** Orderly and neat. *—v.* **-died, -dying.** To put in order. **—ti′di•ly** *adv.* **—ti′di•ness** *n.*

**tie** (tī) *v.* **tied, tying. 1.** To fasten with a cord, rope, etc. **2.** To draw together and knot. **3.** To equal (an opponent) in a contest. *—n.* **1.** Something used to tie. **2.** A bond. **3.** A necktie. **4.** A beam or rod that joins parts. **5.** An equality of scores, votes, etc.

**tier** (tîr) *n.* One of a series of rows placed 1 above another.

**ti•ger** (tī′gər) *n.* A large, wild Asian cat with transverse black stripes. **—ti′gress** *fem.n.*

**tight** (tīt) *adj.* **1.** Impermeable, esp. by water or air. **2.** Fastened or closed securely. **3.** Taut. **4.** Snug. **5.** Closely contested. *—adv.* Firmly; securely. **—tight′en** *v.* **—tight′ly** *adv.* **—tight′ness** *n.*

**tile** (tīl) *n.* A slab of baked clay for covering walls, floors, and roofs. *—v.* **tiled, tiling.** To cover with tiles.

**till**[1] (tĭl) *v.* To prepare (land) for planting.

**till**[2] (tĭl) *prep.* Until. *—conj.* Until.

**tilt** (tĭlt) *v.* To slope or cause to slope; incline; tip. *—n.* **1.** A slant; slope. **2.** A verbal duel.

**tim•ber** (tĭm′bər) *n.* **1.** Wooded land. **2.** Wood for building. **3.** A wooden beam.

**tim•bre** (tĭm′bər, tăm′-) *n.* The distinguishing quality of an individual sound.

**time** (tīm) *n.* **1.** A continuum in which events occur; duration. **2.** An interval; a period of time. **3.** Often **times.** A span of years. **4.** An opportune or designated moment. **5.** An occasion. **6.** The rate of speed of a measured activity. **7.** The beat of musical rhythm. *—adj.* **1.** Of time. **2.** Of installment buying. *—v.* **timed, timing. 1.** To set the time for; schedule. **2.** To regulate for orderly sequence. **3.** To record the speed or duration of. **—time′less** *adj.* **—time′ly** *adj.* **—tim′er** *n.*

**time•ta•ble** (tīm′tā′bəl) *n.* A table listing the arrival and departure times of trains, buses, etc.

**tim•id** (tĭm′ĭd) *adj.* **1.** Hesitant or fearful. **2.** Shy. **—ti•mid′i•ty** *n.* **—tim′id•ly** *adv.*

**tim•or•ous** (tĭm′ər-əs) *adj.* Apprehensive; timid.

**tin** (tĭn) *n.* **1.** A malleable metallic element used to coat other metals to prevent corrosion. **2.** A tin container. *—v.* **tinned, tinning. 1.** To coat with tin. **2.** To pack in tins; can. **—tin′ny** *adj.*

**tin•der** (tĭn′dər) *n.* Readily combustible material. **—tin′der•box′** *n.*

**tine** (tīn) *n.* A pointed prong, as of a fork.

**tinge** (tĭnj) *v.* **tinged, tingeing** or **tinging. 1.** To color slightly. **2.** To affect slightly. *—n.* A faint trace.

**tin•gle** (tĭng′gəl) *v.* **-gled, -gling.** To have a prickling sensation. **—tin′gle** *n.* **—tin′gly** *adj.*

**tin•ker** (tĭng′kər) *v.* To play experimentally with a mechanical device.

**tin•kle** (tĭng′kəl) *v.* **-kled, -kling.** To make or cause to make light metallic sounds. **—tin′kle** *n.*

**tint** (tĭnt) *n.* **1.** A shade of a color. **2.** A slight coloration. *—v.* To give a tint to.

**ti•ny** (tī′nē) *adj.* **-nier, -niest.** Extremely small.

**tip**[1] (tĭp) *n.* **1.** An end or extremity. **2.** A piece fitted to the end of something. *—v.* **tipped, tipping.** To furnish with a tip.

**tip**[2] (tĭp) *v.* **tipped, tipping. 1.** To knock over. **2.** To tilt. *—n.* A slant or tilt.

**tip**[3] (tĭp) *n.* **1.** A sum of money given for services rendered. **2.** Useful information. **—tip** *v.* **—tip'per** *n.*

**tip•toe** (tĭp'tō') *v.* **-toed, -toeing.** To walk stealthily or softly, as on the tips of the toes.

**ti•rade** (tī'răd', tī-răd') *n.* A long, harshly critical speech.

**tire[1]** (tīr) *v.* **tired, tiring. 1.** To make or become weary. **2.** To make or become bored. **—tire'less** *adj.* **—tire'less•ly** *adv.*

**tire[2]** (tīr) *n.* A round, usually rubber covering for a wheel.

**tire•some** (tīr'səm) *adj.* Causing fatigue or boredom.

**tis•sue** (tĭsh'ōō) *n.* **1.** Cellular matter in organisms. **2.** A soft, absorbent piece of paper. **3.** A thin paper used for packing. **4.** A fine sheer cloth, as gauze.

**ti•tle** (tīt'l) *n.* **1.** A name given to a book, painting, etc. **2.** A formal appellation, as of rank. **3. a.** In law, the right of possession or control. **b.** The evidence of this, as a deed. **4.** In sports, a championship. *—v.* **-tled, -tling.** To give a title to. **—tit'u•lar** *adj.*

**tit•ter** (tĭt'ər) *v.* To utter a nervous giggle. **—tit'ter** *n.*

**to** (tōō; *unstressed* tə) *prep.* **1.** Toward. **2.** As far as. **3.** Until. **4.** For; of; belonging to. **5.** As compared with.

**toad** (tōd) *n.* A froglike, mostly land-dwelling amphibian.

**toast[1]** (tōst) *v.* To heat and brown (bread, rolls, etc.). *—n.* Sliced bread heated and browned. **—toast'er** *n.*

**toast[2]** (tōst) *n.* **1.** A person or thing in whose honor persons drink. **2.** The act of proposing such an honor. *—v.* To make a toast.

**to•bac•co** (tə-băk'ō) *n., pl.* **-cos** or **coes. 1.** A plant having broad leaves used chiefly for smoking. **2.** The processed leaves of this plant.

**to•bog•gan** (tə-bŏg'ən) *n.* A long, runnerless sled.

**to•day** (tə-dā') *adv.* **1.** On the present day. **2.** At the present time. *—n.* The present day, time, or age.

**tod•dle** (tŏd'l) *v.* **-dled, -dling.** To walk with short, unsteady steps. **—tod'dler** *n.*

**toe** (tō) *n.* **1.** One of the digits of the foot. **2.** The forward part of something worn on the foot.

**tof•fee** (tô'fē, tŏf'ē) *n.* Hard, chewy candy made of brown sugar and butter.

**to•geth•er** (tə-gĕth'ər) *adv.* **1.** In or into a single group or place. **2.** In total. **3.** Simultaneously. **4.** In harmony or cooperation.

**toil** (toil) *v.* To work strenuously. *—n.* Exhausting labor.

**toi•let** (toi'lĭt) *n.* **1.** A disposal apparatus used to receive body waste. **2.** A bathroom. **3.** The act or process of grooming and dressing oneself.

**to•ken** (tō'kən) *n.* **1.** A sign; symbol. **2.** A keepsake. **3.** A metal disk used as a substitute for currency. *—adj.* Done as an indication or pledge.

**told** (tōld) *v.* p.t. & p.p. of **tell.**

**tol•er•a•ble** (tŏl'ər-ə-bəl) *adj.* **1.** Endurable. **2.** Adequate; passable. **—tol'er•a•bly** *adv.*

**tol•er•ance** (tŏl'ər-əns) *n.* **1.** The capacity for respecting the opinions or practices of others. **2.** The capacity to endure hardship, pain, etc. **—tol'er•ant** *adj.*

**tol•er•ate** (tŏl'ə-rāt') *v.* **-ated, -ating. 1.** To allow; permit. **2.** To respect the opinions, practices, or behavior of others. **3.** To put up with. **—tol'er•a'tion** *n.*

**toll[1]** (tōl) *n.* **1.** A fixed tax, as for passage across a bridge. **2.** A charge for a service, as a telephone call.

**toll[2]** (tōl) *v.* To sound (a bell) slowly at regular intervals. **—toll** *n.*

**tom•a•hawk** (tŏm'ə-hôk') *n.* A light ax used by certain Native American peoples.

**to•ma•to** (tə-mā'tō, -mä'-) *n., pl.* **-toes.** An edible, fleshy red fruit.

**tomb** (tōōm) *n.* A vault for the dead.

**tome** (tōm) *n.* A large scholarly book.

**to•mor•row** (tə-môr'ō, -mŏr'ō) *n.* The day following today. *—adv.* On the day following today.

**ton** (tŭn) *n.* **1.** A unit of weight equal to 2,240 pounds; long ton. **2.** A unit of weight equal to 2,000 pounds; short ton.

**tone** (tōn) *n.* **1.** A distinct sound. **2.** Quality of sound. **3.** Manner of expression. **4.** A general quality or atmosphere. **5.** A color or shade of color. **6.** Normal muscular firmness. **—to'nal** *adj.*

**tongs** (tôngz, tŏngz) *n. (takes sing. v.).* A 2-armed grasping device.

**tongue** (tŭng) *n.* **1.** The fleshy muscular organ in the mouth. **2.** Anything resembling a tongue. **3.** A spoken language.

**ton•ic** (tŏn'ĭk) *n.* Anything that invigorates.

**to•night** (tə-nīt') *adv.* On the present night. —*n.* This night.

**ton•sil** (tŏn'səl) *n.* A mass of tissue between the mouth and pharynx.

**too** (tōō) *adv.* **1.** In addition. **2.** Excessively. **3.** Very.

**took** (tŏŏk) *v.* p.t. of **take.**

**tool** (tōōl) *n.* **1.** A hand instrument. **2.** A mechanical device. **3.** A servile helper; stooge. —*v.* To form or work with a tool.

**tooth** (tōōth) *n., pl.* **teeth. 1.** A hard, bonelike structure rooted in the jaw. **2.** A toothlike structure or projection. **—toothed** *adj.*

**top** (tŏp) *n.* **1.** The uppermost part, point, or end. **2.** A lid or cap. **3.** The highest rank or degree. —*adj.* Of, at, or forming the top. —*v.* **topped, topping. 1.** To go over the top of. **2.** To surpass.

**top•ic** (tŏp'ĭk) *n.* A subject treated in a speech, essay, or conversation.

**top•i•cal** (tŏp'ĭ-kəl) *adj.* **1.** Of current interest; contemporary. **2.** For application to an isolated part of the body.

**to•pog•ra•phy** (tə-pŏg'rə-fē) *n., pl.* **-phies. 1.** The art of representing on a map the physical configuration of a place or region. **2.** The features of a place or region. **—to•pog'ra•pher** *n.* **—top'o•graph'ic, top'o•graph'i•cal** *adj.*

**top•ple** (tŏp'əl) *v.* **-pled, -pling. 1.** To push over. **2.** To fall.

**torch** (tôrch) *n.* A portable light or flame.

**tore** (tôr, tōr) *v.* p.t. of **tear[1].**

**tor•ment** (tôr'mĕnt') *n.* Great pain or anguish. —*v.* (tôr-mĕnt'). **1.** To afflict with great pain or anguish. **2.** To annoy or harass. **—tor•men'tor** *n.*

**torn** (tôrn, tōrn) *v.* p.p. of **tear[1].**

**tor•na•do** (tôr-nā'dō) *n., pl.* **-does** or **-dos.** A funnel-shaped, whirling, destructive storm.

**tor•pe•do** (tôr-pē'dō) *n., pl.* **-does.** A cigar-shaped, self-propelled underwater projectile. —*v.* To attack with a torpedo.

**tor•pid** (tôr'pĭd) *adj.* Sluggishly inactive; lethargic. **—tor'por** *n.*

**torque** (tôrk) *n.* A turning or twisting force.

**tor•rent** (tôr'ənt, tŏr'-) *n.* **1.** A turbulent, rapid stream. **2.** A raging flood. **—tor•ren'tial** *adj.*

**tor•rid** (tôr'ĭd, tŏr'-) *adj.* **1.** Parched by the sun. **2.** Scorching.

**tor•so** (tôr'sō) *n., pl.* **-sos** or **-si.** The trunk of the human body.

**tort** (tôrt) *n.* A wrongful act for which a civil suit can be brought.

**tor•toise** (tôr'tĭs) *n.* A turtle, esp. a land turtle.

**tor•tu•ous** (tôr'chōō-əs) *adj.* **1.** Winding; twisting. **2.** Complex.

**tor•ture** (tôr'chər) *n.* **1.** The intentional infliction of severe pain. **2.** Pain or mental anguish. —*v.* **-tured, -turing.** To subject to torture. **—tor'tur•ous** *adj.*

**toss** (tôs, tŏs) *v.* **1.** To throw or be thrown to and fro. **2.** To throw lightly. **3.** To flip a coin to decide something. —*n.* An act of tossing.

**to•tal** (tōt'l) *n.* The whole amount. —*adj.* Complete; utter. —*v.* **1.** To find the sum of. **2.** To amount to. **—to•tal'i•ty** *n.* **—to'tal•ly** *adv.*

**tote** (tōt) *v.* **toted, toting.** To carry.

**to•tem** (tō'təm) *n.* An emblem or symbol of a family or clan.

**tot•ter** (tŏt'ər) *v.* **1.** To sway as if about to fall. **2.** To walk unsteadily.

**touch** (tŭch) *v.* **1.** To cause a part of the body to come in contact with so as to feel. **2.** To be or come into contact. **3.** To tap lightly. **4.** To come up to; equal. **5.** To move or affect. —*n.* **1.** The act of touching. **2.** The sense by which bodily contact is registered. **3.** The sensation from contact. **4.** A mark or effect left by a specific contact. **5.** A small amount. **6.** A knack.

**touch•down** (tŭch'doun') *n.* In football, a scoring play worth 6 points.

**tough** (tŭf) *adj.* **1.** Strong and resilient. **2.** Hard to cut or chew. **3.** Rugged. **4.** Difficult; demanding. **5.** Having a determined will. **—tough'en** *v.* **—tough'ness** *n.*

**tou•pee** (tōō-pā') *n.* A partial wig or hair piece.

**tour** (tŏŏr) *n.* **1.** A trip with visits to different places. **2.** A brief trip to or through a place. **3.** A period of duty at a single place. —*v.* To make a tour of. **—tour′ism′** *n.* **—tour′ist** *n.*

**tour de force** (to͝or′də-fôrs′, -fōrs′) *n., pl.* **tours de force.** A feat of strength or virtuosity.

**tour•na•ment** (to͝or′nə-mənt, tûr′-) *n.* A contest composed of a series of games.

**tour•ni•quet** (to͝or′nĭ-kĭt, tûr′-) *n.* A bandage or other device to stop bleeding.

**tou•sle** (tou′zəl) *v.* **-sled, -sling.** To rumple.

**tout** (tout) *v.* **1.** To publicize as being of great worth. **2.** To solicit brazenly.

**tow** (tō) *v.* To pull along by a chain or line. —*n.* **1.** An act of towing or being towed. **2.** Something being towed.

**to•ward** (tôrd, tōrd, tə-wôrd′) *prep.* Also **to•wards. 1.** In the direction of. **2.** With regard to. **3.** In furtherance of.

**tow•el** (tou′əl) *n.* An absorbent cloth or paper used for drying.

**tow•er** (tou′ər) *n.* A tall building or part of a building. —*v.* To rise to a great height.

**town** (toun) *n.* A population center smaller than a city.

**town•ship** (toun′shĭp′) *n.* **1.** A subdivision of a county. **2.** A public land surveying unit of 36 square miles.

**tox•ic** (tŏk′sĭk) *adj.* **1.** Of a toxin. **2.** Harmful; poisonous. **—tox•ic′i•ty** *n.*

**tox•in** (tŏk′sĭn) *n.* A poisonous organic substance.

**toy** (toi) *n.* A thing to play with. —*v.* To trifle (with *with*). —*adj.* **1.** Designed as a toy. **2.** Very small.

**trace** (trās) *n.* **1.** A visible sign of the former presence of something. **2.** A touch. **3.** A minute quantity. —*v.* **traced, tracing. 1.** To follow the trail of. **2.** To locate or discover. **3.** To sketch. **4.** To copy by following lines seen through transparent paper.

**tra•che•a** (trā′kē-ə) *n.* An air-carrying tube descending from the larynx to the bronchi.

**track** (trăk) *n.* **1.** A mark, as a footprint; a trace. **2.** A path, route, or course. **3.** A road laid out for racing. **4.** A set of parallel rails for a train. —*v.* To follow; trail.

**tract**[1] (trăkt) *n.* **1.** An expanse of land. **2.** A system of related bodily organs.

**tract**[2] (trăkt) *n.* A propaganda pamphlet.

**tract•a•ble** (trăk′tə-bəl) *adj.* Easily controlled.

**trac•tion** (trăk′shən) *n.* **1.** The act of drawing or of being drawn. **2.** Adhesive friction.

**trac•tor** (trăk′tər) *n.* A vehicle designed for pulling machinery.

**trade** (trād) *n.* **1.** An occupation; a craft. **2.** The business of buying and selling commodities; commerce. **3.** An exchange. —*v.* **traded, trading. 1.** To buy and sell. **2.** To exchange. **—trad′er** *n.*

**trade•mark** (trād′märk′) *n.* A registered name, symbol, or other device identifying a product.

**tra•di•tion** (trə-dĭsh′ən) *n.* **1.** The passing down of elements of a culture from generation to generation. **2.** A set of cultural customs and usages. **—tra•di′tion•al** *adj.* **—tra•di′tion•al•ly** *adv.*

**traf•fic** (trăf′ĭk) *n.* **1.** The commercial exchange of goods; trade. **2.** The passage of persons or vehicles through travel routes. **3.** The amount, as of vehicles, in transit. —*v.* **-ficked, -ficking.** To carry on trade in. **—traf′fick•er** *n.*

**trag•e•dy** (trăj′ĭ-dē) *n., pl.* **-dies. 1.** A dramatic work dealing with human misfortune and profound unhappiness. **2.** A disastrous event. **—trag′ic, trag′i•cal** *adj.* **—trag′i•cal•ly** *adv.*

**trail** (trāl) *v.* **1.** To drag or allow to drag behind. **2.** To follow the trail of; track. **3.** To become gradually fainter. —*n.* **1.** Something that trails, esp. something that hangs loose and long. **2.** A mark, trace, or scent left. **3.** A path.

**trail•er** (trā′lər) *n.* **1.** One that trails. **2.** A large vehicle or van drawn by a truck or automobile and sometimes used as a home.

**train** (trān) *n.* **1.** Something that follows or is drawn along. **2.** A staff of followers; retinue. **3.** A line of moving persons, vehicles, etc. **4.** A string of connected railroad cars. **5.** A succession of related events or thoughts. —*v.* **1.** To make or become proficient with instruction. **2.** To prepare physically. **3.** To focus (on); aim. **—train′a•ble** *adj.* **—train•ee′** *n.* **—train′er** *n.* **—train′ing** *n.*

**traipse** (trāps) *v.* **traipsed, traipsing.** To walk about idly.

**trait** (trāt) *n.* A distinguishing feature.

**trai•tor** (trā′tər) *n.* One who betrays one's country, a cause, etc., esp. one who has committed treason. —**trai′tor•ous** *adj.*

**tra•jec•to•ry** (trə-jĕk′tə-rē) *n., pl.* **-ries.** The path of a moving object.

**tramp** (trămp) *v.* **1.** To walk with a heavy step. **2.** To travel on foot. —*n.* **1.** The sound of heavy walking or marching. **2.** A walking trip. **3.** A vagrant.

**tram•ple** (trăm′pəl) *v.* **-pled, -pling. 1.** To tread heavily or destructively. **2.** To treat harshly.

**tram•po•line** (trăm′pə-lēn′) *n.* Acrobatic equipment made of canvas held taut by springs to a metal frame.

**trance** (trăns) *n.* A hypnotic, semiconscious, or ecstatic state.

**tran•quil** (trăng′kwəl, trăn′-) *adj.* Peaceful; calm. —**tran•quil′li•ty** *n.* —**tran′quil•ize′, tran′quil•lize′** *v.*

**trans•ac•tion** (trăn-săk′shən, -zăk′-) *n.* **1.** The act of doing business. **2.** The business conducted. **3. transactions.** The proceedings of a meeting. —**trans•act′** *v.*

**tran•scend** (trăn-sĕnd′) *v.* **1.** To exist above and independent of. **2.** To rise above; surpass. —**tran•scen′dent** *adj.*

**tran•scribe** (trăn-skrīb′) *v.* **-scribed, -scribing.** To write or type a copy of. —**tran′script′** *n.* —**tran•scrip′tion** *n.*

**trans•fer** (trăns-fûr′, trăns′fər) *v.* **-ferred, -ferring.** To convey or change from 1 person or place to another. —*n.* **1.** The act or means of transferring. **2.** Any person or thing transferred. —**trans•fer′a•ble** *adj.* —**trans•fer′ence** *n.*

**trans•form** (trăns-fôrm′) *v.* **1.** To change markedly in appearance. **2.** To change the nature or function of. —**trans′for•ma′tion** *n.*

**trans•fu•sion** (trăns-fyo͞o′zhən) *n.* The injection of whole blood, plasma, etc., into the bloodstream.

**trans•gress** (trăns-grĕs′, trănz-) *v.* **1.** To go beyond (a limit). **2.** To violate (a law). —**trans•gres′sion** *n.* —**trans•gres′sor** *n.*

**tran•si•ent** (trăn′shənt, -zhənt, -zē-ənt) *adj.* **1.** Passing away with time; transitory. **2.** Passing through from one place to another. —*n.* One that is transient. —**tran′si•ence** *n.* —**tran′si•ent•ly** *adv.*

**tran•sis•tor** (trăn-zĭs′tər, -sĭs′-) *n.* An electrical device used for amplification, switching, etc.

**tran•sit** (trăn′sĭt, -zĭt) *n.* **1.** Passage; crossing. **2.** The conveying of persons or goods, esp. on a local transportation system.

**tran•si•tion** (trăn-zĭsh′ən, -sĭsh′-) *n.* The changing or passing from one form, state, or place to another. —**tran•si′tion•al** *adj.*

**tran•si•tive** (trăn′sĭ-tĭv, -zĭ-) *adj.* Designating a verb that requires a direct object.

**tran•si•to•ry** (trăn′sĭ-tôr′ē, -tōr′ē, trăn′zĭ-) *adj.* Brief; short-lived.

**trans•late** (trăns-lāt′, trănz-, trăns′lāt′, trănz′-) *v.* **-lated, -lating. 1.** To express or render in another language. **2.** To explain. —**trans•lat′a•ble** *adj.* —**trans•la′tion** *n.* —**trans•la′tor** *n.*

**trans•lu•cent** (trăns-lo͞o′sənt, trănz-) *adj.* Letting light pass through diffusely. —**trans•lu′cence, trans•lu′cen•cy** *n.*

**trans•mis•sion** (trăns-mĭsh′ən, trănz-) *n.* **1.** The act of transmitting. **2.** Something transmitted. **3.** An assembly or system of gears linking an engine to a driving axle.

**trans•mit** (trăns-mĭt′, trănz-) *v.* **-mitted, -mitting. 1.** To send or pass along. **2.** To cause to spread. **3.** To impart by heredity. **4.** To send (a signal). —**trans•mis′si•ble, trans•mit′ta•ble** *adj.* —**trans•mit′tal** *n.* —**trans•mit′ter** *n.*

**tran•som** (trăn′səm) *n.* A small window above a door or another window.

**trans•par•ent** (trăns-pâr′ənt, -păr′-) *adj.* Letting light pass through without distortion; clear.

**tran•spire** (trăn-spīr′) *v.* **-spired, -spiring. 1.** To become known; come to light. **2.** To happen; occur.

**trans•plant** (trăns-plănt′) *v.* **1.** To uproot and replant. **2.** To transfer from 1 place to another. —**trans′plant′** *n.*

**trans•port** (trăns-pôrt′, -pōrt′) *v.* **1.** To carry from 1 place to another. **2.** To enrapture. —*n.* (trăns′pôrt′, -pōrt′). **1.** The act of transporting; conveyance. **2.** A vehicle used to transport. —**trans′por•ta′tion** *n.*

**trans•pose** (trăns-pōz′) *v.* **-posed, -posing. 1.** To change the order of. **2.** In music, to write or perform (a composition) in a different key. **—trans′po•si′tion** *n.*

**trans•verse** (trăns-vûrs′, trănz-, trăns′vûrs′, trănz′-) *adj.* Lying across; crosswise. **—trans•verse′** *n.* **—trans•verse′ly** *adv.*

**trap** (trăp) *n.* **1.** A device for catching animals. **2.** A stratagem for tricking an unsuspecting person. *—v.* **trapped, trapping.** To catch in a trap. **—trap′per** *n.*

**tra•peze** (tră-pēz′) *n.* A short swinglike bar used for acrobatics.

**trash** (trăsh) *n.* Garbage. **—trash′y** *adj.*

**trau•ma** (trou′mə, trô-) *n.* **1.** A wound, esp. one produced by sudden physical injury. **2.** An emotional shock. **—trau•mat′ic** *adj.* **—trau′ma•tize′** *v.*

**tra•vail** (trə-vāl′, trăv′āl′) *n.* **1.** Strenuous exertion. **2.** Agony; anguish. **3.** The labor of childbirth. *—v.* **1.** To toil. **2.** To labor in childbirth.

**trav•el** (trăv′əl) *v.* **1.** To go from one place to another. **2.** To be transmitted. *—n.* The act of traveling. **—trav′el•er** *n.*

**tra•verse** (trăv′ərs, trə-vûrs′) *v.* **-ersed, -ersing. 1.** To travel across or through. **2.** To extend across. *—n.* A structural crosspiece. *—adj.* Lying across.

**trav•es•ty** (trăv′ĭ-stē) *n., pl.* **-ties.** A grotesque parody. *—v.* **-tied, -tying.** To make a travesty of.

**trawl** (trôl) *n.* A large fishing net towed along the sea bottom. *—v.* To fish with a trawl. **—trawl′er** *n.*

**tray** (trā) *n.* A flat, shallow receptacle for carrying, holding, etc.

**treach•er•ous** (trĕch′ər-əs) *adj.* **1.** Disloyal. **2.** Not dependable. **3.** Dangerous. **—treach′er•y** *n.*

**tread** (trĕd) *v.* **trod** (trŏd), **trodden** (trŏd′n), or **trod, treading. 1.** To walk on. **2.** To press beneath the foot; stamp. *—n.* **1.** The act or manner of walking. **2.** The horizontal part of a staircase step. **3.** The grooved face of an automobile tire.

**trea•son** (trē′zən) *n.* Violation of allegiance toward one's country or sovereign. **—trea′son•a•ble** *adj.* **—trea′son•ous** *adj.*

**treas•ure** (trĕzh′ər) *n.* **1.** Accumulated wealth in the form of valuables. **2.** One considered precious. *—v.* **-ured, -uring.** To value highly.

**treas•ur•y** (trĕzh′ə-rē) *n., pl.* **-ies. 1.** A place where private or public funds are kept. **2.** A governmental department in charge of public revenue. **—treas′ur•er** *n.*

**treat** (trēt) *v.* **1.** To act or behave toward. **2.** To regard or consider. **3.** To deal with. **4.** To entertain. **5.** To subject to a process. **6.** To give medical aid to. *—n.* **1.** Something paid for by another. **2.** A special delight; pleasure. **—treat′er** *n.* **—treat′ment** *n.*

**trea•tise** (trē′tĭs) *n.* A formal written account on some subject.

**trea•ty** (trē′tē) *n., pl.* **-ties.** A formal agreement between 2 or more states.

**treb•le** (trĕb′əl) *adj.* **1.** Triple. **2.** In music, of the highest range. *—n.* In music, the highest part, voice, instrument, or range; soprano. *—v.* **-led, -ling.** To triple. **—treb′ly** *adv.*

**tree** (trē) *n.* A tall woody plant with a single main trunk.

**trek** (trĕk) *v.* **trekked, trekking.** To make a long, arduous journey. **—trek** *n.*

**trel•lis** (trĕl′ĭs) *n.* A frame for training climbing vines.

**trem•ble** (trĕm′bəl) *v.* **-bled, -bling.** To shake involuntarily; quiver. **—trem′ble** *n.*

**tre•men•dous** (trĭ-mĕn′dəs) *adj.* **1.** Awesome; terrible. **2. a.** Enormous. **b.** Wonderful. **—tre•men′dous•ly** *adv.*

**trem•or** (trĕm′ər) *n.* **1.** A vibration. **2.** An involuntary trembling; shiver.

**trem•u•lous** (trĕm′yə-ləs) *adj.* **1.** Trembling; shaking. **2.** Timid; fearful.

**trench** (trĕnch) *n.* A deep furrow or ditch.

**trench•ant** (trĕn′chənt) *adj.* Keen; incisive. **—trench′ant•ly** *adv.*

**trend** (trĕnd) *n.* **1.** A direction or course. **2.** A tendency.

**trep•i•da•tion** (trĕp′ĭ-dā′shən) *n.* A state of apprehension.

**tres•pass** (trĕs′pəs, -păs′) *v.* **1.** To invade the property or rights of another. **2.** To commit an offense. *—n.* **1.** The act of trespassing. **2.** An offense. **—tres′pass•er** *n.*

**tres•tle** (trĕs′əl) *n.* **1.** A horizontal bar held up by legs and used as a support. **2.** A framework of such construction for supporting a bridge.

**tri•ad** (trī′ăd′) *n.* A group of 3.
**tri•age** (trē-äzh′, trē′äzh′) *n.* A system for sorting patients or allocating limited resources.
**tri•al** (trī′əl, trīl) *n.* **1.** A legal examination of evidence in a judicial procedure. **2.** The act of testing and trying. **3.** An attempt. **4.** Suffering or adversity. **5.** A test of patience or endurance. —*adj.* Made or done during a test.
**tri•an•gle** (trī′ăng′gəl) *n.* A plane figure with 3 angles. **—tri•an′gu•lar** *adj.*
**tri•ath•lon** (trī-ăth′lən, -lŏn′) *n.* An athletic competition with 3 parts. **—tri•ath′lete** *n.*
**tribe** (trīb) *n.* **1.** A social organization or division. **2.** A group having a common distinguishing characteristic. **—trib′al** *adj.*
**trib•u•la•tion** (trĭb′yə-lā′shən) *n.* **1.** Great affliction. **2.** A cause of such affliction.
**tri•bu•nal** (trī-byo͞o′nəl, trĭ-) A court of justice.
**trib•u•tar•y** (trĭb′yə-tĕr′ē) *adj.* **1.** Subsidiary. **2.** Paying tribute. —*n., pl.* **-ies.** A stream or river flowing into a larger one.
**trib•ute** (trĭb′yo͞ot) *n.* **1.** A gift or act as acknowledgment of respect. **2.** A payment, often forced, from 1 nation to another as acknowledgment of submission.
**trick** (trĭk) *n.* **1.** A deception; stratagem. **2.** A prank. **3.** A knack or ability. **4.** All the cards played in a single round. —*v.* To swindle or cheat; deceive. **—trick′er•y** *n.* **—trick′y** *adj.*
**trick•le** (trĭk′əl) *v.* **-led, -ling. 1.** To flow in drops or a thin stream. **2.** To move bit by bit. **—trick′le** *n.*
**tri•dent** (trīd′nt) *n.* A long, 3-pronged weapon.
**tri•en•ni•al** (trī-ĕn′ē-əl) *adj.* **1.** Occurring every 3rd year. **2.** Lasting 3 years. —*n.* A 3rd anniversary.
**tri•fle** (trī′fəl) *n.* **1.** Something of little value. **2.** A small amount. —*v.* **-fled, -fling. 1.** To deal with something as if it were of little value. **2.** To deal insincerely with someone. **—tri′fler** *n.* **—tri′fling** *adj.*
**trig•ger** (trĭg′ər) *n.* **1.** The lever pressed to discharge a firearm. **2.** A device to release a mechanism. **3.** A stimulus. —*v.* To initiate; set off.
**trill** (trĭl) *n.* **1.** A fluttering sound. **2.** In music, the rapid alternation of 2 tones. —*v.* To sound, sing, or play with a trill.
**tril•lion** (trĭl′yən) *n.* The cardinal number represented by 1 followed by 12 zeros. **—tril′lion** *adj. & pron.* **—tril′lionth** *n. & adj.*
**tril•o•gy** (trĭl′ə-jē) *n., pl.* **-gies.** A group of 3 related dramatic or literary works.
**trim** (trĭm) *v.* **trimmed, trimming. 1.** To make neat by clipping or pruning. **2.** To ornament; decorate. **3. a.** To adjust (the sails and yards). **b.** To balance (a ship). —*n.* **1.** Appearance; condition. **2.** Ornamentation. **3.** The readiness or balance of a ship. —*adj.* **trimmer, trimmest.** In good or neat order. **—trim′ly** *adv.* **—trim′mer** *n.* **—trim′ness** *n.*
**trin•i•ty** (trĭn′ĭ-tē) *n., pl.* **-ties. 1.** Any 3 parts in union. **2. Trinity.** The 3-person godhead of orthodox Christian belief.
**trin•ket** (trĭng′kĭt) *n.* **1.** Any small ornament, esp. a piece of jewelry. **2.** A trivial thing.
**tri•o** (trē′ō) *n., pl.* **-os. 1.** A group of 3. **2. a.** A musical composition for 3 performers. **b.** The people who perform this composition.
**trip** (trĭp) *n.* **1.** A journey. **2.** A stumble. —*v.* **tripped, tripping. 1.** To stumble or cause to stumble. **2.** To move quickly or nimbly.
**trip•le** (trĭp′əl) *adj.* **1.** Of 3 parts. **2.** Thrice multiplied. —*v.* **-led, -ling.** To make or become 3 times as great. **—trip′ly** *adv.*
**trip•let** (trĭp′lĭt) *n.* **1.** A set of 3 of 1 kind. **2.** One of 3 siblings born together.
**trip•li•cate** (trĭp′lĭ-kĭt) *adj.* Triple. —*n.* One of a set of 3 copies.
**tri•pod** (trī′pŏd′) *n.* A 3-legged stool, support, etc.
**trite** (trīt) *adj.* **triter, tritest.** Overused and commonplace; lacking originality. **—trite′ness** *n.*
**tri•umph** (trī′əmf) *v.* **1.** To be victorious. **2.** To rejoice over a victory. —*n.* **1.** Victory; success. **2.** Exultation derived from victory. **—tri•um′phal** *adj.* **—tri•um′phant** *adj.* **—tri•um′phant•ly** *adv.*
**triv•et** (trĭv′ĭt) *n.* A metal stand under a hot dish.

**triv•i•al** (trĭv′ē-əl) *adj.* **1.** Trifling. **2.** Ordinary. **—triv′i•a** *pl.n.* **—triv′i•al′i•ty** *n.* **—triv′i•al•ly** *adv.*

**trod** (trŏd) *v.* p.t. & a p.p. of **tread.**

**trod•den** (trŏd′n) *v.* A p.p. of **tread.**

**troll** (trōl) *n.* A supernatural creature in Scandinavian folklore.

**trol•ley** (trŏl′ē) *n., pl.* **-leys. 1.** A streetcar. **2.** A carriage suspended from an overhead track.

**trom•bone** (trŏm-bōn′, trəm-, trŏm′-bōn′) *n.* A low-pitched brass musical instrument. **—trom•bon′ist** *n.*

**troop** (tro͞op) *n.* **1.** A group of people, animals, or things. **2. troops.** Military units. *—v.* To move as a throng. **—troop′er** *n.*

**tro•phy** (trō′fē) *n., pl.* **-phies.** A prize received as a symbol of victory.

**trop•ic** (trŏp′ĭk) *n.* **1.** One of 2 latitudes north and south of the equator that are the boundaries of the Torrid Zone. **2. tropics.** The region of the earth's surface lying between these latitudes. **—trop′i•cal** *adj.*

**trot** (trŏt) *n.* **1.** A gait of a 4-footed animal. **2.** A gait faster than a walk. *—v.* **trotted, trotting. 1.** To move at a trot. **2.** To proceed rapidly. **—trot′ter** *n.*

**troub•le** (trŭb′əl) *n.* **1.** Severe distress, affliction, or danger. **2.** A disturbance or annoyance. **3.** Pain, disease, or malfunction. *—v.* **-led, -ling. 1.** To afflict with pain or discomfort. **2.** To perturb. **3.** To inconvenience. **4.** To take pains. **—troub′le•some** *adj.*

**trough** (trôf, trŏf) *n.* **1.** A long, narrow receptacle, esp. for water or feed for animals. **2.** A long, narrow depression.

**trounce** (trouns) *v.* **trounced, trouncing. 1.** To thrash. **2.** To beat decisively.

**troupe** (tro͞op) *n.* A company, esp. of touring performers. **—troup′er** *n.*

**trou•sers** (trou′zərz) *pl.n.* A 2-legged outer garment covering the body from the waist to the ankles.

**trove** (trōv) *n.* Something of value discovered or found.

**trow•el** (trou′əl) *n.* **1.** A flat-bladed hand tool for spreading cement, mortar, etc. **2.** A small gardening implement with a scoop-shaped blade.

**tru•ant** (tro͞o′ənt) *n.* One who is absent without permission, esp. from school. *—adj.* **1.** Absent without permission. **2.** Lazy or neglectful. **—tru′an•cy** *n.*

**truce** (tro͞os) *n.* An agreement to cease hostilities temporarily.

**truck** (trŭk) *n.* **1.** A heavy automotive vehicle for transporting loads. **2.** A 2-wheeled hand barrow. *—v.* To transport by or drive a truck.

**truc•u•lent** (trŭk′yə-lənt) *adj.* **1.** Savage and cruel; fierce. **2.** Defiant. **—truc′u•lence** *n.*

**trudge** (trŭj) *v.* **trudged, trudging.** To walk wearily; plod. *—n.* A long, tedious walk. **—trudg′er** *n.*

**true** (tro͞o) *adj.* **truer, truest. 1.** Consistent with fact. **2.** Correct. **3.** Genuine. **4.** Faithful. *—adv.* **1.** Rightly; truthfully. **2.** Exactly. **—tru′ly** *adv.*

**tru•ism** (tro͞o′ĭz′əm) *n.* An obvious truth.

**trum•pet** (trŭm′pĭt) *n.* A brass instrument consisting of a long tube ending in a flared bell. *—v.* **1.** To play a trumpet. **2.** To give forth a resounding call. **—trum′pet•er** *n.*

**trun•cate** (trŭng′kāt′) *v.* **-cated, -cating.** To shorten by cutting. **—trun•ca′tion** *n.*

**trunk** (trŭngk) *n.* **1.** The main stem of a tree. **2.** The human body excluding the head and limbs. **3.** A main body of anything. **4.** A large packing case used as luggage or for storage. **5.** A covered compartment of an automobile. **6.** A flexible snout, esp. of an elephant. **7. trunks.** Shorts worn for swimming or athletics.

**truss** (trŭs) *n.* **1.** A supportive device worn to prevent enlargement of a hernia. **2.** A framework used to support a roof, bridge, etc. *—v.* **1.** To tie up or bind. **2.** To support with a truss.

**trust** (trŭst) *n.* **1.** Firm reliance; confident belief. **2.** Custody; care. **3.** One committed into the care of another. **4.** The condition of having confidence placed in one; responsibility. **5.** Future hope. **6.** A legal title to property held by 1 party for the benefit of another. **7.** An often monopolistic combination of firms. *—v.* **1.** To rely; depend. **2.** To hope. **3.** To expect; assume. **4.** To believe. **5.** To entrust. **6.** To extend credit to. *—adj.* Maintained in trust. **—trust′ful** *adj.* **—trust′wor′thy** *adj.*

**trus•tee** (trŭ-stē′) *n.* **1.** A person holding and administering a trust. **2.** A member of a board that directs an institution. **—trus•tee'ship'** *n.*

**truth** (trōōth) *n., pl.* **truths. 1.** Conformity to knowledge, fact, etc. **2.** Fidelity to a standard. **3.** Reality. **4.** A true statement. **5.** Sincerity; integrity. **—truth'ful** *adj.* **—truth'ful•ly** *adv.* **—truth'ful•ness** *n.*

**try** (trī) *v.* **tried, trying. 1.** To test. **2. a.** To examine by judicial process. **b.** To put on trial. **3.** To subject to great strain; tax. **4.** To attempt. *—n., pl.* **tries.** An attempt; effort. **—try'ing** *adj.*

**tryst** (trĭst) *n.* **1.** An agreement between lovers to meet. **2.** The arranged meeting place.

**tub** (tŭb) *n.* **1.** A round, open, flat-bottomed vessel. **2.** A bathtub.

**tu•ba** (t/y/ōō'bə) *n.* A large brass musical wind instrument.

**tube** (t/y/ōōb) *n.* **1.** A hollow cylinder for fluids **2.** A flexible cylindrical container for pigments, toothpaste, etc. **—tu'bu•lar** *adj.*

**tu•ber** (t/y/ōō'bər) *n.* A swollen, usually underground stem, as a potato. **—tu'ber•ous** *adj.*

**tuck** (tŭk) *v.* **1.** To make folds in. **2.** To turn in the end or edge of. **3.** To draw in; contract. *—n.* A flattened pleat or fold.

**Tues•day** (t/y/ōōz'dē, -dā') *n.* The 3rd day of the week.

**tuft** (tŭft) *n.* A cluster of yarn, hair, grass, etc., held or growing close together.

**tug** (tŭg) *v.* **tugged, tugging. 1.** To pull at vigorously. **2.** To move by pulling with great effort. *—n.* **1.** A strong pull. **2.** A tugboat.

**tug•boat** (tŭg'bōt') *n.* A powerful small boat for towing larger vessels.

**tu•i•tion** (t/y/ōō-ĭsh'ən) *n.* A fee for instruction.

**tum•ble** (tŭm'bəl) *v.* **-bled, -bling. 1.** To perform acrobatic feats. **2.** To fall or roll end over end. **3.** To fall headlong. **4.** To cause to fall; bring down. *—n.* A fall.

**tum•bler** (tŭm'blər) *n.* **1.** An acrobat. **2.** A drinking glass having no handle or stem. **3.** The part in a lock that engages the bolt.

**tu•mid** (t/y/ōō'mĭd) *adj.* **1.** Swollen. **2.** Bombastic. **—tu•mid'i•ty** *n.*

**tu•mor** (t/y/ōō'mər) *n.* A noninflammatory bodily growth.

**tu•mult** (t/y/ōō'mŭlt') *n.* Din and commotion. **—tu•mul'tu•ous** *adj.*

**tun•dra** (tŭn'drə) *n.* A treeless area of arctic regions.

**tune** (t/y/ōōn) *n.* **1.** A simple arrangement of pleasing musical tones. **2.** Correct musical pitch or agreement with respect to pitch. **3.** Harmony. *—v.* **tuned, tuning. 1.** To put into tune. **2.** To adjust for maximum performance. **3.** To adjust a radio or television receiver to receive signals. **—tune'ful** *adj.*

**tune•up** (t/y/ōōn'ŭp') *n.* An adjustment of an engine.

**tun•nel** (tŭn'əl) *n.* An underground passage. *—v.* To make a tunnel.

**tur•ban** (tûr'bən) *n.* A headdress made of a scarf wound around the head.

**tur•bid** (tûr'bĭd) *adj.* **1.** Having stirred-up sediment. **2.** In turmoil; muddled. **—tur'bid•ness, tur•bid'i•ty** *n.*

**tur•bine** (tûr'bĭn, -bīn') *n.* A machine that converts the energy of a moving fluid to mechanical power.

**tur•bu•lent** (tûr'byə-lənt) *adj.* **1.** Violently agitated; stormy. **2.** Causing disturbance; unruly. **—tur'bu•lence** *n.*

**tu•reen** (t/y/ōō-rēn') *n.* A broad, covered dish for serving soups, stews, etc.

**turf** (tûrf) *n.* Surface ground covering of grass and roots.

**tur•gid** (tûr'jĭd) *adj.* **1.** Swollen. **2.** Overornate.

**tur•key** (tûr'kē) *n., pl.* **-keys. 1.** A large North American bird. **2.** A foolish person.

**tur•moil** (tûr'moil') *n.* Utter confusion; agitation.

**turn** (tûrn) *v.* **1.** To rotate; revolve. **2.** To shape (something) on a lathe. **3.** To change the position of. **4.** To upset; nauseate. **5.** To change the direction of. **6.** To make a course around. **7.** To direct (the attention, interest, etc.) toward or away from. **8.** To change. **9.** To become. **10.** To depend upon. **11.** To change color. **12.** To sour; ferment. *—n.* **1.** A rotation; revolution. **2.** A change of direction. **3.** A departure or deviation. **4.** An opportunity to do something determined by a scheduled order. **5.** Natural inclination. **6.** A short excursion. **7.** A single wind or convolution.

**turn•pike** (tûrn′pīk′) *n.* A road, esp. a wide highway with tollgates.

**turn•stile** (tûrn′stīl′) *n.* A device used to control passage, consisting of revolving horizontal arms projecting from a central post.

**turn•ta•ble** (tûrn′tā′bəl) *n.* A record player without an amplifier or speakers.

**tur•pen•tine** (tûr′pən-tīn′) *n.* A thin, volatile oil from certain pine trees, used as a paint thinner, solvent, etc.

**tur•pi•tude** (tûr′pĭ-t/y/o͞od′) *n.* Depravity.

**tur•quoise** (tûr′kwoiz′, -koiz′) *n.* **1.** A blue-green mineral valued as a gemstone. **2.** Bluish green.

**tur•ret** (tûr′ĭt) *n.* **1.** A small tower-shaped projection on a building. **2.** A projecting armored structure, usually rotating, for mounted guns.

**tur•tle** (tûr′tl) *n.* A reptile with the body enclosed in a shell.

**tusk** (tŭsk) *n.* A long pointed tooth, as of an elephant or walrus.

**tus•sle** (tŭs′əl) *v.* **-sled, -sling.** To struggle; scuffle. **—tus′sle** *n.*

**tu•te•lage** (t/y/o͞ot′l-ĭj) *n.* **1.** Guardianship. **2.** Instruction.

**tu•tor** (t/y/o͞o′tər) *n.* A private instructor. *—v.* To act as a tutor to. **—tu•to′ri•al** *adj.*

**tux•e•do** (tŭk-sē′dō) *n., pl.* **-dos** or **-does.** A formal men's suit worn with a bow tie.

**twang** (twăng) *v.* **1.** To emit or cause to emit a sharp, vibrating sound. **2.** To utter with a nasal tone. *—n.* **1.** A sharp, vibrating sound. **2.** A nasal tone of voice. **—twang′y** *adj.*

**tweak** (twēk) *v.* To pinch or twist sharply. **—tweak** *n.*

**tweed** (twēd) *n.* A rough-textured woolen fabric. **—tweed′y** *adj.*

**tweez•ers** (twē′zərz) *pl.n.* A small pincerlike tool.

**twelve** (twĕlv) *n.* The cardinal number written 12. **—twelve** *adj. & pron.* **—twelfth** *n. & adj.*

**twen•ty** (twĕn′tē) *n.* The cardinal number written 20. **—twen′ty** *adj. & pron.* **—twen′ti•eth** *n. & adj.*

**twice** (twīs) *adv.* Two times; doubled.

**twig** (twĭg) *n.* A small branch.

**twi•light** (twī′līt′) *n.* **1.** The time interval during which the sun is at a small angle below the horizon. **2.** The illumination of the atmosphere during this interval.

**twill** (twĭl) *n.* A fabric with diagonal parallel ribs.

**twin** (twĭn) *n.* **1.** One of 2 siblings born together. **2.** One of 2 identical things. **—twin** *adj.*

**twine** (twīn) *v.* **twined, twining. 1.** To twist together. **2.** To encircle. *—n.* A strong cord of threads twisted together.

**twinge** (twĭnj) *n.* A sharp and sudden physical or emotional pain.

**twin•kle** (twĭng′kəl) *v.* **-kled, -kling.** To shine with slight, intermittent gleams. *—n.* **1.** A slight, intermittent gleam of light. **2.** A sparkle of delight in the eye.

**twirl** (twûrl) *v.* To spin. **—twirl** *n.*

**twist** (twĭst) *v.* **1.** To entwine (2 or more threads) so as to produce a single strand. **2.** To coil about. **3.** To impart or assume a spiral shape. **4.** To turn or break by turning. **5.** To wrench or sprain. **6.** To distort the meaning of. **7.** To rotate or turn. *—n.* **1.** A spin or twirl. **2.** A spiral curve or turn. **3.** A sprain or wrench. **4.** An unexpected change. **—twist′er** *n.*

**twitch** (twĭch) *v.* To move or cause to move jerkily. *—n.* A sudden involuntary muscular movement.

**two** (to͞o) *n.* The cardinal number written 2. **—two** *adj. & pron.*

**ty•coon** (tī-ko͞on′) *n.* A wealthy and powerful businessperson.

**tyke** (tīk) *n.* A small child.

**type** (tīp) *n.* **.1** A category of persons or things sharing common distinguishing characteristics. **2.** One belonging to such a category. **3.** An example. **4. a.** A small metal block bearing a raised character, used in printing. **b.** Such pieces collectively. *—v.* **typed, typing. 1.** To typewrite. **2.** To classify.

**type•writ•er** (tīp′rī′tər) *n.* A keyboard machine that prints characters on paper. **—type′write′** *v.*

**ty•phoon** (tī-fo͞on′) *n.* A hurricane of the western Pacific.

**typ•i•cal** (tĭp′ĭ-kəl) *adj.* **1.** Exhibiting the characteristics peculiar to a kind or category. **2.** Characteristic. **—typ'i•cal•ly** *adv.*

**typ•i•fy** (tĭp'ə-fī') *v.* **-fied, -fying.** To serve as an example of.

**ty•pog•ra•phy** (tī-pŏg'rə-fē) *n.* **1.** The composition of printed material from movable type. **2.** The arrangement and appearance of such matter. **—ty•pog'ra•pher** *n.* **—ty'po•graph'i•cal** *adj.*

**tyr•an•ny** (tĭr'ə-nē) *n., pl.* **-nies. 1.** A government in which a single ruler wields absolute, oppressive power. **2.** Absolute power, esp. when exercised unjustly or cruelly. **3.** A cruel or despotic act. **—ty•ran'ni•cal** *adj.* **—tyr'an•nize'** *v.*

**ty•rant** (tī'rənt) *n.* **1.** A harsh, cruel, despotic ruler; an oppressor. **2.** Any despotic person.

**ty•ro** (tī'rō) *n., pl.* **-ros.** A beginner.

# — U —

**u, U** (yōō) *n.* The 21st letter of the English alphabet.

**u•biq•ui•tous** (yōō-bĭk'wĭ-təs) *adj.* Being everywhere at the same time. **—u•biq'ui•tous•ly** *adv.* **—u•biq'ui•ty** *n.*

**ud•der** (ŭd'ər) *n.* The mammary organ of cows, goats, etc.

**ug•ly** (ŭg'lē) *adj.* **-lier, -liest. 1.** Unsightly. **2.** Repulsive or offensive. **—ug'li•ness** *n.*

**u•kase** (yōō-kās', -kāz', yōō'kās', -kāz') *n.* **1.** A proclamation of the czar having the force of law in Russia. **2.** An authoritative decree.

**u•ku•le•le** (/y/ōō'kə-lā'lē) *n.* A small 4-stringed guitar.

**ul•cer** (ŭl'sər) *n.* An inflammatory lesion, as on the skin. **—ul'cer•ate'** *v.*

**ul•na** (ŭl'nə) *n.,pl.* **-nae** (-nē') or **-nas.** The forearm bone on the side opposite the thumb. **—ul'nar** *adj.*

**ul•te•ri•or** (ŭl'tîr'ē-ər) *adj.* **1.** Beyond what is evident or admitted. **2.** Beyond or outside a certain area or region. **—ul'te'ri•or•ly** *adv.*

**ul•ti•mate** (ŭl'tə-mĭt) *adj.* **1.** Final; conclusive. **2.** Fundamental; elemental. **—ul'ti•mate** *n.* **—ul'ti•mate•ly** *adv.*

**ul•ti•ma•tum** (ŭl'tə-mā'təm, -mä'-) *n., pl.* **-tums** or **-ta.** A final demand or offer.

**ul•tra•vi•o•let** (ŭl'trə-vī'ə-lĭt) *adj.* Of the range of radiation wavelengths beyond violet in the visible spectrum to the x-ray region. **—ul'tra•vi'o•let** *n.*

**um•bil•i•cus** (ŭm-bĭl'ĭ-kəs, ŭm'bə-lī'kəs) *n.* The navel. **—um'bil'i•cal** *adj.*

**um•brage** (ŭm'brĭj) *n.* Offense.

**um•brel•la** (ŭm-brĕl'ə) *n.* A device consisting of a cloth cover on a collapsible frame mounted on a handle, for protection from the weather.

**um•pire** (ŭm'pīr') *n.* A judge, esp. one who rules in sports. **—um'pire'** *v.*

**un•a•bashed** (ŭn'ə-băsht') *adj.* **1.** Not embarrassed; poised. **2.** Not disguised; open. **—un'a•bash'ed•ly** *adv.*

**un•a•bat•ed** (ŭn'ə-bā'tĭd) *adj.* At original full force. **—un'a•bat'ed•ly** *adv.*

**un•a•ble** (ŭn-ā'bəl) *adj.* **1.** Lacking the necessary power or authority. **2.** Lacking the necessary ability or competence.

**un•a•bridged** (ŭn'ə-brĭjd') *adj.* Having the full original content; not shortened.

**un•ac•count•a•ble** (ŭn'ə-koun'tə-bəl) *adj.* Inexplicable; mysterious. **—un'ac•count'a•bly** *adv.*

**un•ac•cus•tomed** (ŭn'ə-kŭs'təmd) *adj.* Unfamiliar or unusual.

**un•af•fect•ed** (ŭn'ə-fĕk'tĭd) *adj.* Natural; sincere. **—un'af•fect'ed•ly** *adv.*

**u•nan•i•mous** (yōō-năn'ə-məs) *adj.* **1.** Sharing the same opinion. **2.** Based on complete agreement. **—u'na•nim'i•ty** *n.* **—u•nan'i•mous•ly** *adv.*

**un•as•sum•ing** (ŭn'ə-sōō'mĭng) *adj.* Modest. **—un'as•sum'ing•ly** *adv.*

**un•be•known** (ŭn'bĭ-nōn') *adj.* Occurring or existing without the knowledge of; unknown.

**un•bound•ed** (ŭn-boun'dĭd) *adj.* Having no limits. **—un'bound'ed•ly** *adv.*

**un•bowed** (ŭn-boud') *adj.* Not subdued.

**un•bri•dled** (ŭn-brīd'ld) *adj.* Unrestrained; uncontrolled.

**un•bur•den** (ŭn-bûr'dn) *v.* To relieve, as from a burden.

**un•can•ny** (ŭn-kăn'ē) *adj.* **-nier, -niest. 1.** Arousing wonder and fear; strange. **2.** So perceptive as to seem supernatural. **—un'can'ni•ly** *adv.*

**un•cer•tain** (ŭn-sûr'tn) *adj.* **1.** Doubtful; not sure. **2.** Not definite; vague. **3.** Subject to change; variable. **—un′cer′tain•ly** *adv.* **—un′cer′tain•ty** *n.*

**un•civ•il** (ŭn-sĭv′əl) *adj.* Impolite; rude. **—un′civ′il•ly** *adv.*

**un•cle** (ŭng′kəl) *n.* **1.** The brother of one's mother or father. **2.** The husband of one's aunt.

**un•con•scion•a•ble** (ŭn-kŏn′shə-nə-bəl) *adj.* Unreasonable; immoderate; excessive. **—un′con′scion•a•bly** *adv.*

**un•con•scious** (ŭn-kŏn′shəs) *adj.* **1.** Without conscious awareness, esp. psychological rather than physiological. **2.** Temporarily lacking consciousness. **—un′con′scious•ly** *adv.* **—un′con′scious•ness** *n.*

**un•couth** (ŭn-ko͞oth′) *adj.* **1.** Not refined; crude. **2.** Awkward.

**unc•tion** (ŭngk′shən) *n.* **1.** The act of anointing as part of a religious or healing ritual. **2.** Something that soothes; balm.

**unc•tu•ous** (ŭngk′cho͞o-əs) *adj.* **1.** Oily; greasy. **2.** Showing excessive, insincere earnestness. **—unc′tu•ous•ly** *adv.* **—unc′tu•ous•ness** *n.*

**un•daunt•ed** (ŭn-dôn′tĭd, -dän′-) *adj.* Resolute; fearless. **—un′daunt′ed•ly** *adv.*

**un•de•ni•a•ble** (ŭn′dĭ-nī′ə-bəl) *adj.* **1.** Irrefutable. **2.** Excellent. **—un′de•ni′a•bly** *adv.*

**un•der** (ŭn′dər) *prep.* **1.** In a lower position or place than. **2.** Beneath the surface of. **3.** Less than; smaller than. **—un′der** *adj. & adv.*

**un•der•cov•er** (ŭn′dər-kŭv′ər) *adj.* Secret.

**un•der•cut** (ŭn′dər-kŭt′) *v.* **1.** To make a cut under or below. **2.** To sell at a lower price than (a competitor). **—un′der•cut′** *n.*

**un•der•de•vel•oped** (ŭn′dər-dĭ-vĕl′əpt) *adj.* **1.** Immature. **2.** Economically backward.

**un•der•dog** (ŭn′dər-dôg′, -dŏg′) *n.* One who is expected to lose a contest.

**un•der•go** (ŭn′dər-gō′) *v.* **1.** To experience; be subjected to. **2.** To endure; suffer.

**un•der•grad•u•ate** (ŭn′dər-grăj′o͞o-ĭt) *n.* A college student who has not yet received a degree.

**un•der•ground** (ŭn′dər-ground′) *adj.* **1.** Below the surface of the earth. **2.** Hidden; secret. *—n.* A clandestine subversive organization. *—adv.* **1.** Below the surface of the earth. **2.** In secret; stealthily.

**un•der•hand** (ŭn′dər-hănd′) *adj.* Deceitful; sneaky. *—adv.* Slyly; secretly.

**un•der•hand•ed** (ŭn′dər-hăn′dĭd) *adj.* Sly; secret; underhand. **—un′der•hand′ed•ly** *adv.* **—un′der•hand′ed•ness** *n.*

**un•der•mine** (ŭn′dər-mīn′) *v.* **1.** To dig a tunnel beneath. **2.** To weaken or impair by or as if by wearing away.

**un•der•neath** (ŭn′dər-nēth′) *adv.* In a place beneath; below. *—prep.* Beneath; below; under.

**un•der•pin•ning** (ŭn′dər-pĭn′ĭng) *n.* Often **underpinnings.** Something serving as a support or foundation.

**un•der•score** (ŭn′dər-skôr′, -skōr′) *v.* **-scored, -scoring. 1.** To underline. **2.** To emphasize or stress. **—un′der•score′** *n.*

**un•der•stand** (ŭn′dər-stănd′) *v.* **-stood** (-sto͝od), **-standing.** To perceive and comprehend the nature and significance of; know. **—un′der•stand′a•ble** *adj.*

**un•der•stand•ing** (ŭn′dər-stăn′dĭng) *n.* Comprehension; discernment. *—adj.* Compassionate and sympathetic.

**un•der•state** (ŭn′dər-stāt′) *v.* **-stated, -stating. 1.** To state with less truth than the facts warrant. **2.** To express with restraint, esp. ironically. **—un′der•state′ment** *n.*

**un•der•stood** (ŭn′dər-sto͝od′) *adj.* **1.** Agreed upon. **2.** Not expressed in writing; implied.

**un•der•stud•y** (ŭn′dər-stŭd′ē) *n., pl.* **-ies.** A performer trained to substitute for the regular performer.

**un•der•take** (ŭn′dər-tāk′) *v.* **1.** To take upon oneself. **2.** To pledge or commit oneself to doing (something).

**un•der•tak•er** (ŭn′dər-tā′kər) *n.* One who prepares the dead for burial or cremation and makes funeral arrangements.

**un•der•tow** (ŭn′dər-tō′) *n.* The seaward pull of waves breaking on a shore.

**un•der•world** (ŭn′dər-wûrld′) *n.* The part of society engaged in crime and vice.

**un•do** (ŭn-do͞o′) *v.* **1.** To reverse; cancel; annul. **2.** To untie or loosen. **3.** To ruin or destroy.

**un•doubt•ed** (ŭn-dou′tĭd) *adj.* Accepted as beyond question. **—un•doubt′ed•ly** *adv.*

**un•due** (ŭn-d/y/o͞o′) *adj.* **1.** Excessive. **2.** Not just, proper, or legal. **—un•du′ly** *adv.*

**un•du•late** (ŭn′jə-lāt′, ŭn′d/y/ə-) *v.* **-lated, -lating.** To move or cause to move in a smooth wavelike motion. **—un′du•lant** *adj.* **—un′du•la′tion** *n.*

**un•earth** (ŭn-ûrth′) *v.* To bring to public notice; reveal.

**un•eas•y** (ŭn-ē′zē) *adj.* **1.** Lacking ease, comfort, etc. **2.** Awkward in manner; constrained. **—un′eas′i•ly** *adv.* **—un′-eas′i•ness** *n.*

**un•e•quiv•o•cal** (ŭn′ĭ-kwĭv′ə-kəl) *adj.* Clear; plain. **—un′e•quiv′o•cal•ly** *adv.*

**un•err•ing** (ŭn-ûr′ĭng, -ĕr′-) *adj.* Consistently accurate; without error. **—un′-err′ing•ly** *adv.*

**un•ex•pect•ed** (ŭn′ĭk-spĕk′tĭd) *adj.* Coming without warning; unforeseen. **—un′ex•pect′ed•ly** *adv.* **—un′ex•pect′ed•ness** *n.*

**un•fail•ing** (ŭn-fā′lĭng) *adj.* **1.** Inexhaustible. **2.** Constant; reliable. **—un′fail′-ing•ly** *adv.*

**un•fair** (ŭn-fâr′) *adj.* Not fair, right, or just. **—un′fair′ly** *adv.* **—un′fair′ness** *n.*

**un•faith•ful** (ŭn-fāth′fəl) *adj.* **1.** Disloyal. **2.** Not reflecting the original; inaccurate. **—un′faith′ful•ly** *adv.* **—un′-faith′ful•ness** *n.*

**un•fit** (ŭn-fĭt′) *adj.* **1.** Inappropriate. **2.** Unqualified. **3.** Not in good health. **—un′fit′ly** *adv.* **—un′fit′ness** *n.*

**un•fold** (ŭn-fōld′) *v.* **1.** To open and spread out. **2.** To reveal or be revealed gradually.

**un•for•tu•nate** (ŭn-fôr′chə-nĭt) *adj.* **1.** Causing misfortune; disastrous. **2.** Regrettable; deplorable. *—n.* A victim of disaster, poverty, etc. **—un•for′tu•nate•ly** *adv.* **—un•for′tu•nate•ness** *n.*

**un•friend•ly** (ŭn-frĕnd′lē) *adj.* Not disposed to friendship; hostile. **—un′-friend′li•ness** *n.*

**un•god•ly** (ŭn-gŏd′lē) *adj.* **-lier, -liest. 1.** Not revering God. **2.** Sinful; wicked. **3.** Outrageous. **—un′god′li•ness** *n.*

**un•guent** (ŭng′gwənt) *n.* Salve; ointment.

**un•hap•py** (ŭn-hăp′ē) *adj.* **1.** Sad. **2.** Unlucky. **3.** Inappropriate. **—un•hap′pi•ly** *adv.* **—un•hap′pi•ness** *n.*

**un•ho•ly** (ŭn-hō′lē) *adj.* **1.** Not consecrated. **2.** Wicked; immoral. **3.** Outrageous.

**u•ni•corn** (yo͞o′nĭ-kôrn′) *n.* A fabled horselike creature with a single horn on its forehead.

**u•ni•form** (yo͞o′nə-fôrm′) *adj.* **1.** Consistent. **2.** Being the same everywhere; identical. *—n.* An outfit identifying those who wear it as members of a special group, organization, etc. **—u′ni•for′mi•ty, u′ni•form′ness** *n.* **—u′ni•form′ly** *adv.*

**u•ni•fy** (yo͞o′nə-fī′) *v.* **-fied, -fying.** To make into a unit; consolidate. **—u′ni•fi•ca′tion** *n.* **—u′ni•fi′er** *n.*

**u•ni•lat•er•al** (yo͞o′nə-lăt′ər-əl) *adj.* **1.** Of only one side. **2.** Having only one side. **—u′ni•lat′er•al•ly** *adv.*

**un•im•peach•a•ble** (ŭn′ĭm-pē′chə-bəl) *adj.* Beyond doubt or reproach. **—un′-im•peach′a•bly** *adv.*

**un•ion** (yo͞on′yən) *n.* **1.** The act of uniting. **2.** A combination; an alliance or confederation. **3.** A labor organization for the purpose of serving class interests with respect to wages, etc. *—adj.* Of a union, esp. a labor union. **—un′-ion•i•za′tion** *n.* **—un′ion•ize′** *v.*

**u•nique** (yo͞o-nēk′) *adj.* Being the only one, esp. in kind, excellence, etc. **—u•nique′ly** *adv.* **—u•nique′ness** *n.*

**u•ni•son** (yo͞o′nĭ-sən, -zən) *n.* Agreement; concord.

**u•nit** (yo͞o′nĭt) *n.* A thing, group, person, etc., regarded as part of a whole.

**u•nite** (yo͞o-nīt′) *v.* **united, uniting.** To bring together or become joined, formed, or combined into a unit.

**u•ni•ty** (yo͞o′nĭ-tē) *n., pl.* **-ties. 1.** The state of being one. **2.** Accord, as of aims, feelings, etc.; agreement.

**u•ni•ver•sal** (yo͞o′nə-vûr′səl) *adj.* **1.** Of, for, done by, or affecting all. **2.** Of the universe; cosmic. **—u′ni•ver•sal′i•ty** *n.* **—u′ni•ver′sal•ly** *adv.*

**u•ni•verse** (yo͞o′nə-vûrs′) *n.* All the matter and space that exists, considered as a whole.

**u•ni•ver•si•ty** (yo͞o′nə-vûr′sĭ-tē) *n., pl.* **-ties.** An institution that includes a graduate school, professional schools, and an undergraduate division.

**un•kempt** (ŭn-kĕmpt′) *adj.* Messy.

**un•less** (ŭn-lĕs′) *conj.* Except on the condition that.

**un•like** (ŭn-līk′) *adj.* Different; dissimilar.

**un•like•ly** (ŭn-līk′lē) *adj.* **1.** Improbable. **2.** Likely to fail. **—un•like′li•hood′, un•like′li•ness** *n.*

**un•load** (ŭn-lōd′) *v.* **1.** To remove the load or cargo from. **2.** To remove the charge from (a firearm). **3.** To dispose of.

**un•mis•tak•a•ble** (ŭn′mĭ-stā′kə-bəl) *adj.* Obvious; evident. **—un′mis•tak′a•bly** *adv.*

**un•nerve** (ŭn-nûrv′) *v.* **-nerved, -nerving.** To cause to lose courage, composure, etc.

**un•pack** (ŭn-păk′) *v.* **1.** To remove the contents of (a suitcase, etc.). **2.** To remove from a container.

**un•rav•el** (ŭn-răv′əl) *v.* **1.** To undo (a knitted fabric). **2.** To solve.

**un•rest** (ŭn-rĕst′) *n.* Uneasiness; disquiet.

**un•ru•ly** (ŭn-ro͞o′lē) *adj.* **-lier, -liest.** Difficult to discipline or control. **—un•ru′li•ness** *n.*

**un•sa•vor•y** (ŭn-sā′və-rē) *adj.* **1.** Distasteful; disagreeable. **2.** Morally offensive. **—un•sa′vor•i•ness** *n.*

**un•set•tled** (ŭn-sĕt′ld) *adj.* **1.** Disordered; disturbed. **2.** Not determined or resolved.

**un•sight•ly** (ŭn-sīt′lē) *adj.* Offensive to look at; not attractive. **—un′sight′li•ness** *n.*

**un•sung** (ŭn-sŭng′) *adj.* **1.** Not sung. **2.** Not honored; uncelebrated.

**un•tan•gle** (ŭn-tăng′gəl) *v.* **1.** To disentangle. **2.** To clarify; resolve.

**un•tie** (ŭn-tī′) *v.* **1.** To undo or loosen (a knot). **2.** To free from something that binds or restrains.

**un•til** (ŭn-tĭl′) *prep.* **1.** Up to the time of. **2.** Before a specified time. *—conj.* **1.** Up to the time that. **2.** Before. **3.** To the point or extent that.

**un•to** (ŭn′to͞o) *prep.* To.

**un•told** (ŭn-tōld′) *adj.* **1.** Not revealed. **2.** Without limit.

**un•to•ward** (ŭn-tôrd′, -tōrd′) *adj.* **1.** Unfortunate. **2.** Hard to control.

**un•true** (ŭn-tro͞o′) *adj.* **1.** False. **2.** Disloyal. **—un•truth′** *n.* **—un•truth′ful** *adj.* **—un•truth′ful•ness** *n.*

**un•used** (ŭn-yo͞ozd′) *adj.* **1.** Not used or never having been used. **2.** Not accustomed.

**un•u•su•al** (ŭn-yo͞o′zho͞o-əl) *adj.* Not usual, common, or ordinary.

**un•veil** (ŭn-vāl′) *v.* **1.** To remove a veil from. **2.** To disclose or reveal.

**un•wield•y** (ŭn-wēl′dē) *adj.* **-ier, -iest.** Difficult to carry or handle because of shape or size.

**un•wind** (ŭn-wīnd′) *v.* **1.** To open (something rolled up). **2.** To become free of tension, etc.

**un•wise** (ŭn-wīz′) *adj.* Lacking wisdom; foolish. **—un•wise′ly** *adv.*

**un•wit•ting** (ŭn-wĭt′ĭng) *adj.* **1.** Not knowing; unaware. **2.** Not intended or intentional. **—un•wit′ting•ly** *adv.*

**un•wont•ed** (ŭn-wôn′tĭd, -wōn′-, -wŭn′-) *adj.* Not habitual or ordinary.

**un•wor•thy** (ŭn-wûr′*th*ē) *adj.* **1.** Not deserving. **2.** Not suiting or befitting. **—un•wor′thi•ness** *n.*

**up** (ŭp) *adv.* **1.** From a lower to a higher position. **2.** In or toward a higher position. **3.** From a reclining to an upright position. **4.** Out of bed. *—prep.* **1.** Toward or at a point farther along. **2.** In a direction toward the source of. *—n.* A rise or ascent. *—v.* **upped, upping.** To increase or improve.

**up•braid** (ŭp-brād′) *v.* To scold or chide vehemently. **—up•braid′er** *n.*

**up•date** (ŭp-dāt′) *v.* **-dated, -dating.** To make conform to the latest facts or style. *—n.* Information that updates.

**up•heav•al** (ŭp-hē′vəl) *n.* A sudden and violent disruption.

**up•hill** (ŭp′hĭl′) *adj.* Going up a hill or slope. *—n.* An upward incline. *—adv.* (ŭp′hĭl′). Toward higher ground; upward.

**up•hold** (ŭp-hōld′) *v.* To support.

**up•hol•ster** (ŭp-hōl′stər) *v.* To supply furniture with stuffing, covering fabric, etc. **—up•hol′ster•er** *n.* **—up•hol′ster•y** *n.*

**up•keep** (ŭp′kēp′) *n.* Maintenance in proper condition.

**up•lift** (ŭp-lĭft′) *v.* To raise to a higher social, intellectual, or moral level. **—up′lift′** *n.*

**up•on** (ə-pŏn′, ə-pôn′) *prep.* On.

**up•per** (ŭp′ər) *adj.* Higher in place, position, or rank. **—up′per•most′** *adj.*

**up•per•case** (ŭp′ər-kās′) *adj.* Pertaining to or printed in capital letters. **—up′-per•case′** *v.*

**up•pi•ty** (ŭp′ĭ-tē) *adj.* Snobbish or arrogant.

**up•right** (ŭp′rīt′) *adj.* **1.** Erect. **2.** Morally respectable; honorable. **—up′right′-ness** *n.*

**up•ris•ing** (ŭp′rī′zĭng) *n.* A revolt; insurrection.

**up•roar** (ŭp′rôr′, -rōr′) *n.* Noisy excitement and confusion; tumult. **—up•roar′i•ous** *adj.* **—up•roar′i•ous•ly** *adv.*

**up•scale** (ŭp′skāl′) *adj.* Of or relating to high-income consumers. *—v.* **-scaled, -scaling.** Upgrade.

**up•set** (ŭp-sĕt′) *v.* **-set, -setting. 1.** To overturn or capsize; tip over. **2.** To disturb the usual or normal functioning of. **3.** To distress or perturb mentally or emotionally. **4.** To defeat unexpectedly. *—n.* (ŭp′sĕt′). **1. a.** An act of upsetting. **b.** The condition of being upset. **2.** A disturbance, disorder, or agitation. **3.** A game or contest in which the favorite is defeated. *—adj.* (ŭp-sĕt′). **1.** Overturned; capsized. **2.** Disordered; disturbed. **3.** Distressed; distraught; agitated. **—up•set′ter** *n.*

**up•shot** (ŭp′shŏt′) *n.* The final result or outcome.

**up•stage** (ŭp′stāj′) *adj.* Located at the rear of a stage. *—adv.* Toward or at the rear of a stage. *—v.* **-staged, -staging.** To divert attention or praise from.

**up•stairs** (ŭp′stârz′) *adv.* In, on, or to an upper floor; up the stairs. *—n.* (ŭp′-stârz′). A floor above the ground level. *—adj.* (ŭp′stârz′). Of an upper floor or floors.

**up•start** (ŭp′stärt′) *n.* A person who attains sudden wealth or prominence, esp. one who becomes arrogant.

**up tight.** Also **up•tight** (ŭp′tīt′) *adj.* Tense; nervous.

**up•ward** (ŭp′wərd) *adv.* Also **up•wards.** In, to, or toward a higher place, level, or position. *—adj.* Ascending.

**u•ra•ni•um** (yo͝o-rā′nē-əm) *n.* A heavy radioactive metallic element.

**U•ra•nus** (yo͝or′ə-nəs, yo͝o-rā′nəs) *n.* The 7th planet from the sun.

**ur•ban** (ûr′bən) *adj.* Of a city or city life. **—ur′ban•i•za′tion** *n.* **—ur′ban•ize′** *v.*

**ur•bane** (ûr-bān′) *adj.* Polite; suave. **—ur•bane′ly** *adv.* **—ur•ban′i•ty** *n.*

**ur•chin** (ûr′chĭn) *n.* A small, mischievous, or needy child.

**urge** (ûrj) *v.* **urged, urging. 1.** To push, force, or drive onward; impel. **2.** To plead with; exhort. *—n.* An irresistible desire, etc.

**ur•gent** (ûr′jənt) *adj.* Calling for immediate action or attention; pressing. **—ur′gen•cy** *n.* **—ur′gent•ly** *adv.*

**u•ri•nate** (yo͝or′ə-nāt′) *v.* **-nated, -nating.** To excrete urine. **—u′ri•na′tion** *n.*

**u•rine** (yo͝or′ĭn) *n.* A solution containing wastes extracted by the kidneys and excreted from the body.

**urn** (ûrn) *n.* **1.** A vase with a pedestal. **2.** A pot used for serving tea or coffee.

**us** (ŭs) *pron.* The objective case of *we.*

**us•age** (yo͞o′sĭj, -zĭj) *n.* **1.** The act or manner of using something. **2.** Customary practice; habitual use. **3.** The actual way the elements of a language are used, interrelated, or pronounced.

**use** (yo͞oz) *v.* **used, using. 1.** To employ for some purpose. **2.** To consume or expend. **3.** To make a habit of. **4.** To exploit. *—n.* (yo͞os). **1.** The act of using. **2.** Usage. **3.** The goal, object, or purpose for which something is used. **—us′a•ble** *adj.* **—us′a•ble•ness** *n.* **—use′ful** *adj.* **—use′ful•ly** *adv.* **—use′ful•ness** *n.* **—use′less** *adj.* **—use′less•ly** *adv.* **—use′less•ness** *n.* **—us′er** *n.*

**ush•er** (ŭsh′ər) *n.* One who escorts people to their seats, as in a theater. **—ush′er** *v.*

**u•su•al** (yo͞o′zho͞o-əl) *adj.* **1.** Ordinary or normal. **2.** Habitual or customary. **—u′su•al•ly** *adv.* **—u′su•al•ness** *n.*

**u•surp** (yo͞o-sûrp′, -zûrp′) *v.* To seize and hold without legal right. **—u′sur•pa′tion** *n.* **—u•surp′er** *n.*

**u•su•ry** (yo͞o′zhə-rē) *n., pl.* **-ries.** The lending of money at an exorbitant rate of interest. **—u′su•rer** *n.* **—u•su′ri•ous** *adj.*

**u•ten•sil** (yo͞o-tĕn′səl) *n.* An instrument or container, esp. one used in a kitchen.

**u•ter•us** (yo͞o′tər-əs) *n.* An organ of female mammals that holds the fertilized ovum during the development of the fetus. **—u′ter•ine** *adj.*

**u•til•i•tar•i•an** (yo͞o-tĭl′ĭ-târ′ē-ən) *adj.* Useful or practical.

**u•til•i•ty** (yo͞o-tĭl′ĭ-tē) *n., pl.* **-ties. 1.** Usefulness. **2.** A public service, such as electricity, water, etc.

**u•til•ize** (yo͞ot′l-īz′) *v.* **-ized, -izing.** To put to use. **—u′til•i•za′tion** *n.*

**ut•most** (ŭt′mōst′) *adj.* Of the highest or greatest degree, amount, or intensity. *—n.* The maximum.

**u•to•pi•a** (yo͞o-tō′pē-ə) *n.* A condition or place of perfection. **—u•to′pi•an** *adj.*

**ut•ter¹** (ŭt′ər) *v.* To express audibly; pronounce; say. **—ut′ter•ance** *n.* **—ut′ter•er** *n.*

**ut•ter²** (ŭt′ər) *adj.* Complete; absolute. **—ut′ter•ly** *adv.*

**u•vu•la** (yo͞o′vyə-lə) *n.* The small mass of tissue that hangs from the soft palate. **—u′vu•lar** *adj.*

# — V —

**v, V** (vē) *n.* The 22nd letter of the English alphabet.

**va•cant** (vā′kənt) *adj.* **1.** Empty. **2.** Not occupied. **3.** Expressionless; blank. **—va′can•cy** *n.* **—va′cant•ly** *adv.*

**va•cate** (vā′kāt′) *v.* **-cated, -cating.** To cease to occupy or hold; give up; leave.

**va•ca•tion** (vā-kā′shən) *n.* An interval of time devoted to rest or relaxation from work, study, etc. *—v.* To take or spend a vacation. **—va•ca′tion•er** *n.*

**vac•ci•nate** (văk′sə-nāt′) *v.* **-nated, -nating.** To inoculate with a disease-producing agent to immunize against a disease. **—vac′ci•na′tion** *n.* **—vac•cine′** *n.*

**vac•il•late** (văs′ə-lāt′) *v.* **-lated, -lating. 1.** To oscillate. **2.** To change one's mind often; waver. **—vac′il•la′tion** *n.* **—vac′il•la′tor** *n.*

**va•cu•i•ty** (vă-kyo͞o′ĭ-tē) *n., pl.* **-ties. 1.** Emptiness. **2.** Emptiness of mind; stupidity. **—vac′u•ous** *adj.* **—vac′u•ous•ly** *adv.*

**vac•u•um** (văk′yo͞o-əm, -yo͞om) *n.* **1.** A space that is empty of matter. **2.** A void.

**vag•a•bond** (văg′ə-bŏnd′) *n.* A person who wanders from place to place; vagrant. **—vag′a•bond′** *adj.*

**va•ga•ry** (vā′gə-rē, və-gâr′ē) *n., pl.* **-ries.** An extravagant or erratic notion or action.

**va•gi•na** (və-jī′nə) *n.* The passage leading from the uterus to the outside of the body. **—vag′i•nal** *adj.*

**va•grant** (vā′grənt) *n.* A person who wanders from place to place and lives by begging, etc.; tramp. **—va′gran•cy** *n.* **—va′grant** *adj.*

**vague** (vāg) *adj.* **vaguer, vaguest. 1.** Not clearly expressed. **2.** Lacking definite form or character. **—vague′ly** *adv.* **—vague′ness** *n.*

**vain** (vān) *adj.* **1.** Unsuccessful; futile. **2.** Conceited. **—vain′ly** *adv.* **—vain′ness** *n.*

**va•lence** (vā′ləns) *n., pl.* **-lences** or **-lencies.** The capacity of something to unite, react, or interact with something else.

**val•et** (vă-lā′, văl′ā) *n.* **1.** A man's male servant. **2.** An employee, as in a hotel, who performs personal services.

**val•iant** (văl′yənt) *adj.* Brave or courageous. **—val′iance, val′ian•cy** *n.* **—val′iant•ly** *adv.*

**val•id** (văl′ĭd) *adj.* **1.** Well-grounded; sound. **2.** Having legal force. **—val′i•date′** *v.* **—val′i•da′tion** *n.* **—va•lid′i•ty** *n.*

**va•lise** (və-lēs′) *n.* A small piece of hand luggage.

**val•ley** (văl′ē) *n., pl.* **-leys.** A region of lowland between mountains or hills.

**val•or** (văl′ər) *n.* Courage; bravery. **—val′or•ous** *adj.* **—val′or•ous•ly** *adv.*

**val•u•a•ble** (văl′yo͞o-ə-bəl, văl′yə-) *adj.* **1.** Having high monetary or material value. **2.** Of importance, use, or service. *—n.* Often **valuables.** A valuable possession. **—val′u•a•bly** *adv.*

**val•ue** (văl′yo͞o) *n.* **1.** Monetary or material worth. **2.** Worth or importance; merit. **3.** A worthwhile principle or quality. *—v.* **-ued, -uing. 1.** To estimate the worth of; appraise. **2.** To prize; esteem. **—val′u•a′tion** *n.*

**valve** (vălv) *n.* A device that regulates gas or liquid flow.

**van** (văn) *n.* A covered truck for transporting goods, etc.

**van•dal** (văn'dl) *n.* One who maliciously destroys property. **—van'dal•ism'** *n.*

**vane** (vān) *n.* A thin wooden or metal plate that pivots on a spindle, used esp. to indicate wind direction.

**van•guard** (văn'gärd) *n.* **1.** The foremost position in an army or fleet. **2.** The leading position in a trend or movement.

**van•ish** (văn'ĭsh) *v.* To disappear or become invisible.

**van•i•ty** (văn'ĭ-tē) *n., pl.* **-ties.** Excessive pride; conceit.

**van•quish** (văng'kwĭsh, văn'-) *v.* To defeat thoroughly; subjugate. **—van'quish•er** *n.*

**van•tage** (văn'tĭj) *n.* Something providing superiority or advantage.

**vap•id** (văp'ĭd) *adj.* Insipid; flat.

**va•por** (vā'pər) *n.* **1.** Any fine particles of matter in the air, as mist, fumes, etc. **2.** The gaseous state of a substance. **—va'por•ize'** *v.* **—va'por•iz'er** *n.* **—va'por•ous** *adj.* **—va'por•ous•ness** *n.*

**var•i•a•ble** (vâr'ē-ə-bəl) *adj.* **1.** Subject to variation; changeable. **2.** Fickle. *—n.* Something that varies. **—var'i•a•bil'i•ty, var'i•a•ble•ness** *n.* **—var'i•a•bly** *adv.*

**var•i•a•tion** (vâr'ē-ā'shən) *n.* **1.** The act, process, or result of varying; change or deviation. **2.** The extent or degree of such change. **3.** Something that is slightly different from another of the same type.

**var•i•e•gat•ed** (vâr'ē-ĭ-gā'tĭd) *adj.* Having a variety of colors.

**va•ri•e•ty** (və-rī'ĭ-tē) *n., pl.* **-ties. 1.** Diversity. **2.** A number of different kinds of things; assortment. **3.** A kind, sort, or form.

**var•i•ous** (vâr'ē-əs) *adj.* **1.** Of different kinds. **2.** More than 1; several. **—var'i•ous•ly** *adv.*

**var•nish** (vär'nĭsh) *n.* An oil-based liquid that dries with a hard, glossy finish. **—var'nish** *v.*

**var•y** (vâr'ē) *v.* **-ied, -ying. 1.** To cause or undergo change. **2.** To give variety to; diversify. **3.** To differ. **—var'i•ance** *n.* **—var'i•ant** *adj. & n.*

**vase** (vās, vāz, väz) *n.* An open container for holding flowers.

**vast** (văst) *adj.* Very great in size; immense. **—vast'ly** *adv.* **—vast'ness** *n.*

**vat** (văt) *n.* A tank or tub used for storing liquids.

**vault**[1] (vôlt) *n.* **1.** An arched structure forming a ceiling or roof. **2.** An arched room, esp. an underground storeroom or burial chamber. *—v.* To construct or cover with a vault.

**vault**[2] (vôlt) *v.* To jump or leap over. *—n.* A leap. **—vault'er** *n.*

**vaunt** (vônt, vŏnt) *v.* **vaunted, vaunting.** To boast; brag. *—n.* A boastful remark.

**veal** (vēl) *n.* The meat of a calf.

**veer** (vîr) *v.* To change direction; swerve. **—veer** *n.*

**veg•e•ta•ble** (vĕj'tə-bəl, vĕj'ĭ-tə-) *n.* **1.** A plant cultivated for an edible part, as roots, leaves, etc. **2.** A plant as distinguished from an animal or mineral. *—adj.* Of plants.

**veg•e•tar•i•an** (vĕj'ĭ-târ'ē-ən) *n.* One whose diet does not include meat. **—veg'e•tar'i•an** *adj.*

**veg•e•tate** (vĕj'ĭ-tāt') *v.* **-tated, -tating. 1.** To grow as a plant does. **2.** To lead a passive existence.

**veg•e•ta•tion** (vĕj'ĭ-tā'shən) *n.* **1.** The process of vegetating. **2.** Plant life collectively. **—veg'e•ta'tive** *adj.*

**ve•he•ment** (vē'ə-mənt) *adj.* **1.** Intense or ardent. **2.** Strong or violent. **—ve'he•mence** *n.* **—ve'he•ment•ly** *adv.*

**ve•hi•cle** (vē'ĭ-kəl) *n.* A device for carrying passengers, goods, etc.; conveyance. **—ve•hic'u•lar** *adj.*

**veil** (vāl) *n.* **1.** A piece of thin fabric worn over the head or face. **2.** Anything that covers or conceals. **—veil** *v.*

**vein** (vān) *n.* **1.** A blood vessel through which blood returns to the heart. **2.** A branching structure forming a leaf's framework or an insect's wing. **3.** Style or mode of expression. *—v.* To fill or mark with veins.

**vel•lum** (vĕl'əm) *n.* **1.** A fine parchment made from the skins of calf, lamb, or kid and used for fine books. **2.** A paper resembling vellum.

**ve•loc•i•ty** (və-lŏs'ĭ-tē) *n., pl.* **-ties.** Rapidity or speed.

**vel•vet** (vĕl′vĭt) *n.* A fabric having a smooth, dense pile. —*adj.* Made of or resembling velvet. **—vel′vet•y** *adj.*

**ve•nal** (vē′nəl) *adj.* Corrupt or corruptible. **—ve•nal′i•ty** *n.*

**ven•dor** (vĕn′dər) *n.* **1.** One that sells or vends. **2.** A vending machine.

**ve•neer** (və-nîr′) *n.* **1.** A thin surface layer covering an inferior material. **2.** A surface show. —*v.* To cover with a veneer.

**ven•er•a•ble** (vĕn′ər-ə-bəl) *adj.* Worthy of reverence or respect. **—ven′er•a•bil′i•ty** *n.* **—ven′er•ate′** *v.* **—ven′er•a′tion** *n.*

**ve•ne•re•al** (və-nîr′ē-əl) *adj.* Of or transmitted by sexual intercourse.

**ven•geance** (vĕn′jəns) *n.* Retaliation or retribution.

**venge•ful** (vĕnj′fəl) *adj.* Desiring or seeking vengeance; vindictive. **—venge′ful•ly** *adv.* **—venge′ful•ness** *n.*

**ven•i•son** (vĕn′ĭ-sən, -zən) *n.* The flesh of a deer used for food.

**ven•om** (vĕn′əm) *n.* **1.** A poisonous secretion of some animals, esp. some snakes or spiders. **2.** Malice; spite. **—ven′om•ous** *adj.*

**vent** (vĕnt) *n.* An opening for the passage of liquids or gases. —*v.* **1.** To give expression to. **2.** To provide with a vent.

**ven•ti•late** (vĕn′tl-āt′) *v.* **-lated, -lating. 1.** To admit fresh air into. **2.** To expose to public discussion. **—ven′ti•la′tion** *n.* **—ven′ti•la′tor** *n.*

**ven•tri•cle** (vĕn′trĭ-kəl) *n.* A cavity or chamber in an organ, esp. either of the main chambers of the heart. **—ven•tric′u•lar** *adj.*

**ven•ture** (vĕn′chər) *n.* A speculative or risky undertaking. —*v.* **-tured, -turing.** To risk; stake. **—ven′tur•er** *n.* **—ven′ture•some, ven′tur•ous** *adj.*

**ven•ue** (vĕn′yo͞o) *n.* **1.** The locality where a crime is committed or a legal action occurs. **2.** The locality of a gathering.

**Ve•nus** (vē′nəs) *n.* The 2nd planet from the sun.

**ve•ra•cious** (və-rā′shəs) *adj.* Honest; truthful. **—ve•ra′cious•ness, ve•rac′i•ty** *n.*

**verb** (vûrb) *n.* A word functioning to express existence, action, or occurrence.

**ver•bal** (vûr′bəl) *adj.* **1.** Of words. **2.** Expressed in speech. **3.** Word for word; literal. **4.** Of a verb. —*n.* A verb functioning as a noun, adjective, or adverb. **—ver′bal•ize′** *v.* **—ver′bal•i•za′tion** *n.* **—ver′bal•ly** *adv.*

**ver•bose** (vər-bōs′) *adj.* Wordy. **—ver•bose′ly** *adv.* **—ver•bose′ness, ver•bos′i•ty** *n.*

**ver•dant** (vûr′dnt) *adj.* **1.** Green with vegetation. **2.** Inexperienced; unsophisticated.

**ver•dict** (vûr′dĭkt) *n.* **1.** The decision reached by a jury. **2.** A conclusion or judgment.

**ver•i•fy** (vĕr′ə-fī′) *v.* **-fied, -fying. 1.** To prove the truth of. **2.** To test the truth of. **—ver′i•fi′a•ble** *adj.* **—ver′i•fi•ca′tion** *n.*

**ver•i•ta•ble** (vĕr′ĭ-tə-bəl) *adj.* Unquestionable; true. **—ver′i•ta•bly** *adv.*

**ver•i•ty** (vĕr′ĭ-tē) *n.* Truth.

**ver•mil•ion** (vər-mĭl′yən) *n.* A bright red. **—ver•mil′ion** *adj.*

**ver•min** (vûr′mĭn) *n., pl.* **vermin.** A small destructive animal, as a cockroach or rat. **—ver′min•ous** *adj.*

**ver•nac•u•lar** (vər-năk′yə-lər) *n.* **1.** The spoken language of a country or region. **2.** The idiom of a profession, etc. **—ver•nac′u•lar** *adj.*

**ver•sant** (vûr′sənt) *n.* The slope of 1 side of a mountain.

**ver•sa•tile** (vûr′sə-təl) *adj.* **1.** Capable of doing many things well. **2.** Having varied uses. **—ver′sa•til′i•ty** *n.*

**verse** (vûrs) *n.* **1.** A line of poetry. **2.** A stanza. **3.** Poetry. **4.** A division of a Biblical chapter. **—ver′si•fy′** *v.*

**ver•sion** (vûr′zhən, -shən) *n.* **1.** A description or account. **2.** A translation.

**ver•sus** (vûr′səs, -səz) *prep.* **1.** Against. **2.** In contrast with.

**ver•te•bra** (vûr′tə-brə) *n., pl.* **-brae** (-brē) or **-bras.** A bone or segment of cartilage of the spinal column. **—ver′te•bral** *adj.*

**ver•te•brate** (vûr′tə-brāt′, -brĭt) *adj.* **1.** Having a backbone or spinal column. **2.** Of vertebrates. —*n.* A vertebrate animal.

**ver•tex** (vûr′tĕks′) *n., pl.* **-texes** or **-tices. 1.** The highest point of something. **2.** The point at which the sides of an angle intersect.

**ver•ti•cal** (vûr′tĭ-kəl) *adj.* At right angles to the horizon. —*n.* A vertical line, plane, circle, etc. —**ver′ti•cal•ly** *adv.*

**verve** (vûrv) *n.* Energy and enthusiasm; vitality.

**ver•y** (vĕr′ē) *adv.* **1.** Extremely; exceedingly. **2.** Truly. **3.** Precisely. —*adj.* **1.** Absolute; utter. **2.** Identical; selfsame. **3.** Mere. **4.** Actual.

**ves•sel** (vĕs′əl) *n.* **1.** A container. **2.** A ship. **3.** A bodily duct, canal, etc., for the flow of fluid.

**vest** (vĕst) *n.* A sleeveless garment worn over a shirt. —*v.* **1.** To dress, esp. in ecclesiastical robes. **2.** To place (authority, power, etc.) in the control of.

**ves•ti•bule** (vĕs′tə-byo͞ol′) *n.* An entrance hall; lobby. —**ves•tib′u•lar** *adj.*

**ves•tige** (vĕs′tĭj) *n.* A remaining trace, sign, or part. —**ves•tig′i•al** *adj.*

**vest•ment** (vĕst′mənt) *n.* A garment, esp. a robe, gown, etc., worn by a clergyman.

**vet•er•an** (vĕt′ər-ən, vĕt′rən) *n.* A person of long exprience in an activity, esp. a former member of the armed forces. —**vet′er•an** *adj.*

**vet•er•i•nar•i•an** (vĕt′ər-ə-nâr′ē-ən, vĕt′rə-) *n.* A doctor qualified to treat animals.

**ve•to** (vē′tō) *n., pl.* **-toes. 1.** The power or right, esp. of a chief executive, to reject a bill passed by a legislature. **2.** A prohibition or rejection. —**ve′to** *v.*

**vex** (vĕks) *v.* To irritate or annoy. —**vex•a′tion** *n.* —**vex•a′tious** *adj.*

**vi•a•ble** (vī′ə-bəl) *adj.* Capable of living or developing. —**vi′a•bil′i•ty** *n.*

**vi•a•duct** (vī′ə-dŭkt′) *n.* A series of spans or arches used to carry a road or railroad over something, as a valley or road.

**vi•al** (vī′əl) *n.* A small container for liquids.

**vi•brant** (vī′brənt) *adj.* **1.** Of vibration; vibrating. **2.** Energetic or active. —**vi′bran•cy** *n.* —**vi′brant•ly** *adv.*

**vi•brate** (vī′brāt′) *v.* **-brated, -brating. 1.** To move or cause to move back and forth rapidly. **2.** To produce a sound; resonate. —**vi•bra′tion** *n.* —**vi′bra′tor** *n.* —**vi′bra•to′ry** *adj.*

**vic•ar** (vĭk′ər) *n.* **1.** A cleric in charge of a parish. **2.** A substitute or deputy. —**vic′ar•age** *n.*

**vi•car•i•ous** (vī-kâr′ē-əs, vĭ-) *adj.* **1.** Endured or done by 1 person substituting for another. **2.** Felt or undergone as if taking part in the experience or feelings of another. —**vi•car′i•ous•ly** *adv.* —**vi•car′i•ous•ness** *n.*

**vice**[1] (vīs) *n.* **1.** An immoral practice or habit. **2.** Corruption.

**vice**[2] (vīs) *adj.* Substituting for; deputy.

**vi•ce ver•sa** (vī′sə vûr′sə, vīs′) *adv.* With the order or meaning reversed; conversely.

**vi•cin•i•ty** (vĭ-sĭn′ĭ-tē) *n., pl.* **-ties.** A nearby region or place.

**vi•cious** (vĭsh′əs) *adj.* **1.** Cruel; mean; malicious. **2.** Marked by evil or vice; wicked. **3.** Savage and dangerous. —**vi′cious•ly** *adv.* —**vi′cious•ness** *n.*

**vi•cis•si•tude** (vĭ-sĭs′ĭ-t/y/o͞od′) *n.* **1.** Changeability. **2. vicissitudes.** A sudden or unexpected change in a person's life.

**vic•tim** (vĭk′tĭm) *n.* **1.** A living creature sacrificed to a deity. **2.** One harmed or killed by accident, disease, etc. **3.** A person who is tricked, swindled, etc. —**vic′tim•ize′** *v.* —**vic′tim•i•za′tion** *n.*

**vic•tor** (vĭk′tər) *n.* The winner in a war, contest, struggle, etc. —**vic•to′ri•ous** *adj.* —**vic′to•ry** *n.*

**vict•ual** (vĭt′l) *n.* **1.** Food fit for human consumption. **2. victuals.** Food supplies; provisions.

**vid•e•o** (vĭd′ē-ō′) *adj.* Of television. —*n.* **1.** The visual part of a televised broadcast. **2.** Television. **3.** A videotape.

**vid•e•o•tape** (vĭd′ē-ō-tāp′) *n.* A magnetic tape used to record television images. —*v.* **-taped, -taping.** To make a videotape of.

**vie** (vī) *v.* **vied, vying.** To contend or compete.

**view** (vyo͞o) *n.* **1.** An examination or inspection. **2.** The act of seeing something; sight. **3.** An opinion. **4.** Range of sight. **5.** A scene or vista. **6.** An aspect, as from a particular position or angle. **7.** An aim; intention. —*v.* **1.** To look at; see. **2.** To examine or inspect. **3.** To regard or consider. —**view′less** *adj.* —**view′point′** *n.*

**vig•il** (vĭj′əl) *n.* A period of alert watchfulness, esp. at night.

**vig•i•lant** (vĭj′ə-lənt) *adj.* On the alert; watchful. **—vig′i•lance** *n.*

**vi•gnette** (vĭn-yĕt′) *n.* **1.** A short literary sketch. **2.** A short scene or incident, as from a movie.

**vig•or** (vĭg′ər) *n.* **1.** Active physical or mental strength. **2.** Effectiveness or force. **—vig′or•ous** *adj.* **—vig′or•ous•ly** *adv.* **—vig′or•ous•ness** *n.*

**vile** (vīl) *adj.* **viler, vilest. 1.** Miserable; wretched. **2.** Morally low or base. **3.** Hateful. **4.** Unpleasant or objectionable. **—vile′ness** *n.*

**vil•i•fy** (vĭl′ə-fī′) *v.* **-fied, -fying.** To defame; denigrate. **—vil′i•fi•ca′tion** *n.*

**vil•lage** (vĭl′ĭj) *n.* **1.** A community smaller than a town. **2.** The inhabitants of a village. **—vil′lag•er** *n.*

**vil•lain** (vĭl′ən) *n.* An evil person; scoundrel. **—vil′lain•ous** *adj.* **—vil′lain•y** *n.*

**vim** (vĭm) *n.* Ebullient vitality and energy.

**vin•di•cate** (vĭn′dĭ-kāt′) *v.* **-cated, -cating. 1.** To clear of accusation, blame, etc. **2.** To justify. **—vin′di•ca′tion** *n.* **—vin′di•ca′tor** *n.*

**vin•dic•tive** (vĭn-dĭk′tĭv) *adj.* Showing a desire for revenge; vengeful. **—vin•dic′tive•ly** *adv.* **—vin•dic′tive•ness** *n.*

**vine** (vīn) *n.* A plant whose stem is supported by climbing, twining, or creeping.

**vin•e•gar** (vĭn′ĭ-gər) *n.* An acid liquid obtained by fermentation, used as a flavoring and preservative.

**vine•yard** (vĭn′yərd) *n.* Ground planted with cultivated grapevines.

**vin•tage** (vĭn′tĭj) *n.* **1.** The yield of wine from a particular vineyard in a single season. **2.** A year or period of origin. *—adj.* Characterized by excellence; classic.

**vi•nyl** (vī′nəl) *n.* A tough, flexible plastic.

**vi•o•la** (vē-ō′lə) *n.* A musical instrument of the violin family. **—vi•o′list** *n.*

**vi•o•late** (vī′ə-lāt′) *v.* **-lated, -lating. 1.** To break (a law or regulation); disregard. **2.** To profane; desecrate. **3.** To rape. **—vi′o•la′tion** *n.* **—vi′o•la′tor** *n.*

**vi•o•lent** (vī′ə-lənt) *adj.* **1.** Displaying great physical force or rough action. **2.** Showing great emotional force. **3.** Severe; harsh. **—vi′o•lence** *n.* **—vi′o•lent•ly** *adv.*

**vi•o•let** (vī′ə-lĭt) *n.* **1.** A plant with usually purplish-blue flowers. **2.** A bluish purple. **—vi′o•let** *adj.*

**vi•o•lin** (vī′ə-lĭn′) *n.* A stringed instrument played with a bow. **—vi′o•lin′ist** *n.*

**vir•gin** (vûr′jĭn) *n.* One who has not experienced sexual intercourse. *—adj.* **1.** Chaste. **2.** In a pure or natural state. **—vir′gin•al** *adj.* **—vir•gin′i•ty** *n.*

**vir•ile** (vĭr′əl) *adj.* **1.** Having masculine strength and vigor. **2.** Of male sexual functions. **—vi•ril′i•ty** *n.*

**vir•tu•al** (vûr′cho͞o-əl) *adj.* Existing in effect though not in actual fact. **—vir′tu•al•ly** *adv.*

**vir•tue** (vûr′cho͞o) *n.* **1.** Moral excellence and righteousness. **2.** Chastity. **3.** A beneficial quality. **—vir′tu•ous** *adj.* **—vir′tu•ous•ly** *adv.* **—vir′tu•ous•ness** *n.*

**vir•tu•o•so** (vûr′cho͞o-ō′sō) *n., pl.* **-sos** or **-si.** A person with masterly skill or technique, esp. in music. **—vir′tu•os′i•ty** *n.*

**vir•u•lent** (vĭr′/y/ə-lənt) *adj.* **1.** Extremely poisonous or harmful, as a disease. **2.** Bitterly hostile. **—vir′u•lence** *n.* **—vir′u•lent•ly** *adv.*

**vi•rus** (vī′rəs) *n.* A submicroscopic disease-causing agent. **—vi′ral** *adj.*

**vi•sa** (vē′zə) *n.* An authorization stamped on a passport, permitting travel within a country or region.

**vis•age** (vĭz′ĭj) *n.* **1.** The face of a person; countenance. **2.** Appearance; aspect.

**vis•cid** (vĭs′ĭd) *adj.* Thick and sticky; resembling glue. **—vis•cos′i•ty, vis′cous•ness** *n.* **—vis′cous** *adj.*

**vise** (vīs) *n.* Also **vice.** A clamping device used to hold work in position, as in carpentry.

**vis•i•ble** (vĭz′ə-bəl) *adj.* **1.** Capable of being seen. **2.** Apparent. **—vis′i•bil′i•ty** *n.* **—vis′i•bly** *adv.*

**vi•sion** (vĭzh′ən) *n.* **1.** The sense of sight. **2.** Unusual or supernatural perception. **3.** A mental image produced by the imagination.

**vi•sion•ar•y** (vĭzh′ə-nĕr′ē) *adj.* **1.** Of vision or the nature of a vision. **2.** Not practicable. *—n., pl.* **-ies. 1.** One who has visions. **2.** One who has impractical ideas.

**vis•it** (vĭz'ĭt) *v.* **1.** To go to see for business, pleasure, etc. **2.** To afflict; assail. —*n.* **1.** An act of visiting. **2.** A stay or call as a guest. —**vis'i•tor** *n.*

**vi•sor** (vī'zər) *n.* **1.** A piece on the front of a cap that shades the eyes. **2.** The movable front part of a helmet.

**vi•su•al** (vĭzh'ōō-əl) *adj.* **1.** Of the sense of sight. **2.** Capable of being seen; visible. —**vi'su•al•ly** *adv.*

**vi•su•al•ize** (vĭzh'ōō-ə-līz') *v.* **-ized, -izing.** To form a mental image of. —**vi'su•al•i•za'tion** *n.*

**vi•tal** (vīt'l) *adj.* **1.** Of life. **2.** Necessary for life. **3.** Having great importance; essential. —**vi'tal•ly** *adv.*

**vi•tal•i•ty** (vī-tăl'ĭ-tē) *n., pl.* **-ties. 1.** The capacity to grow; living force. **2.** Vigor; energy.

**vi•ta•min** (vī'tə-mĭn) *n.* Any organic substance found in plants and animals, essential for life maintenance and growth.

**vit•re•ous** (vĭt'rē-əs) *adj.* Of glass; glassy.

**vi•tu•per•ate** (vī-t/y/ōō'pə-rāt', vĭ-) *v.* **-ated, -ating.** To revile or berate. —**vi•tu'per•a'tion** *n.* —**vi•tu'per•a•tive** *adj.*

**vi•va•cious** (vĭ-vā'shəs, vī-) *adj.* Animated; lively. —**vi•va'cious•ly** *adv.* —**vi•vac'i•ty** *n.*

**viv•id** (vĭv'ĭd) *adj.* **1.** Perceived as bright and distinct; brilliant. **2.** Full of the freshness of immediate experience. —**viv'id•ly** *adv.* —**viv'id•ness** *n.*

**viv•i•sect** (vĭv'ĭ-sĕkt) *v.* To dissect a living animal, esp. for scientific investigation. —**viv'i•sec'tion** *n.*

**vo•cab•u•lar•y** (vō-kăb'yə-lĕr'ē) *n., pl.* **-ies. 1.** A list of words, usually arranged alphabetically. **2.** All the words of a language. **3.** The words used by a particular person, profession, etc.

**vo•cal** (vō'kəl) *adj.* **1.** Of or produced by the voice. **2.** Meant to be sung. **3.** Speaking freely; outspoken. —**vo'cal•ist** *n.* —**vo'cal•ize'** *v.* —**vo'cal•ly** *adv.*

**vo•ca•tion** (vō-kā'shən) *n.* A profession, trade, or occupation. —**vo•ca'tion•al** *adj.*

**vo•cif•er•ous** (vō-sĭf'ər-əs) *adj.* Making an outcry; clamorous. —**vo•cif'er•ous•ly** *adv.*

**vogue** (vōg) *n.* **1.** The current fashion, practice, etc. **2.** Popularity.

**voice** (vois) *n.* **1.** The sound produced by the vocal organs. **2.** This sound used in singing. **3.** A medium of expression. **4.** The right to express a choice or opinion. **5.** A verb form indicating the relation between the subject and the action the verb expresses. —*v.* **voiced, voicing.** To express or utter; give voice to. —**voice'less** *adj.*

**void** (void) *adj.* **1.** Empty. **2.** Having no legal force. **3.** Ineffective; useless. —*n.* **1.** An empty space. **2.** A feeling of emptiness, loneliness, or loss. —*v.* **1.** To invalidate or annul. **2.** To empty.

**vol•a•tile** (vŏl'ə-tl) *adj.* **1.** Changing to vapor readily at normal temperature. **2.** Changeable, esp. fickle or explosive. —**vol'a•til'i•ty** *n.*

**vol•ca•no** (vŏl-kā'nō) *n., pl.* **-noes** or **nos. 1.** A vent in the earth through which molten lava and hot gases are thrown forth. **2.** A mountain formed by the material thrown forth. —**vol•can'ic** *adj.*

**vo•li•tion** (və-lĭsh'ən) *n.* The power of choosing; the will. —**vo•li'tion•al** *adj.*

**vol•ley** (vŏl'ē) *n., pl.* **-leys.** The simultaneous discharge of a number of missiles. —**vol'ley** *v.*

**volt** (vōlt) *n.* A unit of electronic potential or electromotive force. —**volt'age** *n.*

**vol•u•ble** (vŏl'yə-bəl) *adj.* Talking easily; fluent; glib. —**vol'u•bil'i•ty** *n.* —**vol'u•bly** *adv.*

**vol•ume** (vŏl'yōōm, -yəm) *n.* **1.** A book. **2.** One book of a set. **3.** The measure or size of a 3-dimensional object. **4.** Quantity; amount. **5.** The loudness of a sound. —**vo•lu'mi•nous** *adj.* —**vo•lu'mi•nous•ly** *adv.*

**vol•un•tar•y** (vŏl'ən-tĕr'ē) *adj.* **1.** Arising from an act of choice. **2.** Acting by choice or guarantee of reward. —**vol'un•tar'i•ly** *adv.*

**vol•un•teer** (vŏl'ən-tîr') *n.* **1.** One who performs or gives services voluntarily. **2.** A person who enlists in the armed forces. —*v.* To give or offer of one's own accord.

**vo•lup•tu•ous** (və-lŭp'chōō-əs) *adj.* **1.** Of sensual pleasures. **2.** Full in form.

**—vo•lup'tu•ar'y** *n.* **—vo•lup'tu•ous•ly** *adv.* **—vo•lup'tu•ous•ness** *n.*

**vom•it** (vŏm'ĭt) *v.* To eject (the contents of the stomach) through the mouth. *—n.* Matter ejected from the stomach.

**vo•ra•cious** (vô-rā'shəs, və-) *adj.* **1.** Greedy for food; ravenous. **2.** Too eager; avid. **—vo•rac'i•ty, vo•ra'cious•ness** *n.* **—vo•ra'cious•ly** *adv.*

**vor•tex** (vôr'tĕks') *n.* A flow of fluid that rotates around an axis.

**vote** (vōt) *n.* **1.** A formal expression of preference for a candidate or a proposed resolution. **2.** The result of an election, referendum, etc. **3.** Suffrage. *—v.* **voted, voting.** To express preference by a vote. **—vot'er** *n.*

**vouch** (vouch) *v.* **1.** To supply assurance; verify. **2.** To give or serve as a guarantee. **—vouch'er** *n.*

**vow** (vou) *n.* A solemn pledge. *—v.* To promise or pledge solemnly.

**vow•el** (vou'əl) *n.* **1.** A speech sound made by the relatively free passage of breath through the larynx and mouth. **2.** A letter that represents such a sound.

**voy•age** (voi'ĭj) *n.* A long journey to a distant place. *—v.* **-aged, -aging.** To travel. **—voy'ag•er** *n.*

**vul•gar** (vŭl'gər) *adj.* **1.** Ill-bred. **2.** Obscene; offensive. **3.** Of the common people. **—vul•gar'i•ty** *n.* **—vul'gar•ly** *adv.*

**vul•ner•a•ble** (vŭl'nər-ə-bəl) *adj.* **1.** Capable of being harmed or injured. **2.** Easily affected or hurt. **—vul'ner•a•bil'i•ty** *n.*

# — W —

**w, W** (dŭb'əl-yo͞o, -yo͞o) *n.* The 23rd letter of the English alphabet.

**wad** (wŏd) *n.* **1.** A small soft mass. **2.** A compressed ball. *—v.* **wadded, wadding.** To pad or stuff. **—wad'ding** *n.*

**wad•dle** (wŏd'l) *v.* **-dled, -dling.** To walk with a swaying motion. *—n.* A waddling gait. **—wad'dler** *n.*

**wade** (wād) *v.* **waded, wading. 1.** To walk through water. **2.** To make one's way arduously.

**wa•fer** (wā'fər) *n.* A thin, crisp biscuit.

**waf•fle** (wŏf'əl) *n.* A batter cake baked in a 2-sided griddle.

**waft** (wäft, wăft) *v.* To carry gently through the air. *—n.* **1.** An odor or whiff. **2.** A light breeze.

**wag** (wăg) *v.* **wagged, wagging.** To move repeatedly to and fro. **—wag** *n.*

**wage** (wāj) *n.* Pay; salary. *—v.* **waged, waging.** To carry on (a war or campaign).

**wa•ger** (wā'jər) *n.* A bet. *—v.* To bet.

**wag•on** (wăg'ən) *n.* **1.** A 4-wheeled vehicle with a large rectangular body. **2.** A child's low 4-wheeled cart.

**waif** (wāf) *n.* A homeless child.

**wail** (wāl) *v.* **1.** To grieve audibly; to lament. **2.** To make a high-pitched mournful sound. **—wail** *n.*

**waist** (wāst) *n.* **1.** The part of the body between the ribs and the pelvis. **2.** A middle part of a garment. **—waist'line'** *n.*

**wait** (wāt) *v.* **1.** To remain in anticipation. **2.** To delay. **3.** To serve or attend, as a clerk or waitress. *—n.* The act of or time spent waiting.

**wait•er** (wā'tər) *n.* A boy or man who waits on tables.

**wait•ress** (wā'trĭs) *n.* A girl or woman who waits on tables.

**waive** (wāv) *v.* **waived, waiving.** To relinquish voluntarily. **—waiv'er** *n.*

**wake¹** (wāk) *v.* **woke** (wōk) or **waked, waking. 1.** To awaken or rouse from sleep. **2.** To stir up. *—n.* A vigil beside a corpse. **—wak'en** *v.*

**wake²** (wāk) *n.* The track left in water by a moving boat.

**walk** (wôk) *v.* To go or cause to go on foot. *—n.* **1.** The act of walking. **2.** A slow gait. **3.** A sidewalk, path, etc. **—walk'er** *n.*

**wall** (wôl) *n.* **1.** A vertical structure forming an inner partition or exterior siding of a building. **2.** Something resembling a wall. *—v.* To enclose, divide, or fortify with or as if with a wall.

**wal•let** (wŏl'ĭt) *n.* A small, flat case for paper money, cards, etc.

**wal•lop** (wŏl'əp) *v.* To beat soundly; thrash. *—n.* A severe blow.

**wal•low** (wŏl'ō) *v.* **1.** To roll about in water, mud, etc. **2.** To luxuriate.

**wal•nut** (wôl'nŭt', -nət) *n.* **1.** An edible nut with a hard shell. **2.** A tree bearing such nuts. **3.** The hard, dark wood of this tree.

**wal•rus** (wôl′rəs, wŏl′-) *n., pl.* **-ruses** or **-rus.** A large, tusked Arctic marine mammal.

**waltz** (wôlts) *n.* A dance in triple time. —*v.* To dance a waltz. **—waltz′er** *n.*

**wan** (wŏn) *adj.* Pale; sickly. **—wan′ly** *adv.*

**wand** (wŏnd) *n.* A slender rod used by a magician or conjurer.

**wan•der** (wŏn′dər) *v.* **1.** To roam aimlessly. **2.** To go astray. **3.** To think or express oneself incoherently. **—wan′der•er** *n.*

**wane** (wān) *v.* **waned, waning.** To decrease gradually. —*n.* A decline or dwindling.

**wan•gle** (wăng′gəl) *v.* **-gled, -gling. 1.** To get or achieve by contrivance. **2.** To manipulate fraudulently.

**want** (wŏnt, wônt) *v.* **1.** To lack. **2.** To desire. **3.** To need or require. —*n.* **1.** Poverty. **2.** A need or desire. **—want′ing** *adj.*

**wan•ton** (wŏn′tən) *adj.* **1.** Lewd. **2.** Maliciously cruel. **3.** Freely extravagant; capricious. **—wan′ton•ly** *adv.* **—wan′ton•ness** *n.*

**war** (wôr) *n.* **1.** Armed conflict. **2.** Active antagonism or hostility. —*v.* **warred, warring.** To wage war. **—war′fare′** *n.*

**war•ble** (wôr′bəl) *v.* **-bled, -bling.** To sing with trills, as a bird. **—war′ble** *n.*

**ward** (wôrd) *n.* **1.** An administrative division of a city. **2.** A division in a hospital, prison, etc. **3.** In law, a person placed under the care of a guardian or court. —*v.* To turn aside; repel.

**war•den** (wôr′dn) *n.* **1.** The administrative official of a prison. **2.** An official who enforces certain laws and regulations.

**ward•robe** (wôr′drōb′) *n.* **1.** A clothes cabinet or closet. **2.** Garments collectively; esp. of one person.

**wares** (wârz) *pl.n.* Goods for sale.

**warm** (wôrm) *adj.* **1.** Moderately hot. **2.** Preserving or imparting heat. **3.** Having a sensation of bodily heat, as from exercise. **4.** Enthusiastic. **5.** Cordial. **6.** Loving. —*v.* To make or become warm. **—warm′ly** *adv.* **—warmth** *n.*

**warn** (wôrn) *v.* **1.** To make aware of potential danger. **2.** To admonish. **—warn′ing** *n. & adj.*

**warp** (wôrp) *v.* **1.** To twist or become twisted out of shape. **2.** To corrupt. —*n.* A distortion or twist.

**war•rant** (wôr′ənt, wŏr′-) *n.* **1.** Authorization or certification. **2.** Justification for an action. **3.** A writ, esp. a judicial writ, authorizing something. —*v.* **1.** To guarantee. **2.** To deserve. **3.** To authorize.

**war•ran•ty** (wôr′ən-tē, wŏr′-) *n., pl.* **-ties. 1.** An official authorization. **2.** A guarantee.

**war•ri•or** (wôr′ē-ər, wŏr′-) *n.* One engaged or experienced in battle.

**wart** (wôrt) *n.* A small, hard growth on the skin. **—wart′y** *adj.*

**war•y** (wâr′ē) *adj.* **-ier, -iest.** Cautious; watchful. **—war′i•ly** *adv.* **—war′i•ness** *n.*

**was** (wŏz, wŭz; *unstressed* wəz) *v.* 1st and 3rd person sing. past indicative of **be.**

**wash** (wŏsh, wôsh) *v.* **1.** To cleanse using water or other liquid and usually soap. **2.** To flow over or past. **3.** To carry away or erode. —*n.* **1.** The act of cleansing. **2.** Articles to be washed. **3.** A light hue. **4.** The surge of water or waves. **—wash′a•ble** *adj.* **—wash′ing** *n.*

**wash•er** (wŏsh′ər, wô′shər) *n.* **1.** A small perforated disk of metal or rubber placed beneath a nut to relieve friction, etc. **2.** A machine for washing.

**was•n't** (wŏz′ənt, wŭz′-) *v.* Contraction of *was not.*

**wasp** (wŏsp, wôsp) *n.* A stinging insect.

**waste** (wāst) *v.* **wasted, wasting. 1.** To use carelessly; squander. **2.** To become weak. **3.** To fail to take advantage of. —*n.* **1.** An unnecessary expenditure. **2.** Destruction. **3.** A useless byproduct or remainder. —*adj.* Worthless or useless. **—waste′ful** *adj.* **—waste′ful•ly** *adv.* **—waste′ful•ness** *n.*

**wast•rel** (wā′strəl) *n.* **1.** One who wastes money. **2.** A loafer or good-for-nothing.

**watch** (wŏch) *v.* **1.** To observe carefully. **2.** To guard or tend. —*n.* **1.** Careful, continuous observation. **2.** A period of observation or guard duty. **3.** A guard or watchman. **4.** A small timepiece. **5.** A period of duty on a ship. **—watch′-**

**ful** *adj.*

**wa•ter** (wô′tər, wŏt′ər) *n.* **1.** A clear, tasteless liquid essential for life. **2.** Any form of water, as rain. **3.** Any body of water. —*v.* **1.** To pour water upon. **2.** To supply with drinking water. **3.** To dilute. **4.** To discharge fluid. —**wa′ter•fall′** *n.* —**wa′ter•y** *adj.*

**wa•ter•log** (wô′tər-lôg′, -lŏg′, wŏt′ər-) *v.* **-logged, -logging.** To soak with water, causing loss of buoyancy.

**wa•ter•shed** (wô′tər-shĕd′, wŏt′ər-) *n.* **1.** A ridge that divides 2 areas drained by different rivers. **2.** A critical point that serves as a dividing line.

**watt** (wŏt) *n.* A unit of electric power. —**watt′age** *n.*

**wat•tle** (wŏt′l) *n.* A fleshy, dangling skin fold on the neck.

**wave** (wāv) *v.* **waved, waving. 1.** To move or cause to move back and forth in the air. **2.** To signal by waving the hand. **3.** To curve. —*n.* **1.** A ridge on the surface of water. **2.** A curve or curl. **3.** A back and forth movement. **4.** A surge. —**wav′y** *adj.*

**wa•ver** (wā′vər) *v.* **1.** To sway. **2.** To hesitate. **3.** To fluctuate.

**wax**[1] (wăks) *n.* **1.** A natural, semisolid, heat-sensitive substance, as beeswax. **2.** A substance found in the ears. —*v.* To coat with wax. —**wax′en, wax′y** *adj.*

**wax**[2] (wăks) *v.* To grow greater gradually.

**way** (wā) *n.* **1.** A road or path. **2.** A course of action. **3.** A method. **4.** A mode of living. **5.** A distance. **6.** A direction. —*adv.* **1.** Far. **2.** Away.

**way•lay** (wā′lā′) *v.* **-laid, -laying. 1.** To accost suddenly. **2.** To intercept or delay the progress of.

**way•ward** (wā′wərd) *adj.* **1.** Willful. **2.** Erratic. —**way′ward•ly** *adv.* —**way′ward•ness** *n.*

**we** (wē) *pron.* The 1st person pl. pronoun in the subjective case.

**weak** (wēk) *adj.* **1.** Lacking strength; frail. **2.** Lacking strength of character. **3.** Unsound; deficient. —**weak′en** *v.* —**weak′ly** *adj. & adv.* —**weak′ness** *n.*

**wealth** (wĕlth) *n.* **1.** A great quantity of possessions or resources. **2.** A profusion. —**wealth′y** *adj.*

**wean** (wēn) *v.* **1.** To switch a baby from mother's milk to other nourishment. **2.** To cause to give up a habit or interest.

**weap•on** (wĕp′ən) *n.* An instrument used in combat. —**weap′on•ry** *n.*

**wear** (wâr) *v.* **wore** (wôr, wōr), **worn** (wôrn, wōrn), **wearing. 1.** To be clothed in. **2.** To bear. **3.** To impair by use. **4.** To fatigue. —*n.* **1.** The act of wearing; use. **2.** Clothing. **3.** Gradual impairment or diminution. —**wear′er** *n.*

**wea•ry** (wîr′ē) *adj.* **-rier, -riest. 1.** Tired. **2.** Bored or resigned. —*v.* **-ried, -rying.** To make or become weary. —**wea′ri•ly** *adv.* —**wea′ri•ness** *n.* —**wea′ri•some** *adj.*

**wea•sel** (wē′zəl) *n.* A small carnivorous mammal. —*v.* To be evasive.

**weath•er** (wĕ*th*′ər) *n.* Atmospheric conditions such as temperature, moisture, etc. —*v.* **1.** To expose to or show the effects of weather. **2.** To pass through safely; survive.

**weave** (wēv) *v.* **wove** (wōv), **woven** (wō′vən), **weaving. 1.** To interlace threads into cloth. **2.** To construct by interlacing. **3.** To wind or curve in and out. —*n.* The pattern or method of weaving. —**weav′er** *n.*

**web** (wĕb) *n.* **1.** A woven fabric. **2.** A latticed structure. **3.** A threadlike structure spun by spiders. **4.** A complex network. **5.** A membranous tissue between the toes of ducks, frogs, etc. **6.** Also **Web**. The World Wide Web. —**webbed** *adj.*

**web•cam** (wĕb′kăm′) *n.* A digital camera that sends images to a computer for transmission over the Internet or other network.

**web•cast** (wĕb′kăst′) *n.* A broadcast of an event over the World Wide Web.

**web•log** (wĕb′lôg′, -lŏg′) *n.* A website that displays messages chronologically by one or more people, often with links to comments about specific messages.

**web•mas•ter** (wĕb′măs′tər) *n.* A person who develops, markets, or maintains websites.

**web•page, Web page** (wĕb′pāj′) *n.* A document on the World Wide Web, often linked to other documents.

**web•site, Web site** (wĕb′sīt′) *n.* A set of interconnected webpages prepared as a collection of information by a person or organization.

**wed** (wĕd) *v.* **wedded, wed** or **wedded, wedding. 1.** To marry. **2.** To unite. **—wed′ding** *n.* **—wed′lock′** *n.*

**we'd** (wēd) *v.* **1.** Contraction of *we had.* **2.** Contraction of *we would.*

**wedge** (wĕj) *n.* **1.** A V-shaped piece of metal or wood for splitting, securing, etc. **2.** Anything shaped like a wedge. *—v.* **wedged, wedging. 1.** To split or fix in place with a wedge. **2.** To crowd into a limited space.

**Wednes•day** (wĕnz′dē, -dā′) *n.* The 4th day of the week.

**weed** (wēd) *n.* A troublesome or useless plant. *—v.* **1.** To remove weeds from. **2.** To eliminate as unsuitable. **—weed′er** *n.* **—weed′y** *adj.*

**week** (wēk) *n.* A period of 7 days. **—week′day′** *n.* **—week′end′** *n.* **—week′ly** *adv., adj., & n.*

**weep** (wēp) *v.* **wept** (wĕpt), **weeping. 1.** To mourn (with *for*). **2.** To shed (tears). **—weep′er** *n.* **—weep′ing** *n.*

**weigh** (wā) *v.* **1.** To measure the weight of. **2.** To consider or ponder. **3.** To burden (with *down*). **4.** To have a specific weight. **5.** To be important. **—weigh′er** *n.*

**weight** (wāt) *n.* **1.** A measure of the heaviness or mass of an object. **2.** A system of unit measures of heaviness or mass. **3.** Burden; oppressiveness. **4.** Preponderance. **5.** Influence; importance. *—v.* To add heaviness to. **—weight′y** *adj.*

**weird** (wîrd) *adj.* Strange; uncanny. **—weird′ness** *n.*

**wel•come** (wĕl′kəm) *adj.* **1.** Received with hospitality. **2.** Gratifying. **3.** Permitted to do or enjoy. *—n.* A cordial reception. *—v.* **-comed, -coming. 1.** To greet cordially. **2.** To accept gladly.

**weld** (wĕld) *v.* To join (metals) by heat and pressure. **—weld′er** *n.*

**wel•fare** (wĕl′fâr′) *n.* **1.** Well-being. **2.** Public relief.

**well¹** (wĕl) *n.* **1.** A deep hole dug to obtain water, oil, etc. **2.** A vertical opening through floors, as for stairs. **3.** A source to be drawn upon. *—v.* To rise or surge.

**well²** (wĕl) *adv.* **better** (bĕt′ər), **best** (bĕst). **1.** Satisfactorily. **2.** With skill. **3.** Properly. **4.** Favorably. **5.** Thoroughly. *—adj.* **1.** Satisfactory. **2.** In good health. **3.** Fortunate; good. *—interj.* Expressive of surprise. **—well′ness** *n.*

**we'll** (wēl) *v.* Contraction of *we will.*

**welt** (wĕlt) *n.* **1.** A strip stitched into a shoe between the sole and upper. **2.** A decorative or supporting cord sewn into a seam. **3.** A bump on the skin from a blow or allergy.

**wend** (wĕnd) *v.* To proceed along.

**went** (wĕnt) *v.* p.t. of **go.**

**wept** (wĕpt) *v.* p.t. & p.p. of **weep.**

**were** (wûr) *v.* **1.** Pl. & 2nd person sing. of the past indicative of **be. 2.** Past subjunctive of **be.**

**we're** (wîr) *v.* Contraction of *we are.*

**wer•en't** (wûrnt, wûr′ənt) *v.* Contraction of *were not.*

**west** (wĕst) *n.* **1.** The direction opposite that of the earth's rotation. **2.** Often **West.** The W part of any country or region. **3. West.** Europe and the W Hemisphere; the Occident. *—adj. & adv.* To, from, or in the west. **—west′er•ly** *adj. & adv.* **—west′ern, West′ern** *adj.* **—west′ern•er, West′ern•er** *n.* **—west′ward** *adv. & adj.*

**wet** (wĕt) *adj.* **wetter, wettest. 1.** Covered or saturated with a liquid. **2.** Not yet dry. **3.** Rainy. *—n.* **1.** Moisture. **2.** Rainy weather. *—v.* **wetted, wetting.** To make or become wet. **—wet′ly** *adv.* **—wet′ness** *n.*

**we've** (wēv) *v.* Contraction of *we have.*

**whack** (hwăk) *v.* To strike with a sharp blow. **—whack** *n.*

**whale** (hwāl) *n.* A large marine mammal with horizontal flukes. *—v.* **whaled, whaling.** To hunt whales.

**wharf** (hwôrf) *n., pl.* **wharves** or **wharfs.** A place for loading or mooring vessels.

**what** (hwŏt, hwŭt; *unstressed* hwət) *pron.* **1.** Which thing or things. **2.** That or those which. *—adj.* **1.** Which or which kind of. **2.** Whatever. **3.** How great. *—adv.* **1.** How. **2.** Why (with *for*). **—what•ev′er** *pron. & adj.*

**wheat** (hwēt) *n.* The grain of a cereal plant, ground for flour.

**wheel** (hwēl) *n.* A solid disk or spoked ring that turns around a center axle.

—*v.* **1.** To move on wheels. **2.** To turn around.

**wheeze** (hwēz) *v.* **wheezed, wheezing.** To breathe with a hoarse whistling sound. —*n.* A wheezing breath. **—wheez'y** *adj.*

**whelp** (hwĕlp) *n.* A young offspring of a dog, wolf, etc. —*v.* To bear whelps.

**when** (hwĕn) *adv.* At what time. —*conj.* **1.** At the time that. **2.** Since. **—when•ev'er** *adv. & conj.*

**whence** (hwĕns) *adv.* From where. —*conj.* From which.

**where** (hwâr) *adv.* **1.** To, at, or in what place. **2.** In what situation. —*conj.* **1.** At what or which place. **2.** In or to a place in which. **3.** Wherever. —*pron.* Which place. —*n.* The place or occasion.

**where•as** (hwâr-ăz') *conj.* **1.** Inasmuch as. **2.** While on the contrary.

**whet** (hwĕt) *v.* **whetted, whetting. 1.** To sharpen; hone. **2.** To stimulate. **—whet'stone'** *n.*

**wheth•er** (hwĕ*th*'ər) *conj.* **1.** If it is so that. **2.** In case. **3.** Either.

**whey** (hwā) *n.* The watery part of milk that separates out during cheesemaking.

**which** (hwĭch) *pron.* **1.** What one or ones. **2.** Whichever or whatever. **3.** The one or ones that. **4.** Something that. —*adj.* **1.** What one or ones. **2.** Whichever or whatever. **—which•ev'er** *pron. & adj.*

**whiff** (hwĭf) *n.* **1.** A slight gust. **2.** A breath of air, smoke, etc. —*v.* **1.** To be carried in gusts. **2.** To breathe in. **3.** To sniff.

**while** (hwīl) *n.* A period of time. —*conj.* **1.** As long as. **2.** Whereas. —*v.* **whiled, whiling.** To spend (time) pleasantly.

**whim** (hwĭm) *n.* **1.** A capricious idea. **2.** An impulse.

**whim•per** (hwĭm'pər) *v.* To cry or sob softly. —*n.* A whine.

**whim•si•cal** (hwĭm'zĭ-kəl) *adj.* Capricious; playful. **—whim'si•cal•ly** *adv.*

**whim•sy** (hwĭm'zē) *n., pl.* **-sies** also **-seys. 1.** An odd or capricious idea. **2.** Something odd, fanciful, or quaint.

**whine** (hwīn) *v.* **whined, whining. 1.** To complain in an annoying fashion. **2.** To produce a sustained high-pitched noise. **—whine** *n.* **—whin'y** *adj.*

**whip** (hwĭp) *v.* **whipped, whipping. 1.** To strike with repeated strokes; flog. **2.** To move quickly. **3.** To beat (cream or eggs). **4.** To defeat. —*n.* **1.** A flexible instrument for whipping. **2.** A legislator charged by his or her party with insuring attendance. **—whip'per** *n.*

**whir** (hwûr) *v.* **whirred, whirring.** To move with a buzzing sound. —*n.* A buzzing sound.

**whirl** (hwûrl) *v.* **1.** To revolve or spin rapidly. **2.** To move rapidly. —*n.* **1.** A spinning motion. **2.** Confusion; tumult.

**whisk** (hwĭsk) *v.* **1.** To move or cause to move with quick, sweeping motions. **2.** To whip (eggs or cream). —*n.* **1.** A small broom. **2.** A kitchen utensil for whipping.

**whisk•er** (hwĭs'kər) *n.* **1. whiskers.** A man's facial hair. **2.** A bristle near the mouth of certain animals.

**whis•key** (hwĭs'kē) *n., pl.* **-keys.** Also **whis•ky** *pl.* **-kies.** An alcoholic liquor distilled from grain.

**whis•per** (hwĭs'pər) *v.* **1.** To speak softly. **2.** To tell secretly. —*n.* **1.** Soft speech. **2.** A soft, rustling sound.

**whis•tle** (hwĭs'əl) *v.* **-tled, -tling.** To make a high-pitched, often musical sound by forcing air through pursed lips or a device. —*n.* **1.** A device for making whistling sounds. **2.** A whistling sound. **—whis'tler** *n.*

**white** (hwīt) *n.* **1.** The color of snow. **2.** The white part of something, as the albumen of an egg. —*adj.* **whiter, whitest. 1.** Of the color white. **2.** Pale. **3.** Having light skin. **—whit'en** *v.* **—white'ness** *n.* **—whit'ish** *adj.*

**whith•er** (hwĭ*th*'ər) *adv.* **1.** To what place. **2.** To whatever place.

**whit•tle** (hwĭt'l) *v.* **-tled, -tling. 1.** To cut or pare shavings from (wood). **2.** To reduce gradually. **—whit'tler** *n.*

**who** (ho͞o) *pron.* **1.** What person or persons. **2.** The person or persons that. **—who•ev'er** *pron.*

**whole** (hōl) *adj.* **1.** Complete. **2.** Not divided; intact. **3.** In mathematics, integral; not fractional. —*n.* **1.** All the parts of a thing. **2.** A complete entity. **—whole'ness** *n.* **—whol'ly** *adv.*

**whole•sale** (hōl'sāl') *n.* The sale of goods in quantity, as for resale. —*adj.* **1.** Of or engaged in the sale of goods at wholesale. **2.** Extensive and indiscriminate. **—whole'sal'er** *n.*

**whole•some** (hōl'səm) *adj.* Healthy. **—whole'some•ly** *adv.* **—whole'some•ness** *n.*

**whom** (hōōm) *pron.* The objective case of *who.* **—whom•ev'er** *pron.*

**whore** (hôr, hōr) *n.* A prostitute.

**who're** (hōōr) *v.* Contraction of *who are.*

**who's** (hōōz) *v.* **1.** Contraction of *who is.* **2.** Contraction of *who has.*

**whose** (hōōz) *pron.* The possessive case of *who* or *which,* used as an adjective.

**who've** (hōōv) *v.* Contraction of *who have.*

**why** (hwī) *adv.* **1.** For what reason. **2.** Because of which. *—n.* The cause or intention.

**wick** (wĭk) *n.* A cord of fibers, as in a candle, that draws up fuel to the flame.

**wick•ed** (wĭk'ĭd) *adj.* **1.** Vicious; depraved. **2.** Harmful. **—wick'ed•ly** *adv.* **—wick'ed•ness** *n.*

**wide** (wīd) *adj.* **wider, widest. 1.** Extensive; broad. **2.** Of great scope. **3.** Fully open. **4.** Landing away from a desired goal. *—adv.* **1.** Extensively. **2.** Completely. **—wide'ly** *adv.* **—wid'en** *v.* **—wide'ness** *n.*

**wid•ow** (wĭd'ō) *n.* A woman whose husband has died.

**wid•ow•er** (wĭd'ō-ər) *n.* A man whose wife has died.

**width** (wĭdth, wĭth) *n.* The measurement of something from side to side; breadth.

**wield** (wēld) *v.* **1.** To handle (a weapon, etc.). **2.** To exercise (power).

**wife** (wīf) *n., pl.* **wives.** A female spouse. **—wife'ly** *adj.*

**wig** (wĭg) *n.* A hairpiece.

**wig•gle** (wĭg'əl) *v.* **-gled, -gling.** To move or cause to move quickly from side to side.

**wild** (wīld) *adj.* **1.** Not domesticated or cultivated. **2.** Reckless. **3.** Disordered. **4.** Violent. **5.** Demented. *—n.* An uninhabited or uncultivated region. **—wild, wild'ly** *adv.* **—wild'ness** *n.*

**wil•der•ness** (wĭl'dər-nĭs) *n.* A wild or desolate region.

**wile** (wīl) *n.* A cunning or seductive manner or stratagem.

**will¹** (wĭl) *n.* **1.** The mental faculty of deciding upon a course of action; volition. **2.** An intention or wish. **3.** Attitude toward others. **4.** Determination. **5.** A declaration specifying the disposition of one's possessions after death. *—v.* **1.** To decide upon. **2.** To bequeath.

**will²** (wĭl) *v.* **1.** Used to indicate (often with future reference) willingness, intention, etc. **2.** To wish. **—will'ing** *adj.* **—will'ing•ly** *adv.* **—will'ing•ness** *n.*

**will•ful** (wĭl'fəl) *adj.* Also **wil•ful. 1.** Deliberate. **2.** Obstinate. **—will'ful•ly** *adv.* **—will'ful•ness** *n.*

**wilt** (wĭlt) *v.* To make or become limp.

**wi•ly** (wī'lē) *adj.* **-lier, -liest.** Guileful; calculating. **—wi'li•ness** *n.*

**wimp** (wĭmp) *n.* A weak, ineffectual person.

**win** (wĭn) *v.* **won** (wŭn), **winning. 1.** To achieve victory. **2.** To receive as a prize. **3.** To gain the support of. *—n.* A victory. **—win'ner** *n.*

**wince** (wĭns) *v.* **winced, wincing.** To shrink, as in pain. *—n.* A wincing movement.

**wind¹** (wĭnd) *n.* **1.** Moving air. **2.** Respiration; breath. *—v.* To cause to be out of breath. **—wind'y** *adj.*

**wind²** (wīnd) *v.* **wound** (wound), **winding. 1.** To wrap (something) around an object. **2.** To turn repeatedly, as a crank.

**wind•fall** (wĭnd'fôl') *n.* **1.** Something blown down. **2.** An unexpected piece of good fortune.

**wind•mill** (wĭnd'mĭl') *n.* A mill that runs on wind.

**win•dow** (wĭn'dō) *n.* A wall opening that admits light or air, usually framed and spanned with glass. **—win'dow•pane'** *n.*

**wind•pipe** (wĭnd'pīp') *n.* The trachea.

**wind•shield** (wĭnd'shēld') *n.* A framed glass shield in the front of a vehicle.

**wine** (wīn) *n.* The fermented juice of grapes or other fruits.

**wing** (wĭng) *n.* **1.** An organ of flight, as of a bird, bat, etc. **2.** A winglike structure. **3.** A side projection of an airplane. **4.** An extension of a house, building, etc. *—v.* **1.** To fly. **2.** To wound superficially.

**wink** (wĭngk) *v.* **1.** To close and open (the eyelid) deliberately. **2.** To twinkle. *—n.* The act of winking.

**win•ning** (wĭn′ĭng) *adj.* **1.** Successful; victorious. **2.** Charming. —*n.* **1.** The act of one that wins. **2. winnings.** Something won, esp. money.

**win•now** (wĭn′ō) *v.* **1.** To separate grain from chaff. **2.** To examine closely to separate the good from the bad.

**win•some** (wĭn′səm) *adj.* Pleasant; charming. **—win′some•ly** *adv.* **—win′some•ness** *n.*

**win•ter** (wĭn′tər) *n.* The coldest season of the year. —*adj.* Of, like, or occurring in winter. **—win′try, win′ter•y** *adj.*

**wipe** (wīp) *v.* **wiped, wiping. 1.** To rub, as with a cloth, in order to clean or dry. **2.** To remove by rubbing. **—wip′er** *n.*

**wire** (wīr) *n.* **1.** A pliable metallic strand or rod. **2.** A telegram. —*adj.* Made of wire. —*v.* **wired, wiring. 1.** To connect or provide with a wire. **2.** To send a telegram to.

**wir•y** (wīr′ē) *adj.* **-ier, -iest. 1.** Wirelike; kinky. **2.** Slender but tough.

**wis•dom** (wĭz′dəm) *n.* **1.** Understanding and knowledge. **2.** Common sense; judgment.

**wise** (wīz) *adj.* **wiser, wisest. 1.** Judicious. **2.** Prudent; sensible. **3.** Shrewd. **4.** Having knowledge or information. **5.** Arrogant. **—wise′ly** *adv.*

**wise•a•cre** (wīz′ā′kər) *n.* An offensively self-assured person.

**wish** (wĭsh) *n.* **1.** A desire. **2.** Something desired. —*v.* **1.** To desire; want. **2.** To express wishes for. **—wish′ful** *adj.* **—wish′ful•ly** *adv.*

**wisp** (wĭsp) *n.* **1.** A small bunch or tuft. **2.** A faint streak, as of smoke. **—wisp′y** *adj.*

**wist•ful** (wĭst′fəl) *adj.* Melancholy. **—wist′ful•ly** *adv.* **—wist′ful•ness** *n.*

**wit** (wĭt) *n.* **1.** Understanding; resourcefulness. **2.** The ability to express perceptions in an ingeniously humorous manner. **3.** One with this ability.

**witch** (wĭch) *n.* A person who practices sorcery. **—witch′craft′** *n.*

**with** (wĭ*th*, wĭth) *prep.* **1.** Accompanying. **2.** Next to. **3.** Possessed of. **4.** In support of. **5.** By the means of. **6.** And; plus. **7.** Against.

**with•draw** (wĭ*th*-drô′, wĭth-) *v.* **-drew** (-dro͞o), **-drawn, -drawing. 1.** To take back. **2.** To draw back; retreat. **—with•draw′al** *n.*

**with•drawn** (wĭ*th*-drôn′, wĭth-) *adj.* Shy.

**with•er** (wĭ*th*′ər) *v.* **1.** To dry up or shrivel. **2.** To fade; droop.

**with•hold** (wĭth-hōld′) *v.* **-held** (-hĕld), **-holding.** To refrain from giving or permitting.

**with•in** (wĭ*th*-ĭn′, wĭth-) *adv.* **1.** Inside. **2.** Inwardly. —*prep.* **1.** Inside. **2.** Inside the fixed limits of.

**with•out** (wĭ*th*-out′, wĭth-) *adv.* Outside. —*prep.* **1.** Lacking. **2.** With none of.

**with•stand** (wĭth-stănd′, wĭ*th*-) *v.* **-stood** (-sto͝od), **-standing.** To resist or endure.

**wit•ness** (wĭt′nĭs) *n.* **1.** One who has seen something. **2.** A sign. **3.** One called upon to testify before a court. —*v.* **1.** To see. **2.** To testify. **3.** To attest to by signing one's name.

**wit•ty** (wĭt′ē) *adj.* **-tier, -tiest.** Cleverly humorous. **—wit′ti•ly** *adv.* **—wit′ti•ness** *n.*

**wives** (wīvz) *n.* pl. of **wife.**

**wiz•ard** (wĭz′ərd) *n.* A magician. **—wiz′ard•ry** *n.*

**wiz•ened** (wĭz′ənd) *adj.* Shriveled.

**wob•ble** (wŏb′əl) *v.* **-bled, -bling. 1.** To move erratically from side to side. **2.** To vacillate. **—wob′ble** *n.* **—wob′bly** *adj.*

**woe** (wō) *n.* **1.** Deep sorrow. **2.** Misfortune. **—woe′ful** *adj.* **—woe′ful•ly** *adv.*

**woke** (wōk) *v.* A p.t. of **wake.**

**wolf** (wo͝olf) *n., pl.* **wolves.** A carnivorous mammal related to the dog. —*v.* To eat voraciously.

**wom•an** (wo͝om′ən) *n., pl.* **women** (wĭm′ĭn). An adult female human being. **—wom′an•hood′** *n.* **—wom′an•li•ness** *n.* **—wom′an•ly** *adj.*

**womb** (wo͞om) *n.* The uterus.

**won** (wŭn) *v.* p.t. & p.p. of **win.**

**won•der** (wŭn′dər) *n.* **1.** A marvel. **2.** Awe. **3.** Curiosity or doubt. —*v.* **1.** To feel awe or admiration. **2.** To be curious. **—won′der•ful** *adj.* **—won′drous** *adj.*

**wont** (wônt, wōnt, wŭnt) *adj.* **1.** Accustomed. **2.** Apt or likely. —*n.* Usage or custom. **—wont′ed** *adj.*

**won't** (wōnt) *v.* Contraction of *will not.*

**woo** (wo͞o) *v.* **1.** To seek the affection of, esp. with hopes of marrying. **2.** To entreat.

**wood** (wo͝od) *n.* **1.** The tough substance beneath the bark of trees. **2.** Such a substance used for building material or fuel. **3.** Often **woods.** A forest. —*adj.* Made of wood. **—wood'ed** *adj.* **—wood'y** *adj.*

**wood•cut** (wo͝od'kŭt') *n.* A print made from an engraved piece of wood.

**wood•en** (wo͝od'n) *adj.* **1.** Made of wood. **2.** Lifeless. **3.** Clumsy.

**wood•wind** (wo͝od'wĭnd') *n.* Any of a group of musical wind instruments. **—wood'wind'** *adj.*

**wood•work** (wo͝od'wûrk') *n.* Wooden interior fittings.

**woof•er** (wo͝of'ər) *n.* A bass loudspeaker.

**wool** (wo͝ol) *n.* **1.** Dense, soft, curly hair, esp. of a sheep. **2.** A material or garment made of wool. **3.** A woollike substance. **—wool** *adj.* **—wool'en** *adj. & n.* **—wool'ly** *adj.*

**word** (wûrd) *n.* **1.** A combination of sounds or letters that symbolizes a meaning. **2.** A discourse or talk. **3.** A promise. **4.** News. **5. words.** A dispute. —*v.* To express in words.

**word•y** (wûr'dē) *adj.* **-ier, -iest.** Using more words than necessary. **—word'i•ly** *adv.* **—word'i•ness** *n.*

**wore** (wôr, wōr) *v.* p.t. of **wear.**

**work** (wûrk) *n.* **1.** Toil; labor. **2.** Employment. **3.** A duty or task. **4.** Something produced as a result of effort. **5. works.** *(takes sing. v.).* A factory, plant, etc. **6. works.** Machinery. —*v.* **1.** To labor. **2.** To be employed. **3.** To operate. **4.** To prove successful. **5.** To change or move, esp. by repeated movement. **6.** To cause; bring about. **7.** To solve (an arithmetic problem). **8.** To make productive. **9.** To excite. **—work'a•ble** *adj.* **—work'er** *n.*

**world** (wûrld) *n.* **1.** The earth. **2.** The universe. **3.** Humankind. **4.** A particular part of the earth. **5.** A sphere, realm, or kingdom. **6.** A large amount.

**world•ly** (wûrld'lē) *adj.* **-lier, -liest. 1.** Secular. **2.** Sophisticated or cosmopolitan. **—world'li•ness** *n.*

**World Wide Web** *n.* The set of electronic documents stored on computers that are connected over the Internet and are made available by the process known as HTTP (Hypertext Transfer Protocol).

**worm** (wûrm) *n.* **1.** An invertebrate with a long, flexible body. **2.** A contemptible person. **3. worms.** An intestinal infestation with worms. —*v.* **1.** To move with the crawling motion of a worm. **2.** To elicit deviously. **3.** To cure of intestinal worms. **—worm'y** *adj.*

**worn** (wôrn, wōrn) *v.* p.p. of **wear.**

**wor•ry** (wûr'ē) *v.* **-ried, -rying. 1.** To feel or cause to feel uneasy or troubled. **2.** To grasp and tug at repeatedly. —*n., pl.* **-ries. 1.** Anxiety. **2.** A source of concern. **—wor'ri•er** *n.* **—wor'ri•some** *adj.*

**worse** (wûrs) *adv. & adj.* compar. of **bad** and **ill. 1.** More inferior. **2.** More unfavorable. —*n.* Something that is worse. **—wors'en** *v.*

**wor•ship** (wûr'shĭp) *n.* **1.** The reverence accorded a deity. **2.** The prayers by which this is expressed. **3.** Ardent devotion. —*v.* **-shiped** or **-shipped, -shiping** or **-shipping. 1.** To honor as a deity. **2.** To love devotedly. **3.** To participate in religious worship. **—wor'ship•er** *n.*

**worst** (wûrst) *adv. & adj.* superl. of **bad** and **ill. 1.** Most inferior. **2.** Most unfavorable. —*n.* Something that is worst. —*v.* To defeat.

**worth** (wûrth) *n.* **1.** Value or importance. **2.** The material value of something. **3.** The quantity of something that can be purchased for a specific sum. —*adj.* **1.** Equal in value to. **2.** Deserving of. **—worth'less** *adj.* **—worth'less•ness** *n.* **—worth'while'** *adj.*

**wor•thy** (wûr'*th*ē) *adj.* **-thier, -thiest. 1.** Having merit or value. **2.** Honorable. **3.** Deserving. —*n., pl.* **-thies.** A worthy person. **—wor'thi•ly** *adv.* **—wor'thi•ness** *n.*

**would** (wo͝od) *v.* p.t. of **will**[2].

**would•n't** (wo͝od'nt) *v.* Contraction of *would not.*

**wound**[1] (wo͞ond) *n.* An injury, esp. a cut. —*v.* To inflict a wound upon.

**wound**[2] (wound) *v.* p.t. & p.p. of **wind**[2].

**wove** (wōv) *v.* p.t. of **weave.**

**wo•ven** (wō'vən) *v.* p.p. of **weave.**

**wrack** (răk) *n.* Damage or destruction.

**wran•gle** (răng'gəl) *v.* **-gled, -gling. 1.** To dispute angrily. **2.** To obtain by argument. —*n.* A dispute. —**wran'gler** *n.*

**wrap** (răp) *v.* **wrapped** or **wrapt, wrapping. 1.** To arrange or fold about. **2.** To cover or envelop. —*n.* An outer garment. —**wrap'per** *n.* —**wrap'ping** *n.*

**wrath** (răth, räth) *n.* **1.** Violent, resentful anger. **2.** Retribution. —**wrath'ful** *adj.* —**wrath'ful•ly** *adv.*

**wreak** (rēk) *v.* To inflict (vengeance or punishment).

**wreath** (rēth) *n., pl.* **wreaths. 1.** A ring of flowers or leaves. **2.** Something resembling this.

**wreck** (rĕk) *v.* **1.** To destroy or dismantle. **2.** To bring to ruin. —*n.* **1.** The state of being wrecked. **2.** Something in a worn-out state. —**wreck'age** *n.* —**wreck'er** *n.*

**wrench** (rĕnch) *n.* **1.** A forcible twist. **2.** An injury from straining. **3.** A tool with jaws for gripping. —*v.* **1.** To twist forcibly. **2.** To sprain.

**wrest** (rĕst) *v.* **1.** To obtain by or as by pulling violently. **2.** To usurp.

**wres•tle** (rĕs'əl) *v.* **-tled, -tling. 1.** To contend by attempting to throw one's opponent. **2.** To struggle with. —**wres'tler** *n.* —**wres'tling** *n.*

**wretch** (rĕch) *n.* **1.** An unfortunate person. **2.** A despicable person.

**wretch•ed** (rĕch'ĭd) *adj.* **1.** Pitiable; woeful. **2.** Contemptible. **3.** Inferior. —**wretch'ed•ly** *adv.*

**wrig•gle** (rĭg'əl) *v.* **-gled, -gling. 1.** To squirm. **2.** To insinuate oneself by sly means. —**wrig'gle** *n.* —**wrig'gly** *adj.*

**wring** (rĭng) *v.* **wrung** (rŭng), **wringing. 1.** To twist and squeeze; compress. **2.** To extract by twisting. —**wring'er** *n.*

**wrin•kle** (rĭng'kəl) *n.* A small furrow or crease. —*v.* **-kled, -kling. 1.** To make a wrinkle in. **2.** To become wrinkled. —**wrin'kly** *adj.*

**wrist** (rĭst) *n.* The junction between the hand and arm.

**writ** (rĭt) *n.* A written order issued by a court.

**write** (rīt) *v.* **wrote** (rōt), **written** (rĭt'n), **writing. 1.** To form (letters, etc.) with a pen, pencil, etc. **2.** To compose, esp. as an author. **3.** To communicate by writing. —**writ'er** *n.*

**writhe** (rī*th*) *v.* **writhed, writhing.** To twist, as in pain.

**writ•ten** (rĭt'n) *v.* p.p. of **write.**

**wrong** (rông, rŏng) *adj.* **1.** Not correct. **2.** Contrary to conscience or law. **3.** Not suitable. **4.** Out of order; awry. —*adv.* **1.** Erroneously. **2.** Unjustly. —*n.* **1.** That which is wrong. **2.** The condition of being wrong. —*v.* To treat unjustly. —**wrong'ful** *adj.* —**wrong'ful•ly** *adv.* —**wrong'ly** *adv.*

**wrote** (rōt) *v.* p.t. of **write.**

**wrought** (rôt) *adj.* **1.** Put together. **2.** Shaped by hammering.

**wrung** (rŭng) *v.* p.t. & p.p. of **wring.**

**wry** (rī) *adj.* **wrier** or **wryer, wriest** or **wryest. 1.** Twisted, as facial features. **2.** Dryly humorous. —**wry'ly** *adv.*

# – XYZ –

**x, X** (ĕks) *n.* The 24th letter of the English alphabet.

**xe•non** (zē'nŏn') *n.* A colorless, odorless, highly unreactive gaseous element.

**xen•o•phile** (zĕn'ə-fīl', zē'nə-) *n.* A person attracted to foreign cultures and people. —**xen'o•phil'ic** *adj.*

**xen•o•phobe** (zĕn'ə-fōb') *n.* One unduly fearful of or hostile to strangers or foreigners. —**xen'o•pho'bi•a** *n.*

**xer•ic** (zĕr'ĭk, zîr'-) *adj.* Relating to an extremely dry habitat.

**x-ray. 1.** A relatively high-energy photon with a very short wavelength. **2.** Also **X-ray.** A photograph taken with x-rays. —**x'-ray'** *v. & adj.*

**xy•lo•phone** (zī'lə-fōn') *n.* A musical percussion instrument consisting of a mounted row of graduated wooden bars played with 2 small mallets.

**y, Y** (wī) *n.* The 25th letter of the English alphabet.

**yacht** (yät) *n.* A small sailing vessel, used for pleasure cruises or racing.

**ya•hoo** (yä'hōō, yā'-) *n.* A crude or brutish person.

**yak** (yăk) *n.* A long-haired Asian ox.

**yam** (yăm) *n.* The edible potato-like root of a tropical vine.

**yam•mer** (yăm'ər) *v.* **1.** To complain whimperingly. **2.** To talk volubly and loudly.

**yang** (yăng) *n.* The active, male cosmic principle in Chinese dualistic philosophy.

**yank** (yăngk) *v.* To pull suddenly; jerk. —*n.* A sudden vigorous pull; a jerk.

**Yan•kee** (yăng'kē) *n.* A native or inhabitant of a New England or northern state of the U.S. —**Yan'kee** *adj.*

**yap** (yăp) *v.* **yapped, yapping. 1.** To bark sharply; yelp. **2.** To talk noisily or stupidly. —*n.* A sharp, shrill bark; yelp.

**yard[1]** (yärd) *n.* **1.** A measure of length equal to 3 feet or 0.9144 meter. **2.** A long spar used to support a sail.

**yard[2]** (yärd) *n.* **1.** A tract of ground adjacent to a building. **2.** An enclosed area used for a specific purpose.

**yard•age** (yär'dĭj) *n.* An amount measured in yards.

**yard•stick** (yärd'stĭk') *n.* **1.** A measuring stick one yard in length. **2.** A standard; criterion.

**yarn** (yärn) *n.* **1.** A continuous strand of twisted threads of wool, etc. **2.** A long story.

**yaw** (yô) *v.* To deviate from the intended course, as a ship. —*n.* The action of yawing.

**yawl** (yôl) *n.* A 2-masted sailing vessel.

**yawn** (yôn) *v.* To open the mouth wide from drowsiness or boredom. —*n.* An act of yawning.

**yea** (yā) *adv.* Yes; aye. —*n.* An affirmative vote.

**year** (yîr) *n.* A period of time consisting of 365 days. —**year'ly** *adj. & adv.*

**year•ling** (yîr'lĭng) *n.* An animal that is 1 year old.

**yearn** (yûrn) *v.* To have a strong or deep desire. —**yearn'ing** *n.*

**yeast** (yēst) *n.* A fungus capable of fermenting carbohydrates, used esp. as a leavening agent. —**yeast'y** *adj.*

**yell** (yĕl) *v.* To cry out loudly. —*n.* **1.** A loud cry; a shriek; shout. **2.** A rhythmic cheer uttered in unison.

**yel•low** (yĕl'ō) *n.* A color resembling that of ripe lemons. —*adj.* **1.** Of the color yellow. **2.** Cowardly. —**yel'low•ish** *adj.*

**yellow jacket** *n.* A small, yellow and black wasp.

**yelp** (yĕlp) *v.* To utter a sharp, short cry. —*n.* A sharp, short cry or bark.

**yen** (yĕn) *n.* A yearning; a longing.

**yes** (yĕs) *adv.* Expressive of affirmation, agreement, or consent. —*n.* An affirmative reply or vote.

**yes•ter•day** (yĕs'tər-dā', -dē) *n.* The day before today. —*adv.* On the day before today.

**yet** (yĕt) *adv.* **1.** At this time; now. **2.** Thus far. **3.** In the time remaining; still. **4.** Besides; in addition. —*conj.* Nevertheless; and despite this.

**yew** (yo͞o) *n.* An evergreen tree or shrub with poisonous berries.

**yield** (yēld) *v.* **1.** To give forth; produce. **2.** To furnish or give in return. **3.** To relinquish or concede. **4.** To surrender; submit. **5.** To give way, as to pressure, force, or persuasion. —*n.* **1.** The amount yielded. **2.** The profit obtained from investment; a return.

**yin** (yĭn) *n.* The passive, female cosmic principle in Chinese dualistic philosophy.

**yo•del** (yōd'l) *v.* To sing so that the voice fluctuates between the normal chest voice and a falsetto.

**yo•ga** (yō'gə) *n.* A Hindu discipline aimed at training the consciousness for a state of perfect spiritual insight. —**yo'gi** *n.*

**yo•gurt** (yō'gərt) *n.* A custardlike food prepared from curdled milk.

**yoke** (yōk) *n.* A crossbar that encircles the necks of a pair of draft animals. —*v.* **yoked, yoking.** To fit or join with a yoke.

**yo•kel** (yō'kəl) *n.* A country bumpkin.

**yolk** (yōk) *n.* The yellow inner mass of an egg.

**yon•der** (yŏn'dər) *adv.* Over there.

**yore** (yôr, yōr) *n.* Time long past.

**you** (yo͞o) *pron.* The 2nd person sing. or pl. pronoun in the subjective or objective case.

**you'd** (yo͞od) *v.* **1.** Contraction of *you had.* **2.** Contraction of *you would.*

**you'll** (yo͞ol) *v.* Contraction of *you will.*

**young** (yŭng) *adj.* **1.** In the early period of life; not old. **2.** Vigorous or fresh. —*n.* **1.** Young persons collectively; youth. **2.** Offspring. —**young'ster** *n.*

**your** (yo͝or, yôr, yōr; *unstressed* yər) *pron.* The possessive case of *you,* used before a noun as an attributive adjective.

**you're** (yo͝or; *unstressed* yər) *v.* Contraction of *you are.*

**yours** (yo͝orz, yôrz, yōrz) *pron.* The possessive case of *you,* used by itself or as a predicate adjective.

**your•self** (yo͝or-sĕlf′, yôr-, yōr-, yər-) *pron., pl.* **-selves.** The reflexive and emphatic form of *you.*

**youth** (yo͞oth) *n., pl.* **youths. 1.** The condition of being young. **2.** An early period of development. **3. a.** Young people collectively. **b.** A young person. **—youth′ful** *adj.* **—youth′ful•ness** *n.*

**you've** (yo͞ov) *v.* Contraction of *you have.*

**yowl** (youl) *v.* To howl; wail. *—n.* A howl; a wail.

**yo-yo** (yō′yō′) *n., pl.* **-yos.** A toy consisting of a flattened spool wound with string. *—v.* **-yoed, -yoing.** To vacillate.

**yuc•ca** (yŭk′ə) *n.* A tall New World plant with a cluster of white flowers.

**z, Z** (zē) *n.* The 26th letter of the English alphabet.

**za•ny** (zā′nē) *n., pl.* **-nies.** A clown; buffoon. *—adj.* **-nier, -niest. 1.** Clownish; droll. **2.** Silly; absurd.

**zap** (zăp) *v.* **zapped, zapping. 1.** To destroy with a burst of gunfire, flames, or electric current. **2.** To move swiftly; zoom.

**zeal** (zēl) *n.* Enthusiastic and diligent devotion. **—zeal′ous** *adj.* **—zeal′-ous•ly** *adv.* **—zeal′ous•ness** *n.*

**zeal•ot** (zĕl′ət) *n.* One who is fanatically committed.

**ze•bra** (zē′brə) *n.* A striped, horselike African mammal.

**Zeit•geist** (tsīt′gīst′) *n.* The spirit and outlook characteristic of a period.

**Zen** (zĕn) *n.* A school of Buddhism that asserts that enlightenment can be attained through direct intuition rather than through intellectual studies.

**ze•nith** (zē′nĭth) *n.* **1.** The celestial point that is directly above the observer. **2.** Any culmination or high point.

**zeph•yr** (zĕf′ər) *n.* **1.** The west wind. **2.** A gentle breeze. **3.** Any of various light, soft fabrics or yarns.

**zep•pe•lin** (zĕp′ə-lĭn) *n.* A rigid airship or dirigible.

**ze•ro** (zîr′ō, zē′rō) *n., pl.* **-ros** or **-roes. 1.** The numerical symbol '0.' **2.** A number indicating the absence of any or all units under consideration. **3.** The lowest point. **4.** Nothing; nil.

**zest** (zĕst) *n.* **1.** Piquancy; charm. **2.** Spirited enjoyment; gusto. **3.** The outermost layer of a lemon or orange peel, used as a flavoring. **—zest′ful** *adj.* **—zest′y** *adj.*

**zig•zag** (zĭg′zăg′) *n.* A line that proceeds by sharp turns in alternating directions. *—adj.* Having or moving in a zigzag. *—adv.* In a zigzag manner or pattern. *—v.* **-zagged, -zagging.** To form into or move in a zigzag.

**zinc** (zĭngk) *n.* A bluish-white, lustrous metallic element.

**zing** (zĭng) *n.* A brief, high-pitched humming sound. **—zing** *v.*

**zin•ni•a** (zĭn′ē-ə) *n.* An annual plant with variously colored flowers.

**zip** (zĭp) *n.* **1.** A brief, sharp, hissing sound. **2.** Alacrity; speed. *—v.* **zipped, zipping. 1.** To move swiftly. **2.** To fasten with a zipper.

**zip•per** (zĭp′ər) *n.* A fastening device consisting of interlocking rows of teeth on adjacent edges controlled by a sliding tab. **—zip′per** *v.*

**zith•er** (zĭth′ər) *n.* A stringed musical instrument with a flat sounding box.

**zo•di•ac** (zō′dē-ăk′) *n.* **1.** An imaginary band of the celestial sphere that represents the path of the principal planets. **2.** In astrology, this band divided into 12 equal parts called signs, each bearing the name of the constellation for which it was named. **—zo•di′a•cal** *adj.*

**zom•bie** (zŏm′bē) *n.* **1.** A corpse revived by a voodoo spell. **2.** One who behaves like an automaton.

**zone** (zōn) *n.* **1.** An area, region, or division distinguished from adjacent parts by some distinctive feature. **2.** Any of the 5 regions of the surface of the earth divided according to prevailing climate. **3.** A division of an area or territory.

**zoo** (zo͞o) *n.* A park in which living animals are kept and exhibited.

**zo•ol•o•gy** (zō-ŏl′ə-jē) *n.* The biological science of animals. **—zo′o•log′i•cal** *adj.* **—zo•ol′o•gist** *n.*

**zoom** (zo͞om) *v.* **1.** To climb suddenly and sharply in an airplane. **2.** To move about rapidly; swoop.

**zuc•chi•ni** (zo͞o-kē′nē) *n., pl.* **-ni.** A narrow, green-skinned variety of squash.

# States of the United States

| State | Capital | Admitted to the Union | Population |
|---|---|---|---|
| Alabama | Montgomery | 1819 | 4,450,000 |
| Alaska | Juneau | 1959 | 627,000 |
| Arizona | Phoenix | 1912 | 5,130,000 |
| Arkansas | Little Rock | 1836 | 2,670,000 |
| California | Sacramento | 1850 | 33,900,000 |
| Colorado | Denver | 1876 | 4,300,000 |
| Connecticut* | Hartford | 1788 | 3,410,000 |
| Delaware* | Dover | 1787 | 784,000 |
| Florida | Tallahassee | 1845 | 16,000,000 |
| Georgia* | Atlanta | 1788 | 8,190,000 |
| Hawaii | Honolulu | 1959 | 1,210,000 |
| Idaho | Boise | 1890 | 1,290,000 |
| Illinois | Springfield | 1818 | 12,400,000 |
| Indiana | Indianapolis | 1816 | 6,080,000 |
| Iowa | Des Moines | 1846 | 2,930,000 |
| Kansas | Topeka | 1861 | 2,690,000 |
| Kentucky | Frankfort | 1792 | 4,040,000 |
| Louisiana | Baton Rouge | 1812 | 4,470,000 |
| Maine | Augusta | 1820 | 1,270,000 |
| Maryland* | Annapolis | 1788 | 5,300,000 |
| Massachusetts* | Boston | 1788 | 6,350,000 |
| Michigan | Lansing | 1837 | 9,940,000 |
| Minnesota | St. Paul | 1858 | 4,920,000 |

| | | | |
|---|---|---|---|
| Mississippi | Jackson | 1817 | 2,840,000 |
| Missouri | Jefferson City | 1821 | 5,600,000 |
| Montana | Helena | 1889 | 902,000 |
| Nebraska | Lincoln | 1867 | 1,710,000 |
| Nevada | Carson City | 1864 | 2,000,000 |
| New Hampshire* | Concord | 1788 | 1,240,000 |
| New Jersey* | Trenton | 1787 | 8,410,000 |
| New Mexico | Santa Fe | 1912 | 1,820,000 |
| New York* | Albany | 1788 | 19,000,000 |
| North Carolina* | Raleigh | 1789 | 8,050,000 |
| North Dakota | Bismarck | 1889 | 642,000 |
| Ohio | Columbus | 1803 | 11,400,000 |
| Oklahoma | Oklahoma City | 1907 | 3,450,000 |
| Oregon | Salem | 1859 | 3,420,000 |
| Pennsylvania* | Harrisburg | 1787 | 12,300,000 |
| Rhode Island* | Providence | 1790 | 1,050,000 |
| South Carolina* | Columbia | 1788 | 4,010,000 |
| South Dakota | Pierre | 1889 | 755,000 |
| Tennessee | Nashville | 1796 | 5,690,000 |
| Texas | Austin | 1845 | 20,900,000 |
| Utah | Salt Lake City | 1896 | 2,230,000 |
| Vermont | Montpelier | 1791 | 609,000 |
| Virginia* | Richmond | 1788 | 7,080,000 |
| Washington | Olympia | 1889 | 5,890,000 |
| West Virginia | Charleston | 1863 | 1,810,000 |
| Wisconsin | Madison | 1848 | 5,360,000 |
| Wyoming | Cheyenne | 1890 | 494,000 |

*One of the thirteen original states

# Punctuation

The rules of punctuation listed in this section, although far from comprehensive, cover the most important usages.

**Apostrophe:** The apostrophe is used:

1. To form the possessive case of nouns and some pronouns: *the man's hat; men's clothes; the planets' orbits; each other's books; someone's coat; somebody else's package.*
2. To indicate the omission of figures or letters: *don't; it's; class of '92.*
3. To form the plural of single letters, figures, and symbols: *three R's; 2 by 4's; dot the i's; 8's; &'s.*

**Brackets:** Brackets, in pairs, are used:

1. To indicate a word or phrase that is extraneous, incidental, or explanatory, especially within quoted material: *The emperor* [*Napoleon*] *ordered him to leave. She wrote: "I recieved* [sic] *your package."*
2. To set off parenthetical material within other parenthetical material: *Act of August 5, 1882 (ch. 4. sec.* [or §] *284).*

**Colon:** The colon is used:

1. To introduce a series: *Four items were sold: a painting, two sculptures, and a rare book.*
2. To introduce a clause or phrase that extends, illustrates, or amplifies preceding matter: *Forestry is not an outdoor sport: it is a science.*
3. To introduce formally any material that forms a complete sentence, question, or quotation: *A topic came up for discussion: Which monetary policy should be pursued?*
4. After a salutation in formal correspondence: *Dear Sir:*
5. In expressing clock time: *2:40.*
6. In Biblical and bibliographic references: *Luke 4:3; Boston: Houghton Mifflin Company.*
7. To separate book titles and subtitles: *The Strong Brown God: The Story of the Niger River.*
8. In ratios: *Mix oil and vinegar in the proportion 3:1.*

**Comma:** The comma is used:

1. To separate independent clauses joined by a coordinate or correlative conjunction *(as, and, but, for, nor,* and *or): It snowed yesterday, and today the road is closed.*
2. To separate independent clauses not joined by a conjunction when the clauses are short, closely related, and have no commas within: *I came, I saw, I conquered.*
3. After a dependent clause that precedes the main clause: *If there is any error, please let us know.*
4. To set off a nonrestrictive clause, phrase, or word: *Joan Smith, who lives next door, is ill. (*But *not* in the case of a restrictive clause as in: *The girl who lives next door is ill.)*
5. To set off parenthetical expressions, whether words, phrases, or clauses: *Our host, Bill Martin, is an excellent cook.*
6. To set off words or phrases expressing contrast: *Mr. Smith, not Mr. Jones, was elected.*
7. To set off transitional words and expressions (as *in short, of course*) or conjunctive adverbs (as *however, consequently, therefore*): *We found, in short, many errors in his work. Your question, however, remained unanswered.*
8. After expressions that introduce an example or illustration (as *namely, i.e., for example*): *Some of the writers, for example, Jackson, Riley, Jeffries, are also critics.*
9. To separate words, phrases, or clauses in a series: *Mary, Louise, and Rachel are sisters. He stalked out of the room, turned around, came back, and resumed the argument.*
10. To separate two words or figures that might otherwise be misunderstood: *To Mary, Louise was kind. Instead of hundreds, thousands came.*
11. To separate two adjectives that modify the same noun and can be interchanged in position: *an eager, restless young man.* (But *not* in: *three silver spoons; a rare second chance.*)
12. To set off a short direct quotation: *He said, "Now or never."*
13. To set off a word or phrase in direct address: *Thank you, Mary for the invitation.*
14. To indicate the omission of a word or words: *Then we had much, now nothing.*
15. After a statement followed by a direct question: *You are sure*

*of what you are saying, are you not?*

16. To set off items in dates, addresses, names of places: *She was born on June 5, 1976, at 64 Main Street, York, Maine.*
17. To separate a proper noun from a title: *Phillip Smith, Esq.*
18. After the salutation in informal correspondence: *Dear Mary,*
19. After the complimentary close of a letter: *Very truly yours,*
20. To separate an inverted name or phrase: *Jones, Kristy.*
21. To separate thousands, millions, etc., in numbers of four or more digits: *5,256; 1,000,000.*

**Dash:** The dash is used:

1. To indicate a sudden break or abrupt change in continuity: *"If—if you'll just let me explain," the student stammered.*
2. To set apart an explanatory, defining, or emphatic phrase: *Foods rich in protein—meat, fish, and eggs—should be eaten daily.*
3. To set apart parenthetical matter: *Wilson, in spite of his flaws—and he had many—was a great President.*
4. To mark an unfinished sentence: *"But if my bus is late—" he began.*
5. To set off a summarizing phrase or clause: *Abraham Lincoln, Mark Twain, Francis Parkman—these are among America's most prominent prose writers of the 19th century.*
6. To set off the name of an author or source, as at the end of a quotation: *A poet can survive everything but a misprint.* —*Oscar Wilde*

**Exclamation Point:** The exclamation point is used:

To mark surprise, incredulity, admiration, or other strong emotion: *What! How beautiful! "Excellent!" he shouted. Who shouted, "All aboard!"*

**Hyphen:** The hyphen is used:

1. To indicate that part of a word of more than one syllable has been carried over from one line to the next: *This young nation was beset with many internal problems such as fighting, dis-ease, and famine.*
2. To join the elements of some compounds: *attorney-at-law; great-grandparent; ex-governor; self-defense.*

3. To join the elements of compound modifiers preceding nouns: *a well-dressed executive; high-school students.*
4. To indicate that two or more compounds share a single base: *4- and 6-volume sets.*
5. To substitute for the word *to* between words or figures in print: *pp. 10–15, the Chicago-Philadelphia flight.*
6. In written-out compound numbers from 21 through 99: *forty-six years old; a person who is forty-six.*

**Parentheses:** Parentheses are used:

1. To set off nonessential, supplementary, or explanatory material: *She bought two dresses for £10 (about $16.00). The result (see fig. 2) proves your theory. Ms. Jones belongs to the Portland (Ore.) Chamber of Commerce.*
2. To enclose parenthetical material where the interruption is too great to be indicated by commas: *You can find it neither in American catalogues (at any rate, not in Sears') nor in European.*
3. To enclose letters or numbers in a series: *The order of deliveries will be (a) mail, (b) groceries, and (c) laundry, if any. The cars are (1) old-fashioned, (2) still in good condition, and (3) quite expensive.*

**Period:** The period is used:

1. To mark the end of a sentence or sentence fragment that is neither exclamatory nor interrogatory: *Lobsters are crustaceans. Do not be late.*
2. After some abbreviations: *U.S.A.; Dr.*
3. Before a decimal and between dollars and cents in figures: *90 pounds; 14.5 feet; $9.95.*

**Question Mark:** The question mark is used:

1. To mark the end of a direct query, even if not in the form of a question: *"Did she do it?" he asked. Can the money be raised? is the question.*
2. To express uncertainty or doubt: *Pocahontas (1595?–1617), American Indian princess; The mail clerk said the book weighed 50 (?) pounds.*

**Quotation Marks:** Double quotation marks are used:

1. To enclose direct quotations: *"Karen," asked Kathy, "why are you singing?"*
2. To enclose titles of speeches or lectures, articles, short poems, short stories, chapters of books, songs, short musical compositions, radio and TV programs: *a lecture entitled "The Atomic Era"; The article "The Gypsies" appeared in the last issue. She read Shirley Jackson's "The Lottery" and Keats's "Ode on a Grecian Urn." The chorus sang "God Bless America." We watched "Nova" on PBS.*
3. To enclose coined words, slang expressions, or ordinary words, etc., used ironically or in some other unusual way: *references to the "imperial Presidency" of Richard Nixon; George Herman "Babe" Ruth; His report was "bunk."*

**Semicolon:** The semicolon is used:

1. To separate clauses containing commas: *Rachel Smith, president of the National Bank, was also a director of Acme Lumber Co.; Harvey Jones, chairman of the board of Williams & Sons, was also on the board of American Steel Co. No, sir; I do not recall.*
2. To separate independent clauses joined by conjunctive adverbs: *The supervisor praised his work highly; therefore, he was given a raise.*
3. To separate statements that are too closely related to be written as separate sentences, and also contrasting statements: *War is destructive; peace, constructive.*

# Metric Prefixes

These prefixes are used with metric measurements (such as gram, meter, liter). Abbreviations are formed by taking prefix symbols and appending the abbreviations of the unit (*g* for gram, *l* for liter, *m* for mass). For example, a *kilogram* is 1,000 grams, and *kg* is the abbreviation for kilogram.

| *Prefix* | *Symbol* | *Amount* |
|---|---|---|
| yotta- | Y | $10^{24}$ |
| one septillion | | 1,000,000,000,000,000,000,000,000 |
| zetta- | Z | $10^{21}$ |
| one sextillion | | 1,000,000,000,000,000,000,000 |
| exa- | E | $10^{18}$ |
| one quintillion | | 1,000,000,000,000,000,000 |
| peta- | P | $10^{15}$ |
| one quadrillion | | 1,000,000,000,000,000 |
| tera- | T | $10^{12}$ |
| one trillion | | 1,000,000,000,000 |
| giga- | G | $10^{9}$ |
| one billion | | 1,000,000,000 |
| mega- | M | $10^{6}$ |
| one million | | 1,000,000 |
| kilo- | k | $10^{3}$ |
| one thousand | | 1,000 |
| hecto- | h | $10^{2}$ |
| one hundred | | 100 |
| deka-/deca- | da | $10^{1}$ |
| ten | | 10 |
| deci- | d | $10^{-1}$ |
| one tenth | | 0.1 |
| centi- | c | $10^{-2}$ |
| one hundredth | | 0.01 |
| milli- | m | $10^{-3}$ |
| one thousandth | | 0.001 |
| micro- | µ | $10^{-6}$ |
| one millionth | | 0.000 001 |
| nano- | n | $10^{-9}$ |
| one billionth | | 0.000 000 001 |
| pico- | p | $10^{-12}$ |
| one trillionth | | 0.000 000 000 001 |
| femto- | f | $10^{-15}$ |
| one quadrillionth | | 0.000 000 000 000 001 |
| atto- | a | $10^{-18}$ |
| one quintillionth | | 0.000 000 000 000 000 001 |
| zepto- | z | $10^{-21}$ |
| one sextillionth | | 0.000 000 000 000 000 000 001 |
| yocto- | y | $10^{-24}$ |
| one septillionth | | 0.000 000 000 000 000 000 000 001 |

# Metric Conversion Chart

| *When You Know* | *Multiply by* | *To Find* |
|---|---|---|
| millimeters | 0.04 | inches |
| centimeters | 0.39 | inches |
| meters | 3.28 | feet |
| meters | 1.09 | yards |
| kilometers | 0.62 | miles |
| inches | 2.54 | centimeters |
| feet | 30.48 | centimeters |
| yards | 0.91 | meters |
| miles | 1.61 | kilometers |
| grams | 0.035 | ounces |
| kilograms | 2.20 | pounds |
| metric tons | 1.10 | short tons |
| ounces | 28.35 | grams |
| pounds | 0.45 | kilograms |
| short tons | 0.91 | metric tons |
| milliliters | 0.03 | fluid ounces |
| liters | 2.12 | pints |
| liters | 1.06 | quarts |
| liters | 0.26 | gallons |
| fluid ounces | 29.57 | milliliters |
| pints | 0.47 | liters |
| quarts | 0.95 | liters |
| gallons | 3.79 | liters |
| square centimeters | 0.16 | square inches |
| square meters | 1.20 | square yards |
| square kilometers | 0.39 | square miles |
| hectares | 2.47 | acres |
| cubic meters | 35.31 | cubic feet |
| cubic meters | 1.35 | cubic yards |
| square inches | 6.45 | square centimeters |
| square feet | 0.09 | square meters |
| square yards | 0.84 | square meters |
| square miles | 2.59 | square kilometers |
| acres | 0.40 | hectares |
| cubic feet | 0.03 | cubic meters |
| cubic yards | 0.76 | cubic meters |

Fahrenheit to Celsius: (F – 32) ÷ 1.8 = C
Celsius to Fahrenheit: (C × 1.8) + 32 = F